The History of Economic Thought & Analysis:
A Selective International Bibliography

by
Emma Lila Fundaburk

Volume I:
Development of Economic Thought
and Analysis

The Scarecrow Press, Inc.
Metuchen, N.J.   1973

Library of Congress Cataloging in Publication Data

Fundaburk, Emma Lila, 1922-
  Development of economic thought and analysis.

  (Her The history of economic thought & analysis: a selective international bibliography, v. 1)
  1. Economics--History--Bibliography. 2. Economics--Bibliography. I. Title. II. Series.
Z7164.E2F82 vol. 1   016.330'09s   [016.330'09]   72-13158
ISBN 0-8108-0580-4

Copyright 1973 by Emma Lila Fundaburk

Dedicated to the Professors of Economics
With Whom I Studied at Ohio State University
1958-1963

    Robert D. Patton, Ph.D.
    Glenn W. Miller, Ph.D.
    Clifford L. James, Ph.D.
    David M. Harrison, Ph.D.
    Arthur D. Lynn, Ph.D.

and the late:

    Edison L. Bowers, Ph.D.
    L. Edwin Smart, Ph.D.
    Alvin E. Coons, Ph.D.
    Mikhail V. Condoide, Ph.D.

CHENG-SAN (oil on linen), by Marjorie S. Wright. Photography by Instructional Media, Bowling Green State University

CONTENTS

	Page
Preface	vii
Introduction	xi

PART I: GENERAL WORKS

A.	Chronological and Subject Surveys	1
B.	Collections: Essays, Lectures, Addresses, and Others	47
C.	Summary Works in Economic Thought and Analysis	71

PART II: SPECIFIC WORKS

D.	Economists and Economics	152
E.	Countries and Areas	166
F.	Supply, Demand, Value, and Price	212
G.	Method and Scope	237

PART III: PERIODS AND SCHOOLS

H. Pre-Classical Period
    Section I.   General Works   268
    Section II. Specific Works   316
        1. Primitive, Ancient, and Medieval   316
        2. Mercantilism, Cameralism, and Colbertism   332
        3. Physiocracy   346

J. Classical Period
    Section I.   General Works   355
    Section II. Specific Works   447
        1. Smithian Economics   447

K. Post-Classical Period
    Section I.   General Works   457
    Section II. Specific Works   508
        1. Historicism   508
        2. Institutionalism   512
        3. Socialism and Marxism   518
        4. Marginalism   562
        5. Marshallian Economics   571
        6. Keynesian Economics   576

Appendix (Supplement to Part II, E). L'Economia Politica nella Spagna, nel Portogallo, nel Belgio e nei Paesi Bassi [1891]   595

Indexes
  I. Author and Subject Index   611
  II. Short Title Index   737

PREFACE

This is the first of a six-volume series to be entitled <u>The History of Economic Thought and Analysis: A Selective International Bibliography</u>. Volume I is a chronological survey of contemporary and retrospective writings in economic thought and analysis. It is identified as <u>Development of Economic Thought and Analysis: General and Specific Works by Subject, Country, School, and Period</u>. Volume II will be <u>Specialization of Economic Thought and Analysis: Principles, Problems, and Policies of the Late Nineteenth and the Twentieth Centuries</u>. Since the United Nations has some 130 members now, and the more developed countries of the world are vying with each other to impress their economic views upon the less-developed countries, the third volume will be entitled <u>Comparative Economic Systems: Conditions and Policies</u>. Economics is not a subject which can be entirely set apart, or extracted from the social, political and other forces in the total ideological complex of society. Thus, Volume IV will be concerned with the <u>Interdisciplinary Relationships of Economics</u>. The material in Volume V covers the economic facts and ideas of history which have been both a cause and a result of economic thought and analysis. It will be termed <u>Economic History: The Background of Economic Thought and Analysis</u>. Volume VI will be <u>Bibliographies of the Works of Selected Economists</u>.

It is hoped that this effort in bibliography not only will aid researchers and librarians in identifying sources of materials and in accomplishing investigations, but also that it will point-up the many common economic problems existing in all economic systems. The time has come for the countries of the world to stop fighting about economic and related political and social problems. It now is urgent that countries place increasing emphasis on economic cooperation and peaceful solutions to common domestic and international economic problems.

The six volumes described above are designed to include information selected to cover particular parts of the vast subject matter of economics. In its broadest context as a social and applied science, economics includes agriculture, business, industry, commerce, and related subjects, such as labor, banking, government, and consumption. In more recent years, ecology, pollution, welfare and other more interdisciplinary subjects have become important to policymakers and to economists seeking alternatives for the solution of such problems. The growing complexity of economic studies, policies and activities has required intensive narrowing and specializing of economic investigations and writings. The increasing complexity of economic problems and policies has made it necessary for the quantitative tools of economics to become more numerous and sophisticated. This is epitomized in the quantitative devices necessary to coordinate a planned economic system. The branching out of general economic subject matter into more definite areas of investigation has been accompanied by a mushrooming of printed materials in every form, including books, periodicals, pamphlets, and various types of serials. This increases the difficulty of bringing together a meaningful selection of works in economics in a restricted framework for publication. The great proliferation of economic materials from countries throughout the world has created problems in collections, identification and storage of the material.

By its very nature, a bibliography such as this is incomplete and tentative. Not only is it dated, but since it is selective, it excludes many publications which also are useful. A selective work is only a sampling of materials, which gives examples of works of particular types. In compiling this bibliography, the selected entries were primarily limited to books, pamphlets, and the like. A few articles have been included to remind the reader that periodical literature is and has been a basic part of the development of economic thought and analysis. It is especially important in the development of concepts and theories of particular types. Indexes of articles, such as that of the American Economic Association, are invaluable as sources for locating economic subject matter in periodical literature.

Because of the prominence of the Western world in developing the academic science of economics, especially in the eighteenth and nineteenth centuries, the emphasis in the selection of materials has been from those works produced in continental Europe, Great Britain and the United States. German economists made great contributions to developing the discipline of economic history in the nineteenth century. English, American, French and other economists have continued and elaborated that discipline. French, German and English economists produced nineteenth-century works in the history of economic thought. Economists from throughout Europe produced notable works in economic principles in the nineteenth century. Although American economists in the nineteenth century were prominent in shaping American economic thought, and in some instances won international acclaim, the greatest contributions of American economists have been in the twentieth century. Marxian economists, beginning their elaborations in the nineteenth century, have made an ever-increasing impact upon economic debate throughout the world in the twentieth century, as the Soviet Union, China, and several other countries have adopted administered economic systems.

Entries in this volume, when surveyed together, indicate the interrelated nature of economic problems and their frequent international scope. Although most items included were published in languages using a Roman alphabet, some selections appear in transliteration from other languages. The contents of many publications appearing in countries using languages in the Roman alphabet refer to developments in various other parts of the world. Thinking in Western Europe and America has influenced economic thought, analysis, and activity throughout the globe, and in turn it has been influenced by economic thought and analysis from other areas. Such has been the case during the Middle Ages, the commercial or colonial period, the Industrial Revolution, the nineteenth-century expansion, and even during the past fifty years, when economic planning, government regulation, administered pricing, and government ownership of the means of production in varying degrees have become dominant characteristics of the economic structure of many countries.

The initial work on this series of economic bibliographies, which occurred in 1967-68, was financed by a loan from the College of Business Administration, Bowling Green State University, Bowling Green, Ohio. I am grateful to Dr. Raymond F. Barker, Director of Research for the College, and to the former Deans, Dr. William Schmeltz and Dr. Warren Waterhouse. The Department of Economics at the same university has given limited support to the project, primarily through making available a part-time student assistant, who for the past two years has been Mr. Jim Sorg. In 1967-68, when the initial work began, Dr. L. R. Wynar, then Assistant Director of the University Library, gave useful advice on style, nature, and publication of the bibliographical materials. The help of Professor Beryl M. Parrish, Department of English, in reading the preface and introduction has been much appreciated. I am grateful to the artist, Marjorie S. Wright, M.F.A., School of Art, for permission to reproduce her painting, CHENG-SAN, which appears as the frontispiece of this volume. The Department of Instructional Media produced the black and white photograph of the painting. For exercising patience and care in typing and retyping the manuscript, I am grateful to Mrs. Edward I-Te Chen. The facilities of the Computer Center have been helpful for indexing. I want to thank Jim Hoy for his aid there. This work has required the use of several libraries including the libraries of Bowling Green State University, the Ohio State University, the Library of Congress, and others. I appreciate the aid and services of the various librarians at those institutions. This has been an enormously time-consuming project. I am grateful for the help of everyone who has worked with it or given aid in any way.

Emma Lila Fundaburk, Ph.D.
Associate Professor of Economics
Bowling Green State University

INTRODUCTION

This volume is organized into three major parts. The first, General Works, is designed to contain summary, survey, and collected works in economic thought and analysis. These are primarily retrospective in content. The first sub-part (A) of Part I includes comprehensive histories of economic thought and analysis which are referred to as Chronological and Subject Surveys. Some of the books describe a long span of years, such as from the Middle Ages through the twentieth century. Others focus on shorter periods, such as the nineteenth century. The second sub-part (B) in Part I contains collections of works, including essays, lectures, and addresses. It also includes works of selected and abridged writings of groups of economists. Summary works in economic principles are organized alphabetically by authors in sub-part C of Part I.

The second part of this volume is entitled Specific Works, and includes four sub-parts. The first in Part II (sub-part D) lists books and articles referring to particular economists and to conditions relating to economists. The second (E) organizes major works in economic thought and analysis by countries and areas to which they pertain. The third (F) is devoted to a very basic subject area in economics: the conditions and principles influencing the allocation of scarce resources. This sub-part is entitled Supply, Demand, Value, and Price. The fourth sub-part (G) in Part II covers another basic area of economic thought and analysis, and is entitled Method and Scope.

Historical periods and schools are the basis for division of bibliographical entries in Part III. There are three major sub-parts, identified as (H) the Pre-Classical Period, (J) the Classical Period, and (K) the Post-Classical Period. Each of these has a Section I, called General Works, and a Section II, called Specific Works. Section II of sub-part H, the Pre-Classical Period, has the following three sub-sections: Primitive, Ancient, and Medieval; Mercantilism, Cameralism, and Colbertism; and Physiocracy. Smithian economics is the only sub-section of Section II under J, the Classical Period. In the Post-Classical Period (sub-part K), there were many dissents to Classical economics. The roots of most of the dissents were evidenced within the Classical Period (1776-1859). However, the dissenting economic thought and analysis came to more complete and distinct elaboration following the Classical Period. In the Post-Classical Period (late nineteenth and twentieth centuries) economic thought and analysis became evidently splintered in method and scope. In addition to the Section I on General Works in the Post-Classical Period, the Section II (Specific Works) includes six-sub-sections: they are Historicism, Institutionalism, Socialism and Marxism, Marginalism, Marshallian Economics, and Keynesian Economics.

There is one appendix: a reprint of an article by Professor Luigi Cossa entitled "L'Economia Politica nella Spagna, nel Portogallo, nel Belgio e nei Paesi Bassi." It appeared in the Giornale degli Economisti, and was published as a reprint in pamphlet form in Bologna in 1891. It is included to supplement sub-part E, Countries and Areas, under Part II. There are two indexes--an author and subject index, and a short title index. The author and subject index has been combined because economists are both the authors and the subjects in various works.

The entries in this volume include the following types of identifying information: author or authors; title of publication; series number, if any; edition information; place of publication; publisher; date; and number of pages in the publication. Occasionally there is other brief definitional information pertaining to the entry, such as reference to an association, publisher, or the languages in which the publication is available. There may be also information about editions other than the one listed. This enables a reader to locate, identify, and order additional materials which otherwise might be unknown or unavailable to the reader.

The number of abbreviations has been held to a minimum. However, there are a few which might be explained. The lower case "v" is used for two purposes. One purpose is its part in the page-number complex. As an uncapitalized roman numeral, it represents a page number. In that position it is part of a number which usually refers to pre-text pages, that is, those pages composing the preface, introduction, contents, and the like. This is demonstrated in entry number 15. The second purpose of the lower case "v" is its use in place of the word "volume." It has been employed to mean volume, such as in entry number 78, where it follows the number of volumes issued. Where an entry is a particular volume in a series of volumes, one or more of which have been or will be issued, the "v" precedes the particular volume number. Where the entry is a current bibliography, periodical or index which was begun and continued in periodic publication thereafter, the "v" is used to indicate a continuing series of volumes, such as in entry number 344. In identification of paging, the letter "l" stands for "leaf" or an unnumbered page.

Many of the books and articles in this bibliography contain bibliographies in the form of specialized listings at the back of the books, in footnotes, in connection with various chapters or parts, or in reference notes. Some of the entries which have bibliographies have that identifying information included. Bibliographies listed in books included in Part I, in particular, should prove useful in identifying a broad scope of material on economic thought and analysis.

Notable Bibliographies in Economics

The first comprehensive and annotated bibliography of economic thought was published by Professor John Ramsay McCulloch in 1840 and was entitled The Literature of Political Economy: A Classified Catalogue. As explained in the subtitle, it consisted of "select publications in the different departments of that science, with historical, critical, and bibliographical notices." A large part of his preface is quoted below, since many of the things he mentioned at that time are still appropriate considerations relating to the literature of economics, and in particular to economic policy:

> Those who have got together a considerable number of works in any department of science or literature, or who

have bestowed any pains in tracing its history, can hardly
fail to be struck, on the one hand, with the indications
and explanations of sound principles and doctrines to be
found among its earlier cultivators, and on the other, with
the continued revival of exploded errors and fallacies.
But if this be true in general, it is most especially so in
all that relates to politics and national economy. Writers
on such subjects, like those who undertake to instruct or
lead the public in other departments of human knowledge,
are sometimes imperfectly informed, and sometimes prejudiced, and incapable of communicating any useful information. Exclusive, however, of the common sources
of error, there is another which, if not peculiar to those
who discuss political questions, is found in them more
frequently than in most others, and is far more productive of deceptive and unprincipled works. We allude to
the discrepancy which sometimes exists between the real
or supposed interests of the writers, or of their employers, and those of the public. Those who cultivate mathematical and physical sciences, or who devote themselves
to literature or metaphysics, have rarely any selfish motive to bias their judgment, and to tempt them to conceal
or pervert the truth. But it is not so with those who engage in political and economical discussions. Every abuse,
and every inexpedient or unjust institution or regulation,
operates as a bounty on the production of false theories
and sophistical publications; for, though injurious to the
public, abuses are almost always productive of advantage
to a greater or smaller number of individuals, who, when
they are attacked, undertake their defence; and having enlisted a portion of the press, and probably, also a corps
of itinerant orators, into their service, labour by means
of fallacious representations to make it appear that the
abuses are beneficial to and should be supported by the
public. Party influence is another copious source of
delusion and error: measures being consistent with or
adverse to the public interests, but because they happen
to have been proposed or opposed by the leaders of the
party to which the writer or speaker is attached. And
though in the end truth is sure to prevail over error, the
history of this and most other countries shows that these
attempts to make the worse appear the better cause--to
make what is injurious be regarded as beneficial--and
what is beneficial be regarded as injurious--have not unfrequently been attended with long-continued success.
Hence, while the knowledge of the books that may be advantageously consulted is of considerable use in most
departments of study, it is of paramount importance in
those having relation to the conduct of public affairs.

Besides contributing to hinder the public judgment from
being misled in matters that may deeply affect the national
interests, such knowledge may be of material service to
those about to engage in this field of inquiry. Whether a

writer or a speaker undertakes to unfold principles, to set them in a novel and more striking light, or to recommend their application, he should know what has been already undertaken, what has been accomplished, and what remains for discovery and elucidation. The following work gives sundry examples of the inconveniences resulting from the want of this information, by exhibiting able men engaged in the investigation of principles and the development of laws which had been previously established and traced, and putting forward speculation as original which had been long before the public.

No attempt, that we are aware of, has hitherto been made to supply English readers with this knowledge. So that in endeavouring to furnish the public with an index to the select and really useful Literature of Political Economy, we may not unreasonably, perhaps, expect to meet with some indulgence for the defects unavoidable in a first attempt in a matter so extensive and so difficult.

It will be seen from the preceding remarks that no one needs take up this book in the expectation of finding in it anything like a complete list or catalogue of the various publications in the different departments of this science. Such a work would be bulky in the extreme; and would also, we incline to think, be of little value. We have proceeded on a principle of selection; and neglecting the others, have, with few exceptions, noticed those works only which appear to have contributed to develope sound principles, or to facilitate their adoption. It would, however, be idle to suppose, considering the myriads that have been published on commerce, corn-laws, money, the poor, and other subjects, that we have specified all the English works (for we have been less particular about the others) which deserved notice, or which have promoted the improvement of the science. At the same time we can safely say that our deficiencies in this respect have not been the result of carelessness and inattention. For many years past we have taken every means in our power, by collecting books and otherwise, to become acquainted with the history of the science, and with the leading publications in its different departments. And we have not omitted any work, of the existence of which we were aware, or which was present to our recollection, that appeared to be of any material importance. Perhaps, indeed, it may be thought by some that we have noticed too many rather than too few publications.

In addition to those that have conduced to elicit true principles, or to facilitate their application, we have specified a few of the works in which erroneous theories and opinions have been most ingeniously and ably defended, or which have had considerable practical influence. But we

> have been sparing in our references to this class of publications, and have taken no notice of those recommending a reduction of the standard of money, the issue of inconvertible paper, and the employment of a double standard of value, and similar crudities. Neither have we referred to any work merely because it happened to be scarce: it must have had something else than rarity to recommend it to a place in our pages....
>
> If we have succeeded in our object, this work will be in some measure a history of Political Economy, as well as a critical catalogue of the principal economical works. It contains short notices of the rise of some of the principle theories, and of the circumstances which appear at different periods to have strongly determined public opinion upon economical questions, and given birth to classes of books. Without such notices, indeed, no just estimate could be formed of the latter.
>
> But apart from these considerations, the history of this science has peculiar claims to attention. It is for the most part conversant with matters that belong to the everyday occupations and business of mankind; and some of its more important conclusions appear to be opposed to the most obvious deductions. Under such circumstances it cannot be uninteresting to trace the rise of new opinions, to observe the strong prejudices with which they have to contend, the errors that are often engrafted upon them, the mode in which one idea leads to another, and the generally slow and difficult process by which true doctrines come to be finally established, and their justness universally admitted.

McCulloch's book is an excellent source of bibliography and background information for the period prior to 1840. In it the literature of political economy is arranged into twenty "classes or divisions." McCulloch admits that "it is difficult to say to which of these some books really belong." The entries are arranged primarily in "chronological order, according to the date of their publication, separating between the English, French, Italian, etc." The twenty major divisions of the literature used by McCulloch reflect the economic thinking of the times. They were as follows:

> Political economy in general, or some of its fundamental principles; commerce and commercial policy; money, banks, exchanges, etc.; prices--influence of enclosures on prices; roads, canals, railways, etc.; political arithmetic, statistics, and agricultural economy; coal trade; Herring and other fisheries; manufactures, arts, etc.;

insurance of lives, ships, houses, etc.; interest and annuities, usury, etc.; progress of population; foundlings and foundling hospitals; naturalization; bills of mortality, and works having reference to health and mortality; wages, pauperism, poor laws, saving banks, friendly societies, etc.; right of property, law or succession, copyrights, etc.; slavery; revenue and finance; and miscellaneous.

Approximately contemporary with McCulloch's listing of the literature of political economy was the work of Professor J. A. Blanqui, Histoire de l'Economie Politique en Europe, which appeared in several successive editions, beginning in 1838. In the edition of 1860, a comprehensive bibliography of the literature of political economy was included in the appendix. It indicates the variety and complexity of economic thinking at that time.

A number of other bibliographies of economic literature were published in the nineteenth century. Among the more notable was a bibliography by Dr. Benjamin Rand, professor at Harvard University. It appeared in 1895 and was entitled, A Bibliography of Economics. It includes selected works, arranged in alphabetical author order. Dr. Rand's bibliography was published at a time when the dissents to Classical economics already had become clearly evidenced in economic writing. His selections include works in economic analysis especially pertinent to market-oriented economic systems. At that time Socialism and Marxism had not made a dominant impact upon academic economic thinking as it did later in the twentieth century. Thus, his bibliography neglects the forceful impact of that developing trend.

A more recent annotated bibliography of economics was that of Professor Harold E. Batson of the London School of Economics. It was published in 1930, and was entitled A Select Bibliography of Modern Economic Theory, 1870-1929. It contains an introduction by Lionel Robbins who concluded that, although "theoretical economics" had been developing for some 150 years as a "branch of scientific knowledge," through books, articles, etc., the "main tendencies" of "modern economic theory" were not greatly evidenced until the latter part of the nineteenth and the early twentieth centuries. Robbins called attention to the fact that pamphlets and historical documents pertaining to economic subjects (i.e., economic thought as opposed to analysis) "have never been inconsiderable." This dichotomy between materials relating to economic thought and those relating to economic analysis has often been referred to by twentieth-century authors surveying the history of economic thought and analysis. Joseph Schumpeter's writings on the history of economic doctrines and analysis remind the student of the distinction between thought and analysis. Robbins describes Batson's bibliography as excluding "descriptive economics" and "economic history" and focusing on "modern economic theory."

In the introduction to Batson's bibliography, Lionel Robbins indicates that by 1930 the teaching of economics as a university or academic subject had become widespread, as had the employment of persons in economic research. Those circumstances were resulting in a growing flow of monographs, articles, and other treatises from Departments of Economics in universities around the world. Academic economics had been developing throughout the nineteenth century. A number of textbooks were written in the subject almost every decade of the nineteenth century. However, it was not until the influence and eclecticism of Alfred Marshall's Principles of Economics in 1890 that study, writing, teaching, and research in economics began to develop at an accelerated rate. Lionel Robbins commented that in the first three decades of the twentieth century "at least a dozen journals" were devoted to economics. He refers to journal articles as "valuable" and a "matter of first class importance." It was his view that by 1930 the subject matter of economics and the writings in it had become "so vast" that a student could read for many years and still be ignorant of "vitally important contributions."

Many bibliographies in economics have emerged in the twentieth century in various languages. Because the subject matter of economic thought and analysis is so broad, the bibliographies of economic literature have primarily covered particular periods of thought and analysis, or they have focused upon particular countries of areas of the world. Some of the bibliographies have consisted of books, pamphlets, reprints, and the like, while others have included articles. This volume, while it is primarily books and complete treatises, includes a few articles as evidence of the importance of the vast reservoir of periodical literature in economics. The number of periodicals and serials dealing with economic material has greatly increased during the past fifty years, and especially during the past decade. This reflects not only the "publish or perish" attitude of universities but, more importantly, the economist's and the public's growing awareness of economic problems, of the need for more and better theories and policies to deal with them, and of the need for more trained persons to cope with the growing complexity and involvement of economic activities.

Specialized Economic Libraries

A library shelf-list is a type of bibliography. Famous economists who were collectors of books and whose library shelf-lists have been published have left imprinted upon the history of economic thought their views of books worthy of collection. One of the earliest contributions was the work of Joseph Massie in the eighteenth century. About the middle of that century he published an Alphabetical and Chronological Index of Commercial Books and Pamphlets. Massie's original list is said to be in the British Museum "among the Lansdowne" manuscript materials. It has been reported that Massie's library of 1,500 or more books, pamphlets, and the like, regarding "the commerce, coin and colonies of Great Britain," was sold about 1760. He indicated that it had taken him about twelve years to collect these, and that in so doing he "was not sparing in either time or money."

Economist Jacob Hollander, who was a great collector of early economic materials, attributed his interest in building a collection of economic works, and in particular the "pre-Adamite" economic pamphlets, etc. to the inspiration of Professor E.R.A. Seligman and to his personal library of economic materials. In 1937, E.A.G. Marsh published a list of the library collection of Jacob Hollander. In the introduction of this work Marsh describes Hollander's finding Massie's original list in the manuscripts of the British Museum. Marsh states that Hollander and one of his colleagues from Johns Hopkins University, Charles M. Andrews, both made transcripts of Massie's list. Hollander said that he checked off the list those things which he already owned, and then made an "ardent pursuit" for other "Massie items." He described his search as made partly with the thought of "reconstructing a great collection." Hollander stated that he spent much time browsing in bookstores in Great Britain and often referred to Massie's list because he thought the "reliance is sound." Marsh reported that Hollander thought that Massie's list was revised one or more times, and that by 1764, the list contained about 2300 entries.

In Marsh's publication, <u>The Economic Library of Jacob Harry Hollander</u>, the books, pamphlets, and other materials are classified into three periods: 1574-1750; 1751-1797; 1798-1936. This 300-page listing of the library of Jacob Hollander contains many notable publications. Marsh indicates that when referring to economic literature, Hollander observed that it was in the "eighteenth century, when tracts gave way to treatises and monographs to systems," and that his purpose in collecting works in economics was "to document the doctrinal growth of the science."

Many economists have collected libraries of various sizes over the years. Some of these were to supplement inadequate collections in institutions; others were acquired to obtain more specialized information on particular periods or areas. Among the famous collectors of economics books have been J.R. McCulloch, W.S. Jevons, H.S. Foxwell, J.F. Bell, and A. Wagner. Adam Smith's library has probably received more publicity than that of any other economist. James Bonar's work, <u>A Catalogue of the Library of Adam Smith, Author of the 'Moral Sentiments' and 'The Wealth of Nations,'</u> was published in London and New York in 1894. A second edition was published in 1932, and was prepared by James Bonar with an introduction and appendices for the Royal Economic Society of Great Britain. This has been reprinted a number of times and translated into several languages. In 1967 Hiroshi Mizuta prepared a book entitled, <u>Adam Smith's Library; A Supplement to Bonar's Catalogue with a Checklist on the Whole Library.</u> This was published by the Cambridge University Press for the Royal Economic Society of Great Britain.

Authorities cited by Adam Smith in the Wealth of Nations are listed in the Modern Library edition by Edwin Cannan with an introduction by Max Lerner (1937). Authorities cited by James Steuart in Principles of Political Oeconomy are listed in the edition edited by Andrew S. Skinner and published by the University of Chicago (1966). Some of the private library collections of economists have been acquired by college and university libraries. Throughout the world in the twentieth century libraries at major educational institutions have built notable collections of generalized and specialized works in economics. Two such examples are those of Harvard University and the London School of Economics.

Early Works in the History of Economic Thought and Analysis

Although economic historians attempt to view past economic events and analyses objectively, they are not able entirely to accomplish that objective. In some measure they bring to bear upon the past their own views and environment, as their own thoughts are conditioned by the world in which they live and the problems and policies contemporary to them. In the selection of economic thought and analysis from the past, in the discussion of this, in the placing of more or less emphasis upon particular concepts, and in interpreting the events and ideas of the past, the historian of economics bases his work upon his own insights and understandings of the present. Thus, successive histories of economic thought and analysis are not just up-datings of prior volumes. They offer to students of economics new insights and approaches to present problems and policies based upon selected economic thought and analysis from the past, as well as teach the student something of the sequence and development of economic ideas.

Books and articles describing the development of the history of economic thought and analysis have been written by and about economists and others who have participated in the creating and shaping of doctrines, theories, concepts, principles, and methods of economics. The first comprehensive treatist which explored the history of economic thought was published in 1838. It was written by a French professor, Jérôme Adolphe Blanqui, and was entitled Histoire de l'Economie Politique en Europe. The fifth French edition was published in Paris in 1882. A translation of the fourth French edition was published in New York in 1880. Blanqui was not a theoretician, like Malthus, Ricardo, and others who added an array of new ideas to the emerging discipline of economics. He was a teacher, who also wrote textbooks and brought together ideas for further dissemination and propagation through the medium of teaching. In 1840, Professor John Ramsay McCulloch's work, entitled The Literature of Political Economy; A Classified Catalogue, was an annotated bibliography which was in some measure a contribution both to economic history and to the history of economic thought.

    A concise treatment of the development of the early literature of the history of economic thought and analysis may be found in the "Bibliographical Preface" of Joseph A. Schumpeter's Economic Doctrine and Method, A Historical Sketch (First English edition, 1954, Oxford University Press). This primarily refers to German contributions, but also mentions several French, English and American works. Since German economists in the nineteenth century were leaders in the development of the historical school of economics, this contributed to their prominence in exploring and recording the history of economic thought, as well as accounted for their development of economic history. Although Schumpeter refers to Blanqui's 1838 treatise in the history of economic thought as "rather superficial," he does acknowledge that Blanqui's book was "the first attempt to produce a genuine history" of the science of economics. It was Schumpeter's view that, although Blanqui's work was the first comprehensive attempt to trace the history of economic thought, the early German efforts, though more fragmentary, were, when viewed together, more outstanding than works from other areas. This statement may be substantiated in the work of the following early German economists and their treatises: Rossig, Versuch einer Geschichte der Oekonomie und Kameralwissenschaft, 1781; Weitzel, Geschichte der Staatswissenschaften, 1832-33; and von Mohl, Geschichte und Literatur der Staatswissenschaften, 1855-58.

    In 1851 the German historical economist, Wilhelm Roscher,

produced Geschichte der Englischen Volkswirtschaftslehre. Roscher was a major contributor to the development of the historical school in Germany in the nineteenth century. In 1860, Roscher's student, Kautz, published Die Geschichtliche Entwicklung der Nationalökonomik und Ihrer Literatur. In 1874, Wilhelm Roscher completed a major treatise on the history of economic thought entitled Geschichte der Nationalökonomie in Deutschland. Although it treated the history of economic thought in Germany, it was an example of a carefully produced work and had a wide influence. The same year, another German, Dühring, completed a timely work entitled Kritische Geschichte der Nationalökonomie und des Sozialismus. Karl Marx's Das Kapital, the first volume of which was published in 1867 with volumes two and three edited in the 1880's, surveyed a spectrum of the history of economic thought.

In 1876 Luigi Cossa published Guida allo Studio dell'Economica Politica. It was translated into English with an introduction by W.S. Jevons in 1880. The third Italian edition was published in 1892. In addition to these and other book-length treatises, the early economic journals were substantial contributors to the history of economic thought. One specialized journal in France of particular value was the Revue d'Histoire des Doctrines Economiques.

Some of the other European publications in the history of economic thought and analysis in the late nineteenth and early twentieth centuries included an article by Luigi Cossa reprinted in 1891 and entitled, "L'Economia Politica nella Spagna, nel Portogallo, nel Belgio e nei Paesi Bassi"; Eisenhart, Geschichte der Nationalökonomik in 1881; Oncken, Geschichte der Nationalökonomie; A.V. Espinas, Histoire des doctrines économiques, 1891; Palgrave, Dictionary of Political Economy; J. Bonar, Philosophy and Political Economy in Some of Their Historical Relations, 1893; Zuckerkandl, Zur Theorie des Preises, 1889; Graziani, Storia critica della teoria del valore, 1889; Bergmann, Geschichte der nationalökonomischen Krisentheorieen, 1899; and Schmoller's article, "Volkswirtschaftslehre," in Handwörterbuch der Staatswissenschaften, 3d., 1911.

A major treatise on the history of economics, published in the nineteenth century, was that of John Kells Ingram. It was entitled History of Political Economy, and was first published in 1888. It was translated into German in 1905, and a new and enlarged English edition was published in 1915.

In the early part of the twentieth century there were a number of contributions to the development of the history of economic doctrine in America, Russia, and some other parts of the world, as well as in Western Europe. Among those were Sewall, The Theory of Value Before Adam Smith, 1901; Whittaker, History and Criticism of the Labour Theory of Value in English Political Economy, 1903; Liebknecht, Zur Geschichte der Werttheorie in England, 1902; Salz, Beiträge zur Geschichte und Kritik der Lohnfondstheorie, 1905; Rost, Die Wert-und Preistheorie mit Berücksichtigung Ihrer Dogmengeschichtlichen Entwicklung, 1908; and Karl Marx, Theorien über den Mehrwert, 1910.

Several French treatises in the history of economic thought and analysis were published in the late nineteenth and early twentieth centuries. These include the works of Rambaud, DuBois, and Denis. The latter did not finish the Histoire des Systèmes Economiques et Socialistes on which he worked during the early years of the twentieth century. The French efforts culminated in a famous work by Charles Gide and Charles Rist entitled Histoire des Doctrines Economiques. It was first published in 1908, and has since been translated into English and various other languages, and has been published in several editions. Another comprehensive general work in the history of economic thought and analysis published by an American in the early twentieth century was the work of Lewis Henry Haney entitled History of Economic Thought. The book was first published in 1911, and had its fourth edition in 1949.

General Works. Nineteenth and Twentieth Century Economic Analysis

Among the many general works which include discussions of nineteenth-century economic analysis are the following: J. F. Bell, A History of Economic Thought (1953 and revisions); Witt Bowden, An Economic History of Europe since 1750 (1970); Edwin Cannan, A Review of Economic Theory (1929); Jean Guillaume C. A. H. Colins, L'Economie Politique; Source des Révolutions et des Utopies Prétendues Socialistes (1856-   ); Hans Freyer, Die Bewertung der

Wirtschaft im Philosophischen Denken des 19. Jahrhunderts (1921, 1966); R. N. Ghosh, Classical Macroeconomics and the Case for Colonies (1967); Terence Wilmot Hutchison, A Review of Economic Doctrines, 1870-1929 (1953); Jacob Oser, The Evolution of Economic Thought (1963); Gaston Richard, La Question Sociale et le Mouvement Philosophique au XIXe Siècle (1914); Lionel C. Robbins, The Evolution of Modern Economic Theory (1960); Joseph Schumpeter, History of Economic Analysis (1954, 1966); and Edmund Silberner, The Problem of War in Nineteenth Century Economic Thought (1946).

The more recent histories of economic thought include twentieth-century information and bring the story of the development of economic analysis to contemporary times. Most of those listed above which discuss nineteenth-century thought also include some part of the twentieth century in the survey. Some of the general histories of economic thought and analysis which include twentieth-century material are Iraida Vasil'evna Aleshina, Fal'sifikatory Sotsializma (Transliterated, 1963); Alain Barrère, Cours d'Analyse Economique Contemporaine, Rédigé d'après les Notes, 1964-65 (1965); 1965-66 (1966); 1967-68 (1968); Mark Blaug, Economic Theory in Retrospect (1962, 1968); Roberto de Oliveira Campos, Ensaios de História Economica e Sociologia (1963); Jacques Dartan, Histoire de Fous (1959); Luigi Einaudi, Scienza Economica ed Economisti nel Momento Presente, Discorso Pronunciato il 5 Novembre 1949 per l'Inaugurazione dell'Anno Accademico 1949-1950 della Università di Torino (1950); Janusz Górski, Historia Powszechnej Myśli Ekonomicznej, 1870-1950 (1967); Allan G. Gruchy, Modern Economic Thought. The American Contribution (1947, 1967); Influence des Expériences Communistes sur les Doctrines; Semaine d'Etudes, 27-31 Octobre 1958. Centre d'Etude des Pays de l'Est, Institut de Sociologie Solvay, Université Libre de Bruxelles en Collaboration avec le Centre National pour l'Etude des Pays à Régime Communiste (1959); Murli Dhar Joshi, Arthika Paddhatiyam (Transliterated, 1963); Takeyasu Kimura, Gendai Keizai Riron no Essensu (1969); Alfred Kruse, Wo Steht die Nationalökonomie Heute? (1951); Kenneth K. Kurihara, Post-Keynesian Economics (1954); Claudio Napoleoni, Ekonomické Myšlení Dvacátého Století Z Ital.

Orig. Il Pensiero Economico del přel. a předml. Lumír Smetana (1968); Giuseppe di Nardi, Il Controllo Sociale dell'economia (1967); François Perroux, L'Economie du XXe Siecle... (1969); André Piettre, Histoire de la Pensée Economique et Analyse des Théories Contemporaines (1969); I. H. Rima, Development of Economic Analysis (1967); Marc Riviere, Economie Bourgeoise et Pensee Technocratique (1965); Erich Schneider, Das Gesicht der Wirtschaftstheorie Unserer Zeit und das Studium der Wirtschaftswissenschaften (1947); George L. S. Shackle, The Years of High Theory; Invention and Tradition in Economic Thought, 1926-1939 (1967); Theo Surány-Unger, Economics in the Twentieth Century; the History of Its International Development (1931); Theo Suranyi-Unger, Wirtschafts-philosophie des 20. Jahrhunderts (1967); and Seweryn Zurawicki, Wspólczesna Myśl Ekonomiczna; Prolegomena (1969).

Collections of Works

Collected works in economics have originated from several sources. On a number of occasions during or after the expiration of the life of an economist, the economist's colleagues, friends, and sometimes an economic association have brought together and published in a collected work their own articles in honor of or in memory of the particular economist. Other collected works have resulted when an institution at which an economist has lectured as professor or guest lecturer has brought together a series of lectures, essays, or addresses. Some economists, publishers, and associations have produced collections of their own or some other economist's essays, articles, monographs, or selected works.

A number of books now available in the history of economic thought are anthologies. An editor, who might be an economist, publisher, or association, brings together into book form selections from the works of many economists. Some of these are survey volumes and represent a chronological presentation of the development of economic thought and analysis, others have the material arranged by subjects. In the first quarter of the twentieth century, a very few collections of works in economics gradually came into print. These were primarily developed by professors for use in connection with particular courses which they were teaching. The number of such books in circulation significantly increased in the 1950's and even more in the 1960's. The growing competition for the sale of textbooks, the "publish or perish" policies of universities, the intensified search for relevancy of materials, and the increasing emphasis on problems and policies have accounted for the more frequent classroom use of collected works in recent years. The most numerous types of collected works in economics in the past decade have been books concerning economic problems and policies. Many of them have been designed to supplement and/or accompany more traditional textbooks; others have been produced to take the place of textbooks; still others have been designed for general public distribution. A few of the more recent collections have brought together cases in economics, demonstrating problems and possible alternative policies for solving them. The trend toward a more intensive and complete combination of principles, problems, and policies in elementary economics courses is currently evidenced in the contents of many collected works. The collected works included in sub-part B of Part I are varied in content. Increased frequency of this style of publication has characterized the flow of academic economic materials during the past decade.

Summary Works and Textbooks in Economics

The first organized, systematic treatises describing economic activities were those of Richard Cantillon and Sir James Steuart. Cantillon's Essai sur la Nature du Commerce en Général is thought to have been written between 1730 and 1734. It was published in France in 1755. In 1931 it was edited with an English translation and other material by Henry Higgs. After W. S. Jevons, the famous nineteenth-century English marginalist, discovered the work of Cantillon, he wrote an article entitled "Richard Cantillon and the Nationality of Political Economy" that was printed in the Contemporary Review in January 1881. It later appeared in Jevons' Principles of Economics, which was published in London in 1905. The article was edited with prefatory notes by Henry Higgs for inclusion in the appendix of his translation of Cantillon's Essay on the Nature of Trade. In the article Jevons criticizes the bibliography of McCulloch for an erroneous listing and comment on Cantillon's work, and refutes McCulloch's statement that Cantillon was influenced by David Hume's Political Essays, published in 1752. Although Jevons agrees that Hume was an important early contributor to the history of economic thought, he did not conceive of Hume as a source of Cantillon's ideas. Henry Higgs points out that after Jevons died in 1882 (had he lived, he possibly would have continued his investigations of Cantillon's life), Professor H.S. Foxwell included in his lectures in the 1880's the writing of Cantillon, and interested Higgs in further research regarding Cantillon. Higgs noted that one of the first histories of economic thought which gave "serious attention" to Cantillon was M. Espina's Histoire des Doctrines Economiques, published in Paris in 1891. Before engaging in editing Cantillon's Essai, Higgs wrote a number of articles regarding Cantillon, one of the first of which was published in Harvard's Quarterly Journal of Economics in 1892 (Vol. II, 436-456). In the appendix of Cantillon's book, edited by Henry Higgs, Higgs points out the chief parallels between Cantillon's Essai and Postlethwayt's Dictionary.

The next comprehensive treatise on economics was first published in England in 1767. It was the work of Sir James Steuart and was entitled An Inquiry into the Principles of Political Oeconomy. The book was reprinted with the author's corrections up to the time of his death in 1780. The last edition appeared in 1805, in his Collected Works, edited by his son, General Sir James Steuart. In the reprint of Steuart's Principles of Political Oeconomy which was edited by Andrew S. Skinner and published by the University of Chicago Press in 1966, the edited attempts to trace "Steuart's authorities" and to point out "parallel passages" from the works of succeeding economists, including Smith, Quesnay, Turgot and others. In the appendix Skinner brings together a list of the main authorities cited by Steuart in his Principles. In the back of the second volume of this work, there is a limited bibliography of pre-Smithian, or seventeenth-and-eighteenth-century writings in economics. Steuart experienced a wide range of political, economic, and social activities during his lifetime. He was well acquainted with agriculture, and with government control and operation. His book thus reflects more the mercantilist attitude and views than did the work of his successor, Adam Smith. Steuart lacked Smith's insight into industrial, business and commercial activities, and the division of labor. Also, Steuart did not share Smith's advocacy of severe limitation on the role of government in economic activity, an attitude which was emerging persistently among merchants and other business men, and was being slowly reflected in legislative action in the last quarter of the eighteenth century. Thus, Steuart's comprehensive work was relatively quickly overshadowed by the more comprehensive and more timely work of Adam Smith published in 1776.

Although Cantillon's and Steuart's work, together with that of the Physiocrats in France (1756-1770), is acknowledged to be very important in the early systematizing of economic thought and analysis, Adam Smith's book, An Inquiry into the Nature and Causes of the Wealth of Nations, 1776, was the publication which gave the solid foundation for the beginning of economics as a separate academic discipline. It gained quick acceptance, precipitated much discussion and debate, and was reprinted several times before the end of the eighteenth century. Although Smith inadequately identified the sources which he consulted, his work is undoubtedly that of an eclectic. His long years of study, his experiences in living and traveling in Great Britain and on the continent, and his acquaintance with many great minds of the time are reflected in the broad scope of economic activity to which he gives consideration, and which he draws together into an organized relationship. His theorizing and terminology, and even his often rambling descriptions, were not surpassed in eighteenth-century literature of economics. In the nineteenth and twentieth centuries Smith's work has been reprinted, quoted, abridged, and translated into many languages. It has inspired and incited not only writers in a tradition similar to his, but also writers who were dissenters from some or all of his economic and philosophical views.

Following Adam Smith's Wealth of Nations, many textbooks in political economy appeared. On the continent the work of J. B. Say elaborated and explained the writings of Smith. In England,

Thomas Malthus, David Ricardo, J. R. McCulloch, Nassau Senior, and John S. Mill had produced textbooks in political economy before the middle of the nineteenth century. In the 1870's Stanley Jevons added his textbook to the continually accumulating number of works of academic economists. Alfred Marshall's Principles, first published in 1890, was the culmination and most important effort at summarizing, clarifying, and elaborating economic principles in the nineteenth century.

Many of the summary works on economic principles published in the nineteenth century, and especially those published prior to 1870, were entitled principles of political economy. The increasing awareness of economics as an academic discipline and attempts to make economics a science, stimulated in economic thought of the mid-nineteenth century the search for more objectivity in economics. That attitude led to attempts to extract economic principles from interdisciplinary relationships, and especially from the political connections which were often affected by subjectivity and which had been closely related to economic activity in the mercantile, colonial, or commercial period. The introduction of the marginal principle and increased use of mathematics in explaining certain economic theories hastened the move of economics toward more objectivity, and therefore away from the designation, "political economy."

In the Encyclopedia of Social Sciences, in 1963, with E. R. A. Seligman as editor, there appears in volume V (p. 345-46) an article which traces the development of the use of the phrase "political economy," and the changing emphasis in scope and method of economics toward the middle and end of the nineteenth century. Initial use of this terminology to identify an economic treatise is attributed to Montchrétian de Watteoille who, in 1615, published his Traicté de l'oeconomie politique. He viewed the word as representing a "science of government" and considered "economy" to be inseparable from "policy," since the acquisition of wealth is common both to the state and to individuals. Control of economic activity by the state was universal in Western Europe. The Greeks had thought of "Oeconomy" as pertaining to the household. Some early economists appeared to associate the term "political economy" with the "public household." In general the view of political economy in the seventeenth century included government finance, money, and the regulation of agriculture, trade and industry by the government. In the eighteenth century as the agricultural changes spread throughout England, and Sir William Petty, an agriculturalist, began writing about agricultural and other economic problems and conditions, the word "political economy" gained more widespread recognition. This evidenced itself in Sir James Steuart's selection of the title of his book, <u>Inquiry into the Principles of Political Oeconomy,</u> which was published in 1757 and continued through several editions until 1805. In <u>The Wealth of Nations</u> Adam Smith refers in several places to the term "political oeconomy." In the Introduction of Book IV, entitled "Of Systems of Political Oeconomy," he states:

> Political oeconomy, considered as a branch of the science of a statesman or legislator, proposes two distinct objects: first, to provide a plentiful revenue or subsistence for the people, or more properly to enable them to provide such a revenue or subsistence for themselves; and secondly, to supply the state or commonwealth with a revenue sufficient for the public services. It proposes to enrich both the people and the sovereign.
>
> The different progress of opulence in different ages and nations, has given occasion to two different systems of political oeconomy, with regard to enriching the people. The one may be called the system of commerce, the other that of agriculture. I shall endeavour to explain both as fully and distinctly as I can, and shall begin with the system of commerce. It is the modern system, and is best understood in our own country and in our own times.

All the various writers of textbooks in the nineteenth century added their definitions of political economy. Among these was the definition by John Elliot Cairnes, which appeared in 1857, in his publication entitled <u>The Character and Logical Method of Political Economy</u>. He viewed political economy as "the science which traces the phenomena of the production and distribution of wealth up to their causes in the principles of human nature and the laws and events, physical, political, and social, of the external world." In Cairnes' more widely recognized work in 1874, <u>Some Leading Prin-</u>

ciples of Political Economy Newly Expounded, he continued to hold to the basic views of political economy found in the Classical writings of Smith, Malthus, Ricardo, McCulloch, and Mill.

Nassau Senior, who produced An Outline of the Science of Political Economy slightly prior to the middle of the nineteenth century and shortly before the summary of classical economics by J. S. Mill, was a chief advocate of narrowing the field of concern and investigation of economics, improving the terminology, and becoming more objective. In his treatise, An Outline of the Science of Political Economy, he states:

> We believe that by confining our own and the reader's attention to the Nature, Production, and Distribution of Wealth, we shall produce a more clear, and complete, and instructive work than if we allowed ourselves to wander into the more interesting and more important, but far less definite, fields by which the comparatively narrow path of Political Economy is surrounded. The questions, To what extent and under what circumstances the possession of Wealth is, on the whole, beneficial or injurious to its possessor, or to the society of which he is a member? What distribution of Wealth is more desirable in each different state of society? And What are the means by which any given Country can facilitate such a distribution?--all these are questions of great interest and difficulty, but no more form part of the Science of Political Economy, in the sense in which we use that term, than Navigation forms part of the Science of Astronomy.... The writer who pursues such investigations is in fact engaged on the great Science of legislation; a Science which requires a knowledge of the general principles supplied by Political Economy, but differs from it essentially in its subject, its premises, and its conclusions. The subject of legislation is not Wealth, but human Welfare.

In an effort to further distinguish between the subjective and the objective nature of economics, Senior comments regarding the role of the economist:

> But his conclusions, whatever be their generality and their truth, do not authorize him in adding a single syllable of advice. That privilege belongs to the writer or the statesman who has considered all the causes which may promote or impede the general welfare of those whom he addresses, not to the theorist who has considered only one, though among the most important, of those causes. The business of a Political Economist is neither

to recommend nor to dissuade, but to state general principles, which it is fatal to neglect, but neither advisable, nor perhaps practicable, to use as the sole, or even the principal, guides in the actual conduct of affairs.

When Senior made those and other statements in an effort to present the case for a more scientific approach to economics, he was one of the few who espoused the views so clearly and determinedly. But it was the gradual recognition and elaboration of such new views of the scope and method of economics which ultimately led to changing the name of this discipline from political economy to economics.

W. S. Jevons elaborated the marginal principle of economics in 1871 in his book entitled, The Theory of Political Economy. Further development of marginalism in economics and its application to the principles of production in the 1880's, together with the use of more mathematical and statistical tools, led to designating the science as "Economics," instead of "Political Economy." In the last half of the nineteenth century, in a scientific sense, the scope and method of economics broadened, but in an interdisciplinary sense it was narrowed. The economist and others associated with the economist began to view the economist's role as more objective, and more theoretical. In the 1880's and the 1890's various books appeared using the new title, "Economics." Among them were Statistica and Economics, by Mayo-Smith in 1888; Institutes of Economics, by E. B. Andrews in 1889; and Principles of Economics, by Alfred Marshall in 1890. Marshall attempted to separate the science of economics from the discipline of political economy.

It is interesting that while this determined scientific approach to economics was becoming increasingly dominant in the last quarter of the nineteenth century, dissents to Classical and Neo-Classical economics were emerging and were setting the stage for the resurfacing of "political economy" in the twentieth century. This began to occur in the writings of the Institutionalists in the United States; in the continued development of historical economics in Europe; in the gradual development of welfare economics in the Western world; and in the writings of socialists and Marxists. The trend back toward a science of "political economy" was accelerated by the economic crises of the twentieth-century industrial nations, and notably by the depression of the late twenties and early thirties. It was further promoted by the emergence of fiscal and monetary policy as stabilization tools in capitalistic economies; the taking of economists into the government in advisory capacities in ever-increasing numbers during and since the depression years; the growing size and complexity of economic specialization and interdependence; and the emergence of administered economic systems.

In 1962, M. E. Dimock's book, The New American Political Economy, observed the need for government and business to work in cooperation to provide the things needed for man's happiness. In some measure this is a new assertion of the utilitarian attitude which affected the emerging discipline of political economy in the early nineteenth century. The terms "policy," "public interest," "values," "happiness," "standard of living," "interrelationships," and others relating to a broad scope of economic concern have begun to emerge in connection with a diverging definition of economics and the proper role of the science in the developing twentieth century. In discussing the roles of public policy and political economy, Dimock suggests several possible aims for political economy, including those of creating a high standard of living; encouraging ambition and discouraging indolence; maintaining a balance of power, and avoiding an over-concentration of power; creating an environment which stimulates entrepreneurship and invention; working toward peace in the world; promoting economic stability, etc.

Walter Heller, a member of the Council of Economic Advisors to the Executive Branch of the United States government in the early 1960's, later wrote a book entitled New Dimensions of Political Economy. In it he refers to the advisory role of the Council and suggests ways that it might become more effective in policy-making. The view was expressed that the role of the political economist in the present framework could be more effective if the public and the executive officers who seek the advice of political economists were better informed on economic topics. In short, both of the recent writers on political economy in the United

States appear to believe that the role of economics could be made more effective by giving the economists in government more voice in actual policy-making. Dimock suggests a "managerial" approach which would emphasize, not manipulation of economic activity, but a type of husbandry, where a team of policy-making economists would be a permanent part of the executive decision-making process of government. He suggests coupling this with some decentralization, planning, and a safeguard for stabilization in case of emergency problems.

Those and other growing dissents to traditional economics of the twentieth century have made their imprints in some measure on the total trend in economic thinking which has been toward an ever-broadening view of the role of economics and the economist. Throughout the twentieth century this enlarging view of the scope and method of economics can be observed in summary works in economics. The contents of principles textbooks has been gradually enlarged, especially in the past two decades, to include information on problems and policies as well as principles of economics. As institutions such as labor, management, corporations, government, industries, and others have received increasingly widespread attention in the writings of economic monographs, articles, pamphlets, and other materials, these subjects have gradually created changes in the nature of standard textbooks in economics. As early as 1923, the second edition of the textbook, <u>Principles of Economics,</u> by Professor Henry Rogers Seager of Columbia University, included sections dealing with tariffs, monopolies, railways, and socialism. Since the second world war and especially in the decades of the nineteen-fifties and nineteen-sixties, textbooks have moved toward a continual broadening of their scope to include interdisciplinary subjects and increasingly to emphasize the application of economic principles to actual contemporary problems and policy. Information on problems and policy has not only been included in textbooks, but has been spotlighted in separate books of readings to accompany or supplement textbooks. This trend emphasizes growing public awareness of the economic processes and increased academic emphasis on interdisciplinary and human relationships in economics.

Microeconomics was developed in principles textbooks in the nineteenth and early twentieth centuries. Alfred Marshall's Principles synthesized into a unified whole the nineteenth century's best in economic logic and organization. Others elaborated this in the first quarter of the twentieth century, as Marshall's own work went through a series of revisions until its last edition in 1924. The publication in 1936 of John Maynard Keynes' work, The General Theory of Employment, Interest, and Money, had a very significant impact upon the content of summary works in economic analysis. In the following decade, principles textbooks began to distinguish between his macroeconomics and the traditional microeconomics, and to present both the aggregate and the atomistic approaches to economic principles. Thus, most textbooks since the 1940's have clearly evidenced a dichotomy of subject matter. This distinction in arrangement and contents of textbooks of beginning, intermediate, and advanced principles became increasingly evident in the nineteen-fifties and the sixties. This has resulted in an increasing number of separate principles publications for microeconomics and macroeconomics. Entire courses are now designed for the teaching of one or the other. This situation is evidenced at the beginning, the intermediate, and the advanced levels of principles courses. A few courses for special groups of students, such as for two-year graduates, combine micro and macro into an abbreviated treatment in one term. The separation of these approaches to analysis not only reflects the different subject matter in each, but also the vastness of each method of analyzing the economic process. During the past two decades this has caused economists to become specialized in one or the other approaches, especially at advanced levels of theorizing and where intensive mathematical or quantitative approaches have characterized the textbook and classroom presentations. A basic theoretical concern of some economic theorists now appears to be the need for integrating the two approaches into a more complete and unified theoretical system. Another contemporary concern is that of interpreting economic principles, both macro and micro, within a framework of interdisciplinary relationships, while at the same time seeking both more quantitative precision and more interpretation of human behavior.

In the nineteen-fifties and sixties principles courses have been increasingly designed to meet the needs of various types of students, such as those for engineers, educators, business majors, junior college students and others. During the nineteen-sixties, the trend toward accompanying principles books with books of readings, study guides, instructor's manuals, programmed learning books, and test-banks has accelerated. In some measure this has stemmed from the competition among publishers of textbooks, but more importantly it represents the broadening view of the scope and method of economics. The emergence of many new countries with new economic systems, and the competition between traditional market economic systems and planned or administered economic systems has caused a broadened perspective of economics and of the subject matter incorporated into textbooks. The increased public awareness of problems such as pollution, ecology, and welfare has focused the attention of many economists on the need for developing alternative policies for the solution of contemporary economic problems. The competition among economists to "publish or perish" and among publishers to sell textbooks has created competition among writers of textbooks, and caused them to broaden the scope of contents to appeal to students, the public, and professors. All of those influences together have created changes in summary works in economic analysis which make such treatises vastly different today from what they were in the first quarter of the twentieth century. Now they are more complex and more concerned with contemporary problems and policy than were textbooks in the nineteenth and early twentieth centuries.

Economists and Economics
<u></u>

Biographies and autobiographies generally include information concerning the contemporary economic conditions which have influenced or shaped the development of the thought and analysis of the economist in question. While some biographies and autobiographies focus on the life and environment of the economist or economists, others place primary emphasis on one or more ideas or theories held by the economist. Biographers of economists, as historians, are not always entirely objective in their presentation and interpretation of events and circumstances. Thus, they sometimes exercise a selective bias in presenting personal characteristics, theoretical concepts, and sequences of events. The facts of a person's life, which influence their views and ideas, include those which are both obvious and obscure. A biographer may bias the selection, presentation, and interpretation of these by his own complex of experience. Thus, the reader should be cognizant of the possibility for bias, and consider that in studying biographical material.

Many short biographical sketches of economists can be found in general works on the history of economic thought and analysis, including some of the books of readings. Biographical sketches are also included in various editions of an economist's publications, and especially the collected works of various economists. A notable example of biographical material in an editor's preface is Edwin Cannon's introduction to the 1904 edition of Adam Smith's The Wealth of Nations. Another example is in the editorial comments of Henry Higgs in the 1931 publication of Cantillon's Essai. The Encyclopedia of the Social Sciences is a useful source of biographies of economists. Articles which may be located through journal indexes are also sources of biographies of economists.

In Part II, in the sub-part (D) entitled "Economists and Economics," there are a variety of types of publications. Both articles and books are included. While most of the entries refer to a particular economist or economists, others refer to economists in general. Many of the entries cover all or a portion of the lifespan and conceptual range of a particular person. Some refer to two or more economists. A few refer to the number of economists in a particular country or period of development. Still others pertain to the conditions and nature of the work of economists in particular periods, or particular countries or areas. Also included in this sub-part are a few bibliographies. Several of these include the works of particular economists. A few refer to catalogues of the collections of private libraries of economists. In addition to including full-time economists, some of the works refer to the economic ideas of politicians, statesmen, philosophers, and others who, though not primarily economists, dealt with economic ideas, analysis and policy.

Method and Scope in Economics

A cardinal value of general and specialized histories of economic thought is their emphasis upon the development of method and scope in economics. The primary purpose of the entries in the sub-part (G), entitled "Method and Scope," found in Part II, is to demonstrate the great variety of subjects which must be considered in a comprehensive coverage of the scope and method of economics. The attitude of economists toward scope of economics was broad in the pre-Classical and early Classical periods. In an effort to make economics more scientific and more objective in the middle and late nineteenth century, the scope of ecoomics was narrowed. At the same time the methods were extended through the use of mathematical tools, marginal analysis, improved historical analysis, development of institutional analysis, and the emerging of socialist-marxist interdisciplinary approaches. The development of new methods, the elaboration of old methods, the changing nature of social and political institutions, the increased efforts to understand economic institutions, goals, problems, and policies rapidly enlarged the previously narrowed views of the scope of economics. The twentieth-century industrial developments, intermittent economic crises, political revolutions, and social demands quickly spread the teaching of academic economics throughout the world and gave rise to the need for more textbooks, monographs, articles, government economic documents, economic laws, economic research, and trained economists. This gave further impetus to the steady expansion of method and scope in economics.

To a student of economics the word "method" has the traditional connotation of referring to a way of arriving at a description or generalization concerning an economic phenomenon or a way of testing an economic hypothesis. Over the past two centuries of the development of economic thought and analysis, the word "method" in economics not only has been augmented in terms of its traditional connotation by the application of new tools of analysis, but it has taken on a complex of new implications. Not the least among these refers to the way in which economics, as an academic discipline, is taught or presented to students. "Method" in study and teaching in the mid-twentieth century carries the further consideration of the types of materials and instructional media aids which might be used to expand and accelerate the learning process.

Included in this sub-part G are articles pertaining to the roles of the economists, economic societies, and economic periodicals. Some books and articles on scope refer to the relationship between economics and other disciplines. Some treatises on scope and method refer to the relationships between principles, problems, and policies. Other treatises explain methodology in generalized and abstract terms. Still others apply a particular method to an economic problem. Some of the works describe alternative methods of conceptualizing about a particular problem.

Methods and methodological debates in economics have involved inductive methods, deductive methods, historical methods, mathematical methods, institutional methods, and various combinations of these. When the serious debates on method and scope of economics began in the middle of the nineteenth century and accelerated toward the end of the century, the names of Schmoller and Menger were prominent in writings which ensued. The historical method versus the abstract analytical method became a well-known subject of controversy in economic literature. Some of the entries in this sub-part of Part II were selected to review the controversy between the closely related historical and institutional methods on the one hand and the abstract, mathematical, and marginal methods which were swiftly gaining adherents in the latter part of the nineteenth and the early twentieth centuries. The debate over deductive method and inductive method was accelerated by an increasing reliance on mathematical or quantitative methods in the late nineteenth and early twentieth centuries. Most economists who have written textbooks or done other serious research and writing in economics have produced one or more articles, essays, lectures, or addresses relating to method and/or scope or analysis, or devoted some space in a textbook or economic monograph to one or both of those subjects. Among the economists who were especially active in early writings on scope and method were Nassau Senior, J. S. Mill, F. Y. Edgeworth, Gustav Schmoller, Cliffe Leslie, Carl Menger, Karl Knies, Frank Knight, Alfred Marshall, John Kells Ingram, Vilfredo Pareto, Irving Fisher, and John A. Hobson. The chronological gamut of authors of general and specialized histories of economic thought and analysis have also been concerned with elaborating ideas on method and scope in economics. While the deductive method was defended by J. N. Keynes, F. B. Hawley, Cliffe Leslie, and earlier economists, the accelerating inroads of quantitative analysis led to a reconciliation between the deductive advocates and the inductive advocates in writings by some economists, such as Frank Knight, Alfred Marshall, Jacob Viner and others in the late nineteenth and in the early twentieth century. They contended that the scope of economic thought is such that both the deductive and inductive methods, the historical and abstract methods, and various others have their own unique contributions to make to the total analysis of economic processes, institutions, and phenomena.

Other debates in scope and method of economics have involved such questions as the static versus dynamic theorizing in economics, in which such economists as H. Honegger, J. B. Clark, Joseph Schumpeter and others have expressed concern. The question of abstract reasoning as opposed to empirical investigation and factual evidence concerned Menger and Schmoller. Other controversies have centered around welfare versus price theories in economics, where such economists as J. A. Hobson, A. C. Pigou, R. G. Hawtrey, John Maurice Clark and others have debated. The question of considering economics as a science versus economics as an art has been a subject of debate both in the nineteenth and twentieth centuries, as has the relationship of economics to other sciences. Beginning with writings in the late Classical period, before and immediately following the middle of the nineteenth century rumblings of dissatisfaction with economic method and scope began to appear in the writings of H. J. Von Thunen, H. H. Gossen and

A. Cournot, and later became increasingly prominent in the writings of the Austrian, Lausanne, and Swedish schools of economics.

While it is impossible to cover all the ramifications of the various controversies and debates of economists concerning methods and scope, the articles and books listed should call to the attention of the researcher some of the principles and people involved in the continuously moving panorama of economic thought and analysis in the nineteenth and twentieth centuries. Most of the debate culminated in the early twentieth century in the agreement that economics is not bound to one or a few methods, but that many have validity for various purposes. As late as the nineteen-twenties, debate on economic scope and method was a relatively frequent subject of articles in journals and of lectures, essays, and addresses. In 1924 R. G. Tugwell edited The Trend of Economics, which contained thirteen essays by American economists on subjects related to scope and method of economics. In 1925 M. Pantaleoni brought together several essays on these subjects in his book, Erotemi di Economia. In 1930 H. E. Batson's bibliography, entitled A Select Bibliography of Modern Economic Theory, contained a scholarly annotated listing of works, including a section on scope and method in economics. In the 1930's the Econometric Society was founded. Since that time quantitative methods and mathematical approaches have increasingly over-shadowed and been incorporated into historical and institutional methodologies, so that approaches to methodology have become amalgamated rather than remained separated as they had when they were originating in the nineteenth century. There is still widespread concern about scope and method in economics, but it now more often evidences itself in the specialized treatments of particular subject areas in economics than in the more generalized debate which took place in the late nineteenth and early twentieth centuries.

In addition to the separately published books and articles, such as are listed in this sub-part G, all the materials listed in Part I, General Works, will have information on the scope and method of economics, as will the various publications listed in Part III, in sections relating to particular schools of economic thought and analysis. Works pertaining to the development of mathematical and statistical methods in economics will be treated more completely in Volume II, Specialization in Economic Works. A long list of prominent economists were early experimenters and innovators in mathematical and quantitative methods in economics. Among them were A. Cournot, H. H. Gossen, F. Y. Edgeworth, W. Launhart, R. Lieben, R. Auspitz, G. Cassel, K. Wicksell, G. F. Knapp, A. Wagner, and others. An extensive bibliography of writings relating to the use of mathematical methods in the nineteenth century was presented by Irving Fisher in N. T. Bacon's translation of A. Cournot's Researches into Mathematical Principles of the Theory of Wealth, published in 1897.

Pre-Classical Period

As defined for the purpose of this bibliographical collection, the pre-Classical Period encompasses a very long period of time, including the primitive, ancient, medieval, and colonial or commercial period of the history of Western Europe.

Primitive Period. At archaeological excavations throughout the world caches of materials in burials and at particular locations in town sites have evidenced the existence of economic thought and organization in primitive societies. Former village, camp, and ceremonial sites which have been excavated have yielded artifacts, imprints of structures, petrographs, carbon fragments, tools and weapons, kitchen middens, ovens, firepits, and other traces of well-defined and integrated political, economic, and social systems, many of which tended to be maintained with relatively little change over long periods of time. Ancient documents describing emerging primitive societies, together with descriptions of existing primitive societies contemporary with modern industrial economies, have indicated the existence of economic regulation as between men and women, old and young, warriors and agriculturalists and others. Primitive villages and tribes have often evidenced relationships to each other through trade over hundreds and thousands of miles, involving the transportation of raw materials and finished goods, such as stone, metal, shells, food, pipes, weapons and other articles.

Primitive, nomadic, gathering, and agricultural systems were mainly based upon productions of extractive industries. Trapping, fishing, gathering food and fibers for fabrics from the forests, and cultivating grain consumed the greater part of the day for many primitive peoples. Production of cut stone and excavated minerals at mines and quarries required economic thought and organization. The production of bowls, tools, gorgets, pipes, and a vast array of weapons and ceremonial objects required not only artistic ability and manual dexterity, but a high degree of technical skill which was only possible through specialization of economic processes and a resulting interdependence of economic activity. Such rudimentary economic systems used barter as a means of exchange and expressed economic values in terms of the relationship of one commodity to another. The study of some primitive societies indicates that they selected a particular commodity, such as shells, to serve as a medium of exchange.

Their primitive tools and weapons, plus their lack of power sources other than human or animal, often required joint efforts in the hunt and in agricultural production. That further resulted in communal systems where the land was claimed by the clan, tribe, or village, as a unit, and joint production was often engaged in, sometimes with joint storage houses. Generally there was no employment of one person by another to produce for a third; thus a wage and profit system had not developed, but there was frequently the distribution of certain goods in kind from the communal supplies of the tribe to those engaged in war or special missions or to the general populace, especially in times of ceremonial events. Fixed capital was scarce and often existed mainly in the form of personal property, such as structures, tools and weapons. Sometimes these were tribal possessions other than structures and land. Where there was trade with distant areas there was evidence of production of surplus products, over and beyond those needed for immediate consumption. There were family and tribal structures, the tools and implements of craftsmen and households, and weapons which required an initial investment of human energy and skill and materials, plus later periodic reconstruction and repair. Land for agricultural purposes was relatively more abundant for some primitive peoples than for others. The sedentary or agricultural system appears to have provided a basis upon which the highest primitive cultures were achieved, possibly because it not only made available more food, but also because it increased the diversity of products and the possibility of the accumulation of a surplus for trade.

The most common characteristic of primitive economies was their constant dependent relationship on their environments. Resources were scarce, either because of their absence, their distance, or their difficulty in acquisition. Simultaneously primitive economic systems were adapting their needs to their environments and at the same time using their environments to fill their needs. Primitive economies have differed in various parts of the earth, and at different stages of their development. Archaeological generalizations and observations about primitive economic activities are often focused on activities at particular sites during specific stages of primitive development. In the twentieth century, and particularly in the last two decades, the study of primitive economics has become more popular and scientifically pursued.

Ancient Period. This period of economic development is a popular beginning point for general histories of economic thought and analysis, which typically exclude the primitive period of development. Economic thought in the Ancient Period was expressed in the interdisciplinary writings of philosophers, politicians, historians and others. It appeared in the laws of states, in the policies and problems of governments, in the activities of households, and in the activities and administration of commercial, industrial (often craft as opposed to factory), and agricultural institutions. In the Ancient Period, the history of economic thought is advanced beyond that of primitive economies. While barter was still frequent, particular commodities, such as grain, animals, fish, metal, and others, were often designed as official mediums of exchange, were recognized easily, and were acceptable in payment of debts and taxes. The financing of government bureaucracies and wars required increasing outlays of resources and more time and emphasis on securing adequate revenues. Specialization of economic activity was widespread in commercial, industrial craft, government, and agricultural employment. Political and social orders were more complex, often influencing and being influenced by material or economic requirements. The evidence of the need for organizational structures to control and allocate scarce resources created strong city, state, and regional political affiliations. The lack of materials in regions of strong political power, and their presence in other regions of weaker political power, gave rise to migrations, wars, and expansion of trade. The presence in increasing numbers of specialized craftsmen in towns resulted in the accumulation of more fixed capital in the form of tools, structures, and inventories. Foreign trade increased the need for money for investment in ships and cargoes and to facilitate domestic exchange. Land and labor remained the major factors of production although the importance of capital increased.

It was in the Ancient Period that the beginning of the history of the roots of economic analysis took place. However, most of the economic information considered and recorded was descriptive. The Bible refers to many economic practices including the institutions of property, slavery, prices, money, inheritance, control of agricultural operations, taxation, public relief, loans and credit, commerce, tribute, usury, wealth, and others. Economic teachings in the Ancient Period were intermixed with law, ethics, religion, metaphysics, philosophy, politics, social views, and a total complex of varying ideological structures.

Writers of general histories of economic thought have been primarily concerned with exploring and explaining the economic thought of the ancient Greek philosophers, not only because their writings regarding economic observations were more advanced, but also because they later influenced the economic thought of the schoolmen of the Middle Ages. Economic doctrines expressed by the ancient Greek writers were interdisciplinary in nature, and closely related to politics, ethics and philosophical treatises. The writings of Plato which are most useful in explaining Greek economic thought are the <u>Laws</u> and the <u>Republic</u>. He recognized the existence of the division of labor and wrote about economic classes and occupations. He noted specialization in productive methods and was aware of economic interdependence. He appeared to recognize a relationship between foreign trade and surplus products. He described the institutions of slavery, money, taxation, government, wealth, commerce, and various other economic activities, but his observations were primarily descriptive rather than analytical. Though Aristotle did not produce specialized economic treatises, he displayed greater insight into economic activities and relations and gave these more logical generalizations and arrangements than previous writers had done. His observations on economics are considered to be the beginnings of the analytical approach to economic thought. In Book II of Politics and in the Nicomachaean Ethics Aristotle states his most cogent economic ideas and philosophy. His observations of general economic conditions and relationships, his discussions of the nature and uses of money, and his attempts to describe and define value are the fundamentals of his contribution to economic thought. Another Greek writer, Xenophon, who had studied with Socrates, contributed to economic thought through descriptions and observations of production, labor, commerce, public revenue, agriculture, and other subjects. His insights on economics are contained in his Oeconomicus and in The Ways and Means to Increase the Revenue of Athens.

The economic life of the Romans was more complex and widespread than that of the Greeks, but most of their writings were concerned with descriptive rather than with analytical economics. Commercial expansion, latifundia, agricultural development, land tenure, public revenue, taxation, public expenditures, property, public works, mining, quarrying, trade, handicraft industries, money, and other institutions were an everyday part of Roman economic activity. Historians who described agricultural conditions included Cato, who wrote De Re Rustica, Pliny, who produced Natural History, and others. An important source of information about economics in the Roman period is found in Roman law, such as in the Justinian Code.

Middle Ages. The Medieval or Scholastic period was another interdisciplinary era in the history of economic thought.

Economic views emerged from writings on religion, canon law, civil law, natural law, philosophy, ethics, sociology, and politics. St. Thomas Aquinas, the leading writer on and interpreter of canon law, was the major exponent of economic doctrines and their interpretation in terms of Medieval examples. He was influenced by the Greek thought in regard to value and usury in particular, but gave some original interpretations and analysis as well. These appeared in his Summa Theologica. Thomas Gilby's The Political Thought of Thomas Aquinas, published in 1958, includes information on economic thought. In 1924 A. E. Moore edited a book entitled Early Economic Thought, which remains one of the major sources of collected information about economic thought in the Middle Ages. In this he reproduces material from Nicòle Oresme's Traictie de la Première Invention des Monnoies, a famous work of Medieval economic thought. A general history of economic thought which places particular emphasis on an explanation of Medieval economic thought is Joseph A. Schumpeter's History of Economic Analysis, 1954 (reprinted, 1966). Chapter two in that work is entitled "The Scholastic Doctors and the Philosophers of Natural Law."

It was during the Middle Ages in Western Europe that the fundamental institutions of capitalism and a market economy were beginning to emerge. The guild system controlled production and pricing of commodities and services in towns. This institution probably had its roots in the Roman collegia. Laws were developing to protect private property and enforce contracts. Trade routes were being lengthened, and there was a growing need for money. The banking institutions which were emerging in Italy were extending branches into northern Europe. Credit instruments gradually came into being. The borrowing of money and the charging of interest was prevalent at trade fairs and in the towns. The various political, social, and economic changes which were causing movement were creating dissatisfaction with the institutions of feudalism, serfdom, and local control.

Commercial Period. As the Crusades, the bubonic plague, wars, and trade swept through Europe during the Middle Ages, they began to upset static institutions. Major changes were provoked by the development of towns, growth of the use of money, and the movement of people, goods, and ideas that accompanied trade. The productive, political, and social institutions of the Middle Ages began to break down as the countries of Western Europe moved into the Commercial or Colonial Period. The Hanseatic League, a German trading company of the Middle Ages which had special trading privileges in Great Britain and various other countries, was a basic step in the emergence of the joint stock companies of the Commercial Period. The guild system's inability to be flexible enough to gear production to meet the needs of growing trade led to its gradual replacement by the domestic or putting-out system, and finally by the factory system. The institutions of money, credit, the stock exchange, insurance, and fixed capital resources became increasingly important. Though labor and land still dominated in total factor use, it was during the Commercial Period that capital, interest, entrepreneurship, profit, the wage system, and other capitalistic institutions gained in strength and acceptance. It was also in this period that the influx of gold from America raised price levels in Western Europe, and created more concern for the role of money and its relationship to prices.

  The number of writings about economic subjects greatly increased in the sixteenth, seventeenth, and eighteenth centuries. These works were by traders, jurists, teachers, and others, and often took the form of pamphlets, sometimes undated. One of the more notable jurists in the sixteenth century was Carlos Molinaeus (Charles Dumoulin). Among his several publications was one entitled <u>Tractatus Contractuum et Usurarum,</u> 1546. Another sixteenth-century jurist who included in his writings observations regarding economic institutions was Jean Bodin. In his work, <u>Les Six Livres de la République</u>, 1576, he comments on public finance and mentions price changes of the sixteenth century which reflected the influx of precious metals from America. Antonio Serra of the seventeenth century produced one of the first systematic treatises reflecting Mercantilist attitudes: <u>A Brief Treatise on the Causes Which Can Make Gold and Silver Plentiful in Kingdoms Where There Are No Mines.</u> It is thought to have been written as a rebuttal, clarification and enlargement of Discorso Intorno Alli Effetti, che fa il Cambio in Regno by Marc' Antonio de Santis'. A more famous writer of the seventeenth century was Thomas Mun, a director of the East India Company of England. His first work, in 1621, was A Discourse of Trade from England into the East Indies. A better known work, possibly produced soon afterward, but not published until 1664, was entitled England's Treasure by Forraign Trade.

Another important contributor to the history of economic thought in the seventeenth century was Sir William Petty. The main subjects of his inquiries were taxes, quantification of economic matters, money, and agriculture. His most famous work is his Discourses on Political Arithmetic, 1691. Others which are primarily economic in concern were A Treatise of Taxes and Contributions, 1662; and Quantulumcunque Concerning Money, 1682. A seventeenth-century Austrian contributor to the history of economic thought was Philipp Wilhelm von Hornick. He is best known in economics for his Oesterreich über Alles. In this he proposed nine rules of national economy, and showed a perceptive understanding of the working of an economic system, i.e., some notion of the flow and interrelationship of a country's aggregate economic activity as well as some notion about inputs and outputs of productive activity. A German cameralist of the eighteenth century was Johann Heinrich Gottlob von Justi. He produced several notable works; among them was System des Finanzwesens, 1766. Richard Cantillon's Essai sur la Commerce was a notable contribution to eighteenth-century economic thought. In 1751 Ferdinanco Galiani's Della Moneta was published anonymously. In 1770 his Dialogues sur le Commerce des Blés refuted Physiocracy. David Hume, the philosopher, had an impact on economic thought in the eighteenth century through various of his writings, and in particular in passages contained in his Political Discourses, 1752. Another philosophical writing in the eighteenth century which is thought to have influenced Adam Smith's thought was Bernard de Mandeville's Fable of the Bees, 1704, 1714.

The first school of economic thought emerged in the eighteenth century in France, and is referred to as the Physiocrats.

The leader of this effort to systematize economic activities was Francois Quesnay, whose work, Tableau Economique, became the most famous single contribution and identifying symbol of the school. Among the better known economists associated with Physiocracy, but also going beyond the restrictions of their system, was Ann Robert Jacques Turgot. His best known work was Reflexions sur la Formation et la Distribution des Richesses, 1766.

The above-mentioned are some of the many works on natural law, moral philosophy, economic thought, and related subjects which probably shaped the thinking and writing of Adam Smith and led to his systematic and comprehensive treatise on political economy in 1776.

In the General Works section of sub-part H, The Pre-Classical Period, many of the entries are from the nineteenth-century bibliographies of McCulloch and Blanqui, and all pertain to that period of time following the Middle Ages and preceding the publication of Adam Smith's synthesis of economics in 1776. It is the period sometimes referred to as the "commercial revolution" from approximately 1450-1775, which includes the seventeenth and eighteenth century advances in agricultural methods in England and Western Europe.

Mercantile practices controlled economic activity. These included the body of laws, rules, charters, duties, taxes, and other regulations of economic activity by national and local control. While much of the local control of economic activity present in the Middle Ages had been broken by growing national power, some of it remained. Summary works describing the loose-knit, but relatively total system of economic control are listed under the section entitled Mercantilism. Major among them is the comprehensive work of Eli Heckscher entitled Mercantilism, first published in 1931.

During those several centuries of awakening world trade and colonialism, as new areas were discovered and colonized, more capital was required, the need for credit expanded, money became essential, new means of production were sought to increase the flow of goods for foreign and domestic trade, new social classes were formed, towns grew, and the factory system gradually emerged. The concept of a system of economics also slowly emerged, and the discipline of political economy began to be separated from the interdisciplinary maze in which it had theretofore been entangled. This emergence of political economy was a product of jurists, philosophers, moneylenders, politicians, traders, and professors.

In the beginning of the commercial period, publications tend to relate more to fragmentary economic activity and to activity important to particular persons or groups. By the middle of the eighteenth century, the total aspect of economic activity as associated with nations had come to the attention of government officials, legislators, and businessmen. There was an awareness of the division of labor, the use of new power sources, such as steam, and an international perspective replaced the more restricted national views.

Among the general works in the history of economic thought which describe economic thought and analysis prior to 1800 are the following: Heinrich Contzen, Geschichte der Volkswirthschaftlichen Literatur im Mittelalter unter Berücksichtigung der Mittelalterlichen Staatslehre. (2d ed., 1872); Vito Cusumano, Saggi di Economia Politica e di Scienza delle Finanze (2d. ed., 1887); Pierre Dockès, L'Espace dans la Pensée Economique du XVIe au XVIIIe Siècle (1969); Wilhelm Endemann, Studien in der Romanisch-Kanonistischen Wirtschafts- und Rechtslehre bis Gegen Ende des Siebenzehnten Jahrhunderts (1874); Jan Stanislaw Lewiński, Twórcy Economji Politycznej (Fizjokraci--Smith--Ricardo) Wstep do Historji Doktryn Ekonomicznych (1920); Lev Matveevich Mordukhovich, Ocherki Istorii Ekonomicheskikh Uchenii (1957); and Otto Neurath, Zur Anschauung der Antike über Handel, Gewerbe und Landwirtschaft (1906).

Classical Period

The term "Classical Period" is used here to refer to that period of time from 1776-1859, when under the influence of Adam Smith's Wealth of Nations and other doctrines emerging from the Classical School, England, in particular, moved gradually away from the controls of mercantilism toward freer trade. Business men, parliament, government officials, and the public became increasingly aware of the numerousness and complexity of economic problems. Contemporary writings in this period described economic conditions and theorized about them, in simple as well as complex reasoning. In this period political economists first attempted to describe the history of economic thought in summary works, first produced text books on the principles of political economy, and first wrote general and institutional works of economic history.

It was a period when there were many conflicts of interest between colonial powers and new nations, which produced domestic and international tensions not entirely unlike those of today. The new nations, freed from colonial power and old nations, then recently united or at an early stage in economic development, needed capital to develop their resources, to become specialized in production and trade, and to make possible jobs and income for their unemployed. Changes in techniques and processes were introduced into many industries, including the textile and iron industries. Water and steam power were being rapidly substituted for horse and human power. The discovery of the efficiency of interchangeable parts was revolutionizing production.

England was jealous of her supremacy in industrialization and attempted to protect her know-how. At the same time she needed and attempted to impose freer international trade to accommodate her growing flow of manufactured trade goods and services. Young nations, being sensitive to their independence and knowing the need for industrialization, pressed for policies of protection for infant industries. Agricultural changes were making possible greater production of farm products in Europe which together with mounting supplies from virgin lands in America began to give rise to surpluses in the world markets and to demands for and debates regarding protection of agricultural as well as industrial production.

Although the specific economic problems in Europe and America were different because of different environmental conditions and different stages in economic development, there were many basic similarities. While American and German economic thought frequently focused on the question of industrial protection,

England was torn by disputes for protection to agriculture, as symbolized in the corn law debates. Everywhere governments needed revenue, and surveyed the tariff as a possible source of funds. Expanding transportation and communication facilities internally and externally presented worldwide challenges. Already the ideological debate had begun, as to the necessary and desirable extent of the role of government in the control and ownership of the means of production. Employees were becoming isolated from their employers and the final products they produced as the size of economic units expanded. Labor in industrializing nations was beginning to organize and to express its resistance to unfettered private enterprise.

Financial institutions were increasingly requiring special treatment in statutory and administrative pronouncements, as protection of capital and the public interest were fostered. Human and mechanical division of labor was making possible specialization of production and trade and becoming the universal symbol of economic development based on the application of capital to industrial processes. The growing need for occupational skills and the growing national economic competition evidenced the need for the rapid development of human resources through public as well as private educational systems. Free versus slave labor was a particular problem of the Americas. It had ordered the economic system, was creating a growing surplus of raw cotton and inciting a resultant speculation and fluctuation in world commodity prices. Money, credit, and banking were major economic concerns everywhere as distortions in price levels and fluctuations in economic activity developed with the transfer of economic activities from primarily agricultural to industrial bases.

The growth of cities progressed with the attendant problems of housing, transportation, communication, public services and increase of government expenses. As major nations throughout the earth entered the race to industrialize, the need to strengthen their ties of colonialism as a means of expanding the dimensions of their domestic markets for industrial products was an anachronism in a world in which the philosophy of laissez-faire began to pervade the thoughts of the public and the statutes of government. The scope of commercial treaties expanded and bilateral negotiations rather than armed intervention into economic affairs of other nations became the more realistic course of action for major powers.

In the period 1776-1860, the world was growing closer together. At the same time, there was the increasing demand for the adoption of the new economic philosophy--laissez-faire; nations were confronted by the rapidly growing need for prudent regulation of economic activity to increase the realities of freedom within an increasingly close-knit economic structure. Nations were depending more and more on specialization to increase productivity, raise the standard of living, and make possible the accumulation of fixed capital assets to be used in further moving the bases of economic activity to higher levels of production.

Post-Classical Period

This refers to the period of time from approximately 1860 to the present. It includes that part of the nineteenth century when economics textbooks and other general treatises began to reflect the influence of the dissents to classical doctrines. A diverse body of economic literature has been produced during this period which greatly widened the scope and method of economic thought. The nineteenth-century writings culminated in the work of Alfred Marshall. His eclectic approach to the mainstream of economic thinking was carried forward into the twentieth-century through reprints of his textbook and the work of his students and admirers. Other forces moving economic thought and analysis swiftly into a twentieth-century environment of more rapid change were the many dissenting views which had their roots in the early nineteenth century. These included Historicism, Institutionalism, Socialism and Marxism, Mathematical economics, Marginalism, Marshallian economics and Keynesian economics. Since many references have been made to post-Classical economists and their writings in other parts of this Introduction, there will be no further elaboration of the post-Classical Period, as many of the treatises and ideas which have characterized it have already been mentioned in various parts of the foregoing material. For clarity in presenting the dissents to Classical economics, six sub-sections under Specific Works have been added to the section on General Works under the main sub-part K, Post-Classical Period.

PART I

GENERAL WORKS

A. CHRONOLOGICAL AND SUBJECT SURVEYS

1. ABE, Gen'ichi. Keizaigaku hattatsu-shi; Kodai yari Gendai. (Transliterated.) Tôkyô, Hakutô-shobô, 1958. 375 p. (First edition, 1950: Keizaigaku shi Gairon. Edition, 1962: Keigaigaku hattatsu shi. 401 p.)
2. AGUILAR, Monteverde, Alonso. Economía política y lucha social. México, Editorial nuestro tiempo, 1970. 292 p.
3. AGUIRRE, Manuel Agustín. Apuntes para el estudio de la historia del pensamiento económico. Quito, Editorial universitaria, 1958-62. 2 v. (v. 2: Los clásicos y Marx.)
4. AKERMAN, Johan Henrick. "Instrumental doktrinhistoria." In, Ekonomiska samfundets tidskrift (July, 1955) 79-100.
5. _____. Nationalekonomiens utveckling. (Samhällsvetenskapliga studier, 6.) Lund, C. W. K. Gleerup, 1951. 180 p. Bibliographical notes.
6. ALBERT, H. "Zur interpretation des ökonomischen modelldenkens." In, Jahrbücher für nationalökonomie und statistik 180, 6 (July, 1967) 520-532.
7. ALBREGTS, A. H. M. De leer der maatschappelijk economische organisatievormen, een onderzoek naar de inhoud van de leer der maatschappelijk economische organisatievormen in de economische wetenschap, en meer in het bijzonder naar de factoren, die de wijzigingen in de organisatievormen bepalen. Amsterdam, Elsevier, 1949. 332 p. Bibliography, 323-330. (Also issued as a thesis: Roomsch katholieke handelshoogeschool. Tilburg, Netherlands.)
8. AL-FAKKAK, Muhammad Ahmad. Usūl 'ilm al-iqtisād. (Transliterated.) 1964. 143 p. Bibliography, 141-142.
9. ALTHEIM, F. Utopie und wirtschaft; eine geschichtliche Betrachtung. Frankfurt am Main, Klostermann, 1957. 266 p.
10. ALTMANN, Sally. Studien zur lehre vom geldwert. Beiträge zur geschichte und kritik der geld- und werttheorie. (Abschnitt 2, kapitel 2, 2.) Berlin, Druck von E. Ebering, g. m. b. h., 1906. 34 p., 1 l. (Inaugural dissertation, Berlin.)
11. ALVIM, Decio Ferraz. História das doutrimas econômicas. 2 ed. Petrópolis, Vôzes, 1965. 111 p.
12. AMONN, Alfred. Die klassische und die moderne nationalökonomie; rektoratsrede. (Berner rektoratsreden.) Bern, P. Haupt, 1949. 21 p.
13. ANTONELLI, Etienne. Etudes d'économie humaiste. Paris, Sirey, 1957, i. e. 1958. v. Bibliographical footnotes.
14. ARNDT, Heinz Wolfgang. Gli insegnamenti economici del decennio 1930-1940. Traduzione di Bruno de Angelis. (Biblioteca di cultura economica, 10) Torino, 1949. xi, 510 p.

15. ASSER, Tobias Michael Carel. Verhandeling over het staathuishoudkundig begrip der waarde. (Faculteit der regtsgeleerdheid aan de Hoogeschool te Leiden.) Amsterdam, J. Muller, 1858. viii, 287 p. Bibliographical footnotes.
16. AUDIGIER, Pierre. Economie politique et politique économique. Paris, Editions technip, 1970. 275 p.
17. AUVERT, Enrique. Democracia militante. Caracas, Editorial Arte, 1963. 239 p.
18. BAKASOVA, R. Iz istorii ekonomischeskoĭ mysli v Turkmenistane.) Ashkabad, Turkmenistan, 1961. 89 p. Bibliography.
19. BALDWIN, Armand Jean. A history of economic thought. Latrobe, Pennsylvania, Archabbey press, 1963. 210 l. Bibliography.
20. BARBER, William J. A history of economic thought. (Pelican.) Harmondsworth, Penguin, 1967. 266 p. Paperback. Bibliography, 261-265. (New York, Praeger, 1968, c1967.)
21. BARBIERI, Gino. Problemi economici di ieri e di oggi. (Classe unica, 49.) Torino, Edizioni radio italiana, 1956. 83, 5 p. Bibliography, 85.
22. BARRERE, Alain. Cours d'analyse économique contemporaine, rédigé d'après les notes, D. E. S. 1967-1968. Sciences économiques. Paris, les Cours de droit, 1968. 130 p. Bibliography, 8-16. (D. E. S. 1965-1966. Paris, 1966. 220 p.)
23. ———. Cours d'histoire de la pensée économique. Les Relations de fonctionnement dans l'analyse contemporaine. Rédigé d'après les notes et avec l'autorisation de Alain Barrère. D. E. S., sciences économiques, histoire du droit, 1964-1965. Paris, Cours de droit, 1965. 229 p. Bibliography, 7. (D. E. S. 1963-1964. Paris, 1964. 167 p.)
24. BARTOLI, Henri. "Chronique de la pensée économique en Italie." In, Revue économique (Paris) 8, 1 (January, 1957) 146-152; 3, 8 (May, 1957) 490-493; 8, 6 (November, 1957) 1075-1080; 12, 4 (July, 1961) 645-654.
25. ———. Cours d'histoire de la pensée économique, rédigé d'après la sténotypie du cours et avec l'autorisation. Licence 3e année, 1959-1960. Paris, Cours de droit, 1960. 988 p.
26. BARTOS, E. and J. Dančo. "Nové javy v súčasnej buržoáznej politickej ekonómii." In, Eknomicky casopis, 9, 1 (1961) 63-85.
27. BAUDIN, Jean Pierre Louis. Précis d'histoire des doctrines économiques, conformé au programme de la partie générale du Diplôme d'études supérieures d'économie politique de la Faculté de droit de Paris. 3. edition. Paris, Domat-Montchrestien, 1943. 3, 9-280 p. Bibliography, 271-273.
28. BAUMOL, William J. Welfare economics and the theory of the state. (London school of economics and political science publications series.) 2nd edition. Cambridge, Harvard university press, 1965.
29. BAXA, Jakob. Geschichte der produktivitätstheorie Jena, G. Fischer, 1926. 3 p., 1, 159, 1 p. Bibliographical footnotes.

30. BECKWITH, Burnham Putnam. The economic theory of a Socialist economy. New York, Greenwood press, 1968. viii, 444 p. (First edition: Stanford, California, Stanford university press, c 1949. viii, 444. Bibliography, 431-435.)
31. BEGANDO, Joseph Sheridan. A study of the refinements in the incidents of business ownership from the medieval period to the twentieth century. Urbana, 1951. 16 p. (Thesis abstract. University of Illinois.)
32. BEHRENS, H. H. De ontwikkeling in het economisch denken (Aula-boeken, 427.) Utrecht, Het Spectram, 1969. 512 p. Bibliographical references.
33. BELL, John Fred. A history of economic thought. New York, Ronald press company, 1953. x, 696 p. (2nd edition, 1967. iii, 745 p. Bibliographical references.)
34. BELTRAN Flórez, Lucas. Economistas modernos. (Colección "Duran y Bas"; textos de derecho, legislación y economia, 1.) Barcelona, Editorial teide, 1951. 179 p.
35. ———. Historia de las doctrinas económicas. Barcelona, Teide, 1961. 376 p. Bibliography, 373-376.
36. BERCKUM, Joh. Jos. Das staatsschuldenproblem im liche der klassischen nationalökonomie. Ein beitrag zur geschichte und theorie des staatsschuldenwesens. Leipzig, A. Deichert, 1911. x, 243 p. Bibliography, 239-243.
37. BERGMANN, Eugen Von. Die wirtschaftskrisen. Geschichte der nationalökonomischen krisentheorieen. Stuttgart, W. Kohlhammer, 1895. viii, 440 p. Bibliographical footnotes.
38. BERLIN, Pavel Abramovich. Ocherk razvitiia ekonomicheskikh uchenii. (Transliterated.) Saint Petersburg, 1906. 77 p.
39. BERLIN-NEUBART, Ilse Veronika. Die stellung des Hugo Grotius in der geschichte der national-ökonomie. Erlangen, K. B. Hof- und universität-sbuchdruckerei von Junge & Sohn, 1912. vi, 57. Bibliography, iii-iv.
40. BERNARD, Michel. Introduction à une sociologie des doctrines économiques; des physiocrates à Stuart Mill. (Société mouvements sociaux et ideologies. 1. ser.: Etudes, 7.) Paris, Mouton, 1963. 270 p. Bibliography, 257-261.
41. BEUTIN, L. Einführung in die wirtschaftsgeschichte. Köln, Böhlau, 1958. 179 p.
42. BHATNAGAR, K. P. A history of economic thought. Kanpur, Kishore publishing house, 1957. 421 p.
43. BIANCHINI, Lodovico. Della scienza del ben vivere sociale e della economia degli stati. Parte storica e di preliminari dottrine. Palermo, Stamperia di F. Lao, 1845. xvi, 508 p. Bibliographical text. (Continued by the author's Principi della scienza del ben vivere sociale e della economia pubblica d degli stati, 1855.)
44. BINDER, Hanni. Das sozialitäre system Eugen Dührings. (Beiträge zur geschichte der nationalökonomie. . . . 8.hft.) Jena, G. Fischer, 1933. viii, 112 p. Bibliography, 109-112.

45. BLAUG, Mark. Economic theory in retrospect. Homewood, Illinois, R. D. Irwin, 1962. 633 p. (Reviewed by W. R. Allen, American economic review, 53-1, Part I (March, 1963) 173-174. Bibliographical references. (2nd edition, London, Heinemann Educational, 1968. xxiv, 710 p. Bibliographical references.)
46. BLEDEL, Rodolfo. Ideología y método en la ciencia económica. (Centroplan ediciones, 1.) Buenos Aires, Centroplan ediciones, 1968. 109 p. Bibliographical references.
47. BLIUMIN, Izrail Grigor'evich. Istoriia ekonomicheskikh uchenii. (Transliterated.) Moscow, 1961. 266 p. Bibliography.
48. _____. Istorija ekonomičeskih učenij; očerki teorii. (Transliterated.) Moscow, 1961. 268 p.
49. _____. Krizis sovremennoj buržuaznoj političeskoj ekonomii. (Transliterated.) Moscow, Izdatel'stvo instituta meždunarodnyh otnošenij, 1959. 563 p.
50. _____. O sovremennoj buržuaznoj političeskoj ekonomii. (Transliterated.) Moscow, Socekgiz, 1958. 160 p.
51. _____. Sub'ektivnaia shkola v politicheskoi ekonomii. (Transliterated.) Moscow, 1928. 2 v.
52. BLOCK, Maurice. Les progrès de la science économique depuis Adam Smith; revision des doctrines économiques. 2. édition considérablement augm. Paris, Guillaumin & Cie company, 1897. 2 v.
53. BOARDMAN, Fon Wyman. Economics; ideas and men. New York, H. Z. Walck, 1966. 133 p. Bibliographies.
54. BOCCARDO, Gerolamo. L'economia politica moderna e la sociologia; raccolta delle prefazioni dettate per la biblioteca dell' economista. Torino, Unione tipografico-editrice, 1883. 447 p.
55. _____. Historia del comercio, de la industria y de la economía política. 1. ed. argentina, ajustada a su texto original. Buenos Aires, Rep. Arg., Editorial impulso, 1942. 448 p. Bibliography, 443-448. (Translation of: Manuale di storia del commercio, delle industrie e dell' economia politica.)
56. BODDA, Piero e Arturo Masoero. Economia e diritto nello stato fascista. Ad uso delle scuole medie superiori. Torino, Editrice libraria italiana, 1941. 191 p. Bibliography, 119-125.
57. BONAR, James. Philosophy and political economy in some of their historical relations. London: Swann, Sonnerschein and company; New York, The Macmillan company, 1893. (2nd. edition, 1909. 3rd. edition, London, George Allen and Unwin limited, 1922. 2, vii-xvii, 3-424 p. Bibliographical footnotes. Reprinted: Reprints of Economics classics. New York, A. M. Kelley, 1966. xvi, 410 p. Bibliographical footnotes. Reprinted: Muirhead library of philosophy series, Humanities, 1967. London, Allen and Unwin; New York, Humanities press, 1967. 5, v-xvi, 410 p. Bibliographical references.)
58. BONNER, T. N., D. W. Hill, and G. L. Wilber. The

contemporary world; the social sciences in historical perspective. Englewood Cliffs, New Jersey, Prentice-Hall, 1960. 594 p.
59. BORCHARDT, Ralph Waldo. Grundzüge der wirtschaftsgeschichte. 6., durchges Aufl. Wolfenbüttel, Heckner, 1967. 164 p.
60. BORDEWIJK, Hugo Willem Constantijn. Theoretischhistorische inleiding tot de economie. Groningen, J. B. Wolters, 1931. 3, 652 p. Bibliography, 639-650.
61. BOTS, Aloysius Cornelis Antonius Maria. De vervolmaking van de maatschappij volgens de klassieke economen. Helmond, Drukkerij Helmond, 1968. 232 p. Bibliography, 213-220.
62. BOUCKE, Oswald Fred. The development of economics, 1750-1900. New York, The Macmillan company, 1921. vi, 348 p. Bibliography, 329-342.
63. BOULDING, K. E. "La grande trasformazione economica del tempo nostro." In, Mondo aperto II, 6, (December 1957) 353-359.
64. BOURTHOUMIEUX, Charles. Le mythe de l'ordre naturel en economie politique depuis Quesnay. Paris, M. Riviere, 1935. 3, iii-viii, 140 p. Bibliography, 137-140. (Published also under title: Essai sur le fondement philosophique des doctrines économiques, Rousseau contre Quesnay. Paris, 1936. Thèse, Universite de Paris.)
65. BOUSQUET, Georges Henri. Evolución del pensamiento económico; con una crítica científica de las ideas económicas de Carlos Marx. México, D. F., Editorial "Cosmos," 1938. 157 p.
66. BOUVIER-AJAM, Maurice Jean. Traite d'economie politique et d'histoire de doctrines économiques. Paris, Plon, 1950-54. 3 v.
67. BOWMAN, M. J. "The human investment revolution in economic thought." In, Sociology of education, 39, 2, (Spring, 1966) 111-137.
68. BRAHMANANDA, P. R. The new classical versus the neoclassical economics. Standpoints at the glow of a circular revolution. (1st edition. Mysore.) Prasaranga, University of Mysore, 1967. xxxvii, 287 p. Bibliography, 284-288.
69. BRIEFS, Goetz. Untersuchungen zur klassischen nationalökonomie, mit be-sonderer berücksichtigung des problems der durchschnitts-profitrate. Jena, G. Fischer, 1915. 5, 3-283 p.
70. BROUILHET, Charles. Le conflit des doctrines dans l'économie politique contemporaine. Paris, F. Alcan, 1910. viii, 306 p.
71. BRUGELMANN, Hermann. Politische ökonomie in kritischen Jahren: die Friedrich List-Gesellschaft e. V. von 1925-1935. Mit einer einleitung von Edgar Salin: In memoriam Bernard Harms. (Veröffentlichungen der List Gesellschaft, Bd. 1.) Tübingen, Mohr, 1956. xix, 192 p.
72. BRUGMANS, Izaak Johannes. Wendingen in de economische geschiedenis, rede uitgesproken bij de aanvaarding van het ambt van hoogleraar aan de universiteit van Amsterdam op

20 October 1947. Groningen, J. B. Wolters, 1947. 27 p. Bibliographical references, 25-27.
73. BRUSCA, Vittorio Emanuele. Dol mercantilismo al corporativismo fascista, con un' appendice sull' ordinamento costituzionale e amministrativo dello stato italiano e sulla dottrina fascista dello stato. Catania, Anonima editionale italiana, 1937. 190 p., 1 l.
74. BRUTON, H. J. "Contemporary theorizing on economic growth." In, B. F. Hoselitz, et al. Theories of economic growth. Glencoe, Illinois, The Free press, 1960. pp. 239-298.
75. BUCHANAN, James M. Cost and choice. An inquiry into economic theory. (Markham economics series.) Chicago, Markham publishing company, 1969. xv, 104 p. Bibliographical footnotes.
76. BUCKINGHAM, W. S. Theoretical economic systems; a comparative analysis. New York, Ronald press company, 1958. 518 p.
77. BUDGE, Siegfried. Das Malthus 'sche bevölkerungsgesetz und die theoretische nationalökonomie der letzten jahrzehnte. Karlsruhe i. B., G. Braun, 1912. 2, 221 p.
78. BUDINOVA, Rita, Oldrich Kýn and Václav Müller. Kapitoly ke studiu dějin ekonomických teorií. Vyd. I. Praha, Státní pedagogické nakl., 1964. 2 v. Bibliographical footnotes.
79. BUDISH, Jacob M. Is communism the next stage? A reply to Kremlinologists. New York, International publishers, 1965. 128 p. Bibliography.
80. BUKHARIN, Nikolai Ivanovich. The economic theory of the leisure class. London, Martin Lawrence, 1927? 220 p. Bibliography, 211-215.
81. BUNGE, Nikolai Khristianovich. Esquisses de littérature politico-économique. Translated: du russe, avec un portrait de l'auteur. Bâle et Genève, Georg et company, 1898. xliii, 455 p. Bibliographical footnotes. Bibliography (xxxv-xxxviii). (Saint Petersburg, 1895. 1 p. l., vi, 465 p. Bibliographical footnotes.) (Reprinted: Research and source works series, no. 204, B. Franklin, 1969.)
82. BUNKE, Harvey Charles. The liberal dilemma. Englewood Cliffs, New Jersey, Prentice-Hall, 1964. xii, 339 p.
83. CADET, Félix. Histoire de l'économie politique. Les précurseurs. Boisguilbert. Vauban. Quesnay. Turgot. Reims, H. Gérard; Paris, E. Lacroix, 1869. 3, 248 p. (Reprinted: Research and source series, No. 503, B. Franklin, 1970. Similar title reprinted by B. Franklin, 1969.)
84. CAFFE, F. Economisti moderni. Milano, Garzanti, 1962. 306 p.
85. CAIRNES, John Elliott. Some leading principles of political economy newly expounded. New York, Harper and brothers, 1874. 2, 421 p.
86. CALKINS, Robert De Blois. Economics as an aid to policy. Los Angeles, University of Southern California, Graduate school of business administration, 1963. 28 p. Bibliographical footnotes.

87. CAMPOS, Roberto de Oliveira. Ensaios de história econômica e sociologia. Rio de Janeiro, APEC editôra, 1963. 198 p.
88. CANNAN, Edwin. The economic outlook. London, T. F. Unwin, 1912. 312 p.
89. _____. A review of economic theory. London, P. S. King and son, limited, 1929. x, 448 p. (Reprinted: With a new introduction by B. A. Corry. London, Frank Cass and company, 1964. 448 p. Spanish edition entitled: Repaso a la teoría económica versión de Javier Marquez. México, Fondo de cultura económica, 1940. 2, vii-viii, 423 p. Reprint of economic classics, New York, A. M. Kelley, 1969?)
90. CAPODAGLIO, Giulio. Breve storia dell'economica. Milano, A. Giuffrè, 1968- . v. Bibliography: v. 1 (259-280). (Previous editions entitled: Sommario di storia delle dottrine economiche.)
91. _____. Sommario di storia delle dottrine economiche. 3. ed. Milano, A. Giuffrè, 1945. 1 p. l., v-vi p. 1 l., 257 p. Bibliografica, 227-249. (4th revised edition, 1958. 259 p.)
92. CARLI, Filippo. Studi di storia delle dottrine economiche. Padova, A. Milani, 1932. 2, 147 p. Bibliographical footnotes.
93. CARLIN, Edward Augustine. The relationships between the major economic philosophies since Adam Smith and those expressed by the Supreme court. (Thesis--New York university.) Ann Arbor, University microfilms, 1950, i.e. 1951. Publication no. 2175. Bibliography, 538-549.
94. CARRERA Pujal, Jaime. La evolución de las ideas y las luchas sociales; prólogo de Pedro Gual Villalbí. Barcelona, Bosch, 1940. 454 p.
95. _____. Per un ordre polític i econòmic; democràcia o dictadura? Economia individual o corporativa? Pròleg de Bartomeu Amengual. Barcelona, Llibreria catalònia, 1935. 2, vii-xx, 398 p.
96. CASAS GRIEVE, Luis Felipe de las. Liberalismo económico; mito y realidad de una doctrine. Lima Secretariado nacional de propaganda del P. A. P., 1959. 75 p.
97. CASTELAIN, L. Economie politique et sociale. L'évolution de la pensée économique, essai de théorie positive des valeurs et des prix. Préface du vicomte van de Vijvere. 1953. 180 p. Bibliography, 172-173.
98. CASTELOT, E. Introduction to Rogers, Interprétation économique de l'histoire. Paris, 1892.
99. CATLIN, W. B. The progress of economics; a history of economic thought. New York, Bookman associates, 1962. 788 p.
100. CETTI, Carlo. Dell'economia politica. (Scritti, 7). Como, 1958. 79 p.
101. CHALK, A. F. "Relativist and absolutist approaches to the history of economic theory." In, Southwestern social science quarterly, 48, 1 (June, 1967) 5-12.
102. CHAMBERLAIN, Neil W. A general theory of economic process. New York, Harper, 1955. 370 p.

Chronological and Subject Surveys 9

103. CHANG, Yu-shan. Ching chi ssu hsiang shih. (Transliterated). China, 1940. 4, 2, 274 p.
104. CHASE, Stuart. The economy of abundance. (Kennikat press scholarly reprints. Series on economic thought, history and challenge.) Port Washington, N. Y., Kennikat press, 1971. vii, 327 p.
105. CHATAWAY, Helen Drinkwater. Economics and life. Toronto, Ryerson press, 1948. xiv, 222 p.
106. CHEVALIER, Jean. Doctrines économiques. Paris, Perspectives, 1945. vii-viii, 371 p.
107. CHIGUSA, Yoshindo, Keizai genron. (Transliterated.) Japan, 1948. 2, 6, 333 p. Bibliographical footnotes.
108. CHIKARAISHI, Sadakuzu. Tenkeiki no keizai shisō. (Transliterated.) Japan, 1967. 254 p. Bibliographical references.
109. CHIN, T'ien-hsi. Ching chi ssu hsiang fa chan shih. (Transliterated.) China, 1937. 3, 9, 7, 575, 37 p. Bibliography, 33-36.
110. CHO, Ki-Jun. Sin kyŏngjesa. (Transliterated.) 1961. 346, 10 p. Bibliography, 333-346. (Previously published under another title.)
111. CHO, Moriyoshi. Keizaigaku shi. (Transliterated.) Japan, 1963. xi, 369, 4 p. Bibliography, 104.
112. _____. Kyoshi no tame no keizaigaki kōgi. (Transliterated.) Japan, 1950-51. 2 v.
113. CHO, S. Nihon keizai shisô-shi kenkyu. (Transliterated.) Tokyo, Mirai-sha, 1963. 277 p.
114. CHO, Tong-p'il. Sin kyongjehak sa. (Transliterated.) Korea, 1962. 452, 5 p. Bibliography.
115. CHODKIEWICZ, Zygmunt and Seweryn Zurawicki. Historia myśli ekonomicznej; zagadnienia wybrane. SKRYPT. Warszawa, Państwowe wydawn. naukowe, 1962. 208 p.
116. CH'OE, Mun-hwan. Kyŏngjesa. (Transliterated.) Korea, 1960. 515 p.
117. CHOUMANIDES, Lazaros Th. Ta dogmata tēs oikonomikés. (Transliterated.) 1959. 67 p. Bibliography, 5-6.
118. _____. Hē theórēsis tou oikonomikou problematos. 1958. 66 p.
119. CHRIST, Werner. Allgemeine volkswirtschaftslehre. Geschichte der volkswirtschaftslehre. Geldkredit-bank-börse. Berlin, M. Galle, 1929. 2 p. l., 3-176 p. Bibliography, 168.
120. CHUPROV, Aleksandr Ivanovich. (History of economics.) 1898. 1, 122 p. (Published 1889-1891.)
121. _____. Istoriia politicheskoi ekonomii. (Transliterated.) 7th edition. 1913. 2 l., 223 p. Bibliographical footnotes. (8th edition, 1918. 2 l., 223 p.)
122. CLAEYS, R. H. Overzicht van de evolutie der economische theorieëm van de oudheid tot heden. Gent, Leuven, E. Story-Scientia, 1970. xi, 417 p. Bibliography, 407, 408.
123. CLARK, J. M. "Recent developments in economics." In, Recent developments in the social sciences, (Philadelphia, Lippincott, 1927) 213-306.

124. COHN, Gustav. A history of political economy. Translated by Dr. Joseph Adna Hill. With an introductory note by Edmund Janes James. Philadelphia, 1894. 142 p. (Supplement to the Annals of the American academy of political and social science. March 1894.)
125. ———. Zur geschichte und politik des verkehrswesens. Stuttgart, F. Enke, 1900. vi, 524 p.
126. COLE, Arthur Harrison. The historical development of economic and business literature. (Publication of the Kress library of business and economics, no. 12.) Boston, Baker Library, Harvard graduate school of business administration, 1957. 56 p.
127. COLE, Charles L. Economic fabric of society. New York, Harcourt, Brace and world, 1969. x, 246 p.
128. COLE, George Douglas Howard. Economic tracts for the times. London, Macmillan and company, limited, 1932. 327 p.
129. ———. "Towards a new economic theory." A: In, Economic tracts for the times, 1932. B: In, Studies in world economics, 1934.
130. COLINS, Jean Guillaume César Alexandre Hippolyte. L'économie politique; source des révolutions et des utopies prétendues socialistes. Paris, Librairie générale, 1856- . v.
131. CONACCALAM, K. S. Porulātārac cintanai varalāru. (In Tamil.) 1962. 223 p.
132. CONRAD, Ernst Johannes. Grandriss zum studium der politischen oekonomie. Jena, G. Fischer, 1900. v. (1910 publication, with bibliographies.)
133. ———. Historia de la economía; trad. directa del alemán por el prof. dr. J. Algarra. Madrid, V. Suárez, 1941. 301 p. Bibliographies.
134. CONTZEN, Karl Wilhelm Heinrich. Geschichte der volkswirthschaftlichen literatur im mittelalter unter berücksichtigung der mittelalterlichen staatslehre. 2. verm. aufl. Berlin, L. Heimann, 1872. 4 p., l. 246 p.
135. CORRADO, G. Baccio. La bomba H dell'economia. Genova, Società editrice mercantile, 1955. xiii, 310 p. (English edition entitled: The H-bomb of economics. Illustrated by Andel. London, distributed by W. Dawson, 1957. 247 p.
136. COSSA, Luigi. L'economia politica nella spegna, nel Portogallo, nel Belgio e nei Paesi Bassi. Bologna, Tipografia fava e garagnani, 1891. 24 p. Bibliography.
137. ———. Guida allo studio dell' economia politica. Milano, U. Hoepli, 1876. viii, 261 p. (3rd edition revised and enlarged, subtitled: Introduzione allo studio dell' economia politica. Milan, 1892. English edition entitled: Guide to the study of political economy. Translated from the 2nd Italian edition with a preface by W. Stanley Jevons. London, Macmillan and company, 1880. xvi, 237 p. Bibliographies. English edition entitled: An introduction to the study of political economy. Revised by the author and translated from the Italian by Louis Dyer. London and New York,

Chronological and Subject Surveys 11

Macmillan and company, 1893. x, 587 p. Bibliography, 4-5.)
138. _____. Histoire des doctrines economiques. Avec une preface de A. Deschamps. Paris, V. Giard et E. Brière, 1899. xii, 574 p. Bibliography, 7-8.
139. COSTA, Augusto de Macedo Sá da. Sobre alguns problemas da teoria das cadeias de mercados. Lisboa, 1947. 93 p.
140. COURCELLE Seneuil, Jean Gustave. Traité theórique et pratique d'economie politique. Paris, 1858. 2 v. (2nd edition, 1867. 2 v.; 3rd edition, 1891. 2 v.)
141. COURTIN, René. Cours de théorie économique rédigé d'après la sténotypie du cours et avec l'authorisation de M. Courtin. Diplômes d'études supérieures, économie politique, sciences économiques, 1955-56. Paris, Cours de droit, 1956. 534 p.
142. CRACCO, W. Schets eener geschiedenis der economie. 2. uitgave. Brussel, Bernaerts uitgeverij "De Phalanx," 1943. pp. 7-252. Bibliographies.
143. CRAIG, John. Remarks on some fundamental doctrines in political economy; illustrated by a brief enquiry into the commercial state of Britain, since the year 1815. Edinburgh, 1821. 95 p.
144. CRONIN, John Francis. History of Catholic social thought. Copyright. Baltimore, Maryland, 1943. 2 p. l., 45, 47-59. numb. l. Bibliographies.
145. CROSSER, Paul K. Economic fictions. A critique of subjectivistic economic theory. New York, Philosophical library, 1957. 322 p. (Reprinted: New York, Greenwood press, 1969. xxiii, 322 p. Bibliography, 319.)
146. CROZIER, John Beattie. The wheel of wealth; being a reconstruction of the science and art of political economy on the lines of modern evolution. London, New York and Bombay, Longmans, Green and company, 1906. xix, 526 p.
147. CUNNINGHAM, William. Christianity and economic science. London, J. Murray, 1914. xiii, 111 p. (Five lectures, October 1913, London school of economics.)
148. CUNOW, Heinrich. Allgemeine wirtschaftgeschichte; eine übersicht über die wirtschaftsentwicklung von der primitiven sammelwirtschaft bis zum hochkapitalismus. Berlin, J. H. W. Dietz nachfolger, 1926. v.
149. CURTH, Hermann. Volk und wirtschaft in lehre und geschichte. Hamburg, Hanseatische verlagsanstalt, 1934. 190 p. Bibliography, 189-190.
150. CUSACK, Mary Thomasine. The significance of a changing concept of ownership in social and economic planning. (Studies in economics, Vol. 1.) Washington, Catholic university of America press, 1940. x, 146 p.
151. CUSTARD, Harry Lewis and Edith May Custard. Orientation in the spheres of economics and business: a brief review of the development of economic thought, and a graphic picture of the "major elements" in the production, distribution, exchange, and consumption of wealth . . . Arlington, Virginia, University of knowledge publications, 1959. 66 p.

152. CUSUMANO, Vito. Saggi di economia politica e di scienza delle finanze. 2. ed. Palermo, Tipografia dello "Statuto," 1887. 145 p.
153. CZECH, Z. "Współczesne burzuazyjne teorie przeobrażeń społecznych." In, Zeszyty naukowe wyższej szkoły ekonomicznej w katowicach, 3 (1967) 61-82.
154. DALENCOUR, Francois Stanislas Ranier. Les pays ne sort pays prospères en raison de leur fertilité ou de leur industrie mais en raison de leur liberté. . . . Essai d'une synthèse de sociologie économique. Paris, Librairie des sciences politiques et sociales, M. Rivière, 1937. 2 p. l., iii, 322, ii p.
155. DAMASCHKE, Adolf Wilhelm Ferdinand. Geschichte der nationalökonomie; eine erste einführung. 86-100. tausend; 14., durchgesehene und erweiterte aufl. Jena, G. Fischer, 1929. 2 v. (First published in 1905.)
156. DARTAN, Jacques. Histoire de fous. (A la recherche du XXe siècle, 1.) Paris, La Colombe, 1959. 254 p.
157. DAYRE, Jean. Les faux dilemmes libéralisme ou dirigisme? Inflation ou récession? Paris, 1959. 305 p.
158. DEGUCHI, Yûzô. Gendai no keizaigakushi. (Transliterated.) Japan, 1968. 197 p.
159. _____. "Keizaigaku no rekishi-teki kenkyû no igi." (Transliterated.) In, Keizai ronso, 75, 4 (April 1955.) 9-24.
160. DE JOINT, George. La politique économique du directoire. Paris, Bibliothèque d'histoire économique et sociale, 1951. 280 p.
161. DELFGAAUW, G. Th. J. De economische theorie en enkele economische bevolkings problemen. Amsterdam, Noord-Hollandsche Uitg. Mij., 1947. 34 p.
162. DEMARIA, Giovanni. Materiali per una logica del movimento economico. Milano, La Goliardica, 1953- . v.
163. DENIS, Hector. Histoire des systèmes économiques et socialistes. Vol. I-II. Paris, V. Giard et E. Brière, 1904-07. 2 v. Bibliographies.
164. DENIS, Henri. Cours d'histoire de la pensée économique. Rédigé d'après les notes et avec l'autorisation. Licence 3e année, 1962-63. Paris, Cours de droit, 1963. 423 p.
165. _____. La crise de la pensée économique. (Que sais-je? Le point des connaissances actuelles, 483.) Paris, Presses universitaires de France, 1951. 126 p. Bibliographic footnotes.
166. _____. Histoire de la penséé économique. 2e édition, rev. augm. Paris, Presses universitaires de France, 1967. 804 p. Bibliographies. (1st edition, 1966. 756 p.)
167. DESAI, S. S. M. Economic doctrines: being an account of the development of Western economic thought from ancient times to the present day. Bombay, C. Jamnadas, 1956. xvi, 522 p.
168. _____. History of economic thought. Being an account of the development of Western economic thought from mercantilism to Alfred Marshall. 2d. revised edition. Poona, Continental, 1967. 2, 7, 382 p. Biographical sketches, 365-382.

169. DEUTSCHE akademie der wissenschaften. Institut für wirtschaftswissenschaften. Wirtschaft und wirtschaftswissenschaften in West-deutschland. Berlin, Akademieverlag, 1956. 350 p.
170. DEVAS, Charles Stanton. Political economy. 3rd edition. (7th to 9th thousand.) (Stonyhurst philosophical series.) London, New York, Longmans, Green and company, 1907. vii, xxii, 672, xxiv p.
171. DE VILLENEUVE-BARGEMONT, A. Histoire de l'economie politique du, Etudes historiques, philosophiques. 2 Vols. B. Franklin, 1967. (1st edition, 1841.)
172. DEWE, Joseph Adalbert. History of economics; or, economics as a factor in the making of history. New York, Cincinnati, Benziger brothers, 1908. 334 p.
173. DICKINSON, Zenas Clark. Economic motives; a study in the psychological foundation of economic theory with some reference to other social sciences. Cambridge. Harvard university press. 1922. vii, 3-304.
174. DIGLIO, G. Evoluzione ed unità della teoria economica. Firenze, Davite, 1961. 276 p.
175. DIMOCK, Marshall E. The new American political economy. New York Harper and Brothers, 1962.
176. DOBB, Maurice Herbert. Capitalist enterprise and social progress. (No. 81 in series of monographs by writers connected with London school of economics and political science.) London, G. Routledge and sons, limited, 1925. x, 409 p.
177. _____. Political economy and capitalism. New York, International publishers, 1945.
178. DOCKES, Pierre. L'Espace dans la pensée économique du XVIe and XVIIIe siècle. (Nouvelle bibliothèque scientifique.) Paris, Flammarion, 1969. 461 p. Bibliography.
179. DOPSCH, Alfons. Beiträge zur sozial- und wirtschaftsgeschichte; gesammelte aufsätze, zweite reihe; herausgegeben von univ. professor Erna Patzelt, mit einem gesamtschriftenverzeichnis. Wien, L. W. Seidel und sohn, 1938. ix, 360 p.
180. _____. Naturalwirtschaft und geldwirtschaft in der weltgeschichte. Wien, L. W. Seidel und sohn, 1930. xii, 294 p. Bibliographical footnotes. (Spanish edition entitled: Economía natural y economía monetaria; versión española de José Rovira. México, Fondo de cultura económica, 1943. 3, 9-323 p. Bibliographical footnotes. Italian edition entitled: Economia naturale ed economia monetaria nella storia universale. Traduzione di B. Paradisi. Firenze, Sansoni, 1949. vii, 246 p. Bibliographical footnotes. Reprinted: Aalen, Scientia-verlag, 1968. xii, 294 p. Bibliographical footnotes.)
181. _____. Verfassujngs- und wirtschaftsgeschichte des mittelalters, gesammelte aufsätze. Wien, L. W. Seidel und sohn, 1928. ix, 620 p. Bibliographical footnotes.
182. DUHRING, Eugen Karl. Kritische geschichte der nationalökonomie und des socialismus. 2., theilweise umgearb. auf.

Berlin, T. Grieben, 1875. v-xii, 595 p.
183. _____. Kritische grundlegung der volkswirthschaftslehre. Berlin, 1866.
184. DUPIN, Claude. Economiques, 1745. Pub. avec introduction et table analytique, par Marc Aucuy. Paris, M. Rivière et cie., 1913. 2 v.
185. DU PUYNODE, Michel Gustave Partounau. Etudes sur les principaux économistes: Turgot--Adam Smith--Ricardo--Malthus--J. B. Say--Rossi. Paris, Guillaumin et cie., 1868. xiv, 493 p.
186. DVORKIN, Il'ia Naumovich. "O revizionistskih teorijah 'slijanija' buržnaznoj politiceskoj ekonomii s marksistskoj." In, Voprosy ekonomiki, 8 (August, 1960) 78-88.
187. EAGLY, Robert V. Events, ideology and economic theory. Detroit, Wayne state university press, 1968.
188. EINAUDI, Luigi. Il buongoverno; saggi di economia e politica, 1897-1954. A cura di Ernesto Rossi. (Collezione storica.) Bari, Laterza, 1954. xxxii, 652 p.
189. _____. Saggi bibliografica e storici interno alle dottrine economiche. (Storia di economia; studi, testi, documenti, quaderni, 1.) Roma, Edizioni di storia e letteraturs, 1953. xiii, 367 p.
190. _____. Scienza economica ed economisti nel momento presente, discorso pronunciato il 5 novembre 1949 per l'inaugurazione dell'anno accademico 1949-1950 della università di Torino. (Università di Torino. Memorie dell'Istituto giuridico, ser. 2, memoria 65.) Torino, G. Giappichelli, 1950. 37 p.
191. EISENHART, Hugo. Geschichte der nationalökonomik, 2. verm. aufl., 2. unveranderter abdruck. Jena, G. Fischer, 1901. vii, 278 p. (1st edition, 1881.)
192. EISERMANN, Gottfried. Die grundlagen des historismus in der deutschen nationalökonomie. Stuttgart, F. Enke, 1956. xv, 249 p. Bibliographical footnotes.
193. ELLIOT, G. A. "On some fashions in economic theory." In, Canadian economic political science, 20, 4 (November 1954) 478-492.
194. ELLIS, Howard Sylvester. A survey of contemporary economics. Published for American economics association. Philadelphia, Blakiston company, 1948. xv, 490 p. Bibliographical footnotes.
195. ELY, Richard Theodore. The past and the present in political economy. (Studies in historical and political science. 2d. series, III.) Baltimore, N. Murray, publication agent, Johns Hopkins university, 1884. 64 p.
196. EMEL'ianov, Ivan Vasil'evich. Economic theory of cooperation; economic structure of cooperative organizations. (Thesis, Columbia university.) Washington, D. C., Edwards Brothers, inc., 1942. ix, 269 p. Bibliography, 255-269.
197. ENDEMANN, Wilhelm. Studien in der romanisch-kanonistischen wirtschaftsund rechtslehre bis gegen ende des siebenzehnten jahrhunderts. Berlin, J. Guttentag (D. Collin), 1874. 2 v.

198. EPZTIEN, Léon. L'économie et la morale aux débuts du capitalisme industriel en France et en Grande-Bretagne. (Etudes et mémoires, 62.) Paris, A. Colin, 1966. 355 p.
199. ERGANG, Carl. Untersuchungen zum maschinenproblem in der volkswirtschaftslehre, rückblick und ausblick; eine dogmengeschichtliche studie mit besonderer berücksichtigung der klassischen schule. Karlsruhe i. B., G. Braun, 1911. xi, 186 p.
200. ESHAG, Eprime. From Marshall to Keynes. New York, A. M. Kelley, 1963.
201. ESPINAS, Alfred Victor. Histoire des doctrines économiques. Paris, A. Colin et Cie., 1891. 2, l., 359 p.
202. EUCKEN, Walter and Kurt Heinrich. The foundations of economics; history and theory in the analysis of economic reality. Translated by T. W. Hutchison. London, W. Hodge, 1950. 358 p. Bibliographical references.
203. EYSKENS, Gaston, Economische theorie en economische politiek. (Geschriften, 1929-1956, deel). Leuven, 1956. 415 p.
204. EYSKENS, Mark. Inleiding tot de economische wetenschap (Katholieke universiteit Leuven). Leuven, L. Wouters, 1966- . v.
205. al-FAKKAK, Muhammad Ahmad. Usul 'ilm al-iqtisād. (Transliterated.) 1964. 143 p. Bibliography, 141-142.
206. FANFANI, Amintore. Introduzione allo studio della storia economica. 3. ed. Milano, A. Giuffre, 1960. viii, 106 p. Bibliographical footnotes.
207. _____. Storia delle dottrine economiche. 2. ed. Como, Cavalleri, 1939. v. (Storia delle dottrine economiche dall'antichità al XIX secolo 4th ed. Milano, G. Principate, 1955. xvi, 527 p.)
208. FAURE-SOULET, Jean Francois. Economie politique et progrès au "siècle des lumières," Prèface de Paul Harsin. Avantpropos d'André Piatier. (Serie Histoire et pensée économiques, 1.) Paris, Gauthier-Villars, 1964. xv, 252 p. Bibliography, 239-245.
209. FELLNER, William John. Emergence and content of modern economic analysis. New York, McGraw-Hill, 1960. 459 p.
210. FENOGLIO, Giulio. Corso di storia delle dottrine economiche. Torino, Società tipografico-editrice nazionale, 1931. v. p. Bibliography, 179-188.
211. FERGUSON, John Maxwell. Landmarks of economic thought. New York, London, Longmans, Green and company, 1938. 4, 1, 295 p. (2nd edition, 1950. xvi, 320 p. Bibliography, xii-xvi.)
212. FERRARA, Francesco. Esame storico-critico di economisti e dottrine economiche del secolo XVIII e prima metà del XIX; raccolta delle prefazioni dettate dal professore Ferrara alla 1a e 2a serie della biblioteca degli economisti. Torino, Unione tipografico-editrice, 1889-91. 2 v. in 4.
213. _____. Memorie di statistica. (Ser. iv, N. 39.) Roma, Tipografia eredi botta, 1890. x, 318 p.

214. FETTER, F. A. "The relation of the history of economic thought to economic history." In, American economic review, Papers and proceedings, 55, 2 (May, 1965) 136-142.
215. FLUBACHER, Joseph Francis. The concept of ethics in the history of economics. (Thesis. Temple university.) New York, Vantage press, 1950. iv, 460, iv-ix p. Bibliography, 442-460.
216. FORSTMANN, A. Neue wirtschaftslehren, theorien und hypothesen. Berlin, Duncker und Humblot, 1954. xxi, 512 p.
217. FOSSATI, Eraldo. "Considérations sur les tendance actuelles de la science économique." In, Revue d'economie politique, Paris (November-December, 1958) 1007-1025.
218. FRANCE. Ministère de l'économie et des finances. Centre de formation professionnelle et de perfectionnement. Economie politique. Paris, Direction du personnel et des services généraux, Centre de formation professionnelle et de perfectionnement, 1966. 2 v. Bibliography, v. i., p. xiii.
219. FRANK-OSSIPOFF, Z. "La multiplication des manuels d'économie politique et l'évolution des concepts en union soviétique: objet et rôle de l'economie politique--marchandise--valeur." In, Bulletin du centre d'etudes des pays de l'est, Paris, (April, 1964) 41-59.
220. FRASER, Lindley MacNaghten. Economic thought and language; a critique of some fundamental economic concepts. London, A. &C. Black, limited, 1937. xx, 411 p. Bibliography, 401-406.
221. FREYER, Hans. Die bewertung der wirtschaft im philosophischen denken des 19. jahrhunderts. (Forschungsinstitut für psychologie. Abhandlungen, Nr. 6.) Leipzig, W. Englemann, 1921. 4, 174 p. Bibliographical references, 162-174. (Arbeiten zur entwicklungspsychologie, heft 5. Hildesheim, Gg. Olms, 1966. 174 p.)
222. FRIDRICHOWICZ, Eugen. Grundriss einer geschichte der volkswirtschaftslehre. München und Leipzig, Duncker und Humblot, 1912. vii, 267 p.
223. FRIEDERISCHSEN, Vittoro Cristiano. Epoche svolgimenti tendenze nella storia delle dottrine economiche; compendio esegetico. Udine, Del Bianco, 1958. 277 p. Bibliography.
224. FRIEDMAN, Milton. A theory of the consumption function. (National Bureau of economic research. General series, no. 63.) Princeton, New Jersey, Princeton university press, 1957. 243 p.
225. FRISCH, Ragnar Anton Kittill. Theory of production. Translated from Norwegian by R. I. Christophersen. Dordrecht, Holland, D. Riedel publishing company; Chicago, Rand McNally, 1965. xiv, 370. (Translation of Innledning til produksjonsteorien.)
226. FUJIHARA, Ginjiro. Yowatari kujunen. (Transliterated.) Japan, 1960. 302 p.
227. FURFEY, Paul Hanly. A history of social thought. New York, Macmillan company, 1942. xiii, 468 p. Bibliography.

228. FURTADO, Celso. Development and underdevelopment. Translated by Ricardo W. de Aguiar and Eric Charles Drysdale. Berkeley, University of California press, 1964. xii, 181 p. Bibliographical footnotes.
229. _____. Développement et sous-développement. ... Avant propos de J.- R. Boudeville. ... Préface de Maurice Byé. ... Paris, Presses universitaires de France, 1966. xii, 227 p. Bibliographical footnotes.
230. FUSFELD, Daniel Roland. The age of the economist. Glenview, Illinois, Scott, Foresman, 1966. 147 p. Bibliography. (Reprinted: Morrow, 1968. xii, 209 p. Bibliography, 197-206.)
231. GALBRAITH, John Kenneth. Economics and the art of controversy. New Brunswick, Rutgers university press, 1955. 111 p.
232. GANGEMI, Lello. Svolgimento del pensiero economico. Milano-Roma, Treves-Teccani-Tumminelli, 1932. v. p. Bibliographical notes.
233. GAY Y FORNER, Vincente. Para comprender la economía política e historia de las doctrinas económicas y sociales. Madrid, 1945. 1 v.
234. GEMAHLING, Paul. Büyük ekonomistler, tekrar gözden geçirilmis ve coğaltilmis, metinler ve serhler. 2. tab., türkçeye, çeviren: Zühtü Uray. Istanbut, Devlet basimevi, 1939. 3, 345 p. Bibliographies.
235. _____. Les grands économists. Textes et commentaires. 2nd edition. Paris, Librairie du Recueil Sirey, 1933. ix-xv, 372 p. Bibliographies.
236. GERSCHENKRON, A. "History of economic doctrines and economic history." In, American economic review. Papers and proceedings, 59, 2 (May, 1969) 1-17.
237. GESCHICHTE der ökonomischen Lehrmeinungen übersetzung aus dem Russischen (von W. Tuchscheerer). Berlin, Verlag die wirtschaft, 1965. 540 p. Bibliography, 517-536.
238. GHIO, Paul. La formation historique de l'economie politique. 2. edition rev. Paris, M. Rivière, 1926. xii, 173 p.
239. GHOSH, R. N. Classical macroeconomics and the case for colonies. 1st ed. Calcutta, New age publishers, 1967. 318, xxi p.
240. GIDE, Paul Henri Charles and Charles Rist. Cours d'économie politique, 7th edition, 1921. (English translation, 1914.)
241. _____. Histoire des doctrines économiques depuis les physiocrates jusqu'à nos jours. Paris, L. Larose et L. Tenin, 1909. xix, 766 p. (1st. édition, 1908?) 3rd édition, 1920. 4th édition, 5th édition, Société anonyme du Recueil Sirey, 1926. xvi, 814 p. Bibliography. 7th édition, rev. et augm. Recueil Sirey, 1947. 2 v. xx, 901 p. Bibliographical footnotes. Chinese edition entitled: Ching chi ssu hsiang shih. Transliterated. 1956-58. 5 v. Bibliographical references. English edition entitled: A history of economic doctrines from the time of the physiocrats to the present day. Translated by R. Richards from 2nd French edition. Boston, London, 1915. Bibliographical

footnotes. 2nd English edition, with additional matter from the latest French editions. Translated by Ernest F. Row. Boston, D. C. Heath, 1948. 800 p. Bibliographical footnotes. German edition entitled: Geschichte der volkswirtschaftlichen lehrmeinungen. 3. aufl. nach der vierten durchgesehenen und verbesserten französischen ausgabe, herausgegeben ron Franz Oppenheimer deutsch von R. W. Horn. Jena, G. Fischer, 1923. xx, 811 p. Bibliographical footnotes. Spanish edition entitled: Historia de las doctrinas economicas. Traducción directa de la 7. ed. francesa, ampliada y actualizada por Carlos M. Giuliani Fonrouge. Buenos Aires, Editorial depalma, 1949. 2 v., xxiv, 1103 p.)

242. _____. Principes d'économie politique, 24th edition, 1923. (English edition entitled: Principles of political economy, 1911. Also edition translated from 23rd French edition by Ernest F. Row. Boston, New York, etc., D. C. Heath and company, 1924. xiii, 555 p.

243. _____. Les sciences économiques. Paris, Larousse, 1915. 19 p. Bibliography.

244. GILL, Richard T. Evolution of modern economics. Englewood Cliffs, New Jersey, Prentice-Hall, 1967. viii, 119 p. Bibliography, 111-112.

245. GLASTETTER, Werner. Das integrations problem in den ökonomischen Grundwissenschaften. Stuttgart, Berlin, Koln, Mainz, Köhl-hammer, 1966. 252 p. Bibliography, 245-252.

246. GOETZ, Girey Robert. Cours d'histoire des doctrines économiques, rédigé d'après la sténotypie du cours et avec l'autorisation. Droit romain et histoire du droit, économie politique. D. E. S., 1958-59. Paris, Cours de droit, 1959. 382 p.

247. _____. Croissance et progrès à l'originedes sociétés industrielles. Paris, Montchrestien, 1966. vi, 316 p. Bibliographical footnotes.

248. GOLOB, Eugene Owen. The "isms." A history and evaluation. (Essay index reprint series.) New York, Harper, 1954. 681 p. (Reissued: Freeport, New York. Books for libraries press, 1968. xii, 681 p. Bibliographical references.)

249. GOMES, A. Introducão à economia; subsidios historicos e doutrinários. Rio de Janeiro, Livraria agir editória, 1958. 217 p.

250. GONDRA, Luis Roque. Estudios de historia y economía. 2. ser. Buenos Aires, Imprenta de la universidad, 1938. xx, 503 p.

251. GONNARD, Charles René. Histoire des doctrines économiques. Paris, Librairie valois, 1930. 5, iii-viii, 709 p. (Paris, 1921-22. Librarie générale de droit et de jurisprudence, 1941. x, 723 p. Bibliographical footnotes. Portuguese ed. entitled: História das doutrinas económicas. Traducão e prefácio de Moses Bensabat Amzalak. Lisboa, Depósito, Libraria sá di costas, 1942. 3 v. Spanish ed. entitled:

Historia de las doctrinas económicas; traducción de J. Campo Mareno; rev. y ampliada con arreglo á la última ed. francesa, de 1947, por Inocencia Rodríquez-Mellado. 4. ed. Madrid, Aguilar, 1952. 664 p.)

252. _____. Histoire des doctrines monétaires dans ses rapports avec l'histoire des monnaies. Paris, Librarie du Recueil Sirey, 1935- . v.

253. GOODMAN, Gilbert. The poverty of nations; presenting a new system of economic thought. Ann Arbor, Michigan, Ann Arbor press, 1960. 122 p.

254. GORDON, D. F. "The role of the history of economic thought in the understanding of modern economic theory." In, American economic review, Papers and proceedings, 55, 2 (May, 1965) 119-127.

255. GORNER, A. Die volkswirtschaft; die wandlungen alter grundsätze und die lehre von heute. Berlin, Safari-verlag, 1959. 399 p.

256. GORSKI, Janusz. Polska myśl ekonomiczna a rozwój gospodarczy, 1807-1830; studia nad poczatkami teorii zacofania gospodarczego. Wyd. 1. Warszawa, Państwowe Wydawn. Naukowe, 1963. 357 p. Bibliography.

257. _____. Wybrane zagadnienia z historii myśli ekonomicznej (po 1870 roku.) Warszawa, 196- . v.

258. _____. Zarys historii ekonomii politycznej. Warszawa, Książka i Wiedza, 1967. 464 p.

259. _____, A. Łukaszewicz and W. Sierpinski. "Niektóre metodologiczne problemy historii ekonomii." In, Ekonomista I (1960) 84-108.

260. _____, T. Kowalik, and W. Sierpinski. Historia powszechnej myśli ekonomicznej 1870-1950. Warszawa, Państwowe wydawnictwo naukowe, 1967. 527 p.

261. GRAAF, J. de V. Theoretical welfare economics. Cambridge, England, University press, 1957. 178 p.

262. GRAMPP, William Dyer. Economic liberalism. New York, Random House, 1965. 2 v. Bibliographical references. (Volume 1: Beginnings. Volume 2: Classical view.)

263. _____. "On the history of thought and policy." In, American economic review, Papers and proceedings, 55, 2 (May, 1965) 128-135.

264. GRAY, Alexander. The development of economic doctrine; an introductory survey. London, New York, Longmans, Green and company, 1931. 384 p. Bibliography. (Reprinted: Wiley.) [Indian edition entitled: Arthashastra siddhanta ka vikas. (Transliterated.) Delhi, S. Chand and company, 1958. iv, 422 p.]

265. GRAZIANI, Augusto. "Nuove linee di pensiero della scienza economica." In, Rassegna economica (Napoli) 29, 1 (January-April, 1965) 37-65.

266. _____. Saggi di storia del pensiero economico. Napoli, Morano, 1966. xxvi, 235 p.

267. _____. Storia delle dottrine economiche; saggi. Napoli, A. Morano, 1949. x, 318 p. Bibliography.

268. GRIZIOTTI Kretschmann, Jenny. Storia delle dottrine

economiche. Torino, Unione tipografico-editrice torinese, 1949. xvi, 473 p. Bibliography. (2. ed. riv. e completata. 1954. xii, 408 p.)

269. _____. Storia delle dottrine economiche moderne. (Serie Sapertutto, 144-146.) Milano, Garzanti, 1959. 195 p. Bibliography.

270. GROSSMAN, Henry K. "The evolutionist revolt against classical economics." In, The journal of political economy, LI (October, December, 1943.)

271. GUARESTI, Juan José. Economía política: las doctrinas económicas hijo. Prólogo del Dr. Ricardo Zorraquin Becú. Buenos Aires, G. Kraft, 1963. 476 p. Bibliographies.

272. GULANIAN, Khachik Grigor'evich. Ocherki istorii armianskoi ekonomicheskoi mysii. (Transliterated.) 1955. 350 p.

273. GUTSCHE, Heinz. Die entwicklung der volkswirtschaftslehre. Berlin, Colloquim-verlag, 1949. 252 p. Bibliography.

274. HAAVELMO, Trygve. A study in the theory of economic evolution. Amsterdam, North-Holland publishing company, 1954. 114. Bibliographical footnotes.

275. HABA, Zdeněk. Stúdia o ekonomichkých zákonoch a ich posobení v prechodnom období k socializmu. 1. vyd. Bratislava, Vydavalel'stvo Slovenskej akadémie vied, 1962. 277 p. Bibliography.

276. HALL, Robert Lowe. The economic system in a socialist state. London, Macmillan and company, limited, 1937. xv, 262, 1 p.

277. HAMELIN, André. Les doctrines économiques. Paris, Editions ouvrières, 1959. 188 p.

278. HAMILTON, David Boyce. Evolutionary economics; a study of change in economic thought. Revised edition. Albuquerque, University of New Mexico press, 1970. xi, 132 p. (1953 edition: Newtonian classicism and Darwinian institutionalism.) Bibliography, 124-129.

279. _____. Newtonian classicism and Darwinian institutionalism; a study of change in economic theory. (Publications in economics, no. 1.) Albuquerque, University of New Mexico press, 1953. 138 p. Bibliography.

280. HAMILTON, Gustaf Axel Knut och Georg August Gottman. Om politiska ekonomiens utveckling och begrepp. Upsala, C. A. Leffler, Kongl. akad. boktryckare, 1858. 94 p.

281. HANEY, Lewis Henry. History of economic thought; a critical account of the origin and development of the economic theories of the leading thinkers in the leading nations. 4th and enlarged edition. New York, Macmillan, 1949. xxii, 996 p. Bibliographical notes. (1st edition, 1911. Revised edition, 1920. xix, 677 p. Bibliographical notes, 966-974. 3rd edition, 1936.)

282. HARMS, Bernhard. Volkswirtschaft und weltwirtschaft, versuch der begründung einer weltwirtschaftslehre. Mit zwei lithographischen tafeln. Jena, G. Fischer, 1912. xv, 495 p.

283. HARRIS, Abram Lincoln. Economics and social reform. New York, Harper, 1958. 357 p.

Chronological and Subject Surveys 21

284. HARTOG, F. Hoofdlijnen der moderne economie. (Pallas reeks, 8.) Assen, Born, 1956. 126 p.
285. _____. "Neo-normativisme of oude dwalingen?" In, Economist (Haarlem, 113, 4 (April, 1965) 259-264.
286. HASBACH, Wilhelm. Die allgemeinen philosophischen grundlagen der von François Quesnay und Adam Smith begründeten politischen ökonomie. Leipzig, Duncker und Humblot, 1890. x, 177 p.
287. _____. Untersuchungen über Adam Smith und die entwicklung der politischen ökonomie. Leipzig, Duncker und Humblot, 1891. ix, 440 p.
288. HEADLEY, R. A. Pessimism in economic thought. (Publication no. 11, 411; microfilm AC-1) University microfilms, 1955. xvi, 193 p.
289. HEATH, M. S. "Freedom, economics and corporate organization." In, Southern economics journal, 24, 3 (January, 1958) 251-258.
290. HECKSCHER, Eli Filip. Ekonomisk-historiska studier. Stockholm, A. Bonnier, 1936. 3, 9-320 p.
291. HEIMANN, Eduard. History of economic doctrines; an introduction to economic theory. London, New York, Oxford University press, 1945. ix, 3-263 p. Bibliographical references in notes, 241-254. Bibliography, 255-256. (Reprinted: Galaxy books, 1964. Paperback.)
292. HEINIG, Kurt. Einführung zur geschichte der volkswirtschaft. Hannover, J. H. W. Dietz Nachf. Schmidt-Kuster, 1954. 400 p.
293. HEITMULLER, Wilhelm. Problematische wirtschaftstheorie, versuch zu einer ideengeschichtlichen analyse der liberalen wirtschaftstheorie und zur erneuerung des wirtschaftsdenkens. Berlin, Duncker und Humblot, 1941. 72 p. Bibliographical footnotes.
294. HELLER, Farkas Henrik. A közgazdasági elmélet története. Budapest, Gergely R. Könyvkereskedése, 1943. 602 p.
295. HELLER, Walter W. New dimensions of political economy. Cambridge, Massachusetts, Harvard university press, 1966.
296. HERETIK, S. "Nové tendencie v protimarxizme súčasnej politickej ekonómie." In, Ekonomický časopís, 8, 6 (1960) 576-594.
297. HERKNER, Heinrich. Das frauenstudium der nationalökonomie. Berlin, C. Heymann, 1899. 55 p.
298. HICKS, John Richard. A theory of economic history. Oxford, Clarendon press, 1969. ix, 181 p. Bibliographical footnotes.
299. HIJIKATA, Seibi. Keizai taisei ron. (Transliterated.) Japan, 1969. 370 p. Bibliographical references.
300. _____. Keizaigaku no kiso chishiki. (Transliterated.) Japan, 1969. 220 p.
301. HILDEBRAND, Bruno. Die nationalökonomie der gegenwart und zukunft, und andere gesammelte schriften, herausgegeben und eingeleitet von prof. dr. Hans Gehrig. Jena, G. Fischer, 1922. v.

302. HILLEBRECHT, Arno. Geschichte der volkswirtschaftlichen lehrmeinungen. Stuttgart, W. Kohlhammer, 1950. 119 p. Bibliography, 111-112.
303. HIRATA, Kiyoaki. Keizai kagaku no sōzō. (Transliterated.) Japan, xvii, 565 p. Bibliography, 11-30.
304. HIRAYAMA, Shizuka. Kindai keizai riron no tenkai. (Transliterated.) Japan, 1963. 2, 2, 197 p. (Previously published under another title.)
305. HIRST, Francis W. Free trade and other fundamental doctrines of the Manchester school. London, 1903.
306. HISTOIRE de la pensée économique. Notes. 1. édition. Bruxelles, les Presses universitaires de Bruxelles, 1968. 71 l.
307. HISTORIA myśli ekonomicznej do roku 1970. Edited by Wiktor Boniecki et al. Warszawa, Państwowe wydawn. naukowe, 1967. 165 p.
308. HISTORY of political economy. Durham, North Carolina, Duke University press, 1969- . v. Quarterly.
309. HOFMANN, Werner. Theorie der wirtschaftsentwicklung. Vom Merkantilismus bis zur Gegemwart. Berlin, Duncker und Humblot, 1966. 321 p. Bibliographies.
310. HOMAN, Paul Thomas. Contemporary economic thought. New York and London, Harper and brothers, 1928. x, 3-475 p. (Essay index reprint series. Freeport, New York, Books for libraries press, 1968. x, 475 p. Bibliographical footnotes.
311. HONG, Sŏng-yu. Kŭndae kyŏngjehak sa. (Transliterated.) Korea, 1959. 269 p. Bibliographical references.
312. HONG, U. Kyŏngjehak sa. (Transliterated.) Korea, 1961. 394 p.
313. HON'IDEN Yoshio Hakushi koki kinen rombunshū kankokai. Hon'iden Yoshio Hakushi koki kinen rombun shū. (Transliterated.) 1962. 4, 3, 413 p.
314. HORI, Tsuneo. Keizai shisō shi jiten. (Transliterated.) Japan, 1951. 7, 690, 60 p. Bibliographies.
315. _____. Keizaigaku shi tsuron. (Transliterated.) Japan, 1950. 447 p. (1st edition, 1948.)
316. _____. Kinsei keizaigaku shi taiko. (Transliterated.) Japan, 1948. 178 p.
317. HORN, I. Economie politique avant les physiocrates. New York, B. Franklin, 1967.
318. HOSELITZ, Bert F. and Joseph J. Spengler. Theories of Economic growth. Glencoe, Illinois, Free press of Glencoe, inc., 1960.
319. HSU, Ti-Hsin. Ching chi ssū hsiang hsiao shih. (Transliterated.) China, 1950. 114 p.
320. HUBERMAN, Leo. Man's worldly goods; the story of the wealth of nations. New York and London, Harper and brothers, 1936-1937. [3d impression. London, V. Gollancz, limited, July, 1945. 256 p. Bibliography, 224-256. Israeli edition entitled: Nikhse ha-'amim. (Transliterated.) Tel-Aviv, 1953/54. 276 p. Bibliographical footnotes. Spanish edition entitled: Los bienes terrenales

Chronological and Subject Surveys 23

del hombre; historia de la riqueza de las naciones. Habana, Impr. nacional de cobo, 1961. 312 p.]
321. HUGO, N. P. F. História das doutrinas econômicas. São Paulo, Ed. Atlas, 1959. 518 p.
322. HUGON, Paul. Les doctrines économiques. Préface de Jean Désy. (Bibliothèque économique et sociale, 4.) Montréal, Fides, 1947. 413 p. Bibliography.
323. HULSMANN, Paul. Der wirtschaftsständische gedanke in der englischen literatur, eine ideemgeschichtliche untersuchung. Borna-Leipzig, Spezialbetrieb für dissertationsdruck von R. Noske, 1938. viii, 59 p.
324. HUMMEL, Georg. Die theorie des internationalen handels; ihre entwicklung von David Ricardo bis zu Frank William Taussig. Hamburg, H. Christian, 1937. 95 p. Bibliography, 5-6.
325. HUNTER, Merlin Harold and Gordon S. Watkins. The background of economics. New York, McGraw-Hill book company, incorporated, 1923. x, 514 p. Bibliographical references.
326. HUTCHISON, Terence Wilmot. "Berkeley's querist and its place in the economic thought of the eighteenth century." In, the British journal for the philosophy of science, IV, May, 1953. pp. 52-77.
327. ———. "Insularity and cosmopolitanism in economic ideas, 1870-1914." In, American economic review, Papers and Proceedings, 45, 2 (May, 1955) 1-16. (Comments by J. M. Letiche, G. H. Hildebrand, and W. Jaffé. pp. 29-39.)
328. ———. "Positive" economics and policy objectives. Cambridge, Harvard university press, 1964. 199 p. Bibliography, 198-199.
329. ———. A review of economic doctrines, 1870-1929. Oxford, Clarendon press, 1953. xiv, 456 p. Bibliography, 432-437. [Korean edition entitled: Geun'dae gyeong'je'hag' seol'sa. (Transliterated.) Translated by Gim Yun Hwan and Ro Ji-son. Seoul, Bo'mun'gag, 1959. 346 p.]
330. ———. The significance and basic postulates of economic theory. New York, A. M. Kelley, 1960. 191, 13 p.
331. IMBERT, Jean. Cours d'histoire des faits économiques jusqu'à la fin du XVIII siècle, rédigé d'après les notes et avec l'autorisation de Jean Imbert. Licence 2me année, 1961-62. Paris, Cours de droit, 1962. 355 p.
332. INABA, Shiro. Keizaigaku no kontei. Japan, Osaka Furitsu Daigaku keizai kenkyū sōsho. 1967. 5, 148 p. Bibliographical notes.
333. INFLUENCE des expériences communistes sur les doctrines; semaine d'études, 27-31 octobre 1958. Centre d'étude des pays de l'Est, Institut de sociologie solvay, Université libre de Bruxelles en collaboration avec le Centre national pour l'étude des pays à régime communiste. Bruxelles, 1959. xi, 187 p.
334. INGRAM, John Kells. A history of political economy. With a preface by Professor E. J. James. New York, Macmillan and company, 1888. xv, 250 p. Bibliographical

notes. (Russian edition. 1891. xi, 322 p. Bibliographical notes, 1-4.) (New and enlarged edition, with a supplementary chapter by William A. Scott and an introduction by Richard T. Ely. London, A. and C. Black, limited, 1915. xix, 315 p. New and enlarged edition, London, 1923. Reprinted: A. M. Kelley, from 1915 edition.)

335. ISTORIJA ėkonomičeskih učenij. Moskva, Socekgiz, 1963. 550 p.
336. ISTORIJA ekonomičeskoj mysli. Moskva, Moskovskij universitet, 1961. 512 p.
337. JAMES, Emile. Cours d'histoire des doctrines économiques, rédigé d'après les notes et avec l'autorisation. Diplômes d'études supérieures, economie politique, sciences economiques, 1954-55. Paris, Cours de droit, 1955. 415 p. (Revised edition: Avec l'autorisation de Emile James. License 3 année, 1958-59. Paris, Cours de droit, 1959. 496 p.
338. _____. Histoire de la pensée économique au XX siècle. Bibliotheque de la science économique. Paris, Presses universitaires de France, 1955. 2 v. 712 p.
339. _____. Histoire des théories économiques. Paris, Flammarion, 1950. 329 p. Bibliography, 325-326.
340. _____. Histoire sommaire de la pensée économique. Paris, Editions Montchrestien, 1955. 334 p. (2. édition rev. et augmentée, 1959, 420 p. Bibliography. 4. édition rev. et completée. Paris, Editions Montchrestien, 1969. 453 p. Bibliography, 447.)
341. JOHR, W. A. "Gedanken über die wirtschaft in hundert Jehren." In Schweizerische zeitschrift für volkswirtschaft und statistik, 100, 3 (September, 1964) 369-398.
342. JOSHI, Murli Dhar. Arthika paddhatiyām. (Transliterated.) India, 1963. 12, 269 p. (In Hindi.)
343. JOSTOCK, Paul. Der ausgang des kapitalismus, ideengeschichte seiner überwindung. München und Leipzig, Duncker und Humblot, 1928. vii, 301 p.
344. JOURNAL of economic theory. v. 1-. June 1969- . New York, Academic press. v.
345. JOVASEVIC, V. "Medunarodna konferencija o savremenim teorijama burzoaske ekonomije." In, Ekonomist, Beograd, 17, 2-3 (1964) 398-412.
346. KAUDER, Emill. Repetitorium der theoretischen nationalökonomie. Mit 9 abbildungen. Wien, J. Springer, 1932. vii, 165 p. Bibliography, 153-156.
347. KAULLA, Rudolf. Die geschichtliche entwicklung der modernen werttheorien. Tübingen, H. Laupp, 1906. viii, 282 p.
348. KAUTZ, Gyula. Die geschichtliche entwicklung der nationaloekonomik und ihrer literatur, I. Vienna, 1960.
349. _____. Theorie und geschichte der national-oekonomik. Propyläen zum volks-und staatswirthschaftlichen studium. Wien, C. Gerold's sohn, 1858-60. 2 v.
350. KAWAKAMI, Hajime. Bannen no seikatsu kiroku. (Transliterated.) 1958. 2 v.

351. _____. Keizaigaku taikō. (Transliterated.) 1928.
902 p.
352. _____. Kinsei keizai shisō shi ron. (Transliterated.) 1920.
4, 3, 357 p. Bibliographical footnotes.
353. KAZGAN, Gülten. Iktisadî düsünce; veya Politik iktisadm, evrimi. (Iktical: no. 246.) Istanbul, Istanbul üniversitesi, Iktisat fakültesi, 1969. xxiv, 523 p. Bibliographical footnotes.
354. KELLER, Willy. Tableaux synchroniques, 1800-1955; les événements les plus importants: technique, économie, politique, mouvement syndical, politique et législation sociales, mouvement ouvrier à l'étranger et en Suisse. Zurich, Union syndicale suisse, 1955. 83 p.
355. KERSCHAGL, Richard. Einführung in die methodenlehre der nationalökonomie. 3. auf. Wien, Holder-Pichler-Tempsky, 1948. 121 p.
356. _____. Volkswirtschaftslehre; eine darstellung ihrer wichtigsten lehrmeinungen. f 2., univeränderte aufl. Wien und Leipzig, Manz, 1927. vi, 150 p. Bibliography, 131-145. (4th edition entitled: Volkswirtschaftslehre; ein abriss dec wichtigsten lehrmeinungen. 4 aufl. Wien, Manz, 1947. xii, 218 p. Bibliography, 170-204. 5th edition, 1952. 293 p. Bibliography.)
357. KHATRI, J. D. Modern economic theory. Allahabad, Kitab Mahal, 1957. 490 p.
358. KIKER, B. F. Human capital; in retrospect. Columbia, University of South Carolina, Bureau of Business and economic research, 1968. xi, 142 p. Bibliography, 135-142.
359. KIM, Sam-su. Kyŏngjehak yŏn'gu. (Transliterated.) Korea, 1964. 343 p.
360. KIMURA, Takeyasu. Gendai keizai riron no essensu. (Transliterated.) Japan, 1969. 383 p. Bibliographies.
361. KISHIMOTO, Seijiro. Keizai gaku shi. (Transliterated.) Japan, 1954. 552 p. Bibliography.
362. KNIRSCH, P. "Ideologische einflüsse auf die entwicklung der sowjetischen wirtschaftswissenschaft der gegenwart." In, Schmollers jahrbuch fur gesetzgebung, verwaltung und volkswirtschaft, 81, 5 (1961) 28-51.
363. KOBATSCH, Rudolf. Internationale wirtschaftspolitik, ein versuch ihrer wissenschaftlichen erklärung, auf entwicklungsgeschichtlicher grundlage. Wien, Manz, 1907. xxv, 473 p. Bibliography, 459-473.
364. _____. Politica economica internazionale, traduzione dal tedesco del dott. Guido Palati. Torino, Frantelli Bocca, 1912. xxiv, 362 p.
365. KOBAYASHI, Noboru. Jūshō shugi kaitaiki no kenkyū. (Transliterated.) Japan, 1955. 3, 343, 6 p. Bibliographical footnotes.
366. _____. Genshi chikuseki-ki no keizai shoriron. Tokyo, Miraisha, 1965. 310 p.
367. KOBAYASHI, Yaroku. Keizaigaku hihan taikei no seisei. (Transliterated.) Japan, 1967. iii, 367 p. Bibliographical notes.

368. KOIZUMI, Shinzō. Keizaigaku shi. (Transliterated.) (Keizaigaku zenshu, dai 49-kan.) Japan, 1934. Bibliographies. 491 p.
369. _____. Kindai keizai shichō gaikan. (Transliterated.) Japan, 1949. 3, 2, 226 p. Bibliographies.
370. _____. Kindai keizai shiso shi. (Transliterated.) Japan, 1952. 227 p. (First edition published in 1949.)
371. _____ and Tetsuji Kada. Keizaigaku shi. (Transliterated.) Japan, 1934. 491 p. Bibliographies.
372. KOMMUNISTICHESKAIA partiia sovetskogo soiuza. Vysshaia partūnaia shkola. Kafedra politicheskoĭ ekonomii. Dokapitalisticheskie sposoby proizvodstva. (Transliterated.) 1960. 138 p. Bibliographical footnotes.
373. KORNIENKO, Aleksandr Antonovich. O nekotorykh sovremennykh burzhuaznykh ekonomicheskikh teoriiakh. (Transliterated.) 1957. 88 p.
374. KOSHIMURA, S. Keizai-gaku-shi. (Transliterated.) Tokyo, Shinjūsha, 1962. 300 p.
375. KOTOV, V. "Neoliberal'noe napravlenie v sovremennoj burzuaznoj politékonomii." In, Voprosy ekonomiki, 4 (April, 1961) 45-58.
376. KOTZSCHKE, Karl Rudolf. Allgemeine wirtschaftsgeschichte des mittelalters. Jena, G. Fischer, 1924. xiv, 626 p. Bibliography, xi-xii. Bibliographical footnotes.
377. KOWALIK, T. "Z dziejów polskiej myśli spoŀeczno-ekonomicznej. 'Ekonomista' kwartalnik poświecony nauce i potrazebom zycia, 1901-1918." In, Ekonomista, 3 (1961) 636-661.
378. KRUSE, Alfred. Geschichte der volkswirtschaftlichen theorien. München, R. Pflaum, 1948. 208 p. Bibliographies. (3rd edition, 1953. 319 p. 4. verb. und erweiterte aufl. Berlin, Duncker und Humblot, 1959. 366 p. Bibliographies.)
379. _____. Nationalökonomie; ausgewählte texte zur Geschichte einer wissenschaft. Stuttgart, K. F. Koehler, 1960. 306 p. Bio-bibliographical notes.
380. _____. Wo steht die nationalökonomie heute? München, R. Pflaum, 1951. 103 p.
381. KUHN, William Ernest. The evolution of economic thought. Cincinnati, Southwestern publishing company, 1963. 451 p. (2nd edition, 1970. x, 500 p. Bibliographical references.)
382. _____. Textbooks on economic thought. An analysis of some of their short comings. (Annals.) Washington, Public affairs press, 1956. 13 p.
383. KUHNE, Otto. Die mathematische schule in der nationalökonomie. Berlin und Leipzig, W. de Gruyter und company, 1928. v.
384. KULA, Witold. Problemy i metody historii gospodarczej. Wyd. 1. Warszawa, Państwowe wydawn, naukowe, 1963. 786 p. Bibliographical footnotes.
385. KULISHER Iosif Mikhaĭlovich. Istoriiâ ekonomicheskogo. (Transliterated.) 1916. 512 p. Bibliographies.
386. KUO, Ta-li. Hsi yang ching chi ssu hsiang. (Transliterated.) China, 1950. 2, 1, 2, 224 p.
387. KURIHARA, Kenneth K. Post-Keynesian economics. New

Chronological and Subject Surveys 27

> Brunswick, New Jersey, Rutgers university press, 1954. xviii, 442 p. Bibliographical footnotes. (Reprinted, Humanities, 1970?)

388. KURUMA, Samezō and Yoshiro Tamano. Keizaigaku shi. (Transliterated.) 1954. 7, 367 p. Bibliographical footnotes.
389. KURYU, M. "Keizai riron no takei-teki kōsatsu." (Transliterated.) In, Keizai Ronshū (Oita) 14, 1 (June 1962) 1-17.
390. LACHMANN, L. M. "Some notes on economic thought, 1933-1953" In, South African journal economics, 22, 1 (March 1954) 22-31.
391. LAGUNILLA Iñarritu, Alfredo. Historia económica general. (Biblioteca profesional del economista, del contador publico y del administrador de negocios, 5.) México, Ediciones galaxia; distribuidores exclusivos: Libería patria, 1960. 227 p.
392. LAJUGIE, Joseph. Les doctrines économiques. Paris, Presses universitaires de France, 1949. 134 p. Bibliography. (2e édition, 1952. 136 p. 3e édition, 1954. 136 p. 9e édition, 1967. 136 p. Bibliography, 135.)
393. LANDAUER, Carl. Contemporary economic systems, a comparative analysis. Philadelphia, Lippincott, 1964. x, 560 p. Bibliography, 541-548.
394. LECCE, M. Sommario storico del pensiero economico. Milano, Giuffrè, 1965. 322 p.
395. LEFTWICH, R. H. An introduction to economic thinking. New York, Holt, Rinehart and Winston, 1969. xii, 686 p.
396. LEKACHMAN, Robert. A history of economic ideas. New York, Harper and Row, 1959. 427 p. Bibliography. (French edition entitled: Histoire des doctrines economiques de l'antiquité à nos jours. Translated by Bernard de Zelicourt. Paris, Payot, 1960. 437 p. Spanish edition entitled: Historia de las doctrinas económicas. Translated by Edgardo Guimerans. Buenos Aires, Editorial Victor Lerú, 1962. 419 p.)
397. LEONT'EV, Lev Abramovich. Revoliutsionnyi perevorot v politicheskoĭ ekonomii. (Transliterated.) 1955. 95 p.
398. LEONTIEF, Wassily W. Saggi di economia. Presentazione dell'edizione italiana a cura di Giorgio Lunghini. (Biblioteca di studi economici, 12.) Milano, ETAS Kompass, 1968. xii, 292 p.
399. LESOURD, Jean-Alain and Claude Gérard. Histoire économique, XIXe et XXe siècles. Paris, Librairie A. Colin, 1963. 2 v.
400. LEVITSKII, Vladimir Favstovich. Istoriia politicheskoĭ ekonomii. (Transliterated.) 1914. 493 p. Bibliographies.
401. LEWINSKI, Jan Stanisław. The founders of political economy. London, P. S. King and son, limited, 1922. viii, 173 p.
402. ———. Twórcy economji politycznej (fizjokraci--Smith--Ricardo) wstep do historji doktryn ekonomicznych. (Biblioteka uniwersytetu lubelskiego, wydzial prawa i nauk społecznoekonomicznych, nr. 1.) Lublin, Nakładem,

Uniwersytetu lubelskiego, 1920. 155, 5 p. (Cover dated, 1921.)
403. LI, Chêng-wên. Chan hou ching chi hsüeh shuo. (Transliterated.) China, 1950. 73 p.
404. LIFSCHITZ, Fietel. Die historische schule der wirtschaftswissenschaft. Bern, Stämpfli et cie, 1914. 2, 291 p.
405. ———. Repetitorium der geschichte der nationalökonomie, von dr. Bernhard Siegfried, pseudonym. 2. aufl. Bern, P. Haupt, 1922. 104 p.
406. LIMA, Alceu Amoroso. Introducão à economia moderna. (Tristão de athayde.) 2. ed. (Biblioteca Brasileira de cultura.) Rio de Janeiro, Civilizacão Brasileira, 1933. Bibliography, 389-399.
407. LINDBECK, Assar. The political economy of the new left-- an outsider's view. New York, Harper & Row, 1971. 128 p.
408. LIU, Chi-ch'ên. Chin tai tsu pên chu i ching chi ssū ch'ao. China, 1948. 6, 1, 338 p.
409. LLUCH y Capdevila, Pedro. Historia de las doctrinas económicas. 2. ed. Barcelona, Bosch, 1941. 290 p. Bibliographies, 283-284.
410. LOBO, Roberto Jorge Haddock. Pequeña história da economia. 2. ed. São Paulo, Martins, 1959. 376 p.
411. LOHMANN, Friedrich. Vauban, seine stellung in der geschichte der national-ökonomie und sein reformplan. Leipzig, Duncker und Humblot, 1895. 4, 172 p.
412. LOPEZ, Gento, José. El hombre y la riqueza; sintesis comparativa de doctrinas económicas. Prólogo del prof. Luis Jiménez de Asúa. Buenos Aires, "El Anteneo," 1943. 192 p. Bibliography, 188-190.
413. LOWE, Adolph. On economic knowledge; toward a science of political economics. (World perspectives, v. 35.) New York, Harper and Row, 1965. xxi, 329 p. Bibliographical footnotes.
414. LUKASZEWICZ, Aleksander. Socjalizm ricardiański w historii ekonomii politycznej; poglądy społeczno-ekonomiczne W. Thompsona, J. F. Braya, J. Graya, T. Hodgskins. Wyd. 1. Warszawa, Państwowe wydawn. Naukowe, 1961. 309 p.
415. LUNT, Edward Clark. The present condition of economic science and the demand for a radical change in its methods and aims. New York and London, G. P. Putnam's sons, 1888. ix, 114 p.
416. LUTFALLA, Michel. L'état stationnaire; prix vouters. Préface d'Emile James. (Techniques économiques modernes, 7.-Série analyse économique, 1.) Paris, Gauthier-Villars, 1964. vii, 369 p. Bibliography, 349-359.
417. MACCHIORO, Aurelio. Studi di storia del pensiero economico e altri saggi. Milano, Feltrinelli, 1970. 855 p. Bibliography, 827-850.
418. MACFIE, Alec Lawrence. Individual in society. (University of Glasgow social and economic series.) 1968.
419. MACGREGOR, David Hutchison. Economic thought and

policy. (The home university library of modern knowledge, 216.) London, New York, Oxford university press, 1949. vii, 182 p.
420. MACLEOD, Henry Dunning. The history of economics. London, Bliss, Sands and company, 1896. xv, 690 p.
421. MADAN, Gurmuk R. and H. S. Dhooria. The history and development of economic thought; an introductory analysis. With a foreword by Radhakamal Mukerjee. Delhi, S. Chand, 1963. iii, ii, 311 p. Bibliographical footnotes.
422. MADRAZO, Santiago Diego. Lecciones de économía política. Madrid, P. Calleja y c.ª, 1874-76. 3 v.
423. MAHIEU, Jaime María de. La economía comunitaria. (Publicaciones 2.) Buenos Aires, Editorial universidad Argentina de Ciencias sociales, 1964. 143 p.
424. MAIDE, C. and M. Yokoyama. Keizaigaku-shi. Tokyo, Kobundo, 1955. 272 p.
425. MAIER, Gustav. Soziale bewegungen und theorien bis zur modernen arbeiterbewegung. 7. aufl., 33-37. Tausend, Leipzig und Berlin, B. G. Teubner, 1919. iv, 132 p. Bibliographies.
426. MAILLET, J. Histoire des faits économiques des origines au XXe siècle. (Bibliothèque historique.) Paris, payot, 1952. 362 p.
427. MAKSIMOVIC, I. "Naucne tendencije i valgarno-apologetski elementi u savremenoj ekonomskoj teoriji." In, Ekonomist (Beograd) 14(1), 1961. pp. 1-18.
428. MANTILLA Pérez de Ayala, José María. Apostillas sobre economía; un esquema de historia de la economía. (Publicaciones de la Inspección general de comercio y política arancelaria, Sección de información y propaganda, serie "Divulgación.") Madrid, 1941. 63 p. Madrid, 1941. 63 p.
429. MARCHAL, André. "Bilan d'un demi-siècle de pensée économique." In, Revue de philos., 70, 10-12 (October-December, 1954) 544-570.
430. MARCHAL, Jean et Jacques Lecaillon. Théorie des flux monétaires. Paris, Editions Cujas, 1967. v. Bibliographical footnotes.
431. MARMATAKES, Nikolaos G. Ho kratikos parembatismos. (Transliterated.) 1953. 79 p. Bibliography, 78-79.
432. MARNEF, Ernest. Propos économiques. Bruxelles, Editions "Le Rail," 1961. 64 p.
433. MARNOCO e Souza, José Ferreira. Economia nacional; preleções feitas ao curso do segundo anno juridico de 1908-1909. Coimbra, França Amado, 1909. 422 p.
434. MARRIOTT, Sir John Arthur Ransome. Economics and ethics; a treatise on wealth and life. New York, Dutton, 1923. x, 293 p. Bibliography.
435. MARSHALL, Howard Drake. The great economists. A history of economic thought. New York, Pitman publishing company, 1967. 397 p. Bibliography, 377-383. [Reviewed: A. G. Gruchy, American economic review, 58, I (June, 1968) 208-211.]
436. MARTIN, Richard S. and Reuben G. Miller. Economics and

its significance. Kenneth E. Boulding, consultant. Columbus, Ohio, C. E. Merrill books, 1965. x, 165 p. Bibliography, 86-97. (Includes: Methods for teachers, by Raymond Muessig and Vincent Robert Rogers, 98-163.)
437. MARTINEZ Candia, Marcelo. El pensamiento social-cristiano en la economía. Santiago de Chile imp. "América," 1947. 89, 4 p. Bibliography, 190.
438. MASAI, K. "Eikoku tetsugaku-sha no keizai-ron." (Transliterated.) In, Keizai Ronshū (Oita) 6, 1 (April 1956) 1-23.
439. MASAMURA, Kimihiro. Keizai shisō no kakushin. (Transliterated.) Japan, 1969. 209 p. Bibliography, 203-206.
440. MASOIN, M. "Propos à bâtons rompus sur les doctrines économiques." In, Annales de sciences économiques appliquées, 12, 3 (Juil 1954) 191-202.
441. MASUDA, Shiro. Keizaigaku e no susume. (Transliterated.) Japan, 1968. 385 p. Bibliographies.
442. MATEEV, Evgeni. Subektivnata shkola. (Transliterated.) 1949. 430 p.
443. MATYAS, A. A polgari közgazdasagtan rövid története a marxizmus létrejötte előtt. Budapest, Közgazdasági és Jogi Kiadó, 1961. 327 p.
444. MAULNIER, Thierry. La révolution du XXe siècle. (Tribune libre, 17.) Paris, Plon, 1958. 48 p.
445. McCONNELL, John Wilkinson. Basic teachings of the great economists; summaries of the ideas and the theories of Malthus and others. (Everyday handbook series.) New York, Barnes and Noble, 1947. xiii, 367 p. Bibliographical notes, 343-361. (1st edition, 1943. Spanish edition entitled: Enseñanzas básicas de los grandes economistas. Translated by Delia A. Garcia Daireaux. Tipográfica editora Argentina, 1961. 427 p.)
446. McCULLOCH, James Ramsay. The literature of political economy. A classified catalogue. Select publications in the different departments of that science with historical, critical, and bibliographical notes. London, Longman, Brown, Green, and Longmans, 1845. xiii, 407 p. (Reprinted: London school of economics and political science, 1938. xii, 407 p. New York, A. M. Kelley, 1964. xii9, 407 p.
447. ———. The principles of political economy; with some inquiries respecting their application, and a sketch of the rise and progress of the science. 4th edition, corrected, enlarged, and improved. Edinburgh, A. and C. Black; London, Longman, Brown, Green, and Longmans, 1849. xxiv, 646 p. (5th edition. reprinted: A. M. Kelley, 1965, xxiv, 517 p. Bibliographical footnotes. 1st edition in 1864.)
448. McISAAC, A. M. Elements of economic analysis. New York, Prentice-Hall, 1950.
449. MEINANDER, N. "Den ekonomiska doktrinhistoriens stora bok." In, Ekonomiska samfundets tidskrift, 8, 4 (1955) 237-245.
450. MENGER, Anton. Das recht auf den vollen arbeitsertrag in geschichtlisher darstellung. 2. verb. aufl. Stuttgart, J. G. Cotta, 1891. x, 178 p. (4. aufl., Stuttgart, J. G. Cotta'sche buchhandlung nachfolger, 1910. x, 172 p. Bibliograph-

ical footnotes. English edition entitled: The right to the whole produce of labour; the origin and development of the theory of labour's claim to the whole product of industry. Translated by M. E. Tanner with an introduction and bibliography by H. S. Foxwell. London, Macmillan and company; New York, The Macmillan company, 1899. cxviii, 1, 271 p. Bibliography. Spanish edition entitled: El derecho al producto integro del trabajo en su desarrollo historico; traducción de Adolfo Posada. Buenos Aires, editorial americalec, 1944. 2, 7-173 p. Bibliographical footnotes. Russian edition, 1905. ii, 222. Bibliography.)

451. MEYER, Moritz. Die neuere nationalökonomie in ihren hauptrichtungen. Germany, 1891. xii, 379 p. (Russian edition: St. Petersburg, 1891. xii, 379 p.)
452. MIKLASHEVSKII, Aleksandr Nikolaevich. (History of economics.) Russia, 1909. viii, 638 p.
453. MINC, Bronisław. Problemy i kierunki rozwoju ekonomii politiycznej. Wyd. 1. Warszawa, Państwowe wydawn. Naukowe, 1965. 401 p. Bibliographical footnotes.
454. MIRA, Giuseppe. Lezioni di storia delle dottrine e dei fatti economici. Roma, Soc. poligrafica commerciale, 1949.
455. MISES, Ludwig von. The free and prosperous commonwealth; an exposition of the ideas of classical liberalism. Translated by Ralph Raico. Edited by Arthur Goddard. (The William Volker fund series in the humane studies.) Princeton, New Jersey, Van Nostrand, 1962. 207 p.
456. _____. Theory and history; an interpretation of social and economic evolution. New Haven, Yale university press, 1957. ix, 384.
457. MITCHELL, Wesley Clair. Business cycles and their causes. A new edition of Mitchell's business cycles, part III. Berkeley and Los Angeles, University of California press, 1941. xii, 226.
458. _____. "Economics, 1904-1929." In, A quarter century of learning. New York, Columbia university press, 1931.
459. _____. Lecture notes on types of economic theory. New York, A. M. Kelley, 1949. 2 v.
460. _____. Types of economic theory. From mercantilism to institutionalism. New York, A. M. Kelley, 1967-69. Bibliographical footnotes. (Published in 1949 as Lecture notes. . . .)
461. MITSCHERLICH, Waldemar Oskar Eihard. Der wirtschaftliche fortschritt sein verlauf und wesen. Leipzig, C. L. Hirschfeld, 1912. viii, 262.
462. MITTALA, S. C. Arthika vicāromkā itihāsa. (Transliterated.) India, 1962. 608 p. (In Hindi)
463. MOLNAR, M. and A. Berényi. "Doctrina economica a fiziocratilor." In, Probleme economice (Bucuresti) 10, 2 (February, 1957) 104-116.
464. MOMBERT, Paul. Geschichte der nationalökonomie. Jena, G. Fischer, 1927. ix, 557 p. Bibliographies.
465. MONTENEGRO, Walter E. Introducción a las doctrinas político-económicas. 2. ed. (Breviarios, 122. Psicología

y ciencias sociales.) México, Fondo de cultura económica, 1961. 202 p. (1st edition, 1956.)
466. MORAZE, Charles. Histoire des faits économiques et sociaux. Paris, Les cours de droit, 1951. 3 v. (399 p.)
467. MORDUKHOVICH, Lev Matveevich. Ocherki istorii "ekonomicheskikh" unchenii. Moscow, Gospolitizdat, 1957. 180 p. (Reprinted, 1957, 178 p. 2d. revised and enlarged edition, 1957. 183 p.)
468. MORITO, Tatsuo. Jōyo kachi gakusetsu ryakushi. (Transliteration.) (Series: Keizaigaku zenshū, dai 50-kan.) 1933. 5, 443 p.
469. MUHS, Karl. Kurzgefasste geschichte der volkswirtschaftslehre. Hauptströmungen der nationalökonomie. Wiesbaden, Gabler, 1963. 161 p. Bibliography 147-156.
470. MULLER, Johannes. Abriss einer geschichte der theorie von den produktionsfaktoren. Jena, G. Fischer, 1911. 4, 53 p.
471. MULLER-ARMACK, Alfred. Genealogie der wirtschaftsstile, die geisteschichtlichen ursprünge der staats- und wirtschaftsformen bis zum ausgang des 18. jahrhunderts. Stuttgart, W. Kohlhammer, 1944. 282 p. Bibliographical footnotes.
472. ———. Religion und wirtschaft; geistesgeschichtliche Hintergründe unserer europäischen lebensform. Stuttgart, W. Kohlhammer, 1959. xv, 605 p. Bibliographical footnotes.
473. MUÑOZ, Casillas, Juan. La evolución económica. 1. ed. Madrid, Sociedad general Española de librería, 1952 - . v.
474. MYRDAL, Gunnar Karl. Vetenskap och politik i nationalekonomien. Sweden. [English edition entitled: The political element in the development of economic theory. Translated from the German by Paul Streeten. London, Routledge and Paul, 1953; New York, Harvard university press, 1954. xvii, 248 p. Bibliographical notes. Italian edition entitled: L'elemento politico nella formazione delle dottrine dell' economia pura. (Biblioteca Sansoni di economia, diretta da Giusepe Bruguier Pacini.) Firenze, G. C. Sansoni, 1943. xiii, 340 p. Bibliographical notes.]
475. NAPOLEONI, Claudio. Ekonomické myšlení dvacátého století Z. ital. orig. Il pensiero economico del 900 prel. a předml. naps. Lumír Smetana. 1. vyd. Praha, Academia, 1968. 191, 1 p. Bibliographical footnotes.
476. ———. Il pensiero economico del 900. Torino, Edizioni RAI, 1961. 200 p.
477. NAPOLITANO, G. Gli sviluppi storici della economia politica. Milano, Giuffrè, 1960. 194 p.
478. NARASAKI, Toshio. Keizai shisō shi. (Transliterated.) Japan, 1955. 357 p.
479. ———. Shakai keizai shisō shi. (Transliterated.) Japan, 1949. 246, 119 p.
480. NARDI, Giuseppe di. Il controllo sociale dell'economia. . . . Milano, Giuffrè, 1967. xi, 369 p. Bibliographical footnotes.
481. NASH'AT, Muhammad 'Ali. Fikr al-iqtiṣādī fī Muqaddimat

Ibn Khaldūn. (Transliterated.) 1944. 223 p.
482. NATAN, Zhak. Istoriia na ikonomicheskite ucheniia. (Transliterated.) Sophia, 1949. v.
483. _____. Razvitieto na ikonomicheskata misui sied Rikardo. (Transliterated.) Sophia, 1948. 530 p.
484. NEFF, Frank Amandus. Economic doctrines. Wichita, Kansas, McGuin publishing company, 1946. 3, ix, xiii, 439 p. Bibliography. (2d edition, New York, McGraw-Hill book company, incorporated, 1950. xii, 532 p. Bibliography.)
485. NESIC, Dvagoljub. Historija ekonomiskih doktrina. Sarajevo, Univerzitel, 1967- . v. Bibliographical footnotes.
486. NEUMARK, Fritz. Iktisadi düsünce tarihi. Tercüme: Ahmet Ali Ozeken. (Istanbul universitesi yayinlarindan, no. 201 Iktisat fakütesi nesriyati no. 19.) Istanbul, Güven Basimevi, 1943. v. Bibliographical references.
487. NEURATH, Otto. Zur anschauung der antike über handel, gewerbe und landwirtschaft. Jena, G. Fischer, 1906. 32, 2, p. (Dissertation, Berlin.)
488. NEWMAN, Philip Charles. The development of economic thought. New York, Prentice-Hall, 1952. xiv, 456 p. Bibliographical footnotes. Bibliography. (Dutch edition entitled: Economie. De ontwikkeling van het economisch denken. The Hague, Maandbald succes, 1955. 494 p. Spanish edition entitled: Historia de las doctrinas económicas. Translated by Jose Rico Godoy and Joaquín Muns. Barcelona, Editorial juventud, S. A., 1963. 588 p. Swedish edition entitled: De ekonomiska idéernas historia. Trans. Ulrich Herz. Stockholm, Kooperativa Förbundet, 1953. 367 p.
489. NOGARO, Pierre Gabriel Bertrand. Le développement de la pensée économique. Paris, Libraire générale de droit et de jurisprudence, 1944. 2, 345 p. Bibliography.
490. NOYES, Charles Reineld. Economic man in relation to his natural environment. New York, Columbia university press, 1948. 2 v. xiv, 1443. Bibliographical references.
491. NYS, Ernest. Recherches sur l'histoire de l'économie politique. Bruxelles, A. Castaigne, 1898. 3, xv, 247 p. (English edition entitled: Researches in the history of economics. Translated by N. F. and Albert Robert Dryhurst. London, A. and C. Black, 1899. xxviii, 343 p.)
492. O, Tŏg-yŏng. Sŏyang kyŏngje sa. (Transliterated.) Korea, 1965. 285 p. Bibliographies included.
493. OKOCHI, Kazuo. Keizai shisō shi. (Transliterated.) Japan, 1950-58. 2 v.
494. ONCKEN, August. Geschichte der nationalökonomie. In zwei teilen. Erster teil: Die zeit vor Adam Smith. Mit zwei tafeln. 3., unveränderte aufl. Leipzig, C. L. Hirschfeld, 1922. iv, 516 p. Bibliography. (1st edition, 1902.)
495. ORENSTEIN, Z. "Gîndirea social-economică înaintată din tărîle rommesti la mijlocul secolului XIX." In, Probleme economice (Bucuresti) 9, 7 (July, 1956) 119-133.
496. ORNATI, O. "Problemi e pensiero economico negli stati uniti dal 1929 al 1956." In, Riv. polit. econ., 46, 7-8

(July-August 1956) 593-604.
497. ORITZ R. M. El pensamiento económico de echeverria. Buenos Aires, Editorial Raigal, 1953. 185 p.
498. OSER, Jacob. The evolution of economic thought. New York, Harcourt Brace and World, 1963. 399 p. Bibliography. (2nd edition, 1970. xiii, 458 p. Bibliographies.)
499. OTTONE, Piero. Potere economico. (La Fronda, v. 84.) Milano, Longanesi, 1968. 168 p.
500. OUCHI, Hyōe. Keizai-gaku 50 nen. (Transliterated.) Tokyo Daigaku shippan-kai, 1959. 2 vols. 292, 522 p.
501. ———. Keizaigaku sampo. (Transliterated.) Japan. 1948. 408 p. Bibliography. (1952 edition. 408 p.)
502. PANTALEONI, Maffeo. Scritti varii di economia. Milano, R. Sandron, 1904. 2, 1, 532 p.
503. PAPANDREOU, Andreas George. "Il corso del pensiero economico." In, Rivista internazionale di scienze economiche comerciali (Padova). 7, 4 (April, 1960) 325-335.
504. ———. Hē poreia tēs oikonomikēs skepseōs. Greece, 1960. 33 p.
505. PAQUET, André. Le conflit historique entre la loi des débouchés et le principe de la demande effective. (Centre d'études économiques. Etudes et mémoires, 7.) Paris, A. Colin, 1953. 368 p.
506. PARRILLO, Francesco. Contributo alla teoria della politica economica. (Storia e dottrine economiche, 2.) Torino, Unione tipografico-editrice torinese, 1957. 303 p.
507. PARRISH, J. B. "Rise of economics as an academic discipline; the formative years to 1900." In, Southern economic journal, 34, 1 (July, 1967) 1-16.
508. PASQUALAGGI, G. "Une histoire de la pensée économique contemporaine." In, Cahiers économiques (September, 1955) 15-22.
509. PATTEN, Simon Nelson. The reconstruction of economic theory. Philadelphia, The American academy of political and social science, 1912. 2, 99 p.
510. PEARCE, Alan. Great ideas in economics. London, Maxwell, 1969. xiii, 226 p. Bibliography, 219-220.
511. PEN, Jan. Het aardige van de economie. 5 druk. Utrecht, Het spectrum, 1966. 256 p. Bibliography, 251.
512. ———. Modern economics. Translated from the Dutch by Trevor S. Preston, Baltimore, Penguin books, 1965. c1958. 272 p.
513. PENTY, Arthur Joseph. Protection and the social problem. London, Methune and company, limited, 1926. 4 p., 248 p.
514. PEREIRA, Armando Temperani. Lições de economica política. Rio de Janeiro, Civilização Brasileira, 1967. 538 p. Bibliographical footnotes.
515. PERPIÑA Grau, Román. La crisis de la economía liberal del "ethos" económico al de seguridad. Madrid, Ediciones cultura hispánica, 1953. 158 p.
516. PERROUX, François. L'économie du XXe siècle. . . . 3e édition augmentée. Paris, Presses universitaires de France, 1969. 765 p. Bibliographical footnotes.

517. _____. Le néo-marginalisme. 2. édition. Conférences données à l'école pratique des hautes études de la Sorbonne. Paris, Damat-Montchrestien, 1945. v.
518. PETER, Kattadyil Chacko. Dhanaśāstra purogati jivacaritṛannalilute. (Transliterated.) 1965. viii, 275, ii, iv p. Bibliography, i-ii.
519. PHILIP, André. Cours d'histoire des faits économiques contemporains. Rédigé d'après la sténotypie du cours et avec l'autorisation de André Philip. Licence 2. année, 1961-1962. Paris, Les cours de droit, 1962. 594 p.
520. PHILIPPE, Jules Aime. Las doctrinas economicas. Traducción del capitán A. Ponce; compendio destinado al uso de los oficiales de todas las armas y todos los servicios. Cochabamba, Bolivia universidad autónoma de Cochabamba. 1939. viii, 84, 2 p.
521. PIETTRE, André. Cours d'histoire des doctrines économiques. Rédigé d'après la sténotypie du cours et avec l'autorisation de M. Piettre. Diplômes d'études supérieures, économie politique, histoire du droit, et droit romain, 1955-56. Paris, Cours de droit, 1956. 552 p.
522. _____. Histoire de la pensée économique et analyse des théories contemporaines. Paris, Dalloz, 1958. 520 p. Bibliographical footnotes. (Précis Dalloz, 1959. 517 p. 4e edition, 1966. 558 p. Bibliographical footnotes. 5 éd. rev. et mise à jour., 1970, c1969. 562 p.)
523. _____. Histoire économique, essai de synthèse, faits et idées. Paris, Edition Cujos, 1969. 272 p. Bibliography, 257-258. Bibliographical footnotes.
524. _____. "Tentavivo di bilancio del pensiero economico." In, Rassegna economica (Napoli) 23, 1 (January, 1959) 63-74.
525. PIGOU, A. C. The economics of welfare. London, Macmillan and Company, ltd. 1920. (3rd edition, 1929. 4th edition, 1932. xxxi, 837 p. Reprinted, 1950.)
526. PINEDA de Castro, Alvaro. Introducción a la economía social. Bogotá, Edit. Cahur, 1949. 235 p. Bibliography, 233-235.
527. PJANIC, Zoran. Savremene buržoaske teorije vrednosti i cena. Beograd, 1965. 280 p.
528. POLAK, Siegfried. Beknopte geschiedenis der staathuishoudkunde in theorie en praktijk. Amsterdam, Mij. voor Geode en Goedkope lectuur, 1919. 2 v. in 1.
529. POLANYI, Karl. The great transformation. The political and economic origins of our time. New York, Toronto, Farrar and Rinehart, incorporated, 1944, xiii, 1, 305 p. Bibliographical footnotes. (Reprinted: Beacon press, 1957. 315 p. Paperback, 45.)
530. POLIANSKII, Fedor Iakovlevich. Plekhanov i russkaia ekonomicheskaia mysl'. (Transliterated.) Moscow, 1965. 471 p. Bibliographical footnotes.
531. PONSARD, C. Histoire des théories économiques spatiales. (Centre d'études économiques. Etudes et mémoires, no. 41.) Paris, A. Colin, 1958. 203 p.
532. POPESCU, Oreste. "Contribution à une histoire de l'histoire

de la pensée économique. In, Acta scientiarum socialium, 2 (1965) 167-219.
533. _____. "Periodization in the history of economic thought." In, International social science journal, 17, 4 (1965) 607-634.
534. _____. El sistema económico en las misiones jesuíticas. Bahía Blanca, Editorial "Pampa-Mar," 1952. 125 p. (2 ed. Barcelona, Edicione Ariel, 1967. 198 p.)
535. POPPER, A. "Caracterul antistiintific al conceptiilor burgheze contemporane despre istoria gindirii economice." In, Probleme economice (Bucuresti) 14, 5 (May, 1961) 88-103.
536. PRATO, Giuseppe. Lezioni di storia delle dottrine economiche A stampa, con note e indici a cura di Antonio Fossati. Torino, G. Giappichelli, 1945. ix, 205 p. Bibliographical footnotes.
537. PREISER, Erich. Probleme der wohlstandsgesellschaft. Vorgetragen am 8, Nov. 1963. München, Verlag der Bayerischen akademie der Urssenschaften, in Kommission bei C. H. Beck, 1964. 25 p. Bibliographical footnotes.
538. PRIBRAM, K. "Patterns of economic reasoning." In, American economic review, Papers and proceedings, 43, 2 (May, 1953) 243-258.
539. PROBST, Georges. Das Zwangssparen in der älteren und neueren literatur. Winterthur, P. G. Keller, 1960. ix, 11 p. Bibliography.
540. RAMBAUD, Joseph. Histoire des doctrines économiques. Paris, L. Larousse, 1899.) (3. edition, rev., mise à jour et augm. Paris, L. Larose; Lyon, P. Phily, 1909. 2, 816 p.)
541. RAUSCHER, Anton. Die soziale rechtsidee und die überwindung des wirtschaftsliberalen denkens. Hermann Roesler u. sein Begtr. z Verstandnis von wirtschaft u. gesellschaft. München, Paderborn; Wien, Schöningh, 1969. 313 p. Bibliography, 291-304.
542. RECKTENWALD, Horst Claus. Lebensbilder grosser nationalökonomen, einführung in die geschichte der politischen ökonomie. Köln, Kiepenheuer und Witsch, 1965. 665. Bibliographical references, 587-649.
543. REVIEW of radical political economics. v. 1-. May, 1969- . Ann Arbor, Michigan, Union for radical political economics. v. Quarterly.
544. REVUE d'histoire economique et sociale. v. 1-. 1908- . Paris P. Geuthner, 1908-1913. Quarterly.
545. REVUE économique. Mai 1950- . Paris, A. Colin. 5 per year.
546. RICHARD, Gaston. La question sociale et le mouvement philosophique au XIXe siècle. Paris, A. Colin, 1914. xii, 363 p. Bibliography, 351-356.
547. RIMA, I. H. Development of economic analysis. Homewood, Illinois, R. D. Irwin, 1967. xvi, 422. (2nd edition, revised, 1972.)
548. RIST, Charles. Histoire des doctrines relatives au crédit et à la monnaie depuis John Law jusqu'à nos jours. Paris,

Librairie du recueil sirey, 1938. 4, 471 p. (English edition entitled: History of monetary and credit theory from John Law to the present day. Translated by Jane Degras, 1940. Reprinted: New York, A. M. Kelley, 1966. 442 p. Bibliographical footnotes.)
549. RIVIERE, Marc. Economie bourgeoise et pensée technocratique, contribution à l'étude de la pensée économique universitaire bourgeoise au XXe siècle. (Problèmes.) Paris, Editions sociales, 1965. 239 p. Bibliography.
550. ROBBINS, Lionel Charles. Saggio sulla natura e l'importanza della scienza economica. (Storia e dottrine economiche, 4.) Torino, Unione tip.-editrice torinese, 1947. xxiii, 199 p.
551. ROBINSON, E. V. "War and economics in history and in theory." In, Political science quarterly, xv (1900), 581-622.
552. ROBINSON, J. Doktrinen der wirtschaftswissenschaft. Eine auseinandersetzung mit ihren grandgedanken und ideology. München, C. H. Beck, 1965. 181 p.
553. ROBINSON, Joan. Economic heresies, some old-fashioned questions in economic theory. New York, Basic books, 1971. xix, 150 p.
554. ———. Economic philosophy. Chicago, Aldine publishing company, 1962. 150 p.
555. ROCA, Raymond. Résumé d'histoire des doctrines économiques. Paris, Domat-Montchrestien, 1946. 101, 3 p. Bibliography.
556. RODRIGUEZ, Luis Dantón. Intervención del estado en la economía nacional. México, 1961. 198 p. Bibliography.
557. ROGIN, Leo. The meaning and validity of economic theory; a historical approach. New York, Harper, 1956. xviii, 697 p. (Reprinted: Freeport, New York, Books for Libraries, 1971.)
558. ROLL, Erich. A history of economic thought. London, Faber and Faber, limited, 1938. 3, 9-430 p. Bibliography. New York, (?), 1939. [Revised and enlarged, New York, Prentice-Hall, 1942. Bibliography. Reprinted, 1946. 2. edition, London, 1945. 535 p. 3d edition, revised and enlarged, London, 1954. Englewood Cliffs, New Jersey, Prentice-Hall, 1956. 540 p. Reprinted, London, 1961. Italian edition entitled: Storia del pensiero economico. 2d edition. Torino, Einaudi edizioni scientifiche, 1954. xiii, 658 p. Japanese edition entitled: Keizai gakusetsu-shi. (Transliterated.) Translated by Mikio Sumiya. Tokyo, Yûhikaku company, incorporated, 1951. v. I. 327 p. 1952. v. II. 359 p. Portuguese edition entitled: História das doctrinas econômicas. Translated by Cid Silveira. 2d edition. São Paulo, Companhia editôra nacional, 1962. 576 p. Spanish editions entitled: Historia de las doctrinas economicas . . . versión española de Daniel Cosío Villegas y Javier Márquez. México, Fondo de cultura económica, 1942. 2 v. Bibliography. Historia de las doctrinas economicas. Translated by Florentino M. Torner, Mexico,

Fondo de cultura economica, 1955. 549 p. 4th edition, 1961. 492 p.]
559. RONCHI, Ennio. Economia liberale, economia socialista, economia corporativa, con prefazione di s. e. Dino Alfieri. Monografia premiata al concorso nazionale di diritto ed economia corporativa bandito sotto gli auspici del Ministero per le corporazioni. Roma-Milano, Avgvstea, 1932. 340 p.
560. ROSCHER, Wilhelm Georg Friedrich. Ansichten der volkswirthschaft aus dem geschichtlichen standpunkte. Leipzig und Heidelberg, C. F. Winter, 1861. vi, 495 p.
561. ROSS, E. A. "The sociological frontier of economics." In, Quarterly journal of economics (July, 1899.)
562. ROSSI, Pellegrino. Cours d'économie politique, 1840-1851. 5th édition. Paris, 1884. 4 v.
563. ROSTOW, W. W. "A historian's perspective on modern economic theory." In, American economic review, Papers and proceedings, 42, 2 (May, 1952) 16-29.
564. ROTHENBERG, Jerome. The social welfare function; foundation of welfare economics. (University microfilms, Ann Arbor, Michigan, Publication no. 8813, Microfilm AC-1.) Ann Arbor, University microfilms, 1954.
565. ROZENBERG, David Iokhelevich. Chêng chih ching chi hsüeh shih. (Transliterated.) 1959. 575 p.
566. _____. Istoriia politicheskoi ekonomii. (Transliterated.) 1934. v. Bibliography. (1940 edition. v. Bibliography.)
567. RUBIN, Isaak Il'ich. Istoriia ekonomicheskoi mysli. (Transliterated.) 1929. 380 p.
568. _____. Istoriia ekonomichnoi dumky. (Transliterated.) Microfilm AC-99. 1930.
569. RYBARSKI, Roman. Idea gospodarstwa narodowego. Kraków, Nakł. Akademji umiejętności, 1919. 2, 343 p. Bibliographical footnotes.
570. RYNDINA, M. N. "Kritika sovremennyh burżuaznyh i reformistskih ëkonomičeskih teorij." In, Naučnye doklady vysšej školy. Ekonomika nauki, 12, 8 (August, 1969) 7-80.
571. _____. Kritika osnovyh napravlenij souremennoj burzuaznoj politiceskoj ekonomii. Moscow, Mysl', 1964. 187 p.
572. SACHDEVA, T. N. History of economic thought; full view at a glance. 2d edition, radically revised and elaborately enlarged. New Delhi, Sudha publicationa, 1962. 280 p. Bibliography.
573. SALIN, Edgar. Geschichte der volkswirtschaftslehre. 4. erweiterte aufl. Bern, A. Francke, 1951. 205 p. (3. erweiterte aufl., 1944. 224 p. Bibliographies. Spanish edition entitled: Historia de la doctrina económica. Traducción de la 3. ed., corr. y rev. por su autor, por C. de las Cuevas. Buenos Aires, Editorial Atalaya, 1948. 283 p.)
574. _____. Politische ökonomie-geschichte der wirtschaftspolitischen ideen von Platon bis zur gegenwart. Tübingen, J. C. B. Mohr, 1967. viii, 205 p. [Reviewed: J. E. Barthel, American economic review, 58, 3, Pt. I (June, 1968) 570-572.)

575. SAMUELS, Warren J. The classical theory of economic policy. With an introduction by Herman Finer. Cleveland, World publishing company, 1966. xvii, 341 p.
576. SANTOLI, S. "Di un recente contributo alla storia della teoria economica." In, Revue internationale des sciences sociales, 72, 2 (March-April, 1964) 189-192.
577. SANZ y Escartín, Eduardo. La cuestión económica; nuevas doctrinas. Socialismo de estado. --Crisis agrícola. Protección arancelaria. Madrid, Impr. de A. Pérez Dubrill, 1890. 319 p.
578. SARRAILH, J. L'espagne éclairée de la seconde moitié du XVIIIe siècle. Paris, Imp. nat., 1954. vi, 779 p.
579. SARTORIUS von Waltershausen, Johann Georg August. Zeittafel zur wirtschaftsgeschichte. 2. aufl. Halberstadt, H. Meyer, 1924. vii, 111 p.
580. SAUVY, Alfred. L'évolution économique: les faits et les opinions. Paris, Les cours de droit, 1951. 3 v. (614 p.)
581. SCHATZ, Albert. L'individualisme économique et social, ses origines--son évolution--ses formes contemporaines. Paris, A. Colin, 1907. 4, 590 p.
582. SCHEIFLER Amezaga, Xavier. Historia del pensamiento económico; apuntes de la cátedra del Lic. México, 1964- . v.
583. SCHELLE, Gustav. L'économie politique et les économistes avec une introduction sur L'économique et la guerre. Paris, O. Doin et fils, 1917. xviii, 396 p. Bibliography.
584. SCHMIDT, Peter Heinrich. Wirtschaftsforschung und geographie. Jena, G. Fischer, 1925. ix, 239 p.
585. SCHMOLDERS, G. Geschichte der volkswirtschaftslehre. Reinbekbei-Hamburg, Rowohlt, Taschenbuch verlag, 1967. 360 p.
586. SCHMOLLER, Gustave Friedrich von. Zur litteraturgeschichte der staats- und sozialwissenschaften. Leipzig, Duncker und Humblot, 1888. x, 304 p. (Reprinted: B. Franklin, 1967.)
587. SCHNEIDER, Erich. "Avances de la teoria económica en nuestro tiempo." In, Rivista di politica economica, 51, 4 (April, 1961) 555-556.
588. ———. Einführung in die wirtschaftstheorie. 1. Augsewählte kapitel der geschichte der wirtschaftstheorie. Tübingen, J. C. B. Mohr, 1962. viii, 423 p.
589. ———. Das gesicht der wirtschaftstheorie unserer zeit und das studium der wirtschaftswissenschaften. Tübingen, J. C. B. Mohr, 1947. 31 p.
590. ———. "Rückblick auf ein halbes jahrhundert der wirtschaftswissenschaft." In, Welturrtschaftliches archiv, 102, 2 (1969) 157-167.
591. SCHULLER, Richard. Die wirtschaftspolitik der historischen schule. Berlin, C. Heymann, 1899. vi, 131 p.
592. SCHUMPETER, Joseph Alois. Dogmenhistorische und biographische aufsätze. Tübingen, Mohr, 1954. viii, 383 p.
593. ———. Epochen der dogmen- und methodengeschichte J. C. B. Mohr, (Paul Siebeck) verlag, 1912. (2d. edition

entitled: Epochen der dogmen- und methodengeschichte."
In, Grundriss der sozialökonomik. Tübingen, 1924. vol. 1.
pp. 19-124. English edition entitled: Economic doctrine
and method. An historical sketch. Translated by R. Aris.
New York, Oxford university press, 1954. 207 p. Bibliographical preface and footnotes. New York, Oxford university press, 1967.)

594. _____. History of economic analysis; edited from manuscript by Elizabeth Boody Schumpeter. New York, Oxford university press, 1954. xxv, 1260 p. Bibliographical footnotes. Bibliography. (Italian edition entitled: Storia dell'analisi economica. Translated by Paolo Sylos-Labini and Luigi Occhionero. Turin, Giulio Einaudi, 1960. 3 v. Japanese edition entitled: Keizai bunseki no rekishi. (Transliterated.) Translated by Seiichi Tôhata. Tokyo, Iwanami Shoten, 1955. v. I. 438 p. 1957. v. II, 410 p. 1960? 384 p. 1962. v. III. 138 p.

595. SCOTT, William Amasa. The development of economics. New York, London, The century company, 1933. xii, 540 p. Bibliography. (Chinese edition entitled: Ching chi szu hsiang shih. (Transliterated.) Taipei, San Ming book company, 1960. xviii, 592, xxiii.

596. SEE, Henri Eugène. The economic interpretation of history. Translated and with an introduction by Melvin M. Knight. New York, Adelphi company, 1929. viii, 9-154. Bibliography. (New York, A. M. Kelley, 1968. viii, 154 p. New York, Burt Franklin, 1968. 154 p.)

597. SEKI, Miyosaku. Keizai shakai shiso shi. (Transliterated.) Japan, 1957. 436 p.

598. SELIGMAN, Ben B. Main currents in modern economics. Economic thought since 1870. New York, Free press of Glencoe, 1962. xiv, 887 p. Bibliographical notes.

599. SELIGMAN, Edwin Robert Anderson. Curiosities of early economic literature. An address to his fellow members of the hobby club of New York. San Francisco, priv. print. by J. H. Nash, 1920. xxvi, 1.

600. _____. The economic interpretation of history. 2d. revised edition. New York, Columbia university press, 1961. 166 p. Spanish edition entitled: La interpretación económica de la historia. (Compendios nova de iniciación cultural, 7.) Buenos Aires, Editorial nova, 1957. 135 p.

601. SHACKLE, George Lennox Sherman. The years of high theory. Invention and tradition in economic thought, 1926-1939. Cambridge, England, Cambridge university press, 1967. viii, 328 p. Bibliographical footnotes. [Reviewed: R. F. Harrod, Economic journal, 78, 311 (September, 1968) 660-664; W. J. Baumol, American economic review, 58, 3, I (June, 1968) 565-566.]

602. SHAKAI Keizaishi gakkai. Sengo ni okeru shakaikeizaishigaku no hattatsu. (Transliterated.) Japan, 1955. 2, 2, 284 p. Bibliographies.

603. SHEN, Chih-yuan. Chin tai ching chi hsiieh shuo shih kang. (Transliterated.) 1950. 316 p. (1st edition, 1936.)

604. SHIRASUGI, S. Keizai-gaku-shi gaisetsu. (Transliterated.) Kyoto, Minerva shobo, 1960. 480 p.
605. _____. Keizaigakushi gaisetsu jo. (Transliterated.) Kyôto, Minerva shobô, 1956. 8, 276 p.
606. SIEVEKING, Heinrich Johann. Grundzüge der neueren wirtschaftsgeschichte vom 17. jahrhundert bis zur gegenwart. 2. verb. aufl. Leipzig, B. G. Teubner, 1915. 2, 104 p. (Grundriss der geschichtswissenschaft, reihe II, abt, 2. 5.verb. aufl. Leipzig, B. G. Teubner, 1928. 126 p.)
607. SIK, J. "Polemika med ekonomisti preteklosti in sedanjosti." In Ekonomska revija (Ljubljana) 1 (1954) 1-11.)
608. SIK, O. "Znovu subjektivismus v ekonomické teorii." In, Ekonomický casopis, 15, 5 (November, 1967) 434-448.
609. SILBERNER, Edmund. The problem of war in nineteenth century economic thought. Translated by Alexander Haggerty Krappe. Princeton, New Jersey, Princeton university press, 1946. xiv, 332 p. Bibliography, 299-324. (A continuation of the author's La guerre dans la pensée économique du XVIe au XVIIIe siècle.)
610. SILVA HERZOG, Jesús. Historia y antología del pensamiento económico: antiguedad y edad media. México, Fondo de cultura económica, 1939. 2 ed., 1945. 2, 7-276 p. Bibliography (4. edition corr. y aumentada, Entitled: Historia del pensamiento económico-social; de la antigüedad al siglo XVI, 1961. 285 p. Bibliography.
611. _____. Tres siglos de pensamiento economico, 1518-1817. Mexico, Fondo de cultura economica, 1950. 316 p. Bibliography.
612. SINCLAIR, Huntly MacDonald. A preface to economic history. New York and London, Harper & brothers, 1934. vii, 3-232. Bibliography.
613. SINHA, A. K. and K. Klostermaier. Masters of social thought. Agra, Lakshmi narain agarwal, 1966. 394 p.
614. SMIT, M. N. Očerki istorii buržuaznoj političeskoj ekonomii (seredina XIX--seredina XX vv.) Moskva, Socekgiz, 1961. 296 p.
615. SOBAJIMA, S. Keizai-gaku shi shinkô. (Transliterated.) Kyôto, Seki shoin, 1960. 401 p.
616. SOMBART, Werner. Die drei nationalökonomien; geschichte und system der lehre von der wirtschaft. München und Leipzig, Duncker & Humblot, 1930. xii, 352. Bibliographical footnotes.
617. SOMMERLAD, Theo. Das wirtschaftsprogramm der kirche des mittelalters, ein beitrag zur geschichte der nationalökonomie und zur wirtschaftsgeschichte des ausgehenden altertums. Leipzig, J. J. Weber, 1903. 3, ix-xv, 223.
618. SOSKIC, Branislav. Razvoj ekonomske misli. Beograd, Rad, 1965. 328 p. Bibliographies.
619. SOULE, George Henry. Ideas of the great economists. New York, Viking press, 1952. 218 p. [Reprinted: New York, New American library, 1955. 160 p. Egyptian edition entitled: Al mathahib al iktesadiah al kobra. Translated by

Rashed. al-Barrawi. Cairo, Maktabat al-Nadhat al-Mīsriah, 1957. 228 p. Al-madhāhib al-iqtisādiyyah al-kubrā. Translated by Räshid al-Barrâwi. Cairo, Matba-at Misr, 1962. 226 p. French edition entitled: Qu'est-ce que l'économie politique? Translated by Claude Lefarge. Strasbourg, Istra, 1963. 208 p. German edition entitled: Die ideen der grossen nationalökonomen. Translated by Erwin Schuhmacher. Frankfurt, A. M. Nest-verlag, 1955. 280 p. Indonesian edition entitled: Pikiran sardjana besar ahli economi. Translated by L. M. Sitorus and Oey Hang Lee. Djakarta, Pustaka rakjat, 1958. 305 p. Iranian editions entitled: A'quāyed-e bozorgtarin olamaye eqtesad. (Transliterated.) Translated by Hossem Pirniya. Tehran, Ebn-e Sina, 1955. 224 p. 'Aqāyed-e borzorgtarīn-e 'olamā-ye eqteşād. Tehran, 1961. 224 p. Japanese edition entitled: Idai naru keizai gakusha no shisô. (Transliterated.) Translated by Kiyoshi Kóno. Tokyo, Hôsai Daigaku shuppankoyku, 1962. 114 p. Pakistani editions entitled: Jaleel-ul-qadar mahereen-i-muáshiyat ke afkar. (Transliterated.) Translated by Sardar Mohammed Akhtar. Lehore, Franklin publications, 1957. Ozama ke siyas nazriat. (Transliterated.) Translated by S. M. Akhtar and Gulam Raul Mehr. Lahore, Board for advancement of literature, 1960. 356 p. Spanish editions entitled: Storia del pensiero economico. Translated by Gualtiero da via. L. Cappelli, 1960. 228 p. Ideas de los grades economistas. Translated by Aníbal Leal. Buenos Aires, Compañía general fabril editoria, 1961. 292 p.]

620. SOUSA, Antonio de e Flausino Tôrres. Primeiro império comercial. (Colecção construindo 1. sér.: Construção da sociedade, no. 5.) Lisboa, Empresa contemporanea de edicões, 1946. v. Bibliography.

621. SOUZA, J. C. Martins de. Economia política. Históris dos fatas econômicos, conceitos fundamentais. Sao Paulo, J. Bushatsky, 1969. 541 p.

622. SPANN, Othmar. Die hauptheorien der volkswirtschaftslehre, auf lehrgeschichtlicher grundlage, mit einem anhang: wie studiert man volkswirtschaftslehre? 20., neuerdings durchgesehene aufl, 96.-100. tausend, jubelausgabe, mit sechs bildnissen und dem bildnisse des verfassers. (Wissenschaft und bildung. 193/194.) Leipzig, Quelle & Meyer, 1930. xvi, 232. Bibliography. (25., durchgesehene aufl. Heidelbert, Quelle & Meyer, 1949. xv, 259 p. Bibliography Bibliographical footnotes. English editions entitled: The history of economics. Translated from the nineteenth German edition by Eden and Cedar Paul. New York, W. W. Norton & company, inc., 1930. 3, 9-328. Bibliography. Types of economic theory. Same translation. London, G. Allen & Unwin ltd., 1930. 3, 9-328. Bibliography. Spanish edition entitled: Historia de las doctrinas económicas Traducción de José Ramón Pérez Bances. Revisado por Lorenzo de la Madrid. Madrid, editorial revista de derecho privado, 1934. 3, ix-xv, 324. Bibliography.)

623. SPIEGEL, Henry William. The development of economic thought. New York, John Wiley and sons, inc.; London, Chapman & Hall, ltd., 1952. xii, 811 p.
624. _____. The growth of economic thought. Englewood Cliffs, New Jersey, Prentice-Hall, 1971. 816 p. Bibliographical notes, 664-794.
625. SRIVASTAVA, Shri Krishna. History of economic thought. Delhi, Atma Ram, 1963. xiii, 423. Bibliography. (Hindi edition entitled: Arthika cintana ka vikasa. (Transliterated.) India, 1963. 14, 532 p.
626. STARK, Werner. History of economics in its relation to social development. London, K. Paul, Trench, Trubner & company, ltd., 1944. viii, 80 p. Bibliography. (German edition entitled: Die geschichte der volkswirtschaftslehre in ihrer beziehung zur sozialen entwicklung. Translated by Erich Abt. Dordrecht, Reidel, 1960. viii, 86.) Italian edition entitled: La storia dell-economia in relazione allo sviluppo sociale. Milan, Editrice l'industria, 1950. 82 p. Spanish edition entitled: Historia de la economía en su relación com el desarrollo social. Translated by Rubén Pimentel and José Manuel Sobrino. México, Fondo de cultural, económica, 1961. 112 p.
627. _____. The ideal foundations of economic thought. London, Routledge & Kegan Paul, 1948.
628. STAVENHAGEN, Gerhard. Geschichte der wirtschaftstheorie. 2., völlig neubearb. Aufl. Göttingen, Vandenhoeck & Ruprecht, 1957. 536 p.
629. STEINLEIN, Karl. Handbuch der volks-wirthschafts-lehre, mit drei synoptischen tafeln. Erster band, enthaltend die enleitung mit der literature, die grundlehren, und einen theil der lehre von der production. München, In Commission der literarisch-artistischen anstalt, 1831. lvi, 510 p.
630. STIGLER, George Joseph. Production and distribution theories, 1870-1895. New York, The Macmillan company, 1941. vii, 392 p. (Expansion of Ph.D. thesis, University of Chicago, 1938. Published also without thesis note under title: Production and distribution theories, the formative period.)
631. _____. "The influence of events and policies on economic theory." In American economic review, Papers and proceedings 59, 2 (May, 1960) 36-45; discussed by P. T. Homan, F. Machlup, and J. J. Spengler, 46-54.
632. STOLLBERG, Rudhard. Geschichte der bürgerlichen politischen Okonomie; eine allgemeinverständliche einführung. Berlin, Verlag die wirtschaft, 1960. 242 p. Bibliography.
633. STUDIES in the history of economic thought. v. 1. New York, Distributed by John Day company, 1943. v.
634. SUBRAHMANYAM, A. N. An inquiry into economics. (University of Mysore. Studies in economics and politics, no. 4.) Mysore, Printed by the Assistant Superintendent at the government branch press, 1948. viii, 115 p. Bibliography.
635. SUGIHARA, S. Miru to Marukusu. (Transliterated.) Kyoto, Minerubashobo, 1957. 260 p.
636. SUGIMOTO, Eiichi. Kindai keizaigaku shi. (Transliterated.)

Japan, 1953. 17, 326, 10. Bibliographical footnotes.
637. SUNKEL, O. "El renacimiento de la economía política." In Economía (Santiago de Chile) 19, 71, II (1961) 12-19.
638. SURANYI-UNGER, Theo. Die entwicklung der theoretischen volkswirtschaftslehre im ersten viertel des 20. Jahrhunderts. Jena, G. Fischer, 1927. xii, 320 p. Bibliographical references. (English edition entitled: Economics in the twentieth century; the history of its international development. . . . Edited by Edwin Robert Anderson Seligman. Translated from the German by Noel D. Moulton. New York, W. W. Norton & Company, inc., 1931. xix, 397 p. (Bibliographical notes.)
639. _____. Philosophie in der volkswirtschaftslehre; ein beitrag zur geschichte der volkswirtschaftslehre. Jena, G. Fischer, 1923-26. 2 v. Bibliographical footnotes.
640. _____. Wirtschaftsphilosophie des 20. Jahrhunderts. Stuttgart, G. Fischer, 1967. xiii, 312 p.
641. SVIATLOVSKII, Vladimir Vladimirovich. Ocherki po istorii ekonomicheskikh vozzrienii. (Transliterated.) 1910. viii, 534 p.
642. TAKAGI, M. "Keizai-gaku-shi no Kosei ni tsuite." In Shôdai ronshû (Kôbe) 4-6 (March, 1960) 163-222.
643. TAKAHASHI, Seiichirō. Keizaigaku shi. (Transliterated.) Gemdai keizaigakū zenshu. dai 7-kan.) Japan, 1929. 464 p. Bibliographical footnotes.
644. _____. Keizaigaku zenshi. (Transliterated.) Keizaigaku zenshu, dai 23-kan.) (Japan, 1929. 745 p. Bibliographies.
645. _____. Keizaigaku; waga shi, waga tomo. (Transliterated.) Japan, 1956. 230 p.
646. TAKASHIMA, Z. "Keizai-shisô-shi no atarashii mikata ni tsuite; rekishiteki na mono to riron-teki na mono tono toitsu no kokoromi." In Hitotsubashi ronshû (Tôkyô) 36, 4 (October, 1956) 19-37.
647. TAPFER, Friederike. Der wirtschaftspolitische beitrag der klassik. Meisenheim am Glan, A. Hain, 1956. 157 p. Bibliography.
648. TAUTSCHER, Anton. Geschichte der volkswirtschaftslehre. Wien, A. Sexl, 1950. xii, 279 p. Bibliographies.
649. TAYLOR, E. Historia rozwoju ekonomiki. Poznan, Panistwowe wydawnictwa naukowe, 1957-58. 2 v. (1957: v. I, 258 p. 1958: v. II, 385 p.)
650. TAYLOR, Overton H. "Philosophies and economic theories in modern western civilization." In, Economics and liberalism. Cambridge, Massachusetts, Harvard university press, 1955.
651. _____. A history of economic thought. Social ideals and economic theories from Quesnay to Keynes. New York, McGraw-Hill, 1960. 524 p. Bibliography.
652. TEILHAC, Ernest. L'économie politique perdue et retrouvée. Préf. de André Marchal. (Bibliothéque d'économie politique, v. 2.) Paris, Librairie générale de droit et de jurisprudence, 1962. 171 p.
653. THRUPP, S. S. "The role of comparison in the development

Chronological and Subject Surveys 45

of economic theory." In Journal of economic history, 17, 4 (December, 1957) 554-570.
654. TINBERGEN, Jan. On the theory of economic policy. Amsterdam, North-Holland publishing company, 1952. 78 p. (2nd edition, Humanities press, 1963.)
655. TOKINAGA, Fukashi. Keizaigakushi. (Transliterated.) Japan, 1970. 468 p.
656. ———. "Keizaigakushi no kenkyū hōtō ni tsuite." Transliterated.) In, Keizai shirin (Tokyo) 3, 1 (January, 1962.) 33-68.
657. TOMITA, S. "Keizai-riron no rekishi-sei." (Transliterated.) In, Mita Gakkai Zasshi (Tokyo) 49, 9 (September, 1956) 12-24.
658. ———. Seito gakuha, genkaishugi oyobi markukushizumu no taikeiteki rikai. (Transliterated.) (Keio gijuku keizai keizalgaku kenkyu sosho.) Tokyo, Keio gijuku daigaku, 1961. v, 180 p. Bibliographical footnotes.
659. TOTOMIANTS, Vakhan Fomich. Geschichte der national-ökonomie und des sozialismus im zusammehhang mit der wirtschaftsgeschichte. 2 verb. aufl., 4. bis 6. tausend. Berlin, C. Heymann, 1929. vii, 179 p. (French edition entitled: Histoire des doctrines économiques et sociales, préface de C. Rist. Paris, M. Giard, 1922. x, 238 p. Italian edition entitled: Storia delle dottrine economiche e sociali. Prefazione di Achille Loria. 2. edition, Milano, Fratelli bocca, 1943 ? x, 198 p. Spanish edition entitled: Historia de las doctrinas económicas y sociales. Versión de la 2.ª edición alemana por Vicente Gay. Barcelona, G. Gili, 1934. 3, 3-278.)
660. TRESÇA, Petre. Prolégomènes à une mécanique sociale. Paris, F. Alcan, 1923. 3 v. Bibliographie.
661. TREUB, Marie Willem Frederic. De ontwikkeling der staathuisoudkunde tot sociale economie. Amsterdam, Scheltema en Holkema, 1896. 47 p.
662. TRUSEN, Winfried. Spätmittelalterliche jurisprudenz und wirtschaftsethik, dargestellt an wiener gutachten des 14. Jahrhunderts. (Vierteljahrschrift fur social- und wirtschaftsgeschichte. Beihefte, nr. 43.) Wiesbaden, F. Steiner, 1961. 245 p. Bibliography.
663. TSUCHIYA, Takao. Nihon keizai shi. (Transliterated.) (Keizaigaku zenshu 6.) Japan, 1955. 4, 4, 189, 9 p.
664. TSUKATANI, Akihiro. Kindai nihon keizai shisō shi kenkyū. (Transliterated.) Japan, 1960. 265 p.
665. VEREIN für sozialpolitik, gesellschaft für wirtschaft-und sozialwissenschaften. Die hochschullehrer der wirtschaftswissenschaften in der bundesrepublik deutschland einschl. Westberlin, österreich und der deutschsprachigen schweiz; werdegand und schriften. Berlin, Duncker & Humblot, 1959. xx, 515 p.
666. VERLINDEN, Charles. Introduction à l'histoire économique général Coimbra, 1948. 241 p.
667. VIDELA L, Mario. El pensamiento económico social y las transformaciones del derecho. Santiago do Chile, Talleres

gráficos "San Francisco," 1942. 71 p. Bibliografia.
668. VILLEY, Daniel. Notes de philosophie économique, rédigées d'après le cours et avec l'autorisation de Daniel Villey. D. E. S., 1958-1959. Paris, Cours de droit, 1959. 260 p.
669. _____. Petite histoire des grandes doctrines économiques. Paris, Presses universitaires de France, 1944. xv, 230 p. (Nouv. éd. rev. et précédée d'une prèf. Paris, Librairie de médicis, 1954. 302 p.
670. VITELLO, V. Il pensiero economico moderno. Roma, Editori riuniti, 1963. 130 p.
671. VON MOHL. Geschichte und literatur der staatswissenschaften. 1855-8.
672. WAGENFUHR, Horst. Geschichte der wirtschaftlichen lehrmeinungen und der wirtschaftspolitischen systeme (Mit zwei darstellungen.); ein leitfaden. Leipzig, P. Reclam jun., 1934. 77 p. Bibliographies.
673. WALCKER, Karl. Geschichte der nationalökonomie, insbesondere der neueren und neuesten. Leipzig, Rossberg, 1884. 2, ix-xviii, 324.
674. WANG, Ya-nan. Ching chi hsüeh shih. (Transliterated.) China, 1933. 16, 20, 492 p.
675. WEBER, Max. Gesammelte aufsätze zur sozial- und wirtschaftsgeschichte. Tübingen, Mohr, 1924. iv, 556 p. Bibliographies.
676. _____. Wirtschaftsgeschichte. Abriss der universalen social- und wirtschafts-geschichte. Aus den nachgelassenen vorlesungen, hrsg. von S. Hellmann, und dr. M. Palyi. 2., univeränderte aufl. München und Leipzig, Duncker & Humblot, 1924. xiv, 348 p. Bibliographische.
677. WEBER, Wilhelm. Wirtschaftswissenschaft und wirtschaftspolitik in Osterreich. Wien, Springer, 1949. 85 p.
678. WEILLER, Jean. "Les cadres sociaux de la pensée économique contemporaine." In, Cahiers internationaux de sociologie, 26 (Janv.-Juin, 1959) 103-118.
679. _____. Cours d'histoire des doctrines économiques; rédigé d'apres les notes et avec l'autorisation de Jean Weiller. D. E. S., droit romain et histoire du droit, économie politique, sciences economiques, 1957-58. Paris, Cours de droit, 1958. 253 p.
680. WEISS, Francis Joseph. Grundlagen der volkswirtschaftspolitik in ihrer geschichtlichen entiwicklung. Wien, Manz, 1929. 2, 215 p.
681. WHITTAKER, Edmund. A history of economic ideas. New York, London, Longmans, Green and company, 1940. xii, 766. Bibliography.
682. _____. Schools and streams of economic thought. Chicago, Rand McNally, 1960. 416 p. Bibliography.
683. WIEDENFELD, Kurt. Zwischen wirtschaft und staat; aus den lebenserinnerungen. Aus dem nachgelassenen manuskript. (Kurt Wiedenfelds hrsg. von Friedrich Bülow.) Berlin, W. de Gruyter, 1960. 238 p.
684. WINCH, D. N. "What price the history of economic thought?"

Chronological and Subject Surveys 47

(Comment by H. Hamilton.) In, Scottish journal of political economy, 9, 3 (November, 1962) 193-207.
685. WU, Chên-Hsiung. Chin tai hsi yang ching chi shih. (Transliterated.) 1957. 424 p.
686. YAMADA, Y. Gendai keizaigaku no kontei ni arumono. (Transliterated.) Tôkyô, Hakutô shobô, 1955. 240 p.
687. YAMAGUCHI, Kazuo. Nihon keizai shi kōgi. (Transliterated.) Japan, 1960. 3, 243, 15 p. Bibliography.
688. YOSHIDA, Yoshizō. Keizai seichō. (Transliterated.) Japan, 1961. iv, v, 229 p. Bibliographical footnotes.
689. ZAMIATNIN, V. N. Istoriia ekonomicheskikh uchenii. (Transliterated.) 1964. 547 p. Bibliographies.
690. ZAUBERMAN, A. "Changes in economic thought." In, Survey; a journal of Soviet and East European studies, 64 (1967) 159-168.
691. ZIMMERMAN, Louis Jacques. Sparen, beleggen en investern in de economische literatuur. 's-Gravenhage, M. Nijhoff, 1941. 91 p.
692. _____. Geschiedenis van het economisch denken. 2., herziene druk. Den haag, Albani, 1950. 276 p. Bibliography. (3rd. edition 's-Gravenhage, Albani, 1953. 298 p.)
693. ZURAWICKI, Seweryn. Wspołczesna mysl ekonomiczna. Prolegomena. Wrocław, Zakład narodowy im. Ossolińskich, 1969. 369 p.
694. ZWANZIGER, M. Ha-mahashavah ha-kaikalit. (Transliterated.) Jerusalem, 1957. 175 p. Bibliography.
695. ZWEIG, Ferdynand. Economic ideas. A study of historical perspectives. New York, Prentice-Hall, 1950. 197 p. (Spanish edition entitled: El pensamiento económico y su perspectiva histórica. México, Fondo de Cultura econ., 1954. 216 p.)
696. ZWIEDINECK-Südenhorst, O. von. Von der älteren zur neueren theorie der politischen ökonomie. München, Verlag der bayerischen akademie der wissenschaften, in Komission bei C. H. Beck, 1952. 96 p.

B. COLLECTIONS: ESSAYS, LECTURES, ADDRESSES, AND OTHERS

697. ABBOTT, Leonard Dalton, editor. Masterworks of economics. Digests of 10 great classics. Garden City, New York, Doubleday and company, incorporated, 1946. ix, 754 p.
698. ACADEMISCHE economische Kring, Tilburg, Netherlands. Economische wetenschap en economische politiek. Een bundel opstellen sangeboden aan de Academische senaat ter gelegenheid van het vijfentwintigjarig bestaan van de Katholieke economische hogeschool. Leiden, H. E. Stenfert Kroese, 1952. viii, 443 p.
699. ADAMS, Walter and Leland Eldridge Traywick, editors. Readings in economics, principles and problems. With an introduction by H. F. Williamson. New York, Macmillan company, 1948. xi, 520 p.
700. ALLAIS, Maurice. Economics as a science. (Etudes et travaux l'Institut universitaire de hautes études internationales, no. 7.) Genève, Droz, 1968. 26 p.
701. _____. L'économique en tant que science. (Etudes et travaux de l'Institut universitaire de hautes études internationales, no. 6.) Genève, Droz, 1968. 26 p.
702. AMATO, Luigi d'. Da Cantillon a Pareto. Roma, A. Belardetti, 1955. 83 p.
703. AMERICAN economic association. A survey of contemporary economics. V. I: Howard S. Ellis, editor; V. II: Bernard F. Haley, editor. Philadelphia, Blakiston, 1948. xv. 490 p. (Homewood, Illinois, R. D. Irwin, 1948-52. 2 v.
704. _____. Readings in the theory of income distribution. New York, McGraw-Hill book company, 1946.
705. _____. Surveys of economic theory prepared for the American economic association and the Royal economic society. London, Macmillan; New York, Saint Martin's press, 1965. v. Bibliographies.
706. AMMER, Dean S., editor. Readings and cases in economics. Boston, Ginn, 1966. v, 330 p. Bibliographical footnotes.
707. ANDERSON, Thomas Joel, Jr., Abraham L. Gitlow and Daniel E. Diamond, editors. General economics; a book of readings. (Irwin series in economics.) Homewood, Illinois, R. D. Irwin, 1959. 489 p. (Revised edition, 1963. 519 p.)
708. ANDREANO, Ralph L. The new economic history. Recent papers on methodology. (Collection of essays which first appeared in Explorations of entrepreneurial history, 2d series.) New York, Wiley, 1970. xiv, 178 p.
709. BAGEHOT, Walter. Economic studies. Edited by Richard Holt Hutton. Stanford, California, Academic reprints,

Collections

1953. 236 p. (From volume V of The works of Walter Bagehot, edited by Forrest Morgan.)
710. BALSLEY, Howard Lloyd, editor. Economic doctrines; a book of readings. (The New Littlefield college outlines, no. 74-75.) Paterson, New Jersey, Littlefield, Adams, 1961. 2 v.
711. BARBIERI, Gino, editor. Fonti per la storia delle dottrine economiche. Milano, C. Marzorati, 1958- . v.
712. BARI (City). Università. Facoltà di economia e commercio. Studi in memoria di Rodolfo Benini. Bari, 1956. 236 p.
713. BASTIAT, Frederic. Selected essays on political economy. Edited by George B. de Huszar; translated from French by S. Cain. Princeton, D. Van Nostrand, 1964.
714. BAUDIN, Louis. Traité d'économie politique. Paris, Dalloz, 1951- . v.
715. BEITRAGE zu wirtschaftspolitik und wirtschaftswissenschaft. 1- . (Schriftenreihe der Wiener kammer für arbeiter und angestellte.) Wien, Verlag des Osterreichischen gewerkschaftsbundes, 1969- .
716. BENN, Sir Ernest John Pickstone. Why freedom works; passages from books, 1924-1953. London, E. Benn, limited, 1964. 127 p.
717. BERLIN, Deutsches institut für wirtschaftsforschung. Wirtschafts forschung und wirtschaftsführung; vorträge und aufsätze. Festgabe für Ferdinand Friedensburg zum 70. geburtstage, überreicht von dom Kollegium der abteilungsleiter des Deutschen instituts für wirtschaftsforschung. Berlin, Duncker und Humblot, 1956. xvi, 222 p. Bibliographical footnotes.
718. _____. Freie universität. Wirtschafts- und sozialwissenschaftliche fakultät. Grundsatzfragen der wirtschaftsordnung; ein Vortrags- zyklus veranstaltet von der Wirtschafts- und sozialwissenschaftlichen fakultät der Freien universität Berlin, Sommersemester 1953. (Its Wirtschaftswissenschaftliche abhandlunges; Volks- und betriebswirtschaftliche schriftenreihe, Heft 2.) Berlin, Duncker und Humblot, 1954. 251 p.
719. _____. Universität. Wirtschaftswissenschaftliche fakultät. Lehrbriefe für das fernstudium. Politische ökonomie des sozialismus. 1- ; Feb. 1954- . Berlin? Irregular.
720. BERLE, Adolf Augustus. The motive power of political economy. (Felix Adler lecture, 1960.) New York, New York society for ethical culture, 1960. 14 p.
721. BLACK. R. D. C., editor. Readings in the development of economic analysis, 1776-1848. (Sources for social and economic history.) London, David and C. Blackwell's, 1971.
722. BLUMNER, Sidney M., editor. Readings in microeconomics. (International's series in economics.) Scranton, International textbook company, 1969. xii, 383 p.
723. BONAR, James. Theories of population from Raleigh to Arthur Young; lectures delivered in the Galtonian laboratory, University of London, under the Newmarch foundation,

February 11 to March 18, 1929, with two additional lectures and with references to authorities. 1st edition, new impression. London, Cass, 1966. 3-253. (Reprinted: New York, A. M. Kelley, 1966. 253 p.)
724. BONN, M. J. and M. Palyi, editors. Die wirtschaftswissenschaft nach dem Kriege. Munich, 1925. 2 v.
725. BOSERUP, Mogens. Deres egne ord. (Økonomiske institut. Memorandum, 21.) Københavns universitets fond til Tilvejebringelse of Laeremidler, 1968- . Bibliography, 120-124. (Fra Platon til Stuart Mill. Udvolg og kommentar.
726. BOUSQUET, Georges Henri. Essai sur l'evolution de la pensee economique. Paris, M. Giard, 1927. xv, 314 p. Bibliography, 305-308.
727. BOWDITCH, John and Clement Ramsland, editors. Voices of the industrial revolution. Selected readings from the liberal economists and their critics. Ann Arbor, University of Michigan press, 1961. 187 p.
728. BOWEN, Ian. Acceptable inequalities: an essay on the distribution of income. London, McGill-Queen's; Blackwell's, 1971.
729. BRADFER, Alfred. Essai d'économique. Bruxelles, Editions du Parthénon, 1958. 142 p.
730. BRENNAN, Michael Joseph, editor. Patterns of market behavior; essays in honor of Philip Taft. Providence, Brown university press, 1965. viii, 258 p. Bibliographica references.
731. BROOKINGS institution, Washington, D. C. Economic reasoning series. Washington, 1955. 10 parts in 1 v.
732. BULLOCK, Charles Jesse. Economic essays. Cambridge, Massachusetts, Harvard university press, c1936. viii, 2 l, 550 p. "Book and articles by Professor Bullock": 545-550.
733. _____. Selected readings in economics. Boston, New York, Ginn and company, 1907. ix, 705 p.
734. BURNS, Arthur Frank. The frontiers of economic knowledge; essays. (General series, no. 57.) Princeton, Published for the National bureau of economic research, New York, by Princeton university press, 1954. ix, 367 p.
735. CAIRNCROSS, Alec. Essays in economic management. London, Allen and Unwin, 1971.
736. CANNAN, Edwin. An economist's protest. . . . New York, Adelphi company, 1928. xx, 438 p.
737. CENTRO di studi filosofici cristiani di Gallarate. 13. convegno, Gallarate, 1957. Economia, politica e morale; atti del XIII convegno del Dentro di studi filosofici tra professori universitari, Gallarate, 1957. Collaboratori, Antonelli, et al. Brescia, Morcelliana, 1958. 302 p.
738. CHAMBER of commerce of the United States of America. Understanding economics; materials for the Understanding economics discussion course. Prepared under the direction of Carl H. Madden. Washington, 1966-68. (Discussion leader's guide. 1967. 67 p.)
739. CHENG chih chis chi hstieh chiao ch'êng. (Transliterated.)

Collections 51

China, 1951-52. 16 v. in 2.
740. CHRISTOFFEL, Tom, David Finkelhor and Dan Gilbarg. Up against the American myth. A radical critique of corporate capitalism. . . . New York, Holt, Rinehard and Winston, 1970. xii, 464 p.
741. CLAPHAM, John Harold. The study of economic history; an inaugural lecture. Cambridge, England, The University press, 1929. 39 p.
742. CLARK, John J. and Morris Cohen, editors. Business fluctuations, growth, and economic stabilization; a reader. New York, Random house, c1963. 682 p. Bibliography.
743. CLARK, John Maurice. Alternative to serfdom; five lectures delivered . . . at the University of Michigan, March 1947. (William W. Cook foundation. Lectures, v. 3.) New York, A. A. Knopf, c1948. xii, 153, vi p. Bibliographical footnotes.
744. _____ Guideposts in time of change; some essentials for a sound American economy. Six lectures delivered at Amherst college in the winter of 1947-48. 1st edition. New York, Harper, c1949. x, 210 p.
745. _____. Preface to social economics; essays on economic theory and social problems. New York, Farrar and Rinehart, incorporated, c1936. xxi, 435 p. Bibliography, 434.
746. _____. Studies in the economics of overhead costs. Chicago, Illinois, The University of Chicago press, c1923. xiii, 502 p.
747. CLASSICS in economics. A course of selected reading by authorities. Introductory reading guide by George Douglas Howard Cole. New York, Philosophical library, c1960. 324 p. (English edition was published by International university society under title: Economics.)
748. CLEMENCE, Richard Vernon, editor. Readings in economic analysis. Cambridge, Massachusetts, Addison-Wesley press, 1950. 2 v. Bibliographical footnotes.
749. COLE, George Douglas Howard. Economic tracts for the times. London, Macmillan and company, limited, 1932. vii, 327, 1 p.
750. _____. Some relations between political and economic theory. London, Macmillan and company, limited, 1934. vii, 92 p.
751. COMITATO per il potenziamento in Venezia degli studi economici. Rendiconti del Comitato per il potenziamento in Venezia degli studi economici. A cura di G. Franco. . . . Padova, CEDAM, 1969- . v.
752. CONDLIFFE, John Bell. Technological progress and economic development; three lectures. (Delhi school of economics. Occasional papers, no. 2.) Delhi, Ranjit printers and publishers, by arrangement with Delhi school of economics, 1951. 62 p.
753. CONTEMPORARY economic problems. By Paul Fleming Gemmill and associates, Department of economics, University of Pennsylvania. 1st edition. New York and London, Harper and brothers, c1932. xv p., 1 l., 673 p. Bibliographical

references, 652-659.
754. CORNELIUS, Friedrich. Wirtschaftsgeschichte. (Schaeffers Grundriss des rechts und der wirtschaft. Abt. 2: Offentliches recht und volkswirtschaft, 34 Bd., 2 T.) Stuttgart, Kohlhammer, 1950. 118 p.
755. DEGUCHI, Y., editor. Keizaigaku-shi. (Transliterated.) 3d revised and enlarged edition. Kyôto, Mineruba-shobô, 1958. 508 p.
756. DENIS, Henri. Le crise de la pensée économique. Coll. "Que sais-je?" Paris, 1951. 128 p.
757. DE RYCKE, Laurence and Alvin H. Thompson, editors. Beginning readings in economics. (Study on economic education.) Washington, Council for advancement of secondary education, 1961. 367 p. 2d edition. (C. A. S. E. economic literacy series, 5.) St. Louis, Webster Division, McGraw-Hill, 1968. vi, 378 p.
758. DEVONS, Ely. Essays in economics. London, Allen and Unwin, 1961. 203 p.
759. DOUBLET, Eugène. Yves Guyot" son action, sa pensée, multigr. Rennes, 1955. 193 p. (Thèse, Droit, Rennes, 1955.)
760. DUBOIN, Jacques. L'économie distributive s'impose; troisièm lettre. Paris, Editions Lecdis, 1950. 93 p.
761. DUNBAR, Charles Franklin. Economic essays. Edited by O. M. W. Sprague with an introductory biographical sketch by F. W. Taussig. New York, The Macmillan company; London, Macmillan and company, limited, 1904. xvii, 372 p.
762. EAGLY, Robert V. and others. Events, ideology, and economic theory. The determinants of progress in the development of economic analysis. (Papers presented at a symposium, Wayne state university, May 2nd and 3rd, 1966.) Detroit, Wayne state university press, 1968. 205 p. Bibliographical references.
763. EASTHAM, J. K., editor. Economic essays in commemoration of the Dundee school of economics, 1931-1955. By Duncan Black and others, Coupar Angus, Perthshire, Printed by W. Culross; distributed by the Economists' bookshop London, for the School of economics, Dundee, 1955. 103 p.
764. ECONOMIC essays. Contributed in honor of John Bates Clark Edited by Jacob Harry Hollander. Published in behalf of the American economic association. New York, The Macmillan company, 1927. viii, 368 p. Bibliography.
765. ECONOMIC essays in honor of Wesley Clair Mitchell, presented to him by his former students on the occasion of his sixtieth birthday. New York, Columbia university press, 1935. ix, 519 p.
766. ECONOMIC essays in honour of Gustav Cassel, October 20th, 1933. London, G. Allen and Unwin limited, 1933. 2, 7-720 p.
767. ECONOMIC theory in review, by James S. Earley and others. Edited by C. Lawrence Christenson. (Indiana university publications. Social science series, no. 8.) Bloomington,

68. EDGEWORTH, Francis Ysidro. Papers relating to political economy. London, Macmillan, 1925. 3 v. (New York, Burt Franklin, 1963.)
69. EDWARDS, C. D., E. S. Mason, M. W. Watkins, A. R. Burns, and others. Readings in the social control of industry. Selected by a committee of the American economics association. New York, McGraw-Hill book company, incorporated, Blakiston division, 1942.
70. EKONOMISK tidskrift. 25 economic essays in English, German, and Scandinavian languages, in honour of Erik Lindahl, 21 November 1956. Stockholm, 1956. 412 p.
71. ENNES ULRICH, Ruy. Economía (circulação). Lições proferidas na Faculdade de direito da Universidade de Lisboa no ano lectivo de 1946-1947. Publicadas por: António Luiz R. da Silva Branco e Luiz Manuel R. Tomé. Lisboa, 1947. 293 p.
72. EPSTEIN, Ralph Cecil and Arthur D. Butler, editors. Selections in economics. (Economics books on economics, politics, and business, E-13-13A.) Buffalo, Smith, Keynes and Marshall, c1958. 2 v.
73. ESSAYS in social economics. Presented to Alvin Saunders Johnson on the occasion of his eightieth birthday by the Graduate faculty of political and social science of the New school of social research. New York, 1954. 191 p.
74. ETUDES d'économie politique et sociale à la mémoire de Eugène Duthoit, doyen de la Faculté catholique de droit de Lille, president des Semaines sociales, par ses collègues, ses disciples et ses amis. Paris, Librarie générale de droit et de jurisprudence, 1949. 280 p.
75. EXPLORATIONS in economics; notes and essays contributed in honor of F. W. Taussig. New York and London, McGraw-Hill book company, incorporated, c1936. xii, 539 p. ("Bibliography of Professor Taussig's writings": 535-539.)
76. FAIRCHILD, Fred Rogers and Ralph Theodore Compton, editors. Economic problems, a book of selected readings. Revised edition. New York, The Macmillan company, 1930. xiii, 693 p.
77. FELLNER, William, and Bernard F. Haley, editors. Readings in the theory of income distribution. American economic association, Philadelphia, McGraw-Hill book company, incorporated, Blakiston division; Homewood, Illinois, R. D. Irwin, 1946.
78. FETTER, Frank Albert. Versuch einer bevölkerungslehre ausgebend von einer kritik des Malthus' schen bevölkerungsprincips. Jena, G. Fischer, 1894. 4 p. 1., v-vii, 97, 1 p. 1 l.
79. FIELD, James Anthony. Essays on population. Edited by H. F. Hohnmann. Chicago, University of Chicago press, 1931.
80. FOSSATI, Eraldo. Oeconomica varia, excerpta. (Studi, del Laboratorio di econimia, "Vilfredo Pareto" dell'Università di Genova, ser. A, v. 2.) Milano, Giuffrè, 1960. 253 p.

781. ———. Oeconomica varia; theoricae notulae. Saggi appars in pubblicazioni periodiche italiene e straniere negli anni 1923-1957. Genova, Istituto di politica economica dell'Università di Genova, 1957. 2 v.
782. FRANCO López, Gabriel, editor. Historia de la economía por los grandes maestros; selección de capítulos, artículos relatos y documentos. (Biblioteca de ciencias sociales. Sección 1: Economía.) Madrid, Aguilar, 1965. xxxix, 654 p.
783. FRANKEL, Sally Herbert. The economic impact on underdeveloped societies; essays on international investment and social change. Cambridge, Harvard university press, 1953. vii, 179 p.
784. FRIEDMAN, Milton. Essays in positive economics. Chicago University of Chicago press, c1953. 328 p.
785. ———. The optimum quantity of money and other essays. Chicago, Aldine publishing company, 1969. vi, 296 p. Bibliographical footnotes.
786. FRIEDMAN, Milton and others. The ethics of competition and other essays by Frank Hyneman Knight. New York and London, Harper and brothers, 1936. 2 p., l., 7-363. (1st edition, 1935; 2d edition, 1936.)
787. ———. Studies in the quantity theory of money. With essays by Milton Friedman and others. Chicago, University of Chicago press, 1956. 265 p.
788. GADGIL, Dhananjaya Ramchandra. Economic policy and development; a collection of writings. (Gokhole institute of politics and economic publications, no. 30.) Poona, 1955. 248 p.
789. GALBRAITH, John Kenneth. A contemporary guide to economics, peace and laughter. Deutsch; London, Blackwells 1967.
790. ———. Economics and the art of controversy. (The Brow and Haley lectures, 1954.) New Brunswick, Rutgers university press, c1955. 111 p.
791. GAYER, Arthur David, C. Lowell Harriss and Milton H. Spencer, editors. Basic economics, a book of readings. New York, Prentice-Hall, 1951. xv, 624 p.
792. GEMAHLING, Paul, editor. . . . Les grands économistes; textes et commentaires. Deuxième édition revue et augmentée. Paris, Librairie du recueil sirey (société anonyme), 1933. 2 p. l., ix-xv, 372 p.
793. GEMMILL, Paul Fleming and Ralph Hamilton Blodgett, editors Current economic problems. New York, London, Harper and brothers, c1939. vii p., 2 l., 753 p. ("A complete re vision of 'Contemporary economic problems.' ")
794. GHERITY, James Arthur. Economic thought. A historical anthology. New York, Random house, 1965. xv, 554 p. Bibliographical footnotes.
795. GOMES, Francisco Luiz. Essai sur la théorie de l'économie politique et de ses rapports avec la morale et le droit. (Burt Franklin research and source works series, 602. Philosophy monograph series, 42.) New York, B. Franklir

1970. xii, 232 p.
796. GOURVITCH, Alexander. Survey of economic theory on technological change and employment. Philadelphia, Works project administration, 1940.
797. GRAMPP, William Dyer and Emanuel T. Weiler. Economic policy; readings in political economy. Homewood, Illinois, R. D. Irwin, 1953. 393 p. (Revised edition, 1956. 427 p.)
798. GREY, Arthur L. and John E. Elliott, editors. Economic issues and policies; readings in introductory economics. Boston, Houghton Mifflin, 1961. 420 p. (2d edition, 1965. xvi, 548 p. Bibliographical footnotes.)
799. GUAL VILLALBI, Pedro. La remodelación del orden económico actual; ensayo de revisión de los valores de la economía teórica en la actividad político-económica. Discurso de recepción del académico de número Excmo. Sr. D. Pedro Gual Villalbí y contestación del Excmo. Sr. D. José Larraz. Sesión del martes 30 de enero de 1962. Madrid, 1962. 120 p.
800. HAESELE, Kurt Werner. Weltwirtschaftliche essays. Innsbruck, Universitätsverlag Wagner, 1956. 264 p.
801. HAHN, Lucien Albert. The economics of illusion; a critical analysis of contemporary economic theory and policy. New York, Distributor: New York institute of finance, Publications division, for Squier publishing company, c1949. viii, 273 p.
802. HAILSTONES, Thomas J., editor. Readings in economics. Cincinnati, South-western publishing company, 1963. 512 p. Bibliography.
803. HAILSTONES, Thomas J., Bernard L. Martin and Frank V. Mastrianna. Contemporary economic problems and issues. Cincinnati, South-western publishing company, 1970. iv, 508 p.
804. HAMILTON, Earl Jefferson, Albert Rees and Harry G. Johnson, editors. Landmarks in political economy; selections from the Journal of political economy. Chicago, University of Chicago press, 1962. 622 p. Bibliography.
805. HAMILTON, Walton Hale. Current economic problems; a series of readings in the control of industrial development. Chicago, Illinois, The University of Chicago press, 1915. xxxix, 789 p. (Revised edition, 1919. xxxi, 955 p.)
806. HARLAN, Homer Charles, editor. Readings in economics and politics. New York, Oxford university press, 1961. 751 p.
807. HARRIS, Seymour Edwin. Economic reconstruction. 1st edition. New York, London, McGraw-Hill book company, incorporated, 1945. xii, 424 p. Bibliographical footnotes.
808. _____, editor. New economics. 1947. New York, Alfred A. Knopf, incorporated, 1950; A. M. Kelley, 1970?
809. HARRISS, Clement Lowell, editor. Selected readings in economics. Englewood Cliffs, New Jersey, Prentice-Hall, 1958. 546 p.
810. HARROD, Henry Roy Forbes. Economic essays. New York, Harcourt, Brace, 1952? 300 p.

811. _____. An essay in dynamic theory. In, Economic journal 49 (1939), 14-33.
812. _____. Topical comment; essays in dynamic economics applied. London, Macmillan; New York, Saint Martin's press, c1961. 265 p. Bibliography.
813. _____. Towards a dynamic economics, some recent developments of economic theory and their application to policy. (Lectures, University of London, 1947.) London, Macmillan, 1948. ix, 168 p.
814. HARWOOD, Edward Crosby. Reconstruction of economics. Including papers by May Brodbeck and Richard S. Rudner. Great Barrington, Massachusetts, American Institute for economic research, c1955. 112 p.
815. HAUSER, Henri. Les origines historiques des problemes economiques actuels. (Six lectures, Postgraduate institute on international studies, Geneva, February 1-7, 1928, plus three other papers.) Paris, Vuibert, 1930. vi, 104 p.
816. HAYEK, Friedrich August von, editor. Capitalism and the historians; essays by T. S. Ashton and others. Chicago, University of Chicago press, 1954. vii, 187 p. Bibliographical footnotes.
817. _____. Individualism and economics order. Essays. Chicago, University of Chicago press, c1948. vii, 272 p. Bibliographical footnotes.
818. HENDRICKS, Henry George, editor. Masterpieces in economics. San Antonio? 1950. 102 p.
819. HERZOG, J. S., editor. Antologia del pensamiento económico social. México, Fondo de cultura económica, 1963. 606 p.
820. HESS, Arleigh Porter, editor. Outside readings in economics. New York, Crowell, 1951. 877 p. (2d edition, 1956. 502 p.
821. HIGGINS, Benjamin Howard. What do economists know? Six lectures on economics in the crisis of democracy. Melbourne, Melbourne university press, 1951. viii, 166 p.
822. HISTORY of political economy. v. 1- Spring 1969- . Durham, North Carolina, Duke university press. v. semiannual.
823. HOFMAN, W. Theorie der wirtschaftsentwicklung. Vom merkantilismus bis zur gegenwart. Berlin, Duncker und Humblot, 1966. 321 p.
824. HOLLANDER, Jacob Henry. Economic essays, contributed in honor of John Bates Clark. Published on behalf of the American economics association. New York, The Macmillan company, 1927. viii, 368 p. Bibliography.
825. HON'IDEN Yoshio hakushi koki kinen rombunshū kankōkai. Hon'iden Yoshio hakushi koki kinen rombun shū. Seiyō keizai shi, shisōshi kenkyū. (Transliterated.) Japan, 1962. 4, 3, 423 p.
826. HOOVER, Glenn E., editor. Twentieth century economic thought. New York, Philosophical library, 1950. xiii, 819 p. Bibliographies.
827. HOSELITZ, Berthold Frank, editor. Economics and the idea of mankind. New York, Columbia university press, 1965. xxiv, 277 p. Bibliographical footnotes. (Prepared under the auspices of the Council for the study of mankind.)

Collections 57

828. INCOME, employment and public policy; essays in honor of Alvin H. Hansen. By Lloyd A. Metzler and others. 1st edition. New York, W. W. Norton, c1948. 379 p.
829. INSTITUTE of economic affairs, London. Economics, business and government: addresses given at a dinner on 13 January 1966 to mark the I. E. A.'s 10th year. By John Jewkes, Sir Paul Chambers, Lord Robbins. (IEA occasional paper, no. 8.) London, I.E.A., 1966. 31 p.
830. INTERNATIONAL economic association. Economic progress; papers and proceedings of a round table held by the International economic association. Edited by Léon H. Dupriez with the assistance of Douglas C. Hague. Louvain, Institut de recherches économiques et sociales, 1955. 574 p.
831. INTERNATIONAL economic papers. no. 1- . London, New York, Macmillan, 1951. v. (Translations for the International economic association.)
832. ISAACS, Asher, C. W. McKee and R. E. Slesinger, editors. Selected readings in modern economics. New York, Dryden press, 1952. 700 p.
833. ISTITUTO di cultura bancaria, Milan. Studi in memoria di Gino Borgatta. Bologna, Arti grafiche, 1953. 2 v.
834. ITO, Nobufumi, Economic problems of Asia. Tokyo, Asia cooperation, 1955. 114 p.
835. JEANNENEY, Jean Marcel et al. Documents économiques. 1. édition. ("Thémis," textes et documents.) Paris, Presses universitaires de France, 1958-59. 2 v.
836. JOHNSON, Harry Gordon. Money, trade and economic growth; survey lectures in economic theory. Cambridge, Harvard university press, c1962. 199 p. Bibliography.
837. JOINT council on economic education. Economics in general education; proceedings of conferences on economics in general education sponsored by Joint council on economic education, Riverdale, New York, August 22-September 3, 1954. Edited by James Gemmell, Seymour E. Harris and S. P. McCutchen. New York, 1954. 151 p.
838. JONES, Richard. Literary remains; consisting of lectures and tracts on political economy, 1859. (Reprints of economic classics.) New York, A. M. Kelley, 1965. xl, 620 p.
839. JOVASEVIC, V. "Medunarodna konferencija o savremenim teorijama buržoaśke ekonomije." Ekonomist (Beograd) 17, 2-3 (1964) 298-412.
840. el-KAISSI, Fawzi and Anwar Kassira. Writings of great economists. Bagdad, Matba'at al-Zahra, 1964. 277, 3 p. Bibliographies.
841. KALDOR, Nicholas, editor. Conflicts in policy objectives. London, Blackwell's, 1971.
842. KAMINSKY, Ralph, editor. Introduction to economic issues. 1st edition. Garden City, New York, Anchor books, 1970. x, 270 p.
843. KAPP, Karl William and Lore L. Kapp, editors. Readings in economics. (College outline series, 62.) New York, Barnes and Noble, 1949. vi, 444 p. (2d edition, 1963. viii, 437 p.

844. KARVE, Dattatraya Gopal, editor. Historical and economic studies; published on the occasion of the Silver jubilee of the Historical and economic association of the Fergusson college, Poona. Poona, 1941. 2 p. l., v, ii, 238, vi p.
845. KEYES, Scott, editor. Economics: trends and issues, a book of readings. New York, R. F. Moore company, c1952. 508 p. (2d edition, revised. New York, Whittier books, 1954. 496 p.)
846. KIRZNER, Israel M. The economic point of view; an essay in the history of economic thought. (The William Volker fund series in the humane studies.) Princeton, New Jersey, Van Nostrand, 1960. 228 p. Bibliography.
847. KISHIMOTO, Seijirō, editor. Keizaigaku shi. (Transliterated.) Tokyo, Seirin-Shoin, 1954. 552 p. Bibliography. (Reprint: 1960?)
848. KISHIMOTO Seijirō hakushi kanreki kinen rombunshū henshū iinkai. Keizaigaku ni okeru koten to gendal. (Transliterated.) 1965. 4, 329, 13 p. Bibliographical references in notes.
849. KNIGHT, Frank Hyneman. The ethics of competition, and other essays. 2d edition. New York, London, Harper and brothers, 1936. 2 p. l., 7-363 p. Bibliography, 11-18. (Essays selected by Milton Friedman and others.) [1st edition, 1935. 2d edition, 1926. Reprinted: (Essay index reprint series.) Freeport, New York, Books for libraries press, 1969. 363 p.]
850. _____. On the history and method of economics; selected essays. Chicago, University of Chicago press, 1956. 308 p.
851. KOLLNER, Lutz. Von Marx bis Erhard. Propheten und magier der wirtschaftspolitik. Mit einem geleitwort von Thomas Dehler. Velbert und Kettwig, Blick und Bild verlag, 1967. 376 p.
852. KOMUNISTICKA strana Ceskoslovenska. Ustředni výbor. Osnovy politického skolenî. V. Praze. v.
853. KOOPMANS, Johan Gerbrand. De budgetvergelijking als verbindingeschakel tussen micro- en macro-economie. Haarlem, Erven F. Bohn, 1955. 40 p.
854. KOOPMANS, Tjalling C. Three essays on the state of economic science. New York, McGraw-Hill, 1957. 231 p.
855. KOOY, Tjalling Pieter van der. De zin van het economische. Kampen, J. H. Kok, 1950. 32 p.
856. _____. Tussen beginsel en belang. (Sociaaleconomische boekerij.) Wageningen.
857. KORTEWEG, S. Enige opmerkingen over de grenzen der economische wetenschap; rede uitgesproken bij de aanvaarding van het ambt van hoogleraar aan de Rijksuniversiteit te Groningen op 11 Juni 1949. Amsterdam, Noord-Hollandsche Uitg. Mij., 1949. 32 p.
858. KOSIK, Karel. Dialektika konkrétního; studie o problematice člověka a svčta. Vyd. 1. Praha, Nakl. Ceskoslovenské akademie věd, 1963. 191 p.
859. KRUSE, Alfred, editor. Wirtschaftstheorie und wirtschaftspolitik. Festgabe für Adolf Weber. Zur vollendung seines

Collections 59

        75. Lebensjahres am 29. Dezember 1951, dargebracht von habilitierten Schülern und Münchener kollegen. Eine sammlung von abhandlungen unter mitarbeit von Erich Carell et al. Berlin, Duncker und Humblot, 1951. 364 p.

860. KUHLMAN, John M., editor. Economic problems and policies. Pacific Palisades, California, Goodyear publishing company, 1969. xii, 349 p.

861. KURUMA, K. et al. Keizaigaku-shi. (Transliterated.) Tôkyô, Iwanami shinsho, 1954. 367 p.

862. KUZ'MINOV, I. I., editor. Razvitie ekonomicheskoi teorii v svete reshenii XXII s"ezda. (Transliterated.) Moscow, 1962. 249 p. Bibliography.

863. KUZNETS, Simon Smith. Economic change; selected essays in business cycles, national income, and economic growth. 1st edition. New York, Norton, 1953. 333 p.

864. ———. Economic growth and structure; selected essays. 1st edition. New York, Norton, c1965. viii, 378 p. Bibliographical footnotes.

865. ———. Postwar economic growth, four lectures. Cambridge, Massachusetts, Belknap press of Harvard university press, c1964. 148 p. Bibliographical footnotes. ("Lectures... delivered under the auspices of the John Randolph and Dora Haynes foundation during the week of March 30, 1964... at the Town hall forum of Los Angeles... and the University of California, Riverside.")

866. LAGLER, Ernest. Wirtschaftliche entwicklung und soziale ordnung hrsg. von Ernst Lagler und Johannes Messner. Mit beiträgen von L., Adamovich et al. Ferdinand Degenfeld-Schonburg zum 70. Geburtstag gewidmet. Wien, Verlag Herold, 1952. 456 p.

867. LANE, Frederic Chapin and Jelle C. Riemersma, editors. Enterprise and secular change; readings in economic history. Edited for the American economic association and the Economic history association. Homewood, Illinois, R. D. Irwin, 1953. 556 p.

868. LEBLANC, Marguerite. De Thomas More á Chaptal. Contribution bibliographique à l'histoire economique: inventaire d'un fonds d'ouvrages anciens conservés aux Salles d'études économiques et statistiques de la faculté de droit de Paris. Avant-propos de Robert Goetz-Girey. (Catalogue of the Fonds depitre.) Paris, Editions Cujas, 1961. vi, 169 p. Bibliography, 161-162.

869. LEKACHMAN, Robert, editor. The varieties of economics: documents, examples and manifestoes. (Meridian books, MG46A-B.) Cleveland, World publishing company, 1962. 2 v.

870. LEONTIEF, Wassily W. Essays in economics; theories and theorizing. New York, Oxford university press, 1966. xii, 252 p.

871. LERNER, Abba Ptachya. Essays in economic analysis. London, Macmillan, 1953. 394 p.

872. LESLIE, Thomas Edward Cliffe. Essays in political economy. 2d edition. Dublin, Hodges, Figgis and company, 1888.

[(Reprints of economic classics.) New York, A. M. Kelley, 1969. xii, 437 p.]
873. LHOMME, Jean. La grande bourgeoisie au pouvoir (1830-1880); essai sur l'histoire sociale de la France. (Bibliothèque de la Science economique.) Paris, Presses universitaires de France, c1960. 378 p.
874. LIEGE, Université. Faculté de droit. Problèmes économiques contemporains: colloquia de la chaire Francqui, 1951-1952. (Its Collection scientifique, 1.) Liège, 1953. viii, 150 p.
875. LIIKETALOUSTIETEELLINEN tutkimuslaitos, Helsingfors. Liiketaloustiellisten tutkimuslaitoksen julkaisuja. Helsinki, Kauppatieteellinen Yhdistys, 19- . v.
876. LONGFIELD, Mountifort. Lectures on political economy, delivered in Trinity and Michaelmas terms, 1833. Dublin, R. Milliken and son, 1834. (Series of reprints of scarce tracts in economic and political science. no. 8) London, The London school of economics and political science, 1931. v-xii, 267 p.
877. LOVEDAY, A. and others. The world's economic future. With an introduction by D. H. Robertson. London, G. Allen and Unwin limited, 1938. 134 p.
878. LUNDBERG, Erik. Studies in the theory of economic expansion. (Reprints of economic classics.) New York, Kelley and Millman, 1955. 265 p.
879. MacEWAN, Arthur and Thomas E. Weisskopf, editors. Perspectives on the economic problem; a book of readings in political economy. Englewood Cliffs, New Jersey, Prentice-Hall, 1970. xvii, 333 p.
880. MACHLUP, Fritz. Essays on economic semantics. Edited by Merton H. Miller. Englewood Cliffs, New Jersey, Prentice-Hall, c1963, 304 p.
881. _____. Der wettstreit zwischen mikro- und makrotheorien in der nationalökonomie. (Walter Eucken institut. Vorträge und aufsätze, 4.) Tübingen, Mohr, 1960. 54 p.
882. MACKENZIE, Thomas Findley. Planned society, yesterday, today and tomorrow. A symposium by thirty-five economists, sociologists, and statesmen. Forward by Lewis Mumford. New York, Prentice-Hall, 1937. xxvii, 989 p. Bibliography, 939-978; and at the end of chapters.
883. MAHR, Alexander. Neue beiträge zur wirtschaftstheorie; festschrift anlässlich des 70. Geburtstages von Hans Mayer, unter den Auspizien von Luigi Einaudi in verbindung mit Jean Marchal, Theo Surányi-Unger und Francesco Vito hrsg. von Alexander Mahr. Wien, Springer, 1949. vi, 445 p.
884. MALTHUS, Thomas Robert. The pamphlets of Thomas Robert Malthus. (Reprints of economic classics.) New York, A. M. Kelley, 1970. v, 320 p.
885. The MANCHESTER school of economics and social studies. v. 1- . 1930- . Manchester, England, Department of economics, University of Manchester, 1930. Semiannual (irregular). (Title varies: 1930-31, The Manchester

Collections 61

school of economics, commerce and administration. --1932-38, The Manchester school.)
886. MARK, Shelley M., editor. Economics in action. Readings in current economic issues. 3rd edition. Belmont, California, Wadsworth publishing company, incorporated, 1966?
887. MARKERT, Werner, editor. Sowjetunion. Das wirtschaftssystem. In Zusammenarbeit mit zahlreichen Fachgelehrten. (Osteuropa-Handbuch.) Köln, Graz, Böhlau, 1965. xvii, 587 p. Bibliographical footnotes.
888. MARRIS, Robin and Adrian Wood, editors. The corporate economy. Growth, competition, and innovative potential. Cambridge, Harvard university press, 1971. 595 p.
889. MARSHALL, Howard Drake and Natalie J. Marshall, editors. The history of economic thought. A book of readings. New York, Pitman publishing corporation, 1967, c1968. xvii, 408 p.
890. MARSHALL, Leon Carroll, editor. Industrial society. Chicago, The University of Chicago press, c1929. (Published in 1918 under title: Readings in industrial society. xxiv, 1082 p.
891. MAYER, Hans, editor. Die wirtschaftstheorie der gegenwart. Vienna, 1927-1928. 4 v.
892. McCONNELL, Campbell and Robert C. Bingham, editors. Economic issues: readings and cases. New York, McGraw-Hill, 1963. 318 p. (2d edition, 1966. xii, 426 p.)
893. McCULLOCH, John Ramsay. Treatises and essays on money, exchange, interest, the letting of land, absenteeism, the history of commerce, manufactures, etc. with accounts of the lives and writings of Quesnay, Adam Smith, and Ricardo. 2d edition. enlarged and improved. Edinburgh, A. and C. Black, 1859. vii, 564 p.
894. McNAIR, Malcolm Perrine and Howard T. Lewis, editors. Business and modern society; papers by members of the faculty of the Graduate school of business administration, Harvard university. Cambridge, Massachusetts, Harvard university press, 1938. viii, 411 p. Bibliographical footnotes.
895. MEEK, Ronald L. Economics and ideology and other essays. Studies in the development of economic thought. London, Chapman and Hall, 1967. iii-ix, 227 p. Bibliographical footnotes. (Reviewed: M. Dobb, Economic journal, 78, 310 (June, 1968) 421-423; R. V. Eagly, American economic review, 58, 3, I (June, 1968) 566-568.
896. MEHTA, Jamshed Kaikhusroo. Lectures on modern economic theory. 2d edition. Allahabad, Chaitanya publishing house, 1962. 255 p.
897. MELANGES, economiques dedies a M. le professeur Rene Gonnard. Paris, Librairie generale de droit et de jurisprudence, 1946. 426 p.
898. MENNICKEN, Peter, editor. Technik, wirtschaft, kultur. Carl-Max Maedge zum 70. geburtstag; hrsg. von Peter Mennicken und Fritz Ottel. Düsseldorf, Triltsch, 1954. 101 p.

899. MERMELSTEIN, David, editor. Economics: mainstream readings and radical critiques, edited, with introductions by the author. Special introduction by Robert Lekachman. 1st edition. New York, Random house, 1970. xx, 620 p.
900. MESSMANN, Horst. Anschauliche theorie der verbundenen produktion. Meisenheim-Wien, Westkulturverlag A. Hain, 1952. 69 p.
901. MIEDZYUCZELNIANE zeszyty naukowe. Studia z historii mysli społeczno-ekonomicznej. nr. 1- . Kraków, Nakł. Wyzszej szkoły ekonomicznej w Krakowie, 1961- .
902. MILAN. Università commerciale Luigi Bocconi. Istituto di economia e di politica economica e finanziaria. Studi in onore di Giorgio Mortara di L. Amoroso et al. Padova, CEDAM, 1954. c1955. 489 p.
903. MILL, James. Selected economic writings. Edited and with an introduction by Donald Winch. Chicago, University of Chicago press, 1966. 452 p.
904. MILL, John Stuart. Essays on some unsettled questions of political economy. (Series of reprints of scarce works on political economy, no. 7.) Aldwych, London, Reprinted by the London school of economics and political science, 1948. vi, 164 p.
905. MIRABELLA, Giuseppe. Duplicità dei limiti della attività economica. Palermo, Seminario di economia politica e scienza delle finance dell'Università degli studi di Palermo, 1953. 154 p.
906. MITCHELL, Wesley Clair. Lecture notes on types of economic theory. New York, A. M. Kelley, 1949. 2 v.
907. MOHORTYNSKI, Piotr. Essai sur l'évolution du syndicalisme depuis 1918 sous l'aspect de la collaboration entre le capital et le travail. Strasbourg, 1951. 199 p.
908. MONEY, trade, and economic growth, in honor of John Henry Williams. New York, Macmillan, 1951. xi, 343 p. Bibliographical footnotes.
909. MONROE, Arthur Eli, editor. Early economic thought. Selections from economic literature prior to Adam Smith. Cambridge, Harvard university press, 1924. vii, 400 p. Bibliographical footnotes. (3rd printing, 1930. viii, 399 p. Bibliographical footnotes. Reprinted: 1951.)
910. MONTANER, A. Geschichte des volkswirtschaftslehre. Köhn-Berlin, Kiepenheuer und Witsch, 1967. 476 p. Bibliography, 435-53.
911. MONTEIL, Jacques. Surplus du consommateur et bien-être économique. Toulouse, 1956. 191 l.
912. MORGENSTERN, Oskar, editor. Economic activity analysis. New York, Wiley, 1954. xviii, 554 p.
913. MOUNT Holyoke college. "Those having torches. . . . " Economic essays in honor of Alzada Comstock, presented by her former students. Edited by Lucile Tomlinson Wessmann. South Hadley, Massachusetts, 1954. 134 p. [Reprinted: (Essay index reprint series.) Freeport, New York, Books for libraries press, 1968. 134 p.]
914. MUHS, Karl, editor. Festgabe für Georg Jahn zur

vollendung seines 70. Lebensjahres am 28. Februar 1955. Berlin, Duncker und Humblot, 1955. xvi, 635 p.
915. MULCAHY, Richard E., editor. Readings in economics; selected with introduction and commentary. (The college readings series, no. 5.) Westminster, Maryland, Newman press, 1959. 356 p.
916. MUZIKOVA-NOSILOVA, Ludmila. Národní hospodářství; učební text pro IV. ročník obchodních akademií. V. Praze, Státní nakl., 1948. 73 p.
917. NAKANO, Tadashi, editor. Keizaigaku no hoho. (Transliterated.) Japan, 1968. 354 p. Bibliographical references.
918. NANIWADA, Haruo. Nihon keizai kenkyū. (Transliterated.) Japan, 1970. 311 p.
919. _____. Staat und wirtschaft; Grundlegung der nationalökonomie als der Logik der bürgerlichen gesellschaft. (Science council of Japan. Division of economics, commerce and business administration. Economic series, no. 16.) Tokyo, 1957. 76 p.
920. NARDUZZI, Nestore. Un comune fondamento razionale dei problemi concernenti la utilità collettiva. Milano, A. Giuffrè, 1959. 71 p.
921. NATIONAL industrial conference board. Studies in business economics. no. 1- . New York, 1945- .
922. NELL-BREUNING, Oswald von. Wirtschaft und gesellschaft. Freiburg, Herder, 1956- . v.
923. NEVIN, Edward. Economics: waiting for Godot; inaugural lecture of the Professor of economics delivered at the College on February 25, 1969. (University college of Swansea, Inaugural lecture.) Swansea (Glam.), University college of Swansea, 1969. 3, 27 p.
924. NEWMAN, Philip Charles, Arthur D. Gayer and Milton H. Spencer. Source readings in economic thought. 1st edition. (Norton readings in economics.) New York, Norton, 1954. 762 p.
925. NINAGAWA, Torazō. Ninagawa Torazō Sensei koki kinen. (Transliterated.) Japan, 1968. 2, 402 p. Bibliographical notes.
926. NØGAARD, Ivar, editor. Din økonomi og samfundets. København, Arbejdernes oplysningsforbund, 1960. 188 p.
927. NORTH, Douglass C. and Roger LeRoy Miller, editors. The economics of public issues. New York, Harper and Row publishers, incorporated, 1971. 158 p.
928. NOVACK, David E. and Robert Lekachman, editors. Development and society; the dynamics of economic change. New York, Saint Martin's press, c1964. xiii, 433 p. Bibliography, 431-433.
929. NOVAK, Mijo, editor. Politička ekonomija; skripta za stručne ispite državnih službenika. Sastavili Ivo Vrančic, et al. 2. izd. Zagreb, 1951. 194 p.
930. NURKSE, Ragnar. Equilibrium and growth in the world economy; economic essays. Edited by Gottfried Haberler and Robert M. Stern. With an introduction by Gottfried Haberler. (Harvard economic studies, v. 118.) Cambridge,

Harvard university press, c1961. xiii, 380 p. ("The writings of Ragnar Nurkse": 365-369.)
931. OULES, Firmin, editor. L'ecole de Lausanne. Textes choisis de L. Walras et V. Pareto. (Collection des grands economistes.) Paris, Dalloz, 1950.
932. ———. Pour une économie eclairée capable d'affronter la plus grande révolution industrielle qui a commencé. (Collection de la Nouvelle école de Lausanne.) Lausanne, 1957. 184 p.
933. OXFORD. University. Institute of statistics. The economics of full employment; six studies in applied economics, prepared at the Oxford university Institute of statistics. Oxford, B. Blackwell, 1944. vii, 213 p.
934. OZGA, S. Andrew. Expectations in economic theory. Chicago, Aldine publishing company, 1965. 303 p.
935. PALERMO, Università. Facoltà di economia e commercio. Studi in memoria di Giovanni de Francisci Gerbino. (Its Annali, anno III, 1949, n. 1.) Palermo, Lilia, 1950. xix, 248 p.
936. PARETO, Vilfredo and Ettore Ciccotti. Biblioteca di storia economica. Milan, Società editrice libraria, 1903-29. 6 v. in 8. Bibliographies.
937. PATTEN, Simon Nelson. Essays in economic theory. Edited by Rexford Guy Tugwell, with an introduction by Henry Rogers Seager. New York, Alfred A. Knopf, c1924. xvii p., 1 l., 399 p.
938. PATTERSON, Samuel Howard, editor. Readings in the history of economic thought. 1st edition. New York and London, McGraw-Hill book company, incorporated, 1932. xi, 745 p.
939. PFOUTS, Ralph William, editor. Essays in economics and econometrics; a volume in honor of Harold Hotelling. (Studies in economics and business administration.) Chapel Hill, Published for the School of business administration, University of North Carolina by the University of North Carolina press, 1960. xi, 240 p.
940. PIETTRE, Andre. Les trois âges de l'économie; essai sur les relations de l'économie et de la civilisation de l'antiquité classique à nos jours; économie subordonnée, économie indépendante, économie dirigée. (Economie et humanisme.) Paris, Editions ouvrieres, 1955. 430 p.
941. PIGOU, Arthur Cecil. Essays in economics. London, Macmillan, 1952. 240 p.
942. PJANIC, Zoran. O raspodeli u prelaznom periodu. (Popularna biblioteka politička ekonomije, 21.) Beograd, Rad, 1954. 74 p.
943. POLAK, Nico Jacob, H. T. Go en J. P. Kikkert. Verspreide geschriften, verzameld . . . Purmerend, J. Muusses, 1953. 2 v.
944. POLIER, Léon. . . . L'idée du juste salaire; essai d'histoire dogmatique et critique. Paris, V. Giard et E. Brière, 190? 3 p. 1., 388 p. Bibliographie: 373-384.
945. PRINGLE, William Henderson, editor. Economic problems in

Collections 65

Europe today, With an introduction by Sir Charles Grant Robertson. London, A. and C. Black, limited, 1928. xi, 146 p.
946. PROCHNOW, Herbert Victor, editor. World economic problems and policies. 1st edition. New York, Harper and Row, 1965. xxv, 382 p. Bibliographical footnotes.
947. RAEVSKAIA, E. S. Ocherki istorii ékonomicheskoĭ mysli vengrii. Moscow, 1962. 211 p.
948. RAMAKRISHNA, Kothapalli Tatachar. Lectures on advanced economic theory. New York, Asia publishing house, 1965. xii, 315 p.
949. RAND, Benjamin. Selections illustrating economic history since the seven years' war, 1888. 3rd edition. Cambridge, J. Wilson and son, 1895. viii, 641 p. Bibliography, 545-630.
950. RECKTENWALD, Horst Claus, editor. Lebensbilder grosser nationalökonomen; einführung in die geschichte der politischen ökonomie. Köln, Kiepenheuer und Witsch, 1965. 666 p. Bibliographical references, 587-649.
951. REYNOLDS, Lloyd George. Western economics in non-Western economics. (Edward Shann memorial lecture in economics, 10.) Nedlands, University of Western Australia press, 1970. 37 p.
952. RIMA, Ingrid H., editor. Readings in the history of economic theory. (Holt, Rinehart, and Winston series in economics.) New York, Holt, Rinehart and Winston, 1970. viii, 303 p. Bibliographical footnotes.
953. ROADS to freedom: essays in honour of Friedrich A. von Hayek; edited by Erich Streissler and others. London, Routledge and K. Paul; New York, A. M. Kelley, 1969. xix, 315 p.
954. ROBBINS, Lionel Charles. The evolution of modern economic theory and other papers on the history of economic thought. London, Macmillan; Chicago, Aldine publishing company, 1970. 265 p. Bibliographical references.
955. _____. Politics and economics; papers in political economy. New York, Saint Martin's press, 1963. 230 p.
956. ROBINSON, Joan Violet (Maurice). Collected economic papers. Oxford, B. Blackwell; New York, A. M. Kelley, c1951. 236 p.
957. _____. Essays in the theory of economic growth. New York, Saint Martin's press, 1962. 137 p.
958. _____. Essays in the theory of employment. 2d. edition. Oxford, Blackwell, 1947. vii, 190 p. (1st edition, 1937?)
959. _____. The rate of interest, and other essays. London, Macmillan, 1952. 170 p.
960. ROBERTSON, Sir Dennis Holme. Economic commentaries. London, Staples press, c1956. 174 p.
961. _____. Lectures on economic principles. London, Staples press, 1957-1959. 3 v.
962. ROSARIO, Argentine republic (Santa Fé). Universidad nacional del litoral. Instituto de investigaciones económicas.

963. Serie económica. Rosario, 19- . v.
RUDZKI, Adam, editor. Zatrudnienie i rozwój gospodarczy; wybór rozpraw. Max F. Millikan et al. Nowy Jork, Fundacja Kosciuszkowska, 1958. xiv, 321 p.
964. RUSSETT, Bruce M., editor. Economic theories of international politics. (Markham political science series.) Chicago, Markham publishing company, 1968. ix, 542 p.
965. SALLES, Pierre, editor. Initiation économique et sociale. 5e édition refondue. Enseignements techniques supérieurs, instituts universitaires de technologie, écoles supérieures de commerce. (Université et technique, 3-4.) Paris, Dunod, 1968. 2 v.
966. SAMUELSON, Paul Anthony, Robert L. Bishop and John R. Coleman. Readings in economics. 1st edition. New York, McGraw-Hill, 1952. 484 p. (2d edition, 1955; 488 p.; 3d edition, 1958. 474 p.; 4th edition, 1964. x, 475 p.)
967. SCHLEIFFER, Hedwig and Ruth Crandall. Index to economic history essays in Festschiften, 1900-1950. Preface by Arthur H. Cole. Cambridge, A. H. Cole; distributed by Harvard university press, 1953. 68 p.
968. SCHNEIDER, Erich. Entwicklungen und wandlungen der wirtschaftstheorie. (Veröffentlichungen der Schleswig-Holsteinischen universitätsgesellschaft, n. F., Nr. 25.) Kiel, F. Hirt, 1959. 21 p.
969. SCHUMPETER, Joseph Alois. Essays. Edited by Richard V. Clemence. Cambridge, Addison-Wesley press, 1951. 327 p. [(Essay and general literature index reprint series.) Port Washington, New York, Kennikat press, 1969. 327 p.]
970. SELIGMAN, E. R. A. Essays in economics. Macmillan, 1925.
971. SENIOR, Nassau W. Selected writings on economics. 1827-1852. New York, A. M. Kelley, 1966.
972. SEWELL, William Arthur, editor. 1840 and after. Essays written on the occasion of the New Zealand centenary. Foreword by W. H. Cocker. Auckland, Auckland university college, 1940. 5, 242 p.
973. SHACKLE, George Lennox Sharman. Uncertainty in economics, and other reflections. Cambridge, England, University press, 1955. 267 p.
974. SHELL, Karl. Essays on the theory of optimal economic growth. Cambridge, Massachusetts, M. I. T. press, 1967. xii, 303 p.
975. SINGH, V. B., editor. On political economy. Bombay, New York, Allied publishers private, 1964. vi, 143 p.
976. SMART, William. Second thoughts of an economist. With a biographical sketch by Thomas Jones, M. A. 2d edition. London, Macmillan and company, limited, 1924. lxxix, 189 p. (1st edition, c1916).
977. SMITH, James Haldane. Economic moralism; an essay in constructive economics. London, G. Allen and Unwin, limited, 1916. 287 p.

Collections

978. SMITH, Warren Lounsbury, editor. Readings in money, national income and stabilization policy. Homewood, Illinois, R. D. Irwin, 1965.
979. SOCIETY today, By Edwin Emery Slosson, Walter Dill Scott, Frederick Shipp Deibler and others. New York, D. Van Nostrand company, incorporated, c1929. 6 p. 1., 3-185 p., 1 l.
980. SOCIETY tomorrow. By George Henry Soule, Earl Dean Howard, Ralph Emerson Heilman and others. New York, D. Van Nostrand company, incorporated, c1929. 6 p. 1, 3-185 p., 1 l.
981. SODDY, Frederick. Cartesian economics; the bearing of physical science upon state stewardship. London, Hendersons, 1922. 32 p. (Two lectures to Student unions of Birbeck college and London school of economics, November 10 and 17, 1921.)
982. SOLO, Robert A., editor. Economics and the public interest. Essays written in honor of Eugene Ewald Agger. New Brunswick, New Jersey, Rutgers university press, c1955. xiv, 318 p. Bibliographical footnotes.
983. SPAHR, Walter Earl, editor. Economic principles and problems. By Louis Bader, Jules I. Bogen, Kenneth Dameron . . . and others. Department of economics, School of commerce, accounts and finance, New York university. New York, R. Long & R. R. Smith, inc., 1932. 2 v. Bibliographies. (Published also under title, The economic foundation of business. 3rd edition. By Walter Earl Spahr, Edward Berman, David F. Jordan, A. G. Black, and others. New York, Farrar and Rinehart, inc., 1936. 2 v. Bibliographies.)
984. _____. Economic principles and problems. 4th edition. New York, Farrar and Rinehard, incorporated, 1940. Bibliography.
985. SPENGLER, Joseph John and William Richard Allen, editor. Essays in economic thought: Aristotle to Marshall. (Rand McNally economics series.) Chicago, Rand McNally, 1960. 800 p. Bibliography.
986. SPIEGEL, Henry William, editor. The development of economic thought. Great economists in perspective. (A Wiley publication in economics.) New York, J. Wiley, 1952. 811 p. [Japanese edition entitled: Keizaishisô hatten-shi. (Transliterated.) Translated by Shinzaburô Koshimura and others. Tôkyô, Tôyô Keizai Shimpô-sha, 1954. 4 v. Kindai keizaigaku In Keizaishisô hatten-shi, v. 5. Translated by Shinzaburô Koshimura and others. Tôkyô, Tôyô Keizai Shimpô-sha, 1955. 337 p.]
987. STAMMER, Otto, editor. Festgabe fur Friedrich Bülow zum 70. geburtstag, hrsg. von Otto Stammer und Karl C. Thalheim. Berlin, Duncker und Humblot, 1960. 428 p.
988. STAMPAR, Slobodan. Ekonomisti XVII i XVIII stoljeća. Uredio i uvodnu raspravu napisao Slobodan Stampar. U Zagrebu, Kultura, 1952. 448 p. (Translations from English, French and Italian.)

989. STEINER, George Albert, editor. Economic problems of national defense; a symposium. Foreword by Herman B. Wells. Bloomington, The School of business and department of economics, Indian university, 1941. 1, 214 p. Bibliography.
990. _____, editor. Economic problems of war. New York, J. Wiley and sons, incorporated; London, Chapman and hall, limited, 1942. 692 p. Bibliography.
991. STIGLER, George Joseph. Essays in the history of economics. Chicago, University of Chicago press, 1965. viii, 391 p. Bibliographical references.
992. _____. Five lectures on economic problems; five lectures delivered at the London school of economics and political science on the invitation of the Senate of the University of London. London, London school of economics and political science; New York, Macmillan, c1949. 3 p. 1., 65 p.
993. _____. The intellectual and the market place, and other essays. New York, Free press of Glencoe, c1963. ix, 99 p.
994. STUDI in onore di Amintore Fanfani nel venticinquennio di cattedra universitaria. Milano, Giuffrè, 1962. 6 vol.
995. SUMNER, William Graham. The forgotten man, and other essays, edited by Albert Galloway Keller. Unaltered and unabridged edition. (Essay index reprint series.) Freeport, New York, Books for libraries press, 1969, c1919. 559 p.
996. TAGLIACOZZA, Giorgio, editor. Economisti napoletani dei sec. XVII e XVIII, a cura di Giorgio Tagliacozzo. Bologna, L. Cappelli, 1937. 3 p. 1, v-lxvii, 456 p.
997. TAKAHASHI, Seiichirō. Keizai shisō shi zuihitsu. (Transliterated.) Japan, 1950. 3, 4, 260 p.
998. _____. Zoku keizai shiso shi zuihitsu. (Transliterated.) 1949. 268 p.
999. TAYLOR, Overton H. Economics and liberalism, collected papers. (Harvard economic studies, v. 96. Cambridge, Massachusetts, Harvard university press, 1955. 321 p.
1000. TAYMANS, Adrien. L'homme, agent du développement économique. (Series: Louvain. Université catholique. Ecole des sciences économiques. Collection, no. 39.) Louvain, E. Nauwelaerts, 1951. xv, 326 p. Bibliographie, 299-311. ("Thèses annexes": leaf inserted.)
1001. THOMPSON, Charles Manfred. Principles and practices of economics, an introductory course. Chicago, New York, B. H. Sanborn and company, 1928. ix, 578 p. Bibliography
1002. THORP, Willard Long, editor. Economic problems in a changing world. New York, Farrar and Rinehart, incorporated, 1939. xviii, 820 p. Bibliography.
1003. TINBERGEN, Jan. Selected papers. Edited by L. H. Klaasse L. M. Koyck and H. J. Witteveen. Amsterdam, North-Holland publishing company, 1959. xii, 318 p.
1004. TUGWELL, Rexford Guy. The Trend of economics. By Morris Albert Copeland, Sumner Huber Slichter and others. Edited, with an introduction by R. G. Tugwell. New York,

Collections 69

        F. S. Crofts and company, 1924. xi, 556 p. Bibliography.
        (Reprinted: 1930 and 1935. xi, 556 p. Bibliography.
1005. TURIN, Guido. Der begriff des unternehmers. Zurich? Buchdr.
        Turbenthal, R. Furrers Erben, 1948. xxiv, 223. Bib-
        liography. (Dissertation, Zürich. Also published as Mit-
        tellungen aus dem handelswissenschaftlichen seminar der
        universität. Zürich, n. F., Heft 84.)
1006. UCHIDA, Yoshihiko. Keizaigakushi kōza. (Transliterated.)
        Japan, 1965. (v. 1, c1964.) 3 v. Bibliographies.
1007. _____, editor. Shihonshugi no shisō-kōzō. (Transliterated.)
        Japan, 1968. 582 p. Bibliographical references.
1008. UDAL'TSOV, Ivan Dmitrievich and Fedor IAkovlevich Polianskii,
        editors. Istoriía ekonomicheskoĭ mysli. (Transliterated.)
        1961-64. 2 v. Bibliography, v. 1, 503-509.
1009. UDVIKINGSLINIER i makroøkonomisk teori. Red. af Niels
        Thygesen og P. Nørregaard Rasmussen. (Studier fra
        Københavns universitets Økonomiske institut, 13.) Køben-
        havn, Københavns universitets fond til tilvejebringelse af
        Laeremidler, (Gad), 1969. 415 p.
1010. UNION of Soviet Socialist Republics, Ministerstvo vysshego
        i srednego spetsial'nogo obrazovaniía. Ordel prepodavaniía
        obshchestvennykh nauk. Programma kursa istorii
        ekonomicheskikh uchenii. (Transliterated.) Moscow, 1967.
        36, 3 p. Bibliography, 30-38.
1011. VALKO, Laszlo, Essays on modern cooperation. Pullman,
        Washington State university press, 1964. 143 p.
1012. VEREIN für sozialpolitik, gesellschaft für wirtschaftsund
        sozialwissenschaften. Schristen. Bd. 1- . Berlin,
        Duncker und Humblot, 1949- . v.
1013. VINER, Jacob. The long view and the short; studies in eco-
        nomic theory and policy. Glencoe, Illinois, Free press,
        c1958. 462 p.
1014. VYGOSKIJ, S. L., V. S. Afanas'ev and V. I. Gromeka.
        Istorija ekonomićeskih učenij. (Transliterated.) Moscow,
        Mysl', 1965. 479 p.
1015. WAGNER, Donald Owen, editor. Social reformers. Adam
        Smith to John Dewey. With a foreword by Carlton J. H.
        Hayes. New York, The Macmillan company, 1934. xvii,
        749 p.
1016. WAGNER, Valentin Fritz, editor. Wirtschaftstheorie und wirt-
        schaftspolitik; festschrift für Alfred Amonn zum 70.
        geburtstag. Hrsg. von Valentin F. Wagner und Fritz Mar-
        bach. Bern, Francke verlag, 1953. 371 p.
1017. WARD, Alfred Dudley, editor. Goals of economic life by
        John Maurice Clark and others. 1st edition. (The Ethics
        and economics of society.) New York, Harper, 1953.
        470 p.
1018. WEBER, Max. From Max Weber, Essays in sociology.
        Translated by H. H. Gerth and C. Wright Mills. New
        York, Oxford university press, 1946. 490 p.
1019. WEULERSSE, Georges, editor. Les manuscrits économiques
        de François Quesnay et du marquis de Mirabeau aux Ar-
        chives nationales (M. 778 à M. 785.) Inventaire, extraits

et notes, par Georges Weulersse. Paris, P. Geuthner, 1910. vii, 150 p. 1 l.
1020. WHITE, Zane. Unearned economic benefits; an analysis of the basic problem in a free economy; profits and who should receive them. 1st edition. New York, Exposition press, 1962. 87 p.
1021. WICKSELL, Knut. Lectures on political economy. Translated by E. Classen. London, Macmillan and company, limited, 1934. 2 v.
1022. ———. Selected papers on economic theory. Edited with an introduction by Erik Lindahl. Cambridge, Harvard university press, 1958. 292 p. [(Reprints of Economic classics.) New York, A. M. Kelley, 1969. 292 p.]
1023. WILLIAMS, John Henry. Economic stability in a changing world; essays in economic theory and policy. New York, Oxford university press, c1953. 284 p.
1024. WILSON, George Wilton, editor. Classics of economic theory. Bloomington, Indiana university press, 1964. 637 p. Bibliographical references, 35-36.
1025. WIRTSCHAFT und gesellschaft; beiträge zur oekonomik und soziologie der gegenwart, von R. Wilbrandt et al. Festschrift für Franz Oppenheimer zu seinen 60. geburtstag. Frankfurt am Main, Sauer und Auvermann, 1969. 484 p.
1026. WISKEMANN, Erwin und Heinz Lütke, editors. Der weg deutschen volkswirtschaftslehre, ihre schöpfer und gestalter im 19. jahrhundert, herausgegeben. Berlin, Junker und Dünnhaupt, 1937. 193 p.
1027. WRIGHT, Chester Whitney, editor. Economic problems of war and its aftermath. Chicago, Illinois, The University of Chicago press, 1942. xi, 197 p. Bibliographical footnotes.
1028. YAMADA, Y., editor. Kindai keizaigaku no seisei. Tôkyô, Kawade Shobô, 1955. 327 p.

C. SUMMARY WORKS IN ECONOMIC THOUGHT AND ANALYSIS

1029. AARONS, Eric. Economics for workers. 2d edition. (Current books.) Sydney, Current book distributors, 1961. 80 p.
1030. ABAD-CONDE y Sevilla, Gerardo. Manual de derecho y economía. 9. ed. Madrid, Graficas Orbe, 1951. 252 p.
1031. ABALO, Luis José. El camino del bienestar; introducción a la teoría general del continuo económico. Prólogo de Manuel de Torres. Habana, Editorial Lex, 1958. 595 p.
1032. ABBOTT, Lawrence. Economics and the modern world. New York, Harcourt, Brace, 1960. 880 p. [2nd edition. Under the general editorship of William J. Baumol. (The Harbrace series in business and economics.) 1967. xx, 876 p.]
1033. ABDULLAH Taib dan Zaihar Bachik. Memahami ekonomi. Chetakan 1. Kuala Lampur, Penerbitan Utusan Melayu, 1969. 214 p. Bibliography.
1034. ACKLEY, Gardner. Macroeconomic theory. New York, The Macmillan company, 1961. 597 p.
1035. ADAMS, Henry Carter. Description of industry; an introduction to economics. New York, H. Holt and company, 1918. x, 270 p.
1036. AGAZZINI, Michele. La science de l'économie politique. Ristampa anastatica della prima edizione del 1822. A cura di Oscar Nuccio. (Ristampe anastatiche di opere antiche e rare, 1.) Roma, Bizzarri, 1970. xv, 389 p.
1037. AKADEMIIA nauk SSSR. Institut ékonomiki. Ekonomia polityczna; podręcznik. Wyd. 3. Warszawa, Książka i Wiedza, 1955. 839 p.
1038. _____. _____. Manuel d'économie politique. Texte conforme à la 2. édition, 1955. La 2. édition de ce manuel a été mise au point par K. Ostrovitianov et al. Paris, Editions sociales, 1956. 701 p.
1039. _____. _____. Political economy, a textbook. Moscow, State publishing house of political literature, 1954. n. p., 1955? 401 p.
1040. _____. _____. Politische ökonomie; lehrbuch. Die deutsche ausg. wurde vom Marx-Engels-Lenin-Stalin-Institut beim Zentralkomitee der sozialistischen einheitspartei deutschlands besorgt. Berlin, Dietz, 1955. 3., überarb. russischen ausg. (1 ausg.) 1959. 791 p. 2., ergäntze aufl. 1960. 835 p. Nach der 4., überarb. und ergäntzen russischen ausg. 5. Aufl., Berlin, Dietz, 1964. 767 p.)

1041. _____. _____. Sachwortverzeichnis. Von Hans Schönherr. Berlin, Verlag die wirtschaft, 1956. 40 p.
1042. AKHTAR, Sardar Mohammad. Essentials of economics, according to the new syllabus. New revised edition. Lahore, Publishers united, 1961-62. 2 v. in 3.
1043. AKTIONSGEMEINSCHAFT soziale marktwirtschaft. Wirtschaftsordnung und menschenbild; geburtstagsgabe für Alexander Rüstow. (Its Schriftenreibe, Heft 4.) Köln, Verlag für politik und wirtschaft, 1960. 152 p.
1044. ALBARET, Claude. De la nature des lois économiques. Genève, Château de confignon, 1956. 161 p.
1045. ALBERT, Hans. Okonomische ideologie und politische theorie; das ökonomische argument in der ordnungspolitischen debatte. Mit einem Geleitwort von Gerhard Weisser. (Monographien zur politik, Heft. 4.) Göttingen, O. Schwartz, 1954. 156 p.
1046. ALBERTINI, Jean Marie. Les rouages de l'économie nationale . . . avec le concours de A. Kéréver, L. Turin, et F. Lerouge. (Initiation économique.) Paris, Economie et humanisme, Editions ouvrières, 1960. 215 p.
1047. ALCHIAN, Armen Albert and William R. Allen. University economics. Belmont, California, Wadsworth publishing company, 1964. xv, 924 p. (2nd edition, 1967. xx, 825 p. Accompanied by, A Study guide for University economics. Second edition, by Richard Newcomb and David Ramsey. Belmont, California, Wadsworth publishing company, 1967. 208 p.)
1048. ALCOCER, Mariano. Economia social, curso general. 2. edition. (Biblioteca de economía politica, 15.) México, Editorial América, 1947. 357 p. (3. edition reformada. 1951. 372 p. 4. edition revised. 1954. 366 p.)
1049. ALEMANN, Roberto T. Sistemas económicos. Buenos Aires, Ediciones Arayú, 1953. 250 p.
1050. ALEXANDER, Albert. The challenge of economics; a guide for the perplexed. New York, Pitman publishing corporation, 1970. viii, 227 p.
1051. _____. Economics. (The Young adult library.) New York, F. Watts, c1963. 66 p.
1052. ALEXANDER, Albert, Edward C. Prehn and Arnold W. Sametz. The modern economy in action; an analytical approach. New York, Pitman publishing corporation, 1968. x, 530 p.
1053. ALLAIS, Maurice. Les fondements comptables de la macroéconomique; les équations comptables entre quantités globales et leurs applicatiens. Paris, Presses universitaires de France, 1954. 91 p.
1054. ALLEN, Clark Lee. The framework of price theory. Belmont, California, Wadsworth, 1967.
1055. _____, Aurelius Morgner and Robert H. Strotz. Problems in the theory of price. Englewood Cliffs, New Jersey, Prentice-Hall, 1954.
1056. ALT, Richard M. and William C. Bradford. Business

economics, principles and cases. Chicago, R. D. Irwin, 1951. xii, 581 p. (Revised edition, By Marshall R. Colberg, W. C. Bradford and R. M. Alt. 1957. 537 p.)

1057. ALTMANN, Eva. Uber den gegenstand der politischen ökonomie und über die ökonomischen gesetze. 1. aufl. Berlin, Dietz, 1955. 115 p. (2., durchgeschene aufl. 1959. 114 p. 3., durchgeschene aufl. 1960. 114 p.)

1058. ALVIN, Décio Ferraz. Economia politica. São Palo, Edição Saraiva, 1963, i. e. 1962. 114 p. (Revised edition. Biblioteca mentor cultural. Rio de Janeiro, Edição de ouro, 1968. 118 p.)

1059. AMERICAN institute of banking. Economics. New York, 1951. 470 p. (Revised edition by A. Anton Friedrich, John A. Bryson and Weldon Welfling. New York, 1961. 524 p.)

1060. AMIN, R. K. Economics for engineers; a text book for engineering students. 1st edition. Anand (W. R.), India, Charotar book stall, 1963. 412 p.

1061. AMONN, Alfred. Cemiyet iktisadinda ana mefhumlar, ana meseleler. Türkçeye çeviren: Asim Süreyya Iloglu. (Istanbul üniversitesi yayinlarindan, 538.) Istanbul, I. Akgun Matbaasi, 1953. xi, 251 p.

1062. ———. Nationalökonomie und philosophie. (Erfahrung und denken, Bd. 7.) Berlin, Duncker und Humblot, 1961. 266 p.

1063. AMORE, Giordano dell'. Aspetti aziendali e sociali della politica economica a finanziaria; moneta, resparmio, credito e banche, agricoltura, industria e commercio. (Instituto di economia aziendale dell'Università commerciale "L. Bocconi," Milano. Pubblicazioni: Ser. 1. n. 1.) Milano, A. Giuffrè, 1955. x, 686 p.

1064. AMOROSO, Luigi. Economia di mercato. Bologna, C. Zuffi, 1949. 466 p.

1065. ANDERSEN, Poul Nyboe. Den økonomiske sammenhaeng. København, Danske forlag, 1947. 155 p. (2. revid. udg. 1952. 144 p.)

1066. ———, Bjarke Fog og Poul Winding. Nationaløkonomie. (Foreningen til unge handelamaende uddannelse. Handelshøjskolen i København. Skriftraekke A. 6.) København, E. Harck, 1952. 431 p. (2. udg. 1961. 384 p.)

1067. ANDERSSON, Lars O. och Margit Gennser. Företagets ekonomi. Grundkomponent. Malmö, Hermods, 1967. 4, 282 p.

1068. ANDREAE, Wilhelm Friedrich. Vom Geiste der ordnung in gesellschaft und wirtschaft; ausgewählte aufsätze und abhandlungen. Als festschrift zum 70. Geburtstage angeregt und unterstützt vom Rektor der Karl-Franzens-Universität in Graz, hrsg. vom Walter Heinrich, Hans Riehl und Anton Tautscher. Stuttgart, G. Fischer, 1959. 208 p.

1069. ANDRES Alvarez, Valentin. Más allá de la economía. (Universidad de Madrid. Facultad de Ciencias politicas,

económicas y commerciales. Publicación no. 4.) Madrid, 1962. 98 p.
1070. ANDRIESSEN, Jacobus Eije. Economie in theorie en praktijk. 3 de herz. druk. Bewerkt door A. Heertje en R. Schöndorff. Amsterdam, Brussel, Agon Eisevier, 1968. 480 p.
1071. ANGERS, François Albert. Initiation à l'économie politique (avec applications au Canada); cours abrégé préparé à l'intention des secrétaires de chambres de commerce. 3. édition rev. et augm. (Bibliothèque économique et sociale.) Paris, Fides, 1958. 397 p. (4. éd. rev. et augm. Paris, 1963. 444 p.)
1072. ANSTEY, Vera (Powell). An introduction to economics for students in India and Pakistan. With contributions by Anne Martin. London, Allen and Unwin, 1964. 224 p. Bibliographies.
1073. ANTOINE, Jean Claude. Introduction à l'analyse macroéconomique. Paris, Presses, universitaires de France, 1953- . v. (Bibliothèques de la science économique.)
1074. ARANEDA Dörr, Hugo. Curso de economía política. Santiago de Chile, Editorial jurídica de Chile, 1967, c1966. 521 p.
1075. ARENA, Celestino. Principi di economia politica e nozioni di statistica ad uso delle scuole medie superiori. 1. ed. Torino, G. B. Paravia, 1948. 304 p.
1076. ARIZAWA, H. et al. Gendai keizaigaku nyûmon. (Transliterated.) Tôkyô, Kawade Shobô. 1955. 206 p.
1077. ARNDT, Helmut. Mikroökonomische theorie. Tübingen, Mohr (Siebeck), 1966. 2 v.
1078. ARNOU, André. Eléments d'économie politique. Paris, Editions spes, 1950. 733 p.
1079. AROMOLARAN, Adekunle. Modern economic analysis for West African students. Ibadan, Progresso economic research centre, 1968. v, 332 p.
1080. AROMOLARAN, Adekunle and Areoye Oyebola. Economic theory for West African students. Ibadan, Nigerian economic and social studies syndicate, 1966? 254 p.
1081. ARUNACHALAM, Aiyanperumal. Valluvar vakutta porul valvu. (Transliterated.) 1969. 90 p. (In Tamil.)
1082. ASSOCIAZIONI cristiane lavoratori italiani. Economia politica. Roma, Edizioni ACLI, 1957. 524 p.
1083. AYRES, Clarence Edwin. The industrial economy; its technological basis and institutional destiny. Boston, Houghton Mifflin, 1952. 433 p.
1084. ———. The theory of economic progress; a study of the fundamentals of economic development and cultural change. 2. edition. (Schocken paperbacks. SB33.) New York, Schocken books, 1962. 317 p.
1085. AZMATULLAH Khān. Theoretical problems of economics. 1963. 400 p. (In Urdu.)

Summary Works

1086. BABY, Jean. Principes fondamentaux d'economie politique. Paris, Editions sociales, 1949. 348 p. [Italian edition entitled: Principî fondamentali di economia politica. Traduzione del prof. Arturo Lazzari. (Collana documenti.) Milano, Edizioni sociali ,1950. 278 p.]
1087. BACH, George Leland. Economics, an introduction to analysis and policy. New York, Prentice-Hall, c1954. 720 p. (2d. edition, 1957. 846 p. 3d edition, 1960. 850 p. Bibliography. 4th edition, 1963. 797 p. 5th edition, 1966. xv, 728 p. 6th edition, 1968. xiv, 594 p. 7th edition, 1971. xiii, 722 p.)
1088. BACHMANN, Herbert. Wirtschafts-wille und wert. Bern, A. Francke, 1945. 213 p.
1089. BAGLEY, William Chandler, Jr., and Richard M. Perdew. Understanding economics. New York, Macmillan, 1951. viii, 535 p. Bibliographies.
1090. BAIER, Carl Georg. Allgemeine volkswirtschaftslehre. Neubearb. aufl. (Schaeffers grundriss des rechts und der wirtschaft. Abt. 2: Offentliches recht und volkswirtschaft, 35. Bd.) Stuttgart, W. Kohlhammer, 1950. 219 p.
1091. BAILEY, Martin J. National income and the price level: a study in macro-theory. McGraw-Hill book company, New York, 1962.
1092. BAIN, Joe S. Price theory. New York, Holt, 1952.
1093. BAJT, Aleksandar. Osnovi ekonomike. (Ekonomska biblioteka, 4. kolo, br. 1-2.) Zagreb, "Informator," 1967. xv, 406 p.
1094. _____. Temelji politične ekonomije; uvod y teoretično ekonomsko analizo. Ljubljana, 1963. 504 p.
1095. BALLVE, Faustino, Diez lecciones de economía. (Serie "Temas contemporaneos.") México, Instituto de investigaciones sociales y económicas, 1956. 112 p. (2. ed., 1961. 119 p.)
1096. _____. Essentials of economics; a brief survey of principles and policies. Translated from the Spanish and edited by Arthur Goddard. (The William Volker fund series in the humane studies.) Princeton, New Jersey, Van Nostrand, 1963. 109 p.
1097. BALTRA Cortés, Alberto. Teoria económica. Santiago de Chile, Editorial Andrés Bello, 1963- . v.
1098. BANDT, Jacques de. Dimension du marché et optimum de production. (Université catholique de Louvain. Faculté des sciences économiques et sociales. Collection de l'Ecole des sciences économiques, no. 83.) Louvain, E. Nauwelaerts, 1962. xi, 299 p.
1099. BARBOSA, Daniel Maria Vieira. Análise econômica; apontamentos para seguimento das lições de economia no Instituto superior técnico. Lisboa, Editorial Aster, 1960- . v.
1100. BARISH, Norman N. Economic analysis for engineering and managerial decision-making. New York, McGraw-Hill,

c1962. 729 p. Bibliography.
1101. BARJONET, André. Qu'est-ce que l'économie politique? (Notre temps.) Paris, Editions sociales, 1962. 86 p.
1102. BALLIVIAN Calderón, René. Aspectos de la economía contemporánes. 1. ed. La Paz, Facultad de economía, Universidad Mayor de San Andrés, 1964. 310 p.
1103. BALOGH, Thomas. Obstáculos al desarrollo económico. 1. ed. (Conferencias.) México, Centro de estudios monetarios Latinoamericanos, 1963. 244 p.
1104. BARBERI, Benedetto. Macromeccanica economica. (Studi sulla dinamica economica.) Roma, Ceres, 1968. 178 p.
1105. BARBIERI, Gino. Introduzione all'economia. (Classe unica, 6.) Torino, Edizioni radio italiana, 1954. 76, 4 p.
1106. BARNES, Robert Johnson. Fundamentals of economics. 2nd edition. London, Butterworths, 1967. xiii, 209 p.
1107. BARONE, Enrico. Principi di economia politica. 1908. vi, 269 p. (5th edition, 1920.)
1108. BARRATT Brown, Michael. What economics is about: worker, consumer, government and corporation. (Sheffield series.) London, Weidenfeld and Nicolson, 1970. xvii, 347 p.
1109. BARRE, Raymond. Economie politique. Sous la direction de André Marchal. 2. édition. ("Thémis": manuels juridiques, économiques et politiques.) Paris, Presses universitaires de France, 1957- . v. (8e édition refondue. Paris, 1969- . v.)
1110. _____. La période dans l'analyse économique, une approche à l'étude du temps. Préface d'André Marchal. (Observation économique, 3.) Paris, Société d'édition d'enseignement supérieur, 1950. 260 p.
1111. _____. Principes d'analyse économique. . . . Paris, les Cours de droit, 1966. 2 v. in 6.
1112. BARRERE, Alain. Cours de théorie économique, rédigé d'après les notes et avec l'autorisation de Alain Barrère. D. E. S., sciences économiques, 1960-1961. Paris, Les Cours de droit, 1961. 238 p.
1113. _____. Théorie économique et impulsion keynésienne. Préface de Jean Marchal. (Etudes politiques, économiques et sociales, 5.) Paris, Dalloz, 1952. viii, 762 p.
1114. BARROS, Alamiro Bica Buys de. Instituições de economia política. 2. ed. atualizada. Rio de Janeiro, J. Konfino, 1957. 2 v.
1115. BARTOLI, Henri. Science économique et travail. (Essais et travaux: collection pub. par la Faculté de droit et al. de l'Université de Grenoble, 9.) Paris, Librairie Dalloz, 1957. 308 p.
1116. BASU, Praphullachandra. Economic principles for Indian readers; a course in the elements of economics. London, New York, Sir Pitman and sons, limited, 1927. viii, 348 p.
1117. BATES, James A. and J. R. Parkinson. Business economics. New York, A. M. Kelley, 1969. xv, 316 p.
1118. BAUDHUIN, Fernand. Déontologie des affaires. 4. édition

Summary Works 77

refondue. (Etudes morales, sociales et juridiques.)
Louvain, Société d'études morales, sociales et juridiques,
1950. 227 p. (5. édition refondue, 1960. 246 p.)
1119. _____. Principes d'économie contemporaine. Nouv. édition entièrement mise à jour. (Marabout service, 42.)
Verviers, Editions Gerard et co., 1969- . v.
1120. BAUDIN, Louis. Cours d'économie politique, rédigé d'après les notes et avec l'autorisation de Louis Baudin. Capacité 2e année, 1958-1959. Paris, Cours de droit, 1959. 219 p.
1121. _____. Manuel d'économie politique. 6. édition mise à jour. Paris, Librairie générale de droit et de jurisprudence, 1950- . v. (7. édition complétée et rev. 1953, i. e. 1952- . v.)
1122. BAUER, Leonhard. Wissenschaftstheoretische überlegungen zu grundannahmen der nationalökonomie insbesondere des mikroökonomischen anatzes. (Volkswirtschaftliche schriften, Heft. 136.) Berlin, Duncker und Humblot, 1969. 153 p.
1123. BAUER, Otto. Einführung in die volkswirtschaftslehre. Mit einer einleitung von Ernst Winkler und einem nachwort von Benedikt Kautsky. Wien, Verlag der wiener volksbuchhandlung, 1956. 388 p.
1124. BAUMOL, William J. Economic dynamics, an introduction; with a contribution by Ralph Turvey. New York, Macmillan, 1951. xiii, 262 p. (2nd edition, 1959. 396 p. Bibliography.)
1125. _____. Economic theory and operations analysis. (Prentice-Hall international series in management.) Englewood Cliffs, New Jersey, Prentice-Hall, 1961. 438 p. (2d edition, 1965. xiv, 606 p. Bibliographies.
1126. _____, and Lester Vernon Chandler. Economic processes and policies. New York, Harper, c1954. 690 p.
1127. BAYER, Hans. Wirtschaftsgestaltung. Berlin, Duncker und Humblot, 1958. xvi, 758 p.
1128. BECKWITH, Burnham Putnam. The economic theory of a socialist economy. New York, Greenwood press, 1968, c1949. viii, 444 p.
1129. BELLAN, Ruben C. Principles of economics and the Canadian economy. 2d edition. Toronto, New York, McGraw-Hill company of Canada, 1963. 536 p. (3rd edition, 1967. xii, 593 p.)
1130. BELTLE, Theodor. Die funktion der wirtschaft in theorie und praxis. Berlin, Duncker und Humblot, 1962. 182 p.
1131. BENEMY, F. W. G. Industry, income, and investment: the common sense of economics. London, G. G. Harrap, 1962. 376 p.
1132. BENHAM, Frederic Charles Courtenay. Economics; a general textbook. . . . Adapted to American student use by Friedrich A. Lutz. . . . New York, Pitman publishing corporation, c1941. xv, 525 p. (5th edition entitled: Economics: a general introduction. 1955. 568 p. 6th edition, 1960.)
1133. BENHAM, Frederic Charles Courtenay and Francis Murray

Boddy. Principles of economics. . . . New York, Chicago, Pitman publishing corporation, c1947. xi, 430 p. Bibliographies.
1134. BERLIN. Deutsches institut für wirtschaftsforschung. Wirtschaftsforschung und wirtschaftsführung; vorträge und aufsätze. Festgabe für Ferdinand Friedensburg zum 70. Geburtstage, überreicht von dem Kollegium der abteilungsleiter des Deutschen institute für wirtschaftsforschung. Berlin, Duncker und Humblot, 1956. xvi, 222 p.
1135. BERNACER Tormo, Germán. Una economía libre sin crisis y sin paro. (Biblioteca de ciencias sociales. Sección I: Economía.) Madrid, Aguilar, 1955. xix, 315 p.
1136. BERNARDO, Héctor. Para una economía humana. Buenos Aires, Frontispicio, 1949. 243 p.
1137. BERNHARD, Richard C. Economics. Boston, Heath, 1954. 801 p.
1138. BHANAGE, B. S. Economic analysis; an introduction. 3d edition, revised and enlarged. Bombay, Vora, 1962. 295 p. Bibliography.
1139. BHATTACHARYYA, Sudhendra Kumar. Modern economics; an introduction to price theory. Calcutta, Dass publishing concern, 1962. 424 p.
1140. BILAS, Richard A. Microeconomic theory; a graphical analysis. New York, McGraw-Hill, 1967. 308 p.
1141. BIRMINGHAM, Walter Barr. Economics: an introduction. Revised edition. London, Allen and Unwin, 1966. 3-122 p.
1142. BIVEN, W. Carl. An introduction to economics. Columbus, Ohio, Merrill, 1970. xiii, 400 p.
1143. BJØRNSEN, Mette Koefoed. Orientering i samfundsøkonomien. København, J. H. Schultz, 1958. 106 p. (Tegninger af Ragna Larsen. 6. udg. København, Gyldendal, 1969. 144 p.
1144. ──────. Samfundsøkonomi for den daglige avislaeser. (Statsradiofeniens grundbøger.) København, Fremad, 1956. 180 p.
1145. BJORNSON, Gordon B. Twentieth-century economics; an analysis and prediction of the Nation's economy. 1st edition. (An Exposition-banner book.) New York, Exposition press, c1968. 171 p.
1146. BLADEN, Vincent Wheeler. An introduction to political economy. Revised and edited by Alison Kemp. 2d edition. Toronto, University of Toronto press, 1951. viii, 303 p. (Revised 3d edition, 1956. 319 p.)
1147. BLODGETT, Ralph Hamilton. Principles of economics. Champaign, Illinois, Stipes publishing company, c1940. 1 p. 1., ii, 449 p. Bibliographical footnotes. (3d edition, New York, Rinehart, 1951. xx, 698 p.) Bibliography.
1148. BODDY, Francis Murray. Applied economic analysis. New York, Pitman publishing corporation, c1948. xvi, 573 p. Bibliography.
1149. BOHLER, Eugen. Nationalökonomie; grundlagen und grundle-

hren. 3. vollständig umgearb. aufl. Zürich, Polygraphischer verlag, 1957. 296 p. (4., durchgesehene aufl., 1960. 206 p. 5., durchgesehene aufl., 1964. 206 p.)

1150. BOHM-BAWERK, Eugen von. Gesammelte schriften. Hrsg. von Franz X. Weiss. Frankfurt am Main, Sauer und Auvermann, 1968. 2 v.

1151. ———. Kapital und kapitalzins. (1884-89.) 3rd 1909-14. 2 v. (Contents: Vol. 1, Geschichte und kritik der kapitalzinstheorien, 3rd 1914. xxxv, 747 p. Theorie des kapitales. 3rd 1909-12. xxii, vii, 652, 477 p.

1152. BOITEUX, Marcel. Economie politique. . . . (Ecole supérieure d'électricité. Publications no. 2071.) Malakoff, Ecole supérieure d'électricité, 1966. 178 p.

1153. BONIECKI, Wiktor. Ekonomia polityczna dla wyzszych szkól technicznych. Praca zbiorowa pod red. Wiktora Bonieckiego, Leszka Guzickiego i Stanisława Szefiera. Warszawa, Panstwowe wydawn. Naukowe, 1962- . v.

1154. BORDIN, Arrigo. Lezioni di economia politica (corso superiore) raccolte ed annotate dall'assistente Sergio Ricossa. (Corsi universitari.) Torino, G. Giappichelli, 1959. 255 p.

1155. ———. Principi di scienza economica; introduzione, lo scambio, la produzione. 2. ed. riv. e. ampliata. Torino, Giappichelli, 1947. 255 p. (3. ed., riv. e ampliata. 1953. viii, 293 p.

1156. BOUCKE, Oswald Fred. Principles of economics. New York, The Macmillan company, 1925. 2 v. Bibliographical notes: v. 1, 24-28.

1157. BOULDING, Kenneth Ewart. Economic analysis. New York, Harper and Row, 1948. (3d edition, 1955. 905 p. 4th edition, 1966. 2 v. Bibliographical footnotes. v. 1: Microeconomics. v. 2: Macroeconomics.)

1158. ———. Economics as a science. New York, McGraw-Hill, 1970.

1159. ———. A reconstruction of economics. New York, Wiley, 1950. xiii, 311 p.

1160. BOURCIER DE CARBON, Luc. Analyse économique; deuxième année de licence. Paris, Editions Montchrestien, 1970. v.

1161. BOVET, Eric David. L'organisation rationnelle de la distribution, moyen de stabilisation économique. (Bibliothèque professionnelle et sociale.) Neuchâtel, Delachaux et Niestlé, 1954. 268 p.

1162. BOWMAN, Mary Jean and George Leland Bach. . . . Economic analysis and public policy, an introduction. (Prentice-Hall economic series; E. A. J. Johnson, editor.) New York, Prentice-Hall, incorporated, c1943. xix, 935 p. Bibliographical foot-notes. (Supplement, c1948. 308 p.)

1163. BRAFF, Allan James. Microeconomic analysis. New York, Wiley, 1968, c1969. xii, 295 p.

1164. BRAINARD, Harry Gray. Economics in action. New York, Oxford university press, c1959. 441 p.

1165. BRANDIS, Royall. Economics: principles and policy. (The Irwin series in economics.) Homewood, Illinois, R. D. Irwin, 1959. 340 p. (Revised edition, 1963. 388 p.)
1166. ———. Principles of economics. Homewood, Illinois, R. D. Irwin, 1968. xix, 693 p. (Revised edition, 1972.)
1167. BRANDT, Karl. Das elastizitätsproblem, seine Darstellung und volkswirtschaftliche bedeutung. Heidelberg, 1948. 244 1.
1168. ———. Struktur der wirtschaftsdynamik. (Mannheimer schriftenreihe "Angewandte wirtschaftswissenschaft, " Heft. 4.) Frankfurt am Main, F. Knapp, c1952. 198 p.
1169. BRANSON, William H. Macroeconomic theory and policy. New York, Harper and Row, Publishers, Inc., 1971.
1170. BREMS, Hans. Output, employment, capital and growth; a quantitative analysis. New York, Harper, 1959. 349 p.
1171. BRENNAN, Michael Joseph. Theory of economic statics. Englewood Cliffs, New Jersey, Prentice-Hall, c1965. viii, 535 p. Bibliographies.
1172. BRESCIANI-TURRONI, Costantine. Corso di economia politica. Milano, Giuffrè, 1949- . v (5. ed. aggiornata, 1960- .)
1173. ———. Saggi di economia. Milano, Giuffrè, 1961. 634 p
1174. BRIGGS, Milton and Percy Jordan. Textbook of economics. 5th edition. London, University tutorial press, 1949. vii, 799 p.
1175. BRINKMANN, Carl. Wirtschaftsformen und lebensformen; gesammelte Schriften zur wirtschaftswissenschaft und wirtschaftspolitik. 2 aufl. Tübingen, Mohr, 1950. 549 p.
1176. ———. Wirtschaftstheorie. (Grundries der sozialwissenschaft, Bd. 1.) Göttingen, Vandenhoeck und Ruprecht, 1948. 135 p.
1177. BRISKA, Rudolf. Národné hospodárstvo; teória a politika. 2. doplnené vyd. Bratislava, Druzstevne vydavatel'stvo a knihkupectvo, 1948. 2 v.
1178. BRISMAN, Sven Bernhard. Nationalekonomins grunder. 7. omarb. uppl. Stockholm, Svenska bokförlaget, 1950. 155 p.
1179. BRKIC, Nikola. Politička ekonomija. 2., ism. i dop. izd. (Biblioteka stručnih izdanja.) Beograd, Savremena administracija, 1964. 235 p. (5. izd. Beograd, "Naučna knjiga, " 1969. x, 255, 1 p.)
1180. BROCARD, Lucien. Principles d'economie nationale et internationale. Paris, Recueil Sirey (Societé anonym), 1929 2 v.
1181. BROOMAN, F. S. Macroeconomia. Traduzione di Roberto Zaneletti. Milano, Giuffrè, 1967. xxi, 441 p.
1182. BROULHIET, Georges. Travail et richesses. Paris, J. Oliven, c1945. 255 p.
1183. BROWN, Arthur Joseph. Introduction to the world economy. London, Allen and Unwin, 1959. 212 p.
1184. BROWN, Ernest Henry Phelps. A course in applied economics. London, Pitman, 1951. xiii, 434 p. Bibliographies.

1185. BROWN, James Earl and Harold A. Wolf. Economics: principles and practices. S. Stowell Symmes, consultant. Columbus, Ohio, C. E. Merrill publishing company, 1968. xi, 528 p.
1186. BRUGUIER Pacini, Giuseppe. Economia politica. Bologna, R. Pàtron, 1949- . v.
1187. _____. Lezioni di economia politica per il II anno. Pisa, Libreria goliardica, 1949? 190 p.
1188. BRUIN, P. H. de. Economie, een geesteswetenschap. (Berchmanianum serie.) Roermond, J. J. Romen, 1946. 242 p.
1189. BRUS, Włodzimierz. Ogolne problemy funkcjonowania gospodarki socjalistycznej. Wyd. 1. Warszawa, Panstwowe wydawn. naukowe, 1961. 353 p.
1190. _____. Zarys ekonomii politycznej socjalizmu; skrypt wykładow. Wyd. 2. Warszawa, Panstwowe wydawn. Naukowe, 1951- . v.
1191. BUCKLEY, Helen and Kenneth Buckley. Economics for Canadians. Toronto, Macmillan, c1960. ix, 224 p.
1192. BUITENDIJK, B. Grondbeginselen der moderne economie. Haarlem, H. Stam, 1955. 174 p.
1193. _____. Inleiding tot de moderne economie. Haarlem-Culemborg, Antwerpen, Keulen, H. Stam, 1966. 312 p.
1194. BULAJIC, Zarko. Uvod u politicku ekonomiju. 2., izm. i dop. izd. (Biblioteka drustvenih nauka.) Beograd, Savremena administracija, 1965. 173 p.
1195. BULLOCK, Charles Jesse. Introduction to the study of economics. New edition, revised and enlarged. Boston, New York, etc., Sivler, Burdett and company, c1900. 581 p. Bibliography: 553-571.
1196. BULOW, Friedrich. Volkswirtschaftslehre; eine Einführung in das wirtschafts- und sozialwissenschaftliche Denken. Berlin, F. Vahlen, 1957. ix, 517 p.
1197. BUNTE, Peter. Produktionstechnik, kapital und fortschritt; eine Studie über kapital- und einkommensrechnung. (Volkswirtschaftliche schriften, Heft 62.) Berlin, Duncker und Humblot, 1961. 107 p.
1198. BURNS, Arthur Edward, Alfred Clarence Neal and Donald Stevenson Watson. Modern economics. With an introduction by Howard S. Ellis. New York, Harcourt, Brace, c1948. xvi, 954 p. "Selected references," 933-935. (2nd edition. Same authors; under the general editorship of Albert Gailord Hart. 1953. 790 p.)
1199. BURSTEIN, Meyer Louis. Economic theory; equilibrium and change. London, New York, J. Wiley, 1968. xiv, 335 p.
1200. BURTON, John Hill. Political and social economy: its practical applications. 1884. With an introductory essay "John Hill Burton and popular economic thought in the age of John Stuart Mill," by Joseph Dorfman. (Reprints of economic classics.) New York, A. M. Kelley, 1970. 40, v-xii, 11-345 p.

1201. BYE, Raymond Taylor. Principles of economics. New York, A. A. Knopf, 1924. vii, 508 p. Bibliography. (Revised edition, 1932. 3d edition, 1934. 5th edition, New York, Appleton-Century-Crofts, 1956. 691 p.)
1202. ———— and William Wallace Hewett. Applied economics; the application of economic principles to problems of policy. 5th edition. New York, Appleton-Century-Crofts, 1960. 595 p.
1203. ————. The economic process; its principles and problems. New York, Appleton-Century-Crofts, 1952. 1050 p. (2nd edition, 1963. 895 p.)
1204. CAFFE, Federico. Economisti moderni. 1. ed. (La Cultura moderna: antologie.) Milano, Garzanti, 1962. 306 p.
1205. ————. Saggi critici di economia. Roma, De Luca, 1958. 136 p.
1206. CAIRNCROSS, Alexander Kirkland. Introduction to economics. 2d edition. London, Butterworth, 1951. 502 p. (4th edition, 1966. xii, 606 p.)
1207. CAIRNES, John Elliott. The character and logical method of political economy. 2d edition. (Reprints of economic classics.) New York, A. M. Kelley, 1965. 235 p.
1208. ————. Some leading principles of political economy newly expounded. (Reprints of economic classics.) New York, A. M. Kelley, 1967. 421 p. (1st edition, 1874.)
1209. CALDERWOOD, James D. and George L. Fersh. Economics in action. Teacher's annotated edition. New York, Macmillan, 1968. xi, 531, 96 p.
1210. CAMPBELL, Ernest William. Political economy; a simple outline. Sydney, Current book distributors, 1954. 71 p.
1211. CAMPOLONGO, Alberto. Corso di politica economica e finanziaria. Milano, La goliardica, 1969. 391 p.
1212. CANARD, Nicholas François. Grundsätze der staatswirtschaft. Principes d'économie politique. Deutsch-französisch, mit einer interpretierenden einleitung von W. G. Waffenschmidt. (Veröffentlichungen der wirtschaftshochschule Mannheim. Reihe 1: Abhandlungen, Bd. 5.) Stuttgart, Kohlhammer, 1958. 248 p.
1213. CANNAN, Edwin. Elementary political economy. London, 1888. 152 p.
1214. CANTILLON, Richard. Essai sur la nature du commerce en général. Texte de l'édition originale de 1755, avec des études et commentaires par Alfred Sauvy et al. Paris, Institut national d'études démographiques, 1952. lxxii, 192 p. (Reprint of economic classics: Edited with an English translation and other material by Henry Higgs. London, Macmillan for Royal economic society, 1931. 394 p. New York, A. M. Kelley, bookseller, 1964. vii, 394 p.)
1215. CAPODAGLIO, Giulio. Lezioni di economia politica; a cura ed uso degli studenti. Bari, F. Cacucci, 1950. 293 p.

Summary Works 83

1216. CAPPUCCIO, Athos. Nozioni di scienza economica. Firenze, Sansoni, 1969. 433 p.
1217. _____. Principi di economia politica. Firenze, Sansoni, 1964. 583 p.
1218. CARELL, Erich. Allgemeine volkswirtschaftslehre; eine Einführung. 4. neubearb. aufl. München, R. Pflaum, 1949. 419 p. [5. verb. und erweiterte aufl., 1951. 476 p. 6., durchgesehene und ergänzt aufl. (Hochschulwissen in einzeldarstellungen.) Heidelberg, Quelle und Meyer, 1954. xii, 318 p. 7. verb. und erweiterte aufl., 1956. xii, 386 p. 8., durchgesehene und ergäntze aufl., 1958. xii, 434 p. 10. ergäntze aufl., 1963. 476 p. 12. verb. und erweiterte aufl. (Hochschulwissen in einzeldarstellungen.) Heidelberg, Quelle und Meyer, 1966. 555 p. 13., verb. und erw. aufl., 1968. 631 p.]
1219. CAREY, Henry Charles. Principles of political economy. (Reprints of economic classics.) New York, A. M. Kelly, bookseller, 1965. 4 parts in 3 v.
1220. CARLSON, Valdemar. An introduction to modern economics. (Blakiston books on economics.) Philadelphia, Toronto, The Blakiston company, c1946. xvii, 337 p. Bibliography.
1221. CARLTON, Frank Tracy. Economics. (Economics and business series.) Boston, New York, etc., D. C. Heath and company, c1931. ix, 371 p. Bibliography.
1222. CARREIRO, Carlos Porto. Lições de economia política e noções de finanças e extensas notas sôbre economia matemática pelo Prof. J. F. Kafuri. 7. ed. Rio de Janeiro, F. Briguiet, 1957. 597 p.
1223. CARREL, Jean et Christian Deglin. Eléments d'économie politique, d'organisation administrative tunisienne, de législation financière tunisienne; à l'usage des candidats aux concours administratifs tunisiens. 2. édition rev. et mise à jour au 1er octobre 1959. Tunis, 1960? 65, 68, 51 p.
1224. CARREÑO, Alberto María. Economía política, principios generales. Neuva ed. rev. y aumentada. México, Ediciones Botas, 1953. 319 p.
1225. CARTER, Charles Frederick. The science of wealth; an elementary textbook of economics. 2nd edition, revised. London, Edward Arnold, 1967. vii, 183 p.
1226. CARTER, William Harrison. Economic analysis. Storrs, Connecticut, 1952. 123 p. (Originally published as Economic theory syllabus and workbook. 1948.)
1227. CARTER, William Harrison and William P. Snavely. Intermediate economic analysis. New York, McGraw-Hill, 1961. 424 p.
1228. CARVER, Thomas Nixon. Principles of national economy. Boston, New York, etc., Ginn and company, c1921. vi, 773 p.
1229. _____. Principles of political economy. Boston, New York, etc., Ginn and company, c1919. ix, 588 p.
1230. CASSEL, Gustav. Economía social teórica. Traducida por

Miguel Paredes. 3. ed. rev. Madrid, M. Aguilar, 1946. 637 p.
1231. _____. Fundamental thoughts in economics. 1925. 159 p.
1232. _____. Theoretische sozialökonomie. (6., unveränderte aufl. Reprografischer nachdruck der 5., neubearb. aufl. Leipzig, 1932.) Darmstadt, Wissenschaftliche buchgesellschaft, 1968. xi, 657 p. [1st edition, 1918. 3rd edition, 1923. x, 595 p. English edition entitled: The theory of social economy. Translated by Joseph McCabe. London, T. F. Unwin, ltd. 1923 2 v. English reprint: Revised edition, New York, Harcourt, 1931. Translated by S. L. Barron. New revised edition. (Reprints of eco nomic classics.) New York, A. M. Kelley, 1967. viii, 708 p.]
1233. CASTRO, Antônio Barros de e Carlos Francisco Lessa. Introdução à economia; uma abordagem estructuralista. Rio, Forense, 1967. 160 p.
1234. CASTRO, Armando. Estudos de economia teórica e aplicada. (Colecção seara nova, 3. Secção 3: Economia.) Lisboa, Seara nova, 1968. 350 p.
1235. CASTRO, Diego de. Lezioni su alcuni argomenti di statistica economica. (Corsi universitari.) Torino, G. Giappichelli, 1950? 32, 128, 96, 112 p.
1236. CAULEY, Troy Jesse. Economics; principles and institutions. Scranton, International textbook company, 1968. xi, 368 p.
1237. CAZES, Bernard. La vie économique. (Collection U. série "Société politique.") Paris, A. Colin, 1965. 445 p.
1238. CERNE, Franc. Ekonomija iz novega zornega kota. Ljubljana, Cankarjeva zalozba, 1966. 334, 6 p.
1239. _____. Politična ekonomija, primerjalna analiza ekonomskih problemov i ekonomiskih sistemov. Ljubljana, 1963- . v.
1240. _____. Politična ekonomija; priročnik za študij. Ljubljana, Uradni list LRS, 1958. 148 p.
1241. CHALMERS, Eric Brownlie. Economics for managers. London, Griffith, 1967. ix, 201 p.
1242. CHALMERS, James A. and Fred H. Leonard. Economic principles. Macroeconomic theory. New York, The Macmillan company, 1971. xi, 460 p.
1243. CHAMBERLAIN, Neil W. A general theory of economic process. New York, Harper, c1955. 370 p.
1244. CHAND, Tara. Engineering economics; a study of the general economic principles, industrial law and contracts. 1st edition. Roorkee, Nem Chand, 1952. 336 p.
1245. CHANDLER, Lester Vernon. A preface to economics. New York and London, Harper and brothers, c1947. ix, p., 1 l., 289 p.
1246. NO ENTRY
1247. CHAO, Lan-p'ing. Ching chi hsüeh. (Transliterated.) 1946.

Summary Works 85

          3, 10, 339 p. (Revised edition, 1969. 2, 10, 209 p.)
1248. CHESSA, Federico. L'attività umana e le teorie economiche. (Collana di saggi di economia e storia economica a cura della Facoltà di economia e commercio dell'Università di Genova, 1.) Milano, A. Giuffrè, 1956. viii, 359 p.
1249. _____. Elementi di economia politica. Firenze, Sansoni, 1950. 271 p.
1250. _____. Principî di economia, Ristampa stereotipa con aggiunta del capitolo L'unione economica degli stati. Torino, G. Giappichelli, 1950. 608 p.
1251. CHEVROT, Jean Marc et Maurice Sallée. Initiation à l'économie générale. Paris, Dunod, 1971, c1970. vi, 246 p.
1252. CHIGUSA, Yoshindo. Keizai genron. (Transliterated.) Japan. 1968. 2, 5, 382 p. Bibliography, 365.
1253. _____. Keizaigaku nyūmon. (Transliterated.) Japan. 1955. 3, 12, 485 p. (2nd edition, 1958. 3, 13, 552 p.)
1254. CHIN, Se-in. Kŭndae kyŏngjehak. (Transliterated.) Korea, 1964. 302 p. Bibliographies.
1255. _____. Kyŏngje wŏllon. (Transliterated.) 1966. 408 p. Bibliographies.
1256. CHO, Chin-ha. Sin kyŏngje wŏllon. (Transliterated.) 1964. 322 p. (1st edition, 1959.)
1257. CH'OE, Ho-jin. Kyŏngje wŏllon. (Transliterated.) 1954. 1, 311 p. Bibliography, 309-311. (Second edition, 1964. 380 p. Bibliography, 361-363.)
1258. CH'OE, Ho-jin and Tong-ho Pak. Hyŏndae ŭi kyŏngjehak. (Transliterated.) 1956. 186 p. Bibliographies.
1259. CH'OE, Hwan-nyŏi. Kyongjehak wŏllon. (Transliterated.) 1962. 3, 266, 6 p.
1260. CICHERO, Mario Alberto y Rafael V. Portela Barillatti. Manual de economía política y argentina, con un apéndice sobre ahorro y previsión. 8. ed. corr., aumentada y puesta al día. Buenos Aires, El Ateneo, 1950. 366 p. (9. ed. corr., aumentada y puesta al día, 1952. 359 p.)
1261. CLARK, Harold Florian. Economics. New York, American book company, 1951. 508 p.
1262. CLARK, John Bates. Essentials of economic theory as applied to modern problems of industry and public policy. New York, The Macmillan company, c1907. xiv p., 1 l., 566 p. [(Reprinted: New York, 1915.) (Reprints of economic classics.) New York, A. M. Kelley, 1968. xiv, 566 p.]
1263. _____. The philosophy of wealth; economic principles newly formulated. (Reprints of economic classics.) New York, A. M. Kelley publishers, 1967. xv, 236 p.
1264. CLAY, Henry. Economics. An introduction for the general reader. London, 1916. (New York, The Macmillan company, 1918. xviii, 456 p.)
1265. CLEMENCE, Richard Vernon. Readings in economic analysis. Cambridge, Massachusetts, Addison-Wesley press, 1950. 2 v. Bibliographical footnotes. (V. I: General theory; V. II: Prices and production.)

1266. COGNETTI, Ferdinando. Elementi di economia politica. 2 ed. riv. e ampliata. Roma, Perrella, 1951. 306 p.
1267. COHEN, Bernard Lande. Introduction to the new economics New York, Philosophical library, 1959. 176 p.
1268. COHEN, Victor. Economic society; an introductory survey of economic theory. 4th edition. London, Heinemann, 1955. x, 511 p.
1269. COHN, Gustav. System der nationalökonomie. 1885-9. 2 v.
1270. COLARUSSO, Alfonso. Principi di economia politica. Roma 1950. 187 p.
1271. COLBERG, Marshall Rudolph, Dascomb R. Forbush and Gilbert R. Whitaker, Jr. Business economics; principles and cases. Assisted by the contribution to previous editions of William C. Bradford. 3d edition. Homewood, Illinois, R. D. Irwin, 1964. x, 717 p. (4th edition, 1970. xi, 601 p.)
1272. COLE, George Douglas Howard. Socialist economics. London, Gollancz, 1950. 158 p.
1273. COLSON, C. Cours d'économie politique. 3rd edition, 1916-24. 6 v. First published 1901-07. (Contents: 1: Théorie générale des phénomènes économiques. 2: Le travail et les questions ouvrières. 3: La propriété des capitaux, des agents naturels et des biens incorporels. 4 Les entreprises, le commerce et la circulation. 5: Les finances publiques et le budget de la France. 6: Les travaux publiques et les transports.)
1274. COLTON, Calvin. Public economy for the United States. With an introduction by Michael Hudson. (Reprints of economic classics.) New York, A. M. Kelley, 1969. xvi, 536 p.
1275. COMMITTEE on principles of economics. Principles of economics. (A Pitman collaborative textbook.) New York Pitman publishing corporation, 1959. 873 p.
1276. COMMONS, John Rogers. The economics of collective action. With a biographical sketch by Selig Perlman. Manuscript edited, introduction and supplemental essay contributed by Kenneth H. Parsons. New York, Macmillan, 1950. xii, 414 p. (Reprinted: Madison, University of Wisconsin press, 1970. xxi, 382 p.)
1277. CONDE, Mario. La economía clásica en la defensa de Occidente. Barcelona, BYBLOS, 1951. xxi, 331 p.
1278. CONSERVA, GIOVANNI. Elementi di economia politica. 7. edizione completamente rinnovata. Roma, V. Bonacci 1968. 413 p.
1279. COONS, Alvin E. The income of nations and persons; an introduction to economics. (Rand McNally economics series.) Chicago, Rand McNally, 1959. 672 p.
1280. CORBINO, Epicarmo. Elementi di economia politica. Milano, A. Giuffrè, 1954. 256 p.
1281. CORNA Pellegrini, Giacomo. Introduzione alla politica economica. (Quaderni di formazione sociale, n. 1.) Milano, Istituto sociale ambrosiano, 1959. xi, 302 p.
1282. CORREA Machado, Bernardo. Comprimidos económicos.

Medellín, Colombia, 1950. 197 p.
1283. COSCIANI, Cesare. Elementi di economia politica. 4. ed. rielaborata ed accresciuta. Padova, CEDAM, 1954. 367 p. (8. ed., 1965. xi, 428 p.)
1284. COURNOT, Antoine Augustin. Revue sommaire des doctrines economiques, 1877. (Reprints of economic classics.) New York, A. M. Kelley, 1968. viii, 339 p.
1285. COURTIN, René. Cours d'économie politique, rédigé d'après les notes et avec l'autorisation de René Courtin. Licence 3e année, 1962-1963. Paris, Cours de droit, 1963. 665 p.
1286. ———. Cours d'économie politique, rédigé d'après les notes et avec l'autorisation de René Courtin. Licence 3e année, 1963-1964. Paris, Cours de droit, 1964. 747 p.
1287. CRANE, Burton. Getting and spending; an informal guide to national economics. 1st edition. New York, Harcourt, Brace, 1956. 303 p.
1288. CROBAUGH, Mervyn. Economics for everybody, from the pyramids to the sit-down strike. New York, W. Morrow and company, 1937. 293 p. Bibliography, 285-287. (Reprinted: 1939.)
1289. CRONIN, John Francis. Economic analysis and problems. New York, Cincinnati, etc., American book company, c1945. xv, 623 p. Bibliography, 593-600. (Based on his Economics and society c1939.)
1290. CROOME, Honor Minturn (Scott) and Gordon King. The livelihood of man; economics in theory and practice. London, Christophers, 1953. 329 p.
1291. CRUTZEN, Albert. Cours d'économie politique. A l'usage de l'enseignement moyen, normal et technique commercial. 3e edition. Namur, A. Wesmael-Charlier, 1967. 271 p.
1292. CRUZ SANTOS, Abel. Temas de economía. Bogotá, Editorial Minerva, 1953. 263 p.
1293. CULMANN, Henri. Les mécanismes économiques. 5. édition. ("Que said-je?" Le point des connaissances actuelles, no. 27.) Paris, Presses universitaires de France, 1963. 135 p. (6e édition entièrement refondue, 1967. 128 p.)
1294. CUNHA, Tristão da. Ilusões economicas e a lição dos economistas. São Paulo, Editora Atlas, 1946? 2 v.
1295. CUNYNGHAME, H. A geometrical political economy. London? 1904. 128 p.
1296. CURTIS, Charles Ralph. Economics for everyone. (Foyles handbooks.) London, W. and G. Foyle, 1950. 104 p.
1297. ———. Economics for the student. London, Sweet and Maxwell, 1952. 286 p.
1298. ———. A first primer in economics. London, Cassell, 1954. 285 p.
1299. DABCEVIC-KUCAR, Savka, Alemka Grgurić, Mijo Novak. Politicka ekonomija. 3. izd. Zagreb, Skolska knjiga, 1954- . v. (4., nepromijenjeno izd., 1957- . v.)
1300. DAHL, Dieter. Volkswirtschaftstheorie und volkswirtschafts-

politik. Wiesbaden, Betriebswirtschaftlicher verlag Th. Gabler, 1968. 370 p.

1301. DARGENT, E. Les modèles macroéconomiques de séquence. L'exemple de Lundberg. Préface d'André Marchal. (Centre d'études économiques. Etudes et mémoires, 11.) Paris, A. Colin, 1953. ix, 150 p.

1302. DATE, Kuniharu and Ichiro Okuma. Riron-keizaigaku kogi. (Transliterated.) 1970. 372 p. Bibliographies.

1303. DATT, Ruddar. Understanding an economy; according to the paper on "Economic organisation and development" for the B. A. (Pass) course of the Delhi university for the year 1966 and onwards. 1st edition. Agra, Ratan Prakashan Mandir, 1963. v, 441 p.

1304. DAUGHERTY, Carroll Roop and Marion Roberts Daugherty. Principles of political economy. Boston, Houghton Mifflin, c1950. 2 v., xv, 1125, xi p.

1305. DAUGHERTY, Marion Roberts and Carl H. Madden. The economic process. Gerald Unks, special education consultant. Glenview, Illinois, Scott, Foresman, 1969. 504 p.

1306. DAUPHIN-MEUNIER, Achille. Principes de science économique. Edition conforme au programme relatif à la formation professionnelle des experts-comptables: décrets des 19 juillet 1948 et 9 juillet 1951. Paris, Dunod, 1958, c1957. 331 p.

1307. DAVENPORT, Herbert Joseph. The economics of enterprise 1913. xvi, 544 p.

1308. _____. Outlines of economic theory. (Reprints of economic classics.) New York, A. M. Kelley, 1968. xii, 381 p.

1309. DAVIDSON, Ralph K., Vernon L. Smith, and Jay W. Wiley. Economics: an analytical approach. Homewood, Illinois, R. D. Irwin, 1958. 393 p. (Revised edition, 1962. 460 p.)

1310. DAVISSON, William I. and John G. Ranlett. An introduction to microeconomic theory. New York, Harcourt, Brace and World, 1965. xiii, 226 p. Bibliographical footnotes.

1311. DAWSON, George Glenn and Russell H. McClain. The Collier quick and easy guide to economics. 1st edition. (A Collier books original.) New York, Collier books, 1963. 128 p.

1312. DEARLE, Norman Burrell. Economics; an introduction for the student and for everyman. 3d edition. London, New York, Longmans, Green, 1951. 560 p.

1313. DE GARIS, M. C. Elements of economics; introduction to economics from a new point of view. Geelong, Australia, 1952. 128 p.

1314. DE GARMO, Ernest Paul. Engineering economy. New York, Macmillan, 1960. 580 p.

1315. DEHEM, Roger. Eléments de science économique. Louvain, Institut de recherches économiques et sociales, 1957. 218 p.

1316. _____. Initiation à l'économique. Paris, Dunod, 1967.

	273 p. (Edition canadienne. Québec, Les presses de l'université Laval, 1967. 284 p.)
1317.	_____. Principes d'économie politique. Paris, Dunod, 1962. 197 p.
1318.	_____. Traité d'analyse économique. Paris, Dunod, 1958. 222 p. (2e édition, 1967. 224 p.)
1319.	DEIBLER, Frederick Shipp. . . . Principles of economics. 1st edition. New York, etc., McGraw-Hill book company, incorporated, c1929. xvi, 552 p. Bibliography.
1320.	DEMARIA, Giovanni. Principi gererali di logica economica. 2. ed. Milano, R. Malfasi, pref. 1948. xvi, 479 p.
1321.	DEMPSEY, Bernard William. The functional economy; the bases of economic organization. Englewood Cliffs, New Jersey, Prentice-Hall, 1958. 515 p.
1322.	DERNBURG, Thomas Frederick and Duncan M. McDougall. Macro-economics. The measurement, analysis and control of aggregate economic activity. New York, McGraw-Hill book company, 1960. (Revised and enlarged edition, 1963. x, 310 p.)
1323.	_____ and Judith Dukler Dernberg. Macroeconomic analysis; an introduction to comparative statics and dynamics. Reading, Massachusetts, Addison-Wesley publishing company, 1969. x, 292 p.
1324.	DE WELZ, Giuseppe. La magia del credito svelata. . . . A cura di F. Renda. (Storia economica di Sicilia. Testi e ricerche, 12/13-14/15.) Caltanisetta-Roma, S. Sciascia,
1325.	DEWETT, Kewal Krishan. Modern economic theory; micro and macro analysis. 12th revised edition. New Delhi, Shyam Lal charitable trust; sole distributors: S. Chand, 1966. xii, 824 p.
1326.	_____. Text book of economic theory; theory of price, employment and development for the new B. A. course of the Delhi university. Delhi, Premier publishing company, for Shyam Lal charitable trust, New Delhi, 1963. x, 547 p.
1327.	_____ and J. D. Varma. Refresher course in economic theory, for B. A. and B. com. students, 9th edition, thoroughly revised and brought up-to-date. Delhi, Premier publishing company, 1962. 513 p.
1328.	_____, Gurucharan Singh and Jai Dev Verma. Introductory economics, for intermediate students: elementary theory. 2d edition revised and enlarged. Delhi, Premier publishing company, 1950. 323 p.
1329.	DICK, John Reid. The engineer's approach to the economics of production. London, Pitman, 1952. 248 p.
1330.	DICKSON, Harald. Nationalekonomisk teori; en inledande översikt. Stockholm, Svenska bokförlaget, 1955. 304 p.
1331.	DIEHL, Karl. Theoretische nationalökonomie. 1916-27. 3 v. [Volume 1: Einleitung in die nationalökonomie, 1916. ix, 500 p. (2nd, 1922.) Volume 2: Die lehre von der produktion, 1924. viii, 372 p. Volume 3: Die lehre von der zirkulation: i: "Wert und preis," ii: "Geld und kredit."]
1332.	DIEPENHORST, Pieter Arie. Grondbeginselen der economie.

7. Druk. Zutphen, G. J. A. Ruys, 1945. 339 p.
1333. DIETERLEN, Pierre. L'idéologie économique. Paris, Editions Cujas, 1964. 281 p.
1334. DIETZEL, Heinrich. Theoretische socialökonomik. 1895. xi, 297 p. (Volume II. In, Adolf Wagner, Lehr- und handbuch der politischen oekonomie. 1876- . v.)
1335. DIGLIO, Giovanni. Note elementari di scienza economica (con un'appendice di diritto finanziario). Firenze, Editrice universitaria, 1957. 170 p.
1336. DJOJOHADIKUSUMO, Sumitro. Eknomi umum, azas-azas teori dan kebidjaksanaan. Tjetakan 3. (Pustaka ekonomi, no. 4.) Djakarta, Pembangunan, 1960. v.
1337. DODD, James Harvey. Applied economics; introductory principles of economics applied to everyday problems. 4th edition. Cincinnati, South-western publishing company, 1951. 568 p. (1st edition published, 1936 under title: Introductory Economics. 5th Edition, 1956. 566 p. 7th edition. By John W. Kennedy, Arthur R. Olsen and James Harvey Dodd. 1967. x, 566 p.
1338. _____. Introductory economics. Revised edition. Cincinnati, New York, etc., South-western publishing company, c1940. x, 596 p. Bibliography.
1339. _____, and Carl W. Hasek. Economics; principles and applications. 2d edition. Cincinnati, South-western publishing company, 1952. 775 p. (3rd edition by J. H. Dodd and C. W. Hasek. Consulting editor: T. J. Hailstones. 1957. 817 p. 4th edition J. H. Dodd and Thomas J. Hailstones. 1961. 849 p. 5th edition entitled: Economics; an analysis of principles and policies, by J. H. Dodd and T. J. Hailstones. 1965. ix, 850 p. Bibliographies.)
1340. DOMINGUEZ Vargas, Sergio. Teoría económica; nociones elementales. Prólogo de Manuel R. Palacios. 1. ed. México, Editorial jurídica mexicana, 1960. 298 p.
1341. DOOLEY, Peter C. Elementary price theory. New York, Appleton-Century-Crofts, 1967.
1342. DORANTES, A. Elementos de economía. México, Herrero, 1954. 270 p.
1343. DUBOIN, Jacques. Libération; des bras à la machine, de la disette à l'abondance, de l'échange à la distribution. 2. édition. Paris, Editions OCIA, 1946. 247 p.
1344. DUE, John Fitzgerald. Intermediate economic analysis. Chicago, R. D. Irwin, c1947. xii, 445 p. Bibliographies. [Revised edition, 1950. (Irwin series in economics.) xv, 566 p. 3rd edition. Homewood, Illinois, 1956. 588 p. 4th edition. By John F. Due and Robert W. Clower. Homewood, Illinois, 1961. 545 p. 5th edition entitled: Intermediate economic analysis; resources allocation, factor pricing and welfare. By John F. Due and Robert W. Clower. 1966. xiii, 481 p.]
1345. DUFTY, Norman Francis. Managerial economics. (Essays in social sciences, no. 3.) London and New York, Asia publishing house; 1966. viii, 287 p.

Summary Works 91

1346. DUMONTIER, Jacques. Observation économiqe; cours professé à l'Ecole nationale d'organisation économique et sociale et à l'Ecole d'application de l'Institut nationale de la statistique et des études économiques. 1. édition. (Bibliothèque de l'Ecole nationale d'organisation économique et sociale. Grande série.) Paris, Presses universitaires de France, 1950. 248 p.
1347. DYE, Howard S., John R. Moore and J. Fred Holly. Economics: principles, problems, and perspectives. Boston, Allyn and Bacon, 1962. 627 p. (2d edition, 1966. xiv, 655 p.)
1348. DYKMANS, Gommaire Louis. Introduction critique à la science économique. (Bibliothèque générale des sciences économiques, 12, 14, 36.) Bruxelles, Editions comptables, commerciales et financières, 1944-50. 3 v.
1349. EASTHAM, J. K. An introduction to economic analysis. London, English universities press, 1950. vii, 392 p. Bibliographies.
1350. EATON, John. Political economy; a Marxist textbook. New York, International publishers, 1949. 230, 4 p. (Revised edition. London, Lawrence and Wishart, 1952. 235 p. New revised edition. London, 1963. New York, 1966. 254 p.
1351. EBER, Manuel. Tools of economic analysis. Washington, American association for public information, education and research, 1953. 40 p.
1352. ECONOMIE politică; manual pentru învătămîntul universitar şi tehnic superior. Bucureşti, Editura politică, 1967- . v.
1353. EDIE, Lionel Danforth. Economics; principles and problems. New York, Thomas Y. Crowell company, c1926. xx, 799 p. Bibliography.
1354. ———. Principles of the new economics. (Crowell's social science series, edited by S. Elbridge.) New York, Thomas Y. Crowell company, c1922. xiii, 525 p. Bibliography.
1355. ———, James Ernest Moffat, Carroll Lawrence Christenson, Mark Carter Mills and others. Economics, principles and problems. Based on the original text by Lionel D. Edie. New York, Thomas Y. Crowell company, c1942. xiv, 1022 p. Bibliography. [Fifteenth printing, August 1942 (first printing of third edition).]
1356. EDWARDS, Graham J. The framework of economics. New York, McGraw-Hill, c1964. 317 p.
1357. EELLS, Richard Sedric Fox and Clarence Walton. Conceptual foundations of business. Revised edition. (The Irwin series in management.) Homewood, Illinois, R. D. Irwin, 1969.) viii, 648 p.
1358. EGGERS, Melvin A. and A. Dale Tussing. Economic processes; the composition of economic activity. New York, Holt, Rinehart and Winston, 1965. xi, 435 p.
1359. ———. Economic processes; the level of economic activity. New York, Holt, Rinehart and Winston, 1965. xi, 403 p.

1360. EGNER, Erich. Der haushalt; eine Darstellung seiner volkswirtschaftlichen gestalt. Berlin, Duncker und Humblot, 1952. 516 p.
1361. EINARSEN, Johan og Torgrim Barding. Sosialøkonomie. 3. utg. Oslo, Aschehoug, 1950. 275 p.
1362. EIRIKSSON, Benjamin H. J. Outline of an economic theory. (Based on thesis, Harvard university.) Reykjavik, Helgafell publishing company, 1954. 493 p.
1363. EISERMANN, Gottfried. Wirtschaft und gesellschaft. (Bonner beiträge zur soziologie, Nr. 1.) Stuttgart, F. Enke, 1964. vii, 256 p.
1364. EKONOMIZ polityczna. Wyd. 2. Warszawa, Panstwowe wydawn. Naukowe, 1967-68. 2 v.
1365. EKONOMIA polityczna; zarys popularny. Wyd. 1. Warszawa, Książka i Wiedza, 1964. 567 p. (Wyd. 4., zmienione i rozsz. 1967. 679 p.)
1366. ELIOT, Gerald, Basic contemporary economics. Belmont, California, Dickenson publishing company, 1969. xii, 239 p.
1367. ELLIS, Howard S. and W. Fellner. "External economies and diseconomies." In, Readings in price theory. London, Allen and Unwin, 1953.
1368. ELLIS, Howard S. and others. A survey of contemporary economics. London? Blakiston company for the American economic association, 1948.
1369. ELY, Richard Theodor. An introduction to political economy. New York, 1889. 358 p.
1370. _____. . . . . Outlines of economics. (Chautauqua reading circle literature.) Meadville, Pennsylvania, Flood and Vincent, c1893. 1 p. 1., v-xi, 347 p. (Began issuing it with colleagues, 1908. Richard T. Ely, Thomas S. Adams and Max O. Lorenz. 3rd edition. New York, 1916. xiii, 767 p. 4th edition by Richard Theodore Ely, Thomas Sewall Adams, Max Otto Lorenz, and Allyn Abbott Young. 1923. 729 p. 5th revised edition by Richard Theodore Ely, Thomas Sewall Adams, Max Otto Lorenz, and Allyn Abbott Young. New York, The Macmillan company, 1930. xviii, 868 p. Bibliography. 6th edition, (and last) By Richard Theodore Ely and Ralph H. Hess. 1937.)
1371. EMPOLI, Attilio da. Lezioni di economic politica, anno accademico 1945-46. Napoli, E. Jovene, 1946- . v.
1372. ENKE, Stephen. Intermediate economic theory. (Prentice-Hall economics series.) New York, Prentice-Hall, c1950. xx, 588 p. Bibliographies.
1373. ERGIN, Feridun. Iktisat. Gözden geçirilmiş ve genişletilmiş 3. baski. (Istanbul universitesi yayinlarindan, no. 977.) Istanbul, Hamle Matbaasi, 1962. xvi, 878 p.
1374. ESSEN. Rheinisch-westfälisches institut für wirtschaftsforschung. Beiträge zur wirtschaftsforschung; Festgabe für Walther Däbritz. Beiträge von Fritz Baade et al. Essen, 1951. 358 p. (2. durchgesehene aufl., 1952. 358 p.)
1375. EUCKEN, Walter Kurt Heinrich. Die grundlagen der

nationalökonomie. 6. durchgesehene aufl. (Enzyklopädie der rechts- und staatswissenschaft. Abt. Staatswissenschaft, 1.) Berlin, Springer, 1950. xvii, 279 p. Bibliographical notes. (English edition entitled: The foundations of economics; history and theory in the analysis of economic reality. Translated by T. W. Hutchison. London, W. Hodge, 1950; Chicago, University of Chicago press, 1951. 358 p. 8. aufl. Berlin, New York, Springer-verlag, 1965. xvii, 279 p.)

1376. _____. Kapitaltheoretische untersuchungen. 2. aufl., ergänzt durch 3 aufsätze. Mit einer einleitung von Friedrich A. Lutz: Die Entwicklung die zinstheorie seit Böhm-Bawerk. (Hand- und lehrbücher aus dem Gebeit der sozialwissenschaften.) Tübingen, Mohr, 1954. xxvii, 336 p.

1377. EVANS, George Heberton. Basic economics; a macro- and micro-analysis. 1st edition. New York, Knopf, 1950. xix, 381, xiii p.

1378. EYNERN, Gert von. Grundriss der politischen wirtschaftlehre. (Die Wissenschaft von der politik, 14. Bd.) Köln, West-deutscher verlag, 1968. 307 p.

1379. FAIRCHILD, Fred Rogers and Thomas J. Shelly. Understanding our free economy; an introduction to economics. New York, Van Nostrand, c1952. 589 p. (4th edition, 1965. xxii, 580 p.)

1380. FAIRCHILD, Fred Rogers, Edgar Stevenson Furniss, and Norman Sydney Buck. Elementary economics. New York, The Macmillan company, 1926. (3d edition, 1936. 2 v. 4th edition, 1939? 2 v.)

1381. FAIRCHILD, Fred Rogers, Norman Sydney Buck and Reuben Emanuel Slesinger. Principles of economics. New York, Macmillan, 1954. 780 p.

1382. FALLON, Valère. Principes d'économie sociale. 7. éd. rev. et augm. (Museum Lessianum. Section philosophique.) Bruxelles, Edition universelle, 1949. xv, 554 p.

1383. FANNO, Marco. Elementi di scienza economica. 3. ed. riv. e modificata. Torino, S. Lattes, 1951. 440 p. (5th edition revised, 1953. 448 p.)

1384. _____. Principii di scienza economica. 4. ed. riv. e aggiornata. Padova, CEDAM, 1952- . v.

1385. _____. Scritti vari di economia e finanza. Pubblicati a cura della Facoltà di giurisprudenza dell'Università di Padova. Padova, CEDAM, 1954. viii, 274 p.

1386. FANTINI, Oddone. Scritti economici vari. (Pubblicazioni dell'Istituto di politica economica e finanziaria della Facolta di economia e commercio dell'Universita di Roma.) Milano, Giuffrè, 1962. xii, 348 p.

1387. _____. Strategia economica; principi e aspetti operativi. Milano, Giuffrè, 1966. vii, 228 p.

1388. FAROPPA, Luis A. El pensamiento económico y la evolución social. (Facultad de ciencias económicas y de administración. Instituto de teoria y politica económicas Publicaciones, no. 6.) Montevideo, 1955. 45 p.

1389. FARRAR, Donald Eugene and John R. Meyer. Managerial economics. (Foundations of modern economics series.) Englewood Cliffs, New Jersey, Prentice-Hall, 1970. 115 p.
1390. FASCIANI, F. Leonida. Elementi di economia politica. Bologna, R. Pàtron, 1969. x, 297 p.
1391. FAWCETT, Henry. Manual of political economy. London, 1863. (2d edition, 1865. 7th edition, London, 1885.)
1392. FAY, Charles Ralph. Elements of economics; a textbook for secondary schools. New York, The Macmillan company, 1926. xviii, 631 p. Bibliography, 595-615.
1393. FEIER, Richard. Economics for modern living. New York, College entrance book company, 1958. 468 p.
1394. FELLNER, William John. Emergence and content of modern economic analysis. New York, McGraw-Hill, 1960. 459 p.
1395. FELS, Rendigs. Challenge to the American economy; an introduction to economics. Boston, Allyn and Bacon, 1961. 708 p. (2d edition entitled: An introduction to economics; the challenge to the American economy. 1966, xvi, 698 p.)
1396. FENIZIO, Ferdinando di. Economia politica. Milano, Hoepli, 1949. 523 p. (3rd edition, riscritta. Milano, Editrice l'industria, 1957- . v.)
1397. _____. Le leggi dell'economia: il metodo dell'economia politica e della politica economica. 3. ed. ampliata. Milano, Editrice l'industria, 1961. 405 p.
1398. _____. Le leggi dell'economia: il sistema economico. Lezioni, 3. ed. ampliata. Milano, editrice l'industria, 1960. 237 p.
1399. _____. Lezioni sul metodo dell'economia politica. Milano, Editrice l'industria, c1957. 296 p.
1400. FERGUSON, Charles E. Microeconomic theory. (Irwin series in economics.) Homewood, Illinois, R. D. Irwin, c1966. xiv, 439 p. Bibliographies. (Revised edition, 1969. xv, 521 p.)
1401. _____, and Juanita Morris Kreps. Principles of economics. New York, Holt, Rinehart and Winston, c1962. 352 p. Bibliography. (2d edition, 1965. xii, 863 p. Bibliographies.)
1402. FERGUSON, Charles E. and S. Charles Maurice. Economic analysis. Homewood, Illinois, R. D. Irwin, 1970. ix, 293 p.
1403. FERNANDEZ Pirla, José María. Curso general de economía. Madrid, Editorial estudios jurídicos, económicos y sociales, 1962. 428 p.
1404. FETTER, Frank Albert. Economics. . . . New York, The century company, 1915-16. 2 v. [(v. 1: Economic principles. v. 2: Modern economic problems. Manual of references and exercises in economics for use with volume 1 Economic principles. 1916. 1 p. 1., v-vii, 46 p. Manual . . . for volume 2. 1917. 59 p.) (2d edition, revised. 1922. 6 p. 1., 3-611 p. Bibliography.)]

1405. _____. The principles of economics with applications to practical problems. 1904. xv, 610 p.
1406. FIACCAVENTO, Corrado. Saggi di economia politica. Milano, A. Giuffrè, 1970. 174 p.
1407. FISHER, Irving. Elementary principles of economics. 3d edition. New York, The Macmillan company, 1912. xxvii p., 1 1., 531 p. (First edition published 1910 under title: Introduction to economic science.)
1408. FISHMAN, Betty G., Leo Fishman, Jules Backman and others. The American economy. (Van Nostrand series in business administration and economics.) Princeton, New Jersey, Van Nostrand, c1962. 822 p.
1409. FLAMANT, Maurice. Cours d'économie politique générale, rédigé d'après les notes . . . de M. Maurice Flamant. . . . Licence 1ère année. 1966-1967. Paris, les Cours de droit, 1967. 411 p.
1410. _____. Lexique de termes économiques. Paris, les Cours de droit, 1967. 42 p.
1411. FLECK, Florian H. Untersuchungen zur ökonomischen theorie vom technischen fortschritt; eine dogmengeschichtliche und wirtschaftstheoretische betrachtung. (Veröffentlichungen des wirtschafts- und sozialwissenschaftlichen Institutes der universität Freiburg Schweiz, 4.) Freiburg, Schweiz, Universitätsverlag, 1957. x, 186 p.
1412. FLINK, Salomon J. The American economy, a functional analysis of economic principles and practices. New York, Dryden press, 1948. xviii, 746 p.
1413. FLORIN, Raymond. Dynamique économique. Soissons, Impr. Saint-Antoine, 1948. vi, 115 p.
1414. FLOUZAT, Denise. Analyse économique; première année. (Premier cycle. Droit, sciences économiques.) Paris, Masson et c^{ie}., 1969. 257 p.
1415. FLUX, Alfred William. Economic principles, an introductory study. 2d edition, revised. London, Methuen and company, limited, 1923. xxii, 305 p. (1st edition, 1904.)
1416. FORD, Percy. Economics of modern industry; an introduction for business students. With supplementary material for Indian students by E. R. Dhongde. Bombay, Orient Longmans, 1952. 264 p.
1417. FORSTMANN, Albrecht. Neue wirtschaftslehren, theorien und hypothesen. Berlin, Duncker und Humblot, 1954. xxi, 512 p.
1418. FORTE Francesco. Introdução à política económica. Tradução de Alfredo Margarido. (Perspectivas, 11, 13.) Lisboa, Editorial presença, 1965- . v.
1419. FOSSATI, Antonio. Lezioni di economia politica. (Corsi universitari.) Torino, G. Giappichelli, 1948. 257 p.
1420. FOSSATI, Eraldo. Elementi di politica economica razionale. Milano, A. Giuffrè, 1955. xi, 292 p.
1421. _____. The theory of general static equilibrium. Edited by G. L. S. Shackle. New York, Kelley and Millman, 1957. xvi, 247 p. Bibliographies. (Prepared from the

fourth Italian enlarged edition of Professor Fossati's Elementi di economia razionale.)

1422. FOURGEAUD, Andre. L'homme et les richesses; cours d'économie politique, licence 1ère année. Aix-en-Provence, Pensée universitaire, 1954- , cover 1955- . v.

1423. FRAIN, Hummel La Rue. An introduction to economics. (Under the editorship of Edgar S. Furniss.) Boston, New York, etc., Houghton Mifflin company, c1937. xvii, 1, 693 p.

1424. FRANCE. Ministère de l'économie et des finances. Centre de formation professionnelle et de perfectionnement. Economie politique. (Its Cours.) Paris, Direction du personnel et des services généraux, Centre de formation professionnelle et de perfectionnement, 1966. 2 v.

1425. _____. _____. _____. Eléments d'économie. Paris, Direction du personnel et des services généraux, Centre de formation professionnelle et de perfectionnement, 1968? 2 v.

1426. FRANCHINI-STAPPO, Alessandro. Riassunti di politica economica. Firenze, Editrice universitaria, 1951? 2 v.

1427. FRASER, Lindley Macnaghten. Economic thought and language; a critique of some fundamental economic concepts. London, A. and C. Black, limited, 1937. xx, 411 p. Bibliography, 401-406.

1428. FRISCH, Heinz und Lothar Surkau. Volkswirtschaft in unserer zeit. Volkswirtschaftstheorie und wirtschaftspolitik. 2., durchgesehene aufl. (Gehlenbuch, 20.) Bad Homburg v. d. H., Berlin, Zürich, Gehlen, 1967. 275 p.

1429. FRISELLA Vella, Giuseppe. Appunti dalle lezioni d'economica, anno accademico, 1948-49. Palermo? 1949. v.

1430. FROMAN, Lewis Acrelius. Principles of economics. Revised edition. Chicago, Illinois, R. D. Irwin, incorporated, c1946. xi, 1009 p. Bibliographies, 24-28. (First printing, July 1946.)

1431. FURSTENBERG, Friedrich. Wirtschaftssoziologie. 2., neubearb. u. erg. aufl. (Sammlung Göschen, Bd. 1193/1193a.) Berlin, de Gruyter, 1970. 141 p.

1432. FYOT, Jean Louis. Dimensions de l'homme et science économique. 1. édition. (Bibliothèque de philosophie contemporaine.) Paris, Presses universitaires de France, 1952. 355 p.

1433. GADGIL, G. G. Outline of economic theory. 1st edition. Bombay, Lakhani book depot, 1951. 399 p.

1434. GALLI, Renate. Economic politica. (Valore, produzione, scambio, impress, profitto.) Milano, Giuffrè, 1956- . v. (3. ed. riv. Torino, Unione tipografico-editrice torinese, 1966- . v.

1435. GALVES, Carlos. Elementos de economia política atual. São Paulo, Editôra, F. T. D., 1966. 227 p.

1436. _____. Manual de economia política. 3. ed. Rio, Forense, 1967. 425 p.

1437. GAMBS, John Saké. Man, money, and goods. New York, Columbia university press, 1952. 339 p.

Summary Works

1438. _____, and Sidney Wertimer, Jr. Economics and man. (The Irwin series in economics.) Homewood, Illinois, R. D. Irwin, 1959. 353 p. (Revised edition, 1964. xiii, 433 p.)
1439. GARAU Riu, Miguel. Ciencia económica, mecánica de la producción. Barcelona, Ariel, 1958. 475 p.
1440. GARB, Gerald. Introduction to microeconomic theory. New York, Ronald press company, 1968. viii, 234 p.
1441. GARCIA González, Adolfo. Nueva economía fundamental, hacienda pública y derecho transcendental inmobiliario. Madrid, Instituto editorial Reus, 1947. 672 p.
1442. _____. Polémica en torno a "Nueva economía fundamental." Madrid, 1951. 839 p.
1443. GARINO Canina, Attilio. Scritti varî di economia e finanza. (Università di Torino. Facoltà di economia e commercio. Istituto di finanza. Pubblicazioni, 8.) Torino, G. Giappichelli, 1952. 470 p.
1444. GARVER, Frederic Benjamin . . . and Alvin Harvey Hansen. . . . Principles of economics. Boston, New York, etc., Ginn and company, c1928. x, 726 p. (Revised edition, 1937. x, 686 p.)
1445. GAY y Forner, Vicente. Para comprender la economía política e historia de las doctrinas económicas y sociales. Madrid, 1945. 1 v.
1446. GAZITUA Navarrete, Victor Manuel. Economía política. (Colección de apuntes de clases, no. 6.) Santiago, Editorial jurídica de Chile, 1952. 330 p.
1447. GEMMELL, James and Howard L. Balsley. Principles of economics. Boston, Heath, 1953. 589 p.
1448. GEMMILL, Paul Fleming. Current introductory economics, New York, Harper, 1955. 711 p.
1449. _____. Fundamentals of economics; a textbook for introductory college courses in economic principles. 1st edition. New York and London, Harper and brothers, c1930. xii, 489 p. Bibliography, 470-476. (Revised edition, 1935. xiv, 608 p. 6th edition, 1960. 724 p.)
1450. _____, and Ralph H. Blodgett. Economics, principles and problems. 1st edition. New York, Harper, c1937. 2 v.
1451. GEORGE, Henry. Progress and poverty; an inquiry into the causes of industrial depressions and of increase of want with increase of wealth; the remedy. 1879. (New York, Robert Schalkenbach foundation, 1954. xxix, 599 p. 75th anniversary edition, 1955. xxix, 599 p.)
1452. _____. The science of political economy. New York, 1898.
1453. GERA, Giovanni. Elementi di economia politica. 3. ed. riv. e. modificata. Roma, Libreria ricerche, 1954. 291 p. (7. edizione rivedata e modificata. Roma, A. Signorelli, 1969. 411 p.)
1454. GERHARD, Ingemar. Samhällsekonomi. 3. upp. (Scandinavian university books.) Göteberg, Läromedelsförlagen: (Akademiförlaget), 1968. viii, 320 p.

1455. GESELL, Silvio. The natural economic order. Translated by Philip Pye. Revised English edition. London, P. Owen, 1958. 452 p.
1456. GEYER, Herbert. Untersuchungen über die theorie des dynamischen makro-ökonomischen Kernprozesses. (Frankfurter wirtschafts- und sozialwissenschaftliche studien, Heft. 2.) Berlin, Duncker und Humblot, 1958, c1957. 170 p.
1457. _____, und W. Oppelt. Volkswirtschaftliche regelungsvorgänge im Vergleich zu regelungsvorgängen der technik; vorträge . . . zusammengestellt von. . . . (Beihefte zur regelungstechnik.) München, R. Oldenbourg, 1957. 143 p.
1458. GIDE, Charles. Principles of political economy. Translated from the 23d French edition by Ernest F. Row. Westport, Connecticut, Greenwood press, 1970. xiii, 555 p.
1459. GILBEY, Elizabeth W. A primer on economics of consumption. New York, Random house, 1968.
1460. GILL, Richard T. Economics and the public interest. Pacific Palisades, California, Goodyear publishing company, 1968. 306 p.
1461. GINI, Corrado. Patologia economica. 5. ed. riv. e accresciuta. (Sociologi ed economisti, 2.) Torino, Unione tipografico-editrice torinese, 1952. 630 p.
1462. GIORGI, Giacomo. Principî di economia politica. 2. e. riv. e. aggiornata. Firenze, L. Macrî, 1951. viii, 304 p.
1463. GISLASON, Conrad. Stagnation or growth: America must choose. 1st edition. New York, Vantage press, 1964. 222 p.
1464. GITLOW, Abraham Leo. Economics. New York, Oxford university press, c1962. 748 p. Bibliography.
1465. GLIGORIJEVIC, Slobodan. Osnovi iz politicke ekonomije. 2. izd. (Politicka skola.) Beograd, Rad, 1963. 220 p.
1466. GOBBI, Ulisse. Trattato di economia. Italy, 1919. 653 p.
1467. GOMES, Luiz Souza. O que devemos conhecer da economia política e das finanças; uma introdução ao estudo da economia e finanças. A economia política e finanças divulgadas em linguagem acessível acrescida com uma síntese da teoria geral, de J. M. Keynes. 6. ed. revista e atualizada. Rio de Janeiro, Editôra civilização Brasileira, 1961. 421 p. (8th ed. rev. e atual. Rio de Janeiro, Fundação Getúlio Vargas, 1968. 430 p. 9th ed. rev. e atualizada. Rio de Janeiro, Fundação Getúlio Vargas, Servico de publicações, 1970. xxx, 382 p.)
1468. GONZALES, Antonio J. Tratado moderno de economía general. Cincinnati, South-Western publishing company, 1969. viii, 494 p.
1469. GOODMAN, Kennard Everett and William L. Moore. Economics in everyday life. Photos. by Robert Yarnall Richie, drawings by Forrest Orr. Boston, New York, Ginn and Company, 1938. vi, 488 p. (1943. vi. 557 p. Bibliography. Rev. ed. Boston, Ginn, 1950. vi, 576 p.

Revised edition, 1952. 576 p. Revised edition, 1955. 576 p.
1470. _____. Today's economics. Boston, Ginn, 1957. 631 p.
1471. GOOTJES, Pieter. Sociale economie voor handelswetenschappelijke en andere examens; bewerkt naar Staathuishoudkunde door M. Spaander. Groningen, P. Noordhoff, 1950-51. 2 v.
1472. GORDON, Leland James. Elementary economics. New York, American book company, 1950. xxx, 576 p.
1473. GORDON, Sanford D. and Jess Witchel. An introduction to the American economy; analysis and policy. Boston, Heath, 1967. xvii, 460 p.
1474. GORDON, Sanford D., George G. Dawson and Jess Witchel. The American economy; analysis and policy. Lexington, Massachusetts, Heath, 1969. 1 v.
1475. GOTO, Fumitoshi. Seicho keizaigaku. (Transliterated.) 1964. 2, 4, 207 p.
1476. GOUDRIAAN, Jan. Economie in zestien bladzijden; of, Inleiding tot de analytische economie. Amsterdam, J. H. de Bussy, 1952, c1951. 249 p.
1477. GRAYSON, Henry and Philipp H. Lohman. Principles of economics. New York, American book company, 1958. 720 p.
1478. GRAZIADEI, Antonio. Compendio di economia politica. 1. ed. (Piccola biblioteca di scienze moderne, v. 503. Sezione di economia.) Milano, Fratelli, Bocca, 1951. 118 p.
1479. _____. Scritti scelti di economia. A cura di Mauro Ridolfi. (Sociologi ed economisti, 39.) Torino, Unione tipogravico-editrice torinese, 1969. xxxi, 505 p.
1480. GRAZIANI, Augusto. Istituzioni di economia politica. (Biblioteca del "Foro italiano.") Roma, Soc. ed. del "Foro italiano," 1951. xvi, 720 p. Bibliographical footnotes. (1st edition, 1904. 4th edition, 1925. xix, 803 p.)
1481. _____. Teoria economica. Macroeconomia. 2. edizione ampliata. Napoli, Edizioni scientifiche italiane, 1970. 499 p.
1482. _____. Teoria economica. Testo collazionato da Giuliana Barchiesi. Napoli, Edizioni scientifiche italiane, 1967. 685 p.
1483. GUARESTI, Juan José. Economía política: intercambio internacional, las oscilaciones económicas, producto e ingreso, crecimiento y desarrollo. Prólogo del Dr. José Heriberto Martínez. Buenos Aires, Editorial G. Kraft, 1965. 424 p.
1484. GUERRA Cepeda, Roberto. Economía política contemporánea; conceptos básicos. Texto para el primer curso de economía política, de acuerdo con el programa oficial de la Facultad de comercio y administración de la UNAM. Xochimilco, Argrin, 1967. 462 p.
1485. GUIGNABAUDET, Philippe. De las teorías ideológicas a la realidad económica. Quito, Editorial Casa de la cultura ecuatoriana, 1963. 2 v.

1486. GUILLAUME, Edouard et G. Guillaume. Energétique générale, base rationnelle de la résolution des conflits; la solution pratique de la paix dans l'ère atomique. (Travaux du Centre d'analyse économique.) Paris, 1946. v.

1487. GUITTON, Henri. Analyse économique, 1re année... avec la collaboration de Pierre Buchaillard.... (Travaux dirigés.) Paris, Sirey, 1968. 452 p.

1488. ———. Economie politique. (Petits précis Dalloz.) Paris, Dalloz, 1956- . v. (3. édition, 1962- . v. 6. édition, 1967- . v. 7. édition, 1970. v. 8. édition, 1971, c1970- . v.)

1489. ———. Economie politique générale, notes de cours... Licence, 1re année. 1965-1966. Paris, les Cours de droit, 1966. 746, 20 p.

1490. ———. Economie politique, générale, notes de cours. ... Licence, 1ère année. 1966-1967. Paris, les Cours de droit, 1967. 687 p.

1491. ———. L'objet de l'économie politique. Observations de Léon Dupriez et Francesco Vito. (Bilans de la connaissance économique, 2.) Paris, M. Rivière, 1951. 196 p.

1492. GUTHRIE, John Alexander. Economics. (The Irwin series in economics.) Homewood, Illinois, 1957. 537 p. [Revised edition, 1961. 678 p. 3d edition. By John Alexander Guthrie and Robert F. Wallace, 1965. xix, 750 p. 4th edition, (Same authors) 1969. xxii, 824 p.]

1493. GUTIERREZ G., Victor Manuel y Gabriel Alvarado. Breves resúmenes de economía politica. (Biblioteca de cultura popular, v. 3.) Guatemala, Ministerio de educación pública, 1950. 107 p.

1494. HAAVELMO, Trygve. Generell markedsteori. Haavelmo's forelesninger i vårsemestret 1959. Referert og bearb. av Gunnar Bramness. Oslo, Universitetsforlaget, 1967. 3, 118 p.

1495. HADAR, Josef. Elementary theory of economic behavior. (Addison-Wesley series in management science and economics.) Reading, Massachusetts, Addison-Wesley publishing company, 1966. ix, 332 p.

1496. HADIBROTO, Suhadji. Peladjaran ekonomi; untuk sekolah menengah atas atau jang sederadjad. Tjet. 2. Medan, Islamyah, 1951. 125 p.

1497. HAGENBUCH, Walter. Social economics. (The Cambridge economic handbooks.) Welwyn, Herts., J. Nisbet, 1959, c1958. xv, 320 p.

1498. HAGUE, Dougles Chalmers and Alfred W. Stonier. The essentials of economics; an introduction and outline for students and for the general reader. London, New York, Longmans, Green, 1965. 173 p.

1499. HAHN, Albert. Common sense economics. London, New York, Abelard-Schuman, 1956. xvi, 244 p.

1500. ———. De economie van de illusie. (Serie, "Vraagstukken van heden en morgen," no. 12.) Voorburg, Comité

Summary Works 101

        de bestudering van ordeningsvraagstukken, 194- ? 24 p.
1501. _____. Wirtschaftswissenschaft des gesunden Menschenverstandes. Frankfurt am Main, F. Knapp, 1954. 280 p. (2., neubearb. und erweiterte aufl., 1955. 295 p.)
1502. HAILSTONES, Thomas J. Basic economics. Cincinnati, South-western publishing company, 1960. 513 p. (2nd edition, 1964. xii, 533 p. 3rd edition, 1968. xii, 607 p. 3rd edition. Garden City, New York, Doubleday, 1969. xii, 607 p.)
1503. _____. Readings in economics. Cincinnati, South-western publishing company, 1963. 512 p.
1504. HAILSTONES, Thomas J. and Michael J. Brennan. Economics; an analysis of principles and policies. Cincinnati, South-western publishing company, c1970. ix, 932 p.
1505. HALEY, Bernard F. A survey of contemporary economics. Volume 2. Homewood, Illinois, Richard D. Irwin, for the American economic association, 1952.
1506. HAMBERG, Daniel. Principles of a growing economy. With three introductory chapters on American economic institutions, contributed by Douglas F. Dowd. 1st edition. New York, Norton, 1961. 879 p.
1507. HANSEN, Alvin Harvey. The American economy. (Economics handbook series.) New York, McGraw-Hill, 1957. 199 p.
1508. HANSEN, Michael. A citizen of today; an introduction to the economic aspects of the everyday life of ordinary people. London, Oxford university press, 1957. 143 p. (3rd edition, 1967. 143 p.)
1509. HANSON, John Lloyd. Economic aspects of industry and commerce. London, Macdonald and Evans, 1958. 369 p. (2d edition, 1962. xvi, 369 p. 3rd edition, 1966. xvi, 369 p.)
1510. _____. A textbook of economics. London, Macdonald and Evans, 1953. 596 p. (4th edition, 1966. xxviii, 571 p.)
1511. _____. The world of industry and commerce. 2nd edition. London, Macdonald and Evans, 1966. x, 166 p.
1512. HARDING, Fred O. Politisches modell zur wirtschaftstheorie; theorie der bestimmungsfaktoren finanzwirtschaftlicher staatstätigkeit. Freiburg im Breisgau, 1959. xi, 130 p.
1513. HARRIS, Walter A. Introductory economics; analysis and practice. Minneapolis, Burgess publishing company, 1970. viii, 331 p.
1514. HARRISS, Clement Lowell. The American economy; principles, practices, and policies. 4th edition. (The Irwin series in economics.) Homewood, Illinois, R. D. Irwin, 1962. 895 p. Bibliographical footnotes. (5th edition, 1965. xiv, 876 p. 6th edition, 1968. xv, 998 p.)
1515. _____. Economics: an analytical approach. New edition. Boston, Ginn, 1969. viii, 566 p.
1516. _____. Selected readings in economics. 2d edition. Englewood Cliffs, New Jersey, Prentice-Hall, 1962. 557 p.

1517. HARSIN, Paul. Economie politique et sociale. Liège, Desoer 1947? 425 p.
1518. HARTOG, F. Economische stelsels. Groningen, Wolters-Noordhoff, 1968. 248 p.
1519. ───. Redelijke economie. Leiden, H. E. Stenfert Kroese, 1966. 268 p.
1520. HARVEY, Jack. Modern economics: an introduction for business and professional students. London, Macmillan, 1969. 523 p.
1521. HAUSER, Karl. Volkswirtschaftslehre. (Funk-Kolleg zum verständnis der modernen gesellschaft, Bd. 2.) Frankfurt am Main, Hamburg, Fischer-Bücherei, 1967. 308 p.
1522. HAVENS, Ralph Murray, John S. Henderson and Dale L. Cramer. Economics: principles of income, prices, and growth. New York, Macmillan, 1966. xvi, 623 p.
1523. HAWTREY, Ralph George. The economic problem. London, New York, etc., Longmans, Green and company, limited, 1926. 2 p. l., vii-xii, 417 p.
1524. HAYEK, F. A. von. Prices and production. 2d edition. London, Routledge and Kegan Paul, limited, 1951.
1525. HAYES, Harry Gordon. Our economic system. New York, H. Holt and company, c1928. 2 v. Bibliography.
1526. HAYNES, William Warren. Managerial economics, analysis and cases. (The Dorsey series in economics.) Homewood, Illinois, Dorsey press, 1963. 618 p. (Revised edition. Austin, Texas, Business publications, 1969. xiii, 726 p.)
1527. HAZLITT, Henry. Economics in one lesson. First edition. New York and London, Harper and brothers, c1946. xi, 222 p.
1528. HEERTJE, Arnold. Grundbegriffe der volkswirtschaftslehre. Ubers. von Peter Huber. (Heidelberger taschenbücher, Bd. 78.) Berlin, New York, Springer-Verlag, 1970. x, 207 p.
1529. HEILBRONER, Robert L. The economic problem. Englewood Cliffs, New Jersey, Prentice-Hall, 1968. xx, 652 p. (2d edition, 1970. xxii, 682 p.)
1530. ───. Understanding microeconomics. Englewood Cliffs, New Jersey, Prentice-Hall, 1968. xvii, 141 p.
1531. HEINIG, Kurt. Nationalökonomie des Alltags. Hamburg, Union-Verlag, 1948. 317 p. (4. aufl. Hamburg, Octinger Vorwort, 1952. 359 p.)
1532. HENDERSON, John S. Production and consumption. (University of Alabama studies, no. 7.) University, Alabama, University of alabama press, c1952. 83 p.
1533. HERDER-DORNEICH, Philipp. Der markt und seine alternativen in der freien gesellschaft; ökonomische theorie des pluralismus. Mit Vorworten von Karl Schiller und Goetz Briefs. Hannover, J. H. W. Dietz, 1968. 137p.
1534. HERRERA Lane, Felipe. Política económica. (Colección de apuntes de clases, n. 4.) Santiago, Editorial jurídica de Chile, 1950. 242 p.
1535. HESSE, Albert Hermann. Allgemeine und angewandte

volkswirtschaftslehre; ein leitfaden. 3., völlig neugestaltete aufl. Offenburg, Lehrmittel-verlag, 1948. ix, 210 p.
1536. _____. Lehrbuch der nationalökonomie. 4., völlig neugestaltete aufl. Offenburg, Lehrmittel-verlag, 1949- . v.
1537. HEUSS, Ernst. Grundelemente der wirtschaftstheorie. Eine einf. in d. wirtschaftstheoret. Denken. Göttingen, Vandenhoeck und Ruprecht, 1970. 223 p.
1538. HEWETT, William Wallace. Rudiments of economics. New York, Thomas Y. Crowell company, c1927. 1 p. 1., v-x, 247 p. Bibliographies.
1539. HIBDON, James E. Price and welfare theory. New York, McGraw-Hill, 1969. xv, 492 p.
1540. HIC, Mükerrem. Büjüme teorileri ve az gelişmiş ekonomiler. (Iktisat fakültesi neşriyati, no. 202.) Istanbul, Istanbul üniversitesi, Iktisat fakültesi, 1967. xi, 182 p.
1541. HICKS, John Richard. Einführung in die volkswirtschaftslehre. Deutsche übersetzung von Helmut Maneval. (Rowohlts deutsche enzyklopädie, 155/156. Sachgebiet: Wirtschaftswissenschaften.) Reinbeck bei Hamburg, Rowohlt, 1962. 317 p.
1542. _____, Albert Gailord Hart and James W. Ford. The social framework of the American economy; an introduction to economics. 2d edition. New York, Oxford university press, 1955. 309 p. (3rd edition, 1960.)
1543. HIDAKA, Hiroshi. Keizai genron. (Transliterated.) Japan, 1964. 2, 6, 261 p.
1544. HIJIKATA, Seibi. Keisaigaku genri. (Transliterated.) Japan, 1957. 5, 335 p.
1545. HIRADATE, Toshio. Keizaigaku gairon. (Transliterated.) Japan, 1963. ix, 230, 9 p. Bibliography, i-ii.
1546. HIRASE, Minokichi. Keizaigaku no koten to kindai. (Transliterated.) Japan, 1954. 4, 4, 406 p. Bibliographical footnotes.
1547. _____. Keizaigaku yottsu no miketsu mondai. (Transliterated.) Japan, 1967. 383, iv p. Bibliographical footnotes.
1548. HOAG, Malcolm W. The content of economics. (Rand corporation. Paper, P-1692.) Santa Monica, California, Rand corporation, 1959. ii, 9 1.
1549. HOBSON, John Atkinson. The science of wealth. London, Williams and Norgate, 1911. vii, 1, 9-256 p. [4th edition. (The Home university library of modern knowledge, 16.) London, New York, Oxford university press, 1950. ix, 214 p.]
1550. _____. Work and wealth: a human valuation. New York, The Macmillan company, c1914. xvi, 1 1., 367 p. (2d edition. London, 1933.)
1551. HODGSKIN, Thomas. Popular political economy. With an appendix. A lecture on free trade, in connection with the Corn laws. (Reprints of economic classics.) New York, A. M. Kelley, 1966. xxxi, 268, 23 p.

1552. HOFMANN, Werner. Die volkswirtschaftliche gesamtrechnun (Volkswirtschaftliche schriften, Heft 11.) Berlin, Duncker und Humblot, 1954. 217 p.
1553. HOLT, Solomon. Economics and you. H. L. McCracken, consulting editor. New York, Scribner, 1954. 550 p. (Reprinted, 1956. 550 p. Revised edition, 1962. 598 p. 3rd edition, Chicago, Follett publishing company, 1964. viii, 598 p.
1554. HOLTE, Fritz C. Sosialøkonomi. (Scandinavian university books.) Oslo, Universitets-forlaget, 1965. 433 p. (2. utg., 1967. 307 p.)
1555. HOMAN, Paul Thomas, Albert Gailord Hart and Arnold W. Sametz. The economic order; an introduction to theory and policy. New York, Harcourt, Brace, 1958. 839 p.
1556. HONG, U. Sin kyongje wŏllen. (Transliterated.) Korea, 1964. 12, 627, 28 p.
1557. HOWARD, Willard W. and Edwin L. Dale, Jr. Contemporary economics. Lexington, Massachusetts, Heath, 1971. 537 p.
1558. HOYT, Elizabeth Ellis. The income of society, an introduction to economics. New York, Ronald press company, 1950. xii, 753 p.
1559. HSUEH hsi i ts'ung. Shê hui chu i ching chi wên t'i. (Trans literated.) China, 1954. 312 p.
1560. HUANG, K'ai-lu. General economics. China, 1963. 33, 648, 142, 55 p. Bibliographies.
1561. HUBBARD, Joshua Clapp. Basic ideas of economics. Harrisburg, Pennsylvania, Stackpole company, 1953. 418 p.
1562. HURWITZ, Howard Lawrence and Frederick Shaw. Economics in a free society. Editorial consultant: E. C. Alft. New York, Oxford book company, 1962. 640, xxvi p. (Reprinted, 1964.)
1563. ———. Mastering basic economics. Editorial consultant: E. C. Alft. 1966 revised edition. New York, Oxford book company, 1966. xviii, 509 p.
1564. INABA, Shirō. Kihon keizaigaku. (Transliterated.) 1964. 2, 4, 250 p. Bibliography, 247-250.
1565. ———. Yōsetsu keizaigaku. (Transliterated.) 1958. 269, 1 p. Bibliography, 270.
1566. INTERNATIONAL correspondence schools, Scranton, Pennsylvania. Economics. By ICS staff. Serial 6578A- . Edition 1. Scranton, c1970. v.
1567. IQBAL, Sir Muhammad. 'Ilm al-iqtisād. (Transliterated.) 1961. 3, 26, 221 p.
1568. ISE, John. Economics. First edition. New York and London, Harper and brothers, c1946. x, 731 p. Bibliography, 695-703. (Revised edition, 1950. x, 872 p. Bibliography.)
1569. ISHIKURA, Ichiro. Kagaku, gijutsu jidai no keizaigaku nyumon. (Transliterated.) 1965. vi, 242 p. Bibliographical notes. (First edition, 1963.)
1570. IZHBOLDIN, Boris S. Economic synthesis. 1st edition. New

Delhi, New book society of India, 1958. 543 p.
1571. JAHN, Gunnar. Litt av hvert. Artikler, foredrag og taler. Oslo, Gyldendal, 1949. 290 p.
1572. JAIN, Prakash Chandra. A textbook of modern economics. Allahabad, Chaitanya publishing house, 1956- . v. (3rd edition, 1964. xi, 614 p.)
1573. JAMES, Clifford Lester. . . . An outline of the principles of economics. 4th edition. (College outline series.) New York, Barnes and Noble, incorporated, c1938. 6 p. 1., 274 p. Bibliography. (8th edition, 1952. 359 p. 9th edition, 1954. 367 p. Reprinted, 1956.)
1574. _____, James D. Calderwood and Frances W. Quantius. Economics; basic problems and analysis. (Prentice-Hall economic series.) New York, Prentice-Hall, 1951. xxiii, 611 p.
1575. JANNACCONE, Pasquale. Discussioni ed indagini economiche e finanziarie. (Università di Torino. Miscellanea dell'Istituto giuridico, 4.) Torino, G. Giappichelli, 1953-54. 2 v.
1576. _____. Manuale di economia politica. (Storia e dottrine economiche, 12.) Torino, Unione tipografico-editrice torinese, 1959. xv, 578 p.
1577. JATHAR, Ganesh Bhaskar and S. G. Beri. Elementary economics. 8th edition. Bombay, London, Oxford university press, 1967. ix, 265 p.
1578. _____. Introduction to economics. 10th edition. London, Oxford university press, 1966- . v.
1579. JAWED, H. K. Fundamentals of economics. 1st edition. Dacca, Ideal publications, 1963. ii, 467, 40 p.
1580. JEANNENEY, Jean Marcel. Economie politique. 1. édition, (Thémis"; manuels de capacité.) Paris, Presses universitaires de France, 1959. 304 p.
1581. _____. Eléments d'économie politique. 4e édition mise à jour. (Thémis. Sciences économiques, 14.) Paris, Presses universitaires de France, 1969. vii, 313 p.
1582. JENKS, Jorian E. F. From the ground up; an outline of real economy. With an introduction by H. J. Massingham. London, Hollis and Carter, 1950. xiii, 226 p.
1583. JENNINGS, Richard. Natural elements of political economy. (Reprints of economic classics.) New York, A. M. Kelley, 1969. 275 p.
1584. JENSENIUS, Olav Holten. Samfunnslaere med arbeidsoppgaver. Større utg. 2. revid. oppl. Oslo, Fabritius, 1946. 165 p. (Mindre utg., 3. oppl., 1947. 104 p.)
1585. JIRANEK, Slavomir. World economics. Světová ekonomika. (Ucební texty vysokych skol.) Praha, Statni pedagogicke nakladatelstvi, 1968. 129 p.
1586. JOHANSEN, Arne Dag. Mikroøkonomikk. Utg. av. Norges handelshøyskoles kursvirksomhet. Bergen, 1967. 2 v., 186 1.
1587. JOHANSEN, Leif. Public economics. Reprint. New York, American Elsevier publishing company, 1971. (1st edition, 1965.)

1588. JOHNSON, Albert. Economic theory. (Man and society series.) London, F. Muller, 1954. 144 p.
1589. JOHNSON, Alvin Saunders. Introduction to economics. Revised. (Kennikat press scholarly reprints. Series on economic thought, history and challenge.) Port Washington, New York, Kennikat press, 1971. xiv, 481 p.
1590. JONES, Idris Glyn. Essentials of economics. London, Macdonald, 1949. 294 p.
1591. JONG, Frits J. de. De werking van een volkshuishouding; een eerste inleiding tot het economische denken. (Theorie en practijk; leerboeken voor elementaire en voortgezette studie op economisch, juridisch en comptabel gebied.) Leiden, H. E. Stenfert Kroese, 1953. 2 v.
1592. JOSEPH, Myron L., Norton C. Seeber, and George Leland Bach. Economic analysis and policy. Englewood Cliffs, New Jersey, Prentice-Hall, 1971. xii, 612 p.
1593. JOSSA, Bruno. Analisi economica del progresso technico; primi elementi di una teoria neoclassica. Ed. definitiva. (Pubblicazioni dell'Istituto di science giuridiche, economiche, politiche e sociali della Università di Messina, n. 68.) Milano, Giuffrè, 1966. 390 p.
1594. KAMIENSKI, Henryk Korwin. Filozofia ekonomii materialnej ludzkiego społeczenstwa z dodaniem mniejszych pism filozoficznych. Opracował oraz wstępem i posłowiem opatrzył Bronisław Baczko. Wyd. 1. (Biblioteka klaskyow filozofil. Pisarze polscy.) Warszawa, Panstwowe wydawn. Naukowe, 1959. 592 p.
1595. KANEKO, Kō. Keizai taisei no mondai. (Transliterated.) Series: Kwansei Gakuin Daigaku, Nishinomiya, Japan. Kwansei Gakuin Daigaku sōsho, 5.) Japan, 1957. 2, 364 p. Bibliographical notes.
1596. KANG, O-jŏn. Kyongje wŏllon. (Transliterated.) Korea, 1965. 489 p. Bibliography, 487-489.
1597. KANTO gakuin daigaku keizai gakkai. Keizaigaku keieigaku o manabu tame ni. (Transliterated.) Japan, 1970. 312 p. Bibliographies.
1598. KARATAEV, Nikolaĭ Konstantinovich. Economics. Moscow, 1966. 269 p.
1599. KARIM, Sajedul and M. A. Jalil Khan. An introduction to economic theory, for degree students. 1st edition. Dacca, Mullick brothers, 1965. 16, vi, 401 p.
1600. KARVAS, Imrich A. Základy hospodárskej vedy. Vyd. 1. Turčiansky sv. Martin Matica slovenská, 1947. 2 v.
1601. KAZDA, Josef. Politická ekonomie socialismu. Vyd. 2. (Učebni texty vysokých škol.) Praha, Státní nakl. učebnic, 195- . v.
1602. KEEZER, Dexter Merriam, Addison Thayer Cutler, and Frank Richardson Garfield. Problem economics. New York and London, Harper and brothers, c1928. viii p., 1 l., 719 p.
1603. KEIL, Günter. Vorlesung über mikroökonomische theorie. Meisenheim a. Glan, Hain, 1969. 193 p.
1604. KEILHAU, Wilhelm Christian. Riktig og gal planøkonomi;

innlegg i den sosialøkonomiske idédebatt. (Statsøkonomisk forenings skriftserie om etterkrigstidens økonomiske problemer.) Oslo, I kommisjon hos Aschehoug, 1953. 204 p.

1605. KEIRSTEAD, Burton Seeley. The theory of economic change. Toronto, Macmillan company of Canada, c1948. xi, 386 p. Bibliographical footnotes.

1606. KEISER, Norman Fred. Economics: analysis and policy. New York, Wiley, c1965. xviii, 720 p. Bibliographies.

1607. _____. Introductory economics. New York, Wiley, c1961. 545 p. Bibliography. (Instructor's manual. 56 p. Student workbook. 98 p.)

1608. KEIZAIGAKU e no susume. Japan, 1968. 385 p. Bibliographies.

1609. KERBER, Walter. Die verteilungstheorie von Kenneth E. Boulding. (Volkswirtschaftliche schriften, Heft 103.) Berlin, Duncker und Humblot, 1966. 178 p.

1610. KHAN, M. A. Jalil. Elements of economics. 2d edition. dacca, Mullick brothers, 1965. xii, 404 p.

1611. KHATRI, Jaman Dass and G. C. Jangir. Economics at work. Delhi, Kitab Mahal, 1962. 438 p.

1612. KIEKHOFER, William Henry. . . . Economic principles, problems, and policies. Revised edition. (The Century studies in economics, W. H. Kiekhofer, editor.) New York, London, D. Appleton-Century company, incorporated, c1941. xxxi, 906 p. (3rd edition, 1946. xxxiii, 910 p. 4th edition, 1951. xix, 957 p. Bibliographies.)

1613. KIENZL, Heinz. Wirtschaftstheorie und wirtschaftspolitik; eine Einführung in die nationalökonomie für betriebsräte and gewerkschaftsfunktionäre. 2., verb. aufl. Wien, Verlag des Osterreichischen gewerkschaftsbundes, 1961. 104 p. [Revised edition: Mit diagramman. (Zeit und wissen.) 1967. 118 p.]

1614. KIGA, Kenzō. Shakaiteki shimpo no genri. (Transliterated.) Japan, 1956. 3, 20, 338 p. Bibliographical footnotes.

1615. KILICBAY, Ahmet. Iktisadin prensipleri. (Iktisat fakültesi nesriyati, no. 216.) Istanbul, Istanbul üniversitesi, Iktisat fakültesi, 1968. xiv, 560 p.

1616. _____. Iktisat teorisi. Istanbul, Sermet Matbaasi, 1964. xv, 446 p.

1617. KIM, Chun-bo. Ilban kyŏngjehak. (Transliterated.) Korea, 1963. 384, viii p.

1618. KIM, Sŏ-bong. Kyŏngjehak wŏllon. (Transliterated.) 1966. 386 p. Bibliographical footnotes.

1619. KIM, Yun-hwan. Sin kyŏngje wŏllon. (Transliterated.) Korea, 1963. 623 p. Bibliographies.

1620. KINK, Kurt. Wertschöpfungsprozess und verrechnungslehre; zum problem des system- und stilbegriffs in der betriebswirtschafts- und verrechnungslehre. (Staatswissenschaftliche studien, n. F., Bd. 22.) Zürich, Polygraphischer verlag, 1955. 220 p.

1621. KISHIMOTO, Seijirō. Keizaigaku yōron. (Transliterated.) Japan, 1965. 11, 204 p. Bibliography, 199-204.

1622. KLEINWACHTER, Friedrich von. Lehrbuch der nationalökonomie. 3rd edition. 1921. xvii, 560 p. (1st edition, 1902.)
1623. KLUNDERT, Th. van de. Grondslagen van de economische analyse. (Academische paperbacks.) Amsterdam, J. H. de Bussy, 1968. 272 p. (2^e herz. dr., 1970. 270 p.)
1624. KNIGHT, Bruce Winton. Economic principles in practice. Revised edition. New York, Farrar and Rinehart, incorporated, c1939. xvii, 606 p. Bibliographies. (Reprinted, 1942. xiv, 659 p.)
1625. _____, and Lawrence Gregory Hines. Economics; an introductory analysis of the level, composition, and distribution of economic income. 1st edition. New York, Knopf, 1952. 917 p.
1626. KNIGHT, Bruce Winton and Nelson Lee Smith. Economics. New York, The Ronald press company, c1929-30. 2 v. Bibliography.
1627. KNIGHT, Frank Hyneman. The economic organization. With an article, Notes on cost and utility. New York, A. M. Kelley, 1951. 179 p.
1628. _____. Risk, uncertainty and profit. 1921. xiv, 381 p.
1629. KNORR, Klaus Eugen. Basic principles of economics. Washington, National war college, 1952? 177 p.
1630. KOH, Sung Jae. Kyŏngjehak. (Transliterated.) Korea, 1955. 3, 6, 296 p. Bibliographies.
1631. KOHLER, Heinz. Economics: the science of scarcity. Hinsdale, Illinois, Dryden press, 1970. xxix, 742 p.
1632. _____. Scarcity challenged; an introduction to economics. New York, Holt, Rinehart and Winston, 1968. xxviii, 660 p.
1633. KOIVISTO, William A. Principles and problems of modern economics. New York, Wiley, c1957. 834 p.
1634. KOIZUMI, Shinzō. Keizai genron. (Transliterated.) Japan, 1948. 3, 345 p.
1635. KOLHATKAR, Vasudeo Yeshwant and S. V. Kogekar. An introduction to economics. 4th edition, Bombay, Macmillan, 1950. x, 240 p.
1636. KOMPENDIUM der volkswirtschaftslehre. Hrsg. von Werner Ehrlicher u. a. Göttingen, Vandenhoeck und Ruprecht, 1967-68. 2 v. (2., durchges, aufl. 1969- . v.)
1637. KONEVSKI, Trajko. Osnovi nauke o drustvu i ekonomije. 2., neizm. izd. (Universitetski udzbenici.) Beograd, "Naučna knjiga," 1966. 7, 245 p.
1638. KOPLIN, H. T. Microeconomic analysis. Welfare and efficiency in private and public sectors. New York, Harper and Rowe, Publishers, Inc., 1971, 337 p.
1639. KORAC, Miladin M. Produkcioni odnosi i njihove primene u prelaznom periodu. 2. izd. (Političko-ekonomska biblioteka.) Beograd, Rad, 1952. 97 p.
1640. KORENJAK, Franz. Nationalökonomie; grundlagen für eine exakte theorie. Wien, Springer, 1960. 374 p.
1641. KOREY, Edward Lawrence and Edmond J. Runge. Economics.

1642. KOSIK, Karel. Dialektika konkrétního; studie o problematice človĕka a svĕta. 2., upravené vyd. Praha, Nakl. Ceskoslovenské akademie vĕd, 1965. 191 p.
1443. KOSTIC, Zivko K. Ekonomika Jugoslavije i privredno pravo; priručnik za polaganje stručnog ispita za visokokvalifikovanog radnika u trgovini. (Stručni priručnici za kadrove u trgovini.) Beograd, 1957. 202 p.
1644. _____. Osnovi teorije mezoekonomije. (Organizacija i ekonomika poduzeca, god. 9, br. 8-9.) Zagreb, "Informator," 1968. 280 p.
1645. KOWALIK, Tadeusz. O Ludwiku krzywickim; studium spoleczno-ekonomiczne. Wyd. 1. Warszawa, Panstwowe wydawn. Naukowe, 1959. 382 p.
1646. KRASENSKY, Hans. Wirtschaftskunde. 5 abbildungen und 89 tabellen. 2., durchges. aufl. Wien, Verlag für geschichte und politik, 1966. 237 p.
1647. KRAUS, Willy. Wirtschaftswachstum und gleichgewicht. Frankfurt am Main, F. Knapp, 1955. 297 p.
1648. KRIER, Henri et Jacques Le Bourva. Economie politique. . . . (Collection U. Série sciences économiques.) Paris, A. Colin, 1968- . v.
1649. KRISTERSSON, Helge. De socialekonomiska grupperna och samhällsekonomia. Stockholm, LT:s förlag, 1951. 270 p.
1650. KROLL, Michael. Die volkswirtschaft, das wirtschaftswissen der gegenwart. 2., neubearb. aufl. Wien, Osterreichischer bundesverlag für unterricht, wissenschaft und kunst, 1951. 323 p.
1651. KUDSIA, Jitendra. A text-book of economic theory; pricing, employment, and economic development. 1st edition. Delhi, Metropolitan book company, 1964. viii, 645 p.
1652. KUENNE, Robert E. The theory of general economic equilibrium. Princeton, New Jersey, Princeton university, press, c1963. xv, 590 p. Bibliography, 571-580.
1653. KUHLMAN, John M. and Gordon S. Skinner. The economic system. (The Irwin series in economics.) Homewood, Illinois, R. D. Irwin, 1959. 509 p. Bibliography. (Revised edition, 1964. xiii, 522 p. Bibliographies.)
1654. KUNG, Emil. Wirtschaft und gerechtigkeit. Sozialethische problems im lichte der volkswirtschaftslehre. (St. Galler wirtschaftswissenschaftliche forschungen, Bd. 24.) Tübingen, Mohr [Siebeck], 1967. xii, 315 p.
1655. KURIHARA, Kenneth K. Applied dynamic economics. London, Allen and Unwin, 1963. 122 p.
1656. _____. Macroeconomics and programming. London, Allen & Unwin, 1964. 100 p. Bibliography.
1657. KURODA, Hirokazu. Uno keizaigaku hoho ron hihan. (Transliterated.) Japan, 1968. 302 p. Bibliographical notes.
1658. KUWAHARA, Susumu. Gendai keizaigaku ron. (Transliterated.) Japan, 1964. xi, 199 p. Bibliographical notes.
1659. KUYUCAK, Hazim Atif. Iktisat dersleri. (Istanbul üniversitesi yayinlarindan, 443, 591.) Istanbul, I. Akgün Matbaasi, 1950-54. 2 v.

1660. KWON, Hyŏk-so. Sin Ryongje taeüi. (Transliterated.) Korea, 1966. 370 p. Bibliography, 369-370.
1661. LAGO, Armando V. Microeconomía. (Colección ciencias económicas.) Buenos Aires, Ediciones Macchi, 1969. 370 p.)
1662. LAHERRERE, Raymond. La traición de los técnicos. Santiago de Chile, 1954. 197 p.
1663. LAING, Graham Allan. An introduction to economics. New York, Boston, etc., The Gregg publishing company, c1919. xi, 468 p. Bibliography, 463-464.
1664. LAMPE, Hans. Grundzüge der volkswirtschaftslehre. Göttingen, Vandenhoeck und Ruprecht, 1957. 172 p.
1665. LANCASTER, Kelvin. Introduction to modern microeconomics. Chicago, Rand McNally, 1969. viii, 326 p.
1666. LANDRY, Adolphe. Manuel d'économique. Paris, 1908. 889 p.
1667. LANG, Rikard. Politicka ekonomija. Uvod i osnove. (Ekonomska biblioteka, 4 kolo, br. 3-4.) Zagreb, "Informator," 1968. xiv, 528 p.
1668. LANGE, Oscar Richard. Ekonomia polityczna. Wyd. 1. Warszawa, Państwowe wydawn. Naukowe, 1959- . v. (Wyd. 2., 1961- . v. French edition entitled: Economie politique. Traduit du polonais par Anna Posner. Texte conforme à la 2. édition polonaise. 1. édition. Paris, Presses universitaires de France, 1962- . v. English edition entitled: Political economy. Translated from Polish by A. H. Walker. Oxford, New York, Pergamon press, distributed by Macmillan company, 1963- . v.)
1669. _____. Pisma ekonomiczne i społeczne, 1930-1960. Wyd. 1. Warszawa, Panstwowe wydawn. Naukowe, 1961. 468 p.
1670. _____. Politicka ekonomie; obecné otázky. Z polskeho originalu prel. Ivan Figura. Vyd. 1. Praha, Academia, 1966. 334 p.
1671. _____. Zarys ekonomii politycznej. Warszawa, 195- .
1672. LAUDERDALE, James Maitland. An inquiry into the nature and origin of public wealth and into the means and causes of its increase, 1804. Edited, with an introduction and revisions appearing in the 2d edition, 1819, by Morton Paglin. (The Adam Smith library.) New York, A. M. Kelley, 1966. xxvii, 482 p.
1673. LAUGHLIN, James Laurence. The elements of political economy, with some applications to questions of the day. Revised edition. New York, Cincinnati, etc., American book company, c1902. xxiv, 384 p. ("A teacher's library": xxi-xxiv.)
1674. LAVERGNE, Bernard. L'hégémonie du consommateur; vers une rénovation de la science économique. 1. edition. Paris, Presses universitaires de France, 1958. 359 p.
1675. LA VOLPE, Giulio. Economica. Venezia, Libreria universitaria, 1960- . v.
1676. LECAILLON, Jacques. Analyse microéconomique, initiation. (Collection initiation, 3.) Paris, Editions Cujas, 1967. 263 p.

1677. _____. Les mécanismes de l'économie. . . . (Collection initiation.) Paris, Editions Cujas, 1966. 220 p.
1678. LEE, Maurice W. Macroeconomics; fluctuations, growth and stability. 4th edition. Homewood, Illinois, R. D. Irwin, 1967.
1679. LEFTWICH, Richard H. An introduction to economic thinking. New York, Holt, Rinehart and Winston, 1969. xii, 686 p.
1680. _____. The price system and resource allocation. Revised edition. New York, Holt, Rinehart and Winston, 1960.
1681. LEGITIMO, Gianfranco. Il fondamento strutturale della politica economica. Milano, A. Giuffrè, 1968. viii, 304 p.
1682. LEIBENSTEIN, Harvey. Economic theory and organizational analysis. New York, Harper, 1960. 349 p.
1683. LEITE, João Pinto de Costa. Economia política; spontamentos das lições proferidas ao curso do 2e ano jurídico de 1955-56, pelo Exmo. Senhor Professor Doutor João da Costa Leite (Lumbrales) e coligidos por Lopes Alves e M. da Costa Leão. Lisboa, Associação académica da faculdade de Direito, 1955. 302 p. (Revised: Coimbra, 1963- . v.)
1684. LEITER, Robert David. Modern economics. (Barnes and Noble college outline series, no. 81.) New York, Barnes and Noble, 1968. xiii, 304 p.
1685. LERAT, Eugène. Les structures économiques et la monnaie. Bruxelles, Editions de la librairie encyclopédique, 1961. 178 p.
1686. LERNER, Abba Ptachya. Economics of employment. (Economics handbook series.) New York, McGraw-Hill, 1951. xv, 397 p.
1687. LESOURNE, Jacques. Economic analysis and industrial management. Translated by Scripta technica, incorporated. (Prentice-Hall international series in management.) Englewood Cliffs, New Jersey, Prentice-Hall, 1963. 631 p.
1688. _____. L'étude économique dans l'entreprise. (Marabout-service. Economie moderne, v. 81.) Verviers, Gérard and company, 1968. 200 p.
1689. _____. Technique économique et gestion industrielle. Préface de M. Allais. (Finance et économie appliquée, v. 5.) Paris, Dunod, 1958. 619 p.
1690. LI, Yen-lin. Ching chi hsüeh yüan li hsin lun. (Transliterated.) China, 1967. 2, 18, 480 p.
1691. LIEFMANN, Robert. Grundsätze der volkswirtschaftslehre. 2nd edition. 1920-2?. 2 v. (1st edition, 1919.)
1692. LINDBERG, Niels. Grundtraek af økonomikken. København, Teknisk forlag, 1961. 371 p.
1693. _____. Idealer og regler i anvendt økonomik. Kjøbenhavn, Nyt nordisk forlag, 1951. 470 p.
1694. LIPINSKI, Edward. Teoria ekonomii i aktualne zagadnienia gospodarcze. Wyd. 1. Warszawa, Panstwowe wydawn. Naukowe, 1961. 246 p.
1695. LIPSEY, Richard G. An introduction to positive economics.

London, Wiedenfeld and Nicolson, 1963. xvi, 559 p. (2nd edition, 1966. xxiii, 872 p.)
1696. _____, and Peter O. Steiner. Economics. New York, Harper and Row, 1966. xxxii, 760 p. (2d edition, 1969. xvii, 845 p.)
1697. LIST, Friedrich. Das natürliche system der politischen ökonomie. Nach der französischen handschrift übers. und eingeleitet von Günter Fabiunke. (Okonomische studientexte, Bd. 2.) Berlin, Akademie-verlag, 1961. cviii, 259 p. [English edition entitled: The national system of political economy. (Reprints of economic classics.) New York, A. M. Kelley, 1966. xxxi, 454 p.]
1698. LITTLE, Ian Malcolm David. A critique of welfare economics. Oxford, Clarendon press, 1950. 275 p. [2nd edition (Oxford paperbacks, no. 4.) London, Oxford university press, 1960. 302 p.]
1699. LITTLE, Leo Thomas. Handbook for economics students. London, Jordan, 1955. 181 p.
1700. LIVINGSTONE, Ian and H. W. Ord. An introduction to economics for East Africa. London, Nairobi, Heinemann, educational, 1968. xi, 459 p.
1701. LLOYD, Cliff. Microeconomic analysis. (The Irwin series in economics.) Homewood, Illinois, R. D. Irwin, 1967. xii, 273 p.
1702. LOBL, Eugen. Geistige arbeit, die wahre quelle des reichtums. Entwurf eines neuen sozialistischen ordnungsbildes. (Aus dem Slowakischen von Leopold Grünwald.) Mit einem vorwort von K. Paul Hensel. Wien, Düsseldorf, Econ-verlag, 1968. 299 p.
1703. _____. Úvahy o duševnej práci a bohatstve národa. 1. vy Bratislava, Vydavatel'stvo Slovenskej akadémie vied, 1967. 212 p.
1704. ŁODZ, Poland. Wyzsza szkoła ekoncmiczna. Ekonomia polityczna. nr. 1.- (Its Zeszyty na kowe.) Łódź, 1960- . v.
1705. LOGAN, Harold Amos and Mark K. Inman. A social approach to economics. 2d edition, revised and enlarged. Toronto, University of Toronto press, 1949, c1948. xix, 757 p.
1706. LOHSER, Oskar. Energie, produktivität und geistige arbeit in neuer sicht; der weg zur sicherung der zukunft der welt. Wien, G. Fromme, 1956. xii, 268 p.
1707. LOMBARDINI, Siro. Appunti dalle lezioni di economia politica. Milano, La Goliardica, 1958- . v.
1708. _____. Fondamenti e problemi dell'economia del benessere (Saggi di teoria e politica economica, 1.) Milano, Giuffrè, 1954. xii, 128 p.
1709. LONGO, Gino. Il metodo dell'economia politica. 1. ed. (Quaderni dell'Istituto Gramsci.) Roma, Editori riuniti, 1965. 235 p.
1710. LOPEZ, Rosado, Felipe. Economía política. 5. ed. México, Editorial Porrúa, 1953. 206 p.
1711. _____. El hombre y la economía. 7. ed. corr. y au-

Summary Works 113

1712. mentada. México, Editorial Porrúa, 1953. 302 p.
LOPEZ Sanz, Salvador y Felipe Domingo Muro. Rudimentos de derecho y de economía. Logroño, Editorial Ochoa, 1952. 207 p.
1713. LORIA, Achille. Corso di economia politica. 2nd edition. 1919. xi, 761 p. (1st edition, (1909.)
1714. LOWE, Adolph. On economic knowledge; toward a science of political economics. 1st edition. (World perspectives, v. 35.) New York, Harper and Row, 1965. xxii, 329 p.
1715. LU, Min-jên. Ching chi hsüeh. (Transliterated.) China, 1968. 2, 11, 476 p.
1716. LUCA, Mario de. Istituzioni di scienza economica: produzione, mercato, reddito. Napoli, Morano, 1957. 407 p.
1717. LUGLI, Luigi. Nuovo schema del processo economico. Padova, CEDAM, 1953. 152 p.
1718. LUTZ, Friedrich and Vera Lutz. The theory of investment of the firm. Princeton, Princeton university press, 1951.
1719. LUWEL, A. Inleiding tot de economie, handboek voor schoolgebruik en zelfstudie. Turnhout, Brepols, 194- . 206 p. (2. druk., 1949? 220 p.)
1720. LUXEMBURG, Rosa. Wstęp de ekonomii politycznej. Warszawa, Książka i Wiedza, 1959. 343 p.
1721. LYNN, Robert Athan. Basic economic principles. New York, McGraw-Hill, c1965. viii, 428 p. (2d edition, 1970. xiii, 375 p.)
1722. MACHINEK, Peter. Behandlung und erkenntniswert der erwartungen in der wirtschaftstheorie. (Volkswirtschaftliche schriften, Heft, 118.) Berlin, Duncker und Humblot, 1968. 205 p.
1723. MAGAUD, Charles. L'équilibre économique à travers la pensée moderne. (Observation économique, 2.) Paris, Société d'édition d'enseignement supérieur, 1950. 203 p.
1724. MAGGI, Raffaello. Momenti dinamici dell'economia, con una sezione su economia e psicanalisi. Milano, A. Giuffrè, 1958. 797 p.
1725. MAHER, John Edward. What is economics? New York, Wiley, 1968, c1969. viii, 174 p.
1726. MAHR, Alexander. Volkswirtschaftslehre. 2., wesentlich erweiterte aufl. Wien, Springer, 1959. 491 p.
1727. MAHR, Werner. Einführung in die allgemeine volkswirtschaftslehre. Wiesbaden, Betriebswirtschaftlicher verlag Gabler, 1966. 235 p.
1728. MAISEL, Sherman J. Fluctuations, growth, and forecasting: the principles of dynamic business economics. New York, Wiley, 1957. 552 p.
1729. MAKOWER, Helen. Activity analysis and the theory of economic equilibrium. London, Macmillan; New York, Saint Martin's press, 1957. 192 p.
1730. MAKSIMOVIC, Ivan. O savremenoj ekonomskoj teoriji. Beograd, Kultura, 1961. 180 p.
1731. MALANOS, George J. Intermediate economic theory. (The Lippincott college economics series.) Chicago, Lippincott, c1962. 540 p.

1732. MALTHUS, Thomas Robert. Definitions in political economy preceded by an inquiry into the rules which ought to guide political economists in the definition and use of their terms, with remarks on the deviation from these rules in their writings. (Reprints of economic classics.) London, J. Murray, 1827. New York, Kelley and Millman, 1954. viii, 261 p.

1733. ———. Principles of political economy considered with a view to their practical application. 2d edition with considerable additions from the author's own manuscript and an original memoir. New York, A. M. Kelley, 1951. liv, 446 p. [English reprint: 2nd edition, 1836. With an introduction by Morton Paglin. (Reprints of economic classics.) New York, A. M. Kelley, 1964. ix, iiv, 446 p. French editions entitled: Principes d'économie politique. Réimpression de l'édition 1846. (Collection des principaux économistes, t. 8.) Osnabrück, Zeller, 1966. xxxvi, 550 p. Principes d'économie politique, considérés sous le rapport de leur application pratique. Préface de J.-F. Faure-Soulet. (Perspectives économiques Les Fondateurs de l'économie.) Paris, Calmann-Lévy, 1969. xxxii, 366 p.]

1734. MANES, Pietro. Principi di dinamica economica. Padova, CEDAM, 1956. xxiii, 271 p.

1735. MANGOLDT, Hans Karl Emil von. Grundriss der volkswirtschaftslehre; ein Leitfaden für vorlesungen an hochschulen und für das privatstudium. 1st edition republished. Farnborough, Gregg, 1968. xvi, 224 p.

1736. ———. Die Lehre vom unternehmergewinn. Ein beitrag zur volkswirtschaftslehre. Nachdruck der ausg. Leipzig, Teubner, 1855. Frankfurt am Main, Sauer und Auvermann, 1966. vi, 174 p.

1737. MANNE, Alan Sussmann. Economic analysis for business decisions. New York, McGraw-Hill, c1961. 177 p.

1738. MARANO, Ignazio. Manuale di economia politica, statistica e financa; concetti fondamentali secondo i programmi ministeriali di insegnamento per le classi IV e V degli istituti tecnici commerciali ad indirizzo amministrativo e mercantile. Catania, Casa del libro, 1949. 124 p.

1739. MARCHAL, André. Cours de structures et systèmes économiques, rédigé d'après les notes et avec l'autorisation de André Marchal; licence 3me année, 1954-1955. Paris, Cours de droit, 1955. 208 p.

1740. ———. Systèmes et structures économiques. (Thémis sciences économiques, 11.) Paris, Presses universitaires de France, 1969. 724 p.

1741. MARCHAL, Jean. Cours d'économie politique. Paris, Librairie de Médicis, 1950- . v. (3. édition, 1956- . v.)

1742. ———. Leçons d'économie politique, rédigées d'après les notes et avec l'autorisation de Jean Marchal. Licence 1re année, 1952-1953. Paris, Cours de droit, 1953. 653 p.

743. _____. Problèmes économiques contemporains. Paris, Les Cours de droit, 1950. 3 v, 331 p. (Problèmes économiques. 1955. 3 v. in 1.)
744. MARGET, A. W. The theory of prices. Englewood Cliffs, New Jersey, Prentice Hall, 1938. 2 v.
745. MARKOVIC, Ljubisav. Osnovi politicke ekonomije. ("Univerzum," osnovi savremenih znanja, 14-17.) Sarajevo, Narodna prosvjeta, 1957. 2 v. in 1.
746. MARRAMA, Vittorio. Consumo e produzione. (Corsi universitari.) Roma, Edizioni ricerche, 1966. vi, 206 p.
747. MARRANI, Pelio. Lineamenti di economia. Milano, A. Giuffrè, 1955-56. v. 1, 1956. 3 v. (8. ed., 1966. 3 v.)
748. MARRIS, Robin. The economic theory of managerial capitalism. New York, Free press of Glencoe, 1964. xviii, 346 p. Bibliography, 325-330.
749. MARSHALL, Alfred. Principles of economics. 8th edition, 1920. xxxii, 871 p. [1st edition, 1890. 9th edition, 1924. Reprint: 9th (valiorum) edition, with annotations by C. W. Guillebaud. London, New York, Macmillan for the Royal economic society, 1961. 2 v.]
750. MARSHALL, B. V. Comprehensive economics: descriptive, theoretical and applied. London, Longmans, 1967. xxii, 762 p.
751. MARSILI Libelli del Collechio, Mario. Elementi di economia politica. Firenze, Società editrice universitaria, 1948. 70 p.
752. MARTIN, Richard S. and Reuben G. Miller. Economics and its significance. Kenneth E. Boulding, consultant. (Charles E. Merrill social science seminar series.) Columbus, Ohio, C. E. Merrill books, 1965. x, 165 p.
753. _____. Prologue to economic understanding. Kenneth E. Boulding, consultant. (Social science perspectives.) Columbus, Ohio, C. E. Merrill books, 1966. vi, 98 p.
754. MARTINEZ, Pedro Soares. Curso de economia política; apontamentos das lições proferidas no curso do 3e. ano jurídico de 1955-56. Lisboa, Edição de associação académica, 1956. 250 p.
755. MARTINEZ Val, José María. Manual de derecho y economía política; iniciación jurídico-económica a los estudios mercantiles. Barcelona, Ediciones alma mater, 1950. 393 p.
756. MARX, Karl. Kapitał; krytyka ekonomii politycznej. Wyd. 3. Warszawa, Książka i Wiedza, 1951- . v. (Das Kapital. 1867. 4th edition, 1890-94. 3 v.)
757. MASOIN, Maurice. Précis d'économie politique. (Bibliothèque générale des sciences économiques, 38.) Bruxelles, Editions comptables, commerciales et financières, 1951. 388 p.
758. MASSA, José Luis. La economía del futuro. Madrid, A. Aguado, 1959. 442 p.
759. MAURELL Lobo, Ari. Tratado de economia política realista e de etonômica. . . . Rio de Janeiro, Jornal de commercio, 1945. 832 p.

1760. McCONNELL, Campbell R. Elementary economics: principles, problems, and policies. New York, McGraw-Hill, c1960. 759 p. Bibliography. (2nd edition, 1963. 773 3rd edition entitled: Economics; principles, problems, and policies. 1966. xxv, 792 p. 4th edition, 1969. xxvii, 815 p.)

1761. _____. Instructor's Manual to accompany Economics. Fourth edition. New York, McGraw-Hill, 1969. 219 p.

1762. McCULLOCH, John Ramsay. Outlines of political economy Edited by John McVickar, 1825. With an introductory essay, On the naturalization of Ricardian economics in the United States, by Joseph Dorfman. With notes on McVickar's Outlines by James A. Kent, and the addition of McVickar's pamphlet, Hints on banking in a letter to a gentleman in Albany by a New Yorker, 1827. (Reprints of economic classics.) New York, A. M. Kelley, 1966. 17, 199, 43 p.

1763. McISAAC, Archibald MacDonald. Elements of economic analysis. (Prentice-Hall economics series.) New York, Prentice-Hall, c1950. ix, 240 p.

1764. McISAAC, Archibald MacDonald and James Gerald Smith. . . . Essential economic principles. (Economics and social institutions.) Boston, Heath; New York, Little Brown and Company, c1941. x, 504 p.

1765. _____. . . . Introduction to economic analysis. (Economics and social institutions, volume II.) Boston, Little, Brown and company, c1937. x, 444 p.

1766. McKENNA, Joseph P. Aggregate economic analysis. (Dryden press series in economics.) New York, Dryder press, 1955. 244 p. Bibliographical references. (Revised edition, New York, Holt, Rinehart and Wilson, 1965. xii, 195 p. Bibliographical references. 3rd edition, 1969, xx, 266 p.)

1767. _____. Intermediate economic theory. (The Dryden press series in economics.) New York, Dryden press, 1958. 319 p.

1768. MEADE, James Edward. The growing economy, (His Principles of political economy, v. 2.) London, G. Allen and Unwin; Chicago, Aldine publishing company, 1968. 512 p.

1769. _____. An introduction to economic analysis and policy American edition edited by C. J. Hitch . . . with an introduction by A. H. Hansen. . . New York, Oxford university press, c1938. xxi, 428 p.

1770. _____. Principles of political economy. London, Allen and Unwin; Chicago, Aldine publishing company, 1965- . v.

1771. _____. The stationary economy. (His principles of political economy, v. 1.) London, Allen and Unwin; Chicago, Aldine publishing company, 1965. 238 p.

1772. MEDEIROS, Tarquinio de. Elementos de economia política 4. ed. revista. Rio de Janeiro, Freitas Bastos, 1960. 191 p.

1773. MEDICI, Giuseppe. Lezioni di politica economica. Bologna, Calderini, 1967. x, 392 p.
1774. MEERHAEGHE, M. van. Handboek van de economie. Brussel, Elsevier, 1952. 275 p. (2. uitg. Brussel, F. Larcier, 1958. 345 p.)
1775. MEHTA, D. D. Theory of economic organisation and growth. Agra, Ram Prasad, c1965. xv, 472 p.
1776. MEHTA, Jamshed Kaikhusroo. A philosophical interpretation of economics. London, Allen and Unwin, 1962. 288 p.
1777. _____. Rhyme, rhythm and truth in economics. London, Bombay, New York, Asia publishing house, 1967. vii, 229 p.
1778. _____. Studies in advanced economic theory. 4th edition. Delhi, S. Chand, 1964. viii, 390 p.
1779. MEHTA, Jamshed Kaikhusroo and Mahesh Chand. A guide to modern economics. Bombay, Somaiya publications, 1970. xvi, 359 p.
1780. MEHTA, Satish C. Economic organisation and development. New Delhi, Sudha publications, 1962. 265 p.
1781. MEINANDER, Nils. Folkhushallningens grundfrågor. Helsingfors, Söderström, 1948. 135 p.
1782. MEINHOLD, Wilheim. Grundzüge der allgemeinen volkswirtschaftslehre. München, M. Hueber, 1954. 279 p. (3., durchgesehene und erg. aufl., 1967. 322 p.)
1783. MEINVIELLE, Julio. Conceptos fundamentales de la economía. (Colección ensayistas argentinos.) Buenos Aires, Libreria-editorial nuestro tiempo, 1953. 226 p.
1784. MEJIA-RICART G., Marcio Antonio. Principios fundamentales de economía política. Ciudad Trujillo, Editorial librería Dominicana, 1954, i. e. 1955. 208 p.
1785. MELANGES économiques; doctrines, travail, finances. (Annales de l'Université de Lyon. 3. ser. Droit, fasc. 9.) Paris, Recueil Sirey, 1947. 99 p.)
1786. MELLO, Olbiano de. Economia política; fundamento básicos, doutrinas economicas, direito economico. 2. ed. rev. e ampl. São Paulo, Revista dos Tribunais, 1968. xiv, 217 p.
1787. MENEZES, Djacir. Iniciação à economica. 2. ed., rev. e aumentada. (Iniciaçao cientifica, v. 27.) Sao Paulo, Companhia editôra nacional, 1965. xiv, 211 p.
1788. _____. Das leis econômicas; sua estrutura lógica analisada particularmente nas relações da oferta e procura; sua "naturalidade" e "historicidade." 2. ed. Rio de Janeiro, Gráfico editôra Aurora, 1955. 143 p.
1789. _____. Tratado de economia política. 2. ed. corr. e muito aumentada. Rio de Janeiro, Freitas Bastos, 1956. 622 p.
1790. MENGER, Karl. Gesammelte werke. Hrsg. mit einer einleitung und einem Schriftenverzeichnis von F. A. Hayek. 2. aufl., verb. neuaufl. Tübingen, Mohr (Siebeck), 1968- .
1791. MERKEL, Hans Günter. Theorie der kapitalmarktpolitik.

(Die Unternehmung im markt, Bd. 1.) Berlin, Duncker und Humblot, 1955. xi, 196 p.
1792. MERKLE, Franz. Produktivität und rentabilität. 2. aufl. Stuttgart, C. E. Poeschel, 1951. 168 p.
1793. MEYERS, Albert Leonard. Elements of modern economics Revised edition. (Prentice-Hall economics series; E. A. J. Johnson, editor.) New York, Prentice-Hall, incorporated, c1941. xvii p., 1 1., 425 p. (3rd ed., 1948. xx, 456 p. 4th edition, 1956. 518 p.)
1794. _____. Modern economic problems. 2d edition. (Prentice-Hall economics series.) New York, Prentice-Hall, c1948. xvii, 350 p.
1795. MEYNAUD, Jean. Eléments d'économiques. Paris, Les Cours de droit, 1950. 3 v., 696 p.
1796. _____. Introduction à l'étude des problèmes économique Paris, Les Cours de droit, 1949. 3 v., 735 p.
1797. MEZEI, Stevan. Osnovi politicke ekonomije. (Biblioteka strucnih izdanja.) Beograd, Savremena administracija, 1963. x, 354 p.)
1798. MICHELON, Leno Ceno. Basic economics. In collaboration with Richard T. Thornbury and associates of the Industrial relations center, the University of Chicago. Cleveland, World publishing company, c1960. 223 p.
1799. MICHELON, Leno Ceno and Reuben E. Slesinger. Understanding basic economics. Revised edition. (World continuing education series.) Cleveland, World publishing company, 1968. viii, 277 p.
1800. MILL, James. Elements of political economy. 3d . edition, revised and corrected. (Reprints of economic classics.) New York, A. M. Kelley, 1965. viii, 304 p
1801. MILL, John Stuart. Principles of political economy, with some of their applications to social philosophy. Edited with an introduction by Sir W. J. Ashley. (Reprints of economic classics.) New York, A. M. Kelley, bookseller, 1965. liii, 1013 p.
1802. MINC, Bronisław. Ekonomia polityczna socjalismu. Wyd. 2., popr. i. znacznie rozsz. Warszawa, Panstwowe wydawn. Naukowe, 1963. 883 p.
1803. _____. Studia i polemiki ekonomiczne. Wyd. 1. Warsza wa, Polskie wydawn. Gospodarczem 1959, 181 p.
1804. MINO, Sadao. Koten keizaigaku no tenkai katei. (Transliterated.) 1968. 5, 374, 10 p. Bibliographical references.
1805. MIRANDES Miranda, Francisco de. Los dos valores de la materia y la atomocracia. São Paulo, Editora revista Hispano-Americana, 1961. 212 p.
1806. MISES, Ludwig von. Human action; a treatise on economics New Haven, Yale university press, 1949. xv, 889 p. (New revised edition, 1963. xix, 907 p. 3rd revised edition. Chicago, H. Regnery company, 1966, xvii, 907 p.)
1807. MISZEWSKI, Bronisław. Ekonomia polityczna; wybór zagad nien dla pracowników przemysłu. Wyd. 1. (Polskie

towarzystwo ekonomiczne. Oddział w Katowicach. Wydawnictwa, Seria B., 1959/60.) Katowice, Wydawn. "Slask," 1959. 186 p. (Wyd. 3., popr., 1964. 134 p.)

1808. MITCHELL, John Broadus and others. Basic economics. In collaboration with Harold H. Hutcheson and Norman Leonard. New York, W. Sloane associates, 1951. vi, 502 p.

1809. _____. Economics: experience and analysis. In collaboration with Harold H. Hutcheson and others. New York, Sloane, 1950. viii, 884 p. Bibliographies.

1810. MITCHELL, Waldo F. Economic forces and institutions. Preliminary edition. Ames, Iowa, Littlefield, Adams, c1950. 2 v.

1811. MITRA, Jitendra Kumar. Economics; an introduction to its basic principles; for three-year degree course. 3d revised and enlarged edition. Calcutta, World press, 1962. 578 p.

1812. MITTALA, S. C. Edavāmsda ikonomika thyauri. (Transliterated.) (Advanced economic theory.) Saudi Arabia, 1964. 1 v. In Hindi. Bibliographical footnotes.

1813. MIWA, Masao. Keizaigaku gaisetsu. (Transliterated.) Japan, 1970. 272 p.

1814. MIYADE, Hideo. Keizaigaku. (Transliterated.) Japan, 1968. vii, 188, 6 p.

1815. MOCKERS, Jean Pierre. Dynamique et structures, la méthode structurale comme fondement de l'analyse dynamique en économie. Préface de Gérard Marcy. (Recherches économiques et financières, 12.) Paris, Sirey, 1965. iv, 412 p.

1816. MONSAROFF, Boris. Economics, science, and production; science as a politico-economic factor of production. 1st edition. New York, Vantage press, 1958. 196 p.

1817. MOORE, Henry Ludwell. Synthetic economics. (Reprints of economic classics.) New York, A. M. Kelley, 1967. vii, 186 p.

1818. MOORE, Justin Hartley, William Howard Steiner, Herbert Arkin, and Raymond Roosevelt Colton. Modern economics, its principles and practices. New York, T. Nelson and sons, c1940. 3 p. 1., v-xiii, 486 p.

1819. MORATO, Octavio. El mecanismo de la vida económica. 2. ed. Prólogo por Raúl Montero Bustamante. Montevideo, 1953. 119 p.

1820. MORDASINI, Sergio. Elementi di economic commerciale per i ginnasie le scuole di commercio inferiori. Bellinzona, Tip. grafica Bellinzona, 1947. 242 p.

1821. MORGAN, Edward Victor. A first approach to economics. London, Pitman and sons, 1955. 456 p. (2d edition, 1967. viii, 470 p. Reprint 2nd edition, 1968. viii, 470 p.)

1822. MORGAN, Theodore. Introduction to economics. (Prentice-Hall economics series.) New York, Prentice-Hall, 1950. xxix, 857 p. (2nd edition, 1956. 799 p.)

1823. MORRIS, Ruby (Turner.) Fundamentals of economics. New

York, Ronald press company, 1961. 878 p. (Student workbook. 1961. 1 v. Instructor's manual. 1961. 211 p.)
1824. MORSELLI, Emanuele e Giorgio Stefani. Economia politica. 4. ed. migliorata. Padova, CEDAM, 1967. 367 p. (5. edizione enteramente riveduta, 1969. 334 p.)
1825. MORTENSON, William Peter, Donald T. Krider and Roy J. Sampson. Understanding our economy; analysis, issues, principles. With the editorial assistance of Howard R. Anderson. (Houghton Mifflin social studies program: economics.) Boston, Houghton Mifflin company, 1964. ix, 502 p. (Teacher's edition, 1967. 14, ix, 502 p.)
1826. MOSCARDINO, Mario. Economia politica. Aggiornato con le decisioni del vertice monetario di Washington del marzo 1968. Ad uso degli istituti tecnici commerciali e per concorsi. Bari, Gemma, 1968. 208 p.
1827. MOSSE, Robert. Introduction à l'économie. (Petite bibliothèque Payot, 118.) Paris, Payot, 1968. 286 p.
1828. MOURA, Francisco Pereira de. Lições de economia. (Colecção "Estudos de economia moderna," 3.) Lisboa, Livraria clássica editora, 1964. xv, 447 p.
1829. ———. Problemas fundamentais da economia. 2. ed. (Colecção "Estudos de economia moderna.") Lisboa, Livraria clássica editora A. M. Teixeira, 1963. 254 p.
1830. MUJZEL, Jan. Stosunki towarowe w gospodarce socjalistycznej. Wyd. 1. Warszawa, Panstwowe wydawn. Ekonomiczne, 1963. 233 p.
1831. MULLER, Adam Heinrich, Ritter von Nitterdorf. Die elemente der staatskunst. 36 vorlesungen. Ungekürate ausg. (Neuausgabe des neudrucks Meersburg, Hendel, 1936 der original-ausgabe 1808-1809.) Berlin, Haude und Spener, 1968. 445 p.
1832. MULLER, Richard. Grundriss der volkswirtschaftslehre. 2., durchges. und erg aufl. Zürich, Verlad des Schweizerischen Kaufmännischen vereins, 1965. 181 p. (3. erw. und teilweise neu beard. aufl., 1969. 227 p.)
1833. MUNDELL, Robert A. Man and economics. New York, McGraw-Hill, c1968. 200 p.
1834. MURAD, Anatol. Economics; principles and problems. (Littlefield college outlines, 13.) Ames, Iowa, Littlefield, Adams, c1953. (Revised edition, 1954. 322 p. New, completely revised edition, 1958. 354 p. New, completely revised 4th edition. Paterson, New Jersey, Littlefield Adams, 1963. 354 p.)
1835. MURAT, Auguste. Notions essentielles d'économie politique. Paris, Sirey, 1962. 388 p. (2e édition, 1967. 424 p.)
1836. MUSGRAVE, Anthony. Studies in political economy. (Reprints of economic classics.) New York, A. M. Kelley, 1968. viii, 185 p.
1837. MUSSEY, Henry Raymond and Elizabeth Donnan. Economic principles and modern practice. Boston, New York, etc., Ginn and company, c1942. viii, 840 p. Bibliographies.

(1944. vii, 840, 44 p.)
1838. MUTHESIUS, Volkmar. Müssen wir arm bleiben? Dichtung und wahrheit in der wirtschaftspolitik. Frankfurt am Main, F. Knapp, c1952. 147 p.
1839. MYRDAL, Gunnar. Economic theory and under-developed regions. London, G. Duckworth, 1957. 167 p. (Revision of, Development and under-development, 1956.)
1840. NAKAYAMA, Ichirō. Kinkō riron to shihon riron. (Transliterated.) Japan, 1948. 7, 4, 403 p. Bibliographical footnotes.
1841. ———. Shoto keizaigaku kōgi. (Transliterated.) Japan, 1955. 3, 8, 287, 3 p.
1842. ———. Tsuron keizaigaku. (Transliterated.) Japan, 1954. 2, 3, 208 p.
1843. NAPOLEONI, Claudio. Elementi di economia politica. (His Corso di scienza economica.) Firenze, La nuova Italia, 1967. vi, 423 p. (2. ed., 1968. vi, 433 p.)
1844. ———. Grundzüge der modernen ökonomischen theorien. (Aus dem Italienischen übers. von Karin Monte.) (Edition Suhrkamp, 244.) Frankfurt am Main, Suhrkamp, 1968. 140 p.
1845. NAPOLITANO, Gaetano. Le vie del benessere: fatti, teorie e sistemi economici. Milano, Giuffrè, 1961. 348 p.
1846. NARASAKI, Toshio. Keizai genron. (Transliterated.) Japan, 1962. 341 p.
1847. ———. Keizai tetsugaku. (Transliterated.) 1964. Japan, 5, 4, 6, 255, 9 p. Bibliography, 1-9 (5th group).
1848. NARDI, Giuseppe di. Il controllo sociale dell'economia. ... Milano, Giuffrè, 1967. xi, 369 p.
1849. ———. Economia dello scambio. 2. ed. Bologna, C. Zuffi, 1952. x, 312 p. (3. ed. riv. Napoli, E. Jovene, 1955. x, 326 p.)
1850. ———. Lezioni di economia politica. Bari, Istituto di economia politica, Università degli studi, 1950- . v.
1851. NASIR, M. Saeed. Elements of economics. Lyallpur, Majid book depot, 1963. 2 v., 473 p.
1852. NATIONALØKONOMISK forening. Til Frederik Zeuthen, 9. september 1958. Redigeret af Poul Milhøj. København, 1958. 411 p.
1853. NEARING, Scott. Economics for the power age, a statement of first principles. New York, J. Day company, 1952. 190 p.
1854. NEMMERS, Erwin Esser. Managerial economics; text and cases. New York, Wiley, 1962. 498 p.
1855. NESIC, Dragoljub. Tečaj političke ekonomije; ekonomska teorija Karla Marksa. (Zadružna knjižnica.) Zagreb, Zadružna štampa, 1952. 375 p. (3. izd., 1955. 375 p.)
1856. NEVIN, Edward. Textbook of economic analysis. London, Macmillan; New York, Saint Martin's press, c1958. xiv, 422 p. Bibliographies. (3rd edition. London, Mel-

bourne, etc., Macmillan; New York, Saint Martin's press, 1967. xvi, 488 p.)
1857. NEWBURY, Frank D. The American economic system. New York, McGraw-Hill, 1950. xii, 558 p.
1858. NEWCOMB, Simon. Principles of political economy. 1886. xvi, 548 p. (Reprints of economic classics: New York, A. M. Kelley, 1966. xvi, 548 p.)
1859. NEYT, R. Economie. Basisbegrippen. Leuven, J. B. Wolters, 1968. 159 p.
1860. NICHOLS, Donald A. and Clark W. Reynolds. Principles of economics. New York, Holt, Rinehart and Winston, 1971. xvii, 556 p.
1861. NICHOLSON, J. S. Principles of political economy. 1893. (2nd. edition, Elements of political economy. 1923.)
1862. NIKITIN, Petr Ivanovich. Fundamentals of political economy. Translated and edited by Violet Dutt and Murad Saifulin. Revised. Moscow, Foreign languages publishing house, 1963? 403 p. (2nd revised edition. Translated from the Russian by Violet Dutt and Vic Schneierson. Edited by Murad Saifulin. Moscow, Progress publishers, 1966. 412 p.)
1863. ———. Politische ökonomie, leichtverständlich. Berlin, Verlag die wirtschaft, 1960. 297 p. (3., völlig neubearb. und erweiterte aufl. Ubersetzung: Hermann Mertens, Gerhard Möchel und Ingrid Stolte Redaktion: Fredo Müller und Gerda Tuchscherer. 1963. 357 p.)
1864. NIKL, Miroslav. Kritika ekonomickych koncepci českého reformismu. Vyd. 1. Praha, Nakl. Ceskoslovenske akademie ved, 1964. 225 p.
1865. NOGARO, Bertrand. I grandi problemi dell'economia contemporanea. Traduzione dal francese di Andrea Zanchi. (Saper tutto, 5.) Milano, Garzanti, 1950. 111 p.
1866. NORDIN, John A. and Virgil Salera. Elementary economics (Prentice-Hall economics series.) New York, Prentice-Hall, 1950. xvi, 844 p. (2d edition, 1954. 783 p.)
1867. NØRGARD, Ivar. Focus på nationaløkonomien. 2. udg. København, Arbejdernes oplysningsforbund, 1967. 163 p.
1868. ———. Nationaløkonomi. Tilrettelagt og udg. af Arbejdernes oplysningsforbund. København, Forlaget Fremad, 1949. 144 p.
1869. NOVAK, Mije. Uvod u političku ekonomiju socijalizma. (Izdanje "Ekonomaki pregled," broj 2.) Zagreb, Tisak grafickog zavoda Hrvatske, 1955- . v.
1870. NOVAKOVIC, Stojan D. Priručnik za spremanje stručnih ispita iz političke ekonomije. Beograd, Uredništvo železničkog stručnog časopisa "Zeleznice," 1953. 221 p.
1871. NOVOTNY, Jan Maria. Elementary economics, synopsis of fundamental theory. 2d edition. Rockford, Illinois, Available at Rockford college bookstore, 1958. 179 p.
1872. ———. A library of public finance and economics. Montreal, Available from the McGill university book store, 1953. xii, 383 p.
1873. NYSTROM, Paul Henry. Economic principles of consump-

tion. (Merchandising and distribution series.) New York, The Ronald press company, 1931. xi, 586 p. Bibliography, 548-559.
1874. OELSSNER, Fred. Eine neue Etappe der marxistischen politischen Okonomie; über die bedeutung des werkes J. W. Stalins "Okonomische probleme des sozialismus in der UdSSR." Berlin, Dietz, 1953. 194 p.
1875. OKADA, Jun'ichi. Keizaigaku ni okeru ningenzō. (Transliterated.) Japan, 1964. 242, 3 p. Bibliographical footnotes.
1876. OKOCHI, Kazuo. Keizaigzku kogi. (Transliterated.) Japan, 1968. 307, 7 p. Bibliographical references.
1877. ———. Keizaigaku nyumon. (Transliterated.) Japan, 1956. 2, 281 p. (Editions, 1960, 1968.)
1878. OKUMA, Nobuyuki. Keizai honshitsu ron. (Transliterated.) Japan, 1954. 6, 7, 258, 8 p. Bibliographical footnotes. (1957. 32, 324, 12 p. Bibliographies.)
1879. OLIVA, Felix. Politicka economie; pro učební potřeby Vysoké školy politickych a hospodářskych věd v Praze podle přednašek proslovenych r. 1948-49 v Praze. Vyd. 2. (Cesta mladé vědy, sv. 1.) V Praze, Rovnost, 1950. 133 p.
1880. OLOZAGA y BUSTAMENTE, José Marie de. Tratado de economía politica. Madrid, 1888-1889. 2 v.
1881. OPPENHEIMER, Franz. System der soziologie. III Band: Theorie der reinen politischen ökonomie. 5th edition. 1923-4. xxv, xiii, 1148 p. (1st edition, 1910.)
1882. OPSTELLENBUNDEL ter huldiging van Prof. Dr. J. Wisselink hem angeboden op 20 Oktober 1960. Haarlem, Erven F. Bohn, 1960. 275 p.
1883. ORD, H. W. and I. Livingstone. An introduction to West African economics. London, Ibadan, Heinemann educational, 1969. x, 457 p.
1884. OSTERKAMP, Karl. Kleine wirtschaftskunde. Stuttgart, Ring-verlag, 1958. 193 p.
1885. OSTLIND, Anders Elof. ABC i nationalekonomi. Stockholm, Tidens förlag, 1954. 224 p.
1886. OSWALT, H. Vorträge über wirtschaftliche grundbegriffe. 4th edition. 1922. vi, 169 p. (1st edition, 1905.)
1887. OUCHI, Hyōe. Keizaigaku. (Transliterated.) Japan, 1951. 4, 204 p.
1888. OXENFELDT, Alfred Richard. Economic principles and public issues. By A. F. Oxenfeldt with the assistance of Charles Hoffmann. New York, Rinehart, 1959. 618 p. Bibliography. (Portions are revisions of Economics for the citizen.)
1889. ———. Ecomomics for the citizen. New York, Rinehart, 1953. 746 p.
1890. OXENFELDT, Alfred Richard and Charles Hoffmann. Economic principles and public issues. New York, Rinehart, c1959. 618 p. Bibliography. (Portions of this book consist of revisions of material in the author's Economics for the citizen.)

1891. PAE, Pok-sok. Sin kyongje wŏllon. (Transliterated.)
Korea, 1964. 422 p. Bibliography, 419-422.
1892. PAGE, André Henri Charles. Economie politique, 1re année
de licence. (Mémentos Dalloz.) Paris, Dalloz, 1966.
140 p. (2e édition. 1968. 151 p. 3e édition, 1970.
151 p.)
1893. _____. Economie politique, licence en droit, 2e année.
(Mémentos Dalloz.) Paris, 1967. répartition, relations
internationales. (2e année, monnaie, 2e édition. 1970.
160 p.)
1894. PAK, Hyo-sam. Kyŏngje wŏllon. (Transliterated.) Korea,
1965. 344 p.
1895. PALOMBA, Giuseppe. Cicli storici e cicli economici.
Napoli, Giannini, 1952. xxv, 383 p.
1896. _____. Fisica economica. (Studi economici, v. 2.)
Napoli, Giannini, 1959. xxxi, 563 p.
1897. _____. Introduzione all'economica. Napoli, Pellerano-
Del Gaudio, 1950. xv, 340 p.
1898. _____. Morfologia economica. (Studi economici, v. 1.)
Napoli, Giannini, 1956. xxxix, 531 p.
1899. PANTALEONI, Maffeo. Erotemi di economia. (Raccolta
di scritti a cura dell'Istituto di studi economici, finanziari
e statistici dell'Universita di Roma, ser. 2, v. 2-3.)
Padova, CEDAM, 1964-64. 2 v.
1900. _____. Manuale di economia pura. 2nd edition. 1894.
376 p. (1st edition entitled: Principii di economia pura.
1889. English edition entitled: Pure economics. 1898.)
1901. PAPI, Giuseppe Ugo. Principii di economia. 11. ed.
Padova, CEDAM, 1952- . v.
1902. PARDO González, Nicanor Samuel del. Introducción a la
economía; sus bases lógicas, históricas y filosóficas.
(Universidad de Los Andes. Publicaciones de la facultad
de derecho, no. 2.) Mérida, Venezuela, 1953. 366 p.
1903. PARSONS, Talcott and Neil J. Smelser. Economy and society; a study in the integration of economic and social
theory. Glencoe, Illinois, Free press, 1956. 322 p.
1904. PARTITO comunista italiano. Introduzione allo studio dell'
economia politica. Corso popolare di studio a cura della
Sezione centrale scuole del P. C. I. Roma, Riuniti, 1959?
282 p.
1905. PASCHKE, Werner. Allgemeine volkswirtschaftslehre; einführung in die grundlagen und methodik. Stuttgart,
Deutscher Sparkassenverlag, 1962. 162 p.
1906. PATON, William Andrew. Shirtsleeve economics; a common-
sense survey. New York, Appleton-Century-Crofts, 1952.
460 p.
1907. PATTEN, Simon Nelson. The premises of political economy;
being a re-examination of certain fundamental principles of
economic science. (Reprints of economic classics.) New
York, A. M. Kelley, 1968. 244 p.
1908. PAULHAC, François. Structures et perspectives économiques
du XXe siècle; production et répartition des biens,
mécanismes élémenatires. Paris, J. Vrin, 1957. 301 p.

1909. PAULSEN, Andreas. Neue wirtschaftslehre; einführung in die wirtschaftstheorie von John Maynard Keynes und die Wirtschaftspolitik der vollbeschäftigung. Berlin, Verlag für rechtswissenschaft, 1950. viii, 262 p. (2. neubearb. und erweiterte aufl. Berlin, F. Vahlen, 1952. ix, 272 p. 3. neugefasste und erweiterte aufl., 1954. xi, 387 p. 4. unveränderte aufl., 1958. xi, 387 p. 4., unveränderte aufl. Nachdruck. Berlin und Frankfurt am Main, Vahlen, 1967. xi, 387 p.)

1910. PAUWELS, Marcel. Handboek van de bedrijfseconomie. Brussel, A. de Boeck, 1951. 190 p.

1911. PAVAN, Pietre. L'ordine economico. Roma, Figlie della Chiesa, 1957. 314 p.

1912. PAVLAT, Vladislav a Jiří Vojtíšek. Předmet a metoda politické ekonomie. Vyd. 1. (Učební texty vysokých škol.) Praha, Státní pedagogické nakl., 1954. 105 p.

1913. ———. Předmět politické ekonomie; úvod do studia politické ekonomie. Vyd. 1. (Velká knihovna politické ekonomie, sv. 36.) V Praze, Státní nakl. politické literatury, 1957. 140 p.

1914. PEACH, William Nelson. Principles of economics. Homewood, Illinois, R. D. Irwin, 1955. 704 p. (Revised edition, 1960. 736 p. Bibliography. 3rd edition, 1965. xiv, 741 p. Bibliographical footnotes.)

1915. PEDERSEN, Jørgen. Udvalgte kronikker og artikler. København, I kommission hos Berlingske forlag, 1960. 124, 1 p.

1916. PEDRAGOSA, Salvador. Introducción al estugio de la dimensión económica. 1. ed. Barcelona, Editorial Estela, 1961. 119 p.

1917. PEN, Jan. Het aardige van de economie. 5. druk. (Aulaboeken, 80.) Utrecht, Het spectrum, 1966. 256 p.

1918. ———. Harmonie en conflict. (Kritlese bibliotheek.) Amsterdam, De Bezige Bij, 1968. 336 p.

1919. ———. Harmony and conflict in modern society. Translated from the Dutch by Trevor S. Preston. London, New York, etc., McGraw-Hill, 1966. 7, 294 p.

1920. ———. Modern economics. Translated from the Dutch by Trevor S. Preston. (A Pelican book, A710.) Baltimore, Penguin books, 1965. 265 p.

1921. PEÑA Guzmán, Solano. La economía y sus fundamentos sociológicos. Buenos Aires, EDIAR, 1956. 276 p.

1922. PEÑALOZA, Luis. Curso de economía política: ingreso nacional, desarrollo económico. Cochabamba, Bolivia, 1955. 307 1. (2. ed. corregida. La Paz, Libreria-editorial "Juventud," 1956. 306 p.)

1923. PERALES García, Lorenzo. Derecho usual y nociones de economía; bachillerato laboral, modalidad administrativa. Madrid, 1962. 242 p.

1924. PEREIRA, Armando Temperani. Lições de economia política. Rio di Janeiro, Civilização Brasileira, 1967. 538 p.

1925. PERNAUT Ardanaz, Manuel. Apuntes de teoria económica. Caracas, 1957- . v.

1926. _____. Teoría economica. Madrid, Compañía bibliográfica española, 1958. Prólogo, v. 1, 1959. 2 v. (1. ed., Caracas, Universidad católica Andrés Bello, Facultad de economía, 1960- . v.)
1927. PEROVIC, Mirko. Osnovi političke ekonomije. 2., prečišćeno i dop. izd. (Biblioteka stručnih izdanja.) Beograd, Savremena administracija, 1960. (3., preradeno i dop. izd., 1961. 331 p.)
1928. _____. Politička ekonomija. 3., prerađeno i dop. izd. (Biblioteka društvenih nauka.) Beograd, Savremena administracija, predgover, 1964. xvi, 508 p.
1929. _____. Roba, novac i zakon vrednosti. (Političkoekonomska biblioteka.) Beograd, Rad, 1952. 265 p.
1930. PERROUX, François. L'économie du XXe siècle. 1. édition. Paris, Presses universitaires de France, 1961. 598 p.
1931. _____. Economie et société; contrainte, échange, don. 1. édition. (Initiation philosophique.) Paris, Presses universitaires de France, 1960. 186 p.
1932. PESENTI, Antonio Mario. Lezioni di economia politica. 1. ed. Roma, Editori riunti, 1959- . v.
1933. _____. Manuale di economia politica. . . . (Nuova biblioteca di cultura, 97.) Roma, Editori riuniti, 1970. 2 v.
1934. PETER, Hans. Einführung in die politische ökonomie. Stuttgart, W. Kohlhammer, 1950. xvi, 314 p.
1935. _____. Strukturlehre der volkswirtschaft. Hrsg. von Woldemar Koch, unter mitwirkung von Ursula Schleehauf. Göttingen, O. Schwartz, 1963. xviii, 378 p.
1936. PETERSON, George Shorey. Economics. Revised edition. New York, Holt, 1954. 827 p.
1937. PETERSON, Wallace C. Income, employment, and economic growth. Revised edition. New York, W. W. Norton and company, 1967.
1938. PETERSON, Willis L. Principles of economics. Macro. Homewood, Illinois, Irwin, 1971. xi, 257 p.
1939. PETRE, Gunnel. Ordnad ekonomi. Stockholm, Bonnier, 1955. 156 p.
1940. PETROVIC, Jovan. Politička ekonomija. Opšti pojmovi, kategorije i zakoni. Kapitalizam. Niš, "Prosveta," 1968. 440 p. (2. izd. Beograd, "Savremena administracija," 1970. xi, 404 p.
1941. PETROVIC, Vojislav J. Razvitak privrednog sistema FNRJ, posmatran kroz pravne propise. (Ekonomski institut FNRJ. Serija 4: Prilozi privrednoj istoriji, knj. 1, sv. 1- .) Beograd, 1954- . v.
1942. PHILIP, Grethe. Staten og vore hjems økonomi. Med tegninger af Svend Otto. (Folkevirke-seriea.) København, Gyldendal, 1949. 92 p.
1943. PHILIPPOVITCH, Eugen von. Grundriss der politischen oekonomie. 1893-9. 2 v.
1944. PHILLIPS, Willard. A manual of political economy, with particular reference to the institutions, resources, and condition of the United States. 1828. With an introduc-

tion, "Willard Phillips: a pre-Civil War theorist on economic development," by Joseph Dorfman. (Reprints of economic classics.) New York, A. M. Kelly, 1968. 11, 278 p.
1945. PICHLER, Hanns. Leitfaden zur wirtschaftskunde. Einführung in die volkswirtschaftslehre. Hrsg. vom Arbeitskreis "Wirtschaft und schule" der Niederösterreichischen Volkswirtschaftlichen gesellschaft. Wien, München, Osterreichischer bundesverlag, 1965. 208 p. (Revised edition, 1967- . v.)
1946. PICK, Felice. Dinamica dell'occupazione. Il lavoro come fattore produttivo nell'economia nazionale. Presentazione del ministro del bilancio, Giuseppe Pella. Milano, Stampa commerciale, 1951. viii, 242 p.
1947. PIERSON, N. G. Principles of economics. Translated by A. A. Wotzel. (Leerboek der staathuishoudkunde, 1896-1902.) 1902-12. 2 v.
1948. PIGOU, Arthur Cecil. The economics of welfare. London, 1920. xxxvi, 976 p. (2nd edition, 1924. xxviii, 783 p. 3rd edition, 1929. xxxi, 835 p.)
1949. ———. Income; an introduction to economics. London, Macmillan and company, limited, 1946. Bibliographical footnotes. vii, 117 p. (London, Macmillan, 1960. 114 p.)
1950. ———. Income revisited, being a sequel to Income. An introduction to economics. London, Macmillan; New York, Saint Martin's press, 1955. 86 p.
1951. ———. Wealth and welfare. 1912. xxxi, 493 p.
1952. PILKINGTON, E. C. A. The economic problem in outline. 1st edition. (The Commonwealth and international library of science, technology, engineering, and liberal studies. Social administration, training, economics, and production division.) Oxford, New York, Pergamon press, 1966. viii, 201 p.
1953. PINEDA Alcalá, Francisco. Derecho y economía. 1. ed. México, 1961. 248 p.
1954. PINEDA de Castro, Alvaro. Introducción a la economía social. Bogotá, Edit. Cahur, 1949. 235 p.
1955. PINTO Santa Cruz, Francisco A. Política económica; curso del professor Francisco A. Pinto. Apuntes de clases. Santiago de Chile, Editorial universitaria, 1952. 112 p.
1956. ———. Política económica; notes sinópticas del curso 1960, revisadas en 1961. Santiago, Editorial universitaria, 1962-63, c1961. v. 1, 1963. 2 v.
1957. PIROU, Gaëtan. Les théories de l'équilibre économique: Walras et Pareto. Conférences faites à l'Ecole pratique des hautes études en 1932-33 et 1933-34. 3. édition. Paris, Domat Montchrestien, 1946. 468 p.
1958. ———. Umumî iktisada giriş. Türkçeye çevi: Turhan Feyzioğlu. (Istanbul üniversitesi yayinlari, no. 253.) Istanbul, Kenan Matbaasi, 1945. viii, 264 p.
1959. PITANZA, Lorenzo. Appunti di economia politica. Roma, Edizioni di cultura professionale finanziaria, 1958. 135 p.

1960. PLATTEEUW, O. L. Beginselen van economie. 2. druk.
(V. O. B. O. uitgaven.) Gent, Uitgeverij Norma, 1948.
445 p.
1961. POLAK, Frederik Lodewijk. Kennen en keuren in de sociale
wetenschappen, een onderzoek naar de afbakening van objectieve en subjectieve oordelen in de economie, tevens
proeve van critiek op de wetenschapsleer van Max Weber.
Leiden, H. E. Stenfert Kroese, 1948. 293 p.
1962. _____. Om het behoud van ons bestaan; cultuursociologische voorstudies. Leiden, H. E. Stenfert Kroese,
1951. xi, 287 p.
1963. POLITICKA ekonomia; popularni ucebnice. Zprac.: Josef Sladek
et al. Praha, Svoboda, 1966. 511 p.
1964. POLITICKA ekonomie socializmu. Kolektiv autorů. pod
vedením Viktora Pavlendu. 1. vyd. Bratislava, Vydavatel'
stvo politickej literatúry, 1965. 618 p.
1965. POLITICKA ekonomie socialismu. Kolektiv autorú. Redigovali
František Loula et al. (Učebni texty vysokých škol.)
Praha, Státní nakl. technické literatury, 1961. 411 p.
1966. POLITICKA ekonomija kapitalizma. Napisali, Dušan Calić
i dr. Redackcija: Ivan Vrančić. (Ekonomska biblioteka,
3 kolo, br. 6-7.) Zagreb, "Informator," 1967. 420 p.
1967. POLSKIE towarzystwo ekonomiczne. Oddział w szczecinie.
Kronika szczecińskiego oddbiału polskiego towarzystwa
ekonomicznego za lata 1952-1958. Wyd. 1. Szczecin ,
Wydawn. Poznańskie, 1959. 171 p.
1968. POLY, Jean et J. Roche. Précis d'économie politique.
Ouvrage conforme aux programmes officiels de l'enseignement technique. (Bibliothèque de l'enseignement technique.)
Paris, Dunod, 1954- . v. (2. édition, 1959- . v. Classe
de 2. économique. Lycées techniques, cours commerciaux.
5. édition, 1964. viii, 186 p. Lycées techniques, cours
commerciaux. 6. dé. 1966- . v. 6e édition. Classes terminales T. E., lycées techniques, cours commerciaux,
préparation aux brevets d'études commerciales. 1967.
viii, 326 p.)
1969. POND, Alonzo Smith. Essential economics, an introduction.
Under the general editorship of Albert Gailord Hart. New
York, Harcourt, Brace, 1956. 534 p.
1970. POPIEL, Julian. Towar i pieniądz; zagadnienia wybrane. Wyd.
2., poszerzone i przerobione. Poznań, 1960. 106 p.
1971. POUND, Ezra Loomis. ABC of economics. 2d edition. Tunbridge Wells, England, P. Russell, 1953. 74 p.
1972. POWICKE, John Colyer. Economic theory. London, Edward
Arnold, 1968. 312 p.
1973. POWICKE, John Colyer and Peter H. May. An introduction
to economics. 2nd edition. London, Edward Arnold,
1969. 208 p.
1974. PRADO, Caio. Esbôco dos fundamentosda teoria econômica.
2. ed. São Paulo, Editôra Brasiliense, 1960. 227 p.
1975. PRADOS Arrarte, Jesús. Problemas básicos de la doctrina
económica. (Biblioteca de orientación económica: Problemas
económicos del presente.) Buenos Aires, Editorial

Sudamericana, 1950. 179 p.
1976. PRAGUE. Vysoká škola ekonomická. Proti projevum burzoažní ideologie a revisionismu. Vyd. 1. (Its Vědecký sbornik, 9.) Praha, Státní pedagogické nakl., 1960. 164 p.
1977. ———. ———. Katedra politické ekonomie. Politická ekonomie socializmu; záznam přednášek pro posluchače III. ročníku. Zprac. kolektiv Sekce politické ekonomie socialismu. Vedoucí katedry: Josef Brčák. 2. vyd. (Učebni texty vysokých škol.) Praha, Státní pedagogicke nakl., 1962- . v.
1978. PREISER, Erich. Probleme der wohlstandsgesellschaft. Vorgetragen am 8. November 1963. (Bayerische akademie der wissenschaften. Philosophisch-historische klasse. Sitzungsberichte, Jahrg. 1964, Heft 7.) München, Verlag der Bayerischen akademie der wissenschaften, in Kommission bei C. H. Beck, 1964. 25 p.
1979. ———. Die Zukunft unserer wirtschaftsordnung; probleme und möglichkeiten. Stuttgart, Kreuz-Verlag, 1949. 156 p.
1980. PREOBRAZHENSKII, Evgenii Alekseevich. The new economics. Translated by Brian Pearce. With an introduction by A. Nove. Oxford, Clarendon press, 1965. xx, 310 p.
1981. ———. La nouvelle économique. Traduit du russe par Bernard Joly. Préface de Pierre Naville. Introduction de Ernst Mandel. . . . Paris, Etudes et documentation internationales, 1966. 404 p.
1982. PRIMS, Floris. Beknopte staathuishoudkunde naar de organische beginselen van "Rerum novarum." 5. herziene uitg. bijgewerkt door Ferd. van Blade. Antwerpen, "Lux" drukkerij, 1948. 236 p.
1983. RAAIJMAKERS, Ch. Beginselen der staathuishoudkunde. 14. druk. 's-Hertogenbosch, L. C. G. Malmberg, 1948. 209 p.
1984. RAE, John. Statement of some new principles on the subject of political economy. (Reprints of economic classics.) New York, A. M. Kelley, bookseller, 1964. xvi, 414 p.
1985. RAHMAN, Hafiz Habibur and T. S. Deba. Dhanabijñana pariciti. (Transliterated.) Dacca, Pakistan, Ideal publication, 1966. 7, 636 p. In Bengali.
1986. RAHMAN, Mofizur. Substance of economics, for B. A. & B. Com. students. 3d revised and enlarged edition. Dacca, Pakistan book corporation, 1966. xii, 332, 176 p.
1987. RAYMOND, Daniel. The elements of political economy, in two parts. 2d edition, 1823, with additions from the 3d edition of 1836, and the pamphlet The Bankrupt law, fiscal agent, and auction duties, 1841? (Reprints of economic classics.) New York, A. M. Kelley, bookseller, 1964. 2 v. Bibliography. (First published in 1820 under title: Thoughts on political economy.)
1988. REBOUD, Paul et Henri Guitton. Précis d'économie politique. 9. édition. (Petits précis Dalloz.) Paris, Dalloz, 1951- . v.
1989. RENAUD, Albert. Cours d'économie politique. Paris, 1961. vi, 238 p.

1990. RENDON, Jorge. Fundamentos de la evolución económica; teoría y crítica. 1. ed. Lima, Ediciones "Cumbre," 1963. 158 p.
1991. RENWICK, Cyril and G. A. J. Simpson-Lee. The economic pattern; an elementary textbook for Australian readers. With a foreword by S. J. Butlin. London, New York, Longmans, Green, 1950. xix, 338 p.
1992. RESTA, Manlio. Principî di logica economica. Padova, CEDAM, 1970. xvi, 410 p.
1993. REYNOLDS, Lloyd George. Economics; a general introduction. (The Irwin series in economics.) Homewood, Illinois. R. D. Irwin, c1963. 739 p. Bibliography. (Revised edition, 1966. xxi, 964 p. 3d edition, 1969. xx, 834 p.)
1994. RICARDO, David. The principles of political economy and taxation. With an introduction by William Fellner. (Irwin paperback classics in economics.) Homewood, Illinois, R. D. Irwin, 1963. xiv, 260 p.)
1995. ———. Wert, rente, lohn und profit. On the principles of political economy and taxation, ch. 1-6. (Sozialökonomische texte, Heft 4.) Frankfurt am Main, V. Klostermann, 1946. 103 p.
1996. RICHARDS, Richard David and Percy Jordan. Groundwork of economics. 6th edition. London, University tutorial press, 1951. 331 p.
1997. RICHARDSON, George Barclay. Economic theory. (Hutchinson university library: Economics.) London, Hutchinson, 1964. 207 p.
1998. RICOSSA, Sergio. Misure di una economia moderna. (Corsi universitari.) Torino, G. Giappichelli, 1967. 200 p.
1999. RILEY, Eugene Boniface. Economics for secondary schools. Under the editorial supervision of Allyn A. Young. . . . Boston, New York, etc., Houghton Mifflin company, c1924. iv p., 1 l., 318 p.
2000. RIMINI, Bruno. Money, money, and money again. London, B. Rimini, limited, 1947. 197 p.
2001. RITSCHI, Hans. Theoretische volkswirtschaftslehre. Tübingen, Mohr, 194- . v.
2002. RITTMANNSBERGER, Alfred. Ausgewählte kapitel der volkswirtschaftslehre, für den unterricht au höheren lehranstalten. Stuttgart, Holland und Josenhans, Vorwort, 1959. 126 p.
2003. ROBINSON, Joan. Exercises in economic analysis. London, Macmillan; New York, Saint Martin's press, 1960, i.e. 1961. 242 p.
2004. ———. Introduction to the theory of employment. London, Macmillan and company, c1937. ix, 101 p. Reprinted: 1949. French edition: Introduction à la théorie de l'emploi. Traduction de Jacques Delons. (France, Direction de la conjoncture et des études économiques. Etudes et documents, sér. Th. 2.) Paris, Presses universitaires de France, 1948. 90 p.
2005. ROBINSON, Leland Rex, John F. Adams and Harry L. Dillin. An introduction to modern economics. New York,

Dryden press, 1952. 942 p. (2nd pre-publication edition. Philadelphia, 1951. 632 p.)
2006. ROBLES Alvarez de Sotomayor, Alfredo. Derecho y economía. Oviedo, 1951. 151 p.
2007. ———. Economía política. Oviedo, 1953. 159 p.
2008. ROCHA, Edgar Aquino. Princípios de economia. 30 ed., completamente atualizada. São Paulo, Companhia editôra nacional, 1969. 382 p.
2009. ROCHE, John Ward and Gomer Rhidian James. Getting and spending; an introduction to the market economy. London, Published for the Institute of economic affairs by A. Deutsch, 1963. 226 p. (2nd edition, 1965. x, 236 p. 3rd edition. Harlow, Longmans in association with the Institute of economic affairs, 1968. xii, 260 p.)
2010. RØGIND, Sven. Samfundets økonomiske forhold; en fremstilling of national økonomiens grundsynspunkter. 2. udg. København, Munksgaard, 1951. 346 p.
2011. ROLL, Erich. Elements of economic theory. London, H. Milford, Oxford university press, 1937. viii, 276 p. Bibliography, 269-272.
2012. ROMIG, Friedrich. Theorie der wirtschaftlichen zusammenarbeit. (Beiträge zur ganzheitlichen wirtschafts- und gesellschaftslehre, Bd. 1.) Berlin, Duncker und Humblot, 1966. 312 p.
2013. ROOKE, John. An inquiry into the principles of national wealth, illustrated by the political economy of the British Empire. (Reprints of economic classics.) New York, A. M. Kelley, 1969. xii, iii, 476 p.
2014. ROPKE, Wilhelm. Economics of the free society. Translated by Patrick M. Boarman. Chicago, H. Regnery company, 1963. 273 p.
2015. ———. Ekonomi för miljoner. Stockholm, Natur och kultur, 1946. 200 p.
2016. ———. Die lehre von der wirtschaft. 4. veränderte und verm. aufl. Erlenbach-Zürich, E. Rentsch, 1946, c1943. 303 p. (11., durchgesehene aufl., 1968. 349 p.)
2017. ———. Spiegazione economica del mondo moderno. Unica traduzione autorizzata a cura di Luigi Federici. 1. ed. (Politeia; collezione di scritti di politica e di economia.) Milano, Rizzoli, 1949. xiii, 210 p.
2018. ROSCOE, Edwin Scott. Project economy. (The Irwin series in management.) Homewood, Illinois, R. D. Irwin, 1960, i. e. 1961. 365 p.
2019. ROSSETTI, José Paschoal. Introducão à economia. Apresentação de Jamil Munhoz Bailão. (Série economia.) São Paulo, Ed. atlas, 1969. 420 p.
2020. ROSSI, Lionello. Elementi di economica. Padova, CEDAM, 1959- . v.
2021. ROTHBARD, Murray Newton. Man, economy, and state; a treatise on economic principles. (The William Volker fund series in the humane studies.) Princeton, New Jersey, Van Nostrand, c1962- . v. Bibliography.
2022. RUFENER, Louis August. Principles of economics. Boston,

New York, etc., Houghton Mifflin company, c1930. xix, 842 p. Bibliography.
2023. RUIZ y G. de Linares, Ernesto. Curso de economía política. Burgos, Hijos de S. Rodríguez, 1952-53. 2 v.
2024. RUSTOW, Hanns Joachim. Theorie der vollbeschäftigung in der freien marktwirtschaft. Tübingen, J. C. B. Mohr, 1951. 329 p.
2025. SABOLOVIC, Dusan. Suvremena buržoaska politička ekonomija; uvodni teme: historijski uvjeti nastanka, osnovni pravci, predmet i metoda. (Udžbenici Zagrebačkog sveučilista.) Zagreb, Skolska knj., 1959. 135 p.
2026. SACHDEVA, T. N. Public economics; full view at a glance. 3d edition, radically revised and elaborately enlarged. (Full view at a glance series.) New Delhi, Sudha publications, 1962. 224, 144 p.
2027. ———. Theory of employment and fluctuations; full view at a glance. 2d edition, radically revised and elaborately enlarged. (Full view at a glance series.) New Delhi, Sudha publications, 1963. 150 p.
2028. SADZIKOWSKI, Wiesław. Ekonomia polityczna kapitalizmu. Warszawa, 1965- . v. (Wyd. 2., Warszawa, Państwowe wydawn. Naukowe, 19- . v.)
2029. SAKAMOTO, Ichirō. Keizai genron. (Transliterated.) Japan, 1968. 210 p.
2030. SAKAMOTO, Ichirō and Hidehiro Ichikawa. Kindai heizaigak yōron. (Transliterated.) Japan, 1968. 245 p.
2031. SALLEE, M. Initiation à l'économie générale. Préface de J. Poly. Paris, Dunod, 1970, c1969. x, 243 p.
2032. SALLES, Pierre et J. Wolff. Hommes, besoins, activités, initiation aux faits économiques et sociaux. 2e édition. Classes de 2de AB. Paris, Dunod, 1968. 2 v.
2033. ———. La vie économique et sociale de la nation. Classes de première B. Paris, Dunod, 1969. 2 v.
2034. SAMHABER, Ernst. Wirtschaft verständlich gemacht. (Das Moderne sachbuch, Bd. 69.) Frankfurt am Main, Scheffler, 1968. 333 p.
2035. SAMPAIO, Alde. Lições de economia circulatória e de economia repartitiva. 2. ed., rev. e grandemente aumentada na parte referente à economia repartitiva. Rio de Janeiro, J. Olympio, 1948. 2 v.
2036. SAMPEDRO, José Luis. Realidad económica y análisis estructural. (Biblioteca de ciencias sociales. Sección 1: Economía.) Madrid, Aguilar, 1959. xvi, 277 p.
2037. SAMUELSON, Paul Anthony. Economics, an introductory analysis. 1st edition. New York, McGraw-Hill book company, c1948. xx, 622 p. Bibliographical footnotes. (2d edition, 1951. xxii, 762 p. 3rd edition, 1955. 753 p. 4th edition, 1958. 810 p. 5th edition, 1961. 853 p. 6th edition, 1964. xxii, 838 p. 7th edition, 1967. xxi, 821 p 8th edition, 1970. xxiii, 868 p.)
2038. ———. L'Economique, techniques modernes de l'analyse économique. Traduction de Gaël Fain. . . . (Collection U.) Paris, A. Colin, 1967. 2 v. 1007 p.

Summary Works 133

2039. _____. Foundations of economic analysis. (Economic studies series, no. 80.) Cambridge, Harvard university press, 1947. (Reprinted, 1958. xii, 447 p. Polish edition entitled: Zasady analizy ekonomicznej. Translated by Egon Vielrose. Warsaw, Państwowe wydawnictwo naukowe, 1959. 427 p. Spanish edition entitled: Fundamentos del análisis económico. Translated by José Mameli Cascarini. Buenos Aires, E. L. Ateneo editorial, 1957. xxi, 461 p. Paper edition: Atheneum, 1965.)

2040. _____. Volkswirtschaftslehre; eine einführende analyse. Die Übersetzung besorgte das wirtschaftswissenschaftliche Institut der gewerkschaften Köln-Braunsfeld. Köln, Bund-verlag, 1952. 712 p.

2041. SAMUELSON, Paul Anthony and Anthony Scott. Economics; an introductory analysis. Canadian edition. Toronto, New York, McGraw-Hill company of Canada, 1966. xxiv, 962 p. (2nd Canadian edition, 1968. xxiii, 945 p.)

2042. SANCHEZ-Ventura y Pascual, Francisco. Curso de economía política. (Publicaciones del Centro de estudios juridicos "San Francisco Javier." Monografias, 1.) Zaragoza, 1954- . v.

2043. SANTOS, Ernesto Schop. Elementos de economía política. Barcelona, Bosch, 1950. 2 v.

2044. SANTOS, Theobaldo Miranda. Manual de economia; introdução didática ao estudo da economia política. (Curso de filosofia e ciências, v. 4.) São Paulo, Companhia editora nacional, 1966. 398 p.

2045. SASTRE, Pastor. Economía política para les carreras de abogacía y ciencias económicas. Buenos Aires, Cirodia y Rodríguez, 1951. 255 p.

2046. _____. Economía política para las escuelas nacionales de comercio, 5º año diurno y 6º año nocturno, de conformidad con el nuevo plan de estudios. 6. ed., actualizada. Buenos Aires, Editorial Ciordia, 1966. 281 p.

2047. SATO, Toyosaburō. Kindai heizaigaku gairon. (Transliterated.) Japan, 1968. 302 p. Bibliography.

2048. SAY, Jean Baptiste. A treatise on political economy; or, The production, distribution and consumption of wealth. (Reprints of economic classics.) New York, A. M. Kelley, bookseller, 1964. 488 p.

2049. SCALZO, Antonio. Manuale per la preparazione ai concorsi di gruppo B. Materie trattate: Economia politica, scienza delle finanze, statistica. (Enciclopedia "Trinacria.") Roma, Stab. tip. L. Ambrosini, 1950. 182 p.

2050. SCHERF, Charles Henry. Our standard of living; a first course in economics. New York, Globe book company, 1950. 536 p.

2051. SCHERMAN, Harry. The promises men live by; a new approach to economics. New York, Random house, c1938. 5 p. 1., ix-xxvi, 492 p.

2052. SCHILLER, Karl. Aufgaben und versuche zur neuen ordnung von gesellschaft und wirtschaft; reden und aufsätze. Hamburg, Hansischer Gildenverlag, 1953. 161 p.

2053. SCHMIDT, Ronald. Die theorie der dynamik in der volkswirtschaft. München, 1949. 150 1.
2054. SCHMOLLER, Gustav Friederich von. Grundriss der allgemeinen volkswirtschaftslehre. 2nd edition. 1919-23. 2 v. (1st edition, 1900-04.)
2055. _____. Die volkswirtschaft, die volkswirtschaftslehre und ihre methode, 1893. Hrsg. von August Skalweit. (Sozialökonomische texte, Heft 16-17.) Frankfurt am Main, V. Klostermann, 1949. 107 p.
2056. SCHNEIDER, Erich. Einführung in die wirtschaftstheorie. Tübingen, Mohr, 1949-52. 3 v. (Reprinted: 1953. 3 v. 1955- . v. 1960- . v.)
2057. _____. Pricing and equilibrium; an introduction to static and dynamic analysis. Translated from the original German by T. W. Hutchison. London, W. Hodge; New York, Macmillan, 1952. xii, 327 p. (English 1962. 375 p.)
2058. SCHOBER, Kurt. Grundfragen der volkswirtschaftslehre. 3 aufl. (Maximilian-Bücher für wirtschaft und recht, Nr. 2.) Herford, Maximilian-verlag, 1952, c1949. 143 p.
2059. SCHULTZE, Charles L. National income analysis. 2d edition. Englewood Cliffs, New Jersey, Prentice-Hall, 1967.
2060. SCHUMPETER, Joseph Alois. Aufsätze zur ökonomischen theorie. Tübingen, J. C. B. Mohr, 1952. 608 p.
2061. _____. Theorie der wirtschaftlichen entwicklung, 1912. 2nd edition, 1926. xiv, 369 p.
2062. _____. Das wesen und der hauptinhalt der theoretischen nationalökonomie. 1908. xxxii, 626 p.
2063. SCHWARTZ, Rudolph. Economics for today. Edited by Joseph A. Rueff. Bronxville, New York, Cambridge book company, 1969. xii, 435 p.
2064. SCHWEYER, Herbert English. Process engineering economics. (McGraw-Hill series in chemical engineering.) New York, McGraw-Hill, 1955. 409 p.
2065. SCROPE, George Julius Duncombe Poulett. Principles of political economy, deduced from the natural laws of social welfare and applied to the present state of Britain. (Reprints of economic classics.) New York, A. M. Kelley, 1969. xxiv, 457 p.
2066. SEAGER, Henry Rogers. Economics; briefer course. New York, H. Holt and company, 1909. xii p., 1 l., 476 p. Bibliography. (Although based on the author's larger Introduction to economics, it is an independent work.)
2067. _____. Principles of economics. 2d edition, revised and enlarged. New York, H. Holt and company, c1917. xx, 662 p. Bibliography. (1st edition, 1913. 3rd edition?, 1923. xx, 698 p.
2068. SEGAL, Lev Khonanovich. Principios de economía política. 2. ed. (Colección Marxismo.) Montevideo, Ediciones Pueblos Unidos, 1947. 396 p.
2069. SELIGMAN, Edwin Robert Anderson. . . . Principles of economics, with special reference to American conditions. 10th edition, revised. (American citizen series, edited by Albert Bushnell Hart.) New York, London, etc., Long-

mans, Green and company, 1923. 1x, 711 p. Bibliographies. (1st edition, 1905. 7th edition, 1917.)
2070. SELLIER, François. Morale et vie économique. 1. édition. (Initiation philosophique.) Paris, Presses universitaires de France, 1953. 112 p.
2071. SENIOR, Nassau William. An outline of the science of political economy. (Reprints of economic classics.) New York, A. M. Kelley, 1965. xii, 249 p.
2072. SENSINI, Guido. Corso di economia pura. Roma, P. Maglione, 1955. viii, 409 p.
2073. SERAPHIM, Hans Jürgen. Theorie der allgemeinen volkswirtschaftspolitik. Göttingen, Vandenhoeck und Ruprecht, 1955. 351 p.
2074. SHACKLE, George Lennox Sharman. Economics for pleasure. Cambridge, England, University press, 1959. 268 p.
2075. ———. A new prospect of economics; an introductory textbook by members of the staff of the Department of economics in the University of Liverpool. Chairman of the group: Francis E. Hyde. Liverpool, Liverpool university press, 1958. 498 p.
2076. ———. A scheme of economic theory. Cambridge, England, University press, 1965. x, 209 p.
2077. SHAFER, Joseph E. Analysis of the business system. Durham, University of New Hampshire, 1956. 2 v.
2078. SHAFTO, Thomas Anthony Cheshire and W. R. Cook. Economics in the modern world: an analytical introduction. London, Nelson, 1969. xiii, 418 p.
2079. SHAPIRO, Edward. Macroeconomic analysis. 2d edition. New York, Harcourt, Brace and World, 1970.
2080. SHEPHERD, Ronald William. Cost and production functions. Princeton, Princeton university press, 1953. 104 p.
2081. ———. Theory of cost and production functions. (Princeton studies in mathematical economics, no. 4.) Princeton, New Jersey, Princeton university press, 1970. xi, 308 p.
2082. SHERMAN, Howard J. Elementary aggregate economics. New York, Appleton-Century-Crofts, 1966. xvi, 249 p.
2083. ———. Introduction to the economics of growth, unemployment and inflation. New York, Appleton-Century-Crofts, 1964. xvii, 225 p.
2084. ———. Macrodynamic economics: growth, employment and prices. New York, Appleton-Century-Crofts, 1964. xvii, 257 p.
2085. SHIMIZUGAWA, Shigeo. Kindai keizaigaku kōgi. (Transliterated.) Japan, 1968. 209 p.
2086. SHINOHARA, Miyohei, Yoshio Hayashi and Yoshikazu Miyazaki. Kindai keizaigaku kōza, kiso riron hen. (Transliterated.) Japan, 1967-68. 4 v. Bibliographies.
2087. SIDGWICK, Henry. The principles of political economy. 3rd edition. London, Macmillan? 1901. xxiv, 592 p. [1st edition, The Principles of political economy. 1883. 1968 edition. (Ristampe anastatiche di opere antiche e rare, 132.) Roma, Edizioni Bizzarri. xxiv, 592 p.]

2088. SIEBERT, Horst. Einführung in die volkswirtschaftslehre. (Verwaltung und wirtschaft, Heft, 38, 41.) Stuttgart, Kohlhammer, 1969- . v.
2089. SIEVERS, Allen Morris. General economics, an introduction. Philadelphia, Lippincott, c1952. 812 p. Bibliography.
2090. _____. Revolution, evolution, and the economic order. (A Spectrum book, S-23.) Englewood Cliffs, New Jersey, Prentice-Hall, 1962. 173 p.
2091. SIK, Ota. Ekonomika, zájmy, politika; jejich vzájemné vztahy do socialismu. Vyd. 1. Praha, Nakl. politické literatury, 1962. 587 p.
2092. _____. K problematice socialistických zbožních vztahů. Vyd. 1. Praha, Nakl. Československé akademie věd, 1964. 400 p. (Vyd. 2., 1965. 400 p.)
2093. _____. Okonomie, interessen, politik. (Wissenschaftlich bearb. von Otto Reinhold.) Berlin, Dietz, 1966. 506 p.
2094. _____. Plan und markt im sozialismus. (Aus dem tscheckischen übertragen von Ingrid Kondrkova.) Mit tabellen und diagrammen. Wien, Molden, 1967. 384 p.
2095. SILK, Leonard Solomon. Contemporary economics; principles and issues. New York, McGraw-Hill, 1970. viii, 407 p.
2096. SILK, Leonard Solomon and Phillip Saunders. The world of economics. Saint Louis, McGraw-Hill, 1969. xv, 560 p.
2097. SILVERMAN, Herbert Albert. The substance of economics for the student and the general reader. 13th edition. London, I. Pitman, 1950. xvii, 387 p. Bibliography, 349-353.
2098. SILVERSTOLPE, Gunnar Westin. Företagsekonomi för alla. Stockholm, Kooperativa förbundets bokförlag, 1952. 181 p.
2099. _____. Nationalekonomi för alla. 12. uppl. Stockholm, Kooperativa förbundets bokförlag, 1947. 229 p. (13. uppl., 1950. 261 p.)
2100. SIMONDE de Sismondi, Jean Charles Léonard. Nouveaux principes d'économie politique; ou, De la richesse dans ses rapports avec la population. 3. édition, Genève, Edition Jeheber, 1951- . v.
2101. _____. Political economy and the philosophy of government; selections. (Reprints of economic classics.) New York, A. M. Kelley, 1966. 459 p.
2102. SIMONSEN, Mario Henrique. Teoria microeconômica. 1 ed. Rio de Janeiro, Fundação Getúlio Vargas, Serviço de publiçãoes, 1967-69. 4 v.
2103. SINGER, Leslie P. Economics made simple. (The "Made simple" series.) New York, Made simple books; distributed by Garden City Books, Garden City, New York, 1958. 189 p.
2104. SIRKIN, Gerald. Introduction to macroeconomic theory. (The Irwin series in economics.) Homewood, Illinois, R. D. Irwin, 1961. 252 p. (Revised edition, 1965. x, 278 p.)

2105. SLADEN, Edward. Everyday economics. 3rd edition. London, Pitman, 1966, i.e. 1967. vii, 236 p.
2106. SLATER, Ronald Albert. Economics: fact and theory: an introductory course. (Methuen general studies books, 35/ .) London, Methuen, 1968. viii, 332 p.
2107. SLEJSKA, Dragoslav. Dialektika výrobních sil a socialistických ekonomických vztahů, ve všelidovém sektoru. Vyd. 1. Praha, Nakl. Ceskoslovenské akademie věd, 1962. 338 p.
2108. SLESINGER, Reuben E. Chapters in basic economics. Berkeley, McCutchan publishing corporation, 1969. v, 365 p.
2109. SLESINGER, Reuben E. and Asher Isaacs. Contemporary economics; selected readings. Boston, Allyn and Bacon, 1963. 551 p.
2110. SLOVENIA (Federated republic, 1945-). Sekretariat za personalno službo. Politična ekonomija; gradivo za strokovne izpite. Ljubljana, 1950. 303 p.
2111. SMEJKAL, Miroslav, J. Závada, J. Katz. Několik kapitol z dějin ekonomických teorii. Vyd. 1. (Učebni texty vysokých škol.) Praha, Státní pedagogické nakl., 1960. 282 p.
2112. SMITH, Augustus H. Economics for our times. Consulting editor, S. Howard Patterson. 2d edition. New York, McGraw-Hill, 1950. xii, 534p. (2d edition, revised, 1953. 534 p. 3rd edition, 1959. 596 p. Student activities, Ruth E. Miller, 3rd edition, revised. Saint Louis, Webster publishing division, 1963. xii, 628 p. Recent trends in economics, William Wolman. 4th edition. Saint Louis, Webster division, McGraw-Hill, 1966. xii, 628 p.
2113. SMITH, Erasmus Peshine. A manual of political economy. (Reprints of economic classics.) New York, A. M. Kelley, 1966. 278 p.
2114. SMITH, Henry. The economics of socialism reconsidered. London, New York, Oxford university press, 1962. 225 p.
2115. ———. Introduction to the study of economics. (Sylvan books on modern studies.) London, Sylvan press, 1949. 224 p.
2116. ———. A prospect of political economy. London, Allen and Unwin, 1968. 3-314 p.
2117. SNIDER, Delbert A. Economics: principles and issues. (The Dorsey series in economics.) Homewood, Illinois, Dorsey press, c1962. 654 p.
2118. SOARES, Rosinethe Monteiro. Introdução à economia. Pref. de Adolfo Oliveira. (Coleção estudos universitários, 1. Economia.) Brasília, Ebrasa, 1968. 101 p.
2119. SODDY, Frederick. Wealth, virtual wealth and debt; the solution of the economic paradox. 3d edition. Hawthorne, California, Omni publications, 1961. 352 p.
2120. SOIGNIE, Philippe de. Eléments d'économie politique, économie générale. Bruxelles, Editions L'Avenir, 1955. 282 p.

2121. SOLERI, Giacomo. Economia e morale; storia e teoria del problema. (Collana convergenze.) Torino, Borla, 1960. 381 p.
2122. SOMBART, Werner. Allgemeine nationalökonomie; nach vorlesungen und seminarübungen bearb. und hrsg. von Walter Chemnitz. Berlin, Duncker und Humblot, 1960. 237 p.
2123. _____. Die drei nationalökonomien. Geschichte und system der lehre von der wirtschaft. 2. (unveränderte aufl. Berlin, Duncker und Humblot, 1967. xii, 352 p.
2124. SONG, Ch'ang-Hwan. Kyŏngje wŏllon. (Transliterated.) Korea, 1963. 549 p.
2125. _____. Kyŏngjehak immun. (Transliterated.) Korea, 1957. 3, 4, 279 p.
2126. SOSKIC, Branislav. Marginalistička i kejnsijanski pravac ekonomske misli. Beograd, (Udruženje studenata ekonomskog fakulteta), 1968. 4, 182 p.
2127. _____. Proizvodnja, zaposlenost i stabilizacija. Savremena makro-ekonomska analiza. Beograd, Institut za ekonomska istraživanja, 1970. 276 p.
2128. SOULE, George Henry. Economics for living; illustrated by Bunji Tagawa. New York, Abelard-Schuman, 1954. 161 p. (Revised edition, 1961. 159 p.)
2129. _____. Economics: measurement, theories, case studies. With the editorial assistance of Leland E. Traywick and Francis C. Boddy. New York, Holt, Rinehart and Winston, 1961. 446 p.
2130. _____. Introduction to economic science. New York, Viking press, c1948. 154 p. Bibliography, 153-154. (A Mentor book, M58. New York, New American library, 1951. 138 p.)
2131. _____. The new science of economics, an introduction. New York, Viking press, 1964. xi, 211 p.
2132. SOUZA Gonçalves, Reynaldo de. Elementos de economia (súmulas de economia política) para os cursos técnicos de comércio e os candidatos às faculdades de economia. Rio de Janeiro, Forense, 1968. 157 p.
2133. SOWELL, Thomas. Economics: analysis and issues. Glenview, Illinois, Scott, Foresman, 1971. 349 p.
2134. SPADARO, Louis M. Economics: an introductory view. (Ma and his world.) Milwaukee, Bruce publishing company, 1968, c1969. ix, 209 p.
2135. SPANN, Othmar. Fundament der volkswirtschaftslehre. 2nd edition. 1921. xvi, 872 p. [1st edition, 1918. 5., durchgesehene aufl., eingerichtet Oskar Müllern. Mit einem nachwort von Walter Heinrich. (His Gesamtausgabe, Bd. 3.) Graz, Akademische druck- und verlagsanstalt, 1967. xv, 470 p.]
2136. _____. Tote und lebendige wissenschaft; kleines lehrbuch der volkswirtschaft in fünf abhandlungen. 5., durchgesehene aufl., eingerichtet von Oskar Müllern. Mit einem nachwort von Walter Heinrich. (His Gesamtausgabe, Bd. 6.) Graz, Akademische druck- und verlagsanstalt, 1967. xiii, 442 p.

Summary Works

2137. SPEIGHT, H. Economics and industrial efficiencv. London, Macmillan; New York, Saint Martin's press, c1962. 262 p. Bibliography.
2138. _____. Economics; the science of prices and incomes. London, Methuen, 1960. 671 p. (3rd edition, 1968. 3-750 p.)
2139. SPENCER, Milton H. Contemporary economics. New York, Worth publishers, inc., 1971. xxv, 714.
2140. _____. and Louis Siegelman. Managerial economics; decision making and forward planning. Revised edition. (The Irwin series in economics.) Homewood, Illinois, R. D. Irwin, 1964. xiii, 614 p. (3rd edition, 1968.)
2141. SPIEGEL, Henry William. Introduction to economics. New York, Blakiston, 1951. x, 605 p.
2142. STARK, Albert. Nationalekonomi för nybörjare. Stockholm, Vepe, 1947. 236 p.
2143. STAS, Jules. Manuel d'économie politique. Liège, Sciences et lettres, 1953? 316 p.
2144. STEFANI, Giörgio. Problemi tributari nell'economia del benessere; la copertura dei costi di produzione. (Studi di finanza pubblica, 3.) Padova, CEDAM, 1958. 145 p.
2145. STEUART-Denham, Sir James. An inquiry into the principles of political economy. Edited and with an introduction by Andrew S. Skinner. (Scottish economic classics.) Chicago, University of Chicago press; Edinburgh, London, published for the Scottish economic society by Oliver and Boyd, 1966. 2 v., lxxxiv, 755 p.; 2 v. Bibliography, 744-46.
2146. STIGLER, George Joseph. The theory of price. Revised edition. New York, Macmillan, 1952. 310 p. (3rd edition, 1966. viii, 355 p.)
2147. STIGUM, Bernt P. and Marcia Stigum. Economics. Reading, Massachusetts, Addison-Wesley publishing company, 1968. xxi, 793 p. (Instructor's manual by Marcia Stigum. 1968. 257 p.)
2148. STIKKER, A. H. Leerboek der economie voor Indonesië. 5. druk. Groningen, J. B. Wolters, 1949. 258 p.
2149. STOJANOVIC, Radmila. Savremeni problemi privrednog razvoja u socijalizmu; zbornik radova. (Ekonomska biblioteka "Socijalistička privreda.") Beograd, Naučna knj., 1960- . v.
2150. STOKES, Charles J. Managerial economics; a textbook on the economics of management. Consulting editor: Donald Dewey. New York, Random house, 1969. xv, 414 p.
2151. STOLPE, Herman Albert. Ekonomi; privat- och sammhälls-ekonomins grunder. (Folkbildningsserien.) Stockholm, Ehlin, 1950. 108 p.
2152. STONIER, Alfred William and Douglas C. Hague. A textbook of economic theory. London, New York, Longmans, Green, 1953. 513 p. (2nd edition, 1957. 513 p. 3rd edition, New York, Wiley, 1964. x, 574 p.)
2153. STOWE, Heinz. Okonometrie und makroökonomische theorie;

stochastische wirtschaftsforschung als notwendige ergänzung der theorie. (Okonomische studien, Heft 3.) Stuttgart, G. Fischer, 1959. 190 p.
2154. STUART, C. A. Verrijn. Die grundlagen der volkswirtschaft. 1923. viii, 296 p.
2155. STUDIER i ekonomi och historia. Tillägnade Eli F. Heckscher pa 65-årsdagen den 24. november 1944. Uppsala, Almqvist och Wiksells boktr., 1945. 333 p.
2156. STURMEY, S. G. and D. W. Pearce. Economic analysis: an introductory text. London, New York, etc., McGraw-Hill, 1966. 427 p.
2157. SUITS, Daniel Burbidge. Principles of economics. New York, Harper and Row, 1970. xv, 542 p.
2158. SULMICKI, Paweł. Proporcje gospodarcze. Wyd. 1. Warszawa Pánstwowe wydawn. Naukowe, 1962. 204 p.
2159. SUNDHARAM, K. P. M. A text book of economic theory (for graduate classes.) Agra, Ratan Prakashan Mandir, 1964. 2, vi, 709 p.
2160. SUNDHARAM, K. P. M. and M. C. Vaish. Principles of economics. 4th edition revised and enlarged. Agra, Ratan Prakashan Mandir, 1962. 650 p.
2161. SUPINO, Camillo. Principi di economia politica. 6th edition, 1923. ix, 597 p. (1st edition, 1904.)
2162. SWEEZY, Paul Marlor. The theory of capitalist development; principles of Marxian political economy. New York, Monthly review press, 1964, c1942. ix, 398 p. (Spanish edition entitled: Teoría del desarrollo capitalista. Versión española de Hernán Laborde. México, Fondo de cultura económica, 1945. 480 p.)
2163. SZIGETI, Peter Rudolf. Volkswirtschaftslehre für praktiker; Grundlagen für kaufleute und juristen, ingenieure und naturwissenschaftler. (NWB-Buchreibe, Nr. 245.) Herne, Verlag neue wirtschafts-briefe, 1962. 175 p.
2164. TAGWERKER, Helmut. Beiträge zur methode und erkenntnis in der theoretischen nationalökonomie. Wien, Verlag notring der wissenschaftlichen verbände Osterreichs, 1957. 119 p.
2165. TAKATA, Yasuma. Keisaigaku gaisetsu. (Transliterated.) Japan, 1954. 2, 3, 204 p.
2166. ———. Keizaigaku genri. (Transliterated.) Japan, 1949. 2, 11, 408 p.
2167. ———. Shakaishugi keizaigaku nyūmon. (Transliterated.) Japan, 1950. 6, 241 p.
2168. TAKESHIMA, Kazuo. Kyōyō keizaigaku. (Transliterated.) 1969. 315 p. Bibliography, 301-305.
2169. TALAMONA, Mario. Elementi di microeconomia. Appunti dalle lezioni tenute nella Facoltà di giurisprudenza dell' Università di Pavia. Milano, La Goliardica, 1960- . v.
2170. TAMAGNINI, Giulio. Elementi di economia politica; nozioni fondamentali, evoluzione del pensiero economico, concezione oggettiva e soggettiva del valore, le grandi leggi economiche. Firenze, Editrice universitaria, 1950. 294 p.
2171. TARSHIS, Lorie. The elements of economics, an introduction

to the theory of price and employment. Boston, Houghton Mifflin company, c1947. xii, 699 p. Bibliography. (Under the editorship of Edgar S. Furniss.)

2172. _____ Modern economics; an introduction. (The Houghton Mifflin series in economics.) Boston, Houghton Mifflin, c1967. xvi, 814 p.

2173. TAUSSIG, Frank Williams. Principles of economics. 3d edition revised. New York, The Macmillan company, 1921. 2 v. Bibliographies. (1st edition, 1911. Reprint, 3rd edition, 1923. 2 v. 4th edition, 1939. v.)

2174. TAUTSCHER, Anton. Wirtschaftsethik. (Handbuch der moraltheologie, Bd. 11.) München, M. Huber, 1957. 264 p.

2175. TAYLOR, Edward. Historia rozwoju ekonomiki. Vyd. 1. (Polskie towarzystwo ekonomiczne. Oddział w Poznaniu. Rozprawy i monografie, nr. 1.) Poznań, Państwowe wydawn. naukowe, 195- . v.

2176. TAYLOR, Fred Manville. Principles of economics. 8th edition. New York, The Ronald press company, 1921. ix, 577 p. (1st edition, 1911. 2nd edition, 1913. viii, 476 p. 9th edition, 1925. 589 p.)

2177. TAYLOR, Horace. Contemporary economic problems and trends. New York, Harcourt, Brace and company, c1938. xvi, 603 p. (Revised form of Contemporary problems in the United States. 6th edition.)

2178. _____. Main currents in modern economic life. Produced with the collaboration of associates at Columbia university . . . Harold Barger, Goetz A. Briefs, Courtney C. Brown and others. New York, Harcourt, Brace and company, 1941- . 2 v. (Designed to take the place of Contemporary economic problems and trends.)

2179. TAYLOR, Horace and Harold Barger. The modern economy in operation. New York, Harcourt, Brace and company, 1949. xiv, 846 p. (Designed to take the place of a two volume work, Main currents in modern economic life.)

2180. TAYLOR, Horace, J. J. Coss, and Joseph Daniel McGoldrick. Contemporary problems in the United States. Produced with the collaboration of Columbia college associates in economics, government and public law, history, and philosophy. 1932/33; 1936/37 edition. New York, Harcourt, Brace and company, 1932-37. 12 v. in 9. (Superseded by Contemporary economic problems and trends.)

2181. TAYLOR, Horace and Joseph Daniel McGoldrick. Readings in contemporary problems in the United States. New York, Columbia university, 1929-30. 2 v.

2182. THAON di Revel, Paolo. Teorica del bisogno. Saggio di metaeconomia. (Universita di Torino. Studi dei Laboratorie di economia politica S. Cognetti de Martis. 3. ser., v. 10.) Milano, A. Giuffre, 1967. 776 p.

2183. THEIL, Henri. Principles of econometrics. New York, Wiley, 1971. xxxi, 736 p.

2184. THOMAS, A. H. A refresher course in economics. 2d revised edition. (Newnes refresher course series.)

London, Newnes, 1949. 199 p.
2185. THOMPSON, Charles Manfred. Principles and practices of economics, an introductory course. Chicago, New York, etc., B. H. Sanborn and company, c1928. ix, 578 p. Bibliographies.
2186. THOMPSON, William. An inquiry into the principles of the distribution of wealth most conducive to human happiness, 1824. (Reprints of economic classics.) New York, A. M. Kelley, bookseller, 1963. xxiv, 600 p. [Reprint entitled: An inquiry into the principles of the distribution of wealth most conducive to human happiness, applied to the newly proposed system of voluntary equality of wealth. (Selected essays in history, economics and social science, 54.) New York, B. Franklin, 1968. xxiv, 600 p.]
2187. TINBERGEN, Jan. Economic policy. Principles and design. 4th revised printing. Amsterdam, North-Holland publishing company; Chicago, Rand McNally, 1967. xxviii, 276 p. Bibliography, 272-273.
2188. TOBIN, James. National economic policy. New Haven, Yale university press, 1966.
2189. TORRES Martínez, Manuel de. Teoría y práctica en la política económica. Con prólogo del autor. (Biblioteca de ciencias sociales. Sección 1: Economía.) Madrid, Aguilar, 1955. xix, 224 p.
2190. TRENTON, Rudolph W. Basic economics. New York, Appleton-Century-Crofts, 1964. xiv, 410 p. (2nd edition, 1968. xiv, 448 p.)
2191. TROLLE, Ulf af. Distributionsekonomi. Malmö, Hermods, 1955. 1 v.
2192. TRUCHY, Henri et Auguste Murat. Précis d'économie politique. Paris, Nouvelles éditions latines, 1952- . v.
2193. TSURU, Shigeto. Gendai keizaigaku. (Transliterated.) Japan, 1969. 264 p. Bibliographies.
2194. _____. Keizai no ronri to genjitsu. (Transliterated.) Japan, 1959. vi, 256 p. Bibliographical footnotes.
2195. _____. Keizaigaku nyūmon. (Transliterated.) Japan, 1958. 421 p.
2196. _____. Keizaigaku wa muzukashiku nai. (Transliterated.) Japan, 1964. 230 p.
2197. TUCKER, George. The laws of wages, profits and rent, investigated. (Reprints of economic classics.) New York, A. M. Kelley, bookseller, 1964. x, 189 p.
2198. _____. Political economy for the people. (Reprints of economic classics.) New York, A. M. Kelley, 1970. xix, 238 p.
2199. TUCKER, Gilbert Milligan. Common-sense economics. Harrisburg, Pennsylvania, Stackpole company, 1957. 289 p.
2200. TURNER, John Roscoe. Introduction to economics. New York, Chicago, etc., C. Scribner's sons, c1919. xvi 641 p.
2201. TUSTIN, Arnold. The mechanism of economic systems; an

	approach to the problem of economic stabilisation from the point of view of control-system engineering. London, Heinemann, 1953. 161 p.
2202.	UCHIDA, Yoshihiko. Koten keizaigaku kenkyū. (Transliterated.) Japan, 1957. 313 p. Bibliographical notes.
2203.	ULMER, Melville Jack. Economics; theory and practice. Boston, Houghton Mifflin, 1959. 638 p. (2nd edition, 1965. xxiv, 757 p.)
2204.	UMBREIT, Myron Henry, Elgin F. Hunt and Charles V. Kinter. Economics: an introduction to principles and problems. 3d edition. New York, McGraw-Hill, 1957. 637 p.
2205.	_____. Fundamentals of economics. 2d edition. New York, McGraw-Hill, 1952. 506 p.
2206.	_____. Modern economic problems. 1st edition. New York, McGraw-Hill, 1950. xvii, 642 p.
2207.	UPGREN, Arthur Reinhold and Stahrl Edmunds. Economics for you and me. Edited by Robert W. Smith; drawings by Roger Bradfield. New York, Macmillan, 1953. 246 p.
2208.	VALK, Hendrikus Marchinus Hyminus Arnoldus van der. Grondbegrippen grondbeginselen der economie. 2. druk. Arnhem, G. W. van der Wiel, 1946. 208 p. (4. ongewijzigde druk., 1950. 228 p. 5. druk., 1949. 215 p. 6. herziene en uitgebreide druk., 1950. 241 p. 7. herziene druk., 1952. 248 p.)
2209.	_____. Voortgezet elementair leerboek der economie. 4., ongewijzigde druk. Arnhem, G. W. van der Wiel, 1950. 228 p.
2210.	VALLARINO, Juan Carlos. Tratado de economía política. (Biblioteca de ciencias económicas, políticas y sociales, v. 1, 5.) Buenos Aires, Editorial Claridad, s. a., 1945-49. 2 v.
2211.	VAN Niekerk C., D. de V. Brand and P. R. Joubert. Economics. Cape Town, Nasionale boekhandel, 1960. 130 p.
2212.	VAN Sickle, John Valentine and Benjamin A. Rogge. Introduction to economics. New York, Van Nostrand, 1954. 746 p.
2213.	VAN Tassel, Roger Carleton. Economic essentials; a core approach. Boston, Houghton Mifflin, 1969. xvii, 410 p.
2214.	VANDERBLUE, Homer Bews. Economic principles; a case book. With the assistance of Charles I. Grogg. Chicago and New York, A. W. Show company; London, A. W. Show and company, limited, 1927. xvii, 670 p. Bibliography.
2215.	VECCHIO, Gustavo del. Economia generale. (Trattato italiano di economia, v. 1.) Torino, Unione tipografi-coeditrice torinese, 1961. 813 p.
2216.	_____. Scritti di teoria economia e di statistica. (Pubblicazioni dell'Istituto di politica economica e finanziaria della Facoltà di economia e commercia dell'Università di Roma.) Milano, Giuffrè, 1966. vi, 266 p.
2217.	VETHAKE, Henry. The principles of political economy. 2d edition. 1844. With an essay Henry Vethake--Jacksonian

Ricardian, by Joseph Dorfman and Rexford G. Tugwell. (Reprints of economic classics.) New York, A. M. Kelley, 1971. 54, xvi, 13-415 p.
2218. VILLARD, Henry Hilgard. Economic performance; an introduction to economics. New York, Holt, Rinehart and Winston, c1961. 655 p.
2219. VINCI, Felice. I fondamenti dell'economica. Milano, Istituto editoriale cisalpino, 1953. 318 p.
2220. VITO, Francesco. L'economia a servizio dell'uomo; i nuovi orientamenti della politica economica e sociale. 3. ed., riv. Milano, Vita e pensiero, 1949. xi, 156 p.
2221. _____. Economí política. 3. ed. española corr. y notablemente aumentada. Con prólogo de José Zubizarreta Traducción de Carlos Humberto Núñez. Madrid, Editoria Tesoro, 1961. xxiv, 798 p.
2222. _____. Introduzione alla economia politica. 9. ed. riv. Milano, Giuffrè, 1950. 253 p. (11. ed. riv., 1956. 310 p. 14. ed. riv., 1961. 356 p.)
2223. VOLK, Karl H. Ganzheitliche wirtschaftswissenschaft; eine grundlegung. München, R. Pflaum, 1950. 216 p.
2224. VULERT, Pierre. Vers l'avenir; nouvelles conceptions économiques et sociales. Paris, R. Pichon et R. Durand-Auzias, 1959. 199 p.
2225. WAARDHUIZEN, D. D. van. Staatsinrichting, economie en bedrijfswetgeving, voor het middelbare technische onderwijs. Door Jac. Grooten Jr. 3. herziene druk. Haarlem, H. Stam, 1946. 325 p.
2226. WAFFENSCHMIDT, Walter Georg. Anschauliche einführung die allgemeine und theoretische nationalökonomie. Meisen heim am Glan, Westkulturverlag, 1950. xvi, 223 p.
2227. _____. Wirtschaftsmechanik. Stuttgart, W. Kohlhammer, 1957. vii, 301 p.
2228. WAGEMANN, Ernst Friedrich. Berühmte denkfehler der nationalökonomie, ein kritisches repetitorium. Bern, A. Francke; München, L. Lehnen, 1951. 272 p.
2229. _____. Wagen, wägen, wirtschaften; erprobte faustregeln neue wege. Hamburg, Hoffmann und Campe, 1954. 287 p.
2230. WAGNER, Adolf and others. Lehr- und handbuch der politischen oekonomie. 1876. 4 v.
2231. WAITE, Warren Cleland. Economics of consumption. 1st edition. New York, etc., McGraw-Hill book company, incorporated, 1928. xii, 263 p.
2232. WALKER, Francis Amasa. Political economy. 3rd edition. 1888. vi, 537 p. (1st edition, 1883.)
2233. _____. The science of wealth; a manual of political economy, embracing the laws of trade, currency, and finance. 7th edition, revised. Boston, Little, Brown, 1874. New York, Kraus reprint company, 1969. xi, 496 p.
2234. WALKER, Franklin V. Growth, employment and the price level; intermediate macroeconomic measurement, theory and policy. Englewood Cliffs, New Jersey, Prentice-

Summary Works

	Hall, c1963. 342 p. Bibliography.
2235.	WALRAS, Antoine Auguste. . . . De la nature de la richesse et de l'origine de la valeur, augmente de notes inédites de Jean-Baptiste Say, suivi de Memoire sur l'origine de la value d'échange. Présenté par l'auteur a l'Académie des sciences morales et politiques et précédé d'une introduction biographique sur la vie et les travaux de l'auteur, par Gaston Leduc. . . . Et d'une préface de Gaëtan Pirou. Paris, Felix Alcan, 1938. 3 p. 1., ix-xv, 343 p. 1.
2236.	_____. Theorie de la richesse sociale, ou résumé des principes fondamentaux de l'économie politique. Ristampa anastatica della prime edizione del 1849 con introduzione di Oscar Nuccio. (Ristampe anastatiche di opere antiche e rare, 154.) Roma, Bizzarri, 1969. xxiv, 103.
2237.	WALSH, Vivian Charles. Introduction to contemporary microeconomics. New York, McGraw-Hill, 1969, c1970. xxi, 298 p.
2238.	WARD, Benjamin. Elementary price theory. New York, The free press, 1967.
2239.	WARD, Richard Joseph. Economics: its principles and means. Educational consultant: James O'Donnell. (Issues and challenges.) New York, W. H. Sadlier, 1965. viii, 343 p.
2240.	WARE, Caroline Farrar and Gardiner C. Means. The modern economy in action. 1936. (Accompanied by study outline: The modern economy in action; a guide for studying the relation between our economic thinking and current economic facts. By Caroline Ware. (Social studies series.) Washington, American association of university women, c1936. 55 p. Bibliography.
2241.	WARNER, Aaron W. and Victor Robert Fuchs. Concepts and cases in economic analysis. New York, Harcourt, Brace, c1958. 288 p.
2242.	WASSEIGE, Yves de. Les mécanismes de l'économie moderne. (Collection humanisme d'aujourd'hui.) Bruxelles, E.V.O. (Editions "Vie ouvrière"), 1970. 244 p.
2243.	WASSER, Emil. Gesellschaft und wirtschaft. (Schriften zur sozialwissenschaft.) Zürich, Ovrell Füssli, 1965. 324 p.
2244.	WATSON, Donald Stevenson. Price theory and its uses. Boston, Houghton Mifflin, 1963. 431 p. Bibliography. (2d edition, 1968. xii, 443 p. Bibliography.)
2245.	_____. Price theory in action; a book of readings. Boston, Houghton Mifflin, c1965. xi, 355 p. (2d edition, 1969. xi, 400 p. Bibliographical footnotes.)
2246.	WATTS, Vervon Orval. Away from freedom; the revolt of the college economists. (Studies of the Foundation for Social research, v. 1, no. 1.) Los Angeles, Foundation for social research, 1952. iii, 105 p.
2247.	WAUGH, Albert Edmund. Principles of economics. 1st edition. New York, McGraw-Hill book company, c1947. xii, 934 p. Bibliographical footnotes.
2248.	WEBER, Adolf. Kurzgefasste volkswirtschaftslehre. 7.,

neubearb. aufl. Berlin, Duncker und Humblot, 1956. xvi, 304 p.
2249. _____. Schein und wirklichkeit in der volkswirtschaft; sechs jahrzehnte im dienste der volkswirtschaftslehre. Beiträge zur Klärung sozialökonomischer gegenwartsprobleme. Berlin, Duncker und Humblot, 1961. 449 p.
2250. _____. Stand und aufgaben der volkswirtschaftslehre in der gegenwart. Berlin, Duncker und Humblot, 1956. 41 p.
2251. _____. Volkswirtschaftslehre. Berlin, Duncker und Humblot, 1951- . v. 1, 1953. v. (1958- . v.)
2252. WEBER, Fritz S. Kompendium der nationalökonomie. 4. durchgesehene und ergänzte aufl. Düsseldorf, Müller-Albrechts, 1956. 363 p.
2253. WEBER, Hermann Fritz. Kompendium der volkswirtschaftslehre. 6., völlig neue aufl. Düsseldorf(-Wittlaer), Müller-Albrechts, 1969. 405 p.
2254. WEBER, Max. The theory of social and economic organization. Translated by A. M. Henderson and Talcott Parsons. Edited with an introduction by Talcott Parsons. Glencoe, Illinois, Free press, 1957, c1947. 436 p.
2255. _____. Wirtschaft und gesellschaft; grundriss der verstehenden soziologie. Mit einem anhang: die rationalen und soziologischen grundlagen der musik. 4., neu hrsg. aufl., besorgt von Johannes Winckelmann. Tübingen, Mohr, 1956. 2 v., xviii, 1033 p.
2256. WEBER, Siegfried. Kompendium der nationalökonomie. 3. erweiterte aufl. Oldenburg, M. Albrechts, 1952. 351 p.
2257. WEBER, Wilhelm. Wirtschaftswissenschaft von heute; ein Uberblick über moderne ökonomische forschungen. Wien, Springer, 1953. 214 p.
2258. WEDDIGEN, Walter. Theoretische volkswirtschaftslehre als system der wirtschaftstheorie. 2. durchgesehene und ergänzte aufl. Berlin, Duncker und Humblot, 1958. 377 p. (3. durchgesehene und ergänzte aufl., 1964. 388 p.)
2259. _____. Wirtschaftsethik. System humanitärer wirtschaftmoral. Berlin, Duncker und Humblot, 1951. 214 p.
2260. WEILER, Emanuel Thornton. The economic system; an analysis of the flow of economic life. New York, Macmillan, 1952. 869 p.
2261. WEILER, Emanuel Thornton and W. H. Martin. The American economic system. Dubuque, W. C. Brown company, 1955. 428 p. (A revised edition of The economic system. New York, Macmillan, 1957. 623 p.)
2262. WEILLER, Jean. Théorie économique notes et documents à l'appui du cours de Jean Weiller. D. E. S., économie politique, sciences économiques, 1959-1960. Paris, Cours de droit, 1960. 189 p.
2263. WEINBERGER, Otto. Grundriss der allgemeinen wirtschaftsphilosophie. Berlin, Duncker und Humblot, 1958. 177 p.
2264. WEINTRAUB, Sidney. A general theory of the price level,

output and income distribution, and economic growth. Chilton company, Philadelphia, 1959.
2265. ———. Price theory. New York, Pitman, 1956.
2266. WEISS, Leonard W. Economics and American industry. New York, Wiley, 1961. 548 p.
2267. WEISS, Roger. The economic system. New York, Random House, 1969.
2268. WELD, William Ernest and Alvin Samuel Tostlebe. A case book for economics. Boston, New York, etc., Ginn and company, c1927. xiii, 508 p.
2269. WELFLING, Weldon. Principles of economics. New York, McGraw-Hill, 1971. vii, 488 p.
2270. WELFLING, Weldon and K. Laurence Chang. Economics. Homewood, Illinois, Published for American institute of banking, New York, by R. D. Irwin, 1967. xi, 289 p.
2271. WELINDER, Carsten. Ekonomisk teori och politik. Stockholm, Kooperativa förbundets bokförlag, 1947. 542 p. (2., omarb. uppl., 1953. 547 p.)
2272. ———. Företaget och dess ekonomi. Stockholm, Kooperativa förbundets bokförlag, 1950. 222 p.
2273. WESTSTRATE, Cornelis. Beschrijvende economie. 3., herziene druk. Leiden, Stenfert Kroese, 1949. viii, 488 p. (4., herziene druk., 1951. 408 p.)
2274. ———. Kennismaking met het economisch leven, een nieuwe inleiding tot de economie. Leiden, H. E. Stenfert Kroese, 1947. vii, 200 p.
2275. WHITTAKER, Edmund. Economic analysis. New York, Wiley, 1956. 400 p. (National income analysis; supplement to chapter 13. Fort Collins, Colorado, c1957. 14 l.)
2276. ———. Elements of economics. 1st edition. New York, London, etc., Longmans, Green and company, c1946. xvii, 393 p.
2277. WIEGAND, G. Carl. Economics: its nature and importance. (Barron's essentials: the efficient study guides.) Woodbury, New York, Barron's educational series, incorporated, 1968. ix, 532 p.
2278. WIESER, Friedrich, von. Social economics. Translated by A. Ford Hinrichs, with a preface by Wesley Clair Mitchell. (Reprints of economic classics.) New York, A. M. Kelley, 1967. xxii, 470 p.
2279. ———. Theorie der gesellschaftlichen wirtschaft. 2nd edition. 1924. xi, 330 p. (1st edition, 1914.)
2280. WILDER, Ira and Jerome Sherk. Visualized citizenship economics. (Oxford visualized texts.) New York, Oxford book company, 1954. 207 p. (1958. 207 p.)
2281. WILES, Peter John de la Fosse. The political economy of communism. Oxford, Blackwell; Cambridge, Harvard university press, 1962, 1963. xv, 404 p.
2282. WILLIAMSON, Thames Ross. Introduction to economics. Boston, New York, etc., D. C. Heath and company, c1923. x, 538 p. Bibliography, 530-531.
2283. WINDING, Poul. Some aspects of the acceleration principle.

(Foreningen til unge handelsmaends uddannelse. Handelshøjskolen i København. Det Økonomiske forskningsinstitut. Skriftraekke B, 16.) København, E. Harck, 1957. 254 p.

2284. WIRTH, Max. Grundzüge der nationalökonomie, volume II. 1859. (2nd edition. Cologne, 1861.)

2285. WOESTIJNE, W. J. van de. Economie voor iedereen; een inleiding tot practisch economisch denken. Arnhem, Va. Loghum Slaterus, 1954. 218 p. (2., herziene druk., 1957. 219 p.)

2286. _____. Inleiding in het economisch denken. (Aulaboeken, 446.) Utrecht, Het Spectrum, 1970. 265 p.

2287. WOODS, Baldwin Munger and Ernest Paul De Garmo. Introduction to engineering economy. 2d edition. New York, Macmillan, c1953. 519 p.

2288. WORCESTER, Dean Amory. Fundamentals of political economy. New York, Ronald press company, c1953. 594 p.

2289. WRIGHT, David McCord. Growth and the economy; principles of economics. New York, Scribner, 1964. viii, 398 p.

2290. _____. A key to modern economics. New York, Macmillan, 1954. 520 p.

2291. WRIGHT, Frank Joseph. An introduction to the principles of economics. 1st edition. (The Commonwealth and international library of science, technology, engineering, and liberal studies. Commerce, economics, and administration division.) Oxford, New York, Pergamon press, 1965. ix, 194 p.

2292. WRONSKI, Stanley P., Francis S. Doody and Richard V. Clemence. Modern economics. Consultant: Douglas C. Davis. Boston, Allyn and Bacon, 1964. x, 438 p.

2293. WU, Yen-nan. Kuo fu ssū hsiang yü hsien tai ching chi ssū hsiang. (Transliterated.) China, 1965. 2, 176 p. Bibliographical footnotes.

2294. WURZER, Lothar. Die Zunkunft der marktwirtschaft; eine auseinandersetzung mit J. A. Schumpeter. Köln, Druck W. Kleikamp, 1965. vi, 283 p.

2295. WYKSTRA, Ronald A. Introductory economics. New York, Harper and Row, Publishers, 1971. x, 754.

2296. YAJIMA, Kinji. Atarasāii zeikuro-keizaigaku. (Transliterated.) Japan, 1969. 301 p. Bibliography, 302.

2297. YASURI, Takuma and Hideo Aoyama. Gendai keizaigaku. (Transliterated.) Japan, 1968. 315 p. Bibliographies.

2298. YI, Chŏng-hwan. Sin kyŏngje wŏllon. (Transliterated.) Korea, 1962. 507 p.

2299. YI, Man-gi. Kyŏngje wŏllon. (Transliterated.) Korea, 1964. 421 p. Bibliographical footnotes. (2nd edition, 1968. 400 p. Bibliographical footnotes.)

2300. _____. Kyŏngjehak yŏnsúp. (Transliterated.) Korea, 1965. 3, 311 p.

2301. YI, Yŏng-gi. Ilban kyŏngjehak. (Transliterated.) Korea, 1965. 444 p. Bibliography, 419-428.

2302. YOKENO, Nobumichi. Keizaigaku no kiso riron. (Transliterated.) 1969. 197 p. Bibliographical footnotes.
2303. YOKOYAMA, Masahiko. Keizaigaku gairon. (Transliterated.) Japan, 1968. 220 p. Bibliography, 201-205.
2304. YOSHIDA, Keiichi. Ippan keizaigaku. (Transliterated.) Japan, 1950. 2, 9, 223 p. Bibliographical footnotes.
2305. _____. Keizai genron gaisetsu. (Transliterated.) Japan, 1957. 2, 12, 277 p.
2306. _____. Keizaigaku shinkō. (Transliterated.) Japan, 1964. 217 p.
2307. _____. Kihon keizaigaku. (Transliterated.) Japan, 1947. 215 p.
2308. YOSHIDA, Shōzō. Gendai keizai riron nyūmon. (Transliterated.) 1968. 2, 5, 238, 3, 10 p. Bibliography, 3 (4th group).
2309. YOUNG communist international. Executive committee. Das politische grundwissen des jungen kommunisten. Nach d. ausg. d. kommunist. Jugendinternationale von 1927. Frankfurt, März-verlag, 1970. 160 p.
2310. ZABKOWICZ, Leopold. Eksperymenty ekonomiczne, ich wyniki i przyszłość. Wyd. 1. Warszawa, Książka i Wiedza, 1958. 167 p.
2311. ZACCAGNINI, Emilio. Appunti di economia politica. Torino, Gheroni, 1959? 116 p. (Torino, Tirrenia, 1967. 212 p.)
2312. ZAMORA, Francisco. Introducción a la dinámica económica. 1. ed. (Fondo de cultura económica. Sección de obras de economía.) México, Fondo de cultura económica, 1958.
2313. _____. La sociedad económica moderna; capitalismo, planeación y desarrollo. 1. ed. (Sección de obras de economía.) México, Fondo de cultura económica, 1966. 263 p.
2314. _____. Tratado de teoría económica. 1. ed. (Sección de obras de economía del Fondo de cultura económica.) México, Fondo de cultura económica, 1953. 764 p. (3. ed. corr., 1958. 802 p.)
2315. ZARKOVIC, Dragoje. Politička ekonomija. Novi Sad, Viša ekonomsko-komercijalna škola, 1967. 190, 1 p.
2316. ZAWADZKI, Józef. Teorie wzrostu ekonomicznego a współczesny kapitalizm. Napisali: O. Lange . . . J. Zawadzki, et al. Pod red. Józefa Zawadzkiego i Aleksandra Łukaszewicza. Wyd. 1. Warszawa, Książka i Wiedza, 1962. 610 p.
2317. ZEUTHEN, Frederik. Economic theory and method. London, New York, Longmans, Green, 1955. 364 p.
2318. _____. Problems of monopoly and economic warfare. With a preface by Joseph A. Schumpeter. (Reprints of economic classics.) New York, A. M. Kelley, 1968. xv, 152 p.
2319. ZIMMERER, Carl. Kompendium der volkswirtschaftslehre. Düsseldorf, Müller-Albrechts, c1960. 341 p.
2320. ZINKE, George W. The American economy: an introductory analysis. New York, Ronald press company, 1959. 704 p.

2321. ZINN, Karl Georg. Basistheorie des ökonomischen wohlstandes in der demokratie. Die interdependenz von gleichheit, zeit und nutzen und die verteilungspolitische konsequenz. Wiesbaden, F. Steiner, 1970. x, 285 p.
2322. ZUCCHI, Gaetano. Principî del dinamismo economico. La proporzione in economia, di Armando Scagliarini. (Edizioni M. D.) Verbania, Stampa di A. Airoldi, 1946. 346 p.
2323. ZWIEDINECK-SUDENHORST, Otto von. Allgemeine volkswirtschaftslehre. 2. neu bear. aufl. (Enzyklopädie der rechts- und staatswissenschaft. Abt. staatswissenschaft, 33.) Berlin, Springer, 1948. vii, 298 p.
2324. ———. Mensch und wirtschaft; aufsätze und abhandlungen zur wirtschaftstheorie und wirtschaftspolitik. Berlin, Duncker und Humblot, 1955- . v.
2325. ———. Von der älteren zur neueren theorie der politischen ökonomie. (Sitzungsberichte der Bayerischen akademie der wissenschaften. Philosophisch-historische klasse, jahrg. 1951, heft 5.) München, Verlag der Bayerischen akademie der wissenschaften, in kommission bei C. H. Beck, 1952. 96 p.
2326. ZWIJNDREGT, J. van. Fasal-fasal ekonomi, disalin dalam bahasa Indonesia oleh markoem. Tjetakan 2. Djakarta, J. B. Wolters, 1951- . v.
2327. ———. Hoofdstukken der economie. 8. druk. Groningen, J. B. Wolters, 1953- . v.

PART II

SPECIFIC WORKS

D. ECONOMISTS AND ECONOMICS

2328. AFTALION, Albert. Oeuvre èconomique de Simonde de Sismondi. Paris, A. Pedone, 1899. 267 p. Bibliographie. (Reprinted: B. Franklin, 1968.)
2329. ALEM, André. Le marquis d'Argenson et l'économie politique au début du XVIIIe siècle. Pratiques mercantiles et théories libérales. Paris, A. Rousseau, 1900. vii-viii, 188 p. (Reprinted: B. Franklin, 1967. Researc and source works series no. 242.)
2330. ALEXANDER, Kenneth John Wilson, A. G. Kemp and T. M. Rybozynski. The economist in business. Oxford Blackwell; New York, A. M. Kelley, 1967. vi, 199 p.
2331. ALINSKY, Saul David. John L. Lewis. An unauthorized biography. New York, Putnam, 1949. (Reprinted: Vintage press, 1970. 389 p.)
2332. ANANTARAMAN, Venkatraman. Mobility of professional economists in the United States; a report on the survey of patterns and factors in their mobility. Abridged. Madison, Industrial Relations Research Center, University of Wisconsin, 1961. 56 1.
2333. AMONN, Alfred. Simonde de Sismondi als Nationalökonom; darstellung seiner Lehren mit einer einführung und erlaüterungen. Bern, A. Francke, 1945-49. 2 v.
2334. ARKIN, Marcus. Economists and economic historians; uneasy bedfellows or comrades-in-arms? Grahamstown, Rhodes University, 1968. 35 p.
2335. BALLIVIAN Calderón, René. El pensamiento económico en la moderna filosofía de la historia: Oswald Spengler, Alfred Weber, Arnold Toynbee y Karl Jaspers. Buenos Aires, Librería hachette, 1957. 96 p.
2336. BARDEY, Emil. Der volkswirt als manager? Siegeslauf und problematik des volkswirte-berufes. 2. aufl. Nürnberg, N. Stoytscheff, 1952. 174 p.
2337. BARRINGTON, D. "Edmund Burke as an economist," In Economica, 34, 83 (August, 1954) 252-258.
2338. BASTABLE, Charles F. "Leslie." In, Supplement of Nouveau dictionnaire d'economie politique de Léon Say. Paris (1897.)
2339. BAUDIN, Louis. Frédéric Bastiat; textes choisis. (Collection des grands économists.) Paris, Librairie dalloz, 1962. 166 p. Bibliography, 165-166.
2340. BENTHAM, Jeremy. Jeremy Bentham's economic writings. Critical ed. based on his printed works and unprinted mss. By W. Stark. London, Published for the Royal economic society by Allen & Unwin, 1952-54. 3 v.

2341. BEVERIDGE, William Henry. Power and influence. An autobiography. London, Hodder and Stoughton, 1953. xi, 447 p.
2342. BOISGUILLEBERT, Pierre Le Pesant. Pierre de Boisguilbert ou la naissance de l'économie politique. . . . Paris, Institut national d'études démographiques, 1966. 2 v. (xxiv, 1032 p.)(v. 1: Preface. Etudes. Biographie. v. 2: Oeuvres manuscrites et imprimees.)
2343. BOSWELL, J. T. The economics of Simon Nelson Patten. Philadelphia, 1934.
2344. BOWLEY, Marian. Nassau Senior and classical economics. Reprint of 1937 edition. New York, Octagon books, 1967. 358 p. Bibliography, 340-351.
2345. BRAEUER, Walter. Handbuch zur geschichte der volkswirtschaftslehre; ein bibliographisches nachschlagewerk. Frankfurt am Main, Klostermann, 1952. 224 p.
2346. BREIT, William and Roger L. Ranson. The academic scribblers. American economists in collision. New York, Holt, Rinehart and Winston, inc., 1971. x, 275 p.
2347. BRINK, John T. Joseph of Egypt and his managed national economy. 2d edition. Topeka, Kansas, Mid-Continent Publishing Company, 1954. 49 p.
2348. BRUCE, T. W. "The economic theories of John Craig, a forgotten English economist." In, Quarterly Journal of Economics (August, 1938.)
2349. BUENOS AIRES (Federal Capital). Laws, statutes. Reglamento profesional; ciencias económicas para la Capital Federal. Doctor en ciencias económicas, contador público nacional, actuario. Buenos Aires, Distribuidor R. I. Noguera, 195- . 28 p.
2350. CARDOZO, Jacob Newton. Notes on political economy (1826). With the article Political economy--rent from The Southern review, 1828; and an introduction by Joseph S. Dorfman. (Reprint) New York, A. M. Kelley, 1960. xi, facsim.: 125, 192-218 p.
2351. CAREY, Lewis J. Franklin's economic views. (Franklin monographs.) Garden city, New York; Doubleday, Doran & company, 1928. vi p. 2 1., 243 p. Bibliographies.
2352. CAREY, Robert Lincoln. Daniel Webster as an economist. (Studies in history, economics, and public law, ed. by the Faculty of political science of Columbia university, no. 313.) New York, Columbia university press; London, P. S. King & son, ltd., 1929. Bibliography, 213-218. (Thesis, Ph. D., Columbia university.)
2353. CARR, H. J. "John Francis Bray," In, Economica (November, 1940.)
2354. CATTANEO, Cario. Scritti economici, a cura di Alberto Bertolino. Firenze, F. Le Monnier, 1956. 3 v.
2355. CHANDLER, Lester Vernon. Benjamin Strong, central banker. Washington, Brookings Institution, 1958. 495 p.
2356. CHAO, N. Richard Jones. An early English institutionalist. New York, Columbia university press, 1930.
2357. CHARBONNAUD, Roger. Les idées économiques de Vol-

taire. New York, B. Franklin, 1970. viii, 168 p.
2358. CHIGUSA, Yoshindo. Shihonshugi wa dō kawatta ka. (Transliterated.) Japan, 1962. 261 p.
2359. CLARK, Victor Selden. Who's who in economics; an international biographical encyclopedia. Washington, American council on public affairs, 1948.
2360. CLOSON, Francis Louis. Un homme nouveau; l'ingénieur économiste. Paris, Presses universitaires de France, 1961. 38 p.
2361. COBBENHAGEN, Martinus Joseph Hubertus. De economist Cobbenhagen: economische geschriften van Prof. M. J. H. Cobbenhagen. Amsterdam, Elsevier, 1957. 605 p.
2362. COLE, Arthur Harrison. The historical development of economic and business literature. (Kress library of business and economics. Publication no. 12.) Boston, Baker library, Harvard graduate school of business administration, 1957. 56 p.
2363. COLE, G. D. H. and M. Cole. The opinions of William Cobbett. London, Cobbett, 1944.
2364. COLEGIO de economistas del distrito federal. Directorio nacional de economistas. México, Tall. G. y G. Rivero. v.
2365. DANSK økonomstat 1966. Under redaktion af Erik Hjelmar. København, Danske økonomers forening, 1967. 192 p.
2366. DAWSON, William H. Richard Cobden and foreign policy. London, 1926.
2367. DEMUTH, Fritz. F. Th. V. Bernhardi. Ein beitrag zur geschichte der national ökonomie im XIX juhrhundert. Jena, 1900. 68 p.
2368. DESJARDINS, Arthur. Pierre Joseph Proudhon, sa vie, ses oeuvres, sa doctrine. Paris, Perrin et cie, 1896. 2 v.
2369. DEVLETOGLOU, Nicos E. Montesquieu and the wealth of nations. (Lecture series, 10.) Athens, Center of economic research, 1963. 71 p. Bibliographical footnotes.
2370. DIEHL, Karl. Pierre Joseph Proudhon. Seine lehre und sein leben. Jena, G. Fischer, 1888-96. 3 v. in 1.
2371. DOMMANGET, Maurice. Victor considérant, sa vie, son oeuvre. Paris, 1929.
2372. DOVE, Patrick Edward. Account of Andrew Yarranton, the founder of English political economy. Edinburgh, Johnstone and Hunter, 1854. 106 p.
2373. DURAND, Edward Dana. Memoirs. Washington, 1954. 438 p.
2374. DUPRAT, Jeanne. "Le paupérisme, facteur de bellicisme d'après Proudhon." In, Annales de l'Institut international de sociologie, Paris, XVI (1932.)
2375. ECONOMIC history association. Handbook of the Economic history association. New York, Graduate school of business administration of New York university, 1967. 106 p.
2376. EINAUDI, Luigi. Saggi bibliografici e storici intorno alle

dottrine economiche. (Storia ed economia; studi, testi, documenti, quaderni, 1.) Roma, Edizioni di storia e letteratura, 1953. xiii, 367 p.
2377. EKONOMI, politik, samhälle; en bok tillägnad Bertil Ohlin på sextio-årsdagen. Redaktionskommitté: John Bergvall et al. Stockholm, Folk och samhälle, 1959. 305 p.
2378. EKONOMILIITTO. Ekonomimatrikkeli, 1960. Matrikkelitoimikunta: Valter Hämeen-Aalto, et al. Helsinki, 1961. 863 p.
2379. ESCHER, E. Harriet Martineau's sozialpolitischen novellen. Zurich, Thomas & Hubert, 1925.
2380. ESPEJEL Ontiveros, Félix. Algunas reflexiones sobre economía política. México, Escuela nacional de economía, U.N.A., 1957. 146 p.
2381. FESTSKRIFT til professor, dr. polit. Jørgen Pedersen. Aarhus, Universitetsforlaget, 1951. 194 p.
2382. FETTER, Frank Whitson. The economic writings of Francis Homer in the Edinburgh review, 1802-6. London, London school of economics and political science. University of London, 1957. vii, 134 p.
2383. FINER, S. E. The life and times of Sir Edwin Chadwick. London, Methuen, 1952.
2384. FISCHERSTROM, Johan. En gustaviansk dagbok; Johan Fischerströms anteckningar för året 1773. Utg. och kommenterade av Gustaf Näsström. Stockholm, Bröderna Lagerström, 1951. 169 p.
2385. FISHER, Irving Norton. A bibliography of the writings of Irving Fisher. New Haven, Yale university library, 1961. xii, 543 p.
2386. FLOREZ Estrada, Alvaro. Obras. Estudio preliminar y edición de Miguel Artolo Gallego. (Biblioteca de autores españoles desde la formación del lenguaje hasta nuestros dias continuación t. 112-113.) Madrid, Ediciones atlas, 1958. 2 v.
2387. FLOUZAT, Denise. L'etudiant économiste; études, carrières, documentation. Préf. de Jean Marchal. Paris, Cujas, 1962. 550 p.
2388. FLYNN, James J. The modern economists. New York, Distributed by Monarch press, 1965. 128 p.
2389. FRANCE, Conseil economique. Notices et portraits. Paris. v.
2390. FRANKLIN, Burt and G. Legman. David Ricardo and Ricardian Theory; a bibliographical checklist. (Burt Franklin bibliographical series, 10.) New York, Burt Franklin, 1949. vi, 88 p.
2391. FUJIHARA, Ginjirō. Yowatari kujūnen. (Transliterated.) Japan, 1960. 302 p.
2392. GANZONI, Eduard. Ferdinando Galiani; ein verkannter nationalökonom des 18. Jahrhunderts. Zurich, H. Girsberger, 1938. xii, 149. Bibliography, x-xii.
2393. GEARTY, Patrick William. The economic thought of Monsignor John A. Ryan. Washington, Catholic university of America press, 1953. viii, 341 p.
2394. GESELLSCHAFT fur wirtschafts- und sozialwissen-

schaften, verein fur socialpolitik. Die hochschullehrer der wirtschaftswissenschaften in der bundesrepublik Deutschland einschl. Westberlin, Osterreich und der deutschsprachigen Schweiz; Werdegang und Schriften. Berlin, Duncker & Humblot, 1959. xx, 515 p. (2. aufl. 1966. xxii, 842 p.)

2395. GORDON, BARRY J. Non-Ricardian political economy; five neglected contributions. (Kress library of business and economics, publication, no. 20.) Boston, Baker library, 1967. vii, 51 p.

2396. GREAT money reformers. No. 1-. London, Holborn publishing and distributing company, 1946? v.

2397. HARRIS, Seymour E. Schumpeter. Social scientist. Oxford, England. Oxford university press, 1951.

2398. HAYEK, F. A. John Stuart Mill and Harriet Taylor; their correspondence and subsequent marriage. Chicago, University of Chicago press, 1951. 320 p.

2399. HEILBRONER, Robert L. The worldly philosophers; the lives, times, and ideas of the great economic thinkers. New York, Simon and Schuster, 1953. 342 p. Bibliography, 320-326. (Revised for publication in England with two supplementary chapters by Paul Streeten. Entitled: The great economists. Their lives and their conceptions of the world. London, Eyre and Spottiswoode, 1955. 320 p. Revised edition: New York, Simon and Schuster, 1961. 309 p. Egyptian edition entitled: Qādat al-fīkr al-iqtisadī. Translated by Rashīd al-Barāwī. Cairo, Maktabat al-Nahdah al-Misrīyan, 1963. 387 p. French edition entitled: Les grands penseurs de la révolution économique. Paris, La Colombe, 1957. Korean edition entitled Gyeong'je'sa'sang'sa. (Transliterated.) Translated by Gim Yeong-rog. Seoul, Su'do'mun'hwasa, 1959. 356 p. Widaehan gyeongjehagjadeaul. Translated by Yeong-log Kim. Seoul, Sasanggyesa, 1962. 415 p. Swedish edition entitled: Utopister och samhallsomdanare. Stora ekonomiska tänkares liv och idéer. Translated by Anders Byttner. Stockholm, Natur och kultur, 1959. 303. Revised edition, Simon and Schuster, 1961. 309 p. 3rd edition, newly revised edition, Simon and Schuster, 1967. 320 p. New edition: London, Allen Lane, 1969. 320 p. Bibliography, 307-312.)

2400. HELMS, Lloyd Alvin. The contributions of Lord Overstone to the theory of currency and banking. (Illinois studies in social sciences, Volume 24, No. 4.) Urbana, Illinois, University of Illinois press, 1939. 142 p.

2401. HILL, Wilfrid. Footprints on the sands; an autobiography. London, P. R. Macmillan, 1957. 97 p.

2402. HIRST, Margaret E. Life of Friedrich List and selections from his writings. 1909. Reprinted: With an introduction by Joseph Dorfman and the addition of letter XII to Outlines of American political economy. New York, A. M. Kelley, 1965. xii, 335 p. Bibliography, 323-327.

2403. HOBSON, J. A. Confessions of an economic heretic. London, Allen & Unwin, 1938.
2404. HOLLANDER, Jacob H. David Ricardo. A centenary estimate. Baltimore, Johns Hopkins university press, 1910.
2405. ———. Introduction to "Notes on Malthus" by David Ricardo. Baltimore, Johns Hopkins university press, 1928.
2406. HORIE, Tadao. O-Bei no marukusushugi to minshurshugi. Japan, 1966. 262 p. Bibliographical references.
2407. HOUGH, Robbin R. What economists do. New York, Harper & Row, 1971. 128 p.
2408. HOWARD, Louise Ernestine (Matthaei). Sir Albert Howard in India. London, Faber and Faber, 1953. 272 p.
2409. HUME, David. Writings on economics. Edited and introduced by Eugene Rotwein. Madison, University of Wisconsin press, 1955. cxi, 224 p.
2410. HUTT, William Harold. Economists and the public; a study of competition and opinion. London, J. Cape, 1936. 377 p.
2411. ILLINOIS university. Edmund J. James lectures on government. 6th series. Urbana, University of Illinois press, 1954. 88 p.
2412. JAMES, Emile. John Bates Clark, 1847-1938, et John Maurice Clark, né en 1884. (Textes choisis.) (Collection des grands économistes.) Paris, Dalloz, 1947. 334 p.
2413. JESSOP, Thomas. A bibliography of David Hume and of Scottish philosophy. February 22, 1968.
2414. KAPLAN, Abraham David Hannath. Henry Charles Carey; a study in American economic thought. (Johns Hopkins university studies in historical and political science. Series XLIX, no. 4.) Baltimore, The Johns Hopkins press, 1931. 96 p. Bibliography, 91-93.
2415. KEYNES, John Maynard. Essays in biography. London, Macmillan; New York, Harcourt, Brace, 1933. 2 p. 1., vii-ix, 318 p. (New edition, with three additional essays, edited by Geoffrey Keynes. London, R. Hart-Davis; New York, Horizon press, 1951. 354 p. Paperback: New York, Norton, 1963. Enlarged edition: Essays and sketches in biography, including the complete text of Essays in biography, and two memoirs. New York, Meridian books, 1956. 347 p.)
2416. KHAN, Mohamed Shabbir. Schumpeter's theory of capitalist development. Aligiarh, Muslim University, 1957. viii, 175 p.
2417. KIMBALL, Janet. The economic doctrines of John Gray, 1799-1833. Washington, Catholic university of America press, 1948.
2418. KIRMIS, Alfred. August Friedrich Wilhelm Crome. Ein beitrag zur geschichte der deutschen nationalökonomie... Bern, Buchdr. G. Grunau, 1908. 162 p. Bibliography, 5-7. (Dissertation, Bern.)

2419. KLUCZYNSKI, Jan. Zawód ekonomisty w Polsce Ludowej; z prac Instytutu Gospodarstwa Spolecznego. Wyd. 1. Warszawa, Ksiażka i wiedza, 1966. 357 p.
2420. KOIZUMI, Shinzō. Kindai keizai shichō gaikan. Japan, 1949. 3, 2, 226 p. (2d edition, entitled: Kindai keisai shisō shi. 1952. 227 p.)
2421. KNOWLTON, Thomas Anson. The economic theory of Georg Bernard Shaw. (University of Maine studies. Second series, no. 39.) Orono, Maine, University press, 1936. v. 82 p. Bibliography, 76-80. (The Maine bulletin, Vol. xxxix, no. 4.)
2422. KOVER, J. F. Köpfe der wirtschaft; kleines bebildertes "who ist who" über führende persönlichkeiten der schweizerischen wirtschaft. 1 aufl. Zürich, Origo verlag, 1963. 223 p.
2423. LABRACHERIE, Pierre. Michel Chevalier et ses idées économiques. Dissertation, Paris, 1929.
2424. LEANDER, Lasse. Suomen talouselämän johtajia. Who's who in the economic life of Finland. Toimituskunta: Päiviö Hetemäki et al. Toimitus: Lasse Leander, Hillevi Stelander ja Erkki Merimen. Helsinki, Kirjayhtymä, 1965. 403 p.
2425. LEIMON, Melvin. Jacob N. Cardozo; economic thought in the antebellum South. New York, Columbia university press, 1966. 263 p. Bibliography.
2426. LIST of economic books and tracts, from the library of the Earl of Sheffield. University of London. Goldsmiths' library, 1908. 16 p. (Supplementary list, 1908. 4 p.)
2427. LOHMANN, Friedrich. Vauban, seine stellung in der geschichte der nationalökonomie und sein reformplan. Leipzig, Duncker & Humblot, 1895. 4, 172 p.
2428. MANFRA, Modestino Remigio. Pietro Verri e i problemi economici del tempo suo. Milano-Genova. Società anonima editrice Dante Alighieri. Albrighi, Segati & c., 1932. xii, 260 p. Bibliography.
2429. MANN, Fritz Karl. Der Marschall Vauban und die volkswirtschaftslehre des absolutismus, eine kritik des merkantilsystems. Munchen und Leipzig, Duncker & Humblot, 1914. xvi, 526 p. Bibliography.
2430. MARCY, G. Constantin Pecqueur. Fondateur du collectivisme d'Etat. Dissertation. Paris, University of Lille, 1934.
2431. MARSH, A. G. The economic library of Jacob H. Hollander. Baltimore, Private printing, J. H. Furst company, 1937. 3, v-xi, 324 p.
2432. MARSHALL, Alfred. The old generation of economists and the new. Cambridge, England, University press? 1897. 23 p.
2433. MCCOSH, James. The Scottish philosophy; biographical, expository, critical. From Hutcheson to Hamilton. London, Macmillan and company, 1875.
2434. MCCULLOCH, John Ramsay. A catalogue of books, the property of a political economist. With critical and bibliographical notices. London, 1862. vi-viii, 394 p.

2435. MCEVOY, Helena Mitchell. A complete concordance to the twenty-fifth and fiftieth anniversary editions of Progress and poverty by Henry George. Chicago, Ability press, 1959. 729 p.
2436. MEEK, R. L. Thomas Joplin and the rate of interest. In, Review of economic studies, 3rd series, 17, 47 (1950-51).
2437. MILL, John Stuart. The collected works. Edited by J. I. P. Robson. Toronto, University of Toronto press, 1963.
2438. ———. Stuart Mill; textes choisis et préf. par François Trévoux. (Collection des grands économistes.) Paris, Dalloz, 1953. 372 p.
2439. MITCHELL, Broadus. Great economists in their times. (Littlefield quality paperbacks, 56.) Totowa, New Jersey, Littlefield, Adams, 1966. xix, 236 p. Bibliographies.
2440. MITCHELL, Lucy (Sprague.) Two lives; the story of Wesley Clair Mitchell and myself. New York, Simon and Schuster, 1953. 575 p.
2441. MITCHELL, Wesley. "J. Laurance Laughlin." In, the journal of political economy, XL (December, 1941.)
2442. MONTENEGRO, Abelardo Fernando. A missao do economista no Brasil. Fortaleza, 1957. 50 p.
2443. MORLEY, John. The life of Richard Cobden. London, 1881. 2 vols.
2444. MULCAHY, Richard E. The economics of Heinrich Pesch. New York, Holt, c1952. xii, 228 p. Bibliography, 189-206.
2445. MOSSNER, Ernest Campbell. The life of David Hume. Edinburgh, Nelson, 1954.
2446. MURRAY, David. Memories of the old College of Glasgow. (Glasgow university publications, no. III.) Glasgow, Jackson, Wylie and Company, 1927.
2447. NONOMURA, Kazuo. Gakusha shōbal. Japan, 1960. iii, 213 p.
2448. NORTON, Hugh Stanton. The role of the economist in government; a study of economic advice since 1920. Berkeley, California, McCutchan Publishing Corporation, 1969. xii, 241 p.
2449. O'BRIEN, Dennis Patrick. J. R. McCulloch; a study in classical economics. New York, Barnes and Noble, 1970. 452 p.
2450. O'BRIEN, G. "J. S. Mill and J. E. Cairnes." Economica (November, 1943.)
2451. OHARA, Keiji. Amerika keizai shisō no choryu. Japan, 1951. 4, 4, 397, 8 p. Bibliographical footnotes.
2452. OPIE, Redvers. "A neglected British economist. George Poulett Scrope." In, Quarterly journal of economics (November, 1929.)
2453. OTARU Shoka Daigaku. Catalogue de la bibliotheque du professeur Gustave Schelle de l'Universite du commerce d'Otaru. Otaru, Universite du commerce d'Otaru, 1962. 2, 101, 13 p.
2454. OUCHI, Hyoe, Keizaigaku sampo. (Transliterated.) Japan,

1948. 408 p. Bibliography, 405-408. (Reprinted: 1952. 408 p.)

2455. PANKHURST, R. K. P. William Thompson, 1775-1833. London, Watts, 1954.

2456. PAPPE, H. O. "Wakefield and Marx." In, Economic history review. Second series, 4, 1 (1951.)

2457. PARAHYBA, Brazil (State) universidade federal. Faculdade de ciências econômicas de campina grande. Endereços; reitoria de UFPB e unidades filiadas, FACE, reitoria da FURN e unidades filiadas e outras unidades. Campina Grande, 1968. 48 l.

2458. PETTY, Sir William. The economic writings of Sir William Petty. . . . Edited by Charles Henry Hall. New York, A. M. Kelley, 1963-64. 2 v.

2459. PHILIPPE, Jules Aimé. Las doctrinas económicas, traducción del capitán A. Ponce; comprendio destinado al uso de los oficiales de todas las armas y todos los servicios. Cochabamba, Bolivia, Universidad autónoma de Cochabamba 1939. viii, 84 p.

2460. PIGOU, Arthur Cecil. A. C. Pigou. Traduction, introd. et notes par G.-H. Bousquet. (Collection des grands économistes.) Paris, Dalloz, 1958. 415 p.

2461. PLUMMER, A. "Sir Edward West, 1782-1828." In, Journal of political economy. (October, 1929.)

2462. POOL, Arthur George. Economists and social policy; an inaugural lecture delivered at the University College of Leicester, 17th January 1952. Leicester, England, University College, 1952. 20 p.

2463. PROUDHON, Pierre Joseph. Carnets. Texte inédit et intégral établi sur les manuscrits autographes avec annotations et appareil critique de Pierre Haubtmann; préf. de Daniel Halévy, présentation de Suzanne Henneguy et Jeann Fauré-Fremiet. Paris, M. Rivière, 1960. v.

2464. ———. Lettres à sa femme. Préf. de Suzanne Henneguy. Paris, B. Grasset, 1950. 315 p.

2465. ———. P. J. Proudhon; textes choisis, présentés et commentés par J. Lajugie. (Collection des grandes économistes.) Paris, Dalloz, 1953. 492 p.

2466. ———. La proprietà; traduzione e note di A. Klitsche de la Grange. (Scienze politiche e social.) Roma, O. E. T 194- ? 190 p.

2467. QUINTEROS Delgado, Juan Carlos. Andrés Lamas, economista; conferencia dada en el Instituto histórico y Geográfico del Uruguay el 6 de Setiembre del 1949. Montevideo, Florensa & Lafon, 1949. 22 p.

2468. RANDALL, Clarence Belden. Over my shoulder; a reminiscence. Boston, Little, Brown, 1956. 248 p.

2469. RECKTENWALD, Horst Claus. Lebensbilder grosser national ökonomen; einführung in die geschichte der politischen ökonomie. Köln, Kiepenheuer & Witsch, 1965. 666 p.

2470. REID, James MacArthur. James Lithgow; master of work. London, Hutchinson, 1964. 254 p.

2471. RENWICK, Cyril. Economists and their environment. A series of lectures given for the economic society of Australia and New Zealand, N. S. W. branch, Sydney, Economic society of Australia and New Zealand, New South Wales branch, 1947. 50 p.
2472. REYMANN, Heinz. Glaube und wirtschaft bei Luther. Gütersloh, C. Bertelsmann, 1934. 3, 9-116 p. Bibliography, 111-116.
2473. RICARDO, David. Works and correspondence. Edited by Piero Sraffa, with the collaboration of M. H. Dobb. Cambridge, England, University press for the Royal economic society, 1951-55. 10 v.
2474. RICCI, Umberto. Tre economisti Italiani: Pantaleoni, Pareto, Loria. Bari, Guis, Laterza & Figli, 1939.
2475. RING, Mary Ignatius, Sister. Villeneuve-Bargemont, precursor of modern social Catholicism, 1784-1850. Milwaukee, The Bruce publishing company, 1935. xxxiii, 265 p.
2476. RITZEL, Gerhard and Albert Johannes. Schmoller versus Menger; eine analyse des Methodenstreits im Hinblick auf den Historismus in der national oekonomie. Frankfurt am Main, 1950. 148 p. Bibliography, 141-148.
2477. RIVENBERG, N. E. Harriet Martineau. An example of victorian conflict. Philadelphia, 1932.
2478. ROBBINS, Lionel Charles. The autobiography of an economist. London, MacMillan, 1971.
2479. _____. The economist in the twentieth century, and other lectures in political economy. London, Macmillan; New York, Saint Martin's press, 1954. 224 p.
2480. ROBINSON, Joan. Marx, Marshall, and Keynes. (Delhi school of economics. Occasional papers, no. 9.) Delhi, Delhi school of economics, University of Delhi, 1955. 30 p.
2481. RUBEL, Maximilien. Bibliographie des oeuvres de Karl Marx. Avec en appendice repertoire des oeuvres de Friedrich Engels. Ouvrage publie avec le concous du national de la recherche scientifique. Paris, Riviere, 1956. 272 p.
2482. RUS'AN, H. Ibnu Chaldun tentang sosial ekonomi; beberapa teori, disusa Djakarta, Bulan Bintang, 1963. 167 p.
2483. RUSKIN, John. I diritti del lavoro (Unto this last.) Traduzione con uno studio introduttivo e note di F. Villani. (Biblioteca di cultura moderna, n. 395.) Bari, Laterza, 1946. xii, 222 p.
2484. NO ENTRY
2485. SAMUELSON, Paul A. Collected scientific papers. Edited by Joseph E. Stiglitz. Cambridge, Massachusetts, M. I. T. press, 1965. 2 v.
2486. _____. "Economists and the history of ideas." In, American economic review, 52 (March, 1962) 1-18.
2487. SCHULTZ, Bruno Ladislaus. Die grundgedanken des systems der theoretischen volkswirtschaftslehre von Franz Oppenheimer. Jena, G. Fischer, 1948. vi, 32 p.

2488. SCHUMPETER, Joseph Alois. Ten great economists, from Marx to Keynes. New York, Oxford university press, 1951. xiv, 305 p. Bibliographical footnotes. (London, Allen & Unwin, 1952. xiv, 305 p. Egyptian edition entitled: 'Asharah min a'immat al-iqtisad min markis ila kinz. Translated by Husin 'Umar and Muraga'at 'Abd al-Aziz Miri. Cairo, Maktabit al-Sharq bel-Fajjalan, 1959. 273 p. Italian edition entitled: Epoche di storia delle dottrine e dei metodi. Dieci grandi economisti. Translated by Giuseppe Brauguier Pacini. Turin, Unione tipografico-editrice Torinese, 1953. xii, 472. Japanese edition entitled: Ju dai keizai-gakusha. (Transliterated.) Translated by Ichiro Nahayama and Seiichi Tohata. Tokyo, Nihon Hyoron shin-sha, 1952. 450 p. Portuguese edition entitled: 10 grandes economistas. Rio de Janeiro, Editora civilizacao Brasileira, 1958. Spanish edition entitled: Diez grandes economistas. De Marx a Keynes. Translated by Fabian Estapo. Barcelona, Jose Ma. Bosch, 1955. xx, 381 p. Swedish edition entitled: Stora nationalekonomer. Translated by Anders Byttner. Stockholm, Natur och kultur, 1953. 353 p. Reprinted: Galaxy book, 140. Oxford university press, 1965. 305 p. Paperback.)

2489. SCHUTZE, G. H. Die Lehre von der verteilung in der volkwirtschaft bei Thomas Hodgskin. Leipzig, Ernst' sche vertlh., 1930.

2490. SCOTT, W. R. Francis Hutcheson. His life, teaching and position in the history of philosophy. Cambridge, England, University press, 1900.

2491. ———. "William Cunningham." In, Proceedings of the British Academy (1919-1920.)

2492. SEN, Samar Ranjan. The economics of Sir James Steuart. London, London school of economics and political science, University of London, 1957. 207 p.

2493. SHACKLE, George Lennox Sharman. What makes an economist? Liverpool, University press, 1953. 23 p.

2494. SHIH, Chien-shêng. Tang tai ching chi mu ch'ao. (Transliterated.) China, 1956. v.

2495. SICKESZ, W. Het had anders gekund. Mémoires, 1914-1955. Amsterdam, H. J. W. Becht, 1955. 342 p.

2496. SINHA, A. K. and K. Klostermaier. Masters of social thought. Agra, Lakshmi narain agarwal, 1966. 394 p.

2497. SMITH, Norman Kemp. The philosophy of David Hume. A critical study of its origins and central doctrines. London, Macmillan, 1949.

2498. SOMARY, Felix. Erinnerungen aus meinem Leben. Zürich, Manesse verlag, 1959. 415 p.

2499. SOTIROFF, G. "John Barton, 1789-1852." In, Economic journal (March 1953.)

2500. SOVESCHANIE za "kruglym stolom," Moscow, 1964. (Mathematical economists.) Moscow, 1965. 206 p.

2501. SPRING, D. "Earl Fitzwilliam and the corn laws." In, American Historical Review (June, 1954.)

2502. STIGLER, G. J. "The economist and the state." In, American economic review, 55 (March, 1965) 1-18.
2503. STONE, Richard Gabriel. Hezekiah Niles as an economist. (The Johns Hopkins university studies in historical and political science. . . ser. LI, no. 5.) Baltimore, The Johns Hopkins press, 1933. 137 p. Bibliography, 131-133 p. (Dissertation, Johns Hopkins university.)
2504. SWANN E. Christopher North. Edinburgh, Oliver and Boyd, 1934.
2505. SZUBERT, Wacław. Studia o Fryderyku Skarbku jako ekonomiście. Wyd. 1. (Uniwersytet Lodzki. Prace z historii mysli społecznej. t. 3.) Łódź, Zakład im. Ossolińskich we Wrocławiu, 1954. 175 p.
2506. TAKEUCHI, Kenji. Goyaku. (Transliterated.) Japan, 1964. 216 p.
2507. TAKAHASHI, Seiichirō. Keizalgaku; waga shi, waga tomo. (Transliterated.) Japan, 1956. 230 p.
2508. TAYLOR, William Leslie. Francis Hutcheson and David Hume as predecessors of Adam Smith. Durham, North Carolina, Duke university press, 1965. x, 180 p. Bibliography, 171-175.
2509. ———. "Gershom Carmichael; a neglected figure in British political economy." In, The South African journal of economics, XXIII (September, 1955.) 251-255.
2510. ———. "A short life of Sir James Steuart; political economist." In, The South African journal of economics, XXV (September, 1957.) 290-302.
2511. THOMAS, Ernst. Graf Georg von Buquoy; ein beitrag zur geschichte der deutschen nationalökonomie am anfang des 19. jahrhunderts. München and Leipzig, Duncker & Humblot, 1929. 4, 95 p. Bibliography, 92-95.
2512. THOMAS, P. Félix. Pierre Leroux, sa vie, son oeuvre, sa doctrine. Paris, 1904.
2513. THUNEN, Johann Heinrich von. Ausgewählte texte, ausgewählt und kommentiert von Walter Braeuer. (Die grossen sozialökonomen, Bd. 7.) Meisenheim, Glan, A. Hain, c1951. lxii, 309 p.
2514. TOURNYOL Du Clos, Jean. Les idées financières de Montesquieu. New York, Burt Franklin, 1970. 24 p.
2515. UNITED STATES. Bureau of labor statistics. Educational requirements for employment of economists. Washington, Veterans administration, 1955. iii, 11 p.
2516. UPPSALA. Universitet. Inbjudan till de offentliga högtidligheter vid vilka professorn. . . Ragnar Holte, . . . Ragnar Bentzel installeras i sina ambeten av Torgny T. Segerstedt. . . . (Skrifter rörande Uppsala universitet. B: Inbjudningar, 20.) Uppsala, Stockholm, Almquist & Wiksell, 1966. 19 p.
2517. VACIC, Aleksandar M. Pregled radova objavljenih u "Ekonomistu" u periodu 1948-1967. Glavni i odgovorni urednik Jakov Sirotković. Zagreb, "Ekonomist," organ Saveza ekonomista Jugoslavije, 1968. 147 p.
2518. VALERY, Paul Ambroise. Ecrits divers sur Stéphane

Mallarmé. Paris, Editions de la N. R. F., c1950. 158 p.

2519. VALLE, José Cecilio del. El pensamiento economico de José Cecilio del Valle. (Publicaciones del Banco central de Honduras.) Edición commemorativa de la inauguración del edificio del Banco. Tegucigalpa, 1958. 205 p.

2520. VEREIN für sozialpolitik, Gesellschaft für wirtschafts- und sozialwissenschaften. Die hochschullehrer der wirtschaftswissenschaften in der bundesrepublik Deutschland einschl. Westberlin, Osterreich und der deutschsprachigen Schweiz; Werdegang und Schriften. Berlin, Duncker & Humblot, 1959. xx, 515 p.

2521. VIKOR, Desider. Austrian romantic school; Adam Mueller, Spann, and the present universalists. Ann Arbor, Michigan, University microfilms, 1960.

2522. ———. Economic romanticism in the twentieth century. Spann's attempt to revolutionize economic theory. New Delhi, New book society of India, 1964. 200 p. Bibliography.

2523. VILLEY, Daniel. La vie, l'oeuvre et la doctrine de Charles Brook Dupont-White. Caen, University of Caen, 1936. v. 1.

2524. VILLEY-Desmeserets, Edmond Louis. L'oeuvre économique de Charles Dunoyer. (Ouvrage récompensé par l'Institut.) Paris, L. Larose, 1899. 2 p. 1., 388 p.

2525. WADA, Zentrō. Marukusu-shugi no ronsen. (Transliterated.) Japan, 1966. 245 p.

2526. WALCH, Jean. Bibliographie de Saint-Simonisme, avec trois textes inedits. 1967.

2527. WALLAS, Graham. The life of Francis Place. New York, Burt Franklin, 1951.

2528. WATTS, Vervon Orval. Away from freedom; the revolt of the college economists. Los Angeles, Foundation for social research, 1952. iii, 105 p.

2529. WEBER, Hans. Richard Jones. Ein früher englischer abtrunniger der klassischen schule der national ökonomie. Zürich, H. Girsberger, 1939.

2530. WETZEL, William Achenbach. Benjamin Franklin as an economist. (Johns Hopkins university studies in historical and political science. 13th series, ix.) Baltimore, The Johns Hopkins press, 1895. 58 p. Bibliography, 57-58.

2531. WIEDENFELD, Kurt. Zwischen wirtschaft und staat; aus den lebenserinnerungen. Aus dem nachgelassenen manuskript Kurt Wiedenfelds hrsg. von Friedrich Bülow. Berlin, W. de Gruyter, 1960. 238 p.

2532. WILBRANDT, Robert. Ihr glücklichen augen; lebenserinnerungen. Stuttgart, F. Mittelbach, 1947. 358 p.

2533. WILLIAMSON, H. F. "The economics profession today." In, J. R. Coleman, The changing American economy. London, New York, Basic books, 1967.

2534. WILLS, Elbert Vaughan. Dr. Thomas Cooper, economist. Portsmouth, Virginia. National printing company, 1917. 24 p.

2535. WOLFF, Sam de. Voor het land van belofte; een terugblik op mijn leven. Bussum, G. J. A. Ray, 1954. 300 p.
2536. WOYTINSKY, Wladimir S. Writings. 1905-60. 31 v.
2537. WRIGHT, David McCord. The economic library of the president of the Bank of the United States, 1819-23. Charlottesville, Bibliographical society of the University of Virginia, 1950. 15 p.
2538. WURST, Adolf. A. Thiers' volkswirtschaftliche anschauunger. Jena, G. Fischer, 1893. vi, 89 p.
2539. WYROZEMBSKI, Zygmunt Jan. Dawid Ricardo; studium historyczno-teoretyczne. Wyd. 1. Warszawa, Państwowe wydawn. Naukowe, 1959. 660 p.

E. COUNTRIES AND AREAS *

AFRICA

2540. WHETHAM, Edith Holt and Jean T. Currie. The economics of African countries. London, England. Cambridge university press, 1969. x, 288 p.

ARAB COUNTRIES

2541. KHURI, Ra'īf. al-Fikr al-'Arabī al-ḥadīth. (Transliterated.) 1943. 289 p. Bibliographical footnotes.

ARGENTINA

2542. ALVARADO, Carlos M. Doctrinas economicas; compemento al libro de Julio A. Decoud, economia politica y argentina. Buenos Aires, Editorial dovile, 1943. 129, 1 p.
2543. BURGIN, Miron. The economic aspects of Argentine federalism, 1820-1852. Cambridge, Massachusetts, Harvard university press, 1946. xiv, 304 p. Bibliography, 288-294.
2544. RODRIGUEZ, Juan Carlos. Una nueva clasificacion de los sistemas economicos y sus escuelas. Buenos Aires, Imprenta Caporaletti hnos., 1935. 69, 2 p.

ASIA

2545. ALESHINA, Iraida Vasil'evna. Fal'sifikatory sotsiallzma. (Transliterated.) Leningrad, 1963. 294 p.
2546. ONO, Shinzō. Bukkyō shakai-keizaigakusetsu no kenkyū. (Transliterated.) Japan, 1956. iv, v, 640 p. Bibliographical footnotes.

AUSTRALIA

2547. COPLAND, Douglas Berry. William Edward Hearn: first Australian economist; the Murtagh Macrossan lectures in the University of Queensland, 1935. Melbourne, Melbourne university press in association with Oxford university press, London, New York, 1935. 80 p.
2548. GOODWIN, Craufurd D. W. Economic enquiry in Australia. (Duke University Commonwealth-Studies Center. Publi-

---
*See also APPENDIX, at end of book, covering Belgium, the Netherlands, Portugal, and Spain through 1891.

cation no. 24). Durham, North Carolina, published for Duke University Commonwealth-Studies Center by Duke University Press, 1966. xv, 659 p. Bibliographical footnotes.

2549. LA NAUZE, John Andrew. Political economy in Australia; historical studies. Carlton, Melbourne University Press, 1949. 136 p. (19th century: Jevons in Sydney. Hern and economic optimism. Bibliography of David Syme.)

AUSTRIA

2550. COENEN, Etienne. La "Konjunkturforschung" en Allemagne et en Autriche, 1925-1933. Universite catholique de Louvain. Faculté des sciences économiques et sociales. (Collection de l'Ecole des sciences économiques, No. 87.) Louvain, Editions Nauwelaerts, 1964. vii, 352 p. Bibliography: p. 331-341.

2551. HOFMANN, Heinrich. Der produktivitätsbegriff in der modernen deutschen und österreichischen volkswirtschaftslehre. Tübingen, Buchdruckerei E. Göbel, 1929. viii, 61, 1 p. Bibliography, vii-viii. (Inaugural dissertation, Tübingen.)

2552. SCHMACHTENBERG, Barbara. Die Gedanken zur wirtschaftlichen Erziehung in den Schriften der frühen österreichischen Merkantilisten. Frankfurt-am-Main, ? 1968. 242 p. Bibliography, 226-242. (Inaugural dissertation, Frankfurt-am-Main.)

2553. SOMMER, Louise. Die österreichischen Kameralisten in dogmengeschichtlicher Darstellung. Neudruck der Ausg. Wien 1920-1925. Zwei Teile in einem Band. (Studien zur Sozial-, Wirtschafts- und Verwaltungsgeschichte, Heft 12, 13.)Aalen, Scientia-Verlag, 1967. xx, 106, 507 p. Bibliography, 492-507.

2554. VIKOR, Desider. Economic romanticism in the twentieth century; Spann's attempt to revolutionize economic theory. 1st edition. New Delhi, New Book Society of India, 1964. 200 p. Bibliography, 171-188. (List of publications of Othmar Spann. Literature on Spann, 171-181).

2555. WEBER, Wilhelm. Wirtschaftswissenschaft und Wirtschaftspolitik in Osterreich. Wien, Springer, 1949. 85 p.

2556. WIEN-CLAUDI, Franz. Austrian theories of capital, interest, and the trade-cycle. London, S. Nott, ltd., 1936. vi, 7-176 p. Bibliography, 175-176.

BELGIUM

2557. BELGIUM. Ministère des affaires économiques et de l'énergie. Direction générale des études et de la documentation. Organisation du Ministère des affaires économiques et de l'énergie. Inrichting van het Ministerie van Economische Zaken en Energie. 9 éd. Bruxelles, 1963. 131 p.

2558. MICHOTTE, Paul L. Etudes sur les théories économiques

qui dominerent en Belgique de 1830 à 1886. (Bibliothèque de l'Ecole des sciences politiques et sociales de Louvain. 27.) Louvain, C. Peeters, 1904. xxii, 472 p. Bibliographie; xiii-xxii.

BRAZIL

2559. CONGRESSO Brasileiro dos Economistas, 1st, Rio de Janeiro and Recife, 1968. A economia e os economistas brasileiros; a economia a serviço do progresso do humanidade. Rio de Janeiro, Instituto de Politica Econômica, 1968? 194 p.
2560. GRACA, Arnoble. Economia política e economia brasileira. Sao Paulo, Saraiva, 1962. 339 p.
2561. PAULA, Luis Nogueira de. Sintese da evolução do pensamento econômico no Brasil; ciclo de conferências proferidas na Universidade de Montevidéu pelo professor Luiz Nogueira de Paula em missão cultural do governo brasileiro. Rio de Janeiro, Serviço de Estatística da Previdência e Trabalho, Ministério de Trabalho, Indústria e Comércio, 1942. 198 p.
2562. [NO ENTRY]

BULGARIA

2563. GRIGOROV, K. I. Razvitie na buržoaznata ikonômiceska misal v Bălgarija meždu dvete svetovni vojni. Sofija, Nauka i izkustvo, 1960. 193 p.
2564. GOROV, Kiril Zhelev. Ikonomicheskite vŭzgledi na G. S. Rakovski. Sophia, 1962. 183, 3 p. Bibliography, 180-184. (Georgi Stoĭkov Rakovski, 1821-1867).
2565. NATAN, Zhak. Istoriia na ikonomicheskata misui v Bulgariia. (Transliterated.) Sophia, 1964. 359 p. Bibliography, 349-358.

CANADA

2566. GOODWIN, Craufurd D. W. Canadian economic thought; the political economy of a developing nation, 1814-1914. (Duke University, Commonwealth-Studies Center. Publication no. 15.) Durham, North Carolina, Published for the Duke University Commonwealth-Studies Center by Duke University Press, 1961. xvi, 214 p. Bibliographical footnotes. (Thesis, Duke University.)
2567. LOWER, Arthur Reginald Marsden. The development of Canadian economic ideas. In (supplement with) João Frederico Normano, The spirit of American economics; . . . A publication of the Committee on the study of economic thought. (Studies in the history of economic thought, v. 1.) New York, Distributed by the John Day Company, 1943. 5 p. 1., 13-252 p., 2 1. Bibliographical footnotes.

CHILE

2568. SUBERCASEAUX, Guillermo. Historia de las doctrinas económicas en América y en especial en Chile. Santiago de Chile, Soc. imp. y lit. universo, 1924. 143, 2 p. La literatura económica chilena, 123-128.

CHINA

2569. CHEN Huan-chang. The economic principles of Confucius and his school. (Studies in history, economics and public law, ed. by the Faculty of political science of Columbia university, vol. XLIV-XLV; whole no. 112-113). New York, Columbia university, Longmans, Green & Co., agents, 1911. 2 v.

2570. CHIANG, Kai-shek. China's destiny and Chinese economic theory. With notes and commentary by Philip Jaffe. New York, Roy publishers, 1947. 347 p. (French edition entitled: Destin de la Chine et la théorie économique chinoise. . . . Paris, Amiot-Dumont, 1949. 293 p.

2571. ———. Chung-kuo ching chi hsüeh shuo. (Transliterated.) China, 1954. 78 p. (Same title: 1945. 32 p.)

2572. ENCHES, Evelyn Leslie. The economic principles of the Confucian school. Pasadena, California, 1935. 2 p. 1., 29 numb. 1. Bibliography, leaf 29. (Reproduced from typewritten copy. Written, December 1934; revised, June 1935.)

2573. HORI, Shin'ichi. Keizaigaku to Tōyō shisō. (Transliterated.) Japan, 1965. 8, 391 p. Bibliographies.

2574. HSIA, Yen-tê. Chung-kuo chin pai nien ching chi ssŭ hsiang. (Transliterated.) China, 1948. 2, 3, 202 p.

2575. HSIUNG, Meng. Wan Chou chu tzu ching chi ssŭ hsiang shih. (Transliterated.) China, 1936. 1, 1. 176 p.

2576. HU, Chi-ch'uang. Chung-kuo ching chi ssu hsiang shih. (Transliterated.) China, 1962- . v. Bibliographical footnotes.

2577. KAN, Nai-kuang. Hsien Ch'in ching chi ssŭ hsiang shih. (Transliterated.) China, 1927. 138 p.

2578. KUAN, Chang. Economic thought in ancient China; economic selections from Kuan-tsŭ 300 B.C., with modern commentaries by Huang Han and Fan Ping-t'ung. All three translated by T'an Po-fu and Wen Kung-wen (Adam K. W. Wen) the translation directed and the work edited by Lewis A. Maverick, Carbondale. Illinois. 1947-1950. Manuscript presented for publication, 1950. MMS. 586 p. Bibliographies. Made by Photographic Service, Southern Illinois University, Carbondale.

2579. KUO, Yüan. Kuo shih shang ti li ts'ai chia. (Transliterated.) China, 1954. 202 p.

2580. LIU, Shao-fu. Chung-kuo ching chi ssŭ hsiang shih. (Transliterated.) China, 1960. 371 p.

2581. LY, Siou Y. Les grands courants de la pensée économique chinoise dans l'antiquité (du VIe au IIIe siècle avant J.-C.)

et leur influence sur la formation de la doctrine physiocratique. Paris, Jouve & cie, 1936. 107 p. Bibliographie. 95-105. (These--Dijon.)
2582. OTTE, Friedrich W. K. Bemerkungen zur angewandten wirtschaftswissenschaft in China. (Mitteiliunger des Seminars für orientalische sprachen zu Berlin. Jahrgang XXXIII. Ostasiatisch studien. Sonderabdruck.) Berlin, 1930. 1 p. 1., p. 137-154.
2583. T'ANG, Ch'ing-tsêng. Chung-kuo ching chi ssŭ hsiang shih. (Transliterated.) China, 1936. 2, 5, 1, 2, 11, 411 p. (No more published?)
2584. TAZAKI, Masayoshi. Chung-kuo ku tai ching chi ssŭ hsiang chi chih tu. (Transliterated.) China 1936. 2, 4, 346 p. (Translation of: Shina kodai keizai shisō oyobi seido.) (Transliterated.) Translated by Hsueh-wen Wang.
2585. WU, Pao-san, Tse Fêng, and Chao-lin Wu. Chung-kuo chin tai ching chi ssŭ hsiang, 1840-1864. (Transliterated.) China, 1959. x, 512 p.

CHINA (PEOPLE'S REPUBLIC OF CHINA, 1949-)

2586. DONNITHORNE, Audrey. China's economic system. New York, Frederick A. Praeger, inc., 1967.
2587. KOZUMA, Takae. Mō Taku-tō no keizai shisō to kanri kakumei. (Transliterated.) (Tōa keizai kenkyū sōsho, dai 1-shū.) Japan, 1967. 81 p. Bibliographical notes.
2588. PERKINS, Dwight H. Market control and planning in Communist China. Cambridge, Harvard university press, 1966.
2589. PRYBYLA, Jan S. The political economy of Communist China. (Series in economics.) Scranton, Pennsylvania, International textbook company, 1970. ix, 605 p.
2590. SCHURMANN, Herbert F. Ideology and organization in Communist China. Berkeley, University of California press, 1966.
2591. WU, Yuan-Li. The economy of Communist China. New York, Frederic A. Praeger, inc., 1965.

COLOMBIA

2592. ECHAVARRIA Olózaga, Hernán. El sentido común en la economía colombiana. 2. ed. Bogotá, Impr. Nacional, 1958. 404 p.
2593. ESPINOSA, Augusto. El pensamiento económico y político en Colombia (apuntes sobre su evolución.) (Tesis para recibir el grado de doctor en derecho y ciencias políticas y sociales, Universidad national de Colombia.) Bucaramanga, Imprenta del departamento, 1942. 3 p. 1., 198 p. Indice bibliográfico, 191-198.
2594. GOMEZ, Eugenio J. Ideas económicas y fiscales de Colombia. (Problems colombianos, t. 6.) Bogotá, Editorial santafé, 1949. 432 p.
2595. POPESCU, Oreste. Desarrollo y planeamiento en el pensamiento económico colombiano; una nota. (El presente

trabajo fue publicado . . . en la Revista del Colegio major de nuestra Señora del Rosario, Bogotá, vol. LVII, no. 475, julio y agosto de 1967.) Bogotá, 1968. Bibliographical footnotes.

COMMUNIST COUNTRIES

2596. BROMKE, Adam, editor. The communist states at the crossroads. New York, Frederick A. Praeger, inc., 1965.
2597. FEIWEL, George R., editor. New currents in Soviet-type economies. A Reader. Scranton, Pennsylvania, International textbook company, 1968. (Reprinted, 1969.)
2598. HABA, Zdeněk. Stúdia o ekonomických zákonoch a ich pôsobení v prechodnom období k socializmu. (Oeskoslovenská akadémia vied. Ekonomický ústav SAV.) Bratislava, Vydavateľstvo Slovenskej akadémie vied, 1962. 277 p. Bibliography.
2599. KAIDO, Susumu. Shakaishugi kigyō keizaigaku. (Transliterated.) Japan, 1961. 185 p.
2600. WELLISZ, Stanislaus C. The economy of the Soviet bloc. New York, McGraw-Hill book company, 1967.

CUBA

2601. ALVAREZ DIAZ, José R. Cuba. Geopolítica y pensamiento económico. Miami, 1964. 576 p. Bibliographical footnotes.
2602. CASTRO RUZ, Fidel. Political, economic and social thought of Fidel Castro. Havana, Editorial lex, 1959. 219 p.

CZECHOSLOVAK REPUBLIC

2603. STADNIK, Miloš. (Economic history, Czechoslovak Republic.) Theses for Harvard. Translated from the Czech by V. Jindra. Praha, Economic institute of the Czechoslovak academy of sciences, 1968. 171 p. Bibliographical footnotes.

DENMARK

2604. BISGAARD, Holger Ludvig. Den danske nationaløkonomi i det 18. århundrede, et afsnit af nationaløkonomiens historie i Danmark. . . København, H. Hagerup, 1902. 188 p., 1 l. (Inaugural dissertation, Copenhagen.)
2605. GELTING, J. H. "Recent trends in economic thought in Denmark." In American economic review, 54, 4 (June 1964) 65-78.
2606. NIELSEN, Axel Eduard Hjorth, Erik Arup, O. H. Larsen, and Albert Olsen. Dänische wirtschaftsgeschichte, unter mitarbeit. (Handbuch der wirtschaftsgeschichte, hrsg. von dr. Georg Brodnitz.) Jena, G. Fischer, 1933. 4 p. l., 600 p. Bibliographie, 583-593.

ESTONIA

2607. KRINAL, V., Leida Loone, ja I. Soidra. Majundusliku motte pohijooni kodanlikus Eestis, 1920-1940. (Eesti NSV Teaduste Akadeemia majanduse instituut.) Tallinn, Eesti raamat, 1968. 255, 1 p. Bibliographical footnotes.

EUROPE

2608. BEZOBRAZOV, Vladimir Pavlovich. O viĭänïi ékonomicheskoĭ nauki na gosudarstvennufū zhizñ. (Transliterated.) Moscow, 1867. 31 p.
2609. BIRNIE, Arthur. An economic history of Europe, 1760-1930. London, Methuen & company, ltd., 1930. xi, 289, 1 p.
2610. ———. Historia económica de Europa, 1760-1933; versión española revisada por Daniel Cosio Villegas. México, Fondo de cultura económica, 1938. 2 p. l., vii-xii, 365 p., 5 l. Bibliographie 367-371.
2611. ———. Histoire économique de l'Europe, 1760-1932. Préface de Roger Picard. Edition française par Pierre Coste. (Bibliothèque historique.) Paris, Payot, 1932. 390 p. Bibliographie, 385-388.
2612. BLANQUI, Jérôme Adolphe. Histoire de l'économie politique en Europe depuis les anciens jusqu'à nos jours. 5. édition. Paris, Guillaumin et cie, 1882. xvi, 511 p. (1st edition, 1838. English edition entitled: History of political economy in Europe. Translated from the fourth French edition by Emily Josephine Leonard, with a preface by David A. Wells, appendix and index by translator. New York and London, G. P. Putnam's sons, 1885. xxxviii, 585 p. Reprinted: A. M. Kelley, 1968. xxxviii, 585 p. Reprint of 1880 edition. The edition of 1860 contained Blanqui's Bibliographie des principaux ouvrages d'economie politique.)
2613. BOWDEN, Witt, Michael Karpovich, and Abbott Payson Usher. An economic history of Europe since 1750. Cincinnati, American book company, 1937. viii, 948. (Reprint of 1937 edition. New York, H. Fertig; New York, AMS press, 1970. viii, 948. Bibliography, 885-924.)
2614. BREMS, H. "Current economic thought and its application and methodology in continental Europe. The Scandinavian countries." In, American economic review 46, 2 (May, 1956) 352-359.
2615. BURKS, Robert V., editor. The future of Communism in Europe. Detroit, Wayne state university press, 1968.
2616. CH'IEN, I-shih. Ch'an yeh ko ming chiang hua. (Transliterated.) China, 1950. 166 p.
2617. DABROWSKI, Zdzisław. Makroekonomiczny rachunek gospodarki kapitalistycznej. (Wyższa szkoła ekonomiczna w poznaniu. Zeszyty naukowe. Seria II. Prace habilitacyjne i doktorskie, zesz, nr. 30.) Poznań, Nakł. Wyższej szkoły ekonomicznej, 1964. 196 p. Bibliography, 188-196.

Countries and Areas   173

2618. HORI, Shin'ichi. Keizaigaku to Tōyō shisô. (Transliterated.) Japan, 1965. 8, 391 p. Bibliographies.
2619. KADA, Tetsuji. Shakai keizai shisō shi. (Transliterated.) Japan, 1964. 17, 636, 9 p. Bibliographies.
2620. KULISHER, Iosif Mikhaĭlovich. Dzieje gospodarcze Europy zachodniej; przełozył K. Morawski; przejrzał Jan Rutkowski. . . (Bibljoteka wyższej szkoły handlowej.) Warszawa, Gebethner i Wolff; New York, The Polish book importing company, inc., 19- . v. Bibliographies.
2621. _____. Istoriia ėkonomicheskogo byta Zapadnoĭ Evropy. (Transliterated.) Moscow, 1931. 2 v. Bibliographies.
2622. _____. Lektsii po istorii ėkonomicheskago byta Zapadnoĭ Evropy. (Transliterated.) 4th edition. St. Petersburg, 1916. 512 p. Bibliographies.
2623. LINDBERG, Leon N. The political dynamics of European economic integration. Stanford, California, Stanford university press, 1963. xiv, 367 p. Bibliography.
2624. MARIOTTI, Francesco. Delle origini e dei progressi della scienza economica in Europa. (Nel decembre dello scorso anno l'autore lesse questo scritto nell'aula della R. Università di Sassari.) Imola, Tip. d'I. Galeati e figlio, 1875. ix, 106 p.
2625. SOMMER, Louise, editor and translator. Essays in European economic thought. (The William Volker fund series in the humane studies.) Princeton, New Jersey, Van Nostrand, 1960. x, 229 p. Bibliographies.
2626. SPULBER, Nicholas. "Economic thinking and its application and methodology in Eastern Europe outside the Soviet Russia." In, American economic review, Papers and proceedings, 46, 2 (May, 1956) 367-379.
2627. TWISS, Travers. View of the progress of political economy in Europe since the sixteenth century. (A course of lectures delivered before the University of Oxford in Michaelmus term, 1846, and lent term, 1847.) London, Longman, Brown, Green, and Longmans, 1847. v-xv, 298 p.
2628. WEBER, Max. The protestant ethic and the spirit of capitalism. Translated by Talcott Parsons; with foreword by R. H. Tawney. New York, Scribner, 1958. 292 p.

FINLAND

2629. EKONOMILITTO. Ekonomimatrikkeli, 1970. Matrikkelitormikunta: Jorma Lakkonen, et al. publisher?, 1969? 775 p.
2630. JAHNSSON, Yrjö Waldemar. Tutkimuksia Suomen kansantaloustieteen historiasta vousina 1810-1860, erityisesti silmällä pitäen yleisten kansantaloudellisten suuntien kehitystä. . . (Thesis, Helsingfors.) Helsingissä, K. F. Puromiehen kirjapaino, 1907. 1 p. 1., 340 p., 1 1.

FRANCE

2631. BAUDIN, Jean Pierre Louis. "Las tendencias actuales del

pensamiento económico francés." In, Rivista de economia Córdoba, 2nd. quarter (1958) 5-28.
2632. BECHAUX, Auguste Etienne Joseph. L'école économique française. (Les écoles économiques au XXe siècle.) Paris, A. Rousseau, etc., 1902. 2 p. 1., 152 p.
2633. BOUVIER-AJAM, Maurice Jean. Recherches sur l'histoire économique et sociale de la France... (Les cahiers du centre d'études et de recherches marxistes, no. 50.) Paris, Centre d'études et de recherches marxistes, 1967? i, 35 1.
2634. CENTRE d'études et de recherches marxistes. Les principale écoles de la doctrine économique en France. 3e série. Néocapitalisme, socialisme scientifique, principaux courants actuels... Conférences 1964-1965. (Les Cahiers du Centre d'études et de recherches marxistes.) Paris, Centre d'etudes et de recherches marxistes, 1965? 3 v. Bibliographies. (Contents: Le neo-capitalisme, par M. Bouvier-Ajam. Le socialisme scientifique: la pénétration du marxisme en France, par G. Cogniot. Les principaux courants contemporains, par M. Bouvier-Ajam.)
2635. CEPEDE, Michel et Bernard W. Valluis. La pensée agronomique en France, 1510-1930. (Bibliothèque d'économie contemporaine.) Paris, Presses universitaires de France, 1969. 155 p. Bibliographical footnotes.
2636. COLINS, Jean Guillaume César Alexandre Hippolyte, de. L'économie politique; source des révolutions et des utopies prétendues socialistes. Paris, Librairie générale, 1856- . v.
2637. NO ENTRY
2638. DESCHAMPS, Hubert. Méthodes et doctrines coloniales de la France. Paris, 1953. 222 p.
2639. DOLLEANS, Edouard. Le chartisme. (1841-1848.) Nouvelle édition refondue. Paris, 1949. xii, 338 p.
2640. DUPIN, Claude. Oeconomiques, 1745. Pub. avec introduction et table analytique, par Marc Aucuy. (Collection des économistes et des réformateurs sociaux de la France.) Paris, M. Rivière et cie., 1913. 2 v.
2641. GARGALLO di Castel Lentini, Gioacchino. La scoperta dell' utile nel Settecento. La genesi del concetto di economia in Francia dai libertini agli illuministi e l'aspetto economico della storia nella storiografia dell'illuminismo francese. (Letture di pensiero e d'arte.) Roma, Edizioni di storia e letteratura, 1951. 73 p.
2642. GIDE, Charles. Les sciences économiques. Paris, Larousse, 1915. 19 p. Bibliographie, 15-19 p.
2643. GIRSBERGER, Hans. Der utopische sozialismus des 18. jahrhunderts in Frankreich und seine philosophischen und materiellen grundlagen. Zürich, Rascher & cie., a-g., 1924. xv, 253, 1 p. Quellen- und literaturverzeichnis, vii-xv.
2644. LAROCQUE, Denise. La crise et les doctrines libérales française. (Thèse, Caen.) Paris, Lipschutz, 1937. 1 p.1., 5-253 p., 1 1. Bibliographie, 241-249.
2645. LEVASSEUR, Pierre Emile. Aperçu de l'évolution des

doctrines économiques et socialistes en France sous la troisième république. (Extrait du Compte rendu de d'Académie des sciences morales et politiques. Institute de France. Académie des sciences morales et politiques.) Paris, A. Picard et fils, 1906. 109 p., 1 1.

2646. MARCHAL, André. La pensée économique en France depuis 1945. (Bibliothèque de la science économique.) Paris, Presses universitaires de France, 1953. viii, 240 p. Bibliography, 191-228.

2647. MIYAMOTO, Mataji. "France shakai-keizai-shigaku no hattatsu to genjŏ." In, Keizaigaku, 5, 3-4 (March, 1956) 87-117 p.

2648. OBERFOHREN, Ernst. Die idee der universalökonomie in der französischen wirtschaftswissenschaftlichen literatur bis auf Turgot. (Probleme der weltwirtschaft, schriften des Königlichen instituts für seeverkehr und weltwirtschaft an der Universität Kiel . . . 23.) Jena, G. Fischer, 1915. 3 p. 1., 204 p. (First appeared: Kiel, 1914, as part of author's inaugural dissertation, under title: Jean Bodin und seine schule, untersuchungen über die frühzeit der universalökonomik.)

2649. PIERSTORFF, Julius. Die lehre vom unternehmergewinn in Frankreich. 2. theil der schrift: Die lehre vom unternehmergewinn. (Habilitationsschrift, Göttingen.) Berlin, Druck von W. Pormetter, 1875. 49 p.

2650. PIROU, Gaëtan. Les doctrines économiques en France depuis 1870. (Collection Armand Colin, Section d'histoire et sciences économiques, n^e 66.) Paris, A. Colin, 1925. 2, 204 p. Bibliographie sommaire, 201.

2651. POKROVSKII, Aleksandr Ivanovich. Frant͡suzskai͡a burzhuaznai͡a politicheskai͡a ėkonomii͡a. (Transliterated.) Moscow, 1961. 224 p. Bibliography, 212-217.

2652. SEE, Henri Eugène. Französische wirtschaftsgeschichte. (Handbuch der wirtschaftsgeschichte, hrsg. von dr. Georg Brodnitz.) Jena, G. Fischer, 1930- . v. Bibliographie: v. 1, 380-417. [French edition entitled: Histoire économique de la Farnce . . . publiée avec le concours de Robert Schnerb . . . préface de Armand Rébillon. Paris, A. Colin, 1939- . v. Bibliographie: v. 1, 403-432. ("Il ne faudrait pas considérer le présent ouvrage comme une traduction de l'édition allemande. C'est en réalité l'édition allemande qui a été une traduction du texte rédigé en français par Henri Sée." From Préface p. vi.)]

2653. SPENGLER, Joseph John. French predecessors of Malthus. A study in eighteenth-century wage and population theory. (Reprint, c 1942.) New York, Octagon books, 1965. c1942. ix, 398 p. Bibliographical footnotes. [French edition entitled: Economie et population: les doctrines françaises avant 1800. (France. Institut national d'études démographiques. Travaux et documents, cahier no. 21, 28.) Paris, Presses universitaires de France, 1954-56. 2 v. (v. 1: De Budé a Condorcet. Translated, by Georges

Lecarpentier and Anita Fage. v. 2: Bibliographie générale commentée.)

2654. TEFAS, Georges. Les conceptions economiques des groupements d'action française; étude comparée. (Thèse, University of Paris.) Paris, Imprimerie des Presses modernes, 1939. 5 p. 1., 13-798 p. Bibliographie, 771-789.

2655. WAHA, Raymund de. Die nationalökonomie in Frankreich. Stuttgart, F. Enke, 1910. xix, 540 p.

2656. YAMAKAWA, Yoshio. Kinsei Furansu keizaigaku no keisei. (Transliterated.) Japan, 1968. 293 p. Bibliographical references in notes.

GERMANY

2657. AMERICAN Academy of political and social science, Philadelphia. Consumer's coöperation. Edited by J. G. Brainerd. Supplement: German economic thought today. (Annals. v. 191, May, 1937.) Philadelphia, 1937. xvi, 292 p.

2658. ANDLER, Charles Philippe Théodore. Les origines du socialisme d'Etat en Allemagne. 2. éd., augm. d'une pré face et d'un appendice bibliographique. Paris, F. Alcan, 1911. 3 p. 1., vii, 505 p., 1 l. Bibliographie: 479-492.

2659. BAETEMAN, L., H. K. DeLooz, en J. Meganck. Algemene economie. (De Garves, economische bibliotheck.) Antwerpen, De Garve, 1966. 399 p. Bibliographical footnotes.

2660. BECKER, Julius. Das deutsche Manchestertum, eine studie zur geschichte des wirtschaftspolitischen individualismus . . . (Inaug.-dissertation, Bern.) Karlsruche i. B., G. Braun, 1907. 5 p. 1., 135 p. Anmerkungen, 119-131.

2661. BELOW, Georg Anton Hugo von. Die deutsche geschichtschreibung von den befreiungskriegen bis zu unsern tagen; geschichtschreibung und geschichtsauffassung, mit einer beigabe: Die deutsche wirtschaftsgeschichtliche literatur und der ursprung des marxismus. 2. wesentlich erweiterte aufl. (Handbuch der mittelalterlichen und neueren geschichte . . . abt. I. Allgemeines.) München und Berlin, R. Oldenbourg, 1924. xvi, 207 p. Bibliographical footnotes.

2662. ———. Probleme der wirtschaftsgeschichte; eine einführung in das studium der wirtschaftsgeschichte. Tübingen, Mohr, 1920. xx, 710 p., 1 l. Bibliographical footnotes.

2663. BILGER, François. La pensée économique libérale dans d'Allemagne contemporaine. Exposé fait . . . le 25 mai 1965. (Les Dossiers du CEPEC, 19.) Paris, Centre d'études politiques et civiques, 1966. 36 p.

2664. BONDI, Gerhard. Zu einigen Fragen der wirtschaftstheorie in Deutschland. (Hallische universitätsreden, n. F., Heft 1.) Halle (Saale), Martin-Luther-Universität, 1960. 12 p.

Countries and Areas 177

2665. BORN, Karl Erich. Moderne deutsche wirtschaftsgeschichte. (Neue wissenschaftliche Bibliothek, 12. Geschichte.) Köln, Berlin, Kiepenheuer und Witsch, 1966. 535 p. Bibliography, 507-514.

2666. BROOK, Warner Frederick. The road to planned economy, capitalism and socialism in Germany's development. London, Oxford university press, H. Milford, 1934. xii, 148 p. Bibliographical notes.

2667. BRUGELMANN, Hermann. Politische ökonomie in kritischen jahren: die Friedrich List-Gesellschaft e V. von 1925-1935. Mit einer Einleitung von Edgar Salin: In memoriam Bernhard Harms. (Veröffentlichungen der List Gesellschaft, Bd. 1.) Tübingen, Mohr, 1956. xix, 192 p.

2668. COENEN, Etienne. La "Konjunkturforschung" en Allemagne et en Autriche, 1925-1933. (Université catholique de Louvain. Faculté des sciences économiques et sociales. Collection de L'Ecole des sciences économiques, no. 87.) Louvain, Editions nauwelaerts, 1964. vii, 352 p. Bibliography, 331-341.

2669. CRONBACH, Else. Das landwirtschaftliche betriebsproblem in der deutschen nationalökonomie bis zur mitte des XIX, jahrhunderts. (Studien zur sozialwirtschafts- und verwaltungsgeschichte, hrsg. von Dr. Karl Grünberg, II, hft.) Wien, C. Konegen (E. Stülpnagel), 1907. 2 p. 1., vii-x p., 1 l., 338 p. Bibliography, 326-334.

2670. CROOK, James Walter. German wage theories. A history of their development. (Studies in history, economics and public law, edited by the Faculty of political science of Columbia university . . . vol. ix, no. 2.) New York, Columbia university, 1898. v, 7-113 p. (Published also as author's thesis, Columbia university. Reprinted: Columbia university. Studies in the social sciences series, no. 24. 1968?)

2671. CUSUMANO, Vito. Le scuole economiche della Germania in rapporto alla quistione sociale. (Biblioteca delle scienze giuridiche e sociali, vol. XXII.) Napoli, G. Marghieri, 1875. 366, 2 p.

2672. ———. Ueber die gegenwärtige lage der volkswirtschaftlichen studien in Deutschland. Aus dem italienischen mit vorwort und anhang von S. Emele. Sigmaringen, C. Tappen, 1881. viii, 164 p.

2673. EGNER, Erich. Das Schicksal der volkswirtschaft. Berlin, W. de Gruyter, 1950. 72 p. (Sonderdruck aus der Festschrift der Göttinger Rechts' und Staatswissenschaftlichen fakultät für Julius von Gierke.)

2674. Die ENTWICKLUNG der deutschen volkswirtschaftslehre im neunzehnten jahrhundert. Gustav Schmoller zur siebenzigsten wiederkehr seines geburtstages, 24. juni 1908, in verehrung dargebracht von S. P. Altmann, W. J. Ashley, C. Ballod. . . . Leipzig, Duncker & Humblot, 1908. 2 v.

2675. GEHLHOFF, Joachim. Bibliography of books in economic history published in Germany in the period, 1939-1948.

Frankfurt am Main?, 1947? 91, ix 1.

2676. GOTTL-OTTLILIENFELD, Friedrich von. Die Läuterung des nationalökonomischen Denkens als deutsche Aufgabe; Geleitwort der Reihe. (Volkswirtschaftliche Forschungen, Heft 1.) Berlin, Junker und Dünnhaupt, 1934. 80 p.

2677. GRENNER, Karl Heinz. Wirtschaftsliberalismus und katholisches Denken. Ihre Begegnung und Auseinandersetzung im Deutschland des 19. Jahrhunderts. Köln, Bachem, 1967. 364 p. (Issued also as thesis, Munich, with title: Quellen- und literaturverzeichnis, 341-354.)

2678. GRUNFELD, Judith. Die leitenden sozial- und wirtschaftsphilosophischen ideen in der deutschen nationalökonomie und die ueberwindung des Smithianismus bis auf Mohl und Hermann. (Studien zur sozial-, wirtschafts- und verwaltungsgeschichte . . . IX, hft.) Wien, C. Konegen (E. Stülpnagel), 1913. x, 114 p. Verzeichnis der benützten literatur, 111-114.

2679. GUNTHER, Adolf. Krisis der wirtschaft und der wirtschaftswissenschaft. Dresden, Sibyllen-verlag, 1921. 159, 1 p.

2680. HAFFNER, Alexander. Aufzeichnungen. Frankfurt a. M., Verl. Frankfurter Allgemeine zeitung, 1966. 262 p.

2681. HASEK, Carl William. The introduction of Adam Smith's doctrine into Germany. (Studies in history, economics and public law, ed. by the Faculty of political science of Columbia university, vol. CXVII, no. 2; whole no. 261.) New York, Columbia university, 1925. 155 p. Bibliography, 150-152.

2682. HEITZ, Ernst L. Uebersicht der literatur der Preise in Deutschland und der Schweiz aus den Letzten Sechizg jahren Jena, Druck von ed. Frommann, 1876. 71 p.

2683. HESSE, Albert Hermann. Allgemeine und angewandte volkswirtschaftslehre; ein Leitfaden. 3., völlig neugestaltete aufl. Offenburg, Lehrmittel-verlag, 1948. ix, 210 p. (4. aufl. Mit ergänzungen von Peter Heinz Scraphim. Stuttgart, Kohlhammer, 1955. 256 p.)

2684. HESSE, Kurt. Der kriegswirtschaftliche gedanke, (Schriften zur kriegswirtschaftlichen forschung und schulung.) Hamburg, Hanseatische verlagsanstalt, c1935. 52 p. Wichtigste deutsche literatur, 51-52.

2685. HOFMANN, Heinrich. Der produktivitätsbegriff in der modernen deutschen und österreichischen volkswirtschaftslehre. (Inaug. dissertation, Tübingen.) Tübingen, Buchdruckerei E. Göbel, 1929. viii, 61, 1 p. Quellenverzeichnis, vii-viii.

2686. HONEGGER, Hans. Volkswirtschaftliche gedankenströmungen, systeme und theorien der gegenwart, besonders in Deutschland. (Braun's kleine handbücher.) Karlsruhe, G. Braun, 1925. xi, 1, 139 p. Allgemeiner schriftenverweis, vii-viii.

2687. KITAMURA, Jiichi. Shoki shihonshugi no keizai rinri. (Transliterated.) (Kwansei gakuin daigaku, keizaigaku kenkyū sōsho, 6.) Japan, 1964. 4, 4, 217 p. Bibliographical references in notes.

2688. KLEINWACHTER, Friedrich Ludwig von. Der entwicklungsgang der nationalökonomischen wissenschaft in Deutschland. Leipzig, C. L. Hirschfeld, 1926. 2 p. 1., 154 p.
2689. KLUZA-WOLOSIEWICZ, Zenona. Teoria rozwoju kapitalizmu w dyskusjach socjaldemokracji niemieckief, lata 1891-1914. Wyd. 1. Warszawa, Państwowe wydawn. Naukowe, 1963. 322 p. Bibliography, 303-311. (Summaries in English and Russian.)
2690. KOHLER, Julius Paul. Staat und gesellschaft in der deutschen theorie der auswärtigen wirtschaftspolitik und des internationalen handels von Schlettwein bis auf Fr. List und Prince-Smith; mit einer einleitenden untersuchung über den inneren geistigen zusammenhang von politik und wirtschaft. (Beihefte zur vierteljahrschrift für sozial- und wirtschaftsgeschichte. Hrsg. von prof. dr. G. von Below. VII. hft.) Stuttgart, W. Kohlhammer, 1926. vi, 163 p. Literaturübersicht, 158-163. (Dissertation, Giessen.)
2691. KRAUSE, Werner. Wirtschaftstheorie unter dem Hakenkreuz. Die bürgerliche politische ökonomie in Deutschland während der faschistischen herrschaft. (Deutsche Akademie der wissenschaften zu Berlin. Schriften des Instituts für wirtschaftswissenschaften, Nr. 31.) Berlin, Akademie-verlag, 1969. 247 p. Anmerkungen, 207-240.
2692. KRETSCHMAR, Hans. Die einheit der volkswirtschaft in den älteren deutschen wirtschaftslehren. (Probleme der weltwirtschaft; schriften des Instituts für weltwirtschaft und seeverkehr an der Universität Kiel . . . 50.) Jena, G. Fischer, 1930. xxii, 354 p. Literaturverzeichnis, ix-xxii. (Dissertation, Kiel.)
2693. LUERS, Heinz. Volk und Volkswirtschaft in der deutschen nationalökonomie des 19. und beginnenden 20. jahrhunderts. Göttingen, 1941. 116 p. Literaturverzeichnis, 113-115. (Dissertation, Göttingen.)
2694. MEYER, Ernst Wilhelm. Political science and economics in Western Germany. A postwar survey. Washington, Library of Congress, European affairs division, 1950. 23 p. First of a series of surveys of intellectual life in Western Germany sponsored by the Oberlaender trust, Philadelphia.
2695. MOHRMANN, Heinz. Studien über russisch-deutsche Begennungen in der wirtschaftswissenschaft, 1750-1825. (Quellen und studien zur geschichte osteuropas, Bd. 5.) Berlin, Akademie-verlag, 1959. 146 p. Bibliography, 131-136.
2696. MUSSIGGANG, Albert. Die soziale Frage in der historischen schule der deutschen nationalökonomie. (Tübingen wirtschaftswissenschaftliche abhandlungen, Bd. 2.) Tübingen, Mohr Siebeck, 1968. 264 p. Bibliography, 249-258.
2697. OPPENHEIM, Heinrich Bernhard. Der katheder-sozialismus. Berlin, R. Oppenheim, 1872. 2 p. 1., 84 p.
2698. PARSONS, Talcott. "Capitalism in recent German

literature." In, The Journal of political economy, XXXVI, 6 (1928).

2699. PETER, Joachim Heinrich. Die probleme der armut in de lehren der kameralisten (eine dogmengeschichtliche studi Volkswirtschaftliche studien . . . hft. 44.) Berlin, E. Ebering, 1934. 245, 1 p. Bibliography, 241-245.

2700. POHLE, Ludwig. Die gegenwärtige krisis in der deutschen volkswirtschaftslehre. Betrachtungen über das verhältnis zwischen politik und nationalökonomischer wissenschaft. Leipzig, A. Deichert, 1911. xiv, 136 p.

2701. PROESLER, Hans. Die epochen der deutschen wirtschaftsentwicklung. Nürnberg, Krische & co., 1927. 2 p. 1. 173, 2 p. Bibliographical footnotes.

2702. ROPKE, Wilhelm Theodor. Gegen die Brandung; zeugnisse eines gelehrtenlebens unserer zeit. Gesammelt und hrsg von Albert Hunold. Erlenbach, Zürich, E. Rentsch, 1959 418 p. Bibliography, 398-418.

2703. ROSCHER, Wilhelm Georg Friedrich. Geschichte der national-oekonomik in Deutschland. München, R. Oldenbourg, 1874. viii, 1085 p. (Zweite auflage, 1924, in manuldruck. München und Berlin. Reprinted: Johnson.)

2704. ROTHSCHILD, K. W. "The old and the new. Some recent trends in the literature of German economics." In, American economic review, 54, 2 (March, 1964) 1-33.

2705. SALIN, Edgar. "Die deutsche volkswirtschaftliche theorie im 20. jahrhundert." In, Zeitschrift fur schweizerische statistik und volkswirtschaft, LVII (1921) 87-117.

2706. SCHULTZ, Bruno. Der entwicklungsgang der theoretischen der theoretischen volkswirtschaftslehre in Deutschland; ein beitrag zur erklärung ihres gegenwärtigen zustandes. Halberstadt, H. Meyer, 1928. x, 148 p.

2707. SOMBART, Werner. Die juden und das wirtschaftsleben. 1911-12. 2 v. (4th ed., 1922.)

2708. STICH, Anton Otto. Die entwicklung der Betriebswirtschaftslehre zur selbständigen Disziplin; eine dogmenkritische betrachtung der entwicklung im deutschen Sprachgebiet in den jahren 1900 bis 1935, unter besondered berücksichtigung des verhältnisses der betriebswirtschaftslehre zur nationalökonomie. (Erscheint gleichzeitig als Heft 15 der basler betriebswirtschaftlichen studien.) Basel, Helbing & Lichtenhahn, 1956. 80 p. Bibliography, 76-79. (Dissertation. Basel.)

2709. TURNER, Harald. Der wehrgedanke in der deutschen volkswirtschaftslehre zur zeit der deutschen einigung. Leipzig, J. A. Barth, 1940. 2 p. 1., 108 p. Schrifttumverzeichnis, 106-108.

2710. VLEUGELS, Wilhelm. Zur gegenwartslage der deutschen volkswirtschaftslehre, eine sammlung von aufsätzen über gegenwartslage, erbe und heutige aufgaben der deutschen volkswirtschaftlichen theorie. Jena, G. Fischer, 1939. x p., 1 l., 148 p.

2711. VOPELIUS, Marie-Elisabeth. Die altliberalen ökonomen und die reformzeit. (Sozialwissenschaftliche studien, Heft

11.) Stuttgart, G. Fischer, 1968. 195 p. Bibliography, 148-195.
2712. WAGNER, Adolf Heinrich Gotthilf. Die akademische nationalökonomie und der socialismus. (Zum antritt des rectorats. Univ. Berlin.) Berlin, J. Becker, 1895. 37 p.
2713. WISKEMANN, Erwin. Die neue wirtschaftswissenschaft. (Die neue hochschule, hrsg. von prof. dr. Vahlen.) Berlin, Junker und Dünnhaupt, 1936. 86 p.
2714. WISKEMANN, Erwin und Heinz Lütke. Der weg der deutschen volkswirtschaftslehre, ihre schöpfer und gestalter im 19. jahrhundert, herausgegeben. Berlin, Junker und Dünnhaupt, 1937. 193, 1 p.

GERMANY (FEDERAL REPUBLIC, 1949-)

2715. AGRICOLA, Rudolf. Der gegenwärtige stand der ökonomischen wissenschaft in Westdeutschland. (Deutsche Akademie der Wissenschaften zu Berlin. Vorträge und Schriften, Heft 59.) Berlin, Akademie-verlag. 1956. 62 p.
2716. BILGER, François. La pensée économique libérale dans l'Allemagne contemporaine. Exposé fait . . . le 25 mai 1965. (Les dossiers du CEPEC, 19.) Paris, Centre d'études politiques et civiques, 1966. 36 p.
2717. HABER, Adolf. Mity ekonomiczne w NRF. Wyd. 1. Wrocław, Zakład Narodowy im. Ossolińskich, 1963. 231 p. Bibliography, 211-217. (Summaries in English and Russian.)
2718. MEYERS handbuch über die wirtschaft. Hrsg. von der Lexikonredaktion des bibliographischen instituts. Unter leitung von G. Preuss bearb. von U. Bachert und weiteren Mitarbeitern der Fachredaktion wirtschaft. Mannheim, Bibliographisches institut, 1966. 1148 p.
2719. SHEVIAKOV, Fedor Nikolaevich. Ideologi zapadnogermanskogo imperializma. (Transliterated.) Moscow, 1962. 173 p.

GREAT BRITAIN

2720. Allhusen, Desmond. The master problem. London, P. Davies, limited, 1938. 2 p. 1., 9-316 p.
2721. ASHLEY, William James. Histoire et doctrines économiques d l'Angleterre. Tr. sur la 3. ed. anglaise, rev. par l'auteur. (Bibliothèque internationale d'économie politique.) Paris, V. Giard & E. Brière, 1900. 2 v. Bibliographies. (v. I. Le moyen âge; tr. par Paul Bondois. v. II. La fin du moyen âge; tr. par Savinien Bouyssy.
2722. BAGEHOT, Walter. The postulates of English political economy. Student's edition, with a preface by Alfred Marshall. (Questions of the day, no. 28.) New York, London, G. P. Putnam's sons, 1894. vii p., 1 l.,

114 p. (Contents: The postulates of English political economy. I. The transferability of labour; II. The transferability of capital.) (Originally published in the Fortnightly review in 1876 and republished with some other material, as the author's "Economic studies," edited by Richard H. Hutton, 1880.)

2723. BEER, Max. Early British economics from the XIIIth to the middle of the XVIIIth century. London, G. Allen and Unwin, limited, 1938. 250 p. [(Reprints of economic classics.) New York, A. M. Kelley, 1967. 250 p. Bibliographical footnotes.]

2724. BIRNIE, Arthur. An economic history of the British Isles. 8th edition. London, Methuen, 1955. ix, 401 p. Bibliographies.

2725. BLAUG, Mark. The evolution of Ricardian economics in England; a study in discipleship. (Thesis, Columbia university. University microfilms, Publication no. 12,416.) Ann Arbor, University microfilms, 1956. 3, xii, 400 l. (Abstracted in Dissertation abstracts, v. 16 (1956), no. 4, p. 685.)

2726. ———. Ricardian economics; a historical study. New Haven, Yale university press, 1958. x, 269. Bibliography, 243-261. (Developed out of a dissertation, Columbia university.)

2727. BLIUMIN, Izrail' Grigor'evich. Kritika sovremennoĭ burzhuaznoĭ politicheskoĭ ėkonomii Anglii. (Transliterated.) Moscow, 1953. 356 p.

2728. BONAR, James. The tables turned. London, Macmillan, 1931. (Reprint of economic classics.) New York, A. M. Kelley, 1970. vii, 135 p.)

2729. BOUDEVILLE, Jean. Plein emploi & socialisme en Grande Bretagne. Paris, Recueil sirey, 1946. 3 p. l., 3-124 p. Bibliographie des auteurs français, 119; Bibliographie des auteurs anglais, 120-121.

2730. BRINKMANN, Carl. Der wirtschaftliche liberalismus als system der britischen weltanschauung. (Schriften des Deutschen instituts für aussenpolitische forschung und des Hamburger instituts für auswärtige politik, hrsg. in gemeinschaft mit dem Deutschen auslandswissenschaftlichen institut, hft. 22. Das Britische reich in der weltpolitik, hft. 7.) Berlin, Junker und Dünnhaupt, 1940. 50 p.

2731. BROOKS, Collin. Our present discontents. New York, H. Holt and company, c1933. xii p., 2 l., 3-333 p.

2732. BURTT, E. A. The English philosophers from Bacon to Mill. New York, Modern library, 1939.

2733. CANNAN, Edwin. Histoire des théories de la production et de la distribution dans l'économie politique anglaise de 1776 à 1848. Traduction sur la 2me éd. anglaise par Henry-Emile Barrault et Maurice Alfassa avec une introduction par Henry-Emile Barrault. (Bibliothèque international d'économie politique.) Paris, V. Giard & E. Brière, 1910. xxxvii, 577 p. Index bibliographique,

545-573. (Spanish edition entitled: Historia de las teorías de la producción y distribución en la economía política inglesa de 1776 a 1848; versión española de Javier Márquez. Session de obras de economia del Fondo de cultura economica dirigida por Daniel Cosio Villegas. I. Grandes estudios. Primera edición inglesa, 1893 . . . tercera edición inglesa, 1917 . . . primera edición española, 1942. México, Fondo de cultura económica, 1942. 2 p. 1., 7-469, 2 p. Indice analítico bibliográfico, 455-466. English edition entitled: A history of the theories of production and distribution in English political economy, from 1776 to 1848. Reprint of 3d edition, 1917. (Reprints of economic classics.) New York, A. M. Kelley, 1967. xi, 336 p. Bibliography, 323-336.)

2734. CATHERWOOD, Benjamin Franklin. Basic theories of distribution. Reprint of 1939 edition. (Essay index reprint series.) Freeport, New York, Books for Libraries press, 1970. ix, 262 p. Bibliography, 260-262.

2735. CHECKLAND, S. G. "The Birmingham economists, 1815-50." In, Economic history review, second series, 1, 1 (1948).

2736. CHERNYSHEVSKII, Nikolai Gavrilovich. L'économie politique jugée par la science. Critique des principes d'économie politique de John-Stuart Mill, par N. Tchernychewsky (tr. du russe). Tr. by Aleksĭeĭ Tveritinov and César de Paepe. t. 1. Bruxelles, Typografie de D. Brismée, 1874. v-xxxvi, 492 p.

2737. CHO, Moriyoshi. Kotenha keizaigaku no riron taikel. (Transliterated.) Japan, 1949. 232 p.

2738. CLARK, George Norman. Science and social welfare in the age of Newton. 2d edition. Oxford, Clarendon press, 1949. 159 p. (Reprinted: 1970. 8, 161 p. Bibliographical references.)

2739. COOMBES, David. State enterprise. Business or politics. London, Allen & Unwin, 1971.

2740. DUCION, Georges. Pour une économie du bien commun, selon la doctrine sociale de l'Eglise. Paris, P. Lethielleux, 1960. 142 p.

2741. ECONOMICS, commerce, and administration; visual analysis series. (The Commonwealth and international library. Social administration, training, economics, and production division.) Oxford, New York, Pergamon press, 1966- . v. (Contents: v. I. An introductory atlas, by Neil Skene Smith.)

2742. FUZ, J. K. Welfare economics in English utopias from Francis Bacon to Adam Smith. The Hague, M. Nijhoff, 1952. 113 p. Bibliography.

2743. GORDON, Barry J. Non-Ricardian political economy; five neglected contributions. (Kress library of business and economics, Publication no. 20.) Boston, Baker library, 1967. vii, 51 p.

2744. GORDON, S. "The London economist and the high tide of

laissez-faire." In, Journal of political economy (December, 1955.)

2745. GREAT BRITAIN, British council. Economics; a select book list. London, Longmans, Green, 1963. 60 p.

2746. GRAMPP, William Dyer. The Manchester school of economics. Stanford, California, Stanford university press, 1960. viii, 155 p.

2747. HAHL, Albert. Zur geschichte der volkswirtschaftlichen ideen in England gegen ausgang des mittelalters. (Staatswissenschaftliche studien. 5 bd., 2 hft.) Jena, G. Fischer, 1893. 4 p. 1., 58, 2 p. Die benutzten quellenschariften, 6-13.

2748. HALL, Hubert. A select bibliography for the study, sources, and literature of English mediaeval economic history; compiled by a seminar of the London school of economics. (Studies in economics and political science. Ed. by the director of the London school of economics. No. 4 in the series of bibliographies by students connected with the London school of economics and political science.) London, P. S. King & son, 1914. xiii, 350 p. (Reprinted: Burt Franklin bibliographical and reference series no. 22. New York, B. Franklin, 1960. xiii, 350 p.

2749. HOOD, Francis Campbell. British economists. (Pitman's economic series.) London, New York, Sir I. Pitman & sons, ltd., 1931. viii, 97 p.

2750. HULSMANN, Paul. Der wirtschaftsstandische gedanke in der englischen literatur, eine ideengeschichtliche untersuchung. (Inaugural dissertation, Jena.) P. Borna-Leipzig, Spezialbetrieb für dissertationsdruck von R. Noske, 1938. vii, 59 p., 1 l. Literatur, vii-viii.

2751. JAGER, Georg. Das englische recht zur zeit der klassischen nationalökonomie und seine umbildung im neunzehnten jahrhundert. (Staats- und sozialwissenschaftliche forschungen hrsg. von G. Schmoller und M. Sering, hft. 137.) Leipzig, Duncker & Humblot, 1909. viii, 107, 1 p.

2752. JHA, Narmadeshwar. The age of Marshall, aspects of British economic thought, 1890-1915. Foreword by Dennis H. Robertson. Patna, Novelty & Co., 1963. x, 220 p. Bibliography, 207-215.

2753. JOHNSON, Edgar Augustus Jerome. Predecessors of Adam Smith. The growth of British economic thought. (Prentice-Hall economics series, edited by E. A. J. Johnson.) New York, Prentice Hall, inc., 1937. xii, 426 p. [Reprinted: 1937 edition, (Reprints of economic classics.) New York, A. M. Kelley, 1965. xii, 426 p. Bibliographical references (notes to text), 317-384.]

2754. ———. Some origins of the modern economic world. New York, The Macmillan company, 1936. vii, 163 p.

2755. KADLEC, Vladimir. Kritika Engliše a jeho hospodářských soustav. (Nové hospodářstvi. Rada B, sv. 4.) V Praze, Práce, 1948. 69 p.

Countries and Areas 185

2756. KAMADA, Takeharu. Koten-keizaigaku to shoki shakaishugi. (Transliterated.) Japan, 1968. 407, xv p. Bibliography, i-xv.
2757. KEYSER, Jacques de. La politique économique britannique; les faits et la doctrine. (Université catholique de Louvain. Collection de l'Ecole des sciences économiques, no. 41.) Anvers, Impr. & publicité Bernaerts, 1950. 349 p. Bibliography.
2758. KINLOCH, Tom Fleming. Six English economists. 4th edition. London, Gee, 1950. vii, 107 p. Bibliography, 105-107.
2759. KIRKALDY, Adam Willis. The romance of trade. A survey, commercial and economic. New edition, revised. New York, E. P. Dutton & company, 1929. ix, 246 p. (First edition, 1923. The book resulted from a series of addresses given at University college, Nottingham.)
2760. KLEMME, Max. Die volkswirtschaftlichen anschauungen David Hume's. Ein beitrage zur geschichte der volkswirtschaftslehre. (Sammlung nationalökonomischer und statistischer abhandlungen, bd. 25.) Jena, G. Fischer, 1900. 4 p. 1., 100 p.
2761. KRAUS, Johannes Baptist. Scholastik, puritanismus und kapitalismus; eine vergleichende dogmengeschichtliche übergangsstudie. München und Leipzig, Duncker & Humblot, 1930. 5 p. 1., 3-329. Bibliography, 310-329.
2762. LASKI, Harold J. Political thought in England from Locke to Bentham. London, Oxford university press, 1920. New York, Henry Holt and company, 1920.
2763. LETWIN, William. The origins of scientific economics; English economic thought, 1660-1776. London, Methuen, 1963. x, 316 p. (1st edition in the United States: Garden City, New York, Doubleday, 1964, c1963. viii, 345 p. Bibliography, 325-330.)
2764. LEIBKNECKT, Wilhelm. Zur geschichte der werttheorie in England. (Inaugural dissertation, Berlin). Jena, G. Fischer, 1902. iv p., 1 1., 112 p.
2765. LINK, R. G. English theories of economic fluctuations, 1815-1848. New York, Columbia university press, 1959.
2766. LOWENTHAL, Esther. The Ricardian socialists. . . . (Thesis, Columbia university.) (Studies in history, economics and public law, edited by the Faculty of political science of Columbia university, vol. XLVI, no. 1, whole no. 114.) New York, 1911, 107 p.
2767. MACFIE, Alec Lawrence. Theories of the trade cycle. London, Macmillan and co., limited, 1934. ix, 198 p. Bibliography, 195-198.
2768. MARBURG, Jessie. Die sozialökonomischen grundlagen der englischen armenpolitik im ersten drittel des XIX jahrhunderts. (Volkswirtschaftliche abhandlungen der badischen hochschulen . . . n. f. hft. 11.) Karlsruhe i. B., G. Braun, 1912. 2 p. 1., 120, 1, p. Literaturverzeichnis, 116-120.
2769. MAZZEI, Jacopo. Politica economica internazionale inglese

prima di Adamo Smith, con prefazione del prof. Marco Fanno. . . . (Pubblicazioni della Università cattolica del sacro cuore. Ser. 3: Scienze sociali, vol. II.) Milano, Società editrice "Vita e pensiero," 1924. 2 p. 1., vii-xix, 460 p.

2770. PATTEN, Simon Nelson. The development of English thought. A study in the economic interpretation of history. New York, The Macmillan company; London, Macmillan & co., ltd., 1899. xxvii, 415 p.

2771. PIGOU, A. C. "Medio siglo de ciencia económica inglesa. In, Boletín del banco central de Venezuela, 15, 122-124 (April-June, 1955) 16-26.

2772. PRICE, Langford Lovell Frederick Rice. A short history of political economy in England, from Adam Smith to Alfred Marshall. 15th edition. London, Methuen & co., ltd., 1937. xvi, 315, 1 p.

2773. RAFFEL, Friedrich Andreas. Englische friehändler vor Adam Smith. Ein beitrag zur geschichte der politischen oekonomie. (Zeitschrift für die gesamte staatswissenschaft. . . Ergänzungsheft XVIII.) Tübingen, H. Laupp, 1905. v, 193 p.

2774. RYNDINA, M. N. Burzhuaznye ékonomisty Anglii i SShA. (Transliterated.) Moscow, 1954. 141 p.

2775. SAGAN, John. A study of the development of monetary theory of English economists in the classical tradition, 1776-1848. (Thesis, University of Illinois. University microfilms, Publication no. 2742.) Ann Arbor, University microfilms, 1951. vi, 300 l. Bibliography, 292-300. (Abstracted in Microfilm abstracts, v. 11 (1951) no. 4, p. 868-869.)

2776. SAMUELS, Warren J. The classical theory of economic policy. With an introduction by Herman Finer. (World series in economics.) Cleveland, World publishing company, 1966. xvii, 341 p. Bibliographical references

2777. SARIDAKIS, Georges B. L'évolution de la théorie de la valeur en Angleterre. (Thèse, Université de Paris.) Paris, M. Giard, 1924. 218 p. Bibliographie, 215-216.

2778. SCOTT, William Amasa. The development of economics. (The Century studies in economics, W. H. Kiekhofer, editor.) New York, London, The Century company, c1933. xii, 540 p. Bibliography, 527-528.

2779. SCROPE, George Julius Duncombe Poulett. Principles of political economy, deduced from the natural laws of social welfare and applied to the present state of Britain. New York, A. M. Kelley, 1969. xxiv, 457 p.

2780. SELIGMAN, Edwin Robert Anderson. On some neglected British economists. London, 1903. 56 p. Bibliographical footnotes. [(Reprinted from the Economic journal, vol. XIII.) (Japanese edition entitled: Wasurerareta keizai-gakushatachi. (Transliterated.) Translated by Minokochi Hirase. Tokyo, Mirai-sha, 1955. 163 p.)]

2781. SENIOR, Nassau William. Selected writings on economics.

(Reprints of economic classics.) New York, A. M. Kelley, 1966. 1 v.
2782. STADNIK, Miloš. Některé poznatky z návštěvy anglikých a skotských universit. (Zpráva ze studinjí cesty ve dnech 27. list. až 24. pros. 1964. Ekonomický ústav československé akademie věd. Inform. publ., c 20.) Praha, 1965. 63 p.
2783. STANKIEWICZ, Wacław. Rozwój angielskiej myśli wojenoekonomicznej. Wyd. 1. Warszawa, Wydawn. Ministerstwa obrony narodowej, 1966. 377 p. Bibliography, 361-371.
2784. STEPHEN, Leslie. History of English thought in the eighteenth century. 3rd edition. London, 1902. 2 v. (xvii, 466 p.; xi, 469 p.)
2785. ———. The English Utilitarians. New York, G. P. Putnam's sons; London, Duckworth & Company, 1900. 3 v.
2786. SUENAGA, Takasuke. Kindai keizaigaku no keisei. (Transliterated.) Japan, 1969. 300 p. Bibliographical references. [1950 edition entitled: Eikoku kindai keizaigaku josetsu. (Transliterated.)]
2787. THOMPSON, Charles Woody. The development of economics in British philosophy, 1688-1776. Urbana, Illinois, 1926. 12 p.
2788. TOYNBEE, Arnold. Lectures on the industrial revolution of the 18th century in England. Popular addresses, notes and other fragments. Together with a short memoir by Benjamin Jowett. 5th edition, with appendix. London, New York and Bombay, Longmans, Green and company, 1896. xxxvii p., 1 l., 319 p. [First published in 1884. Russian edition entitled: Promyshlennyĭ perevorot v Anglii. (Transliterated.) Moscow, 1898. xix, 329 p. New and cheaper edition, September 1908. Reprinted in 1937 together with a reminiscence by Lord Milner. London, New York, Longmans, Green and company, 1937. xxxv, 282 p. Reprinted as a paperback in 1956, under title, The industrial revolution, with a preface by Arnold J. Toynbee. Boston, Beacon press, 1956. 139 p. Reprinted in 1969, with a new introduction by the late T. S. Ashton. Newton Abbott, David & Charles, 1969. 10, xxix-xxxix, 256 p. Bibliographical footnotes. New York, A. M. Kelley, 1969. XXXVII, 256 p. Bibliographical footnotes. (Pages v-xxxi of the original are omitted.)]
2789. TUCKER, G. S. L. Progress and profits in British economic thought, 1650-1850. (Cambridge studies in economic history.) Cambridge, England, University press, 1960. 205 p. Bibliography.
2790. TUBERVILLE, Arthur Stanley and Frederich Arthur Howe. Great Britain in the latest age, from laissez faire to state control. London, J. Murray, 1921. vii, 342 p.
2791. VOLKOV, Maĭ Iakovlevich. Sovremennaĭa burzhuaznaĭa politicheskaĭa ékonomiĭa Anglii. (Transliterated.) Moscow, 1963. 91 p. Bibliographical footnotes.

2792. WHITAKER, Albert Conser. History and criticism of the labor theory of value in English political economy. (Thesis, Columbia university.) (Studies in history, economics and public law, edited by the faculty of political science of Columbia university, vol. XIX, no. 2.) New York, The Columbia university press, The Macmillan company, agents; London, P. S. King & son, 1904. 194 p., 1 l. (Reprints of economic classics. New York, A. M. Kelley, 1968. 197 p. Bibliographical footnotes.)
2793. WINCH, Donald. Classical political economy and colonies. Cambridge, Harvard university press, 1965. vi, 184 p.
2794. ZABALETA, R. "La ciencia economica en gran bretaña." In, Revista de la faculdad de derecho y ciencias sociales (Montevideo) 4 (October-December, 1955) 905-921.

GREECE

2795. LACOUR-GAYET, Jacques. Platon et l'economie dirigee. Paris, Imprimerie union, 1945. 2 p. l., 9-42 p. 2 l. Bibliographical footnotes.
2796. RIEZLER, Kurt. Uber finanzen und monopole im alten Griechenland; zur theorie und geschichte der antiken stadtwirtschaft. (Von der philosophischen fakultät der Universität München gekrönte preisschrift.) Berlin, Puttkammer & Mühlbrecht, 1907. 98 p. (Published, in part, under the title: Das zweite buch der pseudoaristotelischen ökonomik, as the author's inaugural dissertation, Munich, 1906. cf. Jahresverzeichnis der an den deutschen universitäten erschienenen schriften, vol. xxi, 1907, p. 488.)
2797. TOZZI, Glauco. Economisti greci. Siena, Libreria Ticci succ. Giubbi, 1955. 286 p.
2798. TREVER, Albert Augustus. A history of Greek economic thought. (Thesis, University of Chicago, 1913. 162 p. Bibliography, 151-155. (Private edition distributed by the University of Chicago libraries. A trade edition, published by University of Chicago press.)

GUATEMALA

2799. WOODWARD, Ralph Lee. "Political economy" in Guatemala. (University of Wichita. University studies no. 52. University of Wichita bulletin, v. 37, no. 3.) Wichita, Kansas, University of Wichita, 1962. 15 p. Bibliography.

HUNGARY

2800. FEKETE, József. Zur geschichte der volkswirthschaft in Ungarn, 1000-1700. Budapest, E. Neumayer, 1888. 84 p.
2801. FOSSATI, Eraldo. Economisti ungheresi e economisti italiani del secolo XIX. Prefazione dell'on. prof. dr. Béla de Erödi Harrach . . . 2. ed. Padova, Cedam,

Casa editrice dott. A. Milani, 1933. 65 p., 3 1.
Bibliographical footnotes, 67-68.
2802. KAUTZ, Gyula. Entwickelungs-geschichte der volkswirthschaftlichen ideen in Ungarn und deren einfluss auf das gemeinwesen. Preisschrift der Ungarischen academie der wissenschaften. Nach dem ungarischen, mit einem einleitenden vorworte. Deutsch bearbeitet von dr. Sigmund Schiller. Budapest, C. Grill, 1876. xvi, 232, 3 p.
2803. RAEVSKAIA, E. S. Ocherki istorii ėkonomicheskoĭ mysli vengril. (Transliterated.) Moscow, 1962. 211 p. (Translations from Hungarian.)

INDIA

2804. BEHARI, Bepin. Gandhian economic philosophy. 1st ed. Bombay, Vora, 1963. xi, 157 p. Bibliographical footnotes.
2805. BRUCKER, Egon. Wirtschaft und finanzen im staate kautilyas, unter besonderer berücksichtigung der historischen und sozialen verhältnisse. (Dissertation, Würzburg.) 1966. 158 p. Bibliography, 147-158.
2806. DATTA, Bhabatosh. The evolution of economic thinking in India. (Dr. P. N. Banerjea memorial lectures, 1961.) Calcutta, Federation hall society, 1962. xvi, 52 p.
2807. DUTT, Shib Chandra. Conflicting tendencies in Indian economic thought. Calcutta, N. M. Ray-Chowdhury & company, 1934. 2 p. 1., iii-vii, 225 p. Bibliographies. (Excepting ch. II and ch. VII all chapters were published serially under different titles in Prabuddha bharata from 1929 to 1931. Chapter II appeared in the Insurance and finance review, Calcutta, May-September, 1933.)
2808. _____. Thirty-five years of Indian economic thought, 1898-1932. Calcutta, Monindra mohan moulik, 1933. 20 p. Bibliography.
2809. ECONOMIC strategy and the third plan. (Indian statistical series, no. 21) (Indian statistical institute.) New York, Asia publishing house, 1963. vii, 132 p. Bibliographical footnotes.
2810. GANDHI, Mohandas Karamchand. Economic and industrial life and relations. Compiled and edited by V. B. Kher. 1st edition. Ahmedabad, Navajivan publishing house, 1957. 3 v.
2811. _____. Sarvodaya, the welfare of all. Edited by Bharatan Kumarappa. 1st edition. Ahmedabad, Navajivan publishing house, 1954. xii, 200 p.
2812. _____. Selected writings. Abmedabad, Navajivan publishing house, 1959. 16 v.
2813. GANGULI, B. N. "Rethinking on Indian economics." In, India economics journal, 3, 3 (January 1956) 235-255.
2814. GOPALAKRISHNAN, Panikkanparambil Kesavan. Development of economic ideas in India, 1880-1914. 's Graven-

hage, 1954. 105 p. Bibliography.
2815. GUPTA, Shanti Swarup. The economic philosophy of Mahatma Gandhi. Delhi, Ashok publishing house, 1968. v. 223 p.
2816. JHA, Shiva Nand. A critical study of Ghandian economic thought. With a foreword by J. C. Kumarappa. Agra, Lakshmi narain agarwal, 1961? iv, 276, ii p. Bibliography, i-ii.
2817. KARVE, Dattatraya Gopal. Historical and economic studies, published on the occasion of the Silver jubilee of the Historical and economic association of the Fergusson college, Poona. Poona, The author, 1941. 2 p. 1., v. ii, 238, vi p.
2818. MADAN, Gurmukh Ram. Economic thinking in India. With a foreword by R. K. Mukerjee. Delhi, S. Chand, 1966. xvi, 399 p. Bibliographical footnotes.
2819. MATHUR, J. S. and A. S. Mathur. Economic thought; Mohandas Karamchand Gandhi. Foreword by J. B. Kripalani. Allahabad. Chaitanya publishing house, 1962. 666 p.
2820. MILLIKAN, M. "Economic thought and its application and methodology in India." In, American economic review, Papers and Proceedings, 46, 2 (May, 1956) 399-407. (Includes a discussion by D. H. Taylor and J. M. Clark, 413-418.)
2821. MUKERJEE, Radhakamal. Economic problems of modern India. London, Macmillan, 1939.
2822. MUKHOPADHYAY, Rabindra Nath. Gāndhijīra arthanaltika darśana. (Transliterated.) India, 1965. 8, 237, 2 p. Bibliography, 239 p. (In Bengali.)
2823. NATARAJAN, Balasubrahmanya. Economic ideas of Tiruvalluvar. (The Sornammal endowment lectures, 1960-61.) Madras?, 1962. 46 p. (Tamil edition.)
2824. ———. Valluvar tanta poruliyal. (Transliterated.) India, 1965. v, 108 p. (In Tamil.)
2825. RANGASWAMI Aiyangar, Kumbakonan virarghava. Aspect of ancient Indian economic thought. 2d edition. (Manindra chandra Nandy lectures, 1927.) Varanasi, Banaras Hindu university, 1965. viii, 186 p. Bibliography, 169-179.
2826. RIVETT, Kenneth. Economic thought of Mahatma Gandhi. Bombay, Allied publishers private, 1959. 32 p.
2827. RUSKIN, John. Unto this last, a paraphrase by M. K. Gandhi. Translated from the Gujarati by Valji Govindji Desai. 1st edition. Ahmedabad, Navajivan publishing house, 1951. vi, 64 p.
2828. SEN, Benoychandra. Economics in Kautilya. (Calcutta Sanskrit college research series, no. 53; studies no. 32.) Calcutta, Sanskrit college, 1967. xvi, 251 p.
2829. SHAH, Khushal Talaksi. Ancient foundations of economics in India. 1st edition. (The Maharaja sayajirao Gaekwad honorarium lectures, 1950-1951.) Bibliographical footnotes.

Countries and Areas 191

2830. SINGH, V. B. Essays in Indian political economy. New Delhi, Peoples publishing house, 1967.
2831. SO takā svadesī. (Transliterated.) Jamanādasa Bhagavānadāsa smārakamāja, 23.) India, 1941. 7, 368 p. (In Gujarati.)
2832. VASUDEVAN, A. The strategy of planning in India. Meerut, Meenakshi prakashan, 1970. ix, 332 p. Bibliography 324-330.

INDONESIA

2833. HATTA, Mohammad. Persoalan ekonomi sosialis Indonesia. Djakarta, Djambatan, c1963. v. 49 p.

IRELAND

2834. BLACK, R. D. Collison. Economic thought and the Irish question, 1817-1870. Cambridge, England, University press, 1960. xiv, 298. Bibliography, 249-292.

ISLAMIC COUNTRIES

2835. ABU AL-SU'UD, Mahmūd. Khutūt ra'īsīyah fī al-iqtisād al-Islāmī. (Transliterated.) 1965. 96 p. Bibliographical footnotes.
2836. AHMAD, Shaikh Mahmud. Economics of Islam; a comparative study. Labore, M. Ashraf, 1947. xi, 191 p.
2837. AHMED Moulavi, C. N. Principles and practice of Islamic economy. Translated by K. Hasan. Calicut, Ansari press, 1964. iii, ii, iv, ii, 200 p.
2838. AL-GILANI, Sayyid Manāzar Ahsan. Islāmī ma'āshiyāt. (Transliterated.) 1962. 11, 566 p. (In Urdu.)
2839. ALI, Syed Ahmad. Economic foundations of Islam. A social and economic study. Bombay, Orient Longmans, 1964. x, 203 p. Bibliographical footnotes.

ISRAEL

2840. PATINKIN, D. "Une histoire de la pensee economique contemporaine." In, American economic review, Papers and proceedings, 46, 2 (May, 1956) 408-412.

ITALY

2841. BARONCI, Mario. Il microbo della guerra. (Collana di studi sociali moderni, 4.) Roma, Coletti, 1944. 346 p., 1 l.
2842. BOUSQUET, Georges Henri. Esquisse d'une histoire de la science économique en Italie. Des origines à Francesco Ferrara. (Bibliothèque générale d'économie politique.) Paris, M. Rivière, 1960. 107 p. Bibliography, 5-9.
2843. CAPODAGLIO, Gialio. "La storiografia italiana delle dottrine economiche nella prima meta del secola XX."

In, Rivista di politica economica, 43, 4 (April, 1953) 427-450.
2844. COSSA, Luigi. Saggi bibliografici di economia politica. (Bibliografie e opere classiche di economia politica, n. 1.) Bologna, A. Forni, 1963. xxii, 452 p.
2845. ERRERA, Alberto. Storia dell'economia politica nei secoli XVII e XVIII negli-stati della Repubblica veneta, corredata da documenti inediti. Venezia, Tip. di. G. Antonelli, 1877. 570 p. (Reprinted: Burt Franklin research & source work series, 114. New York, B. Franklin, 1965. 570 p. Bibliography, 314-335.)
2846. FANFANI, Amintore. Le origini dello spirito capitalistico in Italia. (Pubblicazioni della Università cattolica del Sacro cuore. series 3: Scienze sociali, vol. XII.) Milano, Società editrice "Vita e pensiero," 1933. vi, 179, 1 p. Bibliography, 171-176.
2847. FORNARI, Tommaso. Delle teorie economiche nelle provincie napolitane dal secolo XIII al MDCCXXXIV. Studii storici di Tommaso Fornari. (Studi giuridici e politici.) Milano, U. Hoepli, 1882. xi p., 1 1., 375, 1 p. Bibliography, 371-375.
2848. FOSSATI, Eraldo. Economisti ungheresi e economisti italiani del secolo XIX. Prefazione dell' on. prof. dr. Béla de Eródi Harrach. 2. ed. Padova, Cedam, Casa editrice dott. A. Milani, 1933. 65 p., 3 1. Bibliographical footnotes. Bibliography, 67-68.
2849. GIANNESSI, Egidio. Attuali tendenze delle dottrine economico-tecniche italiane. (Università degli studi di Firenze. Facoltà di economia e commercio. Collana di studi economico-aziendali, pubblicazione n. 2.) Pisa, C. Cursi, 1954. xx, 638 p. Bibliography, 573-629.
2850. GRAZIANI, Augusto. Le idee economiche degli scrittori Emiliani e Romagnoli sino al 1848. Memoria premiata al Concorso Cossa (1892) dalla R. Accademia di scienze, lettere ed arti di Modena. Modena, Coi tipi della Società tipografica, 1893. 187 p. 1 1.
2851. ———. Teorie e fatti economici. Torino, Fratelli Bocca, 1912. 2 p. 1., 3-499 p.
2852. LAMPERTICO, Fedele. Giammaria Ortes e la scienza economica al suo tempo; studi storici economici. (Nuova collezione di opere storiche. vol. I.) Venezia e Torino, G. Antonelli e L. Basadonna, 1865. 4 p. 1., 11-350 p.
2853. LUCA, Mario de. Gli economisti napoletani del settecento e la politica dello sviluppo. (Saggio storico-dottrinario sulle vie allo sviluppo. Athenaeum, 15.) Napoli, Morano, 1969? Bibliographical footnotes, 144 p.
2854. LURACHI, Raimondo. Pensiero e azione economica del conte di Cavour. (Pubblicazioni predisposte dal Comitato torinese dell'Istituti per la storia del Risorgimento per il centenario del 1861, 8.) Torino, Museo nazionale del Risorgimento, 1961. 172 p. Bibliography, 163-168.
2855. MANCARELLA, Antonio. Le dottrine di Ricardo e gli economisti italiani della prima metà del secolo XIX. [R. Università di Napoli. Tesi di laurea, pub. dalla Facoltà

di giurisprudenza (fondazione de Pilla), IV.] Napoli, L. Pierro, 1906. viii, 157 p. Bibliographical footnotes.

2856. MANFRA, Modestino Remigio. Pietro Verri e i problemi economici del tempo suo. (Biblioteca storica del risorgimento italinao. n. 1.) Milano-Genova, Società anonima editrice Dante Alighieri (Albrighi, Segati & c.), 1932. xii, 260 p. Bibliografia, 258-260.

2857. MARZANO, Ferruccio. Un'interpretazione del processo di sviluppo economico dualistico in Italia. (Pubblicazioni della Facoltà di economia e commercio dell'Università di Roma, 35.) Milano, A. Giuffré, 1969. iv, 497 p. Bibliography, 477-490.

2858. MICHELS, Robert. Introduzione all storia delle dottrine economiche e politiche, con un saggio sulla economia classica italiana e la sua influenza sulla scienza economica. (Istituto nazionale fascista di cultura. Studi giuridici e storici.) Bologna, N. Zanichelli, 1932. 1 p. 1., v-xiii p., 1 1., 310 p. Bibliographical footnotes.

2859. MORI, Renato. Le riforme leopoldine nel pensiero degli economisti toscani del '700. (Biblioteca storica Sansoni; nuova ser., v. 18.) Firenze, G. C. Sansoni, 1951. 177 p.

2860. PARETO, Vilfredo. Lettere ai Peruzzi, 1872-1900. A cura di Tommaso Giacalone-Monaco. In apprendice: lettere di Raffaele Pareto a Emilia Peruzzi. (Storia ed economia, 14-15.) Roma, Edizioni di storia e letteratura, 1968. 2 v.

2861. PECCHIO, Giuseppe. Histoire de l'économie politique en Italie, ou Abrégé critique des économistes italiens; précédée d'une introduction par el comte Joseph Pecchio. Tr. de l'italien par M. Léonard Gallois, Paris, A. Levavasseur, 1830. viii, 424 p.

2862. _____. Storia della economia pubblica in Italia, ossia Epilogo critico degli economisti italiani, preceduto da un' introduzione. 2. ed. Lugano, Ruggia e c., 1832. 490 p. 1 1.

2863. RADI, Luciano. Potere democratico e forze economiche. Roma, 5 lune, 1969. (Economia e diritto, 5.) 97 p.

2864. RAINONE, C. "Tendenze e richerche degli scrittori italiani di economia pubblica nella seconda netà del secolo XVIII." In, Studi economici, 8, 1 and 2 (January-February and March-April, 1953) 43-58 and 131, 149.

2865. REYNAUD, Pierre. La théorie de la population en Italie du XVIe au XVIIIe ciècle (les précurseurs de Malthus). (Thesis, University of Lyons, 1904. Catalogue des thèses, v. 4., col. 718.) Lyon, A. Rey, 1904. x p., 1 1., 200 p., 1 1. Bibliography, 1-2.

2866. RICCA-SALERNO, Giuseppe. Storia delle dottrine finanziarie in Italia. Col raffronto delle dottrine forestiere e delle istituzioni e condizioni di fatto. 2. ed. Palermo, A. Reber, 1896. 3 p. 1., ix-xvi, 550 p.

2867. _____. La teoria del salario nella storia delle dottrine e dei fatti economici. Palermo. A. Reber, 1900. viii, 687 p.

2868. RICCI, Umberto. Tre economisti italiani: Pantaleoni, Pareto, Loria. (Biblioteca di cultura moderna, n. 328.) Bari, Gius. Laterza & figli, 1939. 239, 1 p.
2869. RUGGIERO Mazzone, Silvana. Un economista pugliese del settecento: Filippo Briganti. Bari, Università degli studi, 1964. 209 p. Bibliographical footnotes. (Appendice: brani dell'Esame analitico del Briganti.)
2870. SCHULLERN zu Schrattennofen, Anton Johann Heinrich Friedrich Hermann, von. Die theoretische national-ökonomie Italiens in neuester zeit. Lepizig, Duncker & Humblot, 1891. ix, 214 p.
2871. SUPINO, Camillo. La scienza economica in Italia dalla seconda metà del secolo XVI alla prima del XVII. (Estr. dalle Memorie della Reale accademia delle scienze di Torino, serie II, t. XXXIX.) Torino, E. Loescher, 1888. 135 p.
2872. TAGLIACOZZO, Giorgio. Economisti napoletani dei sec. XVII e XVIII. (Istituto nazionale fascista di cultura. Classici del pensiero politico, VII.) Bologna, L. Cappelli, 1937. 3 p. 1., v-lxvii, 456 p.
2873. VIANELLO, Carlo Antonio. I valori spirituali della nuova economia. Milano, Ceschina, 1943. 3 p. 1., 9-182, 2 p. Bibliographical footnotes.

JAPAN

2874. BRONFENBRENNER, M. "The state of Japanese economics. In, American economic review 46, 2 (May, 1956) 389-398. (With discussion by O. H. Taylor and J. M. Clark, 413-418.)
2875. FUJII, Sadayoshi. Bakumatsu no keizai shisō. (Transliterated.) Japan, 1963. (Osaka furitsu daigaku, Sakai, Japan. Osaka furitsu daigaku keizai kenkyū sōsho, dai 10-satsu.) 4, 126 p. Bibliographical references.
2876. HONJO, Eijirō. Economic theory and history of Japan in the Tokugawa period. New York, Russell & Russell, 1965. 350 p. Bibliography, 315-324. (First published in 1943 under title: Economic thought and history of Japan in the Tokugawa period.) (Transliterated.)
2877. _____. Edo, Meiji jidai no keizaigukusha. (Transliterated.) 1962. 231 p. Bibliography, 224-225.
2878. _____. Keizaishi kō. (Transliterated.) Japan, 1921. 5, 358 p.
2879. _____. Kinsei no keizai shisō. (Transliterated.) Japan, 1931. 20, 340 p. Bibliographical notes.
2880. _____. Nihon keizai shisō-shi. (Transliterated.) Tōkyō, Yūhikaku, 1958. 8, 210 p.
2881. _____. Nihon heizai shisō shi kenkyū. (Transliterated.) (Osaka keizai daigaku. Nihon keizaishi kenkyūjo. Osaka keizai daigaku nihon keizaishi kenkyūjo sōsho, dai 2-3-satsu.) Japan, 1966. 2 v. Bibliographies.
2882. _____. Nihon no keizaigaku. (Transliterated.) Japan, 1957. v, 134 p. Bibliographical footnotes.

883. HORIE, Yasuzō. Keizaishi. (Transliterated.) Japan, 1958. 2, 149 p.
884. _____. Nihon keizai shi gaiyō. (Transliterated.) Japan, 1956. 327 p.
885. _____. Seiyō keizai shi gaiyō. (Transliterated.) Japan, 1949. 275 p.
886. KADA, Tetsuji. Nihon shakai keizai shisō shi. (Transliterated.) Japan, 1962. 427 p.
887. KEIO gijuku daigaku, Tokyo. Keiō gijuku keizai gakkai. Nihon ni okeru keizaigaku no hyakunen. (Transliterated.) Japan, 1959. 2 v. Bibliographies.
888. KEIZAIGAKUSHI gakkai. Nihon ni okeru keizaigakushi kenkyū jūnen no ayumi. (Transliterated.) Japan, 1961. 2, 131 p.
889. KITAZAWA, Shinjirō. Kaisō hachijūnen rekishi no hagurama. (Transliterated.) Japan, 1969. 272 p. Bibliography, 251-272.
890. KUBOTA, Akiteru. Mere no shikiten. (Transliterated.) Japan, 1967. 202, 45 p. Bibliographical references in notes. Bibliography of author's works, 16-45.
891. MIYAMOTO, Mataji. Gaisetsu nihon keizai shi. (Transliterated.) Japan, 1956. 175 p. (First edition published in 1946 under another title.)
892. MORI, Shōzaburō. Mori Shōzaburō kyōju lei shi. (Transliterated.) Japan, 1968. 134 p. Bibliography of author's works, 91-102.
893. NAKANO, Tōgo. Nihon shakai no shisōshiteki haikei. (Transliterated.) Japan, 1968. 384 p. Bibliographies.
894. NIHON no Marukushu keizaigaku. (Transliterated.) Japan, 1967-68. 2 v.
895. OUCHI, Hyōe. Jitsuryoku wa oshiminaku ubau. (Transliterated.) Japan, 1965. 396 p.
896. SASAKI, Kyohei. A western influence on Japanese economic thought. The Marxian non-Marxian controversies in the 1920's and their significance for today. (Thesis, Columbia university). Ann Arbor, Michigan, University microfilms, 1958. iv, 159 1. Bibliography, 154-159. (Abstracted in Dissertation abstracts, v. 19 (1958) no. 1, p. 68-69. AC-1, no. 58-2245.)
897. SMITH, Neil Skene. An introduction to some Japanese economic writings of the 18th century. London, P. S. King & son ltd., 1935. 2 p. 1., 3-72, 1 p. Bibliography, 73. (Reprinted from the Transactions of the Asiatic society of Japan, vol. XI, second series, 1934.)
898. SUMIYA, Etsuji. Nihon keizaigaku shi. (Transliterated.) (Shakai Seisaku Gakkai.) Japan, 1958. 9, 440 p. Bibliography, 422. (Revised 1967. 9, 454 p. Bibliography, 433.)
899. _____. Nihon keizaigaku shi no isseki. (Transliterated.) (Shakai seisaku gakkai.). Japan, 1948. 324 p.
900. TAKAMURA, Shōhei. Nihon ni okeru keizaishigaku no hattatsu. (Transliterated.) (Jimbun kagaku kenkyu sosho, dai 2-hen.) Japan, 1949. 6, 148, 7 p.
901. TAKENAKA, Yasukazu. Sekimon shingaku no keizai shisō.

(Transliterated.) Japan, 1962. 20, 699, 13 p. Bibliographical footnotes.
2902. TAKEUCHI, Kenji. Goyaku. (Transliterated.) Japan, 1964. 216 p.
2903. TSUCHIYA, Takao. Nihon keizai shi. (Transliterated.) (Keizaigaku zenshū, 6.) Japan, 1955. 4, 4, 189, 9 p.
2904. TSURU, S. "Survey of economic research in postwar Japan. Major issues of theory and public policy arising out of post war economic problems." In, American economic review, 54, 4, II (June, 1964) 79-101.
2905. YAMAGUCHI, Kazuo. Nihon keizai shi kōgi. (Transliterated. Japan, 1960. 3, 243, 15 p. Bibliography, 229-243.

KOREA

2906. HAN, U-gŭn. Yijo hugi ŭi sahoe wa sasang. (Transliterated. (Hanguk munhwa ch'ongsŏ, che 16-jip.) Korea, 1961. 11, 393, 8 p. (Society and culture: the 18th century Korea.)
2907. HONG, I-sop. Chŏng Yag-yong ŭi chongch'i kyŏngje sasang yŏn'gu. (Transliterated.) (Han'guk yon'gu ch'ongsŏ, che 3-jip.) Korea, 1959. viii, 264, 8, 23 p. Bibliography, 1-8. (The political-economic thought of Yak-yong Chong, 1762-1836.)
2908. KIM, Kwang-jin. Chosŏn kyŏngje sasang sa. (Transliterated.) Korea, 1963. v. Bibliographical footnotes.

LATIN AMERICA

2909. HARRIS, Seymour Edwin, editor. Economic problems of Latin America. New York, London, McGraw-Hill book company, inc., 1944. xiv, 465. Bibliographical footnotes.
2910. HARVARD university. Bureau for economic research in Latin America. The economic literature of Latin America a tentative bibliography. Cambridge, Harvard university press, 1935- . v. (Work initiated by João Frederico Normano under the supervision of Professor Clarence Henry Haring.)
2911. EL PENSAMIENTO económico latino-americano. (Sección de obras de economia del Fondo de cultura económica.) Méxi co, Fondo de cultura económica, 1945- . v. (v. 1. Argentina, por L. R. Gondra. Bolivia, por Victor Paz Estenssoro. Brasil, por Luis Nogueira de Paula. Cuba, por Gerardo Portela. Chile, por Carlos Keller R. Haiti, por E. D. Charlier. Paraguay, por Silvio Maldonado. Peru, por Emilio Romero.)
2912. POPESCU, Oreste. El sistema económico en las misiones jesuíticas; un vasto experimento de desarrollo indoamericano. 2 ed. Barcelona, Ediciones Ariel, 1967. 198 p. Bibliography, 185-189.

LATVIA

2913. KIRTOVSKIS, Imants. Latviešu progresivās ekonomiskās domas attīstība XIX gadsimta 80. un 90. gados. (Latvijas PSR Zinātnu akademija. Ekonomikas instituts.) Rīgā, Latvijas PSR zinātnu akademijas izdevniecība, 1956. 66 p. Bibliography.

MEXICO

2914. COLEGIO de economistas del distrito federal. Directorio nacional de economistas. México, Tall. G. Y. G. Rivero. v.
2915. GLADE, William P. and Charles W. Anderson. The political economy of Mexico; two studies. Madison, University of Wisconsin press, 1963. vii, 242 p.
2916. LOZA Macias, Manuel. El pensamiento económico y la constitución de 1857. (Thesis, Universidad nacional autónoma de México.) México, Editorial jus, 1959. 288 p. Bibliography.
2917. SILVA HERZOG, Jesús. El pensamiento económico en México. (Colección tierra firme, 29.) México, Fondo de cultura económica, 1947. 199 p. Bibliografía, 191-196.
2918. ――――. El pensamiento económico, social y político de México, 1810-1964. México, Instituto Mexicano de investigaciones económicas, 1967. 748 p. Bibliography, 655-673.

NETHERLANDS

2919. BAASCH, Ernst. Holländische wirtschaftsgeschichte. Jena, G. Fischer, 1927. vi p., 1 1., 632 p. Bibliography, 592-615. (Handbuch der wirtschaftsgeschichte, hrsg. von dr. Georg Brodnitz.)
2920. BUTTER, Irene Hasenberg. Academic economics in Holland, 1800-1870. (Studies in social life, 13.) The Hague, Nijhoff, 1969, 1970. viii, 162 p. Bibliography, 150-162.
2921. DE ROOVER, Raymond Adrien. Leonardus Lessius als economist. De economische leerstellingen van de latere scholastiek in de Zuidelijke Nederlanden. (Mededelingen van de Koninklijke Vlaamse Academie voor Wetenschappen, Letteren en schone kunsten van België. Klasse der letteren, jaarg. 31, nr. 1.) Brussel, Paleis der academiën, 1969. 27 p. Bibliographical footnotes. (Summary in English and French.)
2922. REES, Otto van. Geschiedenis der staathuishoudkunde in Nederland tot het einde der achttiende eeuw. Utrecht, Kemink en zoon, 1865-68. 2 v.
2923. ――――. Verhandeling over de verdiensten van Gijsbert Karel van Hogendorp, als staatshuishoudkundige, ten aanzien van Nederland. Uitg. door het Provinciaal Utrechtsche genootschap van kunsten en wetenschappen. Utrecht, C. van der Post, j^r., 1854. viii, 226 p. (In Provinciaal

utrechtsch genootschap van kusten en wetenschappen, Utrecht. Geschied- en letterkundige verhandelingen. Utrec 1859. nieuwe reeks, 1. deel.)

2924. THIEL, H. "Some development of economic thought in the Netherlands." In, American economic review, 54, 2, II (March, 1964) 34-55.

2925. VAN DEN BERG, Martin. Enige aspekte van die invloed var ekonomiese navorsung op makro-ekonomiese beleid in Nederland en die verenigde koninkryk gedurende 1945-52. s'Gravenhage, Excelsior, 1954. 115 p. Bibliography.

NORWAY

2926. BONDE, Gjert Edvard. Totalitetsøkonomien. En populaer fremstilling av Samfundslivets nye evangelium, Bertram Dybwad Brochmann's livssyn og samfundslaere. Bergen, Bondes forlag, 1966. xv, 232 p. Bibliography, ii.

PAKISTAN

2927. SHEIKH, Nasir Ahmad. Some aspects of the constitution and the economics of Islam. With foreword by the late Zahid Husain. 3d ed. Woking, England, Woking Muslim mission and literary trust, 1961. 246 p. Bibliographical references.

POLAND

2928. CZARKOWSKI, Jan. "450 lat krakowskiej myśli ekonomicznej." In Probleme economice, Bucuresti (May, 1964) 8-46.

2929. _____. Zarys dziejów myśli ekonomicznej w Polsce. (Polska Akademia umiejętności. Historia nauki polskiej w monografia. 16.) Kraków, Nakł. Polskiej Akademii umiejętności; skł. gł. w ksieg. Gebethnera i Wolffa, 1948. 53 p.

2930. GARGAS, Zygmunt. Geschichte der nationalökonomie im alten Polen. Berlin, R. L. Prager, 1925. 154 p.

2931. GORSKI, Janusz. Polska myśl ekonomiczna a rozwój gospodarczy, 1807-1830; studia nad poczatkami teorii zacofania gospodarczego. Wyd. 1. Warszawa, Panstwowe wydawn. Naukowe, 1963. 357 p. Bibliography, 339-346. (Summaries in English and Russian.)

2932. GRABSKI, Zdzisław. Sytuacja zawodowa i społeczna w latach 1945-1964 studentów tajnego nauchzania ekonomicznego z lat 1940-1945. Wyd. 1. (Wybrane dokumenty i informaeje o szkolnictwie wyższym, 9.) (Ministerstwo szkolnictwa wyższego. Miedzyuczelniany zakład badań nad szkolnictwem wyzszym Warszawa, Państwowe wydawn. Naukowe, 1966. 152 p. Bibliography, 146-151.

2933. GRODEK, Andrzej. Wybór pism. Pisma zebrali, opracowali i wstępem opatrzyli: Jerzy Ciepielewski et al. Wyd. 1. Warszawa, Państwowe wydawn. Naukowe, 1963, 2 v.

	Bibliographical footnotes. Przegląd polskich bibliografii nauk ekonomicznych, v. 2, 85-97. Bibliografia prac prof. Dr. Andrzeja Grodka by H. Uniejewska and A. Miłaszewska, v. 2, 469-484.
2934.	GUZICKI, Leszek and Seweryn Zurawicki. Historia polskiej myśli społecznoekonomicznej do roku 1914. Warszawa państwowe wydawn. Ekonomiczne, 1969. 358 p.
2935.	KLUCZYNSKI, Jan. Der Beruf des ökonomen in der volksrepublik Polen. Gekürzke und vom verfasser autorisierte Fassung seines 1966 in Polen erschienenen Buches. Berlin, Institut für hochschulbildung und-ökonomie, 1970. 179 p.
2936.	LANGE, Oscar Richard. "Aktualne problemy nauk ekonomicznych w Polsce." In, Ekonomista, 5 (1965) 3-16; In, Nowe drogi, Warszawa, 19, 6 (June, 1956) 24-35.
2937.	LIPINSKI, Edward. De Copernic à Stanislas Leszczynski. La pensée économique et démographique en Pologne. (Ecole pratique des hautes études. Institut nationale d'études démographiques.) Paris, Presses universitaires de France, 1961. 342 p. Bibliography. (Abridged translation of the author's Studia nad historia, polskiej myśli ekonomicznej.)
2938.	_____. Historia powszechnej myśli ekonomicznej do roku 1870. Warszawa, Państwowe wydawnictwo naukowe, 1968. 538 p. Bibliography, 523-532.
2939.	_____. Studia nad historia polskiej myśli ekonomicznej. Warszawa, Państwowe wydawn. Naukowe, 1956. 536 p. Bibliography, 517-528.
2940.	_____. "Uwagi do 'zarysu historii polskiej myśli ekonomicznej.'" In, Ekonomista, Warszawa, 3 (1952) 162-168.
2941.	MINC, Bronisław. Zagadnienia dochodu narodowego. Wyd. 2. uzup. Warszawa, Ksiażka i wiedza, 1951. 278 p.
2942.	RADZISZEWSKI, Henryk. Polska idea ekonomiczna. W Warszawie Wydaw. M. Arcta, 1918. viii, 124, 1 p. Bibliographical footnotes.
2943.	"ZARYS historii polskiej mysli ekonomicznej." In, Economista, 3 (1952) 153-161.
2944.	ZURAWICKI, Seweryn. Myśl ekonomiczno-polityczna w Polsce okresu miedzywojennego. Wyd. 1. Warszawa, Państwowe wydawn. Naukowe, 1970. 286 p. Bibliographical reference. (Table of contents also in English and Russian.)

PORTUGAL

2945.	AMZALAK, Moses Bensabat. Anciens économistes portugais. Lisbonne, Institut français au Portugal, 1940. Bibliographical footnotes. (Extrait du Bulletin des études portugaises, numéro spécial, 1940.)
2946.	_____. O economista José Accursio das Neves. (A economia politica em Portugal.) Lisboa, 1920-21. 2 v. (v. 1: Hiobibliografia. v. 2: Doutrinas económicas.)
2947.	_____. Do estudo e da evolução das doutrinas económicas em Portugal. Lisboa, 1928. 277 p. (Comunicação feita

à Academia das sciêntias de Lisboa na sessão da 2.ª classe de 22 março de 1928.)

2948. CALVET de Magalhães, José. História do pensamento econômico em Portugal; da Idade-Média ao mercantilismo. Coimbra, 1967. xvi, 536 p. Bibliography, 517-529. (Separata do Boletim de ciencias econômicas, vols. VIII, IX, X, XI, e XII.)

2949. FERREIRA, Alexandre. Unbekannte portugiesische Merkantilisten. (Inaugural dissertation, Bern.) Bern, 1952. 204 p. Bibliography, 197-204.

2950. LEAL, Raul. Contribution à l'étude des idées politiques et sociales de l'Ecole de Coïmbre. (Thèse, Universite de Paris.) Paris, M. Lavergne, imprimeur, 1941. 2 p. 1., 7-128 p. Bibliographie, 121-126.

2951. MARNOCO e Souza, José Ferreira. Economia nacional; prelecções feitas ao curso do segundo anno juridico de 1908-1909. Coimbra, França Amado, 1909. 422 p.

2952. SA, Victor de. Perspectivas do século XIX; ensaios. (Coleccão Portugalia. 5: Ciências sociológicas e psicológicas, 1.) Lisboa, Portugália editora, 1964. 291 p.

RUMANIA

2953. ACADEMIA Republicii populare Romîne. Institutul de Cercetări economice. Texte din literatura economica în Romînia; secolul XIX. Bucuresti, Editura Academiei republicii populare Romine, 1960- . v.

RUSSIA

2954. AKADEMIIA nauk SSR. Institut ékonomiki. A history of Russian economic thought: ninth through eighteenth centuries. Edited with a foreword by John M. Letiche. Translated with the collaboration of Basil Dmytryshyn and Richard A. Pierce. (Publications of the Institute of business and economic research, University of California.) Berkeley, University of California press, 1964. xvi, 690 p. Bibliography, 641-673. (A translation of v. 1, pt. 1 of the original work edited by A. I. Pashkov.)

2955. ATSKANOV, Mukhamed Khazhismelovich. Ekonomicheskie otnosheniia i ékonomicheskie vzgliady v Kabarde i Balkarii, 1860-1917. 1967. 130 p. Bibliographical footnotes.

2956. BERENDTS, Eduard Nikolaevich. Volks- und staatswirthschaftliche anschauungen in Russland auf der grenzscheide des 18. und 19. jahrhunderts. Archivalische studie. St. Petersburg, Typographie H. Schacht & co., 1888. xiii, 84 p., 1 1.

2957. BLIUMIN, Izrail' Grigor'evich. Ocherki ekonomicheskoĭ v Rosaii. (Transliterated.) Akademiia nauk SSSR. Institut ekonomiki, Moscow, 1940. 286, 2 p.

2958. LYASHCHENKO, Peter I. History of the national economy of Russia to the 1917 revolution. New York, The Macmillan company, 1949.

Countries and Areas

2959. MAVOR, James. An economic history of Russia. 2d ed. rev. and enl. London & Toronto, J. M. Dent & sons, limited; New York, E. P. Dutton & co., 1925. 2 v.
2960. MOHRMANN, Heinz. Studien über russisch-deutsche begegnungen in der wirtschaftswissenschaft, 1750-1825. (Quellen und studien zur geschichte osteuropas, bd. 5.) Berlin, Akademie-verlag, 1959. 146 p. Bibliography, 131-136.
2961. PAZHITNOV, Konstantin Alekseevich. Ekonomicheskie vozzreniĭa dekabristov. (Transliterated.) Edited by Ivan Dmitrievich Udal'tsov. Akademiia nauk SSSR. Institut ékonomiki. Moscow, 1945. 101, 3 p.
2962. POLIANSKII, Fedor Iakovlevich. Plekhanov i russkaĭa ekonomicheskaĭa mysl'. (Transliterated.) Moscow, 1965. 471 p. Bibliographical footnotes.
2963. REUEL', Abram Lazarevich. Ekonomiche-skoe uchenie A. I. Gerfsena. (Transliterated.) Moscow, 1961. 82 p. Bibliographical footnotes.
2964. STRUMILIN, Stanislav Gustavovich. (Economics, 1897-1917.) Moscow, 1957. 287 p.
2965. VYTANOVYCH, Illĭa. Suspil'no-ekonomichni tendenstii v derzhavnomu budivnytstvi. Ivana Mazepy. (Transliterated.) Ukraine, 1959. 16 p. Bibliographical notes. (Social and economic tendencies in state policies of Ivan Stepanovych Mazepa, Hetman of the Cossacks, 1644-1709.)
2966. WAGENFUHR, Rolf. Die konjunkturtheorie in Russland. Mit 1 kurve im text. (Part of author's dissertation, Jena, 1929.) Jena, G. Fischer, 1929. vi, 137 p. Literaturverzeichnis, 133-137.

SPAIN

2967. COLMEIRO, M. Historia de la economía política española. Madrid, Taururs, 1965. 2 v.
2968. GRICE-HUTCHINSON, Marjorie. The school of Salamanca. Readings in Spanish monetary theory, 1544-1605. Oxford, Clarendon press, 1952. xii, 134 p. Bibliography, 128-131.
2969. RAHOLA y Tremols, Federico. Economistas españoles de los siglos XVI y XVII. Barcelona, Impr. de L. Tasso Serra, 1887. 83 p., 1 1. Bibliographical notes.
2970. SUREDA Carrión, José Luis. La hacienda castellana y los economistas del siglo XVII. (Consejo superior de investigaciones cientificas. Instituto de economía "Sancho de Moncada." Publicaciones, Serie C: Historia de las doctrinas e instituciones económicas, no. 4.) Madrid, 1949. 244 p. Bibliography, 229-230.

SWEDEN

2971. BERENDTS, Eduard Nikolaevich. Merkantilisty i fiziokraty. (Transliterated.) 1892. 1 p. 1., 66 p., 1 1.
2972. BJURLING, Oscar. Att studera ekonomisk och social historia En introduktion. (Scandinavian university books.) Stockholm, Svenska bokförlaget, 1966. 7, 78 p.
2973. CHILDS, Marquis William. Sweden. The middle way. New Haven, Yale university press, 1971.
2974. LANDGREN, Karl Gustav. Den'nya ekonomien'i Sverige: J. M. Keynes, E. Wigforss, B. Ohlin och utvecklingen 1927-39. (Ekonomiska studier utg. av nationalekonomiska institutionen vid Göteborgs universitet, 3.) Stockholm, Almqvist & Wiksell, 1960. 320 p. Bibliography, 309-317.
2975. ————. Economics in modern Sweden. Translation by Paul Gekker. Washington, Reference department, Library of congress, 1957. ix, 117 p. Bibliographical references.
2976. PALANDER, T. "On the concepts and methods of the 'Stockholm school.' Some methodological reflections on Myrdal's monetary equilibrium." Translated from Swedish by Stedman. In, International economic papers, no. 3. London, New York, Macmillan, 1953, 5-57. (Original text: "Om, 'Stockholmsskolans' Begrepp och Metoder," Econ. Ts. 1, 191.) Timoteus.
2977. PETANDER, Karl. De nationalekonomiska åskådningarna i Sverige, sådana de framträda i litteraturen, 1718-1765. (Akademisk afhandlung, Stockholms högskola.) Stockholm, Kungl. boktryckeriet, P. A. Norstedt & söner, 1912. xiv, 285 p. Bibliography, vii-xiv.
2978. SCHAUMAN, Georg Carl August. Studier i frihetstidens nationalekonomiska litteratur, idéer och strömningar 1718-1740. (Akademisk afhandling, Helsingfors.) Helsingfors, Finska litteratursällskapets tryckeri, 1910. viii, 173 p.
2979. SCHNITZER, Martin. The economy of Sweden. The model welfare state. New York, Frederick A. Praeger, Inc., 1970.
2980. WESTERLIND, Erik and Rune Beckman. Sweden's economy: Structure and trends. Stockholm, Bokforlaget prisma, 1964.
2981. YOHE, William Poe. The Wicksellian tradition in Swedish macroeconomic theory. (Thesis, University of Michigan.) (Abstracted in Dissertation abstracts, v. 19 (1959) no. 12, p. 3167.) Ann Arbor, Michigan, University microfilms, 1959. xi, 398 p. Bibliography, 379-398.

SWITZERLAND

2982. MEYER, Robert Paul and others. Conrad Cramer-Frey, 1834-1900. (Von Robert P. Meyer.) Eduard Sulzer-Ziegler, 1854-1913. (Von Arthur Straessle.) Karl Friedrich Gegauf, 1860-1926. (Von Maria Dutli-Rutishauser. Hrsg. vom.) Verein für wirtschaftshistorische studien, Zürich. (Schweizer pioniere der wirtschaft und technik, 21.) Zürich, Wetzikon, Buchdruckerei Wetzikon, 1969. 118 p. Bibliography, 117-118.

UNION OF SOVIET SOCIALIST REPUBLICS

2983. AKADEMIIA nauk SSSR. Istoriia ekonomicheskikh uchenii. (Transliterated.) Edited by Nikolai Konstantinovich Karataev. Moscow, 1963. 549 p. Bibliography, 526-543.
2984. ———. Social sciences in the USSR. New York, Basic books, 1965. xii, 297 p. Bibliographies. (Articles prepared at request of UNESCO; prepared under auspices of the International social science council.)
2985. ———. Institut ekonomiki. Istoriiā russkoĭ ėkonomicheskoĭ mysli. (Transliterated.) Moscow, 1955- . v. Bibliographies.
2986. ———. Institut istorii. Ob osobennostīakh imperializma v Rossii. Edited by Ardakiĭ Lavrovich Sidorov. (Transliterated.) Moscow, 1963. 439 p. Bibliographical footnotes.
2987. AKADEMIIA nauk URSR. Kiev. Institut ekonomikĭ. Narysy z istoriĭ ekonomichnoĭ dumky na Ukraini. (Transliterated.) Edited by D. F. Virnyk. Kiev, 1956. 385, 3 p. Bibliography, 365-386.
2988. ———. ———. Z istoriĭ ekonomichnoĭ dumky na Ukraini. (Transliterated.) Edited by Vasyl' Pakhomo Teplyts'kyi. Kiev, 1961. 346 p. Bibliographical footnotes.
2989. AKADEMIIA obshchestvennykh nauk. Istoriīā ekonomicheskikh uchenĭĭ. (Transliterated.) Moscow, 1965. 479 p. Bibliographical footnotes.
2990. BREGEL' Enokh Iakovlevich. Bor'ba V. I. Lenina protiv antimarksistskikh ėkonomicheskikh teoriĭ. (Transliterated.) (Novoe v zhizni, nauke, tekhnike. Seriīā: ėkonomika, 1969, 4.) Moscow, 1969. 64 p. Bibliographical footnotes.
2991. BREUSENKO, D. P. Nekotorye voprosy metodologii istorii ėkonomicheskoĭ mysli. (Transliterated.) Moscow, 1963. 71 p. Bibliography.
2992. BUDISH, Jacob M. Is communism the next stage? A reply to Kremlinologists. (Little new world paperbacks, LNW3.) New York, International publishers, 1965. 128 p. Bibliography, 127-128.
2993. ELLMAN, Michael. Soviet planning today. (University of Cambridge, Department of applied economics, Occasional papers, 25.) Cambridge, England, University press, 1971. xv, 219 p.
2994. GALLUS, Werner. Zur kritik der sowjetischen wirtschaftslehre (Politökonomie) Sonderausg. für das bundesministerium für Gersamtdeutsche fragen. 2 aufl. Pfaffenhofen/Ilm, Ilmgauverlag, c1959. 83 p. Bibliography.
2995. GOWLANYAN, Khach'ik Grigori. Ocherki istorii armīanskoĭ ėkonomicheskoĭ mysli. (Transliterated.) Moscow, 1955. 350 p.
2996. ———. Owrvagster hay tntesagitakan mtk'i patmowt'yan.

(Transliterated.) 1958. 558 p. Bibliographical footnotes.
2997. GUELFAT, Isaac. Economic thought in the Soviet Union. Concepts and aspects. A comparative outline. Liège, International centre of research and information of collective economy; The Hague, Martinus Nijhoff, 1969. 167 p. Bibliography, 151-157.
2998. HOHMANN, Hans-Hermann und Gertraud Seidenstecher. Sowjetische politische ökonomie und konvergenztheorie. (Berichte des Bundesinstituts für ostwissenschaftliche und internationale Studien, 26/1970.) Köln, Bundesinstitut für ostwissenschaftliche und internationale studien, 1970. 23 p. Bibliographical references. (Summary in English.)
2999. HOLZMAN, Franklyn D. Readings on the Soviet economy. Chicago, Rand McNally and company, 1962.
3000. HORIE, Muraichi. Shakaishugi keizaigaku no kihon mondai. (Transliterated.) Japan, 1951. 9, 238 p.
3001. KABDIEV, Duĭsenkhan Kabdievich. Sotsial'no-ekonomicheskie vozzreniia kazakhskikh prosvetiteleĭ-demokratov. (Transliterated.) Alam-Ata, 1966. 150 p. Bibliographical footnotes.
3002. KADOR, Fritz-Jürgen. Normative grundlagen des sowjetischen wirtschaftsdenkens und ihre wirtschaftspolitischen aspekte. (Dissertation, Göttingen.) Göttingen, 1961. ii, 128 p. Bibliography, 120-127.
3003. KARATAEV, Nikolaĭ Konstantinovich. "Buržuaznye koncepcii istorii ékonomičeskoj mysli." In, Voprosy ékonomiki (February, 1963) 93-104.
3004. _____. Ekonomicheskie nauki v Moskovskom universitete 1755-1955. (Transliterated.) Moscow, 1956. 340 p.
3005. _____. "K voprosu o predmete i zadacah istorii ekonomiceskih ucenij." (Transliterated.) In, Naučnye doklady vysscj skoly. Ekonomiceskie nauki (1959) 91-98.
3006. _____. Russkaia ékonomicheskaia mysl'. (Transliterated.) Moscow, 1957. 185 p.
3007. KEYNES, John Maynard. A short view of Russia. (The Hogarth essays. XIII.) London, L. & Virginia Woolf, 1925. 27, 1 p.
3008. KUPRIIANOV, P. M. Kritika vozzreniĭ russkikh burzhuaznykh ékonomistov vo voprosam imperializma. (Transliterated.) 1963. 78 p. Bibliographical footnotes.
3009. KUZ'MINOV, I. I. Razvitie ekonomicheskoi teorii v svete. resheniĭ XXII s'ezda. (Transliterated.) (Kafedra politicheskoĭ ékonomii, Akademiia obshchestvennykh nauk.) Moscow, 1962. 249 p. Bibliography.
3010. LEONT'EV, Lev Abramovich. Leninskoe issledovanie imperializma. (Transliterated.) Moscow, 1964. 371 p. Bibliographical footnotes.
3011. _____. Sotsialisticheskoe stroitel'stvo i ego kritiki. (Transliterated.) Moscow, 1928. 234 p.
3012. MARKERT, Werner. Sowjetunion. Das wirtschaftssystem. In Zusammenarbeit mit zahlreichen Fachgelehrten. (Osteuropa-Handbuch.) Köln, Graz, Böhlau, 1965. xvii, 587 p. Bibliographical footnotes.

3013. MINO, Sadao. Shakaishugi keizaigaku kenkyū josetsu. (Transliterated.) Japan, 212 p. Bibliographical references.
3014. NORMANO, João Frederico. The spirit of Russian economics. London, D. Dobson, 1950. 130 p. Bibliographical footnotes, 120-123.
3015. NOVE, Alec. Economic rationality and Soviet politics. . . . New York, F. A. Praeger, 1964. 316 p. Bibliographical footnotes.
3016. _____. The Soviet economy. An introduction. Revised edition. New York, F. A. Praeger, 1965. c1961. xxvi, 354 p.
3017. OHANYAN, Aram. Arewelahay tntesagitakan mtk'i patmowt' yownits'. (Transliterated.) Armenia, 1960. 178 p. Bibliographical footnotes.
3018. OKAMOTO, Tadashi. Soren keizai ron. (Transliterated.) Japan, 1968. 2 v. Bibliographical references.
3019. OKAZAKI, Takeshi. Marukusu keizaigaku no yōgo. (Transliterated.) Japan, 1951, 2, 6, 283 p.
3020. POLITICAL economy in the Soviet union. Some problems of teaching the subject. Translated from the Russian by Emily G. Kazakévich, with the collaboration of Vladimir D. Kazakévich. New York, International publishers, 1945. 48 p. Reference notes, 47-48. [Unsigned article: "Some problems of the teaching of political economy," Pod znamenem Marksizma, no. 7-8 (July-August, 1943) 5.].
3021. REUEL', Abram Lazarevich. Russkaiā ėkonomicheskaiā mysl'. (Transliterated.) Moscow, 1956. 423 p.
3022. SCHIFFRIN, Alexander. Zur genesis der sozial-ökonomischen ideologien in der russischen wirtschaftswissenschaft. Tübingen 1926. 720-753 p.
3023. SHAFFER, Harry G., editor. The Soviet economy. A collection of Western and Soviet views. 2nd edition. New York, Appleton-Century-Crofts, 1969. xviii, 628 p.
3024. SOROKOVS'KA, S. V. Istoriiā ekonomichnoï dumky na Ukraïni. (Transliterated.) (Akademiiā nauk URSR, Kiev. Tsentral'na naukova biblioteka.) Kiev, 1962. 189 p.
3025. SPULBER, Nicholas. The Soviet economy. Revised edition. New York, W. W. Norton company, inc., 1969. c1962. xiv, 329 p.
3026. TOTOMIANTS, Vakhan Fomich. Iz istorii russkoj ėkonomičeskoj mysli. (Transliterated.) Mjunhen, Institut po izučeniju SSSR, 1956. 52 p.
3027. ZAKAVKAZSKOE koordinatsionnoe soveshchanie po voprosam istorii ėkonomicheskoĭ mysli narodov zakavkaz'iā, Erivan, 1953. K voprosu ob istorii razvitiiā ėkonomicheskoĭ mysli. (Transliterated.) 1955. 193 p.
3028. ZALESKI, Eugene. Planning reforms in the Soviet Union, 1962-1966. Chapel Hill, University of North Carolina press, 1967.
3029. ZAMIATNIN, V. N. Osnovnye ėtapy razvitiiā russkoĭ progressivnoĭ ėkonomicheskoĭ mysli. (Transliterated.) Moscow, 1957. 47 p.
3030. ZLUPKO, Stepan Mykolaĭovych. Ekonomichna dumka na

Ukraïni. (Transliterated.) 1969. 221 p. Bibliographical footnotes.
3031. AL'TER, Lev Benitsianovich. Burzhuaznye ékonomisty SShA. (Transliterated.) Moscow, 1948. 127 p.

UNITED STATES OF AMERICA

3032. ANDREANO, Ralph L. New views on American economic development. A selective anthology of recent work. Cambridge, Massachusetts, Schenkman publishing company, c1965. x, 434 p. Bibliographical footnotes.
3033. BAKER, Clayton. Depression and inflation. 1st ed. New York, Vantage press, c1963. 136 p.
3034. BARNETT, Paul. Business cycle theory in the United States from 1860 to 1900. (Thesis, University of Chicago. Chicago, 1940. v, 286 1. Bibliography, 256-286.
3035. BECKWITH, Burnham Putnam. Contemporary English and American theories concerning the effect of commercial banking on the supply of physical capital. (Portion of thesis, University of Southern California, 1932. The University of Southern California. School of research studies, no. 8.) Los Angeles, The University of Southern California press, 1935. 3 p. 1., 45 p. Bibliography, 39-45.
3036. BERLE, Adolf Augustus. The American economic republic. (A Harvest book, HB83.) New York, Harcourt, Brace & World, 1965. xxi, 247 p. Bibliographical references, 219-238.
3037. BRODIN, Pierre. Les idées politiques des Etats-Unis d'aujourd'hui. Paris, G.-P. Maisonneuve, 1940. 2 p. 1., 7-303 p. Bibliographie, 281-297.
3038. BROWN, Rollo Walter. Lonely Americans. Reprint of 1929 edition. Freeport, New York, Books for libraries press, 1970. 319 p.
3039. CATCHINGS, Waddill. Bias against business. What the economic professors are teaching today; a brief book for businessmen. New York, 1956. 94 p.
3040. CAULEY, Troy Jesse. Our economy. Scranton, International textbook co., 1963. 324 p.
3041. CHAMBER of Commerce of the United States of America. Committee on Economic Policy. Organizing society for freedom; report. Washington, Chamber of Commerce of the United States, 1964. 49 p. Bibliography, 45-47.
3042. CHEPRAKOV, V. A. Burzhuaznye ékonomisty SSA. (Transliterated.) Moscow, 1953-55 p.
3043. ———. "Social'naja demagogija burzuaznyh ékonomistov SSA." In, Soviet profsojuzy, 4, 1 (January, 1956) 73-79.
3044. COLEMAN, Raymond W. Our changing American economy. (Indiana business paper no. 7.) Bloomington? Graduate school of business, Indiana university, 1963. 28 p. Bibliography.
3045. COPELAND, Morris Albert. Our free enterprise economy. New York, Macmillan, 1965. xvii, 302 p. Bibliographical footnotes.

Countries and Areas 207

3046. DAWSON, George Glenn and Russell H. McClain. The Collier quick and easy guide to economics. 1st edition. New York, Collier Books, 1963. 128 p.
3047. DELIUS, Klaus. Der Institutionalismus als Richtung der amerikanischen nationalökonomie. (Inaugural dissertation, Cologne.) Koln?, 1957. 226 p. Bibliography, 216-224.
3048. DORFMAN, Joseph Harry. The economic mind in American civilization, 1606-1933. New York, Viking press, 1946-59. 5 v. Bibliographical notes. [Reprint: (The economic mind in American civilization, 1606-1865. New York, A. M. Kelley, 1966. v. 1, 2.) Spanish edition entitled: El pensamiento económico en la civilización norteamericana: Historia de la contribución norteamericana al pensamiento económico: Un estudio fundamental de la cultura de los estados unidos. Translated by José Rovira Armengol. México, Editorial guaranía, 1957- . 3 v.]
3049. _____, and Rexford Guy Tugwell. Early American policy: six Columbia contributors. New York, Columbia university press, 1960. 356 p. Bibliographical footnotes.
3050. DVORKIN, Il'ia Naumovich. Kritika teorii sovremennykh burzhuaznykh ekonomistov. (Transliterated.) (Akademiia nauk SSSR. Institut mirovoi ekonomiki i mezhdunarodnykh otnoshenii.) Moscow, 1966. 246 p. Bibliographical footnotes. (Kommunisticheskaia partiia sovetskogo soiuza. Vysshaia partiinaia shkola.)
3051. EDWARDS, Richard C., Michael Reich and Thomas E. Weisskopf. The capitalist system. A radical analysis of American society. Englewood Cliffs, New Jersey, Prentice-Hall, Inc., 1971. 539 p.
3052. ELY, Richard Theodore. A decade of economic theory. A paper submitted to the American academy of political and social science. (AAPSS, Publication no. 272.) Philadelphia, American academy of political and social science, 1900. 1, 92-112 p. (Address delivered, 1899.)
3053. FETTER, F. A. "The early history of political economy in the United States." In, Proceedings of American philosophical society (1943).
3054. FLETCHER, Hugh Mackay. History of economic theory in the United States, 1820 to 1866. (Thesis, University of Illinois.) Urbana, Illinois, 1926. ix, 385 p. Bibliographies (Abstract, 1928. 8 p.)
3055. FURBER, Henry Jewett. Geschichte und kritische studien zur entwicklung der ökonomischen theorien in Amerika. (Inaugural dissertation, Halle.) Halle a. S., Druck von A. Holzhausen, 1891. viii, 87, 1 p.
3056. FUSFELD, Daniel Roland. The economic thought of Franklin D. Roosevelt and the origins of the New Deal. (Columbia studies in the social sciences, 586.) New York, Columbia university press, 1956. 337 p. Bibliography, 305-320. (c1954, thesis, Columbia university, entitled, Roots of the New deal; the economic thought of Franklin D. Roosevelt to 1932. Microfilm form. 1956 edition reprinted: New York, AMS press, 1970. 337 p.)

3057. GALBRAITH, John Kenneth. The affluent society. Boston, Houghton Mifflin, 1958. 368 p. (2d edition, revised, 1969. xxxii, 333 p. Bibliographical footnotes.)

3058. _____. American capitalism. Revised edition. Boston, Houghton Mifflin, 1956.

3059. GRUCHY, Allan Garfield. Modern economic thought. The American contribution. New York, Prentice-Hall, 1947. xiii, 670 p. (Reprints of economic classics. New York, A. M. Kelley, 1967. xii, 670 p. Bibliography, 631-655.

3060. HANSEN, Alvin Harvey. The American economy. (Economics handbook series.) New York, McGraw-Hill, 1957. 199 p.

3061. HEILBRONER, Robert L. The limits of American capitalism. 1st ed. New York, Harper & Row, 1966. 148 p. Bibliographical references, 135-141.

3062. HOFSTADTER, Richard. Social Darwinism in American thought, 1860-1915. Philadelphia, University of Pennsylvania press, 1944.

3063. JOHNSON, Edgar Augustus Jerome. American economic thought in the seventeenth century. London, 1932. (New York, Russell & Russell, 1961. 292 p. Bibliography.)

3064. KUBO, Yoshikazu. Amerika keizaigaku shi kenkyū. (Transliterated.) (Kwansei gakuin daigaku. Nishinomiya, Japan. Kenkyū sōsho, 2.) Japan, 1961. 3, 3, 228, 4 p. Bibliographical references.

3065. LEVY, Lester Samuel and Roy J. Sampson. American economic development; growth of the United States in the Western world. Boston, Allyn and Bacon, 1962. 623 p. Bibliography.

3066. LICHTMAN, Richard. Toward community. A criticism of contemporary capitalism. (Center for the study of democratic institutions. Occasional papers.) Santa Barbara, California, Center for the study of democratic institutions, 1966. 58 p. Bibliography, 55-58.

3067. LIST, Friedrich. Outlines of American political economy, in a series of letters addressed by Friederich List . . . to Charles J. Ingersoll . . . To which is added the celebrated letters of Mr. Jefferson to Benjamin Austin, and of Mr. Madison to the editors of the Lynchburg Virginian. Philadelphia, Printed by S. Parker, 1827. 40 p.

3068. MELMAN, Seymour. Pentagon. Capitalism. The political economy of war. New York, McGraw-Hill, 1970. x, 290 p.

3069. MONSEN, R. Joseph. Modern American capitalism: ideologies and issues. Under the editorship of Jesse W. Markham. Boston, Houghton Mifflin, 1963. 142 p. Bibliography.

3070. NEILL, Charles Patrick. Daniel Raymond. An early chapter in the history of economic theory in the United States. (Johns Hopkins university studies in historical and political science, 15th series, vi.) Baltimore, The Johns Hopkins press, 1897. 63 p.

3071. NORMANO, João Frederico. The spirit of American economics. A study in the history of economic ideas in the

	United States prior to the great depression. With a supplement, The development of Canadian economic ideas, by A. R. M. Lower. A publication of the Committee on the study of economic thought. (Studies in the history of economic thought, v. 1.) New York, Distributed by the John Day company, 1943. 5 p. 1., 13-252 p., 2 1. Bibliographical footnotes.
3072.	NOTZ, William Frederick. Friedrich List in America. Hamburg, Druck von Broschek & co., 1925. 1 p. 1., p. 199-293. (Sonderabdruck aus: Weltwirtschaftliches archiv; hrsg. von prof. dr. Bernhard Harms, Kiel; verlag von Gustav Fischer in Jena; 21. bd., helf 2; 22. bd., heft 1. april, juli 1925.)
3073.	O'CONNOR, Michael Joseph Lalor. Origins of academic economics in the United States. (Thesis, Columbia University.) New York, Columbia university press, 1944. x, 367 p. Bibliography, textbooks, 291-329. Bibliography, 333-354.
3074.	OHARA, Keiji. Amerika keizai shisō no chōryū. (Transliterated.) Japan, 1951. 4, 4, 397, 8 p. Bibliographical footnotes.
3075.	PHILLIPS, Ulrich Bonnell. The economic and political essays of the ante-bellum South. (1st edition, 1909.) (Burt Franklin research and source works series, 417. Selected essays in history, economics, & social science, 110.) New York, B. Franklin, 1970. 29 p. Bibliography, 28-29.
3076.	PIROU, Gaétan. Les nouveaux courants de la théorie économique aux Etats-Unis . . . (Conférences faites à L'Ecole pratique des hautes études en 1934-1935.) Paris, Les éditions Domat-Montchrestien, F. Loviton & co., 1935- . v. Bibliographies. [2. ed. (Vols. 1-2, 4, Conferences faites a l'Ecole pratique des hautes etudes, 1934-35, 1935-36, 1936-37.) Paris, Domat-Montchrestien, 1939-43. 4 v.]
3077.	SAMUELSON, Paul A. "La science économique américaine." In, Economie appliquée, 16, 1 (Jan.-Mars, 1963) 117-138.
3078.	———— Problems of the American economy; an economist's view. (The Stamp memorial lecture, 1961.) London, University of London, Athlone press, 1962. 39 p.
3079.	SHEARER, Henry K. The history of economics in Montana. A preliminary report. A paper presented before the Montana Academy of sciences eighteenth annual meeting held at Montana State university, Missoula, Montana, April 11-12, 1958. (Occasional paper, no. 3.) Missoula, Montana, Montana state university, Bureau of business and economic research, 1958. 24 1.
3080.	SHERWOOD, Sidney. Tendencies in American economic thought. (Johns Hopkins university studies in historical and political science . . . 15th series, XII.) Baltimore, The Johns Hopkins press, 1897. 42 p.
3081.	SOUTH Carolina economists. Essays on the evolution of antebellum economic thought. Contributors: James L. Cochrane and others. Edited by B. F. Kiker and Robert

J. Carlsson. 1st ed. (Bureau of Business and Economic Research, Essays in economics, no. 20.) Columbia, South Carolina, University of South Carolina, Bureau of business and economic research, 1969. xi, 139 p. Bibliographical footnotes.
3082. SPIEGEL, Henry William. The rise of American economic thought. 1st edition. Philadelphia, Chilton company, 1960. 202 p. Bibliography.
3083. TEILHAC, Ernest Charles Eugene. Histoire de la pensée économique aux Etats-Unis au dixneuvième siècle. Paris Recueil sirey, 1928. 2 p. 1., 194 p. Bibliographie, 177-191. (English edition entitled: Pioneers of American economic thought in the nineteenth century. Authorized English translation by E. A. J. Johnson. New York, The Macmillan company, 1936. xi, 187 p. Bibliography. Reprinted: New York, Russell and Russell, 1967. xi, 187 p.
3084. VINING, Daniel Rutledge. Economics in the United States of America. A review and interpretation of research. (Documentation in the social sciences.) Paris, United nations educational, scientific and cultural organization, 1956. 62 p. Bibliographical footnotes.
3085. WALKER, Franklin V. Growth, employment and the price level. Intermediate macroeconomic measurement, theory and policy. Englewood Cliffs, New Jersey, Prentice-Hall, 1963. 342 p. Bibliography.
3086. WILHITE, Virgle Glenn. Founders of American economic thought and policy. New York, Bookman associates, 1958. 442 p.
3087. WILKINS, Billy Hughel and Charles B. Friday. The economists of the New Frontier; an anthology. New York, Random house, 1963. ix, 338 p. Bibliography, 325-329.
3088. YAMAGUCHI, Masayuki. Marukusu-shugi to sangyō shakai ron. (Transliterated.) Japan, 1969. 214 p. Bibliographical references.

VENEZUELA

3089. ALFONZO, Ravard, Francisco. La cuestion social; tesis sostenida ante la ilustre universidad central de Venezuela, para optar al titulo de doctor en ciencias politicas. Caracas, C. A. Artes graficas, 1942. xix-xxxi, 454 p. Bibliografia, 441-454.
3090. PUERTA Flores, Ismael. La economía en el pensamiento venezolano. Caracas, Instituto de Filosofía, Facultad de humanidades y educación, Universidad central de Venezuela, 1969? 42 p.

YUGOSLAVIA

3091. BICANIC, Rudolf. Pogled iz svjetske perspektive i naša ekonomska orientacija. Zagreb, 1939. 105 p.
3092. HOFFMAN, George W. and Fred W. Neal. Yugoslavia and the new communism. New York, Twentieth century fund, 1962.

3093. KOLAJA, Jiri. Workers' councils. The Yugoslav experience. New York, Frederick A. Praeger, Inc., 1966.
3094. MACESICH, George. Yugoslavia. The theory and practice of development planning. Charlottesville, University press of Virginia, 1964.
3095. MILENKOVITCH, Deborah D. Plan and market in Yugoslav economic thought. (Yale Russian and East European studies, 9.) New Haven and London, Yale University press, 1971. x, 323.
3096. PEJOVICH, Svetozar. The market planned economy of Yugoslavia. Minneapolis, Minnesota, University of Minnesota press, 1966.
3097. WATERSTON, Albert. Planning in Yugoslavia. Baltimore, Johns Hopkins press, 1962.
3098. ZANINOVICH, George. The development of Socialist Yugoslavia. Baltimore, Johns Hopkins press, 1968.

F. SUPPLY, DEMAND, VALUE, AND PRICE

3099. ADLER, Georg. Die grundlagen der Karl Marxschen kritik der bestehenden volkswirtschaft; kritische und ökonomisch literarische studien. Hildesheim, G. Olms, 1968. x, 294 p.
3100. ALESSANDRO, Luigi d'. Impianti di riserva. Roma, Staderini editore, 1956. 71 p.
3101. ALLEN, Clark Lee. The framework of price theory. Belmont, California, Wadsworth publishing company, 1967. x, 373 p.
3102. ALSTADHEIM, Håvard. En oversikt over betingelser på etterspørselselastisitetene i teorien for konsumentens tilpasning. (Memorandum fra Sosialøkonomisk institutt, Universitetet i Oslo.) Oslo, 1967. 18 l.
3103. AMERICAN economic association. Readings in price theory; selected by a committee of the American economic association. Edited by George Joseph Stigler and Kenneth E. Boulding. (The Series of republished articles on economics, v. 6.) Chicago, Published for the Association by R. D. Irwin, 1952. x, 568 p.
3104. AMONN, Alfred. Grundzüge der theoretischen Nationalökonomie. Bern, A. Francke, 1948. 199 p.
3105. ANDERSON, Benjamin McAlester. Social value; a study in economic theory, critical and constructive. (Reprints of economic classics.) New York, A. M. Kelley, 1966. xviii, 204 p.
3106. ANGELL, James Waterhouse. "Consumers' demand." In, Quarterly journal of economics, 39 (1925), 584-611.
3107. _____. The theory of international prices: history, criticism, and restatement. (Reprint of economic classics.) New York, A. M. Kelley, 1965. xiv, 571 p. Bibliography.
3108. ARROW, Kenneth Joseph. Social choice and individual values. (Cowles commission for research in economics. Monograph no. 12.) New York, Wiley, 1951. xi, 99 p.
3109. ASOBE, Kyūzō. Kachironsō shi. (Transliterated.) Japan, 1949. 7, 264 p. Bibliography: 259-264.
3110. _____. Kotenha keizaigaku to Marukusu. (Transliterated.) Japan, 1955. 3, 3, 300 p. Bibliographical footnotes.
3111. AUSPITZ, R. and R. Lieben. Untersuchungen über die theorie des preises. Germany, 1889, xxxi, 555 p.
3112. BACHMANN, Herbert. Wirtschafts-wille und wert. Bern, A. Francke, 1945. 213 p.
3113. BADOUIN, Robert. L'éclasticité de la demande des biens de consommation. Préface de Jules Milhau. (Centre

d'études économiques. Etudes et mémoires, 6.) Paris, A. Colin, 1953. 264 p.

114. BAILEY, Samuel. A critical dissertation on the nature, measure, i.e. measures, and causes of value. . . . (Reprints of economic classics.) New York, A. M. Kelley, 1967. 1 v.

115. BAJT, Aleksander. Marxov zakon vrednosti. Ljubljana, 1953. 362 p.

116. BARONE, E. "A proposito delle indagini del Fisher." In, Giornale degli economisti, 8 (1894), 413-39.

117. ———. "Sulla 'Consumer's rent.'" In, Giornale degli economisti, 9 (1894), 211-24.

118. BAXA, Jakob. Geschichte der produktivitätstheorie. Jena, G. Fischer, 1926. 3 p. 1., 159, 1 p. Bibliographical footnotes.

119. BECKER, Gary Stanley. Human capital and the personal distribution of income; an analytical approach. (Woytinsky lecture, no. 1.) Ann Arbor, Institute of public administration, 1967. 49 p.

120. BEDDY, James P. Profits; theoretical and practical aspects. Dublin, Hodges, Figgis & co., 1940. xi, 420 p.

121. BEHRENS, Fritz. Ware, wert und wertgesetz; kritische und selbstkritische Betrachtungen zur werttheorie im sozialismus. Berlin, Akademie-verlag, 1961. 123 p.

122. BIANCA, Giovanni A. Il problema di una misurazione dei valori e la funzione della moneta. Catania, V. Muglia, 1953. 298 p.

123. BLACK, R. D. "Trinity college, Dublin, and the theory of value, 1823-63." In, Economica (August, 1945).

124. BOCZAR, Kazimierz. Ekonomika handlu; wybane zagadnienia. Warszawa, 1962, cover 1963. 199 p.

125. BODEKER, Johanna. Liquiditäts-aequivalenz von angebot und nachfrage; die realgesetzlich vorgegebene Lösung der geld-, kredit- und konjunktur-probleme. Vorwort von Paul Meyer. Birgel bei Lissendorf, Kreis Daun/Eifel, Institut der gesellschaft für sozialproblem-forschung, 1962. xvi, 303 p.

126. BOHM-BAWERK, Eugen von. "Grundzüge der theorie des wirtschaftlichen güterwerts." In, Jahrbücher für nationalökonomie und statistik, 46 (1886), 1-82; 477-541.

127. ———. "Positive theorie des kapitales." In, Handworterbuch der staatswissenschaften, 3rd edition, 3 (1909-11), 211-425.

128. ———. Recent literature on interest, 1884-1899. Translated by W. A. Scott and S. Feilbogen. New York, 1903.

129. ———. "Wert." In, Handworterbuch der staatswissenschaften, 4th edition (1928), 3 (1923-29), 988-1007.

130. BOJER, Hilde. Notat om sammenhengen mellom Richard Stones lineaere utgiftsfunksjoner og Ragnar Frisch' "Complete scheme for computing all direct and cross demand elasticities in a model with many sectors." (Memorandum fra Sosialøkonomisk institutt, Universitetet i Oslo.) Oslo, 1966. 35 l.

3131. BOTZ, Hartmut. Der ertragswert als wertbestimmungs- und als kontroll- instrument. Hamburg, 1954. ii, 98 p.
3132. BOWLEY, A. L. "Does mathematical analysis explain?" In Economica, 4 (1924), 135-39.
3133. ———. "The theoretical effects of rationing on prices." In, Economic journal, 30 (1920), 340-47.
3134. BRITISH productivity council. Sixteen case studies in value analysis. London, 1964. 47 p.
3135. BRONFENBRENNER, Martin. Income distribution theory. Chicago, Aldine-Atherton, inc., 1971.
3136. BRONSHTEIN, Mikhail Lazarevich ja H. Metsa. Väärtus, hind ja hinnapoliitika. (Sotsialistikuit majanduselt kommunistlikule majandusele.) Tallinn, Eesti Riiklik Kirjastus, 1964. 133 p.
3137. BROWN, E. H. P. "Demand functions and utility functions." In, Econometrica, II (1934) 51.
3138. BRUGMANS, Izaak Johannes. Welvaart en historie; tien studien. 's-Gravenhage, M. Nijhoff, 1950. 175 p.
3139. BUKHARIN, Nikolaï Ivanovich. L'Economie politique du rentier, la théorie de la valeur et du profit de l'école autrichienne, critique de l'economie marginaliste. . . . Préface de Pierre Naville. . . . Paris, Etudes et documentation internationales, 1967. 204 p.
3140. ———. Die politische Okonomie des rentners. Die Wert- und profittheorie der österreicheschen schule. Autorisiert Übersetzung von Anna Lifschitz. Photomechanischer nachdruck der Ausg. von 1926. (Archiv sozialistischer literatu Frankfurt am Main, Verlag neue kritik, 1966. 200 p.
3141. BUTLER, Jay Grant. An analysis and measurement of value orientations as related to conventional and delinquen behavior. (University microfilms, Ann Arbor, Michigan. Publication no. 25,199.) Ann Arbor, University microfilms 1958. Microfilm AC-1.
3142. CAMPOS, A. Alves de. Teoria marxistz do valor e "plus valor." ("Filosofia," estudos, 9.) Braga, Livraria Cruz, 1956. 100 p.
3143. CANNAN, Edwin. A history of the theories of production and distribution in English political economy from 1776 to 1848. 3d edition. London, New York, Staples press, 19! xi, 336 p.
3144. ———. "The origin of the law of diminishing returns, 1715-1815." In, Economic journal, II (1892) 53-69.
3145. ———. " 'Total utility' and 'Consumer's surplus.' " In, Economica, 4 (1924), 21-26.
3146. CASSEL, G. Fundamental thoughts in economics. New York, Harcourt, Brace, 1925. 153 p.
3147. CASTELAIN, I. Economie politique et sociale; l'évolution de la pensée économique, essai de théorie positive des valeurs et des prix. Préface du vicomte van de Vijvere. Anvers, J.-E. Buschmann, 1953. 180 p. Bibliography, 172-173.
3148. CATHERWOOD, Benjamin Franklin, Basic theories of distribution. London, P. S. King & son, ltd., 1939. ix, 262 p.

3149. CECCHELLA, Aldo. La forza contrattuale dell'impresa in regime di prezzi amministrati. Milano, A. Giuffrè, 1969. 133 p.
3150. CERNE, Franc. Tržište i cijene. Sa slovenskog preveo Milan Rakočević. (Ekonomska biblioteka, kolo 2, br. 5.) Zagreb, "Informator," 1966. 248 p.
3151. CHAINEAU, André. La demande d'encaisses monétaires. Préface de Emile James. (Connaissances économiques, 9.) Paris, Editions Cujas, 1964. ii, 159 p.
3152. CHAMBER of commerce of the United States of America. Domestic distribution department. Value added by distribution, presented by the Domestic distribution committee and the Business statistics committee of the Chamber of commerce of the United States. Washington, 1956. 42 p.
3153. CHAMBERLIN, Edward. The theory of monopolistic competition; a re-orientation of the theory of value. 7th edition. (Harvard economic studies, v. 38.) Cambridge, Harvard university press, 1956. xiv, 350 p. Bibliography, 277-346. (8th edition, 1962. 396 p.)
3154. _____. Towards a more general theory of value. New York, Oxford university press, 1957. 318 p.
3155. CHAO, Lan-p'ing. Ma-k'o-ssǔ ching chi hsüeh shuo p'i p'ing. (Transliterated.) China, 1956. 217 p.
3156. _____. Ma-k'o-ssǔ chu i p'i p'ing. (Transliterated.) China, 1953. 248 p.
3157. CHAO, Tung-yin. Chia chih yü shêng yü chia chih. (Transliterated.) China, 1949. 72 p.
3158. CHU, Chien-nung. Chia chih chi chia chih kuei lü tsai ko chung shê hui chih tu hsia ti tso yung. (Transliterated.) China, 1956. 84 p.
3159. CLARK, John Bates. "On the possibility of a scientific law of wages." In, American economic association publications, IV (1889) 39.
3160. _____. "The ultimate standard of value." In, the Yale review, 1 (1892), 258-74.
3161. CLARK, John Maurice and B. Anderson, Jr. "The concept of value." In, Quarterly journal of economics, 29 (1915), 663-73.
3162. _____. "A contribution to the theory of competitive prices." In, Quarterly journal of economics, 28 (1914), 747-71.
3163. _____. Studies in the economics of overhead costs. New York, 1923. xii, 502 p.
3164. COMMONS, John Rogers. Legal foundations of capitalism. Madison, University of Wisconsin press, 1957. x, 394 p.
3165. CONGARD, Roger Paul. La demande et le monopole. Préface de Gaston Leduc. (Observation économique, 4.) Paris, Société d'édition d'enseignement supérieur, 1953. xii, 384 p.
3166. COONTZ, Sydney H. Productive labour and effective demand, including a critique of Keynesian economics, with an introduction by William J. Blake. London, Routledge and K. Paul; New York, A. M. Kelley, 1965, i.e. 1966. x, 174 p.

3167. COTTERIL, Charles Forster. An examination of the doctrines of value, as set forth by Adam Smith, Ricardo, M'Culloch, Mill, the author of "A critical dissertation," Torrens, Malthus, Say, etc. Being a reply to those distinguished authors. London, 1831.
3168. CROUSE, Robert L. Value engineering/analysis bibliography. Revised edition, no publisher. Available from Society of American value engineers, 1967. xxviii, 198 p.
3169. CUNYNGHAME, H. "Some improvements in simple geometrical methods of treating exchange value, monopoly, and rent." In, Economic journal, 2 (1892), 35-52.
3170. CZECH, Zdzisław. Teoria wartości i problem rozliczenia w szkole austriackiej. (Polskie towarzystwo ekonomiczne. Oddział w Katowicach. Studia i materiały. Seria C.) Katowice, 1961. 215 p.
3171. DAVENPORT, Herbert Joseph. "Cost and its significance." In, American economic review, 1 (1911), 724-52.
3172. _____. Economics of enterprise. 1913. xvi, 544 p.
3173. _____. "Proposed modifications in Austrian theory and terminology." In, Quarterly journal of economics, 16 (1902), 355-84.
3174. _____. Value and distribution; a critical and constructive study. (Reprints of economic classics.) New York, A. M. Kelley, bookseller, 1964. xi, 582 p. Bibliographical footnotes. (First published in 1908. xi, 582.)
3175. DAVIDSON, Paul and Eugene Smolensky. Aggregate supply and demand analysis. With a section on Social accounts: theory and measurement, by Charles L. Leven. New York, Harper and Row, c1964. xiv, 274 p.
3176. DEAN, Edwin. The supply responses of African farmers; theory and measurement in Malawi. (Contributions to economic analysis, 41.) Amsterdam, North-Holland publishing company, 1966, c1965. xiv, 174 p.
3177. DE CINDIO, Flaminio. Le ragioni di scambio in oligopolio. (Pubblicazioni della Facoltà di giurisprudenza della Università di Pisa, 21. Istituto di economia, finanza e diritto finanziario. Pubblicazioni, 2.) Milano, A. Giuffrè, 1967. vi, 122 p.
3178. DE JANOSI, Peter Engel. Factors influencing the demand for new automobiles: a cross-section analysis. (University microfilms, Ann Arbor, Michigan. Publication no. 21,171. Ann Arbor, University microfilms, 1957. Microfilm AC-1.
3179. DEMMER, Karl Hans. Aufgaben und praxis der wertanalyse. München, Verlag moderne industrie, 1969. 221 p.
3180. DENIS, Henri. La valeur. (La Culture et les hommes.) Paris, Editions sociales, 1950. 132 p.
3181. _____. Valeur et capitalisme. (La Culture et les hommes.) Paris, Editions sociales, 1957. 126 p.
3182. DERYCKE, Pierre Henri. Elasticité et analyse économique; essai de méthodologie statistique. Préface d'Henri Guitton. (Connaissances économiques, 12.) Paris, Editions, Cujas, 1964. ix, 505 p.

3183. DEWEY, Donald. The theory of imperfect competition; a radical reconstruction. (Columbia studies in economics, 2.) New York, Columbia university press, 1969. xii, 205 p.
3184. DEWEY, John. The theory of valuation. Chicago, University of Chicago Press, 1939. (In, the International encyclopedia of Unified Science, 1939.)
3185. DIETZEL, H. "Die klassische werttheorie und die theorie vom grenznutzen." In, Jahrbücher für nationalökonomie und statistik, 54 (1890), 561-606.
3186. _____. "Zur klassischen wert- und preistheorie." In, Jahrbücher für nationalökonomie und statistik, 56 (1891), 685-707.
3187. DMITRIEV, V. K. Essais économiques, esquisse de synthèse organique de la théorie de la valeur-travail et de la théorie de l'utilité marginale. Présentation par Alfred Zauberman. Postface par Henri Denis. Traduit du russe par Barnard Joly. Paris, Editions du Centre national de la recherche scientifique, 1968. 273 p.
3188. DOBLER, Martin. Triebkraft Bedürfnis; zur Entwicklung der bedürfnisse der sozialistischen persönlichkeit. 1. Aufl. Berlin, Dietz, 1969. 245 p.
3189. DOODHA, Kersi. Analytical study of value theory. 1st edition. Bombay, Vora, 1962. 168 p.
3190. DOOLEY, Peter C. Elementary price theory. New York, Appleton-Century-Crofts, 1967. vii, 173 p.
3191. DORFMAN, Robert. The price system. (Foundations of modern economic series.) Englewood Cliffs, Prentice-Hall, 1964. viii, 152 p. Bibliography, 147-148.
3192. _____. Prices and markets. (Foundations of modern economics series.) Englewood Cliffs, New Jersey, Prentice-Hall, 1967. viii, 151 p. Bibliography.
3193. DORP, Elisabeth Caroline van. A simple theory of capital, wages and profit or loss; a new and social approach to the problem of economic distribution. London, P. S. King & son, ltd., 1937. xix, 260 p.
3194. DOUGLAS, Clifford Hugh. Social credit. 4th edition. Hawthorne, California, Omni publications, 1966. xi, 212 p.
3195. DOUGLAS, Paul Howard. "Smith's theory of value and distribution." In, Adam Smith, 1766-1926. Edited by J. M. Clark. Chicago, University of Chicago press, 1928.
3196. _____. The theory of wages. New York, Kelley and Millman, 1957. 639 p. 1st edition, New York, Macmillan, 1934. 1964 edition. With a new foreword and the article, Are there laws of production? (Reprints of economic classics.) New York, A. M. Kelley, bookseller, 1964. 41, vii-xx, 3-639 p.]
3197. DRAKE, Albert Estern. Econometric analysis of the demand and supply relationships for lard at the retail level. Ann Arbor, Michigan, University microfilms, 1959. Microfilm AC-1.
3198. DRECHSLER, László. A használati érték és az érték szerepe a volumenindexek szamitasanal. (A Marx Karoly közgazdaságtudományi Egyetem kozlemenyel, 3. sz.)

Budapest, Közgazdasági és Jogi Könyvkiadó, 1962. 91 p.
3199. DYSKUSJI o prawie wartości ciąg dalszy. Wyd. 1. Warszawa, Książka i Wiedza, 1957. 189 p.
3200. EDGEWORTH, F. Y. "Professor J. S. Nicholson on 'Consumer's rent.' " In, Economic journal, 4 (1894), 151-58.
3201. EKONOMISCI dyskutuja o prawie wartości. Wyd. 1. Warszawa, Książka i Wiedza, 1956. 166 p.
3202. ELIAS, Lucien N. J. H. La paix des peuples par la découverte de la vérité économique et monétaire, réalisation par la synthèse de la valeur totale. Bruxelles, 1954. 44 p.
3203. ENGLÄNDER, O. "Fragen des preises." In, Schmollers, jahrbuch für gesctzgebung, verwaltung und volkswirtschaft im deutschen reiche, 43 (1919), 933-81; 1395-1458.
3204. ENTELEK incorporated, Newburyport, Massachusetts. Supply and demand. (Its Programmed instruction in economics.) New York, Macmillan, 1963- . v.
3205. FALCON, William D., editor. Value analysis, value engineering; the implications for managers. Contributors: Merton E. Davis, Jr., and others. (AMA management reports, no. 81.) New York, American management association, 1964. 128 p.
3206. FELS, Eberhard. Zur Theorie und messung nichtadditiver nachfragefunktionen. München, 1953. 186 1.
3207. FELS, Rendigs. The Law of supply and demand. A programmed approach. Boston, Allyn and Bacon, 1962. (Reprinted: 1966.)
3208. FERGUSON, Charles E. The neoclassical theory of production and distribution. London, Cambridge university press, 1969. xviii, 384 p.
3209. FERNANDEZ, Rafael. La jornada; teoría del valor económico Posibilidad de su aplicación en una ordenación sistemática de la economia general. Madrid, Editorial Dossat, 1952. 268 p.
3210. FETTER, Frank Albert. "The determination of price." In, American economic review, 2 (1912), 783-813.
3211. ———. "The exploitation of theories of value in the discussion of the standard of deferred payments." In, The annals of the American academy of political and social science. Philadelphia, v. 6 (1895) 882-896.
3212. ———. "Price economics vs. welfare economics." In, American economic review (1920).
3213. FISHER, Irving. "Is 'Utility' the most suitable term for the concept it is used to denote." In, American economic review, 8 (1918), 335-37.
3214. ———. Mathematical investigations in the theory of value in the theory of value and price, 1892. Appreciation and interest, 1896. (Reprints of economic classics.) New York, A. M. Kelley, 1965. 126, x, 100 p. [New Haven, Yale University press, c1925. xii, 11-126 p. Bibliography 120-124. From thesis, Ph.D., Yale university, 1891. In, Transactions of the Connecticut academy, IX (July, 1892).]
3215. ———. The nature of capital and income. New York, Macmillan, 1906. 427 p.

3216. _____. The theory of interest as determined by impatience to spend income and opportunity to invest it. (Reprints of economic classics. New York, Kelley and Millman, 1954. 566 p. Bibliography, 543-550.

3217. FLUMIANI, Carlo Maria. How to discover unlimited stock market profits by applying the law of supply and demand. 1st edition. Springfield, Massachusetts, Library of Wall Street, 1967. 41 p.

3218. FOOD and agriculture organization of the United Nations. Bibliography on the analysis and projection of demand and production, 1963. (Its Commodity reference series, 2.) Rome, 1963. xii, 279 p.

3219. FOOTE, Richard Jay. Analytical tools for studying demand and price structures. (United States. Department of agriculture. Agriculture handbook no. 146.) Washington, United States, Department of agriculture, 1958. 217 p.

3220. FOOTE, Richard Jay and Karl A. Fox. Analytical tools for measuring demand. (United States. Department of agriculture. Agriculture handbook no. 64.) Washington, United States Department of agriculture, Agricultural marketing service, 1954. ii, 86 p.

3221. FORZAN Dágger, Jorge. Remanentismo, teoría del remanente. Caracas, Tip. Garrido, 1956. 260 p.

3222. FOX, Karl August. The analysis of demand for farm products. (United States. Department of agriculture. Technical bulletin no. 1081.) Washington, United States Department of agriculture, 1953. 90 p.

3223. _____. Econometric analysis for public policy. Ames, Iowa State college press, 1958. 288 p.

3224. FRANCE. Centre national de la recherche scientifique. Centre d'études sociologiques. Aspects modernes de la logique sociale. (Cahiers d'étude des sociétés industrielles et de l'automation, no. 8.) Paris, Editions du Centre national de la recherche scientifique, 1967. 229 p.

3225. FRIEDMAN, Milton. The demand for money; some theoretical and empirical results. (NBER occasional paper no. 68.) New York, Columbia university press for National bureau of economic research, 1959. 25 p. (Reprinted.)

3226. _____, and Robert V. Roosa. The balance of payments: free versus fixed exchange rates. Washington, American enterprise institute for public policy research, 1967. 192 p.

3227. FUA, Giorgio. La valutazione monetaria della vita umana; discussione del problema generale con una applicazione concreta all'assicurazione-vita. Milano, A. Giuffrè, 1946. 94 p.

3228. FUNKTIONSKOSTNADSANALYS. Teknik att studera produkters och tjänsters funktioner och kostnader. Av Jan Ollner m. fl. Stockholm, Sveriges mekanförbund, 1967. (4), 119, (1) p.

3229. GAGE, William Lionel. Value analysis. London, New York, etc., McGraw-Hill, 1967. xi, 185 p.

3230. GAMBS, John. Beyond supply and demand. New York, Columbia university press, 1946.

3231. GANTNER, Paul. Das marktmodell in hinsicht auf das zwischenhandelsphänomen, die besteuerung und den zoll. Heidelberg, 1949. iii, 176 1.
3232. GARCES Molina, Dolcey. La utilidad marginal, el dinero y los precios en una economía socialista. Bogotá, Editorial Pax, 1952. 56 p.
3233. GEYER, Thomas. Der prozess der bedarfsgestaltung in industriellen unternehmungen; insbesondere in Unternehmungen des maschinen- und apparatebaus. (Vertriebswirtschaftliche abhandlungen, Heft 15.) Berlin, Duncker und Humblot, c1970. 146 p.
3234. GLANSDORFF, Maxime. Théorie générale de la valeur et ses applications en esthétique et en économie. (Institut de sociologie Solvay. Collection de sociologie générale et de philosophie sociale.) Bruxelles, Parthenon, 1954. 324 p.
3235. GOLDMAN, S. M. and H. Uzawa. "A note on the separability of demand analysis." In, Econometrica, 32 (July 1964), 387-98.
3236. GORMAN, W. M. "Professor Friedman's consumption function and the theory of choice." In, Econometrica, 32 (January-April 1964), 189-97.
3237. GOSSEN, Herman Heinrich. Entwickelung der Gesetze des menschlichen verkehrs und der daraus fliessenden Regeln für menschliches handeln. Reprint of the Braunschweig edition, 1854. Amsterdam, Nieuwe Herengracht 31, Liberac, 1967. viii, 284 p.
3238. GOTO, Hiroshi. Jitsurei, fuka kachi bunseki. (Transliterated.) 1968. 214 p.
3239. GREEN, D. I. "Pain cost and opportunity cost." In, Quarterly journal of economics, 8 (1894), 218-29.
3240. GREEN, James L. Economic ecology; baselines for urban development. Athens, University of Georgia press, c1969. xii, 167 p.
3241. GUIHENEUF, Robert. Le problème de la théorie marxiste de la valeur. (Centre d'études économiques. Etudes et mémoires, 2.) Paris, A. Colin, 1952. 194 p.
3242. GURRIA Urgell, José María. La moneda-maíz. México, Editorial Pax-México, Librería Carlos Cesarman, 1965. 126 p.
3243. GUTERSOHN, Alfred und Hans- Georg Geisbüsch. Machtungleichgewichte und gegengewichtsbildungen in der wirtschaftswirklichkeit. (Das Gegengewichtsprinzip in der wirtschaftsordnung, Bd. 2.) Köln, Berlin, Bonn, München, Heymann, 1966. 207 p.
3244. HABAKKUK, H. J. "The long-term rate of interest and the price of land in the seventeenth century." In, Economic history review, 2nd series v (1951-52) 26-45.
3245. HADLEY, A. T. "The different meanings of cost." In, Quarterly journal of economics, 11 (1897), 310, 311.
3246. HAEBERLE, Karl Erich. Phänomen nachfrage. Essen, W. Girardet, 1963. 322 p.
3247. HAMILTON, W. H. "The Place of value theory in economics."

Supply, Demand, etc. 221

In, Journal of political economy, 26 (1918), 217-45; 375-407.
3248. HANEY, Lewis Henry. Value and distribution; some leading principles of economic science. (The century studies in economics; W. H. Kiekhofer, editor.) New York, London, D. Appleton-century company, 1939. xvii p. 1., 734 p. Bibliographical footnotes.
3249. HAVEMAN, Robert H. and Kenyon A. Knopf. The market system. (Introduction to economics series.) New York, J. Wiley, 1966. xiv, 223 p. (2d edition. 1970. xvii, 269 p.)
3250. HAYEK, Freidrich August von. Profits, interest and investment, and other essays on the theory of industrial fluctuations. London, G. Routledge and sons, ltd. 1939. vii, 266 p. (1st published, 1939.)
3251. ———. The pure theory of capital. Chicago, University of Chicago press, 1941. 454 p.
3252. HENDERSON, Sir Hubert Douglas. Supply and demand. (The Cambridge economic handbooks.) Chicago, University of Chicago press, 1958. 142 p. (1st edition, 1922. x, 177 p.
3253. HENDERSON, John Patrick. A reinterpretation of Ricardo's theory of value. (University microfilms, Ann Arbor, Michigan. Publication no. 19,658.) Ann Arbor, University microfilms, 1956. Microfilm AC-1.
3254. HENN, Rudolf und O. Opitz. Konsum- und produktionstheorie. (Lecture notes in operations research and mathematical systems, 25.) Berlin, New York, Springer-verlag, 1970- . v.
3255. HERTFORDSHIRE, England. Technical library and information service. Value engineering bibliography. Hatfield, Hertfordshire, Hatfield college of technology, 1966. 1, 28 p.
3256. HICKS, John Richard. "Edgeworth, Marshall, and the indeterminateness of wages." In, Economic journal, XL (1930) 215.
3257. ———. A revision of demand theory. Oxford, Clarendon press, 1956. 196 p.
3258. ———. Value and capital; an inquiry into some fundamental principles of economic theory. Oxford, The Clarendon press, 1939. xi, 331, 1 p. (2d edition. Fair Lawn, New Jersey, Oxford university press, 1946.)
3259. ——— and R. G. D. Allen. "A reconsideration of the theory of value." In, Economics, new series, 1 and 2 (1934) 52, 196.
3260. HOBHOUSE, L. T. "Competitive and social value." In, Economica, 4 (1924), 278-290.
3261. HOBSON, J. A. "The element of monopoly in prices." In, Quarterly journal of economics, 6 (1891), 1-24.
3262. HOFMANN, Werner, editor. Wert- und preislehre. (Sozialökonomische studientexte, Bd. 1.) Berlin, Duncker und Humblot, 1964. 379 p.

3263. HOMER, S. A history of interest rates. New Brunswick, Rutgers university press, 1963.
3264. HOUCK, J. P. "Price elasticities and joint products." In, Journal of farm economics, 46 (August 1964), 652-56.
3265. HOYT, Elizabeth Ellis. Primitive trade; its psychology and economics. (Reprints of economic classics.) New York, A. M. Kelley, 1968. 191 p.
3266. HSUEH, Mu-ch'iao. Chi hua ching chi yü chia chih kuei lu. (Transliterated.) 1957. 44 p.
3267. JACOBS, Alfred und Margaret Jacobs. Die berechnung der marknachfrage. Amtliche statistik im dienste der nachfrageanalyse. (Absatzwirtschaft, Bd. 5.) Köln und Opladen, Westdeutscher verlag, 1968. 82 p.
3268. JESSUA, Claude. Coûts sociaux et coûts privés. . . . Préface de François Perroux. . . . (bibliothèque d'économie contemporaine.) Paris, Presses universitaires de France, 1968. xxiv, 304 p.
3269. JOHANSEN, L. "Labor theory of value and marginal utilities." In, Economics of planning, 3 (September 1963), 89-103.
3270. JOHANSEN, Tore. Etterspørselssammenhenger belyst ved egenskaper ved den marginale substitusjonsbrøk. (Memorandum fra Sosialøkonomisk institutt, Universietet i Oslo.) Oslo, 1968. 2, 49 p.
3271. JOHNSON, W. E. "The pure theory of utility curves." In, Economic journal, 23 (1913), 483-513.
3272. JOUINEAU, Claude. L'analyse de la valeur et ses nouvelles applications industrielles. De la réduction des coûts à la création du produit. Paris, Entreprise moderne d'édition, 1968. 282 p.
3273. KALDOR, Nicholas. "Alternative theories of distribution." In, Review of economic studies, 2d series, 23, 61 (1955-56).
3274. _____. Essays on value and distribution. Glencoe, Illinois, Free press; London, G. Duckworth, 1960. 238 p.
3275. KAMERSCHEN, David R., editor. Readings in microeconomics. (World series in economics.) Cleveland, World publishing company, 1967. xv, 607 p. (1969 edition. New York, Wiley, xv, 607 p.)
3276. KAPLAN, Norman Maurice. The choice among investment alternatives in Soviet theory. 8 February 1951. (Project Rand research memorandum, RM-539.) Santa Monica, California, Rand corporation, c1951. 95 1.
3277. _____. The law of value and Soviet economic planning. (Rand corporation. Research memorandum, RM-488.) Santa Monica, California, Rand corporation, 1950. i, 30 1.
3278. KARRAS, Heinz. Die grundgedanken der sozialistischen pädagogik in Marx' Hauptwerk "Das Kapital." (Diskussionsbeiträge zu Fragen der pädagogik, Heft 5.) Berlin,

Volk und wissen, 1956. 183 p.
3279. KATANO, Hikoji. Seisan to bumpai ni taisuru boeki koka no bunseki. (Transliterated.) (Series: Kobe Diagaku. Keizai keiei Kenkyujo. Kenkyu sosho, 1.) Japan, 1961. 200 p. Bibliographical footnotes.
3280. KATZNER, Donald W. Static demand theory. (Macmillan series in economics.) New York, Macmillan, 1970. x, 242 p.
3281. KAULLA, Rudolf. Staat, stände und der gerechte preis; ein Beitrag zur geschichte und kritik des ökonomischen wertproblems. 2. neubearb. Aufl. Basel, Verlag für recht und gesellschaft, 1951. viii, 176 p.
3282. KAUTSKY, Karl. La doctrina económica de Carlos Marx. Traducción de Anny dell'Erba. . . . y N. Caplán. (Colección El Pensamiento marxista, 4.) Buenos Aires, Lautaro, 1946. 299 p.
3283. KAWAGUCHI, Takehiko. Kachi ronso shi ron. (Transliterated.) Japan, 1964. 4, 183 p. Bibliography: 177-183.
3284. KEASBEY, Lindley M. "Prestige value." In, Quarterly journal of economics, xvii (1903) 456.
3285. KEIZAI Yosoku Kenkyukai. Shohinbetsu ni mita choki juyo yosoku. (Transliterated.) Japan, 1968. 2 v.
3286. KEYNES, John Maynard. "Relative movements of real wages and output." In, Economic journal 49 (1939) 34-51.
3287. KINOSHITA, Etsuji. Ronso, kokusai kachi ron. (Transliterated.) Japan, 1960. 5, 305 p. Includes bibliographical references in notes.
3288. KIPPER, Gerd. Kostensenkung durch wertanalyse. Illustriert. (Schriftenreihe rationalisieren, Heft 35.) Wien, Bundeskammer der gewerblichen wirtschaft, Wirtschaftsförderungsinstitut, 1966. 28 p.
3289. KNIGHT, Frank Hyneman. "The concept of normal price in value and distribution." In, Quarterly journal of economics, 32 (1917), 66-100.
3290. _____. "Cost of production and price over long and short periods." In, Journal of political economy, 29 (1921), 304-35.
3291. _____. The economic organization. With an article, Notes on cost and utility. New York, A. M. Kelley, 1951. 179 p.
3292. _____. "Economic psychology and the value problem." In, Quarterly journal of economics, 39 (1925), 372-409.
3293. _____. The ethics of competition and other essays. (Essay index reprint series.) Freeport, New York, Books for libraries press, 1969. 363 p.
3294. _____. Risk, uncertainty and profit. New York, Harper, 1921. xiv, 381.
3295. KOCMAN, Michael. Hodnota a ceny v socialistickém prumyslu. Vyd. 1. Praha, Nakl. Ceskoslovenske akademie ved, 1963. 328 p.
3296. KOKKALIS, Alexander B. Introduction to the total theory of labor; new positive foundation of economics. Concord? New Hampshire, 1950. 232 p.

3297. _____. Why is the theory of labor the only fundamental and exact economic theory? With an open letter to President Truman. Concord? New Hampshire, 1952. 56 p.
3298. KOIZUMI, Shinzo. Kachiron to shakaishugi. (Transliterated.) Japan, 1949. 318 p.
3299. KOURIM, Günther. Wertanalyse: Grundlagen, methoden, anwendungen. München, R. Oldenbourg, 1968. 118 p.
3300. KOZUSNIK, Cestmir. Problemy teorie hodnoty a ceny za socialismu; vyvoj cenove soustavy v CSSR. Vyd. 1. Praha, Nakl. Ceskoslovenske akademie ved, 1964. 358 p.
3301. KRELLE, Wilhelm. Präferenz- und entscheidungstheorie. Unter mitarbeit von Dieter Coenen. Tübingen, Mohr (Siebeck), 1968, xvi, 400 p.
3302. KRIER, Jane (Aubert). La courbe d'offre. Ouvrage publié avec le concours du Centre national de la recherche scientifique. Préface du professeur R. H. Chamberlin. 1. édition. (Théoria; études sur la théorie moderne de l'économie.) Paris, Presses universitaires de France, 1949. 266 p.
3303. KRONSTEIN, Rudolf. Die Diskussion um die arbeitswerttheorie. Wien, Druckerei H. Weiss, 1946. 79 p.
3304. KUENNE, Robert E. Microeconomic theory of the market mechanism: a general equilibrium approach. (Macmillan series in economics.) New York, Macmillan, 1968. xiii, 411 p.
3305. _____, editor. Monopolistic competition theory: studies in impact; essays in honor of Edward H. Chamberlin. New York, Wiley, 1967. x, 387 p.
3306. KUHLMAN, J. M. and R. G. Thompson. "Substitution and values of elasticities." In, American economic review, 55 (June 1965), 506-10.
3307. KUHNIS, Sylva. Die wert- und preistheoretischen ideen William Pettys. Winterthur, P. G. Keller, 1960. ix, 239 p.
3308. LAGAUSIE, François de. Une Théorie idéologique de la valeur. . . . n. p., 1966. 180 p.
3309. LAIDLER, David E. W. The demand for money: theories and evidence. (International's series in monetary economics.) Scranton, Pennsylvania, International Textbook company, 1969. xiii, 128 p.
3310. LAIRD, John. The idea of value. (Reprints of economic classics.) New York, A. M. Kelley, 1969. xx, 384 p.
3311. LAMBIN, Jean Jacques. La décision commerciale face à l'incertain; analyse économique, recherche commerciale et prise de décision. (Collection de l'Ecole des sciences économiques de l'Université de Louvain, no. 93.) Louvain, Librairie universitaire, 1965. xxiv, 419 p.
3312. LANDAUER, C. "Wert, preis und zurcchnung." In, Schmoller's jahrbuch für gesetzgebung, verwaltung und volkswietschaft im deutschen reiche, 49 (1925), 805-33; 993-1027.
3313. LANGE, O. "The determinateness of the utility function."

Supply, Demand, etc. 225

In, Review of economic studies, I (1934) 218.
3314. LEHMANN, Max Rudolf. Leistungsmessung durch Wertschöpfungsrechnung. (His Industrielle betriebsstatistik, 2. Bd.) Essen, W. Girardet, 1954. 107 p.
3315. LELART, Michel. Les fondements actuels de la valeur de la monnaie. Préface par Achille Dauphin-Meunier. Paris, Nouvelles éditions latines, 1964. 286 p.
2316. LEMMNITZ, Alfred. Die Arbeitskraft und die produktion des mehrwerts; die Ursachen und quellen des reichtums der westdeutschen und Westberliner Konzernherren. Eine kleine lektion von Karl Marx, vermittelt durch Alfred Lemmnitz, Charlotte Schrott und Helmut Faulwetter. (Kleine bibliothek des arbeiters; Schriftenreihe zum Studium des Marxismus-Leninismus, Heft 2.) Berlin, Sozialistische einheitspartei deutschlands, Bezirksleitung Gross-Berlin, 1958. 45 p.
3317. LENDLE, Ottmar. Einige probleme der arbeitswerttheorie. 1. Aufl. (Schriftenreihe des Instituts für gesellschaftswissenschaften beim ZK der SED, Heft 3.) Berlin, Dietz, 1958. 52 p.
3318. LEON Paz, Fausto. Concepto de utilidad y algunos problemas que se presentan en su determinación. México, 1956. 71 p.
3319. LEPONIEMI, Arvi. On the demand and supply of money; the evidence from the quarterly time series in the United States, the United Kingdom and Finland 1949-1962. (Economic studies, 27.) Helsinki, Finnish economic association, 1966. 162 p.
3320. LERVIKS, Alf-Erik. Nagra anteckningar i anknytning till approbaturförelåsningar i efterfrageteori. (Memo-stencil, nr. 5.) Abo, 1967. 25 1.
3321. LI, Yen-lin. Shêng ch'an yin tzu lun. (Transliterated.) China, 1969. 1, 59 p.
3322. LIANG, Ch'i-k'un. T'an t'an chia chih kuei lü. (Transliterated.) China, 1962. 2, 2, 48 p.
3323. LIEBKNECHT, Wilhelm. Zur geschichte der werttheorie in England. Jena, G. Fischer, 1902. iv p., 1 l., 112 p. (Inaugural dissertation, Berlin.)
3324. LINDSAY, Alexander Dunlop, Baron Lindsay of Birker. Karl Marx's Capital; an introductory essay. (The World's manuals.) London, Oxford university press, H. Milford, 1937. 128 p.
3325. LISOWSKY, Peter Uwe. Das Bedürfnis als absatzwirtschaftliches problem. Zürich, Keller, 1968. xii, 109 p.
3326. LLOYD, Cliff. On the falsifiability of traditional demand theory. (Institute for quantitative research in economics and management. Institute paper, no. 68.) Lafayette, Indiana, Herman C. Krannert graduate school of industrial administration, Purdue university, 1964. 10 l.
3327. LOCKE, John. Some considerations of the consequences of the lowering of interest, and raising the value of money. In a letter to a member of parliament. London, A. & J. Churchill, 1692.

3328. LOMBARDINI, Siro. L'analisi della domanda nella teoria economica. (Saggi di teoria e politica economica, 5.) Milano, Giuffrè, 1957. 203 p.
3329. LORIA, A. "Appunti critici alla teoria del costo ai riproduzione." In, Giornale degli economisti, 32 (1906), 218-28.
3330. LYON, Leverett Samuel and Victor Abramson. The economics of open price systems. (B. I., publication, 71.) Washington, D. C., The Brookings institution, 1936. xii, 165 p.
3331. MACFARLANE, C. W. Value and distribution. 2d edition. Philadelphia, 1911.
3332. MACGREGOR, D. H. "Consumer's surplus; a reply." In, Economia, 4 (1924), 131-4.
3333. MAGALLON de la Vega, Alfonso. Apuntes y comentarios sobre el desarrollo de la teoría del valor. México, 1951. 123 p.
3334. MAINGUY, Yves. La Demande et l'offre, ... Préface de J. Ullmo. . . . (Collection sigma, 8.) Paris, Dunod, 1966. xxii, 269 p.
3335. MAKIGUCHI, Tsunesaburo. Kachiron. (Transliterated.) Japan, 1953. 11, 255 p.
3336. MALANOS, George J. Early cardinal utility theory. (Bureau of business and economic research, Georgia state college of business administration. Studies in business and economics, bulletin no. 8.) Atlanta, Bureau of business and economic research, School of business administration, Georgia state college of business administration, 1960. 40 p.
3337. MALTHUS, Thomas Robert. The measure of value stated and illustrated, with an application of it to the alterations in the value of the English currency since 1790. (Reprints of economic classics.) New York, Kelley and Millman, 1957. v, 81 p.
3338. MARGET, Arthur W. The theory of prices. New York, Prentice-Hall, 1942. 2 v.
3339. MARSHALL, Alfred. Kuo wai uiao i ho kuo nei chia chih ch'un li lun. (Transliterated.) 1953. 72 p.
3340. MARX, Karl. A history of economic theories. Edited, with a preface by Karl Kautsky. Translated from the French, with an introduction by Terence McCarthy. 1st edition. New York, Langland press, 1952- . v.
3341. _____. Loon, prijs en winst. (Klassieke schrijvers der komende wereld.) Brussel, Stuurboord, 1946. 60 p. (German edition: Berlin, Dietz, 1948. 64 p.)
3342. _____. Salários, preços e lucros. (Estante do pensamento social, no. 7.) Curitiba, Editora Guaíra, 194- . 78 p. (Spanish edition: Rio de Janeiro, Vitória, 1963. 78 p.)
3343. _____. Theorien über den Mehrwert (vierter Band des "Kapitals"). 1. Aufl. Berlin, Dietz, 1956-62. 3 v.
3344. _____. Theories of surplus value; a selection from the volumes published between 1905 and 1910 as Theorien über

den Mehrwert, edited by Karl Kautsky. . . . Translated from the German by G. A. Bonner and Emile Burns. London, Lawrence and Wishart, 1951. 432 p. (Reprints: New York, International publishers, 1952. 432 p.; Moscow, Foreign languages publishing house, 1963. v.)

3345. _____. Wages, price, and profit. (Library of Marxist-Leninist classics.) Moscow, Foreign languages publishing house, 1952. 94 p.

3346. MASON, E. S. "The doctrine of comparative cost." In, Quarterly journal of economics, 41 (1926), 63-93.

3347. MAY, K. "The structure of classical value theory." In, Review of economic studies, 1st series, 17, 42 (1949-50.)

3348. MEEK, Ronald L. "Some notes on the transformation problem." In, The economic journal, LXVI (March, 1956.)

3349. _____. Studies in the labour theory of value. London, Lawrence and Wishart, 1956. 310 p.

3350. MERIAM, R. S. "Supply curves and maximum satisfaction." In, Quarterly journal of economics, 42 (1928), 169-98.

3351. MICHIGAN. University. Engineering summer conferences. Value analysis and engineering: theory and applications. Ann Arbor, v. Annual.

3352. MILLER, H. E. "Utility curves, total utility, and consumer's surplus." In, Quarterly journal of economics, 41 (1927), 292-316.

3353. MIZUTANI, Kazuo. A system of functional equations for the behavior of the price of stock in a stock exchange. Fundamental laws of "elasticity" as an operator. (Science council of Japan, Division of economics and commerce. Economic series no. 9.) Tokyo, 1956. 27 p.

3354. MODEL, Horst. Bedarf, produktionsprogramm, absatz. Berlin, Verlag die wirtschaft, 1964. 191 p.

3355. MOE, Lyle Eugene. Saudi Arabia; supply and demand projections for farm products to 1975, with implications for United States exports. (United States. Department of agriculture. Economic research service. ERS-foreign 168.) Washington, Economic research service, United States department of agriculture, 1966. vi, 25 p.

3356. MOFFAT, James Ernest. The theory of diminishing returns; a history and criticism. Chicago, 1924. 391 l.

3357. MONIESON, David Danny. Value added as a measure of economic contribution by marketing institutions. (University microfilms, Ann Arbor, Michigan. Publication no. 21,489.) Ann Arbor, University microfilms, 1957. Microfilm AC-1.

3358. MONTEIL, Jacques. Les Théories des surplus. . . . Préface de François Trévoux. . . . (Collection techniques économiques modernes, 19. Série analyse economique, 6.) Paris, Gauthier-Villars, 1966. 179 p.

3359. MOORE, Henry Ludwell. Economic cycles: their law and cause. (Reprints of economic classics.) New York, A. M. Kelley, 1967. viii, 149 p.

3360. _____. "Partial elasticity of demand." In, Quarterly

journal of economics, 40 (1926), 393-401.
3361. MORET, Marc. Modèles de formation des prix; élaboration et critique. Strasbourg, 1951. 92 p.
3362. MORGENSTERN, Oscar. "Professor Hicks on value and capital. In, Journal of political economy, XLIV (1941) 361-393.
3363. _____. Speiltheorie und wirtschaftswissenschaft. Wien, R. Oldenbourg, c1963. 200 p.
3364. MYERS, Milton Linwood. The economics of the product-saturated economy. Ann Arbor, Michigan, University microfilms, 1959. Microfilm AC-1, no. 59-2046.
3365. MYRDAL, Gunnar. Value in social theory. Edited by Paul Streeten. London, Routledge and K. Paul, 1958. 269 p.
3366. NATAF, André. Théorio des choix et fonctions de demande. (Monographies du Centre d'économétrie, 4.) Paris, Centre national de la recherche scientifique, 1964. 87 p.
3367. NERLOVE, Marc. Distributed lags and demand analysis for agricultural and other commodities. (United States. Department of agriculture. Agriculture handbook no. 141. Washington, Government printing office, 1958. 121 p.
3368. NEW YORK university institute of philosophy, 8th, 1966. Human values and economic policy: proceedings of a symposium edited by Sidney Hook. New York, New York university press, 1967. x, 268 p.
3369. NICHOLSON, J. S. "The measurement of utility by money." In, Economic journal, 4 (1894), 342-47.
3370. NORRIS, Ruby (Turner). The theory of consumer's demand. Revised edition. New Haven, Yale university press, 1952. xiv, 237 p.
3371. NOVE, A. "The changing role of Soviet prices." In, Economics of planning, 3 (December, 1963), 185-95.
3372. OKUN, Arthur M. The effects of open inflation on aggregate consumer demand. (University microfilms, Ann Arbor, Michigan. Publication no. 17,073.) Ann Arbor, University microfilms, 1956. Microfilm AC-1, no. 17,07
3373. OLMOVA, Gabriela. Ekonomicke zaklady cen zemedelskych vyrobku v socialismu. Vyd. 1. Praha, Statni nakl. politicke literatury, 1962. 342 p.
3374. ORTH, Heinrich F. Die Wertanalyze als methode industrieller kostensenkung und produktgestaltung. Wiesbaden, Betriebswirtschaftlicher verlag Dr. Th. Gabler, 1968. 149 p.
3375. OSHIMA, Yuichi. Kakaku to shihon no riron. (Transliterated.) 1965. v, 417, 3 p. Includes bibliographical notes.
3376. OUGHTON, Frederick. Value analysis and value engineering. London, Pitman, 1969. x, 118 p.
3377. PAGE, Alfred N., editor. Utility theory; a book of readings compiled by the author. New York, Wiley, 1968. viii, 454 p.
3378. PANTALEONI, Maffeo. Pure economics. Translated by T. Boston Bruce. New York, Kelley and Millman, 1957. xiii, 315 p. (1st edition in Italian, 1889; 1st

edition in English, 1898.)
3379. PARETO, V. "Considerazioni sin principii fondamentali dell'economia politica pura." In, Giornale degli economisti, 4-7 (1892-93) 4: 389-20; 485-521. 5: 119-57. 6: 1-37. 7: 279-321.
3380. PARK, John C. S. Value theory and oligopolistic manufacturing industries; a study of cost-price-output-profit determining behavior of modern manufacturing corporations. Ann Arbor, Michigan, University microfilms, 1960. Microfilm AC-1, no. 60-125.
3381. PATINKIN, Don. Money, interest, and prices; an integration of monetary and value theory. Evanston, Illinois, Row, Peterson, 1956. xix, 510 p.
3382. PAULEY, Eugene Darrel. The long-run supply curve: some factors affecting its shape. (Fort Hays studies. New series. Economics series, no. 1.) Hays, Fort Hays Kansas state college, 1960. v, 28 p.
3383. PEARCE, Ivor F. A contribution to demand analysis. Oxford, Clarendon press, 1964. viii, 258 p.
3384. PERKINS, D. H. "Price stability and development in Mainland China, 1951-63." In, Journal of political economy, 72 (August 1964), 360-75.
3385. PERLMAN, Richard. Wage determination: market or power forces? Boston, Heath and company, 1964.
3386. PIERSTORFF, Julius. Die lehre vom unternehmergewinn in Frankreich. 2. theil der schrift: Die lehre vom unternehmergewinn. Berlin, Druck von W. Pormetter, 1875. 49 p. (Habilitationsschrift, Göttingen.)
3387. PIGOU, A. C. "An analysis of supply." In, Economic journal, 38 (1928), 238-57.
3388. _____. "The interdependence of different sources of demand and supply in a market." In, Economic journal, 23 (1913), 19-24.
3389. _____. "Some remarks on utility." In, Economic journal, 13 (1903), 58-68.
3390. PJANIC, Zoran. Savremene burzoakse teorije vrednosti i cena. (Institut drustvenih nauka. Odeljenje za ekonomske nauke.) Beograd, 1965. 280 p.
3391. POLIER, Léon. L'idée du juste salaire; essai d'histoire dogmatique et critique. Paris, V. Giard et E. Brière 1903. 3 p. 1., 388 p. Bibliography, 373-384.
3392. POPADIUK, K. "Calculating deviations of prices from values." In, Problems of economics, 11 (March 1964), 21-29.
3393. PORTER, R. L. "Value theory as a key to the interpretation of the development of economic thought." In, American journal of economics and sociology, 24, 1 (1965) 39-50.
3394. PRESTON, L. E. and E. C. Keachie. "Cost functions and progress functions: an integration." In, American economic review, 54 (March 1964), 100-07.
3395. PRODUCTIVITY and materials handling symposium, Sydney, 1966. Symposium papers. Sydney, 1966. 1 v.

3396. RAJAOJA, Vieno. A study in the theory of demand functions and price indexes. (Societas scientiarum fennica. Commentationes physico-mathematicae, XXI, 1.) Helsinki, 195 i.e. 1959. 96 p.
3397. RAUNER, Robert M. Samuel Bailey and the classical theory of value. Cambridge, Harvard university press, 1961. 162 p.
3398. RENNER, Karl. Arbeit und kapital; eine volkstümliche einführung in die probleme der modernen wirtschaft mit einem geleitwort von Adolf Schärf. Wien, Verlag der Wiener volksbuchhandlung, c1953. 79 p.
3399. REUTLINGER, Shlmo. Evaluation of some uncertainty hypotheses for predicting supply. (North Carolina agricultural experiment station. Technical bulletin no. 160.) Raleigh, North Carolina agricultural experiment station, 1964. 59 p.
3400. RICCA-SALERNO, Giuseppe. La teoria del salario nella storia delle dottrine e dei fatti economici. Palermo, A. Reber, 1900. viii, 687 p.
3401. RICCI, Umberto. "Curve crescenti di ofelimita elementare e di domanda." In, Giornale degli economisti, 29 (1904), 112-38.
3402. _____. La loi de la demande individuelle et la rente de consommateur." In, Revue d'economic politique, 40 (1926), 5-24.
3403. _____. Théorie de la valeur; éléments d'économie politique pure. Con le biografie di Umberto Ricci scritte de Luigi Einaudi e Costantino Bresciani-Turroni e una completa bibliografia. Milano, Malfasi, 1951. xxii, 225 p.
3404. ROBBINS, L. "The representative firm." In, Economic journal, 38 (1928), 387-404.
3405. ROBERTSON, Dennis Holme. "Alternative theories of the rate of interest." In, Economic journal, XLVII (1937) 428-36. Money. With an introduction by C. W. Guillebaud. 6th edition, revised with additional chapters. (Cambridge economic handbooks.) New York, Pitman publishing corporation; London, Nisbet, 1948. xviii, 223 p.
3406. _____. Utility and all that and other essays. New York, Macmillan, 1952. 206 p.
3407. ROBINSON, Joan. The economics of imperfect competition. 2nd edition. London, Macmillan, 1969. xx, 352 p.
3408. _____. "The labor theory of value." In, Science and society (Spring, 1954).
3409. RODRIGUES, Felix Contreiras. Conceitos de valor e preço; fundamentos para uma ordem democrática-corporativa. Rio de Janeiro, Olimpica, 1951. 490 p.
3410. ROST, Bernhard. Die wert- und preistheorie, mit berücksichtigung ihrer dogmengeschichtlichen entwickelung. Leipzig, Duncker & Humblot, 1908. vii, 207, 1 p.
3411. RUDAS, Ladislaus. Ertektöbbletelmélet. 5, kiad. Budapest, Szikra, 1949? 32 p.
3412. RUDLOFF, Marcel Paul. L'investissement et la demande; essai sur la théorie de l'investissement induit. Préface

de Paul Coulbois. (Ecole pratique des hautes études. Observation économique, 19.) Paris, Société d'édition d'enseignement supérieur, 1960. 280 p.
3413. RUF, Werner. Die Grundlagen eines betriebswirtschaftlichen wertbegriffes. (Unternehmung und betrieb, Bd. 50.) Bern, P. Haupt, 1955. 133, 1 p.
3414. SAKURAI, Tsuyoshi. Seisan kakaku no riron. (Transliterated.) Japan. 1968. 281 p. Bibliography. (A revision of the author's thesis, Tokyo university, 1966.)
3415. SALZ, Arthur. Beiträge zur geschichte und kritik der lohnfondstheorie. (Münchener volkswirtschaftliche studien, hrsg. von L. Brentano und W. Lotz. 70. stück.) Stuttgart und Berlin, J. G. Cotta'sche buchhandlung nachfolger, 1905. 4 p. 1., 200, 2 p.
3416. SARIDAKIS, Georges B. L'évolution de la théorie de la valeur en Angleterre. . . Paris, M. Giard, 1924. 218 p. Bibliographie, 215-216. (Thèse, Univ. de Paris.)
3417. SARIO, Leo and Kiyoshi Noshiro and others. Value distribution theory. . . . In collaboration with Tadashi Kuroda, Kikuji Matsumoto und Mitsuru Nakai. (The University series in higher mathematics.) Princeton, New Jersey, Van Nostrand, 1966. xi, 236 p.
3418. SCHACK, H. "Zur kritik der preistheorie." In, Jahrbücher für nationalökonomie und statistik, 127 (1927), 32-51.
3419. SCHMIDT, Ronald. Die moderne christliche welt: leben, liebe, wirtschaftlicher frieden. Baden-Baden, 1953. 76 p.
3419a. SCHULTZ, Henry. The theory and measurement of demand. 2d edition. Chicago, University of Chicago press, 1957.
3420. SCHUMPETER, Joseph Alois. The theory of economic development. An inquiry into profits, capital, credit, interest and business cycles. Translated from German by Redvers Opie. (Harvard economic studies, v. 46.) Cambridge, Massachusetts, Harvard university press, 1949. 255 p.
3421. _____. "Zur frage der grenzproduktivitat." In, Schmoller's Jahrbuch für gesetzgetbung, verwaltung und volkwirtschaft in deutschen reiche, 51 (1927), 671-80.
3422. SEITZ, Manfred. Probleme der betrieblichen planung bei im zeitablauf wechselnden marktverhältnissen. (Schriften zur theoretischen und angewandten betriebswirtschaftslehre Bd. 3.) Wiesbaden, Betriebswirtschaftlicher verlag Gabler, 1968. 301 p.
3423. SEWALL, Hannah Robie. The theory of value before Adam Smith. New York, Published for the American economic association by Macmillan company, 1901. 127, 1 p. (New York, A. M. Kelley, 1968. 127 p.)
3424. SHARP, Herbert John. Engineering materials: selection and value analysis. London, Heywood books; New York, Elsevier, 1966. 428 p.
3425. SHIRASUGI, Shoichiro. Kachi no riron. (Transliterated.) Japan, 1959. 314 p.
3426. SHOUP, C. S. "Public goods and joint production." In,

Rivista internazionale di scienze economiche e commerciali, 12 (March 1965), 254-64.

3427. SINGH, H. K. Manmohan. Demand theory and economic calculation in a mixed economy. London, Allen and Unwin, 1963. 135 p.

3428. SMART, William. An introduction to the theory of value on the lines of Menger, Wieser, and Böhm-Bawerk. (Reprints of economic classics.) New York, A. M. Kelley, 1966. x, 2, 104 p. (1st edition, 1891. 3rd edition, 1914. xii, 104 p.)

3429. SOCIETY of American value engineers. Proceedings of the national convention. 1- 1966- . Washington, Spartan books. v.

3430. STIGLER, George Joseph. "The development of utility theory." In, The journal of political economy, LVIII (August, 1950)

3431. ———. The theory of competitive price. New York, The Macmillan company, 1942. vii, 197 p. Bibliography. (Enlarged edition, entitled: The theory of price. 1946. vii, 340. Bibliography. Revised edition, 1952. 310 p.)

3432. STOJILJKOVIC, Dragoljub. Teorija i merenje traznje. Beograd, Naucna knjiga, 1969. xi, 200 p.

3433. STUBER, Peter Rolf. Die Entwicklung der theorie der nachfrage seit der Grenznutzenschule. Eine dogmengeschichtliche untersuchung. Zürich, Juris verlag, 1966. 140 p.

3434. SUN, Huai-jen. Tzu pen yü shêng yü chin chih. (Transliterated.) China, 1954. 63 p.

3435. SWEEZY, P. M., A. P. Lerner, R. F. Kahn, J. R. Hicks, L. Tarshis, and J. E. Meade. "Notes on elasticity of substitution." In, Review of economic studies, 1 (1933-34) 67, 144.

3436. TARDE, Alfred de. L'idee du juste prix; essai de psychologie économique. Paris, F. Alcan, 1907. 3, 372. Bibliography.

3437. TAUSSIG, F. W. "Is market price determinate." In, Quarterly journal of economics, 35 (1921), 394-411.

3438. TEMKIN, Gabriel. Marks i idea pieniądza pracy; z problemów teorii wartosci. Wyd. 1. (Biblioteka studiów nad marksizmem, 6.) Warszawa, Ksiazka i Wiedza, 1965. 457 p.

3439. THEIL, Henri. De invloed van de voorraden op het consumentengedrag. Amsterdam, 1951. 129 3 p.

3440. TRESCOTT, Paul B. The logic of the price system. New York, McGraw-Hill, 1970. viii, 455 p.

3441. TREZZA, Bruno. Valore e distribuzione. (Pubblicazioni della Facoltà giuridica del l'Università di Napoli, 65.) Napoli, E. Jovene, 1963. 224 p.

3442. TROISI, Michele. Saggi di teoria e storia delle dottrine economiche. (Studi di economia e vita sociale, 4.) Firenze, Macri, 1948. 331 p.

3443. TUCKER, George. The laws of wages, profits and rent, investigated. (Reprints of economic classics) New York, A. M. Kelley, 1964. x, 189 p. (1st published, 1887).

Supply, Demand, etc. 233

3444. TULLANDER, Boriz. De ekonomiska ideernas utveckling med särskild hänsyn till värdeteorien. Uppsala, Almqvist and Wiksells boktr., 1956. 251 p. Bibliography, 247-248.

3445. TURGEON, Charles I. and C.-H Turgeon. La valeur d'après les économistes anglais et francais. Paris, Librairie du recueil sirey, 1925.

3446. TURVEY, Ralph, editor and translator. Wages policy under full employment. By Erik Lundberg and others. London, W. Hodge, 1952. 87 p.

3447. UNITED States. Congress. Senate. Committee on public works. Value engineering. Hearings, Ninetieth congress, first session . . . August 1 and 2, 1967. Washington, Government printing office, 1967. iii, 94 p.

3448. _____. Department of health, education, and welfare. Office of the Assistant secretary for program coordination. Program analysis. 1966-1-- . Washington. v.

3449. VALUE, capital, and growth; papers in honour of Sir John Hicks. Edited by J. N. Wolfe. Edinburgh, Edinburgh university press; Chicago, Aldine publishing company, 1968. xi, 552 p.

3450. VALUE engineering in manufacturing; a reference book on the theory, principles, application, and administration of value engineering and analysis in industry. (ASTME manufacturing engineering series.) Englewood Cliffs, New Jersey, Prentice-Hall, 1967. xii, 270 p.

3451. VEBLEN, Thorstein B. "Bohm-Bawerk's definition of capital and the source of wages." In, Quarterly journal of economics (January, 1892) 247-252.

3452. VIMER, Jacob. "The utility concept in value theory and its critics." In, Journal of political economy, 33 (1925), 369-87; 638-59.

3453. VLEESCHHOUWER, J. E. Economische rekenvormen, onderzoek naar de grondslagen van economische ordeningen. 's-Gravenhage, M. Nijhoff, 1949. 2 v.

3454. VON Mises, Ludwig. Epistemological problems of economics; translated by George Reisman. (The William Volker fund series in the humane studies.) Princeton, New Jersey, Van Nostrand, 1960. 239 p.

3455. WALDORF, William Harold. Demand for manufactured foods, manufacturers' services, and farm products in food manufacturing; a statistical analysis. (United States. Department of agriculture, Technical bulletin, no. 1317.) Washington, United States department of agriculture, Economic research service, 1964. iv, 60 p.

3456. WALRUS, L. "Geometrical theory of the determination of prices." In, Annals of the American academy of political and social science, 3 (1892), 45-64.

3457. WANG, Hsü-chuang. Chia chih kuei lü tsai wo kuo she hui chu i ti t'ung i shih ch'ang chung ti tso yung. (Transliterated.) China, 1957. 63 p.

3458. _____. Tzŭ pên shêng yü chia chih ho tzŭ pên chi lei. (Transliterated.) China, 1956. 106 p.

3459. WANG, Mao. Kuo chia chien shê ho jên min shêng huo.

(Transliterated.) China, 1957. 72 p.
3460. WARBURTON, Clark. Forces producing disturbances in the value of output." In, Journal of political economy, 69 (1961) 587-604.
3461. WARD, Benjamin. Elementary price theory. New York, Free Press, 1967. viii, 184 p.
3462. WAUGH, Frederick Vail. Demand and price analysis; some examples from agriculture. (United states. Department of agriculture. Technical bulletin no. 1316.) Washington, Economic and statistical analysis division, United States department of agriculture, 1964. vi, 94 p.
3463. WEBER, Hans Hermann. Grundlagen einer quantitativen theorie des Handels. Zugleich ein beitrag zur theorie mehrstufiger marktformen. (Beiträge zur betriebswirtschaftlichen forschung, Bd. 26.) Köln und Opladen, Westdeutscher verlag, 1966. xi, 246 p.
3464. WEGENER, Walther. Die Quellen der wissenschaftsauffassung Max Webers und die Problematik der werturteilsfreiheit der nationalökonomie; ein wissenschaftssoziologischer beitrag. Berlin, Duncker und Humblot, 1962. 300 p.
3465. WEI, Hsün and Shu-t'ang Ku. Chia chih kuei lü tsai tzu pên chu i ko ko chieh tuan chung ti tso yung. (Transliterated. China, 1956. 54 p. (1961. 80 p.
3466. WELFE, Władysław. Popyt i podaz; zakres i metody statystycznych badan rynku. Wyd. 1. Warszawa, Panstwowe wydawn. ekonomiczne, 1962. 293 p.
3467. WHITAKER, Albert Conser. History and criticism of the labor theory of value in English political economy. (Reprints of economic classics.) New York, A. M. Kelley, 1968. 197 p. (New York, Columbia university press, London, P. S. King & son, 1904. 194 p. 1 l.)
3468. WICKSELL, Knut. Uber wert, kapital und rente nach den neueren nationalökonomischen theorien. Aalen, Scientia verlag, 1969. xvi, 143 p. (First edition, 1893. English editions. Value, capital, and rent. With a foreword by G. L. S. Shackle; translated by S. H. Frowein. (The Library of economics.) New York, Rinehart; London, G. Allen and Unwin, 1954. 180 p.
3469. WICKSTEED, Philip Henry. The alphabet of economic science; elements of the theory of value or worth. (Reprints of economic classics.) New York, Kelley and Millman, 1955. 142 p.
3470. _____. An essay on the co-ordination of the laws of distribution. London, 1894. 56 p.
3471. WIESER, Friedrich, Freiherr von. "The Austrian school and the theory of value." In, Economic journal, 1 (1891), 108-21.
3472. _____. Der naturliche wert. Germany, 1889. xvi, 239 p. (English edition: Natural value. Edited by William Smart. London, 1893. xiv, 243 p. Edited with a preface and analysis by William Smart; the translation by Christian A. Malloch. (Reprints of economic classics.) New York, Kelley and Millman, 1956. xiv, 243 p. German

	edition: 1968. Frankfurt am Main, Sauer und Auvermann, xvi, 239 p.)
3473.	_____. Uber den ursprung und die Hauptgesetze des wirtschaftlichen werthes. Germany, 1894. xiv, 214 p.
3474.	WILCZYNSKI, Wacław. Rynek sprzedawcy i rynek nabywcy a optymalne wykorzystanie zasobow. (Wyzsza Szkoła ekonomiczna w Poznaniu. Zeszyty naukowe. Seria II. Prace habilitacyjne i doktorskie, zesz. nr. 28.) Poznan, Nakł. Wyzszej Szkoły ekonomicznej, 1963. 192 p.
3475.	WILLIAMS, Alan H. Output budgeting and the contribution of micro-economics to efficiency in government. (CAS occasional paper no. 4.) London, H. M. Stationery office, 1967. 22 p.
3476.	WITTICH, Hans. Neuere untersuchungen über eindeutige analytische funktionen. Mit 31 abbildungen. 2., korrigierte Aufl. (Ergebnisse der mathematik und ihrer grenzgebiete, Bd. 8.) Berlin, Heidelberg, New York, Springer, 1968. viii, 163 p.
3477.	WITTMANN, Waldemar. Der Wertbegriff in der betriebswirtschaftslehre. (Beiträge zur betriebswirtschaftlichen forschung. Bd. 2.) Köln, Westdeutscher verlag, 1956. 112 p.
3478.	WOESTIJNE, W. J. van de. Een algemene vorm van de vraagfunctie met toepassings-mogelijkheden voor practische marktanalyse en verkoopcontrole. (Capita selecta der economie, 17.) Leiden, H. E. Stenfert Kroese, 1953. 152 p.
3479.	WOLD, Herman O. A. Analisis de la demanda, un estudio de econometria. Con la colaboración de Lars Juréen. Traducción realizada por J. Béjar, Arnaiz y F. Azorin; coordinada por Sixto Rios. Madrid, Consejo superior de investigaciones cientificas, Instituto de investigaciones estadisticas, 1956. 431 p.
3480.	_____. Demand analysis; a study in econometrics. By H. Wold in association with Lars Juréen. (Wiley publications in statistics.) New York, Wiley, 1953. 358 p.
3481.	WOLFE, J. N. Value, capital, and growth; papers in honour of Sir John Hicks. Edinburgh, Edinburgh university press; Chicago, Aldine pub., 1968. xi, 552 p.
3482.	WOLLMAN, Nathaniel. The development and use of the market concept in value analysis. (University microfilms, Ann Arbor, Michigan. Publication no. 3068.) Ann Arbor, University microfilms, 1952. Microfilm AC-1, no. 3068.
3483.	WRIGHT, P. G. "Total utility and consumer's surplus." In, Quarterly journal of economics, 31 (1917), 307-18.
3484.	WU, Shih-yen and Jack A. Pontney. An introduction to modern demand theory. New York, Random house, c1967. ix, 270 p.
3485.	YOKOYAMA, Tamotsu. Juyo riron no kenkyu. (Transliterated.) Japan, 1960. 4, 162 p. Bibliography, 155-57.
3486.	YOUNG, A. A. "Some limitations of the value concept." In, Quarterly journal of economics, 25 (1911), 409-28.

3487. ZAOPATRZENIE i zbyt w przedsiebiorstwie przemysłowym. Praca zbiorowa: V. Kosik et al. Tłumacz Władysław Tomaszewski. Wyd. 1. Warszawa, Panstwowe wydawn. Ekonomiczne, 1965. 198 p.
3488. ZUCKERKANDL, R. "Preis (Theorie.)" In, Handwörterbuch der staatswissenschaften, 4th edn., 6 (1925), 994-1026.
3489. _____. Zur theorie des preises, mit besonderer berücksichtigung der geschichtlichen entwicklung der lehre. Leipzig, Duncker & Humblot, 1889. x, 384 p.

G. METHOD AND SCOPE

3490. ACKLEY, G. "The contribution of economists to policy formation." In, Journal of finance, 21 (May 1966), 169-77.
3491. ALBERTINI, Jean Marie, A. Calleja et al. Premiers pas en économie; initiation économique en méthode semi-programmée. Graphiques de F. Lerouge. Paris, Economie et humanisme, Editions ouvrières. 1969. 239 p.
3492. ALEXANDER, K. J. W., A. G. Kemp and T. M. Rybczn-ski. The economist in business. Oxford, Basil Blackwell, 1967.
3493. ALLEN, Roy George Douglas. Mathematical analysis for economists. (London school of economics and political science . . . studies in statistics and scientifics method, edited by A. L. Bowley and A. Wolf, no. 3.) London, Macmillan and company, limited, 1938. Bibliography. [French edition entitled: Analyse mathématique et theorie economique. Troby H. Bernard. Paris, Presses universitaires de France, 1950. xii, 600 p. Japanese edition entitled (transliterated): Keizai Kenkyûsha no tame no sûgaku kaiseki. (Translated by Shûgen Takagi.) Tokyo, Yuhikaku, 1953. Vol. I, 351 p. Vol. II, 1954, 722 p. Spanish edition entitled: Análysis matemático para economistas. (Translated by Emilio de Figueroa.) Madrid, Aguilar, 1956. 591 p.]
3494. ———. Mathematical economics. London, Macmillan; New York, Saint Martin's press, 1956. 768 p. Bibliography. [2nd edition, 1959. xviii, 812 p. Bibliography; 1963, xviii, 812 p. Bibliography. Japanese edition entitled (transliterated): Suri keizaigaku Tribytakuma yasui and takeyasu kimura. (From English edition, 1956.) Tokyo, Kinokuniya-shoten, 1959. 511 p. Polish edition entitled: Ekonomia matematyczna. (Translated by Egon Vielrose from English, 2nd edition, 1959.) Warsaw, Panstwowe wydawnictwo naukowe, 1961. 889 p.]
3495. ALSTADHEIM, Havard. Konsistent aggregering i økonomisk teori. En oversikt over problemstillinger. (Memorandum fra Sosialøkonomisk institutt, Universitetet i Oslo.) Oslo, 1968. 27 l.
3496. AMONN, Alfred. "Cassels system der theoretischen nationalökonomie." In, Archiv für sozialwissenschaft und sozialpolitik, LI (1923-1924), 1-87, 322-361.
3497. ———. Objekt und grundbegriffe der nationalökonomie. 1911. ix, 424 p. Bibliographies. (2nd 1927.)
3498. AMOROSO, Luigi. "L'Applicazione della matematica alla

economica politica." In, Giornale degli economisti, 40 (1910), 57-63.

3499. _____. Lezioni di economia matematica, 1921. x, 478 p.

3500. _____. Meccanica economica. (Studi economici e sociologici, 5.) Napoli, Giannini, 1969. xxviii, 186 p.

3501. ARAMANOVICH, Isaak Genriklovich and others. Mathematical analysis: differentiation and integration. Translated by H. Moss. Ist English edition edited by I. N. Sneddon. (International series of monographs in pure and applied mathematics, v. 81.) Oxford, New York, Pergamon press, 1965. xi, 322 p.

3502. ARBEITSTAGUNGEN zur erörterung der aufgaben und methoden der wirtschaftswissenschaft in Unserer Zeit, 1st, Garmisch-Partenkirchen, Germany, 1961. Diagnose und prognose als wirtschaftswissenschaftliche methodenprobleme; Verhandlungen auf der arbeitstagung der vereins für socialpolitik, Gesellschaft für wirtschafts- und socialwissenschaften, im Garmisch-Partenkirchen, 1961. Hrsg. von Herbert Giersch und Knut Borchardt. (Schriften des vereins für socialpolitik, Gesellschaft für wirtschafts- und socialwissenschaften, n. F., Bd. 25.) Berlin, Duncker, und Humblot, 1962. xv, 592 p.

3503. ARENDONK, J. A. Basic relations in theoretical models; a socio-economic approach." In, Philippine economic journal, 3 (No. 1, 1964), 1-20.

3504. ARROW, Kenneth Joseph, Leonid Hurwicz and Hirofumi Uzawa. Studies in linear and non-linear programming. With contributions by Hollis B. Chenery and others. (Stanford mathematical studies in the social sciences, 2.) Stanford, California, Stanford university press, 1958. 229 p.

3505. ASHLEY, W. J. "The enlargement of economics." In, Economic journal, 18 (1908), 181-204.

3506. _____. "The present position of political economy." In, Economic journal, 17 (1907), 467-89.

3507. AYRES, C. E. "Ideological responsibility." In, Journal of economic issues. 1 (June 1967), 3-11.

3508. BABA, Keinosuke. Shakai kagaku to shite no keizaigaku. (Transliterated.) Japan, 1969. 268 p. Bibliographical footnotes.

3509. BACH, G. L. and P. Saunders. "Lasting effects of economics courses at different types of institutions." In, American economic review, 56 (June 1966), 505-11.

3510. BAERWALD, Friedrich. Economic system analysis, concepts and perspectives. New York, Fordham university press, 1960. 113 p.

3511. BAGEHOT, W. "The postulates of English political economy." In, Fortnightly review (1867), 215-24. (Also in, Economic studies, 7th edition 1908, 1-94 p. Same volume contains, "The Preliminaries of political economy." 95-124 p.)

3512. BAGIOTTI, Tullio. Studi in onore di Marco Fanno. Padova,

Italy, Edizioni cedam, 1966. 2 v. (Vol. 2. Investigations in economic theory and methodology.)
3513. BASMANN, R. L. and R. J. Rohr. Some formulas encountered in the deductive analysis of third-order autoregressive processes. (Institute for research in the behavioral, economic, and management sciences. Institute paper no. 202.) Lafayette, Indiana, Herman C. Krannert graduate school of industrial administration, Purdue university, 1968. 40 1.
3514. BATTAGLIA, Felice. . . . Problemi metodologici nella storia delle dottrine politiche ed economiche. (Collana di studi "Pietro Rossi." Circolo giuridico della R. Università di Siena. Vol. III.) Roma, Società editrice del "Foro italiano," 1939. 4 p. 1, 7-206 p. 1 1. Bibliographical footnotes.
3515. BAUMOL, William J. Economic theory and operations analysis. Englewood Cliffs, New Jersey, Prentice-Hall, 1961. 438 p. (2nd edition, 1965. xiv, 606 p. Bibliographies. Spanish edition entitled: Teoría económica y análisis de operaciones. Mexico: Herrero Hermanos, 1964. 546 p. French edition entitled: Théorie économique et analyse opérationelle. Translated by P. Patrel. Paris, Dunod, 1962. xiv, 473 p.
3516. BEACH, Earl Francis. Economic models, an exposition. New York, Wiley, 1957. 227 p.
3517. BEAR, D. V. T. and D. Orr. "Logic and expediency in economic theorizing." In, Journal of political economy, 75 (April 1967), 188-96.
3518. BEHRENS, Fritz. Zur Methode der politischen Ökonomie; ein beitrag zur geschichte der politischen Ökonomie. Berlin, Akademie-verlag, 1952. 71 p.
3519. BEUTIN, Ludwig. Die Praxis und die wirtschaftsgeschichte. Dortmund, Gesellschaft für westfälische wirtschaftsgeschichte, 1955. 14 p.
3520. _____. Einführung in die wirtschafteschichte. Köln, Böhlau, 1958. 179 p.
3521. BEVERIDGE, W. "Economics as a liberal education." In, Economica 1 (1921), 2-19.
3522. BIESENBACH, Friedhelm. Die Entwicklung der nationalökonomie an der Universität Freiburg i. Br. 1768-1896; eine Dogmengeschichtliche analyse. (Beiträge zur Freiburger wissenschafts- und universitätsgeschichte, Heft 36.) Freiburg im Breisgau, E. Albert universitätsbuchhandlung, 1969. 256 p.
3523. BINGHAM, Robert C. Economic concepts; a programmed approach. New York, McGraw-Hill, 1966. ix, 322 p.
3524. BOHM-Bawerk, Eugen von. "The Austrian economists." In, Annals of the American academy of political and social science, 1 (1891), 361-84.
3525. _____. "The historical versus the deductive method in political economy." In, Annals of the American academy of political and social science, 1 (1890), 244-71.
3526. BONGARD, Willi. Nationalökonomie, wohin? Realtypen des wirtschaftlichen Verhaltens. Köln und Opladen,

Westdeutscher verlag, 1965. 132 p. Bibliography, 129-132.
3527. BORTOT, Paolo. Sulla ripartizione di una risorsa fra piu processi produttivi, nel caso che la massima quantità accettabile in ogni progresso non sia nota con certezza. . . . Pisa, Editrice tecnico scientifica, 1968. 10 p.
3528. BOULDING, Kenneth E. "The economics of knowledge and the knowledge of economics." In, American economic association papers and proceedings, 56 (May, 1966) 1-13.
3529. ———. "The legitimacy of economics." In, Western economic journal, 5 (September 1967), 299-307.
3530. ———. "The skills of the economist. Cleveland, H. Allen, 1958. 196 p.
3531. BOWLEY, Arthur Lyon. The mathematical groundwork of economics: an introductory treatise. Oxford, Clarendon press, 1924. viii, 98 p.
3532. BRANDIS, R. "On the noxious influence of authority." In, Quarterly review of economics and business, 7, 3 (1967) 37-43.
3533. BRANDT, Karl, editor. Festschrift zum 70. Geburtstag vo] Walter G. Waffenschmidt. Meisenheim am Glan, A. Hain 1958. 196 p.
3534. BRENTANO, L. Die klassische nationalökonomie. 1888. 32
3535. BRESLAU. Wyzsza szkoła ekonomiczna. Zeszyty naukowe. Wrocław, Panstwowe wydawn. naukowe, 195- .
3536. BREWIS, T. N., H. E. English, Anthony Scott, Pauline Jewett, and J. E. Gander. Canadian economic policy. Toronto, Macmillan company, limited, 1961. (2nd edition, revised, 1965.)
3537. BRIEFS, Henry W. Three views of method in economics. (Georgetown economic studies.) Washington, Georgetown university press, 1960. iii, 97 p.
3538. BROWN, Harry Gunnison. Objectives, prejudice and techniques in the teaching of economics. New York, Robert Schalkenbach foundation, 1948. 84 p. (Essays which appeared in American journal of economics and sociology, 1945, 1946.)
3539. BRUNNER, K. A. "Controversy between 'quantity theory' and 'Keynesian theory.'" In, Schweizerischezeitschrift für volkswirtschaft und statistik, 103 (June 1967), 173-90.
3540. BUCK, Robert Creighton. Studies in modern analysis. By E. J. McShane and others. (Mathematical association of America. Studies in mathematics, v. 1.) Buffalo, Mathematical association of America; distributed by Prentice-Hall, Englewood Cliffs, New Jersey, 1962. viii, 182 p. Bibliographies.
3541. BUDAPEST. Magyar. Közgazdasagtudomanyi Egyetem. Központi Könyvtar. Matematikai modszerek alkalmazasa a közgazdasagtudomanyban. Osszeallitotta: A Marx Károly közgazdasagtudomanyi Egyetem központi könyvtara bibliográfiai es dokumentacios osztalya. (Its Idoszeru gazdasagi kérdérek irodalma, 10-.) Budapest, Közgazdasagi es Jogi könyvkiado, 1963- . v.

3542. BUHLMANN, Hans. Mathematical methods in risk theory. Berlin, Heidelberg, 1970. xii, 210 p.
3543. BURFORD, Roger L. A review of regional economics research methodology. Baton Rouge, Gulf South research institute, 1967. iv, 40 1.
3544. BURN, Duncan, J. R. Seale, and A. R. N. Ratcliff. Lessons from central forecasting. London, Institute of Economic affairs, 1965.
3545. CAIRNES, John Elliott. The character and logical method of political economy. 1888. (Reprinted: New York, A. M. Kelley, 1965.
3546. CALKINS, R. D. "The production and use of economic knowledge." In, American economic association paper and proceedings, 56 (May, 1966), 530-37.
3547. CANNAN, E. "The practical utility of economic science." In, Economic journal 12 (1902), 459-71.
3548. ———. "The subject matter of economics." In, Wealth, chapter I (1914), 2-18. (Not in 3rd edition, 1928.)
3549. CARVER, T. N. "Clark's distribution of wealth." In, Quarterly journal of economics, 15 (1901), 578-602.
3550. CASTANEDA, José. La ciencia y las técnicas de la economía; conferencia pronunciada en el acto de inauguración del curso 1959-60 en el Colegio Mayor universitario de San Pablo. Madrid, Colegio. . . , 1960. 25 p.
3551. CHAIT, B. Sur l'économétrie; science du concret, orientée notamment vers la détection 1e des causes des fluctuations et crises économiques, 2e des moyens pour prévenir ou atténuer cellesci. Bruxelles, Office de publicité, 1949. 46 p.
3552. CHAMBERS, Edward J. Economic fluctuations and forecasting. Englewood Cliffs, New Jersey, Prentice-Hall, 1961. 649 p. Bibliography.
3553. CHEN, John-ren. Der Weltbaumwollmarkt; ein ökonometrisches modell. (Frankfurter wirtschafts- und sozialwissenschaftliche studien, Heft 24.) Berlin, Duncker und Humblot, 1970. 170 p.
3554. CHIANG, Alpha C. Fundamental methods of mathematical economics. New York, McGraw-Hill company, 1967. Bibliography.
3555. CHLEBIKOVA, M. Aplikacia matematiky v ekonómii; vyber literatury. Odborne spolupracoval L. Uncovsky. (Ekonomicke aktuality. Bibliograficky zpravodaj, 1960, c. 3.) Bratislava, Ustredna ekonomicka kniznica, 1960. 409 1. in portfolio.
3556. CHMIELEWICZ, Klaus. Forschungskonzeptionen der wirtschaftswissenschaft; zur Problematik einer entscheidungstheoretischen und normativen wirtschaftslehre. Stuttgart, C. E. Poeschel, 1970. viii, 112 p.
3557. CHRIST, C. F. "Econometrics in economics. Some achievements and challenges." In, Australian economic papers, 6 (December 1967), 155-70.
3558. CLAPHAM, J. H. "Of empty economic boxes." In,

Economic journal, 32 (1922), 305-14; 560-63.
3559. CLARK, John Bates. "Divisions in economic theory." In, Quarterly journal of economics, 13 (1899), 187-203.
3560. _____. "The dynamic law of wages." In, Journal of political economy, 7 (1899), 375-82.
3561. _____. "The field of economic dynamics." In, Political science quarterly, 20 (1905), 246-56.
3562. _____. "The future of economic theory." In, Quarterly journal of economics, 13 (1898), 1-14.
3563. CLARK, John Maurice. "Economic theory in an era of social readjustment." In, American economic review, 9 (1919), Supplement.
3564. _____. "Economics and modern psychology." In, Journal of political economy, 26 (1918), 1-30; 136-66.
3565. _____. "Soundings of non-euclidean economics." In, American economic review, 11 (1921), Supplement, 132-43.
3566. COHN, G. "Methodologie der staatswissenschaften und der nationalökonomie insbesondere." In, Chapter 1, System der nationalökonomie: Erster Band, Grundlegung der nationalökonomie, 1885. 23-78.
3567. CONFERENCE on the history of quantification in the sciences. New York, 1959. Quantification; a history of the meaning of measurement in the natural and social sciences. Edited by Harry Woolf. Indianapolis, Bobbs-Merrill, 1961. 224 p. Bibliographical footnotes.
3568. COPELAND, M. A. "Professor Knight on psychology." In, Quarterly journal of economics 40 (1925), 134-51.
3569. COWLES commission for research in economics. Economic theory and measurement; a twenty year research report, 1932-1952. Chicago, 1952, c1952. 180 p.
3570. COZZI, Terenzio. Sviluppo e stabilità dell'economia. . . . (Studi, 6.) Torino, Fondazione Luigi Einaudi, 1969. 194 p.
3571. CROCE, B. "Sul principio economico." In, Giornale degli economist, 21 (1900), 15-26; 22 (1901), 121-30.
3572. CRUM, William Leonard, editor. Introduction to economic statistics. By William Leonard Crum . . . Alson Currie Patton . . . and Arthur Rothwell Tebbutt . . . 1st edition. New York and London, McGraw-Hill book company, inc., 1938. xi, 423. (Revision of Crum and Patton's Introduction to the methods of economic statistics.)
3573. CRUZ, Salviano. Teoria de metodologia e bibliografia de pesquisas econômicas; crítica bibliográfica da ciência economica. (Coleção de pesquisas econômicas e socials.) Rio de Janeiro, Institutio de Pesquisas e análises economicas, 1949. 324 p.
3574. CUNNINGHAM, W. "The Relativity of economic doctrine." In, Economic journal, 2 (1892), 1-16.
3575. _____. "Why had Roscher so little influence in England?" In, Annals of the American academy of political and social science, 5 (1894), 317-34. [Reprinted: In, Jahrbuch für gesetzgebung, verwaltung und volkswirtschaft

3576. CUNYNGHAME, H. A geometrical political economy. 1904. 128 p.
3577. _____. "Some improvements in simple geometrical methods of treating exchange value, monopoly and rent." In, Economic journal, 2 (1892), 35-52.
3578. CZERWINSKI, Zbigniew. Matematyka na usługach, ekonomii. Wyd. 1. Warszawa, Panstwowe wydawn. naukowe, 1969. 441 p.
3579. DANIEL, Coldwell. Mathematical models in microeconomics. Boston, Allyn and Bacon, 1970. x, 228 p.
3580. DASGUPTA, A. K. Methodology of economic research. New York, Asia publishing house, c1968. viii, 169 p.
3581. _____. Planning and economic growth. London, George Allen and Unwin, limited, 1965.
3582. DAVENPORT, H. J. "The Formula of sacrifice." In, Journal of political economy, 2 (1894), 560-73.
3583. DE ALESSI, L. "Economic theory as a language." In, Quarterly journal of economics, 79 (August 1965), 472-77.
3584. DEGUCHI, Yuzo. Gendai no keizaigakushi. (Transliterated.) Japan, 1968. 197 p. Bibliographical references.
3585. _____. Keizaigaku to rekishi ishiki. (Transliterated.) Japan, 1968. 11, 324, 7 p.
3586. DICKINSON, Zenas Clark. Economic motives; a study in the psychological foundations of economic theory, with some reference to other social sciences. (Published under the direction of Department of economics Harvard university, v. XXIV.) Cambridge, Massachusetts, Harvard university press, 1922. vii p., 2 l., 3-304 p., 1 l.
3587. DIEHL, K. Theoretische nationalökonomie. 2nd edition. Germany, 1922. ix, 500 p. (First edition, 1916.)
3588. _____. Einleitung in die nationalökonomie. V. I. In, Theoretische nationalökonomie. 3 v. (V. 1, 1916; 2nd edition, 1922. ix, 500 p.)
3589. DIETZEL, H. "Beiträge zur methodik der wirtschaftswissenschaft." In, Jahrbücher fur nationalökonomie und statistik 43 (1884), 17-44; 193-259.
3590. DOBREV, K. "The state and the tasks of economics in the light of the decisions of the eighth congress of the Bulgarian communist party." In, Eastern European economics, 3, 3 (1963), 47-64.
3591. DORFMAN, Robert. Application of linear programming to the theory of the firm. (Bureau of business research). Berkeley, University of California press, 1951. ix, 98 p.
3592. _____. Measuring benefits of government investments. Paper presented to conference of experts held, November 7-9, 1963. Washington, Brookings Institution, 1965. xv, 429 p.
3593. _____. Paul A. Samuelson and Robert M. Solow.

Linear programming and economic analysis. (The Rand series.) New York, McGraw-Hill, 1958. 527 p.
3594. DOWLING, H. and F. R. Glahe, editors. Readings in econometric theory. Colorado, Associated university press, 1971. 560 p.
3595. DUMONTIER, Jacques. Observation économique; cours professé à l'Ecole nationale d'organization économique et sociale et à l'Ecole statistique et des etudes economiques 1. edition. (Bibliothèque de l'Ecole nationale d'organisation économique et sociale. Grande série.) Paris, Presses universitaires de France, 1950. 248 p.
3596. DUNBAR, C. F. "The Academic study of political economy." In, Quarterly journal of economics, 5 (1891), 397-416.
3597. DYKMANS, Gommaire Louis. . . . La documentation en science économique. . . . (Bibliothèque générale des sciences commerciales, publiée sous la direction de Jules Baude. 5.) Bruxelles, Les Editions comptables, commerciales et financières, 1943. 230 p.
3598. ECONOMETRICA; journal of the econometric society. v. 1- January, 1933- . Menasha, Wisconsin, G. Banta publishing company, 1933- . quarterly.
3599. ECONOMIC means and social ends; essays in political economics. By Adolph Lowe and others. Edited, and with an introduction by Robert L. Heilbroner. Englewood Cliffs, New Jersey, Prentice-Hall, 1969. ix, 204 p.
3600. ECONOMIC models, estimation and risk programming; essays in honor of Gerhard Tintner. Edited by K. A. Fox, J. K. Sengupta, and G. V. L. Narasimham. (Lecture notes in operations research and mathematical economics, 15.) Berlin, New York, Springer-verlag, 1969. viii, 461 p.
3601. EDGEWORTH, F. Y. Mathematical psychics. London? 1881. vii, 150 p.
3602. _____. "The Objects and methods of political economy." In, Economic journal, 1 (1891), 625-34.
3603. _____. Papers relating to political economy. 1925. 3 v.
3604. _____. "Professor Seligman on the mathematical method in political economy." In, Economic journal, 9 (1899), 286-315.
3605. _____. "Recent contributions to mathematical economics." In, Economic journal, (1915). Bibliography.
3606. EKONOMICKO-matematicky obzor. roc. 1- 1965- . Praha, Ceskoslovenska akademie ved v academii, etc. v. 4 numbers a year.
3607. EKONOMILITTO. Ekonomimatrikkeli, 1960. (Matrikkelitoimikunta: Valter Hämeen-Aalto, et al. Helsinki, 1961. 863 p.
3608. EKONOMSKA analiza. Economic analysis. . . . . g. 1.- 1967- . Beograd, Ekonomski biro. v.
3609. EMMER, Robert E. Economic analysis and scientific philosophy. Foreword by C. F. Carter. London, Allen

3610. FABBRINI, Luigi. Istanze statiche ed istanze evolutive nella modellistica contemporanea: Leontief, Hayek, post-Keynesiani. Bologna, Cappelli, 1959. 172 p.
3611. FABIAN, R. G. "An Empirical principle for deductive theory in economics." In, Southern economic journal, 34 (July 1967), 53-66.
3612. FEDORENKO, N. "Basic trends in the development of economic science." In, Problems of economics, 8, 12 (April 1966), 3-10.
3613. FEIN, Erwin. Bilanzbildsequenzen, ein Versuch über die anwendung betriebswirtschaftlicher methoden auf die nationalökonomische forschung. Bern, A. Francke, c1951. 168 p. Bibliographical footnotes.
3614. FETTER, F. A. "Price economics versus welfare economics." In, American economic review, 10 (1920) 467-87; 719-37.
3615. ———. Value and the larger economics." In, Journal of political economy, 31 (1923), 587-605; 790-803.
3616. FINOIA, Massimo. Nozioni di economia. Equilibrio del produttore ed equilibrio macroeconomico. . . . Lezioni tenute al Centro pergli studi sullo sviluppo economico. Roma, Marve, 1968. 134 p.
3617. FISCHER, Hannelore. Modelldenken und operationsforschung al führungsaufgaben. Mit 7 abbildungen. (Schriftenreihe zur sozialistischen wirtschaftsführung.) Berlin, Dietz, 1968. 15 p.
3618. FISHER, Irving. "Capital and interest." In, Political science quarterly, 24 (1909), 504-16.
3619. ———. A. Cournot's researches into the mathematical principles of the theory of wealth. Translated by N. T. Bacon. 1897. Bibliography.
3620. ———. "Economics as a science." In, Science, New series 24 (1906), 257-61.
3621. ———. "Mathematical investigations in the theory of appreciation and interest." In, American economic association publication (1896).
3622. ———. Mathematical investigations in the theory of value and prices. (First published, 1892). Reprinted: 1926. 126 p.
3623. FLUX, A. W. "Laws of political economy." In, Palgrave's Dictionary of political economy. Edited by H. Higgs, Vol. II (1923), 583.
3624. FORECASTING on a scientific basis. Proceedings, International summer institute, Curia, Portugal, September, 1966. (Sponsored by Science committee of NATO and Gulbenkian foundation.) Lisbon, Centro de economia e financas, 1967.
3625. FORSTER, Wolfgang. Zerlegung und lösung diskreter ökonomischer prozess-modelle; neuere Methoden zur analyse zufälliger zeitreihen und linearer dynamischer systeme. (Institut für angewandte wirtschaftsforschung, Tübingen. Schriftenreihe, Bd. 11.) Tübingen, Mohr, 1969. xii, 384 p.

3626. FOSTER, Edward. Economics: an introductory program. New York, McGraw-Hill, 1970. xv, 379 p.
3627. FRANCE, Centre national de la recherche scientifique. Les modèles dynamiques en économétrie. Paris, 23-28 mai 1955. (Its Colloques internationaux, 62.) Paris, En vente au Service des publications du C.N.R.S., 1956. 381 p.
3628. FRASER, L. M. "How do we want economists to behave?" In, Economic journal, XLII (1932), 555.
3629. FRISCH, Ragnar Anton Kittel, editor. Econometrica journal of the Econometric society. Menasha, Wisconsin, G. Banta publishing company, 1933- . v. i- . Quarterly.
3630. ———. Maxima and minima. Theory and economic applications. Written by Ragnar Frisch in collaboration with A. Nataf. Translated from the French by Express translation service, London, Dordrecht, Holland, D. Reidel publishing company; Chicago, Rand McNally, 1966. xii, 176 p. Bibliography, 174.
3631. ———. New methods of measuring marginal utility. 1932. (Reprinted: New York, A. M. Kelley, 1970.)
3632. FUSFELD, D. B. "Economic theory misplaced. Livelihood in primitive society." In, Otto Feinstein, Two worlds of change. Readings in economic development. New York, Anchor books, 1964.
3633. GABRIELSEN, Arne. Planlegging under usikker horisont. Et "certainty equivalence" resultat. Memorandum fra Sosialøkonomisk institutt. Universitetet i Oslo.) Oslo, 1968. 6 1.
3634. GALBRAITH, John Kenneth. Economics and the art of controversey. (The Brown and Haley lectures, 1954.) New Brunswick, Rutgers university press, c1955. 111 p.
3635. GEORGESCU-ROEGEN, Nicholas. Analytical economics. Issues and problems. Cambridge, Massachusetts, Harvard university press, 1966.
3636. GERMAIN-MARTIN, Henry. Cours de documentation et de méthode économiques, Centre d'études supérieures de banque, 1950-1951. Paris, Cours de droit, 195- . 2 v. 375 p.
3637. GEYER, Herbert und W. Oppelt, editors. Volkswirtschaftliche regelungsvorgänge im vergleich zu regelungsvorgängen der technik; Vorträge . . . zusammengestellt von H. Geyer und W. Oppelt. (Beihefte zur Regelungstechnik.) München, R. Oldenbourg, 1957. 143 p.
3638. GIBSON, W. L., Jr., R. J. Hildreth and Gene Wanderlich. Methods for land economics research. Lincoln, University of Nebraska press, 1966.
3639. GORDON, D. F. "The role of the history of economic thought in the understanding of modern economic theory." In, American economic association papers and proceedings, 55 (May 1965), 119-27.
3640. GOSCHEN, G. J. "Ethics and economics." In, Economic journal, 3 (1893), 377-87.
3641. GRAMPP, W. D. "On the history of thought and policy."

In, American economic association papers and proceedings, 55 (May, 1965), 128-35.
3642. GRANGER, Gilles Gaston. Methodologie economique. (Bibliotheque de philosophie contemporaine. Logique et philosophie des sciences.) 1. ed. Paris, Presses universitaires de France, 1955. 422 p.
3643. GRICHTING, Emil. Die privatwirtschaftslehre als wissenschaft, eine methodologische auseinandersetzung. (Unternehmung und betrieb, Bd. 32.) Bern, P. Haupt, 1951. 117 p.
3644. GRILICHES, Zvi, editor. Price indexes and quality change. Studies in new methods of measurement. (Edited for the Price statistics committee, Federal reserve board.) Cambridge, Massachusetts, Harvard university press, 1971. 300 p.
3645. HAAVELMO, Trygve. A study in the theory of economic evolution. (Contributions to economic analysis, 3.) Amsterdam, North-Holland publishing company, c1954. 114 p. Bibliographical footnotes.
3646. HALLER, Heinz. Typus und gesetz in der nationalökonomie; versuch zur klärung einiger methodenfragen der wirtschaftswissenschaften. Stuttgart, W. Kohlhammer, 1950. 175 p. Bibliographical footnotes.
3647. HAMPL, Frantisek a Jan Kadler. Didaktika ekonomickych predmetu. Vyd. 1. (Ucebni texty vysokych skol.) Praha, Statni pedagogicke nakl., 1956- . v. (Vol. V by F. Hampl and Jiri Koudela. Vysoka skola ekonomicka v. Praze. Fakulta vseobecne ekonomicka.)
3648. HARL, N. E. "Modifying institutional-legal relations among private parties to facilitate adjustments in agriculture." In, Journal of farm economics, 46 (December, 1964), 953-61.
3649. HASBACH, W. "Mit welcher methode wurden die gesetze der theoretischen nationalökonomie gefunden?" In, Jahrbücher für nationalökonomie und statistik 82 (1904), 289-317.
3650. _____. "Zur geschichte des methodenstreites in der politischen ökonomie." In, Jahrbuch für gesetzgebung, verwaltung und volkswirtschaft im deutschen reich 19 (1895), 465-90; 751-808.
3651. HAWLEY, F. B. Enterprise and the productive process. New York? 1907.
3652. _____. "A positive theory of economics." In, Quarterly journal of economics, 16 (1902), 233-64.
3653. HAWTREY, R. G. The Economic problem. London, 1926.
3654. HAYEK, F. A. Studies in philosophy, politics and economics. Chicago, University of Chicago press, 1967.
3655. HAYNES, John. Economics in the secondary school. (Riverside educational monographs.) Boston, Houghton, Mifflin, 1914. 93 p.
3656. HECKSCHER, Eli Filip och Carl Erik Knoellinger. De ekonomista studierna och deras hjälpmedel. Helsingfors,

Söderström, 1945. 294 p.
3657. HEILBROMER, R. L. "Is economic theory possible." In, Social research, 33 (June 1966), 272-94.
3658. _____. The making of economic society. Englewood Cliffs, New Jersey, Prentice-Hall, 1962.
3659. HENN, Rudolf. Uber dynamische wirtschaftsmodelle. Mit einem geleitwort von W. G. Waffenschmidt. (Veröffentlichungen der wirtschaftschochschule Mannheim, Reihe 1; Abhandlungen, Bd. 4.) Stuttgart, Kohlhammer, 1957. 120 p.
3660. HERENDEEN, James B. Modern political economy. Ideas and issues. University Park, Pennsylvania, Pennsylvania state university, 1966. (Revised edition, 1968.)
3661. HOBSON, J. A. Free thought in the social sciences. London, 1926. 4-166 p.
3662. _____. Work and wealth. . . . London, 1914. 1-27 p.
3663. HONEGGER, H. "Zur krisis der statischen nationalökonomisk." In, Schmollers jahrbuch für gesctzgebung, verwaltung und volkswirtschaft in deutschen reiche, 48 (1924), 473-90.
3664. HOOD, William C. and Tjalling C. Koopmans. Studies in econometric method. By Cowles commission research staff members. (Monograph no. 14.) New York, Wiley, 1953. Bibliography.
3665. HOOK, Sidney. Human values and economic policy. A symposium. (Proceedings, 8th annual meeting, New York university institute of philosophy, 1966.) New York, New York university press, 1967.
3666. HOOPER, John W. and Marc Nerlove, editors. Selected readings in econometrics from Econometrica. Cambridge, Massachusetts, M.I.T. press, 1970. 498 p.
3667. HOSELITZ, Bert F. Economics and the idea of mankind. (Conference, auspice of Council for the study of mankind, Endicott house, M.I.T., 1960.) New York, Columbia university press, 1965.
3668. HOYT, E. E. "Choice as an interdisciplinary area." In, Quarterly journal of economics, 79 (February 1965), 106-12.
3669. HUANG, David. Introduction to the use of mathematics in economic analysis. New York, Wiley & son, 1964.
3670. HUGON, Paul. Do método em economia politica. (Universidade de são Paulo. Faculdade de filosofia, ciencias e letras. Boletin no. 177. Economia política e história das doutrinas económicas, no. 2.) São Paulo, 1954. 131 p.
3671. HUPPERT, Walter. Gesetzmässigkeit und voraussehbarkeit des wirtschaftlichen wachstums. Berlin, Duncker und Humblot, 1957. 76 p.
3672. HUTCHISON, Terence Wilmot. The significance and basic postulates of economic theory. (Reprints of economic classics.) New York, A. M. Kelley, 1965, c1960. xxviii, 191 p. Bibliographical references. (First published in 1938.

Method and Scope 249

3673. IDEEN, projekte, produktionen; aktuelle fragen in forschung und entwicklung. Hrsg. von Werner Sydow. Berlin, Verlag die wirtschaft, 1969. 236 p.
3674. IGLESIAS, Francisco. Introdução à historiografia economica. Faculdade de Ciencias economicas da universidade de Minas Gerais. Estudos econômicos, políticos e socials, 11. Belo Horizonte, 1959. 97 p.
3675. INGRAM, J. K. On the philosophical method. (Pamphlet.) London, 1876.
3676. ———. The Present position and prospects of political economy. London? 1878. 31 p.
3677. INSTITUTE of economic affairs, London. Economics, business and government. (IEA occasional papers.) London, 1966.
3678. INTERDEPENDENZEN von politik und wirtschaft. Festgabe für gert von eynern. Berlin, Duncker und Humblot, 1967.
3679. INTERNATIONAL conference on input-output techniques, Geneva, 1961. Structural interdependence and economic development; proceedings. Edited by Tibor Barna, in collaboration with William I. Abraham and Zoltan Kenessey. (Secretariat of the United Nations and the Harvard economic research project.) New York, Saint Martin's press, 1963. x, 365 p. Bibliographies.
3680. INTERNATIONAL conference on input-output techniques. 4th, Geneva, 1968. Proceedings. 8-12 January, 1968. Published in honor of Wassily Leontief. Edited by A. P. Carter and A. Brody, Amsterdam, London, North-Holland publishing company, 1970. 2 v. Bibliographies. (Conference sponsored by United National and The Harvard economic research project under a grant from Ford foundation.)
3681. INTERNATIONAL summer school on mathematical systems theory and economics, Varenna, Italy, 1967. Mathematical systems theory and economics. Proceeding of an International summer school held in Varenna, Italy, June 1-12, 1967. Edited by H. W. Kuhn and G. P. Szegö. (Lecture notes in operations research and mathematical economics, 11-12.) Berlin, Heidelberg, New York, Springer, 1969. 2 v.
3682. JAEGER, Arno und Klaus Wenke. Lineare wirtschaftsalgebra. Eine einführung. Mit 45 figuren, 136 aufgaben, 32 tabellen und zahlreichen beispielen. (Leitfäden der angewandten mathematik und mechanik, Bd. 13.) Stuttgart, Teubner, 1969. x, 334 p.
3683. JEVONS, W. S. "Introduction." In, The Theory of political economy, 4th edition 1911. (First published, 1871.)
3684. ———. Principles of economics. London, 1905. 206 p. ?
3685. JOBST, Eberhard Karl Wolfram. Der Joint council on economic education und seine bemühungen auf dem Gebiet der wirtschaftlichen erziehung in den United States of

America. n. p., 1968? 345 p.
3686. JOHNSON, H. G. "The social sciences in the age of opulence." In, Canadian journal of economics and political science, 32 (November 1966), 423-42.
3687. JOHNSON, W. E. "Method of political economy." In, Palgrave's Dictionary of political economy, 2nd edition, (1923) 739-48.
3688. JONAS, Friedrich, Das Selbstverständnis der ökonomischen theorie. (Volkswirtschaftliche schriften, Heft. 73.) Berlin, Duncker und Humblot, 1964. 236 p. Bibliographical footnotes.
3689. KALECKI, M. Theory of economic dynamics. London, George Allen & Unwin, Ltd., 1954.
3690. KANDILAROV, Georgi St. and Aleksandur G. Dimitrov. Tablitsi za izravniavane na statisticheski redove. (Transliterated.) Sofia, 1963. 103 p.
3691. KANN, Achim. Der Aussagewert von makrogrössen in der wirtschaftsstatistik; ein Beitrage zur methodik der aggregation. (Statistische studien, Bd. 2.) Wiesbaden, F. Steiner, 1968. ix, 130 p.
3692. KANTOROVICH, Leonid Vital'evich. The best use of economic resources. Cambridge, Massachusetts, Harvard university press, 1965. 349 p.
3693. KANTOROVICH, L. "Mathematics and economics." In, Problems of economics, 8, 5 (September 1965), 12-15.
3694. KARPINKSI, Marian Stanisław. Nowa postac sporu o metode ekonomiki. (Archiwum towarzystwa naukowego we Lwowie. Dział II., t. 19, zesz. 4.) We Lwowie, Nakł. tow. naukowego; skł/ gł.: Gubrynowicz, 1937. 211 p.
3695. KEIZER, J. M. Economische wiskunde. Met medew. van J. de Jong en J. M. van Velthoven. Leiden, Stenfert Kroese, 1970. x, 252 p.
3696. KENDALL, Maurice George. New prospects in economic analysis. (The Stamp memorial lecture, 1960.) London, Athlone press, 1960. 26 p.
3697. KERSCHAGL, Richard. Die Methodenfrage in der theoretischen nationalökonomie. (Inauguration als rektor. Hochschule für welthandel.) Wien, Verlag: Hochschule für welthandel in Wien, 1948. 19 p.
3698. KEYNES, John Neville. "Deductive method." In, Palgrave's Dictionary of political economy, 1st edition, 1890? 523-26.
3699. ———. The Scope and method of political economy. 4th edition. London, 1917. xiv, 382 p. (London, New York, Macmillan and company, 1891. xiv, 359 p. 3d edition, revised. London, New York, Macmillan and company, limited, 1904. xiv, 382 p. Reprint: 4th edition, Kelley and Millman, 1955. xiv, 283 p.
3700. ———. Studies and exercises in formal logic, including a generalisation of logical processes in their application to complex inferences... 4th edition, re-written and enlarged. London, Macmillan and company, limited; New York, Macmillan company, 1906. xxiv, 548 p.

3701. KIERSTEAD, B. S.　The Theory of economic change. Toronto, Macmillan, 1948.
3702. KITAGAWA, Sozo.　Keizaigaku hohoron. (Transliterated.) Japan, 1954.　3, 3, 311, 4 p.　Bibliographical notes.
3703. KLEINWACHTER, F.　"Wesen, aufgabe, und system der nationalökonomie." In, Jahrbucher für nationalökonomie und statistik, 52 (1889), 601-51.
3704. KNAPP, Reinhart.　Der Wirtschaftsteil der zeitung. Eine anleitung für den leser. 7., neubearb. aufl. Stuttgart, Poeschel, 1969.　183 p.
3705. KNIES, K.　Die politische oekonomie vom geschichtlichen standpuncte.　1882-3.　xii, x, 533 p. (2nd enlarged edition of Die politische oekonomie vom standpunkte der geschichtlichen methode, 1853.)
3706. KNIGHT, Frank Hyneman.　"Economics." In, Encyclopaedia Britannica, 1951.
3707. _____. "Ethics and the economic interpretation." In, Quarterly journal of economics, 36 (1922), 454-81.
3708. _____. "Fact and metaphysics in economic psychology." In, American economic review, 15 (1925), 247-66.
3709. _____. On the history and method of economics; selected essays.　Chicago, University of Chicago press, c1956.　308 p. (Selection of publications made by W. L. Letwin and A. J. Morin in honor of author's seventieth birthday.)
3710. _____. Risk, uncertainty, and profit. (Chapter I.) New York, 1921.　3-21 p.
3711. KOGIKU, Kiichiro.　A critique of world-wide econometric forecasting.　Ann Arbor, Michigan, University Microfilms, 1959.　(Microfilm AC-1, no. 59-3269.)
3712. KOLGANOV, M.　"Political economy and the natural sciences." In, Problems of economics, 7, 7 (November 1964), 3-16.
3713. KOTOV, I.　"Some problems of applying mathematical methods to economics, and the political economy of socialism." In, Problems of economics, 9, 4 (August 1966), 3-14.
3714. KRELLE, Wilhelm.　Produktionstheorie.　Unter mitarbeit von Wilhelm Scheper.　2. Aufl. (His Die Preistheorie, T. 1.) Tübingen, Mohr (Siebeck), 1969.　x, 237 p.
3715. KRUPP, Sherman Roy and others.　The structure of economic science; essays on methodology.　Englewood Cliffs, New Jersey, Prentice-Hall, 1966.　vi, 282 p. Bibliographical footnotes.
3716. KUHNE, O.　"Ueber die mathematische methode in der deutschen theoretischen nationalökonomie." In, Jahrbücher für nationalökonomie und statistik, 123 (1925), 653-88.
3717. KUKOLECA, Stevan M.　Merenje poslovnog. uspeha. Napisao, Stevan Kukoleca. (Organizacija i ekonomika poduzeca, br. 6-7.) Zagreb, "Informator," 1966. xv, 304 p.
3718. KYRER, Alfred.　Das Werkzeug der nationalökonomie:

nationalökonomische propädeutik. Wien, W. Braumüller, 1964. 104 p.
3719. LANDRY, A. Manuel d'economique. (Introduction.) Paris, 1908. 3-64 p.
3720. LANE, Frederic Chapin. Venice and history. The collected papers of Frederic C. Lane. (Edited by a committee of colleagues and former students in honor of his 65th birthday.) Baltimore, Johns Hopkins university press, 1966.
3721. LANGE, Oscar Richard. Introduction to economic cybernetics. Prepared with the collaboration of Antoni Banasinski on the basis of lectures delivered at the University of Warsaw. Translated from Polish by Józef Stadler. Warszawa, Polish scientific publishers, 1970. xv, 183 p.
3722. LANSING, John B. and James N. Morgan. Economic survey methods. (Institute for social research, University of Michigan.) Ann Arbor, Michigan, ISR, 1971.
3723. LAWS, M. "The Difficulty of imputation." In, Economic journal, xliii (1933), 251.
3724. LEONTIEF, Wassily. Essays in economics. Theories and theorizing. New York, Oxford university press, 1966.
3725. _____. Implicit theorizing; a methodological criticism of the neo-Cambridge school." In, Quarterly journal of economics, 51 (1936-37), 337-351.
3726. _____. Input-output economics. New York, Oxford university press, 1966. viii, 257 p.
3727. LERNER, Daniel, Editor. Quantity and quality; the Hayden colloquium on scientific method and concept. New York, Free press of Glencoe, 1961. 221 p. Bibliographical references.
3728. LESLIE, T. E. Cliffe. Essays in political economy. 2nd edition. London, 1888. xii, 437 p. (1st edition, 1879.)
3729. LESZ, Mieczysław. Optymalizacja planow. Pod red. Mieczysława Lesza. Wyd. 1. (Matematyka w przedsiebiorstwie.) Warszawa, Panstwowe wydawn. ekonomiczne, 1968. 239 p.
3730. LIEFMANN, R. Grundsätze der volkswirtschaftslehre. 2nd edition. 1920. 3-227 p. (1st edition, 1919.)
3731. LINDBECK, A. "The method of isolation in economic statics." In, Swedish journal of economics 68 (September 1966), 148-65.
3732. LISMAN, J. H. C. Econometrics, statistics and thermodynamics, a compilation and extension of different statistical papers published i.a. in 'Het PTT-bedrijf' and other journals. (Publicaties van het staatsbedrijf der posterijen, telegrafie en telefonie, 1.) The Hague, The Nederlands postal and telecommunications services, 1949. 104 p.
3733. LORIA, Achille. The Economic synthesis. 1914. (English translation.)
3734. LOSSEAU, Léon. Règles bibliographiques; examen critique de l'ouvrage: La documentation en science

économique par Gommaire Louis Dykmans. Bruxelles, E. Bruylant, 1945. viii, 144 p.
3735. LOWE, Adolph. On economic knowledge; toward a science of political economics. 1st edition. (World perspectives, v. 35.) New York, Harper and Row, c1965. xxi, 329 p. Bibliographical footnotes.
3736. LUMSDEN, Keith G. and others. New developments in Teaching economics. Englewood Cliffs, New Jersey, Prentice-Hall, 1967.
3737. LUNDBERG, Erik. Studies in the theory of economic expansion. London, P. S. King, 1937. 265 p. Bibliography, 262-265. (New York, Kelley and Millman, 1955.)
3738. MACHLUP, F. "Professor Samuelson on theory and realism." In, American economic review, 54 (September 1964), 733-39.
3739. _____. "Theories of the firm: marginalist, behavioral, managerial." In, American economic review, 57 (March 1967), 1-33.
3740. MARCHAL, André. Méthode scientifique et science économique. Paris, M. T. Génin, 1952- . v. (1952: Le conflit traditionnel des méthodes et son renouvellement. 1955: Problèmes actuels de l'analyse économique, ses approches fondamentales. Paris, Librairie de médicis, 1955. 313 p.)
3741. MARSHALL, Alfred. "Distribution and exchange." In, Economic journal, 8 (1898), 37-44.
3742. _____. "The present position of economics." (Cambridge inaugural lectures, 1885.) In, Memorials of Alfred Marshall, edited by A. C. Pigou. London, 1925. 151-174 p.
3743. _____. Principles of economics. (Book I; Appendix C; Appendix D.) 8th edition. London, 1920. xxxii, 871 p. (1st edition, 1890.)
3744. MARTIN, Kurt and John Knapp. The teaching of development economics. (Proceedings of the Manchester conference on teaching economic development, April, 1964.) Chicago, Aldine publishing company, 1967.
3745. MARTIN, Richard S. and Reuben G. Miller. Economics and its significance. Kenneth E. Boulding, consultant. (Charles E. Merrill social science seminar series.) Columbus, Ohio, C. E. Merrill books, c1965. x, 165 p. Bibliography: 86-97. Bibliographical footnotes. ("Suggesting methods for teachers," by R. H. Muessig and V. R. Rogers: 98-163.)
3746. MARTINDALE, Don. Functionalism in the social sciences. The strength and limits of functionalism in anthropology, economics, political science, and sociology. Philadelphia, American academy of political and social science, 1965.
3747. MATHEMATIK und kybernetik und ökonomie. Internationale tagung, Berlin, Oktober 1964. Konferenzprotokoll. (Deutsche akademie der wissenschaften zu Berlin.

Schriften des Instituts für wirtschaftswissenschaften, Nr. 19.) Berlin, Akademie-verlag, 1965. 2 v.
3748. MATTERN, Ernst. Erzeugen, verbrauchen. Wirtschaftskunde. 12. Aufl. Stuttgart, Holland und Josenhans, 1968. 118 p.
3749. MAYER, Joseph. Social science principles in the light of scientific method, with particular application to modern economic thought. (Duke university press sociological series, C. A. Ellwood and H. E. Jensen, consulting editors.) Durham, North Carolina, Duke university press, 1941. xxii, 573 p.
3750. MAZZILLI, Beniamino. Metodologia dell'inchiesta. Bari, F. Cacucci, 1951. 171 p.
3751. McISAAC, Archibald MacDonald. Elements of economic analysis. (Prentice-Hall economics series.) New York, Prentice-Hall, 1950. ix, 240 p.
3752. MENGER, C. "Grundzüge einer klassifikation der wirtschaftswissenschaften." In, Jahrbücher für nationalökonomie und statistik, 53 (1889), 465-96.
3753. _____. Der irrthümer des historismus in der deutschen nationalökonomie. Germany, 1884. 87 p.
3754. _____. Untersuchungen über die methode der socialwissenschaften und der politischen oekonomie insbesondere. 1883. xxxii, 291 p.
3755. MICHIELI, Igino. Estimo con elementi di economia, di matematica finanziaria e contabilità dei lavori. (Testi universitari Calderini.) Bologna, Calderini, 1969. vii, 1030 p.
3756. MICHIGAN. University. Survey research center. Contributions of survey methods to economics. By George Katona and others. Edited with an introduction by Lawrence R. Klein. New York, Columbia university press, 1954. viii, 269 p.
3757. MISES, Ludwig von. Epistemological problems of economics. Translated by George Reisman. (The William Volker fund series in the humane studies.) Princeton, New Jersey, Van Nostrand, 1960. 239 p. (Translation of Grundprobleme der nationalökonomie.)
3758. _____. Objetivos inmediatos de la educatión económica. Traducción del original inglés por Gustavo R. Velasco. Buenos Aires, Centro de estudios sobre la libertad, 1960. 29 p.
3759. _____. The ultimate foundation of economic science; an essay on method. (The William Volker fund series in the humane studies.) Princeton, New Jersey, Van Nostrand, 1962. 148 p.
3760. MITA, Sekisuke. Shihonron no hoho. Japan, 1963. 243 p.
3761. MITCHELL, Wesley C. "Economic resources in economic theory." In, Studies in economics and industrial relations. Philadelphia, University of Pennsylvania press, 1941.
3762. _____. "Quantitative analysis in economic theory." In, American economic review, 16 (1925), 1-12.

3763. _____. "The Rationality of economic activity." In, Journal of political economy, (1910).
3764. MONTANER, Antonio Martin. Der Institutionalismus als epoche amerikanischer geistesgeschichte. Tübingen, J. C. B. Mohr, 1948. 155 p. "Quellenverzeichnis": 147-152.
3765. MOORE, James C. On Pareto Optima and competitive equilibria. (Institute for research in the behavioral, economic, and management sciences. Paper no. 268.) Lafayette, Indiana, Herman C. Krannert graduate school of industrial administration, Purdue university, 1970- . v.
3766. MORAZE, Charles. Introduction a l'histoire économique. Paris, A. Colin, 1943. 2, 212 p. Bibliography.
3767. MORET, Jacques. L'emploi des mathématiques en économie politique. Paris, M. Giard et E. Brière, 1915. 1., 271 p. Bibliography, 152-156.
3768. MORGENSTERN, Oskar. Economic activity analysis. New York, Wiley, c1954. xviii, 554 p. Bibliographical references. (Prepared under contract for Office for naval research.)
3769. _____. On the accuracy of economic observations. Princeton, New Jersey, Princeton university press, 1950. ix, 101 p. (German edition entitled: Uber die genauigkeit wirtschaftlicher" Beobachtungen. Translated by Valentin Trapp. Munich, Deutsche statistische gesellschaft, 1952. 129 p. American edition: 2nd edition, completely revised, 1963. xiv, 322 p.)
3770. MORISHIMA, Michio. Atarashii keizai bunseki. (Transliterated.) Japan, 1960. 320 p.
3771. MOXTER, Adolf. Methodologische grundfragen der betriebswirtschaftslehre. 1. Aufl. (Beiträge zur betriebswirtschaftlichen forschung, Bd. 4.) Köln, Westdeutscher verlag, 1957. 119 p.
3772. MURRAY, R. H. "L'Applicazione dei procedimenti matematici alle scienze sociali nel momente attuale." In, Giornale degli economisti, 51 (1915), 221-9.
3773. MUTH, Jakob. Wirtschafts- und arbeitslehre. Zum Stand der diskussion. (Münsterische beiträge zu pädagogischen zeitfragen, Heft. 15.) Münster, Deutsches inst. für wiss. pädagogik, 1968. 50 p.
3774. MUTHESIUS, Volkmar. Geld und geist; kulturhistorische und wirtschaftspolitische Aufsätze. Frankfurt am Main, F. Knapp, 1961. 180 p.
3775. NARASAKI, Toshio. Keizaigaku hoho ron. (Transliterated.) Japan, 1969. 192 p. Bibliography, 108.
3776. NAYLOR, Thomas H. Computer simulation experiments, with models of economic system. With contributions by: James M. Boughton and others. New York, Wiley, 1971. xviii, 502 p.
3777. NAYLOR, Thomas H. and John M. Vernon. Microeconomics and decision models of the firm. (The Harbrace series in business and economics.) New York,

Harcourt, Brace and World, 1969. xiii, 482 p.
3778. NEISSER, H. "Three views of method in economics." In, Social research, 34, 2 (1967), 322-32.
3779. NEMCHINVO, Vasilii Sergeevich. Anwendung mathematischer methoden in der ökonomie. Deutsche übersetzung und redaktion: Kr. Kluge, Kr. Wintgen and Dipl.-Phil. König, Leipzig, Teubner, 1963. 437 p.
3780. ———. "Economic science must become an exact science." In, Economics of planning, 2 (March 1962), 36-44.
3781. ———. The use of mathematics in economics. Massachusetts institute of technology, 1965.
3782. NEUMANN, F. J. "Naturgesetz und wirtschaftsgesetz." In, Zeitschrift für die gesammte staatswissenschaft 48 (1892), 405-75.
3783. NICOLA, Pier Carlo. Equilibrio economico generale di tipo concurrenziale in condizioni dinamiche. (Collectanea mathematica, n. 355.) Milano, 1969. 27 p.
3784. NOGARO, Pierre Gabriel Bertrand. La méthode de l'économie politique. 2. édition rev. et augm. (L'Economie politique contemporaine, v. 1.) Paris, Librairie générale de droit et de jurisprudence, 1950. 270 p. Bibliography, 38-39. [Spanish edition: El método de la economia politica .... Traduccion de Luis Nuevamena. (Biblioteca de economia politica, dirigida por Rodrigo Garcia Treviño. VII). México, Editorial América, 1943. 2 p. 1., 7-221 p.
3785. NYBLEN, Göran. The problem of summation in economic science; a methodological study with applications to interest, money, and cycles. (Lund social science studies, 4.) Lund, C. W. K. Gleerup, 1951. xii, 289 p.
3786. OPTIMALE zweig- und standortplanung. Modelle und methoden. Ubersetzung aus dem Russischen. (Ubersetzer: Rudolf Holdhaus, u.a.) Berlin, Verlag die wirtschaft, 1969. 317 p.
3787. OXENFELDT, Alfred Richard. Models of markets. Contributing authors: William J. Baumol and others. New York, Columbia university press, 1963. xii, 371 p. Bibliographical footnotes.
3788. PANTALEONI, M. Erotemi di economia. 1925. 2 v. (xi, 382, xi, 345 p.)
3789. PAPANDREOU, Andreas George. Economics as a science. Chicago, Lippincott, 1958. 148 p.
3790. ———. Fundamentals of model construction in macroeconomics. (Center of economic research. Training seminar series, 1.) Athens, 1962. x, 172 p. Bibliography, 171-172.
3791. ———. He oikonomike hos episteme. (transliterated.) Athens, 1960. 14, 145 p.
3792. PARETO, V. "Economia sperimentale." In, Giornale degli economisti, 57 (1918), 1-18.
3793. ———. "Sul fenomeno economico." In, Giornale degli

Method and Scope 257

3794. ———. "The new theories of economics." In, Journal of political economics, 5 (1897), 485-502.
3795. ———. "Sul principio economico." In, Giornale degli economisti, 22 (1901), 131-38.
3796. PASSET, René. Introduction aux mathématiques de l'analyse économique. . . . (Collection initiation, 7.) Paris, Editions cujas, 1969- . v.
3797. PATTEN, S. N. "The scope of political economy." In, The Yale review, 2 (1893), 264-87.
3798. PATTON, R. D. "Evolutionary empiricism and the content of economics." In, Quarterly review of economics and business, 6, 2 (1966), 25-30.
3799. PAWŁOWSKI, Zbigniew. Modele ekonometryczne rowan opisowych. Wyd. 1. Warszawa, Panstwowe wydawn. naukowe, 1963. 273 p.
3800. PERLO, V. "Notes on Marxian economics in the United States. Comment." In, American economic review, 56 (March 1966), 187-88.
3801. PESTON, Maurice H. Elementary matrices for economics. (Library of modern economics.) Beverly Hills, California, Sage publications, c1969. viii, 110, 1 p.
3802. PFOUTS, Ralph William. "Artistic goals, scientific method and economics." In, Southern economic journal, 33 (April 1967), 457-67.
3803. ———. Essays in economics and econometrics; a volume in honor of Harold Hotelling. Chapel Hill, published for the School of business administration, University of North Carolina by the University of North Carolina press, 1960. xi, 240 p. Bibliography.
3804. PHILIPPOVITCH, E. von. Uber aufgabe und methode der politischen ökonomie. (Inaugural address.) 1886. 55 p.
3805. PIGOU, A. C. Economic science in relation to practice. (Cambridge inaugural address.) Cambridge, 1908. 32 p.
3806. PLATTE, Hans Kaspar. Wirtschafts- und arbeitslehre. Eine wertende bibliographie. (Wirtschaft, beruf, gesellschaft.) Wuppertal, Ratingen, Düsseldorf, Henn, 1970. 56 p.
3807. PUU, T. "Reflections on relation between economic theory and empirical reality." In, Swedish journal of economic 69 (June 1967), 85-114.
3808. PYON, Hyong-yun. Hyondae kyonjehak. (Transliterated.) Korea, 1962. 342 p. Bibliographies.
3809. RASMUSSEN, Knud. Oversigt over samfundsøkonomien med noter. 5. udg. København, Store nordiske videnskabsboghandel, 1947. 69 1.
3810. RASMUSSEN, Poul Nørregaard. Om økonomiens metode. (Memorandum fra Københavns universitets økonomiske institut, nr. 8.) København, G. E. C. Gad, 1963. 105 1. Bibliography, 101-105.
3811. RECENT research in economic education. Edited by Keith G. Lumsden. Englewood Cliffs, New Jersey, Prentice-Hall, 1970. xi, 243 p.
3812. RECHERCHES récentes sur la fonction de production. (Pub-

lications du Centre de recherches économiques et sociales 6. Collection économie mathématique et économétrie, no. 2.) Namur, Facultés universitaires N.-D. de la Paix, 1968. iv, 242 p.

3813. RITZEL, Gerhard and Albert Johannes. Schmoller versus Menger; eine analyse des methodenstreits im hinblick auf den historismus in der national oekonomie. Frankfurt am Main, 1950. 148 p. Bibliography, 141-148.

3814. ROBBINS, Lionel Charles. An essay on the nature and significance of economic science. . . . London, Macmillan and company, limited, 1935. xii, 141, 1 p. (2d edition, revised and extended. 1946? xviii, 160 p.)

3815. ———. "Mr. Hawtrey on the scope of economics." In, Economica, 7 (1927), 172-78.

3816. ROBERTSON, D. H. "Those empty boxes." In, Economic journal, 34 (1924), 16-30, 31.

3817. ROBINSON, Joan. Collected economic papers. Oxford, Basil Blackwell, 1965.

3818. ———. Exercises in economic analysis. London, Macmillan; New York, St. Martin's press, 1960. 242 p.

3819. ROBINSON, Marshall A., Herbert C. Morton and James D. Calderwood. An introduction to economic reasoning. Washington, Brookings institution, c1956. 335 p. (Revised edition: 1959. 335 p. Bibliography, 3rd ed., 1962, 298 p. 4th Revised edition, Garden City, New York, Anchor books, Doubleday and company, incorporated, 1967.)

3820. ROMERO, Mario. Ensayo sobre economia cuantitativa. (Publicaciones de la Universidad de Costa Rica. Serie economia y estadistica, no. 18.) San Pedro, 1966. 38 p.

3821. ROSE, Klaus. Gleichgewichtswachstum und stabilität. (Walter Eucken institut. Vorträge und aufsätze, 26.) Tübingen, Mohr, 1970. 36 p.

3822. ROSSI, Napoleone. La moderna economia alla ricerca di una moderna facoltà. Pavia, Fusi, 1969. 64 p.

3823. RUMMEL, J. Francis and Wesley C. Ballaine. Research methodology in business. New York, Harper and Row, 1963. xvi, 359 p. Bibliographies.

3824. SAMPEDRO, José Luis. Realidad económica y análisis estructural. (Biblioteca de ciencias sociales. Sección 1: Economia.) Madrid, Aguilar, 1959. xvi, 277 p.

3825. SAMUELSON, Paul A. "Problems of the American economy An economist's view." In, Joseph E. Stiglitz, The Collected scientific papers of Paul A. Samuelson. Cambridge, Massachusetts, M.I.T. press, 1966. 2 v.

3826. ———. "Professor Samuelson on theory and realism. Reply." In, American economic review, 55 (December 1965), 164-72.

3827. SAX, E. Das Wesen und die aufgaben der nationalökonomie. 1884. vi, 104 p.

3828. NO ENTRY

3829. SCHMOLLER, Gustav. "Die gerechtigkeit in der volkswirtschaft." In, Jahrbuch für gesetzgebung, verwaltung und volkswirtschaft im deutschen reich, 5 (1881), 19-54. [English translation entitled: "The idea of justice in political economy." In, Annals of the American academy of political and social science, 4 (1894), 697-737.]

3830. _____. "Volkswirtschaft, volkswirtschaftslehre, und -methode." In, Handworterbuch der staatswissenschaften, 3rd edition, 1911. Bibliography.

3831. SCHOEFFLER, Sidney. The failures of economics, a diagnostic study. (Based on thesis, New school for social research.) Cambridge, Harvard university press, 1955. 254 p. Bibliography.

3832. SCHOENMAN, Jean Claude. An analog of short-period economic change. Part 2 written jointly with Bo Persson. (Stockholm economic studies. New Series, 7.) Stockholm, Almqvist and Wiksell, distributor, P. A. Norstedt 1966. 2, xxvi, 388 p.

3833. SCHONPFLUG, Fritz. Betriebswirtschaftslehre; methoden und hauptströmungen. 2. erweiterte Aufl. von "Das Methodenproblem in der einzelwirtschaftslehre," hrsg. von Hans Seischab. Stuttgart, C. E. Poeschel, 1954. xvi, 471 p.

3834. SCHULE und wirtschaft. Beiträge für den wirtschaftskundlichen unterricht und für die Wirtschaftserziehung an allgemeinbildenden pflichtschulen und allgemeinbildenden hoheren schulen. Hrsg. von der Salzburger Sparkasse und dem Pädagogischen institut Salzburg. Mit tabellen. (Veröffentlichungen des Pädagogischen instituts Salzburg, Bd. 24.) Salzburg, Wien, P. Storhal, 1968. 195 p.

3835. SCHUMPETER, Joseph. "Epochen der dogmen- und methodengeschichte." In, Vol. I, Part 2, Grundriss der sozialökonomik. Tübingen, 1914. 19-124 p.

3836. _____. "Gustav von Schmoller und die probleme von heute." In, Schmoller's jahrbuch für gesetzgebung, verwaltung und volkswirtschaft in deutschen reiche, 50 (1926), 337-88.

3837. _____. "Introduction. Scope and Method." In, J. A. Schumpeter, History of Economic Analysis, 1954. Part I, Chapters 1-4.

3838. _____. "On the concept of social value." In, Quarterly journal of economics, 23 (1909), 213-32.

3839. _____. Das wesen und der hauptinalt der theoretischen nationalökonomie. Germany, 1908, xxxii, 626 p. [Reviewed: F. von Wieser. (Article has title of book.) In, Schmoller's jahrbuch für gesetzgebung, verwaltung und volkswirtschaft in deutschen reiche, 35 (1911), 909-31.]

3840. SELIGMAN, B. B. "On the question of operationalism." In, American economic review, 57 (March 1967), 146-61.

3841. SHACKLE, George Lennox Sharman. Time in economics. (Professor Dr. F. de Vries lectures, 1957.) Amsterdam, North Holland publishing company, 1958. 111 p. Bibliographical references.

3842. SHUBIK, Martin. Essays in mathematical economics in honor of Oskar Morganstern. Contributors, S. Afriat ar others. Princeton, New Jersey, Princeton university press, 1967. xx, 475 p.

3843. SIDGWICK, H. The scope and method of economic science (British economic association: address.) 1885. 57 p.

3844. SMITH, Robert S. and Frank T. DeVyver. Economic system and public policy. Essays in honor of Calvin Bryce Hoover. Durham, North Carolina, Duke university press, 1966.

3845. SMYTH, Robert Leslie, editor. Essays in economic metho selected papers read to Section F of the British association for the advancement of science, 1860-1913. With a introduction by T. W. Hutchison. London, Duckworth, 1962. 284 p. Bibliography.

3846. SNOW, John W. Perspectives in economics. Readings in economics and economic history. Danville, Illinois, Interstate printers and publishers, 1967.

3847. SOUTER, Ralph William. Prolegomena to relativity economics; an elementary study in the mechanics and organics of an expanding economic universe. (Studies in history, economics and public law, edited by the Faculty of political science of Columbia university. no. 391.) New York, Columbia university press; London, P. S King and son, limited, 1938. xiv, 171 p. [Issued also a thesis (Ph.D.) Columbia university.]

3848. SPENCER, Milton H., Colin G. Clark and Peter W. Hogue Business and economic forecasting, an econometric approach. (The Irwin series in economics.) Homewood, Illinois, R. D. Irwin, 1961. 412 p.

3849. STANFORD symposium on mathematical methods in the social sciences, Stanford university, 1959. Mathematica methods in the social sciences, 1959; proceedings. Edite by Kenneth J. Arrow, Samuel Karlin and Patrick Suppes. (Stanford mathematical studies in the social sciences, 4. Stanford, California, Stanford university press, 1960. viii, 365 p.

3850. STARK, Werner. The Ideal foundations of economic thought. New York, Oxford university press, 1944.

3851. STIGLER, G. J. "Textual exegesis as a scientific problem." In, Economica, New Series, 32 (November 1965), 477-50.

3852. STONE, Richard. Mathematics in the social sciences and other essays. London, Chapman and Hall, 1966.

3853. ———. The role of measurement in economics. (University of Cambridge. Department of applied economics. Monograph 3.) Cambridge, England, University press, 1951. vi, 85 p.

3854. STONE, Richard and Giovanna Croft-Murray. Social accounting and economic models. London, Bowes and Bowes, 1959. 88 p.

3855. STONIER, Alfred William. . . . Der logische charakter der wirtschaftswissenschaft. (Beitrage zur philosophie.

29.) Heidelberg, C. Winter, 1935. 74 p. (Inaugural dissertation, Heidelberg.)
3856. STOWE, Heinz. Okonometrie und makroökonomische theorie; stochastische wirtschaftsforschung als notwendige ergänzung der theorie. (Okonomische studien, Heft. 3.) Stuttgart, G. Fischer, 1959. 190 p.
3857. STREET, J. H. "Latin American 'structuralist' and the institutionalists. Convergence in development theory." In, Journal of economic issues, 1, 1-2 (June 1967), 44-62.
3858. STUDIENPLANUNG und realität, dargestellt am Beispiel der studienbedingungen in den wirtschafts- und sozialwissenschafter an der universität zu Köln; eine empirische untersuchung von Friedrich schiefer et al. Köln, Wison, 1969. 371 p.
3859. SYSTEMATIC economics, book 1. Sydney, Brooks, 1968. 64 p.
3860. TAGLIACOZZO, Giorgio. Croce y la naturaleza de la ciencia económica. Córdoba, Impr. de la universidad Córdoba, 1945. 36 p.
3861. TARASCIO, Vincent J. Pareto's methodological approach to economics; a study in the history of some scientific aspects of economic thought. (Studies in economics and business administration, v. 6.) Chapel Hill, University of North Carolina press, 1968. 153 p.
3862. TAVOLE sinottiche di politica economica. (Corsi universitari.) Torino, G. Giappichelli, 1968. 84 p.
3863. THEIL, Henri, John C. G. Boot and Teun Kleok. Operations research and quantitative economics; an elementary introduction. New York, McGraw-Hill, 1965. xiv, 258 p. Bibliography (Translated from the Dutch, Voorspellen en beslissen.)
3864. THEOCHARES, Reginos D. Early developments in mathematical economics. Foreword by Lord Robbins. London, Macmillan; New York, Saint Martin's press, 1961. 141 p.
3865. THOMAS, J. J. "The reporting of empirical work in economics." In, Applied statistics, 16, 2 (1967), 172-76.
3866. TINBERGEN, Jan. Central planning. (Studies in comparative economics, 4.) New Haven, Yale university press, 1964. x, 150 p. Bibliography, 143-146.
3867. _____. Econometrics. Translated from the Dutch by H. Rijken van Olst. Philadelphia, Blakiston, 1951. xii, 258 p. Bibliography, 247.
3868. _____. L'économetrie. (Centre d'études économiques. Etudes et memoires, 21.) Paris, A. Colin, 1954. 213 p.
3869. _____. In hoeverre kunen economische stellingen zonder wiskunde worden bewezen. (Mededelingen der koninklijke Nederlandse akademie van wetenschappen. Afd. Leterdunde. Nieuwe reeks, deel 13, no. 10.) Amsterdam, Noord-Hollandshe uitg. mij., 1950. 11 p.
3870. _____. Statistical testing of business-cycle theories. (Series of League of nations publications. 2, Economic

and financial. 1938 II. A. 23; 1939 II A. 16.) New York, Agathon press, 1968. 2 v. in 1. Bibliographical references.
3871. TINBERGEN, Jan and Hendricus Cornelis Bos. Mathematical models of economic growth. (Economics handbook series. New York, McGraw-Hill, 1962. 131 p. Bibliography.
3872. TINTNER, Gerhard. Handbuch der ökonometrie. (Enzyklopädie der rechts- und staatswissenschaft. Abt. Staatswissenschaft.) Berlin, Springer, 1960. 328 p.
3873. TOBIN, James. National economic policy. Essays. London and New Haven, Yale university press, 1966.
3874. TOYODA, Shiro. Shakai keizaishigaku no kompon mondai. (Transliterated.) Japan, 1949. 2, 4, 225 p.
3875. TUSTIN, Arnold. The mechanism of economic systems; an approach to the problem of economic stabilisation from the point of view of control-system engineering. Cambridge, Harvard university press, 1953, i.e. 1954. xi, 161 p. (2d edition, London, Heinemann, 1957. 191 p.
3876. ULMER, Melville Jack. The economic theory of cost of living index numbers. (Columbia university. Faculty of political science. Studies in history, economics and public law, no. 550.) New York, Columbia university press, 1949. 106 p. Bibliography, 101-104. (Also issued as thesis, Columbia university.)
3877. UNITED nations. Educational, scientific and cultural organization. The university teaching of social sciences: economics. Based on reports by C. W. Guillebaud and others on behalf of the International economic association. (Teaching in the social sciences.) Paris, 1954. 300 p.
3878. UNITED States. Air force. Office of scientific research. Proceedings of the symposium in linear programming. Washington.
3879. _____. Council of economic advisers. Economic indicators. May 1948- . Washington, Government printing office, 1948- . v. (Historical and descriptive supplement. 1st- . 1953 - . v.)
3880. _____. Congress. 89th 1st Session. Joint economic committee. Current economic indicators for the U.S.S.R.; materials. Washington, Government printing office, 1965. xii, 220 p. Bibliographies.
3881. _____. Congress, 89th, 2nd session. Joint economic committee. Economic policies and practices. (Papers, nos. 8 and 9.) Washington, Government printing office, 1966.
3882. _____. Congress, 90th, 1st session, 1967. House committee on government operations. Subcommittee on research and technical programs. The use of social research in federal domestic programs. Washington, Government printing office, 1967.
3883. _____. _____. Joint economic committee. Subcommittee economic program. Economic education. (Hearings, April, 1967.) Washington, Government printing office, 1967. 2 v.

3884. UNO, Kozo. Shakai kagaku to shite no keizaigaku. (Transliterated.) Japan, 1969. 288 p.
3885. VAN den Berg, Martin. Enige aspekte van die invloed van ekonomiese navorsing op makro-ekonomiese beleid in Nederland en die verenigde koninkryk gedurende 1945-52. s'Gravenhage, Excelsior, 1954. 115 p.
3886. VEBLEN, T. "Why is economics not an evolutionary science?" In, Quarterly journal of economics, 12 (1898), 373-97.
3887. VICKREY, William Spencer. Metastatics and macroeconomics. New York, Harcourt, Brace and World, 1964. x, 314 p. Bibliography, 281-304.
3888. _____. Microstatics. New York, Harcourt, Brace and World, c1964. x, 406 p. Bibliography, 369-95.
3889. VINER, J. "Some problems of logical method in political economy." In, Journal of political economy, 25 (1917), 236-60.
3890. VRIES, François de. De taak der theoretische economi. Haarlem, Erven F. Bohn, 1946. 25 p.
3891. WADA, Sadao. Keizai seicho no kiso riron. (Transliterated.) 1969. 370 p. Bibliography, 351-363.
3892. _____. Tenshugo to keizai bunseki. (Transliterated.) (Series: Osaka furitsu daigaku. Sakai, Japan. Osaka furitsu daigaku keizai kenkyu sosho, dai 3-satsu.) 1960. 147, 4, p. Bibliography, 145-147.
3893. WAFFENSCHMIDT, Walter Georg und Forschungsgruppe. Erweiterte volkswirtschaftliche gesamtrechnung. Magisches Dreieck. Mitarbeiter: K. Elsner, und al. Meisenheim am Glan, Hain, 1968. 253 p.
3894. WAGNER, A. Grundlegung der politischen oekonomie. 3rd. 1892. 137-285 p. Bibliographical notes. (1st part of Lehr- und handbuch.)
3895. WALLIS, Kenneth F. Methods of economic investigation. Introduction to econometrics. London, Gray-Mills, Blackwells, 1971.
3896. WANTY, Jacques. Réflexions sur les modèles économétriques d'entreprise. (Sorca. Publications du Centre de recherche, no. 3.) Bruxelles, SORCA, 1966- . v.
3897. WARSAW. Instytut ekonomiki i organizacji przemysłu. Osrodek informacji i dokumentacji naukowo-technicznej. Zastosowanie metod matematycznych do ekonomiki i organizacji przemysłu. Opracowała J. Kasprzakowa. (Its Tematyczne zestawienie dokumentacyjne, nr. 43.) Warszawa, 1964. 112 p.
3898. WEBER, Max. Max Weber on law in economy and society; edited with introduction and annotations by Max Rheinstein. Translation from Max Weber, Wirtschaft und gesellschaft, 2d edition (1925) by Edward Shils and Max Rheinstein. (20th century legal philosophy series, v.6.) Cambridge, Harvard university press, c1954. 363 p.
3899. _____. The theory of social and economic organization, translated by A. M. Henderson and Talcott Parsons, edited with an introduction by Talcott Parsons. 1st

American edition. New York, Oxford university press, c1947. x, 436 p. ("A translation of part I of Max Weber's Wirtschaft und gesellschaft, which was in turn originally published as Volume III of the collaborative work Grundriss der sozialoekonomik.")

3900. WEISSKOPF, W. A. "Repression and the dialectics of industrial civilization." In, Review of social economy, 23 (September 1965), 116-26.

3901. WICKSTEED, P. H. "The scope and method of political economy in the light of the marginal theory of value and of distribution." In, Economic journal, 24 (1914), 1-23.

3902. WIESER, F. von. "Gesellschaftliche wirtschaft." In, Vol. 1, Part 3, Grundriss der sozialökonomik. Tübingen, 1914.

3903. WINKLER, Wilhelm. Grundfragen der ökonometrie. Wien, Springer, 1951. 220 p.

3904. WIRTSCHAFTS- und arbeitswelt im Unterricht. Materialien z. didakt. diskussion. Mit betir. von Herbert Bath und al. (Pädagogische zentrum. Veröffentlichungen. Reihe C: Berichte, Bd. 9.) Weinheim/Bergstr., Berlin, Basel, Beltz, 1969. 204 p.

3905. WISSLER, Albert Josef. Hauptprobleme und verfahrensfrage der empirischen konjunkturforschung, vorträge und abhandlungne. (Berlin. Deutsches institut für wirtschaftsforschung. Sonderhefte, n. F., Nr. 14, Reihe B: Vorträge.) Berlin, Duncker und Humblot, 1952. 110 p. Bibliographical footnotes. (Lectures and treatises dating from the autumn of 1951 and the beginning of 1952. p. 109.)

3906. WOLD, Herman O. A. Model building in the human sciences. Monaco, Union européene d'éditions, 1967. (Entretiens de monaco, 1964.)

3907. YI, Hong-jun. Kyongje suhak. (Transliterated.) Korea, 1964. 313 p. Bibliography, 313.

3908. YOTOPOULOS, Pan A. "Economic analysis and economic policy." Athens, Center of planning and economic research, 1960.

3909. YOUNG, A. A. Economic problems. New and old. 1927.

3910. ———. "Economics as a field of research." In, Quarterly journal of economics, 42 (1927), 1-25.

3911. ———. "English political economy." In, Economica, 8 (1928), 1-15.

3912. ———. "Pigou's wealth and welfare." In, Quarterly journal of economics, 27 1913), 672-86.

3913. ———. "The trend of economics as seen by some American economists." In, Quarterly journal of economics, 39 (1925), 155-83.

3914. ZASTOSOWANIE metod matematycznych i techniki obliczeniowej w ekonomice: materiały ze Szkoły Letniej, lipiec 1964. Wyd. 1. Warszawa, Panstwowe wydawn. naukowe, 1966. 224 p.

3915. ZAUBERMAN, A. "The rapproachement between East and

West in mathematical-economic thought." In, Manchester school of economic and social studies, 37, 1 (March, 1969) 1-21.
3916. ZAWADZKI, W. Les mathématiques appliquées à l'économie politique. Paris, 1914. 331 p.
3917. ZEUTHEN, Frederick Ludvig Bang. Economic theory and method. Cambridge, Harvard university press, 1957. xii, 364 p. Bibliographical footnotes. [Translation of . . . Økonomisk teori og metode (. . . Copenhage 1942) thoroughly revised and considerably enlarged."]
3918. ZUKOWSKI, Jan. Programowanie lokalizacji produkcji; zastosowanie programowania nieliniowego i elektronowej techniki obliczniowej. Wyd. 1. (Komitet Przestrzennego Zagospodarowania Kraju Polskiej akademii nauk. Studia, t. 28.) Warszawa, Panstwowe wydawn. naukowe, 1968. 169 p.
3919. ZURAWICKI, Seweryn. Ekonomia polityczna a matematyka; zagadnienia metodologiczne. Wyd. 1. Warzawa, Panstwowe wydawn. ekonomiczne, 1961. 268 p.

PART III

PERIODS AND SCHOOLS

H. PRE-CLASSICAL PERIOD

Section I. General Works

3920. ABEILLE, Louis Paul. Effets d'un privilége exclusif sur les droits de propriété, . . . Paris, 1764.
3921. ———. Lettre d'un négociant sur la nature du commerce des grains. Paris, 1763. (Reprint: Paris, 1910. 103 p.)
3922. ———. Principes sur la liberté du commerce des grains. Amsterdam, 1768. 162 p.
3923. ———. Réflexions sur la police des grains en Angleterre et en France. Paris, 1764. (Reprint: Paris, 1910. 128 p.)
3924. ABSTRACT of the charter . . . Company of Merchants of Great Britain, trading to the south-seas. London, 1711. 8 p.
3925. An ABSTRACT of the grievances of trade which oppress our poor. London, 1694. 18 p.
3926. An ACCOUNT of charity-schools lately erected in Great Britain and Ireland. 6th edition. London, 1707. (8th edition, 1709. 12th edition, 1713.)
3927. An ACCOUNT of Denmark, as it was in the year 1692. London, 1694. 271 p.
3928. An ACCOUNT of European settlements in America. London, 1757. 2 v.
3929. An ACCOUNT of the proceedings of the House of Peers, upon the publick accounts. London, 1702. 86 p.
3930. An ACCOUNT of the revenue and national debt of Ireland. London, 1754. 48 p.
3931. An ACCOUNT of some transactions relating to the late East-India Company. London, 1693. 25 p.
3932. An ACCOUNT of several workhouses for employing and maintaining the poor; setting forth the rules by which they are governed. . . . London, 1725. (2nd. edition. 1732. 184 p.)
3933. ACOSTA, Joseph. The naturall and morall histories of the East and West Indies. (Translated from Italian, 1596.) London, 1604. 590 p.
3934. The ACT for permitting the free importations of cattle from Ireland. London, 1760. 43 p.
3935. The ACT of tonnage & poundage, and rates of merchandize. London, 1702. pp. 768.
3936. An ADDRESS to the proprietors of India stock . . . London, 1769. 34 p.
3937. An ADDRESS upon the present state of trade and manufactures. Aberdeen, 1755. 20 p.

3938. The ADVANTAGES of the East-India trade to England considered. . . London, 1720. 128 p.
3939. The ADVANTAGES and disadvantages which will attend the prohibition of the merchandizes of Spain. London, 1740.
3940. The ADVANTAGES to the people of Ireland by raising of flax and flax-seed. Dublin, 1732. 24 p.
3941. The AFRICAN Trade; . . . British plantation trade in America. London, 1745. 44 p.
3942. AICKIN, Joseph. The mysteries of the counterfeiting of the coin . . . London, 1696. 15 p.
3943. ALCOCK, Thomas. Observations on that part of a late act of parliament which lays and additional duty on cider and perry. Plymouth, 1764.
3944. ———. Observations on the defects of the poor-laws, and on the causes and consequences of the great increase and burden of the poor. London, 1752, 96 p.
3945. ALLEN, Robert. An Essay on the nature and methods of trade to the South-Sea. London, 1712. 37 p.
3946. ALLEN, William. Ways and means to raise the value of land. London, 1736. 58 p.
3947. AMEILHON Hubert Pascal. Histoire du commerce et de la navigation des Egyptiens. Paris, 1766. pp. xxiv, 332.
3948. AMHURST, N. An Epistle to Sir John Blount, one of the directors of the South-Sea Co. London, 1720. 15 p.
3949. The ANATOMY of exchange-alley: or a system of stock-jobbing. London, 1719. 64 p.
3950. ANCIENT accounts of India and China. By two Mohammedan travellers of the ninth century. Translated from the Arabic, with notes, illustrations, and inquiries, by Renaudot. London, 1733. 1 v.
3951. ANCIENT Trades decayed repaired again. By a country tradesman. London, 1678.
3952. ANDERSON, Adam. An Historical and Chronological Deduction of the Origin of Commerce, from the Earliest accounts to the Present Time. 2d. ed. London, 1764. 2 v. (London, 1787-89. 4 v.; Riga, 7 Bde, 1773-79.)
3953. ANGLIA RESTAURATA; or the advantages of putting a stop to smuggling wool. London, 1727. 44 p.
3954. ANGLIAE TUTAMEN, or the safety of England; being an account of the banks, lotteries, mines, diving, draining, metallic, salt, linen, lifting, and sundry other engines, and many pernicious projects now of foot, tending to the destruction of trade and commerce, and the impoverishing of this Realm. By a person of honour. London, 1695.
3955. ANNOTATIONS . . . considerations of the proposal for reducing the interest. London, 1750. 29 p.
3956. An ANSWER of the company of Royal adventurers of England trading into Africa . . . London, 1667. 18 p.
3957. The ANSWER of the merchants-petitioners, and trustees for the factory at Legorn, London, 1704. 159 p.
3958. An ANSWER to the case of the Old East-India Co. . . . London, 1700. 21 p.
3959. An ANSWER to the pamphlet entitled 'Thoughts on the causes, &c.' London, 1768.

3960. An ANSWER to the reasons against an African Company . . . London, 1711. 31 p.
3961. An ANSWER to two letters concerning the East-India Co., London, 1676. 14 p.
3962. An ANSWER upon excise . . . as it relates to the tobacco trade. London, 1733. 19 p.
3963. ANTIGUEDAD Maritima de la republica de Cartage, con el periplo de su General Hannon. Traducido del griego è illustrado por Don. P. R. Campomanes. Madrid, 1756. 1 vol.
3964. ANZANO, Thomas. Reflexiones economico-politicas sobre las causas de las alteraciones de precios que ha padecido Aragon, y discursos sobre los medios que pueden facilitar la restauration de Aragon. Zaragoza, 1768.
3965. An APOLOGY for the builder; or, a discourse shewing the causes and effects of the increase of building. London, 1685. 37 p.
3966. An APOLOGY for the business of paan-broking. By a pawn-broker. 2d ed. London, 1744. 73 p.
3967. An APPEAL to facts regarding the home trade and inland manufactures of Great Britain and Ireland. London, 1751 64 p.
3968. An APPEAL to the public in relation to the tobacco . . . London, 1751. 63 p.
3969. APPENDICE a la educacion popular. Madrid, 1775-1777. 4 v
3970. An APPENDIX to "The Present State of the Nation.' containing a reply to the 'Observations' on that pamphlet. By Mr. Grenville. London, 1769. 68 p.
3971. ARBUTHNOT, John. An Inquiry into the connection between the present price of provisions and the size of Farms; with remarks on population, as affected thereby. To which are added, proposals for preventing future scarcity. By A Farmer. London, 1773.
3972. ———. Tables of ancient coins, weights, and measures. 2d ed. with observations on Dr. Arbutnot's work, by Benjamin Langwith. London, 1754. 1 vol.
3973. ARGELLATI, F. De monetis Italiae. Mediolani, 1750-2. 5 v.
3974. An ARGUMENT proving that the design of employing and enobling foreigners, is a treasonable conspiracy . . . London, 1717. 102 p.
3975. An ARGUMENT to shew the disadvantage from obliging the South-Sea Co. to fix what capital stock. 2d. ed. London, 1720. pp. 18. (By Daniel Defoe?)
3976. An ARGUMENT upon the woollen manufacture of Great Britain. Dublin, 1737. 26 p.
3977. ARRIQUIBAR D. Nicholas de. Recreacion politica. Reflexiones sobre el. Amigo de los hombres en su tratado de poblacion, considerado con respecto à nuestros intereses; obra postuma, presentada à la sociedad Bascongada, en 1770. (Victoria, 1779.)
3978. The ART and mystery of vintners and wine-coopers . . . London, 1682. 79 p. (1750. 95 p.)

3979. ARTICLES of the Copartnery of the Feeman-Burgesses of the royal burrows of Scotland, for carrying on a Fishing trade. . . Edinburgh, 1720. 18 p.
3980. ARTICLES and Regulation of the Edinburgh Friendly Insurance against losses by fire . . . Edinburgh, 1728. 24 p.
3981. ASGILL, John. Several assertions proved, in order to create another species of money than gold and silver. London, 1696. 85 p. (2d. ed. 1720, 46 p. Report edited by Jacob H. Hollander. Baltimore, 1906. pp. 38.)
3982. ———. An Essay on a registry, for titles of lands. London, 1698. 43 p. (2nd. edition, 1701. 4th edition, 1758. 51 p.)
3983. ———. Several Assertions proved in order to create another species of money than gold. London, 1696.
3984. ASHLEY, John. The sugar trade with the incumbrances thereon laid open. By a Barbadoes planter. London, 1734.
3985. ———. Some observations on a direct exportation of sugar. From the British Isles. London, 1725. 23 p.
3986. ———. A Supplement to the second part of the Memoirs of John Ashley . . . 2d. ed. London, 1744. 23 p.
3987. The ASSIENTO. Contract consider'd. As also, the advantages and decay of the trade of Jamaica . . . London, 1714. 50 p.
3988. AUGER, Avocat. Mémoires pour servir à l'histoire du droit public de la France en matière d'impôts, ou recueil de ce qui s'est passé de plus intéressant à la cour des aides, depuis 1756 jusqu'au mois de juin 1775; publiés sous l'inspection de M. Gabriel Choart, président de la cour des aides de Paris. Bruxelles, 1779. 776 p.
3989. B. B. The Exorbitant grants of William the III. examin'd and question'd. London, 1702. 30 p. (2d. ed. 1703, 28 p.)
3990. BADE, Margrave de. Abrégé de l'economie politique. Paris, 1772.
3991. BAILEY, William. A Treatise on the better employment . . . of the poor in workhouses . . . London, 1758. 79 p.
3992. BANDINI, Salustio Antonio. Discorso economico scritto dall'arcidiacono. Nell' anno 1737. (Firenze, 1775. In Custodi's Raccolta, 1803.)
3993. BARBA, Albaro Alonso. A Collection of Scarce and Valuable Treatises upon Metals . . . 2d. ed. London, 1740. 319 p.
3994. BARBIER, Stephen. An Expedient to pay the Publick Debts . . . London, 1719. 24 p.
3995. BARBON, Nicholas. A discourse of Trade. London, 1690. 92 p. London, 1691. Reprints: edited with introduction by Jacob H. Hollander. Baltimore, 1905. 1934 London, G. Allen & Unwin, 1938.
3996. ———. A discourse concerning coining the new money lighter, in answer to Mr. Locke's 'Considerations about raising the value of money.' London, 1696. 96 p.
3997. BARNARD, John. Considerations on the proposal for reducing

the interest on the national debt. London, 1750.
3998. BASINGHEN, Abot de. Table des monnaies courantes. Par 1767.
3999. ———. Traité des monnois, et de la jurisdiction de la cour des monnoies, en forme de dictionnaire. Paris, 17.. 2 v.
4000. BAUDEAU, Nicholas, Abbé. Eclaircissements demandés à M. N. (Necker) sur ses principes économiques, et sur ses projets de législation, au nom des propriétaires fonciers et des cultivateurs francais. 1775.
4001. ———. Idées d'un citoyen sur l'administration des finances du roi. Paris et Amsterdam, 1763.
4002. ———. Idée d'une souscription partriotique en faveur de l'agriculture, du commerce et des arts. Paris, 1765.
4003. ———. Idées d'un citoyen sur le commerce d'Orient et sur la Compagnie des Indes. Amsterdam et Paris, 1764.
4004. ———. De l'origine et des progrès d'une science nouvelle. Londres et Paris, 1786.
4005. ———. Première introduction à la philosophie économique par un disciple de l'Ami des hommes. Paris, 1771. (Reprint: Edited by A. Dubois, 1910.)
4006. ———. Principes économiques de Louis XII et du cardinal d'Amboise, de Henri IV et du duc de Sully, sur l'administration des finances, opposés aux systèmes des docteurs modernes, 1785.
4007. BEARDE de l'abbaye. Recherches sur les moyens de supprimer les impôts, précédées de l'examen de la nouvelle science. Amsterdam, 1770. 1 v.
4008. BEAUMONT, Deon de. Mémoires pour servir à l'histoire Génerale des Finances. Amsterdam, 1760. 2 vols.
4009. BEAWES, Windham. Lex Mercatoria Rediviva; or a Complete Code of Commercial Law. London, 1751. 1 vol.
4010. BECCARIA, C. Dei Delitti e delle Pene. Leghorn, 1764. (Trad. p. F. Hélie, Paris, 1856, 2d. éd. 1870; Deutsch v. J. Glaser, 2 Aufl. Wien, 1876; English by J. A. Farrer. London, 1880.)
4011. ———. Elementi di Economia pubblica (1769). In Custodi's Raccolta vols. xi., xii., 1864 and Ferrara's Bibli. dell' Econ., vol. iii., 1852; trad. fr. Paris, 1852. (Milanese, 1793)
4012. BELLERS, John. Proposals for raising a College of Industry of all useful trades and husbandry, &c. London. 1696. 28 p.
4013. ———. Essays about the Poor, manufacturers, trade, plantations . . . London, 1699. 26 p.
4014. BELLONI, Girolamo. Dissertazione sopra il commercio, con alcune note dell' edizione di Bologna, ed una lettera dell' autore sulla moneta imaginiaria. 1776?
4015. ———. Lettre sur la monnaie fictive. 1765.
4016. BENEZET, Amthomy. An Historical account of Guinea: its Situation, Produce, and the General Disposition of its Inhabitants; with an Inquiry into the Rise and Progress of the Slave Trade, its Nature and lamentable effects. London, 1772.

Preclassical Period

4017. BENNET. John. The National Merchant: Or, discourses on commerce. . . London, 1736. 143 p.
4018. ———. Two Letters and several Calculations on the Sugar Colonies and Trade. 2nd edition. London, 1738. 73 p.
4019. BERGIER, Nicolas. Histoire des Grands Chemins de l'Empire Romain; contenant l'Origine, Progrès, et Etendue quasi incroyable de Chemins Militaires, Pavez depuis la Ville de Rome jusques aux extrémités de son Empire. Paris, 1622. (Reprinted, Brussels, 1728, 1736. with the addition of Peutinger's Itinerary Chart. 2 vols.)
4020. BERKELEY, George. Queries relating to a national bank, extracted from the Querist . . . Dublin, 1737. 40 p.
4021. ———. The Querist, containing several queries, proposed to the considerations of the public. Dublin, 1735-37. Two parts. (2nd edition, London, 1751. Reprints: Edited with introduction by Jacob H. Hollander. Baltimore, 1910. 116 p.)
4022. BIGLAND, Ralph. Observations on marriages, baptisms, and burials, as preserved in parochial registers; with sundry specimens of the entries of marriages, &c., in foreign countries. Garter King-at-Arms, London, 1764.
4023. A BILL for repealing several Subsidies and an Impost now payable on Tobacco . . . London, 1733. 39 p.
4024. BINDON, David. An essay on the gold and silver-coin current in Ireland. Dublin, 1729. 28 p.
4025. ———. A letter . . . in which the case of the British and Irish manufacture of linen . . . is fairly stated. London, 1753.
4026. ———. A scheme for supplying industrious men with money to carry on their trades. Dublin, 1729. 22 p.
4027. BLACK, David. Essay upon Industry and Trade. Edinburgh, 1706. pp. 40.
4028. BLACK, William. Some overtures and cautions in relation to trade and taxes. 1707.
4029. BLACKWELL, John. An essay towards New-Coyning of all Our Moneys . . . London, 1695. 30 p.
4030. BLAXTON, John. The English Usurer; or usury condemned. London, 1634. 84 p.
4031. BLITH, Walter. The English Improver, or a New Survey of Husbandry. London, 1649. 168 p. (3rd edition. 1652. 262 p.)
4032. BODIN, Jean. Republique. Paris, 1756.
4033. BOESNIER de l'Orme. Du Rétablissement de l'Impot dans son ordre naturel. Yverdon, 1769. 171 p.
4034. ———. De l'esprit du gouvernement économique. Paris, 1775.
4035. BOISGUILLEBERT, P. O. Le detail de la France sous le règne présent . . . Paris. 1695. (Nouv. édit. Paris, 1707. 2 v.)
4036. ———. Factum de la France, ou Moyens très-faciles de faire recevoir
4037. BOIZARD. Traité des monnoyes, de leurs circonstances et dépendances. Nouv. édit. Paris, 1723. 2 v.

4038. BOLTS, William. Considerations on Indian affairs. By William Bolts. London, 1772.
4039. BOROUGHS, John. The Soveraignty of the British Seas. London, 1651. 165 p.
4040. BOTERO, Giovanni. A treatise concerning the causes of the magnificencie and greatness of cities . . . English by R. Peterson. London, 1606. 108 p.
4041. BOUCHAUD. De l'impôt du vingtième sur les successions, et l'impôt sur les marchandises chez les Romains., nouvelle édition, 1772. 1 v.
4042. BOUGAINVILLE, de. Dissertation sur les droits des métropoles Grecques sur les Colonies, couronnée par l'académie des inscriptions et Belles Lettres. Paris, 1745. 1 vol.
4043. BRADDON, Lawrence. Particular answers . . . for Relieving . . . the Poor of Great Britain. 1722. 104 p.
4044. BREWSTER, Francis. Essays on Trade and Navigation. London, 1695. 126 p. (Revised, 1702.)
4045. BRIDGES, George. A Whip for the smugglers shewing the only way to prevent wool-smuggling. London, 1742. pp. 16.
4046. A BRIEF account of the priviledges and immunities granted by the French King to the East-India Company . . . London 1671. 12 p.
4047. A BRIEF Case of the distillers in England. London, 1726. 52 p.
4048. A BRIEF state of the question, between the printed and painted callicoes. London, 1719. 48 p.
4049. BRISCOE, John. A Discourse on the late funds of the million-act, lottery-act, and bank of England. London, 1694. pp. iv, iv, 5-56. (3d. ed. 1696. 187 p.)
4050. BRITAIN'S golden mines discover'd: or, the fishery trade considered. London, 1720. 80 p.
4051. BRITANNIA LANGUENS, or a discourse of trade: showing the grounds and reasons of the increase and decay of land, rents, national wealth and strength, &c. London, 1680.
4052. The BRITISH Customs, containing an historical and practical account of each branch of that revenue. By Henry Saxby. London, 1757. 1 v.
4053. BROGGIA, C. A. Dei tributi e del governo politico dello sanità. Naples, 1743. In Custodi's raccolta, parte antica, vol. iv.
4054. ———. Trattato delle monete considerate ne' rapporti de legitima ruduziome di circulazione e di deposito. Paris? 2 v.
4055. BROWN, John. An essay on trade in general and in that of Ireland in particular. Dublin, 1723. 119 p.
4056. ———. Seasonable remarks on trade. Dublin, 1728. 70 p.
4057. ———. A scheme of the money-matters of Ireland. Dublin, 1729. 57 p.
4058. BUCHE de PAVILLON. Essai sur les causes de la diversité des taux de l'argent chez les peuples. Londres et Paris, 1756.

Preclassical Period 275

4059. BUDGELL, Eustace. A letter to the merchants and tradesmen of Great Britain in opposing the extension of the excise-laws . . . London, 1733. 38 p.
4060. The BUDGET. Inscribed to the man, who thinks himself minister. 10th. ed. London, 1764. 23 p.
4061. BURKE, Edmund. Observations on a late 'state of the nation.' 2d. ed. London, 1769. 153 p. (4th. ed. 1769) 154 p.)
4062. _____. Thoughts and details on scarcity . . . London, 1800. 48 p.
4063. BURN, Richard. The history of the poor-laws, with observations. By Richard Burn, LL.D. London, 1764. 1 v.
4064. BURRISH, Onslow. Batavia illustrata: or, a view of the policy, and commerce, of the United Provinces . . . London, 1728. 580 p.
4065. BURTREL du Pasquier. Observations sur la déclaration du 30 Oct. 1785, et l'augmentation progressive de prix des matières d'or et d'argent, depuis 1er janvier, 1726.
4066. BUTEL-DUMONT. Recherches historiques et critiques sur l'administration publique et privée des terres chez les Romains, depuis le commencement de la république jusqu' au siècle de Jules-César, Paris, 1779.
4067. _____. Théorie du luxe, ou traité dans lequel on entreprend d'établir que le luxe est un ressort, non-seulement utile, mais même indispensablement nécessaire à la prospérite d'un Etat. Londres, 1771. 1 v.
4068. _____. Traité de la circulation et du crédit. Amsterdam et Paris, 1771.
4069. CAMPBELL, Ilay. Information, addressed to the Lords of Session, Scotland, for Messrs. Donaldson, Wood . . . against John Hinton. London, Edinburgh, 1773. 82 p.
4070. CAMPBELL, John. A political survey of Britain; being a series of reflections on the situation, lands, inhabitants, revenues, colonies, and commerce of this island. London, 1774. 2 v.
4071. CAMPOMANES, Rodriguez. Appendice a la educacion popular; parte prima, que contiene las reflexiones conducentes a entender el origen de la decadencia de los officios y artes en Espana, durante el siglo pasado, segun la domonstraron los escritores coetanos, que se reimprimen en este appendice, o cuyos pasages se dan à la letra. Madrid, 1775. 4 v.
4072. _____. Carta al senor don Pedro Rodriquez Campomanes, remitiendo el proyecto de erarios publicos, impreso en el siglo pasado, 1777.
4073. _____. Discurso preliminar sobre la marina, navegacion, commercio . . . . Madrid, 1756.
4074. _____. Discurso sobre la educacion popular de los artesanos y su fomento. Madrid, 1775.
4075. _____. Discurso subre al fomento de la industria popular, de orden de S. M. y del consejo. Madrid, 1774.
4076. _____. Respuesta fiscal, sobre abolir la tasa y

establecer el commercio de granos. Madrid, 1764.
4077. CANDID and impartial considerations on the nature of the sugar trade. By Dr. Campbell. London, 1763.
4078. CANTILLON, Richard. Essai sur la nature du commerce en général. Londres (Paris), 1755. 430 p. (2nd edition, 1756. 427 p. Reprinted for Harvard university; with note by Henry Higgs. Boston, 1892. 430 p. Edition with and English translation and other material by Henry Higgs. London, Macmillan & co. ltd. for Royal economic society, 1931. 394 p.) Bibliography, 391-392. London, Frank Cass & Co., Ltds., 1959.)
4079. CARLI, Gian Rinaldo. Osservazioni preventive al piano intorno delle monete di Milano. 1766.
4080. CARLIER L'Abbé. Dissertation sur l'état du commerce en France, sous les rois de la première et de la seconde race. Amiens et Paris, 1753. 166 p.
4081. CARTER, William. England's interest by trade asserted. 2d Impression. London, 1671. 44 p.
4082. _____. A Summary of certain papers about wooll. London, 1685. 14 p.
4083. _____. The Usurpations of France upon the trade of the Woollen manufacture. London, 1695. 30 p.
4084. CARY, John. A discourse on trade and other matters relative to it. London, 1745. 204 p. (2nd edition, 1795. Italian edition, Napoli, 1764.)
4085. _____. An essay on the state of England, in relation to its trade . . . Bristoll, 1695. 178 p. (French edition, 1755. 2 v.)
4086. _____. An essay towards regulating the trade, and employing the poor. London, 1717. 162 p. (2nd. edition, London, 1719. 197 p.)
4087. _____. An essay towards the settlement of a national credit. London, 1696. 19 p.
4088. CASAREGIS, Discursus legales de commercio. Florentiae, 1719-29. 3 v. (Venetiis, 1740, 4 v.)
4089. The CASE fairly stated between the Turky Company and the Italian merchants. London, 1720.
4090. The CASE of bankrupts and insolvents considered. London, 1734-5. 2 v. 72, 46 p.
4091. The CASE of the British and Irish manufacture of linen, threads, and tapes fairly stated, and all the objections against the encouragement proposed to be given to that manufacture fully answered. London, 1738.
4092. The CASE of the planters of tobacco in Virginia. London, 1733. 64 p.
4093. The CASE of the revival of the salt duty . . . London, 1732. 65 p.
4094. The CASE of the Royal African Co. of England and their creditors. London, 1730. 47 p. (1748, 16 p.)
4095. The CASE of the salt-duty and land-tax . . . London, 1732. 27 p.
4096. The CASE of the sinking fund and the right of the public creditors to it considered, &c.; being a defence of 'An

enquiry,' &c., and a full reply to a late pamphlet entitled 'Some considerations,' &c. (Ascribed to Mr. Pulteney.) London, 1735. 138 p.

4097. CASTRO, Juan-Francisco de. Discursos creticos sobre las leyes y sus interpretes: Incertidumbres y detrimentos de los mayorazgos, y otras disposiciones analogas en el bien commun: su ofensa à la poblacion, agricultura, artes y comercio: necesidad de remedio: tentativa de algunos medios. Madrid, 1770.

4098. The CAUSE of the greatnesse of cities, from the Italian of Botero. By Sir T. H. London, 1635. 1 vol.

4099. The CAUSES of the dearness of provisions assigned; with effectual methods of reducing the prices of them. Humbly submitted to the consideration of Parliament. Gloucester, 1766.

4100. CERETTI. Histoire des monts-de-piété, avec des réflexions sur la nature de ces établissements. Paris, 1752. 1 v. 153 p.

4101. CERTAIN Considerations relating to the Royal African Company . . . London, 1680. 10 p.

4102. CHAMBERLAYNE, Edward. Englands wants: or several proposals probably beneficial for England. London, 1667. 43 p. (2d. ed. 1668. 47 p.)

4103. CHAMBERLAYNE, John. Magnae Britanniae notitia; or the present state of Great Britain, with divers remarks upon the ancient state thereof, in two parts (England and Scotland). London, 1737. 1 v.

4104. CHAMBERLEN, Hugh. The Constitution of the office of land credit declared in a deed. By Hugh Chamberlen and others. Enrolled in Chancery, A.D. 1696. London, 1698.

4105. CHARTER granted . . . to the East-India Company of England . . . London, 1766. 51 p.

4106. CHARTER and grants of the Company of Stationers of the City of London . . . London, 1741. pp. xvi, 65, 28 p.

4107. CHASSIPOL. Traté des finances et de la fausse monnaie des Romains, auquel on a adjoint une dissertation sur la manière de discerner les médailles antiques d'avec les contrefaites. Par M. Beauvais. Paris, 1740.

4108. CHESHIRE. Anglia restaurata; or the advantages of smuggling wool from England and Ireland to France, etc. London, 1727.

4109. CHILD, Josiah. Considérations sur le commerce et l'intérêt de l'argent; traduit en francais par Gournay. 1742.

4110. ———. A new discourse of trade. London, 1668. (Editions, 1690, 1693; 2nd edition, London, 1694; 5th edition, London, 1751. 184 p.)

4111. ———. Traités sur le commerce avec un petit traité contre l'usure; traduit par le Chevalier Thomas Culpeper . . . Amsterdam, 1754. 483 p.

4112. ———. A treatise that the East-India trade is the most national of all foreign trades. London, 1681. 43 p. (Supplement, 1689.)

4113. CHOMEL. Dictionnaire économique. Paris, 1767. 3 v.
4114. CHRISTIANI, Girolamo di. Delle misure d'ogni genere, anti chesmoderne. Brescia, 1760. 1 v.
4115. CHRONICON Preciosum, or an account of English gold and silver money; the price of corn and other commodities; and of stipends, salaries, wages, jointures, portions, da labour, &c., in England, for six hundred years last past By Bishop Fleetwood. London, 1707. 1 vol. (2d. ed. London, 1745. 1 v.)
4116. CITY corruption and mal-administration displayed. London, 1738. 46 p.
4117. CLARK, William. The connexion of the Roman, Saxon, and English coins, deduced from observations on Saxon weigh and money. London, 1767. 1 v.
4118. CLAUDE, DUPIN. Economiques (1745). Edited with introduction by Marc Aucuy. Paris, 1913. 3 v. in 2.
4119. CLEEVE, Bourchier. A Scheme for preventing a further increase of the national debt. London, 1756. pp. 15.
4120. CLEIRAC, Etienne. Us et coutumes de la mer, contenant les jugemens d'oleron, les ordonnances de wisbuy, de la Hanse Teutonique . . . Bordeaux, 1647. 1 vol. (and with some additional pieces. Rouen, 1671.)
4121. CLIQUOT de BLERVACHE. Dissertation sur l'état du commerce en France, depuis Hugues Capet jusqu'à Francois Ier Paris, 1766.
4122. ―――――. Considérations sur le commerce, et en particulier sur les compagnies, Sociétés et maitrises. Amsterdam, 1758.
4123. ―――――. Dissertations sur l'effet que produit le prix de l'intérêt sur le commerce et sul l'agriculture. Amiens, 1756.
4124. CODE Noir; ou recueil des règlemens concernant les colonies et le commerce des Nègres. Paris, 1752. 1 v. (1767. 1 v.)
4125. COKE, Roger. A discourse on trade. London, 1670.
4126. ―――――. Reflections upon the East-Indy and Royal African company. London, 1695. 25 p.
4127. A COLLECTION of papers relating to the East India trade; wherein are shown the disadvantages to a nation by confining any trade to a corporation with a joint stock. London, 1730. 118 p.
4128. A COLLECTION of tracts, concerning the present state of Ireland with respect to its riches, revenue, trade, and manufactures. London, 1729. 144 p.
4129. COLLINS, John. Salt and fisher. The several ways of making salt in England, and foreign parts. London, 1682. 163 p.
4130. COMBRUNE, Michel. An enquiry into the prices of wheat, malt, and occasionally of other provision; of land cand cattle, . . . as sold in England from the year 1000 to the year 1765. London, 1768. 1 v.
4131. ―――――. Some account of the rise, progress, and the present state of the brewery. London, 1757.

Preclassical Period

4132. COMMENTARII PECKII in tit. Digestorum et codicis ad rem nauticam pertinentes, cum notis vinii. Amstelodami, 1668. 1 v.
4133. Le COMMERCE de la Hollande, ou tableau de commerce des Hollandais dans les quatre parties du monde. Amsterdam, 1768. 3 v.
4134. A COMPARAISON de l'impot de France avec celui d'Angleterre. Londres, 1766. 42 p.
4135. A COMPARISON between the proposals of the bank and the South-Sea Company . . . London, 1720. 18 p.
4136. A COMPENDIOUS history of the taxes of France . . . London, 1694. pp. 34.
4137. A COMPENDIUM of the corn trade. The practice of ingrossing. London, 1757. 62 p.
4138. CONDUIT, John. Observations on the present state of our gold and silver coins. London, 1774.
4139. The CONSEQUENCES of trade, as to the wealth and strength of any nation. London, 1740. (5th edition, 1741.)
4140. CONSIDERATIONS for enabling the South-Sea Company to increase their capital stock . . . 2nd edition. London, 1720. 36 p.
4141. CONSIDERATIONS on money, bullion, and foreign exchange. . . . London, 1772.
4142. CONSIDERATIONS on the acts of Parliament relative to highways in Scotland, and on the new scheme of a tax in lieu of statute labour. Edinburgh, 1764.
4143. CONSIDERATIONS on the expediency of admitting representatives from the American colonies into the British House of Commons. London, 1770.
4144. CONSIDERATIONS on the present state of the nation, as to publick credit . . . London, 1720. 70 p.
4145. CONSIDERATIONS on roads. London, 1734.
4146. CONSIDERATIONS on several proposals lately made for the better management of the poor. 2nd edition. London, 1952.
4147. CONSIDERATIONS on taxes as they are supposed to affect the price of labour in our manufactures: also, some reflections on the general behaviour and disposition of the manufacturing populace of this kingdom; showing, by arguments drawn from experience, that nothing but necessity will enforce labour; and that no state ever did, or ever can make any considerable figure in trade, where the necessaries of life are at a low price. London, 1765. 64 p.
4148. CONSIDERATIONS on the trade and finances of this kingdom . . . London, 1766. 117 p.
4149. CONSIDERATIONS relating to the late order of the two banks established at Edinburgh. Edinburgh, 1762. 15 p.
4150. CONSIDERATIONS sur le commerce, et en particulier sur les compagnies, societes, et maitrises. Amsterdam, 1758. 1 v.
4151. CONSIDERATIONS upon commissions of bankrupts. London, 1727. 27 p.

4152. CONSIDERATIONS upon the East-India trade. London, 1701. 128 p.
4153. The CONSTITUTIONAL right of the legislature of Great Britain to tax the British colonies in America impartially stated. London, 1768.
4154. CONTARENI, de re frumentaria, dissertatio. Vesaliae, 1669. 1 v.
4155. COYER l'Abbé. La noblesse commercante. Londres, Paris, 1756.
4156. _____. Développement et défense du système de la noblesse commercante. Amsterdam et Paris, 1757.
4157. CRADOCK, Francis. An expedient for Taking Away all Impositions, and for Raising a Revenue without Taxes, by creating Banks for the Encouragement of Trade. London, 1660.
4158. _____. Wealth discovered; . . . raising a revenue without taxes. London, 1661. 44 p.
4159. A CRITICAL inquiry into the legality of the proceedings consequent to the late Gold Act. London, 1774.
4160. CROUCH, Henry. A complete view of the British customs. London, 1724. 355 p. (5th ed. 1755. 604 p.)
4161. CULPEPER, Thomas. A Discourse shewing the many advantages which will accrue by the abatement of usury. London, 1668. pp. xii, 34.
4162. _____. The necessity of abating usury re-asserted; in a reply to the discourse of Mr. Thomas Manly. London, 1670. pp. vi, 58.
4163. _____. A tract against the high rate of usurie. Presented to the High Court of Parliament, 1623. London, 1623.
4164. _____. A Tract against usurie. London, 1621. 19 p. (2d. ed. 1641).
4165. CUMBERLAND, Richard. An ESSAY towards the recovery of the Jewish measures and weights, comprehending their moneys, by help of ancient standards, compared with ours of England. By Richard Cumberland. London, 1686. 1 v.
4166. DALRYMPLE, John. CONSIDERATIONS on the policy of entails in a nation. Edinburgh, 1765.
4167. _____. An ESSAY towards a general history of feudal property in Great Britain. London, 1757. 1 vol. (London, 1759.)
4168. DANGUEL, Plumart. Avantages et les désavantages d. 1. France et d. 1. Grande Bretagne. Paris, 1754. (Trad. Ital., Venezia, 1753.)
4169. _____. Remarques sur les avantages et les desavantages de la France et de la Grande Bretagne, par rapport au commerce. Traduit de l'Anglois du Chevalier John Nickolls. 3d. éd. Paris, 1754. 1 v.
4170. DAVANZATI, Bernardo. Lezione delle moneta. 1588?
4171. DAVENANT, Charles. Discourses on the publick revenues, and on the trade of England. London, 1698. 2 v.
4172. _____. An essay on the East-India trade in a letter to the Marquis of Normandy, London, 1696.

4173. _____. An essay upon the probable methods of making a people gainers in the ballance of trade. London, 1699. 312 p.
4174. _____. Reflections upon the constitution and management of the trade to Africa. London, 1709.
4175. _____. The political and commercial works of Charles Davenant. Collected and revised by Sir Charles Whitworth. London, 1771, 5 v.
4176. DAVIES, John. The question concerning impositions, tonnage, poundage, prizage, customs. London, 1656. 166 p.
4177. De la félicité publique; ou, considérations sur le sort des hommes dans les différentes epoques de l'histoire. Par le Marquis de Chastelluz. 1re. éd. 1 v. Amsterdam, 1772. (Nouvelle édition, avec un notice de la vie de l'auteur, Paris, 1822. 2 v.)
4178. DE la saisie des patimens neutres; ou, du droit qu'ont les nations belligérantes d'arrêter les navires des peuples amis. Par M. Hubner. La Haye, 1759. 2 v.
4179. DECKER, Matthew. An essay on the causes of the decline of the foreign trade, consequently of the value of lands in Britain, and on the means to restore both. London, 1744. 1 v. (Edinburgh, 1756. 1 v. French edition, 1757.)
4180. _____. Serious considerations on the high duties; with a proposal for . . . one single tax. London, 1743. 30 p. (7th edition, London, 1756.)
4181. DECUS et Tutamen; or our new money as now coined in full weight and fineness proved to be for the honour, safety, and advantage of England. London, 1696.
4182. A DEFENCE of the Dutch in the herring fishery. London, 1749.
4183. A DEFENCE of an essay on the public debts of this kingdom, &c. in answer to 'A State of the national debt,' &c. By the author of the essay. London, 1727.
4184. A DEFENCE of the observations on the assiento trade. London, 1728.
4185. The DEFENCE of trade: in a letter to Sir Thomas Smith, Knight, Governor of the East India Company, from one of that society, London, 1615.
4186. A DEFENCE of the unanimous refusal of Mr. Wood's copper money. Dublin, 1724.
4187. A DEFENCE of the United Company of merchants of England, trading to the East-Indies . . . London, 1762. pp. 71.
4188. DEFOE, Daniel. An essay upon projects. London, 1697. pp. xiv, 336.
4189. _____. An essay upon publick credit. London, 1710. pp. 28.
4190. _____. Giving alms no charity; and employing the poor a grievance to the nation. Being an Essay, &c. London, 1704.
4191. _____. A plan of the English commerce, being a complete prospect of the trade of this nation, as well the home trade as the foreign. By Daniel Defoe. 3 parts. pp. xvi, viii, 368. 1 vol. London, 1728. (2d. ed. London, 1730. 1 vol.)

4192. DELLA decima e delle altre Gravezze, della moneta, e della mercatura de'Florentini sino al Secolo XVI. Lisbonna e Lucca, 1765-66. 4 v.
4193. DESCRIPTION du royaume de Siam. Par M. de la Loubere, envoyé extraordinaire du roy auprès du roy de Siam en 1687 et 1688. Paris, 1691. 2 v.
4194. DESLANDES. ESSAI sur la marine des anciens, et particulièrement sur leurs Vaisseaux de Guerre. Paris, 1768. 1 vol.
4195. ———. An essay on maritime power and commerce. London, 1743. 163 p.
4196. A DETECTION of the state and situation of the present sugar planters of Barbadoes . . . London, 1732. 99 p.
4197. DICTIONNAIRE des finances. Contenant la définition de tous les termes de finance. Paris, 1727. 395 p.
4198. DICTIONNAIRE universel du commerce, . . . Par. Messrs. Savary. Paris, 1748. 3 v.
4199. DIDEROT, D. et J. Alembert. Encyclopedie. Paris, 1751-65. 17 v. (Supplement, Amsterdam, Paris, 1776-77. 4 v.)
4200. DIGGES, Dudley. The defence of trade. In a letter to Sir Thomas Smith Knight. London, 1615. 50 p.
4201. DISCORSI e relazione sulle monete del regno di Napoli. Di gian donato turbulo. Napoli, 1616, 1618.
4202. A DISCOURSE concerning the currency of the British plantations in America, especially with regard to their paper money. Boston, 1740. (London, 1751.)
4203. A DISCOURSE on the general notions of money, trade and exchanges . . . London, 1695. 38 p.
4204. A DISCOURSE upon usury: or, lending money for increase . . . London, 1692. pp. iv, 36.
4205. DISCURSO sobre la educacion popular de los artesanos, y su fomento. Madrid, 1775. 1 vol.
4206. DISCURSO sobre el fomento de la industria popular. Madrid, 1774.
4207. DISSERTATION concerning the high roads. By Philips. London, 1737.
4208. DISTILLED spiritous liquors the bane of the nation, &c., to which is added an appendix containing the presentments of the grand juries of London, Middlesex, &c. London, 1736. 61, 24 p.
4209. DOBBS, Arthur. An Essay on the trade and improvement of Ireland. Dublin, 1729. Part I. 99 p. (Part II. 1731, 147 p.)
4210. DOUGLASS, William. A Discourse concerning the currencies of the British plantations in America. London, 1740. 54 p. (1751. 62 p.)
4211. ———. A summary, Historical and political, of the first planting, progressive improvements, and present state of the British settlements in North America. Originally published in Boston, New England, and reprinted in London in 1755.
4212. DU BUAT, Comte. Eléments de la politique, ou recherches

des vrais principes de l'économie sociale. Londres, 1773. 6 v.
4213. DU HAUTCHAMP. Histoire du système des finances sous la minorité de Louis XV. La Hay, 1739. 6 v.
4214. _____. Histoire générale et particulière du visa fait en France pour la réduction et l'extinction de tous les papiers royaux et des actions de la compagnie des Indes, que le système des finances avait enfantés. La Haye, 1743. 4 v.
4215. DUFRESNE de Francheville. Histoire du tarif de 1664. Paris? 1766, 3 v.
4216. DUHALDE, Père. Description Geographique, historique, chronologique, politique, et physique de l'Empire de la Chine et de la tartarie chinoise, avec figures et un atlas. Paris, 1735. 2 v.
4217. DUHAMEL, Monceau du. The elements of agriculture . . . London, 1764. 2 v. (445, 343 p.)
4218. _____. Traite General des Peches Maritimes, des Rivières, etc., des Poissons. du Monceau. Paris, 1769-82. 3 vols. pp. 74.
4219. DUTOT, Charles de Ferrare. Réflexions politiques sur les finances et le commerce. La Haye, 1738. 2 v. (1740, 259, 262 p. 1754. 416, 427 p.)
4220. The EAST-INDIA-Trade a most profitable trade to the Kingdom . . . London, 1677. 27 p.
4221. EDGAR, William. Vectigalium systema: or, a complete view of . . . customs . . . . London, 1714. 330 p.
4222. EDWARDUS, Bernard, De mensuris et ponderibus antiquorum. Oxonii, 1683. 1 v.
4223. EIGHT Letters on the custom of vails-giving in England. London, 1760. 64p.
4224. EISENSCHMIDII, J. I. Ponderibus et mensuris veterum Romanorum, Graecorum, Hebraeorum, &c. Argentorati, 1737. 1 v.
4225. The ELEMENTS of Commerce, politics, and finance. By Thomas Mortimer. London, 1774. 1 v.
4226. ELIBANK, Patrick Murray. An Inquiry into the original and consequences of the publick debt. London, 1754. 40 p.
4227. ELKING, Henry. A VIEW of the Greenland trade and whale-fishery, with the national and private advantages thereof. London, 1722.
4228. ELLERING, Henry. The INTEREST of England considered with respect to its manufactures and East-India callicoes imported. 2d. ed. London, 1720. 40 p.
4229. ENGLAND's great happiness, or a dialogue between content and complaint, wherein it is demonstrated that a great part of our complaints are causeless, &c. By a real and hearty lover of his King and country. London, 1677. 22 p.
4230. An ENQUIRY into the causes of the encrease and miseries of the poor . . . London, 1738. 83 p.
4231. An ENQUIRY into the conduct of our domestick affairs from 1721 to Christmas 1733 in the case of our National debts, the sinking fund . . . London, 1734. 68 p. (3d. ed. 72 p.)

4232.	An ENQUIRY into the past and present state of the trade and publick revenues. London, 1717. 276 p. (2d. ed. 183 p.)
4233.	An ENQUIRY into the reasons of the advance of the price of coals . . . London, 1739. 38 p.
4234.	An ENQUIRY whether a general practice of virtue tends to the wealth or poverty . . . London, 1725. 218 p.
4235.	EON de BEAUMOND. Essai historique sur les différentes situations de la France, par rapport aux finances, sous le règne de Louis XIV et la régence du duc d'Orleans. Amsterdam (Paris), 1753.
4236.	ESSAI sur les Colonies Françoises. Paris, 1754. 1 v.
4237.	ESSAI sur l'etat du commerce d'Angleterre. Paris, 1755. 2 v.
4238.	ESSAI sur les monnoies, ou réflexions sur le rapport entre l'argent et les denrées. Par M. Dupré de St. Maur. Paris, 1746. 1 v.
4239.	ESSAI sur les probablités de la durée de la vie humaine. Par M. Deparcieux. Paris, 1746. 1 v.
4240.	ESSAI sur le rapport des poids etrangers avec le marc de France. Par M. Tillet, Paris, 1766. 1 v.
4241.	An ESSAY for lowering the gold and raising the silver coin. London, 1696. 31 p.
4242.	An ESSAY on the causes of the present high price of provisions, as connected with luxury, currency, taxes, and the national debt. By the Rev. Mr. Dickson. London, 1773.
4243.	An ESSAY on insurances, explaining the nature of the various kinds of marine insurance practised by the different commercial states of Europe, and showing their consistency or inconsistency with equity and the public good. By Nicolas Magens. London, 1755. 2 v.
4244.	An ESSAY on the sinking fund. London, Wherein the nature thereof is fully explained . . . 1736. 72 p. (2d. ed. 1737. 85 p.)
4245.	An ESSAY on trade and commerce, containing observations on taxes, &c. London, 1770. 1 v.
4246.	An ESSAY on the treaty of commerce with France, with necessary expositions. London, 1713. pp. 44.
4247.	An ESSAY on ways and means for the advancement of trade . . . London, 1726. 47 p.
4248.	An ESSAY upon the present interest of England . . . London, 1701. 86 p. (2d. ed. 84 p.)
4249.	ESSAYS on the public debt, on paper money, and on frugality. By Patrick, fifth Lord Elibank. Edinburgh, 1753.
4250.	EVELYN, John. Sylva, or a Discourse of Forest-Trees, and the Propagation of Timber. London, 1664. 83 p.
4251.	———. Navigation and commerce, their original and progress. London, 1674. 136 p.
4252.	EVERETT, George. The Path-way to Peace and Profit. London, 1694. 23 p.
4253.	———. Encouragement for Seamen & Mariners. London, 1695. Two Parts. 24 p.

Preclassical Period

4254. The EVIDENT advantages to Great Britain and its Allies from the Approaching War. London, 1727. 44 p.
4255. An EXACT survey of the Affaires of the United Netherlands . . . London, 1665. 208 p.
4256. EXAMEN de la reponse au Memoire de M. l'Abbé Morellet. Par le Même. Paris, 1769.
4257. EXAMINATION of Dr. Franklin at the Bar of the House of Commons. London, 1766.
4258. An EXAMINATION and Explanation of the South-Sea Company's Scheme for taking in the Publick Debts . . . 3d ed. London, 1720. pp. 38.
4259. EXON, John. The Maritime Dicaeology; or Sea Jurisdiction of England. London, 1664. 1 v.
4260. FAIGUET. L'ami des pauvres, ou l'Economie politique. Paris, 1766.
4261. ———. L'Ami des pauvres; Mémoire politique sul la conduite des finances. Amsterdam, 1770. 1 v.
4262. A FAMILIAR Discourse or Dialogue concerning the Mine-Adventure. London, 1700. 160 p.
4263. FARTHER considerations upon a Reduction of the Land-Tax . . . London, 1751. 95 p.
4264. A FARTHER Examination and Explanation of the South-Sea Company's Scheme . . . London, 1720. 39 p.
4265. FAUQUIER, Francis. An essay on ways and means for raising money for the support of the present war, without increasing the public debts. London, 1756. 35 p.
(3d ed. London, 1757. Edited with Introduction by Jacob H. Hollander. Baltimore, 1915. 40 p.)
4266. FENTON, Roger. A Treatise of usurie . . . London, 1611. 155 p.
4267. FERGUSON, Adam. An essay on the history of civil society. Edinburgh, 1767. (French edition: Paris, 1783. 2 v. 1796.)
4268. ———. Principles of moral and political science. Edinburgh, 1792.
4269. FIELDING, Henry. An enquiry into the causes of the late increase fo robbers with some proposals . . . 2d. ed. London, 1751. 203 p.
4270. ———. A proposal for making an effectual provision for the poor, for amending their morals, and for rendering them useful members of society. London, 1753. 91 p.
4271. FILMER, Robert. A discourse whether it may be lawful to take use for money . . . London, 1678. 119 p.
4272. FIRMIN, Thomas. Some proposals for the imploying the poor, especially in and about the City of London; and for the prevention of begging. By Thomas Firmin. London, 1678.
4273. The FISHERIES revived; or, Britain's hidden treasure discovered. London, 1750.
4274. FLEETWOOD, William. Chronicon preciosum: or, an account of English money . . . London, 1707. 181 p.
4275. ———. A Sermon against clipping . . . London, 1694. 29 p.

4276.	FLETCHER, Andrew. Two discourses concerning the affairs of Scotland. Edinburgh, 1698. (Republished Fletcher's works. London, 1737. 1 v.)
4277.	FOERSTER. Versuch einer einleitung in die kameral und polizei-wissenschaft. Halle, 1771.
4278.	———. Entwurf der land-staats und stadtwirthschaft. Berlin, 1793.
4279.	FOLEY, Robert. Laws relating to the poor . . . 3d. ed. 1751. 328 p.
4280.	FOLKES, Martin. Tables of English gold and silver coins, with their weights, intrinsic values &c. London, 1745. 1 v.
4281.	FORBONNAIS, F. Veron de. Analyse des principes sur la circulation des denrées et l'influence du numeraire sur la circulation. Paris, 1800.
4282.	———. Considérations sur les finances d'Espagne, relativement à celles de France. Dresde Paris, 1753. (2d. ed. 1755, 79 p.)
4283.	———. Divers mémoires sur le commerce, etc. Paris, 1756.
4284.	———. Eléments du commerce. Leyde et Paris, 1734. (2d. ed. 1754. 2 v. Nouv. éd. aug mentée. Paris, 1796. 2 v.)
4285.	———. Essai sur l'admission des navires neutres dans nos colonies. Paris, 1759.
4286.	———. Essai sur la partie politique du commerce de terre et de mer, de l'agriculture et des finances. 1751.
4287.	———. Examen des avantages et des désavantages de la prohibition des toiles peintes, Marseille, 1755.
4288.	———. Extrait du livre de l'Esprit des Lois, chapitre par chapitre, avec des observations. 1753.
4289.	———. Lettre à M. F. (Fréron), ou Examen politique des prétendus inconvénients de la faculté de commercer en gros, sans déroger à la noblesse. 1756.
4290.	———. Le Négociant anglais. Dresde Paris, 1753. 2 v. (London, British Merchant, 1913.)
4291.	———. Observations succinctes sur l'émission de deux milliards d'assignats. Paris, 1790.
4292.	———. Principes et observations économiques. Amsterdam, 1707. 2 v.
4293.	———. Prospectus sur les finances, dédié aux bons Francais. 1789.
4294.	———. Question sur le commerce des Francais du Levant. Marseille, Paris, 1755 (1759.)
4295.	———. Recherches et considérations sur les finances de France, depuis 1595 jusqu'a 1721. Basle, 1758. 2 v. (2d. éd. Liége, 1758. 6 v.)
4296.	FOREMAN, Charles. A Letter . . . for re-establishing the Woollen Manufacturies of Great Britain . . . London, 1732. 70 p.
4297.	FORSTER, Nathaniel. An enquiry into the causes of the present high price of provisions. London, 1767. 216 p.
4298.	FORTREY, Samuel. Englands interest and improvement

consisting in the increase of the store and trade of this kingdom. Cambridge, 1663. 43 p. (2d., 1673. 4th ed. London, 1744. 44 p. Reprint: Edited with Introduction by Jacob H. Hollander. Baltimore, 1907. 41 p.)
4299. FRANCKII, J. C. Institutiones Juris Cambialis, Ed. Optima. Jenae, 1751. 1 v.
4300. FRANKLIN, Benjamin. Complete works. Edited by J. Bigelow. New York, 1887-88. (Translated by M. Barbier Dubourg. Paris, 1773.)
4301. ———. Nature and necessity of paper currency. Philadelphia, 1729.
4302. ———. Observations concerning the increase of mankind. Peopling of countries. Boston, 1751. Philadelphia?
4303. ———. The interest of Great Britain considered, with regard to her colonies. London, 1760. 58 p. (2d. ed. 1761.)
4304. ———. La science du bonhomme Richard. -Plusieurs essais qu'on trouve dans ses Oeuvres morales et politiques, notamment sur le luxe, la paresse et le travail; sur l'état de l'Amérique anglaise, ou tableaux des vrais intérets de ce vaste continent; observations sur l'état de l'Ohio; réflexions sur l'augmentation des salaires. Voyez aussi l'interrogatoire qu'il subit devant la chambres des communes en 1776. (Translated from English. Philadelphia, 1777. 151 p.)
4305. A FREE disquisition concerning the law of entails in Scotland, occasioned by some late proposals for amending that law. Edinburgh, 1765.
4306. FRENCH excise: or, a compendious account of the several excises in France. London, 1733. 54 p.
4307. The FRENCH King's declaration for settling the general poll-tax . . . London, 1695. 20 p.
4308. FROUMENTAEU, N. Le secret des finances de France, découvert et départi en trois livres. 1581.
4309. A FULL Answer to the letter from a by-stander, wherein his false calculations, misrepresentations of facts in the time of Charles II, are refuted, &c. By R. H. said to be Thomas Carte, the Jacobite Historian. London, 1742.
4310. A FULL and clear vindication of the 'Full answer to the letter from a by-stander,' &c. London, 1743.
4311. A FULL and exact collection . . . relating to the company of Scotland trading to Africa and the Indies . . . Edinburgh, 1700. 144 p.
4312. GAIRDNER, Andrew. An Historical account of the old people's hospital. Edinburgh, 1728. 56 p.
4313. GALIANI, Fernando. Dialogues sur le commerce des blés. Londres, Paris, 1770; 1790; 1802; 1848.)
4314. ———. Della Moneta, libri cinque. Napoli, 1750. 1 v. (2d. ed. 1780.)
4315. GEE, Joshua. The trade and navigation of Great Britain considered; showing that the surest way for a nation to increase in riches is to prevent the importation of such foreign commodities as may be raised at home . . . Lon-

4316. GELEE, Vincent. Le Guidon generale des Finances . . . Paris, 1743. 872 p.
4317. A GENERAL Treatise of Monies and Exchanges . . . London, 1707. 95, 424 p.
4318. GENERAL Treatise of Naval Trade and commerce founded on the laws and statutes of the Realm. Londor 1753. 2 v.
4319. GENOVESI, Antonio. Lezioni di Commercio . . . economia civile. Napoli, 1764. (2d. ed. Napoli, 1768-70. Deutsch, 1766.)
4320. The GENUINE thoughts of a Merchant . . . London, 1732-3. 32 p.
4321. GLOVER, Richard. The Substance of the Evidence . . . in the Trade to Germany and Holland . . . London, 1774. 72 p.
4322. GODFREY, Michael. A short account of the intended Bank of England. London, 1694.
4323. GORDON, William. The Universal accountant and complete merchant. 3d. ed. Edinburgh, 1774. 2 v.
4324. GOULD, Sir Nathaniel. An essay on the public debts of this kingdom, wherein the importance of discharging them is considered; the provisions for that purpose by the sinking fund, and the progress therein hitherto made, are stated and explained, &c. London, 1726.
4325. GRASLIN, L. F. F. Essai anlytique sur la richesse et sur l'impot. Londres, 1767. 1 v.
4326. GRAUNT, John. Natural and political observations upon the bills of mortality. By Captain John Graunt, F.R.S. Chiefly with reference to the Government, Religion, Trade, Growth, Air, Diseases, &c., of the City of London. London, 1662. (5th ed. London, 1676.)
4327. GRAY'S Proposal fully to prevent the smuggling of wool. 4th ed. London, 1740. pp. 32.
4328. The GRAZIERS Advocate: or, free thoughts of wool. London, 1742. pp. 31.
4329. GREAT BRITAIN arraigned as of Felo de se, and found guilty. London, 1721. pp. 44.
4330. GREAT BRITAIN'S poverty and distress, exemplified by the East-India monopoly . . . London, 1755. 16 p.
4331. GREAVES, John. A discourse on the Roman foot and denarius, from whence, as from two principles, the measures and weights used by the ancients may be deduced. Oxford, 1647 (Reprinted in the 1st vol. of the collection of Greaves' Miscellaneous Works. London, 1737. 2 vols.)
4332. GRENVILLE, E. W. Knox. Mémoire sur l'administration des finances de l'Angleterre, depuis la paix; ouvrage attribué a M. Grenville, ministre d'Etat, chargé de ce département dans les années 1763, 1764 et 1765. Mayence, 1778.
4333. GRENVILLE, George. The Present state of the nation: particularly with respect to its trade, finances . . . London, 1769. 8 v.

Preclassical Period 289

4334. GRIMAUDET, François. Des monnaies, augment et diminution d'icelles. Paris, 1586.
4335. GROANS of the plantation; or a true account of their grievous and extreme sufferings, by the many impositions on sugar. London, 1689.
4336. GROTII, Mare Liberum. Lugd. Batavorum, 1633. 1 vol. (2 ed. trans: 267 and 308.)
4337. GUA DE MALVES, Abbé de. Discours pour et contre la réduction de l'intérêt naturel de l'argent; traduit de l'anglais. Wesel, 1757. 1 v.
4338. Le GUIDON de la Mer. 1647. (Includes Cleirac's Us et coutumes de la mer.) 1647.
4339. HAINES, Richard. The prevention of poverty: or, a discourse of the causes of the decay of trade, fall of lands, and want of money throughout the nation, with certain expedients for remedying the same, and bringing this kingdom to an eminent degree of riches and prosperity . . . London, N. Brooke, 1674.
4340. _____. A method of government for such publick working alms-houses. London, 1679. pp. 8. As the best known expedient for restoring and advancing the woolen manufacture.
4341. HAKLUYT, R. The Principal Navigations, Voyages, Traffiques and Discoveries of the English Nation. London, 1598-1600. 3 v. (New ed. Edinburgh, C. Goldsmid. 1884.)
4342. HALE, Matthew. De successionibus apud anglos: the law of Hereditary descents; showing the Rise, Progress, and successive Alterations thereof. By Sir Matthew Hale. London, 1700. 1 v.
4343. _____. A discourse touching provision for the poor. London, 1683.
4344. _____. The primitive origination of mankind considered and explained. London, 1677.
4345. HALES, John. A Compendious or briefe examination of certayne ordinary complaints of divers of our countrymen in these our days which, although they are in some part unjust and frivolous, yet they are all by way of dialogues thoroughly debated and discussed. By W. S. Gentleman. London, 1581 (also 1587) pp. iv, 55. Edited by Elizabeth Lamond. Cambridge, 1893.
4346. HALL, F. Importance of British Plantations in America to this Kingdom. London, 1731.
4347. HAMILTON, Alexander. A new account of the East Indies. Edinburgh, 1727. 2 v.
4348. HANWAY, Jonas. Letters on the importance of the rising generation of the labouring part of our fellow-subjects. London, 1767. 2 v.
4349. HARRIS, Joseph. An essay upon money and coins. 2 parts. London, 1757-58. 1 v.
4350. HARTE, Walter. Essays on husbandry. By the Rev. 2d. ed. London, 1770. 1 v.
4351. HAWKINS, John. Observations on the state of the highways,

and on the laws for amending and keeping them in repair. London, 1763.

4352. HAYES, Richard. A New Method for valuing of Annuities upon lives. London. 1727. pp. viii, 128. (2nd edition, 1746.)

4353. HAYNES, John. Great Britain's Glory: or, an Account of the great numbers of poor. London, 1715. 95 p.

4354. ———. Provision for the poor; or a view of the decayed state of the woollen manufacture, with remarks on the causes and evil consequences thereof, and a scheme of proper remedies, &c. By John Haynes. 2d ed. London, 1715.

4355. HEGUERTY, A. P. Essai sur les interets du commerce maritime. Le Hay, 1754.

4356. HERBERT, Cl. Jaco. Essai sur la police générale des grains. Londres, 1754; Berlin, 1755.

4357. ———. Observations sur la liberté du commerce des grains. Paris, 1759.

4358. HEWITT, John. A treatise upon money, coins, and exchanges, in regard both to theory and practice. London, 1740. 1 v. (1755).

4359. HIS Majesties gracious patent to the Goldsmiths, for payment and satisfaction of their debt . . . London, 1677. 19 p.

4360. HIS Majesty's royal charter for the Society of the free British Fishery . . . London, 1750. 36 p.

4361. HISTOIRE du Commerce et de la Navigation des Egyptiens, sous le Regne des Ptolemees; Ouvrage qui a remporté le prix ce l'Academie des incriptions et belles lettres. Paris, 1766. 1 v.

4362. HISTORIE du Système des Finances sous la Minorité de Louis XV., pendant les Années 1719 et 1720. (Paris), 1739. 6 v.

4363. An HISTORICAL account of the establishment, progress and state of the Bank of Scotland; and of the several attempts and inconveniences which the company has encountered. Edinburgh, 1728. 54 p.

4364. The HISTORY of Inland Navigations, particularly those of the Duke of Bridgewater, showing their utility and importance. London, 1766.

4365. The HISTORY of our national debts and taxes, from the year 1688 to the present time. Part I. London, 1751. 87 p. Part II, 1751. 165 p. 2d ed. 1753. 1 v. in four parts. Reprinted as: History of our customs, aids . . . 1761. 1 v. in four parts.)

4366. HOBBES, Thomas. Leviathan, or the matter, forme, & power of a Common-Wealth: London, 1651. 396 p. With an introduction by Henry Morley. London, 1887. 320 p. Reprint.)

4367. HODGES, William. The groans of the poor . . . for the spoiling of our money . . . London, 1696. 35 p.

4368. ———. Ruin to Ruin, after misery to misery . . . London, 1699. 43 p.

4369. HOLLAND, John. A short Discourse . . . with respect to

the Indian and African Company . . . Edinburgh, 1696. 22 p.
4370. _____. The ruine of the bank of England. 1715. 13 p.
4371. HOME, Henry. Essays on several subjects concerning British antiquities. 3d. ed., with additions. Edinburgh, 1763. 1 v.
4372. HOMER, Henry. An essay on the nature and method of ascertaining the specific shares of proprietors upon the inclosure of common fields, with an inquiry into the means of preserving and improving the public roads of this Kingdom. London, 1767.
4373. An HONEST scheme for improving the trade and credit of the nation. 1727. (2d. ed. London, 1729, 72 p.)
4374. HOOKE, Andrew. An essay on the national debt and national capital; or, the account truly stated, debtor and creditor . . . London, 1750. 59 p. (2d. ed. London, 1751)
4375. HOUGHTON, John. Husbandy and Trade Improved; being a Collection of many valuable materials relating to corn, cattle, coal, hops, wool . . . 2d. ed. London, 1728. 4 v.
4376. _____. Husbandry and Trade improv'd. 2d. ed. London, 1728. 4 v.
4377. HOUGHTON, Thomas. Proposals for a fund of a hundred and fifty thousand pounds. London, 1694. 10 p.
4378. HUET, P. D. Histoire du commerce et de la navigation des anciens. Paris, 1716. (Lyon, 1763. London, 1717.)
4378a. _____. A view of the Dutch Trade in all the states. 2d. ed. London, 1722. 232 p.
4379. HUME, David. An enquiry concerning the principles of morals. London, 1751. 253 p.
4380. _____. Essais sur le commerce, le luxe, l'argent . . . Paris? 1767.
4381. _____. Essays and treatises on several subjects. New edition. London, 1768. 2 v. (Edinburgh, 1800. 2 v.)
4382. _____. Essays moral and political. Edinburgh, 1741. (3rd edition, London, 1748. 312 p.) Edited by T. H. Green and T. H. Grose. London, 1875. 2 v. entitled: Essays, moral, political, and literary.)
4383. _____. The letters of David Hume. Edited by J. Y. T. Grieg. Oxford, Clarendon press, 1932.
4384. _____. The life. . . . written by D. Hume. London, 1777. 62 p.
4385. _____. Life and correspondence of David Hume. Edited by John H. Burton. Edinburgh, W. Trail, 1846. 2 v.
4386. _____. Philosophical essays concerning human understanding. London? 1748. (2nd edition, London, 1751. 259 p.
4387. _____. Political discourses. Edinburgh, 1752. 304 p.
4388. _____. Writings on economics. Edited and introduced by Eugene Rotwein. Madison, University of Wisconsin press, 1955. 224 p. Bibliographical footnotes.
4389. HUTCHESON, Archibald. An abstract of all the publick

	debts remaining due at Michaelmas, 1722. London, 1723. 27 p.
4390.	———. An abstract of an account of the clerks at the South-Sea House. London, 1723. 15 p.
4391.	———. A collection of treatises relating to the national debts and funds; to which is added a collection of treatises relating to the South Sea stock and scheme. London, 1721. 1 v.
4392.	———. Some computations relating to the fund of the South Sea company. London, 1720. 11 p.
4393.	———. The two last treatises published by Mr. Hutcheson. London, 1723. 33 p.
4394.	HUTCHESON, Francis. Philosophiae moralis institutio compendaria. Rotterdam, 1745.
4395.	———. System of moral philosophy. Glasgow, 1755. 2 v.
4396.	An IMPARTIAL vindication of the English East-India-Company . . . London, 1688. 347 p.
4397.	The IMPORTANCE of effectually supporting the Royal African Co. of England. 1744. (London, 1745. 47 p.)
4398.	IMPORTANT considerations upon the act . . . relative to the assize of bread. London, 1767. 56 p.
4399.	An INQUIRY into the late mercantile distresses, in Scotland and England. London, 1772. 196 p.
4400.	An INQUIRY into the state of the ancient measures, the Attic, the Roman, and especially the Jewish, with an appendix concerning our old English money and measures of content. By Dr. Hooper, Bishop of Bath and Wells. London, 1721. 1 v.
4401.	INTEREST of money mistaken, or a treatise proving that the abatement of interest is the effect and not the cause of the riches of a nation, &c. London, 1668. 24 p.
4402.	Les INTERETS des nations de l'Europe developes relativement au commerce. A Leide, 1766. 2 v.
4403.	INTRODUZIONE alla pratica del commercio. Livorno, 1759
4404.	JACOBS, G. Lex Mercatoria; or the merchant's companion. London, 1718. 1 v.
4405.	JANSSEN, Theodore. General maxims in trade between Great Britain and France. London, 1713. 23 p.
4406.	JENKINSON, Charles. A discourse on the conduct of the government of Great Britain in respect to neutral nations. London, 1758 and 1794.
4407.	JENYNS, Soame. Thoughts on the causes and consequences of the present high price of provisions. London, 1767.
4408.	JONCHERE de la. Systeme d'un nouveau gouvernement en France. Amsterdam, 1720.
4409.	JOSEPH, Don. Tratado juridico-politico sobre pressas de mar, y calidades que deben concurrir para hacerse legitimamente el corso. Cadiz, 1746. 1 v. (Paris, 1758. 2 v.)
4410.	JUSTI, Johann Heinrich G. von. Staatswirthschaft oder systematische abhandlung. Leipzig, 1755.
4411.	KING, Charles. The British merchant; or, commerce

preserv'd. London, 1713. (1721. 3 v.)
4412. KLOCK, Gaspari. Tractatus oeconomicó-politicus de contributionibus. Nuremberg. 1640.
4413. KURICKE, Rein. Diatribe de Assecurationibus. Hamburgi, 1667. 1 v.
4414. ———. Jus maritimum Hanseaticum. Gotting, 1667.
4415. L'ESTRANGE, Roger. A Discourse of the Fishery . . . London, 1674. 10 p. (3rd edition, 1675. Edition, 1695.)
4416. LAFOREST, L'Abbé de. Traité de l'usure et des intérets. Cologne et Paris, 1769. 1 v.
4417. ———. Etat des pauvres, ou histoires des classes travaillantes de la société en Angleterre, depuis la conquete jusqu'à l'époque actuelle, etc.; extrait de l'ouvrage, publié en anglais par Sir Morton Eden, par Larochefoucault-Liancourt. Paris, an VIII. (Londres, 1797. 3 v.)
4418. The LAIRD and Farmer. A Dialogue upon farming, trade, cookery, and their method of living in Scotland, balanc'd with that of England. London, 1740. 118 p.
4419. LAURAGUAIS, Comte de. Mémoire sur la Compagnie des Indes . . . lequel on établit les droits des actionnaires, etc. 1770. 1 v.
4420. LAW, John. Money and trade considered, with a proposal for supplying the nation with money. Edinburgh, 1705. 2d. ed. London, 1720. Glasgow, 1750.
4421. ———. OEuvres . . . Paris, 1790. 432 p.
4422. LAW, William. Remarks upon a late book, entitled, The Fable of the Bees. London, 1724. 106 p.
4423. The LAWS, ordinances, and institutions of the admiralty of Great Britain, civil and military, comprehending, &c. London, 1746. 2 v. (Republished in 1767.)
4424. LEAKE, Stephen Martin. Nummi Britannici historia; or an historical account of English money. London, 1726. 144 p. (2d. edition with great additions and improvements. London, 1745. 3d. edition, London, 1793.)
4425. A LEARNED and necessary argument to prove that each subject hath a propriety in his goods. London, 1641. 66 p.
4426. LEATHER. A discourse, tendered to the High Court of Parliament. Of the general use of leather. London, 1629. 27 p.
4427. LEE, Wyman. An essay to ascertain the value of leases and annuities . . . London, 1738. 470 p.
4428. ———. Prices of things in different ages. London, 1737.
4429. LEIGH, Edward. An Essay upon credit. London, 1715. 32 p. (Edition, 1719.)
4430. LEQUIN de la Neuville. Origine des postes chez les anciens et chez les modernes. Paris, 1708.
4431. LETHINOIS, André. Apologie du système de Colbert, ou observations juridico-politiques sur les jurandes et maitrises d'arts et métiers. Amsterdam, 1771. 1 v.

4432.	A LETTER concerning the consequences of an incorporating union, in Relation to Trade. 1706. 27 p.
4433.	A LETTER . . . concerning the importance of our Sugar-Colonies to Great-Britain . . . London, 1745. 30 p.
4434.	A LETTER . . . concerning the Naval Store-Bill . . . London, 1720. 43 p.
4435.	A LETTER . . . concerning the Parliament's rejecting the French Treaty of Commerce. London, 1713. 28 p.
4436.	A LETTER . . . concerning the South-Sea Company. London, 1720. 15 p.
4437.	A LETTER . . . concerning the Trade and Coin of England London, 1695. 10 p.
4438.	A LETTER . . . concerning the Tyrone Collieries. Dublin, 1752. 23 p.
4439.	A LETTER containing . . . some important hints relating to the Revenue. London, 1765. 39 p.
4440.	A LETTER from a Fyfe gentleman with regard to the Malt-Tax. Edinburgh, 1725. 16 p.
4441.	A LETTER from a merchant upon the affairs and commerce of North America. London 1757. 98 p.
4442.	A LETTER from a merchant who has left off trade. London, 1738. 84 p.
4443.	A LETTER from Sir Richard Cox, Bart. to Thomas Prior, to establish the Linen-Manufacture. Dublin, 1749. 48 p.
4444.	A LETTER of advice to a friend about the currency of clipt-money. J. R. 2nd. edition. London, 1696. 38 p.
4445.	A LETTER on several proposals for the better maintenance of the poor. London, 1752.
4446.	A LETTER . . . on the revival of the salt duty. London, 1732. 30 p.
4447.	A LETTER opposing the farther extension of the excise laws. London, 1733. 28 p.
4448.	A LETTER to the chairman of the East-India Company . . London, 1727. 38 p.
4449.	A LETTER to the merchants of the Portugal committee. London, 1754. 31 p.
4450.	A LETTER to the Rev. Thomas Carte, author of the 'full answer to the letter from a by-stander. By a Gentleman of Cambridge. London, 1743.
4451.	A LETTER to Sir John Barnard, upon his proposals for raising three millions. London, 1746. 24 p.
4452.	A LETTER to Sir Thomas Osborn upon the present interest of England stated. London, 1672. 19 p.
4453.	A LETTER to the West-India merchants. B. M. London, 1751. 27 p.
4454.	A LETTER . . . touching the African trade . . . London, 1709. 31 p.
4455.	A LETTER . . . . towards enjoying the national benefit of any useful branch of manufactures . . . London, 1745. 27 p.
4456.	LETTERS from a farmer in Pennsylvania to the inhabitants of the British colonies. London, 1768. 80 p.
4457.	LETTRES à un ami sur les avantages de la liberté du

	commerce des grains, &c. Amsterdam (Paris), 1768. 1 v.
4458.	LETTRES d'un citoyen à un Magistrat sur les vingtièmes et les autres impots. Par Le Trosne. Amsterdam (Paris), 1768. 1 v.
4459.	LEWIS, Matthew. Proposals to the King and parliament; or a large model of a bank, showing how the fund of a bank may be made without much charge or any hazard, that may give out bills of credit to a vast extent . . . London, 1678.
4460.	La LIBERTE du commerce des grains toujours utile et jamais nuisible. Par M. Le Trosne. Paris, 1765, 1 v.
4461.	LOCKE, John. Further considerations concerning raising the value of money, wherein Mr. Lowndes' arguments for it in his late report are particularly examined. London, 1698. 1 v.
4462.	————. History of navigation. London, 1704. (French edition, Paris, 1722.)
4463.	————. The life of. . . . By H. R. Fox Bourne. London, 1876. 2 v.
4464.	————. Observations upon the growth and culture of vines and olives. London, 1766. 73 p.
4465.	————. Several papers relating to money, interest and trade . . . London, 1696. 112 p.
4466.	————. Some considerations of the consequences of the lowering of interest and raising the value of money, in a letter to a member of Parliament. London, 1691. 1 v.
4467.	LOCKMAN, John. To the long-concealed first promoter of the cambrick and tea-bills . . . London, 1746. 34 p.
4468.	LOCKYER, Charles. An account of the trade in India . . . London, 1711. 340 p.
4469.	LOEN. Entwurf einer staatskunst. Frankfort, 1751.
4470.	LONDON, J. C. Brief observations concerning trade, and the interest of money. 1668.
4471.	LONDON, John. Some considerations on the importance of the woollen manufactures. London, 1740. 28 p.
4472.	LOWNDES, Thomas. Brine-Salt improved. London, 1746. 38 p.
4473.	LOWNDES, William. A report to the Lords of the Treasury, containing an essay for the amendment of the silver coins. London, 1695.
4474.	LUTKEN, F. Oekonomiske Tanker. Kjöbenhaven, 1755-61. 9 vols.
4475.	MABLY, Abbé de. Doutes proposés aux philosophes économistes, sur l'ordre naturel et essentiel des sociétés politiques. La Haye. 1768.
4476.	MACKWORTH, Humphrey. A proposal for payment of the publick debts, for relief of the South-Sea Company. 3d ed. London, 1720. 38 p.
4477.	MACULLA, James. Proposals for a publick coinage of copper half-pence and farthings. Dublin, 1727. 21 p.
4478.	MADDOX, Thomas. The history and antiquities of the exchequer of the Kings of England, from the Norman

Conquest to the end of the reign of Edward II. London, 1711. 1 v. 725 p. (Reprinted 1769. 2 v. with an index.)
4479. ———. Firma Burgi. London, 1726. 297 p.
4480. MAGENS, Nicholas. An essay on insurances, explaining the nature of the various kinds of marine insurance practised by the different commercial states of Europe, and showing their consistency or inconsistency with equity and the public good. London, 1755. 2 v.
4481. MALLORY, John. Objections . . . against passing the Bill. intitled A Bill for the more easy and speedy recovery of small debts, into a law. London, 1730. 61 p.
4482. MALYNES, Gerrard de. Maintenance of free trade. London, 1622.
4483. ———. Consuetudo vel Lex Mercatoria; or the ancient law merchant. London, 1622. 1 v.
4484. ———. A Treatise of the canker of Englands common wealth . . . London, 1601. 125, 11 p.
4485. MANDEVILLE, Bernard. The Fable of the bees: or, private vice publick benefits. London, 1714. 228 p. (2d. ed. 1723. 4th ed. 1725; 6th ed. 1732. 9th ed. Edinburgh, 1772. 2 v. 316, 298 p.; London, 1806. Edited by F. B. Kaye. Oxford, Clarendon press, 1924. 2 v.)
4486. ———. Free thoughts on religion, the church, and national happiness. 1720. 2d. ed. London, 1729. pp. xiv, 409, xxii.
4487. MANLEY, Thomas. Usury at six per cent. examined, and found unjustly charged . . . London, 1669. 69 p.
4488. MARKHAM, Gervase. A way to get wealth 1625. London, 1648-9. 6 parts.
4489. MARRIOT, James. The case of the Dutch ships, considered. 2d. ed. London, 1759. 58 p.
4490. MASSIE, Joseph. Calculations of taxes for a family of each rank, degree, or class, for one year. London, 1756. (2d. edition; title changed, London, 1761.)
4491. ———. An essay on the governing causes of the natural rate of interest. London, 1750. by Jacob H. Hollander. Baltimore, 1912. 57 p.)
4492. ———. Letter to Bourchier Cleeve, concerning his calculations of taxes, from the author of calculations. London, 1757.
4493. ———. Observations on Mr. Fauquier's 'Essay on ways and means for raising,' &c. London, 1756.
4494. ———. Observations relating to the Coin of Great Britain. London, 1760. 40 p.
4495. ———. The proposal, commonly called Sir Matthew Decker's Scheme for one general tax upon houses, laid open . . . London, 1757. 120 p.
4496. ———. A proposal for making a saving to the public of many thousand pounds a year. London, 1758. 74 p.
4497. ———. Reasons humbly offered against laying any further British duties on wrought silks. London, 1758. 14 p.
4498. ———. A representation concerning the knowledge of

Preclassical Period 297

	Commerce as a national concern. London, 1760. 25 p.
4499.	———. A State of the British sugar-colony trade. London, 1759. 40 p.
4500.	———. Ways and means for raising the extraordinary supplies to carry on the war for seven years. Part I. London, 1757. 88 p.
4501.	———. Reasons humbly offered against laying any further British duties on wrought silks. London, 1758. 14 p.
4502.	MAXWELL, Henry. Reasons offer'd for erecting a bank in Ireland. Dublin, 1721. 63 p.
4503.	MELON, Jean François. Essai politique sur le commerce. Rouen ou Bordeaux, 1734. 273 p. (2d. éd. 1736; reprint, Amsterdam, 1735. 251 p. Nouvelle ed. 1726, 1761, 399 p.; translated by D. Bindon. Dublin, 1739. 1 v. 2d. edition Paris, 1754.)
4504.	———. A Political essay upon commerce. Dublin, 1739. 352 p.
4505.	MEMOIRE sur les effets de l'impot indirect, qui a remporté le prix proposé par la société Royale d'Agriculture de Limoges. Par M. Saint Peravy. Paris, 1768. 1 v.
4506.	MEMOIRE sur la situation actuelle de la compagnie des Indes. Par M. l'Abbé Morellet. Paris, 1769. 231 p.
4507.	MEMOIRES sur le commerce des Hollandois. 1717. 283 p. (Nouvelle Ed. Amsterdam, 1718. 215, 103 p.)
4508.	MEMORIES et considerations sur le commerce et les finances d'Espagne. Amsterdam Paris, 1761. 2 v.
4509.	MEMOIRES relating to the State of the Royal Navy of England. London, 1690. 214 p.
4510.	MEMOIRS of the Dutch trade in all the states . . . London, 1700? 232 p.
4511.	The MERCHANT'S complaint against Spain . . . London, 1738. 63 p.
4512.	A METHOD to prevent without a register the running of wool from Ireland to France. London, 1745. 52 p.
4513.	MIGNOT, L'Abbé. Traité des prets du commerce, ou de l'interet légitime et illégitime de l'argent. Amsterdam, 1767. 4 v.
4514.	MILNER, James. Three letters relating to the South-Sea Company and the bank. London, 1720. 37 p.
4515.	MIRABAUD, J. B. de. Systeme de la nature . . . Londres, 1770. 2 v. 366, 408 p.
4516.	A MISCELLANY containing several tracts on various subjects. By the Bishop of Cloyne (Dr. Berkeley). London, 1752. (Includes the "Querist," first published in 1735; reprinted: London, 1829.)
4517.	The MISCHIEF of the five shillings tax upon coal. London, 1698. pp. iv, 27.
4518.	MISSELDEN, Edward. Circle of commerce. London, 1623. 145 p.
4519.	———. Free trade, or the means to make trade flourish. London, 1622. (2d. edition, London, 1822. 135 p.)
4520.	A MODEST proposal for preventing the children of poor people from being a burthen. London, 1730. 25 p.

4521. MOIVRE, Abraham de. Annuities upon lives, or the valuation of annuities upon any number of lives, as also of reversions, &c. By Abraham de Moivre, F. R. S. London, 1725. 1 v. (3d. ed. 1750. 1 v.)
4522. MOLLOY, Charles. De jure maritimo et navili; or a treatise of affairs maritime and of commerce. London, 1682. (7th edition, 1722. 9th edition. London, 1769. 2 v.
4523. MONCADA, Sancho de. Restauracion política de España. Madrid, 1619.
4524. _____. Riqueza firme y establic. de España. Madrid, 1619.
4525. MONGEZ. Considérations sur les monnaies, par Mongez, membre de l'Institut national, suivies d'une notice sur les monnaies françaises, par Dibarrart. Paris, 1 v. (Depuis 1726 jusqu'en 1796.)
4526. MONINO, Don Jose. Respuesta fiscal sobre acopio de trigo para el consumo de Madrid, 1769.
4527. MONTCHRETIEN, Antoyne, Sieur de Vatteville. Traité d'économie politique. Rouen, 1614. Reprint: Edited by Th. Funck-Brentano, Paris 1889. 398 p.)
4528. MONTESQUIEU, Charles Louis, Baron. De l'espirit des lois. Paris, 1648-49. (3rd. edition, London, 1758. 2 v. 7th edition, Edinburgh, 1778. 2 v. Edited by T. Nugent, London, 1878.)
4529. MOORE, Adam. Bread for the poor, and advancement of the English nation promised by enclosure of the wastes and common grounds of England. London, 1653. 28 p.
4530. MOORE, Francis. Considerations on the present exorbitant price of provisions . . . London, 1773.
4531. MORANDIERE, de la. Police sur les mendiants, les vagabonds, etc. Paris, 1764.
4532. MORE, Sir J. Englands interest . . . how land may be improved. 2d. ed. London, 1703. 166 p.
4533. MORE, Sir Thomas. Utopia . . . Translated into English. London, 1684. 206 p.
4534. MOREAU, J. N. Entendons-nous, ou le Radotage du vieux Notaire; sur la richesse de l'état. 1763. pp. 32. (Reprint, 67 p.)
4535. MORELLET, Jacob Nicolas L'Abbé. Analyse de l'ouvrage (de Necker) intitulé: De la législation et du commerce des grains. Amsterdam et Paris, 1775.
4536. _____. Examen de la réponse de M. N. (Necker) à M. Morellet, sur la Compagnie des Indes. Paris, Desaint, 1769.
4537. _____. Prospectus d'un nouveau Dictionnaire de commerce. 1769. 1 v.
4538. _____. Réflexions sur les avantages et les desavantages de la libre fabrication et de l'usage des toiles peintes en France. Bruxelles, 1758.
4539. _____. Réfutation de l'ouvrage (de Galiani) aui a pour titre: Dialogues sur le commerce des blés. Londres (Paris), 1770.
4540. MORRIS, Corbym. An essay towards deciding the question,

whether Britain be permitted by right policy to insure the ships of her enemies? By Corbyn Morris. 2d. ed. London, 1748.

4541. _____. An essay towards illustrating the science of insurance. London, 1747. 61 p.

4542. _____. A Letter balancing the causes of the present scarcity of our silver coin. London, 1757. 20 p.

4543. _____. A Letter from a by-stander; to a member of Parliament, wherein is examined what necessity there is for the maintenance of a large regular land force in this island; and what proportion the revenues of the crown have borne to those of the people, from the restoration to his present Majesty's accession. London, 1741.

4544. _____. Observations on the past growth and present state of the City of London. London, 1751.

4545. MORTIMER, Thomas. Elements of commerce and finances. London, 1773. 1 v.

4546. _____. A new and complete dictionary of trade and commerce . . . London, 1766. 2 v.

4547. MORUS, Thomas. Description de l'ile d'Utopie. Le titre de ce singulier ouvrage, écrit en latin, est celui-ci: De optimo reipulicae statu, deque nova insula Utopia. Louvain, 1516.

4548. MUN, Thomas. A Discourse of trade from England into the East Indies; answering to diverse objections which are usually made against the same. By Thomas Mun. 2d. impression, London, 1621.

4549. _____. The petition and remonstrance of the Governour and company of merchants of London trading to the East Indies. London, 1641. 34 p.

4550. MURRAY, Alexander. An abstract of an essay on the improvement of husbandry . . . London, 1733. 55 p.

4551. MURRAY, Robert. A proposal for a national bank, consisting of land, or any other valuable securities or depositums, &c. By Robert Murray. London, 1695. 8 p.

4552. The NATIONAL debt as it stood at Michaelmas 1730 . . . London, 1731. 31 p.

4553. The NATIONAL and private advantages of the African trade. London, 1746. 128 p.

4554. NATURAL and political observations and conclusions upon the state and condition of England in 1696. By Gregory King. Lancaster Herald.

4555. The NATURE of the charitable corporation, and its relation to trade, consider'd . . . London, 1732. 16 p.

4556. The NATURE of the present excise . . . London, 1733. 60 p.

4557. NAVEAU, J. B. Le financier citoyen. Paris, 1757. 2 v.

4558. NECKER, Jacques. Sur la législation et le commerce des Grains. 2d. edition. Paris, 1775. 2 v.

4559. _____. Compte rendu au Roi. Paris, 1781. 116 p. (Revised and updated as: Sur le compte rendu au Roi en 1781. Nouveau éclaircissemens. Paris, 1788. 1 v.)

4560. _____. Collection complete de tous les ouvrages . . . Utrecht, 1781. 3 v.
4561. _____. De l'administration des finances de la France. Paris, Panckouke, 1784. 3 v.
4562. _____. Sur la législation et le commerce des grains, 2d. éd. Paris, 1755.
4563. _____. Sur l'administration de Necker par lui-meme. Paris, 1791.
4564. NERI, Pompeo. Osservazioni sopra il prezzo legale delle monete. Fiorentino. 1751. 1 v.
4565. NEWTON, Isaac. Report on state of the coinage. London, 1717.
4566. The NORFOLK scheme; or a letter to William Pulteney. London, 1733. 48 p.
4567. NORTH, Dudley. Discourses upon trade; principally directed to the cases of the interest, coynage, clipping, and increase of money. London, 1691. 23 p. (Edinburgh, 1822, 1846. Edited by Jacob Hollander, Baltimore, 1907. 37 p. For an article regarding the treatise see: W. Letwin, "The authorship of Sir Dudley North's Discourses on trade." In, Economica, new series, 18 (1951) 35-36.)
4568. _____. Observations and advices oeconomical. London, 1669.
4569. NORTH, Roger. The life of the Hon. Sir Dudley North . . . London, 1744. 288 p.
4570. _____. The autobiography of the Hon. Roger North. Edited by Augustus Jessopp. London, 1887. 289 p.
4571. OBSERVATIONS on the case of the Northern Colonies. London, 1731. 31 p.
4572. CBSERVATIONS on the conduct of Great-Britain with regard to the negociations abroad. London, 1729. 61 p.
4573. OBSERVATIONS concerning the increase of mankind, peopling of countries, &c. By Benjamin Franklin. Philadelphia, 1751; and since frequently reprinted.
4574. The OBSERVATIONS on the Treaty of Seville examined. London, 1730. 34 p.
4575. ONELY, Richard. An account of the care taken in most civilised nations for the relief of the poor, more particularly in times of scarcity and distress. London, 1758.
4576. The ORIGINAL papers and letters, relating to the Scots Company, trading to Africa and the Indies. 1700. 56 p.
4577. ORIGINE des postes chez les anciens et chez les modernes. Par M. de Neuville. Paris, 1708. 1 v.
4578. ORIGINES gentium antiquissimae; or attempts for discovering the times of the first planting of nations. By Dr. Cumberland, Bishop of Peterborough. London, 1724. 1 v.
4579. PAPILLON, A.F.W. Memoirs of Thomas Papillon, of London, merchant, 1623-1702. Reading, 1887.
4580. PAPILLON, Thomas. A treatise concerning the East-India trade . . . London, 1696. 27 p.
4581. PARIS du Verney, Jos. Examen des réflexions politiques sur le commerce et les finances de M. Dutot. Paris, 1740. 2 v.

4582. ———. Traité des monnaies. Paris, 1724.
4583. PARKER, Henry. Of a free trade. A discourse seriously recommending to the wonderfull benefits of trade. London, 1648. 34 p.
4584. The PARTICULARS of the enquiry into Mr. Benjamin Wooley's conduct . . . London, 1735. 32 p.
4585. PASCOLI, L. Testamento politico d'un Accademico fiorentino. Colonia (Perugia), 1733.
4586. PATERSON, William. Conferences on the public debts by the Wednesday club in Friday street. London, 1695.
4587. ———. Proposals & reasons for constituting a Council of Trade in Scotland. Edinburgh, 1701. 199 p. (Glasgow, 1751. 282 p.)
4588. PECQUET, M. Lois forestières de France. Paris, 1753. 2. v.
4589. PERRIN, William. The present state of the British and French sugar colonies . . . London, 1740. 63 p.
4590. PETIT, Emilien. Droit public ou gouvernement des Colonies francoises. Edited by Arthur Girault. Paris, 1911. 2 v. (1st edition, 1771.)
4591. The PETITION and remonstrance of the Governor and Company of merchants of London, trading to the East Indies. London, 1628. 37 p.
4592. PETTY, William. A discourse of taxes and contributions. London, 1689. 72 p.
4593. ———. An essay concerning the multiplication of mankind. 2d. ed. London, 1686. 50 p.
4594. ———. Political arithmetick, or a discourse concerning the extent and value of lands. London, 1690. 117 p. (1691. 117 p. Glasgow, 1751.)
4595. ———. Political survey (or anatomy) of Ireland, with the establishment of that kingdom when the Duke of Ormond was Lord Lieutenant . . . London, 1691. 1 v. (2d. ed. with additions, London, 1719.)
4596. ———. Quantulumcunque concerning money. Addressed to the Marquis of Halifax, London, 1682.
4597. ———. Tracts, chiefly relating to Ireland. Dublin, 1749.
4598. ———. A Treatise of taxes and contributions; showing the nature and measures of Crown lands, assessments, customs, poll-money, lotteries, benevolence, &c. By Sir William Petty. London, 1662. 78 p. (1679; 3rd. edition, 1685.)
4599. ———. Two essays on political arithmetick concerning the people, housing, hospitals, etc. of London and Paris. London, 1687. pp. iv, 24 p.
4600. PFEIFFER, Von. Lehrbegriff saemtlicher oeconomischer und kameralwissenschaften. Mannheim, 1754-1778. 4 v.
4600a. ———. Grundriss der staatswirthschaft. Francfort, 1782.
4601. PHILIPS, Erasmus. The State of the nation, in respect to her commerce, debts, and money. 1725. 2d. ed. with additions. London, 1726.

4602. PHILIPS, John? A survey of the National debts, the sinking fund, the civil list . . . London, 1745. 67 p.
4603. PHILLIPPI, L. A. Der vertheidigte Kornjude. Berlin, 1765.
4604. PIGNORII, Laur. De servis et eorum apud veteres ministeriis, commentarius Patavii. 1656. 1 v. (Amsteloedami, 1674.)
4605. PINTO, Isaac. Traité de la circulation et du crédit. Amsterdam, 1771. 384 p. (London, 1774. Amsterdam, 1787.)
4606. ———. Essai sur le luxe, considéré relativement à la population et à l'économie. Amsterdam, 1764.
4607. PLAT, Hugh. The Jewel House of Art and Nature: containing divers rare and profitable inventions. London, 1653. 232 p.
4608. PLUMARD de danguel. Remarques sur les avantages et les désavantages de la France et de la Grande-Bretagne, par rapport au commerce, etc. Amsterdam. (Paris, Esteieme) 1545. (Trad. de l'anglais du chevelier John Nickolls.)
4609. ———. Le rétablissement des manufactures et du commerce d'Espagne; traduit de l'espagnol. 1753.
4610. A POLITICAL account of the diminutions of the revenues and trade of France. London, 1702. 31 p.
4611. A POLITICAL essay upon commerce. Written in French by M. M. Translated with annotations by David Bindon. Dublin, 1739. 1 v.
4612. POLLEXFEN, John. England and India inconsistent in their manufactures; being an answer to a treatise entitled 'An essay on the East India trade.' By John Pollexfen. London, 1697. 1 v.
4613. ———. A discourse of trade, coyn, and paper credit; and of ways and means to gain, and retain riches. London, 1697. 77 p.
4614. POPULAR prejudices against the convention and treaty with Spain, examin'd. London, 1739. 30 p.
4615. POSTLETHWAYT, Malachy. Considerations on the making of bar iron with pitt, or sea cole fire. London, 1747. pp. 20 p.
4616. ———. Great Britain's commercial interest explained and improved. 2d. ed. London, 1759. 2 v.
4617. ———. History of the public revenue from the revolution to the present time. London, 1758. 1 v.
4618. ———. The universal dictionary of trade and commerce. 1951. 3d. ed. London, 1766. 2 v. 4th edition, 1774.
4619. POTTER, William. The Tradesman's jewel; or, a safe, easie, speedy, and effectual means for the incredible advancement of trade, and multiplication of riches, &c., by making Bills become current instead of money. London, 1659.
4620. POULAIN, Henri. Traité des monnaies. Paris, 1707.
4621. POWNALL, Thomas. The administration of the colonies. 2d. ed. London, 1765. 1 v.
4622. The PRESENT condition of France, in reference to her

	revenues . . . London, 1692. 30 p.
4623.	The PRESENT state of Ireland consider'd . . . London, 1730. 32 p.
4624.	The PRESENT state of the national debt . . . London, 1740. 25 p.
4625.	The PRESENT state of the revenues and forces by sea and land . . . London, 1740. 62 p.
4626.	PREVOST, de Genève. De l'économie des anciens gouvernements, comparée à celle des modernes. Berlin, 1733.
4627.	PRICE, Richard. An appeal to the public on the subject of the national debt. London, 1772. 52 p.
4628.	_____. An essay on the population of England. 2d. ed. London, 1780. pp. vi, 88.
4629.	_____. Observations on reversionary payments, annuities . . . London, 1769. 1 v. (7th ed. London, 1812. 2 v.)
4630.	_____. The state of the public debts and finances. 2d. ed. London, 1783. pp. 36.
4631.	The PRIMITIVE origination of mankind considered and explained. By Sir Matthew Hale. London, 1677.
4632.	PRINCIPES de la Jurisprudence Francaise, concernant les prises qui se font sur mer. La Rochelle, 1763. 2 v.
4633.	PRINCIPES sur la liberté du commerce des grains. Amsterdam (Paris), 1768.
4634.	A PROPOSAL for establishing life annuities in parishes for the benefit of the industrious poor. By Baron Maseres. London, 1772.
4635.	The PROPOSAL for the raising of the silver coin of England. London, 1696. 12 p.
4636.	PROPOSALS for National Banks; whereby the profits on usury. London, 1696. 19 p.
4637.	PROPOSALS for setling the East-India trade . . . London, 1696. 22 p.
4638.	PROPOSALS made by his late highness the Prince of Orange, to their high mightinesses the States General, and to the States of Holland and West Friezeland, for redressing and amending the trade of the Republic. Translated from the Dutch. London, 1751.
4639.	PROPOSALS offered for the sugar planters' redress, and for reviving the British sugar commerce, in a letter from a gentleman of Barbadoes to his friend in London. London, 1733.
4640.	The PROVERB crossed or a new paradox maintained . . . London, 1677. 25 p.
4641.	PUCKLE, James. England's Path to wealth and honour. In a dialogue between an Englishman and a Dutchman. London, 1707. 60 p. (Reprinted 1750. 53 p.)
4642.	The QUESTION concerning literary property, determined by the court of King's bench on the 20th of April, 1769, in the case between, &c., with the opinions of the judges (Justices Willes, Aston, Yates, and Lord Mansfield), and the reasons given by each in support of his opinion. London, 1773.

4643. The RATES of merchandise, that is to say, the subsidy of tonnage . . . London, 1660. 59 p.
4644. RAYNAL, L'Abbé, Fr. Histoire philosophique et politique des établissements et du commerce des Européens dans les deux-Indes. Paris, A. Coste et comp. 1770. (Dans les deux Indes. Paris, A. Coste et Comp., 1820-21. 12 v.)
4645. REASONS against lowering the interest of the redeemable national debt. London, 1737. 30 p.
4646. REASONS against a registry for lands . . . London, 1678. 22 p.
4647. REASONS for a limited exportation of wooll. London, 1677. 24 p.
4648. REASONS for the more speedy lessening the national debt . . . London, 1737. 30 p.
4649. REASONS for a Registry: shewing briefly the great benefits and advantages. London, 1678. 22 p.
4650. The REASONS of the decay of trade and private credit. London, 1707. 38 p.
4651. RECHERCHES sur la Population des généralites d'Auvergne, de Lyon, de Rouen, &c., depuis 1674 jusqu'en 1764. Par M. Messance. Paris, 1766. 1 v.
4652. RECOPILACION de las leyes de los Reynos de las Indias. Madrid, 1756. 4 v.
4653. REEVE, Gabriel. Directions for the improvement of barren and healthy land, in England and Wales. London, 1670. 34 p.
4654. REFLECTIONS on coin in general, on the coins of gold and silver in Great Britain in particular, on those metals as merchandise; and also on paper passing as money. London, 1762. 16 p.
4655. REFLECTIONS on the present high price of provisions; and the complaints and disturbances arising therefrom. London, 1766.
4656. REFLEXIONS sur la nécessité de comprendre l'étude du commerce et des finances. Amsterdam., 1756. 266 p.
4657. REFUTATION des dialogues sur le commerce des Bleds. Paris, 1770. 1 v.
4658. REMARKS on the celebrated calculations of the value of South-Sea stock. London, 1720. 31 p.
4659. REMARKS on the English Woollen manufactury for exportation. London, 1730. 12 p.
4660. REMARKS on a letter to Sir John Barnard . . . London, 1746. 28 p.
4661. REMARKS on the occurences of the years 1720 and 1721, relating to . . . the South-Sea scheme. 1728. 27 p.
4662. REMARKS on a scandalous libel . . . relating to the Bill of Commerce. 2d. and 3rd. ed. London, 1713. 26 p.
4663. REMARKS upon the Bank of England, with regard more especially to our trade . . . London, 1705. pp. iv, 5-51 p. (London, 1707).
4664. REMARKS upon Dr. Price's appeal to the public on the subject of the National Debt, addressed to the author. London, 1772.

Preclassical Period 305

4665. REMARKS upon Mr. Webber's scheme and the Draper's pamphlet . . . London, 1741. 40 p.
4666. The REPLY of a member of parliament to the mayor of his corporation . . . London, 1733.
4667. The REPORT of the commissioners for taking, examining, and stating, the Publick accounts. London, 1711. 36 p.
4668. REPORT by Sir Isaac Newton on the state of the coinage. London, 1717.
4669. The REPORT of the Lords Committees as relates to the accounts of the Right Honourable Edward Earl of Oxford. London, 1704. 31 p.
4670. A REPORT . . . to enquire into the original standards of weights and measures . . . London 1758. 78 p.
4671. RETABLISSEMENT des manufactures et du commerce d'Espagne. Traduit de l Espagnol de Don Bernardo de Ulloa. Par Forbonnais(?) Amsterdam (Paris), 1753. 1 v.
4672. A REVIEW of the universal remedy for all diseases incident to coin . . . London, 1696. 61 p.
4673. REY, Claudius. Observations on Mr. Asgill's brief answer . . . London, 1719. 21 p.
4674. REYNARDSON, Samuel. A state of the English weights and measures of capacity, as well ancient as modern; with some considerations thereon; being an attempt to prove that the present avoidupois weight is the legal and ancient standard for the weights and measures of this kingdom. London, 1750.
4675. REYNEL, Carew. The true English interest; or an account of the chief national improvements . . . London, 1674. 96 p.
4676. RICARD, J. P. Le negoce d'Amsterdam. Amsterdam, 1722. 1 v.
4677. RICARD, Samuel. Traité general du commerce. 2nd edition. 1706. (4th edition, Amsterdam, 1721. Nouvelle edition, Paris, 1723. 574 p. 5th edition, 1732.)
4678. La RICHESSE de l'Angleterre. Vienne, 1771. 1 v.
4679. The RISE and fall of the late projected Excise. London, 1733. 61 p.
4680. ROBERTS, L. The Merchants mappe of commerce, wherein the universal manner and matter of trade is compendiously handled . . . London, 1638. 1 v. (4th ed., 1700).
4681. _____. The Treasure of trafficke, or a discourse of forraigne trade . . . London, 1641. 103 p.
4682. ROBINSON, Henry. Englands safety in trades encrease. London, 1641. 63 p.
4683. _____. Briefe considerations, concerning the advancement of trade and navigation. London, 1649. 10 p.
4684. ROE, Sir Thomas. His speech . . . wherein he sheweth the cause of the decay of coyne and trade . . . 1640. 10 p. (1641, 1695.)
4685. ROLT, Richard. A new dictionary of trade and commerce. London, 1761. 1 v.
4686. ROUBAUD, L'Abbé. Récréations économiques, ou letters de l'auteur des représentations aux magistrats, à M. le

chevalier Zanobi, principal interlocuteur des dialogues sur le commerce des blés. Amsterdam et Paris, 1770.

4687. ROUSSEAU, J. J. Du social contrat. Amsterdam, 1762. (Nouv. éd., Paris, 1889; deutsch. v. Denhardt, Leipz., 1833; Engl. by B. M. Harrington, N. Y., 1893. The social contract and discourses. London, J. M. Dent & sons, ltd., New York, E. P. Dutton & Co., 1913. 287 p. Bibliography, xiii-xliv.

4688. ROWE, Jacob. All sorts of wheel-carriage, improved . . . London, 1734. 38 p.

4689. RYMER, T. Foedora. London, 1704-1717. 13 v.

4690. S. R. An essay upon trade and publick credit. London, 1714, 32 p.

4691. S. T. Reasons . . . for the hindering the home consumption of East-India silks . . . London, 1697. 36 p.

4692. SABATIER. Les annales politiques. Londres, 1757. 2 v.

4693. ———. Le même ouvrage, abrégé. Rotterdam (Paris), 1729.

4694. ———. Mémoire pour diminuer le nombre des procès. Paris, 1725.

4695. ———. Mémoire pour l'établissement d'une taille proportionelle, 1717.

4696. ———. Mémoire sur les pauvres mendiants et sur les moyens de les faire subsister. 1724.

4697. ———. Projet pour rendre la paix perpétuelle en Europe, etc. Utrecht (Paris), 1713-17, 3 v.

4698. ———. Les rêves d'un homme de bien, qui peuvent être réalisés, ou les Vues et pratiques de M. l'abbé de Saint-Pierre. (Recueillies par Alletz). Paris, Duchesne, 1772.

4699. ST. LO, Captain George. England's safety. Proposing a sure method for encouraging navigation. London, 1693.

4700. ST. MAUR, Dupré de. Essai sur les monnoies, ou réflexions sur le rapport entre l'argent et les denrées. Paris, 1746. 1 v.

4701. ———. Recherches sur la Valeur des Monnois, et sur le Prix des Grains, avant et après le Concile de Francfore (1409) Paris, 1762. 1 v.

4702. SAINT-PERAVI, de. Mémoire sur les effets de l'impot indirect sur le revenu des propriétaires de biens-fonds, qui a remporté le prix proposé par la société royale d'agriculture de Limoges, en 1767. Londres 1768.

4703. ———. Principes du commerce oppose au trafic, développés par un homme d'Etat. 1787. 2 v.

4704. SAUMAISE, Claude. Salmasii de usuris liber. Lugduni batavorum, 1638.

4705. ———. De foenore trapezitico. 1640 820 p.

4706. SCARUFFI, Gaspardo. Discorso sopra le monete, et della vera proporzione tra l'oro e l'argento. Reggiano, 1582.

4707. A SCHEME to prevent the running of Irish wools to France . . . Dublin, 1745. 48 p.

4708. The SCHEMES of the South Sea Co. for the reducing of the national debts. 2d. ed. London, 1720. 10 p.

4709. SCRAFTON, Luke. Reflections on the government of Indostan,

Preclassical Period 307

	with a short sketch of the history of Bengal, from 1738 to 1756. London, 1763. (Reprinted in 1770.)
4710.	SEASONABLE observations on the trade to Africa. London, 1748. 15 p.
4711.	A SEASONABLE proposal to the nation concerning a register of estates in this kingdom. London, 1669. pp. 8 p.
4712.	SECKENDORFF, V. L. Der deutsche Fürstenstaat. 1655. (3 Aufl. 1665.)
4713.	A SECOND letter recommending the improvement of the Irish-fishery. Dublin, 1729. 30 p.
4714.	SELDEN, John Mare Clausim, seu de domino maris, libri duo. Londini, 1635. 1 v. (Translated to English, London, 1662, 1668.)
4715.	SERIOUS considerations on the several high duties which the nation in general, as well as trade in particular, labours under, &c., with a proposal for raising the public supplies by one single tax. By a well-wisher to the good people of Great Britain. London, 1743.
4716.	SERRA, Antonio. Breve trattato delle cause che possono far abondare li regni d'oro e d'argento dove non sono miniere. Naples, 1613.
4717.	The SEVERAL reports . . . relating to the late South-Sea directors. London, 1721. 74 p.
4718.	SHORT, Thomas. A comparative history of the increase and decrease of mankind in England and several countries abroad. London, 1767. 1 v.
4719.	_____. New observations, natural, moral, civil, political, and medical, on city, town, and country bills of mortality . . . London, 1750. 1 v.
4720.	A SHORT history of the Charitable corporation. London, 1732. 30 p.
4721.	A SHORT treatise . . . why our money and bullion have been exported . . . 2d. ed. London, 1697. 20 p.
4722.	A SHORT view of the apparent dangers and mischiefs from the bank of England . . . London, 1707. 24 p.
4723.	A SHORT view of the frauds, abuses, and impositions of parrish officers. London, 1744. 48 p.
4724.	SIMON, James. An essay towards an historical account of Irish coins, and of the currency of foreign monies in Ireland; with an appendix. By James Simon. Dublin, 1749. 1 v.
4725.	SIMPSON, Thomas. The doctrine of annuities and reversions, deduced from general and evident principles, with useful tables, showing the values of single and joint lives, &c. by Thomas Simpson. London, 1742. 1 v.
4726.	SMART, John. Tables of interest, discount, annuities . . . London, 1726. 123 p.
4727.	SMITH, Charles. Three tracts on the corn trade and corn laws. 2d. edition, London, 1766.
4728.	SMITH, George. The nature of fermentation explained. London, 1729. 56 p.
4729.	SMITH, Captain John. Chronicon rusticum commerciale; or, memoirs on wool. London, 1747. 2 v. (2d. ed., 1757.)

4730. _____. England's improvement revived: in a treatise of all manner of husbandry & trade . . . London, 1673. 270 p.
4731. SMITH, Simon. The herring-busse trade: expressed in sundry particulars . . . London, 1641. 44 p.
4732. _____. A true narration of the royall fishings of Great Brittaine and Ireland . . . London, 1641, 8 p.
4733. SMUGGLING laid open in all its extensive and destructive branches, with proposals for the effectual remedy of that most iniquitous practice. (Ascribed to Sir S. T. Janssen, London, 1763. 1 v.
4734. SNELLING, Thomas. The doctrine of gold and silver computations, in which is included that of the price of money, the proportion in value between gold and silver, &c. London, 1766.
4735. _____. Miscellaneous views of the coins struck by English princes in France, counterfeit sterlings, &c. London, 1769.
4736. _____. A supplement to Mr. Simon's essay on Irish coins. London, 1770.
4737. _____. A view of the coins at this time current throughout Europe, exhibiting the figures of more than 300 on 25 copperplates, &c. London, 1766. 25 p.
4738. _____. A view of the copper coin and coinage of England, London, 1766. 46 p.
4739. _____. A view of the gold coin and coinage of England from Henry III to the present time. London, 1763. 36 p.
4740. _____. A view of the origin, nature, and use of jettons or counters, &c. London, 1769.
4741. _____. A view of the silver coin and coinage of England from the Norman conquest to the present time, with plates. London, 1762. 55 p.
4742. _____. A view of the silver coin and coinage of Scotland from Alexander I to the Union of the two kingdoms. London, 1774.
4743. SOME considerations about the raising of coin. London, 1696. 52 p.
4744. SOME considerations concerning the public funds, the public revenues, and the annual supplies, occasioned by a late pamphlet, entitled 'An Enquire,' &c. (Said by Mr. Coxe to be written by Sir Robert Walpole from p. 8 to p. 81). London, 1735. (2d. ed. 1735. 110 p.)
4745. SOME considerations offered against the continuance of the Bank of England . . . London, 1698. (London, 1700.)
4746. SOME considerations on publick credit. London, 1733. 21 p.
4747. SOME considerations relating to the payment of the publick debts. London, 1717. 23 p.
4748. SOME considerations upon the state of our publick debts in general. London, 1720. 39 p.
4749. SOME general considerations concerning the alteration and improvement of the public revenues. London, 1733. 29 p.
4750. SOME observations upon the Bank of England. London, 1695. 26 p.

Preclassical Period 309

4751. SOME observations upon a paper, intituled, The list . . . London, 1733. 31 p.
4752. SOME remarks on the bill for taking, examining and stating the publick accounts . . . London, 1702. 28 p.
4753. SOME seasonable animadversions on excises. London, 1733. 26 p.
4754. SOME thoughts concerning the maintenance of the poor. London, 1700. 32 p.
4755. SOME thoughts on the land-tax, general excises . . . London, 1733. 33 p.
4756. SOME thoughts on the woollen manufactures of England . . . London, 1731. 19 p.
4757. SOMERS, John. Collection of scarce and valuable tracts. London, 1748. 4 v. (2d. ed. 1809-15. 13 v.)
4758. The SOUTH-SEA scheme detected . . . in answer to the South-Sea scheme examined . . . London, 1720. 28 p.
4759. A SPEECH made by Sir Robert Cotton before the Lords of His Majesties most Hon. Privy Council touching the alteration of coyn. (From Cottoni Posthuma.) London, 1679.
4760. STAFFORD, William. A compendious or briefe examination of certayne ordinary complaints of divers of our countrymen in these our days; which, although they are in some part unjust and frivolous, yet they are all by way of dialogues thoroughly debated and discussed. By W.S., William Stafford. London, 1587.
4761. STANDISH, Arthur. The commons complaint . . . London, 1611. 34 p.
4762. The STATE of the Island of Jamaica; chiefly in relation to its commerce . . . London, 1726. 79 p.
4763. The STATE of the Nation consider'd, in a letter . . . London, 1746. pp. vi, 58.
4764. The STATE of the nation with a general balance of the publick accounts. London, 1748. 55 p.
4765. A STATE of the national debt, as it stood in the 24th of December, 1716, with the payments made toward its discharge out of the sinking fund, &c., compared with the debt at Michaelmas, 1725. London, 1727. 83 p.
4766. The STATE of the silk and woollen manufacture, considered . . . London, 1713. 23 p.
4767. The STATE of the sugar trade, showing the dangerous consequences that must attend any additional duty on sugar. London, 1747. 17 p.
4768. The STATE of the trade and manufactory of iron in Great Britain considered. London, 1750.
4769. STEVENS, John. The Royal treasury of England, or, an historical account of all taxes . . . London, 1725. 372 p. (London, 1733.)
4770. STEUART, James. An inquiry into the principles of political economy. London, 1767-77. 2 v. pp. 639, 646. (French, 1789, 5 v.; Deutsch 1769-72; Basil, 1796, 5 v.; Traduit de l'anglais par Senovert. Paris, Didot aîné, 1789. 5 v.)

4771.	STOKAUSEN. Dissertatio de conjunctione jurisprudentiae atque oeconomices, politices et scientiae cameralis in specie. Leipzig, 1768.
4772.	STUBBS, Henry. A further justification of the present war against the United Netherlands. London, 1673. 136 p.
4773.	STYPMANNI, J. F. Jus maritimum. Stralsundi, 1661.
4774.	A SUBSIDY granted to the King, of tonnage and poundage . . . together with a book of rates . . . London, 1660. 140 p.
4775.	The SUBSTANCE of the arguments for prohibiting the exportation of woollen manufacture from Ireland. London, 1698. 16 p.
4776.	SWIFT, Jonathan. A defence of English commodities. Dublin, 1720. 28 p.
4777.	———. A letter to the whole people of Ireland. 2d. ed. Dublin, 1724. 22 p.
4778.	———. Scheme to pay the public debt of this nation in six months. London, 1732. 23 p.
4779.	———. Some observations upon a paper relating to Wood half-pence. 3d. ed. Dublin, 1724. 32 p.
4780.	———. The Swearer's-Bank: or, Parliamentary security for establishing a new bank in Ireland. Dublin, 1720. 19 p.
4781.	SYMPSON, Anthony. A short method to prevent the running of wool. London, 1741. 15 p.
4782.	TABLES for renewing and purchasing of the leases of cathedral-churches. 5th. ed. London, 1735. 72 p.
4783.	TAPIA, Carlo. Trattato dell' Abbondanza. Naples, 1608.
4784.	The TAXES not grievous, and therefore not a reason for an unsafe peace. London, 1711. 22 p.
4785.	TAYLOR, Silvanus. Common-good: or, the improvement of commons, forrests, and chases, by inclosure. London, 1652. 60 p.
4786.	TEMPLE, William. Essay on the trade of Ireland. London, 1673.
4787.	———. Miscellanea. First Part. 2nd edition, London. (4th ed. London, 1693. 232 p. (5th ed. 1709).
4788.	———. Observations upon the United Provinces of Netherlands. London, 1672. (5th edition. 1690).
4789.	TEMPLEMAN, D. The secret history of the late directors of the South-Sea company . . . London, 1735. 62 p.
4790.	TEORICA y practica del comercio y marina: Por Don Geronymo Ustariz. Madrid, 1724. 1 v. (3d. ed. 1753.) Translated by John Kippax, London, 1751. 2 v. Translated in French by Forbonnais, Paris, 1753. 1 v.)
4791.	THEORIE du système. (Animal.) By Mr. Bruckner of Norwich. Leide, 1767. 1 v.
4792.	THOUGHTS on our silver coin. London, 1718. 30 p.
4793.	THURMANN. Bibliotheca statistica. 1701.
4794.	TIFAUT de Lanoeu, Jérôme. Réflexions philosophiques sur l'impôt, où l'on discute les principes des économistes, et où l'on indique un plan de perception patriotique, Paris, 1775.

Preclassical Period 311

4795. TORQUEMADA, Don Juan, de. Monarquia Indiana. Madrid, 1723. 3 v.
4796. TOUSSAINT, F. V. Recueil d'actes et piéces concernant le commerce de divers pays de l'Europe. Londres, 1754. 230 p.
4797. The TRADE and navigation of Great Britain considered; showing that the surest way for a nation to increase in riches is to prevent the importation of such foreign commodities as may be raised at home, &c. by Joshua Gee.
4798. The TRADESMAN'S Jewel; or, a safe, easie, speedy, and effectual means for the incredible advancement of trade, and multiplication of riches, &c, by making bills become current instead of money. By W. Potter. London, 1659.
4799. TRAITE de la circulation et du crédit. Par M. Pinto, Amsterdam, 1771. 1 v. (Translated in English by S. Baggs. London, 1774.)
4800. TRAITE et commerce des Nègres. Paris, 1764. 1 v.
4801. TRAITE de la construction des chemins. Par Gautier. Paris, 1728, 1 v. (Reprint, 1751.)
4802. TRAITE Général du domaine de la mer, et corps complet des loix maritimes; comprenant ce qu'il y a de plus intéressant dans les écrits des anciens et des modernes. Par Leclere. Amsterdam, 1757. 1 v.
4803. TRAITE historique des monnoyes de France, avec leurs figures, depuis le commencement de la monarchie jusqu'à présent. Par M. Le Blanc. Paris, 1690. 1 v. (Reprinted, Amsterdam, 1692, with the addition of a dissertation sur quelques monnois de Charlemagne, Louis le Debonnaire. Lothaire et ses Successeurs, frappees dans Rome.)
4804. TRAITE des mesures itineraires anciennes et modernes. Par M. D'Anville. Paris, 1769. 1 v.
4805. A TREATISE of the diseases of tradesmen . . . Translated from the Latin of Bernard Ramazzini. London, 1705. 1 v.
4806. A TREATISE wherein it is demonstrated that the East India trade is the most national of all foreign trades, &c. By Josiah Child. London, 1681.
4807. A TRUE discovery of the projectors of the wine project . . . London, 1641. 28 p.
4808. A TRUE and impartial account of the rise and progress of the South-Sea company. London, 1743. 33 p.
4809. The TRUE interest and political maxims of the Republic of Holland. By John De Witt. Translated from the original dutch, with memoirs of Cornelius and John de Witt; by John Campbell. London, 1746. 1 v. (Real author believed to be M. Delacourt? Originally published in 1667, in Dutch.)
4810. A TRUE state of the South-Sea scheme, as it was first form'd. London, 1722. 56 p. (1732.)
4811. TUCKER, Josiah. A brief essay on the advantages and disadvantages which respectively attend France and Great Britain with regard to trade and some proposals for removing principal disadvantages of Great Britain; in a new method. London, 1749 (3rd. edition, London, 1753.)

4812. _____. Cui Bono? or an inquiry what benefits can arise to the English or Americans, the French, Spaniards, or Dutch, from the greatest victories or successes in the present war, in letters addressed to M. Necker. Gloucester, 1782.
4813. _____. Four tracts on political and commercial subjects. 3d. ed. London, 1776.
4814. The ELEMENTS of commerce, and theory of taxes. Issued from Bristol, 10 July, 1755. 1 v. 174 p.
4815. _____. An humble address and earnest appeal to the landed interest, whether a connection with or separation from the American Colonies would be most for the benefit of these kingdoms. Gloucester, 1775.
4816. _____. A LETTER to a friend concerning naturalizations . . . London, 1753.
4817. _____. A letter to Edmund Burke, Esq. M.P. for Bristol, agent for the Colony of New York . . . London, 1775.
4818. _____. The Manifold causes of the increase of the poor distinctly put forth; together with a set of proposals for removing and preventing some of the principal evils, and for lessening others. London, 1760.
4819. _____. Reflections on the expediency of a law for the naturalization of foreign protestants: in 2 parts, the first being historical remarks on the late naturalization bill, and the 2d. queries occasioned by the same. London, 1751 & 1752.
4820. _____. Reflections on the expediency of opening the trade to Turkey. London, 1753. 22 p.
4821. _____. The respective pleas and arguments of the mother country and of the colonies. Glocester, 1775.
4822. _____. A second letter to a friend concerning naturalizations, &c. by Josiah Tucker. London, 1753.
4823. _____. A Series of answers to certain popular objections against separating from the rebellious Colonies, and discarding them entirely. Being the concluding tract of the Dean of Gloucester on the subject of American affairs. Gloucester, 1776.
4824. TURNER, Thomas? The case of the bankers and their creditors. London, 1674. (2nd printing, London, 1675. 56 p.
4825. TWO reports from the Select Committee of the House of Commons appointed to inquire into the original standards of weights and measures, and the laws relating thereto. London, 1758, 1759.
4826. ULLOA, Bernado de. Restablecimiento de las fábricas y comercio Español. Madrid, 1740. 2 v. (Amsterdam, 1953. Traduit de l'espagnol, par Plumard de Danguel.)
4827. UNGER, F. Von der ordnung der fruchtpreise. Gottingen, 1752.
4828. The UNIVERSAL merchant; containing the rationale of commerce. London, 1753. 131 p.
4829. The USE and abuses of money by two propositions for

Preclassical Period 313

regulating our coin. London, 1671.
4830. UZTARIZ, Geronimo de. The theory and practice of commerce and maritime affairs. London, 1751. 2 v. (French translation by Forbonnais. Paris, 1753, pp. xii, 206.)
4831. VALIN, René Josué. Nouveau commentaire sur l'ordonnance de la Marine du Mois d'Août, 1681. La Rochelle, 1760. 2 v. (again in 1766.)
4832. VANDERLINT, Jacob. Money answers all things: or an essay to make money sufficiently plentiful amongst all ranks of people, and increase our foreign and domestic trade . . . London, 1734. 170 p. (Edited by Jacob Hollander, Baltimore, 1913. 161 p.)
4833. VAUBAN, Marechal de. Projet d'une dixme royale, qui, supprimant la taille, les aydes, et les douanes d'une province a pautre . . . produiroit au roy un revenu certain et suffisant . . . Rouen, 1707. 1 v.
4834. VAUGHAN, Rice. A discourse of coin and coinage. London, 1675. (2nd edition, 1696.)
4835. VERELST, Henry. A view of the rise, progress, and present state of the English government in Bengal. London, 1772.
4836. VERRI, Pietro. Consulta sulla reforma delle monete dello stato di Milano, 1772.
4837. _____. Estratto del progetto di una tariffa della mercanzia, per lo stato di Milano, 1774.
4838. _____. Memorie storiche sulla economia pubblica dello stato di Milano, 1804.
4839. _____. Meditazioni sull' economia politica, con annotazione de Gian-Rinaldo Carli. Livorno, 1771. (Deutch, 1774.)
4840. _____. Sulle leggi vinvolanti principalmente nel commercio de'grani, riflessioni, scritte l'anno 1769, con applicazione allo stato di Milano, 17--.
4841. VICO, J. B. Principi di una nuova scienza intorno alla natura delle nazione. Napoli, 1725. (Torino, 1852. Paris, 1827.)
4842. A VIEW of the manner in which trade and civil liberty affect each other. London, 1756.
4843. A VINDICATION of the Bank of England from the misrepresentations . . . London, 1707. 96 p.
4844. A VINDICATION of commerce and arts; proving that they are the source of the greatness, power, riches, and populousness of a state, By J. B. London, 1758.
4845. A VINDICATION of some assertions relating to coin and trade. London, 1699. 180 p.
4846. VIOLET, Thomas. An humble declaration touching the transportation of gold and silver. London, 1643. 39 p.
4847. _____. Proposals humbly presented to his Highness Oliver Lord Protector of England. London, 1656. 112 p.
4848. VIVANT de MEZAGUE. Bilan général et raisonné de l'angleterre depuis 1600 jusqu'a la fin de 1761, ou lettre à M. L. C. D. sur le produit des terres et du commerce de l'angleterre. 1762. 1 v.

4849. VOYAGE de Francois Bernier, docteur en médecine, contenant la description des etats du Grand Mogol; où il est traité de la force, de la justice, et des causes principales de la décadence des etats de l'Asie, et de plusieur événemens considérables; et où l'on voit comment l'or et l'argent, après avoir circulé dans le monde, passent dans l'Indostan, d'où ils ne reviennent plus. Amsterdam, 1679. 2 v. (1723, 1725.)

4850. WALLACE, Robert. A dissertation on the numbers of mankind in ancient and modern times. Edinburgh, 1753. 331 p. (French edition: Dissertation historique et politique sur la population des anciens temps, comparée à ce du nôtre, dans laquelle on prouve qu'elle a été plus grand autrefois que de nos jours; traduit par M.E., 1769. 1 v.)

4851. WALLER, Edmund. A free and impartial inquiry of the present administration in domestic affairs. London, 1743. 63 p.

4852. WALLER, William. An essay on the value of the mines. London, 1698. 55 p.

4853. WARD, D. Bernardo. Proyecto economico, en que se proponen varias providentias dirigidas à promover les intereses de Espana. Madrid, 1739.

4854. The WEALTH of Great Britain in the ocean; including an historical and critical state of the British fisheries. London, 1749. 71 p.

4855. WEBBER, Samuel. An account of a scheme for preventing the exportation of our wool. London, 1740. 37 p. (1741.)

4856. ———. A short account of the state of our woollen manufacturies. 2d. ed. London, 1741. 26. (1737).

4857. WEDDERKOPII. Introduction in jus nauticum. Flensburgi, 1757. 1 v.

4858. WHISTON, James. England's calamities discovered ... London, 1696. 40 p.

4859. Whitworth, Charles. Public accounts of services and grants from 1721 to 1771.

4860. WILKINSON, William. Systema Africanum: or a treatise, discovering the intrigues of the Guiney Company. London, 1690. 26 p.

4861. WILSON, Thomas. A discourse upon usurie, by waie of dialogue and oracions. London, 1584. 204 p.

4862. WIMPEY, Joseph. The challenge, or patriotism put to the test, in a letter to the Rev. Dr. Price, occasioned by his late publications on the national debt. London, 1772.

4863. WITH, Jean de. Ses mémoires. La Haye, 1709.

4864. WOOD, William. A survey of trade, in 4 parts; with considerations on money and buillion. London, 1718. 1 v. (2d. ed. 1719.)

4865. WOODWARD, Richard. An address to the public on the expediency of a regular plan for the maintenance and government of the poor, &c. To which is added, an argument in support of the right of the poor of Ireland to a national provision. By Richard Woodward, Dublin, 1775.

4866. WORLIDGE, John. Systema agriculturae; the mystery of

	husbandry discovered. 2nd. ed. London, 1675. (3d. edition London, 1681. 324 p. 4th edition, 1687.)
4867.	YARRINGTON, Andrew. England's improvement by sea and land; to out-do the Dutch without fighting, to pay debts without money . . . London, 1677. (Part II, 1681.)
4868.	YELVERTON, Henry. The rights of the people of England concerning impositions. London, 1679. 117 p.
4869.	YOUNG, Arthur. Annals of agriculture. London, 1784-1815.
4870.	_____. Arithmétique politique, adressée aux sociétés économiques étables en Europe. Traduit de l'anglais par M. Fréville. La Haye, 1775. 2 v.
4871.	_____. The autobiography of . . . Edited M. Betham-Edwards. London, 1898. pp. x, 480.
4872.	_____. The expediency of a free exportation of corn, with some observations on the bounty. By Arthur Young. London, 1772.
4873.	_____. The farmer's letters to the people of England, containing the sentiments of a practical husbandman on various subjects of great importance . . . 3d. ed. London, 1771. 2 v.
4874.	_____. The farmer's tour through the East of England . . . By the author of the 'Farmer's letters,' &c. London, 1771. 4 v.
4875.	_____. Political arithmetic, containing observations on the present state of Great Britain, and the principles of her policy in the encouragement of agriculture. London, 1774. 1 v.
4876.	_____. Political arithmetic. Part II. Containing observations on the means of raising the supplies within the year. London, 1779.
4877.	_____. Proposals to the legislature for numbering the people. By Arthur Young. London, 1771.
4878.	_____. A six months' tour through the North of England, containing an account of the present state of agriculture, manufactures, and population in several counties of this kingdom. 2d. ed. London, 1771. 4 v.
4879.	_____. A six weeks' tour through the southern counties of England and Wales. By the author of the "Farmer's Letters." 2d. ed. London, 1769. 1 v.
4880.	_____. Tour in Ireland, 1776-79. London, 1780. 384 p. (With int. and notes by A. W. Hutton. London, 1892.)
4881.	_____. Tours of the English counties. Southern. London, 1769. 1 v. Northern: 2d. ed. 1770-71. 4 v.; Eastern: 1771. 4 v.)
4882.	_____. Travels in France during the years 1787, 88, 89. Bury St. Edmunds, 1792-94. 2 v. 566 p. (2d. ed. London, 1794. 2 v. New abrid. ed., with int. and biog. sketch, by M. B. Edwards, London, 1884; Trad. Par M. Lesage. Paris, 1860. 2 v.; 2d. ed., 1882.)
4883.	_____. Travels in Italy and Spain, 1787 and 89. London, 1794. (Trad. par M. Lesage, Paris, 1860.)

H. PRE-CLASSICAL PERIOD

Section II. Specific Works

1. PRIMITIVE, ANCIENT, AND MEDIEVAL PERIODS

4884. ANDREADES, A. M. A history of Greek public finance. Cambridge, Massachusetts, Harvard university press, 1933.
4885. AQUINAS, Thomas. Summa theologica. English translation by Dominican fathers. London, 1911-1925. 20 v.
4886. ———. Summa theologia. Editio altera romana, ad emendatores editioned impressa et noviter accuratissme recognita. Rome, Forzani, 1922-23. 6 v.
4887. ARENDT, Hannah. The human condition. Chicago, University of Chicago press, 1958.
4888. ARISTOTELES. O tratado do econômico, atribuído a Aristóteles. Lisboa, 1945. 47 p.
4889. ASHLEY, W. J. Introduction to English economic history and theory. London, 1888, 1893. (4th edition, London, Longmans, Green & C., ltd, 1906-9.)
4890. BAILEY, Cyril. The Greek atomists and epicurus. London, Oxford University press, 1928.
4891. BALDWIN, J. W. The medieval theories of the just price. Romanists, canonists, and theologians in the twelfth and thirteenth centuries. Philadelphia, American philosophical society, 1959. 94 p. (Transactions, APS, new series, 49, 4, 1959.)
4892. BARKER, Ernest. Greek political theory. London, Methuen & company, 1918.
4893. ———. Politica. The politics of Aristotle. Oxford, Clarendon press, 1961. 411 p.
4894. ———. The political thought of Plato and Aristotle. New York, G. P. Putnam, 1906.
4895. ———. Social and political thought in Byzantium. London, Oxford university press, 1957.
4896. BARON, Salo W., editor. Essays on Maimonides. New York, Columbia university press, 1941.
4897. BEER, Max. Social struggles in antiquity. New York, international publishers, 1929.
4898. BESSAIGNET, Pierre. Principes de l'ethnologie économique. Paris, Librairie générale de droit et de jurisprudence, 1966. 191 p.
4899. BLOCH, Marc. Esquisse d'une histoire monétaire de l'Europe. Paris, Librairie Armand Colin, 1954.
4900. BOECKH, August. The public economy of Athens. Translated from the second German edition by A. Lamb.

Boston, Little, Brown and company, 1857.
4901. BOHATEC, Josef. Die cartesianische Scholastik in der philosophie und reformierten dogmatik des 17. jahrhunderts. T. 1. Hildesheim, G. Olms, 1966. 158 p.
4902. BOLKESTEIN, Hendrick. Economic life in Greece's golden age. New edition, revised and annotated by E. J. Jonkers. Leiden, E. J. Brill, 1958. viii, 168 p. Bibliography.
4903. BOUCHAUD, M. De l'impôt du vingtième sur les successions, et de l'impôt sur les marchandises chez les Romains. Paris, 1766.
4904. BOUSQUET, G. H., editor. Iban Khaldoun. Les textes sociologiques et économiques de la Mouqaddima, 1375-1379. Paris, Marcel Rivière et Cie, 1965.
4905. BRANTS, Victor Leopold Jacques Louis. L'economie politique au moyen-age; esquisse des théories économiques professées par les écrivains des XIIIe et XIVe siècles. Louvain, C. Peeters, 1895. vi p., 1 l., 279 p. Bibliography, 18-22, 26-27.
4906. _____. L'économie sociale au moyen-âge. Coup d'oeil sur les débuts de la science économique dans les écoles françaises aux XIIIe et XIVe siècles. Louvain, C. Peeters; Paris, H. Champion, 1881. viii, 87 p. (Originally appeared as articles in Catholique of Louvain.)
4907. BRAS, Gabriel Le. "Conceptions of economy and society." In, The Cambridge economic history of Europe. London, Cambridge university press, 1963. v. 3.
4908. BROWN, Delmer Myers. Money economy in Medieval Japan; a study in the use of coins. (Monograph no. 1.) New Haven, Yale university, Institute of Far Eastern languages, 1951. 128 p. Bibliography.
4909. CAMBRIDGE economic history of Europe. London, Cambridge university press, 1942, 1952, 1963. v. 1-3.
4910. CASSANDRO, Giovanni. La tutela dei diritti nell'alto Medioevo. Bari, F. Cacucci, 1951. 239 p.
4911. CASSIDY, Francis Patrick. Molders of the medieval mind; the influences of the Fathers of the church on the medieval schoolmen. Port Washington, New York, Kennikat press, 1966, 1944. vii, 194 p.
4912. CENTRO italiano di studi sull'alto Medioevo. Moneta e scambi nell'alto Medioevo. Lezioni e discussioni tenute in occasione della VIII Settimana di studio svoltasi a Spoleto. 21-27 Aprile 1960. (Settimane di studio, 8.) Spoleto, 1961. 746 p.
4913. CHASSIPOL, M. Traite des finances et de la fausse monnoie des Romains . . . Paris, 1740. (English edition entitled: A treatise on the revenue and false money of the Romans. London, 1741. 8 v.)
4914. CHESTERTON, G. K. Saint Thomas Aquinas. London, Hodder & Stoughton, 1933.
4915. CHIERA, Edward. They wrote on clay. The Babylonian tables speak today. Chicago, University of Chicago Press, 1938. 234 p.

4916. CHODKIEWICZ, Z. and J. Górski. "W sprawie pogladów ekonomicznych Mikolaja kopernika." In, Ekonomista, 4 (1958) 955-970.
4917. CIBRARIO, G. A. L. Dell'economia politica del Medioevo. 1839.
4918. CICERO, Marcus Tullius. Laws and the republic. Cambridge Harvard university press, 1928.
4919. CIPOLLA, Carlo M. Money, prices and civilization in the Mediterranean world, fifth to seventeenth century. Princeton, Published for the University of Cincinnati by Princeton university press, 1956. 75 p.
4920. CLARK, John Grahame Douglas. Prehistoric Europe; the economic basis. New York, Philosophical library; London, Methuen, 1952. xix, 349 p. Bibliography, 316-336. (Stanford, California, Stanford university press, 1966. xix, xvi, 349 p.)
4921. CORNFORD, F. M. The Republic of Plato. New York, Oxford university press, 1945.
4922. COULTON, G. C. Medieval panorama. New York, The Macmillan company, 1938.
4923. CRAWFORD, V. E. Sumerian economic texts from the first dynasty of Isin. New Haven, Yale university press, 1954. 75 p.
4924. CROSARA, A. A. La dottrina di S. Antonino di Firenze. Rome, Editrice studium, 1960.
4925. DALTON, George, editor. Tribal and peasant economies. Readings in economic anthropology. 1st edition. (American museum sourcebooks in anthropology.) Garden City, New York, Published for the American museum of natural history press, 1967. xv, 584 p.
4926. D'ARCY, M. C. editor. Thomas Aquinas. Selected writings. (Everyman's library) New York, E. P. Dutton company, 1939.
4927. DAVID, Aryeh Ben. Talmudische oekonomie. Hildesheim, George Olms, 1969-70. 2 v.
4928. DEANE, Herbert A. The political and social ideas of St. Augustine. New York, Columbia university press, 1963.
4929. DEMANT, Vigo A., editor. The just price; an outline of the medieval doctrine and an examination of its possible equivalent today. London, Student Christian movement press, 1930.
4930. DEMOS, Raphael, editor. The philosophy of Plato. New York, Charles Scribner's Sons, 1939.
4931. DEMPSEY, Bernard W. Interest and usury. Introduction by Joseph A. Schumpeter. London, Dobson and company, 1948.
4932. _____. "Just price in a functional economy." In, The American economic review, XXV (September, 1935.)
4933. DEUTSCH, Jürgen. Die zahlungsmittel der völker in Afrika. Marburg, Lahn, Herstellung und vertriebskommission G. nolte, 1957. 251 p.
4934. DIESNER, H. J. Wirtschaft und gesellschaft bei Thukydides. Halle, M. Niemeyer, 1956. 198 p.

4935. DIVINE, Thomas F. Interest. An historical and analytical study in economics and modern ethics. Milwaukee, Marquette university press, 1959.
4936. DRIVER, G. R. and John C. Miles. The Babylonian laws. Oxford, Clarendon press, 1960. 2 v.
4937. DU MESNIL-MARIGNY, Jules. Histoire de l'économic politique des anciens peuples de l'Inde, de l'Egypte, de la Judée et de la Grèce. 3. éd., rev., augm. et annotée par l'auteur . . . Paris, E. Plon et c^{ie}, 1878. 3 v.
4938. DUBY, Georges. L'économie rurale et la vie des campagnes dans l'occident médiéval; France, Angleterre, Empire, IXe-XVe siecles; essai de synthèse et perspectives de rechercehs. (Collection historique.) Paris, Aubier, 1962. 2 v. (822 p.). Bibliography, v. 1, 13-52.
4939. DUNAJEWSKI, H. Mikolaj kopernik. Studia nad myśla spoleczno-ekonomiczma i dzialalności gospodarcza. Warszawa, Panstwowe wydawnictwa. Naukowe, 1957. 467 p.
4940. EHRENBERG, Richard. Capital and finance in the age of the renaissance. A study of the Fuggers and their connections. Translated from the German by H. M. Lucas. (The Bedford series of economic handbooks. 2.) New York, Harcourt, 1928. 390 p. (Translation of the author's Das zeitalter der Fugger, with some sections omitted.) (Reprinted: New York, A. M. Kelley, 1963. 390 p.)
4941. EHRENBERG, Victor. The people of Aristophanes. Cambridge, Mass., Harvard university press, 1951.
4942. EINZIG, Paul. Primitive money. London, Eyre & Spottiswoode, 1948.
4943. ELLWOOD, C. A. The story of social philosophy. New York, Prentice-Hall, 1938.
4944. ———. History of social philosophy. New York, Prentice-Hall, 1939.
4945. ENDEMANN, Wilhelm. Studien in der romanisch-kanonistischen wirthschafts-und rechtslehre bis gegen ende des siebenzehnten jahrhunderts. Berlin, J. Guttentag, D. Collin, 1874. 2 v.
4946. FANFANI, Amintore. Poemi omerici ed economia antica. (Biblioteca della revista economia e storia, 4.) Milano, A. Giuffre, 1960. viii, 142 p.
4947. FINLAY, M. I., editor. Slavery in classical antiquity. Cambridge, England, W. Heffer, 1960.
4948. FIRTH, Raymond William. Primitive Polynesian economy. 2d. edition. London, Routledge & K. Paul; Hamden, Connecticut, Archon books, 1965. xiii, 385 p. Bibliographical footnotes.
4949. ———, editor. Themes in economic anthropology. London, New York, Tavistock publications, 1967. x, 292 p. (Reprinted: New York, Barnes and Node, 1970?)
4950. FLUBACHER, Joseph F. The concept of ethics in the history of economics. New York, Vantage press, inc., 1950.
4951. FRANK, Tenney, editor. An economic survey of ancient Rome. Edited in collaboration with T. R. S. Broughton,

R. G. Collingwood, A. Grenier . . . and others. Baltimore, The Johns Hopkins press, 1933- . v. (Paterson, New Jersey, Pageant books, 1959. 6 v. Bibliographies.)

4952. FREEMAN, Kathleen. The pre-Socratic philosophers. Oxford, England, Basil Blackwell & Mott Ltds., 1946.

4953. GABEL, Creighton. Analysis of prehistoric economic patterns. New York, Holt, 1967. viii, 69. Bibliography.

4954. GARDINER, Alan Henderson. Egypt of the Pharaohs. Oxford, England, Clarendon press, 1961. 461 p.

4955. GARNIER, H. L'idee du juste prix. Paris, 1900.

4956. GEBHART, Emile (Nicolas Emile) Les historiens florentins de la renaissance et les commencements de l'economie politique et sociale. Paris, Orléans, Imp. E. Colas, 1875. 56 p.

4957. GEOGHEGAN, Arthur T. The attitude towards labor in early Christianity and ancient culture. Washington, D.C. The Catholic university press, 1945.

4958. GERNET, J. Les aspects economiques du bouddhisme dans la société chinoise du Ve and Xe siècle. Saigon, Ecole franç. d'extrême-orient, 1956. xvi, 331 p.

4959. GERNET, Louis. Droit et société dans la Grèce ancienne. (Publications de l'institut de droit romain de l'université de Paris, 18.) Paris, Recueil Sirey, 1955. 243 p.

4960. GIERKE, O. von. Political theories of the Middle Ages. Translated by F. W. Maitland, Cambridge, 1900.

4961. ———. Natural law and the theory of society, 1500 to 1800. Translated by E. Barker. Cambridge, 1934. 2 v.

4962. GILBY, Thomas. The political thought of Thomas Aquinas. Chicago, University of Chicago press, 1958. xxvi, 357 p.

4963. GILSON, Etienne. The philosophy of St. Thomas Aquinas. St Louis, B. Herder book company, 1939.

4964. GINZBERG, Eli. "Studies in the economics of the Bible." In, Jewish quarterly review, new series, 22, 4 (1932) 343-408.

4965. GIRARD, Eugène de. Histoire de l'économie sociale jusqu'à la fin du XVI siècle; antiquité--moyen âge--renaissance--réforme. Paris, V. Giard et E. Brière, 1900. 2, 3-276 p.

4966. GOODFELLOW, David Martin. Principles of economic sociology. The economics of primitive life as illustrated from the Bantu peoples of South and East Africa. Westport, Connecticut. Negro universites press, 1970. xx, 289 p.

4967. GOPAL, Lallanji. The economic life of Northern India. A.D. 700-1200. 1st edition, Delhi, Motilal Barnarsidass, 1965. xxiv, 305 p. Bibliography.

4968. GORDON, Barry J. "Aristotle and the development of value theory." In, Quarterly journal of economics, 78, 1 (February, 1964) 115-128.

4969. ———. "Aristotle, Schumpeter, and the metallist tradition." In, Quarterly journal of economics, 75 (November, 1961) 608-14.

4970. GORDON, Cyrus Harzl. Hammurabi's code. Quaint or

Preclassical Period

forward-looking? New York, Rinehart, 1957.
4971. GUTHRIE, W. K. C. A history of Greek philosophy. Cambridge, England, University Press, 1962.
4972. HALL, Hubert, editor. A select bibliography for the study, sources, and literature of English medieval economic history. (Studies in economics and political science. Edited by the director of the London school of economics. No. 4 in the series of bibliographies by students connected with the London school of economics and political science.) London, P. S. King & son, 1914. xiii, 350 p. (Reprinted: Burt Franklin bibliographical and reference series no. 22, New York, B. Franklin, 1960. xiii, 350 p.)
4973. HAMILTON, Earl Jefferson. Money, prices, and wages in Valencia, Aragon, and Navarre, 1351-1500. Cambridge, Massachusetts, Harvard university press, 1936. xxviii, 7-310. Bibliography.
4974. HARPER, R. F. Code of Hammurabi. Chicago, University of Chicago press, 1904. 192 p.
4975. HARRISON, F. Roman farm management in the treatises of Cato and Varro. Translations. New York, Macmillan company, 1913.
4976. HASEBROEK, Johannes. Trade and politics in ancient Greece. Translated by L. M. Fraser and D. C. Macgregor. London, G. Bell & sons, 1933.
4977. HAUREAU, Barthélemy. Histoire de la philosophie scholastique. Unveranderter nachdruck. Paris, 1872-1880. Frankfurt-am-Main, Minerva GmbH, 1966. 2 v. in 3. (Reprinted: Burt Franklin research and source works, 115. New York, B. Franklin, 1965. 2 v.
4978. HEALY, James. The just wage, 1750-1890. The Hague, Martinus Nijhoff, 1966.
4979. HEARNSHAW, F. J. C. Medieval contributions to modern civilization. London, G. C. Harrap & company, 1921.
4980. _____. The social and political ideas of some great Medieval thinkers. London, G. C. Harrap & company, 1923.
4981. HEATH, Thomas. Mathematics in Aristotle. London, Oxford university press, 1949.
4982. _____. A history of Greek mathematics. London, Oxford university press, 1921.
4983. HEICHELHEIM, Fritz Moritz. An ancient economic history, from the palaeolithic age to the migrations of the Germanic, Slavic and Arabic nations. Revised and complete English edition. Leiden, A. W. Sijthoff, 1957. Bibliographical references. (Translation of Wirtschaftsgeschichte des altertums.) (Reprinted: Ancient economic history series. New York, Humanities, 1964-1966, 3 v.)
4984. HEITLAND, W. E. Agricola. A study of agriculture and rustic life in the Greco-Roman world from the point of view of labor. London, Cambridge university press, 1921.
4985. HENDERSON, E. F. Historical documents of the Middle Ages. London, 1892.
4986. HERSKOVITS, Melville Jean. The economic life of primitive

peoples. New York, London, A. A. Knopf, 1940. xii, 492, xxviii p. Bibliography, 469-492 p. (2d. edition, revised, enlarged, and rewritten; title changed to: Economic anthropology; a study in comparative economics. New York, Knopf, 1952. xiii, 547, xxiii p. Bibliography, 533-547. Revised edition, Norton, 1965.)

4987. HICKS, R. D. Stoic and epicurean. 1910. (Reprint: New York, Russell and Russell, 1962.)

4988. HOFFNER, Joseph. Wirtschaftsethik und monopole. Stuttgart, Gustav Fischer verlag, 1941.

4989. ———. Statik und dynamik in der Scholastischen wirtschaftsethik. Opladen, Westdeutscher verlag GMBH, 1955.

4990. HOLLANDER, Samuel. "On the interpretation of the just price." In, Kyklos, 18, 4 (1965) 615-634.

4991. HORVATH, A. Eigentumsrecht nach dem heiligen Thomas von Aquin. Graz, Moser, 1929.

4992. HOWELL, A. G. Ferrers. S. Bernardine of Siena. London, Methune & company, ltd., 1913.

4993. HULL, C. H., editor. Economic writings. London, Cambridge university press, 1899.

4994. IBANES, J. La doctrine de l'Eglise et les réalitiés économiques au IIIIe siècle; l'intérêt, les prix et la monnaie. Paris, Travaux et recherches de la faculté de droit et des sciences économiques, 1967.

4995. IBN, Khaldun. Les textes économiques de la Mouqaddima, 1375-1379. Classes, traduits et annotés. Paris, M. Rivière, 1961. 85 p. Bibliographical footnotes.

4996. ———. Les textes sociologiques et économiques de la Mouqaddima, 1375-1379. Paris, Editions M. Riviere, 1965.

4997. JARRETT, Bede. Social theories of the Middle ages, 1200 to 1500. Boston, Little, Brown and Co., 1926.

4998. ———. Mediaeval socialism. 1913. London, Burns and Oates, Ltd., 1935.

4999. ———. S. Antonio and Mediaeval economics. London, B. Herder, 1914.

5000. JOACHIM, H. H. Aristotle, The Nicomachean ethics; a commentary. London, Oxford university press, 1951.

5001. JOHNS, Claude Hermann Walter. The relations between the laws of Babylonia and the laws of the Hebrew peoples. London, Milford, 1917. 102 p.

5002. JOHNSON, Allan Chester. Egypt and the Roman empire. (The Jerome lectures, 2d. series.) Ann Arbor, University of Michigan press, 1951. vii, 183 p. Bibliographical references in "Notes," 160-175.

5003. JOHNSON, E. A. J. "Just price in an unjust world." In, International journal of ethics, 48 (January, 1938) 165-181.

5004. JONES, T. B. and J. W. Snyder. Sumerian economic texts from the third Ur dynasty; a catalogue and discussion of documents from various collections. Minneapolis, University of Minnesota press, 1961. xix, 421 p.

5005. JOURDAIN, Amable Louis Marie Michel Bréchillet. Recherches critiques sur l'age et l'origine des traductions latines d'Aristote et sur des commentaires grecs ou arabes employés par les docteurs scolastiques. Ouvrage couronné par l'Académie des inscriptions et belles-lettres. Nouv. éd. rev. et aug. par Charles Jourdain. (Burt Franklin bibliographical series, 19.) New York, B. Franklin, 1960. xv, 472 p.)

5006. JOURDAIN, Charles Marie Gabriel Bréchillet. Mémoire sur les commencements de l'économie politique dans les écoles du moyen âge. In, Académie des inscriptions et belles-lettres, Paris. Mémoires. Paris, 28, 1 (1874) 1-51 p.

5007. JOWETT, Benjamin, editor. The dialogues of Plato. New York, Scribner, Armstrong and company, 1876. 4 v.

5008. KAUDER, E. "Genesis of the marginal utility theory. From Aristotle to the end of the eighteenth century." In, Economic journal, 63, 351 (September, 1953) 638-650.

5009. KAULLA, Rudolf. Theory of the just price. Translated by Robert D. Hogg. London, George Allen and Unwin, ltds. 1940.

5010. KERR, Albert Boardman. Jacques Coeur, merchant prince of the Middle Ages. New York, Charles Scribner's sons, 1927.

5011. KHALDUN, Ibn. The Muqaddimah. An introduction to history. Translated by Franz Rosenthal. Bollingen foundation. New York, Random House, Pantheon books, 1967. 3 v.

5012. KUAN, Chung. Economic dialogues in ancient China; selections from the Kuan-tzu, a book written probably three centuries before Christ. Translators: t'an Po-fu and Wen Kung-wen (Adam K. W. Wen) Espert critic: Hsiao Kung-chüan. The enterprise directed, the book edited and published by Lewis Maverick. Carbondale, Illinois, 1954. x, 470 p. (Manuscript form under the title: Economic thought in ancient China . . . Carbondale, Illinois, Lewis A. Maverick, 1950.)

5013. KUMAR, Santosh. The economic history of ancient India. Calcutta, Mita press, 1925.

5014. LACOUR-GAYET, Jacques. Platon et l'economie dirigée. Paris, Imprimerie union. 1945. 2 p. 1., 9-42 p., 2 1. Bibliographical footnotes.

5015. LAIDLER, H. W. Social-economic movements. New York, The Thomas Y. Crowell company, 1945. (1st edition entitled: A history of Socialist thought, 1927.)

5016. LAISTNER, Max Ludwig Wolfram, editor. Greek economics. Introduction and translation. The library of Greek thought. London and Toronto, J. M. Dent & sons, ltd.; New York, E. P. Dutton & co., 1923. xlii, 204 p. Bibliography, 198-199.

5017. LATOUCHE, Robert. Les origines de l'économie occidentale, IV-XI siècle. L'evolution de l'humanite, synthese collective, 2. sect., 43. Paris, A. Michel, 1956. (English edition entitled: The birth of Western economy; economic aspects of the Dark Ages. With a foreword by Philip Grierson. Translated by E. M. Wilkinson. New York, Barnes & Noble, 1961. 341 p. Bibliography. Reprinted:

New York, Harper, 1966?)
5018. LEACH, Helen May Keedwell. Subsistence patterns in prehistoric New Zealand; a consideration of the implications of seasonal and regional variability of food resources for the study of prehistoric economics. (Studies in prehistoric anthropology, v. 2.) Dunedin, Anthropology department, University of Otago, 1969. 114 p.
5019. LECLAIR, Edward E. and Harold K. Schneider, editors. Economic anthropology. Readings in theory and analysis. New York, Holt, Rinehart and Winston, 1968. xiii, 523 p.
5020. LEPOINTE, Gabriel. Cours d'histoire des institutions et des faits sociaux, rédigé d'après les notes et avec l'autorisation de Gabriel Lepointed. Licence 1re année, 1959-1960, Paris, Cours de droit, 1960. 956 p.
5021. ———. Cours d'histoire des institutions publiques et des faits sociaux, rédigé d'après les notes et avec l'autorisation de Gabriel Lepointe. Licence 1re année, 1961-1962. Paris, Cours de droit, 1962. 1056 p.
5022. LEVY, Jean-Philippe. The economic life of the ancient world. Chicago, University of Chicago press, 1967.
5023. LEWALTER, Ernst. Spanisch-jesuitische und deutsch-lutherische metaphysik des 17. jahrhunderts. Ein beitrag zur geschichte der iberisch-deutschen kulturbeziehungen und zur vorgeschichte des deutschen idealismus. (Univeränderter reprografischer nachdruck der ausg. Hamburg, 1935.) Sonderausg. Darmstadt, Wissenschaftliche Buchgesellschaft, 1967. 85 p.
5024. LICHTENBERGER, J. P. The development of social theory. New York, Appleton-Century-Crofts, inc., 1923.
5025. LIPINSKI, E. "O interpretacje myśli ekonomicznej Kopernika." In, Ekonomista, 1 (1956) 136-153.
5026. LOT, Ferdinand. The end of the ancient world. New York, Alfred A. Knopf, 1931.
5027. LOUIS, Paul. Ancient Rome at work. New York, Alfred A. Knopf, 1927.
5028. LOWRY, S. Todd. "Aristotle's mathematical analysis of exchange." In, History of political economy, 1, 1 (1969) 44-66.
5029. LUCAS, A. Ancient Egyptian materials and industries. 4th edition. New York, St. Martins, 1962. 539 p.
5030. MAHMASSANI, Sobhi. Les idées économiques d'Ibn Khaldoun. Beirut, Librairie du Foyer, 1935.
5031. MAIER, Anneliese. Zwei grundprobleme der scholastischen naturphilosophie. Das problem der intensiven grösse und die impetustheorie. (2 Aufl. (Storia e letteratura, n. 37.) Roma, Edizioni di storia e letteratura, 1951. 318 p.) [3., erw. aufl. Studien zur naturphilosophie der spätscholastik, Bd. 2.) 1968. 400 p.]
5032. MARINGER, John. Contribution to the prehistory of Mongolia. A study of the prehistoric collections from Inner Mongolia. . . . Stockholm, 1950. xii, 216 p.
5033. MARITAIN, Jacques. St. Thomas Aquinas. Newly translated and revised by Joseph W. Evans and Peter O'Reilly. New

5034. ———. Scholasticism and politics. Translation edited by Mortimer J. Adler. 3d edition. London, G. Bles, 1954. viii, 197 p.
5035. ———. True humanism. New York, Charles Scribner's sons, 1938.
5036. MAURENBRECHER, Max Heinrich. Thomas von Aquino's stellung zum wirtschaftsleben seiner zeit. Einleitung und erster teil . . . Leipzig, Druck von J. J. Weber, 1898, vi p., 1 1., 122 p. (Inaugural-dissertation, Leipzig.)
5037. MCDONALD, William J. The social value of property according to Saint Thomas Aquinas. Washington, D.C., The Catholic university of America press, 1939.
5038. MCKEON, Richard. Introduction to Aristotle. New York, Modern library, 1947. Albert Douglas, editor.
5039. MENUT, Albert Douglas, editor. Maistre Nicole Oresme: Le livre de yconomique d'Aristote; critical edition of the French text from the Avrauches manuscript with the original Latin version, introduction and English translation. (Transactions of the American philosophical society, new series, v. 47, part 5.) Philadelphia, American philosophical society, 1957. 783-803 p.
5040. MISKIMIN, Harry A., Money, prices and foreign exchange in fourteenth century France. (Yale university studies in economics, 15.) New Haven, Yale university press, 1963. 215 p. Bibliography.
5041. MITCHELL, Humfrey. The economics of ancient Greece. Cambridge, England, The University press; New York, The Macmillan company, 1940. 6 p. 1., 415 p. Bibliography, 394-398. (2d. edition. New York, Barnes and Noble; Cambridge, England, W. Heffner, 1963. 1957. 427 p. Bibliographies.
5042. MONIER, Raymond. Histoire des institutions et des faits sociaux des origines à l'aube du Moyen Age. En collaboration avec Guillaume Cardascia et Jean Imbert. Paris, Editions Montchrestien, 1955. 633 p.
5043. MOORE, George F. Judaism in the first centuries of the Christian era. Cambridge, Mass., Harvard university press, 1927.
5044. MORI, Renato. Le riforme leopoldine nel pensiero degli economisti toscani del '700. (Biblioteca storica Sansoni; nuoya ser. v. 18.) Firenze, G. C. Sansoni, 1951. 177 p.
5045. MORROW, Glenn R. Plato's Cretan city; a historical interpretation of the laws. Princeton, New Jersey, Princeton University press, 1960.
5046. MURRAY, Gilbert. Stoic, Christian and Humanist. Boston, Beacon Press, 1950.
5047. NAG, Daya Shankar. Tribal economy, as economic study of the Baiga. Delhi, Bharatiya Adimjati sevak sangh, 1958. 418 p.
5048. NASH, Manning. Primitive and peasant economic systems. (Chandler publications in anthropology and sociology.) San Francisco, Chandler publishing company. 1966. 166 p.

5049. NELSON, Benjamin N. The idea of usury. Princeton, New Jersey, Princeton University press, 1949.
5050. NICOSIA, Giuseppe. Economia e politica di atene attraverso Aristofane. 2nd edition, Milan, Sperling and Kupfer, 1935.
5051. NIPPOLD, W. Die Anfange des Eigentums bei den naturvölkern und die entstehung des privateigentums. s'Gravenhage, Mouton, 1954. 94 p.
5052. NOONAN, John Thomas. Banking and the early scholastic analysis of usury. (Catholic university of America. Philosophical series, v. 134.) Washington, Catholic university press, 1951.
5053. _____. The Scholastic analysis of usury. Cambridge, Mass., Harvard university press, 1957.
5054. OATES, Whitney J., editor. The stoic and epicurean philosophers. New York, Random house, Modern library, 1957.
5055. O'BRIEN, George Augustine Thomas. An essay on Medieval economic teaching. New York, London, Longmans, Green, and co., 1920. viii, 242 p. Bibliographical footnotes. (Reprints of economic classics: New York, A. M. Kelley, 1967. viii, 242 p. Burt Franklin research and source works series, no. 254: New York, B. Franklin, 1968. viii, 242 p.)
5056. OECONOMICA. Translated by E. S. Forester, In, W. D. Ross, The works of Aristotle. London, Oxford university press, 1921.
5057. OLIVER, E. H. Roman economic conditions at the close of the republic. Toronto, University of Toronto library, 1907.
5058. OPRISAN, Mircea. Gindirea economică din Grecia antică: Xenofon, Platon, Aristotel. Bucuresti, Editura Academiei republicii populare Romine, 1964. 297 p. Bibliography, 291-297.
5059. ORESME, Nicolas. The De moneta of Nicholas Oresme, and English Mint documents. Translated from the Latin with introduction and notes by Charles Johnson. (Medieval texts.) London, New York, Nelson, 1956. xii, 96, 96, 97-114 p.
5060. PANNELL, J. P. Techniques of industrial archaeology. New York, A. M. Kelley, 1968. 191 p.
5061. PEGIS, Anton C., editor. Basic writings of Saint Thomas Aquinas. New York, Random house, inc., 1945. 2 v.
5062. PENDZIG, Paul. Pierre Gassendis Metaphysik und ihr Verhältnis zur scholastischen philosophie. (Renaissance und philosophie, 1. Heft.) New York, B. Franklin, 1969. xiv, 176 p.
5063. PICAVET, François Joseph. Esquisse d'une histoire générale et comparée des philosophies médiévales. 2. éd. revue, corrigée et augmentée. Unveränderter nachdruck. Paris, 1907. Frankfurt-am-Main, Minerva GmbH., 1968. xxxiv, 335 p.
5064. PIRENNE, Jean Henri O. L. M. Economic and social history

of medieval Europe. Translated from the French by
I. E. Clegg. London, 1936; New York, 1937. (First published in Volume 8 of Histoire de moyen age, by Henri
Pirenne, Gustave Cohen, and Henri Focillon, 1933. Reprinted: Harvest books, 14.) New York, Harcourt, Brace,
1956. 239 p.

5065. _____. Medieval cities. Princeton, Princeton university press, 1925.

5066. PLATO, The republic. Translated with notes by F. M. Cornford. New York, Oxford University press, 1945.

5067. POLANYI, Karl. Primitive, archaic, and modern economies; essays of Karl Polanyi. Edited by George Dalton. 1st edition. Garden City, New York, Anchor books, 1968. liv. 346 p.

5068. POLANYI, Karl, Conrad M. Arensberg, and Harry W. Pearson, editors. Trade and market in the early empires; economies in history and theory. Glencoe, Illinois, Free press, 1957. xviii, 382 p. Bibliographical references.

5069. POSPISIL, Leopold. Kapauku papuan economy. (Yale university publications in anthropology, no. 67.) New Haven, Department of Anthropology, Yale University, 1963. 503 502 p.

5070. PROPERTY. Its duties and rights. Introduction by the Bishop of Oxford. London, Macmillan & co., 1913.

5071. QUIGGAN, A. Hingston. A survey of primitive money. London, Methuen and company, ltd. 1949.

5072. RANGASWAMI Aiyangar, Kumbakonam Viraraghava. Aspects of ancient Indian economic thought. (Manindra Chandra lectures, 1927, Benares Hindu university.) Benares, 1934. viii, 210 p. Bibliography 193-206.

5073. RASCHE, J. C. Lexicon universe rei numariae veterum, praecipue Graecorum ac Romanorum, cum observationibus, antiquariis, geographicis, chronologicis, Leipzic, 1785-1794. 8 v.

5074. RENAN, Ernest. A history of the people of Israel. Boston, Roberts brothers, 1889-95.

5075. _____. The History of the origins of Christianity. London, Mathieson and company, 18--?

5076. RIEZLER, Kurt. Uber finanzen und monopole in alten Griechenland;zur theorie und geschichte der antiken stadwirtschaft. Berlin, Puttkammer and Mühlbrecht, 1907. 98 p. (In part, published as author's inaugural dissertation, Munich, 1906, under title: Das zweite buch der pseudoaristotelischen Ökonomik.)

5077. OLMEDA, Mauro. Sociedades precapitalistas. 1. ed. Mexico, Distribuidor exclusivo, J. Grijalbo, 1954- . v.

5078. RITZENTHALER, Robert Eugene. Native money of Palau. (Milwaukee. Public museum. Publications in anthropology, no. 1.) Milwaukee, 1954. 46 p.

5079. ROGERS, A. K. A student's history of philosophy. New York, The Macmillan company, 1902. (3d edition, 1933.)

5080. ROOVER, Raymond Adrien de. "Joseph A. Schumpter and

scholastic economics." In, Kyklos, Basel, 10, 2 (1957) 115-146.

5081. ———. Money, banking and credit in medieval burgs. Italian merchant-bankers, Lombards and money-changers. A study in the origins of banking. (Publication no. 51.) Cambridge, Massachusetts, Medieval Academy of America, 1948. xvii, 420 p. Bibliography. [In, Journal of economic history, supplement (December, 1942).]

5082. ———. The rise and decline of the Medici bank, 1437-1494. (Studies in business history, no. 21.) Cambridge, Massachusetts, Harvard university press, 1963.

5083. ———. San Bernardino of Siena and Saint Antonino of Florence. The two great economic thinkers of the Middle Ages. (Publication no., 19.) Boston, Baker library, Harvard graduate school of business administration, 1967. vii, 46 p. Bibliography, 43-46.

5084. ———. "Scholastic economics . . . survival and lasting influence from the sixteenth century to Adam Smith." In, Quarterly journal of economics, 69, 2 (May, 1955) 161-190.

5085. ———. "The scholastics, usury, and foreign exchange." In, Business history review, 41, 3 (1967) 257-271.

5086. ROSENBERG, Jean Randall. The principle of individuation. A comparative study of St. Thomas, Scotus, and Suarez. (Catholic university of America. Philosophical studies, v. 121.) Washington, Catholic university of America press, 1950.

5087. ROSS, W. D. and J. A. Smith. The works of Aristotle. Oxford, Clarendon press, 1908-1931. 11 v.

5088. ROSTOVZEV, M. I. The social and economic history of the Hellenistic empire. London, Oxford university press, 1941. 3 v.

5089. ———. The social and economic history of the Roman empire. London, Oxford university press, 1926. (2nd edition, revised by P. M. Fraser. London, 1957. 2 v.)

5090. RYAN, John A. Alleged socialism of the church fathers. St. Louis, B. Herder, 1913. (2nd edition, revised by P. M. Fraser, London, 1957. 2 v.)

5091. SCHLATTER, Richard. Private property; the history of an idea. New Brunswick, New Jersey, Rutgers university press, 1951.

5092. SCHREIBER, Edmund. Die volkswirtschaftlichen anschauungen der scholastik seit Thomas v. Aquin. (Beiträge zur geschichte der nationalökonomie . . . 1, hft.) Jena, G. Fischer, 1913. 3 p. 1., v-viii, 246 p. 1.1. Bibliography, 243-246.

5093. SCIVOLETTO, Nino. Spiritualità medioevale e tradizione scolastica nel secolo XII in Francia. (Biblioteca del "Giornale italiano di filologia," 2.) Napoli, Armanni, 1954. 230 p.

5094. SILVA HERZOG, J. Historia y antologia del pensamiento economico; antiguedad y edad media. 3d. ed. México, Fondo de cultura económica, 1953, 209 p.

Preclassical Period 329

5095. SIMCOX, E. J. Primitive civilization. Outlines of the history of ownership in Archaic communities. London, 1894. 2 v.
5096. SIMEY, E. "Economic theory among the Greeks." In, Economic review, 10 (October, 1900) 462-481.
5097. SINHA, Dharnidhar Prasad. Culture change in an intertribal market. The role of the Banari intertribal market among the hill peoples of Chotanagpur. London, Asia publishing house, 1968. xvi, 117 p.
5098. SPENGLER, Joseph J. "Herodotus on the subject matter of economics." In, Scientific Monthly, 81, 6 (1955) 276-85.
5099. STARK, W. The contained economy. An interpretation of medieval economic thought. (Paper read to the Aquinas society of London, 1956.) London, Blackfriars, 1956. 22 p.
5100. STOLIAROV, Dmitrii Dmitrievich. Iz historii antichnykh ekonomicheskikh teorii. (Transliterated.) Tashkent, Uzbek, 1966. 78 p.
5101. NO ENTRY
5102. SUCHON, August. Les theories economiques dans la Grece antique. Paris, Librairie de la société du recueil général des lois et des arrets, 1898.
5103. SUNG, Lien. Economic structure of the Yüan dynasty. Translation of chapters 93 and 94 of the Yüan shih, by Herbert Franz Schurmann. (Harvard-Yenching institute studies, 16.) Cambridge, Harvard university press, 1956. xvii, 251 p. Bibliography, 243-248.
5104. SUTHERLAND, Carol Humphrey Vivian. Coinage in Roman imperial policy, 31 B.C.-A.D. 68. London, Methune, 1951. xi, 220 p.
5105. SWEET, Ronald Frank Garfield. On prices, moneys, and money uses in the old Babylonian period. Chicago, Department of photoduplication, University of Chicago Library, 1958.
5106. TAWNEY, Richard H. Religion and the rise of capitalism. New York, Harcourt, Brace and company, 1937. (New York, New American library, 1947.)
5107. TAYLOR, A. E. Plato, the man and his work. 3d edition. London, Methuen and company, 1929.
5108. _____. Aristotle. London, T. Nelson & sons, 1943.
5109. TAUBENSCHLAG, Rafal. The law of Greco-Roman Egypt in the light of the papyri, 332 B.C.-640 A.D. New York, Herald square press, 1944-48. 2 v. (2d edition, revised and enlarged. Warszawa, Panstwowe wydawnictwo naukowe, 1955. xv, 789 p.
5110. TENNY, Frank. Economic history of Rome. Baltimore, Johns Hopkins university press, 1933.
5111. _____. An economic survey of ancient Rome. Baltimore, Johns Hopkins university press, 1933.
5112. THOMAS, Paul. Essai sur quelques théories économiques dans le Corpus juris civilis (de la richesse, de la

valeur, de la circulation des biens, du credit.) (Burt Franklin research & source works series, 547. Selected essays in history, economics, and social science, 172.) New York, B. Franklin, 1970. 124 p. Bibliography, 7-10. (Reprint of the 1899 edition, published in Paris.)

5113. THOMPSON, James Westfall. Economic and social history of the Middle Ages. New York, London, The Century company, 1928. [v. 1:(300-1300) 1928. ix, 900 p. Bibliographies, 809-850. Same title with added: "in the later Middle Ages. (1300-1530.) 1931. viii, 545. Bibliographies, 509-524.]

5114. THOMSON, Donald E. Economic structure and the ceremonial cycle in Arnhem land. Melbourne, Macmillan, 1949. 106 p.

5115. No Entry.

5116. THURNWALD, Richard. Economics in primitive communities. London, Published for the International institute of African languages and cultures by H. Milford, Oxford university press, 1932. xiv, 314 p., 1 l. Bibliography 299-309.

5117. TOUMBOUROS, George. The laws of ancient Greece. (Parallel legislations of England, U.S.A., France, Germany, Italy and comparative law, v. 1.) Munich, Süddeutscher verlag press, 1959. 388 p.

5118. TOUTAIN, Jules François. The economic life of the ancient world. With 6 maps. New York, A. A. Knopf, 1930. 361. xxvii. Bibliography. (Translated by M. R. Dobie, New York, Barnes & Noble, 1951. xxvii, 361 p. Bibliography, 331-335.)

5119. TOZZI, Glauco. Economisti greci. Siena, Libreria ticci succ. Giubbi, 1955. 286 p.

5120. ———. Economisti greci e romani. 1. ed. Milano Feltrinelli, 1961. 514 p. Bibliographical reference.

5121. ———. Economisti romani. Siena, Libreria ticci succ. Giubbi, 1958. 328 p.

5122. TREVER, Albert Augustus. A history of Greek economic thought. University of Chicago, Chicago, Illinois, 1916. 162 p. Bibliography, 151-55. (Dissertation, University of Chicago, 1913. Private edition distributed by University of Chicago libraries.)

5123. TROUWBORST, Albertus Antonius. Vee als voorwerp van rijkdom in Oost Afrika. 's-Gravenhage, Excelsior, 1956. 115 p.

5124. TRUGENBERGER, Alberto E. San Bernardino da Siena; considerazioni sullo sviluppo dell'etica economica cristiana nel primo Rinascimento. (Staatswissenschaftliche studien, hrsg. von L. V. Furlan und Edgar Salin, neue Folge, Bd. 9.) Bern, A. Francke, 1951. xi, 142 p. Bibliography, ix-xi.

5125. TUCCI, Giovanni. Sistemi monetari africani al lume dell'economia primitiva. Napoli, Rivista di etnografia, 1950. 132 p.

5126. USHER, Abbott Payson. The early history of deposit banking in Mediterranean Europe. Cambridge, Mass., Harvard University press, 1943. (v. 1. The structure and functions of the early credit system. Banking in Catalonia, 1240-1723.)

5127. VERNEAUX, Roger. Philosophie de l'homme. (Cours de philosophie thomiste.) Paris, Beauchesne, 1956. 190 p.

5128. VINOGRADOFF, P. Outlnies of historical jurisprudence. Oxford, England, Oxford university press? 1920-1922. 2 v.

5129. WALDRON-SHAH, D'Lynn. The problems of traditional societies in transition to a monetized, market-principle mode of allocation. Ann Arbor, Michigan, Available thru University microfilms, 1967. vii, 225 l.

5130. WALFORD, Edward. Aristotle's politics and economics. London, Bohn's classical library, 1853.

5131. WALLINGA, Herman Tammo. Een centraal probleem in de studie van de antieke economie. Groningen, J. B. Wolters, 1960. 18 p.

5132. WEBER, Max. Ancient Judaism. Translated and edited by Hans H. Gerth and Don Martindale. New York, The Free Press, 1952.

5133. WEINBERGER, Otto. Die wirtschafts-philosophie des alten testaments. Vienna, Springerverlag, 1948.

5134. WELSKOPF, Elisabeth Charlotte. Die produktionsverhältnisse im alten Orient und in der griechisch-römischen antike; ein diskussionsbeitrag. (Deutsche akademie der wissenschaften zu Berlin. Schriften der sektion für altertumswissenschaft, 5.)

5135. WERVEKE, Hans van. Currency manipulation in the Middle ages: the case of Louis de Male, Count of Flanders. In, Royal historical society, London. Transactions, London, 4th series, 31 (1949) 115-127.

5136. WHEELWRIGHT, Philip. Heraclitus. Princeton, New Jersey, Princeton university press, 1959.

5137. WHITE, Lynn, Jr. Medieval technology and social change. London, Oxford university press, 1962.

5138. WILLEKE, Franz-Ulrich. Entwicklung der markttheorie, von der Scholastik bis zur Klassik. Tübingen, J. C. B. Mohr, 1961.

5139. WILSON, J. A. and others. Authority and law in the ancient orient. (Supplement to the Journal of the American Oriental society, no. 17.) Baltimore, American Oriental society, 1954. ii, 55 p.

5140. WORLAND, Stephen Theodore. Scholasticism and welfare economics. Notre Dame, Indiana, University of Notre Dame press, 1967. x, 298 p.

5141. WUELLNER, Bernard. A dictionary of scholastic philosophy. 2d ed. Milwaukee, Bruce publishing company, 1966. xviii, 339 p.

5142. WULF, Maurice M. C. J. de. Histoire de la philosophie medievale; précédée d'un aperçu sur la philosophie ancienne. Louvain, Institute supérieur de philosophie,

1900. viii, 480 p. English translation by Messenger. 1925-26. 5. éd. francaise, 1924-25. 6. éd, 1934- .)

5143. _____. Scholasticism old and new, an introduction to Scholastic philosophy, medieval and modern. Translated by Peter Coffey. (From French, 1904.) Dublin, M. H. Gill & son, ltd. New York, Benziger bros., 1907. xvi, 327.

5144. XENOPHON. L'économique, suivie du projet de finances pour augmenter les revenus de l'attique. Paris, 1756.

5145. _____. Voir aussi les oeuvres complètes de Xénophon, traduites en Français. Paris, 1842. 2 v.

5146. ZIMMERN, Alfred E. The Greek commonwealth. New York, Oxford university press, 1924. (5th edition, revised. London, Oxford university press, 1931.)

5147. ZWANZIGER, M. ha-Mahashavah ha-kalkalit. (Transliterated.) Haifa, 1958. 16 p. (The economic thought in ancient Palestine.)

5148. ZWIEDINECK-SUDENHORST, Otto von. Kollektivismus und kapitalwirtschaft in der Vor- und Frühgeschichte. (Sitzungsberichte der Bayerischen akademie der wissenschaften. Philosophisch-historische klasse, jahrg. 1949, Heft 3.) München, Verlag der Bayerischen akademie der Wissenschaften, 1949. 84 p.)

H. Section II.

2. MERCANTILISM, CAMERALISM, AND COLBERTISM

5149. ADLER, Max. Die anfänge der merkantilistischen gewerbepolitik in Osterreich. (Wiener staatswissenschaftliche studien, hrsg. von E. Bernatzik und E. Philippovich, IV. bd., 3 hft.) Wien und Leipzig, F. Deuticke, 1903. ix, 212 p.

5150. ALEM, André. Le marquis d'Argenson et l'economie politique au début du XVIII siècle. Pratiques mercantiles et théories libérales. Paris, A. Rousseau, 1900. viii, 188. Bibliographical footnotes.

5151. ANGELL, James W. The theory of international prices. Cambridge, Massachusetts, Harvard university press, 1926.

5152. BAST, J. H. Vauban et Boisguillebert. Groningen, P. Noordhoff ltd., 1935.

5153. BAUMSTARK, Eduard. Kameralistische encyclopadie. Handbuch der kameralwissenschaften und ihrer literatur für rechts- und verwaltungsbeamte, landstande, gemeinde-rathe und kameral-candidaten. Heidelberg und Leipzig, K. Gross, 1835. xvi, 799, 1 p. Bibliographies.

5154. BEARDWOOD, Alice. Alien merchants in England, 1350-

5155. 1377, their legal and economic position. (Monographs of the Mediaeval academy of America, no. 3.) Cambridge, The Mediaeval academy of America, 1931. xii, 212 p. Bibliography, xi-xii.
5155. BELLONI, Girolamo. A dissertation on commerce. Clearly demonstrating the true sources of national wealth and power, together with the most rational measures for acquiring and preserving both. The whole deduced from the nature of trade, industry, money and exchanges. Translated from the Italian. London, printed by R. Manby, 1752. xx, 108 p. (Spanish edition: Disertacion sobre la naturaleze, y utilidades del comercio: escrita en italiano. Tr. al frances, y de este al castellano por D. Joseph Labrada. Santiago, I. Aguayo, 1788. 166 p.)
5156. ———. Marchionis hieronymi Belloni de commercio dissertatio. Latin translation by N. Rubbi. Romae, ex typographia Palladis, excudebant N. et M. Palearini, 1750. 7 p.1., 69 p. (German edition: Des marchese Hieronymi Belloni Abhandlung von commercien und muntz-wesen. Aus dem italianischen ubersetzet und mit einigen anmerckungen erlautert von M. Gottlieb Schumann. Frankfurt und Leipzig, Gledit, 1752. 3 p. 1., 3-12, 68 p.)
5157. BELOV, M. I. Merkantilizm i ego glavnye predstaviteli v stranakh Zapadnoi Evropy. (Transliterated.) Moscow, 1955. 35, 3 p. Bibliography, 37.
5158. BERENDTS, Eduard Nikolaevich. Merkantilisty i fiziokraty. (Transliterated.) 1892. 1 p. 1., 66 p., 1 l.
5159. BERTOLINO, Alberto. Locke economista. Siena, Tipografia ex-combattenti cooperativa, 1928.
5160. BIDERMANN, Hermann Ignaz. Uber den merkantilismus. Vortrag gehalten bei veröffentlichung der preisaufgaben für 1869/70 an der K. K. Universität zu Innsbruck . . . Mit zusätzen und anmerkungen des verfassers. Innsbruck, Wagner, 1870. 58 p.
5161. BIERMANN, W. E. Der Abbé Galiani als nationalökonom, politiker un philosoph nach seinem briefwechsel. Leipzig, Veit & companie, 1912.
5162. BOG, Ingomar. Der Reichsmerkantilismus. Studien zur wirtschaftspolitik des Heiligen Römischen Reiches im 17. und 18. Jahrhundert. (Forschungen zur Sozial- und wirtschaftsgeschichte, Bd. 1.) Stuttgart, Fischer, 1959. x, 193 p. Bibliography, 173-185.
5163. BOHLE, Cilly. Die idee der wirtschaftsverfassung im deutschen merkantilismus (Thesis, Freiburg.) (Freiburger staatswissenschaftliche schriften; . . . Hft. 1.) Jena, G. Fischer, 1940. vi, 140 p. Bibliographical footnotes.
5164. BONAR, James. Theories of population from Raleigh to Arthur Young. London, George Allen & Unwin ltd., 1931.
5165. BORNITZ, Jakob. Tractatus politicus. De rerum sufficientia in rep. & civitate procurandâ. I. Cultura: agrorum, metallorum. II. Opificiis omnis generis. III. Mercatura:

nautica, terrestri. IV. Ministeriis variis. Francofurti, impensis G. Tampachii, 1625. 8 p. l., 253, 27 p. 1 l.

5166. BRIDGES, J. H. France under Richelieu and Colbert. London, 1912.

5167. BUCK, Philip Wallenstein. The politics of mercantilism. New York, H. Holt and company, 1942. viii, 240. Bibliographical notes, 195-226. (Reprint: New York, Octagon books, 1964. viii, 240 p. Bibliographical notes, 195-226.)

5168. CAILLEMER, R. and A. Schatz. "Le mercantilisme liberal a la fin du xviie siècle." In, Revue d'économie politique (1906) 29-70, 791-816.

5169. CASPER, Willy. Charles Davenant, ein beitrag zur kenntnis des englischen merkantilismus. (Beiträge zur geschichte der nationalökonomie . . . 7. hft.) Jena, G. Fischer, 1930. Literaturverzeichnis, 137-139. Schriften Davenants, 140.

5170. CASTILLO, Andrés Villegas. Spanish mercantilism. Gerónimo de Uztáriz--economist. (Thesis, Columbia university.) New York, Printed by Ad press ltd., 1930. ix, 193 p. Bibliography, 183-190.

5171. CHANG, Han-yü. Igirisu jushoshugi kenkyu. (Transliterated.) Japan, 1954. 260 p.

5172. CHYDENIUS, Anders. The national gain. Translated from the Swedish original published in 1765; with an introduction by Georg Schuman. London, E. Benn limited, 1931. 92 p. (Den nationalle winsten was first published anonymously in 1765. It was reprinted in the author's Politiska skrifter, Helsingfors, 1880.)

5173. CLEMENT, M. Pierre. L'Histoire de la vie et de l'administration de Colbert. Paris, Guillaumin, 1846.

5174. ———. Histoire de Colbert et de son administration. Paris, Perrin, 1892.

5175. COATS, A. W. "In defense of Heckscher and the idea of mercantilism." In, Scandinavian economic history review, 5, 1 (1957) 173-87.

5176. COLE, Charles Woolsey. Colbert and a century of French mercantilism. New York, Columbia University press, 1939. 2 v. Bibliography. (Reprint: Hamden, Connecticut, Archon books, 1964. 2 v. Bibliography, v. 2, 589-620.)

5177. ———. French mercantilism, 1683-1700. New York, Columbia university press, 1943. (New York, Octagon books, 1965. c 1943. viii, 354 p. Bibliography, 331-337.)

5178. ———. French mercantilist doctrines before Colbert. New York, R. R. Smith, 1931; W. L. Bauhan, inc., Peterborough, New Hampshire, 1931 (New York, Octagon books, 1969. xiv, 243 p. Bibliography, 229-240.)

5179. COLEMAN, Donald Cuthbert. "Labour in the English economy of the seventeenth century." In, Economic history review, 2nd series, 8, 3 (1956) 280-295. Reprinted in, E. M. Carus-Wilson, editor, Essays in Economic history. London, Edward Arnold, ltd., 1962. v. 2, 291-308 p.

5180. _____. Revisions in mercantilism. (Debates in economic history.) New York, Barnes & Noble, 1969. ix, 213 p. Bibliography, 210-213.

5181. CRANSTON, Maurice. John Locke. London, Longmans, Green & Co., ltds., 1957.

5182. CUNNINGHAM, William. The growth of English industry and commerce. 5th edition. Cambridge, England, The University press, 1910-12. 3 v. v. 1, Bibliography. v. 3, Bibliographical index. (6th edition, 1917, 1919? Reprints: Cambridge, England, The University press, 1922-29. 3 v. Vol. 1, 5th edition; Vols. 2-3, 6th edition. List of authorities, v. 1, 657-681; Bibliographical index, v. 3, 943-998. Reprint of economic classics. New York, A. M. Kelley, 1968. 2 v. Vol. 1, 5th edition; Vols. 2-3, 4th edition, 1907. Bibliographies.)

5183. _____. Western civilization in its economic aspects. Cambridge, 1910, 1911. 2 v.

5184. DANIELSSON, Carl. Protektionismens genombrott och tulltaxerevisionerna 1715 och 1718; studier i merkantilistisk tullpolitik i Sverige av Carl Danielsson. (Akademisk avhandling, Stockholms högskola.) Stockholm, Kungl. boktryckeriet. P. A. Norstedt & söner, 1930. vii, 158, 2 p. Käller och litteratur, 153-158.

5185. DEYON, Pierre. Le mercantilisme. (Questions d'histoire, 11.) Paris, Flammarion, 1969. 126 p. Bibliography, 117-120.

5186. DIONNET, Georges. Le néomercantilisme au XVIIIe siècle et au début du XIXe siècle. (Inaugural dissertation, Paris.) Paris, V. Giard & E. Brière, 1901. 2 p., 1., 226 p.

5187. DREISSIG, Wilhelmine. Die geld-und kreditlehre des deutschen merkantilismus. (Volkswirtschaftliche studien, hft. 63.) Berlin, E. Ebering, 1939. 116 p. Literaturverzeichnis, 113-116.

5188. ECKERT, Georg. Der merkantilismus. (Beiträge zum geschichtsunterricht, 16.) Braunschweig, A. Limbach, 1949. 53 p.

5189. EMRICH, Ignaz. Die geldtheoretischen und geldpolitischen anschaungen John Lockes. Munich, B. Heller, 1927.

5190. ESPINAS, Alfred Victor. La troisième phase et la dissolution du mercantilisme (Mandeville, Law, Melon, Voltaire, Berkeley). Paris, V. Giard & E. Brière, 1902. 20 p. (Extrait de la "Revue internationale de sociologie.")

5191. FANFANI, Amintore. Dal mercantilismo al liberismo; le ricerche di R. Cantillon sulla ricchezza delle nazioni. Milano, A. Giuffré, 1936. viii, 174 p.

5192. FAY, C. R. Imperial economy and its place in the formation of economic doctrine, 1600-1932. London, Oxford university press, 1934.

5193. FERREIRA, Alexandre. Unbekannte portugiesische merkantilisten. (Inaugural dissertation, Bern.) Bern, 1952,

204 p. Bibliography, 197-204.
5194. FETTER, Frank W. "Some neglected aspects of Gresham's law." In, Quarterly journal of economics, 46 (1931-32) 480-95.
5195. FITZMAURICE, Edmond. Life of Sir William Petty. London, John Murray, ltd., 1895.
5196. FOCKE, Walther. Die lehrmeinungen der kameralisten Übe den handel. 1650-1750. (Inaugural dissertation, Erlange Erlangen, 1926. 79, 1 p. Literaturverzeichnis, 5-6.
5197. FURNISS, Edgar Stephenson. The position of the laborer in a system of nationalism. A study in the labor theories o later English mercantilists. (Reprints of economic classics.) New York, Kelley & Millman, 1957. 260 p. Bibliography. (Reprint of work first published in 1920. New York, A. M. Kelley, bookseller, 1965. 260 p. Bibliography, 237-256.
5198. GAINES, Ervin James. Merchant and poet. A study of seventeenth century influences. (Thesis, Columbia university.) (University microfilms, Publication 6622.) Ann Arbor, Michigan, University microfilms, 1954. vi, 289, 3 l. Bibliography, 268-289.
5199. GALIANI, Ferdinando. De la monnaie. 1751. Translated with introduction by G. H. Bousquet and J. Crisafulli. Paris Marcel Riviere et cie. 1955.
5200. ———. Dialogues entre M. Marquis de Roquemaure, et Ms. le Chevalier Zanobi- Frankfurt am Main, Vittorio Klostermann, 1968.
5201. GALLMAN, Robert E. Developing of American colonies, 1607-1783. (Economic forces in American history.) Chicago, Scott, Foresman, 1964. 64 p.
5202. GANILH, Charles. Des systèmes d'économie politique, de la valeur comparative de leurs doctrines, et de celle qui parait la plus favorable aux progrès de la richesse. 2. éd., avec de numbreuses additions relatives aux controverses récentes de MM. Malthus, Buchanan, Ricardo sur les points les plus importans de l'économie politique Paris, Treuttel et Würtz, 1821. 2 v. in 1. (American edition: An inquiry into the various systems of political economy; their advantages and disadvantages; and the theory most favourable to the increase of national wealth. Translated from the French by D. Boileau. New York, Published by Peter A. Mesier, no. 107 Pearl-street, 1812. 2 p. 1., 492 p.)
5203. ———. La théorie de l'économie politique, fondée sur les faits résultans des statistiques de la France et de l'Angleterre. Paris, Deterville, 1815. 2 v.
5204. GANZONI, Eduard. Ferdinando Galiani. Ein verkannter nationalokonom des 18. Jahrhunderst. Zurich, H. Girsberger, 1938.
5205. GERVAISE, Isaac. The system or theory of the trade of the world. 1720. (Reprinted. With introduction by J. M. Letiche. Baltimore, The Johns Hopkins press, 1954.)

5206. GIGLIO, Carlo. Mercantilismo. Padova, CEDAM, Casa editrice dott. A. Milani, 1940. 2 p. 1., iii-iv, 125, 1 p.
5207. GONNARD, René. La conquête portugaise; découvreurs et economistes. Paris, Librairie de Médicis, 1947. 162 p.
5208. _____. Histoire des doctrines de la population. Paris, Nouvelle Librairie nationale, 1923.
5209. GORSKI, Janusz. Poglady merkantylistyczne w polskiej mysli ekonomicznej XVI i XVII wieku. Wyd. 1. (Monografie z dziejow nauki i techniki, 6.) Wrocław, Zakład Narodowy im. Ossolinskich, 1958. 280 p. Bibliography, 260-266. (Summaries in Russian and English.)
5210. GRAMPP, William Dyer. "The liberal elements in English mercantilism." In, Quarterly journal of economics, 66 (November, 1952) 465-501.
5211. _____. Mercantilism and laissez faire in American political discussion, 1787-1829. (Part of thesis, University of Chicago, 1944.) Chicago, Illinois, The University of Chicago library, Department of photographic reproduction, 1946. vi, 25 numb. 1.
5212. GREGORY, T. E. "The economics of employment in England, 1660-1713." In, Economica, 1 (January, 1921) 37-51. Reprinted in, Gold, unemployment, and capitalism. London, P. S. King and son, 1933.
5213. GREVEN, Jakobus. Die dynamische geld- und kreditlehre des merkantilismus; eine studie zu John Law. (Neue deutsche forschungen Abt.: Nationalokonomie . . . hrsg. von Erwin Wiskemann. bd. 8.) (Inaugural disseration, Koln.) Berlin, Junker und Dünnhaupt, 1936. 162 p. Bibliography, 160-162.
5214. GUITTON, H. Essai sur la loi de King. Etude des relations entre les mouvements de l'offre et les mouvements des prix. Paris, Editions sirey, 1938.
5215. HAMILTON, Earl J. American treasure and the price revolution in Spain. Cambridge, Massachusetts, Harvard university press, 1934.
5216. _____. "Spanish mercantilism before 1700." In, Fact and factors in economic history. Cambridge, Massachusetts, Harvard university press, 1932. 214-39 p.
5217. HECHT, Otto. Die K. K. Spiegelfabrik zu Neuhaus in Niederösterreich, 1701-1844; ein beitrag zur geschichte des merkantilismus. Wien, C. Konegen (E. Stülpnagel) 1909. viii p., 1 1., 166 p. Bibliography, 165-166.)
5218. HECKSCHER, Eli Filip. Merkantilismen; ett led i den ekonomiska politikens historia. Stockholm, P. A. Norstedt & soner, 1931. 2 v. (2. revid. uppl. Stockholm, Norstedt, 1953. 2 v. German edition: Der merkantilismus. Autorisierte übersetzung aus dem schwedischen von Gerhard Mackenroth. Jena, G. Fischer, 1932. 2 v. English edition: Mercantilism. Authorized translation by Mendel Shapiro; prepared from the German edition and revised by the author. London, G. Allen & Unwin ltd., 1935. 2 v. Spanish edition: La época mercantilista; historia de la organización y las

ideas económicas desde el final de la edad media hasta la sociedad liberal. Versión española de Wenceslao Roces sobre el texto de la edicion alemana. México Fondo de cultura económica, 1943, 3 p. 1., ix-xiv, 871 p., 1 1. English editions: Mercantilism. Authorized translation by Mendel Shapiro. Revised. 2d edition edited by E. F Söderlund. London, Allen & Unwin; New York, Macmillan, 1955. 2 v. Added to Vol. II, chapter entitled: "Keynes and Mercantilism." Reprinted: London, Allen & Unwin; New York, Macmillan; New York, Barnes & Noble, 1962. 2 v. Bibliographical footnotes.)

5219. HEGELAND, Hugo. The quantity theory of money. Göteborg, Elanders Boktryckeri, 1951.

5220. HELANDER, S. "Josiah Child," In, Weltwirtschaftliches archiv, 19 (1923) 233-49.

5221. HELD, Adolf. Carey's socialwissenschaft und das merkantilsystem. Würzburg, F. E. Thein, 1866. xii, 215, 1 p. (Dissertation, Würzburg.)

5222. HERNANDEZ RON, Ramón. El mercantilismo en España y en Francia; influencia del descubrimiento de América. Caracas, Imprenta nacional, 1939. 47 p. Bibliografia, 46-47.

5223. HOFMANN, Werner. Theorie der wirtschaftsen tsentwicklung. Vom merkantilismus bis sur gegenwart. (Sozialökonomische studientexte, bd., 3.) Berlin, Duncker u. Humblot, 1966. 321 p.

5224. HOGBEN, Lancelot, editor. Political arithmetic. London, George Allen & Unwin, 1938.

5225. HORROCKS, John Wesley. A short history of mercantilism. New York, Brentano's, 1924. viii, 249 p. Bibliographical notes, 219-221, 223-242. (London, Methune & company, ltd., 1924. viii, 249, 1 p.)

5226. HORSEFIELD, J. Keith. British monetary experiments, 1650-1710. Cambridge, Massachusetts, Harvard university press, 1960.

5227. HUME, David. Essays. Moral, political, and literary. New York, Oxford university press, 1963.

5228. HUMPERT, Magdalene. Bibliographie der kameralwissenschaften. Cologne, Pick, 1937.

5229. HYDE, H. Montgomery. John Law. The history of an honest adventurer. London, Home and Van Thal, 1948.

5230. JOCELYN, J. An essay on money and bullion. London, 1718. (New York, Johnson reprint corporation, 1971.)

5231. JONES, Richard. "Primitive political economy of England." In, Edinburgh review (April, 1847.) Reprinted in, Richard Jones, Literary Remains. Edited by W. Whewell. London, John Murray, ltd., 1859. 291-335 p.

5232. JOUBLEAU, Felix. Etudes sur Colbert, ou exposition du système d'économie politique suivi en France de 1661 à 1683. Paris, Guillaumin, 1856.

5233. JUSTI, Johann Heinrich Gottlob von. La chimere de l'equilibre du commerce et de la navigation, ou Refutation des theses nouvelles sur les mesûres des mers et de la supériorité en forces navales: avec des reflexions nouvelles et importantes concernant le commerce et la navigation des peuples, de meme que sur le degré suprème de la force et de la felicité. . . . Traduit de l'allemand par D. T. Copenhague et Leipsic, Veuve de Rothe, 1763. 190 p.

5234. KAMMEN, Michael G. Empire and interest: the American colonies and the politics of mercantilism. (Lippincott history series.) Philadelphia, Lippincott, 1970. x, 186 p. Bibliographical references.

5235. KELLENBENZ, Hermann. Der merkantilismus und die soziale mobilität in Europa. (Institut für Europäische geschichte, Mainz. Vorträge, Nr. 42.) Wiesbaden, F. Steiner, 1965. 71 p. Bibliography, 56-71.

5236. KEYNES, John Maynard. "Mercantilism." In Chapter XXIII, General Theory of Employment, Interest and Money. London, MacMillan, 1936. 403 p.

5237. KNORR, Klaus E. British colonial theories, 1570-1850. Canada, Toronto, University of Toronto press, 1944.

5238. KOBAYASHI. Noboru. Jusho shugi kaitaiki no kenkyu. (Transliterated.) Japan, 1955. 3, 343, 6 p. Bibliographical footnotes.

5239. LAMBERT, Paul. La théorie quantitative de la monnaie. Paris, Editions Sirey, 1938.

5240. LANDA, Louis A. Swift's economic views and mercantilism. (Thesis, University of Chicago, 1941.) 1943. 1 p. l., 310-335. Bibliographical footnotes. (Reprinted from a Journal of English literary history, vol. 10, no. 4, December, 1943.)

5241. LARRAZ, López, José. La época del mercantilismo en Castilla (1500-1700). 2. ed. Madrid, Ediciones Atlas, 1943. 2 p. l., 7-222 p., 1 l. Bibliographical footnotes.

5242. LASPEYRES, Etienne. Geschichte der volkswirtschaftlichen anschauunger der niederlander. Stuttgart, S. Hirzel verlag KG., 1863.

5243. LAURES, John. The political economy of Juan de Mariana. Foreword by E. R. A. Seligman. Bronx, New York, Fordham university press, 1928.

5244. LETWIN, William. Sir Josiah Child. (Publication 14, Kress library of business and economics.) Boston, Harvard graduate school of business administration, Baker library, 1949.

5245. LILLE, Axel. Anders Chydenius i förhallande till samtida nationalekonomer. (Inaugural dissertation, Helsingfors.) Helsingfors, J. C. Frenckell & son, 1882. 2 p. l., 122 p., 1 l.

5246. LIPINSKI, Edward. Rozwoj mysli ekonomicznej, od merkantylizmu do socjalizmu utopijnego. Wyd. 2 popr. i uzup. Warszawa, Nakł. Panstwowego wydawn. Naukowego, 1953. 267 p.

5247. LIPSON, Ephraim. The economic history of England. London, A. & C. Black, ltd., 1915-31. 3 v. Bibliography, v. 1, 532-544; v. 3, 489-510. (6th edition, New York, Barnes & Noble, 1956-1961.)

5248. LODGE, E. C. Sully, Colbert, and Turgot. London, Methuen & Co., 1931.
5249. LOPEZ, Jose Larraz. La epoca del mercantilismo en Castilla, 1500-1700. Madrid, Ediciones atlas, 1943.
5250. LU, Yu-chang. Chung shang chu i. (Transliterated.) China, 1964. 110 p.
5251. MANN, Fritz Karl. Der marschall Vauban und die volkswirtschaftslehre des absolutismus, eine kritik des merkantilsystems. München und Leipzig, Duncker & Humblot, 1914. xvi, 526 p. Bibliography, 507-523.
5252. MARCHAL, André. La conception de l'économie nationale et des rapports internationaux chez les mercantilistes français et chez leurs contemporains. Préface de m. Lucien Brocard. Paris, Librairie du Recueil Sirey (société anonyme), 1931. 1 p. 1., v-xi, 181 p. 1 1. Bibliographie, 173-178.
5253. MARCHAND, Jacques. Un paradoxe économique; la renaissance du mercantilisme à l'époque contemporaine. Paris, Libraire technique et économique. 1937. 221 p. 1 1. Bibliographie, 217-18.
5254. ———. La renaissance du mercantilisme à l'époque contemporaine. (Thèse, Universite de Paris.) Paris, Librairie technique et économique, 1937. 3 p. 1., 5-221 p., 1 1. Bibliographie, 217-218. (Also published under title: Un paradoxe economique; la renaissance du mercantilisme à l'époque contemporaine. Paris, 1937.)
5255. MARGET, Arthur W. The theory of prices. Englewood Cliffs, New Jersey, Prentice-Hall, inc., 1938-1942. 2 v.
5256. MAZAN, J. Les doctrines économiques de Colbert. Paris, 1900.
5257. MAZZEI, Jacopo. Politica economica internazionale inglese prima di Adamo Smith, con profazione del prof. Marco Fanno. (Pubblicazioni della Università cattolica del sacro cuore. Ser. 3: Scienze sociali, vol. II.) Milano, Società editrice "Vita e pensiero," 1924. 2 p. 1., vii-xix, 460 p.
5258. MENGOTTI, Francesco. . . . Abhandlung über den kolbertismus, oder Die freyheit des kommerzes. Aus dem italiänischen übersetzt und mit einer vorrede begleitet von Joseph Utzschneider. München, J. B. Strobl, 1794. 8 p. 1., 200 p. Bibliographical footnotes.
5259. ———. Il Colbertismo; dissertazione coronata dalla Reale società economica fiorentina li 13 giugno 1792. E 2., riv. dall' autore. Venezia, T. Bettinelli, 1792. 2 p. 1., cxxxi p.
5260. ———. Del commercio dei Romani di Francesco Mengotti, e il Colbertismo. Firenze, V. Batelli, e. c°., 1828. 152 p., 2 1., 105 p., 1 1.
5261. MERKANTYLIZM i poczatki szkoły klasycznej; wybor pism ekonomicznych XVI i XVII wieku. Koncepcje wyboru przygotował i wstepem opatrzył Edward Lipinski, przekł. Czesław Znamierowski, redagowali: Edward Taylor i

	Stefan Zaleski. Wyd. 1. (Biblioteka dzieł ekonomii politycznej: Merkantylizm.) Warszawa, Panstwowe Wydawn. Naukowe, 1958. 802 p.
5262.	MERLE, M. editor. L'Anticolonialisme européen de las Cazas à Karl Marx. Paris, Librairie Armand Colin, 1969.
5263.	MINCHINTON, Walter E. Mercantilism; system or expediency? (Problems in European civilization.) Lexington, Massachusetts, Heath, 1969. xvi, 98 p. Bibliographical references.
5264.	MONTENEGRO, Abelardo Fernando. Mercantilismo, comércio internacional e bolsas. (Faculdade de ciencias de economicas do ceara para catedrático de comércio internacional e cambios-técnica comercial.) Fortaleza, 1955. 68 p. Bibliographies.
5265.	MOORE, Arthur E. Monetary theory before Adam Smith. Cambridge, Mass., Harvard University press, 1923.
5266.	MORINI-COMBY, Jean. Mercantilisme et protectionnisme. Essai sur les doctrines interventionnistes en politique commerciale du XVe au XIXe siècle. Préface de Alfred Zimmern. (Nouvelle bibliothèque économique.) Paris, F. Alcan, 1930. xx, 217 p., 1 l. Bibliographique, 203-213. (Preface in French and English.)
5267.	MOUNIER, André. Les faits et la doctrine économiques es Espagne sous Philippe v. Gerónimo de Uztáriz (1670-1732.) Bordeaux, Imprimerie de l'université, Y. Cadoret, 1919. 1 p. l., 300 p., 1 l. Bibliographie, 178-183, 293-298.
5268.	MUCHMORE, Lynn. "Gerrard de Malynes and mercantile economics." In, History of political economy, 1, 2 (Fall, 1969) 336-58.
5269.	MUN, Thomas. England's treasure by forraign trade. Reprinted from 1st edition, 1664. Oxford, Published for Economic history society, by R. Blackwell, 1933. 1949. viii, 88. (Reprints of economic classics. Oxford, Blackwell, 1967; New York, Augustus M. Kelley, 1968. vii, 88 p.)
5270.	NIELSEN, Axel Eduard Hjorth. Die entstehung der deutschen kameralwissenschaft im 17. Jahrhundert. Jena, G. Fischer, 1911. 2, 125 p. (Ins Deutsche übertragen von Gustav Bargum. Faksimile-Neudruck. Frankfurt a M. Sauer u. Auvermann, 1966. 125 p. Translation of Den tyske kameralvidenskabs opstaaen i det 17. aarhundrede. Translated from K. Danske videnskabernes selskab, Skrifter, 7. raekke, Hist.-fil. afd. II, 2.)
5271.	NISHIMURA, Takao. Kyariko ronso shi no kenkyu. (Transliterated.) Japan, 1967. 198, 30 p. Bibliographical notes.
5272.	OUDARD, George. John Law. A fantastic financier, 1671-1729. London, Jonathan Cape, ltd., 1928.
5273.	PACKARD, Laurence Bradford. The commercial revolution, 1400-1776. Mercantilism--Colbert--Adam Smith. (The Berkshire studies in European history.) New York,

H. Holt and company, c1927. vii, 105 p.
5274. PETANDER, Karl. De nationalekonomiska askadningarna i sverige, sadana de framträde i litteraturen. I. 1718-1765. (Akademisk afhandlung--Stockholms högskola.) Stockholm, Kungl. boktryckeriet, P. A. Norstedt & söner, 1912. xiv, 285 p. Anförd litteratur, p. vii-xiv.
5275. PINON FILGUEIRA, Evaristo M. Interpretación del mercantilismo. (Biblioteca de economia, 1.) Buenos Aires, Editorial Fides, 1952. 115 p. Apéndice: autores mercantilistas clasificados por nacionalidad, 79-113.
5276. PLOTNIKOV, I. S. Merkantilizm. (Transliterated.) Leningrad, 1935. 339 p.
5277. POTTER, William. The key of wealth, or a new way of improving trade. London, 1650. (New York, Johnson reprint corporation, 1971.)
5278. ROBERTS, Hazel Van Dyke. Boisguilbert. New York, Columbia university press, 1935.
5279. ROBINSON, Joan. The new mercantilism. (Inaugural lecture.) Cambridge, England, Cambridge university press 1966.
5280. ROOVER, Raymond de. Gresham on foreign exchange. Cambridge, Massachusetts, Harvard university press, 1949.
5281. ROSCHER, Wilhelm. Zur geschichte der englischen volkswirtschaftslehre im 16. und 17. Jahrhundert. Leipzig, 1851-52.
5282. ROTHKRUG, Lionel. Opposition to Louis XIV. The political and social origins of the French Enlightenment. (Thesis, University of California, Berkeley.) Princeton, Princeton university press, 1965. xv, 533 p. Bibliography, 471-507.
5283. SCHACHT, Hjalmar Horace Greeley. Der theoretische gehalt des englischen merkantilismus. (Inaugural dissertation, Kiel.) Berlin, Druck von Gebr. Mann, 1900. 106 p (Reprint of author's thesis, Kiel, 1900. Frankfurt am Main, Sauer & Auvermann, 1968. 105 p. Bibliographic footnotes.)
5284. SCHATZ, Albert. L'Oeuvre économique de David Hume. Paris, Arthur Rousseau, 1902.
5285. SCHMIDT, Julius August Fritz. Grundlagen der volkswirtschaft in einer stunde; ein buch über die wirtschaftskräfte und ihr gleichgewicht. (Zellenbücherei, nr. 24.) Leipzig-Gaschwitz, Dürr & Weber, m. b. h., 1920. 94 p.
5286. SCHMOLLER, Gustav Friedrich von. Das merkantilsystem in seiner historischen Bedeutung. Städtische, territoriale und staatliche wirtschaftspolitik. (Wegbereiter deutscher volkswirtschaftslehre, Lesestucke für volkswirtschaftler bei der wehrmacht, heft 2.) Frankfurt am Main, V. Klostermann, 1944. 62 p. (First published as a chapter of the author's Studien über die wirthschaftliche politik Friedrichs des Grossen und Preussens Uberhaupt, in jahrbuch für gesetzgebung, verwaltung und volkswirtschaft

im deutschen reich, 8. jahrg, (1884.) Notes, 61-62. (Reprints of economic classics: The mercantile system and its historical significance. 1884. New York, A. M. Kelley, 1967. ix, 95 p. Bibliographical footnotes. Reprint of the 1897 translation of a chapter from the author's Studien uber die wirthschaftliche politik Friedrichs des Grossen. New York, The Macmillan company; London, Macmillan & company, ltd., 1897.)

5287. SCHOECK and Helmut James W. Wiggins. Central planning and neomercantilism. Papers by Garrett Hardin and others. (The William Volker fund series in the humane studies.) Princeton, New Jersey, Van Nostrand, 1964. Bibliographies.

5288. SCHUYLER, Robert Livingston. The fall of the old colonial system. A study in British free trade, 1770-1870. New York, London, Oxford university press, 1945. vii, 344 p. Bibliography, 327-336. (Reprinted: Hamden, Connecticut, Archon books, 1966. vii, 344 p. Bibliography, 327-336.)

5289. SCHWEIZER, Franz August. Geschichte der nationalökonomik in vier monographien über Colbert, Turgot, Smith, Marx, nebst einer philosoph. systematik der nationalokonomie. Ravensburg, Dorn. 1903-1904. 2 v. Bibliographies. (Contents: Vol. I. Merkantilismus von Colbert. . . 1903. Vol. II. Physiokratismus von Turgot. . . 1904.)

5290. SELIGMAN, E. R. A. "Bullionists." In, Encyclopaedia of the social sciences, 3 (1930) 60-64.

5291. SEN, S. R. The economics of Sir James Steuart. London, G. Bell and sons, ltd., 1957.

5292. SENIOR, Nassau William. Three lectures on the transmission of the precious metals from country to country and the mercantile theory of wealth, delivered before the University of Oxford, in June, 1827. (Series of reprints of scarce tracts in economic and political science. No. 3.) London, J. Murray, 1828. London, The London school of economics and political science, 1931. 1 p. 1., facsim.: 1 2., 96 p. (Facsimile of the 1st edition.)

5293. SERGEANT, A. C. The economic policy of Colbert. London, 1899.

5294. SILBERNER, Edmund. La guerre dans la pensée économique du XVIe au XVIIIe siècle. Préface par William E. Rappard. (Etudes sur l'histoire des théories économiques, publiées sous la direction d m. Gaétan Pirou. . . t. VII.) Paris, Librairie du Recueil Sirey, 1939. 3 p. 1., v, 301 p., 1 l. Bibliographie, 271-294.

5295. SMALL, Albion Woodbury. The cameralists. The pioneers of German social polity. Chicago, The University of Chicago press, 1909. xxv, 606 p.

5296. SMITH, Adam. "Of systems of political economy." In Chapters 1-8, Boox IV, The wealth of nations. London, 1776.

5297. SOME thoughts on the interest of money in general, and particularly in the public funds. London, 1738. (2nd edition. London, 1774. 114 p. New York, Johnson reprint corporation, 1971.)

5298. SOMMER, Louise. Die österreichischen kameralisten. In dogmengeschichtlicher darstellung. (Studien zur sozial-, wirtschafts-und verwaltungsgeschichte. XII. hft.) Wien, C. Konegen, 1920- . v. Literaturverzeichnis, 107-119. [Reprinted: Neudruck der Ausg. Wien 1920-1925. Zwei Jeile in einem band. (Studien zur sozial-, wirtschafts-und verwaltungsgeschichte, heft 12, 13.) Aalen, Scientia-verlag, 1967. xx, 106, 507 p. Bibliography, 492-507.]

5299. SPENGLER, Joseph J. "Richard Cantillon. First of the moderns." In Journal of political economy, LXII (1954.)

5300. ———. Mercantilism and physiocratic growth theory. (By B. F. Hoselitz and J. J. Spengler.) 1960.

5301. ———. et al. Pierre de Boisguilbert et la naissance de l'économie politique. Preface by Alfred Sauvy. Paris, Institut national d'études demographiques Presses universitaires de France, 1966. 2 v.

5302. SRBIK, Heinrich. Der staatliche exporthandel österreichs v Leopold I bis Maria Theresia; untersuchunger zur wirtschaftsgeschichte österreichs im zeitalter des merkantilismus. Mit unterstützung der Kaiserl. Akademie der wissenschaften in Wien. Wien und Leipzig, W. Braumüller, 1907. xxxvi, 432 p.

5303. STAUDTE, Roland. John Law, 1671-1729; ein beitrag zur geld- und kredit-theorie der merkantilisten und wirtschaftspolitik der Régence. (Dissertation, Zürich.) Winterthur, P. G. Keller, 1953. vi, 112 p. Bibliography, 105-110.

5304. STEUART, Sir James. An inquiry into the principles of political oeconomy; being an essay on the science of domestic policy in free nations. London, A. Miller. . ., 1767. (Edited by Andrew Skinner. Chicago, University of Chicago press, 1966. 2 v.)

5305. STRANGELAND, C. E. Pre-Malthusian doctrines of population. New York, Columbia university press, 1904.

5306. STRAUSS, E. Sir William Petty; portrait of a genius. London, Bodley Head ltd., 1954.

5307. SUVIRANTA, Bruno. The theory of the balance of trade in England. A study in mercantilism. Helsingfors, Printed by Suomal. kirjail. seuran kirjap. o.y., Bibliographical index, 167-171. New York, A.M. Kelley, 1967. iv, 171 p. Bibliographical.)

5308. TAUTSCHER, A. Die staatswirtschaftslehre des kameralismus. Munich, A. Francke verlag, 1947.

5309. TAWNEY, R. H. and Eileen Power, editors. Tudor economic documents. London, Longmans, Green & Co., 1924

5310. TEMPLE, William. A vindication of commerce and the arts. London, 1758. (New York, Johnson reprint corporation, 1971.)

5311. THOMAS, Parakunnel Joseph. Mercantilism and the East India trade. (Reprints of economic classics. First published in 1926.) New York, A. M. Kelley, 1965. xii, 176 p. Bibliography, vii-xii.
5312. TUCKER, G. S. L. Progress and profits in British economic thought, 1650-1850. London, Cambridge university press, 1960.
5313. TUCKER, Josiah. Instructions for travellers. London, 1757. (New York, Johnson reprint corporation, 1971.
5314. UJITA, Tomizo. Shihonshugi seiritsuki no shokuminchi mondai. (Transliterated.) Japan, 1964, 222 p. Bibliographical notes.
5315. VICKERS, Douglas. Studies in the theory of money, 1690-1776. Philadelphia. Chilton book company, 1959.
5316. VINER, Jacob. "English theories of foreign trade before Adam Smith." In, Journal of political economy, 38 (1930) 249-301, 404-457.
5317. ———. "Mercantilism." In, Chapters 1-2, Studies in the Theory of International Trade. New York, Harper and Brothers, 1937.
5318. VOORTHUIJSEN, William Dirk. De Repuliek der verenigde Nederlanden en let mercantilisme. 's-Gravenhage, M. Nijhoff, 1964. x; 143 p. Bibliography, 131-134. (Summary in English.)
5319. WEIGAND, Wilhelm. Der Abbe Galiani. Bonn, Ludwig Rohrscheid, 1948.
5320. WEYHMANN, Alfred. Die merkantilistische währungspolitik herzog Leopolds con Lothringen (1697-1729) mit besonderer berucksichtigung der geschichte John Laws. (III. ergänzungsheft zum jahrbuch der gesellschaft für lothringische geschichte und altertumskunde.) Leipzig, Quelle & Meyer, 1910. 2 p. 1., iii, 100 p. Quellen- und litteraturverzeichnis, iii.
5321. WILSON, Charles Henry. Mercantilism. (Historical association. General series no. 37.) London, Published for the Historical Association by Routledge and Paul, 1958. 28 p.
5322. ———. The other face of mercantilism. In, Royal historical society, London. Transactions. London, 5th series, v. 9 (1959) 81-101. Bibliographical footnotes.
5323. WIRMINGHAUS, Alexander. Zwei spanische merkantilisten. (Gerónimo de Uztariz und Bernardo de Ulloa.) Ein beitrag zur geschichte der nationalökonomie. (Sammlung nationalökonomischer und statistischer abhandlungen des staatswissenschaftlichen seminars zu Halle a. d. S. . . . 4. bd. 2. hft.) Jena, G. Fischer, 1886. 3 p. 1., 88 p.
5324. WITTKOWSKY, George Heyman. Jonathan Swift and the age of mercantilism. (Abridgement of thesis, New York university, 1942.) New York, New York university, 1946. 15 p. Bibliographical footnotes.
5325. WU, Chi-Yuen. An outline of international price theories. London, Routledge and Kegan Paul, ltd., 1939.

5326. ZIELENZIGER, Kurt. Die alten deutschen kameralisten; ein beitrage zur geschichte der nationalökonomie und zum problem des merkantilismus. (Beiträge zur geschichte der nationalökonomie . . . 2. hft.) (Appeared in part as the author's inaugural dissertation.) Jena, G. Fischer, 1914- .

H. Section II.

3. PHYSIOCRACY

5327. ASSOCIATION Francaise de science économique. Bi-centenaire du "Tableau économique" de François Quesnay. Paris, 1958. 48 p.
5328. BAUDEAU, Abbe Nicholas. Explication du Tableau economique, a Madame . . . Paris, Delalain, 1776. 2, 172.
5329. ———. "Du marchand de grains." In, Journal de l'agriculture, du commerce, et des finances (December, 1773.)
5330. ———. Premiere introduction a la philosophie economique ou analyse des etats policies. Paris? 1771.
5331. BEER, Max. An inquiry into physiocracy. London, G. Allen and Unwin ltd. 1939. 196 p. (1st edition, new impression. London, Cass, 1966. 196 p. Bibliographical footnotes. New York, Russell & Russell, 1966. 196 p. Bibliographical footnotes.)
5332. BERENDTS, Eduard Nikolaevich. Merkantilisty i fiziokraty. (Transliterated.) Russia, 1892. 1p. 1., 66 p., 1 1.
5333. BLOONFIELD, Arthur I. "The foreign-trade doctrines of the phsiocrats." In, American economic review, 27, 4 (December, 1938) 716-735.
5334. BODIN, Jean. Les six livres de la republique. Translated by R. Knolles. London, Bishop, 1906.
5335. BOSHER, J. F. The single duty project. A study of the movement for a French customs union in the eighteenth century. (University of London historical studies, 16.) London, University of London, Athlone press, 1964. x, 215 p. Bibliography, 189-205.
5336. BOUDEVILLE, J. R. "Les physiocrates et le circuit économique." In, Revue d'économie politique 64, 3 (1954) 456-481.
5337. BOURTHOUMIEUX, Charles. Le mythe de l'ordre naturel en économie politique depuis Quesnay. . . . Paris, M. Rivière, 1935. viii, 140 p. Ouvrages consultés, 137-140. (These, Univ. de Paris.) Published also under title: Essai sur le fondement philosophique des doctrines économiques, Rousseau contre Quesnay. Paris, 1936.)
5338. BOWMAN, Mary Jean. "The consumer in the history of

economic doctrine." In, American economic review, 41, 2 (May, 1951) 1-18.
5339. BREHMER, Albrecht. Die volkswirtschaftlichen artikel der grossen encyklopädie. Eine würdigung. Breslau, A. Schreiber, 1901. 1 p. 1., 112, 2 p. (Inaugural dissertation, Breslau.)
5340. BRETSCHNEIDER, Karl Konrad. Isaak Iselin. Ein schweizer physiokrat des XVIII. jahrhunderts . . . Aachen, Aachener verlags- und druckereigesellschaft m. b. h., 1908. 2 p. 1., 172 p. (Inaugural dissertation, Bern.)
5341. CADET, Felix. Histoire de l'economie politique. Les precurseurs. Boisquilbert. Vauban. Quesnay. Turgot. (Societe industrielle de Reims. Conferences de 1867-1868.) Reims, H. Gerard; Paris, E. Lacroix, 1869. 3, 248 p.
5342. CHINARD, Gilbert. "Jefferson and the Physiocrats." Chronicle, University of California, 33 (1931) 18.
5343. DAIRE, Eugène. Physiocrates. Réimpression de l'éd. 1846. (Collection des principaux economistes, t. 2.) Osnabrück, Zeller, 1966. ixxxviii, 1027 p. Bibliographical footnotes.
5344. DUPONT de Nemours, Pierre Samuel. De l'exploration et de l'importation des grains. Soissons et Paris, 1764. (Edited by Edgard Depitre. Paris, 1911. 86 p.)
5345. ———. De l'origine et des progrès d'une science nouvelle. Londres, 1768. (Edited by A. Dubois. Paris, P. Gehtner, 1910.)
5346. EINAUDI, Mario. The physiocratic doctrine of judicial control. With an introduction by Charles Howard McIlwain. (Harvard political studies, published under the direction of the Department of government in Harvard university, with the aid of the Louis Adams Frothingham fund.) Cambridge, Massachusetts, Harvard university press, 1938. x p., 2 1., 3-96 p.
5347. ———. "The Physiocratic theory of taxation." In, Economic essays in honour of Gustav Cassel. London, George Allen & Unwin, ltd., 1933. 129-142 p.
5348. ESMEIN, M. La science politique des physiocrates. Address, opening session, Congress of Learned Societies. Paris, 1906.
5349. ———. Memoire comptes rendus d l'academic des sciences morales et politiques, 1904. (Regarding assembly of the Physiocrats.)
5350. FAURE-SOULET, Jean François. Economie politique et progrès au "siècle des lumières." Préf. de Paul Harsin. Avant-propos d'André Piatier. (Collection Techniques économiques modernes, t. 4. Serie histoire et pensée économiques, 1.) Paris, Gauthier-Villars, 1964. xv, 252 p. Bibliography, 239-245.
5351. FEILBOGEN, S. Smith and Turgot. Vienna, A. Hölder, 1892.
5352. FISHMAN, Leslie. "A reconsideration of the Tableau Economique." In, Current economic comment. University

of Illinois, 20, 1 (February, 1958) 41-50.
5353. GAZAVE, Jean. La terre ne ment pas, introduction à une physiocratie nouvelle. 6. ed. Villefranche-de-Rouergue, C. Salingardes, 1942. 4 p. 1., 11-237 p.
5354. GILMER, Francis Walker. Sketches, essays and translations. Baltimore, F. Lucas, 1828. xvi, 17-201.
5355. GUNTZBERG, Benedikt Elias. Die gesellschafts-und staatslehre der Physiokraten. (Staats- und völkerrechtliche abhandlungen . . . hrsg. von dr. G. Jellinek und dr. G. Anschütz, VI, 3.) Leipzig, Duncker & Humblot, 1907. 4 p. 1., xi-xv, 144 p. Bibliography, xiii-xv.
5356. HAMBLOCH, George. Die physiokratische lehre von reinertrag und einheitssteuer. Ein beitrag zur darstellung des physiokratischen wirtschafts- und steuersystems . . . Bonn, E. Georgi, universitäts-buchdruckerei, 1905. vi, 84 p. Bibliography, v-vi. (Inaugural dissertation, Heidelberg.)
5357. HASADA, Kiyoshi. Junogakuha chinginsetsu kenkyu. (Transliterated.) (Hiroshima daigaku seiji keikai kenkyu sosho, dai 4-satsu.) Japan, 1966. 273 p. Bibliographical footnotes.
5358. HERLITZ, L. "The tableau économique and the doctrine of sterility." In, Scandinavian economic history review, 9, 1 (1961) 3-55.
5359. HEUSCHLING, Xavier (i.e. Philippe François Xavier Théodose). Des impôts dans leur rapport avec l'agriculture. (Rural economy pamphlets, v. 15, no. 7.) Bruxelles, Sacré-Savary, 185-? 6 p.
5360. HIGGS, Henry. The Physiocrats. (Six lectures on the French économistes of the 18th century) London, New York, Macmillan company, 1897. [Russian edition: 1899. 112, ii, ii p. Bibliography, i-ii (2d group). Spanish edition: Los fisiócratas; versión española de Javier Márques. (Seccion de obras de economia del Fondo de cultura económica dirigida por Daniel Cosio Villegas.) Mexico, Fondo de cultura económica, 1944. American editions: New York, Langland press, 1952. 158 p. Hamden, Connecticut, Archon books, 1963. 158 p. Bibliography. Reprints of Economic classics. Reprint of 1897 edition. New York, A. M. Kelley, 1968. x, 158 p. Bibliography, 153-154.]
5361. JEFFERSON, Thomas. The correspondence of Jefferson and Du Pont de Nemours. With an introduction on Jefferson and the physiocrats, by Gilbert Chinard . . . (John Hopkins studies in international thought.) Baltimore, The Johns Hopkins press; Paris, "Les Belles lettres," 1931. 3 p. 1., ix-cxxiii, 293., 1 1. (Reprinted title: Correspondence between Thomas Jefferson and Pierre Samuel du Pont de Nemours, 1798-1817. Edited by Dumas Malone . . . Translations by Linwood Lehman. Supplement by Gilbert Chinard. New York, Da Capo press, 1970. xxv, 210, cxxiii p.)
5362. JOBERT, Ambroise. Magnats polonais et physiocrates français (1767-1774) Dijon, 1941. 92 p. Bibliography, 7-11. (These complementaire, Lyons. Published also as

Preclassical Period

Collection historique de l'Institut d'études slaves, 10.)
5363. LABRIOLA, Arturo. Le dottrine economiche di F. Quesnay. (Saggio) Napoli, E. Croce, 1897. viii, 198 p., 1 1.
5364. LABROUQUERE, André. Les idées coloniales des Physiocrates. Paris, Presses universitaires de France, 1927.
5365. LACH, Donald F. Asia in the making of Europe. Chicago, The university of Chicago press, 1966.
5366. LANDAUER, Carl. Die theorien der merkantilisten und physiokraten uber die okonomische bedeutung des Luxus. Munich, M. Steinebach, 1915.
5367. LAVERGNE, L. de. Les economistes français du 18 siècle. Paris, Guillaumin, 1860.
5368. LEWINSKI, Jan Stanislaw. Tworcy economji politycznej (fizjokraci--Smith--Ricardo) wstep do historji doktryn ekonomicznych. (Biblioteca uniwersytetu lubelskiego, Wydzial prawa i nauk społeczno-ekonomicznych, nr. 1.) Lublin, Nakładem, Uniwersytetu lubelskiego, 1920. 155, 5 p.
5369. LUNDBERG, I. C. Turgot's unknown translator. The Hague, Martinus Nijhoff, 1964.
5370. LUTFALLA, Michel. "La Chine vue par quelques économistes du xviiie siècle." In, Population, 1962.
5371. _____. "L'évidence, fondement nécessaire et suffisant de l'ordre naturel chez Quesnay et Morelly." In, Revue d'histoire économique et sociale, 41 (1963) 213-249.
5372. LUTHY, Herbert. François Quesnay und die idee der vlokswirtschaft. Zürich, Polygraphischer verlag, 1959. 38 p.
5373. LY, Siou Y. Les grands courants de la pensée économique chinoise dans l'antiquité (du VIe au IIIe siècle avant J.-C.) et leur influence sur la formation de la doctrine physiocratique . . . Paris, Jouve & Cie, 1936. 107 p. Bibliographie, 95-105. (Thèse, Dijon.)
5374. MAVERICK, Lewis A. China: a model for Europe. San Antonio, Texas, P. Anderson company, 1946.
5375. _____. "Chinese influences upon the Physiocrats." In, Economic history, 3, 13 (February, 1938) 54-67.
5376. MEEK, Ronald L. The economics of physiocracy. Essays and translations. (University of Glasgow social and economic studies, new series, 2.) Cambridge, Harvard university press, 1963. c1962. 482 p. London, George Allen & Unwin, ltd., 1962.)
5377. _____. "Physiocracy and the early theories of underconsumption." In, Economica, new series, 18 (1951) 229-69.
5378. MENCK-TICHAUER, Clara. François Quesnay als politischer oekonom. Wertheim a. M., Buchdruckerei E. Bechstein, 1927. 2 p. 1., 82, 2 p. Literaturverzeichnis, 81-82. (Inaugural dissertation, Heidelberg.)
5379. MIRABEAU, Victor de Riquetti, Marquis de. L'Ami des hommes, ou traité de la population. Avignon (Paris) 1756. 6 v. (Nouvelle edition. Amsterdam? 1758-60. 3 v.)
5380. _____. Le consolateur, pour servir de réponse à la

theorie de l'impot. . . . Bruxelles, 1763. 368 p.
5381. _____. Les économiques. Par L.D. H. (l'Ami des hommes.) Amsterdam et Paris, 1769-72. 2 v.
5382. _____. Essais sur les ponts et chaussés, la voirie et les corvées. Amsterdam, 1759. 404 p.
5383. _____. Les finances considerées dans le droit naturel. . . . Amsterdam, 1762. 204 p.
5384. _____. The oeconomical table. An attempt towards ascertaining and exhibiting the source, progress, and employment of riches, with explanations, by the Friends of Mankind. Translated from French. London? 1766.
5385. _____. Philosophie rurale, ou économie génerale et particulière de l'agriculture. Amsterdam (Paris), 1764.
5386. _____. Théorie de l'impôt. Paris, 1760. (Supplément. La Haye, 1776.)
5387. _____. Victors de Riquetti, weyland marquis von Mirabeau . . . Landwirtschafts-philosophie, oder, politische oekonomie der gesammten land- und staats-wirthschaft, gebaut auf die unwandelbare ordnung physischer und moralischer gesetze zu sicherer beforderung des wohlstandes der lander. Aus dem franzosischen frey ubersetzet, und mit anmerkungen versehen von Christian August Wichmann . . Liegnitz und Leipzig, D. Siegert, 1797-98. 2 v. Bibliography, v. ("Das original dieses werkes ist . . . ohne namen des verfassers, unter dem titel, Philosophie rurale, ou économie générale et politique de l'agriculture, reduite à l'ordre immuable des loix physiques et morales, qui assurent la prospérité des empires, im j. 1764 zu Amsterdam, chez les libraires associés, in drey gross-duo-dez-banden erschienen, aus denen ich zween gross-octav bände zu machen für dienlich befunden habe.")
5388. MOSSION, Edouard. Dupont de Nemours et la question de la compagnie des Indes. (Burt Franklin research and source works series, no. 200.) New York, Burt Franklin, 1968. 6, 134 p. Bibliography, 5th prelim. p. (Thèse, Poitiers. Université de Poitiers. Faculté de droit. Originally published, Paris, 1918).
5389. MOURANT, John Arthur. The physiocratic conception of natural law . . . Chicago, Illinois, 1943. ii numb. 1., 72 p. Bibliography, 70-72. (Thesis, Ph.D., University of Chicago, 1940.)
5390. NECKER, Jacques. De l'administration des finances de la France. Paris? 1784. (Nouvelle edition, 1785. 247 p.
5391. _____. Sur la législation et le commerce des grains. Paris, 1775. 2 v. in 1.
5392. NEILL, Thomas Patrick. The physiocrats. A re-evaluation. St. Louis, 1943. x, 347 numb. 1., 1 1. Bibliography, 323-347. (Thesis, Ph.D., St. Louis university, 1943.) [Copy of manuscript made by University microfilms, publication no. 765. Abstracted in Microfilm abstracts, v. 6 (1945) no. 2, p. 29.]
5393. _____. "The Physiocrats' concept of economics." In, Quarterly journal of economics, 63, 4 (November, 1949)

Preclassical Period

532-553.
5394. _____. "Quesnay and physiocracy." In, Journal of the history of ideas, 9, 2 (1948) 153-173.
5395. NEMTCHINOV, V. S. "Le tableau économic de F. Quesnay." Cahiers de l'Institut de science économique appliquée, 23, 173 (May, 1966) 11-37.
5396. NEYMARCK, Alfred. Turgot et ses doctrines. Paris, Guillaumin et c^{ie}., 1885. 2 v. Bibliographical footnotes. (Reprinted: Genève, Slatkine reprints, 1967. 2 v.)
5397. ONCKEN, Auguste. "Physiocrats as founders of the mathematical school." In, Economic journal (June, 1966).
5398. OPALEK, Kazimierz. Prawo natury u polskich fizjokratow. Wyd. 1 Warszawa, Kosiazka i wiedza, 1953. 158, 2 p. Bibliography, 150-159.
5399. OSWALT, Irene. Das laissez-faire der physiokraten. Freiburg i. Br., Rota-Druck J. Krause, 1964. 190 p. Bibliography, 181-190. (Inaugural dissertation, Freiburg i. B.)
5400. PERVINQUIERE, M. Contribution a l'etude de la productivite dans la Physiocratie.
5401. PETZET, Wolfgang. Der physiokratismus und die entdeckung des wirtschaftlichen kreislaufes; versuch einer soziologischen erklärung. (Probleme der staats-und kultursoziologie . . . 3. bd.) Karlsruhe, G. Braun, 1929. viii, 158 p. Bibliography, 155-158. (Imprint covered by label, Berlin, Junker und Dünnhaupt, 1932.)
5402. PHILLIPS, A. "The Tableau économique as a simple Leontief model." In, Quarterly journal of economics 69, 1 (February, 1955) 137-144.
5403. QUESNAY, François. Allgemeine grundsatze der wirtschaftlichen regierung eines acker bautreibenden reiches, aus dem. franzosischen. Original der ausg. Oncken's ins. Deutsche ubertragen von valentine dorn und eingeleitet bon Heinrich Waentig . . . Jena, G. Fischer, 1921. 101 p.
5404. _____. Le droit naturel. Paris, 1765. [Russian edition: Izbrannye ekonomicheskie proizoedeniia. (Transliterated.)] 1960. 549 Bibliography.
5405. _____. François Quesnay et la physiocratie. Paris, Institut national d'études démographiques, Presses universitaires de France, 1958.
5406. _____. "Les grains." Grande Encyclopedie, 1756.
5407. _____ Oeuvres economiques et philosophiques de Francis Quesnay fondateur du systeme physiocratique; accompagnees des eloges et d'autres travaux biographiques sur Quesnay par differents auteurs; publiees avec une introduction et des notes par Auguste Oncken. Francfort s/M.J. Bear & c^{ie}, 1888. (Paris, Jules Peelman and company, 1888.)
5408. _____. Physiocratie, ou constitution naturelle du gouvernement le plus avantageux au genre humain. Recueil pub. par Du Pont . . . Leyde et Paris, Chez Merlin, 1768. 2 v. (v. 1: 2 p. 1., cxx, 172 p. v. 2: 173-520 p.)

5409. _____. Tableau économique des physiocrates. (1758). Préf. de Michel Lutfalla. (Perspectives économiques. Le fondateurs de l'économie.) Paris, Calmann-Lévy, 1969. 270 p. Bibliographical references. (English edition: London, British economic association, 1894. Facsimile of 1st edition.)

5410. QUESSEL, Ludwig. Francois Quesnay's system der politischen okonomie; darstellung und kritik . . . Zurich, Buchdruckerei kirsten & zeisberg, 1903. 3, 136.

5411. RAYNAUD, B. "Les discussions sur l'ordre naturel au xviiie siècle." In, Revue d'économie politique (1905) 132-148.

5412. _____. La loi naturelle en economie politique. Paris, Domat-Montchrestien, 1936.

5413. REICHWEIN, Adolf. China and Europe. Intellectual and artistic concepts in the eighteenth century. Translated by J. C. Powell. New York, Alfred A. Knopf, inc., 1925.

5414. RICHNER, Edmund. Le Mercier de la Rivière; ein führer der physiokratischen bewegung in Frankreich. (Zürcher volkswirtschaftliche forschungen . . . bd. 19.) Zürich, Girsberger & co., 1931. xx, 288 p. Verzeichnis der werke von Le Mercier de la Rivière, xiii-xiv. Literaturverzeichnis, xv-xx.

5415. RIVIERE, Paul-Pierre Le Mercier de la. L'Ordre naturel e essentiel des sociétés politiques. Londres et Paris, 1767. (Edited by E. Deprite, Paris. P. Gehtner, 1910.)

5416. SALLERON, Louis. La terre et le travail . . . (L'Abeille, 4.) Paris, Plon, 1941. 5 p. 1., 3-183 p., 2 1.

5417. SAMUELS, Warren J. "The physiocratic theory of economic policy." In, Quarterly journal of economics, 76 (February, 1962) 145-162.

5418. SAY, Leon. The life of Turgot. Translated by Gustave Masson. London, Routledge & Kegal Paul ltd. 1888. 210 p.

5419. SCHELLE, Gustave. Du Pont de Nemours et l'ecole physiocratique. Paris, Paris, Librairie Guillaumin et c^{ie}, 1888. 2 p. 1., 456 p.

5420. SHAFER, R. J. The economic societies in the Spanish world, 1763-1821. Syracuse, New York, Syracuse university press, 1958.

5421. SOCIETE populaire du canton de Montfort, l'amaury. Francois Quesnay. Livre d'or 1900. Versailles, Imprimerie aubert, 1900. 1, 7-117.

5422. SPENGLER, Joseph J. "The physiocrats and Say's law of Markets." In, Journal of political economy, 53 (September-December, 1945.)

5423. SPIEGEL, Henry W., editor. Pierre Samuel Du Pont de Nemours on economic curves. Baltimore, The Johns Hopkins press, 1955.

5424. STEPHENS, W. Walter. The bibliography and writings of Turgot, comptroller-general of France, 1774-76. London and New York, Longmans, Green and company, 1895. xiv, 325 p.

5425. STYS, Wincenty. Nouveau schéma interprétatif au tableau économique de François Quesnay; ouvrage posthume. (Tłum. z oryginals polskiego Franciszek Longchamps.) (Zeszyty naukowe uniwersytetu wroclawskiego. Seria A. Nauki spoleczne, nr. 34.) Warszawa, Panstwowe wydawn. Naukowe, 1961. 26 p.

5426. SUAUDEAU, René. Les représentations figurées des physiocrates. Paris, Recueil sirey, 1947. 71 p. Bibliographical footnotes.

5427. SUNG, Ch'êng-hsien. Lun chung nung chu i. (Transliterated.) China, 1957. 74.

5428. TAYLOR, O. H. "Economics and the idea of 'Jus naturale.' " In, Quarterly journal of economics, 44, 2 (February, 1930) 205-241. (Reprinted in, O. H. Taylor, 70-99. Economics and liberalism. Cambridge, Massachusetts, Harvard university press, 1955.)

5429. TSUNASAWA, Mitsuaki. Kindai nihon no dochaku shiso. (Transliterated.) Japan, 1969. 217 p.

5430. TURGEON, Charles and Charles-Henri Turgeon. Premières études. La valeur d'après les économistes anglais et francais depuis Adam Smith et les physiocrates jusqu'à nos jours. 3. éd. Paris, Editions sirey, 1925.

5431. TURGOT, Ann Robert Jacques. Oeuvres de Turgot. Précédée d'une notice sur la vie . . . New edition by E. Daire and H. Dussard. Paris, Guillaumin, 1844. 2 v. (Oeuvres. Ed. Du Pont de Nemours. Paris, Delance, 1808-1811 9 v.)

5432. _____. Réflexions sur la formation et la distribution des richesses. Paris, 1770. Paris, 1778. 130 1. [English editions: London, 1793. 77 p. London, 1795. 122 p. American edition. Edited by W. J. Ashley. (Economic classics series.) New York, Macmillan company, 1898. 112 p.]

5433. _____. The use and abuses of money, and the improvements of it, by two propositions for regulating our coin. . . . London, A. Bancks, C. Harper and G. Marriott, 1671.

5434. WARE, Norman J. "The Physiocrats; a study in economic rationalization." In, American Economic Review, 21, 4 (December, 1931) 607-619.

5435. WEULERSSE, Georges. Les manscrits économiques de Francois Quesnay et du marquis de Mirabeau aux archives nationales (M. 778 à M. 785). Inventaire, extraits et notes, par Georges Wenlersse. Paris, P. Geuthner, 1910. vii, 150 p. (Reprinted: Burt Franklin bibliography & reference series, 170.) New York, B. Franklin, 1968. vii, 150 p.)

5436. _____. Le mouvement physiocratique en France (de 1756 à 1770). (Maison des sciences de l'homme. Rééditions, 4.) Paris, 1910. 2 v. (Paris, La Haye, Mouton; New York, Johnson reprint corporation; S. R. Publishers, 1968. 2 v. Bibliography, v. 1, xiii-xxxiv.)

5437. _____. Les physiocrates. (Encyclopedie scientifique . . .

Bibliotheque d'economie politique.) Paris, G. Doin & c^{ie}, 1931. xvi, 332 p. Bibliography, 322-326.

5438. _____. La physiocratie à la fin du règne de Louis xv, 1770-1774. Préf. de Ernest Labrousse. 1. ed. Paris, Presses universitaires de France, 1959. xi, 238 p. Bibliography, 231-235.

5439. _____. La physiocratie sous les ministères de Turgot et de Necker (1774-1781). Préf. de Paul Mantoux; avant-propos de J. Conan. 1. éd. Paris, Presses universitaires de France, 1950. xvi, 374 p. Bibliography, 367-371.

5440. WILL, Robert M. "Economic Thought in the Encyclopédie." In, Southern economic journal, 32, 2 (October, 1965) 191-203.

5441. WOOG, Henri. The tableau économique of François Quesnay; an essay in the explanation of its mechanism and a critical review of the interpretation of Marx, Bilimovic and Oncken. Bern, A. Francke, 1950. 100 p. Bibliography.

5442. YOKOYAMA, Masahiko. Junoshugi bunseki. (Transliterated.) Japan, 1958. xi, 286, 30 p. Bibliography, 21-30 (3d group).

5443. ZAGORSKI, Józef. Ekonomia Franciszka Quesnaya. Wyd. 1. Warszawa, Panstwowe wydawn. Naukowe, 1963. xix, 1., 444 p.

J. CLASSICAL PERIOD

Section I. General Works

5444. ABBOTT, Charles. A treatise of the law relative to merchant ships and seamen. London, 1802. 1 v. (Edited with notes, appendix by Mr. Sergeant Shoe. London, 1844. 1 v.)
5445. ACCOUNT of the Levant company; with some notices of the benefits conferred upon society by its officers, etc. London, 1825.
5446. An ACCOUNT of the proceedings of the merchants, manufacturers, and others concerned in the wool and woollen trade of Great Britain, etc. London, 1800. 1 v.
5447. ACLAND, John. A plan for rendering the poor independent or public contributions, founded on the basis of the friendly societies commonly called clubs. Exeter, 1786.
5448. ADAMS, John Quincy. Report upon weights and measures, 1817. Washington, 1821.
5449. An ADDRESS to the Congress of the United States on the utility and justice of restrictions upon foreign commerce. Philadelphia, 1809. 97 p.
5450. An ADDRESS to the proprietors of bank stock, the London and country bankers, and the public in general, on the affairs of the Bank of England. London, 1828.
5451. ADDRESS to the two Houses of Parliament on the importance of the corn laws. 2d edition. London, 1817. 23 p.
5452. AGAZZINI, Michel. La science de l'économie politique, ou Principes de la formation, du progrès et de la décadence de la richesse, et application de ces principes à l'administration des nation. Paris et Londres, 1822.
5453. AGOULT, D'. Ancien évêque de Pamiers. Des impôts indirects et des droits de consommation, ou Essai sur l'origine et le système des impositions françaises, comparé avec celui de l'Angleterre. Paris, 1817.
5454. ———. Des impôts indirects et des droits de consommation; ou, Essais sur l'origine et le système des impositions francaises, comparé avec cekui d'angleterre. Paris, 1817.
5455. ALBERGO, G. Storia dell'economica politica in Sicilia. Palermo, 1855.
5456. ALCEDO, Don Antonio de. Diccionario geographico-historico de las Indias occidentales o America: es a saber de los Reynos del Peru, Nueva España, Tierra Firme, Chile, y Nueva Reyna de Granada, Madrid, 1786-99. 5 v.
5457. ALISON, Archibald. Free trade and protection, being a tract on the necessity of agricultural protection. Edinburgh and London, 1844.

5458. ———. The principles of population and their connexion with human happiness. Edinburgh, 1840. 2 v.
5459. ALISON, W. P. Observations on the management of the poor in Scotland and its effects on the health of the great towns. Edinburgh, 1844.
5460. ———. Reply to the pamphlet entitled "Proposed alteration of the Scottish poor-law considered and commented on." Edinburgh, 1840.
5461. ALLARDYCE, Alexander. An address to the proprietors of the Bank of England. 3d edition. London, 1798. 156 p.
5462. ALLEN, John. Wealth of Great Britain. London, 1840.
5463. ALMACK, John. Character, motives and proceedings of the Anti-Corn-Law Leaguers, with a few general remarks on the consequences that would result from a free trade in corn. London, 1843.
5464. ANALYSE et examen du systeme des philosophes économistes. Par un solitaire. Genéve, 1787. 294 p.
5465. ANALYSE de l'ouvrage de la legislation et le commerce des grains. Paris, 1776. 1 v.
5466. ANALYSE et tableaux de l'influence de la petite vérole sur la mortalité à chaque âge, et de celle qu'un préservatif tel que la vaccine peut avoir sur la population et la longévité. Par M. Duvillard. Paris, 1806. 1 v.
5467. ANDERSON, James. A calm investigation of the circumstances that have led to the present scarcity of grain in Britain, suggesting the means of alleviating that evil, and of preventing the recurrence of such a calamity in future. London, 1801.
5468. ———. An enquiry into the nature of the corn laws, with a view to the new corn bill proposed for Scotland. Edinburgh, 1777.
5469. ———. Essays relating to agriculture. 3rd edition. Edinburgh, 1784. 2 v. (4th edition. London, 1797. 3 v.
5470. ANNALES d'hygiène publique, et de médecine légale. Paris, 1829-44. 32 v.
5471. ANNALS of banks for savings, containing an account of their rise and progress, with reports and essays on their national importance, constitution, etc. London, 1818.
5472. ANNUAL reports of the registrar-general. London, 1839.
5473. ANSELL, Charles. A treatise on friendly societies, etc. London, 1835. 1 v.
5474. An ANSWER to the reply to the supposed treasury pamphlet. London, 1785.
5475. An ANSWER to 'War in disguise'; or remarks on the new doctrine of England concerning neutral trade. New York, 1806. (Reprinted in London, 1806.)
5476. APERCU statistique de la France. Par M. Girault de St. Fargeau. 2d edition. Paris, 1836.
5477. ARGUELLES, C. Diccionario de hacienda. London, 1826. 3 v. (2d edition. Madrid, 1834-40.)

5478. ARNOULD. De la balance du commerce et des relations commerciales extérieures de la France dans toutes les parties du globe, particulièrement à la fin du règne de Louis XIV, et au moment de la révolution; le tout appuyé de notes et de tables raisonnées, authentiques, sur le commerce et la navigatin, la population, le produit territorial et l'industrie, le prix du blé, le numéraire, le revenu, la dépense et la dette publique de la France à ces deux époques, avel la valeur de ses importations et exportations progressives depuis 1716, jusqu'en 1788 inclusivement. Paris, 1792. 2 v. 1 v.

5479. _____. Histoire générale des finances de France, depuis le commencement de la monarchie; pour servir d'introduction à la annuelle du budget de l'empire francais. Paris, 1806.

5480. _____. Système maritime et politique des Européens dans le dix-huitième siècle, fonde sur leurs traités de paiz, de commerce et de navigation. Paris, 1797. 1 v.

5481. ARRETA de MONTE-SEGURO, Antonio. Dissertation sobre el aprecio que se debe hacer de las artes practicas, y de los que las exercen con honradez, intelligencia y aplicacion. 1781.

5482. ARRIVABENE, Le Comte Jean. Principes fondamentaux de l'économie politique, tirés des leçons édites et inédites de M. N. W. Senior, professeur d'économie politique a l'Université d'Oxford. Paris, 1835.

5483. _____. Sur les colonies agricoles de la Belgique et de la Hollande. Bruxelles, 1830.

5484. _____. Sur les moyens d'améliorer le sort des ouvriers. Bruxelles, 1832.

5485. _____. Situation économique de la Belgique. Bruxelles, 1843.

5486. ATCHISON, Nathaniel. A letter addressed to Rowland Burdon, on the present state of carrying part of the coal trade, with tables of the duties on coal raised by the corporation of the city of London (from 1700 to 1801). London, 1802.

5487. ATKINSON, William. Principles of political economy. . . . London, 1840. (Introduction by Horace Greeley. New York, 1843.)

5488. _____. The state of the science of political economy investigated. London, 1838.

5489. ATTWOOD, G. Review of the statutes and ordinances of assize, which have been established in England from the fourth year of King John, 1202, to the thirty-seventh of his present Majesty (George III). London, 1801.

5490. ATTWOOD, Thomas. Observations on currency, population and pauperism. 1818. 1v.

5491. AUBER, Peter. An analysis of the laws and constitution of the East India company. London, 1827. 1 v.

5492. AUBERT DE VITRY. Recherches sur les varies causes de la misère et de la félicité publiques, ou de la population et des subsistances. Paris, 1815. 1 v.

5493. AUDIFFRET, Marquis de. Système financier de la France. Paris, Dufart, 1841. 2 v. (2d édition. Paris, Guillamin et cie. 5 v.)
5494. AUDIGANNE, A. Les populations ouvrières et les industries de la France. 1854. (2d édition. Paris, 1860. 2 v.)
5495. AUGIER. Du crédit public et de son histoire depuis le temps anciens jusqu'à nos jours. Paris, 1842. 1 v.
5496. AZUNI, A. Origine et progres du droit et de la legislation maritime, etc. Paris, 1810. 1 v.
5497. ———. Systeme universel des armemens en course et des corsiares en tems de guerre. Gênes, 1817. 1 v.
5498. BABBAGE, Charles. Economy of machinery and manufactures. London, 1831. (2d edition. Firenze, 1832; Paris, 1833.)
5499. BADHAM, Charles. The life of James Deacon Hume. . . . London, 1859. 351 p.
5500. BAERT, J. F. B. Adam Smith en zign onderzoek naar den rikedom des volken. Leiden, 1858.
5501. BAILEY, Samuel. A letter to a political economist; occasioned by an article in the Westminster review on the subject of value. London, 1826.
5502. ———. Money and its vicissitudes in value, as they affect national industry and pecuniary contracts. By the author of 'The Rationale of political representation,' etc. London, 1837. 1 v.
5503. ———. On the nature, measure and causes of value. In, Westminster review (January 1826). 157-72.
5504. ———. Questions in political economy. London, 1823.
5505. ———. The right of primogeniture examined, in a letter to a friend. By a younger brother. London, 1837.
5506. BAILLY, A. Exposé de l'administration générale et locale des finances du royaume-uni de Grande-Bretagne et d'Irlande, contenant des documents sur l'échiquier, la dette nationale, les banques, la navigation, les consommations, etc.; sur le produit et l'emploi des contributions, droits, taxes, peages et émoluments percus par l'administration de l'état, le clergé, la magistrature, les comtés, etc., etc. Paris, 1837. 2 v.
5507. ———. Histoire financière de la France depuis l'origine de la monarchie jusquà la fin de 1789, etc. Paris, 1830. 2 v.
5508. BAILY, Francis. An account of the several life-assurance companies established in London; containing a view of their respective merits and advantages. (The Stock exchange.) London, 1811.
5509. ———. Tables for the purchasing and renewing of leases, etc. London, 1802. 1 v.
5510. BAINES, Edward. History of the cotton manufacture in Great Britain; with a notice of its early history in the east, and in all the quarters of the globe, etc. London, 1835. 1 v.
5511. BALD, Robert. A general view of the coal trade of Scotland, chiefly that of the River Forth, and Mid-Lothian, etc. Edinburgh, 1808.

Classical Period 359

5512. BALDASSERONI, Ascanio. Trattato dell'assecurazione maritime, del cambio maritime, dell'avaria, e leggi e costumi, etc. Firenze, 1801, ... 5 v.
5513. BALSAMO, P. Memorie economiche ed agrarie. Palermo, 1803.
5514. _____. Memorie inedite de pubblica economia. Palermo, 1845. 2 v.
5515. BANCROFT, G. History of the United States. Boston, 1834-74. 10 v. (Revised edition. New York, 1883-85. 6 v.)
5516. BANDINEL, James. Some account of the trade in slaves from Africa, as connected with Europe and America; from the introduction of the trade into modern Europe down to the present time; especially with reference to the efforts made by the British government for its extinction. London, 1842. 1 v.
5517. BANFIELD, Thomas C. Four lectures on the organisation of industry; being part of a course delivered in the University of Cambridge in Easter term, 1844. London, 1845. 96 p. (2d edition 1848; Paris, 1851.)
5518. _____. The organization of industry explained. 2d edition. London, 1848.
5519. BANNEFROY. Mémoire sur la mendicité. Paris, 1791.
5520. Des BANQUES publiques de prets sur gages, et de leurs inconveniens. Par M. Beugnot. Paris, 1829.
5521. BARING, Alexander. An inquiry into the causes and consequences of the orders in council, and an examination of the conduct of Great Britain towards the neutral commerce of America. London, 1808.
5522. BARING, Francis. Observations on the establishment of the Bank of England, and on the paper circulation of the country. London, 1797.
5523. _____. Observations on the publication of Walter Boyd. London, 1801.
5524. BARTON, John. An inquiry into the causes of the progressive depreciation of agricultural labour in modern times with suggestions for its remedy. London, 1820.
5525. _____. An inquiry into the expediency of the existing restrictions on the importation of foreign corn; with observations on the present social and political prospects of Great Britain. London, 1833.
5526. _____. Observations on the circumstances which influence the condition of the labouring classes of society. London, 1817. (Reprinted: Edited by J. H. Hollander. Baltimore, Johns Hopkins press, 1934.)
5527. _____. A statement of the consequences likely to ensue from our growing excess of population, if not remedied by colonization. London, 1830. 48 p.
5528. BASCOME, E. History of Epidemics. London, 1851.
5529. BASTIAT, Fréd. Cobden et la ligue, 1845. (4th édition. 1883.)
5530. _____. Essays on political economy. (From the French. 3d edition London, 1874.)

5531. _____. Harmonies économiques, 1850. (8th édition 1881; English by P. J. Stirling; 2d edition Edinburgh, 1880; Deutsch, Berlin, 1852; Spanish por R. M. Lleras, Bogota, 1853.)
5532. _____. Oeuvres complètes, publiées sur manuscrits de l'auteur et précedées d'une notice biographique, par M. R. de Fontenay de Paillotet. Paris, Guillaumin et cie., 1854-1855. 6 v. (Nouv. édition Paris, 1864-84. 7 v.)
5533. _____. Sophismes économiques, 1846-48. (5th édition 1883; England by P. J. Stirling, Edinburgh, 1873; by H. White, New York, New York, 1875.)
5534. _____. Volkswirthschaft und politische Schriften. (Deutsch v. Bergius. Hamburg, 1859.)
5535. BATEMAN, Thomas. A treatise on agistment tithe. 2d edition. London, 1778. 102 p.
5536. BAUDRILLART, Henri. Des rapport de la morale et de l'économie politique. Paris, Guillaumin. 1 v.
5537. _____. Etudes de philosophie morale et d'économie politique. Paris, 1858. 2 v.
5538. _____. Histoire du luxe privé et public. Paris, 1878-80. 4 v.
5539. _____. La liberté du travail. Paris, 1865.
5540. _____. Manuel d'économie politique. Paris, Guillaumin, 1857. (5th édition 1885.)
5541. _____. Philosophie de l'économie politique. Des rapports de l'économie politique et de la morale, 1860. (2d édition Paris, 1883.)
5542. _____. Les populations agricoles de la France. Paris, 1887-89. 2 v.
5543. _____. Traité général des eaux et forêts. Paris, 1821 à 1845.
5544. BAYLE-MOUILLARD. De l'emprisonnement pour dettes, considerations sur ses rapports avec la morale publique, etc. (Ouvrage couronné par l'institut.) Paris, 1836. 1 v.
5545. BAYLEY, John. Summary of the law of bills of exchange, cash bills, and promissory notes. 5th edition, with considerable additions. By F. Bayley. London, 1830. 1 v.
5546. BEALE, Thomas. The natural history of the sperm whale (including an account of the rise and progress of the sperm-whale fishery), with a sketch of a South-Sea whaling voyage. London, 1839. 1 v.
5547. BEAUMONT de BRIVAZAC de. L'Europe et ses colonies en décembre 1819. 2 v. Paris, Brissot-Thivars, 1820. (Signé, a la fin du 2d vol., par un cosmopolite.)
5548. BECHER, John Thomas. The constitution of friendly societies. 2d edition. London, 1824.
5549. _____. Observations upon the report of the select committee of the House of commons, on the laws respecting friendly societies; exemplifying and vindicating the principles of life assurance adopted in calculating the southwell tables. . . . Newark, 1826.
5550. BECHER, S. Das Österreich. Münzwesen (1524-1838). 2 Bde. Wien, 1838.

Classical Period

5551. _____. Die organisation des gewerbewesens. Wien, 1851.
5552. BECHMANN, Thomas. Beiträge zur geschichte der erfindungen. Leipzig, 1780-1805. 5 v. (Translated by W. Johnston. London, 1797-1814. 4 v.; 4th edition. London, 1846. 2 v.)
5553. BECKFORD, William. A descriptive account of the Island of Jamaica, with remarks on slavery. London, 1790. 2 v.
5554. BEEKE, Henry. Observations on the produce of the income tax, and on its proportion to the whole revenue of Great Britain. A new and greatly improved edition. London, 1800.
5555. BELL, Archibald. An inquiry into the policy and justice of the prohibition of the use of grain in the distilleries. Edinburgh, 1808.
5556. BELL, Benjamin. De la disette. Traduit de Prévost, de Geneve. 1804. 1 v.
5557. BELL, G. J. Commentaries on the laws of Scotland, and on the principles of mercantile jurisprudence, considered in relation to bankruptcy, competition of creditors, and imprisonment for debt. 5th edition. Edinburgh, 1826. 2 v.
5558. BELLIGERENT rights asserted and vindicated against neutral encroachment; being an answer to 'An examination of the British doctrine.' London, 1806.
5559. The BENGAL and Agra guide and gazetteer, for 1841 and 1842. Calcutta, 1841-42. 4 v.
5560. BENNETT, John. On the relative importance of agriculture and foreign trade. London, 1827. 53 p.
5561. BENTHAM, Jeremy. Defence of economy against the Right honorable George Ross. In Pamphleteer, London, X (1817), 284.
5562. _____. A defence of usury showing the impolicy of the present restraints on the terms of pecuniary bargains. London, 1787. (2d edition includes letter to Adam Smith. London, 1790. Paris, 1790. Philadelphia. 1796. 3d edition. London, 1816)
5563. _____. Esquisse d'un ouvrage en faveur des pauvres, traduit et publié par Duquesnoy. Paris, 1802.
5564. _____. Life and work. . . . By Charles Milner Atkinson. London, 1905.
5565. _____. Théorie des peines et des récompenses. 2 v.
5566. BERES, Emile. Essai sur les moyens d'accroître la richesse territoriale en France, notamment dans les départements méridionauz. Paris, 1830.
5567. _____. Les classes ouvrières. Moyens d'améliorer leur sort sous le rapport du bien-être matériel et du perfectionnement moral. Paris, 1836.
5568. BERGASSE. Considérations sur la liberté du commerce. Londres, 1788.
5569. BERNARD, Thomas. Case of the salt duties, with proofs and illustrations. London, 1817. 1 v.
5570. _____. On the supply of employment and subsistence for the labouring classes. In Pamphleteer, London, X (1817.)

362   Economic Thought and Analysis

5571. BERNHARDI, Theodor. Versuch einer kritick der grunde, die für grosses und kleines grundeigenthum, St. Petersburg, 1849.
5572. BESSE, L. Die naturgeschichte der arbeit. Leipzig, 1855.
5573. BEUGNOT. Des banques publiques de prets sur gages, et de leurs inconvéniens. Paris, 1829.
5574. BIANCHINI, Lodovico. Della influenza dell'amministrazione pubblica sulla industria nazionale et sulla circulazione delle richezze. Napoli, 1828.
5575. _____. Della storia delle finanze di Napoli libri sette (sotto questo nome: Si volle compendere la storia civile di Napoli). Napoli, 1834 et 1835. 3 v.
5576. _____. Della storia economico-cîvile di Sicilia, due volumini in-ottavo; il primo stampato in Napoli nella stamperia reale, ed il secondo in Palermo, nella tipografia di Lao, nel 1841.
5577. _____. Principi del credito pubblico. Napoli, 1827.
5578. BIBLIOTECA dell' economista; diretta da Fr. Ferrara. 1 e 2 serie; 26 v. Torino, 1850-70. (G. Boccardo, 3 serie, 15 v., 1875-92.)
5579. BIBLIOTECA di gius nautico, contenente le legge delle piu culte nazioni, ed i migliori trattati moderni sopra le materie maritime. Firenze, 1785. 2 v.
5580. BICHINO, J. E. An inquiry into the poor-laws, chiefly with a view to examine them as a scheme of national benevolence, and to elucidate their political economy. 2d edition. London, 1824.
5581. BIEDERMANN, K. Deutschlands politique materie und sociologie, Zustande im 18 Jahrh. Leipzig, 1854-80. 4 bde.
5582. BILHON, J. F. Gouvernement des Romains, considéré sous le rapport de la politique, de la justice, des finances et du commerce. Paris, 1807.
5583. _____. Principes d'administration et d'économie politique des anciens peuples, appliqués aux peuples modernes. Paris, 1819.
5584. BISCHOFF, James. A comprehensive history of the woollen and worsted manufactures, and the natural and commercial history of the sheep. London, 1842. 2 v.
5585. BLACK, William. A comparative view of the mortality of the human species at all ages; and of the diseases and casualties by which they are destroyed or annoyed. London, 1788. 1 v.
5586. BLAIR, William. An inquiry into the state of slavery among the Romans. Edinburgh, 1833.
5587. BLAIZE, A. Des monts de piété. 2d édition. Paris, 1856. 2 v.
5588. BLAKE, William. Observations on the effects produced by the expenditure of government during the restriction of cash payments. London, 1823.
5589. _____. Observations on the principles which regulate the course of exchange and on the present depreciated state of the currency. London, 1810.

Classical Period 363

5590. BLANC, Louis. L'organisation du travail, 1839. (9th edition revised. Paris, 1850.)
5591. _____. Le socialsme. 3d edition. Paris, 1848; London, 1848.
5592. BLANE, Gilbert. Inquiry into the late and present scarcity of provisions. 2d edition. In Pamphleteer, London, IX (1817) 259.
5593. BLANQUI, Jérôme-Adolphe. Histoire de l'économie politique. Paris, 1837-38. (5th édition 1879; Deutsch, 2 bde., Carlsruhe, 1840. Edited by E. J. Leonard, New York, 1880.)
5594. _____. History of political economy in Europe. With preface by David A. Wells. London, 1880.
5595. _____. Les classes ouvrières en France. Paris, 1849. 2 v.
5596. _____. Précis élémentaire d'économie politique. Paris, 1842.
5597. BLISS, Henry. On colonial intercourse; with an appendix, containing a memorial to the Right honourable Board of trade against opening the West Indies to ships of the United States, with tables of comparative prices, tonnage, etc. London, 1826.
5598. _____. On the timber trade. London, 1831.
5599. BOCCARDO, Gerolamo. Dizionario della economia politica e del commercio. Turin, 1858-63. 4 v. (2d ed. Milano, 1875-77.)
5600. _____. Sul riordinamento delle banche in Italia. Torino, 1881.
5601. _____. Trattato teoretico-pratico di economia politica, 1853. 3 v. (6th ed. Turin, 1879; 7th ed. 1885.)
5602. BOCKH, A. Staatshaushaltung der Athener. Berlin, 1817. [3 aufl. (v. Fränkel), 2 bde, 1886; traduit par Laligant, Paris, 1828. 2 v. English by A. Lamb, Boston and London, 1857.]
5603. BOECKH. Economie politique des Athéniens. Traduit de l'allemand par M. Laligant. Paris, 1828. 2 v. (London, 1828. 2 v.)
5604. BOILEAU, David. An introduction to the study of political economy. London, 1811.
5605. BOISLANDRY, Louis de. Des impôts et des charges des peuples en France. Paris, 1824.
5606. _____. Examen des principes les plus favorables aux progrès de l'agriculture, des manufactures et du commerce de France. Paris, 1815.
5607. BOISSY-D'ANGLAS. Observations sur l'ouvrage de M. de Calonne intitulé: De l'Etat présent et à venir de la France. Paris, 1791.
5608. BOLLMAN, Erick. A letter to Thomas Brand on the resumption of specie payment. London, 1819.
5609. _____. Paragraphs on banks. 2d edition. Philadelphia, 1811.
5610. BONNEMERE, E. Histoire des paysans. 1200-1850. Paris, 1856. 2 v.

5611. BONNET, V. Le crédit et les finances. Paris, 1865.
5612. ———. La question des impôts. Paris, 1879.
5613. ———. Questions économiques et financières. Paris, 1859.
5614. BOOTH, Benjamin. A complete system of book-keeping. London, 1799. 1 v.
5615. BOREL. De l'origine et des fonctions des consuls. St. Petersburg, 1807. 2 v.
5616. BOSANQUET, Charles. Practical observations on the report of the bullion committee. London, 1810.
5617. BOSC, J. Considérations sur l'accumulation des capitaux, et les moyèns de circulation chez les peuples modernes. Paris.
5618. ———. Essai sur les moyens d'améliorer l'agriculture, les arts et le commerce en France. Paris, 1800.
5619. BOWEN, F. Principles of political economy. Boston, 1856. (New edition: American political economy. Boston, 1885.)
5620. BOWRING, John. First report on the commercial relations between France and Great Britain. 1834.
5621. ———. Report on the commercial statistics of Syria. 1840.
5622. ———. Report on the Prussian commercial union (including the commercial statistics of Germany). 1840.
5623. ———. Report on the statistics of Tuscany, Lucca, the Pontifical and the Lombardo-Venetian States; with special reference to their commercial relations. 1837.
5624. BOYD, Walter. A letter to the Right honourable William Pitt on the influence of the stoppage of issues in specie at the bank of England on the prices of provisions and other commodities. 2d edition with notes and a preface. London, 1801.
5625. BRAND, J. A determination of the average depression of the price of wheat in war, below that of the preceding peace. . . . London, 1800.
5626. BRAY, John Francis. Labour's wrongs and labour's remedy; or, the age of might and the age of right. Leeds, 1839. 216 p. (London school of economics reprints, no. 6, 1931.)
5627. BREMOND, Jean-Baptiste. Premieres observations au peuple Francois. Versailles, 1789.
5628. BRERETON, C. D. An inquiry into the workhouse system and the law of maintenance in agricultural districts. Norwich, 1825.
5629. ———. A practical inquiry into the number, means of employment, and wages of agricultural labourers. Norwich, 1826.
5630. ———. The subordinate magistracy and parish system, considered in their connexion with the causes and remedies of modern pauperism, etc. Norwich, 1827.
5631. BRESSON, J. Histoire financière de la France, depuis l'origine de la monarchie jusqu'à l'année 1828. Paris, 1829. 2 v. 2d édition. 1843.)

5632. BRIAVOINNE, M. De l'industrie en Belgique; causes de décadence et de prospérité; sa situation actuelle. Bruxelles, 1839. 2 v.
5633. BRICKWOOD, John. A plan for reducing . . . the national debt. 2d edition. London, 1820.
5634. A BRIEF view of the policy and resources of the United States. Philadelphia, 1810.
5635. BRISTED, J. Resources of the United States. New York, 1818.
5636. BROADHURST, John. Political economy. London, 1842.
5637. BROUGHAM, Henry. An inquiry into the colonial policy of European powers. Edinburgh, 1803. 2 v. (Reprinted 1808.)
5638. ———. Political philosophy. London, 1843. 3 v. (New edition, 1861.)
5639. BROWN, Robert. A treatise on agriculture and rural affairs. Edinburgh, 1811. 2 v.
5640. BROWNE-DIGNAN. Essai sur les principes politiques de l'économie publique. Londres, 1776.
5641. BROWNING, G. Domestic and financial condition of Great Britain. London, 1834.
5642. BRUCE, John. Annals of the Honourable East India company, from the establishment of the charter in 1600 to 1707-8. London, 1810. 3 v.
5643. BRYDGES, Egerton. Arguments in favour of the able-bodied poor. London, 1817.
5644. ———. Reasons for a farther amendment of the copyright act. In Pamphleteer, London, X (1817) 495-507.
5645. ———. What are riches? Or an examination of the definitions. Kent, 1822.
5646. BUCHANAN, David. L'édition qu'il a donnée du grand ouvrage d'Adam Smith, en 4 vol. Edinburgh, 1817.
5647. ———. Inquiry into the taxation and commercial policy of Great Britain. Edinburgh, 1844.
5648. BUCHANAN, Francis. A journey from Madras, through the countries of Mysore, Canara, and Malabar. London, 1807. 3 v.
5649. BUCHANAN, George. Tables for converting the weights and measures hitherto in use in Great Britain into those of the imperial standards, etc. Edinburgh, 1829. 1 v.
5650. BULLER, Thomas Wentworth. A reply to a pamphlet, by David Ricardo, on protection to agriculture. London, 1822.
5651. BURET, Eugène. De la misère des classes laborieuses en Angleterre et en France; de la nature de la misère, de son existence, et ses effets, de ses causes, et de l'insuffisance des remèdes qu'on lui a opposés jusqu'ici, etc. Paris, 1840. 2 v.
5652. BURGESS, Henry. A letter to explain internal bills of exchange. London, 1826.
5653. BURGON, John William. The life and times of Sir Thomas Gresham. London, 1839. 2 v.
5654. BURKE, Edmund. Thoughts and details on scarcity,

originally presented to the Right honourable William Pitt, in November, 1795. London, 1800.
5655. BURNS, Robert. Historical dissertations on the law and practice of Great Britain, and particularly of Scotland, with regard to the poor, etc. 2d edition. Edinburgh, 1819. 1 v.
5656. BURTON, John Hill. Political and social economy: its practical application. Edinburgh, 1849.
5657. BUSCH, J. G. Abhandlung von geldumlauf, 1780. (2 aufl. Hamburg, 1800. 2 bde.)
5658. ──────. La banque de Hambourg, rendue facile aux négociants de l'étranger, avec des recherches intéressantes sur son origine, sur les changements qu'elle a éprouvés a différentes époques, etc. Paris, 1801.
5659. ──────. Traité des banques, de leur différence réele, et des effets qui en résultent dans leur usage et leur administration. Paris, 1814.
5660. BUT, Isaac. The poor-law bill for Ireland examined, its provisions, and the report of Mr. Nicholls contrasted with the facts proved by the poor inquiry commission, in a letter to Lord Viscount Morpeth. London, 1837.
5661. CABARRUS, Francisco. Cartas sobre los obstaculos que la naturaleza, la opinion y las leyes oponen à la felicidad publica, escritas por el Conde de Cabarrus al S. D. Gaspar de Jovellanos. Madrid, 1813.
5662. ──────. Memoria presantado à S. M. para la formacion de un banco nacional, por mano del Excellentissimo Senor Conde de Floridablança, su primer secretare de estado. Madrid, 1782.
5663. ──────. Memoria sobre la union del commercio de la America con la Asia. Leida en la junta general de la compania de Caracas, de 3 de Julio de 1784.
5664. CAGNAZZI, L. De S. Elementi di economia politica. Napoli, 1813.
5665. CAIRD, James. English agriculture. London, 1850-51. (2d edition 1852)
5666. ──────. India; the land and the people. 3d edition. London, 1884.
5667. ──────. Landed interest and supply of food. 4th edition. London, 1880.
5668. CALCUL des rentes viagères sur une et sur plusieurs têtes. Par M. de St. Cyran. Paris, 1779. 1 v.
5669. CALENGE. Des différentes banques de l'Europe. Paris, 1806.
5670. CALONNE, Charles Alexander de. De l'état de France, présent et à venir. Nouvelle édition. Londres, 1790.
5671. ──────. Des finances publiques de la France. Londres, 1797.
5672. ──────. Observations sur les finances. Londres, 1790.
5673. ──────. Observations sur l'ouvrage de intitulé de l'état de la France. By M. Boissy D'Anglas. Paris, 1791.
5674. CALVERT, Frederick. Suggestions for a change in the administration of the poor-laws. London, 1831.

Classical Period 367

5675. CAMBON, député à la convention. Lettres à ses concitoyens sur les finances. Paris, 1795.
5676. ———. Rapport à la convention nationale sur le projet de la formation du grand-livre. Paris, 1793.
5677. CANARD, Nicolas-Fréd. Principes d'économie politique. Paris, 1801.
5678. CANDOLLE-BOISSIER, Adolph de. Les caisses d'epargnes de la Suisse. Genève, 1838. 1 v.
5679. ———. Examen de quelques questions d'économie politique. Genève et Paris, 1816.
5680. CANNING, George. Substance of two speeches into the cause of the high price of bullion. London, 1811.
5681. CAPEFIGUE, J. Histoire des grandes opérations financières. Paris, 1855-57. 4 v.
5682. CAPMANI, don Antonio de. Discurso economico politico, en defensa del trabajo mecanico ed los menstrales y de la influencia de sus gremios en las constumbres populares. Madrid, 1778.
5683. ———. Memorias historicas sobre la marina, comercio y artes de la antiqua ciudad de Barcelona, publicadas por disposicion y a expensas de la real junta y consulado de comercio de la misma ciudad. Madrid, 1779-91. 4 v.
5684. CAPPO, E. National debt financially considered. London, 1859.
5685. CARBALLO y WANGUEMERT, Benigno. Curso de economia politica. Madrid, 1855-56. 2 v.
5686. CARDONNEL, Adam de. Numismata Scotiae, or a series of the Scottish coinage from the reign of William the Lion to the Union. Edinburgh, 1786. 1 v.
5687. CARDWELL, Edward. Lectures on the coinage of the Greeks and Romans, delivered in the University of Oxford. Oxford, 1832. 1 v.
5688. CAREY, Henry C. Answers to the questions, What constitutes currency? What are the causes of unsteadiness of the currency? What is the remedy? Philadelphia and London, 1840.
5689. ———. The credit system of France, Great Britain, and the United States. London and Philadelphia, 1838.
5690. ———. Essay on the rate of wages; with an examination of the causes of the difference in the condition of the labouring population throughout the world. Philadelphia, 1835. 1 v.
5691. ———. Principles of political economy. Philadelphia, 1837-40. 3 v. (Deutsch, Adler, 2 Aufl., Wien, 1870; Italien edition.)
5692. ———. Principles of social science. Philadelphia, 1858-59. 3 v. (Traduit per Leduc et Plance, Paris, 1861. 3 v.; deutsch, Adler, 3 bde., München, 1863-64; Manual by K. McKean. Philadelphia, 1879.)
5693. CAREY, M. Essays in Political economy. Philadelphia, 1822.
5694. CARRION-NISAS A. de. Principes d'Economie politique. Paris, 1825.

5695. CARTWRIGHT, Edmund. A memoir of the life. . . . London, 1843.
5696. CASAUX, Le Marquis de. Absurdité de l'impot territorial, et de plusieurs autres impôts, demontrée par l'exposition des effets, ou réactions des différentes espèces de taxes sur tous les prix, tant du travail que de ses produits, soit dans l'agriculture, soit dans l'industrie, 1790.
5697. ———. Considérations sur les effets de l'impôts dans les différents modes de taxation. Londres, 1794.
5698. ———. Considerations sur quelques parties de mechanisme des sociétés. London, 1785.
5699. CASAUX, L. F. G. de. Bases fondamentales de l'économie politique. Paris, 1826.
5700. CASSAGNAC, A. G. de. Histoire des classes ouvrières. Paris, 1838.
5701. La CAUSE des esclaves nègres. Par. M. Frossard. Lyon, 1789. 2 v.
5702. CAYLEY, Edward Stillingfleet. Corn, trade, wages, and rent; or, observations on the leading circumstances of the present financial crisis, as they affect the artisan, the manufacturer, the labourer, the tenant, and the landlord. . . . London, J. Ridgway, 1826.
5703. ———. On commercial economy in six essays; viz, machinery, accumulation of capital, production, consumption, currency, and free trade. London, J. Ridgeway, 1830.
5704. CAZENOVE, John. An elementary treatise on political economy; or, a short exposition of its first and fundamental principles. London, 1840.
5705. CELESTIN, F. J. Russia seit aufhebung der leibeigenschaft. Laibach, 1855.
5706. CENSUSES of the population of Great Britain. 1801, 1811, 1821, 1831, and 1841.
5707. CENZO de la riqueza territorial . . . de España. Por J. Polo y Catalina. Madrid, 1803.
5708. CHALMERS, George. Considerations of commerce. 2d edition. London, 1811.
5709. ———. An estimate of the comparative strength of Great Britain, and of the losses of her trade from every war since the revolution. London, 1783. 1 v. (Last edition Edinburgh, 1812. Edition 1802 has Gregory King's tract included.)
5710. ———. Opinions of eminent lawyers on the various points of English jurisprudence, chiefly concerning the colonies, fisheries, and commerce of Great Britain, collected and digested from the originals in the board of trade, and other depositories. London, 1814. 2 v.
5711. ———. Political annals of the present United Colonies, from their settlement to the Peace of 1763. London, 1780. 1 v. (All that was published.)
5712. CHALMERS, Thomas. The Christian and civic economy of large towns. Glasgow, Chalmers and Collins, 1821-26. 3 v. (1832.)
5713. ———. Memoirs of the life and writings of. . . . Edited

Classical Period 369

5714.   ———. On political economy, in connection with the moral state and progress of society. Glasgow, Edinburgh, New York, 1832. 1840.
5715.   ———. Selected works of Dr. Chalmers. Edited by William Hanna. Edinburgh, 1856.
5716. CHAMBORANT, de. Du pauperisme, ce qu'il était dans l'antiquité, ce qu'il est de nos jours. Paris, 1842. 1 v.
5717. CHANNING, William E. Remarks on the association formed by the working classes of America. London, 1833.
5718. CHAPTAL, Charles. De l'industrie françoise. Paris, 1819. 2 v.
5719. CHARACTER, object, and effects of trades unions. London, 1834.
5720. CHASTELLUX, Comte de. De la félicité publique, ou considérations sur le sort des hommes dans les différentes époques de l'histoire. 4th édition. Paris, 1822. 2 v.
5721. CHATEAUNEUF, Benoiston de. Considérations sur les Enfans-Trouvés dans les Principaux Etats de l'Europe. Paris, 1824.
5722.   ———. Recherches sur les consommations de la Ville de Paris en 1817, comparées à ce qu'elles étaient en 1789.
5723. CHERBULIEZ, Antoine-Elisée. Essai sur les conditions de l'alliance fédérative en général et sur le nouveau projet c'acte fédéral. Geneva, 1833.
5724.   ———. Etudes sur les causes de la misère. Paris, 1853.
5725.   ———. Précis de la science économique. Paris, 1862. 2 v.
5726.   ———. Simples notions de l'ordre social. Paris, 1848. 2d édition 1884.)
5727. CHEVALIER, Michel. La baisse probable de l'or. Paris, Capelle, 1858. 1 v. (Paris, 1859. English translation by R. Cobden, London, 1859.)
5728.   ———. Cours d'économie politique, 1842. (Deuxième année. Paris, 1844. 2nd édition, Paris, 1858. 2 v.)
5729.   ———. Cours d'économie politique fait au College de France. Paris, Capelle, 1858. 3 v.
5730.   ———. Des intérêts matériels en France, travaux publics, routes, camaux et chemins. . . . 1st édition. 1838. (4th édition Paris, 1839. 1 v.)
5731.   ———. Examen du système commercial connu sous le nom de système protecteur. Paris, Guillaumin, 1852. (2d édition, 1857.)
5732.   ———. Lettres sur l'Amérique du Nord. Paris, 1836. 2 v.
5733.   ———. Lettres sur l'organisation du travail. Bruxelles, 1848.
5734.   ———. Organisation industrielle de l'armée. (In, Religion Saint-Simionienne. Politique industrielle et système de la Méditerranée. Paris, 1832. 7-14 p.)
5735. CHICHESTER, Edward. Oppressions and cruelties of Irish revenue officers; being the substance of a letter to a British member of Parliament. London, 1818.

5736. The CHINESE repository of facts and statements respecting the history, statistics, trade, etc., of China and the adjacent countries. Edited by Dr. Morrison. Canton, 1834, etc. 4 v.
5737. CHITTY, Joseph. The law of nations relative to the legal effect of war on the commerce of belligerents and neutrals.
5738. ———. Practical treatise on bills of exchange, checks on bankers, promissory notes, cash notes, etc. 9th and best edition. London, 1840. 1 v.
5739. ———. A practical treatise on the laws of foreign and inland commerce, manufactures, and contracts, with an appendix of treaties, statutes, and precedents relating thereto. London, 1820-24. 4 v.
5740. CHRISTIAN, Edward. General observations on provident banks. In, Pamphleteer, London, xvii (1820). (Reprint. 14 p.)
5741. CHRISTIE, W. D. A plea for a perpetual copyright, in a letter to Lord Monteagle. London, 1840.
5742. CIBRARIO, Louis. Economia politica del medio evo libri III. . . . Torino, 1839. (5th edition 1861. 2 v. Traduit par Barneaud et Wolowski. Paris, 1859. 2 v.)
5743. CICILIA, José. Memoiria sobre los medios de fomentar solidamente la agricultura en un pais, sin detrimento de la cria de ganados, y el modo de remover los obstaculos que puedan impedirla. Ouvrage couronné par la société économique de Madred en 1777.
5744. CIESZOWSKI, A. Du crédit et de la circulation. 2d édition. Paris, Guillaumin, 1847. 1 v. (3d édition 1884.)
5745. The CLAIMS of Labour. An essay on the duties of the employers to the employed. London, 1844. 174 p.
5746. CLARENDON, R. V. A sketch of the revenue and finances of Ireland. London, 1791. 1 v.
5747. CLARK, Charles. A summary of colonial law, with the practice of the court of appeals from the plantations, charters of justice, orders in council, etc. London, 1834. 1 v.
5748. CLARK, M. H. and D. H. Hall. Legislative and documentary history of the bank of the United States. Washington, 1832.
5749. CLARKE. Coup d'oeil sur la force et l'opulence de la Grande-Bretagne, où l'on voit les progres de son commerce, de son agriculture avant et après l'avénement de la maison de Hanovre; traduit de l'anglais par Marchena. Paris, 1802. (Londres, 1801.)
5750. CLARKSON, Thomas. The history of the rise, progress, and accomplishment of the abolition of the slave trade. London, 1808. 2 v. (A new edition, with additions, 1839. 1 v.)
5751. CLARIERE, M. Opinions d'un créancier de l'Etat sur quelques matières de finances importantes dans le moment actuel. Londres, 1789.
5752. CLAY, John. A free trade essential to the welfare of Great Britain. In, Pamphleteer, London, XVII (1820).

Classical Period 371

(Reprinted, 44 p.)
5753. CLEGHORN, James. An essay on the depressed state of agriculture. Published by order of the Highland society. Edinburgh, 1822.
5754. CLEMENT, P. Histoire de Colbert et de son administration. 2d édition. Paris, 1875.
5755. _____. Histoire du système protecteur en France. Paris, 1854.
5756. _____. Jacques Coeur et Charles VII. . . . Arts au XV siècle. Paris, 1853. (4th édition 1874.)
5757. COBBETT, William. The last of the Saxons . . . writings . . . selected by Edwin Paxton Hood. London, 1854.
5758. _____. Paper against gold: or the history and mystery of the Bank of England. London, 1821. 4th edition.
5759. COBDEN, Richard. Political writings. London and New York, 1867. 2 v.
5760. _____. Speeches on questions of public policy. Edited by John Bright and J. E. T. Rogers. London, 1870. 2 v. (1878.)
5761. _____. The three panics. New edition. London, 1884. (Traduit par A. Raymond. Paris, 1862.)
5762. CODE de commerce, précédé des discours de messieurs les orateurs du conseil. . . . Paris, 1807. 1 v.
5763. CODIGO de las costumbres maritimas de Barcelona, hasta aqui vulgarmente llamado libro del consolato, nuevamente traducido al castellano. . . . Por Don Antonio de Capmany. Con un appendice qui contiene uan colleccion de leyes y estatutos de España, relativos a ordenanzas de comercio naval, de seguros maritimos. . . . Madrid, 1791. 2 v.
5764. COELN, F. de. Die neue staatsweisheit. Berlin, 1812.
5765. _____. Materialien für die Preussische staats-wirtschaftliche gesetzgebung. Leipzig, 1811.
5766. COFFINIERES, A. S. G. De la bourse et des spéculations sur les effets publics. Paris, 1824.
5767. COHEN, Bernard. Compendium of the finances of Great Britain and other countries. London, 1822. 1 v.
5768. COHEN, William. An account of the public funds transferable at the Bank of England. . . . By William Fairman. 7th edition revised and enlarged. London, 1824. 1 v.
5769. COLEBROOKE, H. T. Remarks on the husbandry and internal commerce of Bengal. London, 1806. 1 v.
5770. COLINS, A. H. Science sociale. Paris, 1858. 5 v.
5771. A COLLECTION of conflicting opinions upon the corn question. London, 1825. 76 p.
5772. A COLLECTION of interesting and important reports and papers on the navigation and trade of Great Britain. . . . Printed by order of the Society of shipowners. London, 1807. 1 v.
5773. COLLECTION de lois maritimes anterieures au XVIIIme siècle. Par M. Pardessus. Paris, 1828-39. 5 v.
5774. COLLECTION de mémoires et correspondances officielles sur l'administration des colonies. Par M. Malouet. Paris, 1802. 5 v.

Economic Thought and Analysis

5775. COLLECTION des principaux économistes. Oeuvres, traduit en Francois par E. Daire. Paris, 1843-48. 15 v.
5776. A COLLECTION of public acts and papers relative to the principles of armed neutrality brought forward in 1780 and 1781. London, 1801. 1 v.
5777. COLLYER, F. Practical treatise on the law of partnership, with an appendix of forms. 2d edition. London, 1840.
5778. COLMEIRO, Manuel. Principios de economia politica, 1859. (2d ed. Madrid, 1865.)
5779. COLQUHOUN, Patrick. A treatise on indigence, exhibiting a general view of the national resources for productive labour, with propositions for ameliorating the condition of the poor. London, 1808. 1 v.
5780. ———. A treatise on the wealth, power, and resources of the British empire, in every quarter of the world, including the East Indies. . . . London, 1814. (2d edition London, 1815.)
5781. COLTON, Calvin. Public economy for the United States. New York, 1848. 536 p.
5782. COLWELL, S. Ways and means of commercial payment. Philadelphia, 1858.
5783. COMBER, W. T. An inquiry into the state of national subsistence, as connected with the progress of wealth and population; to which is subjoined a digest of the corn laws. London, 1808. 1 v.
5784. Del COMMERCIO dei popoli neutrali in tempo di guerra. Di Lampredi. Firenze, 1788.
5785. A COMPENDIUM of the laws passed from time to time for regulating and restricting the importation, exportation, and consumption of corn from the year 1660, with tables of prices. . . . London, 1826.
5786. A COMPLETE investigation of Mr. Eden's treaty, as it may affect the commerce of Great Britain. London, 1787. 176 p.
5787. COMTE, Auguste. Cours de philosophie positive. Paris, 1830-1842. 6 v. (3d edition Paris, Littré, 1869. English translation by H. Martineau, London, 1858. 2 v. Deutsch v. J. H. von Kirchmann, Leipzig, 1883-84.)
5788. ———. Système de politique positive. Paris, 1851-54. 4 v. (English translation by J. H. Bridges. London, 1875-79. 4 v.)
5789. COMTE, Charles. Traité de législation, ou Exposition des lois générales suivant les quelles les peuples prospèrent, dépérissent ou restent stationnaires. Paris, 1827. 4 v.
5790. ———. Traité de la propriété. Paris, 1834. 2 v.
5791. CONDER, Josiah. A geographical, historical, and topographical description of India. London, 1830. 4 v.
5792. CONDILLAC, L'Abbé de. Le commerce et le gouvernement considérés relativement l'ún à l'autre. Amsterdam, 1776.
5793. CONDORCET, M. J. A. Oeuvres complètes. Paris, 1804. 21 v. (Paris, 1847. 12 v.)
5794. ———. Réflexions sur le commerce des blés. London, 1776.

Classical Period 373

5795. ———. Reflexions sur l'esclavage des négres. Neufchâtel, 1781.
5796. ———. Vie de Monsieur Turgot. London, 1786. (London, 1787.)
5797. CONDY-RAGUET de Philadelphie. Traité des banques et de la circulation. Traduit de l'anglais par Lemaitre. Paris, 1840. 1 v.
5798. CONGREVE, William. Of the impracticability of the resumption of cash payments. In, Pamphleteer, London, XV (1820). (Reprint, 18p.)
5799. CONSIDERANT, Victor. De la politique nouvelle convenant aux intérêts actuels de la société, 1843. (2d édition Paris, 1843.)
5800. ———. Distinée sociale, 1834-1836. 2 v. (2d édition Paris, 1847-49. 2 v.)
5801. ———. Exposition abrégée du systême phalanstérien de Fourier, 1845. (3d édition, 4e tirage. Paris, 1846.)
5802. ———. Petit cours de politique et d'économie sociale, 1844. (2d édition, 4e tirage. Paris, 1847.)
5803. ———. Principes du socialisme, manifeste de la democratie au XIXe siècle. Paris, 1847.
5804. ———. Le socialisme devant le vieux monde. Paris, 1848.
5805. CONSIDERATIONS on the annual million bill, and on the real and imaginary properties of a sinking fund. London, 1787.
5806. CONSIDERATIONS sur l'admission de navires neutres aux colonies Francaises de l'Amerique en tems de guerre. Paris, 1779.
5807. CONSIDERATIONS sur les causes de la grandeur et de la décadence de la monarchie Espagnole. Par M. Semperé. Paris, 1826. 2 v.
5808. CONSIDERATIONS on the corn laws, with remarks on the observations of Lord Sheffield on the corn bill. London, 1791.
5809. CONSIDERATIONS on the East-India bill now depending in parliament. London, 1779.
5810. CONSIDERATIONS générales sur l'évaluation des monnaies Grecques et Romaines, et sur la valeur de l'Or et de l'argent avant la decourverte de l'Amérique. Par M. Letronne. Paris, 1817.
5811. CONSIDERATIONS on the importation of foreign corn. . . . London, 1814.
5812. CONSIDERATIONS sur la Pêche de la Baleine. Par M. de la Jonkaire. Paris, 1830.
5813. CONSIDERATIONS on the propriety of the Bank of England resuming its payments in specie. London, 1802.
5814. The CONSTITUTION of friendly societies, upon legal and scientific principles, exemplified by the rules and tables of calculations adopted under the advice and approbation of William Morgan, and William Frend, for the government of the friendly institution at Southwell. . . . Neward, 1822.

5815. CONSULAT de la mer, ou pandectes du droit commercial. Par Boucher. Paris, 1808. 2 v.
5816. The CONTRAST; or a comparison between the woollen, linen, cotton, and silk manufactures. London, 1782.
5817. COOK, James. Remarks on the state of the sugar trade. . . . London, 1839.
5818. COOKE, Edward. The real cause of the increased price of the necessaries of life. In, Pamphleteer, London, XIV (1819). (Reprint, 31 p.)
5819. _____. Thoughts on the expediency of repealing the usury laws. In, Pamphleteer, London, XIII (1818). (Reprint, 26 p.)
5820. COOKE, Layton. British husbandry. 1688-1827. London, 1828.
5821. COOPER, C. P. An account of most important public records of Great Britain. London, 1832. 2 v.
5822. COOPER, Thomas. Lectures on the elements of political economy. Columbia, 1826. (2d edition 1829.)
5823. _____. A manual of political economy. Washington, 1833. 109 p.
5824. COQ, Paul. La monnaie de banque, ou l'espèce et le portefeuille. Paris, 1857. 1 v.
5825. COQ, Paul et H. Bernard. Résumé . . . sur le régime économique de la France en 1870. Paris, 1872. 2 v.
5826. COQUELIN, Charles. Du crédit et des banques. 2d édition revue et précédée d'une introduction, par M. Courcelle-Seneuil. Paris, Guillaumin, 1859. 1 v.
5827. COQUELIN, Charles et N. G. Guillaumin, éds. Dictionnaire de l'économie politique. . . . 4e edition. Paris, 1873. 2 v.
5828. CORBET, Thomas. An inquiry into the causes and modes of the wealth of individuals; or the principles of trade and speculation explained. London, 1841.
5829. CORDIER, J. Considérations sur les chemins de fer. Paris 1830.
5830. CORN law; an authentic report of the late important discussions in the Manchester Chamber of commerce on the destructive effects of the corn laws upon the trade and manufactures of the country. London, 1839.
5831. CORN laws; the consequences of the sliding scale examined and exposed. Being the substance of a speech delivered in the House of Lords on the 14th of March, 1843. By Lord Monteagle. London, 1843.
5832. CORNISH, J. A view of the present state of the salmon and channel fisheries. London, 1824. 1 v.
5833. CORY, J. P. A practical treatise on accounts mercantile and official. London, 1840. 1 v.
5834. COTTERIL. An examination of the doctrines of value, as set forth by A. Smith, Ricardo, McCulloch, etc. London, 1831. 1 v.
5835. COUP d'OEIL sur les assurances sur la vie des hommes. Par Juvigny. 4me édition. Paris, 1825.
5836. COUP d'OEIL sur l'Isle de Java et les autres possessions

néerlandaises dans l'archipel des indes. Par le Comte Hogendorp. Bruxelles, 1830. 1 v.
5837. COURCELLE-SENEUIL, J. G. La banque libre. Paris, 1867.
5838. ———. Manuel des affaires, ou traité des entreprises industrielles, agricoles. . . . 4th édition. Paris, 1885.
5839. ———. Protections et libre échange. Paris, 1879.
5840. ———. Traité théorique et pratique d'économi politique. Paris, 1858-59. (3e édition, 1890.)
5841. ———. Traité theorique et pratique des opérations de banque. Paris, 1853. (3e edition, Paris, Guillaumin, 1857. 1 v.; 6e edition, 1876.)
5842. COURNOT, A. A. Principes de la théorie des richesses. Paris, 1863.
5843. ———. Traité élémentaire de la théorie des fonctions du calcul infinitésimal. Paris, 1841. 2 v.
5844. ———. Recherches sur les principes mathématiques de la théorie des richesses. Paris, 1838; New York, 1897. Bibliography by Irving Fisher.
5845. COURS de droit commercial. Par M. Pardessus. 4th édition. Paris, 1831. 5 v.
5846. COWELL, J. W. Letters on currency. Addressed to the Right honourable F. T. Baring. London, 1843.
5847. COXE, Tench. United States arts and manufactures, 1810. Philadelphia, 1814.
5848. ———. A view of the United States. Philadelphia, 1794.
5849. CRAIG, John. Elements of political science. Edinburgh, W. Blackwood, 1814. 3 v.
5850. ———. Remarks on some fundamental doctrines of political economy illustrated by a brief inquiry into the commercial state of Britain, since the year 1815. Edinburgh, Constable, 1821.
5851. CRAIK, G. L. History of British commerce. London, 1844. 3 v.
5852. CRAWFORD, William H. Report of the Secretary of the treasury in relation to the condition of the bank of the United States. In, Pamphleteer, London, XVII (1820). (Reprinted, 45 p.)
5853. CRAWFURD, John. Chinese monopoly examined. London, 1830.
5854. ———. The doctrine of equivalents, or an explanation of the nature, the value, and the power of money. Rotterdam, 1794.
5855. ———. History of the Indian archipelago, containing an account of the manners, arts, languages, religions, institutions, and commerce of its inhabitants. Edinburgh, 1820. 3 v.
5856. ———. An inquiry into some of the principal monopolies (especially those of salt and opium) of the East India company. London, 1830.
5857. ———. Journal of an embassy from the governor-general of India to the courts of Siam and Cochin-China, exhibiting a view of the actual state of those kingdoms. 2d

5858. ———. Taxes on knowledge; a financial and historical view of the taxes which impede the education of the people London, 1836.
5859. ———. A view of the present state and future prospects of the free trade and colonization of India. London, 1829.
5860. CROKE, Alexander. An answer to Schlegel on the visitation of neutrals. London, 1801.
5861. CRUMPE, Samuel. An essay on the best means of providing employment for the people; to which was adjudged the prize proposed by the Royal Irish academy for the best dissertation on that subject. London, 1793. 1 v. (1795.)
5862. CRUTTWELL, Richard. A treatise on the state of the currency at the present time, 1824-25. . . . London, 1825.
5863. CUSTODI, Pietro. Scrittori classici italiani di Economia politica. Milano, 1803-16. 50 v.
5864. DALBIAC, James Charles. A few words on the corn laws, wherein are brought under consideration certain of the statements which are to be found in the 3d edition of Mr. M'Culloch's pamphlet on the same subject. London, 1841.
5865. DALRYMPLE, John. The question considered, whether wool should be allowed to be exported when the price is low at home, on paying a duty to the public? London, 1781.
5866. ———. State of the public debts. 6th edition. London, 1783.
5867. DANKWARDT, H. Nationalökonomie und jurisprudenz. Rostock, 1857-59.
5868. DANVILLA, B. J. Lecciones de economia civil, o del comercio. Escritas para el uso de los caballeros del Real Seminario de Nobles. Madrid, 1779.
5869. DARESTE de la Chavanne. Histoire des classes agricoles en France. 2d edition. Paris, 1858. 1 v.
5870. DAVENANT, Charles. An inquiry into those principles, respecting the nature of demand and the necessity of consumption, lately advocated by Mr. Malthus, from which it is concluded, that taxation and maintenance of unproductive consumers can be conducive to the progress of wealth. London, R. Hunter, 1821.
5871. DAVIDSON, John. Considerations on the poor laws. Oxford, 1817. 122 p.
5872. DAVIES, David. Families in different parts of the kingdom. London, 1795.
5873. DAVIS, J. F. The Chinese: a general description of China and its inhabitants. London, 1840. 1 v.
5874. DAVY, John. Account of the interior of Ceylon, and of its inhabitants. . . . London, 1821. 1 v.
5875. DAWSON, William. An inquiry into the causes of the general poverty and dependence of mankind. . . . Edinburgh, 1814. 255 p.
5876. De la BIENFAISANCE publique. Par M. le Baron Degerando. Paris, 1839. 4 v.
5877. De la CHARITE légale, de ses causes, et spécialement des maisons de travail, et de la proscription de la mendicité.

Classical Period 377

Par M. Naville, Pasteur à Genève. Genève, 1836. 2 v.
5878. DE QUINCY, Thomas de la. The collected writings of. . . . Enlarged by David Masson. Edinburgh, Black, 1890.
5879. ———. The logic of Political-economy. Edinburgh, 1844.
5880. DE ROOY, E. W. Geschiedenis der staatshuishandkunde in Europa. Amsterdam, 1851.
5881. DEAN, R. B. Remarks on the revenue of customs; with a few observations on a late work of Sir H. Parnell on financial reform, in a letter to the Right honourable Henry Coulburn. . . . London, 1830.
5882. DEBRAY. Essai sur la force, la puissance et la richesse nationales. 9e édition. Paris, 1814.
5883. A DEFENCE of joint stock banks and country issues. By Bailey, the author of 'Money and vicissitudes in value.' London, 1840.
5884. A DEFENCE of the Perthshire resolutions, in answer to a letter upon the distillery. Edinburgh, 1784.
5885. DELISLE De Sales. Vie littéraire de Forbonnais. 1801. 1 v.
5886. DELLA giurisprudenza maritima commerciale, antica e moderna. Di Piantanida. Milano, 1806. 4 v.
5887. DELLA societa chiamata accomandia. . . . Del Signor Fierli. Firenze, 1803. 2 v.
5888. DELLA storia delle finanze del regno di Napoli. Del Signor Bianchini. Ediz. 2da. Napoli, 1839. 3 v.
5889. DELPIT, J. . . . Documents francaise qui se trouvent en Angleterre. Paris, 1847.
5890. DEPPING, G. B. Histoire du commerce entre le Levant et l'Europe depuis les croisades. . . . Paris, 1830. 2 v.
5891. Des CANAUX de navigation, et spécialement du Canal de Languedoc. Par M. de la Lande. Paris, 1778. 1 v.
5892. DESAUBIEZ. Système de finance et d'économie politique. Paris, 1827.
5893. DESBROSSES, Bonvallet. Richesses et ressources de la France, pour servir de suite aux moyens de simplifier la recette et la comptabilité des deniers royaux. Paris, 1789. 1 v.
5894. DESCRIPTION of the character, manners, and customs of the people of India. By the Abbé Dubois. London, 1817. 1 v.
5895. DESMEUNIERS. Dictionnaire d'économie politique, faisant partie de l'encyclopédie methodique. 1834-38. 4 v.
5896. DESROTOURS. Notice des principaux règlements, publiés en Angleterre, concernant les pauvres. Paris, 1788.
5897. DESTUTT de Tracy (comte). Traité d'économie politique. Paris, 1823.
5898. DEW, Thomas R. Lectures on the restrictive system. . . . Richmond, 1829.
5899. DICCIONARIO georgraphico-historico de las Indias Occidentales o America: es a saber de los Reynos del Peru, Neuva Espana, Tierra Firme, Chile, y Nueva Reyna de Granada. Por Don Antonio de Alcedo. Madrid, 1786-89. 5 v.

5900. DICKSON, Adam. The husbandry of the ancients. Edinburgh, 1788. 2 v. (Paris, 1802. 2 v.)
5901. DICTIONNAIRE de l'administration francaise M. Block. Paris, 1853. (3d édition 1891.)
5902. DICTIONNAIRE du commerce et de marchandises. . . . Par Messrs. Blanqui, A. Chevalier, Parisot, etc. Paris, 1842. 2 v.
5903. DIETERICI, K. F. W. Die bevölkerung der erde. Berlin, 1857.
5904. ———. Handbuch der statistick des preussens Staats. Berlin, 1858-61.
5905. ———. Statistick uebersicht der wichtigsten gegenstande des verkechrs und verbrauchs im preussens Staat und im deutsch Zollverbande, 1831-53. (6th edition Berlin, 1838-57.)
5906. A DIGEST of the existing commercial regulations of foreign countries with which the United States have intercourse, as far as they can be ascertained. Prepared in compliance with a resolution of the House of representatives of the 3rd of March, 1831. Washington, 1833-36. 3 v.
5907. DIODATI, Luigi. Dello stato presente della moneta nel regno di Napoli. Napoli, 1790.
5908. DIROM, Alexander. An inquiry into the corn trade and corn laws of Great Britain, and their influence on the prosperity of the kingdom. London, 1796. 1 v.
5909. DISSERTATION sur l'influence des loix maritimes des Rhodiens. Par M. Pastoret. Paris, 1784.
5910. DIZZIONARIO universale ragionata della giurisprudenza mercantile. Di dom Alb. Azuni. Livorno, 1822. 4 v.
5911. DOE. Traité sur l'indigence. Quelles sont les principales causes de l'indigence? Moyens pour en arrêter les progrès. Paris, 1805.
5912. DOMESDAY book. London, 1783. 2 v. (Southampton, 1861-63. Translated by G. Plantagenet Harrison. London, 1871.)
5913. DONIOL, H. Histoire des classes rurales en France. Paris, 1857. 1 v. (2d édition, Paris, 1865.)
5914. ———. La revolution française et la Féodalité. Paris, 1874.
5915. DONNIGES, W. Die land-kultur-gasetzbebung Preussens seit 1807. (3d ed. 2 abth. Berlin, 1843-48.)
5916. DORI, J. A. Materialien zur aufstellung einer vernunftmaesigen theorie der staatswirthschaft. (Matériaux pour une théorie rationnelle de l'économie politique.) Leipzig, 1797.
5917. DOUBLEDAY, J. The true law of population. . . . London, 1841.
5918. ———. Financial, monetary, and statistical history of England. 2d edition. London, 1858.
5919. DOUGLAS, James. The prospects of Britain. 2d edition. Edinburgh, 1831.
5920. DOUGLASS, Howard. Considerations on the value and importance of the British North American provinces. London, 1831.

Classical Period

5921. DOURSTHER, Horace. Dictionnaire universel des poids et mesures anciens et modernes, contenant des tables des monnaies de tous les pays. Bruxelles, 1840. 1 v.
5922. DOVE, Patrick Edward. The theory of human progression. London, 1850.
5923. DOYLE, James. A letter to Thomas Spring Rice, on the establishment of a legal provision for the Irish poor, and on the nature and destination of church property.
5924. DROIT maritime de l'Europe. Par Dom. A. Azuni. Paris, 1805. 2 v.
5925. DROIT au travail (Le) à l'assemblee nationale. Recueil de tous les discours prononcés dans cette discussion mémorable. Paris, 1848. 1 v.
5926. DROZ, Joseph. Economie politique ou principes de la science des richesses Bruxelles and Paris, 1829. (3d edition, Paris, 1854.
5927. DRUMMOND, Henry. Cheap corn best for farmers, proved in a letter to G. H. Sumner. London, 1826.
5928. DUBOIS-AYME. Examen de quelques questions d'économie politique. . . . Paris, Pélicier, 1824.
5929. DUBOIS, J.-B. Du commerce français dans l'état actuel de l'Europe, ou observations sur le commerce de la France en Italie, dans le Levant, en Russie et dans la mer Noire. . . . Paris, 1806. 1 v.
5930. DU BUAT. Elements de la politique, ou recherches des vrais principes de l'économie sociale. Londres, 1773.
5931. DUCHATEL, T. De la charité dans ses rapports avec l'état moral et le bien-être des classes inférieures de la société. Paris, 1829.
5932. DUFRESNE SAINT-LEON, (L. C. A.). Etude de crédit public et des dettes publiques. Paris, 1824.
5933. DUNCAN, Henry. An essay on the nature and advanteges of parish banks for the savings of the industrious. 2nd and enlarged edition. Edinburgh, 1816.
5934. DUNCAN, John. Collections relative to systematic relief of the poor, at different periods and in different countries, with observations on charity. . . . Bath, 1815.
5935. DUNCKLEY, H. Charter of nations, or free-trade results. London, 1834.
5936. DUNCOMBE, Charles. Duncombe's free banking; an essay on banking. Cleveland, 1841.
5937. DUNLOP, Alexander. A treatise on the law of Scotland relative to the poor. 2d edition. Edinburgh, 1828. 1 v.
5938. DUNLOP, Anthony. Sketches on political economy. In, Pamphleteer, London, XI (1818). Reprint, 39 p.
5939. DUNOYER, B. C. Nouveau traité d'économie sociale, ou Simple exposition des causes sous l'influence desquelles les hommes parviennent à user de leur force avec le plus de liberté, c'est-à-dire avec le plus de facilité et de puissance. Paris, 1830. 2 v.
5940. DUNOYER, Charles. De la liberté de commerce international, 1847-48.
5941. _____. De la liberté du travail, 1845. (2e édition,

1886. 3 v.)
5942. _____. Notice historique sur l'industrialisme, 1827.
5943. _____. Notices d'économie sociale. 1840. (Paris, 1870.)
5944. _____. Oeuvres. Paris, 1885-87. 3 v.
5945. _____. Politique tirée des doctrines économiques, 1818.
5946. DUPIN, Charles. Discours et leçons sur l'industrie, le commerce, la marine, et sur les sciences appliquées aux arts. Paris, Bchelier, 1825. 2 v.
5947. _____. Force productives des nations depuis 1800. Paris, 1851. 4 v.
5948. _____. Forces productives et commerciales de la France. Paris, Bachelier, 1827. 4 v.
5949. _____. Histoire de l'administration des secours publics. . . . Paris, 1821.
5950. _____. Le petit producteur français. Pairs, Bachelier, 1827. 7 v.
5951. DUPONT-WHITE, Charles Brook. La centralisation. Paris, 1860. (2d edition, 1861.)
5952. _____. L'Individu et l'état, 1857. (2d edition, 1865.)
5953. _____. Le libre échange. In, La Liberté de penser, revue démocratique, viii, 1851.
5954. _____. Relations du travail avec le capital. Paris, 1846.
5955. DUPUIT, Jules. De l'utilité et de sa mesure. Paris, 1844. (Edited by Luigi Einaudi. Turin, 1934.)
5956. _____. La liberté commerciale som principe et ses conséquences. Paris, 1860. (1861).
5957. DUQUESNOY. Recueil de mémoires sur les établissements d'humanité; traduit de l'anglais par Labaume de Liancourt et autres; publié par Duquesnoy avec soin. 1794-1804. 15 v.
5958. DUREAU, A. Economie politique des Romains. Paris, 1840 2 v.
5959. DUREAU de LA MALLE. Economie politique des Romains. Paris, 1840. 2 v.
5960. DUTENS, Joseph M. Analyse raisonnée des principes fondamentaux de l'économie politique. 1804. 1 v.
5961. _____. Histoire de la navigation interieure de la France. Paris, 1829. 2 v.
5962. _____. Philosophie de l'économie politique ou nouvelle exposition des principes de cette science. Paris, 1835. 2 v.
5963. DUVERGIER, J. Collection complète des lois, décrets, reglements et avis du conseil d'état. Paris, 1836. (1885.)
5964. DUVILLARD. Analyse et tableaux de l'influence de la petite vérole sur la mortalité à chaque age, et de celle qu'un préservatif tel que la vaccine peut avoir sur la population et la longévité. Paris, 1806. 1 v.
5965. DYER, George. A dissertation on the theory and practice of benevolence. New edition. In, Pamphleteer, London, XIII (1819). Reprint, 38 p.
5966. ECKHEL, J. H. Doctrina numorum veterum. Vindobonae, 1792-98. 8 v. (Supplement, Vienna, 1826. 1 v.)
5967. ECONOMIE politique des Romains. Par M. Dureau de la Malle. Paris, 1841. 2 v.

5968. ECONOMISTES financiers du XVIIIe siècle. . . . Edited by Eugène Daire. Paris, 1843.
5969. EDEN, Frederick Morton. Eight letters on the peace, and on the commerce and manufactures of Great Britain. London, 1802.
5970. ———. An estimate of the number of inhabitants in Great Britain and Ireland. London, 1800.
5971. ———. On the policy and expediency of granting insurance charters. London, 1806.
5972. ———. The state of the poor; or, an history of the labouring classes in England, from the conquest to the present period; in which are particularly considered, their domestic economy, with respect to diet, dress, fuel, and habitation; and the various plans which from time to time have been proposed and adopted for the relief of the poor. . . . London, 1797. 3 v.
5973. EDEN, William. A letter to the Earl of Carlisle respecting a free trade. Dublin, 1779.
5974. ———. A view of the treaty of commerce with France. 2d edition. London, 1787.
5975. EDGEWORTH, R. L. An essay on the construction of roads and carriages. London, 1812. 1 v.
5976. EDINGTON, Robert. A treatise on coal trade. With strictures on its abuses, and hints for their amendment. 2d edition. London, 1814. 1 v.
5977. EDMONDS, T. R. Life tables, founded upon the discovery of a numerical law regulating the existence of every human being: illustrated by a new theory of the causes producing health and longevity. London, 1832. 1 v.
5978. ———. Practical moral and political economy. . . . London, 1828. 304 p.
5979. EDWARDS, Bryan. The history, civil and commercial, of the British colonies in the West Indies. 5th edition. London, 1819. 5 v.
5980. EDWARDS, George. Radical means of counteracting the present scarcity. . . . London, 1801.
5981. EHRENTAL, V. Die staatswirthschaft nach naturgestzen. Leipzig, 1819.
5982. ———. Ueber das oeffentliche schuldenwesen. Leipzig. 1810.
5983. EIKEMEYER. Abhandlungen über gegenstdaende der staats und kriegswissenschaften. Frankfurt, 1816.
5984. EISDELL, John S. A treatise on the industry of nations, or, the principle of national economy and taxation. London, 1839. 2 v.
5985. EISELEN, J. J. H. Grundzuge der staatswirthschaft. Berlin, 1818. 1 v.
5986. ELEMENTARY thoughts on the bullion question, the national debt, the resources of Great Britain. . . . Barnstaple, 1820.
5987. ELLIOT, J. Report on funding system of United States and Great Britain. Washington, 1843. (House document no. 15, 28th congress, 1st session.)

5988. ELLIS, William. (Articles.) Encyclopedia Britannica, 4th edition, v. xvii. 1810. Vol. XVII, 5, 21, 26, 71, etc. (Political Economy, Production, Labor, Wealth; and Adam Smith.)
5989. ──────. An essay on the political economy of nations; or, a view of the intercourse of countries as influencing their wealth. London, Longman, 1821. (Supplement, 1823.)
5990. ──────. Review of the effect of the employment of machinery. . . upon the happiness of the working classes. London, 1824.
5991. EMERIGON, B. M. Traité des assurances et des contrats a la grosse. Marseille, 1782. 2 v.
5992. EMERY, Thomas. An essay on the causes which regulate the wages of labor. London, 1849.
5993. ENCYCLOPAEDIA metropolitana. 2d edition. London, 1849-54.
5994. ENFANTIN, P. Correspondance philosophique et religieuse, 1843-45. Paris, 1847.
5995. ──────. Economie politique et politique. Paris, 1831. (2d edition, 1823.)
5996. ENSOR, George. An inquiry concerning the population of nations. (Recherches sur la population des nations.) 1818. 1 v.
5997. ──────. The poor and their relief. (Des pauvres et des secours.) 1823. 1 v.
5998. ESCHENMAYER. Ueber das formale prinzip der staatswirthschaft. (Du principe formel de l'economie politique comme science et comme doctrine.) Heidelberg. 1815.
5999. ESSAI comparatif sur la formation et la distribution du revenu de la France en 1815 et 1835. Par Dutens. Paris, 1842.
6000. ESSAI concernant les armateurs, les prises, et les reprises. Par Martens. Gottingen, 1795. 1 v. (Translated into English by Mr. T. H. Horne, London, 1801.)
6001. ESSAI historique et moral sur la pauvreté des nations, la population, la mendicité, les hôpitaux, et les enfans-trouvés. Par Foderé. Paris, 1825. 1 v.
6002. ESSAI sur un code maritime général pour la conservation de la liberté de la navigation, et du commerce des nations neutres en tems de guerre. Leipsic, 1782. 1 v.
6003. ESSAI sur les consuls. Par Steck. Berlin, 1790. 1 v.
6004. ESSAI sur l'état actuel de l'administration des finances et de la richesse nationale de la Grande Bretagne. Par Gentz. Hambourg, 1800. 1 v.
6005. ESSAI sur la science des finances. Par Gandillot. Paris, 1840. 1 v.
6006. ESSAY on money; or, an inquiry into the nature of the circulating medium. Glasgow, 1837.
6007. An ESSAY on the nature of colonies and the conduct of the mother country towards them. London, 1811.
6008. An ESSAY on the political economy of nations. . . . London, 1821. 288 p.
6009. An ESSAY on the right of property in land, with respect to

	its foundation in the law of nature; its present establishment by the municipal laws of Europe; and the regulations by which it might be rendered more beneficial to the lower ranks of mankind. By Mr. Ogilvie, University of Aberdeen. London, 1776?
6010.	ESTADO de las Islas Filipinas en 1810, brevemente descrito. Por Thomas De Comyn. Madrid, 1820. 1 v.
6011.	ESTADO de la poblacion . . . de las Islas Filipinas correspondente a el año de 1818. Manila, 1820.
6012.	ESTRADA, don Alvaro Florez. Traité électique d'économie politique; traduit par L. Galibert. Paris, 1833. 3 v.
6013.	ETAT des cononies et du commerce des Européens dans les Deux Indes depuis 1783 jusqu'en 1821. Par Peuchet. Paris, 1821. 2 v.
6014.	ETUDES de crédit public et des dettes publiques. Par M. Dufresne St. Leon. Paris, 1824. 1 v.
6015.	ETUDES d'économie politique sur la proprieté territoriale. Par Dupuynode. Paris, 1840. 1 v.
6016.	ETUDES historiques et critiques sur les Monts-de-Piété en Belgique. Par Decker. Bruxelles, 1844. 1 v.
6017.	EVANS, D. Morier. Commercial crisis; 1847-48. 2d edition. London, 1849.
6018.	———. Commercial crisis; 1857-58. London, 1859.
6019.	EVERETT, Alexander H. Nouvelles idées sur la population, avec des remarques sur les théories de Malthus et de Godwin; traduit de l'anglais par C. J. Ferry. Paris, Renouard, 1826. (English edition: Boston, 1833.)
6020.	EXAMEN du gouvernement d'Angleterre, comparé aux constitutions des Etats-Unis. Londres, 1789.
6021.	An EXAMINATION of the British doctrine which subjects to capture (vessels engaged in) a neutral trade not open in time of peace. Originally published in America. Reprinted in London, 1806.
6022.	An EXAMINATION of the new tariff proposed by the Honourable Henry Baldwin. By one of the people, Cambreleng? New York, 1821.
6023.	On the EXPEDIENCY and necessity of striking off a part of the national debt. In, Pamphleteer, XVII (1821) Reprint, 23 p.
6024.	FABRICIUS. Anfangsgründe der oeconomischen Wissenschaften. Kopenhague, 1783.
6025.	FACTS addressed to the landholders . . . and generally to all the subjects of Great Britain and Ireland. London, 1780.
6026.	FAIRMAN, William. The stocks examined and compared. 3d edition. London, 1798. (4th edition, 1802.)
6027.	———. An account of the public funds. . . . 7th edition. London, 1824.
6028.	FAUCHER, L. J. Etudes sur l'Angleterre. Paris, 1845. 2 v. (2d édition. Paris, 1856. 2 v.)
6029.	———. Recherches sur l'or et l'argent. Paris, 1843.
6030.	FAZY, Jean-James. Du privélege de la Banque de France, considéré comme nuisible aux transactions commerciales. Paris, 1819.

384 Economic Thought and Analysis

6031. _____. L'homme aux proportions ou conversations philosophiques et politiques. Paris, 1821.
6032. _____. Opuscules financiers sur l'effet des privilèges, des emprunts publics et des conversions; sur le crédit et l'industrie en France. Genève et Paris, 1826.
6033. FELICE de. Eléments de la police d'un état. Yverdun, 1781. 2 v.
6034. FELIX, Ludwig. Die arbeiter und der gesellschaft. Leipzig, 1874.
6035. _____. Entwickelungsgeschichte des eigenthums. 3 thl. Leipzig, 1833-89.
6036. FERRARA, Francesco. Biblioteca dell'economista. Serie I: Trattati complessivi. Serie II: Trattati speciali. Torino, 1850-70. 26 v. (Prima serie. Turin, 1855.)
6037. _____. Esame storico-critico di economisti e dottrine economiche. . . . Torino, 1889-92. 2 v.
6038. _____. Oeuvres économiques choisies. Paris, 1938.
6039. FERRIER, F. L. A. Du gouvernement considéré dans ses rapports avec le commerce ou de l'administration commerciale opposée à l'économie politique. Paris, 1821.
6040. FICHTE, Johann Gottlieb. Der geschlossene handelsstaat. Tubingue, 1800. In, Fichte Sammtliche werke, Berlin, 1845. v. III.
6041. FILOSOFIA della statistica. Da Gioja. 2d ed. con Aggiunte di Romagnosi. Milano, 1829. 4 v.
6042. FIRST report of the commissioners for inquiring into the state of large towns and populous districts. London, 1844.
6043. FISCHER. Lehrbegriff und anfang der deutschen staatswissenschaft. Halle, 1783.
6044. FITZWILLIAM, Earl, Viscount Milton. Address to the landowners of England, on the corn laws. London, 1832.
6045. FIVE reports of the committee of the House of commons appointed, in 1808, to inquire into Indian affairs. London, 1810-13.
6046. FLOREZ ESTRADA, Alvaro. Curso de economia politica, 1828. (5th ed. Madrid, 1840. 2 v.)
6047. FODERE, F. E. Essai historique et moral sur la pauvreté des nations, la population, la mendicité, les hopitaux et les enfants-trouvés. Paris, Mme. Huzard, 1825.
6048. FONTENAY, R. de. Du revenu foncier. Paris, 1854. 1 v.
6049. FORBES, William. Memoirs of a banking-house. Edinburgh, 1859.
6050. FORCES productives et commerciales de la France. Par Dupin. Paris, 1827. 2 v.
6051. FORSTER, Nathaniel. An answer to Sir John Dalrymple's pamphlet on the exportation of wool. Colchester, 1782.
6052. FORTUNE, Thomas. Histoire concise et authentique de la banque d'Angleterre. Londres, 1779. (3d edition. London, 1802.)
6053. FOSTER, John Leslie. An essay on the principle of commercial exchanges, and more particularly of the

Classical Period

exchange between Great Britain and Ireland; with an inquiry into the practical effects of the bank restrictions. London, 1804.
6054. FOUR letters to the Earl of Carlisle, from William Eden. (3d edition has a 5th letter.) London, 1780. 1 v.
6055. FOURIER, Charles. Le nouveau monde industriel et sociétaire; ou invention du procédé d'industrie attrayante et naturelle distribuée en séries passionées. Paris, 1829. 1 v.
6056. ———. Oeuvres complètes. Paris, 1841-5. 6 v. (Choises, 1890.)
6057. ———. Traité de l'association domestique agricole. Paris, 1822. 2 v.
6058. ———. Théorie des quatre mouvements. 1808. 1 v.
6059. ———. Theory of social organization. Introduction by A. Brisbane. New York, 1886.
6060. FRANCIS, John. Chronicles and characters of the stock exchange. London, 1849.
6061. ———. History of English railway, 1820-45. London, 1857.
6062. FRASER, Robert. A review of the domestic fisheries of Great Britain, and Ireland. Edinburgh, 1818. 1 v.
6063. FREE trade in corn the real interest of the landlord and the true policy of the state. By a Cumberland landowner. London, 1828.
6064. FREND, William. "The national debt in its true colours." In, Pamphleteer, London, IX (1817) 416-432.
6065. ———. Principles of taxation. London, 1799.
6066. FULDA. Der staatscredit. Tubingue, 1832.
6067. ———. Grundsaetze der Kameralwissenschaften. Tubingue, 1820.
6068. ———. Systematischer abriss der sogenannten Kameralwissenschaften. Tubinque, 1802.
6069. ———. Ueber nationaleinkommen. Stuttgart, 1805.
6070. ———. Ueber production and consumtion. Tubingue, 1820.
6071. FULLARTON, John. On the regulation of currencies, and the working of the New bank charter act. . . . London, 1844. 1 v. (2d edition, London, 1845.)
6072. FURSTENAU. Versuch einer Apologie des physiocratischen systems. Brunswick, 1780.
6073. FUSCO, F. Le banche e l'industria. Napoli, 1834.
6074. ———. Introduzione allo studio dell' economia industriale. Napoli, 1829.
6075. ———. Saggi economici. Pisa, 1825-27. 2 v.
6076. GAETE, Duc de. Notice historique sur les finances de Francs (de l'an 1800 au 1er avril 1814.) Paris, 1818.
6077. GALE, S. An essay on the nature and principles of public credit. London, 1784.
6078. GALLATIN, Albert. Considerations on the currency and banking system of the United States. Philadelphia, 1831.
6079. ———. Views of the public debt, receipts and expenditures of the United States. 2d edition. Philadelphia, 1801.

6080.	———. The writings of Albert Gallatin. Edited by H. Adams. Philadelphia, 1879. 3 v.
6081.	GANDILLOT, Avocat. Essai sur la science des finances. Paris, Joubert, 1840. 1 v.
6082.	GANILH, Charles. De la science des finances. 1825. 1 v.
6083.	———. Dictionnaire analytique d'économie politique. Paris, L'Advocate, 1826.
6084.	———. Essai politique sur le revenu public des peuples de l'antiquité, du moyen-age, des siècles modernes, et spécialement de la France et de l'Angleterre. depuis le XVe siècle jusqu'au XIXe; 2d edition. Paris, Treuttell et Wurtz, 1823. 2 v.
6085.	———. An inquiry into the various systems of political economy. . . . Translated by D. Boileau. London, 1812. (Paris, 1809. 2 v. 2d edition 1823.)
6086.	———. La théorie de l'économie politique fondée sur les faits recueillisen France et en Angleterre. Paris, 1815. 2 v. (Nouvelle édition 1822.)
6087.	GANS, Baron de. System der staatswissenschaft. Système d'économie politique. Leipzig, 1826.
6088.	GARNIER, Germain. Abrégé élémentaire des principes de l'économie politique. Paris, 1796.
6089.	———. De la propriété dans ses rapports avec le droit politique. Paris, 1792.
6090.	———. Histoire de la monnaie, depuis les temps de la plus haute antiquite reculés jusqu'au règne de Charlemagne. Paris, 1819. 2 v.
6091.	———. Théorie des banques d'escompte. Paris, 1806.
6092.	GARNIER, Joseph. Eléments de l'économie politique, 1846. (2d édition Paris, 1848.)
6093.	———. Traité d'économie politique. . . . Paris, Garnier frères et Guillaumin, 1863. (9th édition, 1889.)
6094.	———. Traité des finances. 4th édition. Paris, 1885.
6095.	GASKELL, P. The manufacturing population of England. London, 1833.
6096.	———. Artisans and machinery: the moral and physical condition of the manufacturing population considered with reference to mechanical substitutes for labour. London, 1836. 1 v.
6097.	GASPARIN, A. E. P. de. Considérations sur les machines. Paris, 1835.
6098.	———. Cours complet d'agriculture. 3d édition. Paris, 1863. 6 v.
6099.	GAUME, L'Abbé J. Histoire de la société domestique. 2d edition. Paris, 1854. 2 v.
6100.	GAVARD. Grundlinien der reinen und angewandten staatsoeconomie. Wurtzbourg, 1796.
6101.	GEIER, Pierre-Philippe. Ueber encyclopedie und methodologie der wirthschaftslehre (De l'encyclopédie et de la méthodologie de l'économie politique). Wurtzbourg, 1818. (Du méme auteru: Versuch einer logischen begründung der withschaftslehre. Wurtzbourg, 1822.)
6102.	GEIJER, E. G. The poor-laws, and their bearing on

Classical Period 387

society; being a series of political and historical essays in English. Stockholm, 1840.
6103. GENTZ, Frédéric. Essai sur l'etat actuel de l'administration des finances et de la richesse national de la Grande-Bretagne. Londres et Hambourg, 1800.
6104. GERANDO, Marie de. De la bienfaisance publique traité complet de l'indigence considéré dans ses rapports. Paris, Renouard, 1839. 4 v. (Uebersetzt v. Dr. F. J. Buss, 3 bde. Stuttgart, 1844.)
6105. ———. Du progrès de l'industrie. 2d edition. Paris, 1845.
6106. GERARD de RAYNEVAL. Principes du commerce entre les nations; traduit de l'anglais de B. Vaughan. Paris, 1789.
6107. GERSTNER. Mémoires sur les grandes routes, les chemins de fer et les canaux de navigation; traduit de l'allemand de Gerstner, et précédé d'une introduction par M. P. S. Girard. Paris, 1827.
6108. GIBBON, Alexander. Past and present delusions in the political economy. . . . Edinburgh, 1850.
6109. GIBBONS, J. S. The banks of New York, New York, 1859.
6110. ———. The public debts of the United States. New York and London, 1867.
6111. GILBART, James William. The elements of banking. London, 1852. 97 p.
6112. ———. The history and principles of banking. London, 1834. (2d edition London, 1835.)
6113. ———. History and principles of ancient commerce. London, 1853. (Lectures. . . . Paris, Guillaumin, 1856.)
6114. ———. The history of banking in America; with an inquiry how far the banking institutions of America are adapted to this country; and a review of the causes of the recent pressure on the money market. London, 1837. 1 v.
6115. ———. The history of banking in Ireland. London, 1836. 1 v.
6116. ———. A practical treatise on banking, containing an account of the London and country banks, the joint stock banks. . . . London, 1827. (2d edition, 1828.)
6117. GILBERT, Thomas. Plan for the better relief and employment of the poor. London, 1781.
6118. GILLIES, John. Aristotle's ethics and politics, comprising his practical philosophy. Translated from the Greek. . . . 3d edition. London, 1813. 2 v.
6119. GIOJA, Melchiorre. Nuovo prospetto delle scienze economiche ossia somma totale delle idee teoriche e pratiche in ogni ramo d'amministrazione privata e publica. Milano, 1815-19. 6 v.
6120. GODSON, Richard. A practical treatise on the law of patents for inventions and of copyright, with an introductory book on monopolies. 2d edition. London, 1840. 1 v.
6121. GODWIN, William. The Enquirer. Reflections on education. . . . London, 1797.

388   Economic Thought and Analysis

6122. ———. An enquiry concerning political justice. London, 1793. 2 v. (2d edition, London, 1976. American from 2d London edition Philadelphia, 1796. 2 v.; 3d edition London, 1798. 2 v.)
6123. ———. Of population: an enquiry concerning the power of increase in the numbers of mankind. . . . London, 1820.
6124. ———. On population, an answer to Malthus. London, 1820.
6125. ———. Recherches sur la population, et sur la faculte d'accroissement de l'espèce humaine; contenant une refutation des doctrines de Malthus sur cette matière. Traduit de l'anglais par F. S. Constancio. Paris, 1821. 2 v.
6126. ———. Thoughts on man. . . . London, 1831.
6127. GOODELL, William. Slavery and anti-slavery. 3d edition. New York, 1855.
6128. GORLOF. De valoris natura. Dorpati, 1838.
6129. GOSSEN, Hermann H. Entwickelung der gesetze des menschlicken verkehrs. . . . Braunschweig, 1854. (New edition Berlin, 1889.)
6130. GOUGE, William M. A short history of paper money and banking in the United States. Philadelphia, 1833.
6131. GOUTTES, L'Abbe. Théorie de l'intéret de l'argent . . . l'abus d'imputation d'usure. Paris, 1780. 1 v.
6132. GOW, N. Practical treatise on the law of partnership. 3d edition. London, 1841. 1 v.
6133. GRAHAM. James. Corn and currency . . . address to landowners. London, 1826. (1827.)
6134. GRANT, James. An inquiry into the nature of zemindary tenures, in the landed property of Bengal. 2d edition. London, 1791.
6135. GRANT, Robert. A sketch of the history of the East India company, from its first formation till 1773. . . . London, 1813. 1 v.
6136. GRAUMAN. Lettre concernant les monnaies d'Allemagne. Berlin, 1852.
6137. ———. Lettre sur la proportion entre l'or et l'argent; sur les monnaies de France. . . . Paris, 1788.
6138. GRAY, John. The essential principles of the wealth of nations. London, 1797.
6139. ———. The income-tax scrutinised, and some amendments proposed to render it more agreeable to the British constitution. London, 1802.
6140. ———. A lecture on human happiness. London, 1825. (London school of economics Reprints, 2. London, 1931.)
6141. ———. Lectures on the nature and use of money. Edinburgh, 1844. (1858.)
6142. ———. The social system. Edinburgh, 1831.
6143. GRAY, Simon. All classes productive of national wealth. London, 1817. (Revised edition with 4 letters to a French economist, J. B. Say. London, 1840.)
6144. GREG, William Rathbone. Not over-production, but

Classical Period 389

        deficient consumption, the source of our suffering. London, 1842.
6145. GRELLIER, J. J. History of the national debt, 1688-1800. London, 1810.
6146. ———. Terms of all loans for the last fifty years. London, 1799.
6147. GRENFELL, Pascoc. The speech . . . on certain transactions subsisting betwixt the public and the bank of England. London, 1816.
6148. GRENVILLE, Lord. Essay on the supposed advantages of a sinking fund. London, 1828.
6149. GRESHAM, Thomas. The life and times. . . . By John William Burgon. London, 1839. 2 v.
6150. GREY, Earl. Colonial policy of Lord John Russell's administration. 2d edition. London, 1853. 2 v.
6151. ———. The commercial policy of the British colonies and the McKinley tariff. London and New York, 1892.
6152. GROSIER, L'Abbe. De la Chine, ou description generale de cet empire, rédigee d'après les mémoires et de la Mission de Pekin. La 3me edition, revue et considerablement augmentee. Paris, 1818. 7 v. (Originally appeared in 1786. 1 v.)
6153. GROUBER DE GROUBENTHAL. Théorie générale de l'administration des finances. Paris, 1788. 2 v.
6154. GUDIN de LA BRENELLERIE. Essai sur l'histoire des comices de Rome, des états généraux de France et du parlement d'Angleterre. Paris, Maranda, 1789. 3 v.
6155. GUEPIN, A. Traité d'économie sociale. Paris, 1833.
6156. GUER, de. Considérations sur les finances. Paris, 1803.
6157. ———. Du crédit public. Paris, 1807.
6158. ———. Essai sur le crédit commercial, considéré comme moyen de circulation, et suivi de l'exposition des principes de la science du crédit public, et de celle de l'imposition. Paris, 1801.
6159. ———. Histoire de la banque d'Angleterre, et considérations sur les grandes banques de circulation. Paris, 1810.
6160. GUEST, Richard. History of the cotton manufacture. Manchester, 1823.
6161. GUIZOT, F. P. G. Histoire de la civilisation en Europe. Paris, 1828. (19e édition 1882.)
6162. ———. Histoire des origines du gouvernement représentatif en Europe. Paris, 1851. 2 v. (English translation by A. R. Scolle, London, 1852.)
6163. GULICH, G. V. Geschichtliche darstellung des handels, der gewerbe und des ackerbaues. Jena, 1830-45. 2 v.
6164. GUTZLAFF, Charles. China opened; or, a display of the topography, history, customs, manners, arts, manufactures, commerce, literature, religion, jurisprudence . . . , of the Chinese empire. London, 1838. 2 v.
6165. HAGEN, Von der. Staatslehre. Koenigsberg, 1839.
6166. HALL, Charles. The effects of civilization on the people in European states, 1805. (London, 1850.)

6167. HALL, George Webb. Letters on the importance of encouraging the growth of corn and wool in the United Kingdom, 1815.
6168. HALLAM, H. State of Europe during the middle ages. London, 1818. 2 v. (New edition London, 1877; New York, 1883.)
6169. HAMILTON, Alexander. Report . . . on . . . national bank, 1790.
6170. _____. Report . . . on . . . public credit. 1795.
6171. _____. Report of the Secretary of the treasury of the United States on the subject of manufactures, 1791. (Dublin 1792. In: A. Hamilton papers on public credit, commerce and finance. New York, 1934.)
6172. _____. Works. Edited by H. C. Lodge. New York, 1885-86. 9 v.
6173. HAMILTON, Andrew. An enquiry into the principles of taxation. London, 1790. (Dublin, 1791.)
6174. HAMILTON, Robert. An inquiry concerning the rise and progress, the redemption and present state, and the management of the national debt of Great Britain and Ireland. Edinburgh, 1813. (3d and best edition Edinburgh, 1818. 1 v.)
6175. _____. Introduction to merchandise, containing a complete system of arithmetic, with an account of the trade of Great Britain. Edinburgh, 1777.
6176. _____. Recherches sur l'origine, les progrès, le rachat, l'état actuel et la régie de la dette nationale de la Grande-Bretagne. Traduit de l'anglais par Henri Lasalle. Paris, 1817.
6177. HAMILTON, Walter. The East India gazetteer, containing descriptions of the empires, kingdoms, principalities, cities, towns etc. of Hindostan and the adjacent countries. 2d edition. London, 1828. 2 v.
6178. _____. A geographical, statistical, and historical description of Hindostan and the adjacent countries. London, 1820. 2 v.
6179. HANCOCK, W. Nielson. An introductory lecture on political economy. . . . Dublin, 1849. 36 p.
6180. _____. Three lectures on the questions, should the lessons of political economy be disregarded. . . . Dublin, 1847. 61 p.
6181. HARCOURT, Vicomte D'. Réflexions sur la richesse future de la France et sur la direction qu'il convient de donner à la prospérité du royaume. Paris, 1826.
6182. HARLEY, Robert. An essay upon public credit. London, 1797. 34 p.
6183. HAUER, Joseph V. Beiträge zur geschechte der finanzen. 4 hfte. Wien, 1848.
6184. HAUTERIVE, Comte d'. Eléments d'économie politique, suivis de quelques vues sur l'application des principes de cette science aux règles administratives. Paris, 1817.
6185. _____. Recueil . . . traités de commerce et navigation de la France. Paris, 1838-42. 10 v.

Classical Period

6186. HAWES, Benjamin. The abolition of arrest and imprisonment for debt considered, in six letters addressed to a constituent. London, 1836.
6187. HAWKINS, Edward. The silver coins of England arranged and described, with remarks on British money previous to the Saxon dynasties. London, 1841. 1 v.
6188. HAWKINS, F. B. Elements of medical statistics. . . . London, 1829.
6189. HEATHFIELD, Richard. Elements of a plan for the liquidation of the public debt of the United Kingdom. London, 1820.
6190. ———. Further observations on the practicability and expediency of liquidating the public debt of the United Kingdom. London, 1820.
6191. ———. Observations on trade, in reference, particularly, to the public debt. London, 1822. In, Pamphleteer, London, XX (1822).
6192. HEBERDEN, William. Observations on the increase and decrease of different diseases in London. London, 1801.
6193. HEEREN, A. H. L. Essai sur l'influence des croisades. 1 v.
6194. ———. De la politique et du commerce des peuples de l'antiquité. Traduit de l'allemand, sur la 4e édition, par M. W. Suckau. Paris, Didot, 1830. 6 v.
6195. ———. Ideen . . . die politik, den verkehr. . . . Handel . . . alten Welt. Göttengen, 1793. (Traduit Paris, 1841. Translated, Oxford, 1833. 6 v.)
6196. ———. Manuel de l'histoire ancienne, considerée sous le rapport des constitutions, du commerce et des colonies des divers états de l'antiquité. Traduit de l'allemand par M. Thurot. Paris, F. Didot et fils, 1823. (1837.)
6197. ———. Vermischte historische schriften. 3 bde. Göttengen, 1821-24.
6198. HEINECCIL, F. G. Elementa juris cambialis. Ed. optima. Nuremberg, 1787. 1 v.
6199. HELFERICH, J. Von den periodischen schwankungen in werthe. . . metalle--entdeckung Amerika's bis zum jahre, 1830. Nürmberg, 1843.
6200. HELPS, Arthur. The claims of labour. 2d edition. London, 1845.
6201. HENFNER, J. Introductio in oeconomiam nationalem. Agram, 1831.
6202. HENNET LE CHEVALIER. Essai d'un plan de finances. Paris, Delaunay, 1816.
6203. ———. Théorie du crédit public. Pairs, Delaunay, 1816. 1 v.
6204. HENRION DE BUSSI. De la destruction de la mendicité. Riom, 1790.
6205. HENSON, Gravenor. The civil, political, and mechanical history of the framework knitters in Europe and America. Nottingham, 1831. 1 v.
6206. HERBERT, William. The history of the twelve great livery

	companies of London. London, 1837. 2 v. (2d edition 1846.)
6207.	HERMANN, F. Staatswirthschaftliche untersuchungen. München, 1832. (2d ed. aufl. 1870; new ed. 1874.)
6208.	HERRENSCHWAND, J. F. de. De l'économie politique et morale de l'espèce humaine. Londres, 1796. 2 v.
6209.	———. De l'économie politique moderne, discours fondamental sur la population. Londres, 1786.
6210.	HERTSLET, Lewis. A complete collection of the treaties and conventions and reciprocal regulations at present subsisting between Great Britain and foreign powers, and of the laws, decrees, and orders in council concerning the same, so far as they relate to commerce and navigation; to the repression and abolition of the slave trade; and to the privileges and interests of the subjects of the high contracting parties. Compiled from authentic documents. London, 1820-40. 5 v.
6211.	HERTZBERG, Baron de. Two discourses . . . on the population of states. . . . Translated from the French. London, 1786.
6212.	HEUSCHLING, T. Apercu des principales statistiques belges de 1794. . . . Bruxelles, 1844.
6213.	———. Essai sur le statistique de la Belgique. Bruxelles, 1838.
6214.	HEWITT, A. S. Statistics and geography of the production of iron. New York, 1856.
6215.	HIGHMORE, Anthony. A practical arrangement of the laws relative to the excise, with cases. . . . London, 1796. 2 v.
6216.	HILDRETH, R. Bank, banking and paper currency. Boston, 1840.
6217.	———. History of United States. Revised edition. New York, 1882.
6218.	HILL, John. An inquiry into the causes of the present high price of gold bullion in England. London, 1810.
6219.	HILL, Rowland. Post-office reform, its importance and practicability. London, 1837.
6220.	HISTOIRE des peches, des découvertes, et des établissemens des Hollandois dans les Mers du Nord. Ouvrage traduit du Hollandois, par Bernard de Reste. Paris, 1801. 3 v.
6221.	HISTOIRE philosophique et politique des établissements et du commerce des Européens dans les deux Indes. Par M. l'Abbé Raynal. Avec des planches. Genève, 1780. 4 v. et 10 v.
6222.	HISTOIRE raisonnée du commerce de la Russie. Par Scherer. Paris, 1788. 2 v.
6223.	HISTOIRE statistique et morale des Enfans-Trouvés. Par Terme et Monfalcon. Paris et Lyon, 1837. 1 v.
6224.	HISTORICAL and political remarks upon the tariff of the commercial treaty (with France), with preliminary observations, attributed to Mr. Eden. London, 1787.
6225.	HISTORICAL researches into the politics, intercourse, and trade of the Carthaginians, Ethiopians, and Egyptians.

Classical Period 393

From the German of A. H. L. Heeren, Professor of history. Oxford, 1832. 2 v.

6226. HISTORICAL researches into the politics, intercourse, and trade of the principal nations of antiquity. From the German of A. H. L. Heeren, Professor of history. Oxford, 1833. 3 v.

6227. HISTORY of the colonization of the free states of antiquity, applied to the present contest between Great Britain and her American colonies. By Mr. Barron. London, 1777.

6228. The HISTORY of maritime and inland discovery. London, 1830. 3 v.

6229. The HISTORY of the factory movement. London, 1857. 2 v.

6230. HOCK, C. V. de. Administration financière de la France. Stuttgart, 1857. Traduit de l'allemand par Legentil. Paris, 1859.

6231. ———. Die finanzen und die finanzgeschichte der vereinigten staaten von Amerika. Stuttgart. 1867.

6232. ———. Die öffentlichen abgaben und schuldern. Stuttgart, 1863.

6233. HODGSKIN, Thomas. Labour defended against the claims of capital, or the unproductiveness of capital proved with reference to the present combinations amongst journeymen. By a labourer. London, 1825. (2d edition 1831. Edited by G. D. H. Cole. London, Labour publishing company, 1922.)

6234. ———. Popular political economy. Four lectures delivered at the London mechanics' institution. London, 1827.

6235. HOECK. Materialien zur finanz-statistik der deutschen bundesstaaten. (Matériaux pour servir à la statistique financière de la confédération germanique.) Smalkalde, 1823.

6236. HOFFMAN, J. G. Die lehre vom gelde. Berlin, 1838.

6237. HOLLAND, John. The history and description of fossil fuel--the collieries and coal trade of Great Britain. London, 1841. 1 v.

6238. ———. A treatise on manufactures in metal. London, 1834. 3 v.

6239. HOLLAND, R. H. Life of William Allen, with selections from his correspondence. London, 1846. 3 v.

6240. ———. Some account of the life and writings of Pope Felix de Vega Carpio. London, 1806.

6241. HOLT, F. L. A system of the shipping and navigation laws of Great Britain, and of the laws relative to merchant ships and seamen and maritime contracts. 2d edition. London, 1824. 1 v.

6242. HOPE, John. Letters on credit. 2d edition with a postscript, and a short account of the bank at Amsterdam. London, 1784.

6243. HOPKINS, Thomas. Economical enquiries relative to the laws which regulate rent, profit, wages and the value of money. London, J. Hatchard, 1822.

6244. ———. Great Britain for the last forty years; being a historical and analytical account of its finances, economy, and general condition, during that period. London, 1834.
6245. ———. On the rent of land, and its influences on subsistence and population. London, 1828.
6246. HORN, J. C. Creditwesen in Frankreich. 2 aufl. Leipzig, 1857.
6247. ———. L'économie politique avant les physiocrates. Paris, 1867.
6248. ———. La liberté des banques. Paris, 1866. (Deutsch, 1867.)
6249. HORTON, Robert John Wilmot. Causes and remedies of pauperism in the United Kingdom considered. Fourth series. Explanations of Mr. Wilmot Horton's bill, in a letter and queries addressed to N. W. Senior. With his answer. London, 1830.
6250. HOWLETT, John. Dispersion of gloomy apprehensions with respect to the decline of the corn trade. London, 1797.
6251. ———. Enclosures a cause of improved agriculture, of plenty and cheapness of provisions, of population, and of both private and national wealth; being an examination of two pamphlets. . . . London, 1787.
6252. ———. An enquiry concerning the influence of tithes upon agriculture, whether in the hands of the clergy or the laity, with some thoughts respecting their commutation. . . . London, 1801.
6253. ———. An examination of Dr. Price's essay on the population of England and Wales, and the doctrine of an increased population in this Kingdom established by facts. Maidstone, 1781.
6254. ———. The insufficiency of the causes to which the increase of our poor, and of the poors' rates, have been commonly ascribed. . . . London, 1788.
6255. HUBBARD, de. L'organisation des sociétés de prévoyance ou de secours mutuels. Paris, 1852.
6256. HUBBARD, J. G. The currency and the country. London, 1843.
6257. HUBER, A. Entwickelung des . . . zollwesens vom . . . tarife bis zur bundesverfassung . . . 1848. (Bern, 1890.)
6258. ———. Sociale fragen. 7 hefte. Nordhausen, 1863-69.
6259. HUBNER, Otto. Die banken. Leipzig, 1854.
6260. ———. Die zolltarife aller länder. Iserlohn, 1869.
6261. ———. Statistische tafeln aller länder. Frankfurt, 1865-70.
6262. HUERNE de POMMEUSE. Des colonies agricoles. Paris, 1832.
6263. HUFELAND, Gottlieb. Neue grundlegung der staatswirthschaftskunst, I, Vienna, 1815. (Giessen, 1807 a 1813. 2 v. Neue aufl. 2 bde. Giessen, 1819.)
6264. HULL, William. A history of the glove trade, with the customs connected with the glove. London, 1834. 1 v.

Classical Period 395

6265. HULLMANN, K. R. D. Deutsche finanzgesch des mittelalters. Berlin, 1805.
6266. ———. Handelsgeschichte der Griechen. Bonn, 1839.
6267. ———. Städtewesen des mittelalters. Bonn, 1825-29.
6268. HUMBOLDT, William von. Ideen zu einem versuch die Gränzen der wirksamkeit des staates zu bestimmen. Breslau, 1851. (Translated by J. Coulthard, Jr., London, 1854.)
6269. HUSKISSON, William. The question concerning the depreciation of our currency stated and examined. London, 1810. (New edition, 1819.)
6270. ———. Speeches in the House of commons on the 24th of February, 1826, on the motion for a committee on the state of the silk trade. By Mr. Huskisson and Mr. Canning. London, 1826.
6271. ———. The speeches . . . with a biographical memoir. London, 1831. 3 v.
6272. ———. Substance of two speeches delivered in the House of commons on the 21st and 25th of March, 1825, respecting the colonial policy and foreign commerce of the country. London, 1825.
6273. INFORMATION concerning the cost and supply of various articles of agricultural produce, etc., in various parts of Northern Europe. Obtained by James Meek, under instruction from government. Printed by order of the House of commons. 1842.
6274. INFORME de la Sociedad economica de Madrid al real y supremo consejo de castilla en expediente de ley agraria. Por Don Gaspar M. de Jovellanos. Madrid, 1795. (Palma, 1814.)
6275. INQUIRY into the causes and remedies of the late and present scarcity and high price of provisions, in a letter to Earl Spencer. London, 1800.
6276. An INQUIRY into the expediency of applying the principles of colonial policy to the government of India, etc. London, 1822. 1 v.
6277. INQUIRY into the late and present scarcity and high price of provisions. London, 1800.
6278. An INQUIRY into the principles of taxation. London, 1790. 1 v.
6279. INSTITUTES de droit commercial. Par M. Delvincourt. 2d édition. Paris, 1823. 2 v.
6280. An INVESTIGATION of the cause of the present high price of provisions. By Mr. Malthus. London, 1800.
6281. IRVINE, Patrick. Considerations on the inexpediency of the law of entail in Scotland. Edinburgh, 1826.
6282. ISNARD. Traité des richesses. Londres et Lausanne. 1781. 2 v.
6283. IVERNOIS, Françis D'. Sur la mortalité proportionnelle des peuples considérée comme mesure de leur aisance et de leur civilisation. Analyse des quinze registres de l'état civil en France, pour les années 1817-31.
6284. ———. Tableau historique et politique des pertes que

la révolution et la guerre ont causées au peuple français dans sa population, son agriculture, ses colonies, ses manufactures et son commerce. Mars, 1799. 2 v.

6285. JACINI, S. La proprietà fondiaria e la popolazione agricola in Lombardia. Milano, 1854. (3d edition, 1857.)

6286. JACOB, William. Considerations on the protection required by British agriculture, and on the influence of the price of corn on exportable productions. London?, 1814.

6287. ———. An historical inquiry into the production and consumption of the precious metals. London, 1831. 2 v. (Philadelphia, 1832.)

6288. ———. A letter to Samuel Whitbread, being a sequel to 'Considerations on the protection required by British agriculture,' to which are added remarks on the publications of a fellow of University College, Oxford, of Mr. Ricardo, and Mr. Torrens, Oxford?, 1815.

6289. ———. Production and consumption of the precious metals. London, 1831. 2 v.

6290. ———. Two reports on the trade in corn and on the agriculture of the north of Europe. (Imprimés par ordre de la Chambre des communes.) 1826 et 1827.

6291. JAKOB, Ludwig Heinrich V. Die staatsfinanzwissenschaft. (La science financière, théorique et pratique, éclaircie par des exemples puisés dans l'histoire financière moderne des Etats de l'Europe.) 2d édition, augmentée par J. J. H. Eiselen. Halle, 1837.

6292. ———. Grundsätze der national-öekonomie oder nationalwirtschaftslehre, 1805. (3d ed. Vienna, 1814; 3d ed. Halle, aufle, 1825.)

6293. JAMES, E. J. Studien über den amerikanischen zolltarif. Jena, 1877.

6294. JAMES, Henry. Essays on money, exchanges, and political economy. London, 1820. 2 v.

6295. ———. Essay on currency. In, Pamphleteer, London, xvii (1820).

6296. JAMES, John. History of the worsted manufacture. London, 1857.

6297. JEFFERSON, Thomas. Notes, on the state of Virginia, Baltimore, 1800.

6298. JENNINGS, Richard. Natural elements of political economy. London, 1855.

6299. ———. Social delusions concerning wealth and want. London, 1856.

6300. JOHNSTON, David. A general medical and statistical history of the present condition of public charity in France, comprising a detailed account of all the establishments destined for the sick, the aged, and infirm, children, lunatics. . . . Edinburgh, 1829. 1 v.

6301. JOHNSTON, William. A history of inventions and discoveries. Translated from the German of Beckmann. London, 1797-1814. 4 v.

6302. JOLLIVET, J. B. M. De l'impot progressif, et du morcellement des patrimoines. 1793. 1 v.

Classical Period

6303. JONES, David. On the value of annuities and reversionary payments, with numerous tables. London, 1843. 2 v.
6304. JONES, Jenkin. A series of tables of annuities and assurances, calculated from a new rate of mortality among assured lives. London, 1843. 1 v.
6305. JONES, Richard. An essay on the distribution of wealth and on the sources of taxation. Londres, J. Murray, 1831. 1 v. (London, 1844.)
6306. ———. An introductory lecture on political economy, delivered at King's College, London, 27th February, 1833. To which is added a syllabus of a course of lectures on the wages of labour. London, 1833.
6307. ———. Literary remains, consisting of lectures and tracts on political economy, of the late Rev. Richard Jones. Edited by Rev. William Whewell. London, J. Murray, 1859.
6308. ———. Syllabus of a course of lectures on the wages of labor. London, 1833.
6309. JOPLIN, Thomas. An analysis and history of the currency question. London, 1832.
6310. ———. Outlines of a system of political economy. London, Baldwin, 1823.
6311. JORIO, Michel de. Storia del commercio e della navigazione, dal principio del mondo sino a giorni nostri. Napoli, 1778. 4 v.
6312. JOSSEAU, Chonsky et Delaroy. Des institutions de crédit foncier et agricole dans les divers Etats de l'Europe. Paris, 1851.
6313. JOUBLEAU, Félix. Etudes sur Colbert ou exposition du système d'économie politique suivi en France de 1661 à 1683. Paris, 1856. 2 v.
6314. JOURNEYS through the Upper Provinces of India, and to Madras and the Southern Provinces, with letters written in India. By Bishop Heber. 2d edition. London, 1828. 2 v.
6315. JOVELLANOS, G. Melchior de. Informe de don Gaspar Melchior de Jovellanos en el expediente de la ley agraria. Burdeos, 1820.
6316. ———. Memoria sobre el establecimiento del monte pio de hidalgos de Madrid, leida en la real sociedad de Madrid. 1784.
6317. JUNG. Lehrbuch der finanzwissenschaft. Leipzig, 1788.
6318. ———. Versuch einer grundlehre saemtlicher cameralwissenschaften. Lautern, 1779.
6319. JUVIGNY, B. Exposé des principes élémentaires et raisonnés sur le meilleur système d'emprunts publics, et sur meilleur mode d'amortissement, précédé de notions générales et spéciales sur la dette publique. Paris, 1833.
6320. KANE, Robert. Industrial resources of Ireland. Dublin, 1844. 1 v.
6321. KAUTZ, Jul. Theorie und geschichtlichen de nationalökonomie. 2d edition. Wien, 1858-60.

6322. KAY, J. P. The moral and physical condition of the working classes employed in the cotton manufacture in Manchester. London, 1832.
6323. KAY, Joseph. Free trade in land. 9th edition. London, 1885.
6324. ———. Social condition and education of the people in England and Europe. London, 1850. 2 v.
6325. KELLNER, G. Zur geschichtlichen des physiocratismus. Göttingen, 1847.
6326. KELLY, J. B. Summary of history and law of usury. London, 1835.
6327. KELLY, Patrick. The universal cambist and commercial instructor, being a full and accurate treatise on the exchange, coins, weights and measures of all trading nations and their colonies; with an account of their banks, paper currencies. . . . 2d and best edition. London, 1831. 2 v.
6328. KEMBLE, J. M. Saxons in England. London, 1849. 2 v.
6329. KENNEDY, L. and T. B. Grainger. The present state of the tenancy of land in Great Britain, showing the principal customs and practices between incoming and outgoing tenants, and the usual methods under which land is now held in the several counties. London, 1828. 1 v.
6330. KLEINSCHROD, C. T. von. Der pauperism in England. 2te fortsetz. Augsburg, 1853.
6331. KNIGHT, Charles. The working man's companion. The results of machinery, namely cheap production and increased employment, exhibited. London, 1831.
6332. KNOX, John. A view of the British empire, more especially Scotland, with some proposals for the improvement of that country, the extension of its fisheries, and the relief of the people. 3d edition. Edinburgh, 1785. 2 v.
6333. KOCH, C. G. de et F. Schoell. History abrégée des traités de paix entre les puissances de l'Europe depuis la paix de Westphalie jusqu'au traité de Paris du 20e Nov. 1815. Paris, 1817-46. 15 v.
6334. KRAUS, Christian Jakob. Staatswirthschaft. 1808-11. 5 v. Koenisberg.
6335. KRAUSE, J. F. Versuch eines systems der national und staatsoeconomie. (Essai d'un système d'économie nationale. Leipzig, 1830. 2 v.
6336. KUDLER, Joseph. Die grundlehren der volkwirthschaft. 2 bde. Wien, 1846. (2 aufl., 2 bde., 1853.)
6337. KUTTLINGER, Friedmann. Grundzüge einer allgemeinenrechts und wirthschaftslehre. (Principes généraux de droit et de l'économie politique à l'usage des jurisconsulte et des caméralistes.) Erlangen, 1837. 2 v.
6338. LA FARELLE FEL. de. Plan d'une réorganisation disciplinaire des classes industrielles en France, précédé et suivi d'études historiques sur les formes du travail humain, 1842. 1 v. (Ajouté à la 2e édition de l'ouvrage précédent.)
6339. LABARTHE. Intérêts de la France dans l'Inde, contenant:

1e l'indication des titres de propriété de nos possessions d'Asie; 2° les époques de nos succès et de nos revers dans ces contrées; 3° les actes relatifs à la rétrocession de nos établissements après la paix de 1783. Paris, 1816.
6340. LABORDE le comte Alexandre de. De l'esprit d'association dans tous les intérêts de communauté. Paris, 1818.
6341. LABOULINIERE, P. De la disette et de la surabondance en France; des moyens de prévenir l'une, en metant l'autre à profit, et d'empêcher les trop grandes variations dans le prix des grains. Paris, 1821. 2 v.
6342. ———. De l'influence d'un grande revolution sur le commerce. Paris, 1808. 1 v.
6343. LAFFITTE, J. Opinion sur le projet de loi relatif à l'emprunt de 80 millions. . . . Paris, Bossange, 1828.
6344. ———. Refléxions sur la réduction de la rente, et sur l'état du crédit. Paris, 1824.
6345. LAING, Samuel. National distress, its causes and remedies. Atlas prize essay. London, 1844.
6346. LAIRD, MacGregor. The effect of an alteration of the sugar duties on the condition of the people of England and the negro race considered. London, 1844.
6347. LALOR, John. Money and morals; a book for the times. London, J. Chapman, 1852.
6348. LAMERVILLE, comte de. De l'impot territorial. . . . Strasbourg, 1788.
6349. LARDNER, Dionysius. Railway economy; a treatise on the new art of transport. . . . New York, 1850.
6350. ———. The steam-engine explained and illustrated; with an account of its invention and progressive improvement (including a life of Watt), and its application to navigation and railways. 7th edition. London, 1840. 1 v.
6351. LARRUGIA, Eugene de. Memorias políticas y económicas sobre los frutos, commercio, fabricas y minas de España. Madrid, 1785-1800. 45 v.
6352. LASALLE, Henri. Des finances d'Angleterre. Paris, 1803. 1 v.
6353. LAUDERDALE, J. M. An inquiry into the nature and origin of public wealth and into the means and causes of its increase. Edinburgh, 1804. (Traduit en français Paris, Dentu, 1807. 2 edition, Edinburgh, 1819.)
6354. ———. Considerations on the state of currency. 1813.
6355. ———. Depreciation of the paper currency of Great Britain. London, 1812.
6356. ———. A letter on the corn laws. London, 1814.
6357. LE PLAY, Frederic. L'organisation du travail selon la coutume des ateliers et la loi du décalogue, 1870. (6th édition, Tours, 1893.)
6358. ———. Les ouvriers des deux mondes. Paris, 1858-75. 5 v.
6359. ———. La réforme sociale en France. Paris, 1864. 3 v. (5th edition, Tours, 1874. 3 v.; 1878.)
6360. LEBER, M. C. Essai sur l'appréciation de la fortune privée au moyen âge . . . variations de valeurs

monétaires. 2me édition. London, 1847.
6361. LECHEVALIER, Jules. Etudes de la science social. 1834.
6362. De la LEGISLATION et le commerce des grains. By Necker Paris, 1776. 1 v.
6363. LEIPZIGER. Geist der nationaloeconomie. Berlin, 1813 à 1814. 2 v.
6364. LEITZMANN, J. J. Verzeichniss numismatische werke. Weissensee, 1841.
6365. LEPELLETIER, de la Sarthe. Du système socialo ses applications à l'industrie, à la famille, à la société. Paris, 1855. 2 v.
6366. LEROUX, Pierre. De l'union Européene, 1827. In, Oeuvres de Pierre Leroux, Paris, 1850. v. 1.
6367. ———. Discours sur la situation actuelle de la société et de l'esprit humain. Paris, 1847. 2 v.
6368. ———. Réfutation de l'éclectisme. Nouvelle édition. Paris, 1841.
6369. LETROSNE. De l'administration provinciale et de la réforme de l'impôt. Bâle, 1788. 2 v.
6370. ———. De l'ordre social, ouvrage suivi d'un traité élémentaire sur la valeur, l'argent, la circulation, l'industrie et le commerce intérieur et extérieur. Paris, 1777.
6371. A LETTER on the true principles of advantageous exportation . . . (1818) edited by Arnold Plant. London, 1933.
6372. A LETTER to the Right honourable Lord Althorpe . . . , on the subject of the duty on printed cottons. By a calico printer. London, 1830.
6373. LETTERS on the corn laws and on the rights of the working classes, originally inserted in the Morning chronicle, showing the injustice and also the impolicy, etc. of the corn laws. By H. B. T. (Duncan Hume?) London, 1834.
6374. LETTRE à la Chambre du commerce de Normandie sur le memoire qu'elle a publié relativement au traité de commerce avec l'Angleterre. Par Dupont. Rouen (Paris), 1781.
6375. LEUCHS, L. C. Gewerb und handelsfreiheit. (De la liberté du commerce et de l'industrie, ou exposé des moyens de fonder la prospérité des peuples, la richesse et la puissance des nations.) Wurtemburg, 1827. 1 v.
6376. LEVASSEUR, Emile. Elements of political economy. Translated by Theodore Marburg. New York, 1905.
6377. ———. La France avec ses colonies. Paris, 1867. (2d édition. 1890. 2 v.)
6378. ———. Histoire des classes ouvrières en France depuis Jules César jusqu'à la révolution. Paris, 1859. 2 v. (2d edition, 1867. 2 v.)
6379. ———. La population Française. Paris, 1889-1892. 3 v.
6380. ———. La question de l'or. Paris, 1858. 1 v.
6381. ———. Recherches historiques du système de law. Paris, 1854. 1 v.
6382. LEWIS, G. C. On the government of dependencies. London,

1841. 1 v.
6383. LIFE tables, founded upon the discovery of a numerical law regulating the existence of every human being: illustrated by a new theory of the causes producing health and longevity. By T. R. Edmonds. London, 1832. 1 v.
6384. LINGUET. Du commerce des grains, nouvelle édition, augmentée d'une lettre à M. Tissot, sur le mérite politique et physique du pain et du blé. 1789.
6385. ———. L'impôt territorial, ou la dixme royale avec tous ses avantages. 1787. 1 v.
6386. LIVERPOOL, Charles (Earl of). The speech of . . . on the subject of the agricultural distress of the country. London, 1822.
6387. ———. A treatise on the coines of the realm. . . . Oxford, 1805. (London, 1880.)
6388. LLOYD, William Forster. A lecture on the notion of value, as distinguished not only from utility, but also from value in exchange. Delivered before the University of Oxford in Michaelmas term, 1833. London, 1834. [In, Economic history, Supplement to the Economic journal (May, 1927) 40.]
6389. ———. Two lectures on the checks to population, delivered before the University of Oxford, in Michaelmas term, 1832. Oxford, 1833.
6390. ———. Two lectures on the justice of the poor-laws, and one lecture on rent, delivered in the University of Oxford in Michaelmas term, 1836. London, 1837.
6391. LOCQUEAN. Essai sur l'établissement des hôpitaux dans les grandes villes. Paris, 1797.
6392. LONG, Charles. A temperate discussion of the high price of bread. London, 1817. [Reprint from Pamphleteer, X, (1817).]
6393. LONGFIELD, Mountifort. Four lectures on poor laws, delivered in Trinity term, 1834. Dublin, 1834.
6394. ———. Lectures on political economy, delivered in Trinity and Michaelmas terms, 1833. Dublin, 1834. (London school of economics reprints, No. 8, London, 1931.)
6395. LORD, Eleazor. On credit, currency, and banking. New York, 1834.
6396. LORPENT, George. On protection to West India sugar. 2d edition: reply to Mr. Marryat's tract. London, 1823.
6397. LOUDON, J. C. An encyclopaedia of agriculture, comprising the theory and practice of the management and cultivation of land. . . . Best edition. London, 1844. 1 v.
6398. LOW, David. Elements of practical agriculture. 2d edition. London, 1838. 1 v.
6399. ———. Landed property and the economy of estates. London, 1844.
6400. ———. Observations on the present state of landed property, and on the prospects of the landlords and farmers. Edinburgh, 1823.

6401. LOWE, Joseph. An inquiry into the state of the British West Indies. London, 1807.
6402. ———. The present state of England in regard to agriculture, trade, and finance; with a comparison of the prospects of England and France. London, 1822. (2d edition London and Edinburgh, 1823.)
6403. LOYD, Samuel Jones (Lord Overstone). Effects of the administration of the Bank of England. A 2d letter to J. B. Smith. London, 1840.
6404. ———. Further reflections on the state of the currency, and the action of the Bank of England. London, 1837.
6405. ———. A letter to J. B. Smith, President of the Manchester Chamber of commerce. London, 1840.
6406. ———. Reflections suggested by a perusal of Mr. J. Horsley Palmer's pamphlet on the causes and consequence of the pressure on the money market. London, 1837.
6407. ———. Remarks on the management of the circulation, and on the condition and conduct of the Bank of England, and of the country issuers during the year 1839. London, 1840.
6408. ———. Thoughts on the separation of the departments of the Bank of England. London, 1844.
6409. LUBERSAC, Comte de. Vues politiques et patriotiques sur l'administration des finances de la France. . . . Paris, 1787.
6410. LUEDER, A. F. L'industrie nationale et ses effets. Berlin, 1808.
6411. ———. Ueber national industrie und staatswirthschaft. De l'industrie nationale et de l'economie publique. Berlin, 1800-04. 3 v.
6412. LUPI, C. Storia de' principii delle massime e regole seguite nella formazione del catasto prediale. Milan, 1825.
6413. MABSON, R. R. A fifty years' history of the British iron trade. London, 1851.
6414. MACADAM, J. L. Observations on roads. London, 1822.
6415. MACAULEY, Zachary. East and West India sugar; or, a refutation of the claims of the West India colonists to a protecting duty on East India sugar. London, 1823.
6416. MACCULLOCH, J. R. A dictionary, geographical, statistical, and historical, of the various countries, places, and principal natural objects in the world. London, 1841. 2 v.
6417. ———. A dictionary, practical, theoretical, and historical, of commerce and commercial navigation. A new and much improved edition. London, 1844. 1 v.
6418. ———. An essay on the circumstances which determine the rate of wages, and the condition of the labouring classes. Edinburgh, 1826.
6419. ———. Historical sketch of the Bank of England, with an examination of the question as to the prolongation of the exclusive privileges of that establishment. London, 1831.

Classical Period 403

6420. _____. The literature of political economy. London, 1845.
6421. _____. Observations illustrative of the practical operation and real effect of the duties on paper, showing the expediency of their reduction or repeal. London, 1836.
6422. _____. Observations on the duty on sea-borne coal, and on the peculiar duties and charges on coal in the Port of London, 1830.
6423. _____. Observations on the influence of the East India company's monopoly on the price and supply of tea, and on the commerce with India, China. . . . London, 1831.
6424. _____. On commerce, its principles and history. London, 1833.
6425. _____. Principles of political economy. Edinburgh, 1825. (London, 1830. 2 v. Stuttgart, 1831. Paris, 1864. New York, 1883.)
6426. _____. Statements illustrative of the policy and probable consequences of the proposed repeal of the existing corn laws, and the imposition in their stead of a moderate fixed duty on foreign corn, when entered for consumption. London, 1841.
6427. _____. A statistical account of the British empire, exhibiting its extent, physical capacities, population, industry, and civil and religious institutions. Assisted by numerous contributors. London, 1837. 2 v. (2d edition, London, 1839. 2 v.)
6428. _____. A treatise on the principles and practical influence of taxation and the funding system. London, 1845. 1 v. (3rd edition, Edinburgh, 1863.)
6429. MACDONALD, Thomas. A treatise on civil imprisonment in England, with the history of its progress, and objections to its policy. . . . London, 1791.
6430. MACE DE RICHEBOURG. Essai sur les qualités des monnais étrangères, et sur leurs différents rapports avec les monnaies de France. . . . Paris, Imprimerie royale, 1776.
6431. MACFARLANE, John. Inquiries concerning the poor. Edinburgh, 1782. 1 v.
6432. MACGREGOR, John. Commercial statistics. A digest of the productive resources; commercial legislation; customs tariffs, navigation, port, and quarantine laws and charges, shipping imports and exports, moneys, weights, measures, etc. of all nations. London, 1844. 3 v. (1843-50. 5 v.)
6433. _____. Report to the British government on the commercial statistics of the Kingdom of the two Sicilies. London, 1840.
6434. MACLEAN, J. H. Remarks on fair prices and produce-rents. Edinburgh, 1825.
6435. MACNAB, Henri-Grey. Examen impartial des nouvelles vues de M. Robert Owen et de ses établissements à New-Lanark en Ecosse, pour le soulagement et l'emploi le plus utile des classes ouvrières et des pauvres. . . ;

avec des observations sur l'application de ce système a l'économie politique de tous les gouvernements. . . . Traduit de l'anglais par Laffon de Ladebat. Paris, 1821.

6436. MACPHERSON, David. Annals of commerce, manufactures, fisheries, and navigation. London, 1805. 4 v.

6437. ———. The history of the European commerce with India. London, 1812. 1 v.

6438. MAFFEI, Marquis de. De l'emploi de l'argent, ouvrage dédié au Pape Benoit XIV. Avignon, 1787.

6439. La MAGIA del credito svelata, istituzione fondamentale de pubblica utilita. Di Giuseppe de Welz. Napoli, 1824. 2 v.

6440. MALCHUS, C. A. Freiherrn von. Handbuch der finanzwissenschaft und finanzverwaltung. Stuttgart, 1830. 2 v.

6441. MALCOLM, John. The political history of India from 1784 to 1823. London, 1826. 2 v.

6442. MALLET, J. L. De la Ligue Hanséatique, de son origine, ses progrès sa puissance et sa constitution politique, jusqu'à son déclin, . . . Genève, 1805. 1 v.

6443. ———. Premier commis des finances sous le contrôleur général Desmarets. Comptes rendus de l'administration des finances du royaume de France, pendant les onze dernières années du règne de Henri IV, le règne de Louis XIII et soixante-cinq années du règne de Louis XIV avec des recherches sur l'origine des impôts, sur les revenus et dépenses de nos rois, depuis Philippe le Bel jusqu'à Louis XIV, et différents mémoires sur le numéraire et sa valeur, sous les trois règnes ci-dessus. Paris, Buisson, 1789.

6444. MALO DE LUCQUE, Eduardo. Historia politica de los establecimientos ultramarinos de las naciones Europeas. Madrid, 1784, 1785 et 1786. 3 v.

6445. MALOUET, Baron. Considérations historiques sur l'empire de la mer chez les anciens et les modernes. Anvers, 1810. 1 v.

6446. MALTHUS, Thomas Robert. Definitions of political economy preceded by an inquiry into the rules which ought to guide political economists. . . . London, 1827. (2d edition 1853.)

6447. ———. An essay on the principle of population as it affects the future improvement of society. London, 1798. Paris, 1823. (6th edition, 1826. Edited by G. F. Berrany, London, 1890. Berlin, 1879. French by P. et G. Prévost, Paris, 1845.)

6448. ———. The grounds of an opinion on the policy of restricting the importation of foreign corn. London, 1815.

6449. ———. An inquiry into the nature and progress of rent. London, 1815.

6450. ———. Observations on the effects of the corn laws. London, 1814.

6451. ———. Principles of political economy. Paris, London, 1820. 2 v. (2d edition 1836. French by M. Monjean, Paris, 1846.)

Classical Period

6452. MALVAUX. Les moyens de détruire la mendicité en France, en rendant les mendiants utiles à l'état sans les rendre malheureux. Paris, 1780.
6453. MANGOLDT, H. V. Die lehre vom unternechmergewinn. Leipzig, 1855.
6454. ———. Grundriss der volkswirthschaftslehre. Stuttgart, 1863. (2te aufl. 1872.)
6455. ———. Volkswirthschaftslehre. 1e bd. Stuttgart, 1868.
6456. MANUEL des consuls. Par Miltitz. London et Berlin, 1837-42.
6457. MANUEL pratique et elementaire des poids et mesures, des monnaies, et du calcul decimal. Par Tarbé. Paris, 1799. 1 v.
6458. MANUEL universel, à l'usage des négocians; ou, traité des monnaies, poids, et mesures. Par Nelkenbrecher. Traduit de l'Allemand. Bruxelles, 1830. 1 v.
6459. MANUFACTURES improper subjects of taxation, addressed to the merchants and manufacturers of Great Britain. . . . London, 1785.
6460. MARCET, Jane. Conversations on political-economy in which the elements of the science are familiarly explained. London, Longman, 1816. (Paris, 1817; Philadelphia, 1817. 5th edition London, 1824. 7th edition 1839.)
6461. ———. John Hopkins notions on political economy. London and Paris, 1833. (Translated into French by Mademoiselle Cherbuliez.)
6462. MARESCOTTI, A. Sulla economie sociale discorso. Firenze, 1856-57. 4 v.
6463. MARIN, C. A. Storia civile e politica del commercio de' Veneziani. Venezia, 1798-1800. 8 v.
6464. MARRECA, Antonio d'O. Nocoës elementares. Lisbon, 1838.
6465. MARRYAT, Joseph. A reply to the arguments contained in various publications recommending an equalisation of the duties on East and West India sugar. London, 1823.
6466. MARSDEN, William. The history of Sumatra: containing an account of the government, laws, customs, and manners of the native inhabitants; with a description of the natural productions, and a relation of the ancient political state of the island. London, 1811. 3d edition.
6467. MARSHALL, Samuel. A treatise on the law of insurance. 3d edition with additions, by C. Marshall. London, 1823. 2 v.
6468. MARSHALL, William. A review and complete abstract of the reports to the board of agriculture on the several counties of England. London, 1817. 5 v.
6469. MARTIN, Montgomery. Statistics of the colonies of the British empire in the West Indies, North and South America, Asia, Australia, Africa, and Europe. London, 1839. 1 v.
6470. MARTIN, R. M. Ireland before and after the union with Great Britain. London, 1843.
6471. MARTINEAU, Harriet. Autobiography. Edited by M. W. Chapman. Boston, 1877. 2 v.

6472. _____. Contes sur l'economie politique. Traduit de l'anglais avec des notes et des préfaces par B. Maurice. Paris, C. Gosselin, 1833-39. 8 v.

6473. _____. Illustrations of political economy. London, 1832-34. 9 v. (London, 1859; traduit par de Molinari. Paris, 1880. 2 v.)

6474. _____. Poor laws and paupers illustrated. London, 1833-34. 4 v.

6475. _____. The tendency of strikes and sticks to produce low wages and of unions between masters and men to ensure good wages. Durham, 1834.

6476. MARTINELLI, J. Harmonies et perturbations. Paris, 1853.

6477. MASERES, Francis. The principle of the doctrine of life annuities, with a variety of new tables. London, 1783. 1 v.

6478. MATTHIAS, W. H. Uber posten und postregale in hinsicht auf volksgeschichte, statistik, und erdkunde. 2 bde. Berlin, 1832.

6479. MAUGHAM, R. Treatise on the laws of literary property, comprising the statutes and cases relating to books, manuscripts, lectures. . . . 1826. 1 v.

6480. MAURER, G. L. v. Geschichte der markenverfassung in Deutschland. 1856.

6481. MEES, W. C. Proeve . . . van het bankwezen in Nederlande. Rotterdam, 1838.

6482. MELANGES d'économie politique. Edited by Eugène Daire and G. de Molinari. Paris, 1847-48. 2 v.

6483. MELANGES de morale et d'économie politique. Paris, 1854.

6484. A MEMOIR of central India; including Malwa and the adjoining provinces. By Major-General Sir John Malcolm. London, 1825. 2 v.

6485. A MEMOIR on the visitation of neutral vessels under convoy; or, an impartial examination of a judgment pronounced by the English court of admiralty, June, 1799, in the case of the Swedish convoy. London, 1801.

6486. MEMOIRE sur l'antiquité de la l peche de la baleine. Par Noel. Paris, 1795. 1 v.

6487. MEMOIRE sur les moyens qui ont amené la grand développement que l'industrie Française a pris depuis vingt ans. Par Costaz. Paris, 1816. 1 v.

6488. MEMOIRES concernant les impositions et droits en Europe. Ire édition compiled by M. Moreau de Beaumont. Paris, 1768. 4 v. (2d édition avec des supplémens, Paris, 1787. 5 v.)

6489. MEMOIRES pour servir à l'histoire de la piraterie. Par Azuni. Gênes, 1816. 2 v.

6490. MEMOIRES pour servir a l'histoire du droit de la France. Bruxelles, 1779.

6491. MEMORIAL of the committee appointed by "The Free Trade convention," held at Philadelphia in September and October, 1831. New York, 1832.

Classical Period 407

6492. MEMORIAS historicas sobre la legislacion y gobierno del comercio de los Espanoles con sus colonias en las Indias occidentales. Recopiladas por el Sr. Don Antunez y Acevedo, del supreme consejo de Indias. Madrid, 1797. 1 v.
6493. MENGOTTI, Francesco. Il colbertismo, ossia della liberta di commercio de' prodotti della terra, dissertazione di Francesco Mengotti, coronata dall'accademia di Georgofili di Firenze nel 1791.
6494. ———. Del commercio de'Romani, dalla Prima Guerra Punica a Costantino, dissertazione, di Francesco Mengotti, coronata dall'Accademia della iscrizione e belle lettere di Parigi nel 1787.
6495. MEREDITH, William. Historical remarks on the taxation of free states, in a series of letters to a friend. London, 1781.
6496. MEREWERTHER, H. A. and A. J. Stephens. History of boroughs. London, 1835. 3 v.
6497. MERIVALE, Herman. Five lectures on the principles of a legislative provision for the poor in Ireland. London, 1838.
6498. ———. An introductory lecture on the study of political economy. . . . London, 1837.
6499. ———. Lectures on colonization and colonies. Delivered before the University of Oxford, in 1839, 1840, and 1841. London, Longman, 1841. 2 v.
6500. MERREM. Allgemeine grundsaetze der burgerlichen wirthschaft. Gottingue, 1817.
6501. MERREY, Walter. Remarks on the coinage of England from the earliest to the present times, with a view to point out the causes of the present scarcity of silver coin. . . . Nottingham, 1789.
6502. MESENGE, P. J. Plan de finance et de liquidation générale des dettes de la nation. . . . Paris, 1790.
6503. MESSANCE. Nouvelles recherches sur la population de la France, avec des remarques importantes sur les divers objets d'administration. Lyon, 1788.
6504. MESSEDAGLIA, A. Dei prestiti pubblici e del miglior sistems di consolidazione. Milano, 1850.
6505. ———. Della teoria della popolazione principalmente sotto l'aspetto del metodo. Verona, 1858. 1 v.
6506. ———. L'economia politica in relazione all sociologia. Roma, 1891.
6507. METROLOGIE, ou tables pour servir à l'intelligence des poids et mesures des anciens, et principalement à déterminer la valeur des monnoies Grecques et Romaines, d'après leur rapport avec les poids, les mesures, et le numéraire actuel de la France. Par M. de Rome de L'Isle. Paris, 1789. 1 v.
6508. METROLOGIE, ou traité des mesures, poids, et monnoies des anciens peuples et des módernes. Par M. Paucton. Paris, 1780. 1 v.
6509. MEYNIEU, Madame Mary. Eléments d'économie politique,

exposés dans une suite de dialogues entre un instituteur et son élève. Genève, 1839. 1 v.

6510. MIDDLETON, Henry. The government and the currency. New edition. New York, 1850.

6511. MILBURN, William. Oriental commerce. Containing a geographical description of the principal places in the East Indies, China, and Japan, with their produce, manufactures, trade. . . . London, 1813. 2 v.

6512. MILL, James. Commerce defended. An answer to the arguments by which Mr. Spence, Mr. Cobbett, and others have attempted to prove that commerce is not a source of national wealth. London, 1808.

6513. ———. Elements of political economy. London, 1821. (3d edition. London, 1826. Translated by J. E. Parisot, Paris, 1823.)

6514. ———. An essay on the impolicy of a bounty on the exportation of grain, and on the principles which ought to regulate the commerce of grain. London, 1804.

6515. ———. History of British India. London, 1817-18. 3 v (London, 1820. 6 v.)

6516. MILL, John Stuart. Autobiography. London, 1874. (German edition. Translated by T. Kolb, Stuttgart, 1880.)

6517. ———. Dissertations and discussions. London, 1858-75. (2d edition 1876. 4 v.)

6518. ———. Essay on some unsettled questions of political economy. London, 1844. (2d edition 1874.)

6519. ———. Principles of political economy. 1848. (Principes d'economie politique. . . . Traduit par M. H. Dussard et Courcelle-Seneuil. Paris, 1854. Guillaumin et cie. 2 v. 2 édition, Paris, 1872. New edition, London, 1891. 2 v.; by J. L. Laughlin, New York, 1884; German edition by Soetbeer, Leipzig, 1882-85.)

6520. MILNE, Joshua. A treatise on the valuation of annuities and assurances on lives and survivorships; on the construction of tables of mortality; and on the probabilities and expectations of life . . . with a variety of new tables. London, 1815. 2 v.

6521. The MINISTRY and the sugar duties. London, 1844.

6522. MIRABEAU, le comte de. Etude sur la Banque d'Espagne, dite Saint-Charles. Paris, 1785.

6523. MODESTE, Victor. Du paupérisme en France. Paris, 1858. 1 v.

6524. ———. Le prêt à l'intéret dernière forme de l'esclavage. Paris, 1889.

6525. MOGGRIDGE, J. H. Remarks on the report of the select committee of the House of commons on the poor-laws. By a Monmouthshire magistrate. Bristol, 1818.

6526. MOHEAU, M. Recherches et considérations sur la population de la France. Paris, 1778. (Edited by René Gonnard. Paris, 1912.)

6527. MOHL, R. V. Die polizeiwissenschaft. 3te aufl. 3 bde. Tübingen, 1866.

6528. ———. Encyklopadie die staatswissenschaften. Tubingen,

Classical Period 409

1859. (2 aufl., 1872.)
6529. MOLINARI, Gustave de. Conversations sur le commerce des grains. Bruxelles et Paris, 1855. 1 v.
6530. ———. Cours d'économie politique. 2 tom. Paris, 1855-63.
6531. ———. L'évolution économique au 19e siècle. Paris, 1881.
6532. ———. Histoire du tarif des céréales. Paris, 1847.
6533. ———. Les lois naturelles de l'économie politique. Paris, 1887.
6534. ———. Notions fondamentales d'économie politique. Paris, 1891.
6535. ———. Précis d'économie politique. Paris, 1893.
6536. ———. Questions d'économie politique. 2 tom. Bruxelles, 1861.
6537. MOLSTER, J. A. De geschiednis der staathuiskunde. Amsterdam, 1851.
6538. MONBORGNE, J. M. Tableau général du maximum de la république française, Paris, Belin, 1794. 3 v.
6539. MONDENARD. Considérations sur l'organisation sociale, appliquées à l'état civil, politique et militaire de la France et de l'Angleterre; à leurs moeurs, leur agriculture, leur commerce et leur finances, à l'époque de la paix d'Amiens. Paris, 1802. 3 v.
6540. MONE, histoira statisticae adumbrata. Lovanii, 1828. 1 v.
6541. MONNIER, Alexander. Histoire de l'assistance publique. Paris, 1857. 1 v. (3d edition, 1866.)
6542. MONTAGU, Basil and Scrope Ayrton. The law and practice of bankruptcy, as altered by the new statutes, orders, and decisions. A new edition by Herbert Koe and Samuel Miller. London, 1844. 2 v.
6543. MONTAIGNAC. Réflexions sur la mendicité, ses causes et les moyens de la détruire en France. 1790.
6544. MONTEIL, Alexis de. Histoire des Français des divers états. 4th edition. Paris, 1853. 5 v.
6545. MONTESQUIOU. Du gouvernement des finances de France, d'après les lois constitutionnelles et d'après les principes d'un gouvernement libre et représentatif. Paris, 1797.
6546. MONTGOMERY, J. Practical detail of the cotton manufacture of the United States. Glasgow, 1840.
6547. MONTYON, Baron de. Particularités et observations sur les ministres des finances les plus célèbres, depuis 1660 jusqu'à 1792. . . . Londres, Dulau, 1812.
6548. ———. Quelle influence ont les diverses espèces d'impôts sur la moralité, l'activité et l'industrie des peuples? Paris, 1808.
6549. MONYPENNY, David. Proposed alteration of the Scottish poor-laws, and of the administration thereof, as stated by Dr. Alison in his 'Observations on the management of the poor in Scotland,' considered and commented on. Edinburgh, 1840.

6550. ———. Remarks on the poor-laws, and on the method of providing for the poor of Scotland. 2d edition improved. Edinburgh, 1836. 1 v.
6551. La MORALE et la politique d'Aristote. Traduit de Grec par Thurot. Paris, 1824. 2 v.
6552. MOREAU de Beaumont. Mémoires concernant les impositions et droits en Europe. Paris, nouvelle édition. 1787-89. 5 v.
6553. MOREAU-CHRISTOPHE, L. M. Du problème de la misère et de sa solution chez les peuples anciens et modernes. Paris, 1851. 3 v.
6554. MOREAU de JONNES, A. Le commerce au dix-neuvième siècle; état actuel de ses transactions dans les principles contrées des deux hémisphères. . . . Paris, 1825. 2 v.
6555. ———. Eléments de statistique, principes généraux de cette science, sa classification, sa méthode ses opérations, ses divers degrés de certitude, ses erreurs et ses progrès, avec son application à la constatation des faits naturels, sociaux et politiques, historiques et contemporains. 1856. 1 v.
6556. ———. Recherches statistiques sur l'esclavage colonial et sur les moyens de le supprimer. Paris, 1842. 1 v.
6557. ———. Statistique de la Grande-Bretagne et de l'Irlande. Paris, 1838. 2 v.
6558. ———. Statistique de l'agriculture de la France, comprenant la statistique des cereales, de la vigne, des cultures diverses, des pâturages, des bois et des forêts, et des animaux domestiques avec leur production actuelle, comparée à celle des temps anciens et des principaux pays de l'Europe. 1848.
6559. ———. Statistique de l'Espagne. Paris, 1834. 1 v.
6560. ———. Statistique de l'industrie de la France. 1856. 1 v.
6561. ———. Statistique des peuples de l'antiquité, les Egyptiens, les Hébreux, les Grecs, les Romains et les Gaulois. 1850. 2 v. (1851.)
6562. MORGAN, Augustus de. An essay on probabilities, and on their application to life contingencies and insurance offices. London, 1838. 1 v.
6563. MORGAN, John Mintner. The revolt of the bees. London, 1826. (3d edition, 1839.)
6564. MORGAN, William. On the principles and doctrine of assurances, annuities on lives, and contingent reversions. London, 1821. 1 v.
6565. ———. A review of Dr. Price's writings on the subject of the finances of this Kingdom; to which are added the three plans communicated by him to Mr. Pitt, in 1786, for redeeming the national debt. London, 1792.
6566. MORIN, Théodore. Essai sur l'organisation du travail et sur l'avenir des classes ouvrières. Paris, 1845. 1 v.
6567. MORRIS, Edward. A short inquiry into the nature of monopoly and forestalling. 3d edition with additions. London, 1800.

Classical Period 411

6568. MORRISON, Charles. Essay on relations between labour and capital. London, 1854.
6569. MOSELEY, Benjamin. A treatise concerning the properties and effects of coffee. 5th edition, with considerable additions. London, 1792.
6570. ———. A treatise on sugar, with miscellaneous observations. 2d edition with considerable additions. London, 1800. 1 v.
6571. MOSSE. L'art de Gagner sa vie, ou Encyclopedie industrielle, traitant de toutes les moyens pour faire, conserver, ou augmenter sa fortune dans quelque etat et dans quelque situation gu'on se trouve. Paris, 1826.
6572. MOUNIER et RUBICHON. De l'agriculture en France, d'après les documents officiels. Paris, Guillaumin et cie, 1846. 2 v.
6573. Les MOYENS de détruire la mendicité en France, en rendant les mendians utiles à l'état sans les rendre Malheureux. Tirés des mémoires qui ont concouru pour le Prix accordé en l'année 1777, par l'Académie de Châlons-sur-Marne. Châlons-sur-Marne, 1780. 1 v.
6574. Des MOYENS de soulager et de prévenir l'indigence. Par Ducpetiaux. Bruxelles, 1837.
6575. MUDIE, George. Mr. Owen's proposed arrangements for the distressed working classes, shown to be consistent with sound principles of political-economy. In three letters addressed to David Ricardo. London, 1819.
6576. MUIRON, Just. Nouvelles transactions sociales, religieuses et scientifiques de Virtomnius. Paris, Bossange père, 1832.
6577. ———. Sur les vices de nos procédés industriels; aperçu démontrant l'urgence d'introduire le procédé sociétaire. Paris, Madame Husard, 1834.
6578. MULLER, A. H. Elemente der staatskunst. Berlin, 1809.
6579. ———. Die fortschritte der nationaloeconomie in England. Leipzig, 1817. 1 v.
6580. ———. Versuch einer neuen geldtheorie. Leipzig, 1816.
6581. MUNOZ, Antonio. Discurso sobre la economia politica. Madrid, 1779.
6582. MURHARD, Charles. Théorie des geldes. Leipzig, 1817.
6583. ———. Théorie und politik des Handels (Théorie et politique du commerce). Goettingue, 1831. 2 v.
6584. MURRAY, Hugh and others. An historical and descriptive account of China. Edinburgh, 1836. 3 v.
6585. ———. Narrative of adventure and discovery in the polar seas and regions, including an account of the whale-fishery. Edinburgh, 1830. 1 v.
6586. MURRAY, James. French finances and financiers under Louis XV. London, 1858.
6587. MUSHET, Robert. An attempt to explain from facts the effect of the issues of the Bank of England upon its own interests, public credit, and country banks. London, 1826.

6588.	———. An enquiry into the effects produced on the national currency and rates of exchange by the bank restriction bill, explaining the cause of the high price of bullion. . . . London, 1810.
6589.	———. Inquiry into the effects of bank restriction bill (Recherches sur les effets de la suspension des payments de la Banque). 1810.
6590.	———. A series of tables, exhibiting the gain and loss of the fund holder from the fluctuations in the value of the currency. London, 1826.
6591.	NAPIER, Macvey. Outlines of political economy, being a plain and short view of the laws relating to the production, distribution, and consumption of wealth. London, 1832.
6592.	———. Parliamentary papers, third report from the select committee on the state of the poor in Ireland. London, 1830.
6593.	———. Selections from the correspondence of the late Macvey Napier. London, 1879.
6594.	NAVIGATION laws; speech of the Right honourable William Husselson in the House of commons, on the 12th of May, 1825, on the state of the shipping interest. London, 1825.
6595.	NAVILLE. De la charité légale, de ses causes, de ses effets, et spécialement des maisons de travail et de la proscription de lamendicité. Paris, 1836. 2 v.
6596.	NEBENIUS, Friedrich. Der öffentliche credit (le crédit public). 2d edition. Carlsruhe, 1829.
6597.	———. Ueber die Herabsetzung der zinsen der öffentlichen schulden. Stuttgart, 1837.
6598.	———. Ueber die natur und die ursachen der öffentlichen credits. 1820. (2te aufl. Carlsruhe, 1829. 1 v.)
6599.	NECKER, J. De l'administration des finances de la France. Paris, 1784. 3 v.
6600.	NEW and old principles of trade compared; or a treatise on the principles of commerce between nations. London, 1784. (1788.)
6601.	The NEW statistical account of Scotland, compiled by the ministers of the respective parishes, under the superintendence of a committee of the society for the benefit of the sons and daughters of the clergy. Edinburgh, 1834. 24 v.
6602.	NEWBOLD, T. J. Political and statistical account of the British settlements in the Straits of Malacca, Pinang, Malacca, and Singapore; with a history of the Malay States in the Peninsula of Malacca. London, 1839. 2 v.
6603.	NEWENHAM, Thomas. A statistical and historical inquiry into the progress and magnitude of the population of Ireland. London, 1805. 1 v.
6604.	———. A view of the natural, political, and commercial circumstances of Ireland. London, 1809, 1 v.
6605.	NEWMARCH, William. On the loans raised by Mr. Pitt. 1793-1801. London, 1855.

Classical Period 413

6606. NICHOLLS, George. History of the English poor law. London, 1855. 2 v.
6607. ———. History of the Scottish poor law. London, 1856.
6608. ———. Three reports to her Majesty's principal secretary of state for the home department. 1838.
6609. NIEMEYER. Ueber die ursachen des englischen national-reichthum. Berlin, 1810.
6610. ———. Ueber den einfluss des handels und des handelsystems und national-glück und unglück. Bremen, 1805.
6611. NORMAN, G. Warde. A letter to Charles Wood, M. P., on money and the means of economising the use of it. London, 1840.
6612. ———. Remarks on some prevalent errors with respect to currency and banking. London, 1838.
6613. NORTH American pamphlet on South American affairs. In, Pamphleteer, London, XIII (1818).
6614. NOTICE historique sur les finances de la France, de l'an 1800 au 1er Avril, 1814. Par M. le Duc de Gaete. Paris, 1818.
6615. NOTICES statistiques sur les colonies francaises. Imprimées par ordre du Ministre secretaire d'état de la marine et des colonies. Paris, 1837. 2 v.
6616. NOUVEAU plan de culture, de finance et d'economie. . . . 1790.
6617. NOUVELLE théorie du calcul des intérêts simples et composés, des annuités, des rentes, et des placemens viagers. Par Grémilliet. Paris, 1823. 1 v.
6618. OBERNDORFER, J. Adam. Bases des sciences camérales. Paris? 1818.
6619. ———. System der nationaloeconomie (Système de l'économie politique déduit de la vie nationale). Paris? 1823.
6620. OBSERVATIONS de la Chambre du commerce de Normandie sur le traité de comerce entre la France et l'Angleterre. Rouen, 1787.
6621. OBSERVATIONS on the commerce of the American states with Europe and the West Indies. . . . London, 1783.
6622. OBSERVATIONS on the mortality and physical management of children. By Roberton. London, 1829. 1 v.
6623. OBSERVATIONS on the present state of the highlands of Scotland, with a view of the causes and probable consequences of emigration. By the Earl of Selkirk. 2d edition. Edinburgh, 1806. 1 v.
6624. OBSERVATIONS on the proposed duties (those in the tariff of 1842) on the exportation of coals; with tables and statements from parliamentary returns and other authentic sources. London, 1842.
6625. OBSERVATIONS politiques et morales de finance et de commerce. . . . Lausane, 1780.
6626. OBSERVATIONS respecting the salmon fishery of Scotland, especially with reference to the stake-out mode of fishing. Edinburgh, 1824.

6627. O'CONNOR, Arthur. Etat actuel de la Grande-Bretagne. Paris, 1804. 1 v.
6628. ———. Le monopole cause de tous le maux. Paris, F. Didot, 1843. 3 v.
6629. ODDY, T. T. Manufactures, and commerce of Russia, Prussia, Sweden. . . . London, 1805. 1 v.
6630. OEUVRES de M. Turgot, Ministre d'état, précédées et accompagnées de mémoires et de notes sur sa vie, son administration, et ses ouvrages. Par M. Dupont de Nemours. Paris, 1811. 9 v.
6631. OLUFSEN, C. Grundtraek af den pratiske statsökonomie. 1815.
6632. ON combinations of trades. London, 1830.
6633. ON the debt of the nation, compared with its revenue; and on the impossibility of carrying on the war without public oeconomy. London, 1781.
6634. ORDERS in council; or an examination of the justice, legality, and policy of the new system of commercial regulations, with an appendix of state papers, statutes, and authorities. London, 1808.
6635. ORDNANCE memoir, or survey of the Parish of Templemore, including the City of Londonderry, in the county of the same name. Dublin, 1837. 1 v.
6636. ORTES, Giammaria. Riflessioni sulla populazione delle nazione per rapporto all' economia nazionale. Venezia, 1790. 1 v.
6637. OTT, A. Traité d'économie sociale, ou l'économie politique coordonnée au point de vue du progrès. Paris, 1851. 1 v. (2e édition, 1892. 2 v.)
6638. OUTLINES of political economy. London, 1832.
6639. OWEN, Robert Dale. A biography of Robert Owen. By Frank Podmore. New York, 1907. 2 v.
6640. ———. Book of the new modern world. London, 1836. (French traduit par T. W. Thornton, Paris, 1847; Italy, 1882.)
6641. ———. A new view of society: or, essays on the principle of the formation of the human character. London, 1812; and 1813.
6642. ———. A supplement to the revolution in mind and practice of the human race. London, 1849.
6643. PAGE, Frederick. The principle of the English poor-laws illustrated and defended. . . . Bath, 1822. (3d edition with the addition of a tract on the state of the "Indigent poor of Ireland." London, 1830.)
6644. PAINE, Thomas. The decline and fall of the English system of finance. Paris, 1796.
6645. ———. Dissertations on government, the affairs of the bank, and paper money. London, 1819.
6646. ———. The rights of man. London, 1795.
6647. PALGRAVE, F. Rise and progress of English commonwealth. London, 1831. 2 v.
6648. PALMER, J. Horsley. The causes and consequences of the pressure upon the money market, with a statement

Classical Period 415

of the action of the Bank of England from the 1st of October, 1833, to the 27th of December, 1836. London, 1837.
6649. ———. Reply to the reflections . . . , of Mr. S. Jones Loyd, on the pamphlet entitled 'Causes and consequences of the pressure upon the money market.' London, 1837.
6650. PALMIERI, N. Saggio delle cause e delle Augustie dell' economia agraria della Sicilia. Palermo, 1826.
6651. PAOLINI, G. B. Della legittima libertà del commercio. Firenze, 1785. 2 v.
6652. PAPERS relative to the American tariffs; printed by order of the House of commons. London, 1828.
6653. PAPERS respecting emigration to the different colonies. Printed by order of the House of commons. London, 1842.
6654. PAPERS respecting the negociation with government for a renewal of the company's charter, from the 1st of March, 1814. Printed by order of the Court of directors. London, 1813.
6655. PAPILLON-LATAPY. Anecdote sur la vie politique de Burke et sur sa mort, relativement à ses recherches et à ses calculs sur les finances et le commerce de la France depuis un siècle; avec des rapprochements sur l'état progressif de l'Angleterre, et sur les moyens de ruiner la nation française. Paris, 1808? 1 v.
6656. ———. Réflexions sur le plan d'une régence des impôts indirects réunis. Paris, 1804.
6657. PAPION. Mémoire sur le crédit public. Tours, 1808.
6658. PARENT-DUCHATELET. De la prostitution dans la Ville de Paris, considérée sous le rapport de l'hygiène publique, de la morale, et de l'administration. 2d édition. Paris, 1837. 2 v.
6659. PARIEU, F. de. Histoire des impôts. Paris, 1857.
6660. ———. La politique monétaire en France et Allemagne. 2d édition. 1872.
6661. ———. Traité des impôts. 2d édition. Paris, 1866-67. 4 v.
6662. PARIEU de l'institut. Histoire des impôts généraux sur la propriété et le revenu. Paris, 1856. 1 v.
6663. PARK, J. A. System of marine insurances, with chapters on bottomry, on insurance on lives, and on insurances against fire. 8th edition, with additions, by F. Hildyard. London, 1842. 2 v.
6664. PARKES, Joseph. A statement of the claim of the subscribers to the Birmingham and Liverpool railroad to an act of parliament. London, 1825.
6665. PARLIAMENTARY reports. Report from the Committee of secrecy on the Bank of England charter. . . . London, June, 1833.
6666. ———. Report from the Select committee of the distressed state of the agriculture. London, June, 1821.
6667. ———. Reports from the Lords committee respecting

grain, and the corn laws. London, July, 1814.
6668. _____. Reports from the Select committee on the expediency of the bank resuming cash payments. London, April and May, 1819.
6669. _____. Third report from the Select committee on emigration. London, June, 1827.
6670. PARNELL, Henry. Observations on paper money, banking, overtrading. . . . London, 1827. (Paris, 1832.)
6671. _____. Observations upon the state of currency in Ireland, and upon the course of exchange between Dublin and London. Dublin, 1804.
6672. _____. On financial reform. London, 1830. 1 v. (4th and enlarged edition, London, 1832. 1 v. Paris, 1832.)
6673. _____. A plain statement of the power of the Bank of England, and of the use it has made of it; with a refutation of the objections made to the Scotch system of banking, and a reply to the 'Historical sketch of the Bank of England.' London, 1832.
6674. _____. Principles of currency and exchange. 4th edition. London, 1835.
6675. _____. A treatise on roads, wherein the principles on which they should be made are explained and illustrated. 2d edition. London, 1838. 1 v.
6676. PASHLEY, R. Pauperism and poor laws. London, 1852.
6677. PASLEY, C. W. Observations on the expediency and practicability of simplifying and improving the measures, weights, and money used in this country, without materially altering the present standards. London, 1834. 1 v.
6678. PASSY, Hippolyte? Des systèmes de culture et de leur influence sur l'économie social. 2d édition. Paris, 1852. 1 v.
6679. _____. Lecons d'économie politique. Paris, 1861. 2 v.
6680. _____. Mélanges économiques. Paris, 1857.
6681. PATTON, Robert. The principles of Asiatic monarchies. London, 1801. 1 v.
6682. PEBRER, Pablo. Histoire financière et statistique de l'empire britannique, avec un exposé du système actuel de l'impôt, suivi d'un plan pratique pour la liquidation de la dette; ou impôts, revenus, dépenses, dettes, forces et richesses de l'empire britannique et de ses nombreuses colonies dans toutes les parties du monde. Traduit de l'anglais par M. Jacobi. Paris et Londres, 1834. 2 v.
6683. PECCHIO, le Comte Joseph. Histoire de l'économie politique en Italie, ou abrege critique des economistes italiens. Traduit par Leonard Gallois. Paris, 1830. 1 v. (Storia dell'economia. . . . Lugano, 1829. Turin, 1852.)
6684. PECQUER, Constantin. Des améliorations matérielles dans leurs rapports avec la liberté. Paris, 1840. 1 v.
6685. _____. Des armées dans leurs rapports avec l'industrie, la morale et la liberté. Paris, 1842.
6686. _____. Economie sociale, Paris, 1839. 2 v.
6687. _____. Théorie nouvelle d'économie sociale et politique. Paris, 1842.

Classical Period 417

6688. PEEL, Robert. Speeches of the Right honourable Sir Robert Peel, in the House of commons, May 6th and 20th, 1844, on the renewal of the bank charter, and the state of the law respecting currency and banking. London, 1844.
6689. PENNINGTON, James. A letter to Kirkman Finlay, on the importation of foreign corn, and the value of the precious metals in different countries. London, 1840.
6690. PERCIVAL, Robert. An account of the Island of Ceylon; containing its history, geography, natural history, with the manners and customs of its various inhabitants. London, 1803. 1 v.
6691. PERCIVAL, Thomas. Observations on the state of the population in Manchester and other adjacent places. London, 1778.
6692. PETTY, Henry. Substance of the speech of the Right honourable Lord Henry Petty, in the House of commons on proposing his new plan of finance. London, 1807.
6693. PEUCHET, Jacques. Statistique élementaire de la France, contenant les principes de cette science, et leur application à l'analyse de la richesse, des forces et de la puissance de l'empire français. Paris, 1805.
6694. PHILLIPS, John. General history of inland navigation, foreign and domestic. London, 1792. (4th edition, London, 1804.)
6695. PHILLIPS, Willard. A manual of political economy of the United States. Boston, 1828.
6696. PILLET-WILL, le comte. De la dépense et du produit des canaux et des chemins de fer; de l'influence des voies de communication sur la prospérité industrielle de la France. Paris, 1837. 2 v.
6697. PINKERTON, John. An essay on medals; or an introduction to the knowledge of ancient and modern coins and medals, especially those of Greece, Rome, and Britain. London, 1784. 2 v. (3d edition, London, 1808. 2 v.)
6698. PINSENT, John. Conversations on political economy; or a series of dialogues, with remarks on our present distress, their causes and the remedies applicable to them. London, 1821.
6699. PITCAIRN, George. A retrospective view of the Scots fisheries. . . . Edinburgh, 1785.
6700. PITKIN, Timothy. A statistical view of the commerce of the United States of America, including an account of banks, manufactures, internal trade. . . . New-Haven, 1835. 1 v. (Enlarged edition, 1837.)
6701. PLACE, Francis. Illustrations and proofs of the principles of population. London, 1822. (Introduction by N. E. Himes. London, Houghton, Mifflin, 1930.)
6702. PLAN d'un caisse de prévoyance et de secours. Par M. Mourgues. Paris, 1809.
6703. PLAYFAIR, W. Commercial and political atlas. London, 1786. (3d edition, 1801.)
6704. ―――. An inquiry into the permanent causes of decline and fall of powerful and wealthy nations. London, 1805.

6705. PLOUGH, Patrick. Letters on the rudiments of a science, called formerly, improperly, political economy, recently, more pertinently catallactics. London, 1842.
6706. PLUQUET, L'Abbé. Traité philosophique et politique sur le luxe. Paris, 1785. 2 v.
6707. A POLITICAL enquiry into the consequences of enclosing waste lands, and the causes of the present high price of butchers' meat; being the sentiments of a society of farmers. . . . London, 1785.
6708. PONCELIN. Tableau général du commerce de l'Europe avec l'Afrique, les Indes orientales et l'Amérique, fondé sur les traités de 1763 et 1783. 1787. 1 v.
6709. PONCET de la GRAVE. Considérations sur le célibat, relativement à la politique, à la population et aux bonnes moeurs. 1801. 1 v.
6710. POOLE, B. Commerce and manufactures. London, 1852.
6711. POPE, Charles. The yearly journal of trade for 1844 and several previous years. London, 1844. 1 v.
6712. PORTER, George Richardson. The progress of the nation in its various social . . . relations, from the beginning of the nineteenth century to the present day. London, 1836-43. 3 v. (2d edition, 1846; 3d edition, 1851. Paris, Chemin-Dupontès, 1839.)
6713. _____. The effect of restrictions on the importation of corn, considered with reference to the landowners, farmers, and labourers. London, 1839.
6714. _____. Tables of the revenue, population, commerce..., of the United Kingdom and its dependencies, from 1820 downwards, compiled from official returns. London, 1833, etc. 12 parts.
6715. POSTSCRIPT to a pamphlet by Dr. Price, on the state of the public debts and finances at the signing. . . . London, 1784.
6716. POTERAT, Marquis de. Observations politiques et morales de finance et de commerce, ou examen approfondi d'un ouvrage de M. R. (Rillet) de Genève, sur l'emprunt el l'impôt. Lausanne, 1780.
6717. PRATT, John Tidd. The history of savings banks in England, Wales, Ireland, and Scotland, with the period of the establishment of each institution, the place where it is held, and the number of depositors classed according to the latest official returns. . . . London, 1842. 1 v.
6718. The PRECIPITATION and fall of Messrs. Douglas, Heron, and company. Edinburgh, 1778.
6719. PRESTON, Richard. A review of the present ruined condition of the landed and agriculture interests. London, 1816.
6720. PREVOST de SAINT-LUCIEN. Moyens d'extirper l'usure, ou projet d'établissement d'une caisse de prêt public sur tous les biens et l'homme, contenant lettres patentes de création du Mont-de-Piété de Paris en 1777. Dédié à Henri IV. Paris, 1778.

Classical Period

6721. PRICE, Richard. An essay on the population of England, from the revolution to the present time. . . . London, 1780.
6722. _____. The state of the public debts and finances at signing the preliminary articles of peace, in January, 1783. . . . London, 1783.
6723. _____. Two tracts on civil liberty, the war with America, and the debts and finances of the Kingdom, with a general introduction and supplement. London, 1778. 1 v.
6724. PRICHARD, J. C. Researches into the physical history of mankind. 4th edition. London, 1841-44. 4 v.
6725. PRIESTLEY, Joseph. Historical account of the navigable rivers, canals, and railways throughout Great Britain. London, 1831.
6726. PRINCE-SMITH, John K. Ueber handelsfeindseligkeit. Berlin, 1843.
6727. _____. Gesammelte schriften. Berlin, 1877-80. 3v.
6728. PRINCIPLES of life annuities and assurances practically illustrated. By an accountant. Edinburgh, 1829.
6729. PRINGSHEIM, Otto. Beiträge zur wirthschaftlichen entwickelungsgeschichte der vereinigten Niederlande im 17 un 18 Jahrhundert. Leipzig, 1826.
6730. PRINSEP, C. R. An essay on money. 1818.
6731. _____. A letter to the earl of Liverpool on the present distress of the country, and the efficacy of raising the standard of our silver currency. 1816.
6732. A PROPOSAL for uniformity of weights and measures in Scotland . . . with tables of the English and Scotch standards . . . Edinburgh, 1779.
6733. PROUDHON, P. J. Oeuvres complètes. Paris, 1868-76. 33 v.
6734. _____. Qu'est-ce que la propriété. Paris, 1840. (Deutsch, Berlin, 1844. Translated by B. R. Tucker. Massachusetts, 1876. 2d edition, Paris, 1841. 1 v.
6735. _____. Système des contradictions économiques. Paris, 1846. 2 v.
6736. _____. Théorie de l'impôt. Paris, 1861.
6737. PRYME, George. Autobiographic recollections. . . . Edited by Alicia Bayne. Cambridge, 1870.
6738. _____. An introductory lecture and syllabus . . . on the principles of political economy. Cambridge, 1823.
6739. PULTENEY, William. Considerations on the present state of public affairs, and the means of raising the necessary supplies. 3d edition. London, 1779.
6740. PURVES, Georges. Toutes les classes productives de richesses. 1817. 1 v.
6741. QUELLE influence ont les diverses espèces d'impôts sur la moralité. Par M. Monthion. Paris, 1808. 1 v.
6742. QUESTIONS constitutionelles sur le commerce et l'industrie, et projet d'un impôt direct. . . . Paris, 1790.
6743. QUETELET, A. Du système social et des lois que le régissent. Paris, 1848. 1 v.

6744. RABENIUS, L. G. Lärebok i national-ekonomien. Upsala, 1829.
6745. RAFFLES, Thomas Stamford. The history of Java. London, 1817. 2 v. (London, 1830. 2 v.)
6746. RAGUET, Condy. Principles of free trade. Philadelphia, 1840.
6747. ———. A treatise on currency and banking. London and Philadelphia, 1839.
6748. RAILROADS. Speech by James Morrison in House of commons, 17th May, 1836. . . . London, 1836.
6749. RAILWAY reform, its expediency and practicability considered. . . . London, 1843.
6750. RAMSAY, George. An essay on the distribution of wealth. Edinburgh, 1836.
6751. RAMSAY, James. An essay on the treatment and conversion of African slaves in the British sugar colonies. London, 1784.
6752. RAPET, J. J. Manuel de morale et d'économie politique. Paris, Guillaumin, 1858. 1 v.
6753. RAPPORT fait au nom de la commission chargée par la chambre des députés d'examiner le projet de loi sur les céreales. Par le Baron Dupin. Paris, 1831.
6754. RAPPORTS du comité de mendicité de l'assemblée constituante. Paris, 1790-91.
6755. RASCHE, J. C. Lexicon universae rei numariae veterum, praecipue graecorum ac Romanorum, cum observationibus antiquariis, geographicis, chronologicis. . . . Leipzig, 1785-94. 12 v.
6756. RAU, Karl Heinrich. Archives der politischen oekonomie. 16 bde. Heidelberg, 1834-53.
6757. ———. Grundsätze der volkswirtschaftslehre. 6th edition. Leipzig, 1855.
6758. ———. Lehrbuch der politischen oekonomie. 3 bde. Leipzig, 1826-32. 3 v. (Heidelberg, 1837; 5te aufl., 1862-65; 1 bde. 8te aufl., 1868-69.)
6759. RAVENSTONE, Piercy. A few doubts as to the correctness of some opinions generally entertained on the subjects of population and political-economy. London, 1821.
6760. RAYMOND, Daniel. The elements of political economy. 2d edition. Baltimore, 1823. 2 v.
6761. ———. Thoughts on political economy, in two parts. Baltimore, 1820.
6762. READ, Samuel. Political economy. An inquiry into the natural grounds of right to vendible property, or wealth. Edinburgh, 1829.
6763. RECHERCHES sur le commerce; ou idées relatives aux intérêts des différens peuples de l'Europe. Amsterdam, 1778. 2 v. en 4 part.
6764. RECHERCHES et considérations sur la population de la France. Par M. Moheau. Paris, 1778. 1 v.
6765. RECHERCHES sur les enfans-trouvés et les enfans illégitimes, en Russie, dans le reste de l'Europe, en Asie, et en Amérique, précédés d'un essai sur l'histoire des enfans-

Classical Period 421

trouvés depuis les temps les plus anciens jusqu'à nos jours. Par M. de Gouroff. Paris, 1839. 1 v.
6766. RECHERCHES sur les enfans-trouvés, les enfans naturels, et les orphelins. Par M. l'Abbé Gaillard. Poitiers, 1837. 1 v.
6767. RECHERCHES historiques et critiques sur l'administration publique et privée des terres chez les Romains. Par Butel-Dumont. Paris, 1779. 1 v.
6768. RECHERCHES sur l'origine de la boussole. Par Dom. A. Azuni. 2d édition. Paris, 1809. 1 v.
6769. RECHERCHES sur l'origine de l'impôt en France. Par P. De Thou. Paris, 1838. 1 v.
6770. RECHERCHES sur la population, les naissances, les décès . . . dans le pays bas. Par Quetelet. Bruxelles, 1827.
6771. RECHERCHES sur les rentes, les emprunts, et les remboursements. Par Duvillard. Paris, 1787. 1 v.
6772. RECHERCHES statistiques sur l'esclavage colonial, et sur les moyens de le supprimer. Par Moreau de Jonnès. Paris, 1842. 1 v.
6773. RECHERCHES statistiques sur la Ville de Paris. Par le Comte Chabrol. Paris, 1821 etc. 3 v.
6774. RECHERCHES sur la topographie de Carthage. Paris, 1838. 1 v.
6775. RECUEIL des règlemens et instructions sur l'administration des secours à domicile. Paris, 1829. 1 v.
6776. RECUEIL des traités de commerce et de navigation de la France avec les puissances etrangères depuis la paix de Westphalie en 1648, suivi du recueil des principaux traités de même nature conclus par les puissances etrangères entre elles. Par M. le Comte d'Hauterive et le Chev. de Cussy. Paris, 1834-42. 10 v.
6777. REDDIE, James. Researches historical and critical in maritime international law. Edinburgh, 1844. 1 v.
6778. REES, O. Van. Geschiedenis der staathuiskounde in Nederland. Utrecht, 1865-68. 2 v.
6779. ———. Het welwaren. Utrecht, 1851.
6780. REEVES, John. Law of shipping and navigation. . . . London, 1792. (2d edition, 1807.)
6781. REFUTATION des principes et assertions contenus dans la lettre à la chambre du commerce de Normandie. Par M. D. P. Par la dite Chambre. Rouen, 1788.
6782. REID, Hugo. The steam-engine; being a popular description of the mode of action of that engine, as applied to raising water, machinery, navigation, railways. . . ; with a sketch of its history, and an account of the laws of heat and pneumatics. Illustrated with engravings. London, 1840. 1 v.
6783. REIMARUS, H. Die freiheit des getriedehandels. 2 aufl. Hamburg, 1790.
6784. ———. Nouvelle exposition des principes sur la liberté du commerce des grains. Traduit de l'Allemand. Paris, 1793.
6785. REMARKS on the Philippine Islands, and on their capital,

Manilla. By an Englishman. Calcutta, 1828.
6786. REMARKS upon the history of the landed and commercial policy of England, from the invasion of the Romans to the accession of James I. London, 1785. 2 v.
6787. RENNY, Robert. A demonstration of the necessity and advantages of a free trade to the East Indies. . . . 2d edition. London, 1807.
6788. RENOUARD, A. C. Traité des droits d'auteurs dans la littérature, les sciences, et les beaux-arts. Paris, 1838. 2 tomes.
6789. A REPLY to the treasury pamphlet entitled 'The Proposed system of trade with Ireland explained.' By Mr. Eden, Lord Auckland? London, 1785.
6790. REPORT and evidence from the select committee of the House of commons on the laws relating to the manufacture, sale, and assize of bread. London, 1815.
6791. REPORT and evidence from the select committee of the House of commons on the proposal of Mr. Cadogan Williams, recommending the purchase of life annuities under the authority of government. 1829.
6792. REPORT by a committee of the General assembly (of the Church of Scotland), on the management of the poor in Scotland. 1839.
6793. REPORT by and evidence taken before the Select committee of the House of commons on the usury laws. 1818.
6794. REPORT for the directors of the town's hospital of Glasgow, on the management of the city poor, the suppression of mendicity, and the principles of the plan for the new hospital. Report drawn up by James Ewing. Glasgow, 1818. 1 v.
6795. REPORT from and evidence taken before a committee of the House of commons on marine insurance. London, 1810.
6796. REPORT from and evidence taken before the select committee of the House of commons, on the combination-laws. London, 1825.
6797. REPORT from and evidence taken before the select committee of the House of commons on the poor-laws. London, 1817.
6798. REPORT from and evidence taken before the select committee of the House of commons on the present state of manufactures, commerce, and shipping in the United Kingdom. London, 1833.
6799. REPORT from and evidence taken before the select committee of the House of commons on the state of mendicity in the metropolis. London, 1815.
6800. REPORT from and evidence taken before the select committee of the House of Lords on the price of shipping foreign grain from foreign ports. London, 1827.
6801. REPORT from and minutes of evidence taken before the select committee of the House of commons appointed to inquire into the state of the laws respecting joint stock companies (except those for banking). London, 1844.

Classical Period 423

6802. REPORT from and minutes of evidence taken before the select committee of the House of commons on the depressed state of agriculture. Drawn up by Mr. Huskisson. London, 1821.
6803. REPORT from commissioners on the administration and practical operation of the poor laws. Reports 1834, XXVIII. London, 1834. (Reprinted 1885.)
6804. REPORT from the committee of secrecy appointed by the House of commons to inquire into the expediency of renewing the charter of the Bank of England, and into the system on which the banks of issue in England and Wales are conducted. London, 1832.
6805. REPORT from the secret committee of the House of commons on joint-stock banks, with minutes of evidence, appendix. . . . London, 1837.
6806. REPORT from select committee appointed to enquire into operation of laws affecting the exportation of machinery. Reports 1841, VII. London, 1841.
6807. REPORT from the select committee of the House of commons appointed to inquire into the acts now in force regarding the highways in England and Wales. . . . London, 1810-11.
6808. REPORT from the select committee of the House of commons appointed to inquire into the present state of the British channel fisheries, and the laws affecting the fishery trade of England, with a view to their amendment. London, 1833.
6809. REPORT from the select committee of the House of commons appointed to inquire into the state of the laws affecting aliens, with minutes of evidence. London, 1843.
6810. REPORT from the select committee of British House of commons on the high price of bullion. Reports, 1811. London, 1811.
6811. REPORT from the select committee of the House of commons on import duties, with minutes of evidence, appendix. . . . London, 1840.
6812. REPORT from the select committee of the House of commons on the linen trade of Ireland, 1825. London, 1825.
6813. REPORT from the select committee of the House of commons on the state of the woollen manufacture of England. London, 1806.
6814. REPORT of a committee of the citizens of Boston and its vicinity on duties on importations. Boston, 1827.
6815. REPORT of the committee of the House of representatives of the 8th of February, 1830, on commerce and navigation. (By Mr. Cambreleng.) New York, 1830.
6816. REPORT of the Lords of the committee of council upon the propriety of reducing the duties payable in Great Britain on the importation of goods of the growth and manufacture of Ireland. . . . London, 1785.
6817. REPORT of the Lords of the committee of council for trade;

with the evidence and information collected under an order in council of the 11th of February, 1788, concerning the present state of the trade to Africa, particularly the trade in slaves, and concerning the effects and consequences of this trade, as well on Africa and the West Indies, as on the general commerce of this kingdom. London, 1789. 1 v.

6818. REPORT of John Finlaison, actuary of the national debt, on the evidence and elementary facts on which the tables of life annuities are founded. Printed by order of the House of commons. London, 1829.

6819. REPORT of the Poor law commissioners on the subject of local taxation. London, 1843.

6820. REPORT of the Secretary (General Hamilton) of the United States on the subject of manufactures, presented to the House of representatives on the 5th December, 1791. 1793.

6821. REPORT of the select committee of the House of commons on the silk trade, with minutes of evidence, appendix. . . . London, 1832.

6822. REPORT of select committee on the state of the coal trade. Reports 1830. London, 1830.

6823. REPORT on the commerce of the ports of New Russia, Moldavia, and Wallachia, made to the Russian government in 1835. By M. de Hagemeister. Translated from the original. London, 1836. 1 v.

6824. REPORT on comparison of tariffs. 1789-1812. United States, 29th congress, 1st session. House documents no. 227, Vol. VII. Washington, 1846.

6825. REPORT on friendly or benefit societies, exhibiting the law of sickness as deduced from returns by friendly societies in different parts of Scotland; to which are subjoined tables. . . . By a committee of the Highland society of Scotland. Drawn up by Mr. Oliphant. Edinburgh, 1824. 1 v.

6826. REPORT to her Majesty's principal secretary of state for the Home department, from the poor law commissioners, on an inquiry into the sanitary condition of the labouring population of Great Britain, with appendices, and local and supplemental reports. 1842. 3 v.

6827. REPORTS and documents connected with the proceedings of the East India company in regard to the culture and management of cotton-wool, raw-silk, and indigo. Printed by order of the East India company. London, 1836. 1 v.

6828. REPORTS and evidence from the committees of the Houses of Lords and commons on the corn laws. London, 1814-15.

6829. REPORTS from and evidence taken before the committees of the Houses of Lords and commons on the expediency of the Bank of England resuming cash payments. London, 1819.

6830. REPORTS from and evidence taken before the select committees of the House of commons in 1824 and 1825, on the

Classical Period 425

condition of the manufacturing population, and the exportation of machinery. London, 1824-25.
6831. REPORTS of cases in the High court of admiralty, commencing with the judgments of the Right honourable Sir William Scott (Lord Snowell), from 1798 to 1808. By Sir Christopher Robinson. London, 1798-1808. 6 v.
6832. REPORTS of central board of His Majesty's commission on employment of children in factories. London? 1833.
6833. REPORTS of the select committee on the income and property tax. Reports, 1852. London, 1852.
6834. The REPORTS on the agriculture, etc. of the different counties of Great Britain and Ireland, drawn up for the information of the Board of Agriculture and of the Dublin society. England, Scotland, and Ireland, 1796-1815.
6835. REPORTS from and minutes of evidence taken before the select committee of the House of commons on the state of the salmon fisheries of the United Kingdom, and on the modes of improving them. London, 1824-25.
6836. REPORTS from the select committee of the House of commons of 1817 and 1818, on the petitions of the watchmakers of Coventry, and on the laws relating to watchmakers. London, 1817, 1818.
6837. REPORTS of the select committees of the House of commons of 1819 and 1823, on the highways of the Kingdom. London, 1819. 1823.
6838. REPORTS from the select committees of the Houses of Lords and commons on the state of the coal trade. London, 1830.
6839. REPORTS from the select committee on artisans and machinery. London, 1824.
6840. REPRESENTATION of the Lords of the committee of council appointed for the consideration of all matters relating to trade and foreign plantations, upon the present state of the laws for regulating the importation and exportation of corn. London, 1790.
6841. REVANS, John. Observations on the proposed alteration of the timber duties, with remarks on the pamphlet of Sir Howard Douglass. London, 1831.
6842. REYBAUD, Louis. Etudes sur le régime des manufactures. . . . Paris, 1859-74. 4 v.
6843. ———. Etudes sur les économistes contemporains. . . . Paris, 1862.
6844. ———. Etudes sur les réformateurs contemporains ou socialistes modernes, Saint-Simon, Charles Fourier, Robert Owen. 3d édition, augmentée biographie raisonnée des principaux utopistes. Paris, Guillaumin, 1842-43. (7th édition, 1864. 2 v.)
6845. ———. Etudes sur les socialistes modernes. . . . 3e édition. Paris, 1842. 1 v.
6846. REYNIER, Jean-Louis-Antoine. De l'économie publique et rurale des Arabes et des Juifs. Genève, 1820.
6847. ———. De l'économie publique et rurale des Celtes, des Germains et des autres peuples du nord et du centre

de l'Europe. Genève et Paris, 1818.
6848. _____. De l'économie publique et rurale des Egyptiens et des Carthaginois; précédé de considérations sur les antiquités Ethiopiennes. Genève et Paris, 1823.
6849. _____. De l'économie publique et rurale des Grecse. Genève et Paris, 1825.
6850. _____. De l'économie publique et rurale des Perses et des Phéniciens. Genève et Paris, 1819.
6851. RICARD, Samuel. Traité general du commerce. . . . Amsterdam, 1781. 2 v.
6852. RICARDO, David. An essay on the influence of a low price of corn on the profits of stock, with remarks on Mr. Malthus's last two publications. London, 1815.
6853. _____. The high price of bullion a proof of the depreciation of bank notes. London, 1809. (4th edition, 1811.)
6854. _____. Plan for the establishment of a national bank. London, 1824.
6855. _____. Principles of political economy and taxation. London, 1817. (3d edition, 1821; Paris, 1818; Leipzig, 1877.)
6856. _____. Proposals for an economical and secure currency, with observations on the profits of the Bank of England. London, 1816.
6857. _____. On protection to agriculture. London, 1822.
6858. _____. Reply to Mr. Bosanquet's 'Practical observations on the Report of the bullion committee.' London, 1811.
6859. _____. The works of. . . . Edited by J. R. McCulloch. London, 1846. (New edition, London, 1881; traduit par F. S. Constancio et A. Fonteyraud, Paris, 1847.)
6860. RICCI, Ludovico. Reforma degl' instituti pii della città di Modena. Modena, 1787. (Reprinted in, Economisti Italiani, Vol. XLI.)
6861. RICHELOT, H. Histoire de la réforme commerciale en Angleterre. . . . Paris, 1853-55. 2 v.
6862. _____. Le zollverein. . . . 2d édition. Paris, 1859.
6863. RICKARDS, Robert. India; or, Facts submitted to illustrate the character and condition of the native inhabitants. London, 1832. 2 v.
6864. The RIGHTS of industry. . . . 2d edition. London, 1831.
6865. RILLET de SAUSSURE. Lettres sur l'emprunt et l'impôt, adressées à M. Necker de Germani. 1779.
6866. ROBERTSON, George. Rural recollections, or the progress of improvement in agriculture and rural affairs in Scotland. Irvine, 1829. 1 v.
6867. ROBERTSON, William. An historical disquisition concerning the knowledge which the ancients had of India, and the progress of trade with that country prior to the discovery of the passage to it by the Cape of Good Hope. London, 1791. 1 v.
6868. ROBINSON, Christopher. Collectanea maritima, being a collection of public instruments tending to illustrate the history and practice of prize law. London, 1801. 2

Classical Period

6869. _____ parts in 1 v.
_____. Reports of cases in the high court of admiralty, commencing with the judgments of the Right honourable Sir William Scott (Lord Snowell), from 1798 to 1808. London, 1798-1808. 6 v.
6870. ROBINSON, Thomas. The common law of Kent, or custom of gavelkind. 3d edition with notes by J. Wilson. London, 1821.
6871. ROCCO. Des banques de Naples. Napoli, 1785. 2 v.
6872. ROCHETTE, Raoul. Histoire critique de l'etablissement des colonies Grecques. Paris, 1815. 4 v.
6873. ROCHON L'ABBE. Essai sur les monnaies anciennes et modernes. 1792. 1 v.
6874. RODBERTUS-JAGETZOW, K. Briefe und socialpolitique. Aufsätze. Hrsg. v. Meyer. 2 bde. Berlin, 1882.
6875. _____. Das kapital. Neue aufl. Berlin, 1884.
6876. _____. Zur beleuchtung der sozialen frage. 2 aufl. 2 thle. Berlin, 1890.
6877. _____. Zur erkenntniss unserer staatswirthschaftlichen zustande. Neubrandenburg, 1842.
6878. _____. Zur erklärung und abhulfe de heutigen kreditnoth des grundbesitzes. 2 aufl. Jena, 1876.
6879. ROEDERER, Pierre-Louis. De la propriété considérée dans ses rapports avec les droits politiques. 2d édition. Paris, Hect. Bossange, 1830.
6880. _____. En quoi consiste la prospérité d'un pays. Paris, 1787.
6881. _____. Journal d'économie publique, de morale et de politique. Paris, 1776. (Et années suivantes.) 5 v.
6882. _____. Mémoires d'économie publique, de morale et de politique (faisant suite au journal précédent). Paris, 1799. 1 v. (En tout 6 v.)
6883. ROESSIG. Encyclopoedie der kameralwissenschaften. Leipzig, 1792.
6884. ROGERS, Edward. An essay on some general principles of political economy, on taxes upon raw produce, and on commutation of tithes. London, 1822.
6885. ROMAGNOSI, G. D. Sulle colonie. (In, G. D. Romagnosi, Opere. Florence, 1835. v. 10.)
6886. ROOKE, John. An inquiry into the principles of national wealth. Edinburgh, 1824.
6887. ROSE, George. A brief examination into the increase of the revenue, commerce, and navigation of Great Britain during the administration of the Right honourable William Pitt. London, 1806.
6888. _____. The diaries and correspondence. . . . Edited by Leveson Vernon Harcourt. London, 1860. 2 v.
6889. _____. The proposed system of trade with Ireland explained. London, 1785.
6890. ROSSER, Archibald. Credit pernicious. London, 1823.
6891. ROSSI, Adiotato. Del l'economia della specie umana. Pavia, 1819. 4 v.
6892. ROSSI, P. Cours d'économie politique fait au Collége de

France. Paris, Joubert, 1839-40. 2 v. (3d édition, Paris, 1854. 2 v.)

6893. _____. Oeuvres complètes. . . . Ed. par M. A. Porée. Paris, 1865. 2 v.

6894. _____. Mélanges d'économie politique. Paris, 1857. 2 v.

6895. ROTTECK, Carl von. Lehrbuch der oeconomischen politick. Stuttgart, 1835.

6896. ROUSE, Boughton. Dissertation concerning the landed property of Bengal. London, 1791. 1 v.

6897. ROUX, Vital. De l'influence du gouvernement sur la prospérité du commerce. Paris, 1801.

6898. ROYER, E. De . . . richesses et de . . . statistique en France. Paris, 1843.

6899. _____. Histoire du crédit hypothécaire. . . . Paris, 1845.

6900. RUDING, Rogers. Annals of the coinage of Britain and its dependencies, from the earliest period of authentic history to the end of the 50th year of His Majesty, King George III. London, 1817. 4 v. (2d edition, 1819. 6 v. 1840. 3 v.)

6901. _____. A proposal for restoring the ancient constitution of the mint, so far as relates to the expense of coinage. . . . London, 1799.

6902. RUGGLES, Thomas. The history of the poor; their rights, duties, and the laws respecting them. London, 1793. 2 v. (French translation by A. C. Duquesnoy. Paris, 1802. 2 v.)

6903. RUSSELL, J. S. On the nature, properties, and application of steam, and on steam navigation. London, 1841. 1 v.

6904. _____. A treatise on the steam-engine. London, 1841. 1 v.

6905. RUTHERFORD, A. W. Hints from Holland; or, gold bullion as dear in Dutch currency as in bank-notes. . . . London, 1811.

6906. SABATIER, William. A treatise on poverty, its consequences, and the remedy. London, 1797.

6907. SADDLER, M. T. The law of population: a treatise in six books, in disproof of the superfecundity of human beings, and developing the real principle of their increase. London, 1830. 2 v.

6908. SAGE, M. Analyse des blés, et expériences. Paris, 1776.

6909. SAGGIO sul buon governo della mendicità . . . del conte petitti di Roreto. Torino, 1837. 2 v.

6910. SAINT-AUBIN. Opuscules sur les finances, le papier-monnaie, le credit. . . . 1797. (Avec tables, 20 pieces.) 1 v.

6911. SAINT-CHAMANS le Vicomte de. Dus système d'impôt fondé sur les principes d'économie politique. Paris, 1820.

6912. _____. Nouvel essai sur la richesse des nations. Paris, Lenormant père, 1824.

6913. _____. Traité d'économie publique. Paris, 1852. 3 v.

6914.	SAINT FARGEAU, Girault de. Apercu statistique de la France. 2d édition. Paris, 1836.	
6915.	SAINT JOHN, John. Observations on the land revenue of the crown. London, 1787. 1 v. (2d edition, London, 1792. 1 v.)	
6916.	SAINT LEON, Dufresne A. Etudes de crédit publie et des dettes publiques. Paris, 1824.	
6917.	SAINT-PIERRE, Charles I. C., L'Abbe de. (Membre de l'academie française.) Sa vie et ses oeuvres precedées d'une appreciation et d'un precis historique de l'idée de la paix perpetuelle suivies du jugement de Rousseau sur le projet de la paix perpetuelle et la polysynodie, ainsi que du projet attribue a Henri IV, et du plan d'Emmanuel Kant pour rendre la paix universelle, et . . . , avec des notes et des eclaircissements, par M. Gust. de Molinari. Paris, Guillaumin, 1857. 1 v.	
6918.	———. Système industriel. Paris, 1821-22.	
6919.	SAINT-SIMON, Charles-Henri. Catéchisme des industriels. Paris, 1824-25.	
6920.	———. Considérations sur les contributions et les taxes indirectes. Paris, Imprimerie de P. Gueffier, 1818.	
6921.	———. Du crédit public et particulier, des moyens d'acquitter indistinctement la dépense de tous les services, et d'opérer des améliorations dans les diverses branches de l'économie politique. 1798.	
6922.	———. L'industrie, ou discussions politiques, morales et philosophiques dans l'intérêt de tous les hommes livrés a des travaux utiles et indépendants. Avec cette épigraphe: Tout par l'industrie, tout pour elle. Paris, 1817. 2 v.	
6923.	———. Oeuvres de St. Simon. . . . Paris, 1865-78. 47 v. (Oeuvres. . . . Bruxelles, 1859. 3 v.	
6924.	———. L'Organisateur. (Paru en plusieurs éditions et de la manière la plus confuse.) Pour des mesures à adopter pour que l'agriculture, l'industrie, le commerce de la France et des divers états jouissent de l'avantage de tels établissements. Paris, 1817.	
6925.	———. Reorganisation de la société europeene. Paris, 1814.	
6926.	———. Tableaux comparatifs des dépenses et des contributions de la France et de l'Angleterre, suivis de considérations sur les ressources des deux états, et servant en même temps de réfutation à l'ouvrage de Gentz. Paris, Arthus-Bertrand, 1805.	
6927.	SARGANT, W. L. Economy of the labouring classes. London, 1857.	
6928.	———. Inductive political economy. London, 1887. 1 v.	
6929.	———. Robert Owen and his social philosophy. London, 1860.	
6930.	———. Science of social opulence. London, 1856.	
6931.	———. Taxation: past, present, and future. London, 1874.	

6932. SARTORIUS, George F. Geschichte des hanseatischen. . . . Göettingue, 1802-08.
6933. ———. Handbuch des staatswirthschaft nach A. Smith. Berlin, 1796. (La deuxième édition à été publiée sous le titre suivant; éléments de la richesse nationale. Göettingue, 1806.)
6934. ———. Von den eleménten des nationalreichthums und vond der staatswirthschaftsgeschichte nach A. Smith. Göettingue, 1806-08.
6935. SAVARY des BRULONS. Dictionnaire universel du commerce. Paris, 1823. 3 v.
6936. SAY, Horace. Histoire des relations commerciales entre la France et le Brésil, et considérations sur les monnaies, les changes, les banques et le commerce extérieur. Paris, 1839. 1 v.
6937. SAY, J. B. Catéchisme d'économie politique, ou instruction familière que montre. . . . Paris, 1815. (English translation by J. Richter. London, 1816; 5th edition, Paris, 1835.)
6938. ———. Cours complet d'économie politique pratique ouvrage destiné à mettre sous les yeux. . . . Paris, 1828-30. 3 v. (2d édition, Paris, Guillaumin, 1840. 2 v. 3d édition, Paris, 1852.)
6939. ———. Mélanges et correspondance d'économie politique, ouvrage posthume, publié (avec une notice historique sur la vie et les ouvrages de l'auteur) par Charles Comte, son gendre. Paris, Chamerot, 1833.
6940. ———. Oeuvres complètes. . . . Paris, 1844.
6941. ———. Petit volume, contenant quelques apercus des hommes et de la société. 3e édition publiée par M. Horace Say. Paris, 1839. 1 v.
6942. ———. Traité d'économie politique, ou simple exposition de la manière. . . . Paris, 1803. (Deutsch, 3 bd., Heidelburg, 1831; English translated by C. C. Biddle, London, 1821. New edition, Philadelphia, 1824; 6th edition, Paris, 1841. 1 v.)
6943. SAY, Louis, de Nantes. Etudes sur la richesse des nations et réfutation des principales erreurs en économie politique. Paris, 1836.
6944. ———. Traité de la richesse individuelle et de la richesse publique. Paris, 1827.
6945. SCHENK, K. F. Das bedurfniss der volkswirthschaft. (Les besoins de l'économie politique dans la plupart des états de la confédération germanique.) Stuttgart, 1831. 2 v.
6946. SCHLETTWEIN, J. A. Grundsaetze der staaten odor die politische oeconomie. Giessen, 1777.
6947. SCHLOEZER, C. de. Anfangsgründe der staatwirthschaft. (Eléments d'économie politique.) Riga, 1805. 2 v.
6948. SCHMALZ, H. Economie politique. Traduit de l'Allemand, par Henry Jouffroy. Paris, 1826. 2 v.
6949. SCHMITTHENNER, F. Zwölf Bücher. . . . Giessen, 1843-45.
6950. SCHNEIDER, J. G. Scriptores rei rusticae veterum Latin-

orum. Lipsiae, 1794. 4 v.
6951. SCHNITZLER, J. H. De la création de la richesse, ou des intérêts matériels en France: statistique comparée et raisonée. Paris, 1842. 2 v.
6952. ———. La Russie, la Pologne, et la Finlande; ou tableau statistique, géographique. et historique de toutes les parties de la Monarchie Russe prises insolément. Paris, 1835. 1 v.
6953. ———. Statistique génerale de la France. Paris, 1842-46. 4 v.
6954. ———. Statistique génerale de l'empire de la Russie. Paris, 1829. 1 v.
6955. SCHOEN, Jean. Neue untersuchung der nationaloekonomie. Nouvelles recherches sur l'économie nationale. Stuttgart 1835. 1 v.
6956. SCHOMBERG, Alexander C. A treatise on the maritime laws of Rhodes. Oxford, 1786.
6957. SCHOOLCRAFT, H. R. History, conditions, and prospects of the Indian tribes of the United States. Washington, 1851-55. 6 v.
6958. SCHULTZE-DELITZSCH, H. Cours d'économie politique. (Traduit par B. Rampal.) Paris, 1874.
6959. ———. Entwickelung des Genossenschaftwesens. Berlin, 1870.
6960. SCIALOJA, A. Principes d'économie politique. (Traduits en francais par M. Devillers.) Paris, 1844. 1 v.
6961. ———. Principii dell' economie sociale. . . . Naples, 1840. (Turin, 1846.) (Traduit French par H. Devillers, 1854.)
6962. SCORESBY, W. An account of the Arctic regions, with a history and description of the northern whale-fishery. Edinburgh, 1820. 2 v.
6963. SCRIPTORES rei rusticae veterum latinorum. Illustravit J. G. Schneider. Lipsiae, 1794. 4 v.
6964. SCRITTORI classici Italiani di economia politica. Milano, 1803-1816.
6965. SCRIVENOR, Harry. A comprehensive treatise of the iron trade throughout the world, from the earliest periods to the present time. London, 1839. 1 v. (Revised edition: History of the iron trade. London, 1854.)
6966. SCROPE, George Poulett. Principles of political economy, deduced from the natural laws of social welfare and applied to the present state of Great Britain. London, 1833. (2d edition published as Political economy for plain people applied to the past and present state of Britain. London, 1873.)
6967. SCUDERI. Principi di civile economia. Napoli, 1829. 3 v.
6968. SEALY, Henry Nicholas. A treatise on coins, currency and banking with observations on the Bank act of 1844. London, 1858.
6969. SEMER. Beitrag zur naeheren bestimmung der staatswirthschaft und ihres gebiets. Mannheim, 1794.
6970. SENAC DE MEILAN, G. Considérations sur les richesses.

Paris, 1787. (Amsterdam, 1789.)
6971. SENIOR, N. W. Essays on wealth. Oxford, 1854.
6972. ———. Lectures on political economy. London, 1826.
6973. ———. A letter to Lord Howick on a legal provision for the Irish poor, a commutation of tithes, and a provision for the Catholic clergy. London, 1831.
6974. ———. Letters on the Factory act, as it affects the cotton manufacture. 2d edition. London, 1844.
6975. ———. Principies fondamentaux de l'économie politique. (Traduit par comte Arrivabene.) Paris, 1836.
6976. ———. Three lectures on the rate of wages, with a preface on the causes and remedies of the present disturbances. London, 1830. (2d edition, London, 1831.)
6977. No Entry.
6978. ———. Three lectures on the transmission of the precious metals from country to country, and on the mercantile theory of wealth. London, 1828.
6979. ———. Two lectures on population, to which is added a correspondence between the author and Mr. Malthus. London, 1829.
6980. SERIONNE, Acarias de. La richesse de la Hollande. Amsterdam, 1778. 2 v.
6981. SERIOUS reflections on the high price of provisions, in which is contained a candid inquiry into the true causes of the present scarcity. . . . London, 1768.
6982. SEVEN reports from the same committee on the state of British fisheries; and on the most effectual means for their improvement, encouragement, and extension. 1786.
6983. SEYBERT, Adam. Statistical annals of the United States. Philadelphia, 1818. (1820. 1 v.)
6984. SHEFFIELD, John Lord. Observations on the commerce of the American states. 2d edition. London, 1784.
6985. ———. Observations on the corn bill now pending in Parliament. London, 1791.
6986. ———. Observations on the manufactures, trade, and present state of Ireland. Dublin, 1785. (2d edition, London, 1785.)
6987. ———. Remarks on the deficiency of grain. . . . London, 1800.
6988. ———. Strictures on the necessity of inviolably maintaining the navigation and colonial system of Great Britain. 2d edition greatly enlarged. London, 1806. 1 v.
6989. SHIPPING interest. Speech of the Right honourable William Huskisson in the House of commons on the 7th of May, 1827, on General Gascoyne's motion on the depressed state of the shipping interest. London, 1827.
6990. SHORT account of the Edinburgh bank for saving. Ascribed to Mr. Forbes. 4th edition. Edinburgh, 1816.
6991. SILVA, I. F. D. Diccionario bibliographico portuguez. Lisbon, 1858-87. 14 v.
6992. SINCLAIR, John. An account of the systems of husbandry adopted in the more improved districts of Scotland. 3d

Classical Period

edition. Edinburgh, 1820. 2 v.

6993. _____. An analysis of the statistical account of Scotland, with a general view of the history of that country, and discussions on some important branches of political economy. Edinburgh, 1825. 2 v.

6994. _____. The correspondence of John Sinclair. . . . London, 1831. 2 v.

6995. _____. General report on the agricultural state and political circumstances of Scotland. Drawn up for the consideration of the board of agriculture and internal improvement, under the directions of Sir John Sinclair. Edinburgh, 1814. 5 v.

6996. _____. The history of the public revenue of the British empire, containing an account of the public income and expenditure from the remotest periods recorded in history to Michaelmas, 1802; with an account of the revenue of Scotland and Ireland. . . . London, 1785. (3d edition, London, 1804. 2 v.)

6997. _____. On the approaching crisis of resuming cash payments at the bank. In, Pamphleteer, London, XII (1818).

6998. _____. The statistical account of Scotland, drawn up from the communications of the ministers. Edinburgh, 1791-99. 21 v.

6999. SISMONDI, J. C. L. Simonde de. Etudes sur l'économie politique. Paris, Treuttel et Wurtz, 1837-38. 3 v.

7000. _____. Nouveaux principes d'économie politique, ou de la richesse dans ses rapports avec la population. Paris, 1819. (2d édition, 1827.)

7001. _____. Political economy and the philosophy of government. London, 1847.

7002. _____. Traité de la richesse commerciale on principes d'économie politiques appliqués a la legislation du commerce. Genève, 1803. 2 v. (Paris, 1803.)

7003. SIX reports from, with minutes of evidence taken before the select committee of the House of commons on the renewal of the company's charter, in 1831-32; being 1st, Public; 2nd, Finance and trade; 3rd, Revenue; 4th, Judicial; 5th, Military; and 6th, Political and foreign.

7004. SKARBEK, Le Comte Frédéric. Théorie des richesses sociales. Paris, 1829. 2 v.

7005. SKETCH of the Ryotwar system of revenue administration. London, 1831.

7006. SMITH, E. Peshine. Manual of political economy. New York, 1853. (Paris, 1854.)

7007. SMITH, Sydney. A memoir of . . . by his daughter, Lady Holland. London, 1855. 2 v.

7008. _____. The works. . . . London, 1865. 2 v.

7009. _____. A sketch of the life and times of Sydney Smith. By Stuart J. Reid. London, 1884.

7010. SMITH, Thomas. An attempt to define some of the first principles of political economy. London, 1821.

7011. _____. An essay on the theory of money and exchange. . . . 2d edition. London, 1811.

7012. SMITH, William Prescott. The book of the great railway celebrations of 1857. . . . New York, 1858.
7013. SMITH, Z. Toulmin, editor. English guilds. London, 1870.
7014. SODEN, Julius. Die nationaloeconomie. Ein philosophischer versuch ueber die quellen des nationalreichtum, und ueber die mittel zu dessen befoerderung. 1805-24. Leipzig, Arau, Nuremberg. 9 v.
7015. SOETBEER, A. Beiträge und materialen zur . . . von geld- und bankfragen. Hamburg, 1855.
7016. ───────. Deutsch münzverfassung. 4 thle. 12 bde. Erlangen, 1874-81.
7017. SOLERA, Maurice. Essai sur les valeurs. 1798.
7018. SOLLY, Edward. Considerations on political economy. Berlin, 1814. (English translation by Thomas Wilkinson. London, 1821.)
7019. SONNENFELS, Joseph von. Grundsätze der polizei der handlung und der finanz. 1765. 8te aufl. Wien, 1819-22. 3 bde. 5th ed., 1786-87. 3 v.)
7020. SOPP, A. A. Neueste darstellung der kameralwissenschaften. (Nouvel exposé des sciences camérales.) Vienne, 1808-11. 3 v.
7021. SPEECH of C. Poulett Thomson, in the House of commons, on the 26th of March, 1830, on moving the appointment of a select committee to inquire into the state of the taxation of the United Kingdom. London, 1830.
7022. SPEECHES in the House of commons on the 24th of February, 1826, on the motion for a committee on the state of the silk trade. By Mr. Huskisson and Mr. Canning. London, 1826.
7023. SPENCE, William. Britain independent of commerce; or proofs deduced from an investigation into the true causes of the wealth of nations, that our riches, prosperity, and power are derived from sources inherent in ourselves, and would not be affected even though our commerce were annihilated. London, 1807.
7024. ───────. Tracts on political economy. London, 1882. (Reprinted and edited by Elisha M. Friedman. New York, 1933.)
7025. ───────. The . . . cause of the present distresses of West India planters pointed out. . . . London, 1807.
7026. STANHOPE, Earl. A letter . . . on the corn laws. London, 1826.
7027. ───────. Life of Right honourable William Pitt. London, 1862-63. 4 v.
7028. The STATE of the commerce of Great Britain, with reference to colonial and other produce for the year 1830. (1831-1832.) By Mr. Cook, firm of Trueman and Cook. London, 1831. (1832, 1833.)
7029. A STATEMENT of the claims of the West India colonies to a protecting duty against East India sugar. London, 1823.
7030. STATISTICAL abstract for British India. London, 1867.
7031. STATISTICAL abstract for the colonial and other possessions

Classical Period 435

of the United Kingdom. London, 1862.
7032. STATISTICAL abstract of the United Kingdom. London, 1854- .
7033. STATISTICAL abstract of the United States. Washington, 1879- .
7034. STATISTIQUE générale et particulière de la France et de ses colonies. Par une société de gens de letters et de savans (MM. Peuchet, Herbin, Sonini. . . .) Paris, an XII. 1803. 7 v.
7035. STAUDLIN, K. F. Kirchliche geographie und statistik. 2 bde. Tübingen, 1804.
7036. STEIN-HORSCHELMANN-WAPPAUSG. Handbuch der geographie und statist. 7 aufl. 4 bde. und 4 nachträge. Leipzig, 1854-71.
7037. STEIN, Lorenz von. Der sozialismus und communismus des heutigen Frankreichs. Leipzig, 1847. (2te aufl. 1848.)
7038. ———. Die lehre vom heerwesen. Als theil der staatswissenschaft. Stuttgart, 1872.
7039. ———. Lehrbuch der finanzwissenschaft. Leipzig, 1860. (5 aufl. 1885-86.)
7040. ———. Lehrbuch der nationalökonomie. Wien, 1858. (3 aufl. Wien, 1887; Veronz, 1879.)
7041. ———. System der staatswissenschaft. Stuttgart, 1852. 2 v.
7042. STEPHEN, James. The slavery of the British West India colonies, as it exists both in law and practice. . . . London, 1824-30. 2 v.
7043. ———. War in disguise, or the frauds of neutral flags. London, 1806.
7044. STEPHENS, Henry. The book of the farm. Edinburgh, 1844. 3 v.
7045. STEPHENSON, David. Sketch of the civil engineering of North America; comprising remarks on the harbours, river and lake navigation, lighthouses, steam-navigation, canals, roads, railways . . . of that country. London, 1838. 1 v.
7046. STEVENS, R. Essay on average and other subjects connected with the contract of marine insurance. 5th edition. London, 1835. 1 v.
7047. STEVENSON, William. Historical sketch of the progress of navigation and commerce, from the earliest periods to the beginning of the 19th century. Edinburgh, 1824. 1 v.
7048. STEWART, Dugald. Elements of the philosophy of the human mind. London, 1792. (Vol. I: 2d edition, London, 1802. Brattleborough, Vermont, 1808. Vol. II: Edinburgh, 1814. 2d ed. 1816. Vol. III: includes additions to Vol. I. London, 1827.)
7049. ———. The collected works of Dugald Stewart. . . . Edited by William Hamilton. Edinburgh, 1854-60. 10 v.
7050. ———. Philosophical essays. Edinburgh, 1810.
7051. ———. Principles of moral and political science.

Edinburgh, 1792. 2 v.

7052. ———. The works of Dugald Stewart. . . . Cambridge, England, 1829. 7 v.

7053. STIRLING, Patrick James. Australian and Californian gold discoveries. Edinburgh, 1852.

7054. ———. The philosophy of trade. Edinburgh, 1846.

7055. STORCH, Henri F. Considérations sur la nature du revenu national. Paris, 1824. (German edition, 1825.)

7056. ———. Cours d'économie politique. Saint Petersburgh, 1815. 6 v. (Hamburg, 1820; Edited by J. B. Say. Paris, 1832. 5 v.)

7057. ———. Tableau historique et statistique . . . de Russie. Leipzig, 1803.

7058. STORIA del commercio e navigazione dei Pisani. Di-Signor Lor. Cantini. Firenze, 1797. 2 v.

7059. STORIA della economia pubblica in Italia. . . . Introduzione de Comte. G. Pecchio, Lugano, 1829. Torino, 1852.

7060. STORIA filosofica e politica delle navigazione, del commercio, e delle colonie degli Antichi, nel Mar Negro. Di Formaleoni. Venezia, 1788. 2 v. (French translation Venice, 1789. 2 v.)

7061. STORY, Joseph. Commentaries on the Law of bailments, with illustrations from the Civil and the Foreign law. London, 1839. 1 v.

7062. ———. Commentaries on the Law of partnership, as a branch of commercial and maritime jurisprudence; with occasional illustrations from the civil and foreign law. London, 1842.

7063. STROMEYER, F. Die folgen der aufhebung der englischen korngesetze für Deutschland. Stuttgart, 1846.

7064. SUBSTANCE of a debate in the House of commons on the 22nd of May, 1823, on the motion of Mr. Whitmore, "That a select committee be appointed to inquire into the duties payable on East and West India sugar." London, 1823.

7065. SUDRE, A. Histoire de la souveraineté. . . . Paris, 1854.

7066. ———. Histoire du communisme, ou réfutation historique des utopies sociales. 5ᵉ édition. Paris, 1856. (2 aufl., Berlin, 1887.)

7067. SUGDEN, E. B. Considerations on the rate of interest, redeemable annuities, and foreign loans. London, 1817.

7068. SUMNER, J. B. A treatise on the records of the creation . . . showing the consistency of the principle of population with the wisdom and goodness of the deity. London, 1815. 2 v. (4th edition, London, 1825.)

7069. SYMONDS, John. Remarks on the essay entitled the 'History of the colonization of the free states of antiquity.' London, 1778.

7070. TABLEAU chronologique et moral de l'histoire universelle du commerce des anciens. . . . Par Jullien du Ruet. Paris, 1809. 2 v.

7071. TABLEAU de la population de toutes les provinces de la

Classical Period

France. . . . Par de Pommelles. Paris, 1789.
7072. TABLES showing the total number of persons assured in the Equitable society, from its commencement in September, 1762, to January, 1829 . . . ; to which are added tables of the probabilities and expectations of the duration of human life, deduced from these documents. . . . London, 1834.
7073. TANNER, H. S. A description of the canals and railroads of the United States. New York, 1840. 1 v.
7074. TATE, William. The modern cambist, forming a manual of foreign exchanges. . . . 4th edition. London, 1842. 1 v.
7075. TATHAM, William. The political economy of inland navigation, irrigation, and drainage. London, 1799. 1 v.
7076. TAYLER, James M. History of taxation of England. London, 1853. (2d edition 1858.)
7077. ———. View of money system of England from the conquest. London, 1823.
7078. TAYLOR, George. An enquiry into the principles which ought to regulate the imposition of duties on foreign corn, in answer. . . . Edinburgh, 1842.
7079. TAYLOR, R. W. Cooke. Factories and the factory system. London, 1844.
7080. TEGOBORSKI, L. de. Des finances et du crédit publie de l'autriche. Paris, 1843. 2 v. (Wien, 1845.)
7081. ———. Etudes sur les forces productives de la Russie. Paris, 1852-55. 4 v.
7082. TELLKAMPF, J. L. Neuere . . . bankwesens in Deutschland. 4 aufl. Breslau, 1857.
7083. ———. Principien de geld- und bankwesens. Berlin, 1867.
7084. La TENUE des livres rendue facile. Par Degrange. Paris, 1840. 1 v.
7085. TETENS, Jean N. Considérations sur les droits reciproques des nations belligerantes, et des puissances neutres sur mer. Copenhague, 1805. 1 v.
7086. THACKRAH, C. T. The effects of arts, trades, and professions, and of civic states and habits of living, on health and longevity. London, 1832. 1 v.
7087. The THEORY of money; or, a practical inquiry into the present state of the circulating medium. London, 1811.
7088. The THEORY of money and banks investigated. By George T. Tucker. Boston, 1839. 1 v.
7089. THIERRY, A. Oeuvres. Paris, 1863. 9 v.
7090. THIERS, A. Histoire du consulat et de l'empire. Paris, 1845-63. 2 v. (London, 1845-62.)
7091. ———. De la propriété. Paris, 1848. (Nouvelle édition, 1868.)
7092. THOMAS, Emile. Histoire des ateliers nationaux. Paris, 1848.
7093. THOMAS, F. S. Ancient exchequers of England. London, 1848.
7094. THOMPSON, Thomas Perronet. Exercises, political and

others. . . . London, 1842. 6 v.
7095. ———. The true theory of rent, in opposition to Mr. Ricardo and others. In, Pamphleteer, London, 27 (1826). (Reprinted, 1827.)
7096. THOMPSON, William. An inquiry into the principles of the distribution of wealth most conducive to human happiness. London, 1824. (New edition by William Pare. London, 1850.)
7097. ———. Labor rewarded. The claims of labor and capital conciliated; or, how to secure to labor the whole produce of its exertions. By one of the idle classes. London, 1827.
7098. ———. Practical directions for the speedy and economical establishment of communities. . . . London, 1830.
7099. THOMSON, Poulett. Speech of C. Poulett Thomson, in the House of commons, on the 26th of March, 1830, on moving the appointment of a select committee to inquire into the state of the taxation of the United Kingdom. London, 1830.
7100. THONISSEN, J. J. Le socialisme depuis l'antiquité. Louvan, 1852. 2 v.
7101. THORBURN, J. Scotch statistics. Edinburgh, 1853.
7102. THORNTON, Edward. A gazetteer of the countries adjacent to India on the north-west, including Scinde, Afghanistan, Beloochistan, the Punjab. . . . London, 1844. 2 v.
7103. ———. History of the British empire in India. London, 1843-44. 5 v.
7104. ———. Observations on the report . . . to inquire into the high price of gold bullion. . . . London, 1811.
7105. THORNTON, Henry. An enquiry into the nature and effects of paper credit of Great-Britain. London, 1802. (Philadelphia, 1807.)
7106. ———. Paper credit of Great Britain. London, 1802.
7107. THORNTON, William Thomas. Indian public works. London, 1875.
7108. ———. On labour. Its wrongful claims and rightful dues. London, 1869. (2d edition, London, 1870. Firenze, 1875. Leipzig, 1870.)
7109. ———. Overpopulation and its remedy. London, 1846.
7110. ———. A plea for peasant proprietors in Ireland. London, 1848. (2d edition, 1874.)
7111. THORPE, B. Laws and institutes of Anglo-Saxon kings. London, 1840. 2 v.
7112. THOUGHTS on the effects of the bank restrictions. By Lord King. London, 1803. (2d edition enlarged, with some remarks on the coinage. London, 1804.)
7113. THOUGHTS upon a new coinage of silver more especially as it relates to the alteration in the division of the pound Troy. By a banker. London, 1798.
7114. THOUGHTS upon the principles of banks, and the wisdom of legislative interference. London, 1837.
7115. THREE reports from the select committee on emigration from the United Kingdom. London, 1826-27.

Classical Period 439

7116. THUNEN, J. H. von. Der isolirthe staat in beziehung auf landwirtschaft und nationaloeconomie. . . . Rostock, 1826. 2te aufl. 1842. Hambourg, 1836. Paris, 1851, 1857, 1863.
7117. TISSOT, J. Turgot, sa vie . . . et ses ouvrages. Paris, 1862.
7118. TOCQUEVILLE, Alexander de. De la démocratie en Amérique. 13e édition. Paris, 1850. 2 v.
7119. ———. Oeuvres complètes. Nouvelle édition. Paris, 1862-65. 9 v.
7120. ———. State of society in France before revolution. Translated by H. Reeve. 3d edition. London, 1888.
7121. TOLLENARE, L. E. de. Essai sur les entraves que le commerce éprouve en Europe. Paris, 1820. 1 v.
7122. TOOKE, Thomas. A history of prices, and of the state of the circulation in 1838 and 1839 . . . ; being a sequel to the foregoing work. London, 1840. 1 v.
7123. ———. An inquiry into the currency principle, the connexion of the currency with prices, and the expediency of a separation of issue from banking. London, 1844.
7124. ———. On the currency in connexion with the corn trade, and on the corn laws, in a second letter to Lord Grenville. London, 1829.
7125. ———. Considerations on the state of the currency. 2d edition. London, 1826.
7126. ———. The history of prices, and of the state of the paper circulation from 1798 to 1837. Londres, 1838. 2 v. (Dresden, 1859.)
7127. ———. A letter to Lord Grenville on the effect ascribed to the resumption of cash payments on the value of the currency. London, 1829.
7128. ———. Thoughts and details of the high and low prices of the thirty years from 1793 to 1822. 2d edition. London, 1824.
7129. TOOKE, Thomas and William Newmarch. A history of prices . . . during the nine years 1848-1856. London, 1857. 2 v. (Introduction by T. E. Gregory. London, 1928.)
7130. TORRENS, Robert. The budget. A series of letters on financial, commercial, and colonial policy. By a member of the political economy club (Colonel Torrens). London, 1841-43.
7131. ———. The economists refuted; being a reply to Mr. Spence's 'Britain independent of commerce.' London, 1808.
7132. ———. An essay on money and the paper currency. London, 1812. (4th edition, 1827.)
7133. ———. An essay on the external corn trade. 1815. (4th edition, London, 1827.)
7134. ———. An essay on the production of wealth; with an appendix in which the principles of political economy are applied to the actual circumstances of this country. London, 1821.

7135. ──────. An inquiry into the practical working of the proposed arrangements for the renewal of the charter of the Bank of England, and the regulation of the currency. . . . London, 1844.
7136. ──────. A letter to Lord Ashley, on the principles which regulate wages, and on the manner and degree in which wages would be reduced by the passing of a ten hours' bill. London, 1844.
7137. ──────. A letter to the Right honourable Lord Viscount Melbourne, on the causes of the recent derangement in the money market and on bank reform. London, 1837.
7138. ──────. On wages and combinations. London, 1834.
7139. TOWNSEND, Joseph. A dissertation on the poor laws. London, 1786. (In, Lord Overstone, Select tracts, v: "Miscellaneous." London, 1859.)
7140. ──────. A Journey through Spain in 1786 and 1787; with particular attention to the agriculture, manufactures, commerce, population, taxes, and revenues of that country. London, 1791. London, 1792. 2d edition. 3 v.
7141. TRACY, Destutt de. Traité d'économie politique. Paris, 1815. (English edition, Georgetown, 1817.)
7142. ──────. Commentaire sul l'esprit des loix de Montesquieu, suivi. . . . Paris, 1811. 1 v.
7143. TRAITE des contrats aléatoires. Par Pothier. Paris, 1777. 1 v. (An edition with useful notes. Marseilles, 1810.)
7144. TRAITE du contrat et des lettres de change. Par Pardessus. Paris, 1809. 2 v.
7145. TRAITE des monnaies, poids, mesures. . . . Par Altes. Marseilles, 1832. 1 v.
7146. TRAITE de la propriété. Par M. C. Comte. Paris, 1834. 2 v.
7147. TRAITE de statistique, ou théorie de l'étude des lois d'après lesquelles se développent les faits sociaux. Par M. Dufau. Paris, 1840. 1 v.
7148. TRAVELS during the years 1787, 1788, and 1789; undertaken more particularly with a view of ascertaining the cultivation, wealth, resources, and national prosperity of the Kingdom of France but extending also into parts of Italy and Spain. 2d edition. Bury Saint Edmunds, 1794. 2 v.
7149. The TRAVELS of Marco Polo, a Venetian of the thirteenth century. Translated from the Italian, with notes, by William Marsden. London, 1818. 1 v.
7150. A TREATISE on the coins of the realm, in a letter to the King (George III), by Charles Earl of Liverpool. Oxford, 1805. 1 v.
7151. A TREATISE on contraband, being a continuation of the preceding work. London, 1801.
7152. A TREATISE on political economy. . . . Baltimore, 1824.
7153. TREVELYAN, C. E. A report on the inland customs and town duties of the Bengal presidency. Calcutta, 1835. 1 v.
7154. TROTTER, Alexander. Observations on the financial position and credit of such of the states of the North American union as have contracted public debts. London, 1839.

Classical Period 441

7155. TROTTER, Coutts. The principles of currency and exchanges. . . . 2d edition. London, 1810.
7156. TUCKER, George. Progress of the United States in population and wealth in fifty years, as exhibited by the decennial census. New York, 1843. 1 v. (2d edition, 1855.)
7157. _____. Political economy for the people. Philadelphia, 1859. (Reprinted: New York, A. Kelley, 1970.)
7158. _____. The theory of money and banks investigated. Boston, 1839.
7159. TUCKER, H. Saint George. A review of the financial situation of the East India company in 1824. London, 1825. 1 v.
7160. TUCKER, Josiah. Four tracts on political and commercial subjects. 3d edition. London, 1776. 1 v.
7161. _____. Reflections on the present low price of coarse wools, its immediate causes, and its probable remedies. London, 1782.
7162. _____. Reflections on the present matters in dispute between Great Britain and Ireland, and on the means of converting these articles into mutual benefits to both kingdoms. London, 1785.
7163. TUCKETT, J. D. History of past and present state of labouring population. London, 1846.
7164. TUFNELL, Edward Carlton. Character, objects and effects of trades' unions; with some remarks on the laws concerning them. By "An anti." London, 1834.
7165. TURNER, Samuel. Considerations upon the agriculture of the British Empire. London, 1822.
7166. _____. A letter with reference to the expediency of the resumption of cash payments. London, 1819.
7167. TURTON, Thomas. An address to the good sense and candour of the people in behalf of the dealers in corn, with observations on a late trial for regrating. London, 1800.
7168. TWELVE reports from, with minutes taken before, the committees of the House of Lords and Commons in 1821, 1822, 1823, and 1824, on the foreign trade of the country. London, 1822, 1823, 1824.
7169. TWISS, T. On certain tests of a thriving population. Four lectures delivered before the University of Oxford, in Lent term, 1845. London, 1845.
7170. _____. View of the progress of political economy in Europe. London, 1847.
7171. TWO reports from the select committee of the House of commons, appointed in 1785 to inquire into the state of the British fisheries, on the Pilchard fisheries. London, 1786.
7172. TWO reports from, with the evidence taken before, the select committee of the House of commons, on the laws respecting friendly societies. London, 1825 and 1827.
7173. TYDEMANN, G. G. Disquisitio de oeconomie politique. Leyden, 1838.
7174. TYSON, J. R. The lottery system in the United States. 3d edition. Philadelphia, 1837.

7175. TYTLER, A. F. Considerations on the present political state of India. 2d edition. London, 1816. 2 v.
7176. _____. Henry Home of Kames. Edinburgh, 1807.
7177. UMPFENBACH, K. Lehrbuch der finanzwissenschaft. Stuttgart, 1859-60.
7178. The UNIVERSAL cambist and commercial instructor, being a full and accurate treatise on the exchanges, coins, weights and measures of all trading nations and their colonies; with an account of their banks, paper currencies. . . . By Patrick Kelly. 2d and best edition. London, 1831. 2 v.
7179. URE, Andrew. Cotton manufacture of Great Britain. London, 1836. 2 v. (French edition: Philosophie des manufactures, ou économie industrielle de la fabrication du coton, de la laine, du lin et de la soie, avec la description des diverses machines employées dans les ateliers anglais. Paris et Bruxelles, 1836. 2 v.)
7180. _____. A dictionary of arts, manufactures, and mines; containing a clear exposition of their principles and practice. London, 1839. (2d edition, London, 1843. 1 v.)
7181. VASCO, G. Delle università delle arti e mestieri. Milan 1793.
7182. VAUCHER, J. Guide to marine insurances, containing the policies of the principle commercial towns in the world; with remarks on the mutual relations between insured and insurers, and comparative tables. . . . London, 1834, 1 v.
7183. VAUGHAN, Robert. The age of great cities; or, Modern society viewed in relation to intelligence, morals, and religion. London, 1843. 1 v.
7184. VERNADSKY, Ivan. Historical compendium of political economy. Saint Petersburg, 1858.
7185. VERRI, Pietro. Riflessioni sulle leggi vincolanti, principalmente nel commercio de'grani. Milano, 1796. 1 v.
7186. VETHAKE, Henry. The principles of political economy. 2d edition. Philadelphia, 1844.
7187. VIDAL, François. De la répartition des richesses. Paris, 1846.
7188. VIEBAHN, G. V. Statistik des zollvereinten . . . Deutschlands. 3 thel. Berlin, 1858-68.
7189. A VIEW of the treaty of commerce with France, signed at Versailles, 20th September, 1786. 2d edition. London, 1787.
7190. VILLENEUVE-BARGEMONT, Alban de. Economie politique Chrétienne; ou, recherches sur la nature et les causes du pauperisme en France et en Europe. . . . Paris, 1834. 3 v.
7191. _____. Histoire de l'économie politique; ou études historiques, philosophiques et religieuses. . . . Paris, 1841. 2 v.
7192. VILLERME. Tableau de l'état physique et moral des ouvriers employés dans les manufactures de cotton, de laine et de soie. . . . Paris, Renouard, 1840. 2 v.
7193. VILLIAUME, N. Nouveau traité d'économie politique. 1857. 2 v.
7194. VINCENT, William. The commerce and navigation of the

ancients in the Indian Ocean. London, 1807. 2 v. (v. 1: 1797.)

7195. Le VISITEUR du Pauvre. Par M. Degerando. Ouvrage couronné en 1820 par l'Académie de Lyons, et, en 1821, par l'Académie Française. 4me édition, Paris, 1829. 1 v.

7196. VOLLGRAFF, Charles. Die systeme der praktischen politik im Abendlande. (Les systèmes de la politique pratique en occident.) Giessen, 1828. 4 v.

7197. ———. Ueber den heutigen begriff, anfang und gegenstand der staatswissenschaften. (Considérations sur l'état actuel de l'économie politique.) Marbourg, 1824.

7198. VOLTAIRE. Recueil des particularités curieuses de sa vie et de sa mort. Porrentruy, 1781.

7199. VOSS. Einleitung in die geschichte der litteratur der allgemeinen staatswissenschaft. Leipzig, 1800-02. 2 v.

7200. VOYAGE de M. le Baron Dupin dans la Grande Bretagne, en 1816, 1817, et 1819. (1re Part. Force militaire. Paris, 1821. 2 v. 2de Part. Force navale. Paris, 1821. 2 v. 3me Part. commerciale. Paris, 1824. 2 v.)

7201. VOYAGES a Peking, Manille, et l'Isle de France, faits dans l'intervalle des années 1784 et 1801. Par M. de Guignes. Paris, 1808. 3 v.

7202. VOYAGES d'un philosophe. Par Pierre Poivre. 3me édition. Paris, 1797. 1 v.

7203. WADE, John. History of the middle and working classes. 3d édition. London, 1834.

7204. WAGNER, Adolf. Lehre von den banken. Leipzig, 1857.

7205. ———. Russische papierswährung. Riga, 1868.

7206. ———. System der deutschen zette bankgesetzgebung. Freiburgh, 1870.

7207. WAKEFIELD, Daniel. A letter to Thomas Paine, in reply to his . . . English system of finance. London, 1796.

7208. WAKEFIELD, Edward Gibbon. An account of Ireland, statistical and political. London, 1812. 2 v.

7209. ———. England and America. A comparison of the social and political state of both nations. London, 1833. 2 v.

7210. ———. A view of the art of colonisation. London, 1849.

7211. WALES, William. An inquiry into the present state of population in England and Wales, and the proportion which the present number of inhabitants bears to the number at former periods. London, 1781.

7212. WALKER, Amasa. Nature and uses of money. Boston, 1857.

7213. ———. The science of wealth. Boston, 1866. (7e édition. Paris, 1876.)

7214. WALKER, Thomas. Observations on the nature, extent, and effects of pauperism, and on the means of reducing it. London, 1826.

7215. WALLACE, Thomas. An essay on the manufactures of Ireland. . . . Dublin, 1798. 1 v.

7216. WALRAS, Auguste. De la nature de la richesse et de l'origine de la valeur. Paris, 1831.
7217. _____. Théorie de la richesse sociale, ou résumé des principes fondamentaux de l'économie politique. Paris, 1849.
7218. WALSH, John. Poor-laws in Ireland considered in their probable effects upon the capital, the prosperity, and the progressive improvement of that country. London, 1830.
7219. WAPPAUS, J. E. Bevölkerungsstatistik. Leipzig, 1859-61.
7220. _____. Uber deutsche auswanderung und kolonisation. Leipzig, 1846-49.
7221. WARD, Robert. A treatise of the relative rights and duties of belligerent and neutral powers in maritime affairs. London, 1801.
7222. WARRE, James. The past, present, and probably the future state of the wine trade. . . . 2d edition. London, 1824.
7223. WATHELY, Richard. Archevêque de Dublin, introductory lectures on political economy. (Leçons d'économie politique.) Londres, 1832. 1 v.
7224. WATTEVILLE, A. de. Code de l'administration charitable. Paris, 1841. (2d édition, 1847.)
7225. _____. Essais sur les établissements de bienfaisance. 1846. (2d édition, 1849.)
7226. _____. Legislation charitable. Paris, 1843-46. 2 v.
7227. WAYLAND, Francis. The elements of political economy. New York, 1837. Edited by H. L. Chapin, New York, 1886.)
7228. WEBER, F. Ben. Systematisches handbuch der staatswirthschaft (Manuel systématique de l'économie politique). Berlin, 1804.
7229. _____. Traité d'économie. Berlin. 2 v.
7230. WEBER, G. Lehrbuch der weltgeschichte. 2 bde. Leipzig, 1888.
7231. WEBSTER, Pelatiah. Political essays on the nature and operation of money. Philadelphia, 1791.
7232. WELFORD, C. G. How will free trade in corn affect the farmer? Being an examination of the effects of corn laws upon British agriculture. London, 1843.
7233. WELZ, Giuseppe de. Magia del credito svelata, instituzione fondamentale di publica utilità. Napoli, 1824. 2 v.
7234. WESKETT, F. A complete digest of the theory, law, and practice of insurance. London, 1781. 1 v.
7235. WEST, Edward. Essay on the application of capital to land. London, 1815.
7236. _____. Prices of corn and wages of labour, with observations. . . . London, 1826.
7237. WEUVES M., Le Jeune. Réflexions . . . sur le commerce de France avec ses colonies de l'Amérique. Genève, 1780.
7238. WEYLAND, John J. The principles of population and production. London, 1816.
7239. WHATELY, Richard. Easy lessons on money matters. . . . 4th edition. London, 1837.

Classical Period 445

7240. _____. Introductory lectures on political economy. London, 1831. (3d edition revised and enlarged. 1847; 4th edition, 1855.)
7241. WHEATLEY, John. An essay on the theory of money and principles of commerce. London, 1807-22. 2 v.
7242. _____. Remarks on currency and commerce. London, 1803.
7243. WHEWELL, William. History of the inductive sciences. London, 1837. 3 v.
7244. _____. Six lectures on political economy. Cambridge, 1862.
7245. WHITE, George S. Memoir of Samuel Slater. . . . Philadelphia, 1836.
7246. WHITMORE, W. W. A letter to the agriculturists of the County of Salop on the present state and future prospects of agriculture. London, 1822.
7247. WILBERFORCE, William. A letter on the abolition of the slave trade, addressed to the freeholders and other inhabitants of Yorkshire. London, 1807. 1 v.
7248. WILDA, W. E. Das gildenwesen im mittelalter. Berlin, 1831.
7249. WILLAN, Robert. Reports on the diseases in London, particularly during the years 1796, 1797, 1798, 1799, and 1800. London, 1801. 1 v.
7250. WILLIAMS, Charles Wye. Considerations on the alarming increase of forgery on the Bank of England. London, 1818.
7251. WILSON, James. Capital, currency, and banking. London, 1847. (2d edition. London, 1859.)
7252. _____. Fluctuations of currency, commerce, and manufactures, referable to corn laws. London, 1840.
7253. _____. Influences of the corn laws, as affecting all classes of the community, and particularly the landed interests. London, 1839. (2d edition. London, 1840.)
7254. WILSON, Jasper. A letter commercial and political addressed to the Right honourable William Pitt. London, 1793.
7255. WOLOWSKI, L. F. La banque d'Angleterre et les banques d'écosse. Paris, 1867. (Berlin, 1870.)
7256. _____. La change et la circulation. Paris, 1867.
7257. _____. Etudes d'économie politique et de statistique. Paris, 1848.
7258. _____. Les finances de la Russie. Paris, 1864.
7259. _____. L'or et l'argent. Paris, 1870.
7260. _____. Question monétaire. 2d édition. Paris, 1869.
7261. WOOD, J. Some account of the Shrewsbury house of industry. Shrewsbury, 1791.
7262. WOOD, Nicholas. A treatise on railroads. 3d edition. London, 1839. 1 v.
7263. WOOD, Stuart and J. B. Clark. Contributions to the wages question. Baltimore, 1839.
7264. WOODS, George. Observations on the present price of bullion. . . . London, 1811.

7265. A WOOLEN draper's letter on the French treaty. London, 1786.
7266. WOOLRYCH, H. W. A practical treatise on the commercial and mercantile law of England. London, 1829. 1 v.
7267. WORDWORTH, C. F. F. The law of joint stock companies; containing chapters on banking, railway, canal, mining, insurance, and other companies. . . . 3d edition. London, 1842. 1 v.
7268. WYATT, J. Observations on the question of the corn laws. London, 1826.
7269. YOUNG, Arthur. Annals of agriculture and other useful arts. Bury Saint Edmunds, 1784. 45 v.
7270. ———. An inquiry into the rise of prices in Europe, during the last twenty-five years, compared with that which has taken place in England; with observations on the effects of high and low prices. London, 1815.
7271. ———. The question of scarcity plainly stated, and remedies considered; with observations on permanent measures to keep wheat at a more regular price. London, 1800.
7272. YOUNG, Gavin. A further inquiry into the expediency of applying the principles of colonial policy to the government of India. . . . London, 1827. 1 v.
7273. YOUNG, William. The West India commonplace book, compiled from parliamentary and official documents; showing the interest of Great Britain in the sugar colonies. . . . London, 1807. 1 v.
7274. ZACHARLE, K. G. Staats-wirthschaftslehr principes d'économie politique. Heidelberg, 1832. 2 v.

J. CLASSICAL PERIOD

Section II. Specific Works

SMITHIAN ECONOMICS

7275. ADAM Smith. Translated by Johann Kaspar Schmidt. (Textbucher zu studien uber wirtschaft und staat. Hrsg. von prof. dr. J. Jastrow, Bd. 3.) Berlin, G. Reimer, 1913. viii, 185, 2 p.
7276. ADAM Smith, 1776-1926. Lectures to commemorate the sesquicentennial of the publication of "The Wealth of nations." Edited by J. M. Clark. Chicago, University of Chicago press, 1928.
7277. ADAM Smith's moral and political philosophy. Edited with an introduction by Herbert W. Schneider. (The Hafner library of classics, no. 8.) New York, Hafner publishing company, 1948. xxviii, 484 p.
7278. BAGEHOT, Walter. "Adam Smith as a person." In, Fortnightly review (new series) 115 (July, 1876) 18-42.
7279. BAGOLINI, Luigi. La simpatia nella morale e nel diritto; aspetti del pensiero di Adam Smith. Bologna, C. Zuffi, 1952. 119 p.
7280. BARTH, Hans. "Uber die idee der selbstentfremdung des menschen bei Rousseau." In, Zeitschrift für philosophische forschung, 13 (1959) 16-35.
7281. BITTERMANN, H. J. "Adam Smith's empiricism and the law of nature. In, Journal of political economy, 48 (August-October, 1940) 487-520.
7282. BLADEN, V. W. "Adam Smith on value." In, H. A. Innis, editor, Essays in political economy in honour of E. J. Urwick. Toronto, University of Toronto press, 1938.
7283. BONAR, James. "Adam Smith's library." In, Economic journal, XLVI (March, 1936.)
7284. ———. A catalogue of the library of Adam Smith, author of the 'Moral sentiments' and 'The wealth of nations.' Edited with an introduction by James Bonar . . . London and New York, Macmillan and company, 1894. xxx, 126 p. (2nd edition. Prepared for the Royal economic society by James Bonar, with an introduction and appendices. London, Macmillan, 1932. xxxiv, 218 p.)
7285. BRUNNSCHWEILER von Hauptwil, Arnold. Die beziehung zwischen der individualität bzw. Individualspäre und der sozialwissenschaft im allgemeinen und im besonderen bei Adam Smith und Karl Marx. Lünen in Westfalen, 1949. 137 p.

7286. BULLOCK, Charles J. The Vanderblue memorial collection of Smithiana. (Kress library of business and economics, Publication no. 2.) Boston, Harvard business school, Baker Library, 1939. (Supplement, In, Harvard business school alumni bulletin (Spring, 1949) 2-4.)
7287. CLIFFORD, James L., editor. Man versus society in eighteenth-century Britain. New York, Cambridge university press, 1968.
7288. CROPSEY, Joseph. Polity and economy. An interpretation of the principles of Adam Smith. (University microfilms, Publication no. 3879, Microfilm AC-1, 3879.) Ann Arbor, Michigan, University microfilms, 1952. (International scholars forum; a series of books by American scholars, 8. The Hague, M. Nijhoff, 1957. xii, 101 p.)
7289. ———, and Leo Strauss. "Adam Smith." In, History of political philosophy. Skokie, Illinois, Rand McNally & Co., 1963. 549-572 p.
7290. DAICHES, David. The paradox of Scottish culture; the eighteenth-century experience. London, Oxford university press, 1964.
7291. DANKERT, Clyde E., editor. Thoughts from Adam Smith. Compiled, with introduction and comments by Clyde E. Dankert. Hanover, New Hampshire, 1963. 30 p.
7292. FAY, Charles Ryle. Adam Smith and the Scotland of his day. (Publications of the Department of social and economic research, University of Glasgow. Social and economic studies, 3.) London, Cambridge university press, 1956. 173 p.
7293. ———. The world of Adam Smith. Cambridge, England, W. Heffer, 1960. 97 p.
7294. FRANKLIN, Burt and Francesco Cordasco. Adam Smith. A bibliographical checklist. An international record of critical writings and scholarship relating to Smith and Smithian theory, 1876-1950. (Burt Franklin bibliographical series, 3.) New York, B. Franklin, 1950. 63 p.
7295. FULTON, Robert Brank. Adam Smith speaks to our times. A study of his ethical ideas. Boston, Christopher publishing house, 1963. 143 p.
7296. GARNIER, J. "De l'origine et de la filiation du mot 'Economie politique.'" In, Journal des economistes, 32 (1852); 33 (1852) 11-23.
7297. GINZBERG, Eli. The house of Adam Smith. New York, Columbia university press, 1934. viii p., 2 l., 3-265 p., 2 l. Bibliography, 245-265. (Issued also as thesis (Ph.D.) Columbia university. Reprinted: New York, Octagon books, 1964. xvi, 265 p.)
7298. GONZALES Alberde, Paulino, editor. Los economistas, Adam Smith e David Ricardo. Seleccion. Buenos Aires, Editorial futuro, 1947.
7299. GRAHAM, Malcolm Kintner. The synthetic wealth of nations. An inquiry into the nature and causes of the wealth of nations, as condensed and extended by M. K. Graham. Nashville, Tennessee, The Parthenon press, 1937. 319 p.

Classical Period 449

7300. HALDANE, R. B. Life of Adam Smith. London, Walter Scott, 1887. 141 p.
7301. HALEVY, Elie. The growth of philosophic radicalism. Translated by Mary Morris. London, Faber and Faber, limited, 1928.
7302. HAMILTON, David. Newtonian classicism and Darwinian institutionalism, a study of change in economic theory. Albuquerque, New Mexico, University of New Mexico press, 1953.
7303. HASBACH, Wilhelm. Die allgemeinen philosophischen grundlagen der von François Quesnay und Adam Smith begründeten politischen ökonomie. Berlin, Duncker und Humblot, 1890.
7304. _____. Untersuchunger über Adam Smith und die entwicklung der politischen oekonomie. Berlin, Duncker und Humblot, 1891.
7305. HASEK, C. W. The introduction of Adam Smith's doctrines into Germany. New York, Columbia university press, 1925.
7306. HAYEK, Friedrich A. Individualism and economic order. London, Routledge and Kegan Paul limited, 1949.
7307. _____. Dr. Bernard Mandeville; lecture on a master mind. (British Academy.) London, Oxford university press, 1966.
7308. HIRST, F. W. Adam Smith. London, Macmillan and company, 1904.
7309. HUME, David. Essays; moral, political, and literary. New York, Oxford university press, 1963.
7310. JOYCE, J. A complete analysis of Adam Smith. London, 1797.
7311. KEYNES, J. M. "Adam Smith as student and professor." In, Economic history 3 (February, 1938) 33-46.
7312. _____, and P. Sraffa. "Introduction." In, An abstract of a treatise of human nature. 1740. England, Cambridge university press, 1938.
7313. KING, J. E. "Origin of the term 'Political economy.'" In, Journal of modern history, 20 (1948) 230-231.
7314. KOEBNER, R. "Adam Smith and the industrial revolution." In, Economic history review, 2, 11 (April, 1959) 381-391.
7315. MACGREGOR, D. H. "The laissez-faire doctrine." In, D. H. Macgregor, Economic thought and policy. London, Oxford university press, 1949. Chapter 3.
7316. MANDEVILLE, Bernard. Fable of the bees. Edited by F. B. Kaye. London, Oxford University press, 1924 2 v.
7317. MCCULLOCH, J. R. Sketch of the life and writings of Adam Smith. Edinburgh, 1855. 45 p.
7318. MILL, John Stuart. The collected works. Edited by J. I. P. Robson. Toronto, University of Toronto press, 1963.
7319. MORROW, G. R. Ethical and economic theories of Adam Smith. Ithaca, New York, Cornell university library, 1923. London, Longman, Green, 1923.

7320. NAPIER, Macvey. "The opinions of the late Mr. Ricardo and of Adam Smith on some of the leading doctrines of political economy; stated and compared." In, The pamphleteer, 23 (1824) 518-26.
7321. ONCKEN, August. Die maxime "Laissez-faire, laissez-passer," ihr ursprung, ihr werden. Bern, K. J. Wyss, 1886.
7322. RAE, John. Life of Adam Smith. London, Macmillan and company, 1895. xv, 449 p.
7323. RANDALL, John H. The career of philosophy; from the Middle Ages to the Enlightenment. New York, Columbia university press, 1962.
7324. ROBBINS, Lionel. The theory of economic policy in English classical political economy. New York, Saint Martin's press, incorporated, 1952.
7325. ROBERTSON, Hector Menteith. The Adam Smith tradition. Inaugural lecture delivered before the University of Cape Town on 13 October 1950. (University of Cape Town lecture series, no. 2.) Cape Town, New York, Oxford university press, 1950. 23 p.
7326. _____, and W. L. Taylor. "Adam Smith's approach to the theory of value." In, Economic journal, 67 (June, 1957), 181-198.
7327. SAY, Jean-Baptiste. Jean-Baptiste Say, texts choisis et préface par Pierre-Louis Reynaud. (Collection des grandes économistes.) Paris, Dalloz, 1953. 362 p.
7328. SCHATZ, Albert. L'Individualisme économique et social. Paris, Librairie Armand Colin, 1907.
7329. _____. L'Oeuvre économique de David Hume. Paris, Arthur Rousseau, 1902.
7330. SCHNEIDER, Louis, editor. The Scottish moralists on human nature and society. Chicago, University of Chicago press, 1968.
7331. SCOTT, William Robert. Adam Smith as student and professor. (Glasgow university publications, no. XLVI.) Glasgow, Jackson, Son and company, 1937.
7332. _____. Studies relating to Adam Smith during the last fifty years. Edited by A. L. Macfie. London, Humphrey Milford, 1962. (British academy, Proceedings, XXVI.)
7333. SMALL, Albion W. Adam Smith and modern sociology. Chicago, University of Chicago press, 1907.
7334. SMELLIE, William. "Life of Adam Smith." In, Literary and characteristical lives. . . . Edinburgh, 1800. ix, 450 p.
7335. SMITH, Adam. Essay on colonies. With an introduction by Arthur T. Hadley. (Universal classics library.) Autograph edition de luxe. Washington, London, M. W. Dunne, 1901. vi, 99 p. (Forms the chapter "Of colonies," book IV, chapter VII of the author's "An inquiry into the nature and causes of the wealth of nations.) (. . . With Sir George C. Lewis. Government of dependencies . . . Washington, London, 1901.) (French edition: Fragment sur les colonies en general, et sur celles des Anglois en particulies. Tr. de l'anglois by Elle Salomon Francois

Reverdil. A. Lausanne, Chez la societe typographique, 1778. viii, 170 p.)
7336. _____. Essays on philosophical subjects ... London, 1795. 244 p. (Dublin, 1795. 332 p.)
7337. _____. An inquiry into the nature and causes of the wealth of nations. London, 1776. 2 v. (510; 587 p.) [English edition: 2d ed. London, Printed for W. Strahan; and T. Cadell, 1778. 2 v. (510; 589 p.) English edition: 3d ed., with additions ... London, W. Strahan and T. Cadell, 1784. 3 v. American edition: Printed for T. Dobson, New edition. Philadelphia, 1789. 3 v. English edition: 5th edition. London, A. Strahan and T. Cadell, 1789. 3 v. Swiss edition: Basil, 1791. 4 v. English edition: 7th edition. London, A. Strahan and T. Cadwell, 1793. 3 v. German edition: Translated by Christian Garve. Aus dem englischen der vierten ausgabe neu ubersezt Frankfurt und Leipzig, 1796-99. 4 v. English edition: 9th edition. London, Printed for A. Strahan, and T. Cadell jun. and W. Davies, 1799. 3 v. French edition: Edited by Germain Garnier. Paris, 1802. 5 v. English edition: A new edition, with additions. In two volumes ... Hartford, Printed for Oliver D. Cooke; Lincoln & Gleason printers, 1804. 2 v. English edition: New edition. Glasgow, 1805. 3 v. Edition. With a life of the author. Also, a view of the doctrine of Smith ... from the French of G. Garnier ... London, J. Maynard, 1811. 3 v. English edition: From the 11th London edition; with notes, supplementary chapters, and a life of Dr. Smith by William Playfair. Hartford, O. D. Cooke, 1811. 2 v. English edition: With notes and an additional volume: Observations on the subjects treated of in Dr. Smith's inquiry. By David Buchanan. Edinburgh, 1814. 3 v. English edition: 2nd edition. Edinburgh, 1817. 4 v. English edition. From the 11th London edition, with notes and supplementary chapters, by William Playfair. And an account of Dr. Smith's life, by Dugald Stewart ... In two volumes ... Hartford, Published by Cooke & Hale, 1818. 2 v. English edition: A complete analysis, or abridgement. ... By Jeremiah Joyce ... 2d edition. London, Law and Whittaker, 1818. 324 p. English edition: 2nd edition. Edited by Germain Garnier. Paris, 1822. 6 v. Edition. London, Printed by J. F. Dove, 1826. viii, 9-933 p. English edition: With life of the author ... By J. R. McCulloch. Edinburgh, 1828. 4 v. English edition. With a commentary by Edward Gibbon Wakefield, author of England and America. London, C. Knight, 1835-39. 4 v. English edition. With a life of the author. Also a view of the doctrine of Smith compared with that of the French economists; with a method of facilitating the study of his works; from the French of Germain Garnier ... Edinburgh, P. Brown, 1838. iv, xxx, 404, 25 p. English Edition: With notes from Ricardo, M'Culloch, Chalmers and other eminent political economists. Edited by Edward

Gibbon Wakefield, esq. With life of the author by Dugald Stewart. A new edition . . . London, C. Knight & co., 1843. 4 v. French edition: Traduction du comte Germain Garnier, entierement rev. et cor. et precedee d'une notice biographique par Jerome A. Blanqui . . . avec les commentaires de Buchanan, G. Garnier, MacCulloch, Malthus, J. Mill, Ricardo, Sismondi; augm. de notes inedites de Jean-Baptiste Say, et d'eclaircassements historiques par J. A. Blanqui. Paris, Guillaumin, 1843. 2 v. English edition: With a life of the author, an introductory discourse, notes, and supplemental dissertations. By J. R. M'Culloch, esq. A new ed., cor. throughout and greatly enl. Edinburgh, A. & C. Black, and W. Tait; etc., 1845. 4 p. 1., lxiii, 648 p. English edition: With a life of the author, an introductory discourse, notes and supplemental dissertations. By J. R. M'Culloch, esq. A new edition, cor., throughout and greatly enl. Edinburgh, A. & C. Black, and W. Tait; 1846. 4 p. 1., lxiii, 648 p. French edition: Traduction de Germain Garnier, rev., cor. et precedee d'une notice biographique par A. Blanqui, avec des notes de Buchanan, G. Garnier, MacCulloch, Ricardo, Sismondi, Bentham, Storch, Malthus, Turgot, J. Mill, Dufresne Saint-Leon, A. Blanqui, J. B. Say, Nouv. ed., rev. et augm. de notes explicatives par m. Joseph Garnier . . . Bibliotheque des sciences morales et politiques. Paris, Guillaumin et c^{ie}, 1859. 3 v. English edition: With a life of the author, an introductory discourse, notes, and supplemental dissertations by J. R. McCulloch. New edition, revised, cor., and improved. Edinburgh, A. and C. Black, 1863. 5 p. 1., lxvi, 669 p. (Edition appeared in 1828 in four volumes octavo; a new edition appeared in 1838; edition of 1863 "has been adopted to present conditions." preface.) English edition: With a life of the author. Also a view of the doctrine of Smith, compared with that of the French economists: with a method of facilitating the study of his works; from the French of G. Garnier. London, New York, T. Nelson and sons, 1865. iv, xxx, 429 p. Russian edition: Izsliedovaniia o prirodie i prichinakh bogatstva narodov. (Transliterated.) Translated from the French edition (edited by Jerome Adolphe Blanqui and Joseph Garnier) by Petr Aleksieevich Bibikov. 1866. 3 v. English edition: Edited by James E. Thorold Rogers. Oxford, 1869. 2 v. English edition: A careful reprint of edition (3 volumes) 1812. With notes by J. R. McCulloch. London, Ward, Lock & co., limited, 187-. 831 p. American edition: New York, R. Worthington, 1878. 2 p. 1., xvi, 780 p. German edition: Deutsch von Franz Stopel. (Bibliothek der volkswirthschaftslehre und gesellschaftswissenschaft, hreg. von F. Stopel, III-IV.) Berlin, Expedition des Merkur, 1878. 4 v. in 2. English edition: Edited by James Edwin Thorold Rogers . . . 2d edition. Oxford, Clarendon press, 1880. 2 v. English edition: Reprinted from the 6th edition, with an introduction by Ernest Belfort Bax . . . (Bohn's standard library.) London, G. Bell and sons, 1887. 2 v. English and American edition: Select chapters and passages . . . (Economic classes, edited by W. J. Ashley.) New York, London, Macmillan and company, 1894. xii, 285 p. Russian edition: Translated by Mitroian Pavlovich Shehepkin. Moscow, 1895. 288 p. 1 1. English and American edition: Reprinted from the 6th edition with an introduction by Ernest Belfort Bax . . . (Bohn's standard library.) London and New York, G. Bell & sons, 1896. 2 v. English edition: Reprinted from 6th edition, with an introduction by Ernest Belfort Bax . . . (Bohn's standard library.) London, G. Bell and sons, 1901. 2 v. English edition: With an introduction, notes, marginal summary and an enlarged index, by Edwin Cannan. (Text from fifth edition.) London, Methuen & co., 1904. 2 v. American edition: A new and condensed edition; with preface and introduction by Hector Macpherson . . . New York, T. Y. Crowell and company, 1904. xxvii, 232 p. American edition: Edited by Charles Jesse Bullock . . . With introduction, notes and illustrations. (Harvard classics, edited by C. W. Eliot; vol. X) New York, P. F. Collier & son, 1909. 1 p. 1., 590 p., 1 1. English and American edition: Introduction by Edwin R. A. Seligman (Everyman's library; edited by Ernest Rhys. Science, no. 412-413.) London, J. M. Dent & sons, ltd.; New York, E. P. Dutton & co., 1910. 2 v. Bibliography, v. 1, xvi. German edition: Translated from the English volume edited by E. Cannon, 1904. Translated and edited by Max Stirner and Heinrich Schmidt. Leipzig, A. Kroner, 1910. English edition: With an introduction by Edwin R. A. Seligman. London, 1911. 2 v. English and American edition: London, G. Routledge & sons, ltd.; New York, E. P. Dutton and company, 1913? 2 p. 1., xvi, 780 p. English edition: Reprinted from the sixth edition, with an introduction by William Robert Scott. (Bohn's standard library.) London, G. Bell and sons, ltd., 1921. 2 v. German edition: Unter zugrundelegung der ubersetzung Max Stirners, aus dem englischen original nach der ausgabeletster Hand (4. Aufl. 1786) ins Deutsche ubertragen von Ernst Grunfeld und eingeleitet von Heinrich Waentig. (Sammiung sozialwissenschaftlicher meister, bd. 11-12.) Jena, G. Fischer, 1923. 3 v. (v. 1: 3. ed.; v. 2: 2. ed.) English edition: Edited by Edwin Cannan. London, Methuen and company, 1930. 2 v. English and American edition: Introduction by Edwin R. A. Seligman (Everyman's library; edited by Ernest Rhys. Science, no. 412-413.) London, J. M. Dent & sons, ltd.; New York, E. P. Dutton & co., inc., 1933-34. 2 v. German edition: Deutsch und mit kommentar von Friedrich Bulow; mit bildnis und faksimile des titels der urausgabe. (Kroners taschenausgabe, Bd. 103.) Leipzig, A. Kroner, 1933. xxxviii p. 1., 348 p.

Russian edition: Issledovanie o prirode i prichinakh bogatstva narodov. (Transliterated.) Moscow, 1935. 2 v. (Translated from the 4th edition.) American edition: Edited, with an introduction, notes, marginal summary and an enlarged index, by Edwin Cannan. With an introduction by Max Lerner . . . New York, The modern library, 1937. ix, 976 p. Bibliography, 971-976. (Text from 5th edition, or last prior to A. Smith's death.) Italian edition: Ricerche sopra la natura. . . . Traduzione di Alberto Campolongo. Introd. di Augusto Graziani. (Sociologi ed economisti, 1.) Torino, Unione tip.-editrice turinese, 1948. xxxii, 885 p. American edition: Simplified, shortened and modernized, by Arthur Hugh Jenkins. New York, R. R. Smith, 1948. 480 p. English edition: Edited by Edwin Cannan, 1904. London, Methune, 1950. 2 v. French edition: Adam Smith. Textes choisis et pref. par G. H. Bousquet. (Collection des grands economistes.) Paris, Dalloz, 1950. 303 p. (Abridgment.) Bibliography, 4-5. American edition: Selections. Introduction by Ludwig von Mises. (A gateway edition.) Chicago, H. Regnery company, 1953. xii, 139 p. American edition: (Great books of the Western world, v. 39.) Chicago, Encyclopaedia Britannica, 1955. c1952. viii, 468 p. Bibliographical footnotes. Spanish edition: Investigacion de la naturaleza. . . . Traducion del ingles y prologo por Amando Lazaro Ros. (Biblioteca de ciencias sociales. Seccion primera: economia.) Madrid, Aguilar, 1955. xvi, 847 p. Korean edition: Translated and edited by Min-gi Ch'oe. Kukpuron kwa hyondae kyongjehak. (Transliterated.) Korea, 1966. 325 p. American edition: With an introduction by M. Blaug. (Irwin paperback classic in economics.) Homewood, Illinois, R. D. Irwin, 1963. 2 v. Edited by Edwin Cannan. With an introduction written especially for this heirloom edition by John Chamberlain. (Classics of conservatism.) New Rochelle, New York, Arlington house, 1966. 2 v. New York, A. M. Kelley, 1966. 2 v. French edition reprint: Nature de la richesse. Réimpression de l'édition 1843. (Collection des principaux économistes, t. 5-6.) Osnabrück, Zeller, 1966. 2 v.]

7338. _____. Lectures on justice, police, revenue and arms, delivered in the University of Glasgow by Adam Smith. Reported by a student in 1763, and edited with an introduction and notes by Edwin Cannan. Oxford, England, xxxix, 1 p. 1 l., 293, 1 p.

7339. _____. Lectures on rhetoric and belles lettres. Edited by John M. Lothian. London, Thomas Nelson and sons, ltd., 1963.

7340. _____. Some practical remarks on the effect of the usury laws on the landed interests, in a letter to John Calcraft, esq. M.P. London, J. Ridgway, 1826.

7341. _____. Die theorie des Aussenhandels. Inquiry into the nature and causes of the wealth of nations. B. IV. Ch.

         1-3, 1776. Hrsg. von August Skalweit. (Sozialokono-
         mische texte, heft 1.) Translated by Max Stirner e Johann
         Kaspar Schmidt. Frankfurt-am-Main, V. Klostermann,
         1946. 79 p.
7342.   _____. Theorie der ethischen gefuhle; oder, versuch einer
         analyse der prinzipien, mittels welcher die menschen
         naturgemass zunachst der verhalten und den charakter ih-
         rer nachsten und sodann auch ihr eigenes verhalten und
         ihren eigenen charakter beurteilen; nach der auflage
         letzter hand ubersetzt und mit einleitung, anmerkungen
         und registern hrsg. von dr. Walter Eckstein . . . (Der
         philosophischen bibliotbek bd. 200.) Leipzig, F. Meiner,
         1926. 2 v. Bibliographie, lxxii-lxxviii.
7343.   _____. The theory of moral sentiments. London, A.
         Millar, 1759. 551 p. (English edition: 2d edition. London,
         1761. 436 p. English edition: 3d edition. London,
         Printed for A. Millar, A. Kincaid and J. Bell in Edin-
         burgh: and sold by T. Cadell, 1767. 4 p. 1., 478 p.
         English edition: 6th edition. London, 1790, 2 v. (488;
         462 p.) English edition: The theory of moral sentiments;
         or, An essay towards an analysis of the principles by
         which men naturally judge concerning the conduct and
         character, first of their neighbours, and afterwards of
         themselves. To which is added, a dissertation on the ori-
         gin of languages. By Adam Smith . . . The 7th edition
         . . . London, A. Strahan, T. Cadell, etc. MDCCXCII.
         2 v. English edition: 12th edition. Enriched with a
         portrait and life of the author. Glasgow, R. Chapman,
         1809. 1 p. 1., 5-15, xxviii, 29-494 p. English edition:
         11th edition? London, Printed for Longman, Hurst, Rees,
         Orme, & Brown; 1812. xv, 611 p. American edition:
         From the last English edition . . . Boston, Wells and
         Lilly, 1817. 2 v. in 1. English edition: London, 1822.
         2 v. English edition: Edinburgh, John D. Lowe, 1849.
         English edition: New edition, with a biographical and
         critical memoir of the author, by Dugald Stewart.
         (Bohn's standard library.) London, H. G. Bohn, 1853.
         lxix, 538 p. English edition: New edition. With a bio-
         graphical and critical memoir of the author, by Dugald
         Stewart. (Bohn's standard library.) London, G. Bell &
         sons, 1887. lxix, 538 p. English and American edition:
         New edition. With a biographical and critical memoir of
         the author, by Dugald Stewart. (Bohn's standard library)
         London and New York, G. Bell & sons, 1892. lxix, 533 p.)
7344.   _____. Vorlesungen uber rechts-, polizei-, steuer- u.
         heereswesen gehalten in der Universitat Glasgow von Adam
         Smith, nachgeschrieben von einem studenten im jahre
         1763; nach der ausgabe von Edwin Cannan ins deutsche
         ubertragen von S. Blach, mit einem geleitwort von prof.
         dr. J. Jastrow. (Alte meister der sozialwissenschaften
         . . . bd. 1.) Halberstadt, H. Meyer, 1928. IX, 199 p.
7345.   _____. The whole works of Adam Smith . . . A new edi-
         tion, with a life of the author. London, J. Richardson,
         1822. 5 v.

7346. SMITH, R. S. "The wealth of nations in Spain and Hispanic America, 1780-1830." In, Journal of political economy, 65 (April, 1957) 104-125.
7347. SPENGLER, Joseph J. "Adam Smith's theory of economic growth." In, Southern economic journal, 25 (April, 1959) 397-415.
7348. STAPPERSHOEF, H. van. Het apriorisme der economisten, Adam Smith, E. de Condillac en Othmar Spann. s'Gravenhage, W. P. van Stockum, 1950. 17 p.
7349. STEWART, Dugald. Biographical memoirs of Adam Smith, of William Robertson, and of Thomas Reid. Edinburgh, 1811. 532 p.
7350. TAYLOR, W. L. "Eighteenth-century Scottish political economy. . . . " In, South African journal of economics, 24 (1956) 261-276.
7351. TREUE, Wilhelm. "Adam Smith in Deutschland." In, Werner Conze, Deutschland und Europa; festschrift fur Hans Rothfels. Dusseldorf. Droste verlag, 1951.
7352. VANDERBLUE, Homer B. Adam Smith and the Wealth of nations. Boston, 1936. 14 p.
7353. VINER, Jacob. "Adam Smith and laissez-faire." In, Journal of political economy, 35 (April, 1927). Also in, Adam Smith, 1776-1926. Lectures. . . . Chicago, University press, 1928.
7354. _____. Guide to John Rae's life of Adam Smith. New York, Augustus M. Kelley, 1965. 36 p.
7355. _____. The long view and the short. New York, The Free press, 1958. (Includes, Jacob Viner, "Introduction." In, Bernard Mandeville. A Letter to Dion. 1953.)
7356. WEST, E. G. "Adam Smith's two views on the division of labour." In, Economica (London) 44, 121 (February, 1964) 23-32.
7357. YANAIHARA, T. A full and detailed catalogue of books which belonged to Adam Smith. Tokyo, Iwanami shoten, 1951.
7358. ZARRIN, Pavel Ivanovich. (Adam Smith and David Ricardo.) Moscow, 1958. 140 p.

K. POST-CLASSICAL PERIOD

Section I. General Works

7359. ABOUT, E. Handbook of social economy. New York, 1873.
7360. _____. The Railways and the traders. 2d. ed. London, 1891.
7361. ACWORTH, W. M. The railways of England. 2d. ed. London, 1890.
7362. _____. The Railways of Scotland. London, 1890.
7363. ADAMS, Charles Francis Jr. Notes on railroad accidents. New York, 1886.
7364. _____. Railroad and railroad questions. New York, 1878.
7365. _____. Railroads: their origin and problems. New York, 1893. 230 p. (Revised ed. New York, 1886.)
7366. ADAMS, C. K. A Manual of historical literature, 3d ed. New York, 1889.
7367. ADAMS, Henry Carter. The Essence of finance. New York, 1898. pp. xiii, 573.
7368. _____. Outline of lectures upon political economy. Baltimore, 1881. 76 p.
7369. _____. Public debts. New York, 1892. pp. xi, 399. (2d ed., 1890.)
7370. _____. Relation of the state to industrial action. Baltimore, 1897. 85 p.
7371. _____. Taxation in the United States, 1789-1816. Baltimore, 1884. 79 p. (2d ed. Ann Arbor, 1886.)
7372. ADLER, G. Rodbertus der Begründer des . . . Sozialismus. Leipzig, 1883.
7373. AGUILLON, L. Legislation des mines francaise et étrangère. Paris, 1886. 3 v.
7374. ALBERTI, G. Le corporazioni d'arti e mestieri e la libertà del commercio interno. Milano, 1888.
7375. ALDRICH, N. W. Retail prices and wages. Washington, 1892. (Senate Report no. 986, 52 C. 1S.)
7376. _____. Wholesale prices, wages, and transportation. 3 v. (Senate Report no. 1394, 52 C. 2 S.) Washington, 1893.
7377. ALESSIO, G. Saggio sul sistema tributario in Italia. Torino, 1883, 1887. 2 v.
7378. ALLEN, W. F. Monographs and essays. Boston, 1890.
7379. ALLOCHIO, S. Il Credito fondiario in Italia. Milano, 1880.
7380. ALPHAND, A. Les Promenades de Paris. Paris, 1867-72.
7381. AME, Leon. Etude sur les tarifs de douanes, et sur les traités de commerce. Paris. 1876. 2 v.

7382. ANDREWS, C. M. The old English manor. Baltimore, 1892.
7383. ANDREWS, Elisha Benjamin. An honest dollar. Hartford, 1894. 183 p.
7384. _____. Institutes of Economics. Boston, 1889. (1892, 227 p.)
7385. ANDRIMONT, L. d'. Coopération ouvrière en Belgique. Bruxelles, 1876.
7386. ANSELL, G. F. The royal mint. 3d ed. London, 1871.
7387. ARAGO, E. Les conditions du travail en Suisse. Paris, 1890.
7388. ARCHBOLD, J. F. The Poor law. 13th ed. Edited by W. C. Glen. London, 1878.
7389. ARENDT, O. Die vertragsmäsige Doppelwährung. 2 v. Berlin, 1880.
7390. ARLIDGE, J. L. The hygiene, diseases, and mortality of occupation. London, 1892.
7391. ARNAUNE, A. La Monnaie, le crédit, et le change. Paris, 1894.
7392. ARNBERG, J. W. Anteckningar om Frihetstidens politiska ekonomi. Upsala, 1868.
7393. ARNOLD, Arthur. Free land. London, 1880.
7394. ARNOLD, W. T. Roman system of provincial government. London, 1879.
7395. ASCHROTT, P. F. Das englische armenwesen. Leipzig, 1885. (Translated by H. P. Thomas. London, 1888.)
7396. ASHLEY, W. J. The Early history of the English woollen industry. Philadelphia, 1887.
7397. _____. The Economic organization of England. London, 1914. 213 p.
7398. _____. An introduction to English economic history and theory. London and New York, 1892-93. (New York, 1894. 227 p. Part II: The End of the middle ages. 3d ed. New York, 1898. 501 p.)
7399. ASHWORTH, H. Recollections of Richard Cobden. New ed. London, 1879.
7400. ATKINSON, Edward. The Distribution of products. New York, 1885.
7401. _____. The industrial progress of the nation. New York, 1890.
7402. _____. The Margin of profits. New York, 1887.
7403. _____. Report . . . upon the present state of bimetalism. Washington, 1887.
7404. AUCOC, L. La question des propriétés primitives. Paris, 1885.
7405. _____. Tarifs des chemins de fer et l'autorité de l'état. Paris, 1880.
7406. AUDIFFERT, C. L.S. Système financier de la France. 3d. éd. Paris, 1863-70. 6 v.
7407. AUSPITZ, R. und R. Lieben. Untersuchungen über die theorie des preises. Leipzig, 1889.
7408. AVELING, E. & E. Marx. Working class movement in America. 2d. ed. London, 1891.

Post-Classical Period 459

7409. AZACARETE, G. Estudios políticos y económicos. Madrid, 1876.
7410. BABEAU, Albert. La Vie Rurale dans l'ancienne France. Paris, 1883.
7411. ———. Le village sous l'ancien régime. 3d. ed. Paris, 1882.
7412. BADEN-POWELL, H. Land revenue and its administration in British India. Oxford, 1894.
7413. ———. The Land systems of British India. Oxford, 1892. 2 v.
7414. BAERNREITHER, J. M. English associations of working men. London, 1891. (Tübingen, 1886.)
7415. BAGEHOT, Walter. Economic studies. Edited by R. H. Hutton. London, 1880.
7416. ———. International coinage. London, 1869.
7417. ———. Lombard Street. 10th ed. London, 1892.
7418. ———. The postulates of English political economy. With a preface by Alfred Marshall. London, 1885. 114 p.
7419. ———. Some articles on the depreciation of silver. London, 1877. 136 p.
7420. ———. The works of Walter Bagehot. Edited by Forrest Morgan. Harford, 1891. 5 v.
7421. BAGNALL, W. R. Textile industries of the United States. Vol. I. 1639-1810. Stafford Springs, Connecticut, 1893.
7422. BAHRFELDT, E. Das Münzwesen Mark Brandenburg v. den ältesten Zeiten. Berlin, 1889.
7423. BAKER, C. W. Monopolies and the people. New York, 1889.
7424. BALCHEN, A. R. Grunddragen af den politiska ekonomiens historia. Stockholm, 1869.
7425. BALFOUR, A. J. International bimetallism. (Speech) London, 1896.
7426. BAMBERGER, L. Deutschland und der Sozialismus. 2 Aufl. Leipzig, 1876.
7427. ———. Le metal argent à la Fin du XIXe siècle. Traduit par R. G. Molinari. Paris, 1894.
7428. ———. Reichsgold. 2 Aufl. Leipzig, 1876.
7429. BANCROFT, H. H. Resources and development of Mexico. San Francisco, 1894.
7430. BARBERET, J. Le travail en France. Nancy, 1896-91. 7 v.
7431. BARBOUR, D. Theory of bimetallism. London and New York, 1886.
7432. BARCLAY, R. Silver question and gold question. 3d. ed. Manchester, 1890.
7433. BARLET, Edward. History du commerce et de l'industrie de la Belgique. 3d. éd. Malines, 1885.
7434. BARNES, William E. The Labor problem. New York, 1886.
7435. BAROIS, J. Les Irrigations en Egypte . . . Paris, 1887.
7436. BARON, S. Le Paupérisme, ses causes et ses remèdes. 2d. éd. Neuchâtel, 1882.
7437. BARRAL, J. A. et L. Passy. Enquête sur le crédit

	agricole. Paris, 1883-85. 2 v.
7438.	BARTH, Thomas. La vie économique de l'Amérique. Berlin, 1887.
7439.	BASTABLE, C. F. The Commerce of nations. London, 1892.
7440.	———. Public finance. London, 1892.
7441.	———. The Theory of international trade. Dublin, 1887. (4th ed. London, 1903.)
7442.	BATBIE, A. P. Mélanges d'économique politique. Paris, 1865.
7443.	———. Nouveau cours d'économique politique. Paris, 1864-65. 2 v.
7444.	———. Turgot, philosophie économique et administration. Paris, 1861.
7445.	BAUMANN, J. G. Die Staatslehre des Thomas von Aquinas. Leipzig, 1873.
7446.	BAXTER, R. D. Income and taxation. London, 1871.
7447.	———. National debts. 2d. ed. London, 1871.
7448.	———. Taxation of the United Kingdom. London, 1869.
7449.	BAYARD, E. La cause d'Epargne et de Prévoyance de Paris. Paris, 1892.
7450.	BEACH, C. F. Company law. Chicago, 1891. 2 v.
7451.	———. The Modern law of railways. San Francisco, 1890. 2 v.
7452.	BEAUJON, A. Overzicht der geschiedenis Vende Nederlandsche Zeevisscherijen. Leiden, 1885.
7453.	BEAUREGARD, P. Elements d'économie politique. Paris, 1889.
7454.	———. Essai sur la théorie du salaire. Paris, 1887.
7455.	BEBEL, A. Die Frau und der sozialismus. 14 Aufl. Stuttgart, 1892.
7456.	BECHAUX, A. Le Droit et les faits économiques. Paris, 1889.
7457.	BEDARRIDE, J. Des chemins de fer au point de vue du transport de voyageurs et de marchandises. 3d. éd. par Rivière. Paris, 1891. 2 v.
7458.	BEER, Adam. Die finanzen Oesterreichs im 19 Jahrh. Prague, 1877.
7459.	———. Die österreichische Handelspolitik im 19. Jahrh. Wien, 1891.
7460.	BELLOC, Al. Recherches historie sur les postes francaises. Paris, 1886.
7461.	BELOT, E. Nantucket, étude sur . . . propiétés primitives. Paris, 1884.
7462.	BELOW, G. v. Ursprung der deutschen stadtverfassung. Dusseldorf, 1892.
7463.	BEMIS, E. W. Cooperation in New England. Baltimore, 1886.
7464.	BEMIS, E. W. and others. History of cooperation in the United States. Baltimore, 1888.
7465.	BEQUET, L. Législation de l'assistance publique en France. Paris, 1885.
7466.	BERENDTS, Edward. Volks- und staatswirthschaftliche

anschauungen in Russland. St. Petersburg, 1888.
7467. BERENS, Eduard. Versuch einer kritischen dogmengeschichte der grundrente. Leipzig, 1868.
7468. BERGMANN, Eugen von. Geschichte der nationalökonomischen krisentheorieen. Stuttgart, 1895.
7469. BERNHARDT, A. Geschichte der Waldeigenthums, der waldwirthschaft . . . in Deutschland. 3 Bde. Berlin, 1872-75.
7470. BERNSTEIN, A. Schultze-Delitzsch. Berlin, 1879.
7471. BERNSTEIN, Ed. Die voraussetzungen des sozialismus. Stuttgart, 1899.
7472. BERTAGNOILLI, C. L'Economia dell' agricultura in Italia. Roma, 1886.
7473. BERTHOLD, G. Die deutsche arbeiterkolonien. Berlin, 1893.
7474. BERTILLON, A. Ethnographie moderne. Paris, 1883.
7475. BERTILLON, J. La statistic humaine de la France. Paris, 1884.
7476. BERTINI, M. Del valore. Torino, 1884.
7477. BERTOLINI, A. Cenno sul socialismo . . . in Italia. Firenze, 1889.
7478. ———. Saggio di bibliografia italiana, 1870-90. Roma, 1892.
7479. BESOBRASOFF, William. Etudes sur l'économique nationale du la Russie. St. Petersburg, 1883-86.
7480. BEUTNER. Die Zoll-tariffe der wichitigeren länder aller erdtheile. 2 Bde. Berlin, 1883.
7481. BEWEGUNG, Die wirthschaftl., . . . handel und industrie in Deutschland von 1884 bis 1888. Berlin, 1890.
7482. BIEDERMANN, H. J. Ueber den merkantilismus. Innsbruck, 1870.
7483. BIENENGRABER, A. Statistik der verkehrs und verbrauchs im zollverein . . . 1842-64. Berlin, 1868.
7484. BIGELOW, E. B. Tariff policy of England and United States contrasted. 2d. ed. Boston, 1877.
7485. ———. Tariff question. Boston, 1862.
7486. BILINSKI, Leon. Luxusteuer als correctiv der einkommensteuer. Leipzig, 1875.
7487. ———. System ekononji społecznéj . . . 2 v. Stockholm, 1880-82.
7488. ———. System nauki skarbowéj . . . Stockholm, 1876.
7489. BIOLLAY, L. Le Pact de famine. Paris, 1885.
7490. BIRBECK, W. L. Historical sketch of the distribution of land in England. London, 1885.
7491. BIRCH, W. G. Domesday book. London, 1887.
7492. BIRWOOD, George. The dawn of the British trade to the East Indies, as recorded in court minutes of the East India company. London, 1886.
7493. BISBEE, L. H., and J. C. Simons. Board of trade and produce exchange, history, methods and law. Chicago, 1884.
7494. BISCHOF, A. Katechismus der finanzwissenschaft. 3 Aufl. Leipzig, 1881.

7495. ———. Lehrbuch der nationalokonomie. 2 Thle. Grax, 1873.
7496. BISHOP, J. L. History of American manufactures, 1608-1860. Philadelphia, 1861-64.
7497. BITZER, F. Arbeit und kapital. Stuttgart, 1871.
7498. BLACKIE, J. S. Scottish highlanders and land laws. London, 1885.
7499. BLACKLEY, W. L. Essays on the prevention of pauperism. London, 1800.
7500. BLAKE, W. P. The Production of the precious metals. New York, 1869.
7501. BLANC, Charles. L'Administration des finances municipales. Paris, 1881.
7502. BLANC, Hyp. Bibliographie des corporations ouvrières avant 1789. Paris, 1885.
7503. ———. Les Corporations de metiérs. Paris, 1888.
7504. BLANCHARD, P. Prud'hommes employés. Paris, 1887.
7505. BLANCHE, Armand. Des transports par chemins de . . . Paris, 1866. 2 v.
7506. BLOCH, Maurice. Petit manuel de le Science économique depuis Adam Smith. 3d. éd. Paris, 1880.
7507. ———. Les progrès de la Science économique. Paris, 1890. 2 v.
7508. ———. Statistique de la France comparée. Paris, 1874. 2 v.
7509. BLODIG, H. Der Wucher und seine Gesetzgebung. Wien, 1892.
7510. BLUNTSCHLI, J. C. Lehr v. modernen staat. 3 Bde. Stuttgart, 1875-86. (Trad. fr. par de Riedmatten, 3 ed., Paris, 1891; English by R. Lodge, 2d. ed. London, 1892; versione ital. per Trono, Roma, 1884. 3 v.
7511. BOASE, C. W. Century of banking in Dundee. Dundee, 1864
7512. BODIO, L. Sul Movimento dell' emigrazione dall' Italia. Roma, 1886.
7513. BOHM-BAWERK, E. V. Kapital und Kapitalzins. 2 Abth. Innsbruck, 1884-89. (English by W. Smart, 1890-91.)
7514. BOHMERT,E. V. Socialismus und Arbeiterfrage. Zürich, 1873.
7515. BOILEAU, E. Le Livre des Métiers, 1268; dans Haussmann's histoire générale de Paris. Paris, 1886.
7516. BOISSEVAIN, G. M. Le Problème monétaire et sa solution. Paris et Amsterdam, 1891. (Translated by G. T. Warner, London, 1891.)
7517. BOITEAU, A. Etat de la France en 1689. Paris, 1860. (2d. éd. 1889.)
7518. ———. Fortune publique et finances de la France. Paris, 1866. 2 v.
7519. ———. Les Traités de commerce, texte . . . Paris, 1864.
7520. BOIZARD, E., and H. Tardieu. Histoire de la législation des Sucres, 1664-1891. Paris, 1891.
7521. BOJANOWSKI, Vict. V. Unternehmer und Arbeiter . . . Stuttgart, 1877.

7522. BOLLES, A. S. Chapters in political economy. New York, 1874.
7523. ———. Financial history of the United States from 1774 to 1885. New York, 1879-86. 3 v. (1774 to 1789: 4th edition, 1896. 1789 to 1861: 4th edition 1894. 1861-1885: 2nd edition, 1894.)
7524. ———. Industrial history of the United States with a description of Canadian industries. Norwich, 1889.
7525. ———. Money, banking and finance, New York, 1903.
7526. BONAR, James. The Intellectual virtues. London, 1894.
7527. ———. Malthus and his work, London, and New York, 1885. 2 v.
7528. ———. Philosophy and political economy. London, 1893.
7529. BONHAM, Q. Railway secrecy and trusts. New York, 1888.
7530. BONNASSIEUX, P. Les grandes compagnies de commerce. Paris, 1892.
7531. BONWICK, J. British colonies. London, 1886.
7532. ———. Romance of the wool trade. London, 1887.
7533. BOOTH, A. J. Saint Simon and Saint Simonism. London, 1871.
7534. BOOTH, C. The aged poor in England and Wales. London, 1894. 1 v.
7535. ———. Life and labor of the people. London, 1892-3. 4 v.
7536. BORAIN, J. Les Enormités du libre échange anglais. Bruxelles, 1878.
7537. BORDIER, A. La colonisation scientifique et les colonies francaises. Paris, 1884.
7538. BORIE, V. Etudes sur le crédit agricole et le crédit foncier en France et à l'Etranger. Paris, 1877.
7539. BOSANQUET, Bernard, Mrs. The Standard of life. London, 1898.
7540. BOTELLA, C. El Problema de la emigración. 2d. ed. Madrid, 1888.
7541. BOUCHARD, L. Système financier de l'ancienne monarchie. Paris, 1891.
7542. BOUCTET, J. G. Etude de sociologie; histoire du communisme et socialisme. Paris, 1890.
7543. BOUET-BOLENS, H. L'avenir économique de la Suisse. Paris, 1884. 2 v.
7544. BOURDEAU, Q. Le socialisme allemagne et le nihilisme russe. Paris, 1892.
7545. BOURINOT, J. G. Canadian studies in comparative politics. Montreal, 1890.
7546. BOURNE, E. G. History of the surplus revenue of 1837. New York, 1885.
7547. BOURNE, H. B. F. English merchants; progress of commerce. London, 1866. 2 v.
7548. BOURNE, S. Trade, population, food. London, 1881.
7549. BOUSQUET, G. La Banque de France et les Inst. des crédits. Paris, 1885.

7550. ———. Le Japon de nos Jours. Paris, 1877. 2 v.
7551. BOUTWELL, George S. A manual of the direct and excise tax system. Boston, 1863.
7552. BOWKER, R. R. Economics for the people. 2d. ed. New York, 1890.
7553. BOWKER, R. R. and George Iles. The Reader's guide in economic, social and political science. New York, 1891.
7554. BOWLEY, Arthur L. Elements of statistics. London, 1901.
7555. ———. Prices and earnings in time of war. London.
7556. ———. A short account of England's foreign trade in the 19th century. London, 1893.
7557. BRACHELLI, H. F. Die Staaten's Europa. 4. Aufl. Brünn, 1883-84.
7558. BRANDES, G. Ferdinand Lassalle. 3d. ed. Leipzig, 1894.
7559. BRANTS, V. Coup d'oeil sur les Débuts de le science économique dans les écoles francais. Louvain, 1881.
7560. ———. Essai historique sur la condition des classes rurales en Belgique. Louvain, 1880.
7561. BRASSEY, Thomas. Foreign work and English wages. 6th. ed. London, 1893.
7562. ———. Lectures on the labor question. New ed. New York, 1886.
7563. BREHON CODE. Hiberniae leges et institutiones antiquae. Dublin, 1881.
7564. BRELAY, E. Les chevaliers du travail. Paris, 1891.
7565. BREMNER, F. The industries of Scotland. London, 1869.
7566. BRENTANO, Lujo. Die Arbeitergilden de Gegenwart. 2 Bde. Leipzig, 1871-72.
7567. ———. Arbeitsverhaltnisse . . . Leipzig, 1868. (French edition, 1885; New York, 1891.)
7568. ———. On the history and development of gilds. London, 1870.
7569. BRETON, Jules. La Réorganisation cadastrale et la conservation du Cadastre en France, Paris, 1889.
7570. BRODERICK. G. C. English land and English landlords. London, 1881.
7571. BROICH, Frhr. V. Sozialreform und Genossenschaftswesen. 2 Aufl. Berlin, 1890.
7572. BROMLEY, J. H. Pacific railroad legislation, 1862-65. Boston, 1886.
7573. BROUGH, W. The Natural law of money. New York, 1894.
7574. BROWNE, W. A. Money weights and measures of the chief commercial nations. 6th ed. London, 1882.
7575. BRYAN, Edward. The mark in Europe and America. Boston, 1893.
7576. BRYCE, J. The American commonwealth. 3d. ed. New York, 1895. 2 v.
7577. BRYCE, T. T. Economic crumbs: labor . . . Hampton, Virginia, 1879.
7578. BRYCE, W. Canadian customs tariff. Toronto, 1894.
7579. BUCHER, K. Die Enstehung die Volkswirthschaft. Tubingen, 1893.

Post-Classical Period 465

7580. BUCHERE, A. Traité des opérations de le bourse. 3d. éd. Paris, 1892.
7581. BUCKLE, H. T. History of civilization in England. New ed. London, 1875. (Leipzig, 1868; Berlin, 1870; Paris, 1865. 5 v.)
7582. BUINDI, G. La Economia esposta nei suoi principii ragionati e dedotti. Milano, 1864.
7583. BULLOCK, Charles Jesse. Introduction to the study of economics. New York, 1897. (3d. ed. New York, 1908.)
7584. BURCHARDT-BISCHOFF, A. Die lateinische Munz-convention. Basel, 1886.
7585. BURNLEY, J. History of wool and wool combing. London, 1887.
7586. BURRI, Ant. Il Laboro: Studio sociale. Roma, 1888.
7587. BUSHILL, T. W. Profit sharing and the labor question. London, 1893.
7588. BUTTS, I. Protection and free trade. New York, 1875.
7589. BUXTON, S. Finance and politics, 1783-1885. London, 1888. 2 v.
7590. BYLES, J. B. Sophisms of free trade. 5th ed. Philadelphia, 1873.
7591. CACHEUX, Emile. Etat des habitations ouvrières a la Fin du xixe siècle. Paris, 1891.
7592. CAIRNES, J. The Character and logical method of political economy. Dublin, 1869. (2d. ed. London, 1875. New York, 1875.)
7593. _____. The Slave power; its character. 2d. ed. New York, 1862. (Dublin, 1863.)
7594. _____. Some leading principles of political economy. London, 1874. (New ed. London, 1884.)
7595. CALDECOTT, A. English colonisation and empire. London, 1891.
7596. CALMON, A. Histoire parlementaire des finances de la restauration. Paris, 1868. 2 v.
7597. CAMPBELL, G. D. The Unseen foundations of society. London, 1893.
7598. CANNAN, Edwin. The history of local rates in England. London, 1896.
7599. _____. Modern currency and the regulation of its value. London, 1931.
7600. _____. Money: its connection with rising and falling prices. London, 1918.
7601. _____. The Paper pound . . . 2d. ed. London, 1925.
7602. _____. Wealth: A brief explanation. London, 1914.
7603. CARDEÑOS De. Ensayo sobre la historia de la propriedad territorial en España. Madrid, 1873. 2 v.
7604. CARO, L. Der Wucher: eine socialpolitische studie. Leipzig, 1893.
7605. CARRERAS y GONZALEZ M. Philosophie de la science économique. Paris, 1881.
7606. CARVER, Thomas N. The place of abstinence in the theory of interest. Boston, 1893.
7607. _____. The theory of wages adjusted. Boston, 1894.

7608.	CASANOVA, L. Sul Problema agrario. Milano, 1885.	
7609.	CATHREIN, V. Der Socialismus. 5te Aufl. Freiburg, 1892.	
7610.	CATTANEO, C. Scritti di economia pubblica. Firenze, 1887-88. 2 v.	
7611.	CAUWES, P. Précis du cours d'économie politique. Paris, 1878-80. 2 v. (3d. éd. 1892-93. 4 v.)	
7612.	CAVAGENARI, V. W. Elementi di scienza dell' amministrazione. Firenze, 1890.	
7613.	CERNUSCHI, Henri. The Great metallic powers. London, 1885.	
7614.	———. Nomisma; or, legal tender. New York, 1877.	
7615.	CHAILLEY, J. L'impôt sur le revenu. Paris, 1884.	
7616.	CHAMBERS, R. A history of currency in the British colonies. London, 1893.	
7617.	CHANNING, Francis Allston. The truth about agriculture depression. New York, 1897.	
7618.	CHAPIN, A. L. First principles of political economy. New York, 1880.	
7619.	CHARGUERAUD, A. L'économie politique et l'impôt. Paris, 1864.	
7620.	CHEVALLIER, Emile. De l'assistance dans les campagnes. Paris, 1889.	
7621.	———. Les salaires au xixme siècle. Paris, 1887.	
7622.	CHEYSSON, E. La question des habitations ouvrières en France et à l'étranger. Paris, 1886.	
7623.	CHISHOLM, G. Handbook of commercial geography. London, 1889.	
7624.	CHRISTIANS, W. Rechnen und Usancen im wechsel-geld- und effecten-verkehr. 3 Aufl. Berlin, 1881.	
7625.	CICCONE, Antonio. Della miseria e della carestia. Napoli, 1884.	
7626.	———. Principii d'economia sociale. 3d. ed. Napoli, 1882-83. 3 v.	
7627.	CLAMAGERAN, J. J. Histoire de l'impôt en France. Paris, 1867-76. 3 v.	
7628.	CLARE, George. The A B C of the foreign exchanges. London, 1893.	
7629.	CLARK, J. B. Capital and its earnings. Boston, 1888.	
7630.	———. Distribution of wealth. Boston, 1899.	
7631.	———. The philosophy of wealth. Boston, 1886.	
7632.	———, and J. H. Giddings. Modern distributive process. Boston, 1889.	
7633.	CLARKE, T. C. The American railway. New York, 1889.	
7634.	CLEAVELAND, J. Banking system of New York. 2d. ed. New York, 1864.	
7635.	CLEMENT, A. La Crise économique et sociale en France et en Europe. Paris, 1886.	
7636.	———. Essai sur la science sociale. Paris, 1867. 2 v.	
7637.	CLERCQ, P. H. de. Les finances de l'Empire de Russie. Amsterdam, 1886.	

7638. COBB, A. S. Threadneedle Street; a reply to Lombard Street. London, 1891.
7639. COBDEN, C. Essays. Second Series. London, New York and Paris, 1871-72.
7640. _____. Local government and taxation. London, New York and Paris, 1875.
7641. _____. Systems of land tenures in various countries. London, 1870.
7642. COCHIN, A. Etudes sociales et économiques. Paris, 1880.
7643. COEN, G. Le Grandi strade del Commerce internazione proposte nel Sec. XVI. 2d ed. Livorgno, 1889.
7644. COGNETTE, de Martis S. Della attinenze tra l'economia sociale e la storia. Firenze, 1865.
7645. _____. L'economia come scienza autonoma. Torino, 1886.
7646. _____. Le forme primitive dell' evoluzione economica. Torino, 1881.
7647. _____. Socialismo antico. Torino, 1889.
7648. COHN, Gustav. Nationalökonomische studien. Stuttgart, 1886.
7649. _____. The science of finance. Translated by T. B. Veblen, Chicago, 1895. xi, 800 p.
7650. _____. System der nationalökonomie. 2 Bde. Stuttgart, 1885-89. 2 v. (Philadelphia, 1894.)
7651. COINS and coinage; the United States mint. Philadelphia, 1884.
7652. COIT, Stanton. Neighbourhood Guilds. London, 1891.
7653. COLLINS, C. M. History, law, and practice of banking. London, 1887.
7654. COLMEIRO, M. Biblioteca de los economistas españolas de los siglos xvi, xvii y xviii. Madrid, 1880.
7655. _____. Historia de la economia politica en España. Madrid, 1865. 2 v.
7656. _____. Tratado elementaria de économia politica . . . Madrid, 1875. 2 v.
7657. COLSON, G. Transports et tarifs. Paris, 1890.
7658. COMPENDIUM of Transportation theories. Washington, 1893.
7659. CONANT, Charles A. A history of modern banks of issue. 2d. ed. New York, 1896.
7660. CONIGLIANI, C. A. Dottrine monetarie in Francia . . . Modena, 1890.
7661. _____. Teoria general de effetti economia de imposte. Milano, 1890.
7662. CONROAD, J. Grundriss zum studium der politischen oekonomie. Jena, 1896. 79 p.
7663. _____. Handwörterbuch der staatswissenschaften. 6 Bde. Jena, 1890-4.
7664. _____. Sammlung nationalökonomischer und statischer Abhandlungen der staatswissenschaftlichen seminars zu Halle. Jena, 1877-95.
7665. CONTZEN, K. W. H. Geschichte literatur und Bedeutg.

Nationalökonomie. 2 Auf. Berlin, 1881.
7666. CONVERT, F. La Propriété, constitution, estimation, administration. Paris, 1886.
7667. COOK, W. W. The Corporation problem. New York, 1891.
7668. ———. Trusts. 2d. ed. New York, 1888.
7669. COOLEY, T. C. The American Railway. New York, 1889.
7670. COOLEY, T. M. Constitutional law in the United States. 2d. ed. Boston, 1891.
7671. ———. A treatise on the law of taxation. 2d. ed. Chicago, 1886.
7672. COOTE, H. C. The Romans of Britain. London, 1878.
7673. COPE, Rufus. The distribution of wealth. Philadelphia, 1890.
7674. CORT Van der Linden, P. W. H. Leerboek der financien. 's Gravenhage, 1887.
7675. COSSA, E. Primi elementi di economia agraria. Milano, 1890.
7676. COSSA, Luigi. Elementi di economia politica. 8 ediz. Milano, 1888.
7677. ———. Introduction allo studio dell'economia politica. 3 ed. Milano, 1892. (London, 1893.)
7678. ———. Scienza della finance. 4 ed. Milano, 1887. (New York, 1888.)
7679. COSTA-ROSSETTI, Jul. Grundlagen der nationalökonomie. Freibourg, 1889.
7680. COSTE, A. Hygiène sociale contre le paupérisme. Paris, 1882.
7681. ———. Nouvel exposé d'economie politique, et de physical sociale. Paris, 1889.
7682. ———. La question monétaire en 1889. Paris, 1889.
7683. COULLET, P. J. et C. Juglar. Extraits des enquêtes parlementaires anglaises sur les questions de banque. 1810 à 1858. Paris, 1865. 3 v.
7684. COURTNEY, W. L. Life of John Stuart Mill. London, 1889.
7685. COURTOIS, A. Histoire des banques en France. 2e éd. Paris, 1881.
7686. ———. Traité des opérations de bourse et de change. 10e éd. Paris, 1889.
7687. COWPERTHWAITE, J. H. Money, silver, and finance. New York, 1892.
7688. COX, Harold. Land nationalization. London, 1892.
7689. COX, S. S. Free land and free trade. New York, 1881.
7690. CRAWFORD, J. B. Crédit mobilier of America. Boston, 1880.
7691. CREASY, E. Imperial and colonial constitition of British Empire. London, 1872.
7692. ———. Rise and progress of the English constitution. London and New York, 1881.
7693. CREIGHTON, Charles. A history of epidemics in Britain from A. D. 664 to the extinction of the plague. Cambridge, 1891.
7694. CROCKER, Uriel H. The Cause of hard times. Boston, 1896.

7695. CROMPTON, H. Industrial conciliation. London, 1876. (Bruxelles, 1880.)
7696. CROUZEL, A. Etude historique, économique et juridique sur les coalitions et les grèves dans l'industrie. Paris, 1887.
7697. CROZIER, J. B. Civilization and progress. 3d. ed. London, 1892.
7698. CRUGER, H. Erwerbs- und wirthschaftsgenossenschaften in den einzelnen Ländern. Jena, 1892.
7699. CRUMP, A. Causes of fall in prices . . . London, 1889.
7700. ———. English manual of banking. 3d. ed. London, 1886.
7701. ———. Position and prophecies of bimetallists. London, 1882.
7702. CUCHEVAL CLARIGNY, A. Les finances de la France de 1870 à 1891. Paris, 1891.
7703. ———. Les finances de l'Italie (1866-1885). Paris, 1886.
7704. ———. Primi elementi di scienze delle finanze. 5e éd. Paris, 1890.
7705. CUMMING, A. N. The value of political economy. London, 1881.
7706. CUNNINGHAM, William. Economic problems after the War. n.p., n.d. pp. 254-268.
7707. ———. Growth of English industry and commerce during the early and middle ages. 2d. ed. London and New York, 1890. (3d. ed. Cambridge, 1896.)
7708. ———. Growth of English industry and commerce in modern times. The Mercantile System. Cambridge, England, 1892. (Cambridge, 1907.)
7709. ———. Politics and economics. London, 1885.
7710. ———. The use and abuse of money. New York, 1891.
7711. CUNNINGHAM, W. and Ellen A. McArthur. Outlines of English industrial history. Cambridge, 1895.
7712. CUSUMANO, V. La teoria del commercio dei Grani in Italia. Bologna, 1877.
7713. DABNEY, W. D. The Public regulation of railways. New York, 1889.
7714. DAHL, F. W. Der Handelsverkehr Schwedens . . . 1829-79. Stockholm, 1884.
7715. DANIELL, C. J. Gold in the East. London, 1879.
7716. DANIELS, Winthrop M. The elements of public finance. New York, 1899.
7717. DARKHEIM, R. De la division du travail social. Paris, 1893.
7718. DAUBY, J. Des Grèves ouvriers en Belgique. Nouv. éd., Bruxelles, 1883.
7719. DAVENNE, H. J. B. De l'organisation et du régime des secours publics en France. Paris, 1865. 2 v.
7720. DAVIDSON, D. Bidrag til kapitalbildningen. Upsala, 1878.
7721. ———. Bidrag til lifränteteoriens historia. Upsala, 1880.
7722. DAVIDSON, John. The Bargain theory of wages. New York, 1898.

7723.	DAVIS, J. B. The Union Pacific Railway. Chicago, 1894.	
7724.	DAVIS, J. E. The English labour laws. London, 1875.	
7725.	DAWSON, W. H. Bismark and state socialism. London, 1890.	
7726.	———. German socialism and Ferdinand Lassalle. 2d ed. London, 1888.	
7727.	———. The Unearned increment. London, 1890.	
7728.	DEBAUVE, A. Manuel de l'Ingénieur des Ponts et Chaussées. Paris, 1871-81.	
7729.	DECKERT, E. Kolonialreiche und Kolonisationsobjekte der Gegenwart. 2 Ausg. Leipzig, 1888.	
7730.	DEL MAR, A. History of money in various countries. London, 1885.	
7731.	———. History of the precious metals. London, 1880.	
7732.	———. Money and civilization; a history of the monetary laws and systems of various states. London, 1886.	
7733.	———. The science of money. London, 1885.	
7734.	DELACOUR, A. Adam Smith, sa vie, ses travaux et ses doctrines. Paris, 1886.	
7735.	DENSLOW, V. B. Principles of the economic philosophy of society, government, and industry. New York, 1888.	
7736.	DENTON, William. England in the 15th century. London, 1888.	
7737.	DESCHAMPS, L. Histoire de la question coloniale. Paris, 1891.	
7738.	DESMAREST, E. Législation et organisation des sociétés de secours mutuels en Europe. Paris, 1873. (7th. éd., 1882.)	
7739.	DEVAS, C. S. Groundwork of economics. London, 1883.	
7740.	DEVINE, Edward T. Economics, Philadelphia, 1893.	
7741.	DEWEY, Davis Rich. Financial history of the United States. London, 1903.	
7742.	DICEY, A. V. The law of domicile. London, 1879.	
7743.	———. Study of the law of the constitution. New ed. London, 1885-87.	
7744.	DICTIONARY of political economy. Edited by P. H. MacLeod. London, 1863. 1 v.	
7745.	DICTIONARY of political economy. Edited by R. H. I. Palgrave. London, 1891.	
7746.	DICTIONNAIRE des finances. Edited by Léon Say. Tome I. Paris, 1889.	
7747.	DICTIONNAIRE général de la politique. Edited by M. Block. Paris, 1862. (New ed. 1884. 2 v.)	
7748.	DIEHL, K. P. J. Proudhon, seine lehre und sein leben. Jena, 1888-90.	
7749.	DIETZEL, H. Karl Rodbertus. Jena, 1886-88.	
7750.	———. Ueber das verhältniss der volkswirthschaftslehre zur socialwirthschaftslehre. Berlin, 1882.	
7751.	DIEZMANN, M. Deutschlands aussereuropäischer handel. Chemnitz, 1882.	
7752.	DIGBY, R. E. History of law of real property. 3d. ed. Oxford, 1884.	
7753.	DILLON, M. Banking in Ireland from earliest times to	

7754. present day. Dublin, 1889.
7754. DILLON, W. The dismal science. Dublin, 1882.
7755. DINGLEY, N. Report on American shipping. Washington, 1882.
7756. DITMAR, W. Der deutsche zollverein. 2 Aufl. Leipzig, 1868.
7757. DODGE, J. R. Wages of farm labor in the United States. 1840-92. Washington, 1892.
7758. DOLE, C. F. The American citizen. Boston, 1894.
7759. DOMERGUE, J. La révolution économique. Paris, 1890.
7760. DOMESDAY Studies. Edited by P. E. Dove. London, 1888-91. 2 v.
7761. DOREN, A. Untersuchungen zur Geschichte der Kaufmannsgilden des Mittelalters. Leipzig, 1893.
7762. DORN, Alexander. Eisenbahns-Politik. Berlin, 1876.
7763. DORSEY, E. E. English and American railroads compared. 2d. ed. New York, 1887.
7764. DOS PASSOS, J. R. The Inter-state Commerce Act. New York, 1887.
7765. DOWELL, Stephen. History and explanation of stamp duties. London, 1873.
7766. ———. A History of taxation and taxes in England. 2d. ed. London, 1888. 4 v.
7767. DOYLE, A. Poor laws in foreign countries. London, 1875.
7768. DRAGE, G. The Unemployed. London, 1894.
7769. DRIOUX, J. Etude économique et juridical sur les associations d'ouvriers et de patrons de 1789 à nos Jours. Paris, 1884.
7770. DU PUYNODE, Gust. Etudes sur les principaux économistes. Paris, 1868.
7771. ———. Les grandes crises financières de la France. Paris, 1876.
7772. ———. De la monnaie, du crédit et de l'impôt. 2d. éd. Paris, 1863. 2 v.
7773. ———. Des lois du travail et de la population. Paris, 1861. 2 v.
7774. DUCHATEL, P. Nouvelle traité d'économie politique et monétaire. Paris, 1890.
7775. DUFF, N. Legal obligations of dwellings of the poor. London, 1884.
7776. DUFFART, Charles. Géographie commerciale. Paris, 1894.
7777. DUHRING, E. Cursus die National- und socialökonomie. 3 Aufl. Leipzig, 1892.
7778. ———. Kritische Geschichte du nationale Okonomie und die socialismus. 3 Aufl. Leipzig, 1879.
7779. DULLO, G. Gesetzkunde und Volkwirtschaftslehre. 2 Aufl. Berlin, 1891.
7780. DUMESNIL-MARIGNY, J. History de l'économie politique des anciens peuples. Paris, 1877. 3 v.
7781. ———. Les libre-échangistes et les protectionistes conciles. Paris, 1860.

7782. DUN, F. American farming and food. London, 1881.
7783. ———. Landlord and tenants in Ireland. London, 1881.
7784. DUN, J. British banking statistics. London, 1876.
7785. DUNBAR, Charles F. Chapters on the theory and history of banking. New York, 1891.
7786. ———. Laws of the United States relating to currency, finance and banking from 1789 to 1891, with vetoed bills, Boston, 1891.
7787. DUNCAN, J. The bank charter act . . . 2d. ed. London, 1878.
7788. DUPONT, J. F. Histoire des sociétés coopératives. Paris, 1873.
7789. DURAND, J. Crédit agricole en France et l'étranger. Paris, 1891.
7790. DURKHEIM, E. De la division du travail social. Paris, 1893.
7791. DUVAL, J. L'algérie et les colonies françaises. Paris, 1877.
7792. ———. History de l'émigration européene, asiatic et african au 19e siècle. Paris, 1862.
7793. EARLE, John. Handbook to land charters and other saxonic documents. Oxford, 1888.
7794. EATON, D. B. Civil service in Great Britain. New York, 1880.
7795. EDGEWORTH, Maria. The life and letters . . . Edited by A. J. C. Hare. Boston, 1895.
7796. EFFERTZ, O. Arbeit und boden. 2 Aufl. Berlin, 1890-91.
7797. EGER, George. Die Einführung eines international; Eisenbahnfrachtrechts. Breslau, 1877. (Berlin, 1878.)
7798. EHEBERG, K. T. Agrarische zuständ in Italien. Leipzig, 1886.
7799. EICHTAL, E. D. Socialisme, communisme et collectivisme. Paris, 1892.
7800. EISENHART, Hugo. Geschichte der nationalökonomik. 2d. e Jena, 1891.
7801. ELDER, W. Conversations on principal subjects of political economics. Philadelphia, 1882.
7802. ———. Questions of the day, economic and social. Philadelphia, 1871.
7803. ELLERO, P. La questione sociale. Bologna, 1889.
7804. ELLIOT, J. R. American farms: their condition and future. New York, 1890.
7805. ELLIOT, O. L. The tariff controversy in the United States. 1789-1833. Palo Alto, California, 1892.
7806. ELLISON, T. Cotton trade of Great Britain. London, 1886.
7807. ELY, R. T. French and German socialism. New York, 1883.
7808. ———. An Introduction to political economy. New York, 1889.
7809. ———. Labor movement in America. New York, 1886.

7810. _____. Problems of to-day; tariffs, taxation, monopolies. New York, 1890.
7811. _____. Socialism. New York, 1894.
7812. ELY, R. T. and J. H. Finley. Taxation in American States and Cities. New York, 1888.
7813. ELYTON, R. W. Domesday studies. London, 1880.
7814. EMMINGHAUS, A. Allgemeine Gewerbslehre. Berlin, 1868.
7815. _____. Das Armenwesen und die Armengesetzgebung in Europ. Staaten. Berlin, 1870. (Leipzig, 1873.)
7816. ENGEL, Ernst. Die deutsche industrie. 1861 u. 1875. 2 Aufl. Berlin, 1881.
7817. ENGELS, F. Herrn Eugen Dührings Umwalzung der Wissenschaft. 2 Aufl. Zürich, 1886.
7818. _____. Der Ursprung der familie, des privateigenthums und des Staats. 4^e Aufl. Stuttgart, 1892.
7819. EPPS, W. Land systems of Australia. London, 1894.
7820. ERAS, W. Der Wahrungstreit 1879-1883. Berlin, 1883.
7821. ERERRA, A. Storia dell' economia politica nei Secoli XVII e XVIII negli Stati della Repubblica veneta. Venezia, 1878.
7822. ESCOTT, J. H. S. England; her people, polity, and pursuits. New ed. London, 1885-86.
7823. ESPINAS A. Histoire des doctrines économiques. Paris, 1892. 359 p.
7824. FABER, Rich. Die entstehung des agrarschutzes in England. Strasburg, 1888.
7825. FAGNIEZ, G. Etudes sur l'industrie et la classe industrielle à Paris au XIIe et au XIVe Siècle. Paris, 1877.
7826. FALKE, J. Geschichte du deutsch Zollwesens. Leipzig, 1869.
7827. FARNAM, H. W. Die innere französische gewerbepolitik von Colbert bis Turgot. Leipzig, 1878.
7828. FARR, William. Vital statistics. London, 1885.
7829. FARRER, J. A. Adam Smith. London, 1881.
7830. FARRER, T. H. Free trade vs. fair trade. London, 1885.
7831. _____. The state in its relation to trade. London, and New York, 1883.
7832. FAURE, F. Les budgets contemporains. Paris, 1887.
7833. FAUVEAU, G. Considérations mathématique sur la théorie de l'impot. Paris, 1864.
7834. FAVAREL, Clément. Théorie du crédit. Paris, 1875-80. 3 v.
7835. FAWCETT, Henry. Economic position of English laborer. London, 1865.
7836. _____. Free Trade and protection. 2d. ed. London, 1879. (Leipzig, 1878.)
7837. _____. Manual of political economy. 6th. ed. London, 1886. (7th ed. 1888.)
7838. _____. Pauperism; its causes and remedies. 6th ed. London, 1885.
7839. FAWCETT, Millicent Garrett. Political economy for

beginners. London, 1870. 7th ed., London and New York, 1889. Berlin, 1888.)
7840. FAWCETT, W. L. Gold and debt. Chicago, 1877.
7841. FECHNER, H. Die handelspolit; beziehungen preussens zu oesterreich, 1741-1806. Berlin, 1886.
7842. FELKIN, William. A history of machine wrought hosiery ... London, 1867.
7843. FENN, C. Compendium of English and foreign funds, debts and revenues. 15th ed. London, 1892.
7844. FERRARIS, Carlo F. Saggi di economia, statistica e scienza dell' amministrazione. Torino, 1879-1880.
7845. FETTER, Frank A. The Definition of price. n.p. 1912.
7846. FIELD, C. D. Landholding, and the relation of landlord and tenant in various countries. London, 1883.
7847. FINK, Albert. Railroad problem and its solution. New York, 1882.
7848. FISCHER, P. D. Deutsche Post- und Telegraphiegesetzgebung. 3te Aufl. Berlin, 1886.
7849. FISHER, Irving. A Brief introduction to the infinitesimal calculus. New York, 1897.
7850. FLINT, H. M. Railroads of the United States, history and statistics. Philadelphia, 1868.
7851. FLINT, R. Socialism. Philadelphia and London, 1895.
7852. FOGOWITZ, Joseph. Moderne Eisenbahnpolitik. Ein Beitrag zur Verkehrsfrage in Oesterreich. Wien, 1883.
7853. FORDYCE, William. History of coal, coak, coal-fields. London, 1860.
7854. FORNARI, T. Delle teorie economiche nelle provincie neopoletane, 1735-1830. Milano, 1883.
7855. FOURNIER de Flaix, E. Etudes économique et financières Paris, 1883. 2 v.
7856. _____. L'impôt sur l. pain et la réaction protectioniste. Paris, 1885.
7857. _____. Statistique comparée des institutions financières, systèmes d'impôts et fiscales des divers états au XIX Siècle. Paris, 1888. 2 v.
7858. FOVILLE, Alf. De. Une enquête sur le prix de détail. Paris, 1888.
7859. _____. Etudes économiques et statistique sur la propriété foncière. I. Le Morcellement. Paris, 1885.
7860. _____. La transformation des moyens de transport et ses conséquences economiques et sociales. Paris, 1880.
7861. FOVILLE, A. de, et H. Pigeonneau. L'administration de l'agriculture en contrôle général des finances, 1785-87. Paris, 1884.
7862. FOWLE, T. W. The Poor law. London, 1881.
7863. FOXWELL, H. S. Irregularity of employment and fluctuations of prices. London, 1887.
7864. FRANCIS, J. H. History of the Bank of England. Chicago, 1889.
7865. FRANKLIN, Alf. Corporations ouvrières de Paris du XIIe au XVIIe Siècle. Paris, 1884.
7866. FRANQUEVILLE, C. de. Du régime des travaux publics

en Angleterre. 2d. éd. Paris, 1875. 4 v.
7867. FRANZ, F., von Mensi. Die finanzen oesterreichs von 1701 bis 1740. Wien, 1890.
7868. FREDERIK, E. La Belgique industrielle et commerciale. Bruxelles, 1881. 2 v.
7869. FRERE, Orban. La dette publique belge de 1830 à 1882. Bruxelles, 1885.
7870. FRERE, Orban et de Laveleye. Questions monétaires en Belgique en 1889. Bruxelles, 1890.
7871. FRIGNET, E. Histoire de l'association commerciale. Paris, 1868.
7872. FROMMER, H. Die Gewinnbetheiligung. Leipzig, 1886.
7873. FUCHS, Johannes. Die Handelspolitik Englands und seiner Kolonien in den letzten Jahrzehnten. Leipzig, 1893.
7874. FUNCK, B. T. Nouveau précis d'économique politica. Paris. 1887.
7875. FUNK, F. X. Geschichte des kirchlichen Zinsverbotes. Tübingen, 1876.
7876. ———. Grundzüge der Wirtschaftslehre. 3 Aufl. Berlin, 1892.
7877. FURBER, Henry Jewett, Jun. Geschichte der ökonomischen theorien in Amerika. Halle, 1891.
7878. FURBER, H. W., editor. Which? Protection, free trade or revenue reform? Harford, 1884.
7879. GABAGLIO, A. Teoria generale della statistica. 2 ed. Milano, 1888. 2 v.
7880. GABBA, C. F. Problemi della scienza sociale. Firenze, 1867.
7881. GALLOIS, E. La poste et les moyens de communication des peuples à travers les siècles. Paris, 1894.
7882. GALLUS, W. Grundlagen die gesammten versicherungswesen. Leipzig, 1874.
7883. GAMMAGE, R. G. History of the chartist movement, 1837-54. London, 1894.
7884. GANDILLOT, R. Principes de le science des finances. Paris, 1875. 3 v.
7885. GARELLA DELLA MOREA, E. G. Princippi di economia politica. 2 ed. Torino, 1881.
7886. GARNIER, R. M. History of the English landed interest, its customs, laws and agriculture. London, 1892.
7887. GASCA, C. L. Il codice ferroviario. Milano, 1890. 3 v.
7888. ———. Il credito e l'agricoltura. Torino, 1884.
7889. GASQUET, Amadée. Précis des institutions politiques et sociales de l'ancienne France. Paris, 1885. 2 v.
7890. GEAL, Eug. V. Die fragé der landwirtschaft krise. Budapest, 1885.
7891. GEHRKE, A. Communistiche idealstaaten . . . Bremen, 1878.
7892. GEISTBECH, M. Der weltverkehr. Telegraphie, post, eisenbahnen und schiffahrt in ihrer entwickelung dargestellt. Freiburg, 1887.
7893. GEORGE, Henry. The condition of labor: an open letter to Pope Leo XIII. New York, 1891. 157 p.

7894. ———. The land question. New York, 1884.
7895. ———. Progress and poverty, 1879. (New York, 1889. Paris, 1887; 5th Aufl., Berlin, 1892; New ed. New York, 1898.)
7896. ———. Protection or free trade. 1886. (New York, 1891; Berlin, 1887; Paris, 1890; Kjobenhavn, 1887.)
7897. ———. The science of political economy. New York, 1898.
7898. GEORGE, Henry Jr. The Menace of privilege. New York, 1906.
7899. GEYER, P. Der Wald in nationalen Wirthschaftleben. Leipzig, 1878.
7900. GIBBINS, H. de B. British commerce and colonies from Elizabeth to Victoria. London, 1893.
7901. ———. An Industrial history of England. London, 1891. (3d. ed. 1894. 240 p.)
7902. GIBBONS, John. Tenure and toil. Philadelphia, 1888.
7903. GIBBS, Henry H. and Henry R. Grenfell. Bimetallic Controversy. London, 1885.
7904. GIDE, C. L'Ecole nouvelle. Genève, 1890.
7905. ———. Principes d'economie politique. 4th. éd. Paris, 1893.
7906. GIERKE, O. Die Genossenschaftstheorie. Berlin, 1887.
7907. GIFFEN, Robert. The Case against Bimetallism. London, 1892.
7908. ———. Essays in finance. London, 1880. (2d. series. London, 1886.)
7909. ———. Growth of capital, London, 1889.
7910. GILL, R. Free Trade; nature of its operation. Edinburgh, 1887.
7911. GILMAN, N. P. The Labor problem. New York, 1893.
7912. ———. Profit sharing between employer and employed. Boston, 1889.
7913. ———. Socialism and the American spirit. Boston, 1893.
7914. GIRAULT, A. Crédit foncier et ses privilèges. Paris, 1889.
7915. GLADDEN, W. Tools and the man; property and industry under Christian law. New York, 1893.
7916. GLADSTONE, W. E. Gleanings of past years. London, 1879. 7 v.
7917. GLEN, W. C. Poor law orders. 8th ed. London, 1879.
7918. ———. Statutes in force relating to poor laws. London, 1873. 2 v.
7919. GNEIST, Rud. Communal Verfassung- und Verwaltungs- gerichte in England. 3 Aufl. Berlin, 1871. (Paris, 1868- 70. 5 v.)
7920. ———. Das englische Verfassungsgeschichte. Berlin, 1884. (London, 1892.)
7921. GOBBI, N. L'Economia politica . . . Italia . . . Milano, 1888.
7922. GOBINEAU, J. A. de. Essai sur l'inégalité des races humaines. 2d. éd. Paris, 1884. 2 v.
7923. GODARD, J. G. Poverty; its genesis and exodus. London, 1892.

7924. GODIN, André. Mutualité sociale et association du capital et du travail. Paris, 1880.
7925. GOLDSCHMIDT, L. Die deutsch hypothekenbanken. Jena, 1880.
7926. ———. System des Handelsrechts. 3 Aufl. Stuttgart, 1891.
7927. GOLTZ, F. T. V. Die landlich arbeiterfrage. 2 Aufl. Danzig, 1874.
7928. GOMEL, C. Causes financières de la révolution française. Paris, 1892.
7929. GOMME, G. L. The village community. London, 1890.
7930. GOMPSOWICZ, L. Sociologie und politik. Leipzig, 1892.
7931. GONNER, E. C. K. The social philosophy of Rodbertus. London, 1899.
7932. GONZALEZ de LINARES, G. La agricultura. Madrid, 1882.
7933. GOODNOW, Frank J. Social reform and the constitution. New York, 1911.
7934. GORI, A. Trattato di tasse di registro. 4 ediz. Firenze, 1887.
7935. GOSCHEN, Viscount George Joachim. Reports and speeches on local taxation. London, 1873.
7936. ———. The theory of the foreign exchanges. London, 1861. (Wien, 1876; Paris, 1875.)
7937. GOSS, John Dean. The history of tariff administration in the United States. New York, 1891.
7938. GOTZ, W. Die verkehrswege im dienste die welthandels. Stuttgart, 1888.
7939. GOULD, J. M. and G. F. Tucker. The federal income tax explained. Boston, 1894.
7940. GOWRY DU ROSLAN, J. Histoire économique de l'Espagne. Paris, 1888.
7941. GRAHAM, P. A. The rural exodus. London, 1892.
7942. GRAHAM, William. One pound note in the rise and progress of banking in Scotland and its adaptability to England. Edinburgh, 1886.
7943. ———. Socialism; new and old. 2d. ed. London, 1891.
7944. GRANDEAU, L. La production agricole en France. Paris, 1885.
7945. GRAPHEUS, D. Darstellung der wirtschaftlich funktion des geldes und kredits. Leipzig, 1891.
7946. GRAY, J. H. Die bestellung der privaten beleuchtungsgesellschaften zu stadt und staat. Jena, 1893.
7947. GRAZIANA, Augusto. Instituzioni di scienza della finanze. Torino, 1897.
7948. ———. Storia critica della teoria del valore in Italia. Milano, 1889.
7949. ———. Teoria generale del profitto. Milano, 1887.
7950. GREELEY, Horace. Essays on political economy. New ed. Philadelphia, 1877.
7951. GREEN, Mrs. J. R. Town life in the fifteenth century. New York, 1894. 2 v.
7952. GREGORY, J. M. A new political economy. Cincinnatti, 1883.

7953. GRIER, John A. The Burning question; our silver coinage. 7th ed. Chicago, 1897.
7954. ———. Our silver coinage and its relation to debt and depression of prices. 4th. ed. Philadelphia, 1885.
7955. GRIERSON, J. Railway rates; English and foreign. London, 1886.
7956. GRIFFITHS, G. C. Digest of the stamp duties. New ed. London, 1881-88.
7957. GRONLUND, L. The co-operative commonwealth. 3d. ed. Boston, 1891.
7958. GROSS, C. The gild merchant. Oxford, 1890. 2 v.
7959. GROSS, Gustav. Die lehre vom unternehmergewinn. Leipzig, 1884.
7960. ———. Staatssubventionen für privatbahnen. Wien, 1882.
7961. GROSVENOR, W. M. American securities. 1875-85. New York, 1886.
7962. ———. Does protection protect? New York, 1870.
7963. GROTE, George. History of Greece. 4th. ed. London, 1872. 10 v.
7964. GRUNER, Ed. Congrès international des accidents du travail. Paris, 1890. 2 v.
7965. ———. Les lois d'assistance ouvrière. Paris, 1887.
7966. ———. Les lois de patronage et d'assistance ouvrière en Autriche. Paris, 1887.
7967. GUILBAULT, C. A. Traité d'économie industrielle. Paris, 1876.
7968. GUMPLOWICZ, L. Rechtsstaat und socialismus. Innsbruck, 1881.
7969. GUNTON, George. Principles of social economics. New York, 1891.
7970. ———. Wealth and progress. London and New York, 1888.
7971. GUTHRIE, W. The Laws of trade unions in England and Scotland. Edinburgh, 1873.
7972. GUYOT, Yves. L'Impôt sur le revenu. Paris, 1887.
7973. ———. La Science économique. 2d. éd. Paris, 1887. (2d. ed., London, 1892.)
7974. HAASS, Frdr. Die Post und die charakter ihrer einkunfte. 2 Aufl. Stuttgart, 1890.
7975. HABERER, Theodor. Geschichte des eisenbahnwesens. Wien, 1884.
7976. HADFIELD, R. A. and H. de B. Gibbons. A Shorter working day. London, 1892.
7977. HADLEY, Arthur T. Economics. New York, 1896.
7978. ———. Railroad transportation. New York, 1893.
7979. HAIN, J. Handbook die statistik die Osterreich Kaiserstaats. 2 Bde. Wien, 1883.
7980. HAKE, A. E. and O. E. Wesslau. Free Trade in capital. New York, 1890.
7981. HALL, Hubert. Antiquities and curiosities of the exchequer. London, 1891.
7982. ———. History of the custom revenue in England. London, 1892.

Post-Classical Period 479

7983. HAMAKER, H. J. De historische school in de staathuishoud-kunde. Leiden, 1870.
7984. HAMILTON, G. K. Om arbetsklassen. Lund, 1865.
7985. ———. Om penningar och kredit. Upsala, 1861.
7986. HAMILTON, Rowland. Money and value. London, 1878.
7987. HANAUER, Abbé Aug. Etudes économiques sur l'Alsace ancienne et moderne. Paris, 1876-1878.
7988. HANDWORTERBUCH der Staatswissenschaften. Jena, 1890-92. 3 v.
7989. HANDWORTERBUCH der Volkswirthschaftslehre. Leipzig, 1865.
7990. HANKEY, Th. Principles of banking. 4th. 1867. (London, 1888.)
7991. HANNSEN, G. Agrarhistorische Abhandlungen. 2 Bde. Leipzig, 1880-84.
7992. HANSOER, E. Die Entwickeln die Vichzucht in Preussen, 1816-1883. Jena, 1887.
7993. HANSON, W. Fallacies in progress and poverty. New York, 1884.
7994. HARROWER, George H. Alexander Hamilton als national-ökonom. Halle, 1887.
7995. HARTMANN, Evon. Die sozialen kernfragen. Leipzig, 1894.
7996. HARVEY, James. Paper money. London, 1877.
7997. HASBACH, A. Die englische arbeiterversicherungswesen. Leipzig, 1883.
7998. HAUPT, O. Arbitrages et parités. 6e éd. Paris et Berlin, 1883.
7999. ———. Gold, silber und Währung. Wien, 1878.
8000. ———. L'Histoire monétaire de notre Temps. Paris et Berlin, 1886.
8001. HAUSHOFER, Max. Die deutsche kleingewerbe. Berlin, 1885.
8002. ———. Grundzuge die nationalökonomie. 2 Aufl. Stuttgart, 1883.
8003. ———. Der Industriebetrieb. Stuttgart, 1874.
8004. HAWKINS, E. Silver coins of England. 3d. ed. London, 1887.
8005. HAWLEY, F. B. Capital and population. New York, 1882.
8006. HAYEM et J. Perrin. Du contrat d'apprentissage. Paris, 1869.
8007. HAZARD, R. G. Economics and politics. Boston, 1889.
8008. HAZLITT, W. C. The coinage ot the European continent. London, 1893.
8009. HEARN, William Edward. First Australian economist. By D. B. Copland. Melbourne, 1935. 80 p.
8010. ———. Plutology: or the theory of the efforts to satisfy human wants. London, 1864.
8011. HECHT, Fel. Bankwesen und bankpolitik in Süddeutschl. 1819-75. Jena, 1880.
8012. ———. Die credit-institut auf actien und auf Gegenseitigkeit. Strasb., 1874.

480   Economic Thought and Analysis

8013. ———. Organisation des bodenkredits in Deutschland. Leipzig, 1891.
8014. HEGEL, C. Städte und gilden der germanische völker im mittelalter. Leipzig, 1892.
8015. HELD, Adolf. Carey's socialwissenschaft und das merkantil-system. Wurzburg, 1866.
8016. ———. Grundriss für Vorlesungen über nationalökonomie. 2 Aufl. Bonn, 1878.
8017. ———. Sozialismus, sozialdemokratie und sozialpolitik. Leipzig, 1878.
8018. ———. Zwei Bucher zur socialen geschichte England. Leipzig, 1881.
8019. HERTSLET, E. Treaties and tariffs regulating trade between Great Britain and foreign nations. London, 1879.
8020. HERTZKA, Theodor. Die Gesetze die socialen entwickelung. Leipzig, 1886.
8021. HERVE-BAZIN, F. Traité élémentaire d'économic politique. Paris, 1880.
8022. HERVEY, M. H. The trade policy of imperial federation. London, 1892.
8023. HERZOG, F. B. The transportation question. New York, 1883.
8024. HEUVEL, J. Van Der. De la situation légale des associations sans but lucratif en France et en Belgique. Paris et Bruxelles, 1884.
8025. HEWINS, W. A. S. English trade and finance. London, 1892.
8026. HEYD, W. Geschichte die deutschen handels. Stuttgart, 1890.
8027. ———. Geschichte die Levanthandels im mittelalter. 2 Bde. Stuttgart, 1879. Leipzig, 1885-86. 2 v.
8028. HEYKING, E. v. Zur geschichte der handelbilanztheorie. Berlin, 1880.
8029. HEYL, L. United States duties on imports. New ed. Washington, 1882.
8030. HEYMANS, G. Karakter en methode der staathuishoudkunde. Leiden, 1880.
8031. HIBBERT, F. A. Influence and development of English gilds. London, 1891.
8032. HIGGS, Henry. Bibliography of economics, 1771-1775. New York, 1935.
8033. ———. Family budgets. London, 1896.
8034. HILDEBRAND, R. Theorie des geldes. Jena, 1883.
8035. HILL, Octavia. Homes for London poor. London, 1880.
8036. HILL, William The first stages of the tariff policy of the United States. Boston? 1893.
8037. HILSE, H. Handbuch der strassenbahnkunde. 2 Bde. München, 1893.
8038. HIRTH, George. Freisinnige ansichten der volkswirthschaft und des staats. 3 Aufl. Leipzig, 1876.
8039. HITZE, Frz. Kapital und Arbeit . . . Paderborn, 1881.
8040. ———. Die sociale frage. Paderborn, 1877.
8041. HOBSON, John W. The Economics of distribution. New

York, 1900.
8042. _____. The evolution of modern capitalism. London, 1894.
8043. _____. The problem of the unemployed. London, 1896.
8044. _____. Problems of poverty. London, 1891. (3d. ed. 1896.)
8045. HODGES, W. Law of railways. 7th. edited by J. M. Lely. London, 1889. 2 v.
8046. HODGSON, W. B. The Education of girls and the employment of women. 2d. ed. London, 1869.
8047. _____. On the importance of Economic science. 3d. ed. London, 1870.
8048. _____. Turgot: His life, times, and opinions. London, 1870.
8049. HOLE, James. The homes of the working classes. London, 1866.
8050. _____. State railways: an argument for state purchase. London, 1893.
8051. HOLLANDER, Jacob H. The Cincinnati Southern railway; a study in municipal activity. Baltimore. 1894.
8052. _____. The concept of marginal rent. Cambridge, 1895.
8053. _____. The financial history of Baltimore. Baltimore, 1899. pp. xvi, 397.
8054. _____. Some unpublished letters of Ricardo. Cambridge, 1896.
8055. _____, editor. Studies in state taxation. Baltimore, 1900.
8056. _____. A study of trade unionism. Boston, 1898.
8057. HOLYOAKE, G. J. The Co-operative movement today. London, 1891.
8058. _____. History of co-operation in England. London, 1875-79. 2 v.
8059. _____. Self-help by the people; co-operation in Rochdale. 9th ed. London, 1883. (Leipzig, 1888.)
8060. HORTON, S. Dana. Silver and gold in relation to resumption. Cincinnati, 1877.
8061. _____. Silver in Europe. New York, 1890. (2d. ed. 1892.)
8062. _____. The silver pound and England's monetary policy. London, 1887.
8063. HOUDDARD, A. La question monétaire à la conférence du Bruxelles. Paris, 1893.
8064. HOUTEN, S. Van. De staathuishoudkunde als wetenschap en kunst. Groningen, 1866.
8065. HOWARD, James. Continental farming and peasantry. London, 1870.
8066. HOWARTH, W. Our clearing system and clearing houses. London, 1885.
8067. HOWE, J. B. Monometallism and bimetallism. Boston, 1879.
8068. HOWELL, George. The conflicts of capital and labour. 2d. ed. London, 1890.

8069.	HOYT, H. M. Protection vs. free trade. New York, 1886.
8070.	HUBERT-VALLEROUX, P. Les associations coopératives en France et à l'étranger. Paris, 1885.
8071.	———. Législations de l'Europe concernant les sociétés coopératives. Paris, 1891.
8072.	HUDSON, James F. The railways of the republic. New York, 1886.
8073.	HULL, Charles Henry. Die Deutsche reichspacketpost. Halle, 1892. pp. viii, 70.
8074.	HULL, Edward. The coal fields of Great Britain. 4th. ed. London, 1881.
8075.	HUMBERT, G. Finances et comptabilité publique chez les Romains. Paris, 1887. 2 v.
8076.	HUNT, R. Mineral statistics of Great Britain. London, 1872.
8077.	HURLIMANN, H. Eidgenössische eisenbahngesetzgebung. Zürich, 1887.
8078.	HURTREL, Alice. La femme, sa condition sociale depuis l'antiquité jusqu'à nos jours. Paris, 1887.
8079.	HUTCHESON, J. H. The commercial restraints of Ireland. 1799.
8080.	HUZEL, C. A. System der communalen naturalverpflegung armer reisender. Stuttgart, 1883.
8081.	HYNDMAN, H. M. The commercial crises of the nineteenth century. London, 1892.
8082.	———. Historical basis of socialism in England. London, 1883.
8083.	INAMA-STERNEGG, K. Th. v. Deutsche Wirthschaftsegeschichte. 2 Bde. Leipzig, 1879. (1891.)
8084.	INNES, C. Scotland in the middle ages. Edinburgh, 1860.
8085.	JAGER, E. Der moderne socialismus. Berlin, 1873.
8086.	JANET, Paul. Histoire de la science politique dans ses rapports avec la morale. 2d. éd. Paris, 1872. 2 v.
8087.	———. Les Origines du socialisme contemporain. Paris, 1883.
8088.	JANNASCH, R. Die europäische Baumwollen-industrie. Berlin, 1882.
8089.	JANET, Claude. Le Socialisme d'état. 2d. éd. Paris, 1890.
8090.	———. Le Capital, la spéculation, et la finance au XIX Siècle. Paris, 1892.
8091.	JANSSEN, J. Geschichte des deutschen volkes. 12-15 Aufl. 6 Bde. Freib., 1890.
8092.	JARDINS, P. Principios de financas. 4 ed. Coimbra, 1891.
8093.	JEANS, J. S. Railway problems in different countries. London, 1887.
8094.	———. Trusts, pools, and corners. London, 1894.
8095.	JEANS, Victorine. Factory act legislation. London, 1891.
8096.	JENKS, J. W. H. C. Carey als nationökonomie. Jena, 1885.
8097.	———. Road legislation for the American State. Baltimore, 1889.

Post-Classical Period

8098. JEVONS, W. Stanley. The Coal question. 2d. ed. London, 1866.
8099. ———. Methods of social reform. London, 1833.
8100. ———. Money and the mechanism of exchange. 4th. ed. London, 1878. (3d. éd. Paris, 1881.)
8101. ———. The State in relation to labor. London, 1882.
8102. JOHN, V. Geschichte der statistik. Stuttgart, 1884.
8103. JOHNSON, E. R. Inland waterways; their relation to transportation. Philadelphia, 1893.
8104. JONES, B. Co-operative production. Oxford, 1894.
8105. JONES, John P. The money question. Washington, 1894.
8106. JONES, Lloyd. The life, times, and labours of Robert Owen. London, 1891.
8107. JOSSEAU, J. B. Traité du crédit foncier. 3d. éd. Paris, 1885. 2 v.
8108. JOUBERT, A. Les finances de la France. La rente et l'impôt; leur origine, leur histoire. Paris, 1893.
8109. JOURDAN, A. Cours analytique d'économie politique. Paris, 1882. (2d. éd., 1890.)
8110. ———. Des Rapports entre le droit et l'économie politique. Paris, 1884.
8111. ———. Du rôle de l'état dans l'ordre économique. Paris, 1882.
8112. JUGLAR, Clement. Crises commerciales et de leur retour périodique en France, en Angleterre et aux etats Unis. 2d. éd. Paris, 1890. (A brief history of Panics in England. Edited by DeCourcy W. Thom. New York, 1893.)
8113. ———. Du change et de la liberté d'émission. Paris, 1868.
8114. KAERGER, K. Die Arbeiterspacht. Berlin, 1894.
8115. KANDT, Moritz. Ueber die entwickelung der australischen eisenbahupolitik. Berlin, 1894.
8116. KAUFMANN, G. Deutsche Volkswirthschaftslehre. Hanover, 1880.
8117. KAUFMANN, M. Christian socialism. London, 1888.
8118. ———. Socialism; nature, dangers, and remedies. London, 1874.
8119. KAUFFMANN, R. v. Die Finanzen Frankreichs. Leipzig, 1882. (Paris, 1884.)
8120. ———. Die Zuckerindustrie. Berlin, 1878.
8121. KEARNEY, J. W. Sketch of American finances. 1789-1835. New York, 1887.
8122. KELETI, C. Ernährungs-statistik der bevölkerungs ungarns. Budapest, 1887.
8123. KERR, Andrew William. History of banking in Scotland. Glasgow, 1884.
8124. KETTELER, W. E. F. Arbeiterfrage und christenthum. 4 Aufl. Mainz, 1890.
8125. KEUSSLER, Johann, Von. Zur geschichte und kritik des bäuerlichen gemeindebesitzes in Russland. 3 Thl. St. Petersburg, 1876-87.
8126. KIESSELBACH, W. Der gang des welthandels im mittelalter. Stuttgart, 1860.
8127. KINLEY, David. The history of the independent treasury

of the United States. New York, 1893.
8128. ———. Money: a study of the theory of the medium of exchange. New York, 1904.
8129. KINNEAR, J. B. Principles of property in land. London, 1880.
8130. KIRKMANN, M. M. Railway expenditures. Chicago, 1880. 2 v.
8131. ———. Railway rates and government control. Chicago, 1892.
8132. KIRKUP, T. A history of socialism. London, and New York, 1892.
8133. KLEINWACHTER, Friedrich. Das einkommen und seine verteilung. Leipzig, 1896.
8134. ———. Die kartelle; organisation die volkswirthschaft. Innsbruck, 1883.
8135. KNOX, John Jay. United States notes. 3d. ed. New York, 1892.
8136. KOLB, G. F. Handbuch der vergleichenden statistik. 8te Aufl. Leipzig, 1879.
8137. KONIG, B. E. Geschichte die deutschen Post. Eisenach, 1889.
8138. KOSUB, H. Die organisation die preussen staats eisenbahnen. Berlin, 1881.
8139. KRAATZ, C. Topographisch-statistischer Handbuch des preussischen Staats. 3 Aufl. Berlin, 1880.
8140. KRAMAR, K. Das papiergeld in oesterrich seit 1848. Leipzig, 1886.
8141. KRIEGK, G. D. Deutsches Bürgerthum im Mittelalter. 2 Bde. Frankfurt, 1871.
8142. KRONIG, F. Verwaltung der preussischen staatseisenbahnen. 2 Bde. Breslau, 1892.
8143. KRUGER, H. C. Russlands finanzlage. Berlin, 1887.
8144. KUBEL, F. Eb. Die soziale und volkswirthschaftliche gesetzgebung des alten testaments. Wiesbaden, 1870.
8145. KUPKA, P. F. Die Eisenbahnen Oesterreich-Ungarns (1822-1867). Leipzig, 1888.
8146. LA GOURNERIE, J. De. Etudes économique sur l'exploitation des Chemins de Fer. Paris, 1880.
8147. LABRA, R. M. de. Estudios de economia social. Madrid, 1892.
8148. LAGASSE, Ch. Les Sociétés coopérative. 2d. éd. Bruxelles, 1888.
8149. LALOR, J. J., editor. Cyclopaedia of political science, political economy, and of the political history of the United States. Chicago, 1881-84. 3 v.
8150. LAMBERT, J. Malet. Two thousand years of gild life. Hull, 1891.
8151. LAMBRECHTS H. et G. Phelan. Economia dei popoli e degli stati. Milano, 1874-84. 5 v.
8152. LAMPERTICO, F. La régime douanier des états-unis. Bruxelles, 1890.
8153. LAMPRECHT, K. Deutsches wirthschaftsleben im mittelalter. 4 Bde. Leipzig, 1885-1886.

Post-Classical Period 485

8154. LANCKMANN, J. B. Traités de commerce et de navigation. Bruxelles, 1883. (Supplement, 1885.)
8155. LANESSEAU, J. L. de. L'Expansion coloniale de la France. Paris, 1886.
8156. LANGE, F. A. Die Arbeiterfrage. 4 Aufl. Winterthur, 1879.
8157. LANGFORD, J. H. A century of Birmingham life (1741-1841). Birmingham, 1868.
8158. LAPPARENT, A. de. Le siècle de fer. Paris, 1890.
8159. LARRABEE, William. The railroad question. Chicago, 1893.
8160. LAUGHLIN, J. Laurence. Banking reform. Chicago, 1912.
8161. ———. Elements of political economy. New York, 1887.
8162. ———. History of bimetallism in the United States. New York, 1886.
8163. ———. The study of political economy. New York, 1885.
8164. LAUNHARDT, W. Theorie de tarifbidung de eisenbahnen. Berlin, 1890.
8165. LAURENS, P. Les chambres de commerce français à l'étranger. Bruxelles, 1882.
8166. LAURENT, E. Le paupérisme. Paris, 1865. 2 v.
8167. LAVELEYE, Emile de. De la propriété et de ses formes primitives. Paris, 1874. (4th. ed., 1891; Leipzig, 1879; London, 1878.)
8168. ———. The elements of political economy. New York, 1884. (3d. ed. Paris, 1891.)
8169. ———. La marche monétaire et de crises. Paris, 1865.
8170. ———. La monnaie et le bimétallisme internat. Paris, 1891.
8171. ———. Le Socialisme contemporain. 5 éd. Paris, 1892. (London, 1886; New York, 1885.)
8172. LAVOINNE E., et E. Pontzen. Les chemins de fer en Amérique. Paris, 1800-82. 2 v.
8173. ———. Le développement intellectuel et matériel de la Belgique depuis 1830. Bruxelles, 1880.
8174. LAVOLLEE, C. Les chemins de fer en France. Paris, 1866.
8175. LAVOLLEE, R. Les classes ouvrières en Europe. 2 éd. Paris, 1885. 2 v.
8176. LECOUTEUX, L. Cours d'économie rurale. 2 éd. Paris, 1889. 2 v.
8177. LEGOYT, A. L'émigration européene. Paris, 1862.
8178. ———. La France et l'étranger, études de statistique comparaison. 2d. éd. Strasburg, 1865.
8179. LEHMANN, H. Velstandslaere. Stockholm, 1874.
8180. LEHR, Julius. Eisenbahntarifwesen und Eisenbahnmonopol. Berlin, 1879.
8181. ———. Politische Oekonomie. München, 1892.
8182. LEIGH, Evan. The science of modern cotton spinnery.

	London, 1877. 2 v.
8183.	LELY, J. M. Municipal corporations. London, 1882.
8184.	LENORMANT, F. Essai sur l'organisation politique et économique de la monnaie dans l'antiquité. Paris, 1863.
8185.	LEROY-BEAULIEU, Paul. Le Collectivisme. Paris, 1884. (2d. éd., 1885.)
8186.	———. Essai sur la répartition des richesses. Paris, 1880. (3d. éd. 1887.)
8187.	———. L'Etat moderne et ses fonctions. Paris, 1890. (English, 1891.)
8188.	———. Précis d'économie politique. Paris, 1888. (4th éd. 1893.)
8189.	———. La Question ouvière au xix Siècle. Paris, 1871.
8190.	———. Traité de la Science des finances. Paris, 1877. 2 v. (6th éd. 1899, 2 v.)
8191.	———. Traité théorique et pratique d'économie politique, 1895. (2d. éd. Paris, 1896. 4 v.)
8192.	LESER, Emanuel. Untersuchungen zur Geschichte der nationalökonomie. Jena, 1881.
8193.	LESLIE, Thomas Edward Cliffe. Essays in political economy. 2d. ed. Dublin, 1888.
8194.	———. Land systems and industrial economy of Ireland, England, and the Continent. London, 1870.
8195.	LESSEPS, F. de. Lettres, journal et documents pour servir à l'histoire du Canal de Suez. Paris, 1875-81. 5 v.
8196.	LETOURNEAU, C. Property; its origin and development. London, 1892.
8197.	LEVI, Leone. Delle reforme necessarie alla moneta metallica. Bologna, 1887.
8198.	———. History of British commerce. 2d. ed. London, 1880.
8199.	———. Il problema ferroviario in Italia. Genova, 1884.
8200.	———. Work and pay, or principles of industrial economy. London, 1877.
8201.	LEVY, J. H. Individualism and the land question. London, 1912.
8202.	———. The outcome of individualism. 3d. ed. London, 1890. 48 p.
8203.	———, editor. Taxation and anarchism. London, 1912. pp. ix, 67.
8204.	———, editor. Transactions of political economy circle of national liberal club. London, 1891.
8205.	LEWINS, W. History of savings banks in Great Britain and Ireland. London, 1882.
8206.	LEWIS, G. H. National consolidation of the railways of the United States. New York, 1893.
8207.	LEWIS, Laurence, Jr. A history of the bank of North America. Philadelphia, 1882.
8208.	LEXIS, W. Gewerkvereine u. unternehmerverbände in

Frankreich. Leipzig, 1879.
8209. ———. Handbuch der politisch oekonomie. London, 1882.
8210. LEYEN, A. v. d. Die nordamerikan; eisenbahnen. Leipzig, 1885.
8211. LIBERATORE, M. Principii di economia politica. Roma, 1890. (Innsbruck, 1891; London, 1892; Madrid, 1890.)
8212. LIEBEN, R., et R. Auspitz. Die theorie des preises. Leipzig, 1887-89.
8213. LIEBSCHER, D. G. Japan's landwirthschaftliche verhältnisse. Jena, 1882.
8214. LINDERMAN, H. R. Money and legal tender in the United States. New York, 1878.
8215. LINDHEIM, W. v. Kohle und Eisen im Welthandel. Wien, 1877.
8216. ———. Strassenbahnen in Belgien, Deutschland. Wien, 1888.
8217. LINDSAY, W. S. History of merchant shipping. London, 1874-76. 4 v.
8218. LISBONA Y FABRAT. Organización y operaciones del banco de España. Madrid, 1888.
8219. LLOYD, Demarest Henry. Wealth against commonwealth. New York, 1894.
8220. LONGE, Francis D. A Critical examination of Mr. Georg's "Progress & Poverty." London, 1883.
8221. ———. A Refutation of the wage-fund theory of political economy. London, 1866. (London, 1869. Edited with introduction and notes by Jacob H. Hollander. Baltimore, 1904.)
8222. LONGSTAFF, G. B. Studies in statistics, social, political, and medical. London, 1891.
8223. LORIA, A. Analisi della proprietà capitalista. Torino, 1889. 2 v.
8224. ———. La legge di popolazione ed il sistema sociale. Siena, 1882.
8225. LOUA, T. Les grands faits économiques et sociaux. Paris, 1872-83. 4 v.
8226. LOWELL, J. S., compiler. Industrial arbitration and conciliation. New York, 1893.
8227. LUDEWIG, Jul. Die telegraphie in Staats- und privatrechtl. Beziehung. Leipzig, 1872.
8228. LUDLOW, J. M., and L. Jones. Progress of the working class, 1832-1867. London, 1867. (Berlin, 1868.)
8229. LUMBROSO, Giac. Recherches sur l'économie politique de l'Egypte sous les Lagides. Turn, 1870.
8230. LUNT, E. C. Present condition of economic science . . . New York, 1888.
8231. LUZZATTI, L. Il credito popolare in Italia. Roma, 1882.
8232. MACADAM, G. An alphabet in finance. New York, 1876.
8233. MACDONALD, A. F. Our ocean railways. London, 1893.
8234. MACDONNELL, W. D. A History and criticism of the various theories of Wages. Dublin, 1888.
8235. MACFARLANE, C. W. The History of the general doctrine

of rent in German economics. Leipzig, 1893.
8236. ———. Value and distribution. Philadelphia, 1899.
8237. MACKAY, F. English poor; sketch of their social and economic history. London, 1889.
8238. MACKENZIE, W. W. Poor law guardian. 3d. ed. London, 1892.
8239. MACLAREN, James. A sketch of the history of currency. 2d. ed. London, 1879.
8240. MACLEAN, J. L. The British railway system. London, 1883.
8241. MACLEOD, Henry Dunning. Bimetalism. London, 1894.
8242. ———. A dictionary of political economy. London, 1863. 1 v.
8243. ———. The elements of banking. New ed. London, 1891.
8244. ———. The elements of economics. London, 1886. 2 v.
8245. ———. Elements of political economy. London, 1880.
8246. ———. The history of economics. New York, 1896.
8247. ———. Principles of economical philosophy. 2d. ed. London, 1872-75. 2 v.
8248. ———. The theory of credit. London, 1889-90. 2 v. (2d. ed. 1893.)
8249. MACVANE, S. M. The working principles of political economy. New York, 1892.
8250. MADRAGO, S. D. Lecciones de economía política. Madrid, 1874. 13 v.
8251. MAGLIANI, A. G. La questione monetaria. Firenze, 1874.
8252. MAINE, Henry S. Village communities in the East and West. London, 1871. (3d. ed. 1876.)
8253. MAITLAND, S. R. Dark ages. New ed. London, 1889.
8254. MAKATO, Tenteoro. Japanese notions of European political economy. 3d. ed. Philadelphia, 1898.
8255. MALLET, L. Free exchange papers. London, 1891.
8256. MALLOCK, W. H. Classes and masses. London, 1896.
8257. ———. Labour and the popular welfare. London, 1894.
8258. ———. Property and progress. London, 1884.
8259. ———. Socialism. New York, 1907.
8260. MALON, B. Histoire du socialisme. Paris, 1880-85.
8261. ———. Le socialisme intégral. 2d. éd. Paris, 1892.
8262. MANN, C. A. Paper money the root of evil; an examination of the currency of United States. New York, 1872.
8263. MANNEQUIN, T. Le problème monétaire et la distribution de la richesses. Paris, 1879.
8264. MARCHET, G. Studien über die entwickelung der versaltungslehre in Deutschland. München, 1885.
8265. MARRIOTT, W. F. Grammar of political economy. London, 1874.
8266. MARSHALL, A. Principles of economics. London, 1890. 1 vol. (2d. ed. 1891: "Elements," 1892.)
8267. MARTIIS, S. Cognetti de. Il socialismo negli statu uniti. Torino. 1891.
8268. MARTIN, E. W. History of the grange movement. Philadelphia, 1873.
8269. MARTIN, R. M. Taxation of the British empire. London, 1885.

Post-Classical Period 489

8270. MARTINS, O. O Regime das riquezas. Lisbon, 1883.
8271. MARZANO, Fr. Scienza delle finanze. 2 ediz. Torino, 1887.
8272. MASON, D. H. A short tariff history of the United States. 1783-89. Chicago, 1886.
8273. MASSIP, A. La France commerciale et industrielle comparée aux Puissances étrangères. Paris, 1884.
8274. MASTIER, A. Turgot, sa vie et sa doctrine. Paris, 1861.
8275. MATAJA, Victor. Der Unternehmergewinn. Wien, 1884.
8276. MAYO-SMITH, Richmond. Statistics and economics. New York, 1899.
8277. MAYR, Georg von. Gestzmässigkeit in Gesellschaftsleben, München, 1877. (Torino, 1886.)
8278. ———. Statistik und gesellschaftslehre. Freiburg, 1897. 2 v.
8279. MAZZOLA, Ugo. Dati statistico da finanza pubblica. Roma, 1889.
8280. M'CARTHY, L. P. Annual statistician. San Francisco, 1891.
8281. McDONNEL, W. D. A history and criticism of the various theories of wages. Dublin, 1888. 72 p.
8282. McNEILL, George E., editor. The Labor Movement; the problem today. Boston, 1890.
8283. MEDLEY, G. W. The trade depression. London, 1885.
8284. MEHRING, H. Die deutsche social-demokratie. 3 Aufl. Bremen, 1879.
8285. MEILI, Fr. Das telegraphenrecht . . . 2 Aufl. Zürich, 1873.
8286. ———. Das telephonenrecht . . . Leipzig, 1885.
8287. MEININGHAUS, A. Soziale aufgaben der industriellen Arbeitgeber. Tübingen, 1890.
8288. MEITZEN, August. Geschichte theoretisch und technik der statistik. Berlin, 1886. (Philadelphia, 1891.)
8289. MENGER, Anton. Das recht auf den vollen arbeitsertrag. Stuttgart, 1886. (2te Aufl., 1891. London, 1899.)
8290. MENGER, Carl. Irrthümer des historismus in der deutschen nationalökonomie. Wien, 1884.
8291. MENIER, E. J. L'avenir economique. 2d. éd. Paris, 1880.
8292. MENSI, v. Die finanzen oesterreichs von 1701-40. Wien, 1890.
8293. MEYER, G. Lehrbuch d. deutschen verwaltungsrecht. Leipzig, 1883-85.
8294. MEYER, J. Ein beitrag zur lösung des wahrungsproblems. Berlin, 1887.
8295. MEYER, M. Die neuere nationalokonomie . . . 4 Aufl. Minden i. Paris, 1885.
8296. MEYER, R. Die emancipationkampf des vierten standes. Berlin, 1882.
8297. MEYER, Robert. Das wesen des einkommens. Berlin, 1887.
8298. ———. Die principien der gerechten besteuerung. Berlin, 1884.
8299. MEYER, R., et A. G. Ardant. Le mouvement agraire. Paris, 1889.

8300. MEYER, Rudolf. La crise internationale de l'industrie. Berlin, 1885.
8301. ———. Der socialismus in Dänemark. Berlin, 1874.
8302. MIASKOWSKI, Aug. v. Agrar-politische zeit- und streitfragen. Leipzig, 1889.
8303. ———. Beiträge staats- und socialwissenhschaftliche Leipzig, 1869.
8304. MILLS, Herbert V. Poverty and the state, or work for the unemployed. London, 1886.
8305. MINGHETTI, M. Dell' economia pubblica e delle sur attinenze colla morale e col diritto. Firenze, 1859. (2^e ediz., 1868.)
8306. ———. Opusculoi letterarii ed economici. Firenze, 1872.
8307. MITCHELL, W. Scotch banks, their position and policy. Edinburgh, 1879.
8308. MOFFAT, R. S. The economy of consumption. London, 1878.
8309. MOGLIA, L. Catechismo di economia politica. Bologna, 1880.
8310. MOIREAU, Aug. La banque de France. Paris, 1891.
8311. MOLESWORTH, G. L. Silver and gold the money of the world. London, 1891.
8212. MONGREDIEN, A. History of free trade movement in England. London, 1881.
8313. ———. Wealth-creation. London, 1882.
8314. MONTAGNON, E. Traité sur les sociétés de crédit foncier. Paris, 1886.
8315. MONTANARI, A. Storia critica della teoria del valore in Italia. Milano, 1889.
8316. MONTGOMERY, W. E. History of land tenure in Ireland. Cambridge, England, 1889.
8317. MONY, S. Etude sur le travail. 2d. éd. Paris, 1882. 2 v.
8318. MOODY, W. G. Land and labor in the United States. New York, 1883.
8319. MOORE, H. L. Economic cycles; their law and cause. New York, 1914.
8320. ———. Generating economic cycles. New York, 1923.
8321. ———. Laws of wages. New York, 1911.
8322. ———. Synthetic economics. New York, 1929.
8323. MORPURGO, E. La finanza; studii di economia pubblica. Firenze, 1877.
8324. MORRISON, W. D. Crime and its causes. London, 1891.
8325. MORSE, J. T. Law of banks and banking. 3d. Boston, 1888. 2 v.
8326. MORTARA, L. Doveri della proprietà fondiaria e la questione sociale. Roma, 1885.
8327. MOSLER, C. Die Wasserstrassen in den verenigten staaten. Berlin, 1877.
8328. MUHLBRECHT, O. Wegweiser durch die neuere litteratur der rechts- und staatswissenschaften. 2te Aufl. Berlin, 1893.
8329. MUHLEMAN, Maurice L. Monetary systems of the World.

Post-Classical Period

New York, 1895. 198 p.
8330. MULHALL, M. G. Dictionary of statistics. New ed. London, 1892.
8331. ———. History of prices since 1850. London, 1885.
8332. MULINEN, Comte de. Les finances de l'Autriche. Wien, 1875.
8333. MULLER, E., et E. Cacheux. Hibitations ouvrières en tous Pays. 2 éd. Paris, 1889.
8334. MURRAY, J. B. C. The History of usury. Philadelphia, 1866.
8335. MURRAY, K. B. Commercial geography in relation to British trade. London, 1887.
8336. MUSGRAVE, Anthony. Studies in political economy. London, 1875.
8337. MUZZI, S. Vocabolario geografico-storico-statistico dell' Italia. Bologna, 1873-4. 2 v.
8338. MYER, A. Agrarische verordeningen in Nederlansch-Indie. 3 druk. 's Hage, 1885.
8339. NAGAI, T. Die Landwirthschaft Japans. Dresden, 1887.
8340. NASSE, E. Ueber die mittelalterliche feldgemeinschaft und der einhegungen des 16 Jahrh. in England. Bonn, 1869. (London, 1872.)
8341. NAUDIER, F. Le Socialisme et la révolution sociale. Paris, 1894.
8342. NAZZANI, E. Saggi di economia politica. Milano, 1881.
8343. ———. Sunto di economia politica. Forli, 1873. (4th. ed. Milano, 1886.)
8344. NEEB, J. F. De grootboeken der nationale schuld. 3de. dr. Nykerk, 1889.
8345. NEROM, Van. Lois ouvrières et sociales en Belgique. Bruxelles, 1890.
8346. NERVO, le Baron de. Les Budgets de la Francaises et de l'Angleterre Paris, 1862.
8347. ———. Les finances francaises. Paris, 1861-66. 5 v.
8348. NEUMANN, F. J. Die progressive einkommensteuer im staats- und gemeindehaushalte. Leipzig, 1874.
8349. NEUMANN-SPALLART, Uebersichten der weltwirthschaft. Stuttgart, 1878-1887.
8350. ———. F. v. Volkswirthschaftslehre. Wien, 1873.
8351. NEURATH, Wilh. Elements der Volkswirthschaftslehre. 2 Aufl. Wien, 1892.
8352. ———. Volkswirthschaftslehre. Wien, 1880.
8353. NEWCOMB, Simon. Critical examination of our financial policy during the Southern rebellion. New York, 1865.
8354. ———. Principles of political economy. New York, 1885.
8355. NEWMAN, F. W. Political economy. London, 1890.
8356. NEYMARCK, A. Les chemins de fer et l'impôt. Paris, 1891.
8357. ——— Colbert et son temps. Paris, 1877. 2 v.
8358. ———. Turgot et ses doctrines. Paris, 1885. 2 v.

8359. NICHOLSON, J. Shield. The Effects of machinery on wages. Cambridge, 1878.
8360. ———. Inflation. London, 1919.
8361. ———. A Treatise on money. Edinburgh, 1888. (2d. ed. London, 1893.)
8362. NICOLAI, E. Les chemins de Fer de l'état en Belgique, 1834-1884. Bruxelles, 1885.
8363. NICOLAS, C. Les Budgets d. 1. France, xix Siècle. Paris, 1885.
8364. NIEDERER, G. Statistique du paupérisme en Suisse pendant 1870. Zurich, 1878.
8365. NINSGRADOFF, Paul. Villainage in England. Oxford, 1892.
8366. NITTI, Francesco S. Population and the social system. London, 1894.
8367. ———. Il Socialismo cattolico. 2 ediz. Torino, Roma, 1891. (Trad. fr., Paris, 1894.)
8368. NOBLE, John. Fiscal legislation, 1842-65. London, 1867.
8369. ———. The Queen's taxes. London, 1870.
8370. NOEL, O. Les banques d'émission en Europe. Paris, 1888.
8371. NORDOFF, Charles. The communistic societies of the United States. New York, 1875.
8372. NORTHCOTE, S. H. Twenty years of financial policy, 1842-61. London, 1862.
8373. NORTON, E. National finance and currency. 3d. ed. London, 1873.
8374. NOTCUTT, G. J. Law relating to factories and workshops. 2d. ed. London, 1879. (Berlin, 1876. Moscow, 1880.)
8375. NOURRY, Claudius. La Question laitière. Paris, 1890.
8376. NOUVEAU Dictionnaire de l'économique politica (Léon Say et J. Chailley). Paris, 1891-92.
8377. NOYES, Alexander D. Thirty years of American finance. New York, 1898.
8378. NOYSS, John H. History of American socialism. Philadelphia, 1870.
8379. OERTMANN, P. Volkswirthschaftslehre . . . Berlin, 1891.
8380. OETTINGEN, A. von. Die moralstatistik. 3 Aufl. Erlangen, 1882.
8381. OFFERMANN, Alfred. Das fictive capital als die ursache niedrigen arbeitslohnes. Wien, 1896.
8382. OLUFSEN, W. Die staatslehre des Aristoteles. 2 Bde. Leipzig, 1870-75.
8383. O'MEARA, J. J. Municipal taxation at home and abroad. London, 1894.
8384. ONCKEN, August. Adam Smith und Imanual Kant. Leipzig, 1877.
8385. ———. Der ältere Mirabeau. Bern, 1886.
8386. ———. Die maxime laissez faire. Berne, 1886.
8387. ———. Geschichte der nationalökonomie. Leipzig, 1902.
8388. OPPERMANN, C. A. Traité complet des chemins de fer économiques. Paris, 1873.
8389. OSBORNE, G. P. Principles of economics. Cincinnati, 1893.

8390. PAASCHE, H. Zuckerindustrie und zuckerhandel der welt. Jena, 1891.
8391. PACHER, P. Die österreichisch-ungarische währung Leipzig, 1890.
8392. PAGE, William. Cooperative agriculture. London, 1870.
8393. PAINE, Charles. The elements of railroading. New York, 1885.
8394. PALAA, G. Dictionnaire législatif et réglementaire des chemins de fer. 3 éd. Paris, 1887. 2 v.
8395. PALGRAVE, R. H. Inglis. Analysis of the minutes of evidence on banks of issue, 1875. London, 1876.
8396. _____. Bank rate in England, France, and Germany, 1844-78. London, 1880.
8397. _____, editor. Dictionary of political economy. London, 1894. 3 v. (Appendix. 1909. Edited by Henry Higgs. 1926. 3 v.)
8398. PANTALEONI, Maffeo. Principii di economia pura. Firenze, 1890. (London, 1898.)
8399. PAPONOT, F. L'Egypte, son avenir agricole et financier. Paris, 1884.
8400. PARIS, Comte de. Les associations ouvrières en angleterre, Paris, 1869. (7e éd., 1884.)
8401. PATTEN, Simon Nelson. The consumption of wealth. Philadelphia, 1889. 70 p.
8402. _____. The development of English thought. New York, 1899.
8403. _____. The economic basis of protection. Philadelphia, 1890.
8404. _____. The fundamental idea of capital. Philadelphia, 1889.
8405. _____. The stability of prices. Baltimore, 1889.
8406. _____. The theory of dynamic economics. Philadelphia, 1892.
8407. _____. The theory of prosperity. New York, 1902.
8408. PATTERSON, R. H. The economy of capital. Edinburgh, 1865.
8409. _____. The new gold age; influences of precious metals. London, 1882. 2 v.
8410. PATTON, J. H. Natural resources of the United States. New ed. New York, 1894.
8411. PAULIAT, L. La politique coloniale sous l'ancien régime. Paris, 1887.
8412. PAYNE, E. J. History of American colonies. London and New York, 1877.
8413. PEARSON, J. B. On the theories of usury in Europe, 1100-1400 A.D. London, 1877.
8414. PEEK, F. Social wreckage; laws of England as they affect the poor. 3d. ed. London, 1883-9.
8415. PEREIRE, E. et I. Pereire. Enquête sur la banque de France. Paris, 1866.
8416. PERIN, Charles. De la richesses dans les sociétés chrétiennes. 2 éd. Paris, 1868. 2 v.
8417. _____. Les doctrines économique depuis un siècle. Paris, 1880.

8418.	PERRIQUET, E. Traité théorique et pratique des Travaux publics. Paris, 1883. 2 v.
8419.	PERROT, A. Les cités ouvrières de Mulhouse. 4th ed. Paris, 1889.
8420.	PERROT, F. Der Bank- Borsen- und Actienschwindel. Rostock, 1873-76.
8421.	———. Zur Geschichte der verkehrswesens. Rostock, 1871.
8422.	PERRY, A. L. Elements of political economy. New York, 1866. (20th. ed. 1891: Principles of political economy.)
8423.	———. Introduction to political economy. New York, 1877. (3d. ed., 1882.)
8424.	PESCATORE, M. Logica delle imposte. Torino, 1867.
8425.	PETO, Sir S. M. Taxation, its levy and expenditure. London, 1863.
8426.	PFAU, J. J. Bankwesen der Schweiz und der Auslandes. Zürich, 1875.
8427.	PHILLIPOVICH, Eugen von. Ueber . . . Methode der politischen oekonomie. Freiburg, 1886.
8428.	PHILLIPS, Henry, Jr. Historical sketch of paper currency of American colonies. Roxbury, Massachusetts. 1866. 2 v.
8429.	PHILLIPS, M. History of banks, bankers and banking in the North of England (1755-1894). London, 1894.
8430.	PICARD, A. Traité des chemins de fer. Paris, 1887. 4 v.
8431.	PIERNAS y HURTADO, J. Tratado de hacienda publica; exámen de la española. 4 ed. Madrid, 1891. 2 v.
8432.	———. Vocabulario de la economia. Saragoza, 1882.
8433.	PIERSON, N. G. Leerboek der staathuishoudkunde. 2 Bdn. Haarlem, 1884-90.
8434.	———. Principles of economis. London, 1902. v 1.
8435.	PIERSTORFF, Julius. Die Lehre vom unternehmergewinn. Berlin, 1875.
8436.	PIGEONNEAU, H. Histoire du commerce du la France. Paris, 1885-88. 2 v.
8437.	PIRET, N. J. Traité d'économie rurale. Bruxelles et Paris, 1889.
8438.	PIZZAMIGLIO, L. Le Societe cooperative di consumo. Milano, 1890.
8439.	PLANTEAU, F. E. Réforme des impôts. Paris, 1888.
8440.	PLEBANO, A. Considerazioni sulla moneta e sul Biglietto de banca. Roma, 1884.
8441.	PLEHN, Carl C. Introduction to Public Finance. New York, 1896. (4th ed. 1920.)
8442.	———. Das kreditwesen der staaten und stadte der Nord-Amerikanischen Union. Jena, 1891.
8443.	PLENER, E. E. Ferdinand Lasalle. Leipzig, 1884.
8444.	POIRE, P. La France industrielle. 3e éd. Paris, 1880.
8445.	POLITICAL economy club. (Members, 1821-1860; questions considered.) London, 1860. (1821-1872: London, 1872.)
8446.	POLLOCK, Sir F. The British land laws. London, 1886.

Post-Classical Period

8447. PONSIGLIONI, A. Economia politica. 2 ed. Genova, 1881.
8448. POOR, H. V. Money and its laws. New York, 1877.
8449. ———. Resumption and the silver question. New York, 1878.
8450. ———. Twenty-two years of protection. New York, 1888.
8451. POSNETT, H. M. The historical method in ethics, jurisprudence, and political economy. London, 1882.
8452. POTTER, Beatrice. The co-operative movement in Great Britain. London, 1891.
8453. POWELL, B. H. Baden. Land systems of British India. Oxford, 1892. 3 v.
8454. PRATT, W. T. Law of friendly societies. 16th ed. Edited by G. W. Brabrook. London, 1889.
8455. PREBLE, Henry. History of steam navigation, 1543-1882. Philadelphia, 1883.
8456. PRICE, Bonamy. Chapters on practical political economy. 2d. ed. London, 1882.
8457. ———. Currency and banking. London, and New York, 1876. (Berlin, 1877.)
8458. PRICE, F. G. H. Handbook of London bankers, with some account of their predecessors, the early goldsmiths. Enl. ed. London, 1891.
8459. PRICE, Lanford Lovell Frederich Rice. Money and its relations to prices. London, 1896. (2d. ed. 1900.)
8460. ———. A short history of political economy in England. London, 1891.
8461. PRIETO, G. Breves nociones de economía política. Mexico, 1888.
8462. PRITTWITZ, R. v. Die arbeiterfrage und deren lösung. Berlin, 1874.
8463. PROBYN, J. W., editor. Local government and taxation in the United Kingdom. New ed. London, 1882.
8464. ———. Systems of land tenure in various countries. New ed. London, 1881.
8465. PROBYN, L. C. Indian coinage and currency. London, 1897. 125 p.
8466. PROTHERO, R. E. The pioneers and progress of English farming. London and New York, 1888.
8467. PROUTEAUX, A. Principes d'économie industrielle. Paris, 1888.
8468. PURDY, W. City life; its trade and finance. London, 1876.
8469. QUACK, H. Q. G. De socialisten personen en stelsels. Amsterdam, 1875-79.
8470. QUARITSCH, Du. Compendium du nationalökonomisch. 4 Aufl. Berlin, 1891.
8471. RABBENO, Ugo. The American commercial policy. 2d ed. London, 1895.
8472. ———. La cooperazione in Italia. Milano, 1886.
8473. ———. Il protezionismo americano. Milano, 1892.
8474. ———. Le società cooperative di produzione. Milano, 1889.

496   Economic Thought and Analysis

8475. RAE, G. The country banker. 2d. ed. London, 1886.
8476. RAFFALOVCH, A. Les finances de la Russie, 1887-89.
        Paris, 1889.
8477. _____. Le marché financier en 1893-94. Paris, 1894.
8478. RAMAIX, M. de. Réforme sociale et économie en Europe
        . . . Bruxelles, 1889.
8479. RAMBAUD, Alf. La France coloniale. Paris, 1886.
8480. RAMBAUD, J. Traité elém. d'économie politique. Paris,
        1892.
8481. RAND, Benjamin. Selections illustrating economic history
        since the seven years' war. Cambridge, United States,
        1888.
8482. RANKE, Leop. V. Weltgeschichte. 9 Thl. Leipzig, 1881-
        89.
8483. RATHGEN, K. Japans volkswirthschaft u. staatshaushalt.
        Leipzig, 1891.
8484. RATZINGER, G. Volkswirthschaft . . . Freiburg, 1881.
8485. RAWSON, H. G. Profit sharing precedents. London, 1891.
8486. RAWSON, R. Tariffs and trade of the British Empire.
        London, 1888.
8487. READ, C., et A. Pell. L'Agriculture des états-Unis.
        Paris, 1881.
8488. REDFIELD, I. F. Law of railways; embracing the law of
        corporations . . . 6th ed. Edited by J. K. Kinney,
        Boston, 1888. 2 v.
8489. REDGRAVE, A., and A. Jasper. Factory and workshop
        acts. 1878-1891. London, 1891.
8490. REEVES, J. The Rothschilds. London, 1887.
8491. REINAUD, Em. Les Syndicats professionels. Paris, 1886.
8492. REMONDIERE, L. A. Une chambre des payans. Paris,
        1893.
8493. REPORT on interstate commerce. Washington, 1886.
        49th. Congress, 1st session. Sen. Rep. no . 46.
8494. REPORT on rates of duty on United States imports, 1789-
        1890. Washington, 1891. 51st Congress, 2d. session.
        (Senate Rep. no. 2130.)
8495. REPORT on Tariff laws of 1890 and 1894. Washington, 1894.
        (Senate Report no. 707, 53d Congress, 2d. session.)
8496. REPORT on United States Labor laws. Washington, 1892.
        (House Report no. 1960, 52d. Congress, 1st session.)
8497. REPORT upon Alleged combinations in manufactures, trade,
        and insurance in Canada. Ottawa, 1888. (Parliament,
        6th, 2d. session.)
8498. REPORTS of commissioners appointed to revise the laws
        for assessment and collection of taxes in New York. New
        York, 1871-2.
8499. REPORTS of Consuls on Streets and highways in foreign
        countries. Washington, 1892. (House Mis. Doc. no.
        20, 52d. Congress, 1st session.)
8500. REPORTS of (United States) Interstate commerce
        commission. Washington, 1887.
8501. REPORTS of United States Consuls on Emigration from
        Europe . . . Washington, 1887. (House Mis. Doc. no.

	604, 50th. Congress, 1st session.)
8502.	RESCH, Pet. Aufeinanderfolge der Welthandelsherrschaften. 2 Auf. Graz, 1885, S. 70.
8503.	_____. Entwickelungsstufen der volkswirthschaft. Graz, 1886.
8504.	REYMOND, J. J. Etudes sur l'économie sociale et internationale. Torino, 1860-1861. 2 v.
8505.	REYNAUD, L. Les travaux public du la France. 5 Pts. Paris, 1876-1883.
8506.	RIBTON-TURNER, C. J. History of vagrants and vagrancy. London, 1887.
8507.	RICCA-SALERNO, Giuseppe. Scienza delle finanze. Firenze, 1888.
8508.	_____. La Teoria del valore. Palermo, 1894. 171 p.
8509.	RICHALD, L. Historie du finances publicques du la Belgique depuis 1830. Bruxelles, 1885.
8510.	RICHARDSON, G. G. Corn and cattle producing districts of France. London, 1888.
8511.	RICHEY, A. G. Irish land laws. 2d. ed. London, 1881.
8512.	RICHMOND, W. Christian economics. New York, 1888.
8513.	RICHTER, Emil. Die entwickelung der verkehrsgrundlagen. 2 Aufl. Berlin, 1873.
8514.	_____. Menschheit und kapital. 2 Bde. Leipzig, 1878.
8515.	RICHTER, Gust. Allgemeine wirthschaftslehre. Freiburg, 1881.
8516.	RIDGEWAY, William. The Origin of metallic currency and weight standards. Cambridge, England, 1892.
8517.	RIEHL, W. H. Die deutsche Arbeit. 3 Aufl. Stuttgart, 1884.
8518.	RINGWALT, J. L. Development of transportation system in United States. Philadelphia, 1888.
8519.	RITTER, C. Geschichte der erdkunde und der entdeckungen. Berlin, 1861.
8520.	RIVET, F. Des rapports du droit et de la législation avec l'économie politique. Paris, 1864.
8521.	ROBERTS, E. H. Government revenue; argument for industrial freedom. Boston, 1884.
8522.	ROBINEAU, L. Turgot, administration et oeuvres économique. Paris, 1889.
8523.	ROCCA, F. de. La circulazione monetaria ed il corso forzoso in Russia. Roma, 1881.
8524.	ROCHUSSEN, H. F. Memoire sur le bimétallisme international. La Haye, 1890.
8525.	RODBERTUS, Karl. Overproduction and crises. Introduction by John B. Clark. London, 1898.
8526.	ROESLER, Carl F. H. Grundlehren d. v. Adam Smith . . . Volkswirthschaftstheorie. 2 Aufl. Erlangen, 1871.
8527.	_____. Zur kritik der lehre vom arbeitslohn. Erlangen, 1861.
8528.	ROGERS, James Edwin Thorold. The economic interpretation of history. London and New York, 1888.
8529.	_____. The First nine years of the Bank of England. Oxford, 1887.

8530. _____. History of agriculture and prices in England. London, 1866-87. 6 v.
8531. _____. Industrial and commercial supremacy of England. (A. Rogers.) London, 1891.
8532. _____. A Manual of political economy. Oxford, 1868. (3d. ed. 1876.)
8533. _____. Six Centuries of work and wages. London, 1884. 2 v.
8534. RONNA, A. Les industrielles agricoles. Paris, 1869.
8535. ROSE, H. New political economy: Carlyle, Ruskin, George. London, 1891.
8536. ROSENTHAL, E. Internationales eisenbahnfrachtrecht, auf grund der berner convention. Jena, 1894.
8537. ROSS, D. W. The early history of land-holding among the Germans. Boston, 1883.
8538. ROSS, E. A. Sinking funds. London, 1892.
8539. ROSSI, Egisto. La concorrenza agraria transatlantica. Roma, 1886.
8540. ROSTRAND, Eug. Les questions d'economie sociale dans Marseille. Paris, 1889.
8541. _____. Réforme des caisses d'épargne franc. Paris, 1891.
8542. ROSWAG, C. Les métaux préciuex considérés au point de vue économique. Paris, 1865.
8543. ROTA, C. Principii di scienza bancaria. 2 ediz. Milano, 1885.
8544. ROTHSCHILD, Arth. de. Histoire de la poste. 2e éd. Paris, 1873.
8545. ROTHWELL, R. P., editor. The mineral industry. New York, 1894. 1 v.
8546. ROUGIER, J. C. P. Liberté commerciale, douanes et traités de commerce. Paris, 1878.
8547. ROYER, Mlle. Cl. A. Théorie de l'impôt. Paris, 1862. 2 v.
8548. RUBLO y DORADO. Economía política. Madrid, 1873.
8549. RUSKIN, John. Unto this last. New ed. New York, 1891.
8550. RYAN, D. J. Arbitration between capital and labor. New York, 1885.
8551. SACH, I. L'Italie et son développement économique. 1859-1884. Paris, 1885.
8552. SAINT, Genis, Flour de. Le crédit territorial en France. Le Havre, 1889.
8553. SALMON, C. S. The Crown Colonies of Great Britain. London, 1889.
8554. SALOMON, G. Les coalitions commerciales d'aujourd'hui Paris, 1884.
8555. SALVA, W. Tratado elemental de Estadística. Madrid, 1882.
8556. SAMPAIO, P. Novos elements de economia politica e estadistica. 7 ed. Coimbra, 1874. 2 v.
8557. SANTILLAN, R. Historias de los bancos. Madrid, 1865. 2 v.
8558. SARACCO, J. Storia d. finanza italiana. 1864-68. Firenze, 1868.

8559.	SARTORIUS, F. Der moderne socialismus in den Vereinigten Staaten. Berlin, 1890.	
8560.	SATO, S. History of the land question in United States. Baltimore, 1886.	
8561.	SAUERBECK, A. Prices of commodities and the precious metals. London, 1886.	
8562.	SAX, E. Das wesen und der aufgabe der Nationalökonomie. Wien, 1885.	
8563.	———. Die hausindustrien in Thüringen. 2 aufl. Jena, 1884-88.	
8564.	———. Die wohnungszustande der arbeitenden klassen. Wien, 1869.	
8565.	———, editor. Dictionnaire des finances. Paris, 1889-1894. 2 v.	
8566.	———. Economie sociale. 2e éd. Paris, 1891.	
8567.	SAY, Léon. Le socialisme d'état. Paris, 1884.	
8568.	SCALABRINI, G. B. Il disegno di legge sulla emigrazione Italiana. Piacenza, 1888.	
8569.	SCHAEFER, G. Ursprung und entwickelung der verkehrsmittel. Dresden, 1890.	
8570.	SCHAFER, E. D. Die Hansestädte; Hansische geschichte bis 1376. Jena, 1879.	
8571.	SCHAFFLE, Albert E. Fr. Die aussichtslösigkeit der Sozialdemokratie. Tübingen, 1885. (4 Aufl. 1891. London, 1892.)	
8572.	———. Bau und leben des sozialen korpers. 1875-1878. (2d. ed. Tübingen, 1896. 2 v.)	
8573.	———. Kapitalismus und socialismus. Tübingen, 1870.	
8754.	———. Die nationalökonomie. Tübingen, 1861. 3 Aufl.	
8575.	———. Die quintessenz des sozialismus. 1875. (13te Aufl. 1891. Madrid, 1885. London, 1889. Geneva, 1891.)	
8576.	SCHELLE, G. Du Pont de Nemours et l'école physiocratique. Paris, 1888.	
8577.	SCHERZER, K. v. Studien über der weltindustrien. Stuttgart, 1880.	
8578.	SCHIATTERELLA, R. Del Metodo in economia sociale. Naples, 1873.	
8579.	SCHIFF, W. Organisation der landwirthschaftlich kredits in Deutschland und Oesterreich. Leipzig, 1892.	
8580.	SCHLOSS, David F. Methods of industrial remuneration. New York, 1892.	
8581.	———. Reports on profit sharing. London, 1894.	
8582.	SCHMIDT, L. H. Repetitorium der national-oekonomie. 2 Aufl. Leipzig, 1886.	
8583.	SCHMIDTBERGER, H. Die volkswirthschaftslehre oder national Oekonomie. Innsbruck, 1881.	
8584.	SCHNEIDER, A. Lehrbuch der landwirthschaft. 3 Aufl. Wien, 1890.	
8585.	SCHOBER, H. Katechismus der volkswirtschaftslehre. 4 Aufl. Leipzig, 1888.	
8586.	SCHOENHOF, J. The economy of high wages. New York, 1892.	
8587.	———. The industrial situation. New York, 1885.	

8588.	SCHONBERG, Gustav von. Handbuch der politischen oekonomie. Tubingen, 1882. (4th ed. Tübingen, 1896-98. 5 v.)
8589.	SCHONE, L. Histoire de la population française. Paris, 1893.
8590.	SCHRAUT, M. Die organisation der kredits. Leipzig, 1883.
8591.	SCHROEDER, E. A. Die politische oekonomie. 2 Aufl. Stuttgart, 1885.
8592.	———. Unternehmen- und Unternehmergewinn. Wien, 1884.
8593.	SCHULLERN-SCHRATTENHOFEN, Hermann v. Die theoretisch nationalökonomie Italiens in neuester Zeit. Leipzig, 1891.
8594.	SCHULZE-GAVERNITZ, G. v. Zum socialen Frieden. 2 Bde. Leipzig, 1890. (London, 1893.)
8595.	SCHWAB, J. C. History of the New York property tax. New York, 1890.
8596.	SCOTT, William A. Money and banking. New York, 1903.
8597.	———. Repudiation of state debts in United States. New York, 1893.
8598.	SCRATCHLEY, A. Treatise on saving banks. New ed. London, 1863.
8599.	SEEBOHM, F. The English village community. 2d. ed. London, 1883.
8600.	SEIDLER, Gust. Budget und budgetrecht. Wien, 1885.
8601.	SELIGMEN, E. R. Essays in taxation. New York, 1895. (9th ed. New York, 1921.)
8602.	———. On the shifting and coincidence of taxation. Baltimore, 1892. (3d. ed. New York, 1910.)
8603.	———. Progressive taxation in theory and practice. Baltimore, 1894. (2d. ed. Princeton, 1908.)
8604.	———. Railway tariff and the interstate commerce law. New York, 1887.
8605.	———. Taxation of corporations. New York, 1890.
8606.	SEMENZA, Gaetano. Italian finances and the abolition of customs duties. London, 1870.
8607.	SERING, Max. Die landwirthschaftlich konkurrenz Nordamerikas in gegenwart und zukunft. Leipzig, 1887.
8608.	SEWARD, G. F. Chinese emigration. New York, 1881.
8609.	SEYD, E. Bullion and foreign exchange. London, 1868.
8610.	———. Reform of the Bank of England note issue. London, 1874.
8611.	SHADWELL, John Lancelot. Political economy for the people. London, 1880.
8612.	———. A system of political economy. London, 1877.
8613.	SHALER, N. S., editor. United States of America: its natural resources. New York, 1894. 2 v.
8614.	SHAW, Albert. Co-operation in a Western City. Boston, 1886.
8615.	———. Municipal government in Great Britain. New York, 1895.
8616.	———, editor. National Revenues. Chicago, 1888.

Post-Classical Period 501

8617. SHAW, George Bernard, editor. Fabian essays in socialism. New York, 1891.
8618. SHAW-LEFEVRE, J. Agrarian tenures in England, Ireland, and Scotland, London, 1893.
8619. _____. English and Irish land questions. London, 1881.
8620. SHEA, Hon. G. Life and epoch of Alexander Hamilton. Boston, 1879.
8621. SHERWOOD, Sidney. The history and theory of money. Philadelphia, 1892.
8622. _____. Tendencies in American economic thought. Baltimore, 1897.
8623. SICILIANI, Socialismo, Darwinismo e socialogia moderna. 3 ediz. Bologna, 1885.
8624. SIDGWICK, Henry. The elements of politics. London, 1891.
8625. _____. Philosophy, its scope and relations. London, 1902.
8626. _____. The scope and method of economic science. London, 1885.
8627. SIEBLIST, Otto. Die post im Auslande. 2 Aufl. Berlin, 1892.
8628. SIEGFRIED, J. La misère, son histoire . . . 4e ed. Paris, 1880.
8629. SIMCOX, E. J. Primitive civilization; or, outlines of the history of ownership in archaic communities. London, 1894. 2 v.
8630. SIMON, Jules. L'Ouvrière. 2d. éd. Paris, 1861.
8631. _____. Le Travail. 2d. éd. Paris, 1867.
8632. SIMONDS, J. C. and J. T. McEnnis. The story of manual labor in all lands and in all ages. Chicago, 1887.
8633. SKALKOVSKY, C. F. Les ministres des finances de la Russie (1802-1890). Paris, 1891.
8634. SMART, William. The distribution of income. London, 1899. 341 p.
8635. _____. Economic annals of the nineteenth century 1801-20. London, 1910.
8636. _____. An introduction to the theory of value. London, 1891. 88 p.
8637. _____. Studies in economics. London, 1895. 341 p.
8638. SMILES, Samuel. Industrial biography. London, 1876-79.
8639. SMISSEN, E. Van Der. La population. Paris, 1893.
8640. SMITH, A. M. Subjective political economy. 2d. ed. London, 1883-86.
8641. SMITH, L. Coalitions et grèves d'après l'histoire et l'économie politique avec un appendice de lois pays. Paris, 1886.
8642. SMITH, R. Mayo. Immigration and emigration. New York, 1890.
8643. _____. Statistics and economics. Baltimore, 1888.
8644. SMITH, S. Bimetallic question. London, 1887.
8645. _____. The nationalisation of land. London, 1884.
8646. SOMER, R. The Scotch banks and system of issue.

Edinburgh, 1873.
8647. SOYEDA, Juichi. Finance and budget. Tokyo, 1892. 2 v.
8648. SPELLING, T. C. A treatise on trusts and monopolies. London, 1894.
8649. STAHL, Fr. Wilh. Das deutsche handwerk. Giessen, 1874.
8650. STAMM, Aug. Die erlösung der darbenden menschheit. 3 Aufl. Stuttgart, 1884.
8651. STAMM, Ferd. Geschichte der arbeit. Wien, 1882.
8652. STAMMHAMMER, J. Bibliographie des socialismus und communismus. Jena, 1893.
8653. STEELE, G. M. Outline study of political economy. New York, 1885.
8654. STEFFENHAGEN, H. Die Kommunal-verwaltung. 3 Bdchn. Berlin, 1887-8.
8655. STEINER, Max. Reform der armenpflege in oesterreich. Wien, 1880.
8656. STENGEL, K. Freih. v. Wörterbuch des deutschen verwaltungsrecht. 2 Bde. Freiburg, 1889-90.
8657. STEPHENS, T. A. A contribution to the bibliography of the Bank of England. London, 1897.
8658. STOPEL, Fr. Soziale reform. 9 Beiträge. Leipzig, 1884-85.
8659. STOURM, René. Le budget. 3d. ed. Paris, 1896.
8660. ———. Les finances de l'ancien régime et de la révolution. Paris, 1885. 2 v.
8661. ———. Systèmes généraux d'impôts. Paris, 1893.
8662. STRACHEY, J. Finances and public works of India (1869-1881). London, 1882.
8663. STRAULING, G. Il Commercio internazionale e la circolazione monetaria nello stato. Firenze, 1893.
8664. STRICKLAND, E. Greece: its conditions and resources. London, 1863.
8665. STUBBS, H. Lectures on mediaeval and modern history. Oxford, 1886-87.
8666. ———. Select charters. Oxford, 1870.
8667. STUDIES in history, economics and public law. (Columbia college.) New York, 1891-93. 4 v.
8668. STUDNITZ, A. v. Nordamerikan. Arbeiterverhältnisse. Leipzig, 1879.
8669. STURMER, G. Geschichte der eisenbahnen. Bromberg, 1876.
8670. STURTEVANT, J. M. Economics, or the science of wealth. New York, 1877.
8671. SUDRE, Ch. Finances de la France du XIXe Siècle. Paris, 1883. 2 v.
8672. SUMNER, William G. The financier and the finances of the American Revolution. New York, 1891. 2 v.
8673. ———. A history of American currency. New York, 1884.
8674. ———. Lectures on history of protection in United States. New York, 1877.
8675. ———. Life of Alexander Hamilton. New York, 1890.
8676. ———. Problems in political economy. New York, 1884.

8677. _____. What social classes owe to each other. New York, 1883.
8678. SUPINO, Cam. Il capitale nell' organismo economia. Milano, 1886.
8679. _____. La definizione dell' economia politica. Pisa, 1883.
8680. _____. La science economiche in Italia, Sec. XVI. and XVII. Torino, 1888.
8681. SWANK, J. M. History of the manufacture of iron in all ages. Philadelphia, 1884.
8682. SWOBODA, Otto. Die kaufmannische arbitrage. 7 Aufl. Berlin, 1889.
8683. SYMES, J. E. Short text-book of political economy. London, 1888.
8684. TALLON, M. Lois de protection de l'enfance ouvrière. 3e éd. Paris, 1880.
8685. TARBIER, H. La Belgique; ses ressources. Bruxelles, 1879.
8686. TAUSSIG, F. W. History of the present tariff, 1860-83. New York, 1885.
8687. _____. Protection to young industries. Cambridge, Massachusetts, 1883.
8688. _____. The silver situation in the United States. 2d. ed. New York, 1893.
8689. _____. Some aspects of the tariff question. Cambridge, 1915.
8690. _____. The tariff history of the United States, 1789-93. New York, 1888. (6th ed. 1914.)
8691. _____. Wages and capital. New York, 1896.
8692. TAYLOR, I. N. Treatise on American law of landlord and tenant. 8th. ed. Boston, 1887.
8693. TAYLOR, Sedley. Profit sharing between capital and labour. London, 1884.
8694. TENNANT, Charles. Bank of England and organisation of credit in England. London, 1867.
8695. THEVENIN, Ev. Cours d'économie industrielle. Paris. 1866-68. 7 v.
8696. THOMAS, K. Natinnalökonomie güterlehre. 2 Aufl. v. T. Ziller. Leipzig, 1879.
8697. THOMPSON, Herbert M. The Theory of wages. London, 1892. 140 p.
8698. THOMPSON, P. Politics of labor. New York, 1887.
8699. THOMPSON, Robert E. Elements of political economy. 3d. ed. Philadelphia, 1882.
8700. _____. Social science and national economy. Philadelphia, 1875.
8701. THOMPSON, R. W. History of protective tariff laws. New York, 1888.
8702. TIDMAN, P. F. Gold and silver money. 2d. ed. London, 1882.
8703. TIKHOMIROV, L. Russia, political and social. Translated by E. Avelin. London, 1887. 2 v.
8704. TONIOLO, G. Scholastica ed umanismo nelle dottrine economiche. Pisa, 1887.

8705. TORTORA, E. Nuovi documenti sulla storia del banco di Napoli. Napoli, 1890.
8706. TOTZKE, A. Deutschlands kolonien und seine kolonialpolitik. Minden, 1885.
8707. TOUBEAU, A. Répartition métriques des impôts. Paris, 1880 2 v.
8708. TOYNBEE, Arnold. Lectures on the industrial revolution of the 18th century in England. London, 1884. (4th. ed. 1894.)
8709. TURNER, B. B. Chronicles of the Bank of England. London, 1897.
8710. TURQUAN, V. Densité de la population en France. Paris, 1887.
8711. TWINING, L. Poor relief in foreign countries and outdoor relief in England. London, 1889.
8712. ULRICH, Franz. Das Eisenbahntarifwesen im Allgemeinen. Berlin, 1886.
8713. UPTON, J. K. Money in politics. Introduction by Edward Atkinson. Boston, 1884.
8714. VALENTI, G. La teoria del valore. Roma, 1890.
8715. VALLEROUX, Hubert. Les corporations d'arts et métiers. Paris, 1885.
8716. VAQUETTE, T., et C. Bornot. Cours d'économie politique. Paris, 1883.
8717. VARIGNY, C. de. Les grandes fortunes aux états-unis et en Angleterre. Paris, 1889.
8718. VAUDERVILLE, M. Enquête sur les associations professionnelles d'artisans et d'ouvriers en Belgique. Bruxelles, 1893.
8719. VAVASSEUR, J. L'impôt sur le revenue des valeurs mobilières. Paris, 1887.
8720. VEDIA, A. de. El banco nacional. 1811-1854. Buenos Ayres, 1892.
8721. VERDEIL, F. De l'industrie moderne. Paris, 1861.
8722. VERNEY, Lady F. P. Peasant properties. London, 1885. 2 v.
8723. VERRIJN-STUART, C. A. Ricardo en Marx. Stockholm, 1890.
8724. VESSELOVSKY, A. Annuaire des finances russes. Paris, 1873-83. 4 v.
8725. _____. L'Impôt sur le revenu mobilier en Italie. St. Petersburg, 1879.
8726. VIDARI, E. Corso di Diritto commerciale. Milano, 1877-79. 9 v.
8727. VIGNES, Edouard. Traité des impôts en France. 4th. éd. Paris, 1880. 2 v.
8728. VIGNON, L. Les colonies françaises. Paris, 1886.
8729. VILLARI, P. Nicolo Machivelli e i suoi Tempi. Firenze, 1887-92. 3 v.
8730. VILLEY, ed. Du rôle de l'état dans l'ordre économique. Paris, 1882.
8731. _____. Traité élémentaire d'économie politique. Paris, 1885.

8732.	VILLIERS, C. P. Free trade speeches. London, 1883-84. 2 v.	
8733.	VIRGILII, F. Manuale di statistica. Milano, 1891.	
8734.	VITU, Aug. Les finances de l'empire. 2e éd. Paris, 1868.	
8735.	_____. Guide financier. Paris, 1864.	
8736.	WAAL, E. de. Onze indische financiën. 's Gravenhage, 1876-84.	
8737.	WALCKER, K. Adam Smith. Berlin, 1890.	
8738.	_____. Hanbuch der nationalökonomie. 2 Aufl. 4 Bde. Leipzig, 1888.	
8739.	_____. Lehrbuch der nationalökonomie. Berlin, 1875.	
8740.	WALFORD, C. Insurance cyclopaedia. London, 1871-78. 4 v.	
8741.	_____. Origin, constitution, objects, and later history of gilds. New ed. London, 1888.	
8742.	WALKER, Francis Amasa. An abstract of Walker's political economy. By E. L. Hawkins. Oxford, 1892.	
8743.	_____. Bimetallism; a Tract for the times. Boston, 1894.	
8744.	_____. First lessons in political economy. New York, 1889.	
8745.	_____. Land and its rent. Boston, 1883.	
8746.	_____. Money in its relations to trade and industry. New York, H. Holt, 1879. (New York, 1889.)	
8747.	_____. Money. New York, 1883. (New ed. 1891.)	
8748.	_____. Statistical atlas of the United States. New York, 1874.	
8749.	WALLACE, A. R. Land nationalization. 2d. ed. London, 1882.	
8750.	WALLACE, R. Indian agriculture. London, 1892.	
8751.	WARD, D. Income tax. 4th. ed. London, 1885.	
8752.	WARING, C. State purchase of railways. London, 1887.	
8753.	WARNER, Amos G. American charities. New York, 1894.	
8754.	_____. Three phases of co-operation in the West. Baltimore, 1887.	
8755.	WARSCHAUER, Otto. Geschichte des socialismus. Leipzig, 1892.	
8756.	WASSERHAB, K. Preise und volkswirthschaftliche Krisen aus unseren Tagen. Stuttgart, 1899.	
8757.	WATTS, John. The facts of the cotton famine. London, 1866.	
8758.	WEBB, Sidney and Beatrice Webb. The history of trade unionism. London, 1894. v 1.	
8759.	_____. Industrial democracy. London, 1897. 2 v.	
8760.	_____. Problems of modern industry. London, 1898.	
8761.	_____. The remedy for unemployment. London, 1909.	
8762.	WEBB, S., and H. Cox. The Eight-hours day. London, 1891.	
8763.	WEBER, M. M. v. Nationalität und Eisenbahnpolitik. Wien, 1876.	
8764.	_____. Schule der Eisenbahnwesens. 4 Aufl. v. R. Koch. Leipzig, 1885.	
8765.	_____. Der staatliche Einfluss auf die Entwickelung der

eisenbahnen minderer ordnung. Wien, 1878.
8766. WEBER, Max. Geschichte der handelsgesellschaften im mittelalter. Stuttgart, 1889.
8767. WEBSTER, R. G. Our Present system of trade of the World. London, 1886.
8768. WEBSTER, Richard. Principles of monetary legislation. London, 1874.
8769. WEEDEN, W. B. Economic and social history of New England, 1620-1789. Boston, 1891. 2 v.
8770. ———. Social law of labor. Boston, 1882.
8771. WEEKS, J. D. Industrial arbitration and conciliation in New York, Ohio, and Pennsylvania. Boston, 1881.
8772. WEICHS-GLON, F. Das finanzielle und sociale Wesen der modernen verkehrsmittel. Tübingen, 1894.
8773. WELLS, David A. Practical economics. New York, 1885.
8774. ———. Recent economic changes. New York, 1889.
8775. ———. Robinson Crusoe's money. New York, 1876.
8776. WESTERGAARD, H. Die grundzüge der theorie der statistik. Jena, 1890.
8777. WESTMAN, C. Nationalekonomiens Grunddrag. Stockholm, 1885.
8778. WEYER, O. W. Die englische fabrikinspection. Tübingen, 1888.
8779. WHITE, Arnold. The problems of a great city. New ed. London, 1886-87.
8780. WHITE, Horace. Money and banking. Boston, 1896. (4th. ed. Boston, 1911.)
8781. WHITNEY, J. D. The United States, Physical geography and material resources. Boston, 1889. (Supplement I., 1894.)
8782. WICKSTEED, P. H. The alphabet of economic science. London, 1888. v 1.
8783. WIESER, Friedrich von. Der natürliche werthes. Wien, 1889.
8784. ———. Uber den Ursprung und die Hauptgesetze des Wirthschaftlichen Werthes. Wien, 1884.
8785. WILLCOX, Walter F. Essays in statistics. Washington, 1899.
8786. WILLIAMS, F. S. Our Iron roads, their history . . . 5th. ed. London, 1884.
8787. WILLIAMSON, J. B. Foreign commerce of England under the Tudors. Oxford, 1883.
8788. WILLINK, H. G. Dutch home labour colonies. London, 1889.
8789. WILLKOM, S. Nationalökonomie und finanzwissenschaft. Berlin, 1891.
8790. WILSON, A. J. The national budget. London, 1882.
8791. ———. Resources of modern countries. London, 1878. 2 v.
8792. WILSON, W. D. First principles of political economy. New ed. Philadelphia, 1879.
8793. WINES, E. C. State of prisons and child-saving institutions. Cambridge, Massachusetts, 1880.

8794. WIRMINGHAUS, A. Zwei spanische mercantilisten. Jena, 1886.
8795. WIRTH, Max. Grundzüge der nationaloekonomie. 3 Bde. Köln, 1873-83.
8796. ———. Handbuch der bankwesens. 3 Aufl. Koln, 1883.
8797. WISKEMANN, H. Darstellung der in Deutschland zur Zeit der reformation herrschenden nationalökonomischen Ansichten. Leipzig, 1861.
8798. WITTELSHOFER, Otto. Untersuchungen über das Kapital. Tübingen, 1890.
8799. WOLKOFF, M. Précis d'économic politique ration. Paris, 1868.
8800. WOOD, John. Money panics; their cause and prevention. London, 1874.
8801. WOODS, R. A. English social movements. London, 1892.
8802. WOOLSEY, T. D. Communism and socialism. New York, 1880.
8803. WORMS, Emile. L'Allemagne économique ou histoire du zollverein. Paris, 1874.
8804. ———. Exposé elementaire de l'économic politique. Paris, 1889.
8805. WORMS, G. Essai de législation; le budget de France. Paris, 1893.
8806. WRIGHT, Carrol D. History of wages and prices in Massachusetts, 1752-1883. Boston, 1885.
8807. ———. Industrial conciliation and arbitration. Boston, 1881.
8808. ———. The relation of political economy to the labor question. Boston, 1882. 53 p.
8809. ———. Some ethical phases of the labor question. Boston, 1902.
8810. WYCKOFF, William C. American silk manufacture. New York, 1887.
8811. WYSE, L. Le Canal de Panama. Paris, 1886.
8812. YEATS, John. The growth and vicissitudes of commerce in all ages. 3d. ed. London, 1887.
8813. ———. The natural history of the raw materials of commerce. 3d. ed. London, 1887.
8814. YOUNG, Edward. Labor in Europe and America. Philadelphia, 1875. (House Ex. Doc., no. 21, 44 Congress, 1st session.)
8815. ———. Special report on the customs-tariff legislation of the United States. Washington, 1872.
8816. ZEYSS, R. Adam Smith und der eigennutz. Tübingen, 1890.
8817. ZIMMERN, Helen. Hanse towns. London, 1889.
8818. ZOLLNER, C. W. Lehrgebäude der volkswirthschaft. 2 Aufl. Leipzig, 1877.
8819. ZORLI, A. Sistemi finanzearii. Bologna, 1885.
8820. ZUCKERKANDL, Robert. Zur theorie des preises. Leipzig, 1889.

K. POST-CLASSICAL PERIOD

Section II. Specific Works

1. HISTORICISM

8821. AMMON, A. Objekt und grundbegriffe der theoretischen nationalökonomie. 2nd edition. Leipzig, 1927.
8822. ———. "Wirtschaft, wirtschaftswissenschaft und 'die drei nationalökonomien." In, Schmollers jahrbuch, 54 (1930).
8823. ASHLEY, William J. An introduction to English economic history and theory. New York, 1888-1893. 2 v.
8824. BAGEHOT, Walter. Works and life of Walter Bagehot. Edited by Mr. Russell Barrington. London, Longmans, Green & co. 1915. 10 v.
8825. BAHR, Friedrich. Die politischen anschauungen Friedrich List. . . . Lepizig, 1929. (Dissertation, University of Leipzig.)
8826. BELOW, George von. "Zur würdigung der historischen schule der nationalökonomie." In, Zeitschrift für sozialwissenschaft, 7 (1904) 145-804.
8827. BOUVIER-AJAM, Maurice. "Frédéric List et la nationalisme économique." In, Economie réalitiés mond, 28-37 (Mai, 1952-Fév. 1953.)
8828. ———. Frédéric List; sa vie, son oeuvre, son influence. Avec illus. en hors-texte de Jacques Marmier. Monaco, editions du Rocher, 1953. xx, 317 p.
8829. BRENTANO, Ludwig Joseph. Die arbeitergilden der gegenwart. Leipzig, 1871-72. 2 v.
8830. ———. Der wirtschafende mensch in der geschichte. Leipzig, 1923.
8831. ———. Geschichte der wirtschaftlichen entwicklung Englands. Jena, 1927-29. 3 v.
8832. ———. Ethik und volkswirtschaft in der geschichte. Munich, 1901.
8833. BRINKMANN, Carl. Gustav Schmoller und die volskwirtschaftslehre. Stuttgart, 1937.
8834. BUCHER, Karl. Entstehung der volkswirtschaft. Tübingen, 1893.
8835. ———. "Roscher, Wilhelm." In, Allgemeine deutsche biographie, Leipzig, supplementary, 53 (1907) 486-492.
8836. CUNNINGHAM, William. Civilization in its economic aspects. Cambridge, 1898. 1900. 2 v.
8837. ———. The growth of English industry and commerce. Cambridge, 1882. (5th edition, 1910-12. 3 v.)

Post-Classical Period   509

8838. DEFOURNEY, M. "Karl Knies." In, Revue d'economie politique, 20 (1906).
8839. EISERMANN, Gottfried. Die grundlagen des historismus in der deutschen nationalökonomie. Stuttgart, F. Enke, 1956. xv, 249 p. Bibliographical footnotes.
8840. EULENBURG, Franz. "Uber gesetzmassigkeiten in der geschichte." In, Archiv für sozialwissenschaft und sozialpolitik XXXV (1912) 299-365.
8841. FABIUNKE, G. Zur historischen rolle des deutschen nationalökonomen Friedrich List, 1789-1846. Berlin, Verlag die wirtschaft, 1955. 295 p.
8842. FRANZ, Gottfried. Studien über Bruno Hildebrand. Marburg, 1928.
8843. GEHRIG, Hans. "Bruno Hildebrand gedenkworte." In, Jahrbücher für nationalökonomie und statistik. 3d series, 53 (1912).
8844. ———. Friedrich List und Deutschlands politisch-ökonomische einheit.
8845. HELANDER, Sven. Die ausgangspunkte der wirtschaftswissenschaft. Jena, 1923.
8846. HILDEBRAND, Bruno. Die nationalökonomie der gegenwart und zukunst. Frankfort am Main, 1848.
8847. HIRST, Margaret Esther. Life of Friedrich List and selections from his writings. With an introduction by Joseph Dorfman and the addition of letter XII to Outlines of American political economy. (Reprints of economic classics.) New York, A. M. Kelley, 1965. xii, 355 p. Bibliography, 323-327.
8848. HUTER, Margret. Die methodologie der wirtschaftswissenschaft bei Roscher und Knies. (Beiträge zur geschichte der nationalökonomie, 5. hft.) Jena, G. Fischer, 1928. vii, 108 p. Bibliography, 105-108.
8849. KNAPP, George Frederich. Bauernbefreiung und der ursprung der landarbeiter. Leipzig, 1887. 2 v.
8850. ———. Staatliche theorie des geldes. Leipzig, 1905. Munich, 1923. London, 1924.
8851. KNIES, Karl. Das moderne kriegswesen; ein vortrag. Berlin, 1867.
8852. ———. Der telegraph als verkehrsmittel. Tübingen, 1857.
8853. ———. Die politische oekonomie vom standpunkte der geschichtlichen method. Braunschweig, 1853. (New edition, Brunsweig, 1883.)
8854. ———. Die statistik als selbstandige wissenschaft. Cassel, 1850.
8855. ———. Geld und kredit. Berlin, 1873-79. 2 v.
8856. LENZ, Friedrich. Friedrich List; der Mann und das werk. Munich, Berlin, 1936.
8857. LESLIE, T. E. Cliffe. On the philosophical method of political economy. Dublin, Hodges, Foster & Figgis, 1876.
8858. LIFSCHITZ, F. Die historische schule der wirtschaftswissenschaft. Bern, 1914.
8859. LIST, Friedrich. Das nationale system der politischen

oekonomie. Stuttgart, 1841. Paris, 1851. (English edition: The national system of political economy. Translated by Sampson S. Lloyd. New York, 1904.)

8860. _____. Outlines of American political economy. Philadelphia, 1827.

8861. _____. "Die times und das deutsche schutzsystem. In, Zollvereinsblatt, IV, 44 (1846) 691-694.

8862. _____. Werke. Schriften, reden, briefe. Berlin, 1927-1935.

8863. LOOS, I. A. "Historical approach to economics." In, American economic review, 8 (1918).

8864. MENGER, Karl. Die irrtümer des historismus in der deutschen nationalökonomie. Neudruck der ausg. Wien, 1884. Aalen, Scientia-verlag, 1966. 87 p. Bibliographical footnotes.

8865. _____. Untersuchunger über die methode der sozialwissenschaften. Leipzig, 1883.

8866. MONTAGUE, F. C. "Arnold Toynbee." In, Johns Hopkins University, Studies in historical and political science, 7, 1. Baltimore, 1889.

8867. MULLER, Adam Heinrich. Die elemente der staatskunst. Berlin, 1809. 3 v.

8868. NUSSBAUM, F. L. A history of the economic institutions of modern Europe. New York, 1932. (After, Sombart's Moderne kapitalismus . . .)

8869. OLDENBURG, Ulrich. List--Knies--von Gottl-Ottlilienfield; eine entwicklungslinie der abkehr vom liberalismus in der deutschen volkswirtschaftslehre. (Neue deutsche forschungen. Abt.: Nationalökonomie . . . hrsg. von Erwin Wiskemann. bd. 9.) Berlin, Junker und Dünnhaupt, 1936. 113 p. 1. Literaturverzeichnis, 115 (Inaugural dissertation, Berlin.)

8870. PFISTER, Bernhard. Die entwicklung zum idealtypus. Eine methodologische untersuchung über das verhältismus von theorie und geschichte bei Menger, Schmoller und Max Weber. Tübingen, 1928.

8871. PLOTNIK, M. J. Werner Sombart and his type of economics. New York, 1937.

8872. POLLOCK, F. Sombarts wiederlegung des Marxismus. 1926.

8873. ROSCHER, Wilhelm Georg Friedrich. Ansichten der volkswirthschaft. 2 Bde. Leipzig, 1868.

8874. _____. Grundriss zu vorlesungen über die staatswirthschaft, nach geschichtlicher methode. Göttingen, 1843.

8875. _____. Principles of political economy. From the 13th, 1877, German edition. With additional chapters . . . for this 1st English and American edition . . . and a preliminary essay on the historical method in political economy. (From the French) by L. Wolowski. The whole translation by John J. Lalor. Chicago, Callaghan and company; New York, Holt, 1878. 2 v. (Paris, 1857.)

8876. _____. System der volkswirthschaft. 4 Bde. Stuttgart, 1854-1894. 5 v. (20 aufl., 1892.)

8877. _____. Zur geschichte der englischen volkswirtschaftslehre

Post-Classical Period 511

Leipzig, 1851. Geschichte der national-oekonomik in Deutschland. München, 1874. (Reprinted: München und Berlin, R. Oldenbourg, 1924. viii, 1085 p.)
8878. _____. and R. Jannasch. Kolonien, kolonialpolitik und auswanderung. 3 aufl. Leipzig, 1885.
8879. SCHELTING, A. von. "Die logische theorie der historischen kulturwissenschaft von Max Weber und in besonderen sein begriff des idealtypus." In, Archiv für sozialwissenschaft und sozialpolitik, 49 (1922) 623-752.
8880. SCHMOLLER, Gustav. Grundfragen des Rechts und der volkswirthschaft. Jena, 1875.
8881. _____. Grundriss der allgemeinen volkswirtschaftslehre. Leipzig, 2 v. (v. 1: 1900 v. 2. 1904.)
8882. _____. Umbrisse und untersuchunger. Leipzig, 1898.
8883. _____. "Volkswirtschaft, volkswirtschaftslehre-und-methode." In, Handworterbuch der staatswissenschaften. 3d edition. Jena, 1911.
8884. _____. Zur litteraturgeschichte der staats- und sozial-wissenschaften. Leipzig, Duncker & Humblot, 1888. x p., 1 l., 304 p.
8885. SCHULLER, Richard. Die klassiche nationalökonomie und ihre Gegner. Berlin, 1895.
8886. _____. Die wirtschaftspolitik der historischen Schule. Berlin, 1899.
8887. SCHUMACHER, Hermann. "The historical school." In, Encyclopedia of the social sciences. New York, 1931, v. V.
8888. _____. "Staatswissenschaften." In, Aus fünfzig jahren deutscher wissenschaft. Edited by Gustav Abb. Berlin, 1930. 136-158 p.
8889. _____. "Weber, Max." In, Allgemeine deutsche bio-graphie. Berlin, 1928. v. 1917-20. 593-615 p.
8890. SCHUMPETER, Joseph A. "Gustav von Schmoller und die problems von heute." In, Schmollers Jahrbuch, 1 (1926) 337-388.
8891. _____. "Sozialpolitik and the historical method." In, J. A. Schumpeter, History of economic analysis. New York, Oxford university press, 1954. 1966. Chapter 4. 800-824.
8892. SOMBART, Werner. Der moderne kapitalismus. 1902. 2 v. (Modern capitalism. 1912-27. 6 v.)
8893. _____. "Economic history and economic theory." In, Economic history review (London), II, 1 (1929).
8894. SOMMER, Arthur. Friedrich Lists system der politischen ökonomie. (List-studien, hft. 1.) Jena, G. Fischer, 1927. Bibliographie, 238-240.
8895. SPIETHOFF, A. "The 'historical' character of economic theories." In, Journal of economic history, 12, 2 (Spring, 1952) 131-139.
8896. TOYNBEE, Arnold. Lectures on the industrial revolution of the eighteenth century in England. London, Longmans, Green, 1908.
8897. VEBLEN, Thorstein Bunde. "Gustav Schmoller's Uber einige

grundfragen der sozialpolitik und der volkswirtschaftslehre." (Review) In, Journal of political economy (June, 1898) 416-419.

8898. _____. "Werner Sombart's des moderne kapitalismus." (Review) In, Journal of political economy (March, 1903) 300-305.

8899. _____. "Gustav Schmoller's economics." In, Quarterly journal of economics (November, 1901) 69-93. (Reprinted: In, The place of science in modern civilization and other essays. New York, Huebsch, 1919. 252-278 p.)

8900. WAGNER, Adolf, editor. Lehr- und handbuch der politischen oekonomie. 1876- . 4 v.

8901. WEBER, Max. The protestant ethic and the spirit of capitalism. London, George Allen & Unwin, ltd.; New York, Charles Scribner's sons, 1930.

8902. _____. "Roscher und Knies und die logischen probleme der historischen nationalökonomie." In, Max Weber, Gesammelte aufsätze sur wissenschaftslehre. Tübingen, 1922. 1-145.

8903. _____. The theory of social and economic organization. New York, Oxford university press, 1947.

8904. WILBRANDT, Robert. Der volkswirt als berater der volkswirtschaft. Stuttgart, 1928.

8905. WOLOWSKI, L. Etudes d'économie politique et de statistique. Paris, 1848.

K. Section II

2. INSTITUTIONALISM

8906. ALBERY, M. "Institucionalismo económico." In, R. Econ. polit, Madrid, 6, 3 (1955) 126-141.

8907. ANDERSON, K. L. "The unity of Veblen's theoretical system." In, The quarterly journal of economics, XLVII (August, 1933.)

8908. ATKINS, Willard Earl, editor. Economic behavior. An institutional approach. By members of the Department of economics, New York university: Willard E. Atkins, Donald W. McConnell, Corwin D. Edwards and others . . . Boston, New York, Houghton Mifflin company, c 1933. xv, 548, xxiii p. Bibliography, (Revised edition. Donald W. McConnell, editor. By members of the Department of economics, Washington square college, New York university: Donald W. McConnell, Edith Ayres, Willard E. Atkins and others. 1939. xiv, 923 p. Bibliographies.)

8909. AYRES, Clarence Edwin. "The Co-ordinates of Institutionalism." In, American economic review, XLI, 2, Supplement.

Post-Classical Period	513

8910. _____. "Fifty years' development in ideas of human nature and motivation." In, American economic review, XXVI, 1, Supplement.
8911. _____. The industrial economy. Its technological basis and institutional destiny. Boston, Houghton Mifflin 1952. 433 p.
8912. _____. The problem of economic order. New York, Farrar and Rinehart, 1938.
8913. _____. Science the false messiah. Indianapolis, Bobbs-Merrill, 1927.
8914. _____. The theory of economic progress, Chapel Hill, The University of North Carolina press, 1944. ix, 317 p. Bibliographical footnotes. (2d edition, (Schocken paperbacks, SB33.) New York, Schocken books, 1962. 317 p. Bibliography.)
8915. BANKS, J. A. "Veblen and industrial sociology." In, British journal of sociology, 10, 3 (September, 1959) 231-243.
8916. BOULDING, Kenneth E. "A new look at institutionalism." In, American economic review, Papers and proceedings, 47, 2 (May, 1957) 1-12.
8917. BURNS, E. M. "Institutionalism and orthodox economics." In American Economic Review, XXI (1931).
8918. CHAO, Nai-Tuan. Richard Jones: an early English institutionalist. New York, 1930. 2 p. 1., 7-169. Bibliography, 158-163. (Thesis, Columbia university, 1930.)
8919. CLARK, John Maurice. Alternative to serfdom. Five lectures delivered on the William W. Cook Foundation at the University of Michigan, March, 1947. New York, A. A. Knopf, 1948. xii, 153. (German edition: Sicherheit in freiheit. Unsere gesellschaft zwischen anarchie und planung. Trans. by Marion Caillaud. Frankfurt-am-Main, Humboldt-verlag, 1954. 190 p.)
8920. _____. Economic institutions and human welfare. New York, A. A. Knopf, 1957. 285. (Spanish edition: Cómo influyen las instituciones económicas en el bienestar humano? Trans. by Luis Diaz Cortes. Mexico, Edit. Novaro, 1959. 347 p.)
8921. _____. Preface to social economics. New York, 1936.
8922. _____. "Round table conference on Institutional economics." In, American economic review, XXII, 1, Supplement.
8923. COATS, A. W. "The influence of Veblen's methodology." In, Journal of political economy, 62, 6 (December, 1954) 529-537.
8924. COMMONS, John Rogers. Distribution of wealth. 1893.
8925. _____. The economics of collective action. With a biographical sketch of Selig Perlman. Manuscript edited, introduction and supplemental essay contributed by Kenneth H. Parson. New York, Macmillan, 1950. xii, 414 p. Bibliography of the writings of John R. Commons, 377-407. [Japanese edition: Shûdan kôdô no keizaigaku. (Transliterated.) Translated by Kaoru Kasugai and Takashi

Kasugai. Tokyo, Bungadô Shoten, 1958. 472.] (1936.)
8926. ———. "Institutional economics." In, American economic review, XXI (1931); XXVI (1936).
8927. ———. Institutional economics. Its place in political economy. New York, Macmillan company, 1934. xiii, 921 p. Bibliography, 9-12, 904-907. (Reprinted: Madison, University of Wisconsin press, 1959. 921 p. Bibliography.
8928. ———. The legal foundations of capitalism. New York, Macmillan, 1924.
8929. COMMONS, John Rogers and others. History of Labor in the United States. New York, Macmillan, 1918.
8930. ———. and others. Industrial government. New York, Macmillan, 1921.
8931. COPELAND, Morris Albert. Fact and theory in economics. The testament of an institutionalist. Collected papers. Edited with an introduction by Chandler Morse. Ithaca, New York, Cornell university press, 1958. xviii, 347 p. Bibliography, 343-347.
8932. ———. "Institutional economics and model analysis." In, American economic review, XLI, 2, Supplement.
8933. DAUGERT, S. M. The philosophy of Thorstein Veblen. New York, Columbia university press, 1950.
8934. DELIUS, Klaus. Der institutionalismus als Richtung der amerikanischen nationalökonomie. Koln? 1957. 226 p. Bibliography, 216-224. (Inaugural dissertation, Cologne.)
8935. DEWEY, E. W. "Thorstein Veblen, radical apologist for conservatism." In, American journal of economics and sociology, 18, 2 (January, 1959) 171-180.
8936. DICKINSON, Henry Douglas. Institutional revenue; a study of the influence of social institutions on the distribution of wealth. 1932. (Reprinted: New York, A. M. Kelley, 1966. 264 p.)
8937. DIXON, Russell A. Economic institutions and cultural change. With the assistance of E. Kingman Eberhart. New York and London, McGraw-Hill book company, inc., 1941. xiv, 529 p. Bibliographies.
8938. DOBRIANSKY, L. E. Veblenism. A new critique. Washington, Public affairs press, 1957. xxi, 409 p.
8939. DORFMAN, Joseph. "Source and impact of Veblen." In, American economic review, Papers and proceedings, 48, 2 (May, 1958) 1-10. Includes a discussion by P. N. Vukasin and G. W. Zinke, 30-34.
8940. ———. Thorstein Veblen and his America. New York, The Viking press, 1934. 5 p. 1., 3-556 p. Bibliography, 525-539. Bibliography of Veblen, 519-524. (Reprinted: With new appendices. New York, A. M. Kelley, 1961. 572 p. Reprinted: With corrections. New York, A. M. Kelley, 1966, 572 p.)
8941. DOW, L. A. "Institutionalism and contemporary price theory." In, American journal of economics and sociology, 20, 2 (January, 1961) 181-194.
8942. DOWD, D. F. Thorstein Veblen. New York, Washington square press, 1964. xvii, 205 p.

8943. _____, editor. Thorstein Veblen. A critical reappraisal. Ithaca, New York, Cornell university press, 1958. xii, 328 p.
8944. ELLIS, J. M. "Cannan and Veblen as institutionalists." In, American journal of economics and sociology, 20, 3 (April, 1961) 305-312.
8945. ELY, Richard T. Property and contract in their relation in the distribution of wealth. 1914.
8946. _____. "Round table conference on Institutional economics." In, American economic review, XXII, 1, Supplement.
8947. EUGSTER, C. Thorsten Bunde Veblen, 1857-1929. Darstellung und Deutung amerikanischen institutionellen denkens aus seinem werk heraus. Zürich, Europa verlag, 1952. 116 p.
8948. FISHMAN, L. Book review: "Institutional economics: Veblen, Commons, Mitchell reconsidered." In, Economic journal, 73, 292 (December, 1963) 759-762.
8949. GAMBS, John Saké. Beyond supply and demand. A reappraisal of institutional economics. New York, Columbia university press, 1946. 5 p. l. 105 p. Bibliography, 95-100.
8950. GRAZIANI, Augusto. Istituzioni di economia politica. 5. ed. (Biblioteca del "foro italiano.") Roma, Soc. ed. del "Foro italiano," 1951. xxi, 720 p.
8951. GROSSMAN, H. "Evolutionist revolt against Classical economics." In, The Journal of political economy, LI (October-December, 1943.)
8952. GRUCHY, A. C. "The influence of Veblen on mid-century institutionalism." In, American economic review, Papers and proceedings, 48, 2 (May, 1958) 11-20.
8953. HALL, F. P. "Toward understanding institutionalism." In, Indian journal of economics, 37, 145 (October, 1956) 177-186.
8954. HAMILTON, D. "Why is institutional economics not institutional?" In, American journal of economics and sociology, 21, 3 (July, 1962) 309-317.
8955. HAMILTON, Walton. "The Institutional approach to economic theory." In American economic review, IX (March, 1919).
8956. _____. "Institutionalism." The Encyclopedia of the social sciences, New York, Macmillan, 1932.
8957. HARRIS, A. "Types of institutionalism." In, The Journal of political economy, XL (December, 1932).
8958. HARTER, L. G., Jr. Book review: "Institutional economics: Veblen, Commons, Mitchell reconsidered." In, American economic review, 53, 5 (December, 1963) 1120-1121.
8959. HOBSON, J. A. Veblen. New York, J. Wiley & Sons, 1937.
8960. HOMAN, Paul T. "An appraisal of Institutional economics." In American economic review, XXII (1932).
8961. _____. "The Institutional school." The Encyclopedia of the social sciences. New York, Macmillan, 1932.
8962. _____. "Institutionalism: what it is and what it hopes to become." In, American Economic Review, XXI (1931).
8963. _____. "Thorstein Veblen." In, Contemporary economic

thought. New York, Harper & Brothers, 1928.
8964. INSTITUTIONAL economics: Veblen, Commons, and Mitchell reconsidered; a series of lectures by Joseph Dorfman and others. Berkeley, University of California press, 1963. 183 p. Bibliography.
8965. JAFFE, William. Les théories économiques et sociales de Thorstein Veblen. Contribution à l'histoire des doctrines économiques aux Etats-Unis . . . Paris, M. Giard, 1924. 187 p., 2 1. Bibliographie, 175-187. [(Thèse, Univ. de Paris.) (Reprinted: New York, Burt Franklin, 1970.)]
8966. KAWASAKI, S. "Seido-shugi keizaigaku no kiso." In, Kockijigyo kenkyu, 6, 2 (March, 1955) 84-109.
8967. KNIGHT, Frank H. "Institutionalism and empiricism in economics." In, American economic review, Papers and proceedings, 42, 2 (May, 1952.)
8968. LANDSMAN, R. F. "The philosophy of Veblen's economics." In, Science and Sociology, 21, 4 (Fall, 1957) 333-345.
8969. LERNER, Max, editor. The portable veblen. New York, The Viking press, 1948.
8970. MCCLUNG, Lee A., editor. Thorstein Veblen: selections from his work. New York, T. Y. Crowell, 1963. vi, 100 p.
8971. MITCHELL, Wesley Clair. Business cycles. Berkeley, University of California Press, 1913.
8972. ———. Business cycles. The problem and its setting. 1927.
8973. ———. "Commons on Institutional economics." In, American economic review, XXV (December, 1935.)
8974. ———. "Economics in a unified world." In, Social research, XI (February, 1944.)
8975. ———. A history of the greenbacks. Chicago, 1903.
8976. ———. "Human behavior and economics." In, Quarterly journal of economics, XXIX (November, 1914.)
8977. ———. "Intelligence and the guidance of economic evolution." In, Scientific monthly, XLIII (November, 1936.)
8978. ———. "Introduction." In, What Veblen taught. New York, The Viking Press, 1936.
8979. ———. "The rationality of economic activity." Journal of political economy, XVIII (February, 1910).
8980. ———, and A. F. Burns. Measuring business cycles. New York, National bureau of economic research, 1946.
8981. MUKERJEE, Radhakamal. The institutional theory of economics. (Sir Kikabhai premchand lectures, 1930-40, University of Delhi, publication, no. x.) London, Macmillan & co., limited, 1942. xv, 376 p. Bibliography, 358-366.
8982. MURPHREE, I. Darwinism in Thorstein Veblen's econom-

Post-Classical Period 517

8983. PECK, Harvey Whitefield. Economic thought and its institutional background. New York, Farrar and Rinehart, inc., 1935. 3 p. 1., 9-379 p. Bibliography, 368-370.
8984. REISMAN, D. "The social and psychological setting of Veblen's economic theory." In, Journal of economic history, 13, 4 (1953) 449-461.
8985. ROSENBERG, Bernard, editor. Thorstein Veblen: selections from his work. (Major contributions to social science series.) New York, Crowell, 1963. 100 p.
8986. SCHUMPETER, Joseph A. "Science and ideology." In, American economic review, XXXIX, 2 (March, 1949) 345-359.
8987. STOCKING, G. W. "Institutional factors in economic thinking." In, American economic review, 49, 1 (March, 1959) 1-19.
8988. SWEEZY, P. M. "Veblen's critique of the American economy." In, American economic review, Papers and proceedings, 48, 2 (May, 1958) 21-29.
8989. THOMPSON, Carey C., editor. Institutional adjustment. A challenge to a changing economy. (Papers from a symposium sponsored by Department of Economics, University of Texas.) Austin, Texas, University of Texas press, 1967. viii, 184 p. Bibliographical footnotes.
8990. THORPE, W. L. Economic institutions. New York, Macmillan company, 1928.
8991. VATTER, B. "Veblen, the analyst and his critics." In, American journal of economics and sociology, 23, 2 (April, 1964) 155-164.
8992. VEBLEN, Thorstein Bunde. Absentee ownership and business enterprise in recent times. The case of America. New York, B. W. Huebsch, 1923. 5 p. 1., 3-445 p. (Reprinted: New York, Viking, 1945.)
8993. _____. The engineers and the price system. New York, Viking, 1947.
8994. _____. Essays in our changing order. Edited by Leon Ardzrooni... New York, Viking, 1934. xviii, 472 p. Bibliography of T. Veblen's book reviews for the Journal of political economy, 471-472.
8995. _____. Instinct of workmanship. New York, B. W. Huebsch, 1922.
8996. _____. The place of science in modern civilisation and other essays. New York, B. W. Huebsch, 1919. 4 p. 1., 509 p. [(Reprinted from periodicals, writings covering about twenty years.) (Reprinted: New York, Viking, 1942. New York, Russell and Russell, 1961. 509 p.)]
8997. _____. The theory of business enterprise. New York, C. Scribner's sons, 1904. vi, 400 p. (Reprinted: 1935.)
8998. _____. The theory of the leisure class. New York, Macmillan company, 1912. (Reprinted: New York, Huebsch,

1926. New York, Modern library, 1934.)

8999. ———. The vested interests and the state of the industrial arts. New York, B. W. Huebsch, 1919. (Reprinted: The vested interests and the common man. The modern point of view and the new order. New York, A. M. Kelley, 1964. 183 p.)

9000. VIANELLO, M. Thorstein Veblen. Milano, Comunita, 1962. 405 p.

9001. WATANABE, T. "W. C. Mitchell. Seido-gakuha to junkan-gakuha." (Transliterated.) Keizaigaku kenkyū, 10 (August, 1956) 1-14.

9002. WITTE, E. E. "Institutional economics as seen by an institutional economist." In, Southern economic journal, 21, 2 (October, 1954) 131-140.

K. Section II

3. SOCIALISM AND MARXISM

9003. ACADEMIA Republicii Populare Romîne. Biblioteca. Marx şi Engels în limba romînă, 1871-1944. Bibliografia întocmită in Secţia de bibliografie a bibliotecii academiei R. P. R., de către Ion Crişan şi Octavian Barbosa, redactor principal: George Baiculescu; studiul introductiv de Ion Crisan. (Its Seria de bibliografii retrospective, 1.) Bucureşti, Editura academiei republicii populare Romîne, 1956.

9004. ADAMS, Henry. Karl Marx and his earlier writings. London, Allen and Unwin, 1940. (Reprinted: 1965.) New York, Russell and Russell, 1965. 221 p.

9005. AGUILAR, Luis E., editor. Marxism in Latin America. New York, Knopf, 1968. xii, 271 p. Bibliography, 267-271.

9006. AKADEMIE der wissenschaften, Berlin. Institut für wirtschaftswissenschaften. Probleme der politischen ökonomie. Redaktion: Martliese Mehnert. (Its Jahrbuch, Bd. 10.) Berlin, Akademie-verlag, 1967. 350 p.

9007. ALTHUSSER, Louis. For Marx. Translated from the French by Ben Brewster. New York, Pantheon books, 1969. 271 p.

9008. ———. Lire (Le capital) . . . (Théorie, 2-3.) Paris, F. Maspero, 1965. 2 v.

9009. ALTHUSSER, Louis e Etienne Balibar. Leggere Il capitale. (I Fatti e le idee, 170.) Milano, Feltrinelli, 1968. 356 p.

9010. ———. Lire "Le Capital." Nouvelle édition refondue. (Petite collection Maspero, 30-31.) Paris, F. Maspero, 1968. 2 v.

9011. ALTVATER, Elmar. Gesellschaftliche produktion und ökonomische rationalität; externe Effekte und zentrale planung im wirtschaftssystem des sozialismus. (Politische ökonomie. Geschichte und kritik.) Frankfurt, Europäische verlagsanstalt, c1969. 214 p.

9012. AMATO, Luigi D'. Per la critica dell'economia marxistica. Roma, A. Belardetti, 1955. 135 p. Bibliography, 127-131.

9013. ANDELSON, R. V. "Nicolas Berdyaev's critique of Marxism." American journal of economics and sociology. 21 (3), July 62: 271-284.

9014. APTHEKER, Herbert, editor. Marxism and alienation, a symposium. (American institute for Marxist studies, Monograph no. 2.) New York, Humanities press, 1965. xii, 158 p.

9015. _____. Marxism and democracy; a symposium. 17th edition. (American institute for Marxist studies. Monograph no. 1.) New York, Published for American institute for Marxist studies by Humanities press, c1965. xii, 113 p. (Publication number 2 in the Bernard Edwin Galitz sponsored series.)

9016. ARMYTAGE, W. Heavens below. Utopian experiments in England 1560-1960. London, Routledge and K. Paul, 1961. 458 p.

9017. ASH, William Franklin. Marxism and moral concepts. New York, Monthly review press, c1964. xiv, 204 p. Bibliography, 199-204.

9018. ASOBE, Kyuzo. Marukusu keizaigaku. (Transliterated.) 1968. 6, 300 p. Bibliography, 271-279.

9019. ASPELIN, Gunnar. Karl Marx. Samhällsforskare och samhällskritiker. En kommentar til Kapitalet 1. (Tema.) Lund, Gleerup, 1969. 215, 1 p.

9020. AVINERI, Shlomo. The social and political thought of Karl Marx. London, Cambridge university press, 1968. viii, 269 p.

9021. BAKUNIN, Mikhail Aleksandrovich. Marxism, freedom and the state. Translated and edited with a biographical sketch by K. J. Kenafick. London, Freedom press, 1950. 63 p.

9022. BALEK, Stanislav. Proč a jak studovat ekonomickou teorii. Ze zkušeností Katedry politické ekonomie na Vysoké strancikė školė Institutu společenskych ved pri UV KSC. Vyd. 1. Praha, NPL, 1964. 135, 4 p.

9023. BALETIC, Zvonimir. Marksistička teorija ekonomskih kriza. Zagreb, Naprijed, 1965. 326, 5 p.

9024. BALINKY, Alexander. Marx's economics; origin and development. Lexington, Massachusetts, Heath, 1970. xiv, 178 p. [(Studies in international development and economics.) New York, D. C. Heath, 1971.] (Bibliography of articles on Marxian economics, 173-178.)

9025. BANKS, Joseph Ambrose. Marxist sociology in action; a sociological critique of the Marxist approach to industrial relations. Harrisburg, Pennsylvania, Stackpole books; (Society today and tomorrow. 70/-.) London, Faber, 1970. 324 p.

9026. BANYAI, Mária. Politikai gazdaságtani alapismeretek. Budapest, Közgazdasági és Jogi Könyvkiadó, 1969. 370 p.
9027. BARAN, Paul and Paul M. Sweezy. Monopoly capital; an essay on the American economic and social order. New York, Monthly review press, 1966. ix, 402 p. [French edition: Le Capitalisme monopoliste, un essai sur la societé industrielle américaine. Traduit de l'anglais par Christos Passadéos. (Economie et socialisme, 11.) Paris, F. Maspero, 1968. 344 p.]
9028. BARCA, Luciano. Il meccanismo unico. (Il Punto, 17.) Roma, Editori riuniti, 1968. 132 p.
9029. BARRI, Tomàs. El "problema social" sota el punt de vista mercantil (badada de Karl Marx); reflections industrials. Barcelona, 1963. 283 p.
9030. BARZUN, Jacques Martin. Darwin, Marx, Wagner; critique of a heritage. Boston, Little, Brown and company, c1941. xii, 420 p. Bibliographical footnotes. (Reprinted: 1947.)
9031. BEBER, M. M. Karl Marx's interpretation of history. Cambridge, Massachusetts, Harvard university press, 1927.
9032. BECKER, Werner. Idealistische und materialistische dialektik; das verhältnis von Herrschaft und Knechtschaft bei Hegel und Marx. Stuttgart, W. Kohlhammer, c1970. 142 p.
9033. BEER, Max. Allgemeine geschichte des sozialismus und der sozialen Kämpfe. 6th edition. Berlin, Verlag für sozialwissenschaft, 1929. 789 p.
9034. ———. La doctrina marxista; Karl Marx. Su vida y su obra. Santiago, Chile, Ediciones "Orbe," 1933. 141 p.
9035. ———. Fifty years of international socialism. London, Allen and Unwin, 1935. 239 p.
9036. ———. The general history of socialism and social struggles. New York, Russell and Russell, c1957. 2 v. Bibliography, v. 1: 209-212, 2d group.
9037. ———. A history of British socialism. London, Bell, 1919. (With an introduction by R. H. Tawney. London, Allen and Unwin, 1953. 2 v. Based on German, 1912 value: Geschichte des sozialismus in England.)
9038. ———. The life and teaching of Karl Marx. Translated by T. C. Partington and H. J. Stenning, and revised by the author. (Social studies series, v. 2.) London and Manchester, National labour press, limited, 1921. xxxii, 132 p. (Boston, Small, Maynard, 1924.)
9039. ———. Social struggles in the middle ages. Translated by H. J. Stenning and revised by the author. Boston, Small, Maynard and company, 1924. (New York, International publishers; London, Allen and Unwin, 1929. 215 p.)
9040. BELL, David. Marxian socialism in the United States. Princeton, New Jersey, Princeton university press, 1967. xiii, 212 p.)
9041. BELLAMY, Edward. Equality. 2d edition. New York, Appleton, 1897. viii, 412 p. (3rd edition, 1898. viii, 412 p.)

9042. _____. Looking backward, 2000-1887. 6th edition. Boston, Massachusetts, Tichnor and company, 1888. vi, 7-470 p. Houghton Mifflin, 1926; New York, Modern Library, 1951. xxvi, 276 p.
9043. BENTHAM, Jeremy. A fragment on government and an introduction to the Principles of morals and legislation. Edited with an introduction by Wilfrid Harrison. Oxford, Blackwell, 1960. 435 p.
9044. _____. Works. Edited by John Bowring. New York, Russell and Russell, 1962. 1 v.
9045. BERANGER, Charles. Religion Saint-Simonienne. La guerre détruit tout commerce et toute industrie. Paris, 1832. 4 p. (La propreté. Paris, Everat, 1832. 2 p. These are only 2 of the many subjects covered in the series: Religion Saint-Simonienne.)
9046. BERDIAEV, Nicholas. The origin of Russian communism. London, Geoffrey Bles, 1955. 191 p.
9047. BERGSON, Abram. Essays in normative economics. Cambridge, Belknap press of Harvard university press, 1966. ix, 246 p. Bibliographical footnotes.
9048. BERLIN. Institut für Marxismus-Leninismus. Die erstdrucke der werke von Marx und Engels: Bibliographie der einzelausgaben. 1 aufl. Berlin, Dietz, 1955. 62 p.
9049. BERLIN, Isaiah. Karl Marx, his life and environment. 2d edition. (The Home university library of modern knowledge. London, 189-.) London, New York, Oxford university press, 1948. 280 p. (3rd edition, New York, London, Oxford university press, 1959. 286 p.; 1963, 295 p.)
9050. BERNARD, Philippe J. Planning in the Soviet Union. Translated by I. Nove. 1st English edition. Oxford, New York, Pergamon press, 1966. xxv, 309 p. Bibliography, 301-303.
9051. BERNERI, M. L. Journey through utopia. Boston, Beacon press, 1951. 339 p.
9052. BERNSTEIN, Eduard. Evolutionary socialism, a criticism and affirmation. New York, Huebsch (Viking press), 1909. London, Huebsch, 1912. 224 p.
9053. BESTOR, A. E. Backwoods utopias. The sectarian and Owenite phases. Philadelphia, University of Pennsylvania press, 1950. 288 p.
9054. BETTELHEIM, Charles. La Transition vers l'économie socialiste. (Economie et socialisme, 9.) Paris, F. Maspero, 1968. 271 p.
9055. BIARD, Gustave. Aperçu des vues morales et industrielles des Saint-Simoniens. Blois, 1832.
9056. The BIBLIOGRAPHICAL bulletin of current Marxology; trial issue. Editor: Jerzy Rudzki. Warszawa, Panstwowe wydawn. naukowe, 1965. 176 p.
9057. BIGO, Pierre. Marxismo e humanismo; introdução à obra econômica de Karl Marx. Tradução portuguêsa de Ubiratan de Macedo. (Coleção ciências do comportamento.) São Paulo, Editôra Herder, 1966. 277 p. [3. éd. rev. et

mise à jour. Préface de Jean Marchal. (Bibliothèque de la science économique.) Paris, Presses universitaires de France, 1961. 228 p.]
9058. BLACKSTOCK, Paul W. and Bert F. Hoselitz, editors. The Russian menace to Europe; a collection of articles, speeches, letters, and news dispatches, by Karl Marx and Friedrich Engels. Glencoe, Illinois, Free press, c1952. 288 p. Bibliographical notes and editors' comments, 242-284.
9059. BLAKE, William J. Elements of Marxian theory and its criticism. New York, Cordon company, 1939.
9060. BOBER, Mandell Morton. Karl Marx's interpretation of history. Awarded the David A. Wells prize for the year 1925-26 and published from the income of the David A. Wells fund. Cambridge, Harvard university press, c1927. x, 370 p. Bibliography, 349-353. [2d edition, revised. (Harvard economic studies, v. 31.) c1948. x, 445 p. Bibliography 431-437.]
9061. ———. "Marx and economic calculations." American economic review, June, 1946.
9062. BOCHENSKI, J. M. and G. Niemeyer, editors. Handbook on Communism. New York, Praeger, 1962. 686 p.
9063. BOFFITO, Carlo. Socialismo e mercato in Jugoslavia. Saggi di Boris Kidrič, Joža Vilfan, Adolf Dragičević, . . . Carlo Boffito. (Serie politica, 5.) Torino, Einaudi, 1968. 332 p.
9064. BOHM von BAWERK, Eugen, Ritter. Karl Marx and the close of his system, by Eugen von Böhn-Bawerk; and Böhn-Bawerk's criticism of Marx, by Rudolf Hilferding; together with an appendix consisting of an article by Ladislaus von Bortkiewicz on the transformation of values into prices of production in the Marxian system. Edited with an introduction by Paul M. Sweezy. New York, A. M. Kelley, c1949. xxx, 224 p. (Glasgow, 1898; translation by A. M. Macdonald. New York, 1898; preface by James Bonar. 221 p.)
9065. BOOTH, A. J. Saint-Simon and Saint-Simonism. London, Longmans, Green, Reader and Dyer, 1871.
9066. BORDIGA, Amadeo. Dall'economia capitalistica al comunismo. Conferenza tenuta a Milano il 2 luglio 1921 da Amadeo Bordiga. Libreria editrice del Partito comunista d'Italia, Roma, . . . 1921. (Biblioteca del Partito comunista d'Italia.) Milano, Feltrinelli reprint, 1968? 24 p.
9067. BOUDIN, Louis Boudianoff. Theoretical system of Karl Marx. Chicago, Charles H. Kerr, 1910. [Reprinted: The theoretical system of Karl Marx in the light of recent criticism. (Classics of radical thought series, no. 6.) New York, Monthly review press, c1967? 1968. 286 p.] (Series of articles that appeared in International socialist review, May 1905 to October 1906.)
9068. BOURGIN, Hubert. Fourier. Paris, 1905.
9069. BRAMELD, Theodore Burghard Hurt. A philosophic approach to communism; with a foreword by T. V. Smith, Ph.D.

Post-Classical Period

Chicago, Illinois, The University of Chicago press, c1933. xi p., 2 1., 3-242 p. Bibliography, 225-235.
9070. BRATISLAVA. Univerzita. Knižnica. Marx-Engels-Lenin; Bibliografia, 1913-1962. Zostavili; L'. Herchlová, M. Nováková, Z. Banská. Red. L'. Herchlová. V Martine, Matica slovenská, 1963. 187 p.
9071. BRAVO, Gian Maria. Marx e Engels in lingua italiana, 1848-1960. (Saggi e documentazioni, 10.) Milano, Edizioni Avanti! 1962. 175 p.
9072. BREMEN. Volksbüchereien. Karl Marx, 1818-1968. Mensch, werk, wirkung. Auswahl der neueren literatur. Hrsg.: Volksbüchereien der Freien Hansestadt Bremen.) Hamburg, Hamburger öffentliche bücherhallen, 1968. 63 p.
9073. BRODY, András. Érték és újratemelés; kísérlet a marxi értékelmélet és újratermelési elmélet matematikai modelljének megfogalmazására. Budapest, Közgazdasági és Jogi Könyvkiadó, 1969. 357 p.
9074. BRONFENBRENNER, M. "Marxian influences in bourgeois economics." Papers and proceedings of the 79th annual meeting of the American economic association (December, 1966). In, American economic review (May, 1967).
9075. BROWDER, Earl Russell. Marx and America; a study of the doctrine of impoverishment. 1st edition. New York, Duell, Sloan, and Pearce, c1958. 146 p. (Previously published: c1957. 38 1.)
9076. BROWNE, Alfredo Lisbôa. Leitura básica de O Capital; resumo e crítica da obra de Marx. (Coleção perspectivas do homen. Série economia, v. 32.) Rio de Janeiro, Civilização, Brasileira, 1968. xvi, 487 p.
9077. BRUNHOFF, Suzanne de. La Monnaie chez Marx. (Problèmes.) Paris, Editions sociales, 1967. 192 p.
9078. BRUS, Włodzimierz, editor. Ekonomia polityczna socjalizmu; praca zbiorowa pod red. Włodzimierza Brusa. Dla studentów wszystkich wydziąłow uniwerstytetów, poza Wydziąłem ekonomii. Wyd. 1. Warszawa, Państwowe wydawn. naukowe, 1964. 309 p. (Wyd. 3., popr. i uzup. 1967. 375 p.)
9079. _____. Essays on the theory of economic growth under socialism. (Szkoła Główna planowania i statystyki. The advanced course in national economic planning. Teaching materials, v. 7/9.) Warszawa, 1965. 118 p.
9080. _____. Ogólne problemy funkcjonowania gospodarki socjalistycznej. Wyd. 2. Warszawa, Państwowe wydawn. naukowe, 1964. 369 p.
9081. _____. Problèmes généraux du fonctionnement de l'économie socialiste. Traduit du polonais par B. P. Leblanc, S. Nowocien, Anna Posner. (Economie et socialisme, 10.) Paris, F. Maspero, 1968. 263 p.
9082. BUBER, Martin. Paths in Utopia. Boston, Beacon press, 1958. 152 p.
9083. BUCHAREST. Institutul de Ştiinţe economcice "Vladimir Ilici Lenin." Facultatea de comert. Economia,

organizarea şi planificarea comerţului socialist; curs pentru studenţii facultăţilor de economie generală (secţiile economie politică şi statistică) şi finante, credit şi contabilitate. Bucureşti, Editura didactică şi pedagogică, 1964. 338 p.

9084. BUDRYS, Dzidas. Politinės ekonomijos apybraižos. Leista naudoti mokymo priemone respublikos aukštųjų mokylklų visų specialybių studentams. Vilnius, Mintis, 1964. 326 p.

9085. BUKHARIN, Nikolaĭ Ivanovich. The economic theory of the leisure class. New York, Greenwood press, 1968. 220 p. (First published: c1927. New York, AMS press, 1970. 220 p. New York, A. M. Kelley, 1970, 220 p.)

9086. ———. Historical materialism. New York, International publishers, 1925.

9087. BURNS, Emile, editor. A handbook of Marxism; being a collection of extracts from the writings of Marx, Engels and the greatest of their followers, selected so as to give the reader the most comprehensive account of Marxism possible within the limits of a single volume: the passages being chosen by Emile Burns, who has added in each case a bibliographical note, and an explanation of the circumstances in which the work was written and its special significance in the development of Marxism: as well as the necessary glossaries and index. London, V. Gollancz, 1935. 1087, 1 p.

9088. ———. An introduction to Marxism. New York, International publishers, 1966. (Issued: 1952.)

9089. BUTTINGER, Joseph. In the twilight of socialism, a history of the revolutionary socialists of Austria. 1953.

9090. CADEMARTORI, José. La economía chilena; un enfoque marxista. (Cormorán.) Santiago, Editorial universitaria, 1968. 293 p.

9091. CALOGERO, Guido. Il metodo dell'economia e il marxismo. Introduzione alla lettura di Marx. (Piccola biblioteca filsofica Laterza, 15.) Bari, Laterza, 1967. 129 p.

9092. CALVEZ, Jean Yves. La pensée de Karl Marx. (Politique, 38.) Paris, Editions du Seuil, 1970. 375 p. (Paris, Editions du Seuil, 1956. 663 p.)

9093. CARMICHAEL, Joel. Karl Marx, the passionate logician. New York, Scribner, 1967. viii, 262 p. Bibliography.

9094. CENTRE d'études et de recherches marxistes. Sur le mode de production asiatique. Préface de Roger Garaudy. Paris, Editions sociales, 1969. 347 p.

9095. CERNE, Franc. Ekonomija iz novega zornega kota. Ljubljana, Cankarjeva založba, 1966. 334, 6 p.

9096. CHAIANOV, Aleksandr Vasil'evich. The theory of peasant economy. 1966.

9097. CHAMBERS, R. W. Thomas More. London, Jonathan Cape, 1935.

9098. CHAMBRE, Henri. From Karl Marx to Mao Tse-tung; a systematic survey of Marxism-Leninism. Translated by Robert J. Olsen. Preface by Thurston N. Davis. New

Post-Classical Period 525

York, Kenedy, 1963. 308 p.
9099. ———. Le marxisme en Union soviétique; idéologie et institutions, leur évolution de 1917 à nos jours. (Collections Esprit. Frontière ouverte.) Paris, Editions du Seuil, c1955. 509 p. Bibliographical footnotes.
9100. CHANG, Sherman Hsiao-ming. The Marxian theory of the state. With an introduction by John R. Commons. New York, Russell and Russell, 1965. xv, 230 p. Bibliography, 201-210. (1st edition, 1931.)
9101. CHARLETY, Sébastien. Histoire du saint-simonisme. Paris, 1931.
9102. CH'OE, Kil-sŏng. Hyŏndae sasang yon'gu. (Transliterated.) 1965. 14, 452 p.
9103. CHUNG-KUO ch'ing nien ch'u pan shê, Peking. Hsüeh hsi Ma-k'o-ssū En-ko-ssū, Lieh-ning, Ssū-ta-lin. (Transliterated.) China, 1959. 232 p.
9104. COHN, N. "The Saint-Simonian portent." Twentieth century, 152 (908), October 52: 330-340.
9105. COLE, George Douglas Howard. Fabian socialism. London, Allen and Unwin, 1943.
9106. ———. The Fabian society, past and present (Tract 258). London, The Fabian society, 1942.
9107. ———. A history of socialist thought. London, Macmillan, 1953-60. 5 v. (v. 2: Marxism and anarchism, 1850-1890.)
9108. ———. The meaning of Marxism. London, V. Gollancz, 1948. 301 p. "A note on books": 291-294. ("Largely based on the author's What Marx really meant.")
9109. ———. Persons and periods. New York, The Macmillan company, 1938.
9110. ———. Robert Owen. London, E. Benn; Boston, Little, Brown and company, 1925.
9111. ———. . . . What Marx really meant. (First American edition.) New York, A. A. Knopf, c1934. 4 p. 1., 3-309, vi p. "A note on books": 305-309.
9112. COLLINS, Henry and Chimen Abramsky. Karl Marx and the British labour movement; years of the first International. London, Macmillan; New York, Saint Martin's press, c1965. xi, 356 p. Bibliography, 315-344.
9113. COMPERE-MOREL, A. C. A., editor. Encyclopedie socialiste, syndicale et cooperative de l'internationale Ouvrière. Paris, Publications sociales, 1912-21. 12 v.
9114. ———. Grand dictionnaire socialiste du movement politique et economique, national et international. Paris, Publications sociales, 1924. 1057 p.
9115. CORNFORTH, M. C. The open philosophy and the open society. New York, International publishers, 1969.
9116. CORNU, Augustin. Karl Marx. Paris, Felix Alcan, 1934.
9117. ———. Karl Marx, die ökonomisch-philosophischen manuskripte. (Deutsche akademie der wissenschaften zu Berlin. Vorträge und schriften, Heft. 57.) Berlin, Akademie-verlag, 1955. 54 p.

9118. ──────. Karl Marx et Friedrich Engels; leur vie et leur oeuvre. 1. édition. Paris, Presses universitaires de France, 1955-58. 2 v.
9119. ──────. The origins of Marxian thought. (American lecture series, publication no. 321. A monograph in American lectures in philosophy.) Springfield, Illinois, C. C. Thomas, c1957. 128 p. Bibliography.
9120. CROCE, Benedetto. Essays on Marx and Russia. Selected and translated, with an introduction by Angelo D. De Gennaro. (Milestones of thought in the history of ideas.) New York, F. Ungar publishing company, 1966. xvi, 129 p.
9121. ──────. Historical materialism and the economics of Karl Marx; translated from the Italian, by C. M. Meredith, and with an introduction by A. D. Lindsay. 1st edition new impression. London, Cass; New York, Russell and Russell, 1966. xxiii, 188 p. Bibliographical footnotes. (1st published in 1914. London, George Allen and Unwin.)
9122. ──────. Materialismo storico ed economia marxistica. 10. ed. (His Saggi filosofici, 4.) Bari, Laterza, 1961. xv, 328 p. [(His Opere in edizione economica, 12.) 1968. xv, 300 p.]
9123. CROSSMAN, Richard Howard Stafford, editor. New Fabian essays by the author and others. Preface by C. R. Attlee. (Books that matter.) New York, F. A. Praeger, 1952. 215 p.
9124. CURTIS, Michael. Marxism. 1st edition. New York, Atherton press, 1970. 336 p.
9125. CUVILLIER, A. "Les antagonismes de classes dans la littérature sociale française de Saint-Simon à 1848," Int. r. soc. history, 1(3), 56: 433-463.
9126. DAS GUPTA, Sankar. Marxian economics, a study. Foreword by Prabhat Sarbadhikari. 1st edition. Calcutta, Vidyodaya library, 1963. xiii, 283 p. Bibliography, 278-281.
9127. DEBREAU, G. Theory of value. New York, John Wiley & sons, 1959.
9128. DEBS, Eugene. Writings and speeches of Eugene V. Debs. New York, Hermitage press, 1948. 486 p.
9129. DENCIK, Peter, Lars Herlitz och Bengt-Ake Lundvall. Marxismens politiska ekonomi. En introduktion. (Zenitserien. 6.) Stockholm, Zenit; Staffanstorp, Cavefors; Solna, Seelig, 1969. 262 p.
9130. DESAN, Wilfrid. The Marxism of Jean-Paul Sartre. 1st edition. Garden City, New York, Doubleday, c1965. xiii, 320 p. Bibliography, 310-312.
9131. DESROCHES, M. C. Signification du Marxisme, economie et humanisme. Paris, 1949. 397 p.
9132. DILAS, Milovan. The unperfect society; beyond the new class. Translated by Dorian Cooke. New York, Harcourt, Brace and World, 1969. 267 p.
9133. DOBB, Maurice Herbert. On economic theory and socialism

collected papers. London, Routledge and Paul; New York, International publishers, 1955. 293 p.
9134. DOBLER, Martin. Triebkraft bedürfnis; zur entwicklung der bedürfnisse der sozialistischen persönlichkeit. 1 aufl. Berlin, Dietz, 1969. 245 p.
9135. No Entry.
9136. DODAN, Sime. Ekonomska politika Jugoslavije. (Obzor: Enciklopedija suvremenog znanja: ekonomija.) Zagreb, Skolska knjiga, 1970. 141 p.
9137. _____. Zakon vrijednosti i odnos tržišta i plana. (Matica hrvatska. Izvanredno izdanje.) Zagreb, Matica hrvatska, 1969. 330 p.
9138. DOLLEANS, Edouard and Michael Crozier, editors. Mouvements ouvier et socialiste; chronologie et bibliographie. Paris, Editions ouvières, 1950- .
9139. DOMAR, E., D. Gordon, and H. S. Gordon. "Discussion on papers: Das Kapital--A centennary of appreciation." Papers and proceedings of the 79th Annual meeting of the American Economic Association (December, 1966). In, American economic review, May, 1967.
9140. DORNEMANN, Louise. Jenny Marx; der lebensweg einer sozialistin. 2. durchgesehene aufl. Berlin, Dietz verlag, 1969. 330 p. (3., durchgesehene aufl. Berlin, Dietz verlag, 1970. 330 p.)
9141. DORTMUND, Stadbücherei. Karl Marx, 1818-1968: Mensch, werk, wirkung; auswahl der neueren literatur: stadbücherei, stadt- und landesbibliothek, Institut für zeitungsforschung. Dortmund. Bibliographische bearbeitung: Rudolf Ernemann. Herausgeber: volksbüchereien der freien hansestadt Bremen. Bremen, 1968. 63 p.
9142. DOWIDAR, Mohamed. Les schémas de reproduction et la methodologie de la planification socialiste. Introd. du professeur Ch. Bettelhiem. Alger, Editions Tiers-monde, 1964. 447 p.
9143. DRACHKOVITCH, Milorad M. De Karl Marx à Léon Blum. La Crise de la social-démocratic. Genève, 1954. 180 p.
9144. _____, editor. Marxism in the modern world. Contributors: Raymond Aron and others. Published for the Hoover Institution on War, Revolution, and Peace. (Hoover institution publications.) Stanford, California, Stanford university press, 1965. xv, 293 p. Bibliography, 275-293.
9145. _____. Marxist ideology in the contemporary world. 1966.
9146. _____. Les socialismes français et allemands et le problème de la guerre 1870-1914. Genève, 1953. 385 p. (Thèse, Droit, Genève, 1953.)
9147. DRAGICEVIC, Adolf. Teorija i praksa socijalizma. Zagreb, "Naprijed," 1966. 288, 3 p.
9148. DRAHN, Ernst. Bibliographie des wissenschaftlichen sozialismus. Berlin, 1923. 160 p.

9149.	_____. Friedrich Engels als kriegswissenschaftler. Gantzsch b. Leipzig, 1915.
9150.	DUNAYEVSKAYA, Raya. Marxism and freedom . . . from 1776 until today. Pref. by Herbert Marcuse. 2d ed. New York, Twayne publishers, 1964. 363 p. Bibliography, 351-358. (Chapter on Mao Tse-tung and the Sino-Soviet rift included in 2d ed.)
9151.	DUNCKER, Hermann. Das "Manifest der Kommunistischen partei"; das wissenchaftliche programm der internationalen arbeiterbewegung. Mit dem beitrag: der Marxsche leitfaden zum gerschichtsstudium. 2 aufl. Berlin, Dietz, 1958. 56 p.
9152.	DUPRE, Louis K. The philosophical foundations of Marxism. New York, Harcourt, Brace and World, 1966. xiv, 240 p. Bibliographical footnotes.
9153.	DUTOIT, Bernard. L'union soviétique face à l'intégration européenne. Préf. de Henri Chambre. Lausanne, Centre de recherches européennes, Ecole des H. E. C., Université de Lausanne, 1964. 237 p.
9154.	DVORKIN, Il'ía Naumovich. "Kapital" K. Marksa i sovremennaía burzhuaznaía politekonomiía. (Novoe v zhizni, nauke, tekhnike. Seriía: Ekonomika, 1968, 4.) Moscow, 1968. 48 p.
9155.	EASTMAN, Marx Forrester. Marxism, is it science? 1st edition. New York, W. W. Norton and company, inc. 1940. 394 p.
9156.	EATON, John. Marx against Keynes; a reply to Mr. Morrison's "socialism." London, Lawrence and Wishart, 1951. 142 p.
9157.	_____. Political economy; a Marxist textbook. New revised edition. New York, International publishers, 1966.
9158.	EDELING, Herbert. Prognostik und sozialismus. Zur marxistisch-leninistischen prognostik moderner produktivkräfte in der Deutschen demokratischen republik. (Mit 7 abbildunger.) Berlin, Dietz, 1868. 335 p.
9159.	EKONOMIA polityczna. (Redagował Zbigniew Chrupek.) Wyd. 1. Warszawa, Panstwowe wydawn, Naukowe, 19--. v. (Wyd. 2. 1967-68. 2 v.)
9160.	EKONOMIA polityczna socjalizmu; dla studiów technicznych i rolniczych. Praca zbiorowa pod red. Stanisława Szeflera. Autorzy: Zdzisław Bombera et al. Wyd. 1. Warszawa, Państwowe wydawn. Naukowe, 1969. 546 p. (Another edition: 1969. 472 p.)
9161.	EKONOMIA polityczna socjalizmu; skrypt dla studentów wyższych szkół rolniczych. Praca zbiorowa pod red. Jana Czarkowskiego. Wyd. 2. Warszawa, Państwowe wydawn. Naukowe, 1969. 265 p.
9162.	EKONOMISKAS zināšnas--darbalaudim; krajums. Rīgā, Latvijas valsts izdevniecība, 1961. 47 p.
9163.	ELEMENTS de théorie économique marxiste. (Cahiers "Rouge," no. 1.) Paris, F. Maspero, 1968. 36 p.
9164.	ELIASBERG, George J. Marxism's hostile children;

Leninism and socialism. (The human affairs pamphlets, no. 39.) Hinsdale, Illinois, H. Regnery company, 1949. 30 p.
9165. ELSTER, Jon. Om kapitalen. (En introduksjon til Marx' hovedverk. Pax-bøkene, 201.) Oslo, Pax, 1969. 148 p.
9166. ELY, Richard T. French and German socialism in modern times. New York, 1883. 274 p.
9167. ———. Socialism . . . with suggestions for social reform. New York, 1894. xiii, 449 p.
9168. ENGELS, Friedrich. Condition of the working class in 1844. London, Sonnenschien, 1892. (Stanford university press, 1968.)
9169. ———. Einführunger in "Das Kapital" von Karl Marx. 2 aufl. (Kleine Bücherei des Marxismus-Leninismus.) Berlin, Dietz, 1968. 163 p.
9170. ———. Herr Eugen Dühring's revolution in science (anti-Dühring). Translated by Emile Burns, edited by C. P. Dutt. (Marxist library.) New York, International publishers, 1894. 1939? 364 p. [French edition: Anti-Dühring (M. E. Dühring bouleverse la science). Traduction d'Emile Bottigelli. Paris, Editions sociales, 1950. 541 p. German edition: Herrn Eugen Dührings umwälzung der wissenschaft; "Anti-Dühring." Moskau, Verlag für Fremdsprachige literatur, 1946. 527 p. English edition: Anti-Dühring; Herr Eugen Dühring's revolution in science. Moscow, Foreign languages publishing house, 1962. 541 p.]
9171. ———. Landmarks of scientific socialism. Chicago, Charles H. Kerr, 1907.
9172. ———. On Marx's "Capital." Moscow, Progress publishers, 1965. 125 p.
9173. ———. Socialism, Utopian and scientific. New York, Scribner, 1892. (Translated by E. Aveling. Chicago, Charles H. Kerr, 1912. 139 p. New York, International publishers, 1935.)
9174. ENSOR, Robert Charles K., editor. Modern socialism as set forth by Socialists in their speeches, writings and programmes. 3rd edition. New York, Harper and Brothers, 1910. 396 p.
9175. ESEJE o teoriích ekonomickeho růstu. Rita Budínová et al. Autorský kolektiv pod vedením L. Urbana. Vyd. 1. Praha, Academia, 1967. 371 p.
9176. EXPOSES et entretiens sur le marxisme, Cerisy-la-Salle, 1967. Le centenaire du capital; exposés et entretiens sur le marxisme. (Décades du Centre culturel international de Cerisy-la-Salle, nouv. sér. 10.) Paris, Mouton, 1969. 341 p.
9177. FABIAN society. Where stands democracy? Essays by G. D. H. Cole, Harold J. Laski, et al. New York, Macmillan company, 1940.
9178. FABIAN tracts. London, The Fabian society, 19--? (A bibliography.)
9179. FALK, Erling. Hva er marxisme? Revid. utg. ved Erling

Schreiner. Oslo, Tiden norsk forlag, 1946. 199 p.
9180. FALKOWSKI, Mieczysław. Les problèmes de la croissance du Tiers monde vus par les économistes des pays socialistes. (Bibliothèque économique et politique.) Paris, Payot, 1968. 223 p.
9181. FEDERN, Karl. The materialist conception of history; a critical analysis. London, Macmillan and company, ltd., 1939. xiv, 262, 1 p.
9182. FEUER, Lewis Sammuel. Marx and the intellectuals; a set of post-ideological essays. Garden City, New York, Anchor books, 1969. 301 p.
9183. FLORES, Angel, editor. Literature and Marxism; a controversy by Soviet critics. (Critics group series, 9.) New York, Critics group, 1938. 95.
9184. FÖLDES, Károly. A szocialista tulajdon ás az árutermelés. Budapest, Kosuth könyvkiadó, 1968. 423 p.
9185. FOLGEN einer theorie. Essays über "Das Kapital" von Karl Marx. Beiträge von Ernst Theodor Mohl. (Edition suhrkamp, 226.) Frankfurt a. M., Suhrkamp, 1967. 205 p.
9186. FOURIER, Charles. Oeuvres complètes de Charles Fourier 2d. edition. Paris, 1841-45. 6 v.
9187. ———. Publication des manuscrits de Charles Fourier. Paris, Librairie phalanstérienne, 1851-1858. 4 v.
9188. ———. Theory of social organization. New York, C. P. Somerby, 1876.
9189. FRAGEN der marxistischen soziologie. (Wissenschaftliche zeitschrift der Humbold-universität zu Berlin. Jahrg. 13, 1964. Sonderband.) Berlin, Humboldt-Universität, 1964. v. 2.
9190. FREEDMAN, Robert, editor. Marx on economics. New York, Harcourt, Brace, 1961. 290 p.
9191. ———, editor. Marxist social thought. New York, Harcourt, Brace, 1968.
9192. FRIEDRICH, Manfred. Philosophie und ökonomie beim jungen Marx. (Frankfurter wirtschafts- und sozialwissenschaftliche studien, heft 8.) Berlin, Duncker und Humblo 1960. 202 p.
9193. FRITSCH, Bruno. Die geld- und kredittheorie von Karl Marx; eine Darstellung und kritische Würdingung. Einsiedeln, Benziger, 1954. xv, 184 p.
9194. FROMM, Erich. Beyond the chains of illusion; my encounter with Marx and Freud. (The Credo series.) New York, Simon and Schuster, 1962. 182 p.
9195. ———, editor. Marx's concept of man. With a translation from Marx's Economic and philosophical manuscripts by T. B. Bottomore. (Milestones of thought in the history of ideas.) New York, F. Ungar publishing company, 1961. xii, 260 p. Bibliographical footnotes.
9196. FUCHS, James, editor. The socialism of Shaw. New York, Vanguard press, 1927.
9197. FULTON, Robert Brank. Original Marxism--estranged offspring; a study of points of contact and of conflict

between original Marxism and Christianity. Boston, Christopher publishing house, 1960. 167 p. Bibliography.
9198. GARAUDY, Roger. Karl Marx: the evolution of his thought. Translated from the French by Nan Apotheker. London, Lawrence and Wishart, 1967, 1968. 223 p. Bibliography, 207-218.
9199. ———. Marxism in the twentieth century. Translated from the French, by René Hague. London, Collins, 1970. 224 p. (New York, Scribner, 1970. 224 p. French edition: Marxisme du XXe siècle. Paris, Gèneve, la Palatine, 1966. 237 p.)
9200. GARINA, Virve. Uleminek kommunistlikule valadjuste järgi jaotamisele. Tallinn, 1965. 23 p.
9201. GARVEY, James Emmett. Marxist-Leninist China: military and social doctrine. 1st edition. (An exposition-university book.) New York, Exposition press, 1960. 447 p. Bibliography.
9202. GEMKOW, Heinrich. Karl Marx. A biography. In collaboration with Oskar Hoffmann and others. Edited by the Institute of Marxism-Leninism of the Central Committee of the Socialist unity party of Germany. Dresden, verlag zeit im bild, 1968. 426 p.
9203. GERMANY (Democratic republic, 1949- .) Ministerium für auswörtige angelgenheiten. Sektion bibliothek. Bibliographie über äusserungen von Karl Marx zu fragen der aussenpolitik und der internationalen Beziehungen. Berlin Ministerium für auswärtige angelegenheiten sektion bibliothek der abteilung wissenschaftliches archiv, 1968. 41 p.
9204. ———. Zentralinistitut für bibliothekswesen. Karl Marx, eine empfehlende bibliographie. Bearb. von Werner Rittner. Leipzig, Verlag für Buch- und bibliothekswesen, 1954. 54 p.
9205. GIANNOTTI, José Arthur. Origens da dialética do trabalho. São Paulo, Difusao Européia do livro, 1966. 265 p.
9206. GILLMAN, J. The falling rate of profit. Marx's law and its significance to twentieth-century capitalism. London, Dennis Dobson, 1957.
9207. GODELIER, Maurice. La notion de "mode de production asiatique" et les schémas marxistes d'évolution des sociétés. (Les Cahiers du Centre d'etudes et de recherches marxistes.) Paris, Centre d'études et de recherches marxistes, 1964? 42 l.
9208. ———. Rationalité et irrationalité en économie. (Economie et socialisme, 5.) Paris, F. Maspero, 1966. 296 p.
9209. GOLDENDACH, David B. Karl Marx; man, thinker and revolutionist. London, M. Lawrence, 1927.
9210. GOTTHEIL, Fred M. Marx's economic predictions. Evanston, Illinois, Northwestern university press, 1966. xv, 216 p. Bibliography, 208-210.
9211. GRAY, A. The Socialist tradition; Moses to Lenin.

London and New York, Longmans, Green and company, incorporated, 1946.
9212. GRAZIA, Gennaro di. Del comunismo; l'aspetto economico, filosofico, sociale, religioso. Napoli, M. D'Auria, 1967. 375 p.
9213. GROSSMAN, Henryk. Marx, die klassische nationalökonomi und das problem der dynamik. Mit einem nachwort von Paul Mattick. (Politische ökonomie. Geschichte und kritik.) Frankfurt, Europäischer verlagsanstalt; Wien, Europa verlag, 1969. 133 p.
9214. GUEVARA, Ernesto. Escritos económicos. 1. ed. (Cuadernos de pasado y presente.) Córdoba, Ediciones Pasado y presente, 1969. 250 p.
9215. GULICK, Charles A. et al. History and theories of the working-class movements. A select bibliography. Berkeley, University of California press, 1955. 364 p.
9216. GURVITCH, Georges. Pour le centenaire de la mort de Pierre-Joseph Proudhon. Proudhon et Marx: une confrontation. Cours public 1963-64. ("Les cours de Sorbonne." Sociologie.) Paris, Centre de documentation universitaire, 1964. 144 p.
9217. HADIPRABOWO, M. Dasar-dasar ilmu ekonomi sosialis. Tjet. 1. Jogjakarta, Mpu Tantular, 1965. 206 p.
9218. HADZIC, Muhamed i Hadžiomerović Hasan. Kratak kurs političke ekonomije. (6. izd.) Sarajevo, "Veselin Masleša,"1969. 270, 1 p.
9219. HAGELMAYER, István. Pénz a szocializmusban. Budapest, Közgazdasági és Jogi Könyvkiadó, 1964. 158 p.
9220. HALEVY, Elie. La doctrine économique de Saint-Simon et des saint-simoniens. In, Revue du mois (1907-1908). Reprinted.
9221. HART, Madge A. Utopias--Old and new. London, T. Nelson and sons, 1932.
9222. HAUSTEIN, Heinz-Dieter. Prognoseverfahren in der sozialistischen wirtschaft. Unter mitarbeit von Herbert Kempf. Berlin, Verlag die wirtschaft, 1970. 384 p.
9223. ———. Wirtschaftsprognose. Grundlagen, Elemente, Modelle. Berlin, Verlag die wirtschaft, 1969. 215 p.
9224. HAYEK, Friedrich August von, editor. Collectivist economic planning; critical studies on the possibilities of socialism. By N. G. Pierson and others. Edited, with an introduction and a concluding essay by F. A. Hayek. New York, A. M. Kelley, 1967? v. 293 p.
9225. ———. The road to serfdom. Chicago, University of Chicago press, 1960. 569 p.
9226. HEINZE, Albrecht und S. I. Tjulpanov. Karl Marx, Das Kapital. Erbe und verpflichtung. Beiträge zum 100. Jahrestag der erstausgabe werkes das kapital von Karl Marx. Im auftrag der Karl-Marx-Universität Leipzig. (Redaktionskollegium; Günter Fabiunke.) Leipzig, Karl-Marx-Universität; Berlin, Verlag die wirtschaft in kommission, 1968. viii, 716 p.
9227. HEISS, Robert. Die grossen dialektiker das 19. Jahr-

hunderts: Hegel, Kierkegaard, Marx. Köln, Kiepenheuer und Witsch, 1963. 437 p.
9228. HERETIK, Stefan. Náčrt dejín politickej ekonómie; do vzniku marxizmu. 1 vyd. Bartislava, Slovenské vydavatel'stvo politickej literatury, 1958. 313 p.
9229. HERRESHOFF, David. American disciples of Marx from the Age of Jackson to the progressive era. 1967.
9230. HERTEL, Gertrud. Inhaltsvergleichsregister der Marx-Engels-Gesamtausgaben. Berlin, Deutscher verlag der wissenschaften, 1957. 295 p.
9231. HERTZLER, Joyce O. The history of Utopian thought. New York, Macmillan, 1923. 321 p.
9232. HET radencommunisme. Grondbeginselen van communistische productie en distributie. (Manifesten.) s'Gravenhage L. J. C. Boucher, 1969. 283 p.
9233. HIDAKA, Hiroshi. Nihon no Marukushu keizaigaku. (Transliterated.) Japan, 1967-68. 2 v.
9234. HILFERDING, R. Böhm-Bawerk's criticism of Marx. Glasgow, 1920. (New York, August M. Kelley, 1949.)
9235. HILLQUIT, Morris. History of socialism in the United States. New York, Funk & Wagnalls, 1910.
9236. HINDS, W. A. American communities. Chicago, Charles H. Kerr, 1902.
9237. HOFMANN, Werner. Grundelemente der wirtschaftsgesellschaft; ein leitfaden für lehrende. (Rororo aktueil, 1149 A.) Erstausg. Reinbek bei Hamburg, Rowohlt, 1969. 185 p.
9238. HONG, Man-gi. Chŏngsh'i kyongjehak un muosui yon'gu hanun'ga. (Transliterated.) Korea, 1960. 69 p.
9239. HOOK, Sidney. From Hegel to Marx; studies in the intellectual development of Karl Marx. ("A John Day book.") New York, Reynal and Hitchcock, 1936. 335 p. (Ann Arbor paperbacks for the study of communism and marxism, AA66. Ann Arbor, University of Michigan press, 1962. 335 p.)
9240. _____. Marx and the Marxists; the ambiguous legacy. (An anvil original, no. 7.) Princeton, New Jersey, Van Nostrand, 1955. 254 p. Bibliography.
9241. _____. Reason, social myths and democracy. New York, Humanities press, 1940. 302 p.
9242. _____. Towards the understanding of Karl Marx, a revolutionary interpretation. New York, The John Day company, 1933. xiv, 347, 1 p.
9243. HORIE, Tadao. Marx keizai-gaku nyūmon. (Transliterated.) Tokyo, Nihon hyōron shinsha, 1962. 258 p.
9244. _____. O-bei no marukusushugi to minshushugi. (Transliterated.) Japan, 1966. 262 p. Bibliographical references.
9245. HOROWITZ, David, editor. Marx and modern economics. London, MacGibbon and Kee; New York, Modern reader paperbacks, 1968. 380 p. Bibliography.
9246. HORVAT, Branko. Ekonomska nauka i narodna privreda. Ogledi i studije. Zagreb, "Naprijed," 1968. 361 p.

Economic Thought and Analysis

9247. HUNT, R. N. C. Books on communism. A bibliography. London, Ampersand ltd., 1959. 333 p.
9248. _____. Marxism, past and present. New York, Macmillan, 1954. 180 p.
9249. _____. The theory and practice of Communism. An introduction. Baltimore, Penguin books, 1963. 315 p.
9250. HUSAR, Jozef. Uvod do bibliografie klasikov marxizmu-leninizmu. Vyd. 1. (Edicia: Teória a dokumentácia bibliografie, č. 2.) Martin, Matica slovenská, 1965. 99 p.
9251. HYMAN, Stanley Edgar. The tangled bank; Darwin, Marx, Frazer and Freud as imaginative writers. 1st edition. New York, Atheneum, 1962. xii, 492 p. Bibliography, 449-458.
9252. HYNDMAN, Henry M. Economics of socialism. London, Twentieth century press, 1896. (Boston, Small, Maynard, 1921. 286 p.)
9253. HYPPOLITE, Jean. Studies on Marx and Hegel. Translated, with an introduction, notes and bibliography. New York, Basic books, 1969. xxii, 202 p. Bibliographical references. (Translation of Etudes sur Marx et Hegel.)
9254. IDEAL commonwealths. London, Colonial press, 1901. 416 p.
9255. INTERNATIONALE Karl-Marx-konferenz, Berlin, 1967. Theoretische probleme des ökonomischen wachstums in sozialismus und kapitalismus. (Deutsche akademie der wissenschaften au Berlin. Schriften des Instituts für wirtschaftswissenschaften, Nr. 28-29.) Berlin, Akademie-verlag, 1968. v.
9256. ISAMBERT, Gaston. Les idées socialistes en France de 1815 à 1848. Paris, 1905.
9257. ISCARO, Rubens. Preguntas y respuestas sobre problemas sindicales, politicos y sociales. Buenos Aires, Editorial anteo, 1965. 308 p.
9258. JACKSON, John Hampden. Marx, Proudhon, and European socialism. New York, Collier books, 1962. 155 p. Bibliography, 149-150.
9259. JACKSON, T. A. Dialectics, the logic of Marxism and its critics. London, Lawrence and Wishart, 1936.
9260. JAHN, Wolfgang. Die Marxsche wert- und mehrwertlehre im zerrspiegel bürgerlicher ökonomen. Berlin, Dietz, 1968. 438 p.
9261. JORDAN, L. A. The evolution of dialectical materialism. London, Macmillan co.; New York, St. Martin's press, 1967.
9262. JOVASEVIC, Vladan. Osnovi političke ekonomije socijalizma. Beograd, Zavod za izdavanje udžbenika socijalističke republike srbije, 1966. 202 p.
9262a. JOZSEF, Dóczi and Vilmos József, editors. A socializmus politikai gazdaságtana; a Marxizmus-Leninizmus esti egyetemek tananyaga. Szerk.: Dóczi József és Vilmos József, irták Bara Józsefné, et al. Budapest, Kossuth Könyvkiadó, 1964. 478 p.

9263. KAGI, Paul. Genesis des historischen materialismus. Karl Marx und die dynamik der gesellschaft. Mit einem vorwort von Werner Kaegi. Wien, Frankfurt, Zürich, Europa verlag, 1965. 413 p.
9264. KAMENICKY, Antonín. Základy marxistické ekonomie. 2 vyd. (5 sv. knijhovny "Politika, sociologie , . . . Rada A.) 2 vyd. Praha, Svoboda, 1946. 194, 6 p.
9265. KAMENKA, Eugene. The ethical foundations of Marxism. (Praeger publications in Russian history and world communism, no. 120.) New York, Praeger, 1962. xvi, 208 p. Bibliography, 200-203.
9266. Das KAPITAL centenary volume; a symposium. Edited by Mohit Sen and M. B. Rao. Delhi, People's publishing house, 1968. viii, 229 p.
9267. KARATAEV, N. and M. Ryndina. Istorija ékonomičeski učenij. Ol vozniknovenija marksizma do velikoj oktjabr' skoj revoljucii. (Transliterated.) Moskava, 1961. 744 p.
9268. KARL-Marx-Kolloquium, Freiberg, 1967. Zur bedeutung der ökonomischen theorie von Karl Marx in der gegenwart. Mit 2 bildern und 3 tabellen. (Freiberger forschungshefte. Reihe D, 61. Politische ökonomie.) Leipzig, Deutscher verlag für grundstoffindustrie, 1968. 146 p.
9269. KARRAS, Heinz. Die grundgedanken der sozialistischen pädagogik in Marx' hauptwerk "Das Kapital." (Diskussionsbeiträge zu fragen der pädagogik, heft 5.) Berlin, Volk und wissen, 1956. 183 p.
9270. KAUTSKY, Karl Johann. Bernstein und das sozial democratische programm. Eine antikritik. Stuttgart, 1899.
9271. ———. The economic doctrines of Karl Marx. Translated by H. J. Stenning. New York, The Macmillan company; London, A. and C. Black, Limited., 1936. vi, 252 p. [First published in English in London, 1925? Spanish edition: La doctrina económica de Carlos Marx. Traducción de Anny dell'Erba . . . y N. Caplán. (Colección el pensamiento marxista, 4.) Buenos Aires, Lautaro, 1946. 299 p.]
9272. ———. Ethics and the materialist conception of history. Translated by John B. Askew. Chicago, Charles H. Kerr, 1913. 206 p.
9273. ———. Karl Marx. New York, 1925.
9274. ———. The social revolution. Translated by A. M. and M. W. Simons. Chicago, Charles H. Kerr, 1902. 189 p.
9275. ———. Terrorism and communism. London, National labor press, 1920. 234 p.
9276. ———. Thomas More and his utopia. New York, International publishers, 1926.
9277. KEMP, Tom. Theories of imperialism. London, Dobson, 1967. viii, 202 p.
9278. KERNER, Antonin. Osnovy a literatura ke studiu politické ekonomie. Vyd. 3., přepracované. (Učební texty vysokých škol.) Praha, Státni pedagogické nakl., 1964. 39 p.

9279. KERR, Clark. Marshall, Marx and modern times;the multidimensional society. London, Cambridge university press, 1969. 6, 138 p.
9280. KHROMUSHIN, Gennadiĭ Borisovich. Marxism and Soviet economy. Moscow, Novosti press agency publishing house, 1968. 143 p.
9281. KIM, Myŏng-san. Chŏngch'i kyŏngjehak kaeyo. (Transliterated.) Korea, 1961-63. 2 v.
9282. KIRKUP, T. History of socialism. London, G. Black, 1913.
9283. KLEIM, Manfred. Marx-Engels Verzeichnis. Werke, schriften, arikel. (Zusammengestellt und bearb. von Manfred Kliem, Horst Merbach and Richard Sperl.) Berlin, Dietz, 1966. 358 p. (2., erg. aufl., 1968. 28, 358 p.)
9284. KOIZUMI, Shinzō. Marukusu shigo gojūnen. (Transliterated. Japan, 1969. 400 p.
9285. KOLARZ, Walter. Books on communism. A bibliography. 2d edition. New York, Oxford university press, 1964. 568 p.
9286. KOLLNER, Lutz. Marxistische wirtschaftstheorie und sowjetische wirtschaftspolitik. (Schriftenreihe der bundeszentrale für politische bildung, heft 68.) Bonn, Bundeszentrale für politische bildung, 1965. 91 p.
9287. KORAC, Miladin M. Politička ekonomija. Osnovi teorijske analize kapitalističke i socijalističke robne proizvodnje. Napisali, Miladin Korać i Tihomir Vlaškalić. (Udžbenici za visoke škole.) Beograd, "Rad," 1966. 1, 456, 3 p. (2. izd. 1968. 2, 476, 3 p.)
9288. KOREN, Henry J. Marx and the authentic man; a first introduction to the philosophy of Karl Marx. Pittsburgh, Duquesne university press, 1967. 150 p. Bibliographical footnotes.
9289. KOROCKIN, V. M. Proniknovenie idej K. Marksa i F. Engel'sa v ěkonomičeskuju literaturi revoljucionnyh demokratov Rossii. Moskva, 1961. 91 p.
9290. KORSCH, Karl. Karl Marx. New York, Russell and Russell, 1963. 3, 247 p.
9291. _____. Marxismus und philosophie. (Neuausg.) Hrsg. und eingeleitet von Erich Gerlach. (Politische texte.) Frankfurt am Main, Europäische verlanganstalt; Wien, Europa verlag, 1966. 178 p.
9292. KOSHIMURA, Shinzaburō. Shihouron no tenkai. (Transliterated.) Japan, 1967. 6, 349 p. Bibliographies.
9293. KOUBA, Karel. Ekonomický růst a soustava řízení. Vybrané práce publikované v letech 1962-1969. Praha, Ekonomicky ustav CSAV, rozmn., 1969. 436 p.
9294. _____. Plán a trh za socialismu. (Ekonomický ústav československé akademie věd. výzkumná publikace, č. 34.) Praha, Ekonomický ústav CSAV, 1967. 57 p.
9295. _____, editor. Politická ekonomie socialismu; sbornik. Koletiv autorů pod vedením Karla Kouby. Vyd. 1. Praha, Nakl. politické literatury, 1964. 694 p.

9296. _____. Úvahy o socialistické ekonomice. 1. vyd. (Edice ekonomie a společnost.) 1. vyd. Praha, Svoboda, 1968. 328, 4 p.
9297. KOZODOEV, Ivan Iosifovich, editor. Chrestomathie zur politischen ökonomie, ein nachschlagewerk. (Übersetzung aus dem Russischen.) Berlin, Verlag die wirtschaft, 1964. 720 p.
9298. KRITIK der politischen ökonomie heute; 100 Jahre "Kapital." Hrsg. von Walter Euchner und Alfred Schmidt. (Politische ökonomie, geschichte und kritik.) Frankfurt, Europäische verlagsanstalt, 1968. 358 p.
9299. KURODA, Hirokazu. Shihoron igo hyakunen. (Transliterated.) Japan, 1967. 310 p. Bibliographical references in notes.
9300. KWANT, Remigius C. De wijsbegeerte van Karl Marx. (Mens en medernnes, aspecten van de sociale werkelijkheld, 33.) Utrecht, Het spectrum, 1962. 143 p.
9301. LABRIOLA, Antonio. Essays on the materialist conception of history. 1966.
9302. _____. In memoria del manifesto dei comunisti. Aggiunavi la traduzione del Manifesto di K. Marx e Fr. Engels; a cura e con introd. di Bruno Widmar. (Biblioteca socialista, 19.) Milano, Avanti, 1960. 167 p.
9303. LACHS, John. Marxist philosophy. A bibliographical guide. Chapel Hill, University of North Carolina press, 1967. xiv, 166 p.
9304. LAIDLER, H. W. A history of socialist thought. New York, Thomas Y. Crowell, 1927. (Revised edition: Social-economic movements. New York, Thomas Y. Crowell, 1944. 751 p.)
9305. LANDY, A. Marxism and the democratic tradition. New York, International publishers, 1946. 220, 2 p. Bibliography, 205-214, 221-222.
9306. LANG, Rikard. Politička ekonomija. Uvod i osnove. (Ekonomska biblioteka, 4 kolo, br. 3-4.) Zagreb, "Informator," 1968. xiv, 528 p.
9307. LANGE, Oscar Richard. Entwicklungstendenzen der modernen wirtschaft und gesellschaft; eine sozialistische analyse. (Europäische perspektiven.) Wien, Europa verlag, 1964. 191 p.
9308. _____. Theory of reproduction and accumulation. Prepared with the collaboration of Antoni Banasińksi on the basis of lectures delivered at Warsaw university. Translation from Polish by Józef Stadler. 1st English edition. Oxford, New York, Pergamon press, 1969. viii, 175 p.
9309. LANGER, Paul F. Japanese communism. An annotated bibliography. New York, International secretariat, Institute of Pacific relations, 1953. 95 p.
9310. LASKI, Harold J. Harold J. Laski on the Communist Manifesto, an introduction. . . . Foreword for the American edition by T. B. Bottomore. New York, Pantheon books, 1967. viii, 179 p. Bibliographical footnotes.

9311. _____. Karl Marx with the Communist Manifesto. New York, League for industrial democracy, 1933.
9312. LAURAT, Lucien. Les faits contre la doctrine dans l'economie soviétique. Claude Harmel. Paris, "Est et Ouest," 1967. 40 p.
9313. LAVERGNE, Nestor. El intercambio mercantil en el socialismo. La Habana, Ministerio del comercio exterior, 1964. 255 p.
9314. LEFEBVRE, Henri. Marx, sa vie, son oeuvre, avec un exposé da sa philosophie. 1. édition. (Philosophes.) Paris, Presses universitaires de France, 1964. 131 p. (2e édition mise à jour. Paris, Presses universitaires de France, 1969. 136 p.)
9315. LEKOVIC, Dragutin. Marksistička teorija otuđenja. Preveo sa francuskog Miloš Drobnjak. (Razvoj socijalističke misli. Studije i monografije.) Beograd, Institut za izučavanje radničkog pokreta, 1968. 436, 3 p.
9316. LENIN, Vladimir Il'ich. A characterization of economic romanticism; Sismondi and our native Sismondists. (Library of Marxist-Leninist classics.) Moscow, Foreign languages publishing house, 1951. 231 p.
9317. _____. Marx, Engels, marxime. Moscou, Editions en langues étrangères, 1947. 498 p. (English edition: 8th revised edition. Moscow, Progress, 1968. 517 p.)
9318. _____. Materialism and empiro-criticism; critical notes concerning a reactionary philosophy. 2d edition. Translated from the Russian by David Kvitko. (His collected works, v. 13.) New York, International publishers, 1927. viii, 336 p. Bibliographical index, 383-393. (Italian edition: Materialismo ed empiriocriticismo; note critiche su una filosofia reazionaria. 1. versione italiana, ed. integrale critica. Brescia, Studio editoriale vivi, 1946. 313 p. English edition: 4th rev. ed. Moscow, Progress publishers, 1967. 397 p.)
9319. _____. State and revolution; Marxist teaching about the theory of the state and the tasks of the proletariat in the revolution. Revised translation. (Little Lenin library, v. 14.) New York, International publishers, 1925. [Reprinted from Toward the seizure of power, by V. I. Lenin. Reprinted. 1946. 104 p. English edition: Moscow, Foreign languages publishing house, 19--. German editions: Staat und revolution; die lehre des Marxismus von Staat und die aufgaben des proletariats in der revolution. (Bucherei des Marxismus-Leninismus, Bd. 17.) Berlin, Dietz, 1951. 140 p. Frankfurt am Main, Verl. Marxistische blatter, 1970. 162 p.]
9320. _____. The teachings of Karl Marx. New York, International publishers, 1964. 62 p. Reference notes 59-62. (Includes essay on Marx written for Gramat encyclopedia, 1914 and 3 articles.)
9321. _____. The three sources and the three component parts of Marxism. Karl Marx. Frederick Engels. Moscow, Progress publishers, 1967. 61 p.

9322. _____. V. I. Lenin on Marxism. Moscow, Novosti press agency publishing house, 1969. 78 p.
9323. _____. What the "friends of the people" are and how they fight the social-democrats; a reply to articles in Russkoye Bogatstvo opposing the marxists. Translated from the Russian. Moscow, Progress publishers, 1966. 217 p.
9324. LENINISM. New York, International publishers, 1928. 472 p.
9325. LEONT'EV, Lev Abramovich. Fundamentals of Marxist political economy (Socialism: theory and practice, 1.) Moscow, Novosti press agency publishing house, 1965. 154 p.
9326. _____. A short course of political economy. Translated from the Russian by Don Danemanis; designed by V. Dober. Moscow, Progress, 1968. 414 p.
9327. _____ and O. Yakhot. New World, new outlook. (USSR 1917-1967.) Moscow, Novosti press agency publishing house, 1967. 251 p.
9328. LEOPOLD, Richard W. Robert Dale Owen. Cambridge, Massachusetts, Harvard university press, 1940.
9329. LEWIS, John. The life and teachings of Karl Marx. New York, International publishers, 1965. 286 p. Bibliographical footnotes.
9330. _____. Marxism and the open mind. London, Routledge & K. Paul, 1957. 222 p.
9331. LIBMAN, Georgii Izrailevich. Decisive advantage (on socialist economic growth rates.) (Socialism: theory and practice.) Moscow, Novosti press agency publishing house, 1967. 84 p.
9332. LICHTHEIM, George. Marxism. An historical and critical study. New York, Praeger, 1961. 412 p. Bibliography. (2d ed. rev., London Routledge and K. Paul, 1964. xix, 412 p. Bibliographical footnotes.)
9333. _____. Marxism in modern France. New York, Columbia university press, 1961. Translated by Ernest Untermann. Bibliography, 199-207. ix, 212 p.
9334. LIEBKNECHT, Wilhelm. Karl Marx; biographical memoirs. Chicago, Charles H. Kerr, 1901. (Michigan, Scholarly press, 1969. 181 p.)
9335. LINDSAY, Alexander Dunlop. Karl Marx's capital; an introductory essay. (The world's manuals.) London, Oxford university press, H. Milford, 1937. 128 p.
9336. LINDSAY, Jack. The anatomy of spirit; an inquiry into the origins of religious emotion. London, Methune & co., ltd., 1937. vii, 182, 2 p.
9337. LIPPINCOTT, Benjamin Evans, editor. On the economic theory of socialism. By Oskar Lange and Fred M. Taylor. (Reprints of economic classics.) New York, A. M. Kelley, 1970. vii, 143 p.
9338. LISICHKIN, Gennadiĭ Stepanovich. Plan i tržište. Napisao. G. S. Lisickin. Preveo Svetislav Petrović. (V. Milenkovic: Uvodne napomene). (Dokumenti današnjice. Nova

ser., god. 6, br. 155.) Naslovna strana: Pavle Ristić. Beograd, "Sedma sila," 1966. 80 p.
9339. LIVERGOOD, Norman D. Activity in Marx's philosophy. The Hague, Martinus Nijhoff, c1967, 1968. 109 p. Bibliography, 51-53.
9340. LOBKOWICZ, Nikolaus. Theory and practice: history of a concept from Aristotle to Marx. (International studies of the committee on International relations, University of Notre Dame.) Notre Dame, Indiana, University of Notre Dame press, 1967. xvi, 442 p.
9341. LORIA, Achille. Karl Marx. New York, Thomas Seltzer, 1920.
9342. LOUIS, Paul. Histoire du socialisme en France. 5th edition. Paris, M. Riviere, 1950. 432 p.
9343. LOWE, Donald M. The function of "China" in Marx, Lenin, and Mao. Berkeley, University of California press, 1966. xiv, 200 p. Bibliography, 160-193.
9344. LOWENTHAL, Esther. The Ricardian socialist. . . . (Studies in history, economics and public law, edited by the Faculty of political science of Columbia university, vol. XLV, no. 1, whole no. 114.) New York, 1911. 107 p. (Thesis, Ph. D., Columbia university.)
9345. LUKASZEWICZ, Aleksander. Przyspieszony wzrost gospodarki socjalistycznej w zwiasku z teoria, G. Feldmana. Wyd. 1. Warszawa, Państwowe wydawn. Naukowe, 1965. 315 p.
9346. LUKAWER, Edward. Możliwość funkcjonowania godpodarki socjalistycznej w świetle miedzywojennej dyskusji na zachodzie. (Wyzsza szkoła ekonomiczna w krakowie. Zeszyty naukowe. Seria specjalna: rosprawy habilitacyjne, nr. 12.) Kraków, 1967. 468 p.
9347. LUZICKI, L., W. Kudla, and S. Zurawicki. Rozwój idei socjalistycznych w myśli ekonomicznej. Warszawa, Uniwersytet Warszawski, 1964. 189 p.
9348. LYSKO, Stanisław. Teoria cen w radzieckich dyskusjach ekonomicznych. Wyd. 1. Warszawa, Państwowe wydawn. ekonomiczne, 1967. 333 p.
9349. MACEK, Josef. The impact of Marxism. Pittsburgh, University of Pittsburgh press, 1955. 147 p.
9350. MAKSIMOVIC, Ivan, editor. Politička ekonomija socijalizma. Redaktori: Ivan Maksimović, Zarko Bulajić. Urednik: Ljubinka Krešić. Beograd, Rad, 1966. 727 p.
9351. ———. Predmet ekonomskih nauka. (Predmet društvenih nauka.) Beograd, Institut društvenih nauka, Grupa za metodologiju, 1967, 1968. 95, 1 p.
9352. MALIA, Martin. Alexander Herzen and the birth of Russian socialism, 1812-1855. Cambridge, Massachusetts, Harvard university press, 1961. 486 p.
9353. MANDEL, Ernest. La formation de la pensée économique de Karl Marx, de 1843 qusqu'à la rédaction du "Capital," étude génétique. (Les textes à l'appui.) Paris, F. Maspero, 1967. 216 p.
9354. ———. An introduction to Marxist economic theory.

	New York, Merit publishers, 1969. 78 p.
9355.	_____. Marxist economic theory. Translated from the French by Brian Pearce. Book club edition. London, Merlin, 1968. 2 v. 797 p. Bibliography, 735-771. (Revised edition: New York, Monthly review press, 1969. c1968. 2 v. 797 p.) [Translation of Traité d'economie marxiste. Paris, R. Julliard, 1962. 2 v. (Revised edition: Paris, Union générale d'éditions, 1969. 4 v.)]
9356.	MANETTI-CUSA, Nicolas. Hallesismo y communismo. Buenos Aires, Editorial Hallesint, 1964. 102 p.
9357.	MANNHEIM, Karl. Ideology and Utopia. Preface by Louis Wirth. Translated by Louis Wirth and Edward Shils. New York, Harcourt, Brace, 1946. 318 p.
9358.	MANUEL, F. E. The new world of Henri Saint-Simon. Cambridge, Massachusetts, Harvard university press, 1956.
9359.	MAO Tse-Tung. Miscellaneous works. Peking, Foreign languages publishing house, 1953-61. 21 v.
9360.	_____. Selected works. London, Lawrence and Wishard, 1954-56. 5 v.
9361.	MARINKOVIC, Pribislav. Politička ekonomija socijalizma. 3. izd. Beograd, Viša škola za spolijnu trgovinu, 1967. 202, 2 p.
9362.	MARKHAM, F. M. H., editor, Henri, comte de Saint-Simon, 1760-1825. Selections. Translated and with an introduction by F. M. H. Markham. Oxford, B. Blackwell, 1952. li, 116 p.
9363.	MARKHAM, Sydney Frank. A history of socialism. London, Black, 1930. 328 p.
9364.	MARKOVIC, Milo. Ekonomska teorija u djelima V. L. Lenjina. Titograd, 1969. 274 p.
9365.	MARX, Karl. Address and provisional rules of the international working men's association. London, Labor and socialist international, 1924. (Address, 1864.)
9366.	_____. Basic writings on politics and philosophy. By Karl Marx and Friedrich Engels. Edited by Lewis S. Feuer. 1st edition. (Anchor books.) Garden City, New York, Doubleday, 1959. 497 p.
9367.	_____. Capital. A critique of political economy. Chicago, Charles H. Kerr & company, 1906-09. 3 v. Bibliography, 849-864. (Contents: v. 1. The process of capitalist production. Translated from the 3d German edition., by Samuel Moore and Edward Aveling, and edited by Frederick Engels. Rev. and amplified according to the 4th German edition by Ernest Untermann. v. 2. The process of circulation of capital. Edited by Frederick Engels. Translated from the 2d German edition by Ernest Untermann. v. 3. The process of capitalist production as a whole. Edited by Frederick Engels. Translated from the 1st German edition by Ernest Untermann. v. 1: 1st edition, 1867. By K. Marx. v. 2. 1st edition, 1885. Edited by F. Engels. v. 3: 1st edition, 1894. Edited by F. Engels. German edition: Das kapital,

1867. 4th edition, 1890-94. 3 v. Edited by Friedrich
Engels. English translation in 1887 by Samuel Moore
and Edward Aveling. Among the many editions in
English have been: London, Sonnenschein, 1903. 3 v.
New York, Modern library, 1906. 869 p. Chicago,
Encyclopedia Britannica, 1952, 1955. xi, 434 p. Many
abridged and selected works of materials from the three
volumes have been printed in numerous languages and
many various titles. Among them are, The people's
Marx, 1921, edited by J. Borchart and abridged by
S. L. Traske. Separate volumes of Das Kapital have
been printed, for example, v. II: Berlin, Dietz-verlag,
1953. 639 p.; v. I, New York, New world paperbacks,
International publishers, 1967.)

9368. ———— . . . . Le capital; extraits faits par M. Paul La
Farque. Introduction by Vilfredo Pareto. (Petite
bibliothèque économique française et étrangère.) Paris,
Guillaumin, lxxx, 176 p.

9369. ————. Capital, the communist manifesto and other
writings, by Karl Marx, edited, with an introduction, by
Max Eastman; with an unpublished essay on Marxism by
Lenin . . . (The Modern library of the world's best
books.) New York, The Modern library, c1932. xxvi,
429 p. (Reprinted: 1959.)

9370. ————. Il capitale, brevemente compendiato da Carlo
Cafiero. A cura di Giulio Trevisani. (Universale
economica, v. n. 51. Serie scientifica, v. 6.) Milano,
Universale economica, 1950. 123 p. (1945?, xvi, 528 p.)

9371. ————. The civil war in France; with an introduction
by Frederick Engels. (Marxist library, 9.) New York,
International publishers, 1933. 92 p. (Address of the
General council of the International working men's association.
Originally produced in 1871. Several editions
appeared: including: London, Labor publishing company,
1921.)

9372. ————. The civil war in the United States. By Karl
Marx and Frederich Engels. Centennial (3rd.) edition.
New York, International publishers, 1961. 334 p.

9373. ————. The class struggles in France, 1848-1850. New
York, International publishers, 1964. 158 p.

9374. ————. The Communist manifesto. By Karl Marx and
Friedrich Engels. Principles of communism. By
Friedrich Engels; a new translation by Paul M. Sweezy.
The Communist manifesto after 100 years. By Paul
Marlor Sweezy and Leo Huberman. New York, Monthly
review press, 1964. v, 113 p. [The communist
manifesto after 100 years, was published in the Monthly
review (August, 1949). The Principles of communism
was translated from the text of the Marx-Engels Gesamtausgabe,
1st division, v. 6, pt. 1, 503-522.]

9375. ————. Communist manifesto, socialist landmark. A
new appreciation written for the Labour party by Harold
J. Laski, together with the original text and prefaces.

Post-Classical Period 543

London, G. Allen and Unwin, 1948. 159 p. (Samuel Moore's translation of the work of Marx and Engels as issued in London in 1888.)

9376. _____. A contribution to the critique of political economy. By Karl Marx. Translated from the 2d German edition by N. I. Stone. With an appendix containing Marx's introduction to the Critique recently published among his posthumous papers. Chicago, Charles H. Kerr, 1904. 1 p. 1., 314 p. (German editions: 1st published, 1859. Stuttgart, 1897. 2. aufl. Berlin, Dietz, 1951, c1947. v.)

9377. _____. Critique of Hegel's 'Philosophy of right.' Translated from the German by Annette Jolin and Joseph O'Malley. Edited with an introduction and notes by Joseph O'Malley. (Cambridge studies in the history and theory of politics.) Cambridge, England, University press, 1970. 151 p.

9378. _____. Critique of the Gotha programme. With appendices by Marx, Engels, and Lenin; a revised translation. New York, International publishers, c1938. vii, 116 p. (Revised translation of edition by International publishers in 1944; based upon Russian edition of the Marx-Engels-Lenin institute. German edition: Randglossen zum programm der deutschen arbeiterpartei. 1875. English edition: The Gotha program. New York, Socialist labor party, 1922.)

9379. _____. Critique of political economy. 1859. Chicago, Charles H. Kerr, 1913.

9380. _____. Early texts. Translated and edited by David McLellan. New York, Barnes and Noble, c1971. 223 p.

9381. _____. Early writings. Translated and edited by T. B. Bottomore. London, Watts, 1963. xix, 227 p. Bibliography, 221-223.

9382. _____. The Eastern question; a reprint of letters written 1853-1856 dealing with the events of the Crimean war. By Karl Marx; edited by Eleanor Marx Aveling and Edward Aveling . . . London, S. Sonnenschein and company, limited, 1897. xv, 656 p. (Letters appeared in New York Tribune.)

9383. _____. Economic and philosophic manuscripts of 1844. Translated by Martin Milligan. Moscow, Foreign languages publishing house, 1959. 208 p. (1961. 208 p. London, Lawrence and Wishart? From German text in Marx-Engels, Gesamtausgabe, Abt. I, Bd. 3 . . . Appendix, Outlines of a critique of political economy by F. Engels; translated from German text in Marx-Engels, Gesamtausgabe, Abt. 1, Bd. 2. 1st American edition: Edited with an introduction by Dirk J. Struik. New York, International publishers, 1964. 255 p. Moscow, Progress publishers, 1967. 191 p.)

9384. _____. The eighteenth Brumaire of Louis Bonaparte. With explanatory notes. New York, International publishers, 1963? 161 p. Bibliographical references, 141-50 (1st produced in 1852. Chicago, Charles H. Kerr, 1913.)

9385. ———. The essential left; four classic texts on the principles of socialism. By Marx, Engels and Lenin. London, Allen and Unwin; New York, Barnes and Noble, 1961. 254 p.

9386. ———. Essentials of Marx. The communist manifesto. By Karl Marx and Frederich Engels. Wage-labor and capital; Value, price and profit. By Karl Marx. With introduction and notes by Algernon Lee. Revised 2d edition. New York, Rand school press, 1946. 2 p. l., 185 p.

9387. ———. The first Indian war of independence, 1857-1859. By K. Marx and F. Engels. Moscow, Foreign languages publishing house, 1960? 245 p.

9388. ———. Fondements de la critique de l'économie politique. Grundrisse der kritik der politischen ökonomie. (Ebauche de 1857-1858.) En annexe: Travaux des années 1850-1859. Traduit par Roger Dangeville . . . Paris, Editions anthropos, 1967-1968. 2 v.

9389. ———. Formen, die der kapitalistischen produktion vorhergehen; die analyse jenes "Prozesses, der bildung des kapitalverhältnisses oder der ursprünglichen akkumulation vorhergeht." Besorgt vom Marx-Engels-Lenin-Institut beim ZK der SED. (Kleine bücherei des Marxismus-Leninismus.) Berlin, Dietz, 1952. 58 p.

9390. ———. The German ideology. Parts I and III. By Karl Marx and Friedrich Engels. Edited with an introduction by R. Pascal. New York, International publishers, 1960, c1947. 214 p. [Edited by S. Ryazanskaya. London, Lawrence and Wishart, 1965. 2 v. in 1 (736 p.) Translation of Die Deutsche ideologie.]

9391. ———. Grundrisse der kritik der politischen ökonomie. (Rohentwurf) 1857-1858. Anhang, 1850-1859. (Fotomechanischer Nachdruck der ausg. Moskau 1939 und 1941.) Frankfurt a. M., Europäische verlags-anstalt, 1967. xvi, 1102 p. (Selections, edited and translated by David McLellan. New York, Harper and Row, 1971. 152 1 p. Bibliography.)

9392. ———. Historia crítica de la téoria de la plusvalía . . . Versión directa y prólogo de Wenceslao Roces. 1st Spanish edition. (Sección de obras de economía del Fondo de cultura económica dirigida por Daniel Cosío Villegas.) México, Fondo de cultura económica, 1944-45. 3 v.

9393. ———. A history of economic theories. Edited, with a preface by Karl Kautsky. Translated from the French, with an introduction and notes, by Terence McCarthy. 1st edition. New York, Langland press, 1952- . v. (1st German edition, 1904: Theorien über den mehrwert. New York, Langland press, 1932.)

9394. ———. Das kapital, 1867-1967. Beiträge über "Das kapital" und marxistische politische ökonomie. Veröffentlicht anlässlich des 100. Jahrestages des Erscheinens des hauptwerkes von Karl Marx. (Marxistische Blätter. Sonderheft 2.) Frankfurt/Main, August-Bebel-Gesellschaft, 1967. 88 p.

9395. _____, and Friedrich Engels. Correspondence, 1846-1895. London, Lawrence & Wishart, 1934.

9396. _____. and Frederick Engels. Selected Works. Moscow, Progress publishers, 1969-1970. 3 v.

9397. _____. Karl Marx dictionary. Edited by Morris Stockhammer. New York, Philosophical library, c1965. vii, 273 p.

9398. _____. Karl Marx und Friedrich Engels: ausgewählte schriften. Moskau, Verlag für fremdsprachige literatur, 1950. 2 v.

9399. _____. Kleine ökonomische schriften. von Karl Marx und Friedrich Engels. Ein sammelband, besorgt von Marx-Engels-Lenin-Stalin-Institut beim ZK der SED. 1 aufl. (Bücherei des Marxismus-Leninismus, Bd. 42.) Berlin, Dietz, 1955. 618 p.

9400. _____. Lineamenti fondamentali della critica dell' economia politica. 1857-1858. Presentazione, traduzione e note di Enzo Grillo. (Classici della filosofia, 7.) Firenze, La nouva Italia, 1969--. v.

9401. _____. Manoscritti economico-filosofici del 1844. Nuova edizione. Prefazione e traducione di Norberto Bobbio. (Nuova universale Einaudi, 92.) Torino, G. Einaudi, 1968. xix, 188 p.

9402. _____. Manuskripte über die polnische frage, 1863-1864. Hrsg. und eingeleitet von Werner Conze und Dieter Hertz-Eichenrode. (Quellen und unterschunger zur Geschichte der deutschen und österreichischen arbeiterbewegung, 4.) 's-Gravenhage, Mouton, 1961. 202 p.

9403. _____. Marx on economics. Edited by Robert Freedman. Introduction by Harry Schwartz. 1st edition. (Harvest books, HB39.) New York, Harcourt, Brace, 1961. 290 p.

9404. _____. Marx vs. Russia. Edited, with an introduction by J. A. Doerig. Afterword by Hans Kohn. New York, Ungar, 1962. viii, 198 p. (Selection, articles, New York Daily tribune, March 1853 and April 1856; based on The eastern question, London, 1897. Introduction and running text, translated by Charles M. Stern, from German, Marx contra Russland.)

9405. _____. Okenomisch-philosophische manuskripte, gesechrieben von April bis August 1844. Nach der handschift. Einleitung und Anmerkungen von Joachim Höppner. 1 aufl. (Reclams universal-bibliothek, Bd. 448.) Leipzig, Reclam, 1968. 348, 4 p.

9406. _____. On religion. By Karl Marx and Friedrich Engels. Introduction by Reinhold Niebuhr. (Schocken paperbacks.) New York, Schocken books, 1964, 382 p. Bibliographical references, 348-359.

9407. _____. Opere filosofiche giovanili: 1. Critica della filosofia hegeliana del diritto pubblico. 2. Manoscritti economico-filosofici del 1844. Traduzione di Galvano della Volpe. (1 Classici del marxismo, 24.) Roma, Rinascita, 1950. 314 p.

9408. _____. Le origini della società borghese. Ristampa della traduzione italiana della sezione 8 del 1. volume del "Capitale," con nota espositiva di Giulio Pierangeli. ("I Germogli," le pagine vive, 2.) Citta di Castello, Il Sloco, 1946. 124 p.

9409. _____. Pre-capitalist economic formations. Translated by Jack Cohen. Edited and with an introduction by E. J. Hobsbawm. 1st United States edition. New York, International publishers, 1965, c1964. 153 p. (Translation of Foremen, die de kapitalistischen produktion vorhergehen, 1st published as part of Grundrisse der kritik der politischen ökonomie and later published separately.)

9410. _____. The poverty of philosophy; answer to the "Philosophy of poverty," by M. Proudhon. Preface by Frederick Engels to the first German edition. Moscow, Foreign languages publishing house, 1962. 225 p. (1st published in 1847. Chicago, Charles H. Kerr, 1910. Moscow, Foreign languages publishing house, 1955? 256 p. New York, International publishers, 1963. 233 p.)

9411. _____. Revolution and counter-revolution; or, Germany in 1848. Edited by Eleanor Marx Aveling. London, G. Allen and Unwin, ltd. 1952. 148 p. (1st published 1891; Chicago, Charles H. Kerr, 1914. Reprinted, 1952.)

9412. _____. Selected essays. Translated by H. J. Stenning. London, Leonard Parsons, n. d. 207 p.

9413. _____. Selected works. Prepared by the Marx-Engels-Lenin institute, Moscow. Under the editorship of V. Adoratsky . . . New York, International, 1933. (London, Lawrence and Wishart limited, 1942. 2 v. C. P. Dutt, editor of English edition.)

9414. _____. Selected works of Karl Marx and Frederick Engels. Moscow, Foreign languages publishing house, 1949-50. v. 1, 1950. 2 v.

9415. _____. Selected works of Karl Marx and Frederick Engels. Moscow, Progress, 1968. 800 p., 2 1.

9416. _____. Selected writings in sociology and social philosophy. Edited with an introduction and notes by T. R. Bottomore and Maximilien Rubel. Texts translated by T. B. Bottomore. London, Watts, 1956. 268 p. (Newly translated by T. B. Bottomore. Edited, with an introduction and notes by Mr. Bottomore and Maximilien Rubel, and with a foreword by Erich Fromm. 1st McGraw-Hill edition. New York, McGraw-Hill, 1964. xviii, 268 p.)

9417. _____. Theorien über den mehrwert; aus dem nachgelassenen manuskript "Zur kritik der politischen ökonomie" von Karl Marx, hrsg. von Karl Kautsky . . .

(Internationale bibliothek, bd. 35-37a.) Stuttgart, J. H. W. Dietz nachf., 1910. 3 v. in 4. (1st produced, 1861-63. 5th edition, 1923. Berlin, Dietz, 1956-62. English edition: Theories of surplus values. Edited by S. Ryazanskaya, translated by Renate Simpson. London, Lawrence and Wishart, 1969- . v. Translated by G. A. Bonnar and Emily Burns. London, Lawrence Wishart, 1951. 432 p. New York, International publishers, 1952. 432 p. Moscow, Foreign languages publishing house, 1963. Bibliographies.)

9418. ———. Teoriĩa nakopleniĩa. (Transliterated.) Moscow, 1948. 111 p.

9419. ———. Uvod ke kritice politické ekonomie. (Malá knihovna marxismu-leninismu, 19.) Z německého originálu přel. Ladislav Stoll. Praha, Svoboda, 1946. 22, 2 p.

9420. ———. Value, price and profit. Addressed to workingmen. Edited by Eleanor Marx Aveling. Chicago, Charles H. Kerr, 1913? 128 p. (1st published, 1865. German edition: Leipzig, Reclam-verlag, 1953. 103 p.)

9421. MARX and the western world. Edited by Nicholas Lobkowicz. Contributors: James L. Adams and others. Notre Dame, Indiana, University of Notre Dame press, 1967. xix, 444 p.

9422. MARXISM and modern thought. By N. I. Bukharin, A. M. Deborin, Y. M. Uranovsky, S. I. Valilov, V. L. Komarov, & A. I. Tiumeniev. Translated by Ralph Winston Fox. New York, Harcourt, Brace and company, 1935. viii, 342 p. Notes, 321-335. (Selected material from the Soviet academy of science's memorial volume on the fiftieth anniversary of the death of Karl Marx.)

9423. MARZ, Eduard. Die Marxsche wirtschaftslehre im widerstreit der meinungen; ist sie heute noch gültig? Mit einem Beitrag von Ernst Winkler. (Schriftenreihe des österreichischen gewerkschaftsbundes, Nr. 76.) Wien, Verlag des Österreichischen gewerkschaftsbundes, 1959. 271 p.

9424. MASSERA, José Luis. Marx, Lenin; sus nombres perdurarán por los siglos. Montevideo, Comisión nacional de propaganda del Partido comunista del Uruguay, 1968. 35 p.

9425. MATERIALY do studiowania ekonomii politycznej socjalizmu; wybór tekstów. Wyboru dokonali: W. Brus et al. Wyd. 1. Warszawa, Książka i Wiedza, 1964. 1180 p.

9426. MATTICK, Paul. Marx and Keynes; the limits of the mixed economy. (Extending horizons books.) Boston, P. Sargent, 1969. viii, 364 p.

9427. MATYAS, Antal. A polgári kozgazdaságtan rövid története a marxizmus létrejötte elött. Budapest, Közgazdasági es Jogi Könyvkiadó, 1961. 327 p.

9428. MAYER, Gustav. Friedrich Engels. Eine Biographie. The Hague, 1934. 2 v. (New York, Knopf, 1936.)

9429. MAYER, Henry. Marx, Engels, and Australia. (Sydney studies in politics, 5.) Melbourne, F. W. Cheshire for the Department of government and public administration, University of Sydney, 1964. 149 p.
9430. MAYO, Henry Bertram. Introduction to Marxist theory. New York, Oxford university press, 1960. 334 p. Bibliography.
9431. MAYZ Vallenilla, Ernesto. Del hombre y su alienación. (Colección pensamiento y verdad.) Caracas, Instituto nacional de cultura y bellas artes, 1966. 121 p.
9432. MCBRIAR, A. M. Fabian socialism and English politics, 1884-1918. Cambridge, England, University press, 1962. 387 p.
9433. MCCARRAN, Margaret Patricia. Fabianism in the political life of Britain, 1919-1931. 2nd edition. Washington, Catholic university of America press, 1954. 612 p.
9434. MCLELLAN, David. Marx before Marxism. New York, Harper and Row, 1970. viii, 233 p. Bibliography, 223-229.
9435. ———. The young Hegelians and Karl Marx. London, Melbourne, Macmillan; New York, F. A. Praeger, 1969. ix, 170 p.
9436. The MEANING of Marx, a symposium. By Bertrand Russell, John Dewey, Morris Cohen, Sidney Hook and Sherwood Eddy. New York, Farrar & Rinehart, incorporated, 1934. vi p., 2 l., 144 p.
9437. MEEK, R. L. Studies in the labour theory of value. London, Lawrence and Wishart, 1956.
9438. MEHRING, Franz. Karl Marx; the story of his life. With illustrations and facsimile reproductions, notes by the author, an appendix prepared under the direction of Eduard Fuchs on the basis of the researches of the Marx-Engels institute, a bibliography and an index. Translated by Edward Fitzgerald. London, Allen & Unwin, 1936. 2 p., 1., vii-xxi p., 1 l., 575 p. Bibliography, 557-565. (New edition. Translated by Edward Fitzgerald. New introduction by Max Schactman. Ann Arbor, University of Michigan press, 1962. 575 p. German edition: Karl Marx. Geschichte seines lebens. 4th edition. Leipzig, 1923. Berlin, Dietz, 1960. 16, 619 p. Die Herausgabe des Bandes besorgte Thomas Höhle. Berlin, Dietz, 1964. 606 p. Frankfurt/M, Europäische verlagsanstalt, 1964. 606 p.)
9439. MEISNER, Maurice. Li Ta-Chao and the origins of Chinese Marxism.
9440. MENDEL, Arthur P. Essential works of Marxism. New York, Bantam, 1961. 592 p.
9441. MENEZES, Djacir. Proudhon, Hegel e a dialética. (Bibioteca de ciéncias socials.) Rio de Janeiro, Zahar, 1966. 158 p.
9442. MENGER, Anton. The right to the whole produce of labour. Translated by M. E. Tanner. Introduction by H. S. Foxwell, London, New York, Macmillan, 1899.

Post-Classical Period

9443. MESZAROS, István. Marx's theory of alienation. London, Merlin press, 1970. 352 p.
9444. MEYER, Alfred G. Communism. New York, Random house, 1960. 217 p.
9445. _____. Leninism. Cambridge, Massachusetts, Harvard university press, 1957. 324 p.
9446. _____. Marxism: the unity of theory and practice; a critical essay. (Russian research center studies, 14). Cambridge, Harvard university press, 1954. 181 p. (London, Oxford university press, 1961. 181 p.)
9447. MICHNAK, Karel. Ekonomie a fetišismus. (Živé myšlenky, 9.) Praha, Svobodné slovo, 1965. 259 p.
9448. MILLS, Charles Wright. The Marxists. (A Laurel edition, LX 141.) New York, Dell publishing company, 1962.
9449. MILON, René. Marxisme, communisme, et socialisme africain. Paris, Imp. Edimpra, 1962? 65 p.
9450. MISZEWSKI, Bronisław. Zarys ekonomii politycznej; wybór tematów i pytania sprawdzajace. (Politechnika slaska im. W. Pstrowskiego. Skrypty uczelniane, nr. 180.) Gliwice, 1967. 188 p.
9451. MITA, Sekisuke. Uno riron to marukusu-shugi keizaigaku. (Transliterated.) Japan, 1968. 257 p.
9452. MITRANY, David. Marx against the peasant; a study in social dogmatism. Chapel Hill, University of North Carolina press, 1951. xvi, 301 p. Bibliography, 270-286.
9453. MIYAKAWA, Minoru. Marukusu keizaigaku jiten. (Transliterated.) Japan, 1965. iv, 326 p.
9454. MOLNAR, Erik. L'influence de la philosophie de l'histoire de Hegel sur l'historiographie marxiste. (Studia historica academiae scientiarum Hungaricae, 47.) Budapest, Akadémiai kiadó, 1960. 14 p.
9455. MONDOLFO, Rodolfo. El humanismo de Marx. Tradicción del original en italiano por Oberdan Caletti. 1 ed. México, Fondo de cultura económica, 1964. 125 p.
9456. MORE, Sir Thomas. Utopia and a dialogue of comfort. Introduction by John Warrington. London, New York, Dent, Dutton, 1951. 428 p.
9457. MORF, Otto. Dasverhältnis von wirtschaftstheorie und wirtschaftsgeschichte bei Karl Marx. (Staatswissenschaftliche studien, n. F. Bd. 11.) Bern, A. Francke, 1951. 133 p.
9458. MUMFORD, Lewis. The story of utopias. New York, Boni and Liveright, 1922.
9459. NEGLEY, Glenn and J. Max Patrick. The quest for Utopia. New York, H. Schuman, 1952. 599 p.
9460. NICARD des Rieux, Samuel. Michel Chevalier, saint-simonien. Limoges, 1912. (Dissertation, University of Poitiers.)
9461. NICOLAIEVSKY, Boris, and Otto Maenchen-Helfen. Karl Marx, Man and fighter. Philadelphia, Lippincott, 1936. (German edition: Nikolaevskiĭ, Boris Ivanovich. Karl Marx; eine biographie. von B. Nicolaevsky und O.

Maenchen-Helfen. Hannover, Dietz, 1963. xii, 419 p.)
9462. NICK, Harry. Technische revolution und ökonomie der produktionsfonds. Berlin, Dietz, 1967. 211 p.
9463. NORDHOFF, Charles. The communistic societies of the United States. New York, Harper and brothers, 1875.
9464. OELSSNER, Fred. Die Arbeitswerttheorie als die wissenschaftliche grundlage der Marxschen politischen ökonomie. (Deutsche akademie der wissenschaften zu Berlin. Vorträge und schriften, heft 103.) Berlin, Akademie-verlag, 1967. 19 p.
9465. OI, Tadashi. Yuibutsu shikau no keisei katei. (Transliterated.) Japan, 1968. xii, 419, ix p.
9466. OKONOMISCHE gesetze im gesellschaftlichen system des sozialismus von Georg Ebert et al. 1 aufl. Berlin, Dietz, 1969. 392 p.
9467. OTTO, Hans. Neue aufgaben für die Führungstätigkeit der parteiorganisation im staatsapparat, bei der durchsetzung des ökonomischen systems des sozialismus. (Uberarbeiteter vortrag.) (Der parteiarbeiter.) Berlin, Deitz, 1968. 30 p.
9468. OWEN, Robert. The book of the new moral world. London, E. Wilson, 1836. 104 p.
9469. ———. Dialogue sur le système social. Paris, 1848.
9470. ———. A new view of society. Glencoe, Illinois, Free press, 1948. 184 p. (3rd edition. London, 1817.)
9471. PAEGLIS, Jānis. K. Markss, F. Engelss, V. I. Lenins latviešu valodā. Bibliogrāfija. Rīgā, 1969. 362 p.
9472. PAHLOW, Winfried. Wirtschaftliche entwicklungsgesetze? Eine allgemeine kritik der Idee der zwangsläufigkeit in der wirtschaft. (Nürnberger abhandlungen zu den wirtschafts- und sozialwissenschaften, heft 26.) Berlin, Duncker & Humblot, 1968. 233 p.
9473. PAN, Luis. Justo y Marx; el socialismo en la Argentina; conferencias. Buenos Aires. Ediciones monserrat, 1964. 173 p. Bibliographical footnotes.
9474. PANKHURST, R. K. P. "Saint-Simonism in England." In, Twentieth century, 152, 910 (December, 1952) 498-512.
9475. PAPPENHEIM, Fritz. The alienation of modern man; an interpretation based on Marx and Tönnies. New York, Monthly review press, 1959. 189 p.
9476. PARAIN, Charles. Mode de production féodal et classes sociales en système précolonialiste (précapitaliste). Par Charles Parain et Pierre Vilar . . . (Les cahiers du centre d'études et de recherches marxistes, no. 59.) Paris, Centre d'études et de recherches marxistes, 1968. 39 1.
9477. PARKES, Henry Bamford. Marxism: an autopsy. Boston, Houghton Mifflin company, 1939. 5 p. 1., 299, 1 p. Bibliographical references in notes, 261-290. (Chicago, University of Chicago press, 1964. viii, 299 p.)
9478. PASZTORY, Tibor von. Von marxistischer ideologie zur planwirtschaft. (Darstellung, analyse und kritik.) Berlin, Duncker and Humblot, 1964. 163 p.

9479. PAVLENDA, Viktor, editor. Politická ekonómia sozializmu. Kolektiv autorov pod vedením Viktora Pavlendu. 1 vyd. Bratislava. Vydavateľstvo politickej literatúry, 1965. 618 p.
9480. PEASE, Edward R. History of the Fabian society. London, New York, International publishers, 1925.
9481. PENGANTAR untuk ekonomi politik Marxis. Diterdjemahkan oleh Rollah Sjarifah dan M. H. Lukman. Djarkarta, Japasan "Pembaruan," 1952? 40 p.
9482. PEREIRA, Luiz. Trabalho e desenvolvimento no Brasil. (Corpo e alma do Brasil, 17.) São Paulo, Difusão Europeia do livro, 1965. 320 p.
9483. PEROVIC, Mirko. Politička ekonomija. 7., izm. izd. (Biblioteka društvenih nauka.) Beograd, "Savremena administracija," 1967. xiv, 498 p.
9484. PETROVIC, Gajo. Marx in the mid-twentieth century; a Yugoslav philosopher considers Karl Marx's writings. 1st edition. Garden City, New York, Anchor books, 1967. 237 p.
9485. PETROVIC, Radomir. Društveno-ekonomsko obrazovanje. Beograd, Casopis "Priručnik--propisi i objašnjenja," 1968. 158, 3 p.
9486. PHILOSOPHISCHER kongress der DDR, Berlin, 1968. Die philosophische lehre von Karl Marx und ihre aktuelle bedeutung. Im auftrage der sektion für philosophie der Deutschen akademie der wissenschaften zu Berlin hrsg. von Dieter Bergner, Wolfgang Eichorn I und Günter Héyden. 1. aufl. Berlin, Verlag der wissenschaften, 1968. 830 p.
9487. PIASNY, Janusz. Miejsce konsumpcji w teorii gospodarki socjalistycznej. Wyd. 1. (Wyzsza szkoła ekonomiczna w Poznaniu. Zeszyty naukowe. Seria II. Prace habilitacyjne i doktorskie, zesz. nr. 40.) Poznan, Wydawn. uczelniane wyzszej szkoły ekonomicznej, 1967. 124 p.
9488. PIETTRE, A. Marx et marxisme. Paris, Presses universitaires de France, 1957. viii, 234 p.
9489. PLAINE, Henry L., editor. Darwin, Marx, and Wagner; a symposium. Columbus, Ohio state university press, c1962. viii, 165 p. Bibliographies.
9490. PLEKHANOV, Georgiĭ Valentīnovĭch. Essays in the history of matérialism. Translated by Ralph Fox. London, John Lane, 1934. ix p., 2 l., 3-287, 1 p. (French edition: Essais sur l'histoire du matérialisme: d'Holbach, Helvétius, Marx. Paris, Editions sociales, 1957. 191 p.)
9491. PODMORE, Frank. Robert Owen. A bibliography. London, Hutchinson, 1906. London, Allen & Unwin, 1923.
9492. POLIITOKONOOMIA propagandistile. Metoodili ne oppevahend marksismi-leninismi aluste koolidele. Tallinn, Eesti Raamat, 1967. 256 p.
9493. POLITICAL economy of socialism. Translated from the Russian. Edited by Don Danemanis. Moscow, Progress publishers, 1967. 310 p. [(Ucebni texty vysokych skol.) Praha, SPN, 1968. 214 p.]
9494. POLITICKA ekonomie; populární učebnice. Zprac.: Josef

Sládek et al. Praha, Svoboda, 1966. 511 p.
9495. POLITISCHE ökonomie des sozialismus und ihre anwendung in der DDR. (Mit 17 Grafiken u. 21 Tab.) Berlin, Dietz, 1969. 903 p.
9496. POPELOVA, Jirina. K filosofické problematice Marxova Kapitálu. 1. vyd. (Ceskoslovenska akademie ved. Studie a prameny sekce filosofie a historie, sv. 9.) Praha, Nakl. Ceskoslovenské akademie věd, 1954. 191 p.
9497. POPPER, K. R. The open society and its enemies. Princeton, Princeton university press, 1950.
9498. PORTER, Eugene Oliver. Fallacies of Karl Marx. With an introduction by Samuel Dr. Myres. El Paso, Texas western college, 1962. 96 p.
9499. PRA, Mario dal. Il pensiero filosofico di Marx dal 1835 al 1848 (con particolare riguardo alla filosofia della prassi). Milano, Le Goliardica, 1959. 442 p.
9500. PRAGUE. Universita Karlova. Knihovna. Soupis spisů a článků Karla Marxe a Bedřicha Engelse z fondů universitní knihovny a Slovanské knihovny v Praze. Sest. Miroslav Havránek s kolekitvem pracovníků universitní knihovny. Ridigoval Kamil Groh. (Bibliografické příručky, č. 5, sesit 1-3.) V Praze, 1954. 3 pts. (428 p., in portfolio.)
9501. PRAGUE. Ustav dějin komunistické strany československa. Knihovna. Karel Marx a Bedřich Engels v některých českých a německých dělnických, sociálně demokratickych a komunistickýćh časopisech a novinách, vycházejících na našem území v letech 1867-1938. (Bibliografické pomůcky.) Praha, 1957. 191 p.
9502. PREMIERES sociétés de classes et mode de production asiatique . . . (Recherches internationales à la lumiere du marxisme, 57-58, janvier-avril 1967.) Paris, les Editions de la nouvelle critique, 1967. 344 p.
9503. RANKOVIC, Slavka. Ekonomska efektivnost uvođenja nove tehnike u socijalizmu. (Ekonomska biblioteka, 19.) Beograd Savez ekonomista Jugoslavije, 1963. 228 p.
9504. RELIGION Saint Simonienne. L'Armée guerrière et l'armée pacifique, Paris, 1832.
9505. RIAZANOV, O. Karl Marx and Friedrich Engels. New York, International publishers, 1926.
9506. RICCHETTI, D. Note sul marxismo. Milano, Vita e pensiero, 1964. vi, 159 p.
9507. RIPP, Géza. A gazdasági, növekedés szakaszai és az ipari tarsdalom elmélete. Budapest, Kossuth könyvkiadó, 1967. 321 p.
9508. ROBINSON, Joan Violet (Maurice). An essay on Marxian economics. London, Macmillan and company limited, 1942. ix, 120, 1 p. (2d edition, London, Macmillan; New York, Saint Martin's press, 1966, 1967. xxiv, 104 p.)
9509. ———. On re-reading Marx. Cambridge, England. Student's bookshops, 1953. 23 p.
9510. RODBERTUS, Johann Karl. Aus dem literarischen nachlass von Carl Rodbertus-Jagetzow, Hrsg. von H. Schumacher-Zarchlen und Adolph Wagner. Berlin, Puttkammer und

Mülbrecht, 1878-99. 3 v. in 2.
9511. ———. Die forderungen der arbeitenden klasse. 1837.
9512. ———. Das kapital. Vierter sociales brief an von Kirchmann, von dr. Carl Rodbertus-Jagetzow, Hrsg. und eingeleitet von Theophil Kozak. Berlin, Puttkammer und Mühlbrecht, 1884. xix, 315 p.
9513. ———. Overproduction and crises. Translated by Julia Franklin. With an introduction by John B. Clark. (Social science series, no. 2.) London, S. Sonnenschein and company, limited; New York, C. Scribner's sons, 1898. 140 p.
9514. ———. Soziale briefe au von Kirchman. 1850.
9515. ROSE, Günther. Karl Marx, Schöpfer des wissenschaftlichen sozialismus. Hrsg. vom zentralinstitut für bibliothekswesen, Abt. Ausund weiterbildung. (Studienmaterial für die hauptberuflichen bibliothekarischen mitarbeiter der allgemeinbildenden bibliotheken in der DDR, Heft 6.) Berlin, 1958. 35 p.
9516. ROSENBERG, Arthur. A history of Bolshevism. London, Oxford university press, H. Milford, 1934. 250 p.
9517. ROSSITER, Clinton Lawrence. Marxism: the view from America. 1st edition. (Communism in American life.) New York, Harcourt, Brace, c1960. 338 p. Bibliography.
9518. ROY, Ajit. A Marxist commentary on economic developments in India, 1951-1965; a selection of articles and notes. Calcutta, National publishers, 1967. 160 p.
9519. ROZDOLSKI, Roman. Zur entstehungsgeschichte des Marxschen kapital; der Rohentwurf des kapital 1857-58. 2., überarbeitete aufl. (Politische ökonomie. Geschichte und kritik.) Frankfurt, Europäische verlagsanstalt; Wien, Europa verlag, 1969, c1968. 2 v. in 1. 686 p.
9520. ROZENBERG, David Iokhelevich. Die entwicklung der ökonomischen lehre von Marx und Engels in den vierziger Jahren des 19. Jahrhunderts. Ubersetzt von Wilhelm Fickenscher. 1. aufl. Berlin, Dietz, 1958. 424 p.
9521. ROZENTAL', Mark Moiseevich. Die dialektik in Marx' Kapital. Ubers. von J. Harhammer. Berlin, Dietz, 1957. 446 p. (2., ergäntze und überarb. aufl., 1959. 448 p.)
9522. ———. Die dialektische methode der politischen ökonomie von Karl Marx von M. M. Rosental. Ubers. von Hans Zikmund. 1 aufl. Berlin, Dietz verlag, 1969. 576 p.
9523. ———. Les problèmes de la dialectique dans le capital de Marx. Paris, Editions sociales, 1959. 482 p.
9524. RUBEL, Maximilien. Bibliographie des oeuvres de Karl Marx; avec en appendice un répertoire des oeuvres de Friedrich Engels. Paris, M. Rivière, 1956. 272 p. (Supplément. Paris, M. Rivière, 1960. 74 p.)
9525. ———. Karl Marx devant le bonapartisme. (Ecole pratique des hautes études, Sorbonne. 6. section: Sciences économiques et sociales. Société et idéologies. 2. sér.: Documents et témoignages, 2.) Paris, Mouton, 1960. 164 p.

9526. ———. Karl Marx, essai de biographie intellectuelle. Paris, Librairie M. Rivière, 1957. 463 p.
9527. RUHLE, Otto. Karl Marx. New York, Viking press, 1929.
9528. RUMIANTSEV, Alekseĭ. Categories and laws of the political economy of Communism. Translated from the Russian by D. Danemanis. Moscow, Progress publishers, 1969. 387 p. (French edition: Economie politique du communisme; essai méthodologique. Moscou, Editions du progrès, 1969. 596 p.)
9529. RUSSELL, Bertrand R. Proposed roads to freedom. Socialism, anarchism and syndicalism. New York, Holt, 1919. 218 p.
9530. RUSSELL, Bertrand, John Dewey, et al. The Meaning of Marx. A symposium. New York, Farrar and Rinehart, 1934.
9531. RUYER, R. L'utopie et les utopies. Paris, Presses universitaires de France, 1950. 295 p.
9532. SADZIKOWSKI, Wiesław. Ekonomia polityczna kapitalizmu; podręcznik dla wyższych szkól ekonomicznych. Wyd. 1. Warszawa, Panstwowe wydawn. Naukowe, 1969. 543, 1 p.
9533. SAINT-SIMON, Claude Henri de, Count. Oeuvres. Publiées par les membres de conseul institute par enfantin pour l'execution de ses dernières volontés. 2. ed. Paris, 1865-78. 47 v. (Oeuvres. Paris, F. Alcan, 1925. Paris, Capelle, 1941.)
9534. ———. Selected writings. Translated and edited by F. M Markham. Oxford, Blackwell, 1952. 116 p.
9535. SALTER, Frank Reyner. Karl Marx and modern socialism. London, Macmillan and company, limited, 1921. 5 p. 1., 263 p. Bibliography, 257-260.
9536. SALVADORI, M. La aparición del comunismo moderno. Traducción de la edición inglesa. 1952. por A. Müller Montiel. México, Univ. nacional, 1954. 208 p.
9537. SAMUELSSON, Kurt. Det fördömda kapitalet. En kritik av den nymarxistiska mytologin. Stockholm, Bonnier, 1970. 217, 1 p.
9538. SANTEN, J. van. De Marxistische accumulatietheorie. Leiden, H. E. Stenfert Kroese, 1968. 260 p.
9539. SAUVY, Alfred. Malthus et les deux Marx, le problème de la faim et de la guerre dans le monde. Nouvelle édition. (Bibliothèque médiations, 50.) Paris, Gonthier, 1966. 250 p. (Paris, Gonthier, c1963.)
9540. SAVAGE, Katharine. The story of Marxism and communism. 1st American edition. New York, H. Z. Walck, 1969, c1968. 224 p.
9541. SCALAPINO, R. A. Japanese communist movement, 1920-1966. c1967.
9542. SCHELLENBERG, Walter. Grundkurs zum "Kapital." 2. aufl. Berlin, Dietz, 1968. 137 p.
9543. SCHLESINGER, Rudolf August Joseph. Marx, his time and ours. (International library of sociology and social reconstruction.) London, Routledge and Paul, 1950. xi,

440 p. Bibliography, 434-436.
9544. SCHONMANN, Ernst. Karl Marx; Das Kapital. Die wirtschaftlichen lehren von Karl Marx aufs neue dargeboten und einer Auswahl kritischer Stimmen von Thomas G. Masaryk, Karl Kautsky und Silvio Gesell gegenübergestellt von Ernest Schönmann. Affoltern am Albis, Aehren verlag, 1952. 267 p.
9545. SCHUMPETER, Joseph A. Capitalism, socialism, and democracy. New York, Harper and brothers, 1942. (2nd edition. New York, Harper and brothers, 1947.)
9546. SCHWANK, Karl Heinz. Marx, Lenin und die geheimnisse des staatsmonopolitischen kapitalismus. (ABC des Marxismus-Leninismus.) Berlin, Dietz, 1967. 68 p.
9547. SCOTT, A. M. The anatomy of Comunism. New York, Philosophical library, 1951.
9548. SEE, Henri Eugène. The economic interpretation of history. Translation and introduction by Melvin M. Knight. (Reprints of economic classics.) New York, A. M. Kelley, 1968. viii, 154 p. [(Burt Franklin research and source works no. 225.) New York, B. Franklni, 1968. 154 p.]
9549. SELSAM, Howard. Dynamics of social change; a reader in Marxist social science, from the writings of Marx, Engels and Lenin. Selected and edited, with introduction and notes by Howard Selsam, David Goldway, and Harry Martel. 1st edition. New York, International pub., c1970.
9550. SELSAM, Howard Brillinger, editor. Reader in Marxist philosophy, from the writings of Marx, Engels, and Lenin. Selected and edited with introductions and notes by Howard Selsam and Harry Martel. New York, International publishers, c1963. 384 p.
9551. SHAW, George Bernard. Bernard Shaw and Karl Marx; symposium, 1884-1889. New York, Printed for Random house by R. W. Ellis: The Georgian press, c1930. 3 p. 1., v-ix p., 1 1., 200 p., 1 1.
9552. ———. The Fabian society; its early history. (F. S. Tract 41.) London, Fabian society, 1892.
9553. ———, editor. Fabian essays. London, Fabian society, 1920.
9554. ———. Intelligent woman's guide to socialism and capitalism. New York, Brentano, 1928.
9555. SHIBATA, Shingo. Shakaikau nyūmon. Nihon no kindaika to sono tembō. (Transliterated.) Japan, 1964. 3, 172 p.
9556. SHIRATO, Ichiro and Martin C. Wilbur. Japanese sources on the history of the Chinese Communist movement. New York, East Asian institute, Columbia university, 1953.
9557. SHOUL, Bernice. "Karl Marx and Say's law." In, The quarterly journal of economics, LXXI (November, 1957).
9558. SIEBER, Rolf und Günter Söder. Politik und ökonomie im sozialistischen gesellschafts-system von Rolf Sieber und Gunter Söder. 1 aufl. Berlin, Dietz verlag, 1970. 92 p.
9559. ———, und ———. Die herausbildung der marxistischen politischen ökonomie. von Rolf Sieber u. Horst Richter. Berlin, Dietz, 1969. 386 p.

9560. SIK, Ota. Ekonomika, zájmy, politika; jejich vzájemné vztahy do socialismu. Vyd. 1. Praha, Nakl. politické literatury, 1962. 587 p.
9561. _____. K problematice socialistických zbožních vztahů. Vyd. 1. Praha, Nakl. Ceskoslovenské akademie věd, 1964. 400 p. (Vyd. 2. Praha, Nakl. Ceskoslovenské akademie věd, 1965. 400 p.) (Translated and revised as Plan and market under socialism.)
9562. _____. Okonomie, interessen, politik. (Wissenschaftlich bearb. von Otto Reinhold.) Berlin, Dietz, 1966. 506 p.
9563. _____. Plan und markt im sozialismus. (Aus dem tschechischen übertragen von Ingrid Kondrková.) Mit. Tabellen und diagrammen. Wien, Molden, 1967. 384 p. (Polish edition: Plán a trh za socializmu. Vyd. 3. Praha, Academia, 1968. 362 p. English edition: Plan and market under socialism. White Plains, New York, International arts and sciences press, 1968, c1967. 382 p.)
9564. SILBERNER, E. Western European socialism and the Jewish problem (1800-1918). A selective bibliography. Jerusalem, Eliezer Kaplan school of economics and social science of the Hebrew university, 1955. 62 p.
9565. SILBERSTEIN, Enrique. Dialéctica, economía y desarrollo. Buenos Aires, J. Alvarez, 1965. 156 p.
9566. _____. Marx, su pensamiento economico. (Enciclopedia del pensamiento esenical, 30.) Buenos Aires, Centro Editor de América Latina, 1968. 119 p.
9567. SILHAN, V. V. I. Lenin o řizení a plánování socialistického národního hospodařštvi. Praha, Státní nakl. politické líteratury, 1960. 90 p.
9568. SILVIN, E. Index to periodical literature on Socialism. Santa Barbara, California, Rogers and Morely, 1909. 45 p.
9569. SIMON, B., editor. The challenge of Marxism. London, Lawrence and Wishart, 1963. 206 p.
9570. SLOVNIK světové ekonomiky. Josef Mervart, a kolektiv. Vyd. 1. Praha, Svoboda, 1967. 423 p.
9571. SMITH, H. "Marx and the trade cycle:" In, Review of economic studies, 4 (1936-1937), 192-204.
9572. _____. "Marx and the trade cycle; A reply." In Review of economic studies, 6 (1938-1939), 76-77.
9573. SMITH, Henry. A prospect of political economy. London, Allen and Unwin, 1968. 3-314 p.
9574. SOCIALIST party of Great Britain. The communist manifesto and the last hundred years. London, 1948. 92 p. (Centenary edition.)
9575. SODRE, Nelson Werneck. Fundamentos de economia marxista (a economia capitalista). (Coleção perspectivas do homem, v. 45. Série economia.) Rio de Janeiro, Civilização Brasileira, 1968. xviii, 257 p.
9576. SOEJIMA, Tanenori. Shakaishugi keizai no shomondai. (Transliterated.) Japan, 1967. 222, 18 p. Bibliographical notes.
9577. SOMBART, Werner. Sozialismus und soziale bewegung.

1896. (English edition: Socialism and the social movement. New York, Dutton, 1909. 319 p. 10th German edition: Der proletarische sozialismus. 2 v.)
9578. SOUTHERAN, Charles. Horace Greeley and other pioneers of American socialism. New York, Mitchell Kennerley, 1915.
9579. SPARGO, John. Karl Marx: His life and work. New York, Huebsch, 1910.
9580. ———. Sidelights on contemporary socialism. New York, B. W. Huebsch, 1911. 154 p. (Third lecture appeared in American journal of sociology.)
9581. STALIN, Iosif. Marxism and linguistics. New York, International publishers, 1951. 63 p. ("The Soviet linguistics controversy, by Margaret Schlauch" 57-63.)
9582. ———. Marxism and the national and colonial question. A collection of articles and speeches. (Marxist library. Works of Marxism-Leninism, v. 38.) New York, International publisher, 193-? viii, 304 p.
9583. ———. Works. Moscow, Foreign languages publishing house, 1952-55. 13 v.
9584. STAMMHAMMER, Josef. Bibliographie des sozialismus und communismus. Jena, Gustav Fisher, 1893-1909. 3 v.
9585. STERNBERG, Fritz. Anmerkungen zu Marx--heute. (Sammlung "Res novae"; Veröffentlichungen zur politik, wirtschaft, soziologie und geschichte, Bd. 41.) Frankfurt a. M., Europäische verlagsanstalt, 1965. 86 p.
9586. STOJANOVIC, Radmila. Jugoslávská ekonomie v teorii a praxi; sborník prací jugoslávských ekonomů. Napsali: I. Maksimović et al. za red. R. Stojanovićové. Přel. Jiří procházka. Vyd. 1. Praha, Academia, 1965. 457 p.
9587. STUDIENANLEITUNG. Politische ökonomie des sozialismus. Hrsg. im auftrage des staatssekretariats für das Hoch und fachschulwesen, sektor rechts- und wirtschaftswissenschaften von der Karl-Marx-Universität Leipzig, wirtschaftswissenschaftliche fakultät, abteilung fernstudium. Ausarbeitung des kollektivs der Institute für politische ökonomie der DDR. Redaktion Klaus Steinitz et al. Leipzig, 1962- . v. (v. 1, 1963.)
9588. SUDA, Jyoti Prasad. Manu, Marx & Gandhi. 1st edition. Meerut, Jai Prakash Nath, 1967. vi, 188 p.
9589. SUN Yat-sen. Political and social ideals. Los Angeles, University of southern California press, 1933. 505 p.
9590. SUR les sociétés précapitalistes; textes choisis de Marx, Engels, Lénine. Préf. de Maurice Godelier. Paris, Editions sociales, 1970. 414 p.
9591. SUSLOV, Mikhail Andreevich. Brilliant teacher and leader of the working class: report by M. A. Suslov . . . at a meeting in Moscow on May 5, 1968, to commemorate the 150th anniversary of the birth of Karl Marx. Moscow, Novosti press agency publishing house, 1968. 32 p.
9592. SUZUKI, Kōichirō and Kōzō Uno, editors. Marukusu keizaigaku no kenkyū. (Transliterated.) Japan, 1968. 2 v.

Bibliographical references.
9593. SWARUP, Shanti. A study of the Chinese communist movement, 1966.
9594. SWEEZY, Paul Marlor. Socialism. New York, McGraw-Hill, 1949. 276 p.
9595. _____. The theory of capitalist development; principles of Marxian political economy. New York, Oxford University press, 1942. xiv, 398 p. Bibliography, 379-384. (Spanish edition: Teoría del desarrollo capitalista, versión española de Hernán Laborde. México, Fondo de cultura económica, 1945. 480 p. Reprinted in English: New York, Monthly review press, 1964. ix, 308 p.)
9596. A SZOCIALISMUS politikai gazdaságtana, tankönyv. Berei Andor a szerkesztő bizottsag vezetöje. 2. kiad. Budapest, Kossuth Könyvkiadó, 1968. 556 p.
9597. TAMEDLY, Elisabeth L. Socialism and international economic order. Caldwell, Idaho, Caxton printers, 1969. xviii, 302 p.
9598. TEMKIN, G. Karola Marksa obraz gospodarki komunistycznej. Warszawa, Pánstwowe wydawnictwo Naukowe, 1962. 321 p.
9599. THEORETISCHE und methodologische probleme der marxistischen industriesoziologie. (Schriftenreihe "Soziologie.") (Von einem, autorenkollektiv: Waltraud Bronizkaja.) Berlin, Dietz, 1967. 175 p.
9600. THEORY of profit in socialist economy; a discussion on the recent economic reforms in the USSR by Evsei Liberman, Maurice Dobb and others. New Delhi, People's publishing house, 1966. 98 p.
9601. THOMAS, Norman M. Socialism re-examined. New York, Norton, 1963. 280 p.
9602. TIRONI, Jakov. Politička ekonomija. (Biblioteka udžbenici, 28.) Zagreb, "Narodne novine," 1968. xv, 430, 2 p.
9603. TOKEI, Ferenc. Az ázsiai termelési mód kérdéséhez. Budapest, Kossuth Könyvkiadó, 1965. 133 p.
9604. TOMIZUKA, Ryōzō. Keizaigaku genri. (Transliterated.) Japan, 1970. 415 p. Bibliographical references.
9605. TRAGER, Frank N., editor. Marxism in Southeast Asia. A study of four countries. Edited, with an introduction and conclusion. With contributions by Jeanne S. Mintz and others. Stanford, California, Stanford university press, 1959. 381 p. Bibliography, 357-369.
9606. TRKLJA, Milivoje. Kamata na investicione kredite u uslovima društvenog samoupravljanja. Beograd, Institut društvenih nauka. Centar za istraživanje društvenih odnosa, 1966. 148 p.
9607. TROTSKY, Leon. Basic Writings. Edited and with an introduction by Irving Howe. New York, Random house, 1963. 427 p.
9608. TSURU, Shigeto. Essays on Marxian economics. (Science Council of Japan. Division of Economics & Commerce. Economic series no. 8.) Tokyo, 1956. 79 p.

9609. TUCHSCHEERER, Walter. Bevor "Das Kapital" entstand. Die herausbildung und entwicklung der ökonomischen theorie von Karl Marx in der Zeit von 1843-1858. (Hrsg. von Gerda Tuchscheerer.) Berlin, Akademie-verlag, 1968. 493 p.
9610. TUCKER, Robert C. Philosophy and myth in Karl Marx. Cambridge, England, University press, 1961. 263 p. Bibliography, 254-257. (Dissertation, Harvard university.)
9611. TUGAN-BARANOWSKI. Modern socialism and its historical development. London, S. Sonnenschein, 1910. (Reprinted, 1966.)
9612. TURNER, John Kenneth. Challenge to Karl Marx. New York, Reynal and Hitchcock, 1941. viii, 455 p. Bibliography, 437-446.
9613. UNO, Kōzō. Marukusu-keizaigaku no shomondai. (Transliterated.) Japan, 1969. 281 p. Bibliographical references.
9614. ———. Shakai kagaku to shite no keizaigaku. (Transliterated.) Japan, 1969. 288 p.
9615. ———. Shihonron kenkyū. (Transliterated.) Japan, 1967-68. 5 v. Bibliographies.
9616. ———. Shihonron no keizaigaku. (Transliterated.) Japan, 1969. 192 p. Bibliographical references.
9617. URBAN, Bohumil. Politická ekonomie socialismu; vysokoškolska učebnice. Kolektiv autorů pod redakci B. Urbana. Vyd. 1. Praha, Svoboda, 1966. 376 p.
9618. URBAN, Luděk. Eseje o teoriích ekonomického růstu. Rita Budínová et al. Autorsky kolektiv pod vedením L. Urbana. Vyd. 1. Praha, Academia, 1967. 371 p.
9619. UTILITARIANISM. Edited by Oscar Piest. 2d edition, revised. New York, Liberal arts press, 1957. 79 p.
9620. UYEHARA, Cecil H. Leftwing social movements in Japan. An annotated bibliography. Tokyo, Rutland, Vermont, Published for Tufts university, Fletcher school of law and diplomacy by C. E. Tuttle company, 1959. 444 p.
9621. VACIC, Aleksandar M. Elementi socijalističke ekonomije. Napisao Aleksandar M. Vacić. Beograd, Centar za društveno-političko obrazovanje radničkog univerziteta "Duro salaj," 19--. v.
9622. ———. Uzroci robne proizvodnje u socijalizmu. Beograd, "Naučna knjiga," 1966. vi, 302 p.
9623. VARGA, Eugen. Marxism and the general crisis of capitalism. With an introduction by B. T. Ranadive. Bombay, People's publishing house, 1948. 68 p.
9624. VASQUEZ, Eduardo. En torno al concepto de alienación en Marx et Heidegger. (Colección avance, 17.) Caracas, Ediciones de la biblioteca, Universidad central de Venezuela, 1967. 140 p.
9625. VEBLEN, Thorstein Bunde. "Socialist economics of Karl Marx and his followers. In, Quarterly journal of economics. (August, 1906) 578-595; (February, 1907) 299-322. (Reprinted: In, The place of science in modern civilization and other essays. New York, Huebsch, 1919, 509 p.)

9626. ———. "Some neglected points in the theory of socialism." In, The place of science in modern civilization and other essays. New York, Huebsch, 1919. 509 p.
9627. VIGOR, Peter Hast. A guide to Marxism and its effects on Soviet development. London, Faber; New York, Humanities press, 1966. 3-253 p.
9628. VOLPE, Galvano della. Chiave della dialettica storica. 2. ed. (Saggistica, 2.) Roma, Samonà e Savelli, 1968. 38 p.
9629. ———. Rousseau e Marx e altri saggi di critica materialistica. (Nuova biblioteca di cultura, 18.) Roma, Editorial riuniti, 1957. 162 p.
9630. VOPROSY ékonomičeskoj teorii v trudah V. I. Lenina. (Transliterated.) Moscow, 1962. 373 p.
9631. VUJOSEVIC, Miladin. Zakonitost dohotka u društvenim uslugama. Beograd, 1967. 248 p.
9632. VYGODSKIĬ, Vitaliĭ Solomonovich. Die geschichte einer grossen entdeckung. Uber die entstehung des werkes "Das Kapital" von Karl Marx. Von Witali Solomonowitsch Wygodski. Ubersetzung aus dem Russischen: (Horst Friedrich und Horst Richter.) Berlin, Verlag die wirtschaft, 1967. 158 p., 4 l.
9633. WADA, Zentarō. Marukusu-shugi no rosen. Soren akademikku to no riron tōsō kiroku. (Transliterated.) Japan, 1966. 245 p.
9634. WAGNER, Adolf Heinrich Gotthilf. El capital, Wagner contra Marx. Buenos Aires, 1948. 133 p.
9635. WAGNER, Donald O. Social reformers. New York, The Macmillan company, 1934.
9636. WAKAR, Aleksy. Zarys teorii gospodarki socjalistycznej. Pod kierownictwem naukowym Aleksego Wakara. Wyd. 1. Warszawa, Państwowe wydawn. Naukowe, 1965. 489 p.
9637. WARD, Benjamin N. The socialist economy; a study of organizational alternatives. New York, Random house, 1967. ix, 272 p. Bibliographical footnotes.
9638. WARSAW. Biblioteka Narodowa. Marks i Engels w Polsce; materiały do bibliografii, 1842-1952. Warszawa, 1953. 111 p.
9639. WEBB, Sidney and Beatrice Webb. Soviet communism. A new civilization. New York, 1936.
9640. WEILL, Georges. L'ecole saint-simonienne. Paris, 1896.
9641. ———. Un précurseur du socialisme: Saint-Simon et son oeuvre. Paris, 1894.
9642. WELTER, Gustav A. Dialectical materialism. A historical and systematic survey of the philosophy in the Soviet Union. London, Routledge and K. Paul, 1958. 609 p.
9643. WILES, Peter John de la Fosse. Communist international economics. Oxford, Blackwell, 1968. xiv, 566 p. (New York, Praeger, 1969. xvi, 566 p.) Bibliographical footnotes.
9644. WILLIAM, Maurice. The social interpretation of history; a refutation of the Marxian economic interpretation of history. Long Island City, New York, Sotery publishing

company, 1921. xxxi, 1 1., 397 p.
9645. WILSON, J. D. "Marx and the trade cycle." In, Review of economic studies, 5 (1937-1938) 107-113.
9646. WOLFE, Bertram David. Marxism, one hundred years in the life of a doctrine. 1st edition. New York, Dial press, 1965. xxiii, 404 p. Bibliographical footnotes.
9647. WOLFSON, Murray. Karl Marx. (Columbia essays on great economists, no. 3.) New York, Columbia university press, 1971. 68 p. Bibliography, 67-68.
9648. ———. A reappraisal of Marxian economics. New York, Columbia university press, 1966. xii, 220 p. Bibliographical references in notes, 191-214.
9649. WORTERBUCH der Ökonomie. Sozialismus. Hrsg. von Willi Ehlert, Heinz Joswig und Willi Luchterhand. Unter Mitarbeit von Günter Bähne. Berlin, Dietz, 1967. 539 p. (2., erw. u. überarb. aufl. Berlin, Dietz, 1969. 940 p.)
9650. WRIGHT, David McCord. The trouble with Marx. Introduction by Gottfried Haberler. New Rochelle, New York, Arlington house, 1967. 192 p.
9651. WYBANE zagadnienia ekonomii politicznej; materiały pomocnieze dla słuchaczy wyższych szkól oficerskich. Opracowanie autorskie: Stanisław Lysko et al. Wyd. 2., popr. Warszawa, Wydawn. Ministerstwa obrony narodowej, 1969. 331 p.
9652. YANOWITCH, Murray, editor. Contemporary Soviet economics; a collection of readings from Soviet sources. White Plains, New York, International arts and sciences press, 1969. 2 v.
9653. ZAFFARONI, Juan Carlos. Marxismo y cristianismo; puntos de contacto, puntos de ruptura. Montevideo, Ediciones Ap. O. C. E., 1966. 103 p.
9654. ZELENY, Jindřich. O logické struktuře Marxova Kapitálu; příspěvek ke zkoumání základních logických otázek současného marxismu. Vyd. 1. Praha, Nakl. Ceskoslovenské adademie věd, 1962. 238 p.
9655. ZEITLIN, I. M. Marxism. A reexamination. Princeton, Van Nostrand, 1967.
9656. ZUR anwendung der Marxschen theorie bei der erforschung moderner ökonomischer prozesse und beiträge zur rationalisierung im Bergbau-Teifbau. Mit 17 bildern und 7 tabellen. (Freiberger forschungshefte reihe. A: 442 ingeni-eurökonomie bergbau.) Leipzig, Deutscher verlag für grundstoffindustrie, 1968. 91 p.
9657. ZUR entscheidungsfindung in der sozialistischen Volkswirtschaft. Von einem autorenkollektiv. (Freiberger forschungshefte. Reihe D. 66: Sozialistische wirtschaftsfuhrung.) Leipzig, Deutscher verlag für grundstoffindustrie, 1969. 89 p.

K. Section II

4. MARGINALISM

9658. AMOROSO, Luigi, et al. Cournot nella economia e nella filosofia. Padua, Milani, 1939.
9659. BACHMANN, Verena. Der haushaltplan des konsumenten und seine theoretische erfassung durch die grenznutzenlehre; eine dogmengeschichtiche untersuchung. (Zürcher volkswirtschaftliche forschunger, a. F., Bd. 7.) Zürich, Polygraphischer verlag, 1963. 190 p.
9660. BAUMOL, William J. and Stephen M. Goldfeld, editors. Precursors in mathematical economics. An anthology. London, The London school of economics and political science, 1968.
9661. BEHRENS, F. H. H. Gossen oder die geburt der "wissenschaftlichen apologetik" des kapitalismus. Leipzig, Bibliographisches institut, 1949.
9662. BLOCH, H. S. La théorie des besoins de Carl Menger. Paris, R. Pichon et R. Durand-Auzias, 1937.
9663. BOHM-BAWERK, Eugen von. Capital and interest, a critical history of economical theory. Translated with a preface and analysis by William Smart. London and New York, Macmillan and company, 1890. xiv, 431 p. (London, 1932. Kelley and Millman, 1957. xiv, 431 p. German edition entitled: Kapital und kapitalzins, erste abtheilung; kapitalizins-theorieen. 1884. Capital und capitalzins. 2d edition. Innsbruck, 1900. xxvii, 702 p. Capital and interest: history and critique of interest theories. Translated by George D. Huncke and Hans F. Sennholz. Illinois, Libertarian press, 1959. 3 v.)
9664. ———. Einige strittige fragen der capitalstheorie. Wien, 1900. 127 p.
9665. ———. The positive theory of capital. Translated and with a preface and analysis by William Smart. London and New York, Macmillan and company, 1891. xl, 428 p. [Austrian edition: Positive theorie des kapitales. 3d edition. Innsbruck, 1906. xxiii, 171 p. American edition: (Photographic reprint of edition of 1891.) New York, G. E. Stechert & co., reprint, 1930. xi, 428 p. Bibliography, 427-428.]
9666. ———. Shorter classics of Eugen von Böhm-Bawerk. South Holland, Illinois, Libertarian press, 1962- . v.
9667. BOMPAIRE, F. Economie mathématique. Du principe de la liberté économique dans l'ouvrage de Cournot et dans celle, de l'école de Lausanne. Walras, Pareto. Paris, Editions sirey, 1931.
9668. BOSON, Marcel. Léon Walras, foundateur de la politique économique scientifique. Paris, Librairie générale de droit et de jurisprudence, 1951.
9669. BOUSQUET, G. H. Introduction a l'étude du manuele de v. Pareto. Paris, 1927.

9670. _____. Vilfredo Pareto; sa vie et son oeuvre. Paris, 1928.
9671. BOWLEY, Arthur L. "Francis Ysidro Edgeworth." In, Econometrica, 2 (April, 1934) 113-24.
9672. _____. F. Y. Edgeworth's contributions to mathematical statistics. London, Royal statistical society, 1928.
9673. BROWN, E. H. P., H. Bernardelli, R. G. D. Allen, and O. Lange. "Notes on the determinateness of the utility function." In, Review of economic studies II (1934-35) 66, 155.
9674. BUKHARIN, Nikolaĭ Ivanovich. L'Economie politique du rentier, la théorie de la valeur et du profit de l'école autrichienne, critique de l'economie marginaliste. 1926. Par Nicolas Boukharine. Préface de Pierre Naville . . . Paris, Etudes et documentation internationales, 1967. 204 p. (Die politische ökonomie des rentners. Frankfurt-am-Main, Verlag neue kritik, 1966. 200 p.)
9675. _____. The economic theory of the leisure class. New York, 1927.
9676. CHAMBERLIN, Edward H. The theory of monopolistic competition. Cambridge, Massachusetts, Harvard university press, 1933.
9677. CLARK, John Bates. The distribution of wealth. New York, 1899. xxviii, 445 p. (New York, Kelley and Millman, 1956. 445 p.)
9678. _____. The philosophy of wealth. Boston, 1887. xv, 236 p.
9679. COURNOT, Antoine-Augustin. Considérations sur la marche des idées. Paris, 1872. 2 v.
9680. _____. Principes de la théorie des richesses. Ristampa anastatica cella prima edizione di Parigi del 1863 a cura di Oscar Nuccio. (Ristampe anastatiche di opere antiche e rare, 44.) Roma, Bizzarri, 1969. iv, 527 p.
9681. _____. Recherches sur les principes mathématiques de la théorie des richesses. Paris, 1838. [English editions; Researches into the mathematical principles of the theory of wealth. 1838. Translated by Nathaniel T. Bacon . . . with . . . bibliography of mathematical economics by Irving Fisher. (Economic classics.) New York and London, Macmillan & co., ltd., 1897. ix, 213 p. Bibliography, 173-209. Reprinted: Irwin paperback classics in economics. Homewood, Illinois, R. D. Irwin, 1963. xviii, 174 p. Bibliography, 147-174.]
9682. _____. Revue sommaire des doctrines économiques. Paris, 1877.
9683. CROS, J. Le néo-libéralisme; étude positive et critique. Paris, 1952. 413 p.
9684. CZECH, Zdzisław. Teoria wartości i problem rozliczenia w szkole austriackiej. (Polskie towarzystwo ekonomiczne. Oddział w Katowicách. Studia 1 materiały. Seria C.) Katowice, 1961. 215 p.
9685. DAVENPORT, H. J. Value and distribution. Chicago, 1908.
9686. DICKINSON, Henry Douglas. Institutional revenue; a study

of the influence of social institutions on the distribution of wealth. (Reprints of economic classics.) New York, A. M. Kelley, 1966. 264 p.

9687. DORFMAN, J. "Wicksteed's recantation of the marginal productivity theory." In, Economica (London) 44, 123 (August, 1964) 294-295.

9688. _____, Paul A. Samuelson and Robert M. Solow. Linear programming and economic analysis. New York, McGraw-Hill book company, 1958.

9689. DUE, John F. and Robert W. Clower. Intermediate economic analysis. 5th edition. Homewood, Illinois, Richard D. Irwin, Inc., 1966.

9690. ECKARD, Edwin Woodrow. Economics of W. S. Jevons. Washington, D. C., American council on public affairs, 1940. 4 p., 1., 113 p. (Thesis, Ph.D., Duke university, 1937.)

9691. EDGEWORTH, Francis Ysidro. Currency and finance in time of war. . . . London, 1917. 48 p.

9692. _____. H. H. Gossen. In, Palgrave's dictionary of political economy. 1894-99. Edited by H. Higgs. London, Macmillan, 1923.

9693. _____. "Intrinsic value." In, Palgrave's Dictionary of Political economy. 1894-99. Edited by H. Higgs. London, Macmillan, 1923. v.

9694. _____. Mathematical physics. An essay on the application of mathematics to the social sciences. (Series of reprints of scarce tracts in economic and political science, no. 10.) London, C. K. Paul & company, 1881. London, London school of economics and political science, 1932. viii, 150 p. (Reprint: Reprints of economic classics. 150 p.) New York, A. M. Kelley, 1961.

9695. _____. On the relations of political economy. London, n.d. 36 p.

9696. _____. Papers relating to political economy. (Royal economic society.) London, Macmillan, 1925. 3 v. Bibliographical references. (New York, B. Franklin, 1963?- v. Bibliography. Reviews and articles appearing in Economic journal, 1891-1921.)

9697. EISERMANN, G. Vilfredo Pareto als national-ökonom und soziologe. Tübingen, Mohr, 1961. 76 p.

9698. ENGLANDER, Oskar. "Karl Mengers Grundsätze," In, Schmollers jahrbuch, LI (1927) 271-401.

9699. FEILBOGEN, S. L'école autrichienne d'économie politique." In, Journal des economistes (6th series) 31 (1911) 50-57, 214-230, 375-388.

9700. FISHER, I. "Cournot and mathematical economics." In. Quarterly journal of economics, 12 (1898) 119-38; 238-44.

9701. FITZPATRICK, Paul J. "Leading British statisticians of the nineteenth century." In, Journal of the American statistical association, 55 (March, 1960) 38-70.

9702. FRIEDMAN, Milton. "Leon Walras and his economic system." In, The American economic review, XLV (December, 1955.)

9703.	GIACALONE-MONACO, T. Antonio Agostino Cournot. L'uomo e l'economista. Padova, 1956. 90 p.
9704.	_____. Pareto e Sorel. Padova, A. Milani, 1960. 190 p.
9705.	GILLOT, Frédéric. Algèbre et logique, d'après des textes originaux de G. Boole et W. S. Jevons. Paris, Albert Blanchard, 1962.
9706.	_____. Eléments de logique appliquée d'après Wronski, Jevons, Solvay. Paris, Albert Blanchard, 1964.
9707.	GOSSEN, Hermann Heinrich. Entwicklung der gesetze des menschlichen verkehrs und der daraua fliessenden regeln fur menschliches handeln. Braunschweig, Friedrich vieweg und sohn, 1854. Edition with introduction by F. A. von Hayek. Berlin, Praeger, 1927.
9708.	HARROD, R. F. "Walras, a reappraisal." In, Economic journal, 66, 262 (June, 1956) 307-316.
9709.	HAYASHI, Jiichi. Osutoria gakuha kenkyū josetau. (Transliterated.) (Series: Kōbe keizaigaku sōsho, 4.) Japan, 1966. 3, 248, 2 p. Bibliographical footnotes.
9710.	HAYEK, F. A. Prices and production. London, Routledge and K. Paul, 1931.
9711.	_____. Profits, interest and investments. London, Routledge and K. Paul, 1939.
9712.	_____. Pure theory of capital. London, Routledge and N. Paul, 1941.
9713.	HERFORD, C. H. Philip Henry Wicksteed. London, J. M. Dent, 1931.
9714.	HICKS, J. R. "Pareto revealed." In, Economica (London) 28, 111 (August, 1961) 318-322.
9715.	_____. The theory of wages. London, Macmillan, 1932.
9616.	HITOTSUBASHI university, Tokyo. Katalog der Carl Menger-bibliothek. 1926. 2 v.
9717.	HOLLANDER, Jacob H. "The concept of marginal rent." In, Quarterly journal of economics (January, 1895).
9718.	_____, editor. Economic essays. Contributed in honor of John Bates Clark. New York, 1927.
9719.	HOWEY, R. S. The rise of the marginal utility school, 1870-1889. Lawrence, University of Kansas press, 1960. 271 p. Bibliography.
9720.	JENKIN, Fleeming. The graphic presentation of the laws of supply and demand and other essays on political economy. London, The London school of economics, 1931.
9721.	JESSUA, Claude. Coûts sociaux et couts privés . . . Préface de François Perroux . . . (Bibliotheque d'economie contemporaine.) Paris, Presses universitaires de France, 1968. xxiv, 304 p.
9722.	JEVONS, W. Stanley. Elementary lessons in logic. . . . New edition. London, 1876. xi, 340 p.
9723.	_____. Investigations in currency and finance. London, Macmillan, 1909.
9724.	_____. Letters and journal of W. Stanley Jevons. London, Macmillan, 1886. viii, 473 p.
9725.	_____. Money and the mechanism of exchange. 10th

	edition. London, 1893. 95 p. (New York, D. Appleton & company, inc., 1896.)
9726.	_____. Political economy. London, 1878. (Science primers, edited by Professors Huxley, Roscoe and Balfour Stewart.) New York, D. Appleton and company, 1886. 3 p. l., 5-134 p.
9727.	_____. Principles of economics, and other papers. A fragment of a treatise on the industrial mechanism of society, and other papers. With a preface by Henry Higgs. London, 1905. (Reprints of economic classics. New York, A. M. Kelley, 1965. xxviii, 273 p.)
9728.	_____. The theory of political economy. London and New York, Macmillan and company, 1871. xvi, 267 p. [2d edition, 1879; 3d edition, 1888; Edition, 1898. 4th edition, 1911. lxiv, 339. Bibliography, mathematical economics, 1711-18979. Italian edition: Teoria della economia politica ed altri scritti economici. Introd. di Luigi Amoroso. (Sociologi ed economisti, 4.) Torino, Unione tip-editrice torinese, 1947. xxxv, 395. American edition: with preface and notes and an extension of the bibliography of mathematical economic writings by H. Stanley Jevons. 5th edition. (Reprints of economic classics.) New York, A. M. Kelley, 1965. lxiv, 343 p.]
9729.	KAUDER, Emil. "Genesis of the marginal utility theory from Aristotle to the end of the eighteenth century." In, Economic journal, LXIII (September, 1953).
9730.	_____. A history of marginal utility theory. Princeton, N. J., Princeton university press, 1965. xxii, 248 p.
9731.	_____. "The retarded acceptance of the marginal utility theory." In, Quarterly journal of economics, 67, 4 (November, 1953) 564-575.
9732.	KNIGHT, Frank H. "Marginal utility economics." In, Encyclopaedia of the social sciences. New York, Macmillan company, 1931.
9733.	KUENNE, Robert E. Monopolistic competition theory. Studies in impact. Essays in honor of Edward H. Chamberlin. New York, John Wiley, 1967.
9734.	LACHMANN, L. M. Capital and its structure. London, G. Bell and son, limited, 1956.
9735.	LANGE, Oscar, Francis McIntyre, Theodore O. Yntema, editors. Studies in mathematical economics and econometrics; in memory of Henry Schultz. Chicago, The university of Chicago press, 1942.
9736.	LEIGH, Arthur H. "Von Thünen's theory of distribution and the advent of marginal analysis." In, Journal of political economy, LIV (December, 1946) 481-502.
9737.	LUTZ, A. The theory of interest. Translated by C. Wittich. Dordrecht, Holland, D. Reidel, 1967.
9738.	MALANOS, George J. Early cardinal utility theory. (Bureau of business and economic research, Georgia state college of business administration. Studies in business and economics, bulletin no. 8.) Atlanta, Georgia state college of business administration, 1960. 40 p.

9739. MENGER, Carl. Grundsätze der volkswirthschaftslehre. Erster, allgemeiner theil. (Series of reprints of scarce tracts in economic and political science, no. 17.) Wien, W. Braumüller, 1871. 2nd edition, London, 1923. xxvi, 335 p. The London school of economics and political science, 1934. xlviii, 2, 285 p. (The collected works of Carl Menger, vol. 1. English edition: Principles of economics. First, general part. Translated and edited by James Dingwall and Bert F. Hoselitz, with an introduction by Frank H. Knight. Glencoe, Illinois, Free press, 1950. 328 p. Bibliographical references.)

9740. ———. Kleinere schriften zur methode und geschichte der volkswirtschaftlehre. (Series of reprints of scarce tracts in economic and political science no. 19.) London, The London school of economics and political science, University of London, 1935. 3 p. 1., 3-307 p.

9741. ———. Problems of economics and sociology (Untersuchungen über die Methode der socialwissenschaften und der politischen oekonomie insbesondere.) Edited and with an introduction by Louis Schneider. Translated by Francis J. Nock. Urbana, University of Illinois press, 1963. 237 p. Bibliography. (Leipzig, 1883.)

9742. ———. Untersuchungen über die methode de socialwissenschaften und der politischen ökonomie insbesondere. Leipzig, Duncker und Humblot, 1883.

9743. MISES, Ludwig von. Epistemological problems of economics. New York, 1960.

9744. ———. The historical setting of the Austrian school of economics. New Rochelle, New York, Arlington house, 1969. 47 p.

9745. ———. Theory and history. New Haven, Connecticut, Yale university press, 1957.

9746. ———. The theory of money and credit. New York, 1912.

9747. MURRAY, R. A. Lecons d'économie politique suivant la doctrine de l'école de Lausanne. Paris, Editions payot, 1920.

9748. NICHOL, A. J. "A re-appraisal of Cornot's theory of duopoly price." In, Journal of political economy, XLII (February, 1934) 80-105.

9749. OULES, F. L'école de Lausanne. Textes choisies de L. Walras et Pareto. Paris, Librairie dalloz S. A., 1950.

9750. PAGE, Alfred N., editor. Utility theory. A book of readings. New York, Wiley, 1968. viii, 454 p.

9751. PANTALEONI, M. Pure economics. Translated by T. B. Bruce. London, Macmillan and company, 1898.

9752. PARETO, Vilfredo. Cours d'economie politique. Lausanne, F. Rouge, 1896-97. 2 v.

9753. ———. "Economie mathématique." In, Encyclopédie des sciences mathématiques, v. I (1911) 606.

9754. ———. Lettere a Maffeo Pantaleoni, 1890-1923. A cura di Gabriele de Rosa. Roma, 1960. 3 v.

9755. ———. La liberté économique et les événements d'Italie. Lausanne, 1898.

9756. _____. Manuale di économia politica. 1906. xii, 579 p (French editions: Translated by A. Bonnet. Manuel d'économie politique. 1909. 595 p. 2d edition, 1927. Traduit sur l'edition italienne par Alfred Bonnet (revue par l'auteur 1st AMS edition. New York, AMS press, 1969. 605 p. Introd. del. prof. Luigi Amoroso. Ristampa integrale dell ed. del 1906, con aggiunta la traduzione di Aldo Pacifici e Fabio del Prete, dell'appendice alla 2. ed. francese. Roma, Bizzarri, 1965. xxxix, 507 p.)

9757. _____. Mon journal. Con una pref. di Giovanni Demaria: soliloquio paretiano; uno studio di Tullio Bagiotti: Del "Giornale" paretiano e dell'unità analitica come criterio d'integrazione delle scienze sociali e una nota su Pareto di d'integrazione delle science sociali e una nota su Pareto di Giuseppe La Feria. A cura di Tullio Bagiotti. Padova, CEDAM, 1958. xvi p. 160 p.

9758. _____. Scritti paretiani, con 47 lettere inedite di Vilfredo Pareto ad Alfonso de Pietri-Tonelli, a cura di Pietro de Pietri-Tomelli. Padova, CEDAM, 1961. viii, 158 p.

9759. _____. Scritti teorici. Raccolti da Giovanni Demaria, 3 pubblicati dall'Università Bocconi nel cinquantesimo anniversario della fondazione. Milano, R. Malfasi, 1952. xxx, 651 p.

9760. PERMUTTER, S. Karl Menger und die österreichische schule. Berne, 1902.

9761. PETER, H. Freiheit der wirtschaft; kritik der neoliberalismus. Köln, Bund-verlag, 1953. 170 p.

9762. PETERSEN, Asmus and others. Von Thünens isolierter staat. Die landwirtschaft als glied der volkswirtschaft. Hamburg, Verlag Paul Parey, 1944.

9763. PIROU, Gaëtan. Les théories de l'équilibre économique. Walras et Pareto. Conferences faites à l'école pratique des hautes études en 1932-33 et 1933-34. 3. éd. Paris, Domat Montchrestien, 1946. 468 p.

9764. POLLIS, A. and B. L. Koslin. "On the scientific foundations of marginalism." In, American journal of economics and sociology, 21, 2 (April, 1962) 113-130.

9765. REICHARDT, H. Antoine Augustin Cournot. Sein beitrag zur exakten wirtschaftswissenschaft. Tübingen, J. C. Mohr, 1954. 130 p.

9766. RIEDLE, H. Hermann Heinrich Gossen, 1810-1858, ein wegbereiter der modernen ökonomischen theorie. Winterthur, P. G. Keller, 1953. ix, 137 p.

9767. ROBERTSON, R. M. "Jevons and his precursors." In, Econometrica (July, 1951).

9768. ROBINSON, Joan. Collected economic papers. Oxford, Basil Blackwell, 1951.

9769. _____. The economics of imperfect competition. London, 1933.

9770. ROSENSTEIN-RODAN, Paul. "Marginal utility." In, International economic papers, Number 10. New York, Macmillan company, 1960. 71-106 p.

9771. SCHNEIDER, Erich. Einführung in die wirtschaftstheorie. 4 Teil ausgewählte kapital der gehichte der wirtschaftstheorie, 1. Band. Tübingen, J. C. B. Mohr, 1962.
9772. SENNHOLZ, Mary, editor. On freedom and free enterprise; essays in honor of Ludwig von Mises. New York, Van Nostrand Reinhold company, 1956.
9773. SMART, William. An introduction to the theory of value on the lines of Menger, Wieser, and Böhm-Bawerk. London, 1899. (Reprints of economic classics.) New York, A. M. Kelley, 1966. x, 2, 104 p. (3d. edition. London, 1914.)
9774. SOMMARIN, Emil. "Das lebenswerk von Knut Wicksell." In, Zeitschrift für nationalökonomie. v. II (1930-1931) 221-267.
9775. SPENGLER, Joseph J. "Quantification in economics; its history." In, Daniel Lerner, editor. Quantity and quality. New York, Free Press, 1960. 129-211.
9776. STIGLER, George J. "The development of utility theory." In, Journal of political economy, 58 (August-October) 1950. (In, Essays in the history of economics. Chicago, University of Chicago press, 1965. 66-155 p.
9777. ———. "The economics of Carl Menger." In, Journal of political economy, XLV (April, 1937).
9778. ———. Production and distribution theories. The formative period. New York, 1941.
9779. TABASCIO, Vincent J. Pareto's methodological approach to economics. Chapel Hill, North Carolina, University of North Carolina press, 1967.
9780. TAVIANI, Paolo Emilio. Il concetto di utilità nella teoria economica. . . . Firenze, Le Monnier, 1968--. v.
9781. THIEMEYER, Theo. Grenzkostenpreise bei öffentlichen unternehmen. Köln, Westdeutscher verlag, 1964. 248 p.
9782. THUNEN, J. H. von. Von Thünen's isolated state. Translated by C. M. Wartenberg. Elmsford, New York, Pergamon press, 1966.
9783. UHR, Carl G. "Knut Wicksell. A centennial evaluation." In, American economic review, XLI (December, 1951).
9784. VEBLEN, Thorstein. "The limitations of marginal utility." In, Journal of political economy (November, 1909) 620-636. (Also, in Veblen, T., Place of science in modern civilisation and other essays. New York, Huebsch, 1919. 509 p.)
9785. ———. "Professor Clark's economics." In, Quarterly journal of economics. (February, 1906) 147-195.
9786. VINCI, F. La meccania economica nel pensiero di Vilfredo Pareto. Teoria e pratica dei costi comuni. Milano, Unione tipografica, 1956.
9787. VINER, Jacob. "The utility concept in value theory and its critics." In, Journal of political economy, 33 (1925) 369-387, 638-659.
9788. VLEUGELS, W. Das ende der grenznutzentheorie. Stuttgart, 1925.
9789. WALRAS, Léon. Abrégé des éléments d'économie politique pure. Précédé d'un avertissement et révisé par les

soins de Gaston Leduc. Paris, R. Pichon et R. Durand-Auzias; Lausanne, R. Rouge et Cie, s. a., 1938. 2 p. 1., 399 p.

9790. ———. Eléments d'économie politique pure; ou Théorie de la richesses sociale. Lausanne, L. Corbaz & Cie, 1874. viii, 208 p. (2. ed., rev., cor. et augm. Lausanne, F. Rouge, 1889. xxiv, 523, 1 p. 4th edition, 1900. xxiv, 496 p. Edition définitive rev. et augm par l'auteur. Nouv. tirage. Paris, Librairie générale de droit et de jurisprudence, 1952. 491 p. English edition: Elements of pure economics; or, The theory of social wealth. Translated by William Jaffé. American economic association, translation series. London, Published for the American economic association and the Royal economic society by Allen and Unwin, 1954. 620 p. Reprints of economic classics. New York, A. M. Kelley, 1969. 620 p.)

9791. ———. Etudes d'économie politique appliquée. Ristampa anastatica della prima edizione del 1898 a cura di Oscar Nuccio. (Ristampe anastatiche di opere antiche e rare, 158.) Roma, Bizzarri (R. Pioda), 1969. 499 p. (Lausanne, F. Rouge; Paris, R. Pichon, 1898. 2 p. 1., 499 p.)

9792. ———. Etudes d'économie sociale. (Théorie de la répartition de la richesse sociale.) Ristampa anastatica della prima edizione del 1896 a cura di Oscar Nuccio. (Ristampe anastatiche di opere antiche e rare, 157.) Roma, Bizzarri, 1969. viii, 464 p. (Lausanne, F. Rouge et c^{ie}, s. a.; Paris, R. Pichon et R. Durand-Auzias, 1936. viii p., 2., 3-488 p.)

9793. ———. Théorie mathématique de la richesse sociale. Lausanne, 1883.

9794. ———. "Unpublished papers and letters of Leon Walras." Edited by W. Jaffe. In, Journal of political economy, XLIII (April, 1935) 187-207.

9795. WEINBERGER, O. Mathematische volkswirtschaftslehre. Stuttgart-vaihingen, B. G. Teubner, 1930.

9796. WICKSELL, Knut. "The influence of the rate of interest on prices." In, Economic journal, XVII (1907) 213-220.

9797. ———. Interest and prices (Geldzins und güterpreise.) A study of the causes regulating the value of money. Translated from the German by R. F. Kahn. With an introduction by Bertil Ohlin. London, Published on behalf of the Royal economic society by Macmillan and company, limited, 1936. xxxi, 219. (Appendix: The monetary problem of the Scandinavian countries. In, Ekonomisk tidskrift, 1925. Translated by Mrs. H. Norberg. Reprinted edition includes article: The enigma of business cycles. Translated by Carl G. Uhr. New York, A. M. Kelley, 1965. xxxi, 239. Bibliographical footnotes.)

9798. ———. Lectures on political economy. Translated from the Swedish by E. Classen and edited with an introduction by Lionel Robbins. (Based on 3d Swedish edition.) London, G. Routledge and sons, ltd., 1934-35. 2 v.

Post-Classical Period   571

              Bibliographies. (Appendix to v. 1 (1934) 219 contains
              "Professor Cassel's system of economics." Also In,
              Schmollers Jahrbuch, LII (1928) 771-808.)
9799.   _____. Uber wert, kapital und rente. . . . Jena, 1893.
              143 p. [English edition: Value, capital, and rent. With a
              foreword by G. L. S. Shackle; translated by S. H. Fro-
              wein. (The library of economics.) London, G. Allen &
              Unwin, 1954. 180 p.]
9800.   _____. Vorlesungen über nationalökonomie. Erster
              Band, Theoretische teil. 1913. xi, 290 p.
9801.   WICKSTEED, Philip Henry. Alphabet of economic science.
              London, 1888. New York, A. M. Kelley, 1956.
9802.   _____. The common sense of political economy, and
              selected papers and reviews on economic theory.
              Edited with an introduction by Lionel Robbins . . .
              London, G. Routledge & sons, ltd., 1933. 2 v. Bibliogra-
              phy, v. 2 (863-864). (1st edition, 1910. xi, 702 p. New
              York, A. M. Kelley, 1950. 2 v., xxx, 871 p.)
9803.   _____. An essay on the co-ordination of the laws of
              distribution. London? 1894. (London, London school
              of economics, 1932.)
9804.   WIESER, F. von. Natural value. Translated into English.
              London, 1893.
9805.   YOHE, William Poe. The Wicksellian tradition in Swedish
              macroeconomic theory. (Thesis, University of Michigan.)
              Ann Arbor, Michigan, University microfilms, 1959. xi,
              398 1. Bibliography, leaves 379-398. (Abstracted in
              Dissertation abstracts, v. 19 (1959) no. 12, p. 3167.)
9806.   YOUNG, A. A. "Jevon's 'Theory of political economy.'"
              In, A. A. Young, Economic problems, new and old.
              Boston, 1927.

                              K. Section II

5. MARSHALLIAN ECONOMICS

9807.   AGGARWALA, K. C. "Marshall's concept of quasi-rent."
              In, Indian journal of economics, 28 (April, 1948) 555-561.
9808.   BLADEN, V. W. "Mill to Marshall; the conversion of the
              economists." In, Journal of economic history, series 1
              (December, 1941) 17-29.
9809.   BONER, J. "Alfred Marshall." In, Journal of the Royal
              Statistical Society, Series A, 88 (January, 1925) 152-156.
9810.   BOULDING, Kenneth E. "The concept of economic surplus."
              In, American economic review, 35 (December, 1945)
              851-869. (In, American economic association, Readings
              in the theory of income distribution. Homewood, Illinois,
              Richard D. Irwin, Inc., Blackiston books, 1946. 638-
              659.
9811.   CANNAN, E. "Alfred Marshall, 1842-1924." In, Economica
              (London) 4 (November, 1924) 257-261.

9812. DAVENPORT, Herbert Joseph. The economics of Alfred Marshall. Ithaca, New York, Cornell university press; London, H. Milford, Oxford university press, 1935. 5 p. 1., 481 p. (In foreword: "Prepared for publication by a committee of the Department of economics of Cornell university, consisting of Paul T. Homan and M. Slade Kendrick, in collaboration with Margaret F. Milliken."

9813. FELLNER, William and Howard S. Ellis. "External economies and diseconomies." In, American economic review, 33 (September, 1943) 493-511.

9814. FRIEDMAN, Milton. Essays in positive economics. Chicago, University of Chicago, press, 1953.

9815. ———. "The Marshallian demand curve." In, Journal of political economy, 57 (December, 1949) 463-495.

9816. FRISCH, Ragner. "Alfred Marshall's Theory of value." In, Quarterly journal of economics, 64, 4 (November, 1950) 495-524.

9817. GEORGESCU-Roegen, N. "Revisiting Marshall's constancy of marginal utility of money." In, Southern economic journal, 35 (October, 1968) 176-181.

9818. GLASSBURNER, Bruce. "Alfred Marshall on economic history and historical development." In, Quarterly journal of economics, 69 (November, 1955) 577-595.

9819. GUILLEBAUD, C. W. "The evolution of Marshall's Principles of economics." In, Economic journal, 52 (December, 1942) 330-349.

9820. HANSEN, Alvin H. Monetary theory and fiscal policy. New York, McGraw-Hill, 1949.

9821. HENDERSON, H. D. Supply and demand. New York, Harcourt, Brace and company, 1922. (London, Nisbet and company, 1926. Chicago, University of Chicago press, 1958.)

9822. HICKS, John Richard. "The four consumers' surpluses." In, Review of economic studies, 11, 1 (Winter, 1943) 31-41

9823. ———. "The rehabilitation of consumers' surplus. In, Review of economic studies, 8 (February, 1941) 108-116.

9824. HIGGINS, G. and H. H. Liebhafsky. Pareto and the Marshallian constancy assumption." In, Southern economic journal 35 (October, 1968) 167-75.

9825. HIRSCH, H. Alfred Marshalls beitrag zur modernen theorie der unternehmung. Berlin, Duncher and Humblot, 1966.

9826. HOMAN, Paul Thomas. "Alfred Marshall." In, P. T. Homan, Contemporary economic thought. New York and London, Harper and brothers, 1928. x, 475 p.

9827. JHA, Narmadeshwar. The age of Marshall, aspects of British economic thought, 1800-1915. Foreword by Dennis H. Robertson. Patna, Novelty and company, 1963. x, 220 p.

9828. KERR, Clark. Marshall, Marx and modern times; the multidimensional society. (Marshall lectures, 1967-1968). London, Cambridge university press, c1969. 138 p.

9829. KEYNES, John M. "Alfred Marshall." In, Economic journal, 34 (September, 1924) 311-372. (In, J. M. Keynes,

Essays in biography. London, Macmillan, 1930.)

9830. _____. "Bibliographical list of the writings of Alfred Marshall." In, Economic journal 34 (December, 1924) 627-637.

9831. _____. "Dr. Marshall's eightieth birthday; address presented by members of the Royal economic society." In, Economic journal 32 (September, 1922) 287-289.

9832. KNIGHT, Frank H. The ethics of competition. New York, Harper and Row, 1935.

9833. _____. "Realism and relevance in the theory of demand." In, Journal of political economy, 52, 4 (December, 1944) 289-318.

9834. KRISHNASAWAMI, A. "Marshall's contribution to Indian economics." In, Indian journal of economics, 22 (April, 1942) 875-897.

9835. LAUGHLIN, J.L. "Marshall's theory of value and distribution." In, Quarterly journal of economics, 1 (January, 1887) 227-232.

9836. MACMILLAN, D. "Marshall's principles of economics; a bibliographical note." In, Economic journal 52 (December, 1942) 290-293.

9837. MAJUNDAR, Tapas. The measurement of utility. London, Macmillan and company, limited, 1958.

9838. MARSHALL, Alfred. Distribution and exchange. London, 1898. 23 p.

9839. _____. Elements of economics of industry, being the first volume of Elements of economics. (Abridgement of the first volume of Principles of economics, 2d edition, 1891.) London and New York, Macmillan and company, 1892. xiv, 416 p. (3d edition. London, 1899. xvi, 421 p. 4th edition. London, 1909. xiv, 440 p. Japanese edition: Masharu keizaigaku nyumon. (Transliterated.) 1952. 12, 21, 539, 8 p. London, New York, Macmillan, 1958. xiv, 440 p.)

9840. _____. The fiscal policy of international trade; being a summary of the memorandum by Prof. Alfred Marshall, published as a Parliamentary paper in 1908, by J. M. Robertson, M. P. London, New York, Cassell and company, ltd., 1910. 36 p.

9841. _____. Fiscal policy of international trade. Return to an order of . . . the House of commons, dated 11 November 1908; for, copy "of memorandum by Mr. Alfred Marshall . . . " Ordered, by the House of commons, to be printed, 11 November 1908. (Great Britain. Parliament. H. of C. 1908. Reports and papers, 321.) London, Printed for H. M. Stationery off., by Eyre and Spottiswoode, 1908. 29 p.

9842. _____. Industry and trade; a study of industrial technique and business organization; and of their influences on the conditions of various classes and nations. London, Macmillan and company, limited, 1919. xxiv, 875 p. (London, 1923.)

9843. _____. Memorials of Alfred Marshall. Edited by

A. C. Pigou. London, Macmillan and company, limited, 1925. xi, 518 p. (Reprints of economic classics.) (New York, Kelley & Millman, 1956. ix, 518 p.)

9844. _____. Money, credit and commerce. London, Macmillan & company, ltd.; New York, St. Martin's press, inc., 1923. xv, 369. (Supplements Marshall's "Principles of economics" and "Industry and trade.") (London, 1929. xv, 369 p. Reprints of economic classics. Reprint of 1923 edition. New York, A. M. Kelley, 1960. xv, 369 p.)

9845. _____. The new Cambridge curriculum in economics and associated branches of political science; its purpose and plan. London, New York, Macmillan and company, ltd., 1903. 3 p. 1., 34 p.

9846. _____. Official papers. Alfred Marshall. Published for the Royal economic society. (Editor's preface by J. M. Keynes.) London, Macmillan and company, ltd., 1926. vii, 428 p.

9847. _____. "On rent." In, Economic journal, 3 (March, 1893) 74-90.

9848. _____. The present position of economics. An inaugural lecture given in the senate house at Cambridge, 24 February, 1885. London, Macmillan and company, 1885. 57 p.

9849. _____. Principles of economics. London and New York, Macmillan and company, 1890. V. I. xxviii, 745 p. (No more published, January, 1905.) (2d edition, Vol. 1. London, Macmillan, 1891. xxx p. 1 1., 770 p. no more published. 3d edition, London, 1895. xxxi, 823 p. 4th edition, 1989. xxix, 820 p. 5th edition, London, 1907. xxxvi, 870 p. 6th edition, London, 1910. xxxii, 871 p. 8th edition, London, 1920. xxxiv, 871 p. Reprint, 8th edition, London, 1930. xxxiv, 871, 1 p. Reprint, 8th edition, London, 1936. xxxix, 871, 1 p. Reprint, 8th edition, London, 1948, xxxix, 871 p. Reprint, 8th edition, 1956. xxxii, 731 p. Spanish edition: Principles de economia; un tratado de introduccion. Traduccion directa de la S. edicion inglesa por Emilio de Figueroa; introd. por Manuel de Torres. 3. ed. (Biblioteca de ciencias sociales. Sección primera: economia.) Madrid, Aguilar, 1957. 733 p. 9th variorum edition. With annotations by Claude William Guillebaud. London, New York, Macmillan for the Royal economic society, 1961. 2 v. Bibliographical footnotes.

9850. _____. The pure theory of foreign trade. The pure theory of domestic values. (Series of reprints of scarce tracts in economic and political science, no. 1.) London, The London School of economics and political science, 1930. 2 p. 1., 28, 37, 1 p. (Facsimile reprint of two papers printed for private circulation in 1879.)

9851. _____. "The social possibilities of economic chivalry."

In, Economic journal, 17 (March, 1907) 7-29.
9852. _____. and Mary Paley Marshall. The economics of industry. London, 1879. xiv, 225 p. (2d edition. London, Macmillan and company, 1881, xvi, 231, 1 p. Reprinted, London, 1884. xvi, 231 p. Reprinted, London, 1891, xvi. 231, 1 p.)
9853. MARSHALL, Mary Paley. What I remember. Cambridge, England, Cambridge university press, 1947.
9854. OPIE, R. "Die quasirente in Marshalls Lehrgebäude." Archiv für sozialwissenschaft und sozialpolitik 40 (1928) 251-279.
9855. PARSONS, Talcott. "Economics and sociology; Marshall in relation to the thought of his time." In, Quarterly journal of economics, 46 (February, 1932) 316-347.
9856. _____. The structure of social action. New York, McGraw-Hill, 1937.
9857. _____. "Wants and activities in Marshall." In, Quarterly journal of economics, 46 (November, 1931) 101-140.
9858. PENROSE, Edith T. The theory of growth of the firm. Oxford, Basil Blackwell, 1959.
9859. PFOUTS, R. W. "A critique of some recent contributions to the theory of consumers' surplus." In, Southern economic journal, 19, 3 (January, 1953) 315-333.
9860. PIGOU, Arthur Cecil. Alfred Marshall and current thought. London, Macmillan, 1953.
9861. _____. Employment and equilibrium. 2nd edition. London, Macmillan, 1949.
9862. _____. The theory of unemployment. London, Macmillan, 1933.
9863. PRICE, L. L. "Notes on a recent economic treatise." In, Economic journal, 2 (March, 1892) 17-34.
9864. ROBBINS, Lionel. "The representative firm." In, Economic journal, 38 (1928) 387-404.
9865. _____. The theory of economic development in the history of economic thought. London, 1968.
9866. ROBERTSON, Denis H. Money. London, 1952. (Revised edition, 1928.)
9867. _____. Utility and all that and other essays. London, George Allen and Unwin, 1952.
9868. ROGIN, L. "Davenport on the economics of Alfred Marshall." (Review) In, American economic review, 26 (June, 1936) 248-257.
9869. ROY, Réne. De l'utilité. Paris, Hermann, 1942.
9870. SAMUELSON, Paul A. Collected scientific papers. Edited by J. E. Stiglitz. Cambridge, Massachusetts, M. I. T. press, 1966.
9871. _____. "Constancy of the marginal utility of income." In, Oscar Lange, Francis McIntyre and Theodore O. Yntema, Studies in mathematical economics . . . Chicago, University of Chicago press, 1942. 75-91.
9872. SCHUMPETER, Joseph A. "Alfred Marshall." In, J. A. Schumpeter, Ten economists. New York, Oxford university press, 1951.

9873. ———. "Alfred Marshall's Principles; a semi-centennial appraisal. In, American economic review 31 (June, 1941) 236-248.
9874. SCOTT, W. R. Alfred Marshall. Oxford, England, 1926.
9875. SHIRAI, T. "Alfred Marshall on free competition." Osaka economic papers, Osaka university, 16, 2 (March, 1968) 11-15.
9876. SHOVE, G. F. "The place of Marshall's Principles in the development of economic theory." In, Economic journal, LII (December, 1942) 294-329.
9877. SIMPSON, P. B. "Neoclassical economics and monetary problems." In, American economic review, 39 (September, 1949) 861-882.
9878. STIGLER, G. J. "Production and distribution in the short run." In, Journal of political economy, 47 (1939) 305-327.
9879. TAUSSIG, F. W. "Alfred Marshall." Quarterly journal of economics, 39 (November, 1924) 1-14.
9880. VINER, Jacob. "Cost curves and supply curves." In, Zeitschrift für nationalökonomie, 1931. (In, American economic association, Readings in price theory. Homewood, Illinois, Richard D. Irwin, 1953. 198-232.)
9881. ———. "Marshall's economics, in relation to the man and his times." In, American economic review, 31 (June, 1941) 223-35.
9882. WAGNER, A. "Marshall's Principles of economics." In, Quarterly journal of economics, 5 (April, 1891) 319-338.
9883. WEINTRAUB, Sidney. "The foundations of the demand curve." In, American economic review, 32 (September, 1942) 538-552.
9884. WILSON, E. B. Pareto versus Marshall. In, Quarterly journal of economics, 53 (August, 1939) 645-650.

K. Section II.

6. KEYNESIAN ECONOMICS

9885. ABBATI, Alfred Hendy. Lord Keynes' central thesis and the concept of unclaimed wealth. Cardiff, W. Lewis, 1947?, 25 p.
9886. ACKLEY, Gardner. Macroeconomic theory. New York, Macmillan, 1961.
9887. ALEXANDER, S. S. "Mr. Keynes and Mr. Marx." In, Review of economic studies 8 (February, 1940) 123-135.
9888. AMMON, A. "Keynes' allgemeine theorie der beschaftigung." Jahrbucher für nationalökonomie und statistik, 147 (1938) 1-27.
9889. ANGERS, Francois Albert. Essai sur la centralisation; analyse de principe politique et économique dans les perspections canadiennes. Avec la collaboration de

Pierre Harvey et Jacques Parizeau. Montreal, Presses de l'école des hautes études commerciales, 1960. 331 p. Bibliography.
9890. ASCHHEIM, Joseph and Ching-Yao Hsieh. Macroeconomics. Income and monetary theory. Columbus, Ohio, C. E. Merrill publishing company, 1969. xi, 265 p.
9891. BALOGH, T. et al. The economics of full employment. Studies prepared at the Oxford university institute of statistics. Oxford, Basil Blackwell, 1944.
9892. BARDET, Benjamin. Les contradictions de la General theory (de J. - M. Keynes); ou, Les leçons d'une expérience manquée. Poitiers, Société française d'impr. et de libraire & Impr. M. Texier réunies, 1955. 57 p.
9893. BARRERE, Alain. Théorie économique et impulsion keynésienne. (Etudes politiques, économiques et sociales, 5.) Préf. de Jean Marchal. Paris, Dalloz, 1952. viii, 762 p.
9894. BELL, Quentin. Bloomsbury. London, George Weidenfeld and Nicolson, Limited, 1968.
9895. BENNION, E. G. "Unemployment in the theories of Schumpeter and Keynes." In, American economic review, 33 (1943) 336-347.
9896. BEVERIDGE, William H. Full employment in a free society. New York, W. W. Norton and company, 1945.
9897. BIERI, Hermann Gottlieb. Die neuen konjunkturtheorien von Keynes, Hawtrey und Ohlin in kritisch vergleichender betrachtung. Wollishofen, Buchdruckerei Wollishofen, G. Schürch, 1944. 2 p. 1., 132 p. Literaturverzeichnis, 130-132.
9898. BOER, Abraham Adolf de. Inleiding tot het denken van Keynes. (Born denkers, no. 10.) Assen, Amsterdam, Rotterdam, Born, 1966. 96 p. Bibliografische notities, 92-95.
9899. BOLZA, Hans. Dialektische oder rationale methoden in der nationalökonomie? Eine erwiderung an J. M. Keynes. München und Leipzig, Duncker & Humblot, 1936. 83 p.
9900. BORNER, Silvio. Die Uberbeschäftigung; ansätze zu einer theoretischen Klärung. (Veröffentlichungen der hochschule St. Gallen für wirtschafts- un sozialwissenschaften. Volkswirtschaftlich-wirtschaftsgeographische reihe, bd. 18.) Zürich, Polygraphischer verlag, 1969. 386 p. Bibliography, 17-27. (Dissertation: Hochschule für wirtschafts- und sozialwissenschaften, St. Gall, Switzerland.)
9901. BOWLEY, A. L. and J. M. Keynes. "The measurement of real income." In, Economic journal, 50 (1940) 340-342.
9902. BRENIER, Henri. Le traité de Versailles et le problème des réparations, le point de vue français, une réfutation par les faits du livre de M. Keynes. Marseille, Comité de relations internationales intellectuelles et économiques, 1921. 13 p.
9903. BROWDER, Earl Russell. Keynes, Foster and Marx. Yonkers, New York, 1950- . v.
9904. BUBECK, C. Harry. Vollbeschäftigung ohne inflation. Geldumlaufsicherung und deren darstellung in einem

"Keynesschen" system. (Fsu-informationen für kultur, wirtschaft, politik, 19. Jahrg. aug. 1966. Hamburg, Verlag die "Informationen," 1966. 36 p.

9905. BURNS, Arthur Frank. Economic research and the Keynesian thinking of our times. In, National bureau of economic research, Annual report, v. 26.)

9906. BURNS, Emile. Mr. Keynes answered. An examination of the Keynes plan. London, Lawrence & Wishart ltd., 1940. 80 p.

9907. CAFFE, Federico. L'economia moderna e l'interventismo pubblico. (Classe unica, 51.) Torino, Edizioni radio italiana, 1956. 58 p. Bibliographical footnotes.

9908. CAMBRIDGE university. King's college. John Maynard Keynes, 1883-1946, fellow and bursar. A memoir prepared by direction of the Council of King's college, Cambridge. Cambridge, 1949. 41 p.

9909. CAMERON, Burgess. Input-output analysis and resource allocation. London, Cambridge, Cambridge university press, 1968. vii, 109 p. Bibliography, 1968.

9910. CASSEL, G. "Keynes General theory." In, International labour review, 36 (1937) 437-445.

9911. CHAMLEY, P. "Sir James Steuart, inspirateur de Lord Keynes?" In, Revue d'economie politique (May-June, 1962) 303-313.

9912. CHIANG, Hsüeh-mo. Mo ch'i ti tzǔ pen chu i ching chi. (Transliterated.) China, 1949. 2, 74 p.

9913. COCHRANE, James L. Macroeconomics before Keynes. Glenview, Illinois, Scott, Foresman and company, 1970. 109 p.

9914. COKKINOS, Théodore. Théorie économique et coordination des investissements dans la C. E. C. A. (Communauté européenne du charbon et de l'acier.) (Travaux de droit, d'économie et de sociologie, no. 7.) Genève, Librairie Droz, 1963. 158 p. Bibliography, 147-155. (Thesis, Geneva, under title: Les principes de la coordination des investissements au sein de la communauté européenne du charbon et de l'acier à la lumière de l'évolution de la théorie économique.)

9915. COPELAND, Morris Albert. The Keynesian reformation. Three lectures. (Delhi school of economics. Occasional papers, no. 4.) Delhi, Ranjit by arrangement with the Delhi school of economics, 1952. 62 p.

9916. DAVIDSON, Frank Geoffrey. Economics and economic polity. (La Trobe University. Inaugural lectures.) Melbourne, Canberra, Cheshire for La Trobe university, 1967. 15 p. Bibliographical footnotes.

9917. DAVIDSON, Paul and Eugene Smolensky. Aggregate supply and demand analysis. With a section on social accounts: theory and measurement, by Charles L. Leven. New York, Harper & Row, c 1964. xiv, 274 p. Bibliographical footnotes.

9918. DAVIS, J. Ronnie. The new economics and the old economists. Ames, Iowa, Iowa State University press, 1972.

9919. DEMANDE, Joffre. Les tribulations du général Ken's au pays des économics. Dessins de Claude Gourlet. Toulouse, Impr. du Sud, 1967. 80 p.
9920. DILLARD, Dudley D. The economics of John Maynard Keynes. The theory of a monetary economy. (Prentice-Hall economics series.) London, C. Lockwood, 1948. xv, 364 p. Bibliographies. Bibliography of Keynes writings, 336-351.
9921. _____. "Keynes and Proudhon." In, Journal of economic history, 2 (1942) 63-76.
9922. _____. "On the theory of a monetary economy." In, Nebraska journal of economics and business, 2, 2, (Autumn, 1963) 3-15.
9923. DOMARCHI, Jean. La pensée économique de John-Maynard Keynes et son influence en Angleterre. (L'économie du XXe siècle, collection dirigée par François Perroux.) Paris, Domat-Montchrestien, 1943- . v.
9924. DRAHOTA, Helmut. Sparen, Horten und Zins in der modernen Geltheorie, insbesondere bie John Maynard Keynes. (Forschungen zur Finanzwissenschaft. Schriften des Instituts für finanzwesen der wirtschaftshochschule Berlin, heft 5.) Jena, G. Fischer, 1941. xiv, 178 p. Literaturverzeichnis, 174-178. (Issued also as thesis, Berlin.)
9925. DUESENBERRY, James. Income, saving and the theory of consumer behavior. Cambridge, Massachusetts, Harvard university press, 1949.
9926. EATON, John. Marx against Keynes. A reply to Mr. Morrison's "socialism." London, Lawrence & Wishart, 1951. 142 p.
9927. ELLSWORTH, P. T. "Mr. Keynes on the rate of interest and the marginal efficiency of capital." In, Journal of political economy, 44 (1936) 767-790.
9928. FAN, Hung. K'ai-ên-ssǔ ti "Chiu yeh, li hsi ho huo pi ti i pan li lun" p'i p'an. (Transliterated.) China, 1955. 125 p.
9929. _____. "Keynes and Marx on the theory of capital accumulation, money, and interest." In, Review of economic studies (October, 1939).
9930. FORCHHEIMER, Karl. Keynes' neue wirtschaftslehre; eine einführung. (Schriftenreihe der arbeiterkammer in Wien.) Wien, Verlag des Osterreichischen gewerkschaftsbundes, 1952. 71 p.
9931. FRACCHIA, Charles A. John Maynard Keynes, book collector. (The series of great book collectors, no. 1.) San Francisco, Champion press, 1968. 20, 2 p. Bibliographical reference: in notes, 21-22.
9932. FRIEDMAN, Milton. A theory of the consumption function. Princeton, Princeton University press, 1957.
9933. FURUYA, Yoshisada. Keinzu-ha keizaigaku. (Transliterated.) (Daito bunka daigaku. Toyo kenkyujo. Daito bunka daigaku Toyo kenkyujo sosho, 4.) Japan, 1967. 164 p. Bibliography, 9-11.
9934. FUSCO, A. M. "Gli economisti italiani di fronte alla

'rivoluzione keynesiana.' " In, Cahiers Vilfredo Pareto, Geneve (1964) 187-194.

9935. GARELLO, Jacques. Le contenu de la courbe keynesienne d'offre globale. (Publications des annales de la faculté de droit et des sciences économiques, Aix-en-Provence. Série: Travaux et mémoires, no. 7, 1966.) Paris, Editions cujas, 1966. 116 p. Bibliographical footnotes.

9936. GEIGER, Rudolf. Die entwicklungstendenzen des kapitalismus bei Keynes, Schumpeter und Burnham. (Schriften des schweizerischen wirtschaftsarchivs, bd. 13.) Zürich, Polygraphischer verlag, 1959. 102 p. (Also issued as thesis, Basel.)

9937. GHAUSSY, Abdul Ghanie. Verbrauchen und sparen; versuch einer kritischen überprüfung der Keynes'schen konsumfunktion an hand der langfristigen sparentwicklung in den USA. (Untersuchungen über das spar-, giro- und kreditwesen, bd. 16.) Berlin, Duncker & Humblot, 1964. 236 p. Bibliography, 196-228.

9938. GILLMAN, Joseph Moses. Prosperity in crisis. New York, Marzani & Munsell, 1965. 256 p. Bibliographical references in notes, 238-252.

9939. GOEDHART, Cornelis. Enige theoretisch-economische aspecten van de rentevorming in de moderne volkshuishouding. (Proefschrift, Nederlandsche economische hoogeschool, Rotterdam.) Leiden, H. E. Stenfert Kroese, 1947. viii, 280 p. Bibliography, 273-278. (Published also as: Capita selecta der economie, 4; entitled: De rentevorming in de moderne volkshuishouding. Leiden, H. E. Stenfert Kroese, 1947. x, 280 p.)

9940. GOWDA, Krishnadasa gowda venkatagiri. Keynes-Triffin plans and international liquidity. (A "Kautilya" publication.) Mysore, "Kautilya," Maharaja's College, University of Mysore, 1962. viii, 37 p. Bibliographical footnotes. (Reprinted from Kautilya: a review of international affairs, January, 1962.)

9941. GRASNICK, Peter. Die entwicklung der kritik an der Keynes'schen liquiditäts-theorie des zinses. (Dissertation, Freie universität, Berlin.) Berlin?, 1954? 98 p. Bibliography, 88-98.

9942. GREIDANUS, Tjardus. The development of Keynes' economic theories. London, P. S. King & son, ltd., 1939. v., 40 p.

9943. GRUSON, Claude. Esquisse d'une théorie générale de l'équilibre économique, réflexions sur la Théorie générale de Lord Keynes. 1. éd. (Theoria, études sur la théorie moderne de l'économie, 7.) Paris, Presses universitaires de France, 1949. 328 p.

9944. HABERLER, Gottfried. "Mr. Keynes' theory of the multiplier. A methodological criticism." In, Zeitschrift für nationalökonomie, 7 (1936) 299-305. (In, Readings in business cycle theory. Philadelphia, The Blakiston company, 1944.)

9945. HAJELA, Prayag Das. Keynes' "General Theory" trade cycle

and foreign exchange. Allahabad, Pothishala, 1952? 232, ii p.
9946. HANSEN, Alvin Harvey. "Economic progress and declining population growth." In, American economic review, 29, 1 (March, 1939).
9947. _____. Fiscal policy and business cycles. New York, 1942.
9948. _____. A guide to Keynes. (Economics handbook series.) New York, McGraw-Hill, 1953. 237 p.
9949. _____. Monetary theory and fiscal policy. New York, McGraw-Hill, 1949.
9950. _____. "Mr. Keynes on underemployment equilibrium." In, Journal of political economy, XLIV (1936), 667-86.
9951. _____. "Some notes on Terborgh's The bogey of economic maturity." In, Review of economic statistics, 28, 1 (February, 1946).
9952. HARRIS, Seymour Edwin. John Maynard Keynes, economist and policy maker. (Twentieth century library.) New York, Scribner, 1955. 234 p.
9953. _____, editor. The new economics. Keynes' influence on theory and public policy. 1st edition. New York, A. Knopf, inc., 1947. xxii, 686 p. Bibliography of Keynes' writings by Seymour E. Harris and Margarita Willfort. (Reprint of economic classics. New York, A. M. Kelley, 1965. xxii, 686 p. Bibliography, 663-686.)
9954. HARROD, Roy Forbes. International economics. Chicago, University of Chicago press, 1939.
9955. _____. The life of John Maynard Keynes. New York, Harcourt, Brace, 1951. xvi, 674 p. London, Macmillan & company, ltd., 1951. xvi, 674 p. New York, St. Martin's press, 1963, xvi, 674 p. (Reprints of economic classics. New York, A. M. Kelley, 1969. xvi, 674. Bibliographical footnotes.)
9956. HAYASAKA, Tadashi. Keinzu. (Transliterated.) Japan, 1969. 218 p. Bibliography, 217-218.
9957. HAZLITT, Henry, editor. The critics of Keynesian economics. Princeton, New Jersey, Van Nostrand, 1960. viii, 427 p.
9958. _____. The failure of the "new economics." An analysis of the Keynesian fallacies. Princeton, New Jersey, Van Nostrand, 1959. 458 p.
9959. HEGELAND, Hugo. "The genesis of the multiplier theory." In, Money, growth and methodology, and other essays in economics; in honour of Johan Akerman. Lund, Gleerup bokfoerlag, 1961.
9960. HICKS, J. R. "Mr. Keynes and the 'Classics.' A suggested interpretation." In, Econometrica, New series, 5, 2 (April, 1937) 147-159.
9961. _____. "Mr. Keynes 'Theory of Employment.' In, Economic Journal, XLVI (1936) 238-253.
9962. HIGGINS, Benjamin. "The doctrine of economic maturity." In, American economic review 37, 1 (March, 1946) 133-141.

9963. HIJIKATA, Seibi. Tōmen no bukka mondai to Keinzu seisaku (Transliterated.) (Kansai keizai kenkyū sentā. Kansai keizai kenkyū sentā shiryō, 68-7.) Japan, 1968. 20 p.
9964. HOLLER, Karl Heinz. Der Begriff der investition und seine bedeutung bei W. Eucken und J. M. Keynes. Marburg, 1962. iii, 145, 7 p. Bibliography, 147-149. (Inaugural dissertation, Marburg.)
9965. HOLY, Václav L. Uber die zeitgebundenheit der kreislauftheorien von Quesnay, Marx und Keynes. (Staatswissensschaftliche studien, bd. 28.) Einsiedeln, Benziger, 1957. 199 p. Bibliography, 195-197. (Inaugural dissertation, Basel.)
9966. HSIN, Ying. Kai-yin-ssǔ ching chi hsüeh yüan li. (Transliterated.) China, 1953. 3, 9, 161 p.
9967. HUTT, William Harold. Keynesianism--retrospect and prospect. A critical restatement of basic economic principles. Chicago, H. Regnery company, 1963. 447 p. Bibliography.
9968. _____. The theory of idle resources. London, J. Cape, 1939. 2 p. 1., 7-193 p.
9969. JAMES, Emil. Histoire de la pensée économique an XXe siecle. Paris, Presses universitaires de France, 1955. 2 v.
9970. JOHN Maynard Keynes, 1883-1946. Cambridge, England, The Council of King's College, 1949. 22 p.
9971. "JOHN Maynard Keynes, 1883-1946." In, Economic journal 57, 225 (March, 1947) 43-44.
9972. JOHNSTONE, J. K. The Bloomsbury group. London? Noonday press, 1954.
9973. KAHN, Richard F. "The relation of home investment to unemployment." In, Economic journal, 41 (June, 1931) 173-198.
9974. KALECKI, M. Studies in the theory of business cycles, 1933-1939. Oxford, Basil Blackwell, 1966.
9975. KANAPA, J. et al. Keynes, economista vulgar. (5 ensayos.) Mexico, 1950. 129 p.
9976. KEYNES, John Maynard. "Bibliographical list of the writings of Alfred Marshall." In, Memorials of Alfred Marshall, edited by A. C. Pigou. London, Macmillan and company, limited, 1925. ix p., 1 1., 518 p. Bibliography, 500-508.
9977. _____. Can Lloyd George do it? An examination of the liberal pledge. By J. M. Keynes and H. D. Henderson. London, The nation and athenaeum, 1929. 44 p.
9978. _____. The collected writings of John Maynard Keynes. For the Royal economic society. London, Macmillan, New York, St. Martin's, 1971- . v- .
9979. _____. "An economic analysis of unemployment." In, Unemployment as a world-problem. By John Maynard Keynes, Karl Pribram and E. J. Phelan. Edited by Philip Quincy Wright. (Lectures on the Harris foundation, 1931.) Chicago, Illinois, The University of Chicago Press, c1931. ix, 260, 1 p. (Essay index reprint

series. Freeport, New York, Books for libraries press, 1970. ix, 260 p.)

9980. ———. The economic consequences of Mr. Churchill. London, L. and V. Woolf, 1925. 32 p. (American edition: The economic consequences of sterling parity. New York, Harcourt, Brace and company, 1925. 32 p.

9981. ———. The economic consequences of the peace. London, Macmillan and company, limited, 1919. vii, 279 p. [American edition: New York, Harcourt, Brace and Howe, 1920. 5 p. l., 3-298 p. French edition: Les conséquences économiques de la paix. Traduit de l'anglais par Paul Franck. 7. éd. Paris, Editions de la nouvelle revue française, 1920. 237 p. German edition: Die wirtschaftlichen folgen des friedensvertrages. Übersetzt von M. J. Bonn und C. Brinkmann. Einzig autorisierte Übersetzung aus dem englischen. München und Leipzig, Duncker & Humblot, 1920. v p., 1 l., 243, 1 p. Russian edition: Ekonomicheskiia posliedstviia. (Transliterated.) 1921. 2 p. l., 7-199 p., 1 l. Spanish edition: El tratado de Versalles y sus consecuencias económicas; estractos del libro "The economic consequences of the peace" (London, 1920) comentado por Juan Ernesto Vlademina. Buenos Aires, Empresa editorial "Germania," 1921. 112 p. American edition: (Introduction by Robert Lekachman.) (Harper torchbooks, TB1554) New York, Harper & Row, 1971. xxxvii, 298 p.]

9982. ———, editor. Economic history (a supplement to the economic journal) published by the Royal economic society . . . v. 1- Jan. 1926- . London, New York, Macmillan, 1926- . v. Irregular. (Editors: J. M. Keynes with: F. Y. Edgeworth, January 1926; D. H. Macgregor, May 1927-June 1934.)

9983. ———, editor. The Economic journal, the journal of the Royal economic society. v. 1- (no. 1-); March 1891- London, New York, Macmillan, v. quarterly. [Issues for 1891-1902 were the journal of the society under its earlier name: British economic association. Editors: 1891-1911, F. Y. Edgeworth (with Henry Higgs, 1896-1905)--1912 J. M. Keynes (with F. Y. Edgeworth, September 1919-1925; with D. H. Macgregor, June 1926-June 1934)]

9984. ———. "Editor's preface." In, Official papers. By Alfred Marshall. Published for the Royal economic society. London, Macmillan and company, 1926. vii, 428 p.

9985. ———. The end of laissez-faire. 3d impression. London, L. & Virginia Woolf, 1927. 53, 1 p. (Based on the Sidney Ball lecture delivered before the University of Oxford in 1924, and a lecture delivered before the University of Berlin in 1926.)

9986. ———. Essays in persuasion. New York, Harcourt, Brace and company, 1932. xiii, 376 p. Bibliography, 375-376. (The Norton library edition: New York,

9987. ———. European reconstruction. In, Manchester guardian commercial. Section 1-16; April 20, 1922-July 12, 1923. Manchester, Published by J. R. Scott for the Manchester guardian ltd., 1922-23. 2 v. Irregular. v. 1: 782 p. v. 2: 783-888 p. Title varies: Sec. 1-12 (April 20, 1922-January 4, 1923) Reconstruction in Europe. Section 13 (March 29, 1923) European reconstruction series. Sections 14-16 (April 26-July 12, 1923) European reconstruction. Sections 1-12 edited by J. M. Keynes. Index of contributors, nos. 1-12, p. 780-781.

9988. ———. "Foreword." In, the history of the National mutual life assurance society, 1830-1930. Compiled by Robert Finch, assisted by Alfred Roberts. London, National mutual life assurance society, 1930. 93 p., 1 l.

9989. ———. The general theory of employment, interest and money. London, Macmillan and company, limited, 1936. xii, 403 p. [First edition February, 1936; reprinted, March, 1936, 1942, 1957. American editions: New York, Harcourt, Brace, 1936. xii, 403 p. A Harbinger book. New York, Harcourt, Brace & World, 1965. xii, 403 p. Bibliographical footnotes. French edition: Théorie générale de l'emploi, de l'intérêt, et de la monnaie. Traduit de l'anglais par Jean de Largentaye. (Bibliothèque économique.) Paris, Payot, 1942. 2 p. l., 7-407 p. Spanish editions: Teoría general de la ocupación, el interés y el dinero; versión española de Eduardo Hornedo. (Sección de obras de economía dirigida por Daniel Cosío Villegas. III. Grandes estudios.) México, Fondo de cultura económica, 1943. 2 p. l., 7-379 p., 1 l. Reprinted, 1956. Segunda edicion espanola, 1945. Italian edition: Occupazione, interesse e moneta, teoria generale; traduzione di Alberto Campolongo. (Storia e dottrine economiche, 2.) Torino, Unione tip.-editrice torinese, 1947. xv, 358 p. Bibliographical footnotes. Chinese edition: Chiu yeh li hsi yü huo pi ti i pan li lun. (Transliterated.) China, 1955. 2 v. (1, 2, 341 p.) Polish edition: Ogólna teoria zatrudnienia procentu i pieniadza. Warszawa, Państwowe wydawnictwo naukowe, 1956. 1 v.)]

9990. ———. "The general theory." In, Quarterly journal of economics, 51 (February, 1937).

9991. ———. How to pay for the war. A radical plan for the chancellor of the exchequer. London, Macmillan and company, limited, 1940. vii, 88 p. New York, Harcourt Brace and company, c1940. vii, 88 p. (Spanish edition: Los problemas de la inflación de guerra. Traducción de Omar Dengo O. (Editorial Universitaria. Sección grandes obras contemporáneas, no. 1.) San Jose, Impr. Tormo, 1957. 102 p.

Post-Classical Period 585

9992. _____. Indian currency and finance. London, Macmillan and company, 1913. viii, 263 p. (Reprinted: 1924.)
9993. _____. Laissez-faire and communism. New York, New republic, inc. 1926. 6, 144 p.
9994. _____. The means to prosperity. London, Macmillan and company, limited, 1933. 37 p. (Enlarged from four articles in The Times, London, March, 1933. American editions: New York, Harcourt, Brace and company. c1933. 5 p. 1., 3-37 p. Edition: With a bibliography by Seymour E. Harris. Economica books on economics, politics, and business, E-15. Buffalo, Smith, Keynes & Marshall, 1959. 92 p. Bibliography.)
9995. _____. Mr. Lloyd George's general election. London, Liberal publication department, 1920. 14, 2 p. (An extract from The economic consequences of the peace.)
9996. _____. A revision of the treaty, being a sequel to The economic consequences of the peace. New York, Harcourt, Brace and company, 1922. viii, 242 p. London, Macmillan, 1922. viii, 223 p. German edition: Revision des Friedensvertrages, eine fortsetzung von "Die wirtschaftlichen folgen des friedensvertrages." Ubersetzt von Fritz Ransohoff. München, Duncker & Humblot, 1922. 244 p.
9997. _____. A tract on monetary reform. London, Macmillan and company, limited, 1923. viii, 209 p. (American edition entitled: Monetary reform. New York, Harcourt, Brace and company, 1924. viii, 227 p. German edition entitled: Ein traktat über währungsreform. Ubers. von Ernst Kocherthaler. München, Duncker & Humblot, 1924. viii, 214 p.)
9998. _____. A treatise on money. New York, Harcourt, Brace; London, Macmillan, 1930. 2 v. (English reprints: 1933, 1935, 1958-60. 2 v. German edition: Vom gelde. Translated by Carl Krämer and Louise Krämer. Berlin, Duncker & Humblot, 1955. xx, 635. Japanese edition: Kahei-ron. (Transliterated.) Translated by Nisaburo Kito. Tokyo, Dobun-kan, 1952-53. Japan, 1968. 8, 375 p.)
9999. _____. A treatise on probability. London, Macmillan and company, limited, 1921. xi, 466 p. Bibliography, 429-458. (Reprinted: 1929 and 1957.)
10000. _____. Two memoirs: Dr. Melchior, a defeated enemy, and My early beliefs. Introduced by David Garnett. New York, A. M. Kelley, 1949. 106 p.
10001. _____. The world's economic crisis and the way of escape. By Sir Arthur Salter, Sir Josiah Stamp, J. Maynard Keynes, Sir Basil Blackett, Henry Clay and Sir W. H. Beveridge. (Halley Stewart lecture, 1931.) New York, The Century company, c1932. 5 p. 1., 3-185 p.
10002. KIM, Chun-bo. Iron kyŏngjehak. (Transliterated.) Korea, 1964. 7, 354, 6 p.
10003. KITO, Nisaburō. Keinzu keizaigaku kaisetsu. (Transliterated.) Japan, 1947. 6, 3, 152 p.

10004. _____. Keinzu kenkyū. (Transliterated.) Japan, 1948. 195 p.
10005. KLEIN, Lawrence Robert. The Keynesian revolution. (Based on thesis, Massachusetts institute of technology.) New York, Macmillan, 1947. xii, 218 p. 2d edition. New York, Macmillan, 1966. xiii, 288 p. Bibliographical footnotes. (Based on doctoral thesis, 1944, Massachusetts institute of technology.)
10006. KOBAYASHI, Akira. Keinzu keizaigaku kogi. (Transliterated.) Japan, 1970. 287 p. Bibliographies.
10007. KRISHNAN-KUTTY, G. An essay on Keynesian economics. Vellanad, Mitraniketan, 1969. 84 p. Bibliographical footnotes.
10008. KURIHARA, Kenneth K. Introduction to Keynesian dynamics. London, Allen & Unwin, 1956. 222 p.
10009. _____. The Keynesian theory of economic development. New York, Columbia university press, 1959. 219 p. Bibliography.
10010. _____, editor. Post-Keynesian economics. New Brunswick, New Jersey, Rutgers university press, 1954. xviii, 442. Bibliographical footnotes. (Italian edition entitled Economia post-keynesiana. Translated by Michelangelo Giorda. Turin, Unione tipografico-editrice torinese, 1958. xix, 476 p.
10011. KUZNETS, S. National product since 1869. New York, National bureau of economic research, incorporated, 1946.
10012. LABOUR research department. The Keynes plan; its dangers to the workers. London, The Labour research department, 1940? 15, 1 p.
10013. LAMBERT, Paul. L'oeuvre de John Maynard Keynes. The Hague, Martinus Nijhoff's, N. V., 1963. v. 1.
10014. LANDGREN, Karl Gustav. Den'nya ekonomien' i Sverige: J. M. Keynes, E. Wigforss, B. Ohlin och utvecklingen 1927-39. (Ekonomiska studier utg. av nationalekonomiska institutionen vid Göteborgs universitet, 3.) (Akademisk avhandling, Göteborgs universitet.) Stockholm, Almqvist & Wiksell, 1960. 320 p. Bibliography, 309-317.
10015. LEIJONHUFVUD, Axel. Keynes and the classics: two lectures on Keynes' contribution to economic theory. (Institute of Economic affairs. Occasional paper, 30.) London, Institute of economic affairs, 1969. 46 p. Bibliography, 46.
10016. _____. On Keynesian economics and the economics of Keynes. A study in monetary theory. New York, Oxford university press, 1968. xiv, 431 p. Bibliographical references.
10017. LEKACHMAN, Robert. The age of Keynes. New York, Random house, 1966. vii, 324 p. Bibliography, 305-314. (London, Allen Lane the Penguin press, 1967. 9, 265 p. Bibliographies.)
10018. _____, editor. Keynes and the classics. (Studies in

economics.) Boston, Heath, 1964. xviii, 114 p. Bibliography, 113-114. Bibliographical footnotes.

10019. _____, editor. Keynes' General theory. Reports of three decades. New York, St. Martin's press, 1964. xii, 347 p. Bibliography, 346-347. Bibliographical footnotes.

10020. LIN, Lung-ho. K'ai-ên-ssŭ yü Ma-êrh-sa-ssŭ. (Transliterated.) China, 1967. iii, 2, 87 p. Bibliography, 85-87.

10021. LONG, Clarence Dickinson. The Keynesian economics and its fundamental defect. Baltimore, c1949. 33 l.

10022. LUCK, Willy. Monetäre unabhängigkeit; untersuchung der vorschläge von J. M. Keynes für unabhängige nationale währungssysteme; mit geleitwort von prof. dr. Wilhelm Hasenack. Im anhang: veröffentlichung einer brieflichen stellungnahme von J. M. Keynes. Leipzig, K. F. Koehler, 1939. Literaturverzeichnis, 175-185.

10023. LUTZ, Friedrick A. "The outcome of the saving-investment discussion." In, Quarterly journal of economics, 52 (August, 1938) 588-614. (In, Readings in Business cycle theory. Philadelphia, The Blakiston company, 1944.)

10024. MACGREGOR, D. H. Economic thought and policy. London, 1949.

10025. MANN, Maurice. Keynes and his underconsumption predecessors. (Thesis, Syracuse university.) (University microfilms, Ann Arbor, Michigan. Publication no. 12,692.) Ann Arbor, University microfilms, 1955. iv, 298 l. Bibliography, 291-298 l. (Abstracted in Dissertation abstracts, v. 15 (1955) no. 9, 1522-1523.)

10026. MANTOUX, Etienne. The Carthaginian peace; or, The economic consequences of Mr. Keynes. With an introduction by R. C. K. Ensor and a foreword by Paul Mantoux. London, New York, G. Cumberlege, Oxford University press, 1946. xvii, 210 p. Bibliographical footnotes. [French edition: La paix calomniée; ou, Les conséquences économiques de m. Keynes. Préface de Raymond Aron. (Problèmes et documents.) Paris, Gallimard, 1946. 2 p. l., 7-329 p., 3 l. Bibliographical footnotes. Etienne Mantoux a ecrit un anglais. American reprints: New York, Scribner, c1952. xvii, 210 p. Bibliographical footnotes. With an introduction by Robert G. Colodny. Pittsburgh, University of Pittsburgh press, 1965, c1952. xvii, 236 p. Bibliography, 214-230.

10027. MARGET, A. W. The theory of prices. New York, Prentice-Hall, 1938-42. 2 v.

10028. MARSHALL, Natalie J., editor. Keynes: updated or outdated? (Studies in economics.) Lexington, Massachusetts, Heath, 1970. viii, 142 p.

10029. MATTICK, Paul. Marx and Keynes. The limits of the

mixed economy. (Extending horizons books.) Boston, P. Sargent, 1969. viii, 364 p. Bibliography, 342-344. (London, Merlin press, 1971.)
10030. MCCRACKEN, Harlan Linneus. Keynesian economics in the stream of economic thought. Baton Rouge, Louisiana state university press, 1961. 201 p. Bibliography.
10031. MCKENNA, Joseph P. Aggregate economic analysis. 3d edition. New York, Holt, Rinehart and Winston, 1969. xx, 266 p. Bibliographical references.
10032. MONISSEN, Hans George. Konsum und vermögen. Analyse der konsum-vermögen-relation im makroökonomischen gesamtzusammenhang. (Theorie und politik, bd. 3.) Göttingen, Vandenhoeck & ruprecht, 1968. 284 p. Bibliography, 266-284.
10033. MORGAN, Theodore. Introduction to economics. New York, 1950.
10034. MORIKAWA, Tarō. Keinzu-keizaigaku no kisen. (Transliterated.) Japan, 1951. 3, 3, 177 p. Bibliographical footnotes.
10035. MOULTON, Harold G. The new philosophy of public debt. Washington, 1943.
10036. MURAD, Anatol. What Keynes means. A critical clarification of the economic theories of John Maynard Keynes. New York, Bookman associates, 1962. 223 p. Bibliography.
10037. NAGASU, Kazuji. Gendai to shihonshugi. (Transliterated.) Japan, 1965. viii, 265 p. Bibliographical references in notes.
10038. NASH, R. T. and W. P. Gramm. "A neglected early statement of the paradox of thrift." In, History of political economy, 1, 2 (Fall, 1969) 395-400.
10039. NATIONAL industrial conference board. The economic doctrines of John Maynard Keynes. A series of papers presented at a symposium conducted by the National industrial conference board. New York city, National industrial conference board, inc., c1938. vii, 78, 2 p.
10040. NODA, Isao. Keiki bunseki ABC. (Transliterated.) Japan, 1963. 13, 330 p.
10041. OKAMOTO, Takeyuki. Keinzu-shugi keizai riron josetsu. (Transliterated.) (Osaka Furitsu daigaku. Sakai, Japan. Osaka furitsu daigaku keizai kenkyū sōsho, sai 17-satsu.) Japan, 1965. viii, 144 p. Bibliography, 139-144.
10042. OKYAR, Osman. Neo-klâsik teoriden Keynes teorisine. (Istanbul universitesi yayinlarindan, no. 590.) Istanbul, I. Akgün Matbaasi, 1954. 95, 1 p.
10043. O'LEARY, J. J. "Malthus and Keynes." In, Journal of political economy, 50 (1942) 901-919.
10044. OSTASZEWSKI, Jan, editor. Wstęp do teorii ekonomicznej Johna Maynarda Keynesa. Wybor pism ze wstepem G. L. S. Shackle'a, w przekładzie z języka angielskiego Bohdana Brodzińskiego et al. pod. red. Jana Ostaszewskiego. Londyn, Szkoła nauk politycznych i społecznych, 1961.

xv, 350 p. Noty biograficzne, xiii-xv. Bibliographical footnotes.

10045. PAULSEN, Andreas. Neue wirtschaftslehre. Einführung in die wirtschaftstheorie von John Maynard Keynes und die wirtschaftspolitk der vollbeschäftigung. Berlin, Verlag für rechtswissenschaft, 1950. viii, 262 p. (2. neubearb. und erweiterte Aufl. Berlin, F. Vahlen, 1952. ix, 272 p. 3. neugefasste und erweiterte Aufl. Berlin, F. Vahlen, 1954. xi, 387 p. 4., unveränderte aufl. nachdruck. Berlin u. Frankfurt a. M., Vahlen, 1967. xi, 387 p. Bibliography, 373-374 p.)

10046. PHILLIPS, Helen Anabel. J. M. Keynes, vision and technique. (Stanford honors essays in humanities, no. 1.) Stanford, California, Stanford university press, c1951. 39 p. Bibliography, 39.

10047. PIGOU, Arthur Cecil. Employment and equilibrium. London, Macmillan, 1941.

10048. _____. Keynes's "General theory," a retrospective view. London, Macmillan, 1950. viii, 68 p. (Two lectures given in Cambridge, November, 1949.)

10049. _____. "Mr. J. M. Keynes' general theory of employment, interest and money." In, Economica, 3 (1936) 115-132.

10050. RIEGEL, Robert Dee. Birth of a radical. 1st edition. New York, Vantage press, 1964. 218 p.

10051. ROBERTSON, Dennis Holme. Essays in monetary theory. London, P. S. King & son, ltd., 1940. ix, 234 p. (London, New York, Staples press, 1946. ix, 234 p.)

10052. _____. "Mr. Keynes and finance." In, Economic journal, 48 (1938) 314-318, 555-556.

10053. _____. "Mr. Keynes' theory of money." In, Economic journal, 41 (1931) 395-411.

10054. ROBINSON, Joan. Ensayos de economía poskeynesiana. Mexico, Fondo de cultura económica, 1959.

10055. _____. Essays in the theory of employment. New York, The Macmillan company, 1937. vii, 254, 1 p. (2d edition. Oxford, B. Blackwell, 1947. vi, 190 p.)

10056. _____. Introduction to the theory of employment. 2d edition. London, Macmillan; New York, St. Martin's press, 1969. xvii, 105 p.

10057. ROLL, Erich. The world after Keynes. An examination of the economic order. (Britannica perspective.) New York, F. A. Praeger; London, Pall Mall press, 1968. xiii, 193 p.

10058. ROTHSCHILD, K. W. "The old and the new. Some recent trends in the literature of German economics." In, American economic review, 54, 2, 2 Supplement (March, 1964) 8-11.

10059. ROWSE, Alfred Leslie. Mr. Keynes and the labour movement. London, Macmillan and company, limited, 1936. x, 68 p.

10060. RUMLER, Miroslav. J. M. Keynes a soudobý kapitalismus. Vyd. 1. Praha, Nakl. politické literatury. 1965.

255, 5 p. Bibliography, 255-256.
10061. SA'ID, Jamāl al-Dīn Muhammad. al-Nazarīah al-'āmmah li-Kinz. (Transliterated.) In arabic, 1965. 551, 1 p. Bibliography, 552.
10062. SAMUELSON, Paul A. Economics. New York, 1948.
10063. _____. "Lord Keynes and the general theory." In, Econometrica, 14 (July, 1946) 187-200.
10064. SANCHEZ SARTO, Manuel. Meditaciones sobre Keynes y el keynesianismo. (Divulgaciones del Instituto de estudios económicos.) San Salvador, 1959. 25 l.
10065. SAULNIER, Raymond Joseph. Contemporary monetary theory. Studies of some recent theories of money, prices, and production. (Thesis, Columbia university, 1938.) New York, 1938. 2 p. l., 7-420 p., 1 l. Bibliographical note, 393-416. (Also published as: Studies in history, economics and public law, edited by the Faculty of political science of Columbia university, no. 443.)
10066. SCHMOLDERS, Günter, R. Schröder und H. St. Seidenfus. John Maynard Keynes als "Psychologe." Berlin, Duncker & Humblot, 1956. 167 p. Bibliography, 159-162.
10067. SCHUMPETER, Joseph A. "John Maynard Keynes, 1883-1946." In, American economic review, 37 (September, 1946). (In, J. A. Schumpeter, Ten great economists. London, Oxford university press, 1951.)
10068. SCHWANK, Karl Heinz. Lord Keynes' theorie, weder revolutionär noch wissenschaftlich; zur Kritik der apologetischen behauptung von der renaissance in der modernen bürgerlichen politischen ökonomie. 1. aufl. Berlin, Dietz, 1961. 234 p. (Dieser arbeit liegt eine dissertation zugrunde, die der verfasser am institut für gesellschaftswissenschaften beim ZK der SED, Berlin, verteidigte.)
10069. SETH, Manohar Lal. An introduction to Keynesian economics. The modern theory of employment. With a foreword by K. P. Bhatnagar. 3d rev. and enl. ed. Agra, L. N. Agarwal, 1964. xviii, 329 p. Bibliographical footnotes.
10070. SHACKLE, G. L. S. Expectations in economics. London, Cambridge university press, 1949.
10071. SHIONOYA, Tsukumo. Keinzu nyumon. (Transliterated.) Japan, 1968. 222 p. Bibliography, 216-219.
10072. _____. Keizai hatten to shihon chikuseki. (Transliterated.) Japan, 1951. 386, 11 p.
10073. SILBERSTEIN, Enrique. Keynes. (Enciclopedia del pensamiento esencial, 3.) Buenos Aires, Centro editor de América Latina, 1967. 119 p. Bibliography, 117-119.
10074. SIMONS, Henry C. Economic policy for a free society. Chicago, 1948.
10075. SINGH, V. B., editor. Keynesian economics. A symposium. By Maurice Dobb and others. Delhi, People's publishing house, 1956. 233 p.

10076. SISKIND, George. John Maynard Keynes, ein falscher prophet. Die ursachen des ideologischen einflusses der Keynesschen lehre und ihre Trugschlüsse. Übersetzung nach dem englischen originalmanuskript. 1 Aufl. Berlin, Dietz, 1959. 116 p.
10077. SMITHIES, Arthur. "Keynesian economics; the propensity to consume and the multiplier." In, American economic review, 38, 2 (May, 1948).
10078. ———. "Reflections on the work and influence of John Maynard Keynes." In, Quarterly journal of economics, 45, 4 (November, 1951) 578- .
10079. SOŁDACZUK, Jozef. Teoria ekonomiczna. J. M. Keynesa. Próba krytyki. Wyd. 1. Warszawa, Państwowe wydawn naukowe, 1959. 279 p. Bibliography.
10080. STEIN, Herbert. The fiscal revolution in America. Chicago, University of Chicago Press, 1969.
10081. STEWART, Michael. Keynes and after. Harmondsworth; Baltimore, 1967. 271 p. Bibliographical notes, 263-266.
10082. STUDI keynesiani. Di Celestino Arena et al. Con pref. di G. Ugo Papi. (Istituto di economia e finanza della Facoltà giuridica di Roma.) Milano, A. Giuffrè, 1953. xi, 385 p. Principali pubblicazioni italiane sulla teoria keynesiana, vii-xi.
10083. SUZUKI, Ryōichi. Koyō riron to chingin riron. (Transliterated.) Japan, 1949. 7, 3, 225, 4 p. Bibliographies.
10084. SWANSON, Ernst Werner and Emerson P. Schmidt. Economic stagnation or progress. A critique of recent doctrines on the mature economy, oversavings, and deficit spending. 1st edition. New York, London, McGraw-Hill book company, inc., 1946. xi, 212 p. Bibliography, 199-202. Visual aids, 203-205.
10085. SZIGETI, Peter Rudolf. Die zinsauffassungen John Maynard Keynes'. Darstellung und kritische würdigung unter besonderer berücksichtigung der liquiditätstheorie und der regulierungsfunktion des zinses. (Dissertation, Mainz.) Mainz? 1959. ii, 132 l. Bibliography, 119-132.
10086. TARSHIS, Lorie. The elements of economics. Boston, Houghton-Mifflin, 1947.
10087. TATSUMI, Hirokazu. Keinzu koyō riron no bunseki. (Transliterated.) Japan, 1948. 184 p.
10088. TERBORGH, George. The bogey of economic maturity. Chicago, 1945.
10089. THALBERG, Bjørn. En analytisk presisering av Keynes' "General theory." (Tidligere utg. som memorandum fra sosialøkonomisk institutt, Universitetet i Oslo, 1. okt. 1959.) Oslo, Universitetsforlaget, 1969. 70 l. Bibliography, 70.
10090. ———. A Keynesian model extended by explicit demand and supply functions for investment goods. (Stockholm economic studies. Pamphlet series, 2.) Stockholm, Almqvist & Wiksell, 1964. 60 p. Bibliographical footnotes.

10091. TIMLIN, Mabel Frances. Keynesian economics. (Developed from a dissertation, 1940, University of Washington.) Toronto, Canada, The University of Toronto press, 1942. ix, 198 p. Bibliographical footnotes.

10092. TODOSIA, M. "Antikeynesismul in economia politică burgheză contemporană." In, Probleme economice (Bucuresti) 15, 5 (May, 1962) 103-570.

10093. TOWNSEND, M. Monetarism versus Keynesian. (Macmillan studies in economics.) London, Macmillan, 1971.

10094. TURNER, Carl B. An analysis of Soviet views on John Maynard Keynes. Durham, North Carolina, Duke university press, 1969. vii, 183 p. Bibliography, 167-179.

10095. ULMER, Melville, Jack. The welfare state: U. S. A. An exploration in and beyond the new economics. Boston, Houghton Mifflin, 1969. xiv, 203 p. Bibliographical references in "Notes to chapters," 173-192.

10096. VANDENBORRE, H. J. De geldkringloop in de Keynesiaanse theorie. (Katholieke universiteit te Leuven. Faculteit der economische en sociale wetenschappen. Reeks van de School voor economische wetenschappen, no. 54.) Leuven, Ceuterick, 1956. 171 p.

10097. VERITAS Foundation, New York. Keynes at Harvard. Economic deception as a political credo. New York 1960. 114 p. (Revised edition: 1962.)

10098. VINING, R. "Suggestions of Keynes in the writings of Veblen." In, Journal of political economy, 57 (1939) 692-704.

10099. VOLODIN, Viktor Stepanovich. Keĭns--ideolog monopolisticheskogo kapitala. (Transliterated.) Moscow, 1953. 118 p. (German edition entitled: Keynes; ein ideologe des monopolkapitals. Übers. aus dem Russischen. Ins deutsche übertragen von Wilhelm Fickenscher.) Berlin, Verlag die wirtschaft, 1955. 130 p.

10100. WALSH, Walter. "The economic consequences of the peace;" or, The doom according to Keynes. Delivered by Dr. Walter Walsh on behalf of the Free religious movement of London, on Sunday morning, 18th January 1920, in Steinway hall. (Free religious addresses, no. 142.) London, The Free religious movement towards world religion and world brotherhood, 1920. 15, 1 p.

10101. WATTS, Vervon Orval. Away from freedom. The revolt of the college economists. (Studies of the foundation for social research, v. 1, no. 1.) Los Angeles, Foundation for social research, 1952. iii, 105 p. Bibliography, 104-105.

10102. WEINTRAUB, Sidney. Classical Keynesianism. Monetary theory and the price level. 1st edition. Philadelphia, Chilton company, Book division, 1961. 190 p.

10103. ———. A Keynesian theory of employment, growth & income distribution. 1st edition. Philadelphia, Chilton books, 1966. x, 147 p. Bibliographical footnotes.

10104.	WIENKE, William F. America's Roman circus. Delusions of our time. 1st edition. New York, Exposition press, 1968. 113 p. Bibliographical footnotes.
10105.	WILLIAMS, Harold R. and John D. Huffnagle, editors. Macroeconomic theory. Selected readings. New York, Appleton-Century-Crofts, 1969. viii, 527 p. Bibliographical footnotes.
10106.	WILLIAMS, John H. "An appraisal of Keynesian economics." In, American economic review, 38, 2 (May, 1948) 273-290.
10107.	WINCH, Donald. Economics and policy. A historical study. (Twentieth century studies.) London, Hodder & Stoughton, 1969. 366 p. Bibliographical references. (New York, Walker, 1970. c1969. 366 p. Bibliographical references.)
10108.	WRIGHT, David McCord. The Keynesian system. (Millar lectures, no. 4.) New York, Fordham university press, 1962. 90 p. (Millar lectures, no. 4.)

APPENDIX
(A Supplement to Part II., E. "Countries and Areas")

L'Economia Politica nella Spagna, nel Portogallo, nel Belgio e nei Paesi Bassi [Political Economy in Spain, Portugal, Belgium and the Low Countries]*

by Luigi Cossa

Nelle storie generali dell' economia politica, rivolte specialmente a narrare le vicende di questa scienza presso le nazioni più colte e che se ne occuparono da secoli, sono di regola dimenticate le letterature d' alcuni Stati nei quali gli studii economici, di origine più recente, hanno, negli ultimi decennii, raggiunto un grado di coltura assai elevato. Della Russia quasi nulla sappiamo; quanto agli Stati Uniti si conoscono, da gran tempo. gli scritti del Carey, magnificati nella storia del Dühring, e non si ha notizia degli altri posteriori se non per fuggevoli recensioni, che, di tanto in tanto, compaiono in qualche periodico speciale e pel breve saggio inserito dal dotto Prof. Dunbar nella North American Review (1876), sul quale è in gran parte fondato quello che il Cliffe Leslie pubblicò, pochi anni dopo, nella Fortnightly Review.

Circa allo svolgimento dell' economia politica presso gli Stati d'importanza politica ancor minore, possiamo attingere sufficienti informazioni sulle teorie degli antichi economisti spagnuoli, nelle opere del Campomanes, del Sempere y Guarinos e del Colmeiro. Agli antichi economisti olandesi, si riferiscono le erudite opere del Laspeyres e del Van Rees, e finalmente le varie fasi degli studii economici in Ungheria, sono esposte dai Kautz in apposito volume.

Data questa spiacevole lacuna nelle cognizioni che si hanno generalmente circa alle vicende dell' economia politica nel secolo XIX, presso la maggior parte degli Stati secondarii, ed in attesa che i dotti dei rispettivi paesi, valendosi dei mezzi necessari, che non sono a nostra disposizione, si accingano, come si suol dire a colmarla, non sembra inopportuno che noi, ripresi con maggior lena alcuni studi speciali, già istituiti or sono quindici anni, approfittiamo dell' ospitalità che ci accordano i gentili Direttori del Giornale degli Economisti, per inserirvi un cenno riassuntivo sullo sviluppo della scienza economica, nel secolo presente, cosi nella penisola iberica, come nella regione belgica ed olandese.

---

*Reprinted from the Giornale degli Economisti and published in pamphlet form, Bologna: Tipografia Fava e Garagnani, 1891.

Adempiamo, innanzi tutto, ad un gradito dovere, rendendo pubbliche grazie a quegli eruditi e cortesi Colleghi, i quali coll' invio di libri, di giornali e di notizie, talvolta assai diffuse, ci hanno reso meno arduo il nostro lavoro. E in modo affatto speciale ricordiamo i Professori Colmeiro e Piernas y Hurtado di Madrid, Ledesma di Valladolid, Laranjo, e Pereira Jardim di Coimbra, il sig. Deslandes, Direttore della Stamperia Nazionale di Lisbona, i Professori De Laveleye di Liegi, De Ridder di Gand, Périn e Brañts di Lovanio, Van der Rest e Denis di Bruxelles, i Professori Greven di Leida, Barone D'Aulnis de Bourouill di Utrecht, Cort van der Linden, e Quack d' Amsterdam, gli onorevoli Van Houten, Rochussen, Boissevain, e l'illustre amico Gerardo Nicola Pierson, Ministro delle finanze all' Aja.

I. Spagna

La poca stabilità dei governi che dominarono nella penisola iberica, il dissesto amministrativo, economico e finanziario, i molti ostacoli alla diffusione del sapere, e la scarsa originalità degli scrittori di scienze sociali, avvezzi ad imitare le opere straniere e in ispecie la francesi, bastano a spiegare in parte il fatto della poca importanza relativa degli economisti spagnuoli e portoghesi contemporanei, attenuata però, negli ultimi anni, da alcune onorevoli eccezioni.

Della Spagna puo dirsi, innanzi tutto, che non patisce difetto di libri elementari, i quali pero non vanno segnalati nè par vastità di dottrina, nè per acume di critica, nè per rigore di metodo, a segno da far sentire il bisogno di tradurre compendii dettati in altra lingua. Citiamo tuttavia i Principii del Las Heras Ibarra (1813), il Trattato di Espinosa de los Monteros (1831), i Principii di Paso y Delgado (1841), il Compendio del Gazquez Rubí (1844), il Manuale del Petano y Mazariegos (1859), i Principii del Coll y Masadas (1872), il Trattato del Moreno Villena (1875) e gli Elementi dell'España Lledó (1883).

Un' opera di maggior mole e di merito notevolmente superiore è dovuta ad Alvaro Florez Estrada († 1853) ed ha per titolo: Curso de Economia Politica 1ª ediz. Londra, 1828, 2 vol. 7ª ediz. Oviedo, 1852, trad. francese di L. Galibert, 1833). Essa trovò molto favore, anche fuori di Spagna, perchè riassume, con molta abilità e con svolgimenti talora originali, le teorie degli economisti classici. Ebbero fama alquanto mignore gli Elementi del Marchese di Valle Santoro, non scevri del resto di pregio (1829), il Corso di E. Jaumeandreu (1836, 2 vol.), quello di E. M. Del Valle (1842; 2^a ediz. 1846.) Sono invece più noti i Principii di economia politica del protezionista A Borrego (1844). Ancor più devoto alle idee restrittive fu, nel principio della sua carriera, l'illustre storico e pubblicista vivente D. Manuel Colmeiro (Tratado elemental de economia politica ecléctica. Madrid, 1845, 2 vol), che, convertito più tardi al libero scambio, riepilogò le sur lezioni nei Principios de economia politica (Madrid, 1859; 4ª edizione, 1873). Benigno Carballo y Wanguemert

(† 1864) professò idee più larghe, e più conformi alle teorie ricevute, nel suo Curso de economia politica (Madrid, 1855-56, 2 vol.) E ancora più diffusa l'opera del Prof. Santiago Diego Madrazo, dell' Università di Madrid (Lecciones de econ. polit. Madrid, 1874-75; 3 vol.), seguace delle idee di Bastiat. Teorie analoghe sono professate anche dal senatore Mariano Carreras y Gonzales, noto scrittore drammatico, morto pochi anni or sono, ed autore di un compendio di statistica (1863), e di un trattato di economia, molto adoperato nelle scuole, e che ha il titolo caratteristico di Filosofia del interes personal (Madrid, 1865; 3ª ediz. 1881) e infine di una propedeutica economica dettata in lingua francese (Philosophie de la science économique. Madrid et Paris, 1881). E. parimenti da ascriversi alla scuola degli ottimisti J. M. de Olozaga y Bustamente, autore di una erudita opera (Tratado de economia politica. Ma 1885-86. Due volumi) che fu largamente diffusa oltre i confini della Spagna.

Pregevoli monografie furono inserite nella Gaceta Economista (1860-68, 12 volumi), nelle Memorie della Società Economica di Madrid (1835-77) ed in quelle della Accademia delle Scienze Morali e Politiche (1863-78); altre sono riunite nei volumi di Saggi e di Studi, pubblicati dal Diaz (1855), dal Duran y Bas (1856), e dall' Escudero (1878). Sostennero il libero scambio il Figuerola, il Barzanellana, il de Bona y Ureta, ecc.; scrissero, sul credito territoriale l'Oliver (1874) e l'Isbert y Cuyas (1876); sulla proprietà il Santamaria de Paredes (1874) ed il Martinez (1875); sulla popolazione, il Caballero, che provoco una vivace polemica (1863); sulle crisi industriali, il Pastor y Rodriguez (1879); sulla quistione sociale, l'Arenal (1880), il Ferran, il Menendez (1882) ed i due storici radicali delle classi operaie, F. Garrido (1870) e J. M. Olias (1874-75); sulle casse di risparmio, il Ramirez (1876), sulla beneficenza, l'Aranaz (1859), l Perez Molina (1868), il Montells y Bohigas (1879) ed altri parecchi.

Assai numerose sono le opere concernenti la scienza delle finanze. Oltre al Diccionario de hacienda del Canga Argüelles (Londra, 1826, 2ª ediz. Madrid, 1834-40, 3 vol.), a quello più recente pubblicato nel Chili dall'Ovilo y Canales (Santiago, 1880 e segg.) ed alle opere elementari del La Llave (1840), del Pasaron y Lastra (Elementos de economia fiscal. Madrid, 1846), del Lopez Narvaez (Tratado de Hacienda, ecc. Madrid, 1856), dell'Espinola y Lubize (Madrid, 1959) e del Lozano y Montes (Compendio ecc. Madrid, 1878), si hanno le opere critiche del Pita Pizzarro (Examen economico de la hacienda ecc., Madrid, 1840) e del Conte (Examen ecc., Cadix, 1854-55, 4 vol.) ed i trattati sistematici del Peña y Aguayo (Tratado de la Hacienda, ecc. Madrid, 1838), del Toledano (Curso de instituciones ecc., Madrid, 1859-1860, 2 vol.), e quello più recente e più accreditato del Prof. Piernas y Hurtado e del De Miranda y Eguia (Manual de instituciones de hacienda publica española. Cordoba, 1869, 4ª ediz., Madrid, 1887), ricco di notizie sulla storia e sulla legislazione finanziaria nazionale. Va particolarmente segnalato, tra gli scrittori di finanze, L. Maria Pastor († 1872) autore di tre pregevoli opere sulle imposte (La

Ciencia de la contribucion. Madrid, 1856), sul credito privato e pubblico (Filosofia del credito. Madrid, 1850, 2ª ediz., 1858) e sulla storia del debito pubblico in Ispagna. (Historia de la deuda publica española. Madrid 1863). Sulle imposte scrissero l'Heredia (1813), Lopez de Aedo (1844), il Valdespino (1870), ecc.; sul debito publico si hanno inoltre, un trattato elementare di A. Hernandez Amores (Murcia, 1869) ed uno scritto di L. Sanchez de la Campa (El problema de la deuda, ecc. Madrid, 1874).

Tra i lavori di storia economica sono meritevoli di menzione speciale quello di F. Gallardo Fernandez (Origen, progresos, ecc., de las rentas de España. Madrid, 1806-1832, 7 vol.), l'interessantissima storia delle banche spagnuole di R. Santillan (Historia sobre los bancos, ecc., Madrid, 1865, 2 vol. in 4º) ed il Saggio sulla proprietà fondiaria del De Cardenas (Ensayo sobre la historia de la propriedad territorial en España. Madrid, 1873-75, 2 vol. in 4º).

Le dottrine dei socialisti della cattedra, combattute dal Rodriguez, dal Sanromá, dal Carreras, trovano valenti e temperati sostenitori in F. Giner (Principios elementales del derecho. Madrid, 1871), G. Azcárate (Estudios politicos y economicas. Madrid, 1876) e Sanz y Escartin (La cuestion economica. Madrid, 1890). Un savio eclettismo è invece seguito dal citato Piernas y Hurtado, attualmente professore a Madrid (Vocabulario de la economia 1877, 2ª ediz., 1882), che ha testè pubblicato delle interessanti Conferenze sulla cooperazione (El movimiento cooperativo. Madrid 1890).

II. Portogallo e Brasile

J. F. Da Silva. Diccionario bibliographico portuguez, ecc. (Lisboa, 1858-1884. Dodici volumi in 8º).

J. Fred. Laranjo. Economistas Portuguezes. (O Instituto. Vol. XXIX e segg. Coimbra 1882-84).

Ancor meno propizie che nella Spagna volsero le sorti dell' economia politica nel Portogallo, ed anche nel Brasile, cosi prima che dopo la sua separazione dalla madre patria. Il primo scrittore di qualche importanza è il Vescova di Pernambuco e di Elvas J. J. da Cunha d'Azéredo Coutinho (1742-1821), che pubblico vari saggi di carattere più pratico che teorico, riguardanti il commercio, le miniere, la moneta, la schiavitù. Altre monografie, intorno a questioni d'applicazione, trovansi raccolte nelle Memorie dell' Accademia delle Scienze (1789-1816). Ebbe il merito di diffondere in Portogallo e nel Brasile la teoria di Smith l'illustre giureconsulto ed economista José da Silva Lisboa (1756-1835), scrittore espertissimo, le cui idee trovansi riassunte negli Estudos do bem comum e economia politica. (Rio de Janeiro, 1819-1820, 2 vol.). Altri scrittori sono ecclettici od inclinano alla fisiocrazia, come il Prof. di Coimbra J. J. Rodrigues de Brito (1753-1831), che scrisse: Memorias politicas sobre as verdadeiras bases de la grandeza das

Appendix 599

nações (Lisboa, 1803-1805), oppure si fecero patrocinatori di un moderato protezionismo, come F. S. Constancio, il noto traduttore di Malthus e Ricardo, che fondò e diresse a Londra gli Annaes das Sciencias (1818-22) e José Accursio das Neves (1766-1834) erudito, conoscitore della storia economica portoghese (Variedades sobre objectos relativos as artes, commercio e manufacturas. Lisboa, 1814-1817; 2 vol.)

Il primo compendio portoghese d'economia politica, detato in forma alquanto scolastica dal sacerdote D. Manuel d'Almeida (Lisboa, 1822), doveva servire per la cattedra di cui, nell'anno precedente, il deputato Rodrigues da Brito aveva proposta la fondazione, ma che non venne attivata, perchè l'opinione pubblica subì, ancora per molto tempo, l'influenza del sistema restrittivo, inaugurato nel secolo precedente, con molta energia, dal ministro riformatore Marchese di Pombal Tennero dietro le Instituições (Lisboa, 1834), di José Ferreira-Borges (1786-1838), estratte in gran parte dalle opere di Tracy e di Storch, le Preleçcões (Porto, 1837) di Ag. Alb. da Silveira Pinto (1785-1852), le Noções elementares di Ant. D'Oliveira Marreca (Lisboa, 1838), il brevissimo compendio del noto pubblicista Pinheiro-Ferreira (Précis d'un cours d'économie politique. Paris, 1850; in-12º), e gli altri più recenti di F. L. Gomes (Essai sur la théorie de l'économie politique, etc. Paris 1867), e di L. Aug. Rebello da Silva (Compendio de economia politica, rural, industrial e commercial (Lisboa, 1868, 3 vol.)

Creata poscia, colla riforma degli studi del 5 Dicembre 1836, la cattedra di economia politica nell'Università di Coimbra, ne fu affidato l'insegnamento al Professore Adriano Pereira Foriaz de Sampajo (nato nel 1810) che lo tenne fino al 1871. Egli pubblicò un compendio, seguendo nella prima edizione (1839) il Catechismo del Say e nella seconda (1841) il trattato del Rau. Accresciuta notevolmente nelle ristampe successive, e specialmente nella quinta (Novos elementos de economia politica e estadistica. Coimbra, 1858-59, 3 vol. in 8º), nuovamente corretta ed alquanto abbreviata nella sesta (1867) e nella settima (Elementos, ecc. 1874, 2 vol.), tale opera, pregevole per ordine, perspicuità e ricchezza di notizie, ma poco originale e profonda, formò testo e fece dimenticare le compilazioni precedenti.

Introdotto, più tardi (1865), nell'Università L'insegnamento della scienza della finanza, unito, come in Ispagna, a quello del diritto finanziario nazionale, si ebbero gli Estudos finançeiros del Mendonça Cortez, riassunti (1873) dal Carnido de Figuereido, autore di una Introduçcao a sciencia das finanças (1874). E preferibile il dotto trattato del Professore Antonio dos Sanctos Pereira Jardim (nato nel 1821) col titolo: Principios de Finanças. Coimbra, 1867. (3ª ediz. 1880).

All'influenza delle idee radicali, confinanti col socialismo, è dovuto il libretto di F. M. de Sousa Brandao (O trabalho. Lisboa, 1857). Si ispirarono invece alle teorie della scuola storica ed ai dettami della cosi detta sociologia l'Oliveira Martins (O regime das riquezas. Lisboa, 1883) e l'autore d'un'opera ancor più originale J. J. Rodrigues de Freitas, professore all'Accademia Politecnica di Oporto (Principios de Economia Politica. Porto, 1883).

Tra le monografie, ricordiamo i Principii de Scienza delle finanze (Syntelologia) del Ferreira Borges (Lisboa, 1834), la storia del debito pubblico del Da Silveira Pinto (Divida publica portugueza. Londra, 1831), gli scritti del Morato Roma sulla moneta (De la monnaie. Lisbona, 1861), del Serzedello sulle banche Os bancos, ecc Lisboa, 1867) e gli interessanti studii di Aug. de Carvalho (1874) e del Prof. J. Fred. Laranjo sull'emigrazione e le colonie (Theoria geral da emigração. Tomo I. Coimbra, 1878, in 8°).

III. Belgio

Quantunque nel Belgio non si trovi alcun economista di merito pari a quello di Adolfo Quetélet (1796-1874), l'illustre creatore della statistica moderna, tuttavia gli studi economici vennero sempre coltivati con molto amore, non solo nella Università governativa di Gand, dove insegnarono il Brasseur ed il Walbroeck, autore d'un corso di legislazione industriale e di una monografia sulle coalizioni, e dove professa ora R. De Ridder, che scrisse sulle monete e sul credito, ed in quella di Liegi (De Laveleye) ma ben anche nell'Università cattolica di Louvain (Coux, Périn, Brants) e nell'Università libera di Bruxelles, dove insegnarono Carlo de Brouckere (1796-1860), eminente uomo di Stato, Augusto Orts (1814-1880) ed ora Eugenio van der Rest (nato nel 1841), autore d'alcune interessanti prolusioni sulla sociologia ed Ettore Dénis (nato nel 1848), positivista che scrisse due volumi, l'uno sull'imposta in generale (Bruxelles, 1889) l'altro sull'imposta sul reddito (1881) ed alcuni opuscolo storici e statistici, tra i quali ricordiamo una interessante memoria sui Fisiocrati. Anche in altri istituti d'istruzione venne dato l'insegnamento dell'economia politica, come ad esempio nel Museo Industriale di Bruxelles, nel quale ebbero cattedra l'emigrato napoletano Luigi Chitti (nato nel 1790), che publicò alcune lezioni (Cours d'économie politique Bruxelles 1833) ed una monografia alquanto eccentrica in fatto di credito (Des crises financières et de la réforme du système monétaire. Bruxelles, 1839), e poscia il De Molinari. Nella scuola delle miniere di Mons venne, per alcuni anni, insegnata l'economia dal Professore Carlo Le Hardy de Beaulieu, autore di un Traité élémentaire (Bruxelles 1861) e di due monografie sul salario (2ª edizione 1862) e sulla proprieta (La propriété et sa rente, 1868), nell'ultima dell quali nega l'esistenza della rendita fondiaria. Di tanto in tanto se ne discute, benchè, par verità, non troppo profondamente, nella Société belge d'économie politique.

Scrissero Compendii, ora quasi dimenticati, il Conte Ferninando de Hamal (1844), il De Brouckère (Principes généraux d'économie politique (1851), il Royer de Behr (Traité élementaire, 1854), l'Olivier e il Vanlerberghe nel 1861. Enrico Brasseur, che fu Professore a Gand ed è autore d'una memoria sulle libertà delle

banche (1864), detto anche, con molta erudizione, chiarezza e senso
pratico, ma con poca profondità, un Manuale d'economia, che richi-
ama in parte quelli del Rau, del Roscher e del Garnier. Rimase in-
completo, abbracciando soltanto la teoria della produzione e quella
della circolazione, esposte molto diffusamente e con copiosi riferimenti alla legislazione nazionale (Manuel d'économie politique.
Bruxelles et Gand, 1860-1864. Volumi due.)

I tre economisti più rinomati, che vissero e scrissero, o
sempre o per moltissimi anni, nel Belgio sono i provetti professori
De Molinari, De Laveleye e Périn, ai quali e ora da aggiungere un
altro giovane e valoroso insegnante, Vittorio Brants.

Gustavo De Molinari (nato a Liegi nel 1819) Direttore dell'
Economiste Belge (Bruxelles, 1855-1868. Dodici volumi) ed ora, da
molti anni , del Journal des Economistes di Parigi, è un fecondo e
brillante scrittore, benemerito per i suoi studi sul sistema monetario, sulla servitu in Russia, ecc. (Question d'économie politique.
Bruxelles, 1861. Volumi due), ma seguace alquanto eccentrico del
più estremo individualismo, di cui si hanno traccie nelle Soirées de
le rue Saint-Lazare (Paris, 1849) nelle Conversations familières sur
le commerce des grains, ed in parte anche nelle sue opere principali,
del resto assai pregevali, quali sono, per esempio, la sua Evolution
économique au 19e Siècle (1881), la Morale économique (1888), il
Cours d'économie politique (Paris, 1855-1863. Due volumi), le
Notions fondamentales d' économie politique (1891), ecc. ecc.

Emilio De Laveleye (nato a Bruges nel 1822) letterato e
pubblicista, professore a Liegi fino dal 1864, scrittore elegante e di
una straordinaria attività, collaboratore delle principali riviste
d'Europa e d'America, vuol essere specialmente ricordato per le
sue monografie sul libero scambio. (Etudes historiques, etc., 1857),
sulle crisi commerciali (Le marché monétaire et les crises depuis
cinquante ans. Paris, 1865) e per quelle, ancora migliori, sull'
agricoltura del Belgio (Essai sur l'économie rurale de la Belgique,
1863. Rapport sur l'agricolture belge, etc.), dei Paesi Bassi e della
Svizzera. Egli è parimente conosciuto come uno dei più risoluti ed
estremi sostenitori del bimetallismo internazionale, sul qual tema publico moltissimi opuscoli, riassunti ora in un volume (La monnaie et
le bimétallisme international. Paris, 1891) e sostenne vivaci polemiche col Pirmez e col Frère Orban (La question monétaire, 1874)
propugnatori dell' unimetallismo in oro, e quest' ultimo anche dell'
unita d' emissione bancaria. Diventato, da circa tre lustri, un fautore
ardente delle nuove dottrine tedesche (Les tendances nouvelles de
l'économie politique, nella Revue des Deux Mondes, 1875), attese a
riassumere con molta competenza i risultati delle più recenti inves-
tigazioni fatte in Germania ed in Inghilterra sulle antiche forme di
proprietà collettiva (De la propriété et des ses formes primitives.
Paris, 1874, tradotte in inglese, ed anche in tedesco da H. Bücher,
con molte aggiuute. Quarta edizione, 1891) e scrisse inoltre un
volume sul socialismo (Le socialisme contemporain. Paris, 1881.
Ultima edizione, 1891). Vanno finalmente ricordati, pei loro
pregi estrinseci e per la loro erudizione, i suoi Eléments d'économie

politique (Paris, 1882). Terza edizione, 1891), molto bene accolti, anche all'estero, non ostante le gravi inesalttezze che rivelano nell' illustre autore minore attitadine per le ricerche della scienza pura, che non per la trattazione di singoli questioni d'applicazione. Altri scritti minori del Laveleye trovansi indicati nei Jahrbücher für National Oekonomie di Conrad (Vol. 34.° Jena, 1870).

Il francese Carlo Périn, professore a Lovanio per moltissimi anni, e in Europa il rappresentante piu illustre è più temperato di quella scuola (seguita in Francia dal Corbière, dal De Metz-Noblat, dal Jannet, dall'Hervé-Bazin, ecc.) che si suol chiamare cattolica, e che si accorda, rispetto al metodo ed in alcuni particolari, coi seguaci del benemerito Le-Play, che tendono, in ispecie, alla ricostituzione economicomorale della famiglia. La scuola del Périn riconosce però l'influenza benefica della libertà economica e si studia di armonizzarla colla morale cristiana, dissentendo da un'altra scuola cattolico-sociale (rappresentata in Inghilterra dal cardinale Manning, dal Devas ecc.; in Germania dal defunto Mons. Ketteler Vescovo di Magonza, ecc.; in Francia dal Conte Mun) più proclive alla ricostituzione delle antiche maestranze ed all'intervento dello stato. Le principali opere del Périn (tradotte esse pure in parecchie lingue) sono: De la richesse dans les sociétés chrétiennes (Paris, 1861, 2 volumi. Terza edizione, 1883). Les lois de la société chrétienne. Paris, 1875, 2 volumi. Seconda edizione, 1876), Le socialisme chrétien (1878). L'ultimo suo lavora è una storia critica dell'economia moderna, pur troppo non sempre imparziale (Les doctrines économiques depuis un siècle. Paris, 1880).

Degnissimo successore del Périn nella cattedra, ispirato alle stesse tendenze, pari a lui nella attività a nell'ingegno, ma superiore nella erudizione storica e nella cognizione tecnica delle singole dottrine economiche, Vittorio Brants, dopo d'avere esordito con una monografia interessantissima sulle condizioni degli agricoltori nel Medio Evo (Essai historique sur la condition des classes rurales en Belgique. Louvain, 1880), pubblicò qualche saggio storico-letterario sopra Senofonte (Xénophon économiste, 1881), Filippo di Maizières (1880) ed in generale sull'economia scolastica (Coup d'oeuil sur les débuts de la science économique, 1881). Diventato poscia Professore, il Brants, oltre a piccoli ma interessanti articoli su varii punti della questione operaia, rese un utile servizio alla scienza, pubblicando tre volumetti che riepilogano le sue lezioni e sono, in pari tempo, il miglior compendio delle dottrine della scuola a lui rappresentata. Eccone il titolo: Lois et méthodes de l'économie politique. Louvain, 1883. 2.ᵉ édit., 1887. La lutte pour le pain quotidien, 1885. La circulation des hommes et des choses, 1886.

Un altro Professore di Lovanio, il Thonissen († 1891), il quale fu anche Ministro, e scrisse un Commento assai pregevole alla Carta costituzionale del Belgio, dettò del pari alcuni opuscolo d'economia (Mélanges d'histoire, de droit et d'économie politique, 1873) ed una conscienziosa storia del socialismo (Le socialisme dépuis l'antiquité, etc. 1852. Due volumi).

Meritano parimenti d'essere accennati il Ducpétiaux, che si occupò delle funzioni economiche dello Stato, delle associazioni operaie, e della carità; Aug. Visschers, che scrisse sulle casse di risparmio (Nouvelle étude sur les caisses d'épargne. Bruxelles, 1861), sulle società di mutuo soccorso ed altri istituti di previdenza; l'Haeck, autore di opuscoli sulla Union de crédit di Bruxelles e sulla questione monetaria; Leone D'Andrimont, che studiò le società cooperative, e l'illustre giureconsulto Laurent, Professore a Gand, che istituì e diresse con parecchie monografie popolari le casse di risparmio scolastiche.

Per ultimo ricordiamo il protezionista Jobard, caloroso difensore della proprietà industriale perpetua (Nouvelle économie sociale, 1844), il socialista De Paepe, il noto collettivista Colyns et il suo discepolo Ag. De Potter (Economie sociale, 1874), che ne divulgò le dottrine.

IV. Paesi Bassi

Nella patria di Grozio, di De Witt, dei due De la Court, di Graswinckel, di Usselinx, non venne mai meno il fervore per le discussioni economiche, ed in ispecie per quelle concernenti la moneta, il commercio, il credito, le colonie e il regime tributario. Ne fanno testimonianza le dissertazioni pubblicate in appositi periodici, come la Tijdschrift vor Staathuishoudkunde, redatta dal Barone W. A. F. Sloet tot Oldhuis, (Zwolle, 1841-1875. Volumi 28) e l'Economist, diretto da J. L. De Bruyn Kops, già Professore di Delft, (Amsterdam, 1852 e segg.) e continuato anche dopo la sua morte da valenti collaboratori. Nella revista di coltura generale De Gids (Amsterdam, 1835 e segg.) si leggono pure interessanti articoli del Pierson, del Vissering, ecc, ecc.

Eminenti uomini di Stato, quali il Conte Gisberto Carlo di Hogendorp (1762-1834) e Giovanni Rodolfo Thorbecke (1798-1872) ed altri, essi pure segnalati, come il Gogel, il Van Hall', il Betz coltivarono con amore gli studii economici e in particolare i finanziarii.

Al lodevole intento di risvegliare nel popolo il desiderio di erudirsi nell'economia contribuirono alcuni libri elementari, in generale però piuttosto superficiali. Si possono vedere quelli di H. J. Smidt (1858), i dialoghi del Knottenbelt (1872) ed il libro più largo e più conosciuto del già citato De Bruyn Kops Beginselen der Staathuishoudkunde. Amsterdam, 1850. Cinque edizioni). Hanno un carattere alquanto più scientifico, il breve schizzo del Van Rees (Overzicht, 1861) il brevissimo del Tellegen (Beginselen, 1853. 3a edizione, 1870) e quello di E. J. Kiehl, condotto sulle traccie dello Stuart Mill e del Roscher e destinato agli istituti di istruzione secondaria, o media (middelbaar) come si dice in Olanda (Eérste beginselen, ecc. Middelburgh, 1869. Seconda edizione, 1871). Di gran lunga superiore, ed al corrente della scienza, è l'opera, redatta per il medesimo scopo, dal Pierson (Grondbeginelen der Staathuishoudkunde.

Haarlem, 1875-1876. Due piccoli volumi), notevole in ispecie nella parte riguardante la distribuzione delle ricchezze. L'edizione del 1886 (in un solo volume) è alquanto mutata, con indirizzo più pratico.

Come è ben naturale un impulso più efficace doveva venire dalle Università di Leida, di Utrecht e di Groninga e dall'Ateneo illustre di Amsterdam, trasformato in Università comunale nel 1877.

A Leida insegnò, dal 1815, al 1848, Enrico Guglielmo Tydeman (1778-1863), che tradusse Senior (1839), scrisse sulle Gilde ed ebbe nel 1838 l'idea poco felice di comporre una specie di compendio d'economia con varii frammenti del Corpus Juris. Dal 1850 al 1879 tenne cattedra il Vissering, del quale diremo dopo, e dal 1880 in avanti, H. B. Greven, più profondo dei suoi predecessori, e favorevolmente noto per una dissertazione (De ontwikkeling der bevolkingsleer, Leiden, 1875), nella quale spiega e difende, con singolare chiarezza ed efficacia, la teoria della popolazione di Malthus avuto speciale riguardo alle idee degli evoluzionisti. Spencer, Greg e Galton. Al qual proposito notiamo (astenendoci da ogni commento) che in Olanda ha una certa importanza la cosi detta Lega neo-malthusiana, presieduta dal Van Houten, membro influente della Seconda Camera ed egli pure distinto economista.

Ad Utrecht professò, dal 1849 al 1860, J. Ackersdyk (1790-1861), più noto pei suoi viaggi, per la sua biblioteca, per il suo insegnamento, che per le brevi sue dissertazioni.

Gli succedette Ottone van Rees (1825-1868), anteriormente Professore a Groninga (dal 1858) il quale, più che per i suoi lavori teorici, vuol essere ricordato come insigne storico. Esordi con due monografie su Pietro De la Court (1851) e G. K. v. Hogendorp (1854) e pubblicò poscia, in due volumi, una dotta storia della scienza economica in Olanda sino alla fine del secolo 18.º (Geschiednis der Staathuishoudkunde in Nederland. Utrecht, 1805-1868) Mori affogato in un bagno e non potè compiere il terzo volume. Ad H. P. Quack, professore dal 1868 al 1877, indi segretario generale della Banca, poi nouvamente Professore (ad Amsterdam), sono dovuti una raccolta di Saggi (1877) e tre volumi, testè ristampati, sul socialismo (De socialisten. Personen en stelsels. Amsterdam, 1875-1888), che sono molto pregevoli nel rispetto letterario. L'attuale Professore Barone J. D'Aulnis de Bourouill, autore d'alcuni articoli sulla misura dell'interesse, incominciò la sua carriera, svolgendo con molta competenza (Het inkomen der maatschappy. Leiden, 1874) le teorie degli economisti matematici Jevons e Walras, ch'egli mise tra loro in comunicazione. Più di recente egli confutò, sulle orme del Leroy-Beaulieu, le dottrine dei socialisti contemporanei (Het hedendaagsche socialisme. Amsterdam 1886) e quelle del George.

Nella piccola Università di Groninga professarono lo Star Numan, il van Rees ed il Tellegen, già ricordati il Freseman Viëtor, e per alcuni anni P. W. A. Cort van der Linden, testè passato ad Amsterdam, autore di alcune monografie sulla questione monetaria, e di un buon compendio di scienza della finanza (Leerboek der financien, 1887), ispirato alle teorie del Wagner e di altri scrittori tedeschi contemporanei.

Complete, da poco tempo, colle Università dello Stato, per la Valentia dei suoi insegnanti, quella comunale di Amsterdam, che ebbe professore Gerolamo De Bosch Kemper (morto nel 1876), fondatore della Società statistica olandese, direttore del pregevole suo Annuario (Staatkundig en staathuishoudkundig jaarboekje, 1849 e segg.) ed autore di una dotta monografia storica sulla beneficenza (Geschiedkundig onderzoek naar de armoede in ons vaderland. Amsterdam, 1851) e di un diffuso trattato di sociologia (De wetenschap der samenleving. Amsterdam, 1859-1864. Tre volumi), che comprende anche il diritto pubblico nazionale. Gli succedettero e lo vinsero, così nel campo della scienza pura come in quello delle sue applicazioni, i due Professori N. G. Pierson (1877-1884) ed Antonio Beaujon (1885-1890). L'ultimo di questi, rapito da morte immatura alla scienza ed alla scuola, potè tuttavia darci alcuni saggi luminosi della sua molta dottrina, combinata con squisito senso pratico. Si occupò da principio di lavori statistici, scrisse quindi, ottenendo un premio segnalato, la sua opera principale (History of the dutch sea fisheries. Amsterdam, 1884), dando anche prova di una speciale attitudine nell'uso delle lingue straniere. Pubblicò, per ultimo, un'altra preziosa monografia (Handel en handelspolitiek. Amsterdam, 1888) nella quale, lasciando in disparte alcune ragioni poco concludenti, dedusse correttamente dalla teorica degli scambi internazionali il corollario della libertà del commercio, ch'egli poscia difese (nell'Economist) dalle obbiezioni del protezionista Harte.

Si acquistò fama di buon insegnante e di elegantissimo scrittore, Simone Vissering (1818-1888) Professore a Leida (1850-1878), Ministro delle finanze (1879-1881), autore di Saggi brillanti, che vennero poscia riuniti in tre volumi (Herrinneringen. Amsterdam, 1863-72) e di un dotto Manuale di economia applicata, nel quale tratta con vedute liberali le principali teorie della politica economica e finanziaria, difende l'unico tipo monetario, non teme l'eccesso di popolazione, ecc. Sono pregevoli, in questo trattato, l'ordine, la chiarezza ed i molti ed esatti riferimenti alla legislazione patria. (Handboek van practische Staathuishoudkunde. Amsterdam, 1860-65. Due volumetti. Quarta edizione, 1878). Difettava tuttavia il Vissering di quella profondità scientifica, che contraddistingue i due maggiori economisti olandesi di questo secolo, cioè il Mees ed il Pierson.

Guglielmo Cornelio Mees (1813-1884) fu uno scienziato di primo ordine, che riunì in sè stesso, evitandone i difetti, le attitudini di Ricardo e quelle di Hermann. Incominciò con due tesi, la prima in latino, molto lodata dal Savigny, sulle mutazioni monetarie (De vi mutatae monetae in solutionem pecuniae debitae, 1838), la seconda sulla storia delle antiche banche di deposito, nella quale chiarì la vera natura delle operazioni della banca di Amsterdam, correggendo alcuni errori di Steuart e di Smith (Proeve eener geschiedenis van het bankwezen in Nederland. Rotterdam, 1838). Pubblicò poscia un' altra eccellente monografia sul lavoro negli istituti pii (De Werkinrigtingen van armen, 1844). Per la sua conosciuta competenza in materia di moneta e di credito, comprovata anche da altro suo lavoro (Het muntwezen van Nederlandsch Indie. Amsterdam, 1851), ottenne poi la carica di Presidente della Banca neerlandese, che tenne con molta lode sino alla morte. Diverso in ciò da moltissimi, non pubblicò che negli anni di una maturità già inoltrate, i suoi lavori concernenti la scienza pura, preziosi per la profondità del concetto, la correttezza e perspicuità del dettato, la sodezza e sobrietà dell' erudizione, e la piena e sicura considerazione dei varii aspetti d'un dato problema; difettosi soltanto per l'aridità letteraria della forma. Nel volume intitolato: Overzicht van eenige hoofdstukken der Staathuishoudkunde. Amsterdam, 1866, egli riassunse, con magistrale semplicità e chiarezza, le teorie della scuola classica inglese, e in ispecie quelle di Ricardo e di Stuart Mill, relative alla produzione, al valore, alla distribuzione delle ricchezze, non ommettendo le osservazioni necessarie circa ai limiti della loro applicabilità. Specialmente commendevole è la teorica degli scambi internazionali, da lui arricchita con alcune analisi originali. Altre memorie, pubblicate negli alti della R. Accademia delle Scienze in Amsterdam, possono considerarsi come saggi complementari, essi pure importantissimi. La prima di esse concerne il sistema monetario, del quale il Mees trattò ripetutamente, anche in notevoli rapporti ufficiali. (De munstandaard in verband mit de pogingeu tot invoering van eenheid van munt, 1869). In questo scritto, che servi di modello ad uno analogo del Roscher, l'autore espone con metodo corretto la teoria del bimetallismo internazionale, tenendosi ben lontano dalle esagerazioni del Cernuschi e d'altri fautori incondizionati di quel sistema. Una tale dottrina è accolta dalla maggioranza degli economisti olandesi, tra i quali si segnalarono, trattandone ex professo, il Pierson, poi il Van den Berg. Direttore della Banca di Java e da ultimo il Boissevain, e l'antico ministro Rochussen (1891), autori di due dissertazioni meritamente premiate. Piene d'acute osservazioni sono altre due memorie del Mees sul riparto dei tributi (1874) e sopra i concetti fondamentali dell' economia (utilità, valore, ecc.).

(Cfr. N. G. Pierson, Levensbericht van Mr W. C. Mees. Amsterdam, 1885).

Primeggia tra gli economisti viventi della sua patria, il più volte ricordato Nicolò Gerardo Pierson, nato nel 1839, in gran parte autodidatto, esperto nella pratica degli affari, addetto, come Direttore, alla Banca cei Paesi Bassi, dottore onorario di leggi nel 1875, professore d'economia ad Amsterdam (1877-84), successore del Mees nella presidenza di detta Banca (1884-1891) e chiamato nell' agosto di quest'anno nei consigli della Corona, qual Ministro delle finanze. Fornito di sottile ingegno, di soda e svariata dottrina, conoscitore delle lingue e letterature forestiere, dotato di attitudine singolare alle ricerche storiche, non meno che a quelle di teoria e di applicazione, il Pierson scrisse un gran numero di monografie, concernenti, in ispecie, la moneta, il credito, il valore, il salario, la rendita, e l'imposta, per lo più inserite negli accennati periodici De Gids e De Economist. Tra i lavori storici, meritano particolare elogio i suoi studii sugli antichi economisti italiani raccolti dal

Custodi (1866) e quelli ancor più interessanti sulla scuola fisiocratica, che, nel rispetto critico, sono ancora migliori (Het Physiocratisme nell' Economist, luglio ed Agosto 1880). Ammiratore degli economisti inglesi (in particolare di Ricardo, di Stuart Mill, di Bagehot, di Jevons) e pienamente informato dei progressi della scienza in Germania, persevera nella teoria del libero scambio, senza cascare nell' ottimismo di Bastiat; ammette la necessità dell' intervento dello Stato, ma respinge con energia le teorie del socialismo di piazza, di Stato, e di cattedra. Fra le sue monografie, non pubblicate nelle riviste, accenneremo la traduzione del classico libro del Goschen sul corso dei cambi; il discorso sul concetto della ricchezza (Het begrip van volksrykdom. 'S. Gravenhage, 1864); l'opuscolo Twee advizen over muntwezen (Amsterdam, 1874) e finalmente le brillanti ed erudite sue dissertazioni storico politiche sul governo delle colonie olandesi (Het Kultuur-stelsel, 1868 totalmente rifuse col titolo: Koloniale politiek. Amsterdam, 1877). Il capo lavoro del Pierson è tuttavia il suo trattato di economia politica, nel quale, scostandosi dalle divisioni generalmente seguite, e lasciando da parte ogni apparato di erudizione, egli espone, con profondità pari a quella del Mees, benchè meno sistematicamente, e con una vivacità di stile, che il suo maestro non possedeva, le dottrine dell'economia moderna, spiegate con piena cognizione dello stato odierno della scienza. Esordisce dalla teorica del valore, che gli apre la via a quella della distribuzione e della circolazione, ricca di svolgimenti, per conchiudere poi, dopo di aver discusso i problemi finanziarii con particolare riguardo ai bisogui della pratica, svolgendo le teorie del consumo, della popolazione e della produzione e proclamando l'importanza fondamentale di questa ultima dottrina. Ben a ragione, pertanto, il libro del Pierson è considerato, anche in Germania, come una delle migliori esposizioni dello stato attuale della scienza.

  N. G. Pierson, Leerboek der Staathuishoudkunde. Haarlem, 1884-1890. Due volumi.

  Nel gran numero di monografie pubblicate in Olanda trovano un posto onorevole le dissertazioni di laurea, redatte, d'ordinario, coll'assistenza dei Professori, che suggeriscono i temi ed accennano le fonti migliori. Cosi, per esempio, il noto pubblicista Prof. T. M. C. Asser incominciò la sua carriera scrivendo sul valore (1858) e così, l'anno dopo, anche il van Houten, che riusci superiore (Verhandeling over de waarde. Groningen, 1859), illustrando la teoria dell'utilità. Si occupò testè della stessa materia C. A. Verrijn Stuart (Ricardo en Marx. s'Gravenhage, 1890) per dimostrare, con molto acume, che la dottrina del valore di Ricardo nulla ha a che fare con quella dei moderni collettivisti. Dei rapporti dello Stato colle banche trattò con molta erudizione P. Verloren (De verhouding van den Staat tot het bankwezen. Utrecht, 1869) e sugli errori dei moderni protezionisti, più brevemente, il Godée (1885). J. G. T. Harte è autore d'una buona tesi sull'interesse dei capitali (De rentestand. Utrecht, 1880), tema svolto, in parte, con maggiore originalità, de J. de Haas nel Giornale della Società Statistica di Londra (A third element in the rate of interest, 1889). Discusse invece molto bene sul salario, Ph. Falkenburg (Bijdrage tot de leer van het arbeidsloon.

Rotterdam, 1890), dando occasione ad un cenno critico del Pierson. Sul tema delle imposte dirette aveva scritto E. Van Voorthuysen (De directe belastingen. Utrecht, 1848) e su quelle di successione G. A. Nahuys (De belastingen op de erfopfolging, etc. Utrecht, 1869). Più di recente, e con maggiore profondità, A. J. Cohen Stuart (Bijdrage tot de theorie der progressieve inkomstenbelasting. s'Gravenhage, 1889) ed il Mees juniore, esaminarono il problema dell' imposta progressiva e, per ultimo, J. Rochussen parlò del tributo sul reddito (Die theorie der inkomstenbelasting. 's Gravenhage, 1889).

Lo spazio ci manca per apprezzare parecchi altri lavori special sulle teorie economiche e finanziarie. Basti il dire che il decano dei giureconsulti olandesi, professore J. T. Buys di Leida si occupò delle banche di circolazione (1856) e delle ipotecarie (1861); che scrissero sul commercio il Portielie, il Wynne, i due Muller; sul colonie il Van Hoevell, il Veth, il De Waal, il Quarles van Ufford, ecc., ecc. Non sono poche le monografie sulle banche mutue (van der Heym), sulle casse di risparmio (Fokker), sulle cooperative di produzione e sulla partecipazione al profitto (Kerdijk), sui Monti di pietà (Van Heel) e in generale sulla beneficenza (i due Tydeman, l'Hemskeerk, it Mackay, il Fock, ecc.). Circa alle imposte, considerate sia nel rispetto storico sia nel teorico, si hanno pregevoli lavori dell'Engels, del Sickenga, del Treub e di parecchi altri, ai quali fanno degno riscontro la monografia sui prestiti pubblici del l'Hooft Grafland (De staatschulden. Utrecht, 1851), quella molto più interessante ed erudita di J. J. Weevering (Handleiding tot de geschiednis der staatschulden, 1852. Due vol.) e, per ultimo, gli scritti lodatissimi del Betz.

Non andò immune neppure l'Olanda dalla controversie suscitate in Germania per le dottrine dei così detti socialisti della cattedra, accolte con plauso dal Goeman Borgesius (1878), in parecchi articoli della revista Vragen der Tijds, diretta dal Van Houten, e prolissamente commentate nel libro erudito ma poco profondo dell'Avvocato J. A. Levy (Engelsch Katheder-Socialisme, 1879). Lo confutarono con molta temperanza e senza punto disconoscere i meriti dells scuola storica tedesca, da prima il Pierson (De Gids, settembre 1878 e settembre 1879), e poscia, nei loro discorsi inaugurali, il Greven a Leida e il d'Aulnis de Bourouill ad Utrecht (1880) e quest' ultimo anche in alcuni interessanti articoli dell' Economist di Amsterdam (febbraio e marzo 1880). Coll'ingegnosa dissertazione di laurea di G. Heymans (Karakter en Methode der Staathuishoudkunde. Leiden, 1880), che precorre, in parte, ai lavori più pensati del Menger (1883) e del Keynes (1891) la vivace polemica arrivò al suo termine.

Un' eco ancora più debole ebbero nei Paesi Bassi le accanite battaglie tra gli economisti capitanati in Germania dallo Schmoller e la nuova scuola austriaca, di cui sono capi il Menger, il Sax, ed il Böhm-Bawerk. Ciò era ben naturale, perchè non occorreva una reazione contro dottrine che gli uomini più competenti non avevano accettate. Ed inoltre la teoria del valore fondato sull'utilità subbiettiva, mantenuta nei suoi limiti di regione, non riesciva nuova in Olanda, perchè il D'Aulnis aveva (come già si disse) divulgate le dottrine del Jevons e del Walras (1874) e più tardi il Pierson, nel 1^0 Volume del suo Leerboek (1884), aveva fatta una esposizione magistrale della teoria del valore, nella quale erano armonizzate le dottrine della scuola classica (Ricardo, Mill, Cairnes) e quelle già svolte nella Economia Politica del Jevons e nel primo scritto del Menger (1871). Ed è gran fortuna che siano troncate polemiche, le quali altrove proseguono tuttora, con una utilità non sempre proporzionale al peso dei volumi ed al numero degli articoli ai quali danno occasione.

INDEX I

Author and Subject Index

Aarons, E., 1029
Abad-Conde Y Sevilla, G., 1030
Abalo, L. J., 1031
Abb, G., 8888
Abbati, A. H., 9885
Abbott, C., 5444
Abbott, L., 1032
Abbott, L. D., 697
Abe, G., 1
Abeille, L. P., 3920-3923
Abendlande, 7196
About, E., 7359
Abramsky, 9112
Abramson, V., 3330
Absenteeism, 893
Abstinence, 7606
Abu Al-Su'ud, M., 2835
Academia Republicii Populare Romine, 2953
Academic des Sciences Morales et Politiques, Paris, 5349
Academie de Lyons, 7195
Academie des Inscriptions, 344
Academie Francaise, 6917
Academische Economische Kring, Tilburg, 698
Academy of Political and Social Science, 509
Academy of Science, Soviet Union, 2984
Academy of Science, Soviet Union, 1037
Acceleration Principle, 2283
Accident, Railroad, 7363
Accounting, Social, 3854
Accounts, Public, 3929, 4667, 4752, 4764, 4859
Accumulation, Marxian, 9538
Accumulation, Theory, 2936, 9308
Accursio, J., 2946
Acevedo, A., 6492

Achaeology, Industrial, 5060
Ackley, G., 1034, 3490, 9886
Acland, J., 5447
Acosta, J., 3933
Acta Scientiarum Socialium, 532
Action, Collective, 1276
Action, Human, 1806
Action, Social, 9856
Activity, Economic, 1322, 1359
Acworth, W. M., 7360-7362
Adams, C. F., 7365
Adams, H., 9004
Adams, H. C., 1035, 7367-7371
Adams, J. L., 9421
Adams, J. Q., 5448
Adams, T. S., 1370
Adams, W., 699
Address, 3804, 3843
Adler, G., 3099, 7372
Adler, M., 5149
Adler, M. J., 5035
Administration, 1923, 2741, 7612
Administration, City, 4116
Adoratsky, V., 9413
Advice, Economic, 2448
Afanas'Ev, V. S., 1014
Afghanistan, 7102
Africa, 1817, 2540, 3956, 4174 4311, 4576, 4710, 5123, 5516, 6751
Africa, Bantu, 4966
Africa, Colony, 6469
Africa, East, 1700
Africa, West, 1079-1080, 1883
Africa Company, 3960, 4369
Aftalion, A., 2328
Agarwal, L. N., 10069
Agazzini, M., 1036, 5452
Aggarwala, K. C., 9807
Agger, E. E., 982
Aggregation, 3691

Agoult, D., 5453, 5475
Agra, 5559
Agriculture, 487, 577, 1063, 2635, 2669, 3219, 3355, 3367, 3462, 3648, 4001, 4097, 4123, 4217, 4286, 4566, 4866, 4869, 4878, 4984, 5251, 5359, 5385, 5387, 5469, 5483, 5512, 5560, 5606, 5618, 5628, 5639, 5650, 5665, 5696, 5743, 5749, 5753, 6057, 6098, 6252, 6262, 6284-6285, 6290, 6312, 6315, 6398, 6402, 6468, 6539, 6558, 6572, 6650, 6666, 6719, 6802, 6834, 6857, 6866, 6924, 6995, 7025, 7140, 7165, 7246-7247, 7269, 7472, 7538, 7608, 7675, 7789, 7861, 7932, 8176, 8299, 8302, 8399, 8437, 8487, 8530, 8534, 8539, 8750
Agriculture, Classes, 5869
Agriculture, Credit, 7437, 7888
Agriculture, Depression, 7617
Agriculture, Europe, 7148
Agriculture, France, 7944
Agriculture, Great Britain, 6286, 6288, 7232
Agriculture, Products, Cost, 6273
Agriculture, Protection, Great Britain, 5455
Agriculture, Spain, 7140
Agrucikam, R. M., 2715
Aguiar, R. W., 228
Aguilar, L. E., 9005
Aguilar, M. A., 2
Aguillon, L., 7373
Aguirre, M. A., 3
Ahanyan, A., 2017
Ahmad, S. M., 2836
Ahmed Moulavi, C. N., 2837
Aickin, J., 3942
Akademie der Wissenschaften, Berlin, 9006
Akademisk Avhandling, Stockhoms Hogskola, 5184
Akamoto, T., 3018
Akerman, J. H., 4, 5, 9959

Akgun, I., 10042
Akhtar, S. M., 619, 1042
Al-Fakkak, M. A., 8, 205
Al-Gilani, S. M. A., 2838
Al'ter, L. B., 3031
Albaret, C., 1044
Albebra, 9705
Albergo, G., 5455
Albert, H., 6, 1045
Alberti, G., 7374
Albertini, J. M., 1046, 3491
Albery, M., 8906
Albregts, A. H. M., 7
Alcedo, A., 5456, 5899
Alchain, A. A., 1047
Alcocer, M., 1048
Alcock, T., 3943-3944
Aldrich, N. W., 7375-7376
Alem, A., 2329, 5150
Alemann, R. T., 1049
Alembert, J., 4199
Aleshina, I. V., 2545
Alessandro, L., 3100
Alessio, G., 7377
Alexander, A., 1050-1052
Alexander, K. J. W., 2330, 3492
Alexander, S. S., 9887
Alexander, I., 4742
Alfassa, M., 2733
Alfieri, D., 559
Alfonzo, R. F., 3089
Algarra, J., 133
Algeria, 1223
Ali, S. A. 2839
Alienation, 9014, 9443
Aliens, 6809
Alighieri, D., 2856
Alinsky, S. D., 2331
Alison, 6549
Alison, A., 5457-5458
Alison, W. P., 5459-5460
Allais, M., 700-701, 1053
Allardyce, A., 5461
Allen, C. L., 1054-1055, 3101
Allen, J., 5462
Allen, R., 3945
Allen, R. G. D., 3259, 3493-3494, 9673
Allen, W., 3946, 6239
Allen, W., F., 7378
Allen, W. R., 45, 985, 1047
Allgemeine Deutsche Biographie,

Author and Subject Index 613

8835, 8889
Allhusen, D., 2720
Allocation, Resource, 1680, 5129
Allochio, S., 7379
Almack, J., 5463
Alms House, 4340
Alphand, A., 7380
Alstadheim, H., 3102, 3495
Alt, R. M., 1056
Altheim, F., 9
Althorpe, Lord, 6372
Althusser, L., 9008-9010
Altmann, E., 1057
Altmann, S., 10
Altmann, S. P., 2674
Altvater, E., 9011
Alvarado, C. M., 2542
Alvarado, G., 1493
Alvarez Diaz, R., 2601
Alvin, D. F., 1058
Amato, L., 702, 9012
Amboise, 4006
Ame, L., 7381
Ameilhon, H. P. 3947
America, 3928, 3941, 4143, 4153, 4202, 4210, 4346, 4823, 5201, 5223, 5234, 5454, 5516, 5521, 5806, 5810, 5899, 5920, 6114, 6199, 6205, 6621, 6723, 6765, 6984, 7118, 7438, 7575-7576, 8172, 8442, 8940, 9075, 9517, 10080
America, Colony, 6469
America, Hispanic, 7346
America, Labor, 5717
America, North, 5732, 6613, 7045, 8210
America, South, 6613
America, Working Class, 7408
American Academy of Political and Social Science, 2657, 3052, 3211, 3456, 3575, 3746
American Association for Public Information, 1351
American Association of University Women, 2240,
American Council on Public Affairs, 2359, 9690
American Economic Association, 194, 703-705, 769, 777, 824, 867, 1368, 1505, 3103, 3159, 3423, 3528, 3546, 3621, 3639, 3641, 7629, 9074, 9139, 9810, 9880
American Enterprise Institute, 3226
American Historical Review, 2501
American Institute for Economic Research, 814
American Institute for Marxist Studies, 9015
American Institute of Banking, 1059, 2260
American Journal of Economics and Sociology, 3538, 8941, 8944, 8954, 8936, 8991, 9013, 9764
American Journal of Sociology, 9580
American Management Association, 3205
American Philosophical Society, Proceedings, 3053
Amherst College, 744
Amhurst, N., 3948
Amin, R. K., 1060
Ammer, D. S., 706
Ammon, A. O., 8821-8822, 9888
Amonn, A., 12, 1016, 1061-1062, 2333, 3104, 3496-3497
Amore, G., 1063
Amoroso, L., 902, 1064, 3498-3499, 3500, 9658, 9728, 9756
Ampanella, 7891
Amzalak, M. B., 251, 2945-2947
Analysis, Dynamic, 2057
Analysis, Graphical, 1140
Analysis, Operations, 1125, 1682
Analysis, Quantitative, 1170
Analysis, Static, 2057
Anantaraman, V., 2332
Anarchism, 8203, 9529
Ancient, Economics, Indian, 2829
Ancient, Economics, Portugal, 2945

Ancient History, 6196
Ancient Institutions, 7563
Ancient Period, 167, 2825, 3950, 3963, 3972, 4019, 4103, 4194, 4331, 4378, 4400, 4430, 4577, 4626, 4802, 4804, 4850, 4884, 4892, 4897, 4902-4903, 4918-4919, 4946, 4951, 4958-4959, 4965, 4983, 4984, 4987, 5004, 5012-5014, 5016, 5026-5027, 5029, 5040, 5058, 5072, 5094, 5102, 5117-5118, 5122, 5373, 5495, 5583, 5716, 5810, 5900, 5921, 5958-5959, 5967, 6084, 6113, 6225, 6445, 6507-6508, 6551, 6561, 6697, 6755, 6767, 6774, 6848-6850, 6868, 6867, 6900-6901, 7069-7070, 7100, 7194, 7410-7411, 8184, 8411, 8660
Ancient Period, Rome, 5975
Ancient Period, Trade, 6225
Andelson, R. V., 9013
Andersen, P. N., 1065-1066
Anderson, A., 3952
Anderson, B., 3161
Anderson, B. M., 3105
Anderson, C. W., 2915
Anderson, H. R., 1825
Anderson, J., 5467-5469
Anderson, K. L., 8907
Anderson, T. J., 707
Andersson, L. O., 1067
Andler, C. P. T., 2658
Andreades, A. M., 4884
Andreae, W. F., 1068
Andreano, R. L., 708, 3032
Andres Alvarez, V., 1069
Andrews, C. M., 7382
Andrews, E. B., 7383-7384
Andriessen, J. E., 1070
Andrimont, L., 7385
Angell, J. W., 3106-3107, 5151
Angers, F. A., 1071, 9889
Annales de Sciences Economique, Appliquees, 440
Annuity, 4352, 4427, 4521, 4629, 4634, 4725-4726, 6617
Annuity, Life, 6477, 6564, 6728
Anschutz, G., 5355
Ansell, C., 5473
Anstey, V., 1072

Anthology, 794
Anthropology, Economic, 4925, 4949, 5018-5019, 5049, 5069
Antoine, J. C. 1073
Antonelli, E., 13
Antonio, M., 1784
Aoyama, H., 2297
Apotheker, N., 9198
Apprentice, Contract, 8006
Aptheker, H., 9014-9015
Aquinas, T., 4885-4886, 4914, 4926, 4962-4963, 4991, 5036-5037, 5061, 5092
Arabian Countries, 2541
Arago, E., 7387
Aragon, 3964, 4973
Aramanovich, I. G., 3501
Araneda Dorr, H., 1074
Arbitration, Industrial, 8226, 8550, 8771
Arbuthnot, J., 3971-3972
Archbold, J. F., 7388
Archison, N., 5486
Archiv fur Sozialwissenschaft und Sozialpolitik, 3496, 8840, 8879, 9854
Arctic Regions, 6962
Ardant, A. G., 8299
Ardzrooni, 8994
Arena, C., 1075
Arendonk, J. A, 3503
Arendt, H., 4887
Arendt, O., 7389
Arensberg, C. M., 5068
Argellati, F., 3973
Argenson, Marquis, 2329, 5150
Argentina, 962, 1260, 2542-2543, 9473
Arguelles, C., 5477
Aris, R., 593
Aristophanes, 4941
Aristotle, 985, 4887, 4893-4894, 4968, 4969, 4981, 5005, 5008, 5039, 5050, 5108, 5130, 5928, 5956, 5958, 5987, 6551, 8382, 9340, 9729
Arithmetic, 6175
Arithmetic, Political, 4875
Arizawa, H., 1076
Arkin, H., 1818
Arkin, M., 2334
Arlidge, J. L., 7390
Armenia, 2453, 2996

Arms, 7338
Army, 4543, 6685
Armytage, W., 9016
Arnaune, A., 7391
Arnberg, J. W., 7392
Arndt, A., 14
Arndt, H., 1077
Arnhem Land, 5114
Arnold, A., 7393
Arnold, W. T, 7394
Arnou, A., 1078
Arnould, 5479-5480
Aromolaran, A., 1079-1080
Aron, R., 10026
Arreta de Monte-Seguro, A., 5481
Arriquibar, D. N., 3977
Arrivabene, J., 5482-5484
Arrow, K. J., 3108, 3504, 3849
Artisan, 4074, 4205, 4431, 6096, 6839
Artisan, Dictionary of, 7180
Arunachalam, A., 1081
Arup, E., 2606
Aschrott, P. F., 7395
Asgill, J., 3981, 3983
Ash, W. F., 9017
Asher, C. W., 7005
Ashley, J., 3984-3986
Ashley, Lord, 7136
Ashley, W. J., 1801, 2674, 4889, 5432, 7337, 7396-7398, 8823
Ashton, T. S., 816, 2788
Asia, 834, 2545, 2546, 4849, 5663, 6339, 6765
Asia, Colony, 6469
Asia, Southeast, 9605
Asiatic Society of Japan, 1897
Askew, J. B., 9272
Asobe, K., 3109, 9018
Aspelin, G., 9019
Asser, T. M. C., 15
Assiento, 3987
Assistance, Public, 7465
Assistance, Public, History of, 6541
Assize, 5489, 6790
Assize, Bread, 4398
Association Francaise de Science Economique, 5327
Associazioni Cristiane Lavoratori Italiani, 1082

Asua, L. J., 412
Athens, 5603
Atkins, W. E., 8908
Atkinson, C. M., 5564
Atkinson, E., 7400-7403, 8713
Atkinson, W., 5487-5488
Atlas, Commercial, 6703
Atlas, Political, 6703
Atlas, Statistical, 8748
Atskanov, M. K., 2955
Attlee, C. R., 9123
Attwood, G., 5489
Attwood, T., 5490
Auber, P., 5491
Aubert de Vitry, 5492
Aucoc, L., 7404-7405
Auction Duties, 1987
Aucuy, M., 184, 2637, 2640, 4118
Audiffret, M., 5493
Audiganne, A., 5494
Audigier, P., 16
Auger, A., 3988
Augier, 5495
August, J. G., 579
Aus Funfzig Jahren Deutscher Wissenschaft, 8888
Auspitz, R., 3111, 7407, 8212
Austin, B., 3067
Australia, 1991, 2471, 2547-2549, 8009, 8627, 9429
Australia, Colony, 6469
Austria, 2550-2556, 2668, 2685, 5298, 9089
Austria, Mercantilism, 5149
Austrian School, 2556, 3471, 3524, 9744
Austrian School, Romantic, 2521
Austrian Theory, 3172
Autobiography, 2341, 2401, 2478
Automobile, 3178
Autrichienne, Ecole, 9699
Auvert, E., 17
Aveling, E., 7408, 8703, 9173, 9367
Aveling, E. M., 9382, 9411
Avineri, S., 9020
Awuinas, T., 5086
Ayres, C. E., 1083-1084, 3507, 8909-8914
Ayres, E., 8908
Ayrton, S., 6542
Azmatullah, K., 1085

Azorin, F., 3479
Azuni, A., 5496-5497, 5924, 6489, 6768

Baasch, E., 2919
Baba, K., 3508
Babbage, C., 5498
Babeau, A., 7410-7411
Baden-Powell, H., 7412-7413
Baby, J., 1086
Babylonian Period, 5105
Babylonian Tables, 4915
Bach, G. L., 1087, 1162, 1592, 3509
Bachert, U., 2718
Bachik, Z, 1033
Bachman, V., 9659
Bachmann, H., 1088, 3112
Backman, J., 1408
Bacon, F., 2732, 2742
Bade, M., 3990
Bader, L., 983
Badham, C., 5499
Badouin, R., 3113
Baernreither, J. M., 7414
Baert, J. F. B., 5500
Baerwald, F., 3510
Baeteman, L. H. K. D., 2659
Bagehot, W., 709, 2722, 3511, 7278, 7416-7420, 8824
Baggs, S., 4799
Bagiotti, T., 3512, 9757
Bagley, W. C., 1089
Bagnall, W. R., 7421
Bagolini, L., 7279
Bahne, G., 9649
Bahr, F., 8825
Bahrfeldt, E., 7422
Baier, C. G., 1090
Baiga, 5047
Bailao, J. M., 2019
Bailey, M. J., 1091
Bailey, S., 3114, 3397, 5501-5505
Bailey, W., 3991
Bailly, A., 5508-5509
Bailments, Law, 7061
Baily, F., 5508-5509
Bain, J. S., 1092
Baines, E., 5510
Bajt, A., 1093-1094, 3115
Bakasova, R., 18
Baker, C., 3033

Baker, C. W., 7423
Baker Library, Harvard University, 126, 2395
Bakunin, M. A., 9021
Balance of Payments, 3226
Balance of Trade, 4173, 5165, 5269, 5307, 5478
Balchen, A. R., 7424
Bald, R., 5511
Baldasseroni, A., 5512
Baldwin, A. J., 19
Baldwin, H., 6022
Baldwin, J. W., 4891
Balek, S., 9022
Baletic, Z., 9023
Balfour, A. J., 7425
Balibar, E., 9009
Balinky, A., 9014
Ballaine, W. C., 3823
Ballivian, C., R., 1102, 2335
Ballod, C., 2674
Ballve, F., 1095-1096
Balogh, T., 1103, 9891
Balsamo, P., 5512, 5514
Balsley, H. L., 710, 1447
Baltra Cortes, A., 1097
Balue, 3142
Bamberger, L., 7426-7428
Banari Intertribal Market, 5097
Banasinski, A., 9308
Banco Nacional, 5662
Bancroft, G., 5515
Bancroft, H., 7429
Bandinel, J., 5516
Bandini, S. A., 3992
Bandt, J., 1098
Banfield, T. C., 5517-5518
Bangal, India, 6134
Bank, 1063, 2517, 3035, 3954, 4135, 4149, 4157, 4459, 4780, 5508, 5510, 5573, 5609, 5658, 5740, 5797, 5824, 5841, 5852, 6049, 6053, 6091, 6109, 6216, 6259, 6327, 6589, 6645, 6700, 6804, 6936, 6997, 7015, 7088, 7114, 7158, 7255, 7549, 7659, 7685, 8011, 8325, 8370, 8420, 8426, 8429, 8440, 8458, 8557,
Bank, Country, 6587, 6116
Bank, Europe, 5669
Bank, Industry, 6073
Bank, Joint Stock, 5882

Bank, National, 4020, 4551, 4636, 6170, 6854, 8720
Bank, Parish, 5933
Bank, Saving, 5471, 8205, 8598
Bank, Savings, 6717
Bank, Scotland, 8307, 8646
Bank, Specie Payments, 6668
Bank at Amsterdam, 6242
Bank Charter, 6071, 6688
Bank Charter Act, 7787
Bank in Ireland, 4502
Bank Notes, Depreciation, 6853
Bank Notes, Netherlands, 6905
Bank of England, 4050, 4322, 4370, 4663, 4722, 4745, 4750, 4843, 5450, 5461, 5522, 5624, 5758, 5768, 5813, 6147, 6159, 6403-6404, 6407-6408, 6419, 6587, 6648-6649, 6665, 6673, 6804, 6820, 6856, 7135, 7250, 7255, 7864, 8529, 8694, 8709
Bank of England, Bibliography, 8657
Bank of France, 6030, 8310, 8415
Bank of Naples, 6871
Bank of Napoli, 8705
Bank of North America, 8207
Bank of Scotland, 4363
Bank of Spain, 6522, 8218
Bank of the United States, 1819-1823, 2537
Bank Reform, 7137
Bank Restriction Bill, Great Britain, 6588
Bank Restrictions, 7112
Banker, 4824, 8475
Banker, Italian, 5081
Banking, 1762, 2260, 2355, 2400, 5052, 5081, 5450, 6111, 6130, 6395, 6481, 6612, 6669, 6747, 6968, 7082-7083, 7204-7205, 7251, 7511, 7525, 7653, 7700, 7785-7786, 7990, 8123, 8160, 8243, 8457, 8543, 8596, 8780
Banking, America, 6114
Banking, Commercial, 3035
Banking, Deposit, 5127
Banking, Free, 5936
Banking, Great Britain, 7784, 8429

Banking, History, 6112
Banking, History, Ireland, 6115
Banking House, 6049
Banking, Ireland, 7753
Banking, Joint Stock, 6116
Banking, Origins, 5081
Banking, Scotland, 6672, 7942
Banking, Statistics, 7784
Banking System, 7634
Banking, System, United States, 6078
Bankrupt, 4151, 4909, 5557, 6542
Banks, J. A., 8915, 9025
Bannefory, 5519
Banque de Hambourg, 5658
Bantu People, 4966
Banyai, M., 9026
Baran, P., 9027
Barba, A. A., 3993
Barbados, 4739
Barber, W. J., 20
Barberet, J., 7430
Barberi, B., 1104
Barbier, S., 3994
Barbieri, G., 21, 711, 1105
Barbon, N., 3995
Barbosa, D. M. V., 1099
Barbout, D., 7431
Barca, L., 9028
Barcelona, 5683, 5763
Barchiesi, G., 1482
Barclay, R., 7432
Bardey, E., 2336
Barding, T., 1361
Bargum, G., 5270
Bari, 2474
Barillatti, R. V. P., 1260
Baring, A., 5521
Baring, F., 5522-5523
Baring, F. T., 5846
Barish, N. N., 1100
Barjonet, A., 1101
Barker, E., 4892-4894, 4961
Barlet, E., 7433
Barnard, J., 3997, 4451, 4660
Barneaud, 5742
Barnes, R. J., 1106
Barnes, W. E., 7343
Barnett, P., 3034
Barois, J., 7435
Baron, 6227
Baron, S., 7436

Baron, S. W., 4896
Baronci, M., 2841
Barone, E., 1107, 3116
Barral, J. A., 7437
Barratt Brown, M., 1108
Barrault, H. E., 2733
Barre, R., 1109-1111
Barrere, Alain, 22-23, 1112-1113
Barri, T., 9029
Barrington, D., 2337
Barrington, R., 8824
Barron, S. L., 1232
Barros, A. B. B., 1114
Barth, H., 7280
Barth, T., 7438
Bartoli, H., 24-25, 1115
Barton, J., 2499, 5514-5517, 5525
Bartos, E., 26
Barzun, J. M., 9030
Bascome, E., 5528
Basford, F. A., 7005
Basinghen, A., 3998-3999
Basmann, R. L., 3513
Bast, J. H., 5152
Bastable, C. F., 2338, 7439-7441
Bastiat, F., 713, 2339, 5529-5534
Basu, P., 1116
Batbie, A. P., 7444
Bateman, T., 5535
Bates, J. A., 1117
Battaglia, F., 3514
Batvie, A. P., 7442-7443
Bauban, 5342
Baude, J., 3597
Baudeau, N., 4000-4006, 5328-5330
Baudhuin, F., 1118-1119
Baudin, J. P. L., 27, 714, 1120-1121, 2339, 2631
Baudrillart, H., 5537
Bauer, L., 1122
Bauer, O., 1123
Baumann, J. G., 7445
Baumol, W. J., 28, 601, 1032, 1124-1126, 3515, 3787, 9660
Baumsterk, E., 5153
Bax, E. B., 7337
Baxa, J., 29, 3118
Baxter, R. D., 7446-7448
Bayard, E., 7449

Bayard, E., 7449
Bayer, H., 1127
Bayle-Mouillard, 5544
Bayley, J., 5545
Bayne, A., 6737
Beach, C. F., 7450-7451
Beach, E. F., 3516
Beale, T., 5546
Bear, D. V. T., 3517
Bearde de L'Abbaye, 4007
Beardwood, A., 5154
Beaujon, A., 7452-7453
Beaumont, D., 4008
Beaumont, M., 6488
Beauregard, P., 7454
Beawes, W., 4009
Bebel, A., 7455
Beber, M. M., 9031
Bechaux, A., 7456
Bechaux, A. E. J., 2632
Becher, J. T., 5548-5549
Becher, S., 5550
Bechmann, T., 5552
Beck, C. H., 696
Becker, G. S., 3119
Becker, J., 2660
Becker, W., 9032
Beckford, W., 5553
Beckman, R., 2980
Beckwith, B. P., 1128, 3035
Beckwith, G., P., 30
Becu, R. Z., 271
Bedarride, J., 7457
Beddy, J. P., 3120
Beeke, H., 5554
Beer, A., 7458-7459
Beer, M., 2723, 4897, 5341 9033-9039
Bees, 6563
Bees, Fable of, 4422, 4485, 7316
Begando, J. S., 31
Begging, 4271
Behari, B., 2804
Behavior, Economic, 1495, 8908
Behavior, Functional Equations, 3353
Behrens, F., 3121, 3518, 9661
Behrens, H. H., 32
Bejar, J., 3479
Belgium, 136, 2557-2558, 5483, 5485, 5632, 6016, 6213, 7560, 7718, 7868, 7870, 8024, 8063,

8173, 8216, 8509, 8685, 8718
Bell, A., 5555
Bell, B., 5556
Bell, D., 9040
Bell, G. J., 5557
Bell, J. F., 33
Bell, Q., 9894
Bellamy, E., 9041-9042
Bellan, R. C., 1129
Belloc, A., 7460
Belloni, G., 5155-5156
Belloni, H., 5156
Belot, E., 7461
Belov, M. I., 5157
Below, G., 8826
Below, G. A. H., 2661-2662
Below, G. V., 7462
Beltle, T., 113
Beltran Florez, L., 35-35
Bemis, E. W., 7463-7464
Benares Hindu University, 5072
Benefit Society, 6825
Benefits, Unearned Economic, 1020
Benemy, F. W. G., 1131
Benett, J., 5559
Benevolence, 4598
Benezet, A., 4016
Bengal, 4709, 4835, 5559, 5769, 7153
Benham, F. C. C., 1132-1133
Benini, 712
Benn, E. J. P., 716
Bennathan, E., 2057
Bennet, J., 4017
Bennett, J., 5560
Bennion, E. G., 9895
Bentham, J., 2340, 2762, 5561-5565, 7337, 9043-9044
Bentzel, R., 2516
Bequet, L., 7465
Beranger, C., 9045
Berckum, J. J., 36
Berdiaev, N., 9046
Berdyaev, N., 9013
Berendis, E., 7466
Berendts, E. N., 2956, 5158, 5332
Berens, E., 7467
Berenyi, A., 463
Beres, E., 5566-5567
Bergasse, 5568

Bergier, N., 4019
Bergmann, E., 37, 7468
Bergson, A., 9047
Beri, S. G., 1577
Berkeley, 5190
Berkeley, G., 4020-4021
Berle, A. A., 720, 3036
Berlin, I., 9049
Berlin, P. A., 38
Berlin-Neubart, I. V., 39
Bernacer Tormo, G., 1135
Bernard, E., 4222
Bernard, H., 5825
Bernard, M., 40
Bernard, P. J., 9050
Bernard, R., 5570
Bernard, T., 5569
Bernard, T. H., 3493
Bernardelli, H., 9673
Bernardo, D., 4671
Bernardo, H., 1136
Berneri, M. L., 9051
Bernhard, R. C., 1137
Bernhardi, T., 5571
Bernier, F., 4849
Bernstein, A., 7470
Bernstein, E., 7471, 9052
Berrany, G. F., 6447
Bertagnoilli, C., 7472
Berthold, G., 7473
Bertillon, A., 7474
Bertillon, J., 7475
Bertini, M., 7476
Bertolini, A., 7477-7478
Bertolino, A., 2354, 5159
Besobrasoff, W., 7479
Bessaignet, P., 4898
Besse, L., 5572
Besson, J., 5629-5630
Bestor, A. E., 9053
Betjam-Edwards, 4871
Bettange, 4021
Bettelheim, C., 9054, 9142
Beugnot, 5573
Beutin, L., 41, 3519-3520
Beutner, 7480
Beveridge, W. H., 2341, 3521, 9896, 10001
Bevlen, T., 8964
Bewegung, 7481
Bezobrazov, V. P., 2608
Bhanage, B. S., 1138
Bhatnagar, K. P., 42, 10069

Bhattacharyya, S. K., 1139
Bianca, G. A., 3122
Bianchini, L., 43, 5573, 5575-5576, 5888
Biard, G., 9055
Bibikov, P. A., 7337
Bible, The Economics of, 4964
Bibliographical Bulletin of Current Marxology, 9056
Bibliographical Society of the University of Virginia, 2537
Bibliography, 446, 447, 484-485, 488, 556, 558, 594-596, 598, 609, 625-626, 687-689, 692, 694, 812, 816, 826, 840, 902, 908, 954, 982-985, 1000, 1033, 1124, 1147, 1162, 1184, 1204, 1257, 1265, 1302, 1338, 1344, 1370, 1400, 1421, 1449, 1469, 1480, 1514, 1564-1565, 1568-1569, 1605-1608, 1652, 1656, 1657-1658, 1748, 1766, 1804, 1856, 1873, 1888, 1890, 1914, 1987, 1993, 2037, 2066-2067, 2069, 2086, 2193-2194, 2247, 2296-2297, 2328, 2339, 2342, 2345, 2351, 2385, 2390, 2406, 2413, 2434, 2444-2445, 2451, 2453-2454, 2472, 2476, 2481, 2488, 2508, 2526, 2530, 2541, 2546, 2548-2549, 2551-2554, 2558, 2564-2565, 2567, 2572-2573, 2576, 2581, 2595, 2601, 2612-2613, 2634-2635, 2642, 2646, 2652, 2653, 2659, 2661, 2665-2666, 2669, 2675, 2681, 2699, 2702, 2711, 2717-2718, 2721, 2723-2724, 2726, 2729, 2733-2734, 2738, 2742, 2745, 2748, 2753, 2756, 2763, 2775, 2777-2778, 2780, 2786, 2788-2789, 2795, 2801, 2804-2805, 2807, 2814, 2825, 2829, 2832, 2834-2835, 2839, 2842, 2844, 2845, 2846-2849, 2853, 2855-2858, 2865, 2869, 2875-2876, 2879, 2881-2882, 2889-2890, 2892-2893, 2896-2898, 2905, 2907-2910, 2912, 2918-2921, 2926, 2933, 2937, 2944-2946, 2948-2949, 2954, 2960, 2965, 2974-2975, 2977, 2981-2983, 2986, 2989, 2991-2992, 2997-2998, 3001-3002, 3013-3015, 3030, 3032, 3034, 3036, 3041, 3045, 3050, 3054, 3059, 3063, 3065, 3070, 3071, 3073-3074, 3076, 3081, 3084-3085, 3089, 3107, 3110, 3118, 3147, 3153, 3168, 3174, 3192, 3215, 3218, 3249, 3255, 3279, 3284, 3287, 3403, 3414, 3417, 3431, 3497, 3493, 3508, 3514-3515, 3553-3554, 3567, 3573, 3584, 3605, 3613, 3643, 3672, 3680, 3702, 3727, 3734, 3735, 3745, 3784, 3787, 3806, 3810, 3823, 3830, 3831, 3841, 3866-3867, 3870, 3876, 3880, 3887-3888, 3892, 3907, 3917, 4078, 4687, 4908, 4920, 4951, 4953, 4972-4973, 4986, 5002, 5006, 5014, 5040-5041, 5055, 5068, 5081, 5092, 5099, 5103, 5112, 5118, 5120, 5122, 5150, 5154, 5162-5163, 5167, 5176-5178, 5181-5182, 5185, 5197, 5209, 5214, 5218, 5225, 5228, 5235, 5238, 5240, 5247, 5251-5254, 5258, 5263-5264, 5267, 5283, 5286, 5288, 5289, 5294, 5307, 5311, 5314, 5318, 5322, 5324, 5331, 5343, 5350, 5355-5356, 5360, 5362, 5373-5374, 5388-5389, 5392, 5396-5397, 5399, 5401, 5405, 5407, 5424, 5426, 5436-5438, 5442, 5844, 6420, 7297, 7342, 7343, 7366, 7502, 8839, 8847, 8848, 8864, 8894, 8908, 8914, 8925, 8927, 8931, 8937, 8940, 8949, 8964, 8989, 8994, 9003, 9017, 9018, 9030, 9047, 9048, 9050, 9058, 9060, 9070, 9099, 9100, 9119, 9121, 9126, 9130, 9138, 9144, 9148, 9150, 9152, 9195, 9204, 9215, 9244, 9245, 9247, 9250, 9253, 9285, 9299, 9303, 9309, 9318, 9332, 9334, 9343, 9406, 9417, 9430, 9438, 9448, 9473, 9477, 9489, 9524, 9564, 9576, 9592, 9595, 9604, 9610, 9615, 9620, 9643, 9646, 9661, 9665, 9696, 9705, 9709, 9728, 9739, 9742, 9798, 9802, 9830, 9836, 9898, 9907, 9914, 9916, 9917, 9922, 9931,

9932, 9933, 9935, 9937,
9939, 9940, 9941, 9953,
9956, 9964, 9968, 9976,
9986, 9989, 9993, 9994,
9999, 10005, 10006, 10007,
10009, 10010, 10015,
10016, 10017, 10018, 10019,
10020, 10025, 10026, 10030,
10031, 10034, 10035, 10036,
10041, 10044, 10045, 10046,
10061, 10066, 10069, 10072,
10073, 10081, 10083, 10085,
10089, 10090, 10091, 10094,
10095, 10101, 10104, 10107
Bibliography, A. Smith, 7294
Bibliography, Socialism, 8652
Biblioteca de Ciencias Sociales, Madrid, 1135
Biblioteca de Economia, 5275
Biblioteka Strucnih Izdanja, 1797
Bibliotheque d'Economie Contemporaine, 9721
Bibliotheque d'Economie Politique, 652
Bibliotheque de la Science Economique, 1073, 2646
Bicanic, R., 3091
Bichino, J.E., 5580
Bidermann, H. I., 5160
Biedermann, H. J., 7482
Biedermann, K., 5581
Bienengraber, A., 7483
Bieri, H. G., 9897
Biermann, W. E., 5161
Biesenbach, F., 3522
Bigelow, E. B., 7385, 7484
Bigelow, J., 4300
Bigland, R., 4022
Bigo, P., 9057
Bilas, R. A., 1140
Bilger, F., 2663, 2716
Bilhon, J. F., 5582-5583
Bilimovic, 5441
Bilinski, L., 7486-7488
Bill of Commerce, 4662
Bill of Exchange, 5652, 5738
Bills, Cash, 5545
Bills of Mortality, 4719
Bimetallism, 7403, 7425, 7701, 7903, 7907, 8162, 8170, 8241, 8524, 8743
Binder, H., 44

Bindon, D., 4024-4026, 4503, 4611
Bine, J., 7355
Bingham, R. C., 892, 3523
Biography, 1415, 2331, 2359, 2415, 2433, 8638
Biollay, L., 7489
Birbeck, W. L., 7490
Birbeck College, 981
Birch, W. G., 7491
Birmingham, Economists, 2735
Birmingham, England, Life, 8157
Birmingham, W. B., 1141
Birnie, A., 2609-2611, 2724
Birwood, G., 7492
Bisbee, L. H., 7493
Bischof, A., 7494-7495
Bischoff, J., 5584
Bisgaard, H. L., 2604
Bishop, J. L., 7496
Bishop, R. L., 966
Bishop of Cloyne, 4516
Bishop of Oxford, 5070
Bismark, 7725
Bittermann, H. J., 7281
Bitzer, F., 7497
Biven, W. C., 1142
Bjornsen, M. K., 1143-1144
Bjornson, G. B., 1145
Bjurling, O., 2972
Black, D., 4027
Black, R. D. C., 721, 763, 2834, 3123
Black, W., 4028, 5586
Blackett, B., 10001
Blackie, J. S., 7498
Blackstock, P. W., 9058
Blackwell, J., 4029
Bladen, V. W., 1146, 7282, 9808
Blair, W., 5586
Blaize, A., 5587
Blake, W., 5588-5591
Blake, W. J., 3166, 9059
Blake, W. P., 7500
Blanc, C., 7501
Blanc, H., 7502-7503
Blanc, L., 5590, 5591
Blanc de Volx, J., 5591
Blanchard, P., 7504
Blanche, A., 7507
Blane, G., 5592

Blanqui, J. A., 2612, 5593-5596, 5902, 7337
Blaug, M., 45, 2725-2726, 7337
Blaxton, J., 4030
Bledel, R., 46
Bliss, H., 5597-5598
Bliss, W. D. T., 8533
Blith, W., 4031
Bliumin, I. G., 47-51, 2727
Bloch, H. S., 9662
Bloch, M., 4899, 7506-7508
Block, 5901
Block, M., 52, 7747
Blodgett, R. H., 793, 1147, 1450
Blodig, H., 7509
Bloomsbury Group, 9894, 9972
Bloomfield, A. I., 5333
Blount, J., 3948
Blum, L., 9143
Blumin, I. G., 2957
Blumner, S. M., 722
Bluntschli, J. C., 7510
Board of Agriculture, 6834
Board of Trade, 5710
Boardman, F. W, 53
Boase, C. W, 7511
Bobbio, N., 9401
Bober, M. M., 9060
Boccardo, G., 54-55, 5601
Bochenski, J. M., 9062
Bockh, A., 5602
Boczar, K., 3124
Bodda, P., 56
Boddy, F. M., 1133, 1148
Bodeker, J., 3125
Bodin, J., 2648, 4032
Bodio, 7512
Boeckh, 5603
Boer, A. A. 9898
Boesnier, Orme, 4033-4034
Boffito, C., 9063
Bog, I., 5162
Bogen, J. I., 983
Boggie, C. A., 4053-4054
Bohatec, J., 4901
Bohle, C., 5163
Bohler, E., 1149
Bohm-Bawerk, E., 1150-1151, 3126-3129, 3428, 3451, 3524, 7513, 9064, 9234, 9663, 9666, 9773
Boileau, D., 5202, 5604, 6085

Boileau, E. 7515
Boisguillebert, P. P., 83, 2342, 4035-4036, 5152, 5278, 5301, 5341
Boislandry, L., 5606
Boissevain, G. M., 7516
Boissy d'Anglas, 5607, 5673
Boiteau, A., 7517
Boiteux, M., 1152
Boizard, 4037
Boizard, E., 7520
Bojanowski, V. V., 7521, 8374
Bojer, H., 3130
Bolivia Universidad, 520
Bolkestein, H., 4902
Bolles, A. S., 7522-7524
Bollman, E., 5608-5609
Bolshevism, 9516
Bolts, W., 4038
Bolza, H., 9899
Bompaire, F., 9667
Bonaparte, L., 9384
Bonar, J., 57, 723, 2728, 5164, 7283-7284, 7526-7528, 9064
Bonde, G. E., 2926
Bondi, G., 2664
Bondois, P., 2721
Bonds, Government, United States, 8135
Boner, J., 9809
Bongard, W., 3526
Bonham, Q., 7529
Boniecki, W., 307, 1153
Bonn, M. J., 724, 9981
Bonnar, G. A., 9417
Bonnassieux, P., 7530
Bonnemere, E., 5610
Bonner, G. A., 3344
Bonner, T. N., 58
Bonnet, A., 9756
Bonnet, V., 5613
Bonwick, H., 7531-7532
Book Keeping, 5614
Boole, G., 9705
Boot, J. C. G., 3863
Booth, A. J., 7533, 9065
Booth, B., 5614
Booth, C., 7534-7535
Borain, J., 7536
Borchardt, K., 3502
Borchardt, R. W., 59
Borchart, J., 9367

Bordewijk, H. W. C., 60
Bordier, A., 7537
Bordiga, A., 9066
Bordin, A., 1154
Borel, 5615
Borgatta, G., 833
Borges, J. F., 5616
Borie, V., 7538
Born, K. E., 2665
Borner, S., 9900
Bornitz, J., 5165
Bornot, C., 8716
Boroughs, J., 4039
Bortkiewicz, L., 9064
Bortot, P., 3527
Bos, H. C., 3871
Bosanquet, B., 7539
Bosanquet, C., 5616
Bosc, J., 5617
Boserup, M., 725
Bosher, J. F., 5335
Boson, M., 9668
Boston, 6814
Boswell, J. T., 2343
Botella, C., 7540
Botero, G., 4040
Bots, A. C. A. M., 61
Bottigelli, E., 9170
Bottomore, T. B., 9195, 9381, 9416
Botz, H., 3131
Bouchard, 4041
Bouchard, L., 7541
Bouchaud, M., 4903
Boucher, 5815
Boucke, O. F., 62, 1156
Boudeville, J., 2729
Boudeville, J. R., 229, 5336
Boudin, L. B., 9067
Bouet-Bolens, H., 7543
Bougainville, 4042
Boughton, J. M., 3776
Boukharine, N., 9674
Boulding, K. E., 63, 436, 1157-1158, 1752-1753, 3103, 3528-3530, 3745, 8916, 9810
Bourcier de Carbon, L., 1160
Bourdeau, Q., 7544
Bourgin, H., 9068
Bourinot, J. G., 7545
Bourne, H. R. F., 4463, 7547
Bourne, S., 7548
Bourthoumieux, C., 64, 5337

Bourva, J., 1648
Bousquet, G. H., 65, 726, 2460, 2842, 4903, 7337, 7549-7550, 9699-9670
Boutwell, G. S., 7551
Bouvier-Ajam, M. J., 66, 2633-2634, 8827-8828
Bouyssy, S., 2721
Bovet, E. D., 1161
Bowden, W., 2613
Bowditch, J., 727
Bowen, F., 5619
Bowen, I., 728
Bowker, R. R., 7552-7553
Bowley, A. L., 3132-3133, 3493, 3531, 7554-7556, 9671-9672, 9901
Bowley, A. Y., 3531
Bowley, M., 2344
Bowman, J. J., 67
Bowman, M. J., 1162, 5338
Bowring, J., 5620-5623, 9044
Boyd, W., 5523, 5624
Brachelli, H. F., 7557
Braddon, L., 4043
Bradfer, A., 729
Bradfield, R., 2207
Bradford, W. C., 1056, 1271
Braeuer, W., 2345, 2513
Braff, A. J., 1163
Brahmananda, P. R., 68
Brainard, H. G., 1164
Brainerd, J. G., 2657
Brameld, T. B. H., 9069
Branco, A. L. R., 771
Brand, J., 5625
Brand, T., 5608
Brandis, R., 1165-1166, 3532
Brandt, K., 1167-1168, 3533
Branson, W. H., 1169
Brants, V., 7559-7560
Brants, V. L. J. L., 4905-4906
Bras, G., 4907
Brasil, 2442
Brassey, T., 7561, 7562
Bravo, G. M., 9071
Bray, J. F., 414, 2353, 2766, 5626
Brazil, 1114, 2559-2562, 6936, 9482
Bread, 4529, 6790
Bread, Assize, 4398
Breesenko, D. P., 2991

Bregel, E. I., 2990
Brehmer, A., 5339
Brehon Code, 7563
Breit, W., 2346
Brelay, E., 7564
Bremmer, F., 7565
Bremond, J.-B., 5627
Brems, H., 1170, 2614
Brendis, E. N., 2971
Brenier, H., 9902
Brennan, M. J., 730, 1171, 1504
Brentano, L. J., 2698, 3415, 3534, 7566-7568, 8829-8832
Brereton, C. D., 5628-5629
Bresciani-Turroni, C., 1172, 3403
Bresson, J., 5628
Breton, J., 7569
Bretschneider, K. K., 5340
Brewis, T. N., 3536
Brewster, B., 9007
Brewster, F., 4044
Briavoinne, M., 5632
Brickwood, J., 5633
Bridges, G., 4045
Bridges, J. H., 5166, 5788
Bridgewater, Duke of, 4364
Briefs, A., 2178
Briefs, G., 69
Briefs, H. W., 3537
Briganti, F., 2869
Briggs, M., 1174
Bright, J., 5760
Brink, J. T., 2347
Brinkmann, C., 1175, 2730, 8833, 9981
Brisbane, A., 6059
Briscoe, J., 4049
Briska, R., 1177
Brisman, S. B., 1178
Bristed, J., 5635
British Academy, 7307, 7332
British Association for the Advancement of Science, 3845
British Economic Association, 3843
British Journal for the Philosophy of Science, 326
British Journal of Sociology, 8915
British Productivity Council, 3134

Brivazac, B., 5547
Brkic, N., 1179
Broadhurst, J., 5636
Brocard, L., 1180
Brochmann, B. D., 2926
Brodbeck, M., 814
Brodin, P., 3037
Brodnitz, G., 2652
Brodrick, G. C., 7570
Brody, A., 3670, 9073
Broggia, C. A., 2772, 4053-4054
Broich, F. V., 7571
Bromke, A., 2596
Bromley, J. H., 7572, 7592
Bronfenbrenner, M., 2874, 3135, 9074
Bronshtein, M. L., 3136
Brook, W. F., 2666
Brookings Institution, 731, 3330, 3592, 3819
Brooks, C., 2731
Brooman, F. S., 1181
Brough, W., 7573
Brougham, H., 5637
Broughton, T. R. S., 4951
Broulhiet, G., 1182
Browder, E. R., 9075, 9903
Brown, 5639
Brown, A. J., 1183
Brown, C. C., 2178
Brown, D. M., 4908
Brown, E. H. P., 1184, 3137, 9673
Brown, H. G., 3538
Brown, J., 4055-4057
Brown, J. E., 1185
Brown, R. W., 3038
Brown University, 730
Browne, A. L., 9076
Browne, W. A., 7574
Browne-Dignan, 5640
Browning, G., 5641
Bruce, J., 5642
Bruce, T. B., 8396, 9751
Bruce, T. W., 2348
Brucker, E., 2805
Brugelman, H., 71, 2667
Brugess, H., 5652
Brugmans, I. J., 72, 3138
Bruguier Pacini, G., 1186
Bruin, P. H., 1188
Brunhoff, S., 9077

Brunner, K. A., 3539
Brunnschweiler von Hauptwil, A., 7285
Brus, W., 1189-1190, 9078-9081
Brusca, V. E., 73
Bruton, H. J., 74
Bryan, E., 7575
Bryce, J., 7576
Bryce, T. T., 7577
Bryce, W., 7578
Brydges, Egerton, 5643
Bryson, J. A., 1059
Bubeck, C. H., 9904
Buber, M., 9082
Buchaillard, P., 1487
Buchanan, D., 5202, 5646, 5647, 7337
Buchanan, F., 5648,
Buchanan, G., 5649
Buchanan, J. M., 75
Buche de Pavillion, 4057
Bucher, A., 7579
Bucher, K., 8834-8835
Bucher, Z., 694
Buchere, A., 7580
Buck, N. S., 1380-1381
Buck, P. W., 5167
Buck, R. C., 3540
Buckingham, W. S., 76
Buckle, H. T., 7581
Buckley, H., 1191
Buckley, K., 1191
Buddist, 4958
Budge, S., 77
Budgell, E., 4059
Budget, 4060, 5479, 7832, 8647, 8659
Budget, France, 1273, 8805
Budget, National, 7130, 8346, 8363
Budinova, R., 78, 9175
Budish, J. M., 79, 2992
Budrys, D., 9084
Buenos Aires, 2349
Buindi, G., 7582
Buitendijk, B., 1192-1193
Bukharin, N. I., 80, 3139, 9085-86, 9422, 9674-9675
Bulajic, Z., 1194
Bulet, F., 5651
Bulgaria, 2563-2565, 2955
Bulgarian Communist Party, 3590
Buller, T. W., 5650
Bulletin du Centre d'Etudes des Pays de L'est, 219
Bullion, 4141, 4721, 4864, 5230, 5680, 5986, 6588, 6811, 6858
Bullion, Gold, 6905
Bullion, Price, 6853, 7104, 7264
Bullion Committee, 5616
Bullionists, 5920
Bullock, C., J., 732-733, 1195, 7286, 7583
Bulow, F., 1196, 2531, 7337
Bunge, N. K., 81
Bunke, H. C., 82
Bunte, P., 1197
Buquoy, G. G., 2511
Burchardt-Bischoff, A., 7584
Burdge, 8600
Burdon, R., 5486
Burford, R. L., 3543
Burges, Middle Ages, 5081
Burgin, M., 2543
Burgon, J. W., 5653, 6149
Burke, E., 2337, 4061-4062, 4817, 5654
Burks, R. V., 2615
Burn, D., 3544
Burn, R., 4063
Burnham, 9936
Burnley, J., 7585
Burns, A. E., 1198
Burns, A. F., 734, 8980, 9905
Burns, A. R., 769
Burns, E., 3344, 9087-9088, 9170, 9417, 9906
Burns, E. M., 8917
Burns, R., 5655
Burri, A., 7586
Burrish, O., 5064
Burstein, M. L., 1199
Burton, J. H., 1200, 5656,
Burtrel Du Pasquier, 4065
Burtt, E. A., 2732
Busch, J. G., 5657-5659
Bushill, T. W., 7587
Business, 151, 829, 894, 1221, 1357, 1416, 1520, 1728, 1737, 2330, 2739, 3039, 3492, 3677, 3966,
Business Cycle, 157, 430, 742, 863, 1135, 1451, 1678, 1728, 2027, 2556, 2668, 2765, 2767, 3033-3034, 3071, 3250, 3359, 3372, 3553, 3785, 3870, 4399,

5625, 5761, 6017, 6144, 6345,
6669, 6731, 7161, 7252, 7617,
7694, 7954, 8081, 8169, 8283,
8300, 8319, 8320, 8525, 8800,
8971-8972, 8980, 9513, 9571-
9572, 9645, 9797, 9938, 9944,
9945, 9947, 9974, 10001, 10023
Business Cycles, Austria, 2550
Business History Review, 5085
Business Literature, 126
Business Organization, 9842
But, I., 5659-5660
Butel-Dumont, 4066-4068, 6767
Butler, A. D., 772
Butler, J. G., 3141
Buttringer, J., 9089
Butts, I., 7588
Buxton, S., 7589
Bye, M., 229
Bye, R. T., 1201-1203
Byles, J. B., 7590
Byttner, A., 2488
Byzantium, 4895

Cabarrus, Conde de, 5661
Cabarrus, F., 5662-5663
Cacheux, E., 7591, 8333
Cademartori, J., 9090
Cadet, F., 83, 5341
Caffe, F., 84, 1204-1205, 9907
Cafiero, C., 9370
Cagnazzi, L., 5664
Cahiers de l'Institut de Science
  Economique Appliquee, 5395
Cahiers du Centre D'Etudes et
  de Recherches Marxistes, 9476
Cahiers Economiques, 508
Cahiers Internationaux de
  Sociologie, 678
Cahiers Vilfredo Pareto, 9934
Caillaud, M., 8919
Caird, J., 5665-5667
Cairncross, A. K., 735, 1206
Cairnes, J., 7592-7594
Cairnes, J. E., 85, 1107, 1208,
  2450, 3545,
Calcraft, J., 7340
Calculus, 7849
Calcutta Sanskrit College, 2828
Caldecott, A., 7595
Calderwood, J. D., 1209, 3819
Caletti, O., 9455
Calkins, R. D., 86, 3546

Callemer, R. S., 5168
Calmon, A., 7596
Calogero, G., 9091
Calonne, C. A., 5670-5673
Calude, D., 4118
Calver de Magalhaes, J., 2948
Calvez, J. Y., 9092
Camberalism, 7020
Camberlian, J., 7337
Cambreleng, 6815
Cambrick, 4467
Cambridge Curriculum, 9845
Cambridge Economic History,
  4907
Cambridge University, 741, 10048
Cambridge University, King's
  College, 9908
Cameralism, 2553, 2699, 4277,
  4600, 5153, 5196, 5228, 5270,
  5295, 5298, 5308, 5326, 6066-
  6067, 6318, 6337, 6618, 6883
Cameron, B., 9909
Campbell, 4077
Campbell, D. F., 7090
Campbell, E. W., 1210
Campbell, G. D., 7597
Campbell, I., 4069
Campbell, J., 4070, 4809
Campolongo, A., 1211, 7337,
  9989
Campomanes, P. R., 3963
Campomanes, R., 4071-4076
Campos, A. A., 3142
Campos, R. de O., 87
Canada, 1129, 1191, 2566-2567,
  3071, 3536, 7545, 7578,
  8497, 9889
Canadian Journal of Economics
  and Political Science, 3686
Canal, 6725, 7073
Canal de Languedoc, 5891
Canal de Panama, 8811
Canal de Suez, 8195
Canara, 5648
Canard, N. F., 1212, 5677
Candolle-Boissier, A., 5678-
  5679
Canaan, E., 89, 736, 1213,
  2733, 3143-3144, 3547-3548,
  7337-7338, 7344, 7598-7602,
  8944, 9811
Canning, 6270, 7022
Canning, G., 5680

Cannon Law, 4885-4886
Cans, Baron de, 6087
Cantillon, R., 702, 1214, 4078, 5191, 5299
Cape of Good Hope, 6867
Capefigue, J., 5681
Capital, 907, 1151, 1170, 1273, 1376, 1756, 2002, 2556, 2722, 3085, 3193, 3215, 3251, 3258, 3278, 3324, 3362, 3449, 3451, 3468, 3481, 3618, 5954, 6233, 6568, 6876, 7097, 7218, 7235, 7251, 7497, 7513, 7629, 7909, 7924, 8005, 8090, 8266, 8381, 8404, 8408, 8514, 8550, 8678, 8691, 8693, 8798, 9008-9010, 9027, 9076, 9139, 9154, 9169, 9172, 9176, 9185, 9226, 9335, 9353, 9367-9370, 9394, 9408, 9496, 9519, 9523, 9542, 9544, 9609, 9632, 9634, 9654, 9663, 9712, 9734, 9771, 9799, 9825
Capital, Accumulation, 5617, 5702, 9929
Capital, Fund, 4377
Capital, Human, 358, 3119
Capital, Marginal Efficiency, 9927
Capital, National, 4374
Capital, Physical, 3035
Capital, Positive Theory, 9665
Capital Unproductive, 6233
Capitalism, 148, 176-177, 198, 343, 816-817, 1151, 1940, 1966, 2028, 2162, 2417, 2617, 2666, 2687, 2698, 2731, 2761, 2846, 3010, 3051, 3058, 3061, 3066, 3068, 3181, 5106, 5148, 7513, 7720, 8223, 8521, 8573, 8868, 8892, 8898, 8901, 8928, 9027, 9066, 9165, 9206, 9255, 9389, 9537, 9545, 9546, 9554, 9575, 9623, 9661, 9663, 9636, 10060
Capitalism, Corporate, 740
Capitalism, Legal Foundations, 3164
Capitalism, Managerial, 1748
Caplan, N., 3282, 9271
Capmani, A., 5682-5683
Capodaglio, G., 90-91, 1215, 2843
Cappelli, L., 619
Cappo, E., 5684

Cappuccio, A., 1216-1217
Carballo y Wanguemert, B., 5685
Cardascia, G., 5042
Cardenos de, 7603
Cardonnel, A., 5686
Cardozo, J. N., 2350, 2425
Cardwell, E., 5687
Carell, E., 1218
Carey, H. C., 1219, 2414, 3083, 5688-5693, 8015, 8096
Carey, L. J., 2351
Carey, M., 5693
Carey, R. L., 2352
Carli, F., 92
Carli, G. R., 4079
Carli, G-R., 4839
Carlier, L'Abbe, 4080
Carlin, E. A., 93
Carlson, R. J., 3081
Carlson, V., 1220
Carlton, F. T., 1221
Carmichael, G., 2509
Carmichael, J., 9093
Caro, L., 7604
Carpio, F. V., 6240
Carr, H. J., 2353
Carreiro, C. P., 1222
Carrel, J., 1223
Carreno, A. M., 1224
Carrera Pujal, J., 94-95
Carreras y Gonzalez M., 7605
Carriage, 5975
Carriage, Wheel, 4688
Carrion-Nisas A., 5694
Carro, 4975
Carroll, W. G., 8079
Carte, R., 4450
Carte, T., 4309
Cartel, 8134
Carter, A. P., 3860
Carter, C. F., 1225, 3609
Carter, W., 4081
Carter, W. H., 1226-1227
Carthage, 3963, 6774, 6848
Cartwright, E., 5695
Carus-Wilson, E. M., 5179
Carver, T. N., 1228-1229, 3549, 7606-7607
Cary, J., 4084-4087
Casanova, L., 7608
Casaregis, 4088

Casas Grieve, L. F. de Las., 96
Casauz, L. F. G., 5699
Causuz, C., 5698
Cascarini, J. M., 2039
Case, 706, 1056, 1526, 1854, 2268
Casper, W., 5169
Cassagnac, A. G., 5700
Cassandro, G., 4910
Cassel, G., 766, 1230-1232, 3146, 5347, 9798, 9910
Cassidy, F. P., 4911
Castaneda, J., 3550
Castelain, I., 3147
Castelain, L., 97
Castelot, E., 98
Castillo, A. V., 5170, 5241, 5249
Castro, A., 1234
Castro, A. B., 1233
Castro, D., 1235
Castro, J-F., 4097
Castro Ruz, F., 2602
Catalina, Spain, 5707
Catalonia, Banking in, 5126
Catchings, W., 3039
Catherwood, B. F., 2734, 3148
Catholic Social Thought, 144
Catholic University of America, 150, 2393, 5052, 5086
Catholicism, 2677
Catholicism, Modern Social, 2475
Cathrein, V., 7609
Catlin, W. B., 99
Cato, 4975
Cattaneo, C., 2354, 7610
Cattle, 3934, 4375
Cauley, T. J., 1236, 3040
Causzux, 5696-5698
Cauwes, P., 7611
Cavagenari, V. W., 7612
Cayley, E. S., 5702-5703
Cazenove, J., 5704
Cazes, B., 1237
Cecchella, A., 3149
Cecilio, J., 2519
Celestin, F. J., 5705
Celt, 6847
Census, 5706-5707
Census, Great Britain, 6714

Census, United States, 7156
Center of Planning and Economic Research, 3908
Centre Culturel International de Cerisy-La-Salle, 9176
Centre D'Econometrie, 3366
Centre D'Etudes Economiques, Paris, 505, 531, 3241
Centre D'Etudes et de Recherches Marxistes, 2633-2634, 9094, 9207
Centre de Documentation Universitaire, 9216
Centre National de la Recherche Scientifique, 3302
Centro de Economia e Financas, Portugal, 3624
Centro di Studi Filosofici Cristiani di Gallarate, 737
Centro Italiano di Studi sull'Alto Medioevo, 4912
Century, Twentieth, 516-517
Cepede, M., 2635
Ceretti, 4100
Cerne, F., 1238-1240, 3150, 9095
Cernuschi, H., 7613-7614
Cesar, J., 6378
Ceskoslovenska Akademie ved v Academii, 3606
Cetti, C., 100
Ceylon, 5874, 6690
Ch'ien, I., 2616
Ch'oe, H., 1257, 1259
Ch'oe, K., 9102
Ch'oe, M., 116, 7337
Ch'oe, N., 1258
Chabrol, 6773
Chadwick, E., 2383
Chaianov, A. V., 9096
Chailley, J., 7615, 8376
Chaineau, A., 3151
Chalk, A. F., 101
Chalmers, 7337
Chalmers, E. B., 1241
Chalmers, G., 5708-5711
Chalmers, J. A., 1246-1247
Chalmers, T., 5712-5714
Chamber of Commerce, 6620, 6781
Chamber of Commerce, Normandie, 6374
Chamber of Commerce of the

Author and Subject Index 629

United States of America, 738, 3041, 3152
Chamberlain, N. W., 102, 1243
Chamberlayne, E., 4102
Chamberlen, H., 4104
Chamberlin, E., 3153, 3154
Chamberlin, E. H., 3302, 3305, 9676, 9733
Chambers, E. J., 3353
Chambers, P., 829
Chambers, R., 7616
Chambers, R. W., 9097
Chambre, H., 9098, 9153
Chamley, P., 9911
Chancellor of the Exchequer, 9991
Chand, M., 1779
Chand, T., 1244
Chandler, L. V., 1126, 1245, 2355
Chang, H., 5171
Chang, K. L., 2260
Chang, S. H., 9100
Chang, Y., 103
Change, 1199
Change, Cultural, 1084
Change, Economic, 3701, 8774
Change, Economic, 928
Change, Economics, 1605
Changer of Commerce, 1071
Channing, F. A., 7617
Channing, W. E., 5717
Chao, L., 1246-1247, 3155
Chao, N., 2356, 8918
Chao, T., 3157
Chapin, A. L., 7618
Chapin, H. L., 7227
Chapman, M. W., 6471
Chaptal, 868
Chaptal, C., 5718
Charbonnaud, R., 2357
Chargueraud, A., 7619
Charity, 4190, 4555, 4720, 5934
Charity, American, 8753
Charity, Public, France, 6300
Charles II, 4309
Charlety, S., 9101
Charlier, E. D., 2911
Charter, 4105-4106, 4360, 8666
Charter, Bank, 6071, 6665, 6688

Charter, Bank of England, 7135
Charter, Company, 6654, 7003
Charter, Corporate, 5642
Charter of Justice, 5747
Charter of Nations, 5935
Chartist Movement, 2639, 7883
Chase, S., 104
Chassipol, M., 4107, 4913
Chastellux, Conte de, 4177, 5720
Chataway, H. D., 105
Chateauneuf, B., 5721, 5722
Checkland, S. G., 2735
Chen, J., 3551
Chen Huan-Chang, 2569
Cheprakov, V. A., 3042
Cherbuliez, 6461
Cherbuliez, A-E., 5723-5726
Chernyshevskii, N. G., 2736
Chessa, F., 1248-1250
Chesterton, G. K., 4914
Chevalier, J., 106
Chevalier, M., 2423, 5727-5734, 9460
Chevallier, E., 7620-7621
Chevrot, J. N., 1251
Cheysson, E., 7622
Chiang, A. C., 3554
Chiang, H., 9912
Chiang, K-S, 2570
Chichester, E., 5735
Chiera, E., 4915
Chigusa, Y., 107, 1252-1253, 2358
Chikaraishi, S., 108
Child, J., 4109-4112, 4806, 5220, 5244
Children, 6622, 6765-6766, 6832. 8793
Childs, M. W., 2973
Chile, 1074, 2568, 5456, 9090
Chin, S., 1254-1255
Chin, T., 109
China, 2569-2585, 3384, 4216, 5370, 5374, 5413, 5736, 5873, 6164, 6423, 6584, 7201
China, Ancient, 2578, 5012
China, Ninth Century, 3950
China, People's Republic, 2586-2595, 2589, 9150, 9201, 9343, 9593
Chinard, G., 5342, 5361
Chisholm, G., 7623
Chitty, J., 5737-5739

Chivalry, Economic, 9851
Chlebikova, M., 3555
Chmielewicz, K., 3556
Cho, C., 1256
Cho, J., 111, 112
Cho, K., 110
Cho, M., 2737
Cho, S., 113
Cho, T., 114
Choart, G., 3988
Chodkiewicz, A., 4916
Chodkiewicz, Z., 115
Choice, 75
Choice, Economic, 6038
Choice, Theory of, 3236
Chomel, 4113
Chong, Yak-Yong, 2907
Chotanagpur, 5097
Choumanides, L. T., 117-118
Christ, C. F., 3557
Christ, W., 119
Christenson, C. L., 767, 1355
Christian, E., 5740
Christiani, G., 4114
Christianity, 147, 2687, 2761, 5075, 9197, 9653
Christians, W., 7624
Christie, W. D., 5741
Christoffel, T., 740
Christophersen, R. I., 225
Chronicle, University of California, 5342
Chu, C., 3158
Chuprov, A. I., 120-21
Church, 2677, 4486, 4782
Church Property, 5923
Churchill, W., 9980
Chydenius, A., 5172, 5245
Cibrario, G. A. L., 4917
Cibrario, L., 5742
Ciccone, A., 7626
Ciccotti, E., 936
Cicero, M. T., 4918
Cichero, M. A., 1260
Cicilia, J., 5743
Cider, 3943
Cieszkowski, A., 5744
Cipolla, C. M., 4919
Circulation, 5744
Circulation, Medium, 6158
Citizen, 1889
City, 4041, 4098, 4116, 7183
City, Problems, 8780

Civil Service, 7794
Civil War, Pre, 1944
Civilization, 4919, 6166, 7697, 7732, 8836
Civilization, American, Economic Mind in, 3048
Civilization, England, 7581
Civilization, Industrial, 3900
Civilization, Modern, 4979
Civilization, New, 9639
Civilization, Primitive, 5095
Civilization, Western, 650, 5183
Claeys, R. H., 122
Clamageran, J. J., 7627
Clapham, J. H., 741, 3558
Clare, G., 7628
Clarendon, R. V., 5746
Clark, C., 5747
Clark, C. G., 3848
Clark, G. N., 2738
Clark, H. F., 1261
Clark, J. B., 764, 824, 1262-1263, 2412, 3159, 3160, 3559-3560, 3561-3562, 7265, 7629-7632, 8525, 9513, 9677-9678, 9718, 9785
Clark, J. G. D., 4920
Clark, J. J., 742
Clark, J. M., 123, 743-746, 1017, 2412, 2874, 3076, 3161-3163, 3195, 3563, 3564, 3565, 7276, 8919, 8920-8922
Clark, M. H., 5748
Clark, V. S., 2359
Clark, W., 4117
Clarke, T. C., 7633
Clarkson, T., 5750
Class, 6143, 7253, 8256, 8677, 9213, 9842
Class, Antagonism, 9125
Class, Idle, 7097
Class, Industrial 7815
Class, New, 9132
Class, Productive of Wealth, 6740
Class, Rural, 5913, 7560
Class, Social, 9476, 9502
Class, Struggles, France, 9373
Class, Working, 6322, 6566, 6575, 6927, 7203, 7408, 9168, 9511, 9591
Class, Working, History of, 9215
Class, Working, Rights of, 6373

Classburner, B., 9818
Classen, E., 1021, 9798
Classical Period, 575, 5444-7267
Classicism, Newtonian, 278-279, 7302
Classics, 1024
Claviere, M., 5751
Clay, H., 1264, 10001
Clay, J., 5752
Cleaveland, J., 7634
Cleeve, B., 4119
Clegg, I. E., 5064
Cleghorn, J., 5753
Cleirac, E., 4120
Clemence, R. V., 748, 969, 1265, 2292
Clement, A., 7635-7636
Clement, M. P., 5173-5174
Clement, P, 5754-5756
Clercq, P. H., 7637
Clergy, 6252, 6601
Clergy, Catholic, 6973
Clifford, J. L., 7287
Cliquot de Blervache, 4121-4123
Closon, F. L., 2360
Cloth, 4048, 4228
Clower, R. W., 1344, 9689
Coal, 4233, 4517, 5976, 7853, 8074, 8098
Coal, Duty, 5486, 6422
Coal Trade, 5511
Coats, A. W., 5175, 8923
Cobb, A. S., 7638
Cobbenhagen, M. J. H., 2361
Cobbett, W., 2363, 5757, 5758, 6512
Cobden, R., 2443, 5759-5761, 7399
Cobden Club, 7369-7641, 8464
Cochin, A., 7642
Cochin, China, 5857
Cochrane, J. L., 3081, 9913
Cocker, W. H., 972
Code de Commerce, 5762
Code Noir, 4124
Coeln, F., 5764-5765
Coen, G., 7643
Coene, E., 2550
Coenen, E., 2668
Coeur, J., 5010
Coffee, 6569
Coffinieres, A. S. G., 5766

Cognette, M. S., 7644-7647
Cognetti, F., 1266
Cogniot, G., 2634
Cohen, B., 5767
Cohen, B. L., 1267
Cohen, G, 5064
Cohen, J., 9409
Cohen, M., 742
Cohen, V., 1268
Cohen, W., 5768
Cohn, G., 124-125, 1269, 3566 7650,
Cohn, N., 9104
Coin, 3942, 4117, 4138, 4281, 4349, 4358, 4437, 4495, 4565, 4654, 4672, 4735, 4737, 4743, 4779, 4834, 4845, 5433, 6327, 6387, 6968, 7150, 7178, 7651
Coin, Ancient, 3972, 6697
Coin, Copper, 4477, 4738
Coin, Gold, 4739
Coin, Ireland, 4724, 4274, 4736
Coin, Silver, 4241, 4473, 4542, 4635, 4741-4742, 4792, 6187, 6501, 8004
Coin, Tables of, 4280
Coinage, 3996, 4567, 4668, 4739, 4741, 4834, 5029, 5104, 5687, 6501, 6900-6901, 7112, 7651, 8008
Coinage, Ancient, 5687
Coinage, Europe, 8008
Coinage, India, 8465
Coinage, International, 7416
Coinage, Scottish, 5686
Coinage, Silver, 7953-7954
Coit, S., 7652
Coke, R., 4125-4126
Colarusso, A., 1270
Colberg, M. R., 1056, 1271
Colbert, 4431, 5166, 5173-5174, 5176, 5178, 5232, 5248, 5256, 5273, 5289-5290, 5293, 6313, 7827
Colbert, J. B., 5258-5260
Colbertism, 5258-5260, 6493
Cole, A. H., 126, 967, 2362
Cole, C. L., 127
Cole, C. W, 5176-5178
Cole, G. D. H., 128-129, 747, 749-750, 1272, 2362, 9105-9111

Cole, M., 2362
Colebrooke, H. T., 5769
Coleman, D. C., 5179-5181
Coleman, J. R., 966, 2533
Coleman, R. W., 3044
Colin, A., 2650
Colins, A. H., 5770
Colins, J. G. C. A. H., 130, 2636
Collected Works, 697-1028, 2674, 2710, 2817, 3817, 5277, 5775, 5878, 5889, 7049, 7318, 8931
Collective, 920, 2740, 5148, 8185
Collectivism, 2430, 7799
College of France, 5729
College of Glasgow, 2446
Colley, T. M., 7670-7671
Collingswood, R. G., 4951
Collins, C. M., 7653
Collins, H., 9112
Collins, J., 4129
Collyer, F., 5777
Colmeiro, M., 5778, 7654-7656
Colodny, G., 10026
Colonial Doctrine, 2638
Colonial Question, 9582
Colonial Theories, Great Britain, 5237
Colony, 239, 2973, 2922, 4018, 4036, 4124, 4153, 4236, 4285, 4571, 4589, 4590, 4621, 4821, 4823, 5262, 5364, 5527, 5547, 5710, 5711, 5774, 5806, 5860, 6007, 6013, 6227, 6262, 6339, 6377, 6499, 6556, 6615, 6653, 6772, 6885, 6988, 7028, 7034, 7069, 7130, 7178, 7220, 7335, 7537, 7595, 7729, 7737, 7791, 7873, 8411, 8412, 8479, 8553, 8878
Colony, American, 4143, 4815, 5201, 5234, 7237, 8428
Colony, France, 8727
Colony, Germany, 8706
Colony, Great Britain, 4456, 5979, 6151, 6469, 6751, 7042, 7531, 7616
Colony, Greece, 6867
Colony, Labor, 8788
Colony, Sugar, 4433, 6751
Colouhon, P., 5779-5780

Colson, C., 1273, 7657
Colton, C., 1274, 5781
Colton, R. R., 1818
Columbia, 2592-2595
Columbia University, 196, 458, 827, 2180, 2425, 2569, 2670, 2681, 2792, 3049
Colwell, S., 5782
Comber, W. T., 5783
Combination Laws, 6796
Combinations, Labor, 7138
Commentaries, Economic, 960
Commerce, 55, 143, 893, 932, 935, 965, 1063, 1214, 1291, 1509, 1511, 1820, 2741, 2759, 3921, 3922, 3947, 3952, 3954, 4001, 4003, 4017, 4064, 4070, 4073, 4076, 4088, 4097, 4109, 4111, 4122-4124, 4133, 4151, 4155-4156, 4191, 4195, 4198, 4219, 4225, 4237, 4245, 4246, 4283, 4284, 4286, 4289, 4313, 4318, 4319, 4357, 4378, 4402, 4403, 4411, 4435, 4441, 4457, 4460, 4498, 4503, 4504, 4508, 4513, 4518, 4522, 4539, 4545, 4546, 4558, 4562, 4581, 4602, 4609, 4611, 4618, 4633, 4644, 4656, 4657, 4671, 4677, 4680, 4685, 4686, 4703, 4729, 4762, 4790, 4796, 4800, 4814, 4826, 4828, 4830, 4844, 4848, 5155, 5156, 5233, 5310, 5391, 5465, 5478, 5480, 5521, 5568, 5582, 5599, 5606, 5618, 5623, 5683, 5709, 5710, 5739, 5749, 5763, 5769, 5784, 5786, 5792, 5794, 5850, 5868, 5902, 5940, 5946, 5948, 5956, 5969, 5979, 6013, 6039, 6050, 6106, 6164, 6171, 6185, 6196, 6210, 6222, 6284, 6302, 6311, 6370, 6417, 6423, 6424, 6436, 6463, 6493, 6494, 6539, 6554, 6583, 6600, 6604, 6620, 6621, 6625, 6629, 6651, 6655, 6700, 6710, 6714, 6716, 6742, 6763, 6776, 6784, 6798, 6815, 6817, 6851, 6861, 6887, 6897, 6924, 6936, 6984, 7023, 7028, 7047, 7058, 7140, 7160, 7178, 7185, 7194, 7237, 7241, 7254, 7381, 7519, 7530, 7547, 7574, 7643, 7710, 7712, 8154,

Author and Subject Index 633

    8436, 8663, 8812, 8813, 9045,
    9844
Commerce, Africa, 6708
Commerce, America, 5663, 6708
Commerce, Ancient, 6113
Commerce, Dictionary, 6935
Commerce, English, 4191, 5182,
    7708, 8837
Commerce, Europe, 6708
Commerce, Fluctuations, 7252
Commerce, Foreign, 6272, 8787
Commerce, Foreign, United
    States, 5449
Commerce, France, 4080, 5591,
    8165, 8273,
Commerce, Grain, 6362, 6514
Commerce, Great Britain,
    7131, 7266, 8198
Commerce, History, 4361, 5886
Commerce, Indes, 6708
Commerce, India, 5855
Commerce, Internal, 7374
Commerce, Interstate, United
    States, 8493
Commerce, Nations, 7439
Commerce, Orient, 4003, 6511
Commerce, Spain, 6351
Commerce, Treaty of, 7189
Commercial, 8726
Commercial Association, 7871
Commercial Crises, 8081
Commercial Law, 4009, 5815,
    5845, 6279, 6432
Commercial Policy, 5266, 5647
Commercial Policy, History of,
    6786
Commercial Regulations, 5906
Commercial Regulations, Great
    Britain, 6634
Commercial Revolution, 5273
Commercial System, 5731
Commercial Towns, 7182
Commercial Treaty, 6224
Commercial Union, Prussian, 5622
Committee on Principles of
    Economics, 1275
Commons, J. R., 1276, 3164,
    8924, 8925, 8926-8930, 8948,
    8958, 8964, 8973, 9100
Commons, Land, 4785
Commonwealth, Ideal, 9254
Communaute Europeenne du
    Charbon et de l'Acier, 9914

Communication, 6696, 7881
Communism, 47-51, 79, 333,
    2281, 2588-2591, 2596, 2615,
    2992, 3092, 3136, 7037, 7542,
    7799, 8652, 8802, 9046, 9062,
    9066, 9069, 9150-9151, 9212,
    9232, 9239, 9249, 9265, 9275,
    9285, 9356, 9374, 9444, 9449,
    9463, 9517, 9528, 9536, 9540,
    9547, 9584, 9598, 9993
Communism, Bibliography, 9247
Communism, History, 7066
Communism, Japanese, 9309
Communism, Soviet, 9639
Communist, 2309, 8371
Communist Countries, 2596-2600
Communist International, 9112
Communist International Eco-
    nomics, 9643
Communist Manifesto, 9302,
    9310, 9369, 9374, 9375, 9386,
    9574
Communist Movement, Chinese,
    9556, 9592
Communist Movement, Japan,
    9541
Communist Party, Uruguay, 9424
Communities, 7098
Communities, American, 9236
Compagnie des Indes, 4003, 4214,
    5388
Compagnie des Index, 4536
Company, Constitution of, 5491
Company of Merchants of Great
    Britain, 3942
Company of Merchants of
    London, 4549, 4951
Company of Scotland, 4311
Company of Stationers, London,
    4106
Comparison in Economic Theory,
    653
Compere-Morel, A. C. A.,
    9113
Competition, 786, 849, 888, 2410,
    9832
Competition, Ethics, 3293
Competition, Free, 9875
Competition, Imperfect, 3183,
    3407, 9769
Competition, Monopolistic, 3305,
    9676, 9733
Compsowicz, L., 7930

Compton, R. T., 776
Computer Simulation, 3776
Comstock, Alzada, 913
Comte, A., 5787-5788
Comte, C., 5789-5790
Conaccalam, K. S., 131
Conan, J., 5439
Conant, C. A., 7659
Concepts, Moral, 9017
Concile de Francfore, 4701
Conciliation, Industrial, 7695
Conde, M., 1277
Conder, J., 5791
Condillac, E., 5792-5796, 7348
Conditions, Economic, 1944
Conditions, Social, 2953, 2959, 6324
Condliffe, J. B., 752
Condorcet, D. B., 2654
Condorcet, M. J. A., 5793-5796
Conduit, J., 4138
Condy, Raguet, 5797
Conference, 3567, 3680, 9763
Conference, Institutional Economics, 8946
Conference, Karl Marx, 9255
Conference, Marxian, 9591
Conference, Socialism, 9473, 9486, 9551
Conflict, 1918, 1919, 2477
Confucianism, 2569, 2572
Congard, R. P., 3165
Congress, United States, 8814
Congress of Learned Societies, 5348
Congresso Braisileiro dos Economistas, 2559
Congreve, W., 5798
Conigliani, C. A., 7660-7661
Coninage, 7113
Connecticut Academy, 3216
Conrad, E. J., 132-133, 7662-7664, 7988
Conserva, G., 1278
Conservatism, 8935
Considerant, V., 5799-5804
Conspiracy, 2961
Constancio, F. S., 6125, 6859
Constitution, 7743, 7933
Constitution, Colonial, 7691
Constitution, English, 7692
Constitution, Natural, 5408
Construction, 3965

Consul, 5762, 6003, 8499
Consul, Functions, 5615
Consulate, 7090
Consume, Propensity to, 10077
Consumer, 1108, 2657, 5338, 8438
Consumer Behavior, 9925
Consumer Surplus, 911
Consumer's Demand, 3370
Consumer's Rent, 3200
Consumer's Surplus, 3145, 3332, 3352, 3483, 9822-9823, 9859
Consumption, 151, 1459, 1532, 1741, 1873, 2048, 2231, 5702, 5722, 5870, 6070, 6144, 6289, 8308
Consumption, Function, 224, 3236, 9931
Consumption, Law of, 5475
Conte, A., 5787-5788
Contemporary Economic Thought, 8963
Contraband, 7151
Contract, 5739
Contracts, 1244
Contradictions, Economic, 6735
Control, Judicial, 5346
Control, Market, 2588
Controversy, 231, 790
Contzen, K. W. H., 134, 7665
Convert, F., 7666
Conzalez de Linares, G., 7
Conze, W., 7351
Cook, J., 5817
Cook, W. R., 2078
Cook, W. W., 7667-7668
Cooke, D., 9132
Cooke, E., 5818-5819
Cooke, L., 5820
Cooley, T. C., 6228, 7669
Coombes, D., 2739
Coons, A. E., 1279
Coontz, S. H., 3166
Cooper, C. P., 5821
Cooper, T., 2534, 5822-5823
Cooperative, 196, 559, 1011, 2657, 2756, 7463-7464, 7957, 8104, 8148, 8438, 8452, 8614
Cooperative, Social, 7788
Cooperative, Western United States, 8754
Coote, H. C., 7672
Cope, R., 7673
Copeland, M. A., 99, 1004, 3045,

3568, 8931, 9915
Copland, D. B., 2547
Copyright, 5644, 5741, 6120
Coq, P., 5824, 5825
Coquelin, C., 5826
Corbet, T., 5828
Corbino, E., 1280
Cordasco, F., 7294
Cordier, J., 5829
Corn, 4115, 4375, 4613, 4684, 4727, 4759, 4872, 5461, 5525, 5702, 5771, 5927, 6063, 6133, 6167, 6840, 6852, 7236
Corn, Consumption, 5875
Corn, Foreign, 6426, 7078
Corn, France, 8510
Corn, Free Trade in, 7232
Corn, Importation, 5811, 6689, 6713, 7133
Corn, Price of, 6286
Corn, Trade, 6250, 7124, 7133,
Corn Bill, 5466, 5808
Corn Laws, 1551, 2501, 5451, 5463, 5466, 5783, 5785, 5808, 5830-5831, 5864, 5908, 6044, 6356, 6373, 6426, 6450, 6667, 6828, 7026, 7124, 7232, 7253, 7268
Corn Laws, Business Cycle, 7252
Corna Pellegrini, G., 1281
Cornelius, F., 754
Corner, 8094
Cornford, F. M., 4921, 5066
Cornforth, M. C., 9115
Cornish, T., 5832
Cornu, A., 9116-9119
Corporate Organization, 289
Corporation, 1108, 3380, 4127, 4432, 4666, 5486, 7667, 8715
Corporation, Charitable, 4555, 4720
Corporation, Law, 8488
Corporation, Municipal, 8183
Corporation, Taxation, 8605
Corrado, G. B., 135
Correa Machado, B., 1282
Corry, B. A., 89
Corsi Universitari, 3862
Cort Van Der Linden, P. W. H., 7674

Cortes, L. D., 8922
Cory, J. P., 5833
Cosciani, C., 1283
Coss, J. J., 2180
Cossa, C., 2850
Cossa, E., 7675
Cossa, L., 136-138, 2844, 7676-7678
Cost, 75, 2080, 2081, 2144, 3171, 3245, 3290, 3291, 3329, 3346, 3380
Cost, Agricultural, 6273
Cost, Curves, 9880
Cost, Functions, 3394
Cost, Opportunity, 3239
Cost, Overhead, 3163
Cost, Real, 3239
Costa, A. M. S., 139
Costa-Rossetti, J., 7679
Costaz, 6487
Coste, A., 7680-7682
Cotteril, C. F., 3167, 5833
Cotton, 6287, 8757
Cotton, Manufacture, 5510, 5816, 7179, 7192
Cotton, Spinnery, 8182
Cotton, R., 4759
Coulbois, P., 3412
Coulet, P. J., 7683
Coulton, G. C., 4122
Council for Advancement of Secondary Education, 757
Council for the Study of Mankind, 827, 3667
Counter, 4740
Counterfeiting, 3942
Counties, England, Tours, 4881
Courcelle Seneuil, J. G., 140, 5837-5841
Cournot, 3619, 9658, 9667, 9700, 9748
Cournot, A. A., 1284, 5842-5844, 9703, 9765, 9679-9682
Court, Cases, Maritime, 6869
Court, Supreme, 93
Courtin, R., 141, 1285-1286
Courtney, W. L., 7684
Courtois, A., 7685-7686
Cowell, J. W., 5846
Cowles Commission for Research in Economics, 3569, 3664

Cowperthwaite, J. H., 7687
Cox, H., 7688, 8762
Cox, R., 4443
Cox, S. S., 7689
Coxe, T., 5847-5848
Coyer, L'Abbe, 4155-4156
Cracco, W., 142
Cradock, F., 4157
Craig, J., 143, 2348, 5849-5850
Craik, G. L., 5851
Cramer, D. E., 1522
Cramer-Frey, C., 2982
Crandall, R., 967
Crane, B., 1287
Crawford, J. B., 7690
Crawford, V. E., 4923
Crawfurd, J., 5854-5859
Creasy, E., 7691-7692
Credit, 10, 54, 548, 1063, 3035, 4373, 4429, 4459, 4605, 4799, 5081, 5112, 5187, 5213, 5410, 5571, 5611, 5744, 6032, 6246, 6344, 6395, 6439, 6595, 6598, 6890, 6899, 6910, 7233, 7379, 7391, 7549, 7834, 7914, 7945, 7985, 8012, 8107, 8125, 8231, 8248, 8314, 8442, 8527, 8552, 8579, 8590, 8851, 8855, 9391, 9409, 9746, 9761, 9844, 9937
Credit, Agriculture, 6312, 7538, 7888
Credit, Commercial, 6158
Credit, Early System, 5126
Credit, England, 8694
Credit, Land, 4104
Credit, National, 4987
Credit, Paper, 4613, 7105
Credit, Private, 4650
Credit, Public, 4144, 4189, 4690, 4746, 5495, 5577, 5932, 6077, 6157, 6158, 6170, 6171, 6182, 6203, 6587, 6657, 6916, 6921, 7080
Credit, Social, 3194
Credit Mobilier, America, 7690
Credit System, France, 5689
Credit System, Great Britain, 5689
Credit System, United States, 5689
Credit Union, 6257
Creditor, 4094, 4374, 4824
Creditor, Public, 4096
Creighton, C., 7693
Crime, 8324
Crisis, Commercial, 8112
Croce, B., 9120-9122
Crocker, U. H., 7694
Croft-Murray, G., 3854
Croke, A., 5860
Crome, A. F. W., 2418
Crompton, H., 7695
Cron, 4137
Cronbach, E., 2669
Cronin, J. F., 144, 1289
Crook, J. W., 2670
Croome, H. M., 1290
Cropsey, J., 7288-7289
Cros, J., 9683
Crosara, A. A., 4924
Crosser, P. K., 145
Crossman, R. H. S., 9123
Crouch, H., 4160
Crouse, R. L., 3168
Crouzel, A., 7696
Crown, Land Revenue of, 6915
Crozier, J. B., 146, 7697
Crozier, M., 9138
Cruger, H., 7698
Crum, W. L., 3572
Crump, A., 7699-7701
Crumpe, S., 5861
Cruttwell, R., 5862
Crutzen, A., 1291
Cruz, S., 3573
Cruz Santos, A., 1292
Cuba, 2601-2602, 9313
Cucheval Clarigny, A., 7702-7704
Culmann, H., 1293
Culpepper, T., 4161-4162
Cultural Change, 89737
Culture, 898, 6678
Cumberland, R., 4165
Cumming, A. N., 7705
Cunha, T., 1294
Cunningham, W., 147, 2491, 3574, 5182-5183, 7707-7711, 8836-8837
Cunow, H., 148
Cunynghame, H., 1295, 3169, 3576

Cupin, Baron, 7200
Currency, 2233, 2400, 4210,
 4444, 5135, 5320, 5490,
 5688, 5702, 5846, 5862,
 6071, 6078, 6130, 6133,
 6295, 6327, 6354, 6404,
 6612, 6671, 6674, 6747,
 6856, 6968, 7123, 7125,
 7135, 7155, 7251, 7616,
 7786, 8239, 8262, 8373,
 8457, 8646, 9691, 9723
Currency, American, 8673
Currency, American
 Colonies, 7127, 7166
Currency, Cash Payments,
 7127, 7666
Currency, Circulation, 7122
Currency, Depreciation,
 5589, 6269, 6355
Currency, Fluctuations, 7252
Currency, Indian, 9992
Currency, Metal, 8516
Currency, National, 6588
Currency, Netherlands,
Currency, Paper, 4301, 5522,
 6216, 7126, 7132, 7601,
 8140, 8428
Currency, Silver, 6731
Currency, Value, 6590, 7599
Currency Question, 6309
Currency Question, Germany,
 5187
Current Economic Comment,
 5352
Currie, J. I., 2540
Curth, H., 14
Curtis, C. R., 1296-1298
Curtis, M., 9124
Curves, Economic, 5423
Curves, Utility, 3271
Cusack, M. T., 150
Cussy, C., 6776
Custard, E. M., 151
Custard, H. L., 151
Custodi, P., 5863
Custom, 4598
Custom Union, 6863, 7188,
 7756, 8803
Customs, 4221, 4223
Customs, Great Britain,
 4052
Customs, Inland, 7153
Customs Union, France, 5335

Cusumano, V., 2671-2672, 7712
Cutler, A. T., 1602
Cuvillier, A., 9125
Cybernitics, 3721
Czarkowski, J., 2928-2929
Czech, A., 153
Czech, Z., 3170, 9684
Czechoslovakia, 852, 2091-
 2092, 2603
Czeckslovakia, 9560-9563
Czerwinski, Z., 3578

D'Arcy, M. C., 4926
Dabcevic-Kucar, S., 1299
Dabney, W. D., 7713
Dabritz, W., 1374
Dabrowski, Z., 2617
Dahl, D., 1300
Dahl, F., W., 7714
Daiches, D., 7290
Daire, E., 5343, 5431, 6482
Dalbiac, J. C., 5864
Dale, E. L., 1557
Dalencour, F. S. R., 154
Dalrymple, J., 4166-4167,
 5865-5866, 6051
Dalton, G., 4925
Damaschke, A. W. F., 155
Dameron, K., 983
Danco, J., 26
Danemanis, D., 9326, 9528
Dangeul, P., 4168, 4608-4609
Dangeville, R., 9388
Daniel, C., 3579
Daniel, R., 3083
Daniell, C. J., 7715
Daniels, W. M., 7716
Danielsson, C., 5184
Dankert, C. E., 7291
Dankwardt, H., 5867
Danvilla, B. J., 5868
Dareste de la Chavanne,
 5869
Dargent, E., 1301
Darkheim, R., 7717
Dartan, J., 156
Darwin, 9030, 9251, 9489
Darwinism, 8623, 8982
Dasgupta, A. K., 3580-
 3581
Date, K., 1302
Datt, R., 1303
Datta, B., 2806

Dauby, J., 7718
Daugert, S. M., 8933
Daugherty, C. R., 1304
Daugherty, M. R., 1304-1305
Dauphin-Meunier, A., 1306, 3315
Dautilya, A., 2827
Davanzati, B., 4170
Davenant, C., 4171-4175, 5169, 5870
Davenne, H. J. B., 7719
Davenport, H. J., 1307-1308, 3171, 3174, 3582, 9685, 9812, 9868
David, C. G., 9995
Davidson, D., 7710-7721
Davidson, F. G., 9916
Davidson, J., 7722
Davidson, P., 3175, 9917
Davidson, R. K., 1309
Davies, D., 5872
Davies, J., 4176
Davis, D. C., 2292
Davis, J. B., 7723
Davis, J. E., 7724
Davis, J. F., 5873
Davis, J. R., 9918
Davis, M. E., 3205
Davis, T. N., 9099
Davisson, W. I., 1310
Davy, J., 5874
Dawson, G. G., 1311, 1474, 3046
Dawson, W., 5875
Dawson, W. H., 7725-7727
Dayre, J., 157
De Alessi, L., 3583
De Cindio, F., 3177
De Garis, M. C., 1313
De Garmo, E. P., 1314
De Janosi, P. E., 3178
De Joint, G., 160
De Quincy, T., 5878-5879
De Roover, R. A., 2921
De Rooy, E. W., 5880
De Rycke, L., 757
De Villeneuve-Bargemont, A., 171
De Vyver, F. T., 3844
De Welz, G., 1324
De Witt, C., 4809
De Witt, J., 4809
Dean, E., 3176

Dean, R. B., 5881
Dean of Gloucester, 4823
Deane, H. A., 4928
Dearle, N. B., 1312
Debauve, A., 7728
Deborin, A. M., 9422
Debray, 5882
Debreau, G., 9127
Debs, E., 9128
Debt, 2119, 4601, 6633, 6723, 7840, 7843, 7954
Debt, Goldsmiths, 4359
Debt, Imprisonment, 5557
Debt, National, 3930, 3997, 4183, 4231, 4365, 4374, 4391, 4552, 4602, 4624, 4627, 4630, 4645, 4648, 4664, 4708, 4765, 4862, 5633, 5684, 5986, 6023, 6064, 6145, 6174, 6565, 6818, 7447, 8597
Debt, Personal, 6186
Debt, Public, 36, 3994, 4183, 4226, 4249, 4258, 4265, 4324, 4389, 4476, 4586, 4747, 4748, 4778, 5866, 6079, 6110, 6189-6190, 6196, 6715, 6722, 10035
Debt, Public, States, United States, 7154
Debt, Small, 4481
Deception, Economic, 10097
Decision-Making, Managerial, 1100
Decker, M., 4179-4180, 4495
Deckert, E., 7729
Decoud, J. A., 2542
Deductive Analysis, 3513, 3525, 3611
Defense, National, 989
Defoe, D., 4188-4189
Defourney, M., 8838
Degarando, Baron, 5876
Degarando, 7195
Deglin, C., 1223
Degrange, 7084
Degras, J., 548
Deguchi, M., 3584
Deguchi, Y., 158, 755, 3584
Dehen, R., 1315-1318
Dehler, T., 851
Deibler, F. S., 979, 1319
Del Mar, A., 7731

Delacour, A., 7734
Delacourt, 4809
Delfgaauw, G. T. J., 161
Delhi School of Economics, 752, 2480, 9915
Delhi University, 1303, 1326
Delius, K., 3047, 8934
Dell'Erba, A., 3282
Delpit, J., 5889
Delvincourt, 6279
Demand, 3175, 3197, 3204, 3207, 3218-3220, 3222, 3225, 3230, 3235, 3257, 3280, 3309, 3319, 3326, 3334, 3355, 3360, 3366, 3367, 3383, 3388, 3396, 3402, 3412, 3427, 3455, 3462, 3479, 3480, 3484, 5870, 8949, 9720, 9815, 9821, 9833, 9917
Demand, Aggregate Consumer, 3372
Demand, Consumers, 3106
Demand, Curves, 9883
Demand, Effective, 3166
Demand, Explitit, 10090
Demand, Function, 3137
Demande, J., 9919
Demant, V. A., 4929
Demaria, G., 1320, 9757, 9759
Demaria, G., 162
Demmer, K. H., 3179
Democracy, 95, 821, 2321, 7118, 9015, 9241, 9545
Democracy, Industrial, 8759
Democracy, Social, 8571, 9143
Democratic Tradition, 9305
Democrats, Social, 9323
Demography, 5301, 5405
Demos, R., 4930
Dempsey, B. W., 1321, 4931-4932
Dencik, P., 9129
Denis, H., 164-166
Denis, H., 756, 3180-3181, 3187
Denmark, 1065-1066, 1143-1144, 2010, 2604-2606, 3927, 8301
Dennis, H., 163

Denslow, V. B, 7735
Denton, W., 7736
Deparcieux, 4239
Depitre, E., 4356
Depping, G. B., 5890
Depression, 3033, 5625
Depression, United States, 2567
Deprite, E., 5415
Dernburg, J. D., 1323
Dernburg, T. F., 1322-1323
Derycke, P. H., 3182
Desai, S. S. M., 167-168
Desan, W., 9130
Desaubuez, 5892
Desbrosses, B., 5893
Deschamps, A., 138
Deschamps, H., 2638
Deschamps, L., 7737
Design, 2187
Deslandes, 4194
Desmarest, E., 7738
Desmeuniers, 5895
Desroches, M. C., 9131
Desrotours, 5896
Desy, Jean, 322
Deutsche, A., 2009
Deutsche Akademie der Wissenschaften, 169, 9255
Deutsches Institut für Wirtschaftsforschung, 717-719, 1134, 3905
Devas, C. S., 170, 7739
Development, 752, 788, 928, 1084, 1103, 1303, 1326, 1651, 1780, 1839, 1944, 2566, 2666, 2670, 3632, 3744, 8551, 9865, 10009
Development, American, 3065
Development, Analysis, 762
Development, Capitalist, 2162, 2417, 9595
Development, Economic, American, 3032
Development, Historical, 9611, 9818
Development, Industrial, 805
Development, Marxian, 9726
Development, Social, 626
Development, Urban, 3240
Devillers, H., 6960-6961
Devine, E. T., 7740
Devons, E., 758
Dew, T. R., 5989

Dewe, J. A., 172
Dewer, J., 1015
Dewett, K. K., 1325-1328
Dewey, D., 2150, 3183
Dewey, D. R., 7741
Dewey, E. W., 8935
Dewey, J., 3184, 9436, 9530
Deyon, P., 5185
Dhongde, E. R., 1416
Dhooria, 421
Dialectical Materialism, 9032, 9205, 9227, 9259, 9261, 9263, 9441, 9521-9523, 9565, 9628-9629, 9642
Diamond, D. E., 707
Dicey, A. V., 7742-7743
Dick, J. R., 1329
Dickinson, H. D., 8936, 9686
Dickinson, Z. C., 173, 3586
Dickson, 4242
Dickson, A., 5900
Dickson, H., 1330
Dictionary, 2718, 4113, 4197-4198, 4242, 4546, 4618, 4685, 5456, 5599, 5895, 5899, 5901-5902, 5910, 5921, 6083, 6416-6417, 6935, 6991, 7180, 7744-7747, 8376, 8394, 8565, 9114, 9397
Dictionary, Farming, 5477
Dictionary, Political Economy, 5827
Diderot, D., 4199
Diehl, K., 1331, 2370, 3588, 7748
Diepenhorst, P. A., 1332
Dieterici, K. F. W., 5903-5905
Dieterlen, P., 1333
Dietzel, H., 1334, 3185, 3589, 7750
Diezmann, M., 7751
Digby, R. E., 7752
Digest, 5906
Digests, 697
Digges, D., 4100
Diglio, G., 174, 1335
Dilas, M., 9132
Dillard, D. D., 9920-9922
Dillon, M., 7753
Dillon, W., 7754

Diminishing Returns, 3144, 3356
Dimitrov, A. G., 3690
Dimock, J. E., 175
Dingley, N., 7755
Dingwall, J., 9739
Diodati, L., 5907
Dionnet, G., 5186
Directors, South Sea Company, 4717
Dirom, A., 5908
Discount, 4726
Disease, 4805, 5585, 6192, 7249, 7390
Diseconomies, External, 1367, 9813
Dissertation, 2604, 2644
Dissertation, Basel, 2708, 9965
Dissertation, Berlin, 2764, 3323, 8869, 9924
Dissertation, Bern, 5340
Dissertation, Breslau, 5339
Dissertation, Columbia University, 2725-2726, 2766, 2792, 2896, 3073, 5170, 5198, 7297, 8918, 9344
Dissertation, Duke University, 9690
Dissertation, Erlangen, 5196
Dissertation, Freiburg, 5163, 5399
Dissertation, Freie Universitat, Berlin, 9941
Dissertation, Geneva, 9914
Dissertation, Giessen, 2690
Dissertation, Gottingen, 3002
Dissertation, Harvard University 9610
Dissertation, Heidelberg, 3855, 5356, 5378
Dissertation, Helsingfors, 5245
Dissertation, Jena, 2750, 2966, 5326
Dissertation, Kiel, 2692, 5283
Dissertation, Koln, 5213
Dissertation, Leipzig, 5037, 8825
Dissertation, Lyons, 5362
Dissertation, Mainz, 10085
Dissertation, Marburg, 9964
Dissertation, Massachusetts Institute of Technology, 10005

Dissertation, Munich, 2796, 5076
Dissertation, New York University, 5324
Dissertation, Paris, 5186
Dissertation, St. Louis University, 5392
Dissertation, Syracuse University, 10025
Dissertation, Universidad Nacional Autonoma de Mexico, 2916
Dissertation, Universite de Paris, 2777, 2950, 3417, 5337
Dissertation, University of California, Berkeley, 5281
Dissertation, University of Chicago, 2798, 3034, 5211
Dissertation, University of Illinois, 2775, 3054
Dissertation, University of Michigan, 2981, 9805
Dissertation, University of Poitiers, 9460
Dissertation, University of Southern California, 3035
Dissertation, University of Washington, 10091
Dissertation, Yale University, 3214
Dissertation, Zurich, 5303
Distiller, 4047, 5555, 5884
Distribution, 151, 187, 631, 1161, 1343, 2048, 2733, 2734, 3119, 3135, 3142, 3148, 3174, 3193, 3195, 3208, 3248, 3274, 3331, 3441, 3470, 3901, 5432, 5702, 6750, 7096, 7400, 7630, 7632, 7673, 8236, 8263, 8634, 8924, 8945, 9685, 9736, 9778, 9803, 9835, 9838, 9878,
Distribution, Income, 704, 728, 777, 9810, 10103
Ditmar, W., 7756
Dixon, R. A., 8937
Djojohadikusumo, S., 1336
Dmitriev, V. K., 3187
Dmytryshyh, B., 2954
Dobb, M. H., 176-177, 2473, 9133, 10075
Dobbs, A., 4209

Dober, V., 9326
Dobler, M., 3188, 9134
Dobrev, K., 3590
Dobriansky, L. E., 8938
Dockes, P., 178
Doczi, J., 9135
Dodan, S., 9136
Dodd, J. H., 1337-1339
Dodge, J. R., 7757
Doe, 5911
Doerig, J. A., 9404
Dole, C. F., 7758
Dolleans, E., 2639, 9138
Domar, E., 9139
Domarchi, J., 9923
Domergue, J., 7759
Domesday Book, 5912, 7491
Domesday Studies, 7760
Domestic Affairs, Great Britain, 4851
Dominguez Vargas, S., 1340
Dominican Fathers, 4885
Dommanget, M., 2371
Donaldson, W., 4069
Doniol, H., 5913-5914
Donnan, E., 1837
Donniges, W., 5915
Donnithorne, A., 2586
Doodha, K., 3189
Doody, F. S., 2292
Dooley, P. C., 1341, 3190
Dopsch, A., 179-181
Dorantes, A., 1342
Doren, A., 7761
Dorfman, J., 1200, 1762, 1944, 2217, 2402, 8847, 8939-8940, 8964, 9687-9688
Dorfman, J. H., 3048-3049
Dorfman, R., 3191-3192 3591, 3593
Dori, J. A., 5916
Dorn, A., 7762
Dornemann, L., 9140
Dorp, E. C., 3193
Dorsey, E. E., 7763
Dortmund, S., 9141
Dos Passos, J. R., 7764
Dostrobitopm, 3273
Doubleday, J., 5917-5918
Doubleday, T., 6688
Doublet, E., 759

Douglas, C. H., 3194
Douglas, Heron, and Company, 6718
Douglas, J., 5919
Douglas, P. H., 3195-3196
Douglass, H., 5920, 6841
Douglass, W., 4210
Doursther, H., 5921
Dove, P. E., 2372, 5922, 7760
Dow, L. A., 8941
Dowd, D. F., 1506, 8942
Dowell, S., 7765-7767
Dowidar, M., 9142
Dowling, H., 3594
Doyle, A., 7767
Doyle, J., 5923
Drachkovitch, M. M., 9143-9146
Dragicevic, A., 9063, 9147
Drahn, E., 9148-9149
Drahota, H., 9924
Drainage, 7075
Drake, A. E., 3197
Drechsler, L., 3198
Dreissig, W., 5187
Drioux, J., 7769
Droz, J., 5926
Drummond, H., 5927
Dryhurst, A. R., 491
Drysdale, E. C., 228
Du Buat, 5930
Du Buat, C., 4212
Du Hautchamp, 4213-4214
Du Puynode, G., 7770-7773
Du Puynode, M. G. P., 185
Dublin, 7223
Dublin Society, 6834
Duboin, J., 760, 1343
Dubois, 5894
Dubois, A., 4005, 5345
Dubois, J. B., 5929
Dubois-Ayme, 5928
Duchatel, P., 7774
Duchatel, T., 5931
Ducpetiaux, 6574
Due, J. F., 1344, 9689
Duesenberry, J., 9925
Duff, N., 7775
Duffart, C., 7776-7778
Duffy, N. F., 1345
Dufresne de Francheville, 4215

Dufresne Saint Leon, 5932
Duhalde, P., 4216
Duhamel, M., 4217-4218
Duhring, E., 7817, 9170
Duhring, E. K., 182-183
Duhrings, Eugen, 44
Duke of Ormond, 4595
Duke University, 822, 2508, 2548
Dullo, G., 7779
Dumesnil-Marigny, J., 7781
Dumontier, J., 1346, 3595
Dun, F., 7782
Dun, J., 7784
Dunayevskaya, R., 9150
Dunbar, C. F., 716, 3596, 7785-7786
Duncan, H., 5933
Duncan, J., 5934, 7787
Dunckley, H., 5935
Duncombe, C., 5936
Dundee, 7511
Dundee School of Economics, 763
Dunker, H., 9151
Dunlop, A., 5937-5938
Dunoyer, B. C., 5939
Dunoyer, C., 2524, 5940-5945
Duopoly Price, 9748
Dupin, C., 184, 2637, 2640, 5946-5950
Dupont, J. F., 7788
Dupont de Nemours, P. S., 5344-5345, 5361, 5388, 5419, 5423, 6630, 6374, 8576
Dupont-White, C. B., 2523, 5952-5954
Duprat, J., 2374
Dupre, L. K., 9152
Dupriez, L., 1491
Dupreiz, L. H., 830
Dupuit, J., 5955-5956
Dupuynode, 6015
Duquesnoy, 5957
Duquesnoy, A. C., 6902
Durand, E. D., 2372
Durand, J., 7789
Dureau, A., 5958
Dureau de la Malle, 5959
Durkheim, E., 7790
Dussard, H., 5431
Dutens, J. M., 5960-5962

Dutli-Rutishauser, M., 2982
Dutoit, B., 9153
Dutot, C. F., 4219, 4581
Dutt, C. P., 9170
Dutt, S. C., 2807
Dutt, V., 1862
Duty, 4093, 4095, 4497, 4505, 4702, 4794, 4903, 5359, 5380, 5386, 5452, 5486, 5606, 5612, 5696, 5697, 6302, 6348, 6369, 6385, 6421, 6548, 6624, 6656, 6659, 6661, 6662, 6682, 6716, 6736, 6741, 6742, 6769, 6811, 6814, 6865, 7078, 7153, 7615, 7619, 7627, 7661, 7772, 7833, 7856, 7857, 7972, 8029, 8414, 8439, 8494, 8606, 8661, 8707, 8719, 8720, 8725, 8727
Duty, Coal, 6422
Duty, Printed Cottons, 6372
Duty, Salt, 4446
Duty, Single, 5335
Duty, Stamp, 7765, 7956
Duty, Sugar, 4767, 6306, 6415, 6521
Duty, Timber, 6841
Duval, J., 7791-7792
Duvergier, J., 5963
Duverney, 4362
Duvillard, 5466, 5964, 6771
Dvorkin, I. N., 186, 3050, 9154
Dye, H. S., 1347
Dyer, G., 5965
Dyer, L., 137, 7677
Dykmans, G. L., 1348, 3597, 3734
Dynamics, Economic, 1124
Dynamics, Keynesian, 10008

Eagley, R. V., 187, 762
Eaire, E., 5968
Earl, E., 4669
Earl of Carlisle, 5973, 6054
Earl of Selkirk, 6623
Earle, J., 7793
Earnings, 7629
Earnings, Wartime, 7555
East India Bill, 5809

East India Company, 3931, 3958, 3961, 4046, 4105, 4126, 4127, 4172, 4185, 4220, 4228, 4330, 4369, 4396, 4448, 5272, 5491, 5642, 5856, 6135, 6423, 6827, 7492
East India Gazetteer, 6177
East India Sugar, 6415, 6465
East India Trade, 3938, 4112, 4152, 4580, 4637, 4806, 5311
East Indies, 3933, 4187, 4347, 4548, 4549, 4591, 6787
East Indies, Sugar, 7064,
Eastham, J. K. 763, 1349
Eastman, M. F., 9155, 9369
Eastwick, E. B., 7815,
Eaton, D. B., 7794
Eaton, J., 1350, 9156, 9926
Eber, M., 1351
Eberhart, E. K., 8937
Ebert, G., 9466
Eckard, E. W., 9690
Eckert, G., 5188
Eckhel, J. H., 5966
Eckstein, W., 7342
Ecole de Coimbre, 2950
Ecole des Sciences Economiques, 2668
Ecole des Sciences Politiques et Sociales de Louvain, 2558
Ecole Nationale d'Organisation Economique et Sociale, 3595
Ecole Pratique des Hautes Etudes, 1957, 3076
Ecology, 3240
Econometric Society, 3598
Econometrica, 3137, 3235, 3236, 3598, 3629, 9671, 9767, 9961, 10063
Econometrics, 939, 2183, 3197, 3223, 3479, 3480, 3557, 3594, 3627, 3664, 3666, 3732, 3803, 3848, 3867, 3895, 3896, 9735
Economia, Santiago, 637
Economic Conditions, 43, 2665, 2747, 2817, 2830, 2878, 2920, 2931, 2958, 3044-3045, 3085
Economic Conditions, American Colonies, 5201
Economic Conditions, Australia, 2548

Economic Conditions, China, 2620-2621
Economic Conditions, Cuba, 2601
Economic Conditions, Denmark, 2604
Economic Conditions, Europe, 5165
Economic Conditions, France, 2652
Economic Conditions, Germany, 2681, 2691, 2701
Economic Conditions, Great Britain, 2721, 2731, 2792
Economic Conditions, Guatemala, 2799
Economic Conditions, Hungary, 2800
Economic Conditions, Italy, 2845, 2854
Economic Conditions, Netherlands, 2919, 2922, 2923
Economic Conditions, Pakistan, 2927
Economic Conditions, Poland, 2931, 2933, 2941
Economic Conditions, Portugal, 2951
Economic Conditions, Russia, 2957
Economic Conditions, Soviet Union, 2986, 3001, 3012
Economic Conditions, United States, 3032, 3044, 3057, 3061, 3075, 3087
Economic Dynamics, 3561
Economic History, 214, 236, 298, 529, 551, 596, 612, 666, 721, 741, 850, 867, 949, 967, 991, 2334, 2609, 2675, 2724, 2748, 2789, 3846, 4972, 4983, 5064, 5088-5089, 5110, 5179, 5247, 5375, 6388, 7311, 8237, 8481, 8893, 9808, 9982
Economic History, Ancient India, 5013
Economic History, English, 4889, 8823
Economic History Association, 867, 2375
Economic History Review, 2456, 2735, 3244, 5179, 7314, 8893
Economic History Society, 5269
Economic Institute . . . Czechoslovakia. . . , 2603
Economic Journal, 38, 601, 2499, 2780, 3144, 3169, 3200, 3256, 3271, 3286, 3348, 3369, 3404-3405, 3505-3506, 3547, 3558, 3574, 3577, 3602, 3604-3605, 3628, 3640, 3723, 3741, 3816, 3901, 5008, 6388, 7283, 7326, 9696, 9709, 9729, 9796, 9819, 9829-9831, 9836, 9847, 9851, 9863-9864, 9876, 9901, 9961, 9971, 9973, 9982-9983, 10052-10053
Economic Predictions, Marxist, 9210
Economic Process, 102
Economic Review, 5096
Economic Society of Australia and New Zealand, 2471
Economic Studies, 3511
Economic Thought, American, 2414, 8622
Economic Thought, Modern, 254, 259, 357, 512
Economic Thought, Periodization, 533
Economic Thought, Psychological Foundations, 173
Economic Thought, Western, 168
Economic Tracts, 129
Economica, 2353, 2450, 3123, 3145, 3259, 3260, 3521, 3815, 4567, 5212, 5377, 9687, 10049
Economica, London, 7356, 9714
Economica, New Series, 3851
Economics, 1-10108
Economics, Advanced Theory, 1778
Economics, American, 2567-2568, 3036, 3080
Economics, Applied, 933, 1148, 1184, 1201, 1337, 1655, 3077
Economics, Austrian, 2556, 3173
Economics, Business, 1056, 1117, 1728
Economics, Canadian, 2566

Economics, Cartesian, 981
Economics, Christian, 8512
Economics, Classical, 3, 12,
  36, 61, 68-69, 199, 647,
  1277, 2344, 2449, 2529,
  2751, 2775, 2776, 2793,
  3185, 3186, 3347, 3398,
  3534, 7302, 7324, 8951,
  10015, 10018, 10102
Economics, Classical, Macro-
  economics, 239
Economics, Dynamic, 812-813,
  1413
Economics, Eighteen Eighties,
  9848
Economics, Eighteenth Century,
  2784, 2788, 2954, 5150,
  5420, 7393, 8896, 9729
Economics, Eighteenth Century,
  Japan, 2897
Economics, Eighteenth Century,
  Korea, 2906
Economics, Engineering, 1244
  1314, 1329, 2064, 2287
Economics, Evolution, 6531
Economics, Industrial, 6074
Economics, Institute, 7384
Economics, Intermediate, 1227,
  1372, 1731, 9689
Economics, International, 1180,
  8504
Economics, Keynesian, 3166,
  10007
Economics, Liberal Theories,
  2329
Economics, Macro, 14, 239,
  853, 881, 1034, 1053, 1073,
  1091, 1104, 1157, 1169,
  1181, 1287, 1301, 1325,
  1377, 1481, 1656, 1678,
  1766, 1938, 2079, 2082,
  2084, 2153, 2234, 2617,
  2981, 3790, 3856, 3885,
  3887, 9886, 9913, 10031,
  10105
Economics, Macro, Swedish,
  9805
Economics, Managerial,
  1345, 1389, 1526, 1854,
  2140, 2150
Economics, Manchester School,
  2746
Economics, Marshallian,
  9807-9884
Economics, Marxian, 9608
Economics, Mathematical,
  7, 3493-3494, 9660, 9667,
  9700, 9735, 9753, 9871
Economics, Micro, 722, 853,
  1077, 1122, 1140, 1157,
  1163, 1310, 1325, 1400,
  1440, 1530, 1586, 1603,
  1638, 1661, 1665, 1676,
  1701, 2102, 2169, 2237,
  3275, 3304, 3579, 3777,
Economics, Modern, 598, 670,
  896, 954, 1079, 1139, 1220,
  1325, 1393, 1394, 1404,
  1684, 1723, 1793, 1818,
  1828, 1998, 2078, 2172,
  2178, 2242, 2290, 2292,
  2754
Economics, Modern, Sweden,
  2975
Economics, Neoclassical, 68,
  1593, 3208, 9877
Economics, New, 808, 1267, 1354,
  1980, 1981, 2704, 2758,
  9918, 9953, 9958,
  10095
Economics, Nineteenth Century,
  609, 3083
Economics, Ninth Century,
  2954
Economics, Normative, 9047
Economics, Philosophical Interpretation, 1776
Economics, Positive, 784, 1695,
  3296
Economics, Polynesian, 4948,
  9814
Economics, Post Keynesian,
  387, 10010
Economics, Pre-Capitalistic,
  9409
Economics, Prehistoric, 5018
Economics, Quantitative,
  3863, 9775
Economics, Relativity, 3847
Economics, Ricardian, 2725-
  2726
Economics, Ricardian, 1762
Economics, Scientific, 2763
Economics, Seventeenth
  Century, 3063, 3244, 5192,
  5198, 5294

Economics, Social, 526, 745, 773-774, 1232, 1382, 1497, 1517, 1604, 1649, 1954, 1995, 2220, 2224, 2278, 2379, 2394, 3232, 4212, 4965, 5930, 5944, 6155, 6462, 6686, 6687, 6960, 7359, 7626, 7644, 7969, 8147, 8225, 8504, 8566, 8578, 8921, 9792, 9851

Economics, Sociological, 561, 1272

Economics, Strategy, 1387

Economics, Twentieth Century, 601, 2554, 9967, 1145

Economics, Welfare, 564, 2742, 3212

Economics, Western, 951

Economics and Liberalism, 650

Economics of Planning, 3269, 3371, 3780

Economies, External, 1367, 9813

Economist, 445, 619, 770, 821, 840, 882, 976, 986, 1276, 2328-2539, 2655, 2662, 2690, 2749, 2758, 2776, 2847, 2859, 2872, 2902, 2920, 2946, 2947, 2949, 2969, 2995, 3038, 3445, 3530, 5208, 5501, 6843, 7131, 7327, 7337, 8009, 9002, 9109, 9808, 9872, 9952

Economist, American, 2346, 3913

Economist, Birmingham, 2735

Economist, British, 2452

Economist, Business, 2330

Economist, College, 2528, 10101

Economist, Employment, 2515

Economist, English, 2348

Economist, French, 5360, 6143

Economist, Government, 2448

Economist, Haarlem, 285

Economist, Liberal, 727

Economist, Mobility, 2332

Economist, Modern, 2388

Economist, Occupation of, 2407

Economist, Portugal, 5193

Economist, Professional, 2332

Economist 3081

Economista, 2943

Economisti Italiani, 6860

Economy, American, 744, 1507, 2533, 3050, 8988

Economy, Christian, 7190

Economy, Civic, 5712

Economy, Commercial, 5703

Economy, Corporate, 888

Economy, France, 5252

Economy, Free, 1020, 1379, 3044

Economy, Functional, 1321, 4932

Economy, German, 2551, 2659

Economy, Government, 4034

Economy, Imperial, 5192

Economy, Industrial, 1083, 8200, 8467, 8911

Economy, Mature, 10084 10088

Economy, Mixed, 3427, 9426, 10029

Economy, Modern, 1052, 2685

Economy, Moral, 5978

Economy, National, 1269, 1330, 1331, 1375, 1640, 1867-1868, 1885, 1946, 2010, 2122-2123, 2142, 2252, 2256, 2427, 2469, 2476, 2511, 2604, 2655, 2669, 2676, 2678, 2688, 2751, 5867, 5984, 6069, 6363, 6579, 6618, 6636, 6744, 6955, 7014, 7040, 7116, 7495, 7648, 7650, 7664, 7665, 7679, 7777-7778, 7800, 7994, 8002, 8016, 8096, 8182, 8290, 8295, 8387, 8470, 8562, 8574, 8582-8583, 8593, 8696, 8700, 8738, 8777, 8789, 8795, 8797, 8821-8822, 8826, 8828, 8839, 8841, 8846, 8859, 8864, 8869, 8877, 8902, 8934, 9213, 9697, 9800, 9899

Economy, National, Planned, 2347

Economy, Organization, 8678

Economy, Organizational Alternatives, 9637

Economy, Peasant, 4925
  5048, 9096
Economy, Planned, 2666, 2739,
  2790
Economy, Precapitalist, 5077,
  9476, 9590
Economy, Primitive, 4948,
  5116
Economy, Public, 1274, 5640,
  6631, 6633, 7610, 8232
Economy Public, United States,
  5781
Economy, Railway, 6349
Economy, Social, 1200, 1334,
  2520, 3754, 5656, 5802,
  6678, 6961
Economy, Socialist, 1128, 9600,
  9637
Economy, Soviet, 3276-3277
Economy, Soviet Bloc, 2600
Economy, Soviet-Type, 2597
Economy, Stationary, 1771
Economy, Sweden, 2979-2980
Economy, System, 7196
Economy, Tribal, 5047
Economy, World, 930, 1183
Eddy, S., 9436
Edeling, H., 9158
Eden, F. M., 5971-5972
Eden, M., 4417
Eden, W., 5973-5974
  6054
Edgar, W., 4221
Edgeworth, F. Y., 768, 3200,
  3256, 9671-9672, 9691-
  9696, 9983
Edgeworth, F. Y., 3601-3605
Edgeworth, M., 7795
Edgeworth, R. L., 5975
Edie, L. D., 1353-1355
Edinburgh Bank for Saving,
  6990
Edinburgh Cabinet Library,
  6584
Edinburgh Friendly Insurance,
  3980
Edinburgh Review, 5231
Edington, R., 5976
Edmonds, T. R., 5977-5978
Edmunds, S., 2207
Education, 3969, 4074, 4205,
  6121, 6324
Education, Economic, 837, 3883

Education, Economics, 3811
Edward II, 4478
Edwards, B., 3882
  5979
Edwards, C. D., 769, 8908
Edwards, G., 5980
Edwards, G. J., 1356
Edwards, R. C., 3051
Effertz, O., 7796
Efficiency, 1638
Efficiency, Marginal, 9927
Eger, G., 7797
Eggers, M. A., 1358-1359
Egner, E., 1360, 2673
Egypt, 3947, 4954, 5002, 6561,
  6848, 7435, 8229, 8399
Egypt, Ancient, 4361, 5029
Eheberg, K. T., 7798
Ehlert, W., 9649
Ehrenberg, V., 4941
Ehrental, V., 5981
Eichthal, E. D., 7799
Eight Hour Day, 8762
Eikemeyer, 5983
Einarsen, J., 1361
Einaudi, L., 188-189, 190, 883,
  2376, 3403, 5955
Einaudi, M., 5346-5347
Einzig, P., 4942
Eirksson, B. H. J., 1362
Eisdell, J. S., 5984
Eiselsen, J. J. H., 5985,
  6291
Eisenhart, H., 191, 7800
Eisenschmidii, J. C., 4224
Eisermann, G., 192, 1363,
  8839, 9697
Ekonomia Polityczna, 9159
Ekonomicky Casopis, 26, 296,
  608
Ekonomika Mauki, 570
Ekonomilitto, 2629
Ekonomisk Tidskrift, 9797
Ekonomiska Samfundets Tid-
  skrift, 4, 449
Ekonomist, Beograd, 427, 839
Ekonomista, 2936, 4916
Ekonomska Revija, Ljubljana,
  607
Ekonomski Institut FNRJ,
  Beograd, 1941
El-Kaissi, F., 840
Elasticity, 1167, 3113, 3182,

3306, 3353, 3360, 3435
Elasticity, Price, 3264
Elbridge, S., 1354
Elder, W., 7801-7802
Elias, L. N. J. H., 3202
Eliasberg, G. J., 9164
Elibank, P. M., 4226
Eliezer Kaplan School of Economics and Social Science, 9564
Eliot, C. W., 7337
Eliot, G., 1366
Elking, H., 4227
Ellering, H., 4228
Ellero, P., 7803
Elliot, G. A., 193
Elliot, J., 5987
Elliot, J. R., 7804
Elliot, O.L. 7805
Elliott, J. E., 798
Ellis, H. S., 194, 703, 1367, 1368, 9813
Ellis, J. M., 8944
Ellis, W., 5988-5990
Ellison, T., 7806
Ellman, M., 2993
Ellsworth, P. T., 9927
Ellwood, C. A., 4943-4944
Elster, J., 9165
Elster, L., 7988
Ely, R. T., 195, 334, 1369-1370, 3052, 7807-7811, 7812, 8945, 8946, 9166, 9167
Emel' Ianov, I. V., 196
Emele, S., 2672
Emerigon, B. M., 5991
Emerton, W. P., 7005
Emery, T., 5992
Emigration, 6623, 6653, 6669, 7115, 7512, 7540, 8501, 8642
Emigration, Chinese, 8608
Emigration, Europe, 7792, 8177
Emmer, R. E., 3609
Emminghaus, A., 7814, 7815
Emotion, Religious, 9336
Empiricism, 3798, 8967
Empiricism, A. Smith, 7280
Employer, 5745, 7912
Employment, 796, 828, 958, 1155, 1170, 1326, 1651, 1686, 1937, 2004, 2027, 2084, 2171, 2234, 2515, 5212, 5570, 5629, 5861, 5990, 6832, 7863, 9861, 9989, 10047, 10049, 10056, 10069, 10103
Employment, Full, 933, 3446, 9891, 9896
Employment, Poor, 3991
Employment, Theory, 9961
Empoli, A., 1371
Emrich, I., 5189
Enama-Sternegg, K. T., 8068
Enches, E. L., 2572
Enclosure, 4785
Encyclopedia, 4199, 5339, 5440, 5895, 5988, 5993, 6101, 6528, 6883, 8149
Enclyclopedia, Industrial, 6569
Encyclopedia, Insurance, 8740
Encyclopaedia Britannica, 3706, 7337, 9367
Encyclopedia of the Social Sciences, 5290, 8887, 8956, 8961, 9732
Encyclopedie des Sciences Mathematiques, 9753
Encyclopedie Scientifique, 5437
Encyclopedie Socialiste, Syndicale et Cooperative, 9113
Endemann, W., 197, 4945
Energy, 1706
Enfantin, P., 5994
Engel, E. 7816
Engels, F., 1040, 2481, 7817-7818, 9003, 9048, 9070-9071, 9118, 9149, 9168, 9169-9173, 9230, 9283, 9289, 9302, 9317, 9321, 9366-9367, 9371, 9374, 9378, 9385-9386, 9387, 9390, 9395, 9396, 9398-9399, 9406, 9410, 9414-9415, 9428-9429, 9471, 9500-9501, 9520, 9524, 9549, 9590, 9638
Engine, Steam, 6904
Engineering, 1100, 1952, 3376, 3424, 3447
Engineering, Value, 3205, 3255, 3351, 3450
Engineers, 1060, 8993
England, 770, 4085, 4437, 4612, 4635, 6187, 6402, 6721, 7484, 8618
England, Eighteenth Century, 8708

Englander, O., 3203, 9698
English, H. E., 3536
English Industry, 7708
English Universities, 1349
Enke, S., 1372
Ennes Ulrich, R., 771
Ensor, G., 5996-5997
Ensor, R. C. K., 9174, 10026
Entail, Scotland, 4305
Entelek Incorporated, 3204
Enterprise, 1273, 1307, 1688
Enterprise, Business, 8992, 8997
Enterprise, Free, 9772
Enterprise, State, 2739
Environment, 490, 762, 2471
Eon de Beaumond, D., 4235
Epidemics, 5528
Epps, W., 7819
Epstein, R. C., 772
Epztien, L., 198
Equality, 9041
Equilibrium, 930, 1199, 1652, 1729, 1957, 2057, 2976, 3304, 9861, 10047
Equilibrium, Economic, 9763, 9943
Equilibrium, Monetary, 2976
Equilibrium, Static, 1421
Equilibrium, Underemployment, 9950
Equitable Society, 7072
Eras, W., 7820
Erba, A., 9271
Ererra, W., 7821
Ergang, C., 199
Ergin, F., 1373
Erhard, 851
Erlangen, K. B., 39
Errera, A., 2845
Eschenmayer, 5998
Escher, E., 2379
Escott, J. H. S., 7822
Eshan, E., 200
Esmein, M., 5348-5349
Espejel, O. F., 2380
Espinas A., 7823
Espinas, A. V., 201, 5190
Espinosa, A., 2593
Essays, 523, 708, 713, 728-730, 732, 735, 745, 758, 761, 763, 764, 765-766, 770, 773, 775, 779, 783, 784-787, 795, 800, 810-812, 816-817, 824, 828, 846, 849-850, 854, 863-864, 870-873, 880, 893, 895, 904, 907, 913, 930, 937, 939, 941, 953, 957-958, 967, 969-970, 974, 982, 985, 991, 993, 995, 1011, 1018, 1023, 2415, 3075, 3081, 3293, 3709, 3715, 3803, 3852, 3873, 5227, 5347, 7309, 7378, 7639, 8601, 8994, 8996, 9047, 9079, 9123, 9301, 9335, 9647, 9718, 9733, 9776, 9867, 9959, 9986, 10055
Essays, Political, 3075
Essen, 1374
Estapo, F., 2488
Estate, 4711
Estonia, 2607
Estrade, A. F., 6012
Ethics, 215, 434, 786, 795, 849, 1017, 3293, 3640, 3077, 4950, 6118, 7319, 8451, 8832, 9832
Ethics, Marxism, 9265
Ethnology, 4898
Ethnology, Modern, 7474
Euchner, W., 9298
Eucken, W., 202, 1375-1376, 9964
Eugster, C., 8947
Eulenburg, F., 8840
Europe, 945, 2608-2628, 2623, 3928, 4402, 4480, 4644, 4697, 4737, 4870, 4899, 4907, 5365, 5374, 5413, 5480, 5516, 5547, 5637, 5721, 5880, 5890, 5924, 5929, 6009, 6161-6162, 6166, 6168, 6205, 6291, 6324, 6366, 6437, 6444, 6488, 6552, 6558, 6621, 6763, 6765, 6847, 6925, 7351, 7575, 7635, 7738, 7815, 7987, 8008, 8175, 8254, 8370, 8413, 8478, 8501, 8814, 8868, 9153, 9913
Europe, Eastern, 2626
Europe, Middle Ages, 5064
Europe, Reconstruction, 9987
Europe, War, 9995
Evaluation, 9783
Evans, D. M., 6017-6018
Evans, G. H., 1377

Evans, J. W., 5033
Evelyn, J., 4250-4251
Events, 762
Everett, A. H., 6019
Everett, G., 5252-5253
Evolution, 2090
Evolution, Economic, 456, 1900, 8977
Evolution, Social, 456, 1388
Ewing, J., 6794
Exchange, 151, 893, 1343, 3949, 4203, 4317, 5028, 5155, 5545, 5589, 6327, 6588, 6670, 6674, 7011, 7155, 7178, 8100, 8128, 9725, 9838
Exchange, Commercial, 6053
Exchange, Foreign, 5280, 7074, 7628
Exchange, Free, 8255
Exchange, Rates, 3226
Exchequer, 7981
Exchequer, England, 7093
Excise, 4059, 4447, 4556, 4679, 4753, 6215
Excise, France, 4306
Excise, General, 4755
Exon, J., 4259
Expansion, Economic, 878, 3737
Export, 3355, 3985, 4659, 5344, 5785, 6371, 6806, 6830, 6840
Export, Coal, 6624
Eynern, G., 1378
Eyskens, G., 203
Eyskens, M., 204

Fabrini, L., 3610
Faber, R., 7824
Fabian Essays, 8617, 9553
Fabian Socialism, 9105, 9432
Fabian Society, 9106, 9123, 9178, 9552
Fabian Society, History, 9480
Fabiunke, G., 8841
Fabrian, R. G., 3611
Fabricius, 6024
Factory, 6050, 6229, 6832, 8489
Factory, Laws, 8374
Factory, Legorn, 3957
Factory Act, 6974, 8095
Factory Acts, 2781

Factory System, 7079
Faculte Catholique de Droit de Lille, 774
Fage, A., 2653
Fagniez, G., 7815
Faiget, 4260-4261
Fairchild, F. R., 776, 1379-1381
Fairman, W., 6026-6027
Falcon, W. D., 3205
Falk, E., 9179
Falke, J., 7826
Falkowski, M., 9180
Fallon, V., 1382
Fan, H., 9928-9929
Fanfani, A., 206, 207, 994, 2846, 4946, 5191
Fanno, M., 1382-1385, 2769, 5257
Fantini, O., 1386-1387
Fardin, G., 5287
Farm Management, Roman, 4975
Farm Products, 3355
Farmer, 4418, 4456, 5927, 6400, 6707, 6713
Farmer, African, 3176
Farmer, Corn Trade, 7232
Farmer, Letters, 4783, 4879
Farmer, Tours, 4874
Farming, 4418, 5477, 8065
Farming, English, 8466
Farming, Spain, 6316
Farming, United States, 7782
Farms, 3971, 7043
Farms, American, 7804
Farnam, H. W., 7827
Faroppa, L. A., 1388
Farque, P., 9368
Farr, W., 7828
Farrar, D. E., 1389
Farrer, J. A., 7829
Farrer, T. H., 7830-7831
Fasciani, F. L., 1390
Fascist, 56, 73
Faucher, L. J., 6028-6029
Faulwetter, H., 3316
Fauquier, F., 4265, 4493
Faure, F., 7832
Faure-Fremiet, J., 2463
Faure-Soulet, J. F., 208, 5350
Fauveau, G., 7833
Favarel, C., 7834

Fawcett, H., 1391, 7835-7838
Fawcett, M. G., 7839
Fawcett, W. L., 7840
Fay, C. R., 1392, 5192, 7292-7293
Fazy, J. J., 6030-6032
Fechner, H., 7841
Federal Reserve Board, 3644
Federalism, Argentina, 2543
Federici, L., 2017
Federn, K., 9181
Fedorenko, N., 3612
Feier, R., 1393
Feilbogen, S., 3128, 9699
Fein, E., 3613
Feiwel, G. R., 2597
Fekete, J., 2800-2803
Felice, 6033
Felix, L., 6034-6035
Felkin, W., 7842
Fellner, W., 777, 1367, 1994, 9813
Fellner, W. J., 209, 1394
Fels, E., 3206
Fels, R., 1395, 3207
Feng, T., 2585
Fengels, F., 9505
Feninstein, O., 3632
Fenizion, F., 1396-1397
Fenn, C., 7483
Fenoglio, G., 210
Fenton, R., 4266
Ferguson, A., 4267-4268
Ferguson, C. E., 1400-1402, 3208
Ferguson, J. M., 211
Fergusson College, Poona, 844, 2817
Feria, G., 9757
Fernandez, R., 3209
Fernandez Pirla, J. H., 1403
Ferrara, F., 212-213 2842, 6036, 6038
Ferraris, C. F., 7844
Ferreira, A., 5193
Ferrier, F. L. A., 6039
Ferry, C. J., 6019
Fersh, G. L., 1209
Festschiften, 967
Fetter, F. A., 778, 1404-1405, 3053, 3210-3212, 3614, 7845
Fetter, F. W., 214, 2382, 5194
Feuer, L. S., 9182, 9366

Fiaccavento, C., 1406
Fiance, 5272
Fichte, J. G., 6040
Fickenscher, W., 9520
Field, C. D., 7846
Field, J. A., 779
Fielding, H., 4269-4270
Fierli, 5887
Figli, 2474
Figuerga, E., 3493, 9849
Filangieri, G., 2871
Filmer, R., 4271
Finland, 6952
Finance, 152, 902, 1063, 1211, 1222, 1223, 1467, 1512, 1738, 1785, 1896, 2233, 2514, 2720, 2796, 2856, 2866, 3755, 4002, 4006, 4088, 4148, 4197, 4214, 4219, 4225, 4282, 4293, 4295, 4308, 4316, 4332, 4333, 4508, 4545, 4557, 4561, 4581, 4624, 4656, 5383, 5390, 5479, 5493, 5507, 5582, 5611, 5613, 5672, 5675, 5681, 5746, 5751, 5767, 5888, 5892, 5968, 5981, 6004, 6005, 6032, 6048, 6081, 6082, 6094, 6103, 6153, 6156, 6171, 6183, 6202, 6230, 6231, 6291, 6317, 6352, 6402, 6409, 6644, 6645, 6502, 6539, 6545, 6547, 6565, 6599, 6614, 6616, 6625, 6692, 6715, 6716, 6722, 6723, 6910, 7019, 7039, 7076, 7080, 7130, 7177, 7258, 7406, 7458, 7494, 7518, 7525, 7589, 7596, 7637, 7649, 7674, 7678, 7687, 7702, 7703, 7704, 7771, 7786, 7855, 7857, 7861, 7867, 7884, 7908, 7928, 7947, 8025, 8075, 8090, 8092, 8108, 8119, 8121, 8143, 8190, 8232, 8271, 8279, 8292, 8323, 8332, 8347, 8353, 8372, 8399, 8468, 8477, 8558, 8565, 8633, 8647, 8660, 8662, 8671, 8672, 8724, 8734, 8735, 8736,

8772, 8789, 8819, 9691, 9723, 9992, 10052
Finance, American, 8377
Finance, Ancient, 5144
Finance, French, 6586, 6599
Finance, Germany, 5150
Finance, Great Britain, 5506, 6643, 7207, 9906
Finance, Greek, 4884
Finance, History, 4362, 5628
Finance, History, United States, 7741
Finance, Italian, 8606
Finance, Louis XV, 6586
Finance, Public, 1273, 1872, 2144, 5671, 7440, 7551, 7716, 8373, 8441, 8509, 9905
Finance, Russia, 8476
Finch, R., 9988
Finer, H., 2776
Finer, S. E., 2383
Fink, A., 7487
Finklhor, D., 740
Finlaison, J., 6818
Finland, 2424, 3319
Finlay, K., 6689
Finley, J. H., 7813
Finnish Economic Association, 3319
Finoia, M., 3616
Fire, 3980
Firenze, A., 4924
Firm, 1718, 3404, 3591, 3739, 3777, 9858
Firm, Represenative, 9864
Firmin, R., 4272
Firth, R. W., 4948-4949
Fiscal Agent, 1987
Fiscal History, 8603
Fiscal Legislation, 8368
Fiscal Policy, 9820, 9840-9841, 9947, 9949
Fiscal Revolution, 10080
Fischer, G., 3072, 6043
Fischer, H., 3617
Fischer, P. D., 7848
Fischerstrom, J., 2384
Fish, 4129
Fisher, I., 1407, 3213-3216, 3618, 3620-3622, 5844, 7849, 9700
Fisher, I. N., 2385

Fishery, 3979, 4182, 4273, 4415, 4713, 5710, 5832, 6062, 6220, 6332, 6436, 6486, 6626, 6699, 6808, 7171
Fishery, Great Britain, 6982
Fishery, Salmon, 6385
Fishery, Whale, 5546, 6965
Fishing, Royal, 4732
Fishing, Trade, 4050
Fishman, B. G., 1408
Fishman, L., 5352, 8948
Fitzgerald, E., 9438
Fitzmaurice, E., 5195
Fitzpatrick, P. J., 9701
Fitzwilliam, E., 2501
Fitzwilliam, M., 6044
Flag, Neutral, 7043
Flamant, M., 1409-1410
Flaubacher, J. F., 4950
Flax, 3940
Fleck, F. H., 1411
Fleetwood, W., 4115, 4274
Fletcher, A., 4276
Fletcher, H. M., 3054
Flink, S. J., 1412
Flint, H. M., 7850
Flint, R., 7851
Florence, 4956
Flores, A., 9183
Florez Estrada, A., 2386, 6046
Floridablanca, 5662
Florin, R., 1413
Flouzat, D., 1414, 2387
Flubacher, J. F., 215
Flux, A. W., 1415, 3623
Flynn, J. J., 2388
Focillon, H., 5064
Focke, W., 5196
Fodere, F. E., 6047
Foerster, 4277-4278
Fog, B., 1066
Fogowitz, J., 7852
Foldes, K., 9184
Foley, R., 4279
Folkes, M., 4280
Fondo de Cultura Economica, 2312-2314
Fonrough, C. M. G., 241
Fontenay, R., 5532, 6048
Fonteyraud, A., 6859
Food, 5667, 7548
Foote, R. J., 3219, 3220

Forbes, W., 6049
Forbonnais, F., 4281-4295, 4671, 5885
Forbush, D. R., 1271
Forchheimer, K., 9930
Ford, J. W., 1542
Ford, P., 1416
Fordyce, W., 7853
Forecasting, 1728, 3624, 3848
Forecasting, Central, 3544
Forecasting, Econometric, 3711
Foreign Exchange, 4141, 5085, 7936, 9945, 10022
Foreman, C., 4296
Forest, 4785
Forestalling, 6567
Forester, E. S., 5055
Forestry, 4588
Forgery, 7250
Formaleoni, 7060
Fornari, T., 2847, 7854
Forster, E., 3626
Forster, N., 4297, 6051
Forster, W., 3625
Forstmann, A., 216, 1417
Forte, F., 1418
Fortnightly Review, 3511, 7278
Fortrey, S., 4298
Forzan Dagger, J., 3221
Fossati, A., 536, 1419
Fossati, E., 217, 780-781, 1420-1421, 2801, 2848
Foster, 9903
Foster, J. L., 6053
Foundation for Social Research, 2246
Fourgeaud, A., 1422
Fourier, C., 5801, 6055-6059, 6844, 9068, 9186-9187
Fournier de Flaix, E., 7855
Foville, A., 7858-7861
Fowle, T. W., 7862
Fox, K. A., 3220, 3222-3223, 3600
Fox, R. W., 9422, 9490
Foxwell, H. S., 450, 7863, 9442
Fracchia, C. A., 9931
Frain, H. R., 1423
France, 1112, 1273, 1346, 1424-1425, 2632-2656, 3923, 4035-4037, 4083, 4108, 4134, 4136, 4169, 4214, 4235-4236, 4240, 4246, 4282, 4294, 4306-4308, 4405, 4408, 4512, 4525, 4538, 4561, 4578, 4588-4589, 4608, 4610, 4622, 4707, 4735, 4803, 4806, 4811, 4882, 4892, 5037-5038, 5176-5178, 5222, 5232, 5252, 5436, 5453, 5475-5476, 5493-5494, 5508-5509, 5542, 5566, 5591, 5606-5607, 5618, 5627, 5651, 5670-5671, 5730, 5775, 5806, 5825, 5869, 5893, 5901-5902, 5913, 5948, 5950, 5962, 5999, 6032, 6050, 6076, 6085, 6137, 6143-6154, 6181, 6185, 6211, 6230, 6283, 6300, 6313, 6338-6339, 6341, 6353, 6359, 6377-6378, 6402, 6409, 6430, 6443, 6452, 6487, 6490, 6503, 6524, 6526, 6538, 6539, 6545, 6554-6559, 6560, 6572, 6599, 6614-6615, 6620, 6655, 6660, 6693, 6696, 6764, 6769, 6776, 6892-6894, 6898, 6914, 6926, 6936, 6951, 6953, 6975, 7034, 7071, 7120, 7189, 7195, 7201, 7237, 7265, 7406, 7410, 7430, 7465, 7475, 7508, 7517-7518, 7538, 7549, 7559, 7569, 7591, 7622, 7627, 7635, 7660, 7685, 7702, 7719, 7771, 7789, 7807, 7889, 7928, 8024, 8108, 8112, 8165, 8174, 8178, 8273, 8310, 8346, 8347, 8363, 8415, 8436, 8444, 8479, 8505, 8541, 8552, 8589, 8671, 8727-8728, 9146, 9166, 9333, 9342, 9355, 9371, 9373, 9528
France, Centre d'Etudes Sociologiques, 3224
France, Colony, 7537
France, Commerce, 4435
France, Counseil Economique, 2389
France, Finance, 5507

France, History, 6544
France, Ministere de l'Economie et Des Finances, 218
France, Statistics, 7148
Franchini-Stappo, A., 1426
Francis, J. H., 7864
Franckii, J. C., 4299
Franco Lopez, G., 782
Frank, T., 4951
Frank-Ossipoff, Z., 219
Frankel, A. H., 783
Franklin, A., 7865
Franklin, B., 2351, 2390, 2530, 4257, 4300-4304, 4573, 7294
Franklin, J., 9513
Franqueville, C., 7866
Franz, F., 7867
Franz, G., 8842
Fraser, L. H., 220, 1427, 3628
Fraser, R., 6062
Frederick, E., 7868
Free Religious Movement, London, 10100
Free Trade, 305, 2660, 2773, 3067, 4519, 5184, 5266, 5457, 5461, 5859, 5935
Free Trade, Great Britain, 5288
Freedman, R., 9190, 9403
Freedom, 289, 2246, 2528, 9150
Freight Rates, 4643, 4774, 5597
French, 988, 6461, 9393
French Enlightenment, 5282
Frend, W., 5814, 6064
Frere, O., 7869
Frere, P., 7870
Freville, 4870
Freyer, H., 221 222
Friday, C. B., 3087
Fridrichowicz, E., 222
Friederischsen, V. C., 223
Friedman, M., 224, 784-789, 849, 3225, 3236, 9702, 9814-9815, 9932
Friedrich, A. A., 1059
Friedrich, M., 9192
Friedrichs des Grossen, 5286
Friendly Societies, 5447, 5473, 5548-5549, 5814, 8454

Frignet, E., 7871
Frisch, H., 1428
Frisch, R. A. K., 225, 3629-3630, 9816
Frisella Vella, G., 1429
Fritsche, B., 9193
Froman, L. A., 1430
Fromm, E., 9194, 9416
Frommer, H., 7872
Frossard, 5701
Frothingham, Louis Adams, Fund, 5346
Froumentaeu, N., 4308
Frowein, S. H., 9799
Fua, G., 3227
Fuchs, E., 9438
Fuchs, J., 7873, 9196
Fuchs, V. R., 2241
Fuel, Fossil, 6237
Fujihara, G., 226, 2391
Fujii, S., 2875
Fulda, 6066-6070
Fullarton, J., 6071
Fulton, R. B., 7295, 9197
Funck, B. T., 7875
Funck-Brentano, T., 4527
Function, 3137, 3394
Function, Demand, 3396
Function, Production, 10, 2080
Function, Supply, 10090
Function, Utility, 9673
Funding System, 6428
Funds, Foreign, 7843
Funk, F. X., 7875-7876
Furber, H. J., 3055
Furfey, P. H., 227
Furniss, E. S., 1380, 1423, 5197
Furstenau, 6072
Furstenberg, F., 1431
Furtado, C., 228-229
Furuya, Y., 9933
Fusco, A. M., 9934
Fusco, F., 6073-6075
Fusfeld, D. B., 3632
Fusfeld, D. R., 230, 3056
Fuz, J. K., 2742
Fyot, J. L., 1432

Gabaglio, A., 7879
Gabel, C., 4953
Gabrielsen, A., 3633
Gadgil, D. R., 788
Gadgil, G. G., 1433

Gaete, D., 6076, 6614
Gage, W. L., 3229
Gaillard, 6766
Gaines, E. J., 5198
Gairner, A., 4312
Galbraith, J. K., 231, 789-790, 3057-3058, 3634
Gale, S., 6077
Galiani, A., 4539, 5161, 5319
Galiani, F., 2872, 4313, 5204
Galibert, L., 6012
Galitz, B. E., 9015
Gallatin, A., 6078-6080
Gallego, M. A., 2386
Galli, R., 1434
Gallman, R. E., 5201
Gallois, E., 7881
Gallois, L., 6683
Gallus, W., 2994, 7882
Galves, C., 1435-1436
Gambs, J. S., 1437-1438, 3230, 8949
Gammage, R. G., 7883
Gander, J. E., 3536
Gandhi, M. K., 2804, 2810-2812, 2816, 2826-2827, 9588
Gandillot, A., 6005, 6081
Gandillot, R., 7884
Gangemi, L., 232
Ganguli, B. N., 2813
Ganilh, C., 5202-5203, 6085-6086
Gantner, P., 3231
Ganzoni, E., 2392, 5204
Garau Riu, M., 1439
Garaudy, R., 9094, 9198
Garb, G., 1440
Garces Molina, D., 3232
Garcia Gonzales, A., 1441-1442
Gardiner, A. H., 4954
Garella Della Morea, E. G., 7885
Garello, J., 9935
Garfield, F. R., 1602
Gargallo di Castel Lentini, G., 2641
Gargas, Z., 2930
Garina, V., 9200
Garino Canina, A., 1443
Garmo, E. P., 2287
Garnett, D., 10000
Garnier, G., 6088-6091, 7337
Garnier, H., 4955
Garnier, J., 6092-6094, 7296
Garnier, R. M., 7886
Garve, C., 7337
Garver, F. B., 1444
Garvey, J. E., 92
Gasca, C. L., 7888-7889
Gaskell, P., 6095
Gaspar de Jovellanos, S. D., 5561
Gasparin, A. E. P., 6097-6098
Gasquet, A., 7889
Gaume, J., 6099
Gavard, 6100
Gavelkind, Custom of, Kent, 6873
Gay, V., 659
Gay Y Forner, V., 233, 1445
Gayer, A. D., 791, 924
Gazave, J., 5353
Gazetteer, 7102
Gazetteer, India, 5560
Gazitua Navarrete, V. M., 1446
Geal, E. V., 7890
Gearty, P. W., 2393
Gebhart, E., 4956
Gee, J., 4315
Gegauf, K. F., 2982
Gehlhoff, J., 2675
Gehrig, H., 8843-8844
Gehrig, Hans, 301
Geier, P. P., 6101
Geiger, R., 9936
Geijer, E. G., 6102
Geisbusch, H. G., 3243
Geistbech, M., 7892
Geiter, E. G., 6102
Gekker, P., 2975
Gelee, V., 4316
Gelting, J. H., 2605
Gemahling, P., 234-235, 792
Gemkow, H., 9202
Gemmell, J., 837, 1447
Gemmill, P. F., 753, 793, 1448-1450
General Theory, 10063
Gennaro, A. D., 9120
Gennser, M., 1067
Genovesi, A., 2873, 4319
Gentz, F., 6103
Geography, 584, 6214, 7776
Geography, Commercial, 7623, 8335

George, H., 1451-1452, 2435, 3083, 7893-7897, 8220
George, H., Jr., 7898
George, L., 9977, 9995
George III, 7150
Georgescu-Roegen, N., 3635, 9817
Georgetown University, 3537
Georgia State College, 3336, 9738
Georgofili di Firenze, 6493
Gerando, M., 6104-6105
Gerard, C., 399
Gerard de Rayneval, 6106
Gerbino, G. F., 935
Gerlach, E., 9291
Germain-Martin, H., 3636
German, 770, 2551, 7199, 7220, 9319, 9377
German, Federal Republic, 2715-2719, 9203-9204
Germany, 192, 265, 451, 967, 1134, 2652, 2657-2714, 2960, 3472, 4321, 5187, 5295, 5581, 6194, 6301, 6337, 6480, 6660, 6784, 6847, 7063, 7082, 7188, 7305, 7351, 7426, 7462, 7481, 7624, 7699, 7751, 7807, 8001, 8013, 8073, 8091, 8116, 8137, 8141, 8216, 8235, 8253, 8264, 8293, 8515, 8579, 8649, 8706, 8712, 8797, 8803, 8839, 8844, 8861, 8869, 8877, 9146, 9166, 9202, 9390, 9411, 10058
Gernet, J., 4958
Gernet, L., 4959
Gerschenkron, A., 236
Gerstner, 6107
Gerth, H. H., 1018
Gervaise, I., 5205
Gesammelte Aufsatze sur Wissenschaftslehre, 8902
Gesell, S., 9544
Geyer, H., 1457, 3637
Geyer, P., 7899
Geyer, T., 3233
Ghaussy, A. G., 9937
Gherity, J. A., 794
Ghio, P., 238
Ghosh, R. N., 239

Giacalone-Monaco, T., 2860, 9703
Giannessi, E., 2849
Giannotti, J. A., 9205
Gibbi, U., 1466
Gibbins, H., 7900-7901
Gibbon, A., 6108
Gibbon, J., 7902
Gibbons, B., 7976
Gibbons, J. S., 6109-6110
Gibbs, H. H., 7903
Gibson, W. L., 3638
Giddings, J. H., 7632
Gide, C., 1458, 2642, 7904-790?
Gide, P. H. C., 240-243
Gierke, J., 2673
Gierke, O., 4960-4961, 7906
Giersch, H., 3502
Giffen, R., 7909
Giglio, C., 5206
Gilbarg, D., 740
Gilbart, J. W., 6111- 6116
Gilbert, T., 6117
Gilbey, E. W., 1459
Gilby, T., 4962
Gill, R., 7910
Gill, R. T., 244, 1460
Gillies, J., 6118
Gillman, J., 9206
Gillman, J. M., 9938
Gillot, F., 9705
Gilman, N. P., 7911-7913
Gilmer, F. W., 5354
Gilson, E., 4963
Gini, Co., 1461
Ginzberg, E., 4964, 7297
Giorgi, G., 1462
Giornale Degli Economisti, 3329, 3498, 3571, 3792-3793, 3795
Girard, E., 4965
Girault, A., 4590, 7914
Girsberger, H., 2643
Gislason, C., 1463
Gitlow, A. L., 707, 1464
Gladden, W., 7915
Glade, W. P., 2915
Gladstone, W. E., 7916
Glahe, F. R., 3594
Glansdorff, M., 3234
Glasgow, 6794
Glastetter, W., 245
Glen, W. C., 7918
Gligorijevic, S., 2465

Glover, R., 4321
Gneist, R., 7919
Go, H. T., 943
Goals, 1017
Gobbi, H., 7921
Gobineau, J. A., 7922
Godard, J. G., 7923
Goddard, A., 455, 1096
Godelier, M., 9207, 9590
Godfrey, M., 4322
Godin, A., 7924
Goddy, J. R., 488
Godson, R., 6120
Godwin, W., 6121-6126
Goedhart, C., 9939
Goetz, G. R., 246-247
Goetz, H. B., 2178
Goetz-Givey, R., 868
Gold, 902, 994, 3125, 3512, 3981, 3983, 4024, 4115, 4138, 4241, 4280, 4654, 4706, 4734, 5187, 5189, 5213, 5303, 5657, 5727, 5758, 5810, 6029, 6137, 6218, 6236, 6380, 6580, 6582, 7015, 7083, 7259, 7433, 7624, 7715, 7840, 8068, 8311, 8409, 8458, 8850, 8855
Gold, Australia, 7053
Gold, California, 7053
Gold, Price of, 7104
Gold, Unemployment, and Capitalism, 5212
Gold Act, 4159
Goldendach, D. B., 9209
Goldfeld, S. M., 9660
Goldman, S. M., 3235
Goldschmidt, L., 7926
Goldsmid, C., 4341
Goldsmith, 4359
Gollancz, V., 9108
Golob, E. D., 248
Goltz, F. T. V., 7927
Gomel, C., 7928
Gomes, A., 249
Gomes, F. L., 795
Gomes, L. S., 1467
Gomez, E. J., 2594
Gommer, G. L., 7629
Gondra, L. R., 250
Gonnard, C. R., 251-252, 897, 5207-5208, 6526

Gonner, E. C. K., 7931
Gonzales, A. J., 1468
Gonzales Alberde, P., 7298
Goodell, W., 6127
Goodfellow, D. M., 4966
Goodman, G., 253
Goodman, K. E., 1469-1470
Goodnow, F. J., 7933
Goods, 320
Goods, Investment, 10090
Goods, Public, 3426
Goodwin, C. D. W., 2548, 2566
Gootjes, P., 1471
Gopal, L., 4967
Gopalakrishnan, P. K., 2814
Gordon, B. J., 2395, 2743, 4968-4969
Gordon, C. H., 4970
Gordon, D., 9139
Gordon, D. F., 254, 3639
Gordon, H. S., 9139
Gordon, L. J., 1472
Gordon, S. D., 1473-1474
Gordon, W., 4323
Gori, A., 7934
Gorlof, 6128
Gorman, W. M., 3236
Gorner, A., 255
Gorov, K. Z., 2564
Gorski, H., 4916
Gorski, J., 256-260, 5209
Gorski, M., 2931
Goschen, G. J., 3640, 7936
Goss, J. D., 7937
Gossen, H. H., 3237, 6129, 9661, 9692, 9707, 9766
Gotha Programme, 9378
Goto, F., 1475
Goto, H., 3238
Gottheil, F. M., 9210
Gottl-Ottilienfeld, F., 2676, 8869
Gottman, G. A., 280
Gotz, W., 7938
Goudriaan, J., 1476
Gouge, W. M., 6130
Goulburn, H., 5881
Gould, J. M., 7939
Gould, N., 4324
Gourlet, C., 9919
Gouroff, 6765
Gourvitch, A., 796
Gouttes, 6131
Government, 829, 1108, 2448,

3677, 5234, 5408, 6644,
6897, 7001
Government, British, 5516
Government, Control, 8131
Government, Expenditure, 5588
Government, Great Britain,
5620
Government, Industrial, 892
Government, Local, 7640, 8463
Government, Municipal, 8615
Government, Philosophy, 2101
Government, Regulation, 5792
Government, Roman System,
7394
Gow, N., 6132
Gowda, K. G. V., 9940
Gowlanyan, K. G., 2995
Gowry du Roslan, J., 7940
Graaff, J. V., 261
Grabski, Z., 2932
Graca, A., 2560
Graham, J., 6133
Graham, M. K., 7299
Graham, P. A., 7941
Graham, W., 7942-7943
Grain, 3921-3923, 4356-4357,
 4457, 4460, 4501, 4535,
 4558, 4562, 4633, 4701,
 5329, 5344, 5391, 5406,
 5465, 5466-5469, 5555,
 6341, 6362, 6384, 6514,
 6667, 6784, 6800, 6987, 7185
Grainger, T. B., 6329
Grampp, W. D., 262, 263, 797,
 2746, 3641, 5210
Grande Encyclopedie, 5406
Grandeau, L., 7944
Grange Movement, United States,
 8268
Granger, G. G., 3642
Grant, J., 6134
Grant, R., 6135
Grapheus, D., 7945
Graphic Presentation, 9720
Graslin, L. F. F., 4325
Grasnick, P., 9941
Grauman, 6136-6137
Graunt, J., 4326
Gray, A., 264
Gray, J., 2417, 2766, 6138-
 6142
Gray, J. H., 7946
Grayson, H., 1477

Grazia, G., 9212
Graziadei, A., 1478-1479
Graziani, A., 265-267, 1480-
 1482, 2850, 2851, 7947-
 7949, 8950
Great Britain, 198, 323, 2065,
 2509, 2720-2794, 2834, 3035,
 3323, 3337, 3467, 3511,
 3575, 3911, 3917, 3923-
 3924, 3926, 3938, 3954,
 3967, 3976, 3985, 4025,
 4039, 4043, 4047, 4049-
 4052, 4059, 4070, 4091,
 4094, 4102-4106, 4108,
 4129-4131, 4134, 4139-
 4153, 4157-4165, 4167,
 4169, 4171-4176, 4179-
 4180, 4181-4191, 4223,
 4225-4234, 4237, 4244-
 4254, 4290, 4296-4298,
 4315, 4329-4330, 4341-
 4355, 4399-4401, 4405-
 4406, 4417, 4423, 4433-
 4456, 4510, 4551-4556,
 4564-4576, 4589, 4616,
 4639, 4641, 4653-4654,
 4659, 4675, 4678, 4682,
 4699, 4715, 4718, 4732,
 4734-4772, 4738, 4756,
 4774-4782, 4797-4798,
 4811-4825, 4848, 4854-
 4856, 4858-4883, 5206,
 5210, 5212, 5231, 5247,
 5257, 5281, 5283, 5307,
 5316, 5446, 5452, 5455,
 5453, 5462, 5489, 5506,
 5508, 5510, 5521, 5525,
 5554, 5558, 5641, 5647,
 5649, 5651, 5706, 5709,
 5749, 5752, 5767, 5772,
 5780, 5786, 5821, 5850,
 5888, 5896, 5908, 5918,
 5919, 5969-5970, 5972,
 5986-5987, 6020, 6025,
 6028, 6044, 6053, 6062,
 6086, 6095, 6103, 6139,
 6154, 6167, 6174-6176,
 6189, 6210, 6227, 6237,
 6241, 6249, 6306, 6324,
 6328-6330, 6332, 6352,
 6355, 6374, 6427, 6429,
 6433, 6470, 6485, 6501,
 6539, 6557, 6579, 6620,

6627, 6647, 6655, 6677,
6682, 6717, 6786, 6816,
6826, 6834-6835, 6861,
6887, 6900, 6926, 6966,
6981, 6988, 6996, 7021,
7028, 7030, 7032, 7076-
7078, 7099, 7104-7109,
7162, 7165, 7179, 7200,
7207, 7246, 7272, 7361,
7396-7403, 7412-7413,
7418, 7448, 7536, 7554-
7556, 7672, 7691-7694,
7693, 7765-7767, 7794,
7806, 7814, 7822, 7843,
7866, 7886, 7919, 7920,
7942, 7971, 7982, 8004,
8018-8019, 8074, 8076,
8112, 8205, 8269, 8340,
8346, 8400, 8414, 8452,
8486, 8530, 8531, 8553,
8615, 8618, 8717, 8787,
8831, 8896, 8918, 9037,
9433, 9474, 9536, 9574,
9827, 9841, 9923
Great Britain, Coin, 4495
Great Britain, Colonies,
  America, 5920
Great Britain, Commerce, 143
Great Britain, Commercial Relations, 6712
Great Britain, Emigration, 7115
Great Britain, England, Hertfordshire, 3255
Great Britain, Fourteenth Century, 5154
Great Britain, Sugar Colony, 4499
Greaves, J., 4331
Greece, 2795-2798, 4042, 4902,
  4959, 4984, 5041, 5058,
  5117, 5120, 6507, 6551,
  6849, 7963, 8664
Greek, 4884, 4892, 5016, 5096,
  5102, 5122, 5146, 5687,
  5810, 6118
Greeley, H., 5487, 7950, 9578
Green, D. I., 3239
Green, J. L., 3240
Green, J. R., 7951
Green, T. H., 4382
Greenbacks, History of, 8975
Greenland, 4227

Greenville, Lord, 6148, 7127
Greg, W. R., 6144
Gregory, J. M., 7952
Gregory, T. E., 5212
Greidanus, T., 9942
Grellier, J. J., 6146
Gremilliet, 6617
Grenfell, H. R., 7903
Grenfell, P., 6147
Grenier, A., 4951
Grenner, K. H., 2677
Grenville, E. K., 4332
Grenville, G., 3970, 4333
Gresham, T., 5280, 5653, 6149
Gresham's Law, 5194
Greven, J., 5213
Grey, A. L., 798
Grey, E., 6150-6151
Grice-Hutchinson, M., 2968
Grichting, E., 3643
Grier, J. A., 7954
Grierson, J., 7955
Grierson, P., 5017
Griffiths, G. C., 7956
Grigorov, K. I., 2563
Griliches, Z., 3644
Grillo, E., 9400
Grimaudet, F., 4334
Griziotti, Kretschmann, J.,
  268-269
Grodek, A., 2933
Grogg, C. I., 2214
Gromeka, V. I., 1014
Gronlund, L., 7957
Grooten, J., 2225
Grose, T. H., 4382
Grosier, 6152
Gross, C., 7958
Gross, G., 7959-7960
Grossman, H., 8951, 9213
Grossman, H. K., 270
Grosvenor, W. M., 7961-7963
Grotii, M. L., 4336
Grotius, Hugo, 39
Grouber de Groubenthal, 6153
Growth, 742, 888, 930, 1678, 1728,
  1775, 2083-2084, 2234, 2289,
  3449, 3481, 4544, 8812,
  888, 9858, 9959
Growth, Economic, 836, 863-865,
  908, 957, 974, 1170, 1937,
  2264, 3871, 3581, 5301,
  7347, 9079

Growth, English Industry, 8837
Growth, National, 5172
Growth, Rates, 9331
Gruchy, A. G., 435, 3059, 8952
Grunberg, K., 2669
Gruner, E., 7965
Grunfeld, J., 2678
Gruson, C., 9943
Gua de Malves, Abbe, 4337
Gual Villalbi, P., 799
Guaresti, J. J., 271, 1483
Guatemala, 2799
Gudin de la Brenellerie, 6154
Guelfat, I., 2997
Guepin, A., 6155
Guer, 6156-6159
Guerra Cepeda, R., 1484
Guest, R., 6160
Guevara, E., 9214
Guide, 789, 1050, 1311, 2240, 9948
Guide, Insurance, 7182
Guignabaudet, P, 1485
Guiheneuf, R., 3241
Guilbault, C. A., 7967
Guild, 7568, 7652, 7958, 8150, 8741
Guild, England, 7013, 8031
Guillaume, E., 1486
Guillaume, G., 1486
Guillaumin, N. G., 5827
Guillebaud, C. W., 3877, 9819, 9849
Guimerans, Edgardo, 396
Guinea, 4016
Guiney Company, 4860
Guis, 2474
Guitton, H., 1487-1491, 1988, 3182
Guitton, H., 5214
Guizot, F. P. G., 6161-6162
Gulanian, K. G., 272
Gulbenkian Foundation, 3624
Gulich, G. V., 6163
Gulick, C. A., 9215
Gumplowicz, L., 7968
Gunther, A., 2679
Gunton, G., 7969-7970
Guntzberg, B. E., 5355

Gupta, S., 9126
Gurria Urgell, J. M., 3242
Gurvitch, G., 9216
Gutersohn, A., 3243
Guthrie, J. A., 1492
Guthrie, W., 7971
Gutierrez G., 1493
Gutsche, H., 273
Gutzlaff, C., 6164
Guyot, V., 759, 7973
Guzicki, L., 2934

Haas, F., 7974
Haavelmo, T., 274, 1494, 3643
Haba, Z., 275, 2598
Habakkuk, H. J., 3244
Habdbook, 2652
Haber, A., 2717
Haberer, T., 7975
Haberler, G., 930, 9650, 9944
Hadar, J., 1495
Hadfield, R. A., 7976
Hadibroto, S., 1496
Hadiprabowo, M., 9217
Hadley, A. T., 3245, 7335, 7977-7978
Hadzic, M., 9218
Haeberle, K. E., 3246
Haesele, K. W., 800
Haffner, A., 2680
Hagelmayer, I., 9219
Hagemeister, 6823
Hagen, 6165
Hagenbuch, W., 1497
Hague, D. C., 830, 1498, 2152
Hague, R., 9199
Hahl, A., 2747
Hahn, A., 1499-1501
Hahn, L. A., 801
Hailstones, T. J., 802-803, 1331, 1502-1504
Hain, J., 7979
Hajela, P., 9945
Hake, A. E., 7980
Hakluyt, R., 4341
Haldane, R. B., 7300
Hale, M., 4342-4344, 4631
Halevy, D., 2463
Halevy, E., 7301, 9220
Haley, B. F., 703, 777, 1505
Hall, C., 6166
Hall, C. H., 2458
Hall, D. H., 5748
Hall, F., 4346

Hall, F. P., 8953
Hall, G. W., 6167
Hall, H., 2748, 4972, 7981-7982
Hall, R. L., 276
Hallam, H., 6168
Haller, H., 3646
Hamaker, H. J., 7983
Hambourg, D., 1506
Hambloch, G., 5356
Hamburg, G., 6004
Hameen-Aalto, V., 2378
Hamelin, A., 277
Hamilton, A., 4347, 6169-6172, 6173, 7994, 8620, 8675
Hamilton, D. B., 278-279, 7302, 8954
Hamilton, E., 5215-5216
Hamilton, E. J., 804, 4973
Hamilton, E.m 5215-5216
Hamilton, G. A. K., 280, 7984-7985
Hamilton, H., 684
Hamilton, R., 6174, 7986
Hamilton, W., 6177-6178, 7049, 8955-8956,
Hamilton, W. H., 805, 3247
Hammarabi, Code of, 4974
Hampl, F., 3647
Han, H., 2578
Han, U-G, 2906
Hanauer, A., 7987
Hancock, W. N., 6179-6180
Handbook, 1686, 1699, 1774, 1910, 2174, 2345, 2375, 2606, 2661, 6933, 7036, 7228, 7359, 7623, 7663, 8136, 8139, 8209, 8458, 8738, 8796, 8900, 9087
Handbook, Finance, 6440
Handbook, Insurance, 7234
Handbook, Land Charters, 7793
Handon, J. L., 1509-1511
Handworterbuch der Staatswissenschaften, 3129, 3488, 3830
Haney, L. H., 281, 3248
Hankey, T., 7990
Hanna, W., 5713, 5715
Hannsen, G., 7991
Hanse Towns, 8817
Hanseatic League, 4414, 6442, 6932, 8570
Hansen, A. H., 828, 1444, 1507 1769, 3060, 9820, 9947-9948

Hansen, M., 1508
Hansoer, E., 7992
Hanson, W., 7993
Hanway, J., 4348
Happiness, 6140
Happiness, Human, 2186, 7096
Harcourt, L. V., 6888
Harcourt, Vicomte, 6181
Harding, F. O., 1512
Hare, A. J. C., 7795
Haring, C. H., 2910
Harl, N. E., 3648
Harlan, H. C., 806
Harley, R., 6182
Harms, B., 71, 282, 2667, 3072
Harper, R. F., 4974
Harrach, B. E., 2847
Harrington, E. M., 4687
Harris, A., 8957
Harris, A. L., 283
Harris, J., 4349
Harris, S. E., 807-808, 837, 2397, 2909, 9952-9954, 9994
Harris, W. A., 1513
Harrison, F., 4975
Harrison, G. P., 5912
Harrison, W., 9043
Harriss, C. L.. 791, 809, 1514-1516
Harrod, H. R. F., 810-813
Harrod, R. F., 601, 9708, 9954-9955
Harrower, G. H., 7994
Harsin, P., 1517, 5350
Hart, A. B., 2069
Hart, A. G., 1542, 1555, 1969
Hart, M. A., 9221
Harte, W., 4350
Harter, L. G., 8958
Hartmann, E., 7995
Hartog, F., 284, 1518-1519
Harvard Business School, 7286
Harvard University, 474, 733, 836, 888, 894, 909, 930, 999, 1022, 1362, 2603, 2910, 3586, 5346, 10097
Harvey, J., 1520, 7996
Harvey, P., 9889
Harwood, E. C., 814
Hasada, K., 5357
Hasan, K., 2387
Hasbach, A., 7997
Hasbach, W., 286-287, 3649-3650,

7303-7304
Hasek, C. W., 1339, 2681, 7305
Hasenack, W., 10022
Hatchard, J., 6243
Hatfield College of Technology, 3255
Hatta, M., 2833
Hauer, J. V., 6183
Haupt, O., 7998-8000
Haureau, B., 4977
Hauser, Henri, 815
Hauser, K., 1521
Haushoffer, M., 8001-8003
Haustein, H.-D., 9222
Hauterive, Comte, 6184
Haveman, R. H., 3249
Havens, R. M., 1522
Hawes, B., 6186
Hawkins, E., 6187, 8004
Hawkins, E. L., 8742
Hawkins, F. B., 6188
Hawkins, J., 4351
Hawley, F. B., 3651-3652, 8005
Hawtrey, R. G., 1523, 3653, 3815, 9897
Hayasaka, T., 9956
Hayashi, J., 9709
Hayek, F. A., 815-817, 953, 1524, 2398, 3250, 3251, 3610, 3654, 7306-7307, 9224, 9707, 9710-9712
Hayes, H. G., 1525
Hayes, J. H., 1015
Hayes, R., 4352
Haynes, J., 3655, 4353
Haynes, W. W., 1526
Hazard, R. G., 8007
Hazlitt, H., 1527, 9957-9958
Hazlitt, W., 6161
Hazlitt, W. C., 8008
Headley, R. A., 288
Health, 5468, 5977, 6383
Health, Effects on, 7
Health, France, 6658
Healy, J., 4978
Hearn, W. E., 2547, 8009-8010
Hearnshaw, F. J. C., 4979
Heat, Laws of, 6782
Heath, M. S., 289
Heath, T., 4981-4982
Heathfield, R., 6189, 6190, 6191

Heber, Bishop, 6314
Heberden, W., 6192
Hecht, F., 8011-8013
Hecht, O., 5127
Heckscher, E., 5175
Heckscher, E. F., 290, 2155, 3656, 5218
Heeren, A. H. L., 6194-6197, 6225
Heertje, A., 1528
Hegel, G. W. F., 9032, 9239, 9253, 9377, 9435, 9441, 9454
Hegel, C., 8014
Hegeland, H., 5219
Heguerty, A. F., 4355
Heichelheim, F. M., 4983
Heidegger, 9624
Heilbroner, R. L., 1529-1530, 2399, 3061, 3599, 3657-3658
Heilman, R. E., 980
Heimann, E., 291
Heineccii, F. G., 6198
Heinig, K., 292, 1531
Heinrich, K., 202, 1375-1376
Heinrich, W., 2136
Heinze, A., 9226
Heiss, R., 9227
Heitland, W. E., 4984
Heitmuller, W., 293
Heitz, E. L., 2682
Helander, S., 8845
Held, A., 5221, 8015
Heleland, H., 9959
Helferich, J., 6199
Hellenistic Empire, 5088
Heller, F. H., 294
Heller, W. W., 295
Helms, L. A., 2400
Helps, A., 6200
Helvetius, C., 9490
Henderson, A. M., 2254, 3899
Henderson, E. F., 4985
Henderson, H. D., 9821, 9977
Henderson, J. S., 1522, 1532
Hendricks, H. G., 818
Henfner, J., 6201
Henn, R., 3659
Henneguy, S., 2463-2464
Hennet Le Chevalier, 6202-6203
Henrion de Bussi, 6204
Henry III, 4739
Henry IV, 4006
Henson, G., 6205

Herbert, C. J., 4356
Herbert, W., 6206
Herder-Dorneich, P., 1543, 2894
Herendeen, J. B., 3660
Heresies, Economic, 553
Heretic, Economic, 2403
Heretik, S., 296, 9228
Herford, C. H., 9712
Herkner, H., 297
Herlitz, L., 5358, 9129
Hermann, F. B. W., 2678, 6207
Hernandez Ron, R., 5222
Herrenschwand, J. F., 6208-6209
Herrera Lane, F., 1534
Herreshoff, D., 9229
Herskovits, M. J., 4986
Hertel, G., 9230
Hertslet, E., 8019
Hertslet, L., 6210
Hertz-Eichenrode, D., 9402
Hertzberg, Baron de, 6211
Hertzen, A. K., 2974
Hertzier, J. O., 9231
Hertzka, T., 8020
Herve-Bazin, F., 8021
Hervey, M. H., 8022
Herwins, W. A. S., 8025
Herz, U., 488
Herzen, A., 9352
Herzog, F. B., 8023
Herzog, J. S., 819
Hess, A. P., 820
Hesse, A. H., 1535-1536, 2683
Hesse, K., 2684
Hetemaki, P., 2424
Heuschling, P. F. X. T., 5359, 6212-6213
Heuss, E., 1537
Heuvel, J., 8024
Hewett, W. W., 1202, 1538
Hewitt, A. S., 6214
Hewitt, J., 4358
Heyd, W., 8026-8027
Heyking, E., 8028
Heyl, L., 8029
Heymans, G., 8030
Hibbert, F. A., 8031
Hibdon, J. E., 1539
Hic, M., 1540
Hicks, J., 3449, 3481
Hicks, J. R., 298, 1541-1542, 3256-3257, 3259, 3362, 3435, 3449, 3481, 9714-9715, 9822-9823, 9961
Hicks, R. D., 4987
Hidaka, H., 1543, 2894, 9233
Higgins, B. H., 821, 9962
Higgins, G., 9824
Higgs, H., 1214, 3623, 5360, 9692, 9727, 9793
Highland Society, Edinburgh, 5753
Highmore, A., 6215
Highway, 4142, 4351, 6807, 6837, 8499
Hijikata, S., 299-300, 1544, 9963
Hildebrand, B., 301, 8842-8843, 8846
Hildebrand, G. H., 327
Hildreth, R., 6216-6217
Hildreth, R. J., 3638
Hildyard, F., 6663
Hilferding, R., 9064, 9234
Hill, D. W., 58
Hill, J., 6218
Hill, J. A., 124, 7650
Hill, R., 6219
Hill, W., 2401
Hillebrecht, A., 302
Hillquit, M., 9235
Himes, N. E., 6701
Hindi, 462, 625
Hindostan, 6177-6178
Hinds, W. A., 9236
Hines, L. G., 1625
Hinrichs, A. F., 2278
Hinton, J., 4069
Hiradate, R., 1545
Hirase, M., 1546-1547, 2780,
Hirata, K., 303
Hirayama, S., 304
Hirsch, H., 9825
Hirst, F. W., 305, 7308
Hirst, M. E., 2402, 8847
Histo, Bank, 4363
Historical School, 8887
Historicism, 2476, 8821-8905
Historiography, 2918
History, 1445, 2025, 2661, 2681, 2953, 4362, 4803, 5020-5021, 5721, 5869, 6424, 8667, 9745
History, Constitutional, 2916
History, Economic Interpretation,

600, 2770, 8528, 9548
History, Entrepreneurial, 708
History, Finance, 7523
History, Industrial, 7524
History, Maritime, 6228, 6868
History, Marxian Interpretation, 9031, 9644
History, Materialist Conception, 9181, 9272, 9301
History, Modern, 8665
History, Natural, 8813
History, Political, 529
History, Social, 721, 5064, 5088-5089, 5113, 5115, 8237
History, Social Interpretation, 9644
History, War, 551
History of Political Economy, 822
History of Political Philosophy, 7289
Hitch, C. J., 1769
Hitotsubashi Ronshu, Tokyo, 646
Hitotsubashi University, Tokyo, 9716
Hoag, M. W., 1548
Hobbes, T., 4366
Hobhouse, L. T., 3260
Hobsbawm, E. J., 9409
Hobson, J. A., 1549-1550, 2403, 3261, 3661, 8959
Hock, C. V., 6230-6232
Hodges, W., 4367-4368
Hodgskin, T., 1551, 2489, 2766, 6233
Hodgskins, T., 414
Hoeck, 6235
Hoffman, G. W., 3092
Hoffman, J. G., 6236, 6238
Hoffmann, C., 1888, 1890
Hoffner, J., 4988-4989
Hofman, W., 823
Hofmann, H., 2551, 2685
Hofmann, W., 309, 1552, 3262, 9237
Hofstadter, R., 3062
Hogben, L., 5224
Hogg, R. D., 5009
Hoguet, P. W., 3848
Hohmann, H.-H., 2998
Hohnmann, H. F., 779
Holbach, 9490

Holland, 4321
Holland, J., 4369-4370 6237
Holland, R. H., 6239, 6240
Hollander, J. H., 764, 824, 2404, 2431, 3981, 3995, 4021, 4265, 4298, 4491, 4567, 4832, 5524, 8221, 9717-9718
Hollander, S., 4990
Holler, K. H., 9964
Holly, F., 1347
Holt, F. L., 6241
Holt, S., 1553
Holte, F. C., 1554
Holte, R., 2516
Holy, V. L., 9965
Holy Roman Empire, 5162
Holzman, F. D., 2999
Homan, P. T., 310, 1555, 8960, 8961, 8962, 8963, 9812, 9826,
Home, F., 2382
Home, H., 4371
Homer, H., 4372
Homer, S., 3263
Honduras, 2517
Honegger, H., 2686, 3663
Hong, I-Sop, 2907
Hong, M., 9238
Hong, S., 311
Hong, U., 312, 1556
Honjo, E., 2876-2882
Hood, E. P., 5757
Hood, F. C., 2749
Hood, W. C., 3664
Hodgeschool te Leiden, 15
Hook, E., 3368
Hook, S., 3665, 9239-9242, 9436
Hooke, A., 7409
Hooke, Andrew, 4374
Hooper, 4400
Hooper, J. W., 3666
Hoover, G. E., 826
Hoover Institution on War, Revolution, and Peace, 9144
Hope, J., 6242
Hopkins, T., 6243
Hoppner, J., 9405
Hori, S., 2573, 2618
Hori, T., 314-316

Horie, T., 2406, 9243-9244
Horie, Y., 2883-2885
Hormann, H., 308
Horn, I., 317
Horn, J. C., 6246
Horn, J. C., 6248
Horn, R. W., 241
Horne, T. H., 6000
Hornedo, E., 65, 9989
Horowitz, D., 9245
Horrocks, J. W., 5225
Horsefield, J. K., 5226
Horten, 9924
Horton, R. J. W., 6249
Horton, W., 6249
Horvat, B., 9246
Horvath, A., 4991
Hoselitz, B. F., 318, 827, 3667, 5300, 9058, 9739
Hosiery, Factory, 7842
Hospital, 4312, 4599, 6001, 6391, 6794
Hotelling, H., 939, 3803
Hoty, H. M., 8069
Houck, J. P., 3264
Houddard, A., 8063
Hough, R. R., 2407
Hought, Greek, 5016
Houghton, J., 4375
Houghton, T., 4377
Hours of Work, Ten, 7136
Housing, 4599
Houten, S., 8064
Howard, A., 2408
Howard, E. D., 980
Howard, J., 8065
Howard, L. E., 2408
Howard, W. W., 1557
Howarth, W., 8066
Howe, F. A., 2790
Howe, I., 9607
Howe, J. B., 8067
Howell, A. G. F., 4992
Howell, G., 8068
Howey, R. S., 9719
Howick, Lord, 6973
Howlett, J., 6250-6254
Hoyt, E. E., 1558, 3265, 3668
Hsia, Y., 2574
Hsieh, C., 14
Hsin, Y., 9966
Hsiung, M., 2575

Hsu, T., 319
Hsueh, M., 3266
Hu, C-C., 2576
Huang, D., 3669
Huang, K., 1560
Hubbard, 6255
Hubbard, J. C., 1561
Huber, A. E., 6257, 6258
Huber, P., 1528
Huberman, L., 320, 9374
Hubert-Valleroux, P., 8070-8072
Hubner, 4178
Hubner, O., 6259-6261
Hudson, J. F., 8072
Hudson, M., 1274
Huerne de Pommeuse, 6262
Huet, P. D., 4378-4379
Hufeland, G., 6263
Huffnagle, J. D, 10105
Hugo, N. P. F., 321
Hugon, P., 322, 3670
Hull, C. H., 4993, 8073
Hull, E., 8074
Hull, W., 6264
Hullmann, K. R. D., 6265-6267
Hulsmann, P., 323, 2750
Human Behavior, 8976
Human Beings, Physical History, 6724
Human Character, 6641
Human Condition, 4888
Human Nature, 7330, 8910
Human Race, 6642
Human Welfare, 8920
Humanism, 940, 9057, 9131
Humanism, Marxian, 9455
Humbert, G., 8075
Humbold-Universitat zu Berlin, 9189
Humboldt, W., 6268
Hume, D., 2409, 2413, 2445, 2497, 2508, 2760, 4379-4388, 5227, 5284, 7309, 7329
Hume, J. D., 5499
Hummel, G., 324
Humpert, M., 5228
Huncke, G. D., 9663
Hungary, 2848, 9454
Hunt, E. F., 2204
Hunt, R., 8076
Hunt, R. N. C., 9247-9248

Hunter, M. H., 325
Huppert, W., 3671
Hurlimann, H., 8077
Hurtrel, A., 8078
Hurwicz, L., 3504
Hurwitz, H. L., 1562-1563
Husain, Z., 2917
Husar, J., 9250
Husbandry, 4031, 4350, 4550, 4730, 4866, 5769, 5900, 6992
Husbandry, Great Britain, 5820
Huskisson, W., 6269-6272, 6802, 6989, 7022
Husselson, W., 6594
Huszar, G. B., 713
Hutcheson, 2433, 4393-4395
Hutcheson, A., 4389-4393
Hutcheson, F., 2490, 2508
Hutcheson, H. H., 1809
Hutcheson, J. H., 8079
Hutchison, T. W., 202, 326-330, 2057, 3672, 3845
Hutchisson University Library, 1997
Huter, M., 8848
Hutt, W. H., 2410, 9967-9968
Hutton, A. W., 4880
Hutton, R. H., 709, 2722, 7415
Huxley, 9726
Huzel, C. A., 8080
Hwan, G. Y., 329
Hyde, M. M., 5228-5229
Hyman, S. E., 9251
Hyndman, H. M., 8082, 9252
Hyppolite, J., 9253

Ibanes, J., 4994
Ibn, K., 4995-4996
Ichikawa, H., 2030
Idea, Social, 466
Idealism, 5023
Idealogy, 8879
Ideals, Political, 9589
Ideals, Social, 651, 9589
Ideas, Political, 4980
Ideas, Social, 4980
Ideology, 46, 187, 248, 762, 895, 1045, 1333, 1485, 1976, 2590, 2719, 3069, 3308, 3507, 8870, 8986, 9145, 9182, 9357, 10076, 10099
Ideology, German, 9390
Ideology, Marxian, 9099, 9477
Iglesias, F., 3674
Iles, G., 7553
Ilglu, A. S., 1061
Illinois, University, 2411
Illusion, 801
Imbert, J., 331, 5043
Immigration, 8568, 8642
Imperialism, 2719, 3008, 3010, 9277
Import, 4042, 4315, 4325, 4505, 4797, 5787, 5811, 6432, 6814, 6840, 8029, 8494, 8547
Import, Free, 3934
Import, Grain, 5344-5345
Imports, 4458
Impost, 4023
Imprisonment, Civil, England, 6429
Imputation, 3723
Inaba, S., 332, 1564-1565
Inama-Sternegg, K. T. 8068
Income, 14, 82, 1131, 1558, 1937, 1949, 1950, 2138, 2264, 2617, 3119, 3135, 3215-3216, 6833, 7446, 9871, 9925, 10103
Income, Distribution, 8634, 9810
Income, National, 863, 978, 1091, 1279, 2059, 2275
Income, Public, 6996
Income, Real, 9901
Increment, Unearned, 7727
Indes, 4644, 5836
Index, Numbers, Cost of Living, 3876
India, 1072, 1116, 1416, 1570, 1651, 2159, 2408, 2554, 2804-2832, 4038, 4468, 4612, 4752, 5047, 5072, 5666, 5791, 5857, 5894, 6045, 6177, 6276, 6314, 6423, 6437, 6863, 6867, 7102, 7272, 8338, 8662, 8750, 9387, 9834
India, Ancient, 5013
India, Bengal, 6896
India, Central, 6484
India, Great Britain, 6515, 7030, 7103

Author and Subject Index 667

India, History, 6441
India, N., 4967
India, Ninth Century, 3950
India, Political State, 7175
India, Public Works, 7107
India, Stock, 3936
Indian Archipelago, 5855
Indian Journal of Economics, 2813, 8953, 9807, 9834
Indian Ocean, Navigation, Ancient Period, 7194
Indian Tribes, United States, 6957
Indiana University, 767, 1024
Indicators, Economic, 3879-3880
Indies, 4311, 4576
Indies, West, 5456
Indigo, 6827
Individualism, 581, 817, 2650, 2660, 5086, 5828, 5952, 7285, 7306, 7328, 8201-8202
Indonesia, 2148, 2833
Indostan, 4709
Industrial, 6696
Industrial History, 8603
Industrial Relations, Marxist, 9025, 9029
Industrial Relations Research Center, 2332
Industrial Revolution, 2788, 7314, 8708, 8896
Industrial Technique, 9842
Industries, Canada, 7524
Industries, Infant, Protection, 8687
Industry, 55, 154, 450, 769, 1035, 1063, 1131, 1262, 1416, 1509, 1511, 3039, 3233, 3272, 3374, 3450, 3900, 4027, 4075, 4206, 5029, 5155, 5494, 5517-5518, 5632, 5696, 5734, 5838, 5942, 5946-5948, 6032, 6055, 6073-6074, 6105, 6338, 6365, 6370, 6375, 6427, 6487, 6560, 6569, 6577, 6685, 6742, 6864, 6918-6919, 6922, 6924, 7261, 7481, 7565, 7696, 7735, 7816, 7868, 7967, 8003, 8120, 8200, 8226, 8287, 8300, 8444, 8521, 8563, 8577, 8580, 8587, 8746, 9045, 9599, 9839, 9842, 9844, 9852, 9924, 9992
Industry, American, 2266
Industry, Belgium, 5632
Industry, Biography, 8638
Industry, Fluctuations, 3250
Industry, France, 5718, 8273
Industry, Great Britain, 5182, 7707-7708, 7711, 7901, 8531, 8837
Industry, Mineral, 8545
Industry, Modern, 8721, 8760
Industry, National, 6410-6411
Industry, Soviet Bloc, 2600
Industry, Textiles, 7421
Industry, Vested Interests, 8999
Inflation, 157, 3033, 8360, 9904, 9991
Ingersoll, C. J., 3067
Ingram, J. K., 334, 3675-3676
Inman, M. K., 1705
Innes, C., 8084
Innis, H. A., 7282
Innovative Potential, 888
Input-Output Analysis, 3679, 9909
Instiule de l'Etat de la France, 5673
Institut d'Etudes Slaves, 5362
Institut de Droit Romain, 4959
Institut de Gewerkschaften Koln-Braunsfeld, 2040
Institut de Recherches Economiques et Sociales, 830
Institut de Sociologie Solvay, 3234
Institut fur Angewandte Wirtschaftsforschung, Tubingen, 3625
Institut fur Marxismus-Leninismus, Berlin, 9048
Institut fur Wirtschaftsforschung, 1374
Institut International de Sociologie, 2374
Institut National d'Etudes Demographiques, 1214, 2342, 2653
Institut Nationale de la Statistique . . . , 1346

Institut Universitaire de Hautes
Etudes Internationales, 700,
701
Institut za Izucavanje Radnickog
Pokreta, 9315
Institute for Social Research,
3722
Institute of Economic Affairs,
London, 829, 2009, 3544,
3677, 10015
Institute of Marxism-Leninism,
Germany, 9202
Institute Superieur de Philosophie,
5142
Instituti Tecnici Commerciali e
Per Concorsi, 1826
Institution, 1810, 3648, 5020-
5021, 5814
Institution, Children, 8793
Institution, Religious, 6427
Institutionalism, 460, 1083,
3047, 3076, 3764, 8906-
9002
Institutionalism, Darwinian,
278-279, 7302
Institutionalism, Types, 8957
Institutionalist, 3857
Institutionalist, English, 2356
Institutions, 1236, 1810, 1944
Institutions, American, 1506
Institutions, Economic, 8937
Institutions, Economic, Europe,
8868
Institutions, Social, 8936, 9686
Institutions, Social, France,
7889
Instituto de Economia "Sancho de
Moncada, " 2970
Instituto de Estudios Economicos,
10064
Institutio de Filosofia, 3090
Instituto de Investigaciones
Sociales y Economicas, 1095
Instituto de Politica Economica,
Rio de Janeiro, 2559
Instituto de Teorie y Politica
Economicas, 1388
Instituto di Cultura Bancaria,
Milan, 833
Instituto di Economia e Finanza
. . . Roma, 10082
Instituto di Finanza, 1443

Instituto di Politica Economica
dell'Universita, Genova, 781
Instituto di Politica Economica
e Finanziaria, 1386
Instituto di Studi Economici,
Finanziari . . . , 1899
Instituto Historico y Geografico
del Uruguay, 2467
Instituto Nazionale Fascista di
Cultura, 2858
Instituto Veneto di Scienze,
2845
Institutul de Stiinte Economice,
V. I. Lenin, 9083
Instruction, Programmed, 3204,
3207
Instytut Ekonomiki i Organizacji
Przemyslu, 3897
Instytutu Gospodarstwa Spolecz-
nego, 2419
Insurance, 4480, 4541, 5991,
6303, 6304, 6467, 6477,
6520, 6562, 6564, 6728,
7067, 7738, 8497, 8740
Insurance, Digest, 7234
Insurance, Fire, 6663
Insurance, Life, 5508, 6663,
6791, 6818
Insurance, Marine, 4243, 4480,
6663, 6795, 7046, 7182
Insurance, Tables, 6383, 7072
Insurance and Finance Review,
2807
Insurance Charters, 5971
Integration, European Economic,
2623
Intellectual, 993, 9182, 9239,
9526
Interest, 893, 959, 2556, 3066,
3216, 3244, 3250, 3263,
3327, 3381, 3405, 3618,
3785, 3955, 3997, 4123,
4337, 4401, 4416, 4465,
4567, 4645, 4726, 4931,
4994, 5297, 6131, 6525
6617, 6976, 7606, 9663,
9711, 9737, 9796, 9797,
9927, 9929, 9939, 9989,
10049, 10091
Interest, Natural Rate, 4491
Interest, Rate of, 7067
Internal Improvement, 6995
International Correspondence

Schools, 1566
International Economic Association, 830-831, 3877
International Economic Papers, 2976, 9770
International Encyclopedia of Unified Science, 3184
International Institute of African Languages, 5116
International Journal, 5003
International Labour Review, 9910
International Political Economy, 363-364
International Socialist Review, 9067
International Trade, 324
International University Society, 747
International Working Men's Association, 9365, 9371
Interstate Commerce Act, 7764
Interstate Commerce Commission, 8500
Interstate Commerce Law, 8604
Intervention, Public, 9907
Invention, 4607, 6120, 6301, 6310
Investment, 1131, 1718, 3085 3250, 3412, 9711, 10023
Investment, Alternatives, 3276
Investment, Foreign, Soviet Union, 2986
Investment, Government, 3592
Investment, Home, 9973
Investment, Human, 67
Investment, International, 783
Iqbal, M., 1567
Ireland, 2834, 3926, 3930, 3934, 3940, 3967, 4024-4025, 4055, 4057, 4091, 4108, 4128, 4209, 4512, 4595, 4597, 4623, 4707, 4713, 4724, 4732, 4777, 4780, 4876, 4865, 4880, 5660, 5735, 5746, 5923, 5970, 6025, 6053, 6062, 6115, 6174, 6320, 6470, 6557, 6592, 6603-6604, 6671, 6717, 6788-6789, 6812, 6816, 6834, 6889, 6973, 6986, 6996, 7110, 7162, 7208, 7215, 7218, 7783, 8079, 8205, 8316, 8511, 8618

Iron, 6214, 8786
Iron, Bar, 4615
Iron, Trade, 6413, 6965
Irrigation, 7075, 7435
Irvine, P., 6281
Isaacs, A., 832, 2109
Isambert, G., 9256
Iscaro, R., 9257
Ise, J., 1568
Iselin, I., 5340
Ishida, B., 2901
Ishikura, I., 1569
Isin, 4923
Islamic Countries, 2835-2839, 2927
Isnard, 6282
Israel, 2840, 5074
Issues, 798, 803, 845, 886, 892, 1825, 1890, 2025, 2117, 2122, 3069
Istanbul Universitesi, 353, 486, 1061
Italy, 24, 56, 73, 232, 475-476, 751, 781, 988, 1086, 1466, 2474, 2801, 2841-2873, 3973, 4098, 4836-4840, 4883, 5155, 5600, 5623, 5863, 6636, 6683, 6962, 7181, 7233, 7377, 7379, 7472, 7512, 7712, 7798, 7948, 7958, 8199, 8231, 8315, 8551, 8558, 8568, 8593, 8680, 8725, 9066, 9121, 9455, 9755, 9907, 9934
Italy, Middle Ages, 5044
Italy, Statistics, 7148
Ito, N., 834
Ivernois, F. D., 6284
Izhboldin, B. S., 1570

Jacini, S., 6285
Jackson, J. H., 9258
Jackson, T. A., 9259
Jacob, W., 6286-6289
Jacobi, 6682
Jacobs, A., 3267
Jacobs, G., 4405
Jacobs, M., 3267
Jaeger, A., 3682
Jaffe, W., 327, 8965, 9790, 9794
Jager, E., 8085

Jager, G., 2751
Jahn, G., 914, 1571
Jahn, W., 9260
Jahnsson, Y. W., 2630
Jahrbuch fur Gesetzgebung, 3575
Jahrbucher fur Nationalokonomie, 3589
Jahrbucher fur Nationalokonomie und Statistik, 6, 3703, 3716, 3752, 9888
Jain, P. C., 1572
Jakob, L. H. V., 6292
Jamaica, 3987, 4762, 5553
James, C. L., 1573-1574
James, E., 337-340, 416, 2412, 3151, 9967
James, E. J., 124, 334, 2411, 6293
James, G. R., 2009
James, H., 6294-6295
James, J., 6296
Janet, P., 8086, 8087
Jangir, G. C., 1611
Jannaccone, P., 1575-1576
Jannasch, R., 8088, 8878
Jannet, C., 8089-8090
Janssen, J., 8091
Janssen, S. T., 4405, 4733
Japan, 2193-2916, 2780, 2786, 2874-2905, 3493, 7550, 8019, 8213, 8254, 8337, 8483, 9541, 9556, 9608
Japan, Middle Ages, 4908
Jardins, P., 8092
Jarrett, B., 4997
Jasper, A., 8489
Jaspers, K., 2335
Jastrow, J., 7275, 7344
Jathar, G. B., 1577-1578
Java, 5836, 6745
Jawed, H. K., 1579
Jeanneney, J. M., 835, 1580-1581
Jeans, J. S., 8093-8094
Jefferson, T., 3067, 5342, 5361, 6297
Jellinek, G., 5355
Jenkin, F., 9720
Jenkins, A. H., 7337
Jenkinson, C., 4406
Jenks, J. E. F., 1582
Jenks, J. W., 8096-8097
Jennings, R., 1583, 6298-6299
Jensenius, O. H., 1584
Jenyns, S., 4407

Jessop, T., 2413
Jessopp, A., 4570
Jessua, C., 3268
9721
Jesuits, 2912
Jevons, W. S., 137, 2758, 3683, 8098-8101, 9690, 9706, 9722-9728, 9767
Jewett, P., 3536
Jewish Quarterly Review, 4964
Jewkes, J., 829
Jha, N., 2752, 9827
Jha, S. N., 2816
Ji-son, R., 329
Jindra, V., 2603
Jiranek, S., 1585
Joao, D., 1683
Jobert, A., 5362
Jobst, E. K. W., 3685
Jocelyn, J., 5230
Joggs, J., 4078
Johannes, A., 2476, 3813
Johansen, A. D., 1586
Johansen, L., 1587, 3269
Johansen, T., 3270
Johns, C. H. W., 5001
Johns Hopkins University, 2414, 3070, 5361, 6461, 8866
Johnson, A., 1588
Johnson, A. C., 5002
Johnson, A. S., 773, 1589
Johnson, C., 5059
Johnson, E. A. J., 1162, 1793, 2753, 3063, 5003
Johnson, E. R., 8103
Johnson, H. G., 804, 836, 3686
Johnson, W. E., 3271, 3687
Johnston, D., 6300
Johnston, W., 5552, 6301
Johnstone, J. K., 9972
Johr, W. A., 341
Joint Council on Economic Education, 837
Joint Stock Banks, 6116
Joint Stock Company, 4127, 6801
Jolin, A., 9377
Jollivet, J. B. M., 6302
Joly, B., 1981, 3187
Jonas, F., 3688
Jonchere, 4408
Jones, B., 8104
Jones, D., 6303
Jones, I. G., 1590

Jones, J., 6304
Jones, J. P., 8105
Jones, L., 8106, 8228
Jones, R., 838, 2356, 2529, 5229, 5231, 6305-6308, 8918
Jones, T., 976
Jones, T. B., 5006
Jong, F. J., 1591
Jonkaire, 5812
Jonkers, E. J., 4902
Jonnes, M., 6772
Joplin, T., 2436, 6309-6310
Jordan, L. A., 9261
Jordan, P., 1174, 1996
Jorio, M., 6311
Joseph, D., 4409
Joseph, M. L., 1592
Joseph of Egypt, 2347
Joshi, M. D., 342
Jossa, B., 1593
Josseau, 6312
Josseah, D., 6312
Josseau, J. B., 8107
Jostock, P., 343
Joubert, A., 8108
Joubert, P. R., 2211
Joubleau, F., 5232, 6313
Jouffroy, H., 6948
Jouineau, C., 3272
Jourdain, A. L. M., 5005
Jourdain, C. H. G. B., 344, 5006
Jourdan, A., 8109-8111
Journal de l'Agriculture, du Commerce, et des Finances, 5329
Journal des Economistes, 7296, 9699
Journal of Economic History, 653, 5081, 8895, 8984, 9808, 9921
Journal of Economic Issues, 3507, 3857
Journal of English Literary History, 5240
Journal of Farm Economics, 3624, 3648
Journal of Finance, 3490
Journal of Modern History, 7313
Journal of Political Economy, 804, 2441, 2461, 2698, 2744, 3247, 3290, 3362, 3384 3430, 3452, 3460, 3517, 3560, 3564, 3582, 3615, 3763, 3889, 3894, 5299, 5316, 5422, 7281, 7346, 7353, 8897-8898, 8923, 8951, 8957, 8979, 8994, 9736, 9748, 9776-9777, 9784-9785, 9787, 9794, 9815, 9833, 9778, 9927, 9951, 10098
Journal of the American Oriental Society, 5139
Journal of the American Statistical Association, 9701
Journal of the History of Ideas, 5394
Journal of the Royal Statistical Society, 9809
Journey, India, 5648
Jovasevic, V., 345, 839, 9262
Jovellanos, G. M., 6274, 6315
Jowett, B., 2788, 5007, 8708
Joyce, J., 7310, 7337
Jozsef, D., 9162a
Jozsef, V., 9162a
Jozsefne, B., 9135
Juglar, C., 7683, 8112-8113
Juhrbucher fur Nationalokonomie und Statistik, 8843
Jung, 6317-6318
Jureen, L., 3480
Jurisprudence, Historical, 5128
Justi, J. H., 4410
Justi, J. H. G., 5233
Justice, 7338
Justice, Political, 6122
Justo, 9473
Juvigny, B., 6319

Kabardia, 2955
Kabdiev, D. K., 3001
Kada, T., 2619, 2886
Kadlec, V., 2755
Kadler, J., 3647
Kador, F-J., 3002
Kaegi, W., 9263
Kaerger, K., 8114
Kagi, P., 9263
Kahldoun, Ibn, 5030
Kahn, M. A. J., 1599
Kahn, M. S., 2416
Kahn, R. F., 3435, 9797, 9973

Kaido, S., 2599
Kaldor, N., 841, 3273, 3274
Kalecki, M., 3689, 9974
Kamada, T., 2756
Kamenicky, A., 9264
Kamenka, E., 9265
Kamerschen, D. R., 3275
Kamienski, H. K., 1594
Kaminsky, R., 842
Kammen, M. C., 5234
Kan, N., 2577
Kanapa, J., 9975
Kandilarov, G., 3690
Kandt, M., 8115
Kane, R., 6320
Kaneko, K., 1595
Kang, O., 1596
Kann, A., 3691
Kansas State College, 3382
Kant, E., 6917
Kant, I., 8384
Kantorovich, L. V., 3692-3693
Kaplan, A. D. H., 2414
Kaplan, N. M., 3276, 3277
Kapp, K. W., 843
Kapp, L. L., 843
Karataev, N., 9267
Karataev, N. K., 1598, 3003-3006
Karim, S., 1599
Karl Marx Kolloquium, Freiberg, 9268
Karl Marx Universitat Leipzig, 9226, 9587
Karlin, S., 3849
Karpinski, N. S., 3694
Karpovich, M., 2613
Karras, H., 3278 9269
Karvas, I. A., 1600
Karve, D. G., 844, 2817
Kaspar, J., 7341
Kassira, A., 840
Kasugai, K., 8925
Kasuagi, T., 8925
Katano, H., 3279
Katholieke Universiteit te Leuven, 10096
Katona, G., 3756
Katz, J., 2111
Katzner, D. W., 3280
Kauder, E., 346, 5008, 9729-9231

Kaufman, R., 8119-8120
Kaufmann, G., 8116
Kaufmann, M., 8117-8118
Kaulla, R., 347, 3281, 5009
Kautilya, A Review of International Affairs, 9940
Kautsky, B., 1123
Kautsky, K., 3282, 3340, 3344, 9393, 9417, 9544
Kautsky, K. J., 9270-9276
Kautz, G., 348-349, 2802
Kautz, J., 6321
Kawaguchi, T., 3283
Kawakami, H., 350-352
Kawasaki, S., 8966
Kay, J., 6324
Kay, J. P., 6322-6323
Kaye, F. B., 4485, 7316
Kaynes, J. M., Life, 9952
Kazakevich, E. F., 3020
Kazakevich, V. D., 3020
Kazakstan, 3001
Kazda, J., 1601
Kazgan, G., 353
Keachie, E. C., 3394
Kearney, J. W., 8121
Keasbey, L. M., 3284
Keezer, D. M., 1602
Keil, G., 1603
Keilhau, W. C., 1604
Keid, G. D., 2887
Keirstead, B. S., 1605
Keiser, N. F., 1606-1607
Keisselbach, W., 8126
Keizai Ronshu, Oita, 389, 438
Keizaigaku, 2647
Keizaigakushi Gakkai, 2888
Keizer, J. M., 3695
Keleti, C., 8122
Kellenbenz, H., 5235
Keller, A. G., 995
Keller, W., 354
Kellner, G., 6325
Kelly, J. B., 6326
Kelly, P., 6327
Kemble, J. M., 6328
Kemp, A., 1146
Kemp, A. G., 2330, 3492
Kemp, T., 9277
Kempf, H., 9222
Kenafick, K. J., 9021
Kendall, M. G., 3696
Kendrick, M. S., 9812

Kennedy, J. W., 1336
Kennedy, L., 6329
Kent, J. A., 1762
Kerber, W., 1609
Kerever, A., 1046
Kerner, A., 9278
Kerr, A. B., 5010
Kerr, A. W., 8123
Kerr, C., 9279, 9828
Kerschagl, R., 355-356 3697
Ketteler, W. E. F., 8123
Keupp, S. R., 3715
Keussler, J., 8125
Keyes, S., 845
Keynes, G., 2415
Keynes, J. M., 200, 651, 1909, 2415, 2480, 2488, 2974, 3007, 3286, 3539, 3610, 5236, 7311, 7312, 9426, 9829-9831, 9846, 9895, 9976-10001, 10066
Keynes, J. M., Life, 9955
Keynes, J. N., 772, 3698-3700
Keynesian Economics, 9885-10108
Keynesian Economics, Critics of, 9957
Keynesian Fallacies, 9958
Keynesian Revolution, 9934
Keyser, J., 2757
Khaldun, I., 5011
Khan, J. A. J., 1610
Khan, M. S., 2416
Khatri, J. D., 357, 1611
Kher, V. B., 2810
Khromushin, G. B., 9280
Khuri, R., 2541
Kidric, B., 9063
Kiekhofer, W. H., 1612, 2778, 3248
Kienzl, H., 1613
Kierstead, B. S., 3701
Kiga, K., 1614
Kiker, B. F., 358, 3081
Kikkert, J. P., 943
Kilicbay, A., 1615-1616
Kim, A., 1618
Kim, C., 1617, 10002
Kim, Kwang-Jin, 2908
Kim, M., 9281
Kim, S., 359
Kim, Y., 1619

Kimball, J., 2417
Kimura, T., 360
King, 4459, 7111
King, C., 4411
King, G., 1290, 4554
King, J., 5489
King, J. E., 7313
Kink, K., 1620
Kinley, D., 8127-8128
Kinloch, T. F., 2758
Kinnear, J. B., 8124
Kinoshita, E., 3287
Kinter, C. V., 2204
Kippax, J., 4790
Kipper, G., 3288
Kirchmann, J. H., 5787
Kirkaldy, A. W., 2759
Kirkmann, M. M., 8130-8131
Kirkup, T., 8132, 9282
Kirmis, A., 2418
Kirtovskis, I., 2913
Kirzner, I. M., 846
Kishimoto, S., 848, 361, 847, 1621
Kitagawa, S., 3702
Kitamura, J., 2687
Kitazawa, S., 2889
Kito, N., 9998, 10003-10004
Klassen, L. H., 1003
Kleim, M., 9283
Klein, L. R., 3756, 10005
Kleinschrod, C. T., 6330
Kleinwachter, F., 1622, 3703, 8133-8134
Kleinwachter, F. L., 2688
Klemme, M., 2760
Kleok, T., 3863
Klitsche, A., 2466
Klock, G., 4412
Klostermaier, K., 613, 2496
Kluczynski, H., 2935
Kluczynski, J., 2419
Klundert, T., 1623
Kluza-Wolosiewicz, Z., 2689
Knapp, G. F., 8018, 8849-8850
Knapp, J., 3744
Knapp, R., 3704
Knies, K., 3705, 8838, 8848, 8851-8855, 8869
Knight, B. W., 1624-1626
Knight, C., 6331
Knight, F. H., 786, 849-859,

1627-1628, 3289-3295, 3568, 3706-3710, 8967, 9732, 9740, 9832-8933
Knight, M. M., 9548
Knight, T. S., 4100
Knirsch, P., 362
Kniwes, K., 8902
Knoellinger, C. E., 3656
Knolles, R., 5334
Knopf, K. A., 3249
Knorr, K. E., 1629, 5237
Knowledge, Economic, 3546
Knox, J., 6332
Knox, J. J., 8135
Kobatsch, R., 363-364
Kobayashi, A., 10006
Kobayashi, N., 365-366 5238
Kobayashi, Y., 367
Kφbenhavns Universitets, 725, 3810
Kφbenhavns Universitets Okonomiske Institut, 1009
Koch, C. G., 6333
Kocherthaler, E., 9997
Kockijigyo Kenkyu, 8966
Kocman, M., 3295
Koe, H., 6542
Koebner, R., 7314
Kogekar, S. V., 1635
Kogiku, K., 3711
Koh, S. J., 1630
Kohler, H., 1631-1632
Kohler, J. P, 2690
Kohn, H., 9404
Koivisto, W. A., 1633
Koizumi, S., 368-371, 1634, 2420, 3298, 9284
Kokkalis, A. B., 3296
Kolaja, J., 3093
Kolarz, W., 9285
Kolb, G. F., 8136
Kolganov, M., 3712
Kolhatkar, V. Y., 1635
Kollner, L., 851, 9286
Komarov, V. L., 9422
Kommunisticheskaia Partiia, 372
Konevski, T., 1637
Konig, B. E., 8137
Koniglichen Instituts, 2648
Konstantinovich, N., 2983
Koopmans, J. G., 853

Koopmans, T. C., 854, 3664
Kooy, T. P., 855-856
Koplin, H. T., 1638
Korac, M. M., 9287
Korea, 2906-2908
Koren, H. J., 9288
Korenjak, F., 1640
Korey, E. L., 1641
Kornienki, A. A., 373
Korsch, K., 9290
Korteweg, S., 857
Korzc, M. M., 1639
Koshimura, S., 374, 986, 9292
Kosik, K., 858, 1642
Koslin, B. L., 9764
Kostic, Z. K., 1643-1644
Kosub, H., 8138
Kotov, A., 375
Kotov, I., 3713
Kotzschke, K. R., 376
Kouba, K., 9293, 9296
Koudela, J., 3647
Kourim, G., 3299
Kover, J. F., 2422
Kowalik, T., 377, 1645
Koyck, L. M., 1003
Kozodoev, I. I., 9297
Kozuma, T., 2587-2588
Kozusnik, C., 3300
Kraatz, C., 8139
Kramar, K., 8140
Kramer, C., 9998
Kramer, L., 9998
Krappe, A. H., 609
Krasensky, H., 1646
Kraus, C. J., 6334
Kraus, J. B., 2761
Kraus, W., 1647
Krause, A., 859
Krause, J. F., 6335
Krause, W., 2691
Krelle, W., 3301, 3714
Kremlinologist, 2992
Kreps, J. M., 1401
Kress Library of Business and Economics, Baker Library, 2744
Kretschmar, H., 2692
Krider, D. T., 1825
Kriegk, G. D., 8141
Krier, H., 1648
Krier, J., 3302

Krinal, V., 2607
Krishnan-Kutty, G., 10007
Krishnaswami, A., 9834
Kristersson, H., 1649
Kroll, M., 1650
Kronig, F., 8142
Kronstein, R., 3303
Kruger, H. C., 8143
Kruse, A., 378-380
Ku, S., 3465
Kuan, C., 2578, 5012
Kubel, F. E., 8144
Kubo, Y., 3064
Kubota, A., 2890
Kudla, W., 9347
Kudler, J., 6336
Kudsia, J., 1651
Kuenne, R. E., 1652, 3304-3305, 9733
Kuhlman, J. M., 860, 1652, 3306
Kuhn, H. W., 3681
Kuhn, W. E., 381-382
Kuhne, O., 3716
Kuhnis, S., 3307
Kukoleca, S. M., 3717
Kula, W., 384
Kulisher, I. M., 2620-2622
Kumar, S., 5013
Kumarappa, B., 2811
Kumarappa, J. C., 2816
Kung, E., 1654
Kung-Chuan, J., 5012
Kuo, Y., 2579
Kupka, P. F., 8145
Kupriianov, P. M., 3008
Kuricke, R., 4413-4414
Kurihara, K. K., 387, 1655-1656, 10008-10010
Kuroda, H., 1657, 9299
Kuroda, T., 3416
Kuruma, K., 861
Kuruma, S., 388
Kuryu, M., 389
Kuwahara, S., 1658
Kuyucak, H. A., 1659
Kuz'Minov, I. I., 682, 3009
Kuznets, S. S., 863-865, 10011
Kwant, R. C., 9300
Kwon, H., 1660
Kyn, O., 78
Kyrer, A., 3718

L'Estrange, R., 4415

La Farelle Fel, 6338
La Gournerie, J., 8146
La Nauze, J. A., 2549
La Volpe, G., 1675
Labarthe, 6339
Labor, 617, 1911, 2722, 2788, 2792, 3296-3297, 3409, 4142, 4147, 4348, 5179, 5197, 5514, 5570, 5626, 5651, 5690, 5702, 5745, 5779, 5972, 5992, 6096, 6200, 6233, 6306, 6308, 6357-6358, 6418, 6568, 6713, 6826, 7097, 7108, 7236, 7356, 7434, 7535, 7562, 7577, 7587, 7965-7567, 7997, 8257, 8318, 8550, 8668, 8693, 8698, 8770, 9289
Labor, Agriculture, 5524, 7757,
Labor, Condition, 7893
Labor, Cotton Manufacture, 7192
Labor, Great Britain, 7835, 9112
Labor, Law, 7724, 8496
Labor, Manual, 8632
Labor, Movement, 7809, 8282, 9112, 10059
Labor, Produce of, 450, 9442
Labor, Productive, 3166
Labor, Regulation, 8101
Labor, United States, 7809
Labor, Unproductive, 7909
Labor, Law, 7724, 8496
Laborde, A., 6340
Labouliniere, P., 6341-6342
Labra, R. M., 8147
Labracherie, P., 2423
Labrada, D. J., 5155
Labriola, A., 5363, 9301-9302,
Labrouquere, A., 5364
Lach, D. F., 5365
Lachmann, L. M., 390, 9734
Lachs, J., 9303
Lacour-Gayet, J., 2795, 5014
Lafarge, C., 619
Laffitte, J., 6343-6344
Laffon de Ladebat, 6435
Laforèst, L'Abbe, 4416-4417
Lagasse, C., 8148
Lagausie, F., 3308
Lagides, 8229
Lagler, E., 866
Lago, A., 1661

Lagunilla, Inarritu, A., 391
Laherrere, R., 1662
Laidler, D. E. W., 3309
Laidler, H. W., 9304
Laing, G. A., 1663
Laing, S., 6345
Laird, J., 3310
Laird, Macgregor, 6306
Laissez-Faire, 2660,
   2663, 2730, 2790, 5191,
   5211, 5399, 7321, 8386,
   9985, 9993
Laistner, M. L. W., 5016
Lajugie, J., 2465
Lakkonen, J., 2629
Laligant, 5603
Lalor, J. J., 6347, 8149,
   8875
Lamas, A., 2467
Lambert, J. M., 8150
Lambert, P., 5239, 10013
Lambin, J. J., 3311
Lambrechts, H., 8151
Lamerville, 6348
Lampe, H., 1664
Lampertico, F., 2852, 8152
Lamprecht, K., 8153
Lampredi, 5784
Lancaster, K., 1665
Lanckmann, J. B., 8154
Land, 893, 1995, 3244, 3638,
   3946, 3982, 4051, 4263,
   4551, 4594, 4598, 4625,
   4646, 4755, 4782, 5387,
   5666, 5667, 6009, 6245,
   6399, 6400, 6915, 7490,
   8129, 8213, 8318, 8337,
   8579, 8584, 8607, 8632,
   8745
Land, Bengal, 6134
Land, Capital Application, 7236
Land, Charter, 7793
Land, Credit, 4104
Land, England, 7570, 8619
Land, Free, 7689
Land, Ireland, 8619
Land, Laws, Great Britain, 8446
Land, Nationalization, 8645
Land, Ownership, 7253, 7340, 7886
Land, Question, 7894, 8560
Land, Revenue, 7412
Land, System, Australia, 7819
Land, System, India, 8453
Land, Tenancy, 6329
Land, Tenure, 2834, 7641, 8464, 8618
Land, Tenure, Ireland, 8316
Land, Waste, 6707
Landa, L. A., 5240
Landauer, C., 3312, 5366
Lande, 5891
Landgren, K. G., 2974-2975, 10014
Landlord, 5702, 6400, 7846, 8692
Landlord, England, 7570
Landlord, Ireland, 7783
Landman, R. H., 8968
Landowner, 6044, 6134, 6713
Landry, A., 1666, 3719
Landy, A., 9305
Lane, F. C., 867, 3720
Lanesseau, J. L., 8155
Lang, R., 1667, 9306
Lange, F. A., 8156
Lange, O., 3313, 9337, 9673, 9735, 9871
Lange, O. R., 1668-1671, 2936-2937, 3721, 9308
Langer, P. F., 9309
Langford, J. H., 8157
Language, 220, 3583
Langue, O. R., 9307
Langwith, B., 3972
Lansing, J. B., 3722
Lapparent, A., 8158
Lard, 3197
Lardner, D., 6310
Lardner Dionysius, 6349
Largentaye, J., 9989
Larrabee, W., 8159
Larraz, Lopez, J., 799, 5241
Larrugia, E., 6350
Larsen, O. H., 2606
Lasalle, F., 8443
Lasalle, H., 6176, 6352
Laski, H. J., 2762, 9310-9311, 9375
Laspeyres, E., 5242
Lassalle, F., 7558, 7726
Laterza, 2474
Latin, 5059
Latin America, 2909-2912, 9005
Latouche, R. L., 5017
Latvia, 2913

Lauderdale, J. M., 1672, 6353
Laughlin, J. L., 1673, 2441, 8160-8163, 9835
Lauguage, 1427
Launhardt, W., 8164
Lauraguals, 4419
Laurat, L., 9312
Laurens, P., 8165
Laurent, E., 8166
Laures, J., 5243
Lausanne School, 931, 9667, 9747, 9749
Laveleye, E., 7870, 8167, 8168, 8169, 8170, 8171
Lavergne, B., 1674
Lavergne, L., 5367
Lavergne, N., 9313
Lavoinne, E., 8172
Lavollee, C., 8174
Lavollee, R., 8175
Law, 56, 489, 521, 580, 795, 868, 874, 1115, 2349, 3898, 4288, 4318, 4528, 4918, 5045, 6210, 6381, 6552, 6744, 6753, 6788, 6902, 7147
Law, Admiralty, 4423
Law, American, 8692
Law, Ancient, 5109
Law, Babylonia, 5001
Law, Bailments, 7061
Law, Bankrupt, 1987
Law, Colonial, 5747
Law, Commercial, 5739
Law, Commercial, Great Britain, 5710
Law, Common, 6870
Law, Company, 7450
Law, Constitutional, 7670
Law, Corn, 2501, 5785
Law, Egypt, 5109
Law, Great Britain, 5655
Law, Hebrew, 5001
Law, History, 6490
Law, Industrial, 1244
Law, Insurance, 7234
Law, International, 7221
Law, Maritime, 4522, 4802 5444, 5496, 5763, 5773, 5815, 5909, 5924, 6777, 6868, 6956, 7062, 7085, 7221
Law, Mercantile, Scotland, 4447
Law, Merchant, 4483
Law, Montesquieu, 7142
Law, Moral, 5387
Law, Municipal, 6009
Law, Natural, 64, 2065, 2779, 4961, 5383, 5389, 5404, 5412, 5428, 6966
Law, Partnership, 5777
Law, Physical, 5387
Law, Public, 2681, 2766, 8667
Law, Roman, 246, 679
Law, Scotland, 5557
Law, War, 7085
Law, J., 548, 4410-4421, 5190, 5213, 5229, 5272, 5303, 5320
Law, W., 4422
Laws, M., 3723
Lazzari, A., 1086
Le Play, F., 6357-6358
Leach, H. M. K., 5018
League for Industrial Democracy, 9311
Leake, S. M., 4424
Leal, A., 619
Leal, R., 2950
Leander, L., 2424
Lease, 4427, 5509
Leather, 4426
Leber, M. C., 6360
Leblanc, B. P., 9081
Leblanc, M., 868
Lecaillon, J., 430 1676-1677
Lecarpentier, G., 2653
Lecce, W., 394
Lechevalier, J., 6361
Leclair, E. E., 5019
Lecouteux, L., 8176
Lecture, 459, 720, 723, 741, 743-744, 752, 771, 813, 815, 821, 836, 838, 865, 876, 896, 906, 923, 948, 961, 981, 992, 1021, 1120, 1172, 1742-1743, 1828 2471, 2479, 2627, 2759, 2788, 2825, 6141, 6179, 6479, 7239-7240, 7244, 7276, 7307, 7325, 7338, 7339, 7353, 7368, 7562, 8603, 8674, 8896, 8919, 8964, 8981, 9308, 9828,

9848, 9915-9916, 9979, 9985,
Leduc, G., 3165
Lee, A., 9386
Lee, M. W., 1678
Lee, O. H., 619
Lee, W., 4427
Lefebvre, H., 9314
Left, 407, 1712, 1953, 2006
Leftwich, R. H., 395, 1679, 1680
Legal Tender, 7614, 8214
Legentil, 6230
Legislative Interference, 7114
Legitimo, G., 1681
Legman, G., 2390
Legoyt, A., 8177-8178
Lehman, L., 5361
Lehmann, H., 8179
Lehmann, M. R., 3314
Lehr, J., 8180-8181
Leibenstein, H., 1682
Leibkneckt, W., 2764
Leigh, A. H., 9736
Leigh, E., 4429, 8182
Leijonhufvud, A., 10015-10016
Leimon, M., 2425
Leindberg, N., 1692-1693
Leipziger, 6363
Leisure Class, 80, 8998, 9085, 9675
Leite, C., 1683
Leite, J. P., C., 1683
Leiter, R. D., 1684
Leitzmann, J. J., 6364
Lekachman, R., 869, 899, 928, 10017-10019
Lekovic, D., 9315
Lelart, M., 3315
Lely, J. M., 8183
Lemaitre, 5797
Lemmnitz, A., 3316
Lendle, O., 3317
Lenin, V., 1040, 2990, 3010, 9070, 9083, 9135, 9316-9323, 9343, 9369, 9378, 9385, 9399, 9424, 9471, 9546, 9549, 9590, 9630
Leninism, 3316, 9158, 9164, 9201, 9250, 9324, 9419, 9445
Lenormant, F., 8184
Lenz, F., 8856

Leon Paz, F., 3318
Leonard, E. J., 2612
Leontief, W. W., 398, 870, 3610, 3724, 5402
Leontiev, L. A., 3010-3011, 9325-9327
Leopold, J., 5320
Leopold, R. W., 9328
Leopold I., 5302
Leopolds Con Lothringen, 5320
Lepelletier, S., 6365
Lepointe, G., 5020-5021
Leponiemi, A., 3319
Leppington, C. H., 7973
Lequin de la Neuville, 4430
Lerat, E., 1685
Lerner, A. P., 871, 1686, 3435
Lerner, D., 3726, 9775
Lerner, M., 7337, 8969
Lerouge, F., 1046
Leroux, P., 2512, 6366-6368
Leroy-Beaulieu, P., 8185-8191,
Lerviks, A. E., 3320
Leser, E., 8182
Leslie, C., 2338
Leslie, T. E. C., 872, 3728, 8193-8194, 8857
Lesourd, J. A., 399
Lesourne, J., 1687-1689
Lessa, C. F., 1233
Lesseps, F., 8195
Lessius, L., 2921
Lessons, 1095
Lesz, M., 3729
Lethinois, A., 4431
Letiche, J. M., 327, 2954, 5205
Letourneau, C., 8196
Letrosne, 6369-6370
Letwin, W., 2763, 5244
Letwin, W. L., 3709
Leuchs, L. C., 6375
Levant, 5890
Levant Company, 5445
Levasseur, P. 6377-6381
Levasseur, P. E., 2645
Leven, C. L., 3715, 9917
Levi, L., 8197-8200
Levitskii, V., F., 400
Levy, J. H., 8201-8204
Levy, L. S., 3065
LeWalter, E., 5023
Lewins, W., 8205

Lewinski, J. S., 401-402, 5368
Lewis, G. C., 6382, 7335
Lewis, G. H., 8206
Lewis, H. T., 894
Lewis, J., 9329-9330
Lewis, J. L., 2331
Lewis, L., 8207
Lewis, M., 4459
Lexis, W., 7988, 8208
Leyen, A., 8210
Lhomme, J., 873
Li, C. W., 403
Li, Y., 1690, 3321
Liancourt, L., 5957
Liang, C., 3322
Liberalism, 82, 157, 261, 515, 999, 2644, 2677, 2716, 2730, 2977, 5191, 5294, 5428, 8869
Liberalism, Classical, 445
Liberalism, Economic, 559
Liberatore, M., 8211
Liberman, E., 9600
Libman, G. I., 9331
Librairie Generale de Droit et de Jurisprudence, 897, 1121
Library, A. Smith, 7283
Library of Congress, 2694
Lichtenberger, J. P., 5024
Lichtheim, G., 9332-9333
Lichtman, R., 3066
Lieben, 3111
Lieben, R., 7407, 8212
Liebhafsky, H. H., 9824
Liebknecht, W., 3323, 9334
Liebscher, D. G., 8213
Liefmann, R., 1691, 3730
Lienation, 9475
Life, 434
Life, Duration of, 7072
Life, Economic, 1017, 2033, 2070, 2260
Life, Intellectual, 2694
Life, Moral, 2070
Life, Social, 2033
Lifschitz, F., 404-405, 8858
Lille, A., 5245
Lima, A. A., 406
Lin, L., 10020
Lindahl, E., 770, 1022
Lindbeck, A., 407, 3731
Lindberg, L. N., 2623

Linderman, H. R., 8214
Lindheim, W., 8215-8216
Lindsay, A. D., 3324, 9121, 9335
Lindsay, J., 9336
Lindsay, W. S., 8217
Linear Programming, 9688
Linen, 4091
Linen, Manufacture, 4025, 5816
Linguet, 6384-6385
Linguistics, Marxian, 9581
Lininism, 9320
Link, R. G., 2765
Lipinski, E., 1694, 2937, 5025, 5246, 5261
Lippincott, B. E., 9337
Lipsey, R. G., 1695-1696
Lipson, E., 5247
Liquidity, International, 9940
Liquor, 4208
Lisbona Y Fabrat, 8218
Lisichkin, G. S., 9338
Lisman, J. H. C., 3732
Lisowsky, P. U., 3325
List, F., 71, 1697, 2402, 2667, 2690, 3067, 3072, 8825, 8828, 8841, 8844, 8847, 8856, 8859, 8860-8862, 8869, 8894
Literature, Business, 126, 2362
Literature, Economic, 599, 2362
Literature, German, 2698
Lithgow, J., 2470
Little, I. M. D., 1698
Little, L. T., 1699
Littre, B., 5787
Liu, C., 408
Liu, S., 2580
Livergood, N. D., 9339
Liverpool, C., 6386-6387
Liverpool, Earl of, 6731, 7150
Livery Companies, 6206
Livingstone, I., 1700, 1883
Llarocque, D., 2644
Lloyd, C., 1701, 3326
Lloyd, D. H., 8219
Lloyd, S. S., 8859
Lloyd, W. F., 6388-6390
Lluch Y Capdevila, P., 409
Loans, 6146
Loans, Foreign, 7067

Loaz Macias, M., 2916
Lobkowicz, N., 9340, 9421
Lobl, E., 1702-1703
Lobo, R. J. H., 410
Locke, J., 2762, 3327, 3995, 4461-4466, 5159
Lockman, J., 4467
Lockyer, C., 4468
Locquean, 6391
Lodge, H. C., 5248, 6172
Lodz, P., 1704
Loen, 4469
Loenig, E., 7988
Logan, H. A., 1705
Logic, 9722
Lohman, P. H., 1477
Lohmann, F., 411, 2427
Lohser, O., 1706
Lombard Street, 7417, 7638
Lombardia, 6285
Lombardini, S., 1707-1708, 3328
Lombardo-Venetian State, 5623
Lonbards, 5081
London, 4272, 6192, 6206, 7249
London, City of, 5486
London, J., 4471
London, J. C., 4470
London, J. I., 6786
London Mechanics Institution, 6234
London School of Economics and Political Science, 176, 876, 904, 981, 992, 2382, 2492, 2478, 3493, 4972, 5292, 5626, 6394, 9660, 9694, 9740, 9803, 9850
Londonderry, 6635
Long, C., 6392
Long, C. D., 10021
Longe, F. D., 8220, 8221
Longfield, M., 876
Longo, G., 1709
Longstaff, G. B., 8222
Loone, L., 2607
Loos, I. A., 8863
Lopez, J. L., 5249
Lopez Gento, J., 412
Lopez Rosado, F., 1710-1711
Lopez Sanz, S., 1712
Lord, E., 6395
Lord, O., 4847

Lorenz, M. O., 1370
Loria, 2474
Loria, A., 659, 1713, 2474, 2868, 3329, 3733, 8223-8224, 9341
Lorpent, G., 6396
Losseau, L., 3734
Lot, F., 5026
Lothian, J. M., 7339
Lottery, 3954, 4598
Lottery Act, 4049
Lottery System, United States, 7174
Lotz, W., 3415
Loua, T., 8225
Loubere, 4193
Loudon, J. C., 6397
Louis, P., 5027, 9342
Louis XII, 4006
Louis XIV, 4235, 5281, 5478, 6443
Louis XV, 4213, 4362, 5438
Loula, F., 1965
Loveday, A., 877
Low, D., 6398-6399
Lowe, A., 413, 1714, 3599, 3735
Lowe, D. M., 9343
Lowe, J., 6401-6402
Lowell, J. S., 8226
Lowenthal, E., 2766, 9344
Lower, A. R. M., 3071
Lower, M., 2567
Lowndes, 4461
Lowndes, T., 4472
Lowndes, W., 4473
Lowry, S. T., 5028
Loyd, S. J., 6403, 6649
Loyd, S. M., 6404-6408
Lu, M., 1715
Lu, S. Y., 5373
Lu, Y., 5250
Lubersac, Conte, 6409
Luca, M., 1716, 2853
Lucas, A., 5029
Lucca, 5623
Luchterhand, W. 9649
Lucky, W., 10022
Ludewig, J., 8227
Ludlow, 8228
Lueder, A., 6410-6411
Luers, H., 2693
Lugli, L., 1717
Lukaszewica, A., 259

Lukaszewicz, A., 414, 9345
Lukawer, E., 9346
Lukman, M. H., 9481
Lumbroso, G., 8229
Lumsden, K. G., 3736
Lundberg, 1301
Lundberg, E., 878, 3446, 3737
Lundberg, I. C., 5369
Lundvall, B-A., 9129
Lunghini, G., 398
Lunt, E. C., 8230
Lupi, C., 6412
Lurachi, R., 2854
Lutfalla, M., 416, 5370-5371, 5409
Luther, M., 2472
Lutheran, 5023
Luthy, H., 5372
Lutke, H., 1026, 2714
Lutken, F., 4474
Lutz, A., 9737
Lutz, F. A., 1132, 1718, 10023
Lutz, V., 1718
Luwel, A., 1719
Luxemburg, R., 1720
Luzicki, L., 9347
Luzzatti, L., 8231
Ly, S. Y., 2581
Lynn, R. A., 1721
Lysko, S., 9348, 9651

Mably, A., 4475
Mabson, R. R., 6413
Macadam, G., 8232
Macauley, Z., 6415
Macchioro, A., 417
MacCulloch, J. R., 6416-6428
Macdonald, A. F., 8233
Macdonald, A. M., 9064
Macdonald, T., 6429
Macdonnell, W. D., 8234
Mace de Richebourg, 6430
Macedo, U., 9057
Macek, J., 9349
Macesich, G., 3094
Macewan, A., 879
Macfarlane, C. W., 3331,
Macfarlane, J., 6431
 8235-8236
MacFie, A. L., 418, 2767, 7332
Macgregor, D. H., 3332, 7315, 9983-9984, 10024

Macgregor, J., 6432
Machiavelli, N., 8729
Machinek, P., 1722
Machinery, 1343, 5498, 5990, 6096, 6097, 6331, 6782, 6806, 6830, 6839, 8359
Machlup, F., 880-881, 3738
Mackay, F., 8237
Mackenzie, T. F., 882
Mackworth, H., 4476
Maclaren, J., 8239
Maclean, J. H., 6434
Maclean, J. L., 8240
Macleod, H. D., 4241-4242
 8243-8248
Macleod, H. P., 7744
Macmillan, D., 9836
Macnab, H. G., 6435
Macpherson, D., 6436
Macpherson, H., 7337
Macrossan, M., 2547
Maculla, J., 4477
MacVane, S. M., 8249
Madan, G. R., 421, 2818
Madden, C. H., 738, 1305
Maddox, T., 4478-4479
Madison, J., 3067
Madrago, S. D., 8250
Madras, 5648
Madrazo, S. D., 422
Maedge, C.-M., 898
Maenchen-Helfen, O., 9461
Maffei, Marquis de, 6438
Magallon de La Vega, A., 3333
Magaud, C., 1723
Magens, N., 4243, 4480
Maggi, R., 1724
Magliani, A. G., 8251
Maher, J. E., 1725
Mahieu, J. M., 423
Mahmassani, S., 5030
Mahr, A., 883, 1726
Mahr, W., 1727
Maide, C., 424
Maier, A., 5031
Maillet, J., 426
Maine, H. S., 8252
Mainguy, Y., 3334
Maintenance, Law of, 5628
Maisel, S. J., 1728
Maitland, F. W., 4960
Maitland, S. R., 8253

Majundar, T., 9837
Makano, T., 917
Makato, T., 8254
Makiguchi, T., 3335
Makower, H., 1729
Maksimovic, I., 427, 1730, 9350
Malabar, 5648
Malanos, G. J., 1731, 3336, 9738
Malawi, 3176
Malay States, 6602
Malchus, C. A., 6440
Malcolm, J., 6441, 6484
Male, L., Count of Flanders, 5135
Malia, M., 9352
Mallarme, S., 2518
Mallet, J. L., 6442
Mallet, L., 8255
Mallock, W. H., 8256-8259
Mallory, J., 4481-4484
Malo de Lucque, E., 6444
Malon, B., 8260
Malone, D., 5361
Malquet, 5774
Malquet, Baron, 6445
Malthus, T., 77, 187, 778, 2405, 2758, 2781, 2865, 5202, 5870, 6019, 6124, 6280, 6852, 6979
Malthus, T. R., 77, 185, 445, 778, 884, 1732-1733, 2405, 2653, 2749, 2758, 2781, 2865, 3167, 3337, 5202, 5870, 6019, 6124, 6280, 6446-6451, 6852, 6979, 7337, 7527, 9539
Malvaux, 6452
Malynes, G., 4482-4484 5268
Man, 7287
Management, 1495, 2150
Management, Economic, 735
Management, Industrial, 1687, 2708, 2740, 3045
Manager, 1241, 3205
Mancarella, A., 2855
Manchester, 6691
Manchester, Cotton Manufacture, 6322
Manchester, Chamber of Commerce, 5830, 6405
Manchester Conference on Teaching Economics, 3744

Manchester Guardian, 9987
Manchester School, 305, 2746, 3915
Manchester School of Economic and Social Studies, 885
Mandel, E., 1981, 9353
Mandeville, B., 4485-4486, 5190, 7307, 7316, 7355
Manes, P., 1734
Manetti-Cusa, N., 9356
Manfra, M. R., 2428, 2856
Manger, K., 1790
Mangoldt, H., 6453-6455
Mangoldt, H. K. E., 1735-1736
Manila, 7201
Manilla, 6785
Manindra Chandra Lectures, 2825, 5072
Mankind, 827
Manley, T., 4487
Manly, T., 4162
Mann, C. A., 8262
Mann, F. K., 2429, 5251
Mann, M., 10025
Manne, A. S., 1737
Mannequin, T., 8263
Mannheim, K., 9357
Manor, English, 7382
Mantoux, E., 10026
Mantoux, P., 10026, 5439
Mamu, 9588
Manual, 1038, 1391, 1436, 1576, 1666, 1738, 1755, 1900, 1944, 2044, 2049, 2113, 2143, 2147, 2233, 5823, 5838, 6432, 6457-6458, 6695, 6708, 6752, 7366, 7551, 7728, 9669, 9756
Manual, Banking, 7700
Manual, Commercial, 6327, 7178
Manual, Consul, 6456
Manual, Instructor's, 1761
Manual, Statistics, 6952
Manuel, F. E., 9358
Manuel, V., 1493
Manufacture, 893, 3450, 4083, 4091, 4128, 4147, 4228, 4354, 4471, 4612, 4756, 5606, 5830, 6095, 6700, 6710, 6816, 6817, 6986
Manufacture, Cloth, 4228,

4766, 5816
Manufacture, Cotton, 6160, 6322, 6546, 6974, 7179
Manufacture, Cotton, Workers, 7192
Manufacture, Food, 3455
Manufacture, Iron, 4768, 8681
Manufacture, Linen, 4025, 4443
Manufacture, Wool, 4775, 4856, 6813
Manufacture, Worsted, 6296
Manufacturer, 5446, 5702
Manufactures, 3937, 3967, 4296, 4455, 4609, 4671, 5498, 5584, 5739, 5969, 6171, 6238, 6436, 6459, 6629, 6798, 6820, 6842, 7140
Manufactures, American, 7496
Manufactures, Combination, 8497
Manufactures, Dictionary of, 7180
Manufactures, Fluctuations, 7252
Manufactures, Ireland, 7215
Manufactures, Spain, 7140
Manufal, 8532
Mao Tse-Tung, 9359, 9360
Marano, I., 1738
Marcet, J., 6460-6461
Marchal, A., 429, 652, 1109-1110, 1301, 1739-1740, 2646, 5252
Marchal, Andre, 3740
Marchal, J., 430, 883, 1113 1741-1743
Marchand, J., 5253-5254
Marchet, G., 8264
Marco Polo, 7149
Marcuse, H., 9150
Marcy, G., 2430
Mareno, J., C., 251
Marescotti, A., 6462
Margarido, A., 1418
Marget, A. W., 1744, 3338, 5255, 10027
Marginal Analysis, 9736
Marginal Productivity Theory, 9687
Marginal Utility, 3187

Marginal Utility School, 9719
Marginalism, 2126, 9658-9806
Mariana, J., 5243
Marin, C. A., 6463
Maringer, J., 5032
Marinkovic, P., 9361
Mariotti, F., 2624
Maritain, J., 5033, 5035
Mark, S. M., 886
Markert, W., 887, 3012
Market, 2024, 3095-3096, 3192, 3304, 3385, 3482, 5129, 5422
Market, Behavior, 730
Market Institutions, 3357
Market, Intertribal, 5097
Market, Model, 3787
Market, Place, 993
Market, Socialism, 9563
Markham, F. M. H., 9362, 9534
Markham, G., 4488
Markham, J. W., 2069
Markham, S. F., 9363
Markle, F., 1792
Markovic, L., 1745
Markovic, M., 9364
Marmatakes, N. G., 431
Marmier, J., 8828
Marnef, E., 432
Marnoco E Souza, J. F., 433, 2951
Marquez, J., 2733
Marrama, V., 1746
Marrani, P., 1747
Marreca, A., 6464
Marriot, J., 4489
Marriott, J. A. R., 434
Marriott, W. F., 8265
Marris, R., 888, 1748
Marryat, J., 6465
Marsden, W., 6466, 7149
Marsh, A. G., 2431
Marshall, A., 168, 200, 772, 985, 1749, 2432, 2480, 2722, 2749, 2752, 2758, 2772, 3256, 3339, 3741-3743 8266, 9279, 9807-9884, 9984
Marshall, A., Bibliography, 9976

Marshall, E. V., 1750
Marshall, H. D., 435, 889
Marshall, L. C., 890
Marshall, M. P., 9852-9853
Marshall, N. J., 889, 10028
Marshall, S., 6467
Marshall, W., 6468
Marsili Libelli del Collechio, Mario, 1751
Martel, H., 9549
Martiis, S. C., 8267
Martin, B. L., 803
Martin, E. W., 8268
Martin, I., 1072
Martin, K., 3744
Martin, M., 6469
Martin, R. M., 6470-6472, 8269
Martin, R. S., 436, 1752-1753, 3745
Martin, W. H., 2261
Martindale, D., 3746
Martineau, H., 2379, 2477, 5787, 6471-6475
Martinelli, J., 6476
Martinez, P. S., 1754
Martinez Candia, M., 437
Martinez Val, J. M., 1755
Martins, O., 8270
Marx, J., 9140
Marx, K., 3, 65, 635, 851, 1040, 1756, 1855, 2456, 2480, 2481, 2488, 3282, 3316, 3324, 3340-3345, 3541, 5262, 5289, 5441, 7285, 8612, 8723, 8872, 9003-9004, 9007, 9014, 9019, 9029-9034, 9038, 9048-9049, 9057, 9060, 9064, 9067, 9070-9072, 9075-9077, 9092-9093, 9098, 9111-9112, 9116-9118, 9120-9121, 9135, 9141, 9143, 9165, 9185, 9192-9195, 9198, 9202, 9204, 9206, 9209, 9213, 9216, 9226, 9229-9230, 9239, 9242-9243, 9251, 9253, 9258, 9263, 9269, 9271, 9279, 9283, 9289-9290, 9300, 9302, 9314-9315, 9317, 9320, 9329, 9340-9341, 9343, 9353, 9355, 9365-9422, 9438, 9471, 9473, 9490, 9500-9501, 9521-9522, 9527, 9535, 9543-9544, 9546, 9551, 9566, 9579, 9588, 9590-9591, 9598, 9609, 9624, 9629, 9632, 9634, 9638, 9645, 9647, 9650, 9654, 9656, 9828, 9887, 9903, 9926, 9929, 9965, 10029
Marx-Engels Institute, 9438
Marx-Engels-Lenin Institute, Moscow, 9413
Marxism, 186, 580, 1350, 1874, 2162, 2634, 2894, 2896, 3099, 3110, 3115, 3241, 3278, 3282, 3316, 3800, 9003-9657
Marxism, American, 9229
Marxism, Chinese, 9439
Marz, E., 9423
Marzano, F., 2857, 8271
Masai, K., 438
Masamura, K., 439
Masaryk, T. G., 9544
Maseres, F., 6477
Masdero, A., 56
Masoin, M., 440, 1757
Mason, D. H., 8272
Mason, E. S., 769, 3346
Massa, J. J., 1758
Massera, J. L., 9424
Massie, J., 4490-4500
Massingham, H. J., 1582
Massip, A., 8273
Masson, D., 5878
Masson, G., 5418
Mastier, A., 8274
Mastrianna, F. V., 803
Masuda, S., 441
Mataja, V., 8275
Mateev, E., 442
Material, Raw, 8813
Materialism, 9086, 9121-9122, 9318, 9490
Mathematical Association of America, 3540
Mathematics, 383, 1170, 1222, 3493, 3531, 3540-3542, 3554-3555, 3578-3579, 3600, 3619, 3621, 3669, 3693, 3747, 3755, 3767,

3796, 3842, 3864, 3915-
3916, 3919, 4981, 5028,
5844, 9073, 9660, 9671-
9672, 9681, 9694, 9728,
9735, 9753, 9775, 9793,
9795, 9909, 10032
Mathematics, Greek, 4982
Mathur, A. S., 2819
Mathur, J. S., 2819
Matrix, Economic, 3801
Matsumoto, K., 3416
Mattern, E., 3748
Matthias, W. H., 6478
Mattick, P., 9213, 9426, 10029
Maturity, Economic, 9962
Matyas, A., 443, 9427
Maugham, R., 6479
Maulnier, T., 444
Maurell Lobo, A., 1759
Maurenbrecher, M. H., 5036
Maurer, G. L., 6480
Maurice, S. C., 1402
Maverick, L. A., 2578, 5012, 5374-5375
Mavor, J., 2958
Maxwell, H., 4502
May, K., 3347
May, P. H., 1973
Mayer, G., 9428
Mayer, H., 883, 891, 9429
Mayer, J., 3749
Mayer, R. P., 2982
Mayo, H. B., 9430
Mayo-Smith, R., 8276
Mayr, G., 8277-8278
Mayz Vallenilla, E., 9431
Mazan, J., 5256
Mazepy, I., 2974
Mazzei, J., 2769, 5257
Mazzilli, B., 3750
Mazzola, U., 8279
McAdam, J. L., 6414
McArthur, E. A., 7711
McBriar, A. M., 9432
McCabe, J., 1232
McCarran, M. P., 9433
McCarthy, L. P., 8280
McCarthy, T., 3340, 9393
McClain, R. H., 1311, 3046
McClung, L. A., 8970
McConnell, C., 892

McConnell, C. R., 1760
McConnell, D. W., 8908
McConnell, J. W., 445
McCosh, J., 2433
McCracken, H. L., 1553, 10030
McCulloch, J. R., 446-447, 893, 1762, 2434, 2449, 3167, 5834, 5864, 6005, 6416-6428, 6859, 7317, 7337
McCutchen, S. P., 837
McDonald, W. J., 5037
McDonnel, W. D., 8281
McDougall, D. M., 1322
McEnnis, J. T., 8632
McEvoy, H. M., 2435
McGill University, 1872
McGoldrick, J. D., 2180
McIlwain, C. H., 5346
McIntyre, F., 9735, 9871
McIsaac, A. M., 448, 1763-1764, 3751
McKee, C. W., 832
McKenna, J. P., 1766-1767, 10031
McKinley Tariff, 6151
McLellan, D., 9382, 9391, 9434-9435
McNair, M. P., 894
McNeil, G. E., 8282
McShane, E. J., 3540
McVickar, J., 1762
Meade, J. E., 1768-1769, 3435
Measurement, 3644
Meat, High Price, 6707
Medeiros, T., 1772
Medici, G., 1773
Medici Bank, 5082
Mediterranean, 5734
Mediterranean Area, Middle Ages, 4919
Mediterranean Europe, 5127
Medley, G. W., 8283
Meek, J., 6273
Meek, R. L., 895, 2436, 3348-3349, 5376-5377
Meerhaeghe, M., 1774
Mees, W. C., 6481
Meganck, J., 2659
Mehr, G. R., 619
Mehring, H., 8284

Mehta, D. D., 1775
Mehta, J. K., 896, 1776-1779
Mehta, S. C., 1780
Meili, F., 8285-8286
Meinander, N., 449, 1781
Meinhold, W., 1782
Meininghaus, A., 8287
Meinvielle, J., 1783
Meisner, M., 9439
Meisser, H., 3778
Meitzen, A., 8288
Mejia-Ricart, G. M. A., 1784
Melbourne, Lord Viscount, 7137
Melbourne University, 821, 2549
Melchiore, G., 6119
Mello, O., 1786
Melman, S., 3068
Melon, J. F., 4503-4504, 5190
Menck-Tichauer, C., 5378
Mendel, A. P., 9440
Menezes, D., 1787-1789, 9441
Menger, A., 9289, 9442
Menger, C., 2476, 3428, 3752-3754, 3813, 8290, 8864-8865, 8870, 9662, 9698, 9716 9739-9742, 9760, 9773, 9776
Mengotti, F., 5258-5260, 6493
Menier, E. J., 8291
Mennicken, P., 898
Mensi, V., 8292
Mentchinov, V. S., 5395
Menut, A. D., 5039
Mercantile Treatise, 5833
Mercantilism, 13, 73, 168, 309, 460, 823, 2329, 2429, 2552-2553, 2948-2949, 2971, 2977, 5149-5326, 5332, 5366, 6978, 7843, 8794
Merchandise, 3935, 3939, 4837, 6175
Merchandise, Great Britain, 4776
Merchandising, 1873
Merchant, 4017, 4059, 4320, 4323, 4441-4442, 4449, 4483, 4511, 4680, 4828, 5198, 5446, 6459
Merchant, Alien, 5154
Merchant, English, 7547
Merchant, Great Britain, 4411
Merchant, Italian, 4089
Merchant, Japanese, 2901
Merchant, Petitioners, 3957

Merchant, West India, 4453
Meredith, C. M., 9121
Meredith, W., 6495
Merewerther, H. A., 6496
Meriam, R. W., 3350
Merimen, Erkki, 2424
Merivale, H., 6498-6499
Merle, M., 5262
Merrem, 6500
Merrey, W., 6501
Mervart, J., 9570
Mesenge, P. J., 6502
Mesico, 2380
Messance, 4651, 6503
Messedaglia, A., 6504-6505
Messmann, H., 900
Meszaros, I., 9443
Metal, 3993, 5292, 6328
Metal, Coin, 6697
Metal, Precious, 5293, 6287, 6289, 6978, 7500, 7731, 8409, 8542, 8561
Metals, Precious, Value of, 6689
Metaphysics, 3708
Metastatics, 3887
Method, Dialectical, 9899
Method, Economics, 46, 54, 355, 384, 436, 593, 708, 850, 898, 1815, 1905, 2025, 2476, 2614, 2626, 2638, 2976, 2991, 3299, 3455, 3456, 3490-3919, 5895, 6101, 8578, 8848, 8853, 8874, 8883, 8923, 9073, 9091, 9142, 9492, 9528, 9599, 9742-9743, 9779, 9944, 9959, 10032
Method, Geometrical, 3169
Method, Historical, 2661, 2918, 3674, 3753, 8863, 8887, 8891
Method, Mathematical, 54, 3604, 3849, 9775
Method, Philosophical, 3675, 8857
Method, Problems of, 3889
Method, Schmoller and Menger, 8870
Method, Scientific, 3749
Method, Statistical, 3182
Metzler, L. A., 828
Mexico, 610-611, 1095, 1103,

2733, 2914-2918, 7429
Meyer, A. G., 9444-9446
Meyer, E. W., 2694
Meyer, G., 8293
Meyer, J., 8294
Meyer, J. R., 1389
Meyer, M., 451, 8295
Meyer, P., 3125
Meyer, R., 8296, 8299
Meyer, R. P., 2982
Meyer, Robert, 8297-8298
Meyer, Rudolph, 8300-8301
Meyers, A. L., 1793-1794
Meynaud, J., 1795-1796
Meynieu, M., 6509
Mezague, V., 4848
Mezei, S., 1797
Miaskowski, A., 8302
Michelon, L. C., 1798, 1799
Michels, R., 2858
Michieli, I., 3755
Michnak, K., 9447
Michotte, P. L., 2558
Micolai, E., 8362
Microstatics, 3888
Middle Ages, 13, 31, 344, 2721, 2748, 2761, 4891, 4906, 4908, 4911, 4917, 4922, 4929, 4945, 4960, 4965, 4972, 4978-4980, 4985, 4994, 4997-4999, 5006, 5010, 5017, 5037, 5042, 5055, 5061, 5063-5064, 5080-5085, 5081, 5083, 5086, 5092, 5094, 5099, 5113, 5115, 5135, 5142-5143, 5742, 6084, 6168, 6360, 6932, 7149, 7323, 7660, 7710, 8084, 8253, 8665, 9039
Middle Ages, Banking, 5052
Middle Ages, Chinese, 4958
Middleton, H., 6510
Mignot, 4513
Migrations, Ancient Period, 4983
Mijo, N., 1299
Milan, 4336, 4838
Milburn, W., 6511
Milenkovitch, D. D., 3095
Milford, H., 5116
Milhau, J., 3113
Military Doctrine, 9201
Mill, J., 903, 1800, 7095, 7337

Mill, J. S., 40, 904, 1200, 1801, 2398, 2437-2438, 2450, 2732, 2736, 2758, 3167, 6511-6513, 6516-6519, 7318, 7684, 9808
Mill, Stuart, 725
Miller, H. E., 3352
Miller, M. H., 880
Miller, R. E, 2112
Miller, R. G., 436, 1752, 3745
Miller, R. L., 927
Miller, S., 6542
Milligan, M., 9383
Millikan, M. F., 963
Milliken, M. F., 9812
Mills, C. W., 1018, 9448
Mills, H. V., 8304
Mills, M. C., 1355
Milne, J., 6520
Milner, J., 4514
Milner, L., 2788
Milon, R., 9449
Miltitz, 6456
Minc, B., 453, 1802-1803, 2941
Minchinton, W. E., 5263
Mine, 3954, 4262, 4852
Mine, Dictionary of, 7180
Mine, France, 7373
Minghetti, N., 8305, 8306
Minister, 4060
Ministere de l'Economie et des Finances, 1424
Ministere des Affaires Economiques . . . Belgium, 2557
Mino, S., 1804, 3013
Mint, English, 5059
Mint, Royal, 7386
Mint, United States, 7651
Mintz, J., S., 9605
Mira, C., 454
Mirabaud, J. B., 4514
Mirabeau, V. R., 1019, 5435, 5379-5387, 6522, 8385
Mirabella, G., 905
Mirandes Miranda, F., 1805
Misery, 4368
Mises, L., 455-456, 1806, 3454, 3757-3759, 7337, 9743-9746, 9772
Miskimin, H. A., 5040
Misselden, E., 4518-4519

Miszewski, B., 1807, 9450
Mita, S., 3760, 9451
Mita Gakkai Zasshi, 657
Mitchell, 8948
Mitchell, B., 2439
Mitchell, H., 5041
Mitchell, J. B., 1808-1809
Mitchell, L., 2440
Mitchell, W., 8307
Mitchell, W. C., 457-460, 765, 906, 2278, 2440-2441, 3761-3763, 8958, 8964, 8971-8980, 9001
Mitchell, W. F., 1810
Mitra, J. K., 1811
Mitrany, D., 9452
Mitscherlich, W. O. E., 461
Mittala, S. C., 462, 1812
Miwa, M., 1813
Miyade, H., 1814
Miyakawa, M., 9453
Miyamoto, M., 2647, 2891
Mizutani, K., 3353
Mockers, J. P., 1815
Model, 3600, 3854
Model, Building, 3906
Model, Construction, 3790
Model, Decision, 3777
Model, Mathematical, 3871
Model, H., 3354
Modeste, V., 6523-6524
Moe, L. E., 3355
Moffat, J. E., 1355, 3356
Moffat, R. S., 8308
Moggridge, J. H., 652
Moglia, L., 8309
Mohammedan Traveler, 3950
Moheau, M., 6526, 6764
Mohl, E., 9185
Mohl, R. V., 671, 2678, 6527
Mohortynski, P., 907
Mohrmann, H., 2695, 2960
Moireau, A., 8310
Moivre, A., 4521
Moldavia, 6823
Molesworth, G. L., 8311
Molinari, G., 6482, 6529-6535
Molly, C., 4522
Molnar, E., 9454
Molnar, M., 463
Molster, J. A., 6537
Mombert, P., 464

Monarch, 5509
Monarchy, Asiatic, 6681
Monborgne, J. M., 6538
Moncada, S., 4523-4524
Mondenard, 6539
Mondo Aperto, 63
Mondolfo, R., 9455
Monetary Economics, 9922
Monetary Experiments, Great Britain, 9797
Monetary Problems, 9877
Monetary Problem, Scandinavian Area, 9797
Monetary Reform, 9997
Monetary Theory, 2775, 5265, 9820, 9922, 9949, 10016, 10051, 10065
Monetary Theory, Spanish, 2968
Money, 10, 14, 37, 71, 78, 119, 180, 182-183, 252, 430, 548, 785, 836, 893, 908, 978, 1063, 1685, 1826, 2000, 2396, 2720, 2781, 3122, 3125, 3151, 3202, 3232, 3281, 3309, 3315, 3319, 3327, 3369, 3381, 3415, 3418, 3734, 3785, 3981, 3983, 3995, 3998-3999, 4026, 4029, 4054, 4057, 4058, 4065, 4109, 4117, 4141, 4170, 4181, 4203-4204, 4265, 4271, 4317, 4334, 4337, 4339, 4349, 4358, 4380, 4400-4401, 4465, 4470, 4513 4525, 4567, 4582, 4596, 4601, 4619, 4620, 4701, 4706, 4716, 4721, 4734, 4798, 4803, 4829, 4832 4849, 4864, 4899, 4908, 4912-4913, 4919, 4973, 4994, 5041, 5071, 5078, 5081, 5105, 5125, 5129, 5155-5156, 5230, 5239, 5297, 5315, 5433, 5502, 5617, 5810, 5854, 5883, 5907, 5918, 6006, 6029, 6090, 6131, 6137, 6139, 6141, 6294, 6347, 6430, 6438, 6457-6458, 6507, 6525, 6611, 6660, 6677, 6730, 6829, 6936, 6976, 7011, 7077, 7087-7088,

7132, 7137, 7145, 7158,
7212, 7231, 7239, 7241,
7256, 7259, 7260, 7391,
7525, 7574, 7600, 7660,
7682, 7687, 7710, 7730,
7732-7733, 7870, 7986,
8063, 8100, 8105, 8128,
8170, 8184, 8197, 8214,
8251, 8263, 8311, 8361,
8440, 8459, 8523, 8596,
8621, 8713, 8746-8747,
8768, 8780, 9077, 9725,
9746, 9844, 9866, 9924,
9929, 9939, 9989, 9998,
10049, 10091, 10093, 10102
Money, Circular Velocity, 9904
Money, Copper, 4186
Money, Counterfeit, 4735
Money, Demand, 3225
Money, Foreign, 4724
Money, Functions, 3211
Money, Germany, 6136
Money, Gold, 8702
Money, Great Britain, 4274, 4424, 6187
Money, History, 6868
Money, Marginal Utility, 9817
Money, Market, 6406, 6649
Money, Metal, 6873, 7427
Money, Natural Law of, 7573
Money, Panics, 8800
Money, Paper, 4202, 4249, 6130, 6645, 6670, 6910, 7996, 8262
Money, Policy, 7231
Money, Primitive, 4942 6873
Money, Quantity, 785
Money, Quantity Theory, 787, 5219
Money, Robinson Crusoe, 8775
Money, Silver, 8702
Money, Value, 4461, 4466, 6243, 6360
Money-Changer, 5081
Mongez, 4525
Mongolia, Prehistoric, 5031
Mongredien, A., 8312-8313
Monier, R., 5042
Monieson, D. D., 3357
Monino, J., 4526
Monissen, H. G., 10032
Monnier, A., 6541
Monopolistic Competition, 3153, 3305
Monopoly, 2796, 3165, 3169, 3261, 3577, 4137, 4330, 4988, 6120, 6567, 6628, 7423, 7810, 8648, 9027, 9546, 10099
Monopoly, Chinese, 5853
Monopoly, Trade, 5856, 6423
Monroe, A. E., 909
Monsaroff, B., 1816
Monsen, R. J., 3069
Montagnon, E., 8314
Montagu, B., 6542
Montague, E. C., 8866
Montaignac, 6543
Montana, 3079
Montana Academy of Sciences, 3079
Montana State University, 3079
Montanari, A., 8315
Montaner, A., 910
Montaner, A. M., 3764
Montchretien, A., 4527
Monte de Piete, 6720
Monteagle, Lord, 5741, 5832
Monteil, A., 6544
Monteil, J., 911, 3358
Montenegro, A. F., 2442, 5264
Montenegro, W. E., 465
Montesquieu, C. L., 2514, 4528, 6545, 7142
Montgomery, J., 6546
Montgomery, W. E., 8316
Montyon, Baron de, 6547-6548
Mony, S., 8317
Monypenny, D., 6549
Moody, W. G., 8318
Moore, A., 4529
Moore, A. E., 5265
Moore, F., 4530
Moore, H. L., 1817, 3076, 3359-3360, 8319-8322
Moore, J. C., 3765
Moore, J. H., 1818
Moore, J. R., 1347
Moore, S., 9367
Moore, W. L., 1469
Morals, 977, 4379, 6347, 6625, 7183, 7343
Morals and Legislation, 9043
Morandiere, 4531
Morato, O., 1819
Morawski, K., 2620

Moraze, C., 466, 3766
Mordasini, S., 1820
Mordukhovich, L. M., 467
More, J., 4532
More, T., 868, 9097, 9276, 9456
Moreau, J. N., 4534
Moreau de Beaumont, 6552
Moreau de Jonnes, A., 6554-6559
Moreau-Christophe, L. M., 6553
Morellet, J. N., 4256, 4506, 4535-4539
Morelly, 5370
Moret, J., 3767
Moret, M., 3361
Morf, O., 9457
Morgan, A., 6562
Morgan, E. V., 1821
Morgan, F., 709, 7420
Morgan, J. M., 6563
Morgan, J. N., 3722
Morgan, T., 1822, 10033
Morgan, W., 5814, 6564-6565
Morganstern, O., 912, 3362-3363, 3768, 3842
Morgner, A., 1055
Mori, R., 2859, 5044
Mori, S., 2892
Morikawa, T., 10034
Morin, A. J., 3709
Morin, T., 6566
Morini-Comby, J., 5266
Morishima, M., 3770
Morito, T., 468
Morley, H., 4366
Morley, J., 2443
Morning Chronicle, London, 6373
Morpeth, Lord Viscount, 5660
Morpurgo, E., 8323
Morris, C., 4540-4544
Morris, E., 6567
Morris, M., 7301
Morris, R., 1823
Morrison, C., 6568
Morrison, J., 6748
Morrison, W. D., 8324
Morrow, G. R., 5045, 7319
Morse, C., 8931
Morse, J. T., 8325
Morselli, E., 1824
Mortality Rate, 4326, 5466, 5585, 5964, 6520, 6622, 7390

Mortara, G., 902
Mortara, L., 8326
Mortenson, W. P., 1825
Mortimer, T., 4225, 4545
Morton, H. C., 3891
Morus, T., 4547
Moscardino, M., 1826
Moseley, B., 6569, 6570
Moskovskij Universitet, 336
Mosler, C., 8327
Moss, H., 3501
Mosse, 6571
Mosse, R., 1827
Mossion, E., 5388
Mossner, E. C., 2445
Mother Country, 4821, 6007
Motivation, 8910
Motive, Economic, 3586
Moulton, H. G., 10035
Moulton, N. D., 638
Mounier, A., 5267
Mounier et Rubichon, 6572
Mount Holyoke College, 913
Mouqaddima, 4995-4996
Moura, F. P., 1828
Mourant, J. A., 5389
Movement, Social, 546
Moxter, A., 3771
Muchmore, L., 5268
Mudie, G., 6575
Mueller, A., 2521
Muessig, R. H., 436, 3745
Muhlbrecht, O., 8328
Muhleman, H. L., 8329
Muhs, K., 469, 914
Muiron, J., 6576, 6577
Mujzel, J., 1820
Mukerjee, R., 421, 2821, 8981
Mukerjee, R. K., 2818
Mukhopadhyay, R. N., 2822
Mulcahy, R. E., 915, 2444
Mulhall, M. G., 8330-8331
Mulinen, Comte, 8332
Muller, A. H., 1831, 2554, 6578-6580, 8867
Muller, E., 8333
Muller, J., 470
Muller, R., 1832
Muller, V., 78
Muller-Armack, A., 471-472
Mullern, O., 2135
Multiplier, 9944
Multiplier Theory, 9959

Mumford, L., 882, 9458
Mun, T., 4548-4549, 5269
Munoz, A., 6581
Munoz, C. J., 473
Muns, J., 488
Muqaddimah, 5011
Murad, A., 1834, 10036
Murat, A., 1835, 2192
Murhard, C., 6582-6583
Muro, F. D., 1712
Murphree, I., 8982
Murray, A., 4500
Murray, D., 2446
Murray, H., 6584
Murray, J., 6586
Murray, J. B. C., 8334
Murray, K. B., 8335
Murray, R., 4551
Murray, R. A., 9747
Murray, R. H., 3772
Musgrave, A., 1836, 8336
Mushet, R., 6587-6590
Mussey, H. R., 1837
Mussiggang, A., 2696
Muth, J., 3773
Muthesius, V., 1838, 3774
Muyden, G., 7797
Muzikova-Nosilova, L., 916
Myer, A., 8338
Myers, M. L., 3364
Myrdal, G. K., 474, 1839, 2976, 3365
Myres, S. D., 9498
Mysore, 5648

Nag, D. S., 5047
Nagai, T., 8337
Nagasu, K., 10037
Nakai, M., 3416
Nakano, T., 2893
Nakayama, I., 1840-1842
Naniwada, H., 918-919
Napier, M., 6591-6593, 7320
Naples, 2853
Napoleoni, C., 475-476, 1843-1844
Napoli, 5888, 5907
Napolitani, G., 1845
Napolitano, G., 477
Narasaki, T., 478-479, 1846-1847, 3775
Narasimham, G. V. L., 3600
Nardi, G., 480, 1848-1850
Narduzzi, N., 920
Nash, M., 5048
Nash, R. T., 10038
Nash'at, M. A., 481
Nasir, M. S., 1851
Nasse, E., 8340
Nasstrom, G., 2384
Nataf, A., 3366, 3630
Natan, A., 2565
Natan, Z., 482-483
Natarajan, B., 2823
Nation, 4061, 6600
Nation, Decline and Fall, Causes, 6704
Nation, Poor, 6047
National Bureau of Economic Research, 224, 734, 3225, 9905, 10011
National Industrial Conference Board, 921, 10039
National Liberal Club, 8104
National Mutual Life Assurance Society, 9988
Nationalism, 5197
Nationalization, 7688, 8749
Nationalization, Land, 8645
Nato, 3624
Naturalization, Foreign Protestants, 4819
Nature, 1044, 4515
Nature, Human, 7312
Nature, Law of, 6009, 7281
Naudier, F., 8341
Naval Store Bill, 4434
Navarre, 4973
Naveau, J. B., 4557
Navigation, 3947, 4044, 4251, 4364, 4462, 4683, 4699, 4797, 5480, 5508, 5772 5891, 5961, 6107, 6185, 6310-6311, 6432, 6436, 6782, 6887, 6988, 7045, 7047, 7060, 7075, 7194, 8154
Navigation, Great Britain, 6210
Navigation, Steam, 6903, 8455
Navigation Statutes, 5444, 6241, 6594, 6780
Naville, 5877, 6595
Naville, P., 1981, 9674
Navy, 5233
Navy, Royal, England, 4509
Naylor, T. H., 3776-3777

Nazzani, E., 8342-8343
Neal, A. C., 1198
Neal, F. W., 3092
Nearing, S., 1853
Nebenius, F., 6596-6598
Nebraska Journal of Economics and Business, 9922
Necker, 4812, 5439
Necker, J., 4558-4563, 5390-5391, 6599
Necker de Germani, 6865
Neeb, J. F., 8344
Neff, F. A., 484
Negley, G., 9459
Negro, 4124, 4800, 5795, 6306, 7247
Neill, C. P., 3070
Neill, T. P., 5392-5394
Nell-Breuning, O., 922
Nelson, B. N., 5049
Nemchinvo, V. S., 3779-3781
Neo-Cambridge School, 3715
Neocapitalism, 2634
Neoliberalism, 9683, 9761
Neomercantilism, 5186, 5287
Neri, P., 4564
Nerlove, M., 3367, 3666
Nerom, V., 8345
Nervo, Baron, 8346-8347
Nesic, D., 485, 1855
Netherlands, 72, 2919-2925, 4133, 4182, 4255, 4489, 4638, 4641, 4772, 4809, 5483, 5836, 6220, 6482, 6729, 6778-6779, 6905, 6980, 7452, 8338, 9939
Neumann, F. J., 3782, 8348
Neumann-Spallart, F., 8349-8350
Neumark, F., 486
Neutrality, Armed, 5776
Neves, J. A., 2946
Nevin, E., 923, 1856
Nevsky, 8633
New Deal, 3056
New England, 7463
New England, History, 8769
New Frontier, 3087
New Lanark, 6435
New School of Social Research, 773
New York, 6109, 7634, 8595, 8771
New York Institute of Finance, 801
New York Society for Ethical Culture, 720
New York University, 93, 2375, 8908
New York University Institute of Philosophy, 3368
New Zealand, 972, 2471, 5018
Newbold, T. J., 6602
Newbury, F. D., 1857
Newcomb, S., 1858, 8353-8354
Newenham, T., 6603
Newman, F. W., 8355
Newman, P. C., 488, 924
Newmarch, W., 6605, 7129
Newton, I., 2738, 4565, 4668
Neymarck, A., 5396, 8356-8359
Neyt, R., 1859
Nicard des Rieux, S., 9460
Nichol, A. J., 9748
Nicholls, G., 6608, 6696-6607
Nichols, D. A., 1860
Nicholson, J. S., 3200, 3369, 7005, 8360
Nick, H., 9462
Nickolls, J., 4169, 4608
Nicola, P. C., 3783
Nicolaievsky, B., 9461
Nicosia, G., 5050
Niederer, G., 8364
Nielsen, A. E. H., 2606, 5270
Niemeyer, 6609-6610
Niemeyer, G., 9062
Nigerian Economic and Social Studies Syndicate, 1080
Nikitin, P. I., 1862-1863
Nikl, M., 1864
Ninagawa, T., 925
Ninsgradoff, P., 8365
Nippold, W., 5051
Nishimura, T., 5271
Nishizawa, T., 3000
Nitterdorf, R., 1831
Nitti, F. S., 8366
Nivholson, J. S., 1861
Niyrgyes, 6702
Noble, J., 8368
Nock, F. J., 9741
Noda, I., 10040
Noel, O., 8370
Nogaard, I., 926
Nogaro, P. G. B., 489, 1865, 3784

Nogueira, L., 2561
Non-Marxian, 2896
Non-Ricardian, 2743
Nonomura, K., 2447
Noonan, J. T., 5052
Norberg, H., 9797
Nordhoff, C., 9463
Nordin, J. A., 1866
Nordoff, C., 8371
Norfolk Scheme, 4566
Norgard, I., 1867-1868
Norman, G. W., 6611-6612
Norman Conquest, 4478, 4741
Normandy, 6620, 6781
Normandy, Marquis of, 4172
Normano, J. F., 2910, 3014, 3071
Norris, R., 3370
North, C., 2504
North, D., 4567-4568
North, D. C., 927
North, R., 4569-4570
North America, 4441
Northcote, S. H., 8372
Norton, E., 8373
Norton, H. S., 2448
Norway, 875, 2926
Noshiro, O., 3416
Notcutt, G. J., 8374
Note, Primissory, 5545, 5738
Notz, W. F., 3072
Nourry, C., 8375
Novack, D. E., 928
Novak, M., 929, 1869
Novakovic, S. D., 1870
Nove, A., 1980, 3015-3016, 3371, 9050
Novotny, J. M., 1871-1872
Nowocien, S., 9081
Noyes, A. D., 8377
Noyes, C. R., 490
Noyes, J. H., 8378
Nuccio, O., 1036, 3895, 9791-9792
Nunez, C. H., 2221
Nurkse, R., 930
Nussbaum, F. L., 8868
Nyblen, G., 3785
Nys, E., 491
Nystrom, P. H., 1873

O'Connor, A., 6627

O'Connor, M. J. L., 3073
O'Donnell, J., 2239
O'Mally, 9377
O'Meara, J. J., 8383
O'Reilly, 5033
Oates, W. J., 5054
Oberfohren, E., 2648
Oberlaender Trust, Philadelphia, 2694
Oberdorfer, J. A., 6618-6619
Obrien, D. P., 2449
Obrien, G., 2450
Obrien, G. A. T., 5055
Occhionero, L., 594
Occupation, 7390
Ochen, M., 9436
Oelassner, F., 1874, 9464
Oertmann, P., 8379
Oettingen, A., 8380
Offermann, A., 8381
Ogarev, N. P., 2974
Ogilvie, 6009
Ohara, K., 2451, 3074
Ohlin, B., 2377, 9797, 9897
Oi, T., 9465
Okada, J., 1875
Okamoto, T., 10041
Okazaki, T., 3019
Okuchi, K., 493, 1876-1877
Okuma, N., 1878
Okun, A. M., 3372
Okyar, O., 10042
Oldenburg, U., 8869
Oligopoly, 3177, 3380
Oliphant, 6825
Oliva, F., 1879
Olive, 4464
Oliveira Martins, J. P., 2950
Oliver, E. H., 5057
Oliveria, A., 2118
Ollner, A., 3228
Olmeda, M., 5077
Olmova, G., 3373
Olozaga y Bustamante, J. M., 1880
Olsen, 9098
Olsen, A., 2606
Olsen, A. R., 1337
Olst, H. R., 3867
Olufsen, C., 6631
Olufsen, W., 8382
Oncken, 5403, 5441

Oncken, A., 494, 5407, 7321, 8384-8387
Onely, R., 4575
Ono, S., 2546
Opalek, K., 5397
Operationalism, 3840
Opie, R., 2452, 9854
Opium, 5856
Oppelt, W., 1457, 3637
Oppenheim, H. B., 2697
Oppenheimer, F., 241, 1025, 1881
Oppermann, C. A., 8388
Oprisan, M., 5058
Orange, Prince of, 4638
Ord, H. W., 1700, 1883
Order, Economic, 817, 2090, 7306, 8912, 9597, 10057
Order, Natural, 5337, 5371, 5411, 5415
Order, Social, 6370
Orenstein, Z., 495
Oresme, N., 5039, 5059
Organization, Economic, 1303, 1321, 2590, 3291, 3899, 8903
Organization, Social, 2254, 3899, 6059, 8903
Orient, Ancient, 5139
Oritz, R. M., 497
Ornati, O., 496
Orr, D., 3517
Orr, F., 1469
Ortes, G., 6636
Ortes, G. M., 2852
Orth, H. F., 3374
Osaka University, 9875
Osborn, T., 4452
Osborne, G. P., 8389
Oser, J., 498
Oshima, Y., 3375
Ostaszewksi, J., 10044
Osterkamp, K., 1884
Ostlind, A. E., 1885
Ostrovitianov, K., 1038
Oswalt, H., 1886
Oswalt, I., 5399
Otaru, S. D., 2453
Ott, A., 6637
Otte, F. W. K., 2582
Ottel, F., 898
Otto, H., 9467

Ottone, P., 499
Ouchi, H., 500-501, 1887, 2454,
Oudard, G., 5272
Oughton, F., 3376
Oules, F., 931-932, 9749
Output, 1170, 2264, 3286, 3380, 3460
Overproduction, 6144, 8525, 9513
Oversavings, 10084
Overstone, Lord, 2400, 6403-6408, 7139
Owen, R. D., 6435, 6575, 6638-6642, 6844, 6929, 9053, 9110, 9328, 9468-9470, 9491
Ownership, 150
Ownership, Absentee, 8992
Ownership, Archaic Communities, 8629
Ownership, Business, 31
Oxenfeldt, A. R., 1888-1890, 3787
Oyebola, A., 1080
Ozga, S. A., 934

Paasche, H., 8390
Pacher, P., 8391
Pacifici, A., 9756
Pacini, G. B., 2488
Packard, L. B., 5273
Padagogischen Institut Salzburg, 3834
Pae, P., 1891
Paeglis, J., 9471
Paepe, C., 2736
Page, A. H. C., 1892-1893
Page, A. N., 3377, 9750
Page, F., 6646
Paglin, M., 1672, 1733
Pahlow, W., 9472
Paillotet, 5532
Paine, C., 8392-8393
Paine, T., 6644-6646, 7207
Pak, H., 1894
Pak, T., 1258
Pakistan, 1072, 2927
Palaa, G., 8394
Palacios, M. R., 1340
Palander, T., 2976
Palau, 5078
Palermo, 5576
Palermo Universita, 935
Palgrave, F., 6647

Palgrave, R. H. I., 7745, 8394-8397
Palgrave's Dictionary of Political Economy, 3623, 3687, 9692-9693
Palmer, J. H., 6403, 6648-6649
Palomba, G., 1895-1898
Palyi, M., 724
Pamphlet, 884
Pamphleteer, 60, 5570, 5592, 5644, 5740, 5752, 5798, 5818-5819, 5852, 5938, 6064, 6191, 6295, 6613, 6997, 7320
Pan, L., 9473
Pankhurst, R. K. P., 2455 9474
Pannell, J. P., 5060
Pantaleoni, M., 502, 1899-1900, 2474, 2868, 3378, 3788, 8396, 8398, 9751, 9754
Paolini, G. B., 6651
Papandreou, A. G., 503-504, 3789
Papers, 1003, 1022
Papi, G. U., 1901, 10082
Papillon, A. F. W., 4579
Papillon, T., 4579-4580
Papillon-Latapy, 6655
Papion, 6657
Paponot, F., 8399
Pappe, H. O., 2456
Pappenheim, F., 9475
Paquet, A., 505
Paradox, Economic, 2119
Parahyba, Brazil, 2457
Parain, C., 9476
Pardessus, 5845, 7144
Pardo Gonzalez, N. S., 1902
Pare, W., 7096
Paredes, M., 1230
Parent-Duchatelet, 6658
Pareto, R., 2860
Pareto, V., 702, 780, 931, 936, 1957, 2474, 2860, 2868, 3379, 3792-3793, 3861, 9368, 9667, 9669-9670, 9697, 9704, 9713, 9749, 9752-9759, 9779, 9786, 9824, 9884
Parieu, F., 6661-6663, 6675
Paris, 6658, 6720, 7380, 7449

Paris, Comte, 8400
Paris du Verney, J., 4581-4582
Parish of Templemore, Great Britain, 6635
Parish System, 5630
Paristan, 1985
Parizeau, J., 9889
Park, J. A., 6663
Park, J. C. S., 3380
Parker, H., 4583
Parkes, H. B., 9477
Parkes, J., 6660
Parkinson, J. R., 1117
Parliament, 4099, 4142, 4163, 4257, 4426, 4435, 4459, 4466, 4543-4544, 4666, 4780, 4825, 5451, 5549, 5735, 5809, 6624, 6799-6802, 6805-6813, 6828-6829, 6985, 7274, 9840
Parliament Act, Railroad, 6660
Parliament, House of Commons, 6045, 6270, 6272-6273, 6525, 6594, 6652-6653, 6688, 6692, 6748, 6790, 6796-6797, 6821, 6830, 6836-6837, 7003, 7021, 7064, 7099, 7168, 7171-7172, 9841
Parliament, House of Lords, 5831, 7168
Parliamentary Reports, 6665-6669
Parnell, H., 5881, 6670-6675
Parrillo, F., 506
Parrish, J. B., 507
Parsons, F., 8325
Parsons, K. H., 8925
Parsons, T., 1903, 2254, 3899, 9855-9857
Partington, T. C., 9038
Partito Comunista Italiano, 1904
Partnership, Law of, 5777, 6132
Pascal, R., 9390
Paschke, W., 1905
Pascoli, L., 4585
Pascual, F., 2042
Pashkov, A. I., 2954
Pashley, R., 6676
Pasley, C. W., 6677
Pasqualaggi, G., 508
Passadeos, C., 9027
Passet, R., 3796

Passy, H., 6678-6680
Passy, L., 7437
Pastoret, 5909
Pasztory, T., 9478
Patent, 4359, 6120
Paterson, W., 4586
Patinkin, D., 2840, 3381
Paton, W. A., 1906
Patrick, Fifth Lord Elibank, 4249
Patrick, J. M., 9459
Patten, S. N., 509, 937, 1907, 2343, 2770, 3797, 8401-8407
Pattern, Economic, 1991
Patterson, R. H., 8408-8409
Patterson, S. H., 938, 2112
Patton, A. C., 3572
Patton, J. H., 8410
Patton, R., 6681
Patton, R. D., 3798
Patzelt, E., 179
Paucton, 6508
Paula, L. N., 2561, 2911
Pauley, E. D., 3382
Paulhac, F., 1908
Pauliat, L., 8411
Paulsen, A., 1909, 10045
Pauperism, 5490, 5630, 5716
Pauwels, M., 1910
Pavan, P., 1911
Pavlat, V., 1912-1913
Pavlenda, V., 9479
Pawlowski, Z., 3799
Pawn Broker, 3966
Payment, Cash, 5798
Payment, Commercial, 5782
Payne, E. J., 8412
Pazhitnov, K. A., 2961
Peace, 789, 4252, 10026
Peace, Economic Consequences, 9981, 9996, 10100
Peace of Amiens, 6539
Peace of 1763, Great Britain, 5711
Peach, W. N., 1914
Pearce, A., 510
Pearce, B., 1980, 9355
Pearce, D. W., 2156
Pearce, I. F., 3383
Pearson, H. W., 5068
Peasant, 9452
Peasant Proprietors, 7110
Pease, E. R., 9480

Pebrer, P., 6682
Pecchio, G., 2861-2862
Pecchio, J., 6683
Peck, H. W., 8983
Pecquet, M., 4588
Pecqueur, C., 2430, 6684-6687
Pedersen, J., 1915, 2381
Pedragosa, S., 1916
Peek, F., 8414
Peel, R., 6688
Pegis, A. C., 5061
Pejovich, S., 3096
Peking, 7201
Pell, A., 8487
Pen, J., 511-512, 1917-1920
Pena, G. S., 1921
Penaloza, L., 1922
Pendzig, P., 5062
Pennington, J., 6689
Pennsylvania, 4456
Penrose, E. T., 9858
Pentagon, 3068
Penty, A. J., 513
Perales Garcia, L., 1923
Peravy, 4505
Percival, R., 6690
Perdew, R. M., 1089
Pereira, A. T., 514, 1924
Pereira, L., 9482
Pereire, E., 8415
Pereire, I., 8415
Performance, Economic, 2218
Perimutter, S., 9760
Perin, C., 8416-8417
Periods, Time, 3290
Perkins, D. H., 2588, 3384
Perlman, R., 3385
Perlman, S., 8925
Perlo, V., 3800
Pernaut Ardanaz, M., 1925
Perovic, M., 1927-1929, 9483
Perpena Grau, R., 515
Perrin, J., 8006
Perrin, W., 4589
Perriquet, E., 8418
Perrot, A., 8419
Perrot, F., 8420-8421
Perroux, F., 516-517, 1930, 3268, 9923
Perry, A. L., 8422-8423
Peru, 5454, 5899
Peruzzi, E., 2860

Pervinquiere, M., 5400
Pescatore, M., 8424
Pesch, H., 2444
Pesenti, A. M., 1932-1933
Peston, M. H., 3801
Petander, K. T., 2977, 5274
Peter, H., 1934-1935, 9761
Peter, J. H., 2699
Peter, K. C., 518
Petersen, A., 9762
Peterson, G. S., 1936
Peterson, R., 4040
Peterson, W. C., 1937
Peterson, W. L., 1938
Petit, E., 4590
Peto, S. M., 8425
Petre, G., 1939
Petrovic, G., 9484
Petrovic, J., 1940
Petrovic, P. S., 9338
Petrovic, R., 9485
Petrovic, V. J., 1941
Petty, H., 6692
Petty, W., 2458, 3307, 4592-4594, 5195, 5306
Petzet, W., 5401
Peuchet, J., 6693
Pfau, J. J., 8426
Pfeiffer, 4600-4601
Pfister, B., 8870
Pfouts, R. W., 939, 3802, 9859
Pharaohs, 4954
Phelan, E. J., 9979
Phelan, G., 8151
Philip, A., 519
Philip, G., 1942
Philippe, J. A., 520, 2459
Philippine Economic Journal, 3503
Philippine Islands, 6010-6011, 6785
Philippines, 7201
Philippovitch, E., 1943, 3804
Philips, E., 4601
Philips, J., 4602
Phillipovich, E., 8427
Phillippi, L. A., 4603
Phillips, A., 5402
Phillips, H., 8428
Phillips, H. A., 10046
Phillips, J., 6694
Phillips, M., 8429

Phillips, U. B., 3075
Phillips, W., 1944, 6695
Philosopher, 2732
Philosophers, Worldly, 2399
Philosophy, 57, 93, 171, 221, 286, 546, 639, 640, 737, 1062, 1263, 1594, 1978, 2643, 2770, 3642, 3654, 4005, 4644, 4963, 5079, 5161, 5289, 5330, 5407, 5787, 5962, 5994, 6031, 6118, 6221, 6922, 7048, 7050, 7197, 7202, 7301-7304, 7323, 7336, 7605, 8625, 8968, 9117, 9152, 9192, 9195, 9291, 9314, 9318, 9377, 9405, 9407, 9454, 9484, 9496, 9499, 9610, 9642, 9658, 9678
Philosophy, Economic, 554, 4475, 5464, 7735, 8247
Philosophy, Essay, 4386
Philosophy, Great Britain, 2787
Philosophy, Marxian, 9303, 9339, 9366, 9383, 9401, 9486, 9549
Philosophy, Middle Ages, 5052-5063, 5142
Philosophy, Moral, 4394-4395, 7277
Philosophy, Political, 5638
Philosophy, Rural, 5385
Philosophy, Scholastic, 4977
Philosophy, Scientific, 3609
Philosophy, Scottish, 2413, 2433
Philosophy, Social, 2929, 3234, 4943-4944, 7931, 9416
Philosophy, Wealth, 7631
Phoenicians, 6850
Physiocracy, 40, 64, 2581, 2971, 5158, 5289, 5327-5443, 6072, 6247, 6325, 8576
Physiocracy, Chinese Influence, 5375
Physiocracy, Polish, 5397
Piantanida, 5886
Piasny, J., 9487
Piatier, A., 208, 5350
Picard, A., 8430
Picavet, F. J., 5063
Pichler, H., 1945
Pick, E., 1946

Pierangeli, G., 9408
Pierce, R. A., 2954
Piernas y Hurtado, J., 8431-8432
Pierson, N. G., 1947, 8433-8434, 9224
Pierstorff, J., 2649, 3386, 8435
Piest, O., 9619
Pietri-Tonelli, A., 9758
Pietri-Tonelli, P., 9758
Piettre, A., 521-524, 940, 9488
Piettre, M., 521
Pigeonneau, H., 7861, 8436
Pignorii, L., 4604
Pigou, A. C., 525, 941, 1948-1951, 2460, 2771, 3387, 3742, 3805, 3912, 9843, 9860-9862, 9976, 10047-10049
Pilkington, E. C. A., 1952
Pillet-Will, 6696
Pillexfen, J., 4612
Pineda, C. A., 526
Pineda, Alcala, F., 1953
Pineda de Castro, A., 1954
Ping-T'ung, F., 2578
Pinkerton, J., 6697
Pinmeiro-Ferreira, 6697
Pinon Filgueira, E. M., 5275
Pinsent, J., 6698
Pinto, I., 4605
Pinto Santa Cruz, F. A., 1955-1956
Pirenne, J. H. O. L. M., 5064-5065
Piret, N. J., 8437
Pirou, G., 1957, 2650, 3076, 9763
Pisani, 7058
Pit, W., 5654
Pitanza, L., 1959
Pitcairn, G., 6699
Pitkin, T., 6700
Pitt, W., 5624, 6565, 6605, 6887, 7027, 7254
Pizzamiglio, L., 8438
Pjanic, Z., 527, 942, 3390
Place, F., 2527, 6701
Plaine, H. L., 9489
Planning, 3094-3097, 3276-3277, 3422, 3581, 3729, 9079, 9083, 9142, 9224, 9294, 9478, 9563, 9567
Planning, Central, 3866, 5287
Planning, Economic, 150, 2739
Planning, India, 2832
Planning, Social, 150
Planning, Soviet Union, 2993, 3028, 9050
Plant, A., 6371
Plantation, 1441, 4335, 6840, 8431
Plantation, Court of Appeals, 5747
Plantation, Great Britain, 3941, 4202, 4210, 4346
Planteau, F. E., 8439
Planter, 4092
Planter, Sugar, 4196
Plat, H., 4607
Plate, 5107
Plato, 2795, 4894, 4921, 5007, 5014, 5045, 5058, 5066, 7891
Platon, F., 725
Platte, H. K., 3806
Platteeuw, O. L., 1960
Playfair, W., 6703-6704, 7337
Plebano, A., 8440
Plehn, C. C., 8441-8442
Plekhanov, G., 2963
Plekhanov, G. V., 9490
Plener, E. E., 8443
Plotnik, M. J., 8871
Plotnikov, I. S., 5276
Plough, P., 6705
Plummer, A., 2461
Pluquet, 6706
Plutology, 8010
Po-Fu, T., 2578
Podmore, F., 6639, 9491
Pohle, L., 2700
Poire, P., 8444
Poivre, P., 7202
Pokrovskii, A. L., 2651
Polak, F. L., 1961-1962
Polak, N. J., 943
Polak, S., 528
Poland, 1037, 2783, 2928-2944, 6952, 9638
Polanyi, K., 529, 5067-5068
Polar Seas and Regions, 6585
Polianskii, F. I., 530, 1008, 2962

Author and Subject Index 699

Police, 7338
Policy, 263, 328, 654, 801, 813, 841, 946, 1013, 1023, 1087, 1096, 1126, 1162, 1165, 1169, 1201, 1338, 1514, 1592, 1606, 1769, 2188, 2234, 2448, 2700, 2702, 2709, 2720, 2729, 2739, 2757, 2776, 3086, 3368, 3490, 3641, 3665, 3881, 3908, 4064, 5255, 5293, 5330, 6426, 6429, 6879-6882, 7288, 7315, 10024, 10074, 10107
Policy, American, 3049
Policy, Colonial, 5637, 6151, 6272, 6276, 7130, 7272
Policy, Commercial, 5288, 6151, 7130
Policy, Commercial, Great Britain, 5269
Policy, Economic, 575, 788, 797, 798, 860, 2187, 2922, 5162, 5418, 7315, 7324, 9916
Policy, Economic, France, 5178, 5252
Policy, Economic, Great Britain, 4231
Policy, Economic, India, 2814
Policy, Economic, Ireland, 2834
Policy, Economic, Italy, 2857, 2861-2862
Policy, Economic, Japan, 2895
Policy, Economic, Mexico, 2915, 2918
Policy, Economic, Soviet Union, 3011
Policy, Economic, Spain, 5170
Policy, Economic, United States, 3057
Policy, Public, 828, 1262, 3223, 3844, 5760, 9953
Policy, Rome, 5104
Policy, Social, 5295
Policy, Stabilization, 978, 7231
Policy, Trade, 8022
Polier, L., 944, 3391
Polish, 377

Political Arithmetic, 4875, 5224
Political Economy, 859, 975, 1021, 1200, 1210, 1213, 1219, 1229, 1280-1281, 1283, 1291, 1304, 1350, 1369, 1391, 1397, 1452, 1551, 1648, 1667, 1681, 1697, 1708, 1713-1714, 1732, 1741, 1768, 1772, 1800, 1835-1836, 1843, 1861, 1874, 1924, 1955-1956, 1984, 1987-1988, 1989, 1994, 2007, 2013, 2048, 2068, 2071, 2087, 2100-2101, 2113, 2116, 2120, 2143, 2161, 2192, 2198, 2217, 2221, 2232-2233, 2281, 2325, 2350, 2479, 2589, 2627, 2722, 2733, 2736, 2743, 2779, 2799, 3020, 3053, 3067-3068, 3142, 3576, 3599, 3603, 3623, 3660, 3676, 3683, 3713, 3728, 3797, 3829, 3911, 3990, 4242, 4527, 4770, 5202, 5296, 5304, 5482, 5488, 5530, 5536-5537, 5540-5541, 5580, 5596, 5599, 5601, 5604, 5619, 5636, 5656, 5677-5678, 5682, 5685, 5691, 5963-5694, 5699, 5704, 5714, 5728, 5729, 5742, 5778, 5822-5823, 5840, 5850, 5863, 5878-5778, 5892, 5955, 5897, 5916, 5926, 5928, 5938, 5958, 5960, 5962, 5967, 5978, 5989, 5995, 5998, 6008, 6012, 6015, 6046, 6083, 6085, 6087-6088, 6093, 6094, 6108, 6179-6180, 6184, 6208, 6209, 6234, 6247, 6294, 6298, 6306, 6307, 6310, 6313, 6376, 6425, 6446, 6451, 6460, 6472-6473, 6482, 6499, 6509, 6513, 6518-6519, 6530, 6533-6536, 6575, 6579, 6581, 6591, 6637, 6638-6642, 6678-6679, 6687, 6695, 6697-6698, 6705, 6716, 6737-

6738, 6752, 6756, 6759,
6760, 6762, 6855, 6884,
6894, 6895, 6911, 6913,
6921, 6928, 6937-6939,
6942, 6943, 6945, 6946-
6948, 6957, 6959, 6962,
6966, 6972, 6975, 6993,
6999, 7000, 7006, 7010,
7018, 7024, 7055, 7075,
7134, 7141, 7152, 7157,
7173, 7184, 7186, 7190,
7191, 7197, 7217, 7223,
7227, 7240, 7244, 7257,
7274, 7282, 7296, 7313,
7320, 7250, 7368, 7392,
7418, 7424, 7442-7444,
7454, 7522, 7528, 7592,
7594, 7598, 7611, 7618,
7619, 7655, 7656, 7662,
7676-7677, 7681, 7705,
7744-7745, 7774, 7780,
7801, 7808, 7821, 7837,
7839, 7874, 7884, 7897,
7905, 7921, 7950, 7952,
8021, 8108-8111, 8161,
8163, 8168, 8188, 8204,
8209, 8211, 8221, 8229,
8245, 8249, 8250, 8254,
8265, 8305, 8309, 8336,
8342-8343, 8354-8355,
8376, 8422-8423, 8427,
8447, 8451, 8456, 8461,
8480, 8520, 8532, 8535,
8548, 8556, 8588, 8591,
8603, 8611-8612, 8640-
8641, 8653, 8676, 8679,
8683, 8699, 8731, 8742,
8744, 8792, 8799, 8804,
8844, 8847, 8853, 8857,
8859, 8875, 8880-8881,
8894, 8900, 8905, 8927,
9129, 9278, 9287, 9298,
9376, 9379, 9391, 9394,
9400, 9419, 9425, 9483,
9528, 9573, 9602, 9617,
9668, 9692-9693, 9695-
9696, 9699, 9720, 9726,
9728, 9742, 9747, 9752,
9756, 9789-9790, 9798,
9802, 9806, 10038, 10068
Political Economy, American,
 2402, 8860
Political Economy, Bibliography,
 6420
Political Economy, Capitalism,
 9532
Political Economy, Europe, 7170
Political Economy, Marxian, 9157
 9228, 9325, 9388, 9393,
 9464, 9595,
Political Economy, Non-Ricardian, 2395
Political Economy, Origin, 7296
Political Economy, Socialism,
 9160-9161, 9295, 9297,
 9305-9306, 9350, 9479,
 9493, 9587
Political Economy Club, 8445
Political Science, 2530, 2694, 2950
 3037, 3049, 5849, 7051,
 7553, 8149, 8866, 9845
Political Science Quarterly, 551,
 3561, 3618
Political Thought, 5759, 9020
Politics, 80, 955, 3654, 4225,
 5788, 6031, 7094, 7160,
 7409, 7589, 7709, 8007,
 8624, 9433, 9560
Politics, Comparative, 7545
Politics, International, 964
Politics, Social, 6874, 7604
Politiska Skrifter, 5172
Pollard, A. W., 8168
Pollis, A., 9764
Pollock, F., 8446, 8872
Polo, J., 5707
Population, 7068, 7238
Poly, J., 1968
Pommelles, 7071
Ponce, A., 520, 2459
Poncelin, 6708
Poncet de la Grave, 6709
Pond, A. S., 1969
Ponsard, C., 531
Ponsiglioni, A., 8447
Pontney, J. A., 3484
Pontzen, E., 8172
Pool, 8094
Pool, A. G., 2462
Poole, B., 6710
Poor, 3925, 3932, 3944, 3991,
 4043, 4086, 4146, 4160,
 4230, 4270, 4272, 4279,
 4343, 4353, 4354, 4367,
 4417, 4445, 4510, 4529,
 4575, 4634, 4754, 4518,

4865, 5447, 5459, 5563,
5643, 5779, 5934, 5937,
5965, 5972, 5997, 6001,
6117, 6204, 6249, 6254,
6330, 6382, 6431, 6435,
6452, 6523, 6549, 6553,
6574, 6592, 6754, 6794,
6799, 6902, 6909, 7214,
7436, 7489, 7499, 7534,
7625, 7680, 7838, 8166,
8364

Poor, Causes, 5724
Poor, England, 8237
Poor, France, 6543, 6595, 7190, 7195
Poor, Housing, 7775
Poor, Inquiry Commission, 5660
Poor, Ireland, 5923, 6497, 6643, 6973
Poor, Law, 2768, 3944, 4063,
5458, 5580, 5655, 5660,
6102, 6390, 6393, 6474,
6525, 6550, 6607, 6676,
6797, 7139, 7218, 7388,
7767, 7862, 7918
Poor, Law, Commissioners, 6819, 6826
Poor, Law, English, 6643
Poor, Relief, England, 8711
Poor, Scotland, 6792
Poor, H. V., 8448-8450
Popadiuk, K., 3392
Pope, C., 6711
Popelova, J., 9496
Popescu, O., 532-534, 2595, 2912
Popiel, J., 1970
Popper, A., 535
Popper, K. R., 9497
Population, 460, 723, 779,
2653, 2781, 2937, 4097,
4302, 4573, 4593, 4599, 4628,
4651, 4718, 4844, 5164,
5208, 5370, 5379, 5458,
5466, 5478, 5490, 5492,
5494, 5527, 5666, 5690,
5706, 5783, 5917, 5922,
5964, 5996, 6019, 6042,
6047, 6095, 6123-6124,
6209, 6211, 6251, 6253,
6284-6285, 6379, 6389,
6427, 6447, 6503, 6505,
6526, 6603, 6636, 6691,
6701, 6709, 6714, 6721,
6759, 6764, 6770, 6907,
6979, 7000, 7071, 7140,
7169, 7211, 7548, 7773,
8005, 8224, 8366, 8639,
8710, 9946
Population, Agricultural, 5542
Population, Excessive, 7109
Population, France, 8589
Population, Great Britain, 7211
Population, Labor, 6096
Population, Manufacturing Workers, 6830
Population, Pre-Malthusian Doctrines, 5305
Population, Spain, 7140
Population, United States, 7156
Populism, Russia, 2962
Poree, M. A., 6894
Porrentry, 7198
Port, Great Britain, 6800
Porter, E. O., 9498
Porter, G. R., 6712-6714
Portugal, 136, 2945-2952,
3624, 4449, 5193,
5207, 6991, 9057
Posada, A., 450
Posner, A., 9081
Posnett, H. M., 8451
Pospisil, L., 5069
Post, History of, 8544
Post, Reform, 6219
Postgraduate Institute on International Studies, 815
Postlethwayt, M., 4615
Poterat, 1716
Pothier, 7143
Potter, B., 8452
Potter, W., 4619, 4798, 5277
Poulain, H., 4610
Poulett, J. D., 2065
Pound, E. L., 1971
Poverty, 253, 2699, 4234, 4330,
4339-4340, 5492, 5875,
6906, 7895, 7993, 8304,
8628
Powell, B. H. B., 8453
Powell, J. C., 5413
Power, Age of, 1853
Power, Maritime, 4195
Power, E., 5309
Powicke, J. C., 1972-1973

Pownall, T., 4621
Pra, M., 9499
Prado, C., 1974
Prados Arrarte, J., 1975
Prague, 1976-1977
Prato, G., 536
Pratt, J. T., 6717
Pratt, W. T., 8454
Preble, H., 8455
Prehn, C. E., 1052
Preiser, E., 537, 1978-1979
Preobrazhenskii, E. A., 1980-1981
Preston, L. E., 3394
Preston, R., 6719
Preston, R. S., 1920
Preston, T. S., 1919
Prete, F., 9756
Preuss, G., 2718
Prevost, G., 4626, 5556, 6447
Prevost de Saint-Lucien, 6720
Pribram, K., 538, 9979
Price, 97, 226, 1130, 1326, 1341, 1367 1524, 1539, 1651, 1680, 1744, 2057, 2084, 2138, 2146, 2171, 2234, 2238, 2444-2445, 3103, 3147, 3186, 3190-3192, 3203, 3210, 3212, 3219, 3232, 3244, 3261, 3262, 3268, 3281, 3290, 3307, 3311-3312, 3330, 3338, 3341, 3345, 3361, 3380-3381, 3384, 3392, 3409, 3418, 3436, 3440, 3461-3462, 3489, 3614, 3622, 3714, 3734, 3971, 4099, 4115, 4123, 4147, 4233, 4242, 4297, 4361, 4407, 4428, 4505, 4632, 4655, 4701-4702, 4734, 4827, 4919, 4973, 4994, 5040, 5105, 5214, 5255, 5325, 5597, 5625, 5696, 5725, 5818, 6423, 6434, 6565, 6715, 6810, 7123, 7270, 7407, 7555, 7600, 7611, 7699, 7845, 7858, 7863, 7874, 7954, 8188, 8212, 8459, 8530, 8561, 8756, 8799, 8820, 8941, 9064, 9386, 9420, 9710, 9796-9797, 10027, 10102
Price, Bread, 6392
Price, Bullion, 5680, 6218, 6588, 7264
Price, Competitive, 3162, 3431
Price, Duopoly, 9748
Price, Elasticity, 3264
Price, Europe, 7270
Price, Fluctuations, 7128
Price, High, 6280
Price, History, 7122, 7126, 7129
Price Index, 3396, 3644
Price, International, 3107, 5151
Price, Just, 4891, 4929, 4932, 4955, 4990, 5003, 5009
Price, Market, 3437
Price, Meat, High, 6707
Price, Provisions, 6275
Price, Revolution, 5215
Price, Revolution, Spain, 5215
Price, Soviet, 3371
Price, Stability, 8405
Price, System, 8993
Price, Theory, 1054-1055, 1092 1139, 9880
Price, Wholesale, 7376
Price, Wool, 1761, 5865
Price, B., 8457
Price, F. G. H., 8458
Price, L., 9863
Price, L. L. F. R., 2772
Price, R., 4627-4630, 6721
Prichard, J. C., 6724
Priestley, J., 6725
Prieto, G., 8461
Primitive Period, 3632, 4344, 4948, 4953, 4966, 4986, 5018, 5031, 5067, 5071, 5095, 5097, 5114, 5116, 5125, 5231, 8167
Primogeniture, 5505
Prims, F., 1982
Prince-Smith, J. K., 6726-6727
Princeton University, 724, 1718
Principles, Economic, 699, 961, 1029-2327, 8389, 8434
Pringle, W. H., 945
Pringsheim, O., 6729
Prinsep, C. R., 6731
Prior, T., 4443
Prison, 8793

Prissia, 2681
Prittwitz, R., 8462
Privilege, 7898
Probability, 9999
Problem, Economic, 699, 753, 776, 793, 803, 805, 834, 846, 860, 879, 945, 983-984, 989-990, 992, 1002, 1020, 1027, 1055, 1203, 1262, 1289, 1337, 1353, 1355, 1405, 1602, 1612, 1633, 1743, 1760, 1794, 1829, 1834, 1952, 1979, 2144, 2177, 2180, 2181, 2204, 2206, 2336, 2662, 2904, 3318, 3392, 3612, 3693 3712-3713, 3825, 3909, 7706, 7810, 9806
Problem, Epistemological, 9743
Problem, Great Britain, 4229
Problem, Scientific, 3851
Problem, Social, 513, 745, 2092, 2677, 3089
Probleme Economice, Bucuresti, 463, 495, 535, 2928, 10092
Probst, G., 539
Probyn, J. W., 8463
Probyn, L. C., 8465
Process, Economic, 1203, 1243, 1359
Prochnow, H. V., 946
Produce, Raw, 6884
Production, 29, 151, 225, 308, 470, 630, 1098, 1155, 1329, 1434, 1439, 1524, 1532, 1639, 1706, 1746, 1792, 1816, 1908, 2048, 2080-2081, 2144, 2551, 2685, 2733, 3118, 3142, 3196, 3208, 3218, 3272, 3316, 3329, 3354, 3364, 3374, 3546, 3714, 5134, 5400, 5702, 6070, 6286, 6289, 7134, 7238, 7500, 9389, 9409, 9462, 9502, 9710, 9778, 9878
Production, Colony, 7028
Production, Cost, 3290
Production, Excessive, 9513
Production, Farm, 3222, 3455
Production, Function, 3228, 3812
Production, Joint, 3264, 3426

Productive Forces, 7081
Productivity, 3395
Proesler, H., 2701
Profession, Economics, 2533
Profit, 1020, 1434, 1628, 1995, 2197, 2649, 2789, 3120, 3193, 3250, 3294, 3345, 3380, 3443, 3710, 4253, 4636, 5312, 6341, 6852, 6856, 7402, 7949. 9206, 9386, 9420, 9711
Profit, Sharing, 7587, 7912, 8581, 8693
Profit, Socialist Economy, 9600
Programed Learning, Economics, 3523
Programming, 1656
Programming, Linear, 3504, 3591, 3593, 3878
Programming, Non-Linear, 3504
Programming, Risk, 3600
Progress, Economic, 830, 1084, 8914
Progress, Industrial, 7401
Progress, Technological, 752
Progress and Poverty, 8220
Progresso Economic Research Centre, Ibadan, 1079
Proletariat, 9319
Property, 4642, 5070, 5790, 6009, 6181, 6375, 6479, 6734, 6762, 7091, 7146, 7404, 7461, 7666, 8167, 8196, 8223, 8258, 8945
Property, Feudal, 4167
Property, Land, 6399, 6400, 8129
Property, Land, Bengal, 6896
Property, Law of, 3920
Property, Middle Ages, 5037
Property, Peasant, 8722
Property, Private, 5091
Property, Real, 7752
Prosperity, 9994
Protection, 513, 2660, 2773, 3067, 3923, 5184, 5455, 5650, 6857, 7588, 7781, 7836, 7896, 7962, 8069, 8450, 8674
Protection, Infant Industries, 8687

Protectionism, 5266
Protest, Economist's, 736
Protestant, 4819
Protestant, Ethic, 8901
Prothero, R. E., 8466
Proudhon, P. J., 2370, 2374, 2463-2465, 6733-6736, 7748, 9216, 9258, 9410, 9441, 9921
Prouteaux, A., 8467
Prussia, 5915, 6629
Prussia, Industry, 8273
Prybyla, J. S., 2589
Pryme, G., 6737-6738
Psychics, Mathematical, 3601
Psychology, 173, 3265, 3436, 3564
Psychology, Economic, 3292, 3708
Public, 2410, 4021
Public, Interest, 982, 1460
Public, Works, 3447, 8662
Public, Works, India, 7107
Puckle, J., 4641
Puerta Flores, I., 3090
Pulteney, W., 4566, 6739
Punjab, 7102
Purdue University, 3326, 3513
Purdy, W., 8468
Puritanism, 2761
Purves, G., 6740
Puu, T., 3807
Pyon, H., 3808

Quack, H. Q. G., 8469
Quality Change, 3644
Quantification in Economics, History of, 3864, 9775
Quarantine Laws, 6432
Quaritsch, D., 8470
Quarterly Journal of Economics, 2348, 2432, 2452, 3161-3162, 3173, 3239, 3245, 3261, 3284, 3292, 3346, 3350, 3352, 3360, 3437, 3451, 3483, 3486, 3549, 3559, 3562, 3568, 3583, 3596, 3652, 3668, 3707, 3725, 3838, 3886, 3910, 3912-3913, 4968-4969, 5194, 5211, 5393, 5402, 5428, 8907, 8976, 9557, 9625, 9700, 9718, 9731, 9785, 9816, 9818, 9835, 9847, 9855, 9879, 9882, 9884, 8899, 9990, 10023, 10078
Quarterly Review of Economics and Business, 3532, 3798
Quesnay, F., 83, 286, 651, 893, 1019, 5327, 5337, 5341, 5363, 5370, 5372, 5378, 5394-5395, 5403-5410, 5421, 5425, 5435, 5441, 5443, 9965
Quessel, L., 5410
Queteiet, A., 6743
Quiggan, A. H., 5071
Quinteros Delgado, J. C., 2467

Raaijmakers, C., 1983
Rabbeno, U., 8471-8474
Rabenius, L. G., 6744
Radi, L., 2863
Radical, Birth of, 10050
Radical Critique, 740, 899
Radicalism, Philosophic, 7301
Radziszewski, H., 2942
Rae, G., 8475
Rae, J., 1984, 7322, 7354
Raevskaia, E. S., 2803, 947
Raffalovch, A., 8476-8477
Raffel, F. A., 2773
Raffles, T. S. R., 6745
Raguet, C., 6747
Rahman, H. H., 1985
Rahman, M., 1986
Rahola y Tremols, F., 2969
Railroad, 6310, 6696, 6725, 6748, 6782, 7012, 7073, 7262, 7360-7362, 7364-7365, 7451, 7505, 7529, 7713, 7847, 7850, 7955, 7978, 8093, 8146, 8158, 8199, 8206, 8230, 8231, 8233, 8240, 8388, 8393-8394, 8430, 8488, 8604, 8752, 8786
Railroad, America, 7633, 7669, 8172
Railroad, Brimingham and Liverpool, 6664
Railroad, Great Britain, 7763
Railroad, Legislation, 7572
Railroad, Pacific, 7572

Railroad, Reform, 6749
Rainone, C., 2864
Rajaoja, V., 3396
Rakocevic, M., 3150
Rakovski, G. S., 2564
Raleigh, W., 723, 5164
Ramaix, M., 8478
Ramakrishna, K. T., 948
Ramazzini, B., 4805
Rambaud, A., 8479
Rambaud, J., 8480
Rampal, B., 6958
Ramsay, G., 6750
Ramsland, C., 727
Rand, B., 949, 8481
Randall, C. B., 2468
Randall, J. H., 7323
Rangaswami Aiyangar, K. V., 2825, 5072
Ranke, L. V., 8482
Rankovic, S., 9503
Ranlett, J. G., 1310
Ranson, R. L., 2346
Rao, M. B., 9266
Rapet, J. J., 6752
Rappard, W. E., 5294
Rasche, J. C., 5073, 6755
Rasmussen, K., 3809
Rasmussen, N., 1009
Rasmussen, P. N., 3810
Rassegna Economica, Napoli, 265, 524
Ratcliff, A. R. N., 3544
Rathgen, K., 8483
Rationalization, Economic, 3763, 5434
Ratzinger, G., 8484
Rau, K. H., 6756-6758
Rauner, R. M., 3397
Ravenstone, P., 6759
Rawson, R., 8486
Raye, J. L., 7318
Raymond, A., 5761
Raymond, D., 1987, 3070, 6761
Raynal, F., 4644, 6221
Raynaud, B., 5411
Read, C., 8487
Read, S., 6762
Readings, 699, 704, 706, 707, 710, 721-722, 727, 733, 747-748, 757, 769, 776-777, 782, 791, 794, 797-798, 802, 804-806, 809, 816-820, 826-827, 832, 843, 845, 867, 879, 886, 889, 890, 892, 899, 909, 912, 915, 938, 945-946, 950, 952, 963-966, 971-972, 975, 978, 1265, 1367, 1516, 2181, 2445, 2999, 3103, 3275, 3377, 3594, 3632, 3846, 4925, 5019, 9652, 9750, 9810, 9880, 9944, 10023, 10105
Realism, 3738, 3826
Reasoning, Economic, 538, 731, 3819
Rebillon, A., 2652
Rebound, P., 1988
Recession, 157
Recktenwald, H. C., 542, 950, 2469
Reconstruction, Economic, 807, 814
Records, Public, 5821
Reddie, J., 6777
Redfield, I. F., 8488
Redgrave, A., 8489
Rees, A., 804
Rees, O., 2922-2923, 6779
Reeve, G., 4653
Reeve, H., 7120
Reeves, J., 6780, 8490
Reform, Economic, 8478
Reform, Economic, Soviet Union, 9600
Reform, Financial, 5881, 6672
Reform, Revenue, 7878
Reform, Social, 283, 6359, 7571, 7933, 8658, 9167
Reformation, 4965
Reformer, Money, 2396
Reformer, Social, 1015, 9635
Reginald, A., 2567
Registrar-General, England, 5472
Registry, Land, 4646, 4649
Reichardt, H., 9765
Reichwein, A., 5413
Reid, H., 6782
Reid, J. M., 2470
Reid, S. J., 7009
Reid, T., 7349
Reimarus, H., 6783-6784
Reinaud, E., 8491
Reisman, G., 3454, 3757

Reizier, K., 5076
Relief, 5997
Relief, Outdoor, 8711
Relief, Poor, 8711
Religion, 4486, 5106, 7183, 7197, 9045, 9336, 9406, 9504
Remondiere, L. A., 8492
Renaissance, 4956, 4965, 5253
Renan, E., 5074-5075
Renaud, A., 1989
Renda, F., 1324
Rendon, J., 1990
Renny, R., 6787
Renouard, A. C., 6788
Rent, 1995, 2197, 3169, 3402, 3443, 3468, 3577, 4051, 5702, 6245, 6344, 6390, 6449, 6617, 6771, 7095, 8235, 8745, 9799, 9847
Rent, Marginal, 9717
Rent, Produce, 6434
Rent, Quasi, 9807, 9854
Rentzsch, H., 7989
Renwick, C., 1991, 2471
Reparation, 1908, 9902
Reproduction, 2936, 9308
Republic, 4918
Resch, P., 8502-8503
Research, 3084, 3589, 3910, 9905
Research, Education, 3811
Research, Japan, 2904
Research, Operations, 3863
Resource, 1944, 3692, 3761, 5934, 8791
Resource Allocation, 9909
Resource, Belgium, 8685
Resource, Europe, 7148
Resource, Idle, 9968
Resource, Industrial, 6320
Resource, Material, 8781
Resource, Mexico, 7429
Resource, National, 5779-5780
Resource, Natural, 8410, 8613
Resource, Productive, 6432
Resource, United States, 5634-5635
Resta, M., 1992
Reste, B., 6220
Restraint of Trade, 3066
Retail, 3197
Reuel, A. L., 2964, 3021

Reutlinger, S., 3399
Revans, J., 6841
Revenue, 3930, 4157, 4439, 4544, 4610, 4622, 4625, 4702, 4913, 5746, 5999, 6633, 6662 6714, 6887, 7338, 7615, 7843, 7972, 8725
Revenue, Custom, 7982
Revenue, Institutional, 8936 9686
Revenue, Ireland, 5735
Revenue, Land, 6915, 7412
Revenue, National, 7055, 7140, 8616
Revenue, Public, 4171, 4232, 4543, 4617, 4744, 4749, 5298, 5768, 6027, 6996, 8521, 8719
Reverdil, S. F., 7335
Review of Economic Statistics, 9951
Review of Economic Studies, 2436, 3273, 3313, 3347, 3435, 9645, 9887, 9929
Review of Radical Political Economics, 543
Review of Social Economy, 3900
Revista de Economia, 29
Revista de la Faculdad de Derecho. . . . , 2794
Revolution, 130, 444, 2090, 2636, 2958, 6642, 6721, 8660, 9319
Revolution, American, 8672
Revolution, Economic, 7759
Revolution, France, 5914
Revolution, Germany, 9411
Revolution, Human Mind, 6642
Revloution, Industrial, 727, 932, 2788, 8896
Revolution, Keynesian, 10005
Revolution, Social, 8341
Revue d'Economie Politique, 217, 5336, 5411, 8838, 9911
Revue d'Histoire Economique et Sociale, 544, 5370
Revue de Philosophie, 429
Revue du Mois, 9220
Revue Economique, 545
Revue Internationale de Sociologie 5190
Revue Internationale des Sciences Sociales, 576

Rey, C., 4673
Reybaud, L., 6842-6843, 6844-6845
Reymann, H., 2472
Reymond, J. J., 8504
Reynardson, S., 4674
Reynaud, L., 8505
Reynaud, P. L., 2486, 2865, 7327
Reynel, C., 4675
Reynier, J. L. A., 6846-6850
Reynolds, C. W., 1860
Reynolds, L. G., 951, 1993
Rheinstein, M., 3898
Rhodes, 6064, 6956
Rhys, E., 7337
Riazanov, O., 9505
Ribton-Turner, C. J., 8506
Ricard, J. P., 4676
Ricard, S., 4677, 6851
Ricardian, Jacksonian, 2217
Ricardo, 2758
Ricardo, D., 185, 324, 893, 1994-1995, 2390, 2404-2405, 2473, 2539, 2749, 2766, 2855, 3167, 5202, 5368, 5650, 5834, 6288, 6575, 6852-6859, 7095, 7298, 7320, 7337, 7358, 8723
Ricca-Salerno, G., 2866-2867, 3400, 8507-8508
Ricchetti, D., 9506
Ricci, L., 6860
Ricci, U., 2474, 2868, 3401-3403
Rice, T. S., 5923
Richald, L., 8509
Ricards, G., 546
Richards, R. D., 1996
Richardson, G. B., 1997
Richardson, G. G., 8510
Richelieu, 5166
Richelot, H., 6861-6862
Riches, 4315, 5645
Richey, A. G., 8511
Richie, R. Y., 1469
Richmond, W., 8512
Richner, E., 5414
Richter, E., 8513-8514
Richter, G., 8515
Richter, H., 9559
Rickards, R., 6863
Ricossa, S., 1154, 1998

Ridgeway, W., 8516
Ridolfi, M., 1479
Riedle, H., 9766
Riegel, R. D., 10050
Riehl, W. H., 8517
Riemersma, J. C., 867
Riesman, D., 8984
Riezler, K., 2796
Rights, Man, 6646
Riley, E. B., 1999
Rillet de Saussure, 6865
Rima, I. H., 547, 952
Rimini, B., 2000
Ring, M. I., 2475
Ringwalt, J. L., 8518
Ripp, G., 9507
Riquetti, V., 5387
Risk, 1628, 3294, 3542, 3710
Rist, C., 240-243, 548, 659
Ritschi, H., 2001
Ritter, C., 8519
Rittmannsberger, A., 2002
Ritzanthaler, R. E., 5078
Ritzel, G., 2476, 3813
Rivenberg, N. E., 2477
Rivers, 6725
Rivet, F., 8520
Rivett, K., 2826
Riviere, M., 549, 5414
Riviere, P.-P. M., 5415
Rivista de Economia, 2631
Rivista di Politica Economica, 587
Rivista Internazionale di Scienze Economiche, 503, 3426
Road, 4145, 4207, 5975, 6414, 6675
Road, Iron, 8786
Road, Legislation, 8097
Road, Public, 4372
Robber, 4269
Robbins, L., 829, 3404, 3864, 7324, 9798, 9802, 9864-9865
Robbins, L. C., 550, 954-955, 2478-2479, 3814
Roberts, 9988
Roberts, E. H., 8521
Roberts, H. V. D., 5278
Roberts, L., 4680-4681
Robertson, C. G., 945
Robertson, D. H., 877, 960-961, 2752, 3405, 3406, 3816,

9827, 9866-9867, 10051-10052
Robertson, G., 6866
Robertson, H. M., 7325-7326
Robertson, J. M., 9840
Robertson, R. M., 9767
Robertson, W., 6867, 7349
Robineau, L., 8522
Robinson, E. V., 551
Robinson, C., 6831, 6868-6869
Robinson, H., 4682-4683
Robinson, J., 552-554, 2003-2004, 2480, 3407, 3817-3818, 5279, 9508, 10056
Robinson, J. V., 956-959, 9508-9509
Robinson, M. A., 3819
Robinson, T., 6870
Robinson, J., 9768-9769
Robinson Crusoe's Money, 8775
Robles Alvarez de Sotomayor, A., 2006
Roca, R., 555
Rocca, F., 8523
Rocco, 6871
Roces, W., 5218, 9392
Rocha, E. A., 2008
Roche, J., 1968
Roche, J. W., 2009
Rochette, R., 6872
Rochon L'Abbe, 6873
Rochusson, H. F., 8524
Rockford College, 1871
Rodbertus, J. K., 7749, 7931, 8525, 9510-9513
Rodbertus-Jagetonzow, K., 6877
Rodrigues, F. C., 3409
Rodriguez, L. D., 556
Rodriguez-Mellado, I., 251
Roe, T., 4684
Roederer, P. L., 6879-6882
Roesler, C. F. H., 8526-8527
Roessig, 6883
Rogers, A. K., 5079
Rogers, E., 6884
Rogers, J. E. T., 5760, 7337, 8528-8533
Rogers, V. B., 436
Rogers, V. R., 3745
Rogge, B. A., 2212
Rogin, L., 557, 9868
Rogind, S., 2010
Roll, E., 558, 2011, 10057

Rolt, R., 4685
Romagnosi, A., 6041
Romagnosi, G. D., 6885
Roman, 4041
Romanticism, 668, 2554, 9316
Rome, 4066, 4107, 4117, 4903, 4913, 4951, 4984, 5002, 5027, 5089, 5104, 5110-5111, 5120, 5121, 5162, 5260, 5582, 5586, 5810, 5957-5959, 5967, 6154, 6494, 6507, 6561, 6767, 8074
Romero, M., 3820
Romig, F., 2112
Ronchi, E., 559
Ronna, A., 8534
Rooke, J., 2013, 6886
Roosa, R. V., 3226
Roosevelt, F. D., 3056
Roover, R. A., 5080-5085, 5280
Ropke, W., 2014-2017
Ropke, W. T., 2702
Ros, A. L., 7337
Rosario, A., 962
Roscher, 8848, 8902
Roscher, W. G. F., 560, 2703, 3575, 5281, 8835, 8873-8878
Roscoe, 9726
Roscoe, E. S., 1018
Rose, G., 5561, 6887-6889, 9515, 9754
Rose, H., 8535
Rose, K., 3821
Rosenberg, A., 9516
Rosenberg, B., 8985
Rosenberg, J. R., 5085
Rosenstein-Rodan, P., 9770
Rosenthal, E., 8536
Ross, D. W., 8537
Ross, E. A., 561, 8538
Ross, W. D., 5055, 5087
Rosser, A., 6890
Rossetti, J. P., 2019
Rossi, 185
Rossi, A., 6891
Rossi, E., 188, 8539
Rossi, L., 2020
Rossi, N., 3822
Rossi, P., 562, 3514, 6892-6894

Rossiter, C. L., 9517
Rostovzev, M. I., 5088
Rostow, W. W., 563
Rostrand, E., 8540-8541
Roswag, C., 8542
Rota, C., 8543
Rothbard, M. N., 2021
Rothenberg, J., 564
Rothfels, H., 7351
Rothkrug, L., 5281
Rothschild, 8490
Rothschild, A., 8544
Rothschild, K. W., 2704, 10058
Rothwell, R. P., 8545
Rotteck, C., 6895-6896
Rotwein, E., 2409, 4388
Roubaud, 4686
Rougier, J. C. P., 8546
Rouse, C. B., 6896
Rousseau, J. J., 4687, 5337, 6917, 7280, 9629
Roux, V., 6897-6899
Rovira, J., 180
Row, E. F., 241-242
Rowe, J., 4688
Rowse, A. L., 10059
Roy, R., 9869
Royal Adventures of England, 3956
Royal African Company, 4084, 4101, 4226, 4397
Royal Economic Society, 705, 2340, 2473, 4078, 7284, 9696, 9797, 9831, 9846, 9849, 9978, 9983, 9984,
Royal Historical Society, 5135, 5322
Royal Irish Academy, 5861
Royal Statistical Society, 9809
Royal Statistical Society, London, 9672
Royer, E., 6898-6899
Royer, M. C. A., 8547
Royr, R. J., 3513
Rozdolski, R., 9519
Rozenberg, D. I., 565-566, 9520
Rozental', M. M., 9521-9523
Rturvey, R., 3446
Rubbi, N., 5156
Rubel, M., 2481, 9416, 9524-9526
Rubin, I. I., 567-568

Rublo y Dorado, 8548
Rudas, L., 3411
Ruding, R., 6900-6901
Rudloff, M. P., 3412
Rudner, R. S., 814
Rudzki, A., 963
Rudzki, J., 9056
Rueff, J. A., 2063
Ruet, J., 7070
Ruf, W., 3413
Rufener, L. A., 2022
Ruggiero Mazzone, S., 2869
Ruggles, T., 6902
Ruhle, O., 9527
Ruiz y G., L. E., 2023
Rumania, 2953, 9003
Rumiantsev, A., 9528
Rumler, M., 10061
Rummel, J. F., 3823
Runge, E. J., 1641
Rural Affairs, 5639
Rural Exodus, 7941
Rus'an, H., 2482
Ruskin, J., 2483, 2827, 8549
Russell, B. R., 9436, 9529-9530
Russell, J., 6150
Russell, J. S., 6903
Russett, B. M., 964
Russia, 81, 237, 2954-2966, 6222, 6629, 6765, 6823, 6952, 6954, 7081, 7258, 7466, 7479, 7544, 7637, 8143, 8476, 8523, 8633, 8703, 9404
Russian, 2717
Rustow, A., 1043
Rustow, H. J., 2024
Rutgers University, 231, 790, 982
Rutherford, A. W., 6905
Rutkowski, J., 2620
Ruyer, R., 9531
Ryan, D. J., 8550
Ryan, J. A., 2393, 5090
Ryazanskaya, S., 9390, 9417
Rybarski, R., 569
Rybozynski, T. M., 2330, 3492
Rymer, T., 4689
Ryndina, M., 9267
Ryndina, M. N., 570-571, 2774 9267

Sa, V., 2952
Sa'id, J., 10061
Sabatier, W., 4692-4698, 6906
Sabolovic, D., 2025
Sach, I., 8551
Sachdeva, T. N., 572, 2026-2027
Sacrifice, 3582
Saddler, M. T., 6907
Sadzikowski, W., 2028, 9532
Sagan, J., 2775
Sage, M., 6908
Saifulin, M., 1862
Saint, G. F., 8552
Saint Antonio, 4999, 5083
Saint Aubin, 6910
Saint Augustine, Social and Political Ideas, 4928
Saint Bernardine of Siena, 4992
Saint Cyran, 5668
Saint Fargeau, G., 5476, 6914
Saint John, J., 6915
Saint Leon, D. A., 6014, 6916
Saint Lo, G., 4699
Saint Maur, D., 4700-4701
Saint Peravi, 4702
Saint Seidenfus, H., 10066
Saint-Chamans le Vicomte, 6911-6913
Saint-Pierre, 4698, 6917-6918
Saint-Simon, C. H., 2526, 6844, 6919-6926, 7533, 9045, 9055, 9101, 9104, 9125, 9065, 9220, 9358, 9362, 9460, 9474, 9504, 9533-9534, 9641
Sakamoto, I., 2029-2030
Sakurai, T., 3414
Salamanca, 2968
Salary, 3400, 7621
Salera, V., 1866
Salin, E., 71, 573-574, 2667, 2705
Sallee, M., 1251, 2031
Salleron, 5417
Salles, P., 965, 2032
Salmon, 5832
Salmon, C. S., 8553
Salomon, G., 8554
Salt, 4093, 4095, 4129, 4472, 5569, 5856

Salter, A., 10001
Salter, F. R., 9535
Salva, W., 8555
Salvadori, M., 9536
Salz, A., 3415
Sametz, A. W., 1052, 1055
Sampaio, A., 2035
Sampaio, P., 8556
Sampedro, J. L, 2036, 3824
Sampson, R. J., 1825, 3065
Samuels, W. J., 575, 2776, 5417
Samuelson, P. A., 966, 2037-2041, 2484-2485, 3077, 3593, 3738, 3825, 9688, 9870-9871, 10063
Samuelsson, K. 9537
San Bernardino of Siena, 5083, 5124
Sanchez, Sarto, M., 10064
Sanchez-Ventura, 2042
Sanitary Condition, 6826
Santen, J., 9538
Santillan, R., 8557
Santoli, S., 576
Santos, E. S., 2043
Santos, T. M., 2044
Sanz y Escartin, E., 577
Saracco, J., 8558
Sarbadhikari, P., 9126
Sargant, W. L., 6928-6931
Saridakis, G. B., 2777, 3417
Sario, L., 3416
Sarkar, G. K., 2807
Sarrailh, J., 578
Sartorius, F., 8559
Sartorius, G. F., 6932-6934
Sartre, J-P., 9130
Sasaki, K., 2896
Sastre, P., 2045
Satisfaction, Maximum, 3350
Sato, S., 8560
Sato, T., 2047
Saudi Arabia, 3355
Sauerbeck, A., 8561
Saulneir, R. J., 10065
Saumaise, C., 4704-4705
Saunders, P., 2096, 3509
Sauvy, A., 580, 5301, 9539
Savage, K., 9540
Savory des Bruslons, Jacques, 4198, 6935
Saving, 5933, 9924-9925, 10023
Sax, E., 3827, 8562-8564

Saxon, 5757, 6328, 7794
Saxon Dynasties, 6187
Say, H., 6936
Say, J. B., 185, 2048, 2486, 3167, 5422, 6143, 6937-6944, 7055, 7327, 7337, 9557
Say, L., 5418, 6943-6944, 7746, 8376, 8567
Say's Law, 9557
Sazby, H, 4052
Scagliarini, A., 2322
Scalabrini, G. B., 8568
Scalapino, R. A., 9541
Scalzo, A., 2049
Scandinavia, 770, 2614
Scandinavian Economic History Review, 5175, 5358
Scandinavian University, 1554
Scarcity, 1631-1632, 4063, 4542, 4575, 5465, 5592, 5654, 6275, 6981, 7271
Scarcity, Labor, 5524
Scaruffi, G., 4706
Schacht, H. H. G., 5283
Schack, H., 3418
Schaeffer, G., 8569
Schafer, E. D., 8570
Schaffle, A. E. F., 8571-8575
Schatz, A., 581, 5284, 7328-7329
Schauman, G. C., A., 2978
Scheifler Amezaga, X., 582
Schelle, G., 583, 2453, 5419 8576
Schellenberg, W., 9542
Schelting, A., 3023, 8879
Schenk, K. F., 6945
Scheper, W., 3714
Scherf, C. H., 2050
Scherman, H., 2051
Scherzer, K., 8577
Schiatterella, R., 8578
Schiefer, F., 3838
Schiff, W., 8579
Schiffrin, A., 3022
Schiller, K., 2052
Schlatter, R., 5091
Schlauch, M., 9581
Schleiffer, H., 967
Schlesinger, R. A. J., 9543
Schlettwein, J. A., 6946
Schloezer, C., 6947
Schloss, D. F., 8580-8581

Schmachtenberg, B., 2552
Schmalz, H., 6948
Schmidt, A., 9298
Schmidt, E. P., 10084
Schmidt, F., 5285
Schmidt, J. K., 7275
Schmidt, L. H., 8582
Schmidt, P. J., 584
Schmidt, R., 2053, 3419
Schmidtberger, H., 8583
Schmitthenner, F., 6949
Schmolders, G., 585, 10066
Schmoller, G. F., 586, 2054-2055, 2476, 2674, 3813, 3829, 3830, 3836, 5286, 8833, 8880-8884, 8870, 8897, 8899
Schmollers Jahrbuch, 3203, 3663, 3312, 3421, 8822, 8890, 9698, 9798
Schneider, A., 8584
Schneider, E., 587-590, 968, 2056, 2057, 9771
Schneider, H. K., 5019
Schneider, H. W., 7277
Schneider, J. G., 6950, 6963
Schneider, L., 9741, 7330
Schnerb, R., 2652
Schnitzer, M., 2979
Schnitzler, J. H., 6951-6954
Schober, H., 8585
Schober, K., 2058
Schoeck, H., 5287
Schoeffler, S., 3831
Schoell, F., 6333
Schoen, J., 6955
Schoenhof, J., 8587
Schoenman, J. C., 3832
Scholasticism, 2761, 4901, 4911, 4977, 4989, 5005, 5031, 5034, 5052-5053, 5062, 5080, 5084-5085, 5092, 5140, 5141, 5143, 8704
Schomberg, A. C., 6956
Schonberg, G., 8209, 8588
Schone, L., 8589
Schonherr, Hans, 1040
Schonmann, E., 9544,
Schonpflug, F., 3833
School, 682
School, Austrian, 3173, 9744
School, Charity, 3926
School, Economic, 682
School, Marginal Utility, 9719
School, Salamanca, 2968

School, Secondary, 1999
School, Stockholm, 2976
Schoolcraft, H. R., 6957
Schraut, M., 8590
Schreiber, E., 5092
Schroder, R., 10066
Schroeder, E. A., 8591-8592
Schrott, C., 3316
Schuller, R., 8885-8886
Schullern Zu Schrattenhofen, A. J. H., 2870
Schullern-Schrattenhoffen, H., 8593
Schultz, B., 2705
Schultz, B. L., 2487
Schultz, H., 9735
Schultze, C. L., 2059
Schultze-Delitzsch, H., 6958-6959, 7470
Schulze-Gavernitz, G., 8594
Schumacher, H., 8887-8889
Schumacher-Zarchlin, H., 9510
Schuman, G., 5172
Schuman, G. C. A., 5173
Schumann, G., 5156
Schumpeter, E. B., 594
Schumpeter, J. A., 592-594, 969, 2060-2062, 2294, 2397, 2416-2417, 2488, 3421, 3835-3839, 4931, 4969, 5080, 8890-8891, 8986, 9545, 9872-9873, 9895, 9936, 10067
Schurmann, H. F., 2590, 5103
Schutze, G. H., 2489
Schuyler, R. L., 5288
Schwab, J. C., 8595
Schwank, K. H., 9546, 10068
Schwartz, H., 9403
Schwartz, R., 2063
Schweitzer, F. A., 5289
Schweizerische Zeitschrift fur Volkswirtschaft, 341, 3539
Schweyer, H. E., 2064
Scialoja, A., 6960-6961
Science, 1495, 3620, 8899, 8913
Science, Economics, 700-701, 854, 1158, 1306, 2624, 3708, 3785, 5715, 7507, 7553, 7559, 7645, 8230, 8626, 8782, 9801
Science, Human, 3906
Science, Inductive, History of, 7243

Science, New, 4004
Science, Physical, 981
Science, Political, 7553. 8086
Science, Quantification, 3567
Science, Revolution, 9170
Science, Social, 5770, 7553, 7636
Science and Society, 3408
Science and Sociology, 8968
Science Council of Japan, 3353, 9608
Scientific Monthly, 8977
Scivoletto, N., 5093
Scolle, A. R., 6162
Scope, Economics, 3797, 3815, 3837, 3843, 3901
Scoresby, W., 6962
Scotland, 3979, 4069, 4142, 4276, 4305, 4399, 4587, 4742, 4969, 5459-5460, 5468, 5511, 5557, 5655, 5937, 6281, 6332, 6549-6550, 6601, 6607, 6623, 6626, 6672, 6699, 6732, 6792, 6825, 6869, 6992-6993, 6995-6996, 6998, 7290, 7101, 7290, 7330, 7350, 7362, 7498, 7565, 7971, 8084, 8123, 8618
Scots Company, 4576
Scott, A., 2041, 3536
Scott, A. M., 9547
Scott, W., 6831, 6869
Scott, W. A., 334, 595, 2778, 3128, 8596, 8597
Scott, W. D., 979
Scott, W. R., 2490, 2491, 7331, 7332, 7337, 9874
Scottish Economic Society, 2145
Scottish Journal of Political Economy, 684
Scotus, 5086
Scrafton, L., 4709
Scratchley, A., 8598
Scrivenor, H., 6965
Scrope, G. H., 2065
Scrope, G. J. D. P., 2452, 2779, 6966
Scureri, 3780,
Sea, 4259, 4338, 4625
Sea Power, 5233
Seager, H. R., 937, 2066-2067

Seale, J. R., 3544
Sealy, H. N., 6968
Seamen, 4253
Seckendorff, V. L., 4712
Secondary School, 1392, 3655
Sectors, 1638
Security, Finance, 7961
See, H. E., 596, 2652, 9548
Seeber, N. C., 1592
Seebohm, F., 8599
Segal, L. K., 2068
Segerstedt, T. T., 2516
Seidenstecher, G., 2998
Seidler, G., 8600
Seischab, H., 3833
Seitz, M., 3422
Seki, M., 597
Selden, J., 4714
Seligman, 3604
Seligman, B. B., 598, 3840
Seligman, E. R. A., 599-600, 638, 970, 2069, 2780, 5243, 5290, 7337, 8601-8605
Sellier, F., 2070
Selsam, H. B., 9549
Semantics, Economic, 880
Semenza, G., 8606
Semer, 6969
Sempere, 5807
Sen, B., 2828
Sen, M., 9266
Sen, S. R., 2492, 5291
Senac de Meihan, G., 6970-6977
Sengupta, J. K., 3600
Senior, N. W., 971, 2071, 2344, 2781, 5292, 5482, 6249, 6971-6979
Sennholz, H. F., 9663
Sennholz, M., 9772
Sensini, G., 2072
Seraphim, H. J., 2073
Serfdom, 743, 2957, 8919, 9225
Sergeant, A. C., 5293
Sering, M., 8607
Serionne, A., 6980
Serra, A., 2872, 4716
Seth, M. L., 10069
Seven Years War, 949, 4500, 8481
Seville, Treaty of, 4574

Sewall, H. R., 3423
Seward, G. F., 8608
Sewell, W. A., 972
Seybert, A., 6983
Seyd, E., 8609-8610
Schachtman, M., 9438
Schackle, G. L. S., 601, 973, 1421, 2074-2076, 2493, 3841, 9799, 10044
Shadwell, J. L., 8612
Shafer, J. E., 2077
Shafer, R. J., 5420
Shaffer, H. G., 3023
Shafto, T. A. C., 2078
Shah, K. T., 2829
Shaler, N. S., 8613
Shapiro, E., 2079
Shapiro, M., 5218
Sharp, H. J., 3424
Shaw, A., 8614
Shaw, F., 1562-1563
Shaw, G. B., 8617 9196, 9551-9554
Shaw-Lefevre, J., 8619
Shea, G., 8620
Shearer, H. K., 3079
Sheep, 5584
Sheffield, Earl of, 2426
Sheffield, J., 6984-6988
Sheffield, Lord, 5808
Shehepkin, M. P., 7337
Sheikh, N. A., 2927
Shell, K., 974
Shelly, T. J., 1379
Shen, C., 602
Shephard, R. W., 2080-2081
Sherman, H. J., 2082-2083
Sherwood, S., 3080, 8621-8622
Sheviakov, F. N., 2719
Shibata, S., 9555
Shih, C. S., 2494
Shils, E., 3898, 9357
Shimizugawa, S., 2085
Shinohara, M., 2086
Shionoya, T., 10071-10072
Ship, 6241
Ship, Dutch, 4489
Ship, Interest, 6989
Ship, Merchant, 6241, 8217
Ship, United States, 5597, 7755
Ship, War, 6021
Shirai, T., 9875
Shirasugi, S., 604-605, 3425,

Shirato, I., 9556
Shodai Ronshu, Kobe, 642
Short Run, 9878
Short, T., 4718-4719
Shoul, B., 9557
Shoup, C. S., 3426
Shove, G. F., 9876
Shrewsbury House of Industry, 7261
Shubik, M., 3842
Siam, 4193
Sicily, 5455, 5576, 6650
Sickesz, W., 2495
Sicily, 6433
Sidgwick, H., 2087, 3843, 8624-8626
Sieber, R., 9558, 9559
Siebert, H., 2088
Sieblist, O., 8627
Siegelman, L., 2140
Siegfried, J., 8628
Sierpinski, W., 259-260
Sieveking, H. J., 606
Sievers, A. M., 2089-2090
Sik, J., 607
Sik, O., 608, 2091-2094, 9560-9563
Silberner, E., 609, 5294, 9564
Silberstein, E., 9565-9566, 10073
Silhan, V., 9567
Silk, 4497, 4766, 6827
Silk, Manufacturing, 5816
Silk, Wrought, 4497
Silk, L. S., 2095-2096
Silva, I. F., 6991
Silva Herzog, J., 610-611, 2917-2918, 5094
Silver, 3981, 4024, 4115, 4138, 4654, 4734, 7113, 7432, 7687, 7699, 8068, 8311, 8448
Silver, Depreciation, 7419
Silver, United States, 8688
Silverman, H. A., 2097
Silverstolpe, G. W., 2098-2099
Silvin, E., 9568
Simcox, E. J., 5095, 8629
Simey, E., 5096
Simmel, G., 2496
Simon, B., 9569
Simon, J., 4724, 8630

Simonds, J. C., 8632
Simons, A. M., 9274
Simons, H. C., 10074
Simons, J. C., 7493
Simons, M. W., 9274
Simonsen, M. H., 2102
Simpson, P. B., 9877
Simpson, R., 4725, 9417
Simpson-Lee, G. A. J., 1991
Sinclair, J. H. M., 612
Sinclair, J., 6992-6998
Singer, L. P., 2013
Singh, 1328
Singh, H. K., M., 3417
Singh, V. B., 975, 2830, 10075
Sinha, A. K., 613, 2496
Sinha, D. P., 5097
Sinking Fund, 4096, 4244, 4602, 5805, 6148, 8538
Sinking Fund, National Debt, 4231, 4765
Sinking Fund, Public Debt, 4324
Sirkin, G., 2104
Sirotkovic, J., 2517
Siskind, G, 10076
Sismondi, J. C. L. S., 2100-2101, 2328, 2333, 6999-7002, 7337, 9316
Sitorus, L. M., 619
Sjerk, J., 2280
Skalkovsky, C. F., 8633
Skalweit, A., 7341
Skarbek, F., 7004
Skinner, A., 5304
Skinner, A. S., 2145
Skinner, G. S., 1653
Sladek, J., 9493
Sladen, E., 2105
Slater, R. A., 2106
Slater, S., 7245
Slave, 5516, 5553, 5586, 5701, 5795, 6127, 6817, 7042, 7593
Slave, African, 6751
Slave, Trade, 4016, 5750, 6210, 6817, 7247
Slejska, D., 2107
Slesinger, R. E., 832, 1381, 1799, 2108
Slichter, S. H., 1004
Sliding Scale, Corn Laws, 5831
Slosson, E. E., 979
Small, A. W., 5295, 7333
Smart, J., 4726

Smart, W., 976, 3428, 8634-8637, 9663, 9773
Smejkal, M., 2111
Smellie, W., 7334
Smelser, N. J., 1903
Smiles, S., 8638
Smissen, E., 8639
Smit, M. N., 614
Smit, S., 7007-7009
Smith, A., 52, 93, 185, 286-287, 494, 772, 893, 909, 1015, 2508, 2678, 2681, 2742, 2748, 2753, 2758, 2769, 2772 2773, 3167, 3423, 5257, 5265, 5273, 5289, 5296, 5316, 5368, 5430, 5500, 5646, 5833, 6933-6934, 7005, 7275-7358, 7506, 7734, 7829, 8384, 8526, 8737, 8816
Smith, A., Bibliography, 7294 7297
Smith, A., Library, 7283-7284, 7357
Smith, A., Life, 7278, 7300 7317, 7322, 7334, 7345, 7349
Smith, A., Student and Professor, 7311, 7331
Smith, A. H., 2112
Smith, A. M., 8640
Smith, C., 4727
Smith, E. P., 2113, 7006
Smith, G., 4728
Smith, H., 2114-2116, 9571-9573
Smith, J., 4729-4730
Smith, J. A., 5087
Smith, J. B., 6405
Smith, J. G., 1764
Smith, J. H., 977
Smith, L., 8641
Smith, N. K., 2497
Smith, N. L., 1626
Smith, N. S., 2741, 2897
Smith, N. S., 2741, 2897
Smith, R. M., 8642-8643
Smith, R. S., 3844, 7346
Smith, R. W., 2207
Smith, S., 4731-4732, 8645
Smith, T., 4185, 7010-7011
Smith, T. V., 9069
Smith, V. L., 1309
Smith, W. L., 978

Smith, W. P., 7012
Smith, Z. T., 7013
Smithies, A., 10077-10078
Smolensky, E., 3175, 9917
Smuggling, 4733
Smyth, R. L., 3845
Snavely, W. P., 1227
Sneddon, I. N., 3501
Snelling, T., 4734-4743
Snider, D. A., 2117
Snow, J. W., 3846
Snyder, J. W., 5004
Soares, R. M., 2118
Sobajima, S., 615
Social Accounts, 3175
Social Approach, 3193
Social Change, 783
Social Classes, 8677
Social Control, 769, 1848
Social Darwinism, 3062
Social Doctrine, 233, 659, 5800, 9201
Social Economics, 660-661, 667
Social Ideals, 9589
Social Law, 8770
Social Literature, France, 9125
Social Movement, 9577
Social Movement, English, 8801
Social Movement, Japan, 9620
Social Opulence, 6930
Social Order, 5726
Social Organization, 9188
Social Problem, 9029
Social Question, 2671
Social Reform, 8099
Social Relations, Great Britain, 6712
Social Research, 3778, 8974, 8982
Social Revolution, 9274
Social Science, 58, 123, 173, 675, 767, 2397, 2769, 2984, 3567, 3575, 3586, 3662, 3686, 3746, 3749, 3852, 3877, 5692, 6361, 7880, 8700, 9441, 9694
Social Struggle, 4897, 9036, 9039
Social Studies, 7642
Social System, 9469
Social Theory, 1230, 3365
Social Thought, 9020-9191
Social Thought, Catholic, 144
Social Thought, History of, 227

Social Work, 7717, 7790
Socialism, 30, 163, 182, 414,
  577, 659, 1040, 1128, 1190
  1196, 1272, 1601, 1802, 1830,
  1869, 1963, 1965, 2091,
  2107, 2114, 2149, 2598,
  2634, 2636, 2643, 2645,
  2650, 2658, 2666, 2689,
  2697, 2699, 2711, 2729,
  2756, 2805, 2953, 3022,
  3098, 3121, 3188, 3198-
  3199, 3295, 3300, 3316,
  3373, 3552, 3713, 5246,
  5401, 5591, 5803, 5804,
  6844, 7037, 7100, 7285,
  7372, 7426, 7455, 7471,
  7514, 7542, 7544, 7609,
  7647, 7777-7778, 7799,
  7811, 7851, 7913, 7943,
  8017-8018, 8020, 8082,
  8085, 8087, 8089, 8118,
  8171, 8259, 8260-8261,
  8267, 8301, 8341, 8367,
  8469, 8559, 8567, 8572,
  8573, 8575, 8594, 8617,
  8623, 8652, 8755, 8802,
  9003-9657, 9926
Socialism, African, 9449
Socialism, American, 8378, 9578
Socialism, Argentina, 9473
Socialism, Christian, 8117
Socialism, Economic, 559
Socialism, Europe, 7807
Socialism, Evolutionary, 9052
Socialism, Fabian, 9432-9433
Socialism, France, 9256
Socialism, German, 7726
Socialism, Great Britain, 9574
Socialism, History, 9364
Socialism, Japan, 9620
Socialism, Middle Ages, 4998,
  5090
Socialism, Modern, 6845
Socialism, Periodicals, 9568
Socialism, Revolutionary, 9089
Socialism, Ricardian, 2766,
  9344
Socialism, Russian, 9352
Socialism, Scientific, 9171
Socialism, State, 7725
Socialism, United States, 9235
Socialism, Western European,
  9564

Socialist Thought, 9304
Socialist Tradition, History of,
  9211
Socialist Unity Party, Germany,
  9202
Sociedad Economica, 6274
Societa Anonima Editrice Dante
  Alighieri, 2428
Societa Chiamata Accomandia,
  5887
Societe d'Etudes Morales,
  Sociales et Juridiques, 1118
Societe Populaire du Canton de
  Montfort, 5421
Societe Royale d'Agriculture de
  Limoges, 4505, 4702
Societes et Maitrises, 4122
Society, 418, 928, 979, 980,
  1558, 3898, 4907, 5799,
  6255, 6576, 6641, 7147,
  7330, 7597, 9470, 9497,
Society, Domestic, 6099
Society, Economic, 1017, 1268,
  1529, 2471, 5743
Society, Eighteenth Century,
  Great Britain, 7287
Society, Evolutinn, 9207
Society, France, 7120
Society, Free, 2014, 9896,
  10074
Society, Imperfect, 9132
Society, Industrial, 247, 890,
  9727
Society, Modern, 894, 7183
Society, Modern, Intelligence of,
  7183
Society, Multidimensional, 9278,
  9828
Society, Planned, 882
Society, Theory of, 4961
Society, Traditional, 5129
Society, Underdeveloped, 783
Society of American Value
  Engineers, 3429
Society of Scotland, 6825
Society of Shipowners, 5772
Society of the Free British
  Fishery, 4360
Sociologist, 882
Sociology, 40, 54, 87, 154,
  1018, 1479, 1881, 1921,
  2770, 3088, 4996, 6506,
  7333, 7542, 7930, 8623,

9189, 9416, 9697, 9741, 9855
Sociology, China, 2619
Sociology, Economic, 4966
Sociology, Industrial, 8915, 9599
Sociology, Marxist, 9025
Soddy, F., 981, 2119
Soden, J., 7014
Soder, G., 9558
Soderlund, E. F., 5218
Sodre, N. W., 9575
Soejima, T., 3000, 9576
Soetbeer, A., 7015
Soidra, J. I., 2607
Soignie, P., 2120
Soldaczuk, J., 10079
Solera, M., 7017
Solly, E., 7018
Solo, R. A., 982
Solow, R. M., 3593, 9688
Solvay, 9706
Somary, F., 2498
Sombart, W., 616, 2122-2123, 2707, 8868, 8871-8872, 8892-8893, 8898, 9577
Somer, R., 8646
Somers, J., 4757
Sommarin, E., 9774
Sommer, A., 8894
Sommer, L., 2553, 5298
Sommerlad, T., 617
Song, C., 2124-2125
Sonnenfels, J., 7019
Sopp, A. A., 7020
Sorel, 9704
Sorkovs'ka, S. V., 3024
Soskic, B., 618, 2126
Sotiroff, G., 2499
Soule, G. H. 619, 980, 2128, 2130, 2131
Southern Economic Journal, 3611
Sousa, A., 620
Souter, R. W., 3847
South, Antebellum, 2425, 3075, 3081
South African Journal of Economics, 390, 2509-2510, 7350
South Sea, Trade, 3945
South Sea Company, 3948, 3975, 4135, 4140, 4258, 4264, 4390, 4392, 4436, 4514, 4708, 4717, 4758, 4789, 4808
South Sea Scheme, 4661, 4810
South Sea Stock, 4391
Southern, C., 9578
Southern Economic Journal, 289, 507, 5440, 7347, 9002, 9817, 9825, 9859
Southern Illinois University, 2578
Southwestern Social Science Quarterly, 101
Souza, J. C. M., 621
Souza Goncalves, R., 2132
Soviet Union, 47-51, 219, 530, 1010, 1037-1040, 1862-1863, 1980-1981, 2626, 2695, 2774, 2983-3030, 3276-3277, 3786, 9046, 9050, 9058, 9120, 9153, 9183, 9280, 9313, 9316-9323, 9528, 9600, 9627, 9642, 9652, 10094, 10099
Soviet Union, Academy of Science, 1037, 2984-2986
Soviet Union, Academy of Science, Kiev, 2987-2988
Soviet Union, Economic Indicators, 3880
Sowell, T., 2133
Soyeda, J., 8647
Spadaro, L. M., 2134
Spahr, W. E., 983-984
Spain, 136, 1099, 2967-2970, 3939, 4071, 4282, 4508, 4511, 4523, 4526, 4609, 4614, 4671, 4826, 4853, 4883, 5023, 5170, 5215-5216, 5249, 5267, 5420, 5454, 5678, 5682-5683, 5707, 5763, 5899, 6274, 6351, 6492, 6559, 7603, 7654-7655, 7940, 8218, 8431
Spain, Economic Conditions, 5170
Spain, Journey, 7140
Spain, Monarch, 5807
Spain, Statistics, 7148
Spain, Wealth of Nations, 7346
Spann, O., 622, 2135, 2136, 2521-2422, 2554
Sparen, 9924
Spargo, J., 9579, 9580

Specie Payment, 5813
Speculation, 5828, 8090
Speight, H., 2137-2138
Spelling, T. C., 8648
Spence, 6512, 7131
Spence, W., 7023-7024
Spencer, M. H., 791, 924, 2139-2140, 3848
Spending, 1287
Spending, Deficit, 10084
Spengler, J. J., 318, 985, 2653, 5299, 5300-5301, 5422, 7347, 9775
Spengler, O., 2335
Spiegel, H. W., 623-624, 986-987, 2141, 3082, 5423
Spiethoff, A., 8895
Spirit, Anatomy of, 9336
Sprague, O. M. W., 761
Spring, D., 2501
Spulber, N., 3025
Sraffa, P., 2473, 7312
Srbik, H., 5302
Srivastava, S. K., 625
St. Maur, D., 4238
Stabilization, 742, 1023, 1161, 1678
Stadler, J., 3721, 9308
Stadnik, M., 2603, 2782
Stafford, W., 4760
Stagnation, 10084
Stahl, F. W., 8649
Stalin, J., 1040, 1874, 1964, 9581-9582
Stamm, A., 8650
Stamm, F., 8651
Stammer, O., 987
Stammhammer, J., 8652, 9584
Stamp, J., 10001
Stampar, S., 988
Standish, A., 4761
Stanhope, E., 7026-7027
Stankiewicz, W., 2783
Stappershoef, H., 7348
Stark, A., 2142
Stark, W., 626-627, 2340, 3850, 5099
Stas, J., 2143
State, 2021, 2502, 6063, 8304, 9021
State, Control, 2790
State, Economic Role, 8730
State, Functions of, 8187

State, Industrial, 2731
State, Marxian Theory, 9100
State, Marxian View, 9319
State, Police, 6033
State, Socialist, 276
Statecraft, 9
Statesman, 882
Statics, Economic, 1171, 3731
Statistical Abstract, 7030-7033
Statistician, British, 9701
Statistics, 54, 934, 1075, 1235, 1738, 2216, 2705, 3267, 3493, 3572, 3690, 3732, 4793, 5203, 5323 5476, 5623, 5736, 5904, 5905, 5918, 6041, 6178, 6214, 6223, 6261, 6300, 6416, 6469, 6540, 6555, 6558-6561, 6601, 6615, 6622, 6693, 6700, 6772-6773, 6898, 6951-6954, 6993, 6998, 7036, 7057, 7070-7071, 7140, 7145, 7147, 7188, 7208, 7219, 7257, 7475, 7483, 7506, 7510, 7554, 7664, 7784, 7828, 7844, 7850, 7857, 7859, 7879, 7979, 8122, 8136, 8139, 8178, 8222, 8276, 8278-8280, 8288, 8337, 8364, 8380, 8643, 8748, 8765, 8776, 8785, 8850, 8854, 8905, 9762
Statistics, Agriculture, 6273
Statistics, Applied, 3865
Statistics, Colony, 7034
Statistics, Commercial, 5621, 6432-6433, 7178
Statistics, Finance, 6235
Statistics, France, 6914, 7034
Statistics, Germany, 5622
Statistics, Manufacturing, 3455
Statistics, Mathematical, 9672
Statistics, Medical, 6188
Statistics, Mineral, Great Britain, 8076
Statistics, Nineteenth Century, 9701
Statistics, Population, 5464
Statistics, Scotland, 7101
Staudlin, K. F., 7035
Staudte, R., 5303
Stavenhagen, G., 628

Steam Engine, 6350, 6782
Steele, G. M, 8653
Stefani, G., 1824, 2144
Steffenhagen, H., 8654
Stein, H., 10080
Stein, L., 7037-7041
Stein-Horschelmann-Wappausg, 7036
Steiner, G. A., 989-900
Steiner, M., 8655
Steiner, P. O., 1696
Steiner, W. H., 1818
Steinlein, K., 629
Stelander, H., 2424
Stengel, K., 8656
Stenning, H. J., 9038-9039 9271, 9412
Stephen, J., 7042
Stephen, L., 2784
Stephens, H., 7044
Stephens, T. A., 8657
Stephens, W. W., 5424
Stephenson, D., 7045
Sterility, 5358
Stern, C. M., 9404
Stern, R. M., 930
Sternberg, F., 9585
Steuart, J., 2145, 2492, 2510, 4770, 5291, 5304, 9911
Stevens, J., 4769
Stewardship, State, 981
Stewart, B., 9726
Stewart, D., 7048-7052, 7343, 7349
Stewart, M., 10081
Stich, A. O., 2708
Stigler, G. J., 630-631, 991-993, 2146, 2502, 3103, 3431, 3851, 9776, 9878
Stiglitz, J. E., 2484, 3825, 9870
Stigum, B. P., 2147
Stigum, M., 2147
Stikker, A. H., 2148
Stirling, P. J., 7053-7054
Stirner, M., 7337, 7341
Stock, 6027
Stock, Bank, 5450
Stock, Capital, 4140
Stock, Exchange, 3353, 5508, 7580, 7686
Stock, Jobbing, 3949
Stock, South Sea, 4658

Stockhammer, M., 9397
Stockholm School, 2976
Stocking, G. W., 8987
Stojanovic, R., 2149, 9586
Stojiljkovic, D., 3432
Stokausen, 4771
Stokes, C. J., 2150
Stoliarov, D. D. , 5100
Stollberg, R., 632
Stolpe, H. A., 2151
Stone, N. I., 9376
Stone, R., 3130, 3852-3854
Stone, R. G., 2503
Stonier, A. W., 1498, 2152, 3855
Stonyhurst Philosophical Series, 170
Stopel, F., 7337, 8658
Storch, H. F., 7055-7057
Story, J., 7061-7062
Stourm, R., 8659-8661
Stowe, H., 2153, 3856
Strachey, J., 8662
Straessle, A., 2982
Straits of Malacca, 6602
Strangeland, C. E., 5305
Strauling, G., 8663
Strauss, E., 5306
Strauss, L., 7289
Street, J. H., 3857
Streeten, P., 474, 3365
Streissler, E., 953
Strickland, E., 8664
Strike, Labor, 6475
Stromeyer, F., 7063
Strong, B., 2355
Strotz, R. J., 1055
Struik, D. J., 9383
Strumilin, S. G., 2964
Stuart, C. A. V., 2154
Stubbs, H., 4772, 8665-8666
Stuber, P. R., 3433
Student, 1297
Student, Business, 1986
Student, Professional, 1520
Studi Economici, 2864
Studie nad Historia, 2937
Studies, Liberal, 1952
Studnitz, A., 8668
Study and Teaching, 2712, 2782, 2932, 3039, 3170, 3596, 3758, 3811, 3877

Study and Teaching, United States, 3073
Sturmer, G., 8669
Sturney, S. G., 2156
Sturtevant, J. M., 8670
Stypmanni, J. F., 4773
Stys, W., 5425
Suarez, 5086
Suaudeau, R., 5426
Subercaseaux, G., 2568
Subsidy, 4023, 4643, 4774
Subsistance, 5818
Substitution, 3435
Suchon, A., 5102
Suckau, M. W., 6194
Suda, J. P., 9588
Sudre, A., 7065-7066
Sudre, C., 8671
Suenaga, T., 2786
Sugar, 3984, 3985, 4018, 4335, 6521, 6570, 7520
Sugar Colony, 4499, 4589
Sugar Colony, Great Britain, 7273
Sugar Trade, 4077, 5817
Sugden, E. B., 7067
Sugihara, S., 635
Suginoto, E., 636
Suits, D. B., 2157
Sully, 4006, 5248
Sulmicki, P., 2158
Sulzer-Ziegler, E., 2982
Sumatra, 6466
Sumerian Economic Texts, 4923, 5004
Sumiya, E., 2898, 2899
Summer, W. G., 8672-8680
Sumner, J. B., 7068
Sumner, W. F., 995
Sun, H., 3434
Sun Yat-Sen, 9589
Sundharam, K. P. M., 2159-2160
Sung, C., 5427
Sung, L., 5103
Sunkel, D., 637
Supino, C., 2161-2162, 2871, 8678-8680
Suppes, P., 3849
Supply, 3197, 3204, 3207, 3230, 3319, 3350, 3355, 3382, 3387-3388, 3399, 8949, 9720, 9821
Supply, Aggregate, 3175, 9917

Supply, Curves, 9880
Suranyi-Unger, T., 638-640, 883
Surawicki, S., 3919
Sureda Carrion, J. L., 2970
Surkau, L., 1428
Surplus, Economic, 9810
Survey, Journal of Soviet . . . Studies, 690
Suslov, M. A., 9591
Sutherland, C. H. V., 5104
Suviranta, B., 5307
Suzuki, K., 9592
Suzuki, R., 10083
Sviatlovskii, V. V., 641
Swank, J. M., 8681
Swann, E., 2504
Swanson, E. W., 10084
Swarup, S., 9593
Sweden, 1178, 1939, 2015, 2098-2099, 2377, 2971-2981, 3832, 5172, 5184, 5332, 6485, 6629, 7487-7488, 9537, 9798
Swedish Journal of Economics, 3731, 3807
Swedish Macroeconomic Theory, 9805
Sweet, R. F. G., 5105
Sweezy, P. M., 3435, 8988, 9027, 9064, 9374, 9595
Swift, J., 4776, 5240, 5324
Switzerland, 2982, 5678, 7543, 8364
Swoboda, O., 8682
Sylos-Labini, P., 594
Symes, J., E., 8683
Symmes, S. S., 1185
Symonds, J., 7069
Symposium, 762, 989, 9014-9015, 10039, 10075
Sympson, A., 4781
Syndicalism, 907, 8491, 9257, 9526
Synthesis, 1570, 3733
Syria, 5621
System, Business, 2077
System, Economic, 76, 393, 1049, 1239, 1398, 1525, 1653, 1739, 1740, 2201, 2260, 2267, 2586, 2686, 3510, 9702
System, Economic, American,

2261, 2320
System, Law, 6381
System, Market, 3249
System, Mathematical, 3681
System, Price, 3440
System, Social, 6142, 6365, 6743, 8224, 8366
Szeflera, S., 9160
Szego, G. P., 3681
Szigeti, P. R., 2163, 10085
Szubert, W., 2505

T'ang, C., 2583
Table, Currency, 6590
Table, Insurance, 4725, 5977, 6303-6304, 6520, 6383, 6825, 7182
Table, Lease, 5509
Table, Price of Corn, 5785
Table, Statistical, 6714
Tableau, Economique, 5327, 5328, 5352, 5358, 5384, 5395, 5402, 5409, 5441
Taft, P., 730
Tagawa, B., 2129
Tagliacozzo, G., 996, 2872, 3860
Tagwerker, H., 2164
Taib, A., 1033
Takagi, M., 642
Takahashi, M., 2902
Takahashi, S., 643-645, 997-998, 2507
Takamura, S., 2900
Takashima, Z., 646
Takata, Y., 2165-2167
Takenaka, Y., 2901
Takeshima, K., 2168
Takeuchi, K., 2506, 2902
Talamona, M., 2169
Talleyrand, 7247
Tallon, M., 8684
Tamagnini, G., 2170
Tamano, Y., 388
Tamedly, E. L., 9597
Tamil, 2823
Tanadive, B. T., 9623
Tanner, H. S., 7073
Tanner, M. E., 9442
Tanner, N. E., 450
Tapfer, F., 647
Tapia, C., 4783
Tarascio, V. J., 3861, 9779

Tarbe, 6457
Tarbier, H., 8685
Tarde, A., 3436
Tardieu, H., 7520
Tariff, 4216, 6022, 6224, 6257, 6260, 6652, 6824, 7381, 7405, 7480, 7484-7485, 7578, 7657, 7805, 7810, 7937, 8019, 8164, 8486, 8495, 8604, 8686, 8689
Tariff, America, 6293
Tariff, History, 8690
Tariff, History, Grain, 6532
Tariff, History, United States, 8272
Tariff, Legislation, 8815
Tariff, Protective, 8701
Tariff, Sweden, 5184
Tarshis, L., 2171-2172, 3435, 10086
Tate, W., 7074
Tatsumi, H., 10087
Taubenschlag, R., 5109
Taussig, F. W., 324, 775, 761, 2173, 3437, 8686-8691, 9879
Tautscher, A., 648, 2174, 5308,
Taviani, P. E., 9780
Tawney, R. H., 4861, 5106, 5309, 9037
Tax, 1994, 4028, 4136, 4142, 4147, 4153, 4157-4158, 4242, 4245, 4365, 4490, 4517, 4592, 4598, 4769, 4784, 4814, 5382, 5506, 5647, 5697, 5858, 5870, 5894, 6065, 6278, 6305, 6428-6429, 6495, 6819, 6855, 6884, 6931, 7021, 7076, 7099, 7140, 7448, 7640, 7671, 7766, 7810, 7812, 7935, 8203, 8269, 8369, 8425, 8463, 8498, 8601, 9891
Tax, Corporate, 8605
Tax, Excise, 7551
Tax, Incidence, 8602
Tax, Income, 5554, 6139, 7939, 8751
Tax, Indirect, 6920
Tax, Land, 4095, 4755
Tax, Malt, 4440
Tax, Municipal, 8383

Tax, Poll, 4307
Tax, Progressive, 8603
Tax, Property, 6833, 8595
Tax, Single, 4180, 4715
Tayler, J. M., 7076-7078
Taylor, A. E., 5107-5108
Taylor, E., 649, 2175
Taylor, F. M., 2176, 9337
Taylor, G., 7078
Taylor, H., 2177-2181, 2398
Taylor, I. N., 8692
Taylor, O. H., 650-651, 999, 2874, 5428
Taylor, R. W. C., 7079
Taylor, S., 4785, 8693
Taylor, W. L., 2508, 7326, 7350
Taymans, A., 1000
Tazaki, M., 2584
Tea, 4467, 6423
Teaching, 3538
Tebbutt, A. R., 3572
Technical, 898
Technological Change, 796
Technology, 1952, 2738, 8911, 9462
Tefas, G., 2654
Tegoborski, L., 7080-7081
Tehernyshewsky, N., 2736
Teilhac, C. E., 3038
Teilhac, E., 652
Telegraph, 7848, 7892, 8227, 8852
Tellkampf, J. L., 7082-7083
Temkin, G., 3438, 9598
Temple, W., 4786-4788, 5310
Temple University, 215
Templeman, D., 4789
Tenant, 5702, 7846, 8692
Tenant, Ireland, 7783
Tennant, C., 8694
Tenny, F., 5110-5111
Tenure, 7902
Tenure, Zemindary, Bengal, 6134
Teplyts'kyi, V. P., 2988
Terborgh, G., 9951, 10088
Terminology, Economic, 1410, 8432
Terrorism, 9275
Testing, Statistical, 3870
Tetens, J. N., 7085
Textbook, 382, 1039, 1060, 1132, 1174, 1225, 1326, 1350, 1392, 1449, 1510, 1572, 1651, 1854, 1856, 1991, 2075, 2150, 2152, 2159, 2415
Textile Industry, Great Britain, 5272
Thackrah, C. T., 7086
Thalberg, B., 10089-10090
Thalheim, K. C., 987
Thaon di Revel, P., 2182
Theil, H., 2183, 3439, 3863
Theochares, R. D., 3864
Theodose, P. F. X., 5359
Theologians, 4891
Theology, Moral, 2174
Theory, Dynamic, 811
Theory, Implicit, 3725
Theory, Political, 750, 1045
Theory, Price, 1054-1055, 1092, 1139
Theory, Social, 5024
Theresia, M., 5302
Thermodynamics, 3732
Thesis, 1362
Thevenin, E., 8695
Thiel, H., 2924
Thiemeyer, T., 9781
Thierry, A., 7089
Thiers, A., 7090-7091
Thomas, A. H., 2184
Thomas, E., 2511, 7092
Thomas, F. S., 7093
Thomas, H. P., 7395
Thomas, J. J., 3865
Thomas, K., 8696
Thomas, N. M., 9601
Thomas, P., 5112
Thomas, P. F., 2512
Thomas, P. J., 5311
Thompson, A. H., 757
Thompson, C. C., 8989
Thompson, C. M., 1001, 2185
Thompson, C. W., 2787
Thompson, H. M., 8696
Thompson, J. W., 5113
Thompson, P., 8698
Thompson, R. E., 8699-8700
Thompson, R. G., 3306
Thompson, R. W., 8701
Thompson, T. P., 7094, 7095
Thompson, W., 414, 2186,

2455, 2766, 7096-7098
Thompson, C. P., 7021
Thomson, D. F., 5114
Thomson, P., 7099
Thonissen, J. J., 7099
Thorburn, J., 7101
Thornbury, R. T., 1798
Thornton, E., 7102-7104
Thornton, H., 7105
Thornton, T. W., 6640
Thornton, W. T., 7107-7110
Thorp, W. L., 1002
Thorpe, B., 7111
Thorpe, W. L., 8990
Thought, Christian, 437
Thought, Political, 4894, 4962
Thought, Social, 437, 610, 613, 2496, 2602, 4895
Thought, Socialist, 9107
Thrift, Paradox of, 10038
Thrupp, S. S., 653
Thünen, J. H., 2513, 7116, 9736, 9762, 9782
Thurmann, 4793
Thurnwald, R., 5116
Thurot, 6196, 6551
Thygesen, N., 1009
Tidman, P. F., 8702
Tifaut de Landeu, J., 4794
Tikhomirov, L., 8703
Tillet, 4240
Timber, 4250, 5598
Time, in Economics, 3841
Timlin, M. F., 10091
Tinbergen, J., 654, 1003, 2187, 3866-3871
Tintner, G., 3600, 3872
Tironi, J., 9602
Tiruvalluvar, T., 2823-2824
Tissot, J., 6384, 7117
Tithe, 5535, 6884
Tiumeniev, A. I., 9422
Tjulpanov, S. I., 9226
Tobacco, 3962, 3968, 4023, 4092
Tobin, J., 3873
Tocqueville, A., 7118-7120
Todosia, M., 10092
Tokei, F., 9603
Tokinaga, F., 655-656
Tokyo University, 3414
Tomata, S., 657-658
Tome, L. M. R., 771

Tomizuka, R., 9604
Toniolo, G., 8704
Tonnies, 9475
Tooke, T., 7122-7129
Tools, 7915
Torquemada, D. J., 4795
Torrens, R., 3167, 6288, 7130-7138
Torres, F., 620
Torres, M., 9849
Torres Martinez, M., 2189
Tortora, E., 8705
Tostlebe, A. S., 2268
Totomiants, V. F., 659, 3026
Totzke, A., 8706
Toubeau, A., 8707
Toumbouros, G., 5117
Tournyol du Clos, J., 2514
Toussaint, F. V., 4796
Toutain, J. F., 5118
Town, 6042
Town Life, Fifteenth Century, 7951
Townsend, J., 7139-7140
Townsend, M., 10093
Toynbee, A., 2335, 2788, 8708, 8866, 8896
Toyoda, S., 3874
Tozzi, G., 2797, 5119-5121
Trace, 4137
Tracy, D., 5897, 7141
Trade, 836, 908, 2233, 2759, 3925, 3934, 3937, 3939, 3945, 3954, 3956, 3963, 3987, 3995, 4018, 4026-4028, 4044, 4051-4052, 4055-4056, 4083, 4084-4085, 4100, 4110, 4125, 4127-4128, 4139, 4147-4148, 4157, 4171, 4174, 4184-4185, 4203, 4209, 4220, 4232, 4245, 4247, 4298, 4315, 4321, 4333, 4339, 4373, 4375-4376, 4405, 4432, 4437, 4442, 4465, 4468, 4519, 4546, 4555, 4567, 4583, 4587, 4610, 4613, 4618-4619, 4650, 4663, 4680, 4682-4685, 4690, 4710, 4715, 4738, 4768, 4797-4798, 4842, 4843, 4845, 4849, 4864, 5068, 5155, 5269,

Trade (cont.) 5277, 5317, 5473, 5512, 5559, 5579, 5597, 5702, 5828, 5830, 5908, 6021, 6175, 6191, 6210, 6402, 6600, 6788-6789, 6840, 6889, 6986, 7548, 8019, 8025, 8468, 8486, 8497, 8746, 9842, 9844
Trade, Africa, 3941, 4455, 4553
Trade, Ancient, 3951, 6867
Trade, Carthaginian, 6225
Trade, Coal, 5976, 6237, 6822, 6838
Trade, Corn, 4727, 7124, 7133, 7185
Trade, Cotton, Great Britain, 7806
Trade, Depression of, 8283
Trade, Dutch, 4378, 4510
Trade, East Indies, 3938, 4637, 7492
Trade, Fish, 3979, 4050, 6332
Trade, Foreign, 4112, 4179, 5316, 9850
Trade, Foreign, Doctrine, 5333
Trade, Foreign, England, 5560, 7556
Trade, Free, 1551, 4482, 5752, 5973, 6063, 6323, 6491, 6747, 6787, 7232, 7588, 7590, 7689, 7830, 7836, 7878, 7896, 7910, 8312, 8732
Trade, Glove, 6244
Trade, Great Britain, 3941, 3967
Trade, Greenland 4227
Trade, Herring, 4731
Trade, International, 7441, 8767, 9840-9841
Trade, Iron, 6965
Trade, Iron, British, 6413
Trade, Linen, 6812
Trade, Naval, 4318
Trade, Philosophy of, 7054
Trade, Primitive, 3265
Trade, Regulation, 7831
Trade, Silk, 6270, 6821, 7022
Trade, Statistics, 6711
Trade, Sugar, 3984, 4499, 4767, 5817
Trade, Timber, 5598
Trade, Tobacco, 3962
Trade, Whale, 4227
Trade, Wine, 7222
Trade, Wool, 5446, 7532
Trade, World, 5205
Trades, 7086
Trades, Combinations, 6632
Tradesmen, 4805
Trager, F. N., 9605
Transcaucasia, 3027
Transferability, 2722
Transformation Problem, 3348
Transport, 6349, 7457
Transportation, 1273, 7376, 7860, 8023, 8103, 8518
Transportation, America, 7045
Transportation, Great Britain, 6725
Transportation Theories, 7658
Trapp, V., 3769
Traske, S. L., 9367
Travel, Europe, 7148
Travel, Orient, Marco Polo, 7149
Traveler, 5313
Traywick, L. E., 699
Treasury, 5472
Treasury, United States, 5852, 8127
Treaty of Westphalia, 6776
Tree, 4250
Trends, Economic, 845
Trenton, R. W., 2190
Tresca, P., 660
Trescott, P. B., 3440
Treub, M. W. F., 661
Treue, W., 7351
Trevelyan, C. E., 7153
Trever, A. A., 2798, 5122
Trevisani, G., 9370
Trevoux, F., 2438, 3358
Trezza, B., 3441
Triffin, 9940
Trimestre Economico, 637
Trinity College, Dublin, 3123
Trklja, M., 9606
Trobe University, 9916
Troisi, M., 3441
Trolle, U., 2191
Trosne, 4460
Trotsky, L., 9607
Trotter, A., 7154
Trotter, C., 7155

Trouwborst, A. A., 5123
Trucky, H., 2192
Trugenberger, A. E., 5124
Truman, H., 3297
Trusen, W., 662
Trust, 7529, 8094, 8648
Tse-Tung, M., 9098, 9150
Tsuchiya, T., 663, 2903
Tsukatani, A., 664
Tsunasawa, M., 5429
Tsuru, S., 2193-2196, 2904, 9608
Tuberville, A. S., 2790
Tucci, G., 5125
Tuchscheerer, G., 9609
Tuchscheerer, W., 237, 9609
Tucker, B. R., 6735
Tucker, G., 2197-2198, 3443, 7088, 7155-7158
Tucker, G. F., 7939
Tucker, G. M., 2199
Tucker, G. S. L., 2789, 5312
Tucker, H. S. G., 7159
Tucker, J., 4811-4823, 5313, 7160-7162
Tucker, R. C., 9610
Tuckett, J. D., 7163
Tudor, 5309, 8787
Tufnell, E. C., 7164
Tugan-Baranowski, 9611
Tugwell, R. G., 937, 1004, 2217, 3049
Tullander, B., 3444
Turgeon, C.-H., 3445, 5430
Turgeon, C. I., 3445, 5430
Turgot, A. R. J., 83, 2648, 5248, 5289, 5341, 5369, 5396, 5416, 5424, 5431-5433, 5439, 5796, 6630, 7117, 7444, 7827, 8274, 8522
Turin, G., 1005
Turin, L., 1046
Turkey, 1958, 4820
Turkey Company, 4089
Turkmenistan, 18
Turner, B. B., 8709
Turner, C. B., 10094
Turner, H., 2709
Turner, J. K., 9612
Turner, J. R., 2200

Turner, R., 4824
Turner, S., 7165-7166
Turquan, V., 8710
Turton, T., 7167
Turvey, R., 1124
Tuscany, 5623
Tussing, A. D., 1358
Tustin, A., 2201, 3875
Twentieth Century, 668, 826, 9104, 9674
Twining, L., 8711
Twiss, T., 2627, 7169-7170
Tydemann, G. G., 7173
Tyrone Collieries, 4438
Tyson, J. R., 7174
Tytler, A. F., 7175-7176

Uchida, Y., 1006-1007, 2202
Udal'Tsov, I. D., 1008, 2961
Unemployment, 9979
Uhr, C. G., 9783, 9797
Ujita, T., 5314
Ukraine, 3024
Ulloa, B., 4826, 5323
Ulmer, M. J., 2203, 10095
Ulmer, M. M., 3876
Ulrich, F., 8712
Umar, H., 2488
Umbreit, M. H., 2204-2206
Umpfenbach, K., 7177
Uncertainty, 973, 1628, 3294, 3710
Under-Consumption, 5377, 10025
Unemployment, 7768, 8304, 8761, 9862, 9895, 9973, 9977
Unger, F., 4827
Union Labor, 5717, 5719, 6475, 7971
Union, Labor, History of, 8758
Union Pacific Railway, 7723
United Company of Merchants, 4187
United Nations, 3218, 3877
United States, 175, 1944, 2181, 2261, 2332, 2414, 2537, 3031-3090, 3319, 3355, 3447-3448, 3462, 3800, 5515, 5597, 5634, 5781, 5847-5848, 5852, 5987, 6020, 6078-6080, 6110, 6130, 6217, 6546, 6695, 6700, 6824, 7033, 7073, 7156-7158, 7421, 7464, 7484

7523-7524, 7670, 7741,
7757, 7758, 7782, 7785-
7786, 7805, 7812, 7850,
7913, 7937, 8029, 8097,
8112, 8121, 8127, 8135,
8149, 8151, 8162, 8206-
8207, 8214, 8262, 8272,
8318, 8371, 8410, 8487,
8493-8496, 8501, 8518,
8560, 8597, 8613, 8674,
8688, 8690, 8748, 8771,
8781, 8814-8815, 8965,
9040, 9229, 9235, 9463
United States, Air Force, 3878
United States, Bureau of Labor Statistics, 2515
United States, Congress, 3880-3883, 5449, 5906
United States, Congress, House of Representatives, 6815, 6820
United States, Council of Economic Advisers, 3879
United States, Department of Agriculture, 3219-3220, 3222
United States, Resources, 5634-5635
United States, Secretary of the Treasury, 6171
United States, States, Financial Position, 7154
Universidad Autonoma de Cochabamba, 2459
Universidad Catolica Andres Bello, 1926
Universidad Central de Venezuela, 3090
Universidad de Costa Rica, 3821
Universidad de Madrid, 1069
Universidad Mayor de San Andres, 1102
Universidad Nacional, Argentine Republic, 962
Universidad National de Colombia, 2593
Universidade de Lisboa, 771
Universidade de Montevideu, 2561
Universidade de Sao Paulo, 3670
Universietet i Oslo, 3270
Universita Bari, 712
Universita Bocconi, 9759

Universita Bratislava, 9070
Universita Cattolica, Milano, 2769
Universita Cattolica del Sacro Cuore, 2846, 5257
Universita Commerciale Luigi Bocconi, Milano, 902, 1063,
Universita Degli Studi di Firenze, 2849
Universita Degli Studi di Palermo, 905
Universita di Genova, 780, 1248
Universita di Messina, 1593
Universita di Napoli, 2855, 3441
Universita di Pavia, 2169
Universita di Pisa, 3177
Universita di Roma, 1386, 1899 2857
Universita di Siena, 3514
Universita di Torino, 190, 1443 2182
Universita Karlova, 9500
Universitaires de Bruxelles, 306
Universitaires de France, 338, 835, 1073, 1346, 1930, 2360, 2646, 2653, 3493, 5301, 5405, 9721
Universitaires de France, 392
Universitario de San Pablo, 3550
Universitat Munchen, 2796
Universite Catholique, 1000
Universite Catholique de Louvain, 1098, 2550
Universite Catholique de Louvai 1098, 2550
Universite Catholique de Louvin 2668
Universite de Bruxelles, 333
Universite de Grenoble, 1115
Universite de Lausanne, 9153
Universite de Louvain, 3311
Universite de Lyon, 1785
Universite de Paris, 64, 4959
Universite de Poitiers, 5388
Universite du Commerce d'Otary 2453
Universite Liege, 874
Universitet, Uppsala, 2516
Universitetet i Oslo, 10089
University College of Leicester

2462
University College of Nottingham, 2759
University College of Swansea, 923
University of Aberdeen, 6009
University of Alabama, 1532
University of Berlin, 9985
University of Caen, 2523
University of California, Berkeley, 2954, 5342
University of California, Riverside, 865
University of Cambridge, 2993, 5517
University of Cape Towns, 7325
University of Chicago, 630, 784, 787, 804-805, 816-817, 890, 1027, 1798, 2798, 5122
University of Delhi, 8981
University of Glasgow, 418, 2446, 5376, 7292, 7331, 7344
University of Illinois, 31, 2400, 5352
University of Lille, 2430
University of London, 723, 813, 992, 2382, 2426, 2492
University of Lyons, 2865
University of Maine, 2421
University of Manchester, 885
University of Michigan, 743, 3351, 3722, 3756, 8919
University of Mysore, 9940
University of New Hampshire, 2077
University of New Mexico, 278-279
University of North Carolina, 939
University of Notre Dame, 9340
University of Oxford, 593, 933, 1023, 2627, 2666, 5292, 5428, 5687, 6225, 6288, 6388, 6389, 6499, 7169, 8903, 9891, 9985
University of Paris, 2654
University of Pennsylvania, 753
University of Queensland, 2547
University of Southern California, 86
University of South Carolina, 358, 3081
University of Sydney, 9429
University of Texas, 8989
University of Toronto, 1146, 7282
University of Warsaw, 3721
University of Western Australia, 951
University of Wichita, 2799
University of Wisconsin, 2332, 2409, 3164
Unks, G., 1305
Uno, K., 3884, 9592, 9614, 9615, 9616
Upgren, A. R., 2207
Upton, J. K, 8713
Uranovsky, Y. M., 9422
Urban, B., 9617
Urban, L., 9618
Ure, A., 7179-7180
Uruguay, 9424
Urwick, E. J., 7282
Usher, A. P., 2613, 5126
Ustariz, D. G., 4790
Usury, 2556, 4030, 4104, 4111, 4161-4163, 4204, 4266, 4416, 4487, 4636, 4704, 4861, 4931, 5049, 5053, 5085, 5562, 5819, 6132, 6720, 6793, 7340, 8334, 8413, 9924, 9939
Utilitarianism, 2785, 9619
Utility, 3213, 3271, 3291, 3318, 3336, 3352, 3369, 3377, 3389, 3406, 3430, 3452, 3483, 6388, 9750, 9776, 9780, 9787, 9867, 9869
Utility, Cardinal, 9738
Utility, Function, 3137, 3313, 9673
Utility, Marginal, 3232, 3269, 3631, 5008, 9729-9732, 9770, 9784, 9817, 9871
Utility, Measurement, 9837
Utility, Total, 3145
Utopia, 9, 130, 2636, 2643, 2742, 4533, 4547, 7066, 7276, 9016, 9051, 9053, 9173, 9221, 9231, 9357, 9456, 9458, 9459, 9531
Utzschneider, J., 5258
Uyehara, C. H., 9620

Uzawa, H., 3235, 3504
Uztariz, G., 4830, 5170, 5267, 5323

Vacic, A. M., 2517, 9621-9622
Vagrant, 8506
Vahlen, 2713
Vaish, M. C., 2160
Vakyem, 2777
Valencia, 4973
Valenti, G., 8714
Valery, P. A., 2518
Valin, R. J., 4831
Valk, H. M. H. A., 2208-2209
Valko, L., 1011
Vallarino, J. C., 2210
Valle, J. C., 2519
Valleroux, H., 8715
Valluis, B. W., 2635
Valuation, Money, 3227
Valuation, Theory, 3184
Value, 10, 97, 219, 347, 942, 1088, 1434, 1995, 2170, 2764, 2792, 3112, 3114, 3121, 3122-3123, 3129, 3142, 3147, 3152-3154, 3161, 3167, 3169, 3174, 3179-3181, 3185-3187, 3189, 3195, 3202, 3205, 3209, 3211, 3229, 3234, 3421, 3247-3248, 3255, 3258-3260, 3262, 3272, 3274, 3277, 3281, 3284, 3288, 3292, 3307, 3309, 3310, 3312, 3315, 3323, 3327, 3332-3333, 3337, 3343, 3347, 3351, 3357, 3362, 3365, 3375, 3376, 3380-3381, 3392, 3397, 3403, 3408-3409, 3413, 3416-3417, 3423-3424, 3428, 3441, 3445, 3447, 3449, 3450, 3452, 3460, 3468-3469, 3471-3472, 3481-3482, 3486, 3577, 3615, 3622, 3901, 3946, 4701, 4968, 5112, 5430, 5501-5503, 5833, 5883, 6128, 6370, 6388, 7017, 7282, 7326, 7476, 7705, 7948, 7986, 8236, 8315, 8508, 8636, 8714, 8783-8785, 8843, 8846, 9064, 9127, 9386, 9685, 9693, 9773, 9787, 9799, 9816, 9825, 9835
Value, Domestic Theory of, 9850
Value, Engineering, 3168
Value, Exchange, 6388
Value, Human, 3368, 3665
Value, Individual, 3108
Value, Labor Theory, 2792, 3269, 3349, 3467, 9437
Value, Natural, 9804
Value, Origin, 7216
Value, Social, 5, 3105, 3838
Value, Surplus, 3344, 3358, 9417
Van Den Berg, M., 2925, 3885
Van Niekerk, C., D., 2211
Van Sickle, J. V., 2212
Van Tassel, R. C., 2213
Vandenborre, H. J., 10096
Vanderblue, H. B., 2214, 7352
Vanderlint, J., 4832
Vaquette, T., 8716
Varigny, C., 8717
Varma, J. D., 1327
Vasco, G., 7181
Vasquez, E., 9624
Vasudevan, A., 2832
Vatter, B., 8991
Vauban, 83, 2427, 5152
Vauban, J., 4833
Vauban, M., 2429, 5251
Vauban, S., 5251
Vaucher, J., 7182
Vauderville, M., 8718
Vaughan, R., 4834, 7183
Vaughn, B., 6106
Vavilov, S. I., 9422
Veblen, T. B., 3076, 3451, 3886, 7649, 8897-8899, 8907, 8915, 8923, 8933, 8935, 8938, 8939, 8940, 8943-8944, 8947-8948, 8952, 8958, 8959, 8965, 8968-8970, 8978, 8982, 8984-8985, 8988, 8991-8999, 9000, 9625-9626, 9784-9785, 10098
Vecchio, G., 2215-2216
Vedia, A., 8720
Velasco, G. R., 3758
Venezuela, 2771
Venice, Commerce, 6463

Venice, Middle Ages, 7149
Verdeil, F., 8721
Verelst, H., 4835
Veritas Foundation, New York, 10097
Verlinden, C., 666
Verma, J. D., 1328
Vernadsky, I., 7184
Verneaux, R., 5127
Verney, F. P., 8722
Vernon, J. M., 3777
Verri, P., 2428, 2856, 4836-4840, 7185
Verrijn-Stuart, C. A., 8723
Versailles, 7189, 9902
Vesselovsky, A., 8724, 8725
Vestinik Akademii Nauk SSSR, 175
Vethake, H., 2217, 7186
Vianello, C. A., 2873
Vianello, M., 9000
Vickers, D., 5315
Vickrey, W. S., 3887
Vico, J. B., 4841
Vidal, F., 7187
Vidari, E., 8726
Videla, M., 667
Viebahn, G. V., 7188
Vielrose, E., 2039
Vieweg, F., 9707
Vignes, E., 8727
Vignon, L., 8728
Vigor, P. H., 9627
Vijvere, V., 3147
Vikor, D., 668, 2521, 2522, 2554
Vilar, P., 9476
Vilfan, J., 9063
Village Community, 8252
Village Community, England, 8599
Villages, England, 8365
Villalbi, D. P. G., 94, 799
Villard, H. H., 2218
Villari, P., 8729
Villegas, D. C., 2610, 2733, 5360, 9392, 9989
Villeneuve-Bargemont, A., 2475, 7190-7191
Villerme, 7192
Villey, D., 669, 2523
Villey, E., 8730-8731
Villey-Desmeserets, E. L., 2524

Villiaume, N., 7193
Villiers, C. P., 8732
Vimer, J., 3452
Vincent, W., 7194
Vinci, F., 2219, 9786
Vincolanti, L., 7185
Viner, J., 1013, 3889, 5316-5317, 7353-7355, 9787, 9880-9881
Vining, D. R., 3084, 10098
Vinogradoff, P., 5128
Violet, T., 4486-4847
Virgilii, F., 8733
Virginia, 4092, 6297
Virnyk, D. F., 2987
Vitello, V., 670
Vito, F., 1491, 2220-2222
Vitu, A., 8734-8735
Vlademina, J. E., 9981
Vlaskalic, T., 9287
Vleeschhouwer, J. E., 3453
Vleugels, W., 2710, 9788
Vojtisek, J., 1912
Volk, K. H., 2223
Volkov, M. I., 2791
Vollgraff, C., 7196-7197
Volodin, V. S., 10099
Volpe, G., 9407, 9628-9629
Voltaire, F., 2357, 5190, 7198
Voorthuijsen, W. D., 5318
Vopelius, M-E., 2711
Voprosy Ekonomiki, 186, 375
Voss, 7199
Vossion, L., 7896
Vrancic, I., 1966
Vries, F., 3828, 3841, 3890
Vujosevic, M., 9639
Vukasin, P. N., 8952
Vulert, P., 2224
Vygodskii, V. S., 9632
Vygoskij, S. L., 1014
Vytanovych, I., 2965

Waal, E., 8736
Waardhuizen, D. D., 2225
Wada, A., 3891
Wada, S., 3891
Wada, Z., 2525, 9633
Wade, J., 7203
Waentig, H., 5403, 7337
Waffenschmidt, W. G., 2226-2227, 3659, 3893
Wage, 2197, 2653, 2670, 3159,

3193, 3196, 3342, 3345,
3385, 3443, 3446, 3451,
3560, 4115, 4304, 4973,
5702, 5992, 6243, 6306,
6308, 6418, 6475, 7136,
7138, 7236, 7265, 7607,
8321, 8359, 8533, 8586,
8691, 8697, 9386, 9715
Wage, Bargain Theory, 7722
Wage, Farm Labor, Great
 Britain, 5629
Wage, Farm Labor, United
 States, 7757
Wage, Great Britain, 7561
Wage, Indeterminateness,
 3256
Wage, Just, 944, 3391, 4978
Wage, Rate, 5690, 6977
Wage, Real, 3286
Wage, Subsistence, 5492
Wage, Theory, 8234, 8281
Wage, Theory, Wage-Fund, 8221
Wagemann, E. F., 2228-2229
Wagenfuhr, H., 672
Wagenfuhr, R., 2966
Wagner, 9030, 9489
Wagner, A., 2230, 3894, 7204-7206, 8900, 9510, 9634, 9882
Wagner, A. H. G., 2698, 2712, 9634
Wagner, D. O., 1015, 9635
Wagner, V. F., 1016
Waha, R., 2655
Waite, W. C., 2231
Wakar, A., 9636
Wakefield, D., 7207
Wakefield, E. G., 2456, 7208-7210, 7337
Walch, J., 2526
Walcker, K., 673, 8739
Waldorf, W. H., 3455
Waldron-Shah, D., 5129
Wales, 4653, 4879, 6807, 7211, 7534
Wales, W., 7211
Walfe, J. N., 3449
Walford, C., 8740-8741
Walford, E., 5130
Walker, A., 7212-7213
Walker, F. A., 2232-2233, 8742-8748
Walker, F. V., 2234, 3085

Walker, T., 7214
Wallace, A. R., 8749
Wallace, R., 4850, 8750
Wallace, T., 7215
Waller, E., 4851
Waller, W., 4852
Wallinga, H. T., 5131
Wallis, K. F., 3895
Walls, G., 2527
Walpole, R., 4744
Walras, A. A., 2235-2236, 7216-7217
Walras, M. E. L., 931, 1957, 3456, 9667-9668, 9702, 9708 9749, 9789-9794
Walsh, J., 7218
Walsh, V. C., 2237
Walsh, W., 10100
Walthershausen, A., 8559
Walton, C., 1357
Wanderlich, G., 3638
Wang, H., 3457-3458
Wang, M., 3459
Wang, Y., 674
Want, 6299
Wants, 9857
Wanty, J., 3896
Wappaus, J. E., 7219-7220
War, 551, 583, 609, 990, 1027, 1908, 4265, 5294, 5475, 5497, 5558, 5625, 5709, 5737, 5784, 5806, 6021, 6494, 6633, 7043, 7555, 7706, 9045, 9504, 9539, 9691, 9905, 9991
War, Civil, United States, 9372
War, Civil, United States,
 Finance, 8353
War, Europe, 10000
War, Great Britain and America,
 6723
War, Indian Independence, 9387
War, Nations Involved, 7221
War, Neutral Powers, 7221
Warburton, C., 3460
Ward, A. D., 1017
Ward, B., 2238, 3461
Ward, B. N., 9637
Ward, D., 8751
Ward, D. B., 4853
Ward, R., 7221
Ward, R. J., 2239
Ware, C. F., 2240

Ware, N. J., 5434
Waring, C., 8752
Warner, A. G., 8753, 8754
Warner, A. W., 2241
Warre, J., 7222
Warrington, J., 9456
Warsaw Biblioteka Narodowa, 9638
Warschauer, O., 8755
Wartenberg, C. M., 9782
Wasseige, Y., 2242
Wasser, E., 2243
Wasserhab, K., 8756
Watanabe, T., 9001
Watchmaker, 6936
Waterston, A., 3097
Waterways, Inland, 8103
Wathely, R., 7223
Watkins, G. S., 325
Watkins, M. W., 769
Watson, D. S., 2444-2445
Watt, J., 6310
Watteville, A., 7224-7226
Watts, J., 8757
Watts, V. O., 2246, 2528, 10101
Waugh, A. E., 2247
Waugh, F. V., 3462
Wayland, F., 7227
Wayne State University, 762
Wealth, 146, 151, 320, 434, 1225, 1263, 1451, 1549, 1672, 1951, 2048, 2119, 2186, 2233, 2846, 3548, 3549, 3619, 3662, 3912, 4139, 4158, 4234, 4366, 4401, 4488, 4641, 4854, 5155, 5277, 5384, 5432, 5462, 5780, 5783, 5828, 5842, 5844, 5870, 5927, 5989, 6004, 6181, 6282, 6299, 6305, 6591, 6693, 6750, 6762, 6886, 6912, 6933, 6944-6945, 6951, 6970-6971, 6978, 7000, 7023, 7096, 7134, 7187, 7213, 7216, 7337, 7346, 7602, 7630-7631, 7673, 7909, 7970, 8186, 8219, 8263, 8270, 8313, 8416, 8670, 8924, 8945, 9678, 9680, 9885
Wealth, Distribution, 9677, 9686
Wealth, Europe, 7148
Wealth, National, 2013, 4051, 4483, 5882, 6103, 6138, 6143, 6251, 6512, 7299
Wealth, Netherlands, 6980
Wealth, Public, 6353
Wealth, Social, 7004, 7217, 9790, 9792-9793
Wealth, Synthetic, 7299
Wealth, United States, 7156
Weaving, 7245
Webb, B., 8758, 9639
Webb, S., 8758, 8762, 9639
Webber, S., 4855-4856
Weber, A., 859, 2248-2251, 2335
Weber, F. B., 7228-7229
Weber, F. S., 2252
Weber, G., 7230-7231
Weber, H., 2529
Weber, H. F., 2253
Weber, H. H., 3463
Weber, M., 675-676, 1018, 1961, 2254-2255, 3898-3899, 8766, 8870, 8879, 8889, 8901-8903
Weber, M. M., 8763-8765
Weber, S., 2256
Weber, W., 677, 2257, 2555
Webster, D., 2352
Webster, P., 7231
Webster, R., 8768
Webster, R. G., 8767
Wedderkopii, 4857
Weddigen, W., 2258-2259
Weeden, W. B., 8769-8770
Wegener, W., 3464
Wei, H., 3465
Weichs-Glon, F., 8772
Weigand, W., 5319
Weights and Measures, 3972, 4117, 4165, 4280, 4331, 4670, 4674, 4835, 5448, 5649, 6327, 6457-6458, 6677, 6732, 7145, 7178, 7574, 8516
Weiler, E. T., 797, 2260, 2261
Weiler, P., 7695
Weill, G., 9640-9641
Weiller, J., 678-679, 2262
Weinberger, O., 2263, 9795
Weintraub, S., 2264-2265,

10102-10103
Weiss, F. J., 680
Weiss, L. W., 2266
Weiss, R., 2267
Weisskopf, T. E., 879, 3051
Weisskopf, W. A., 3900
Weitraub, S., 9883
Weld, W. E., 2268
Welfare, 261, 525, 1638, 1639, 1948, 1951, 2742, 2811, 3212, 3614, 3912, 5140, 8257
Welfare, Function, 564
Welfare, Social, 2065, 2738, 2779, 6966
Welfare, State, 10095
Welfare, Theory, 1539
Welfe, W., 3466
Welfling, W., 1059, 2269-2270
Welford, C. G., 7232
Welinder, C., 2271-2272
Wellisz, S. C., 2600
Wells, D. A., 2612, 8773-8775
Wells, D. A., Fund, 9060
Wells, H. B., 989
Welskopf, E. C., 5134
Welter, G. A., 9642
Weltwirtschaftliches Archiv, 5220
Welz, G., 6439, 7233
Wen, A. K. W., 2578, 5012
Wenke, K., 3682
Wertimer, S., 1438
Werveke, H., 5135
Weskett, F., 7234
Wesslau, O. E., 7980
Wessmann, L. T., 913
West, E., 2461, 7235-7236
West, E. G., 7356
West Indies, 662, 3933, 5597, 6469, 6621, 6817, 7029, 7274
West Indies, Great Britain, 6401, 7042
West Indies, Planters, 7025
West Indies, Sugar, 646, 6415, 6465, 7064
Westergaard, H., 8776
Westerlind, E., 2980
Western Economic Journal, 3529

Westman, C., 8777
Westminster Review, 5501, 5503
Weststrate, C., 2273-2274
Wetzel, W. A., 2530
Weulersse, G., 1019, 5435-5439
Weuves, M. J., 7237
Weyer, O. W., 8778
Weyhmann, A., 5320
Weyland, J. J., 7238
Whale Fishery, 4227, 5546, 6585
Whately, R., 7240
Wheat, 5625
Wheatley, J., 7241-7242
Whetham, E. H., 2540
Whewell, W., 5229, 6307, 7423-7244
Whiston, J., 4858
Whitaker, A. C., 3467
Whitaker, G. R., 1271
Whitbread, S., 6288
White, A., 8779
White, G. S., 7245
White, H., 8780
White, Z., 1020
Whitmore, W. W., 7246
Whitney, J. D., 8781
Whittaker, E., 2275-2276
Whitworth, C., 4175
Wichmann, C. A., 5387
Wicksell, K., 1021-1022, 2980, 3468, 9774, 9783, 9796-9801
Wicksellian Tradition, 9805
Wicksteed, 9687
Wicksteed, P. H., 3469, 3901, 8782, 9713, 9801-9803
Widmar, B., 9302
Wiedenfeld, K., 683, 2531
Wiegand, G. C., 2277
Wien-Claudi, F., 2556
Wienke, W. F., 10104
Wieser, F., 2278-2279, 3428, 3471-3473, 3839, 3902, 8784, 9773, 9804
Wigforss, E., 2974
Wiggins, J. W., 5287
Wilber, G. L., 58
Wilberforce, W., 7247
Wilbrandt, R., 1025, 2532, 8904
Wilbur, M. C., 9556

Author and Subject Index

Wilczynski, W., 3474
Wilda, W. E., 7248
Wilder, I, 2280
Wiles, P. I., 2281, 9643
Wiley, J. W., 1309
Wilhite, V. G., 3086
Wilkins, B. H., 3087
Wilkinson, T., 7018
Wilkinson, W., 4860
Will, R. M., 5440
Willcox, W. F., 8785
Willfort, M., 9953
William, C., 9849
William, M., 9644
William, R., 7249
William the Lion, 5686
William The III, 3989
Williams, A. H., 3475
Williams, C., 6791
Williams, C. W., 7250
Williams, F. S., 8786
Williams, H. R., 10105
Williams, J. H., 908, 1023, 10106
Williamson, H. F., 699, 2533
Williamson, J. B., 8787
Williamson, T. R., 2282
Willink, H. G., 8788
Willkom, S., 8789
Wills, E. V., 2534
Wilson, A. J., 8790-8791
Wilson, C. J., 5321-5322
Wilson, E. B., 9884
Wilson, G. W., 1024
Wilson, J., 7251-7253
Wilson, Jasper, 7254
Wilson, J. A., 5139
Wilson, J. D., 9645
Wilson, T., 4861
Wilson, W. D., 8792
Wimpey, J., 4862
Winch, D., 903, 2793, 10107
Winch, D. N., 684
Winding, P., 1066, 2283
Wine, 4807
Wine, Cooper, 3978
Wines, E. C., 8793
Winkler, E., 1123, 9423
Winkler, W., 3903
Wirminghaus, A., 5323, 8794
Wirth, L., 9357
Wirth, M., 2284, 8795-8796
Wiskemann, E., 1026, 2713-2714

Wiskemann, H., 8797
Wiskermann, E., 8869
Wisselink, J., 1882
Wissertation, Wurzburg, 2805
Wissler, A. J., 3905
Witchel, J., 1473-1474
With, J., 4863
Wittaker, E., 681-682
Witte, E. E., 9002
Wittelshofer, O., 8798
Witteveen, H. J., 1003
Wittich, C., 9737
Wittich, H., 3476
Wittkowsky, G. H., 5324
Wittmann, W., 3477
Woestijne, W. J., 2285-2286, 3478
Wold, H. O. A., 3479, 3906
Wolf, A., 3493
Wolf, H. A., 1185
Wolfe, B. D., 9646
Wolfe, J. N., 3481
Wolff, J., 2032
Wolff, S., 2535
Wolfson, M., 9647-9648
Wolkoff, M., 8799
Wollman, N., 3482
Wolman, W., 2112
Wolowski, 5742
Wolowski, L., 8875, 8905
Wolowski, L. F., 7255-7259
Women, 8078
Wood, A., 888
Wood, C., 6611
Wood, J., 7261, 8800
Wood, N., 7262
Wood, S., 7265
Wood, W., 4864
Woods, B. M., 2287
Woods, G., 7264
Woods, R. A., 8801
Woodward, J., 4865
Woodward, R. L., 2799
Woog, H., 5441
Wool, 3953, 3976, 4045, 4082, 4108, 4296, 4327-4328, 4471, 4512, 4647, 4659, 4707, 4729, 4756, 4766, 4775, 4781, 4856, 5446, 5584, 5865, 6167, 7585
Wool, Manufacture, 4354, 5816
Wool, Price, 5865

Wooley, B., 4584
Woolf, H., 3567
Woolrych, H. W., 7266
Woolsey, T. D., 8802
Worcester, D. A., 2288
Wordworth, C. F., 7267
Work, 907, 1115, 1182, 1273, 1550, 1723, 1785, 1915, 1945, 3303, 3316, 3502, 4304, 4693, 5416, 5539, 5563, 5567, 5572, 5590, 5673, 5733, 5925, 5941, 6357, 6566, 7195, 7430, 7564, 7924, 8200, 8317, 8462, 8630
Work, Foreign, 7561
Work, Forms of, 6338
Work, House of, 5877
Work, Laws, 7773
Workbook, 1226, 1607, 1823
Worker, 376, 425, 868, 1029, 1108, 1706, 3317, 3904, 4560, 5463, 5484, 5494, 5700, 6034, 6917, 6926, 7092, 7192, 7473, 7497, 7502-7503, 7514-7515, 7521, 7566, 7591, 7622, 7769, 7796, 8114, 8124, 8126, 8141, 8156, 8175, 8189, 8287, 8333, 8381, 8400, 8419, 8517, 8527, 8682, 8829, 9420
Worker, Belgium, 8718
Worker, Laws, Protective, 8684
Workhouse, 3932, 3991, 5628
Working Class, 6378, 8228
Workmanship, 8995
Works, Public, 1273
Works Progress Administration, 796
Workshop, Act, 8489
Workshop Laws, 8374
Worland, S. T., 5140
World, Modern, 1032
Worlidge, J., 4866
Worms, E., 8803-8804
Worms, G., 8805
Wotzel, A. A., 1947
Woytinsky, W. S., 2536
Wright, C. D., 8806-8809
Wright, C. W., 1027
Wright, D. M., 2289-2290, 2537, 9650, 10108
Wright, F. J., 2291
Wright, G., 3483
Wright, P. Q., 9979
Wronski, 9706
Wronski, S. P., 2292
Wu, C., 2485, 5325
Wu, C.-H., 685
Wu, P., 2585
Wu, S., 3484
Wu, Y., 2293, 2591
Wuellner, B., 5141
Wulf, M., 5142-5143
Wurst, A., 2538
Wurzer, L., 2294
Wyatt, J., 7268
Wyckoff, W. C., 8810
Wygodski, W. S., 9632
Wykstra, R. A., 2295
Wyrozembski, A. J., 2539
Wyse, L., 8811

Xenophon, 5058, 5144-5145

Yajima, K., 2296
Yakhot, O., 9327
Yale Review, 3797
Yale Russian and East European Studies, 3095
Yale University, 4908
Yamada, Y., 686, 1028
Yamaguchi, K., 687, 2905
Yamaguchi, M., 3088
Yamakawa, Y., 2656
Yanaihara, T., 7357
Yanowitch, M., 9652
Yanzhul, I. I., 8374
Yarraton, A., 2372
Yarrington, A., 4867
Yasuri, T., 2297
Yeats, J., 8812-8813
Yelverton, H., 4868
Yi, C., 2298
Yi, H., 3907
Yi, M., 2299-2300
Yi, Y., 2301
Yntema, T. O., 9735, 9871
Yohe, W. P., 2980, 9805
Yokeno, N., 2302
Yokoyama, J., 424
Yokoyama, M., 2303, 5442
Yokoyama, T., 3485
Yoshida, K., 2304-2307
Yoshida, S., 2308

Yoshida, Y., 688
Yotopoulos, P. A., 3908
Young, A., 723, 4869-4883, 5164, 7269-7271
Young, A. A., 1370, 1999, 3486, 3909-3913, 9806
Young, E., 8814, 8815
Young, G., 7272
Young, W., 7273
Young Communist International, 2309
Yuan Dynasty, 5103
Yugoslavia, 3091-3098, 9063, 9136, 9484, 9586

Zabaleta, R., 2794
Zablowicz, L., 2310
Zaccagnini, E., 2311
Zacharle, K. G., 7274
Zaffaroni, J. C., 9653
Zagorski, J., 5443
Zaleski, E., 3028
Zamiatnin, V. N., 689, 3029
Zamora, F., 2312-2314
Zaneletti, R., 1181
Zaninovich, G., 3098
Zarkovic, G., 2315
Zarrin, P. I., 7358
Zauberman, A., 690, 3187, 3915
Zavada, J., 2111
Zawadzki, J., 2316
Zawadski, W., 3916
Zeitlin, I. M., 9655
Zeitschrift fur die gesammte Staatswissenschaft, 3782
Zeitschrift fur Nationalokonomie, 9774, 9880
Zeitschrift fur Schweizerische Statistik. . . , 2705
Zeitschrift fur Sozialwissenschaft, 8826
Zeleny, J., 9654
Zelicourt, Bernard, 396
Zeuthen, F., 1852, 2317-2318
Zeuthen, F. L. B., 3917
Zeyss, R., 8816
Zielenziger, K., 5326
Zimmerer, C., 2319
Zimmerman, L. J., 691-692
Zimmern, A., 5266
Zimmern, A. E., 5146
Zimmern, H., 8817
Zinke, G. W., 2320, 8952
Zinn, K. G., 2321
Zins, 9924
Zlupko, S. M., 3030
Zollner, C. W., 8818
Zollvereinsblatt, 8861
Zorli, A., 8819
Zucchi, G., 2322
Zuckerandl, R. 3488, 8820
Zukowski, H., 3918
Zurawicki, S., 693, 2934, 2944, 9347
Zwanziger, M., 694, 5147
Zweig, F., 695
Zwiedineck-Sudenhorst, O., 696, 2323, 5148
Zwijndregt, J., 2326

INDEX II

Short Title Index

ABC i nationalekonomi 1885
ABC of economics 1971
The A B C of the foreign exchanges 7628
A economia e os economistas 2559
A gazdasagi 9507
A polgári kozgazdaságtan 9427
A proposito delle indagini 3116
A szocializmus politikai 9135
Abhandlung uber den kolbertismus 5258
Abhandlung v. Geldumlauf 5657
Abhandlungen über gegenstdaende 5983
The abolition of arrest 6186
Abrégé de l'economie politique 3990
Abrégé des éléments 9789
Abrégé elémentaire 6088
Abriss einer geschichte der theorie 470
Absentee ownership 8992
An abstract of all the publick debts 4389
An abstract of an account of the clerks 4390
An abstract of an essay on the improvement of husbandry 4550
Abstract of the charter 3924
An abstract of the grievances 3925
Abstract of Walker's political 8742
Absurdité de l'impôt territorial 5696
Academic economics in Holland 2920
The academic scribblers 2346
The academic study of political 3596
Acceptable inequalities 728

Account of Andrew Yarraton, 2372
An account of a scheme 4855
An account of charity-schools 3926
An account of Denmark 3927
An account of European settlements 3928
An account of Ireland 7208
An account of several workhouses 3932
An account of some transactions 3931
An account of the arctic 6962
An account of the care taken in most civilised nations 4575
Account of the interior of Ceylon 5874
An account of the Island of Ceylon 6690
Account of the Levant company 5445
An account of the most important public records 5821
An account of the proceedings of the House of Peers 3929
An account of the proceedings of the merchants 5446
An account of the public funds 5768
An account of the public funds 6027
An account of the revenue 3930
An account of the several life-assurance 5507
An account of the systems of husbandry 6992
An account of the trade in India 4468
The act for permitting the free importations 3934
The act of tonnage 3935
Activity analysis 1729
Activity in Marx's philosophy 9339

Address and provisional rules 9365
An address to the Congress 5449
An address to the good sense 7167
Address to the landowners 6044
An address to the proprietors 3936
An address to the proprietors 5450
An address to the proprietors 5461
An address to the public 4865
Address to the two Houses 5451
An address upon the present state of trade 3937
L'administration de l'agriculture 7861
L'administration des financés 7501
Administration financière 6230
The administration of the colonies 4621
The advantages and disadvantages 3939
The advantages of the East-India trade 3938
The advantages to the people of Ireland 3940
The affluent society 3057
The African trade 3941
The age of great cities 7183
The age of Keynes 10017
The age of Marshall 2752
The age of the economist 230
The aged poor 7534
The age of Marshall 9827
Aggregate economic analysis 1766
Aggregate economic analysis 10031
Aggregate supply and demand 3175
Aggregate supply and demand 9917
Agrarhistorische abhandlungen 7991
Agrarian tenures 8618
Agrarische verordeningen 8338
Agrarische zustand 7798

Economic Thought and Analysis

Agrar-politische 8302
La agricultura 7932
L'agriculture 8487
Die akademische nationalökonomie 2712
Akerika keizai shiso 3074
Aktionsgemeinschaft soziale marktwirtschaft 1043
Aktualne problemy nauk 2936
al-Fikr al-'Arabi al-hadith 2541
Alien merchants 5154
The alienation of modern 9475
al-Nazarīyah al-ʿāmmah li-Kinz 10061
Algèbre et logique 9705
Algemene economie 2659
L'algerie et les colonies 7791
Algunas reflexiones 2380
An alphabet in finance 8232
The alphabet of economic science 3469
The alphabet of economic science 8782
Alphabet of economic science 9801
Die alten deutschen kameralisten 5326
Der ältere Mirabeau 8385
Alternative theories 3405
Alternative theories of distribution 3273
Alternative to serfdom 743
Alternative to serfdom 8919
Die altliberalen okonomen 2711
All classes productive 6143
All sorts of wheel-carriage 4688
Alleged socialism of the church 5090
L'allemagne économie 8803
Allgemeine geschichte 9033
Allgemeine gewerbslehre 7814
Allgemeine grundsatze 5403
Allgemeine grundsaetze 6500
Allgemeine nationalökonomie 2122
Allgemeine und angewandte 1535
Allgemeine und angewandte 2683
Allgemeine volkswirtschaftslehre 119

Short Title Index

Allgemeine volkswirtschaftslehre 1090
Allgemeine volkswirtschaftslehre 1218
Allgemeine volkswirtschaftslehre 1905
Allgemeine volkswirtschaftslehre 2323
Allgemeine wirtschaftgeschichte 148
Allgemeine wirtschaftsgeschichte 376
Allgemeine wirthschaftslehre 8515
Die allgemeinen philosophischen grundlagen 286
Die allgemeinen philosophischen 7303
American capitalism 3058
American charities 8753
The American citizen 7758
The American commercial policy 8471
The American commonwealth 7576
American communities 9236
American disciples of Marx 9229
American economic development 3065
The American economic republic 3036
The American economic system 1857
The American economic system 2261
American economic thought 3063
The American economy 1408
The American economy 1412
The American economy 1474
The American economy 1507
The American economy 1514
The American economy 2320
The American economy 3060
American farming 7782
American farms 7804
The American railway 7633
The American railway 7669
American securities 7961
American silk manufacture 8810
American treasure 5215

America's Roman circus 10104
Amerika keizai shiso 2451
Amerika keizaigaku shi kenkyu 3064
L'ami des hommes 5379
L'ami des pauvres 4260, 4261
Análise económica 1099
L'analisi della domanda 3328
Analisi della proprietà 8223
Analisi economica 1593
Análisis de la demanda 3479
An analog of short-period 3832
L'Analyse de la valeur 3272
Analyse de l'ouvrage 4535
Analyse de l'ouvrage 5465
Analyse des blés 6908
Analyse des principes sur la circulation des denrées 4281
Analyse économique 1160
Analyse économique 1414
Analyse économique 1487
Analyse et examen du systeme 5464
Analyse et tableaux 5964
Analyse et tableaux de influence 5466
Analyse microeconomique 1676
Analyse raisonnée 5960
An analysis and history 6309
An analysis and measurement of value 3141
The analysis of demand 3222
Analysis of prehistoric 4953
An analysis of Soviet views 10094
An analysis of supply 3387
Analysis of the business 2077
An analysis of the laws 5491
Analysis of the minutes of evidence on banks 8395
An analysis of the statistical 6993
Analytical economics 3635
Analytical study of value 3189
Analytical tools 3219, 3220
The anatomy of communism 9547
The anatomy of exchange-alley 3949
The anatomy of spirit 9336
Ancien évêque de Pamiers 5453
Anciens economistes 2945
Ancient accounts of India and

China 3950
An ancient economic history 4983
Ancient Egyptian materials 5029
Ancient exchequers 7093
Ancient foundations of economics in India 2829
Ancient Judaism 5132
Ancient Rome at work 5027
Ancient trades decayed 3951
Anecdote sur la vie politique de Burke 6655
Die anfange der merkantilistischen 5149
Anfangsgründe der staatswirtschaft 6947
Die anfange des eigentums 5051
Anglia restaurata 3953
Anglia restaurata 4108
Angliae tutamen 3954
Anmerkungen zu Marx-heute 9585
Annales d'hygiène publique 5470
Les annales politiques 4692
Annals of agriculture 4869
Annals of agriculture 7269
Annals of banks for savings 5471
Annals of commerce 6436
Annals of the coinage 6900
Annals of the hon. East India 5642
Annals of the present united colonies 5711
Annotations 3955
Annuaire des finances russes 8724
Annual reports of the registrar-general 5472
Annual statistician 8280
Annuities upon lives 4521
Anschauliche einführung 2226
Anschauliche theorie 900
Ansichten der volkswirtschaft 560
Ansichten der volkswirtschaft 8873
An answer of the company of Royal adventurers 3956

The answer of the merchants-petitioners 3957
An answer to Schlegel 5860
An answer to Sir John Dalrymple's pamphlet 6051
An answer to the case of the old East-India company 3958
An answer to the pamphlet entitled 'Thoughts' 3959
An answer to the reasons against an African company 3960
An answer to the reply to the supposed treasury 5474
An answer to two letters 3961
An answer to 'War in disguise' 5475
An answer upon excise 3962
Answers to the questions 5688
Les antagonismes de classes 9125
Anteckningar om Frihetstidens 7392
L'anticolonialisme européen 5262
Antiguedad Maritima de la republica de Cartage 3963
Antikeynesismul 10092
Antiquities and curiosities of the exchequer 7981
Antologia del pensamiento 819
St. Antonio and mediaeval 4999
Anwendung mathematischer methoden 3779
La aparicion del comunismo moderno 9536
Apercu de l'evolution 2645
Apercu des principales 6212
Aperçu des vues morales 9055
Apercu statistique 5476
Apercu statistique 6914
Aplikacia matematiky 3555
Apologie du système de Colbert 4431
An apology for the builder 3965
An apology for the business of pawn-broking 3966
Apostillas sobre economía 428
An appeal to facts regarding the home trade 3967
An appeal to the public 4627
An appeal to the public in relation to the tobacco 3968

Short Title Index 741

Appendice a la educacion
  popular 3969
Appendice a la educacion
  popular 4071
An appendix to 'The Present
  state of the nation' 3970
Application of linear programming 3591
L'Applicazione dei procedimenti matematici 3772
L'Applicazione della matematica 3498
Applied dynamic economics
  1655
Applied economic analysis
  1148
Applied economics 1202
Applied economics 1337
An appraisal of institutional
  8960
An appraisal of Keynesian
  10106
Apuntes de teoria 1925
Apuntes para el estudio 3
Apuntes y comentarios sobre
  3333
Appunti critici alla teoria
  3329
Appunti dalle lezioni 1429
Appunti dalle lezioni 1707
Appunti di economia politica
  1959
Appunti di economia politica
  2311
Saint Thomas Aquinas 4914
Thomas Aquinas 4926
St. Thomas Aquinas 5033
Thomas von Aquino's stellung
  5036
Arbeit und boden 7796
Arbeit und kapital 3398
Arbeit und kapital 7497
Die arbeiter 6034
Arbeiterfrage 8124
Die arbeiterfrage 8156
Die arbeiterfrage 8462
Die arbeitergilden 7566
Die arbeitergilden 8829
Die arbeiterspacht 8114
Die arbeitskraft 3316
Arbeitsverhältnisse 7567
Die arbeitswerttheorie 9464
Arbitrages et parités 7998

Arbitration between capital
  8550
Archeveque de Dublin 7223
Archives der politischen 6756
Arewelahay tntesagitakan 3017
An argument proving the design
  of employing 3974
An argument to shew the disadvantage 3975
An argument upon the woollen
  manufacture 3976
Arguments in favour of the
  able-bodied poor 5643
Aristotle 5108
Aristotle and the development
  of value 4968
Aristotle, Schumpeter 4969
Aristotle, the Nicomachcan
  ethics 5000
Aristotle's ethics 6118
Aristotle's mathematical
  analysis 5028
Aristotle's politics 5130
Arithmétique politique 4870
Das armenwesen 7815
The art and mystery of vintners
  3978
L'art de gagner sa vie 6571
Arthika paddhatiyam 342
Arthika vicaromka itihasa 462
Articles and regulation of the
  Edinburgh 3980
Articles of the copartnery of
  the Feeman-Burgesses 3979
Artisans and machinery 6096
Artistic goals 3802
Asia in the making of Europe
  5365
Aspect of ancient Indian 2825
Aspectos de la economía contemporanes 1102
Les aspects economiques du
  bouddhisme 4958
Aspects of ancient Indian 5072
Aspects modernes de la logique
  3224
Aspetti aziendali e sociali
  della politica economica
  1063
Les associations coopératives
  8070
Les associations ouvrieres
  8400

Austrian romantic school 2521
Atarashii keizai bunseki 3770
Atarsaii zeikuro-keizaigaku 2296
Att studera ekonomisk 2972
An attempt to define 7010
An attempt to explain from facts 6587
The attitude towards labor 4957
L'attivita umana 1248
Attuali tendenze delle dottrine 2849
Aufeinanderfolge der welthandels- herrschaften 8502
Aufgaben und praxis 3179
Aufgaben und versuche 2052
Aufsätze zur ökonomischen 2060
Aufziechnungen 2680
Aus dem literarischen nachlass von Carl Rodbertus- Jagetzow 7510
Die ausgangspunkte 8845
Der ausgang des kapitalismus 343
Ausgewahlte kapitel 2002
Ausgewählte texte 2513
Der aussagewert von makrogrossen 3691
Die aussichtslösigkeit 8571
The Austrian economists 3524
Austrian theories of capital 2556
Authority and law 5139
Australian and Californian gold 7053
The Austrian school 3471
Autobiographic recollections 6737
Autobiography 6471
Autobiography 6516
The autobiography of an economist 2478
The autobiography of Arthur Young 4871
The autobiography of the Hon. Sir Roger North 4570
Avances de la teoria economica 587
Avantages et le desavantages 4168
L'avenir économique 7543
L'avenir economique 8291
Away from freedom 2246

Away from freedom 2528
Away from freedom 10101
Az áziai termelési 9603

The Babylonian laws 4936
The background of economics 325
Backwoods utopias 9053
Samuel Bailey and the classical 3397
La baisse probable 5727
Bakumatsu no keizai shiso 2875
The balance of payments 3226
Le banche 6073
El banco nacional 8720
Bank, banking and paper 6216
The bank charter act 7787
Bank of England 8694
Bank rate in England 8396
Der bank- borsen- und action- schwindel 8420
Die banken 6259
Banking and the early scholastic 5052
Banking in Ireland 7753
Banking reform 8160
Banking system of New York 7634
The banks of New York 6109
Bankwesen der Schweiz 8426
Bankwesen und bankpolitik 8011
Bannen no seikatsu kiroku 350
La banque d'Angleterre 7255
La banque de France 7549
La banque de France 8310
La banque de Hambourg 5658
La banque libre 5837
Les banques d'émission 8370
The bargain theory 7722
John Barton 2499
Bases des sciences camérales 6618
Bases fondamentales 5699
Basic contemporary economics 1366
Basic economic principles 1721
Basic economics 791
Basic economics 1377
Basic economics 1502
Basic economics 1798
Basic economics 1808
Basic economics 2190
Basic ideas 1561

Short Title Index 743

Basic principles 1629
Basic problems 1574
Basic relations in theoretical models 3503
Basic teachings of the great economists 445
Basic theories of distribution 2734
Basic theories of distribution 3148
Basic trends in the development 3612
Basic writings 9607
Basic writings of Saint Thomas Aquinas 5061
Basic writings on politics 9366
Basistheorie 2321
Batavia illustrata 4064
Bau und leben 8572
Bauernbefreiung 8849
Bedarf, produktionsprogram 3354
Das Bedürfnis als absatzwirtschaftliches 3325
Das bedurfniss der volkswirtschaft 6945
Beginning readings 757
Beginselen der staathuishoudkunde 1983
Beginselen van economie 1960
Der begriff der investition 9964
Der begriff des unternehmers 1005
Behandlung und erkenntsiswert 1722
Beitrag zur naeheren bestimmung 6969
Beiträge staats- und socialwissenschaftliche 8303
Beiträge und materialen 7015
Beitrage zu wirtschaftspolitik 715
Beiträge z. geschechte 6183
Beiträge zur geschichte 3415
Beiträge zur geschichte 5552
Beitrage zur methode 2164
Beitrage zur methodik 3589
Beitrage zur sozial- und wirtschaftsgeschichte 179
Beiträge zur wirthschaftlichen 6729

Beiträge zur wirtschaftsforschung 1374
Beknopte geschiedenis der staathuishoudkunde in theorie 528
Beknopte staathuishoudkunde 1982
La Belgique 8685
La Belgique industrielle 7868
Belligerent rights asserted 5558
Bemerkungen zur angewandten 2582
The Bengal and Agra guide 5559
Jeremy Bentham's economic writings 2340
Nicolas Berdyaev's critique 9013
Die berechnung der marknachfrage 3267
Berkeley's querist and its place 326
S. Bernardine of Siena 4992
F. Th. V. Bernhardi 2367
Bernstein und das sozial democratische 9270
Der Beruf des okonomen 2935
Beruhmte denkfehler 2228
Beschrijvende economie 2273
The best use of economic resources 3692
Die bestellung der privaten 7946
Betreibswirtschaftslehre 3833
Die bevolkerung der Erde 5903
Bevolkerungsstatisik 7219
Bevor Das Kapital entstand 9609
Bewegung, die wirthschaftl. 7481
Die bewertung der wirtschaft im philosophischen 221
Beyond supply and demand 3230
Beyond supply and demand 8949
Beyond the chains of illusion 9194
Die beziehung zwischen 7285
Bias against business 3039
The bibliographical bulletin 9056
Bibliographical list 9830
Bibliographical list 9976
Bibliographie 9148
Bibliographie 9584
Bibliographie de Saint-Simonisme 2526
Bibliographie der kameralwissenschaften 5228

Bibliographie des corporations 7502
Bibliographie des oeuvres de Karl Marx 2481
Bibliographie des oeuvres de Karl Marx 9524
Bibliographie des socialismus 8652
Bibliographie über äusserungen von Karl Marx 9203
Bibliography 2339
The bibliography and writings of Turgot 5424
Bibliography of books 2675
A bibliography of David Hume 2413
Bibliography of economics 8032
A bibliography of the writings of Irving Fisher 2385
Bibliography on the analysis 3218
Biblioteca 6036
Biblioteca de los economistas españoles 7654
Biblioteca dell' economista 5578
Biblioteca di Gius Nautico 5579
Biblioteca di storia economica 936
Bibliotheca statistica 4793
Bi-centenaire du "Tableau economique" 5327
Bidrag til kapitalbildningen 7720
Bidrage til lifranteteoriens historia 7721
Bilan d'un demi-siècle de pensée économique 429
Bilan général et raisonné 4848
Bilanzbildsequenzen 3613
A bill for repealing several subsidies 4023
Bimetallic controversy 7903
Bimetallic question 8644
Bimetalism 8241
Bimetalism 8743
Biographical memoirs of Adam Smith 7349
A biography of Robert Owen 6639
The Birmingham economists 2735

Birth of a radical 10050
The birth of western economy 5017
Biamark and state socialism 7725
Bloomsbury 9894
The Bloomsbury group 9972
Board of trade 7493
The bogey of economic maturity 10088
Bohm-Bawerk's criticism 9234
Bohm-Bawerk's definition of capital 3451
Boisguilbert 5278
Pierre de Boisguilbert 5301
Pierre de Boisguilbert ou la naissance 2342
La bomba H dell'economia 135
The book of the farm 7044
The book of the great railway celebrations 7012
The book of the new moral 9468
Book review: Gustav Schmoller's Uber einige grundfragen 8897
Book review: Institutional 8948
Book review: Institutional 8958
Book review: Werner Sombart's des moderne kapitalismus 8898
Books on communism 9247
Books on communism 9285
Boon of the new modern world 6640
Bor'ba V. I. Lenina protiv anti-marksistskikh 2990
John Francis Bray 2353
Bread for the poor 4529
Breve storia dell'economica 90
Breve trattato delle cause che possono 4716
Breves nociones 8461
Breves resúmenes 1493
A brief account of the privileges and immunities 4046
A brief case of the distillers 4047
A brief essay on the advantages 4811
A brief examination into the

increase of the revenue 6887
A brief state of the question 4048
Briefe considerations 4683
Briefe und socialpolitique 6874
British colonies 7531
A brief introduction to the infinitesimal calculus 7849
Brief observations concerning trade 4470
A brief view of the policy 5634
Brilliant teacher 9591
Brine-salt improved 4472
Britain independent of commerce 7023
Britain's golden mines 4050
Britannia languens 4051
British banking 7784
British colonial theories 5237
British commerce and colonies 7900
The British customs 4052
British economists 2749
British husbandry 5820
The British land laws 8446
The British merchant 4411
British monetary experiments 5226
The British railway system 8240
Brundbegriffe der volkswirtschaftslehre 1528
The budget 4060
The budget 7130
Le budget 8659
Budget und budgetrecht 8600
Les budgets 8346
Les budgets 8363
Les budgets contemporains 7832
Bütjüme teorileri 1540
Bukkyo shakai-keizaigakusetsu 2546
Bullion and foreign exchange 8609
Bullionists 5290
Il buongoverno 188
Edmund Burke as an economist 2337
The burning question 7953

Burzhuaznye ekonomisty Anglii 2774
Burzhuaznye ekonomisty SShA 3031
Burzhuazyne ekonomisty SShA 3042
Burzuaznye koncepcii istorii 3003
Business and economic forecasting 3848
Business and modern society 894
Business cycle theory 3034
Business cycles 457
Business cycles 8971, 8972
Business economics 1056
Business economics 1117
Business economics 1271
Business fluctuations 742
Buyuk ekonomistler, tekrar gozden 234

Les cadres socizux 678
Les caisses d'epargnes 5678
Calcul des rentes viagères 5668
Calculating deviations of prices 3392
Calculations of taxes 4490
A calm investigation 5467
Cambridge economic history 4909
The cameralists 5295
El camino del bienestar 1031
Can Lloyd George do it 9977
Canadian customs tariff 7578
Canadian economic policy 3536
Canadian economic thought 2566
Canadian studies in comparative politics 7545
Le Canal de Panama 8811
Candid and impartial considerations 4077
Cannan and Veblen 8944
Richard Cantillon 5299
Capital 9367-9370
Capital and Finance 4940
Capital and interest 3618
Capital and interest 9663
Capital and its earnings 7629
Capital and its structure 9734
Capital and population 8005
Capital, currency 7251

Le capital, la spéculation 8090
El capital, Wagner contra Marx 9634
Il capitale 8678
Capitalism and the historians 816
Capitalism in recent German 2698
Capitalism, socialism 9545
Capitalist enterprise 176
The capitalist system 3051
Caracterul artistiintific 535
Jacob N. Cardozo 2425
The career of philosophy 7323
Henry Charles Carey 2414
H. C. Carey als nationökonomie 8096
Carey's socialwissenschaft 5221
Carey's socialwissenschaft 8015
Gershom Carmichael 2509
Carnets 2463
Carta al senor don Pedro Rodriquez Campomanes 4072
Cartas sobre los obstaculos 5661
Cartesian economics 981
Die cartesianische scholastik 4901
The Carthaginian peace 10026
The case against bimetallism 7907
A case book 2268
The case fairly stated between the Turky company 4089
The case of bankrupts 4090
The case of the British and Irish manufacture of linen 4091
The case of the bankers 4824
The case of the Dutch ships 4489
The case of the planters of tobacco 4092
The case of the revival of the salt duty 4093
The case of the Royal African company 4094
The case of the salt-duty 4095

Case of the salt duties 5569
The case of the sinking fund 4096
Cassels system 3496
Catalogue de la bibliotheque 2453
A catalogue of books 2434
A catalogue of the library of Adam Smith 7284
Catéchisme d'économie politique 6937
Catechisme des industriels 6919
Catechismo di economia politica 8309
Categories and laws of the political economy 9528
La cause d'épargne 7449
The cause of hard times 7694
The cause of the greatnesses of cities 4098
The cause of the present distress 7025
The causes and consequences of the pressure 6648
Causes and remedies of pauperism 6249
Causes financières 7928
Causes of fall in prices 7699
The causes of the dearness of provisions 4099
Cemiyet iktisandinda ana mefhumlar 1061
Cenno sul socialismo 7477
Censuses of the population 5706
Central planning 3866
Central planning 5287
La centralisation 5951
Centro di studi filosofici 737
Century of banking 7511
A century of Birmingham life 8157
Cenzo de la Riqueza territorial 5707
Certain considerations relating to the Royal African 4101
The challenge 4862
The challenge of economics 1050
The challenge of Marxism 9569
Challenge to Karl Marx 9612
Challenge to the American economy 1395
Une chambre des payans 8492

Short Title Index

Les chambres de commerce 8165
Chan hou ching chi hsüeh shuo 403
Ch'an yeh ko ming chiang 2616
La change et la circulation 7256
Changes in economic thought 690
The changing role of Soviet prices 3371
Chapters in basic 2108
Chapters in political 7522
Chapters on practical political 8456
Chapters on the theory and history of banking 7785
The character and logical method 7592
Character, motives and proceedings of the Anti-Corn 5463
Character, object and effects 5719
Character, objects 7164
A characterization of economic romanticism 9316
Charter and grants 4106
The character and logical method 1207
The character and logical method 3545
Charter granted 4105
Charter of nations 5935
Le chartisme 2639
Cheap corn best 5927
Les chemins de fer 8172
Les chemins de fer 8174
Les chemins de fer 8356
Les chemins de fer 8362
Cheng chih ching chi hsueh 565
Cheng chih chin chi hsueh 739
Michel Chevalier 9460
Michel Chevalier et ses idees 2423
Les chevaliers du travail 7564
Chi hua ching chi yü chia 3266
Chia chih chi chia chih 3158

Chia chin kuei lü tsai 3457
Chia chih kuei lü tsai tzū 3465
Chia chih yü shêng 3157
Chiave della dialettica 9628
Josiah Child 5220
Sir Josiah Child 5244
La chimere de l'equilibre 5233
Chin tai ching shi hsüeh 603
Chin tai hsi yang ching chi 685
Chin tai tzu pen chu i ching 408
China a model for Europe 5374
China and Europe 5413
China opened 6164
China's destiny 2570
China's economic system 2586
La Chine vue par quelques 5370
The Chinese 5873
Chinese emigration 8608
Chinese influences 5375
Chinese monopoly examined 5853
The Chinese repository of facts 5736
Ching chi hsueh 1246
Ching chi hsueh 1715
Ching chi hsueh kai yao 1247
Ching chi hsueh shih 674
Ching chi hueh yuan 1690
Ching chi ssu hsiang fa chan shih 109
Ching chi ssu hsiang hsiao shih 319
Ching chi ssū hsiang shih 103
The choice among investment 3276
Choice as an interdisciplinary area 3668
Chong Yag-yong ui chongch'i 2907
Chŏngch'i kyŏngjehak 9238
Chŏngch'i kyŏngjehak kaeyo 9281
Choson kyongje sasang sa 2908
Chrestomathie zur politischen 9297
The Christian and civic economy 5712
Christian economics 8512
Christian socialism 8117
Christianity and economic science 147
Chronicles and characters 6060

Chronicles of the bank 8709
Chronicon preciosum 4115
Chronicon preciosum 4274
Chronicon rusticum commerciale 4729
Chronique de la pensée économique 24
Chung-kuo chin pai nien ching 2574
Chung-kuo chin tai ching 2585
Chung-kuo ching chi hsueh 2571
Chung-kuo ching chi ssu hsiang 2576
Chung-kuo ku tai ching chi 2584
Chung shang chu i 5250
Anders Chydenius i forhallande 5245
Cicli storici 1895
La ciencia economia en gran bretaña 2794
Cinema económica 1439
La ciencia y las técnicas 3550
The Cincinnatti southern railway 8051
Circle of commerce 4518
La circulazione monetaria 8523
Les cités ouvrières de Mulhouse 8419
A citizen of today 1508
City corruption 4116
City life 8468
The civil, political 6205
Civil service in Great Britain 7794
The civil war in France 9371
The civil war in the United States 9372
Civilization 8836
Civilization and progress 7697
The claims of labour 5745
The claims of labour 6200
John Bates Clark 2412
Clark's distribution of wealth 3549
Professor Clark's economics 9785
The class struggles in France 9373
Classes and masses 8256

Les classes ouvrières 5567
Les classes ouvrières 5595
Les classes ouvrières 8175
Classical Keynesianism 10102
Classical macroeconomics 239
Classical political 2793
The classical theory 575
The classical theory of economic 2776
Classics in economics 747
Classics of economic theory 1024
The coal fields of Great 8074
The coal question 8098
Les coalitions 8554
Coalitions 8641
Richard Cobden and foreign 2366
Cobden et la Ligue 5529
Code de commerce 5762
Code de d'administration charitable 7224
Code noir 4124
Code of Hammurabi 4974
Il codice ferroviario 7887
Codigo de las costumbres maritimas 5763
Jacques Coeur et Charles VII 5756
Jacques Coeur, merchant prince 5010
Coinage in Roman imperial 5104
The coinage of the European 8008
Coins and coinage 7651
Colbert and a century of French 5176
Colbert et son temps 8357
Il Colbertismo 5259
Il Colbertismo 6493
Collectanea maritima 6868
Collected economic papers 956
Collected economic papers 3817
Collected economic papers 9768
Collected scientific 9870
Collected scientific papers 2484
The collected works 7318
The collected works of Dugald Stewart 7049
The collected writings 5878
The collected writings of John Maynard Keynes 9978

Short Title Index 749

Collection complete de tous les ouvrages 4560
Collection de lois maritimes 5773
Collection de mémoires 5774
Collection complète des lois 5963
Collection des principaux économistes 5775
A collection of conflicting opinions 5771
A collection of interesting 5772
A collection of papers relating to the East India 4127
A collection of public acts 5776
Collection of scarce 4757
A collection of scarce and valuable treatises 3993
A collection of tracts 4128
A collection of treatises 4391
Collections relative to systematic relief 5934
Le collectivisme 8185
Collectivist economic planning 9224
The Collier quick and easy guide 1311
The Collier quick and easy Guide 3046
Colonial policy 6150
Les colonies francaises 8728
La colonisation scientifique 7537
Commentaries on the law of bailments 7061
Commentarie sul l'esprit des loix 7142
Commentaries on the law of partnership 7062
Commentaries on the laws of Scotland 5557
Commentarii peckii 4132
Commerce and manufactures 6710
The commerce and navigation 7194
Le commerce au dix-neuvième 6544
Le commerce de la Hollande 4133
Commerce defended 6512

Le commerce et le gouvernement 5792
The commerce of nations 7439
Commercial and political atlas 6703
The commercial crises 8081
Commercial crisis 6017, 6018
Commercial geography 8335
The commercial policy 6151
The commercial restraints 8079
The commercial revolution 5273
Commercial statistics 6432
Il commercio internazionale 8663
The common law of Kent 6870
The commons complaint 4761
Commons on institutional 8973
Common-good 4785
Common sense economics 1499
Common-sense economics 2199
The common sense of political 9802
Communal verfassung- und verwaltungsgerichte 7919
Communism 9444
Communism and socialism 8802
Communist international 9643
The communist manifesto 9374, 9375
The communist manifesto 9574
The communistic societies 8371
The communistic societies 9463
Communistiche idealstaaten 7891
The Communists states 2596
Company law 7450
A comparaison de l'impot de France 4134
A comparative history of the increase and decrease 4718
A comparative view of the mortality 5585
A comparison between the proposals of the bank 4135
A comparison of the social 7209
Compendio di economia politica 1478
A compendious 4345
A compendious 4760
A compendious history of the taxes of France 4136
Compendium der national-ökonomisch 8470
Compendium of English and

foreign funds 7843
A compendium of the corn trade 4237
Compendium of the finances 5767
A compendium of the laws passed 5785
Compendium of transportation 7658
Competitive and social value 3260
A complete analysis of Adam Smith 7310
A complete collection of the treaties 6210
A complete concordance 2435
A complete digest of the theory 7234
A complete investigation of Mr. Eden's treaty 5786
A complete system of bookkeeping 5614
A complete view of the British customs 4160
Complete works 4300
Comprehensive economics 1750
A comprehensive history of the woollen 5584
A comprehensive treatise of the iron trade 6965
Comprimidos economicos 1282
Compte rendu au Roi 4559
Computer simulation experiments 3776
Un comune fondamento razionale 920
Conceitos de valor e preço 3409
The concept of economic surplus 9810
The concept of ethics 215
The concept of ethics 4950
The concept of marginal rent 8052
The concept of marginal rent 9717
The concept of normal price 3289
The concept of value 3161
La conception de l'economie nationale 5252
Les conceptions economiques 2654

Conceptions of economy 4907
Concepto de utilidad 3318
Conceptos fundamentales 1783
Concepts and cases 2241
Conceptual foundations 1357
Il concetto di utilità 9780
La concorrenza agraria 8539
The condition of labor 7893
Condition of the working 9168
Les conditions du travail 7387
The connexion of the Roman 4117
Conferences on the public debts 4586
Confessions of an economic heretic 2403
Conflicting tendencies in Indian 2807
Conflicts in policy 841
The conflicts of capital 8068
Le conflit des doctrines 70
Le conflit historique entre la loi des débouchés 505
Congres international des accidents 7964
La conquete portugaise 5207
The consequences of trade 4139
Considerations for enabling the South-Sea company 4140
Considérations générales sur l'évaluation 5810
Considérations historiques 6445
Considérations mathématique 7833
Considerations of commerce 5708
Considerations of the present exorbitant price 4530
Considerations on Indian 4038
Considerations on money 4141
Considerations on political 7018
Considerations on roads 4145
Considerations on several proposals 4146
Considerations on taxes 4147
Considerations on the acts of Parliament 4142
Considerations on the alarming increase 7250
Considerations on the annual million bill 5805
Considerations on the corn laws 5808
Considerations on the currency

Short Title Index 751

6078
Considerations on the East-India 5809
Considerations on the expediency of admitting representatives 4143
Considerations on the importation 5811
Considerations on the inexpediency 6281
Considerations on the making of bar iron 4615
Considerations on the policy of entails 4166
Considerations on the poor 5871
Considerations on the present 7175
Considerations on the present state 4144
Considerations on the present state 6739
Considerations on the proposal for reducing the interest 3997
Considerations on the propriety of the bank 5813
Considerations on the protection 6286
Considerations on the rate of interest 7067
Considerations on the state of currency 6354
Considerations on the state of the currency 7125
Considerations on the trade 4148
Considerations on the value 5920
Considerations sur l'accumulation 5617
Considérations sur l'admission des navires neutres 5806
Considérations sur la liberté 5568
Considérations sur la marche des idées 9679
Considérations sur la nature du revenu 7055
Considérations sur la Pêche de la Baleine 5812
Considérations sur le causes de la grandeur 5807
Considerations sur le célibat 6709
Considérations sur le commerce 4109
Considerations sur le commerce 4150
Considérations sur le commerce 4122
Considérations sur les chemins 5829
Considérations sur les contributions 6920
Considérations sur les droits reciproques 7085
Considérations sur les effets de l'impôt 5697
Considérations sur les enfans-trouvés 5721
Considérations sur les finances d'Espagne 4282
Considerations sur les finances 6156
Considérations sur les machines 6097
Considérations sur les monnaies 4525
Considérations sur les richesses 6970
Considérations sur les tendance actuelles 217
Considérations sur l'organisation sociale 6539
Considérations sur quelques parties 5698
Considerations upon commissions of bankrupts 4151
Considerations upon the agriculture 7165
Considerations upon the East-India trade 4152
Considerazioni sin principii fondamentali 3379
Considerazioni sulla moneta 8440
Le consolateur 5380
The constitution of friendly 5548
The constitution of friendly societies 5814
The constitution of the office of land credit 4104
Constitutional law 7670
The constitutional right of the

legislature 4153
Consuetudo vel lex mercatoria 4483
Consulta sulla reforma 4836
Consulat de la mer 5815
The consumer in the history 5338
Consumer's cooperation 2657
Consumers' demand 3106
Consumer's surplus 3332
Consumo e produzione 1746
The consumption of wealth 8401
The contained economy 5099
Contareni de re frumentaria 4154
Contemporary economic 753
Contemporary economic problems 803
Contemporary economic problems 2177
Contemporary economic systems 393
Contemporary economic thought 310
Contemporary economics 1557
Contemporary economics 2095
Contemporary economics 2109
Contemporary economics 2139
Contemporary English and American theories 3035
A contemporary guide 789
Contemporary monetary theory 10065
Contemporary problems 2180
Contemporary Soviet economics 9652
Contemporary theorizing 74
The contemporary world 58
The content of economics 1548
Le contenu de la courbe keynesienne 9935
Contes sur l'économie politique 6472
Continental farming 8065
Contract consider'd 3987
Les contradictions 9892
The contrast 5816
Contribution a l'etude de la productivite 5400

Contribution à l'étude des idées politiques 2950
Contribution à une histoire 532
A contribution to demand analysis 3383
The contribution of economists to policy 3490
A contribution to the bibliography of the bank 8657
A contribution to the critique of political 9376
Contribution to the prehistory of Mongolia 5032
A contribution to the theory of competitive prices 3162
The contributions of Lord Overstone 2400
Contributions of survey methods 3756
Contributions to the wages 7263
Contributo alla teoria della politica economica 506
Il controllo sociale 480
Il controllo sociale 1848
Controversy between 'quantity theory' 3539
Constancy of the marginal 9871
Conversations on political 6698
Conversations on political-economy 6460
Conversations on principal subjects 7801
Conversations sur le commerce 6529
Dr. Thomas Cooper 2534
Co-operation in a Western city 8614
Cooperation in New England 7463
Coopération ouvrière 7385
Co-operative agriculture 8392
The co-operative commonwealth 7957
The co-operative movement 8057
The co-operative movement 8452
Co-operative production 8104
La cooperazione in Italia 8472
The co-ordinates of institutionalism 8909
Corn and cattle 8510

Short Title Index 753

Corn and currency 6133
Corn Laws 5830, 5831
Corn, trade, wages 5702
The corporate economy 888
The corporation problem 7667
Les corporations 7503
Les corporations d'arts 8715
Corporations ouvrières 7865
Correspondance philosophique 5994
The correspondence of Jefferson 5361
The correspondence of John Sinclair 6994
Il corso del pensiero economico 503
Corso di diritto commerciale 8726
Corso di economia politica 1172
Corso di economia politica 1713
Corso di economia pura 2072
Corso di politica economica 1211
Corso di storia delle dottrine economiche 210
Cost and choice 75
Cost and its significance 3171
Cost and production 2080
Cost curves 9880
Cost functions and progress 3394
Cost of production 3290
Cotton manufacture 7179
Cotton trade of Great Britain 7806
Le corporazioni d'arti 7374
The country banker 8475
Coup d'oeil sur la force 5749
Coup d'oeil sur les assurances 5835
Coup d'oeil sur les debuts 7559
Coup d'oeil sur l'Isle de Java 5836
La courbe d'offre 3302
T. Antonio Agostino Cournot 9703
Antoine Augustin Cournot 9765
Cournot and mathematical 9700

Cournot nella economia 9658
A. Cournot's researches 3619
Cours analytique 8109
Cours complet d'agriculture 6098
Cours complet d'économie politique 6938
Cours d'analyse économique 22
Cours d'économie politique 240
Cours d'economie politique 562
Cours d'économie politique 1120
Cours d'économie politique 1273
Cours d'économie politique 1285, 1286, 1291
Cours d'économie politique 1409
Cours d'économie politique 1741
Cours d'économie politique 1989
Cours d'économie politique 5728, 5729
Cours d'économie politique 6530
Cours d'économie politique 6892
Cours d'économie politique 6958
Cours d'économie politique 7056
Cours d'économie politique 9752
Cours d'économie industrielle 8695
Cours d'économie rurale 8176
Cours de documentation 3636
Cours de droit commercial 5845
Cours de philosophie positive 5787
Cours de structures 1739
Cours de théorie économique 141
Cours de théorie économique 1112
Cours d'histoire des doctrines économiques 337
Cours d'histoire de la pensée 23
Cours d'histoire de la pensée économique 25
Cours d'histoire de la pensée économique 164

Cours d'histoire des doctrines economiques 246
Cours d'histoire des doctrines economiques 521
Cours d'histoire des doctrines economiques 679
Cours d'histoire des faits économiques 331
Cours d'histoire des faits économoqies contemporains 519
Cours d'histoire des institutions 5020
Cours d'histoire des institutions publiques 5021
Cours de l'économie politique 8716
A course in applied economics 1184
Coûts sociaux 3268
Coûts sociaux 9721
Conrad Cramer-Frey 2892
Crédit agricole 7789
Le crédit et les finances 5611
Crédit foncier 7914
Die credit-institut auf actien 8012
Crédit mobilier of America 7690
Credit pernicious 6890
The credit system of France 5689
Le crédit territorial 8552
Il credito e l'agricoltura 7888
Il credito fondiario 7379
Il credito popolare 8231
Creditwesen in Frankreich 6246
Crime and its causes 8324
Le crise de la pensee 756
La crise de la pensée économique 165
La crise économique 7535
La crise et les doctrines 2644
La crise internationale 8300
Crises commerciales 8112
La crisis de la economia liberal 515
A critical dissertation 3114
A critical examination 8220
Critical examination 8353

A critical inquiry 4159
A critical study of Gandhian 2816
The critics of Keynesian 9957
A critique 9859
Critique of Hegel's Philosophy of right 9377
Critique of political 9379
Critique of the Gotha 9378
A critique of welfare 1698
A critique of world-wide econometric forecasting 3711
Croce y la naturaleza 3860
Croissance et progrès a l'originedes societes 247
The crown colonies 8553
Robinson Crusoe's money 8775
La cuase des esclaves nègres 5701
Cuba 2601
La cuestion económica 577
La cuestión social 3089
Cui bono 4812
Culture change 5097
William Cunningham 2491
Curiosities of early economic literature 599
Currency and banking 8457
Currency and finance 9691
The currency and the country 6256
Currency manipulation 5135
Current economic indicators 3886
Current economic problems 793
Current economic problems 805
Current economic thought 2614
Current introductory economics 1448
Currents in modern 2178
Curso de economía política 1074
Curso de economía política 1754
Curso de economía política 1922
Curso de economía política 2023
Curso de economía política 2042
Curso de economía política 5685
Curso de economía política 6046
Curso general de economica 1403
Cursus die national- und socialökonomie 7777
Curve crescenti di ofelimita 3401
Cyclopaedia of political science

Short Title Index

8149

Da cantillon a Pareto 702
Dal mercantilismo 5191
Dall'economia capitalistica 9066
Danische wirtschaftsgeschichte 2606
Dansk økonomstat 1966 2365
Dark ages 8253
Darstellung der in deutschland 8797
Darstellung der wirtschaftlich 7945
Darwin, Marx, Wagner 9030
Darwin, Marx, and Wagner 9489
Darwinism in Thorstein Veblen's 8982
Dasar-dasar ilmu ekonomi sosialis 9217
Dati statistico da finanza 8279
Charles Davenant 5169
Davenport on the economics of Alfred Marshall 9868
The dawn of the British trade 7492
De budgetvergelijking 853
De Copernic a Stanislas Leszczynski 2937
De economie van de illusie 1500
De economische theorie 161
De economist Cobbenhagen 2361
De ekonomiska ideernas utveckling 3444
De ekonomiska studierna 3656
De foenore trapezitico 4705
De geldkringloop in de Keynesiaanse 10096
De geschiednis der staathuiskunde 6537
De grootboeken 8344
De historische school 7983
De invloed van de voorraden 3439
De jure maritimo et navili 4522
De Karl Marx à Léon Blum 9143
De la balance du commerce 5478
De la bienfiasance publique 5876
De la bienfaisance publique 6104
De la bourse 5766
De la charité dans ses rapports 5931
De la charité légale 5877
De la charité légale 6595
De la Chine 6152
De la création de la richesse 6951
De al démocratie 7118
De la dépense et du produit 6696
De la destruction 6204
De la disette 5556
De la disette 6341
De la division du travail social 7717
De la division du travail social 7790
De l'administration des finances 4561
De l'administration des finances 5390
De l'administration des finances 6599
De l'administration provinciale 6369
De la felicité publique 4177
De la félicité publique 5720
De l'agriculture en France 6572
De la législation 6362
De la liberté du commerce 5940
De la liberté du travail 5941
De la Ligue Hanséatique 6442
De la misere des classes labourieuses 5651
De la monnaie 5199
De la monnaie, du crédit 7772
De la nature de la richesse 2235
De la nature de la richesse 7216
De la nature des lois economiques 1044
De la politique 6194
De la politique nouvelle convenant 5799
De la propriété 7091
De la propriété 8167
De la propriété considerée 6879
De la propriété dans ses

rapports 6089
De la prostitution 6658
De la répartition des richesses 7187
De la richesses 8416
De la saisie des patimens neutres 4178
De la science des finances 6082
De la situation légale 8024
De las teorias ideologicas 1485
De l'assistance dans les campagnes 7620
De l'économie des anciens gouvernements 4626
De l'économie politique 6208
De l'économie politique moderne 6209
De l'économie publique 6846-6850
De leer der maatschappelijk economische 7
De l'emploi de l'argent 6438
De l'emprisonnement pour Dettes 5544
De l'esprit d'association 6340
De l'esprit des lois 4528
De l'esprit du gouvernement 4034
De l'état de France 5670
De l'exportation et de l'importation 5344
De l'impot du vingtième 4041
De l'impot du vingtieme 4903
De l'impot progressif 6302
De l'impot territorial 6348
De l'industrie en Belgique 5632
De l'industrie françoise 5718
De l'industrie moderne 8721
De l'influence du gouvernement 6897
De l'influence d'un grande revolution 6342
De l'ordre social 6370
De l'organisation et du regime 7719
De l'origine et de la filiation 7296
De l'origine et des fonctions des consuls 5615
De l'origine et des progrès 400
De l'origine et des progres 5345
De l'union Européenne 6366
De l'utilite 5955
De l'utilité 9869
De Republiek der verenigde Nederlanden 5318
De Marxistische accumulatietheorie 9538
De Mensuris 4222
The de moneta of Nicholas Oresme 5059
De monetis Italiae 3973
De Thomas More a Chaptal 868
De nationalekonomiska askadningarna 5274
De ontwikkeling der staathuisoudkunde 661
De ontwikkeling in het economisch denken 32
De richesse 6898
De servis et eorum apud veteres ministeriis 4604
De socialekonomiska grupperna 1649
De socialisten personen 8469
De successionibus apud anglos 4342
De taak der theoretische 3890
De valoris naturâ 6128
De vervolmaking van de maatschappij volgens 61
De werking van een volkshuishouding 1591
De wijsbegeerte von Karl Marx 9300
De zin van het economische 855
A decade of economic theory 3052
La décision commerciale face 3311
Decisive advantage 9331
The decline and fall of the English system 6644
Decus et Tutamen 4181
Deductive method 3698
A defence of an essay on the public debts 4183
Defence of economy 5561
A defence of English commodities 4776
Defence of joint stock banks 5883

Short Title Index

A defence of the Dutch 4182
A defence of the Perthshire resolutions 5884
A defence of the unanimous refusal of Mr. Wood's copper money 4186
A defence of the United company of merchants 4187
The defence of trade 4185
The defence of trade 4200
A defence of usury 5562
A defence of the observations on the assiento trade 4184
The definition of price 7845
Definitions 1732
Definitions of political 6446
La definizione dell'economia politica 8679
Dei delitti e delle Pene 4010
Dei prestiti pubblici 6504
Dei tributi e del governo politico 4053
Del commercio dei popoli neutrali 5784
Del commercio dei Romani 5260
Del commercio dei Romani 6494
Del comunismo 9212
Del hombre y su alienación 9431
Della attinenze 7644
Della decima e delle altre Gravezze 4192
Della giurisprudenza maritima 5886
Della influenza dell' amminstrazione pubblica 5574
Della legittima liberta 6651
Della miseria 7625
Della moneta 4314
Della scienza del ben vivere sociale 43
Della societa chiamata 5887
Della storia delle finanze 5888
Della storia delle finanze di Napoli 5575
Della storia economico-cívile 5576
Della teoria della popolazione 6505
Dell'economia 6891
Dell'economia politica 100
Dell'economia politica del medioevo 4917
Dell'economia pubblica 8305
Delle misure d'ogni genere 4114
Delle origini e dei progressi 2624
Delle reforme necessarie 8197
Delle teorie economiche 2847
Delle teorie economiche 7854
Delle università delle arti 7181
Dello stato presente della moneta 5907
Del metodo in economia sociale 8578
Del valore 7476
Demand analysis 3480
Demand and price analysis 3462
Demand for manufactured 3455
The demand for money 3225
The demand for money 3309
Demand functions 3137
Demand theory 3427
La demande d'encaisses monétaires 3151
La demande et le monopole 3165
La Demande et l'offre 3334
Democracia militante 17
A demonstration of the necessity 6787
Den danske nationaløkonomi 2604
Den ekonomiska doktrinhistoriens 449
Den økonomiske sammenhaeng 1065
Den'nya ekonomien' i Sverige 2974
Den'nya ekonomien' i Sverige 10014
Densité de la population 8710
Déontologie des affaires 1118
Depreciation of the paper currency 6355
Depression and inflation 3033
Derecho usual y nociones 1923
Derecho y economia 1953
Derecho y economia 2006
Deres egne ord 725
Des améliorations materielles 6684

757

Des armées dans leurs rapport 6685
Desarrollo y planeamiento 2595
Des banques de Naples 6866
Des banques publiques 5520
Des banques publiques 5573
Des canaux de navigation 5891
Des chemins de fer au point de vue du transport 7457
Des colonies agricoles 6262
Des différentes banques 5669
Des finances 7080
Des finances d'angleterre 6352
Des finances publiques 5671
Des grèves ouvriers 7718
Des impots dans leur rapport 5359
Des impots et des charges 5605
Des impots indirects 5453
Des institutions de crédit 6312
Des intérêts matériels 5730
Des lois du travail 7773
Des monnaies 4334
Des monts de piété 5587
Des moyens de soulager 6574
Des rapports de la morale 5536
Des rapports du droit 8520
Des rapports entre le droit 8110
Des systèmes d'économie politique 5202
Des systèmes de culture 6678
Des transports par chemins 7505
Description de l'ile d'Utopie 4547
Description du royaume de Siam 4193
Description geographique 4216
Description of industry 1035
A description of the canals 7073
Description of the character 5894
A descriptive account of the island of Jamaica 5553
Le détail de la France 4035
A detection of the state and situation 4196
The determinateness of the utility 3313
The determination of price 3210
A determination of the average depression 5625
Det fördömda kapitalet 9537
La dette publique belge 7869
Die deutsch hypothekenbanken 7925
Die deutsche arbeit 8517
Die deutsche arbeiterkolonien 7473
Deutsche finanzgesch 6265
Der deutsche fürstenstaat 4712
Die deutsche geschichtschreibur 2661
Das deutsche handwerk 8649
Die deutsche industrie 7816
Die deutsche kleingewerbe 8001
Das deutsche Manchestertum 2660
Deutsche münzverfassung 7016
Deutsche post- und telegraphie- gesetzgebung 7848
Die Deutsche reichspacketetpost 8073
Die Deutsche social-demokratie 8284
Deutsche volkswirthschaftslehre 8116
Die deutsche volkswirthschaftlich theorie 2705
Deutsche wirthschaftsgeschichte 8083
Der deutsche zollverein 7756
Deutsches bürgerthum 8141
Deutsches wirthschaftsleben 8153
Deutschland pol. mater 5581
Deutschland und der sozialis- mus 7426
Deutschlands aussereuropäische handel 7751
Deutschlands kolonien 8706
Developing of American colonies 5201
Development and society 928

Development and underdevelopment 228
The development and use of the market concept 3482
Development et sous-developpement 229
Development of economic analysis 547
The development of economic doctrine 264
Development of economic ideas in India 2814
The development of economic thought 488
The development of economic thought 623
The development of economic thought 986
The development of economics 62
The development of economics 595
The development of economics 2778
The development of economics in British 2787
The development of English thought 2770
The development of English thought 8402
The development of Keynes' 9942
The development of social theory 5024
The development of Socialist Yugoslavia 3098
Development of transportation 8518
The development of utility 3430
The development of utility 9776
Le developpement de la pensee economique 489
Développement et défense 4156
Le développement intellectuel 8173
Dhanabijnana pariciti 1985
Dhanasāstra purōgati jivacarit-rannalilūte 518
Diagnose und prognose 3502
Dialéctica, economía 9565
Dialectical materialism 9642
Dialectics, the logic of Marxism 9259

Die dialektik in Marx' Kapital 9521
Dialektika konkretniho 858
Dialektika konkrétniho 1642
Dialektika vyrobnich 2107
Die dialektische methode 9522
Dialektische oder rationale 9899
Dialogue sur le système social 9469
Dialogues entre M. Marquis de la Roquemaure 5200
The dialogues of Plato 5007
Dialogues sur le commerce 4313
The diaries and correspondence of George Rose 6888
Diatribe de assecurationibus 4413
Diccionario bibliographico 6991
Diccionario de Hacienda 5477
Diccionario geographico-historico 5456
Diccionario geographico-historico 5899
Dictionnaire 5827
Dictionnarie 5895
Dictionnaire analytique 6083
Dictionnaire de l'administration francaise 5901
Dictionnaire des finances 4197
Dictionnaire des finances 7746
Dictionnaire des finances 8565
Dictionnaire du commerce 5902
Dictionnaire économique 4113
Dictionnaire général 7747
A dictionary, geographical 6416
A dictionary of arts 7180
Dictionnaire législatif 8394
Dictionnaire universel 6935
Dictionnaire universel des poids 5921
Dictionnaire universel du commerce 4198
Dictionary of political 7744, 7745
A dictionary of political 8242
Dictionary of political 8397
A dictionary of scholastic 5141
Dictionary of statistics 8330

A dictionary, practical 6417
Di un recente contributo 576
Didaktika ekonomických předmětu 3647
Diez lecciones de economia 1095
The different meanings of cost 3245
The difficulty of imputation 3723
A digest of the existing commercial regulations 5906
Digest of the stamp duties 7956
Dimension du marché et optimum de production 1098
Dimensions de l'homme et science economique 1432
Din økonomi og samfundets 926
Dinamica dell'occupazione 1946
Directorio nacional 2364
Directorio nacional 2914
Direction generale des etudes 2557
Directions for the improvement of barren 4653
Discorsi e realzione sulle monete 4201
Discorso economico scritto 3992
Discorso sopra lemonete 4706
Discours et leçons sur l'industrie 5946
Discours pour et contre la réduction 4337
Discours sur la situation actuelle 6367
A discourse 4271
A discourse concerning coining 3996
A discourse concerning the currency 4202
A discourse concerning the currencies 4210
A discourse of coin 4834
A discourse of taxes 4592
A discourse of the fishery 4415
A discourse of the general notions of money 4203
A discourse of trade 3995

A discourse of trade 4613
A discourse of trade from England 4548
A discourse on the conduct of the government 4406
A discourse on the late funds of the million-act 4049
A discourse on the Roman foot 4331
A discourse on trade 4084
A discourse on trade 4125
A discourse shewing the many advantages 4161
A discourse touching provision 4343
A discourse upon usurie 4861
A discourse upon usury 4204
Discourses on the publick reven 4171
Discourses upon trade 4567
Discurso economico politico 5682
Discurso preliminar sobre la marina 4073
Discurso sobre el fomento 4206
Discurso sobre la economia politica 6581
Discurso sobre la educacion popular 4074
Discurso sobre la educacion popular 4205
Discurso subre el fomento 4075
Discursos creticos sobre las leyes 4097
Discursus legales de commercio 4088
Discussion on papers 9139
Discussioni ed indagini 1575
Les discussions sur l'ordre naturel 5411
Il disegno di legge sulla emigrazione 8568
Die diskussion um die arbeitswerttheorie 3303
The dismal science 7754
Dispersion of gloomy apprehensions 6250
Disquisitio de oeconomie politique 7173
Dissertacion sobre al aprecio 5481

Short Title Index 761

Dissertatio de conjunctione jurisprudentiae atque 4771
Dissertation concerning the high roads 4207
Dissertation concerning the landed 6896
A dissertation on commerce 5155
A dissertation on the numbers of mankind 4850
A dissertation on the poor laws 7139
A dissertation on the theory 5965
Dissertation sur les droits des métropoles Grecques 4042
Dissertation sur l'état du commerce 4121
Dissertation sur l'état du commerce en France 4080
Dissertation sur l'influence des loix maritimes 5909
Dissertations 6517
Dissertations on government 6645
Dissertations sur l'effet que produit le prix 4123
Dissertazione sopra il commercio 4014
Distilled spirituous liquors 4208
Distinée sociale 5800
Distributed lags and demand 3367
Distribution and exchange 3741
Distribution and exchange 9838
The distribution of income 8634
The distribution of products 7400
Distribution of wealth 7630
The distribution of wealth 7673
Distribution of wealth 8924
The distribution of wealth 9677
Distributionsekonomi 2191
Divers mémoires sur le commerce 4283
Divisions in economic theory 3559

Dizionnario della economia politica 5599
Dizzionario universale ragionata 5910
Do estudo e da evolucao 2947
Do método em economia politica 3670
La doctrina economica 3282
Doctrina economica a fiziocratilor 463
La doctrina marxista 9034
Doctrina numorum veterum 5966
Las doctrinas economicas 520
Las doctrinas economicas 2459
Doctrinas ecónomicas 2542
La doctrine de l'église 4994
La doctrine économique de Saint-Simon 9220
The doctrine of annuities 4725
The doctrine of comparative 3346
The doctrine of economic maturity 9962
The doctrine of equivalents 5854
The doctrine of gold 4734
Les doctrines economique 8417
Doctrines economiques 106
Les doctrines economiques 277
Les doctrines économiques 322
Les doctrines economiques 392
Les doctrines économiques 2650
Les doctrines économiques de Colbert 5256
La documentation en science 3597
Documents economiques 835
Documents franc. 5889
Does mathematical analysis 3132
Does protection protect 7962
Dogmenhistorische 592
Dokapitalisticheskie sposoby proizvodstva 372
Doktrinen der wirtschaftswissenschaft 552
Dol mercantilismo al corporativismo fascista 73
Domesday book 5912
Domesday book 7491
Domesday studies 7760
Domesday studies 7813

Domestic and financial 5641
Los dos valores de la materia 1805
La dottrina di S. Antoninoddi Firenze 4924
Le dottrine di Ricardo 2855
Le dottrine economiche di F. Quesnay 5363
Dottrine monetaire 7660
Doutes proposés aux philosophes 4475
Doveri della proprietà 8326
Die drei nationalokonomien 616
Die drei nationalökonomien 2123
Droit au travail 5925
Le droit et les faits 7456
Droit et societe dans la Grece ancienne 4959
Droit maritime de l'Europe 5924
Le droit naturel 5404
Droit public ou gouvernement 4590
Društveno-ekonomsko obrazovanje 9485
Du change et de la liberté 8113
Du commerce des grains 6384
Du commerce français 5929
Du contrat d'apprentissage 8006
Du crédit 5744
Du crédit 5826
Du crédit public 5495
Du crédit public 6157
Du crédit public 6921
Du gouvernement considéré 6039
Du gouvernement des finances 6545
Du marchand de grains 5329
Du pauperisme 5716
Du pauperisme en France 6523
Pierre Samuel Du Pont de Nemours 5423
Du Pont de Nemours 8576
Dupont de Nemours et la question 5388
Du Pont de Nemours et l'ecole physiocratique 5419
Du privilége de la banque 6030

Du problème de la misère 6553
Du progrès de l'industrie 6105
Du régime des travaux publics 7866
Du rétablissement del'Impot 4033
Du revenu foncier 6048
Du rôle de l'état 8111
Du rôle de l'état 8730
Du social contrat 4687
Du système d'impôt fondé 6911
Du système sociale 6365
Du système social 6743
Herr Eugen Dühring's revolution 9170
Herr Eugen Dührings umwalzung 7817
Duncombe's free banking 5936
Duplicità dei limiti 905
Dutch home labour colonies 8788
The dynamic law of wages 3560
Dynamics of social change 9549
Dynamique économique 1413
Dynamique et structures 1815
Die dynamische geld- und kredit-lehre 5213
Dyskusji o prawie wartości 3199
Dziejeogospodarsze Europy 2620

Early American policy 3049
Early British economics 2723
Early cardinal utility 3336
Early cardinal utility 9738
Early developments in mathematical 3864
Early economic thought 909
The early history 7396
The early history of deposit 5126
The early history of land-holding 8537
The early history of political 3053
Early texts 9380
Early writings 9381
East and West India sugar 6415
The East India gazetteer 6177
The East-India-Trade 4220

Short Title Index 763

The Eastern question 9382
Easy lessons on money 7239
Eclaircissements demandes 4000
L'école autrichienne 9699
L'ecole de Lausanne 931
L'école de Lausanne 9749
L'ecole economique francaise 2632
L'école nouvelle 7904
L'ecole saint-simonienne 9640
Econometric analysis 3197
Econometric analysis 3223
Econometrica 3598
Econometrica journal 3629
Econometrics 3867
Econometrics in economics 3557
Econometrics, statistics 3732
L'économétrie 3868
Economia 1675
L'economia a servizio 2220
La economia chilena 9090
Economia (circulação) 771
La economia clásica 1277
L'economia come scienza 7645
Economia dei popoli 8152
La economia del futuro 1758
L'economia dell'agricultura 7472
Economia dello scambio 1849
Economia di mercato 1064
Economia e diritto nello 56
Economia e morale 2121
La economia en el pensamiento venezolano 3090
Economia e politica di atene attraverso Aristofane 5050
La economia esposta 7582
Economia generale 2215
Economia liberale 559
L'economia moderna 9907
Economia nacional 433
Economia nacional 2951
Economia, organizarea 9083
Economia politica 271
Economia politica 621
Economia politica 1058
Economia politica 1082
Economia politica 1186
Economia politica 1224
Economia politica 1396
Economia politica 1446

Economia politica 1483
Economia politica 1683
Economia politica 1710
Economia politica 1786
Economia politica 1824
Economia politica 1826
Economia politica 2007
Economia politica 2045, 2046
Economia politica 2221
Economia politica 2560
L'economia politica 6506
L'economia politica 7921
Economia politica 8447
Economia politica 8548
Economia politica contemporanea 1484
Economia politica del Medio Evo 5742
L'économia politica moderna 54
L'economia politica nella spegna 136
Economia politica y lucha social 2
Economia social 1048
Economia social teorica 1230
Economia sperimentale 3792
La economia y sus fundamentos 1921
Economic activity analysis 912
Economic activity analysis 3768
Economic analysis 1138
Economic analysis 1157
Economic analysis 1162
Economic analysis 1226
Economic analysis 1289
Economic analysis 1402
Economic analysis 1592
Economic analysis 1687
Economic analysis 1737
Economic analysis 2156
Economic analysis 2275
Economic analysis 3609
Economic analysis 3908
Economic analysis for engineering 1100
An economic analysis of unemployment 9979
Economic and industrial life 2810
Economic and philosophic manuscripts 9383
The economic and political

essays 3075
Economic and social history 5064
Economic and social history 8769
Economic and social history of the middle ages 5113
Economic annals 8635
Economic anthropology 5019
The economic aspects 2543
Economic aspects of industry 1509
The economic basis of protection 8403
Economic behavior 8908
Economic change 863
Economic commentaries 960
La economic comunitaria 423
Economic concepts 3523
The economic consequences 9980, 9981
The economic consequences 10100
Economic crumbs 7577
Economic cycles 3359
Economic cycles 8319
Economic dialogues in ancient China 5012
Economic doctrines 167
Economic doctrines 484
Economic doctrines 710
The economic doctrines of John Gray 2417
The economic doctrines of John Maynard Keynes 10039
The economic doctrines of Karl Marx 9271
Economic dynamics 1124
Economic ecology 3240
Economic education 3883
Economic essays 732
Economic essays 761
Economic essays 763-766
Economic essays 810
Economic essays 824
Economic essays 9718
Economic essentials 2213
Economic fabric of society 127
Economic fictions 145
Economic fluctuations 3552
Economic forces 1810
Economic foundations of

Economic Thought and Analysis Islam, 2839
Economic growth 864
Economic heresies 553
Economic history 8893
Economic history 9982
Economic history, Czechslovak 2603
The economic history of ancient India 5013
The economic history of England 5247
An economic history of Europe 2609
An economic history of Europe 2613
Economic history of Rome 5110
An economic history of Russia 2959
An economic history of the British 2724
Economic ideas 695
Economic ideas of Tiruvalluvar 2823
The economic impact 783
Economic in zestien bladzijden 1476
Economic indicators 3879
Economic inquiry in Australia 2548
Economic institutions 8937
Economic institutions 8920
Economic institutions 8990
The economic interpretation 596
The economic interpretation 600
The economic interpretation 8528
The economic interpretation of history 9548
Economic issues 798
Economic issues 892
The Economic journal 9983
Economic liberalism 262
The economic library 2537
The economic library of Jacob H. Hollander 2431
Economic life in Greece's golden 4902
The economic life in Northern India 4967
The economic life of primitive 4986

Short Title Index 765

The economic life of the ancient 5022
The economic life of the ancient 5118
The economic literature of Latin America 2910
Economic man in relation 490
Economic means and social ends 3599
The economic mind 3048
Economic models 3516
Economic models, estimation 3600
Economic moralism 977
Economic motives 173
Economic motives 3586
The economic order 1555
The economic organization 1627
Economic organisation 1780
The economic organization 3291
The economic organization 7397
The economic outlook 88
The economic pattern 1991
Economic performance 2218
Economic philosophy 554
The economic philosophy of Mahatma Gandhi 2815
The economic point of view 846
Economic policy 788
Economic policy 797
Economic policy 2187
Economic policy 10074
The economic policy of Colbert 5293
Economic policies and practices 3881
Economic politica 1434
Economic politique 1517
Economic position of English laborer 7835
Economic principles 983, 984
Economic principles 1404
Economic principles 1415
Economic principles 1624
Economic principles 1837
Economic principles 1873
Economic principles 1888
Economic principles 1890

Economic principles 2214
The economic principles of the Confucian 2572
The economic principles of Confucius 2569
The economic problem 1523
The economic problem 1529
The economic problem 1952
The economic problem 3653
Economic problems 776
Economic problems 860
Economic problems 1002
Economic problems 3909
Economic problems after the war 7706
Economic problems in Europe 945
Economic problems of Asia 834
Economic problems of Latin America 2909
Economic problems of modern India 2821
Economic problems of national defense 989
Economic problems of war 990
Economic problems of war 1027
The economic process 1203
The economic process 1305
Economic processes 1126
Economic processes 1358, 1359
Economic progress 830
Economic progress 9946
Economic psychology 3292
Economic rationality 3015
Economic reconstruction 807
Economic research 9905
Economic reasoning 731
Economic resources 3761
Economic romanticism 2522
Economic romanticism 2554
Economic science 3780
Economic science 3805
The economic societies 5420
Economic society 1268
Economic stability 1023
Economic stagnation 10084
Economic strategy 2809
Economic structure 5114
Economic structure of the Yuan 5103
Economic studies 709
Economic studies 7415

Economic survey methods 3722
An economic survey of ancient Rome 4951
An economic survey of ancient Rome 5111
Economic synthesis 1570
The economic synthesis 3733
The economic system 1653
The economic system 2260
The economic system 2267
Economic system analysis 3510
Economic system and public policy 3844
The economic system in a socialist state 276
Economic theories of international politics 964
The economic theories of John Craig 2348
Economic theory 1080
Economic theory 1125
Economic theory 1588
Economic theory 1682
The economic theory 1748
Economic theory 1839
Economic theory 1972
Economic theory 1997
Economic theory 2317
Economic theory 3515
Economic theory 3563
Economic theory 3917
Economic theory among the Greeks 5096
Economic theory and history of Japan 2876
Economic theory and measurement 3569
Economic theory as a language 3583
Economic theory; equilibrium 1199
Economic theory in retrospect 45
Economic theory in review 767
Economic theory misplaced 3632
The economic theory of a Socialist economy 30
The economic theory of a socialist economy 1128
Economic theory of cooperation 196

The economic theory of cost 3876
The economic theory of George Bernard Shaw 2421
The economic theory of the leisure 9085
The economic theory of the leisure class 80
Economic thinking 2626
Economic thinking in India 2818
Economic thought 794
Economic thought 1427
Economic thought 8983
Economic thought 10024
Economic thought and its application 2820
Economic thought and language 220
Economic thought and policy 419
Economic thought and the Irish 2834
Economic thought in ancient China 2578
Economic thought in the encyclopédie 5440
Economic thought in the Soviet Union 2997
Economic thought; Mohandas Karamchand Gandhi 2819
The economic thought of Franklin D. Roosevelt 3056
Economic thought of Mahatma Gandhi 2826
The economic thought of Monsignor John A. Ryan 2393
Economic tracts 749
Economic tracts for the times 128
Economic voor iedereen 2285
Economic writings 4993
The economic writings of Francis Homer 2382
The economic writings of Sir William Petty 2458
Economical enquiries 6243
Economics 1051
Economics 1059
Economics 1132
Economics 1137
Economics 1221
Economics 1236

Short Title Index 767

Economics 1261, 1264
Economics 1338
Economics 1464
Economics 1492
Economics 1568
Economics 1598
Economics 1626
Economics 1641
Economics 1696
Economics 1936
Economics 1993
Economics 2066
Economics 2211
Economics 2270
Economics 2745
Economics 3626
Economics 3706
Economics 7740
Economics 7977
Economics 8670
Economics 10062
Economics; an analysis 1504
Economics: an analytical 1309
Economics: an analytical 1515
Economics, an introduction 1087
Economics: an introduction 1141
Economics; an introduction 1312
Economics; an introduction 1811
Economics: an introduction 2204
Economics; an introductory 1625
Economics, an introductory 2037
Economics; an introductory 2041
Economics an introductory 2134
Economics: analysis 1606
Economics; analysis 2133
Economics and American industry 2266
Economics and economic polity 9916
Economics and ethics 434
Economics and ideology 895
Economics and industrial 2137
Economics and its significance 436

Economics and its significance 1752
Economics and its significance 3745
Economics and liberalism 999
Economics and life 105
Economics and man 1438
Economics and modern psychology 3564
Economics and policy 10107
Economics and politics 8007
Economics and social reform 283
Economics and sociology 9855
Economics and the art of controversy 231
Economics and the art of controversy 790
Economics and the art of controversy 3634
Economics and the idea 827
Economics and the idea of 'Jus naturale' 5428
Economics and the idea of mankind 3667
Economics and the modern world 1032
Economics and the public 982
Economics and the public 1460
Economics and you 1553
Economics as a field of research 3910
Economics as a liberal education 3521
Economics as a science 700
Economics as a science 1158
Economics as a science 3620
Economics as a science 3789
Economics as on and to policy 86
Economics at work 1611
Economics, business 829
Economics, business 3677
Economics, by ICS staff 1566
Economics by Stigum 2147
Economics, commerce 2741
Economics, 1897-1917 2964
Economics: experience 1809
Economics: fact and theory 2106
Economics for Canadians 1191
Economics for engineers 1060
Economics for everyone 1296

Economics for living 2128
Economics for managers 1241
Economics for modern living 1393
Economics for our times 2112
Economics for pleasure 2074
Economics for secondary schools 1999
Economics for the citizen 1889
Economics for the people 7552
Economics for the power age 1853
Economics for the student 1297
Economics for today 2063
Economics for workers 1029
Economics for you and me 2207
Economics; ideas and men 53
Economics in a free society 1562
Economics in a unified 8974
Economics in action 886
Economics in action 1164
Economics in action 1209
Economics in everyday life 1469
Economics in general education 837
Economics in Kautilya 2828
Economics in modern Sweden 2975
Economics in one lesson 1527
Economics in primitive 5116
Economics in the modern 2078
Economics in the secondary school 3655
Economics in the United States 3084
Economics: its nature 2277
Economics: its principles 2239
Economics made simple 2103
Economics: mainstream readings 899
Economics: measurement 2129
Economics, 458, 1904-1929
The economics of African 2540

Economic Thought and Analysis

The economics of Alfred Marshall 9812
The economics of ancient Greece 5041
The economics of Carl Menger 9777
The economics of collective 1276
The economics of collective 8925
Economics of consumption 2231
The economics of distribution 8041
Economics of employment 1686
The economics of employment 5212
The economics of enterprise 1307
Economics of enterprise 3172
The economics of full employment 933
The economics of full employment 9891
The economics of Heinrich Pesch 2444
The economics of illusion 801
The economics of imperfect 9769
The economics of imperfect competition 3407
The economics of industry 9852
Economics of Islam 2836
The economics of John Maynard Keynes 9920
The economics of knowledge 3528
Economics of modern industry 1416
The economics of open price 3330
The economics of physiocracy 5376
The economics of public issues 927
The economics of Simon Nelson Patten 2343
The economics of Sir James Steuart 5291
The economics of Sir James Stuart 2492

The economics of socialism 2114
Economics of socialism 9252
Economics of the free society 2014
The economics of the product-saturated 3364
The economics of welfare 525
The economics of welfare 1948
Economics of W. S. Jevons 9690
Economics: principles 1116
Economics: principles 1185, 1339
Economics: principles 1347
Economics: principles 1353, 1355
Economics: principles 1450
Economics: principles 1612
Economics: principles 1834
Economics: principles 2117
Economics: principles and 1165
Economics: principles of income 1522
The economics profession 2533
Economics; the science 2138
Economics, the science of scarcity 1631
Economics; theory 2203
Economics: trends and issues 845
Economics: waiting for Godot 923
Economicsti greci e romani 5120
Economie 1859
Economie bourgeoise 549
L'économie distributive 760
L'économie du XXe siècle 516
L'économie du XXe siècle 1930
Economie, een geesteswetenschap 1188
L'economie et la morale 198
Economie et société 1931
Economie in theorie 1070
Economie mathématique 9667
Economie mathématique 9753
Economie politica 1352
L'economie politique 130
Economie politique 218

L'economie politique 583
Economie politique 1109
Economie politique 1152
Economie politique 1424
Economie politique 1580
Economie politique 1648
Economie politique 1892, 1893
Economie politique 2636
L'economie politique 4905
Economie politique 5926
Economie politique 5995
Economie politique 6247
Economie politique 6948
Economie politique 7190
L'économie politique 7619
Economie politique avant les physiocrates 317
Economie politique des Athéniens 5603
Economie politique des Romains 5958, 5959
Economie politique des Romains 5967
L'Economie politique du rentier 3139
L'Economie politique du rentier 9674
Economie politique et politique economique 16
Economie politique et progrès 208
Economie politique et progres 5350
Economie politique et sociale 97
Economie politique et sociale 3147
Economie politique 1488-1490
L'économie politique jugee 2736
L'²economie politique perdue 652
L'economie rurale 4938
L'economie sociale 4906
Economie sociale 6686
Economie sociale 8566
L'economique 5144
L'Economique, techniques, 2038
Les économiques 5381
L'économique en tant que science 701
Economiques 184, 1745
Economis, science 1816
Economische rekenvormen 3453

Economische stelsels 1518
Economische theorie en economische politiek 203
Economische wetenschap 698
Economische wiskunde 3695
The economist and the state 2502
The economist in business 2330
The economist in business 3492
The economist in the twentieth century 2479
Un economista pugliese 2869
Economistas espanoles 2969
Los economistas, Adam Smith 7298
Economistas modernos 34
Economistes financiers 5968
Les economistes français 5367
Economisti greci 2797
Economisti greci 5119
Economisti moderni 84
Economisti moderni 1204
Economisti napoletani 996
Economisti napoletani 2872
Economisti romani 5121
Economisti ungheresi 2801
Economisti ungheresi 2848
Economists and economic historians 2334
Economists and social policy 2462
Economists and the history 2485
Economists and the public 2410
Economists and their environment 2471
The economists of the New Frontier 3087
An economist's protest 736
The economists refuted 7131
Economy and society 1903
The economy of abundance 104
The economy of capital 8408
The economy of Communist China 2591
The economy of consumption 8308
The economy of high wages 8586
Economy of machinery 5498
The economy of Sweden 2979

Economy of the labouring 6927
The economy of the Soviet 2600
The economy theory of the leisure 9675
Ecrits divers sur Stephane Mallarmé 2518
Edavamsda ikonomika thyauri 1812
Francis Ysidro Edgeworth 9671
Edgeworth, Marshall, and the indeterminateness 3256
F. Y. Edgeworth's contributions 9672
L'édition qu'il a donnée 5646
Editor's preface 9984
Edo, Meiji jidai 2877
The education of girls 8046
Educational requirements 2515
Een algemene vorm van de vraagfunctie 3478
Een centraal probleem 5131
The effect of an alteration of the sugar duties 6346
The effect of restrictions 6713
The effects of arts, trades 7086
The effects of civilization 6166
The effects of machinery 8359
The effects of open inflation 3372
Effects of the administration 6403
Effets d'un privilége exclusif 3920
Egypt and the Roman empire 5002
Egypt of the Pharaohs 4954
L'Egypte 8399
Eidgenössische eisenbahngesetzgebung 8077
Eigentumsrecht nach dem heiligen Thomas von Aquin 4991
The eight-hours day 8762
Eight letters on the custom of vails-giving 4223
Eight letters on the peace 5969
1840 and after 972
The eighteenth Brumaire of Louis Bonaparte 9384
Eighteenth-century Scottish 7350
Eikoku tetsugaku-sha no keizai-

ron 438
Ein beitrag zur geschichte 2418
Ein beitrag zur lösung 8294
Eine neue Etappe der marxistischen 1874
Die enführung eines international 7797
Einführung in die allgemeine 1727
Einführung in die methodenlehre 355
Einführung in die politische 1934
Einführung in die volkswirtschaftslehre 1123
Einführung in die volkswirtschaftslehre 1541
Einführung in die volkswirtschaftslehre 2088
Einfuhrung in die wirtschafteschichte 3520
Einführung in die wirtschaftgeschichte 41
Einführung in die wirtschafttheorie 588
Einführung in die wirtschaftstheorie 2056
Einführung in die wirtschaftstheorie 9771
Einführung zur geschichte der volkswirtschaft 292
Einführunger in Das Kapital 9169
Die einheit der volkswritschaft 2692
Einige probleme der arbeitswerttheorie 3317
Einige strittige fragen 9664
Das einkommen 8133
Einleitung in die geschichte 7199
Einleitung in die nationalokonomie 3588
Die eisenbahnen oesterreich-ungarns 8145
Eisenbahns-politik 7762
Eisenbahntarifweseb 8180
Das eisenbahntarifwesen 8712
Ekonomi for miljoner 2015
Ekonomi, politik, samhalle 2377
Ekonomi; privat- och 2151
Ekonomi umum 1336

Ekonomia Franciszka Quesnaya 5443
Ekonomia polityczna 1037
Ekonomia polityczna 1364, 1365
Ekonomia polityczna 1668
Ekonomia polityczna 1704
Ekonomia polityczna 1807
Ekonomia polityczna 9078
Ekonomia polityczna 9159
Ekonomia polityczna a matematyka 3919
Ekonomia polityczna dla wyzszych szkoł technicznych 1153
Ekonomia polityczna kapitalizmu 2028
Ekonomia polityczna kapitalizmu 9532
Ekonomia polityczna socjalizmu 1802
Ekonomia polityczna socjalizmu 9160, 9161
Ekonomiche-skoe uchenie A. I. Gertsena 2963
Ekonomicheskie nauki v Moskovskom 3004
Ekonomicheskie otnosheniia 2955
Ekonomicheskie vozzreniia 2961
Ekonomichna dumka Ukraini 3030
Ekonomicke mysleni duacateho stoleti 475
Ekonomicke základy 3373
Ekonomicko-matematicky 3606
Ekonomický růst 9293
Ekonomie e festišimus 9447
Ekonomija iz novega 9095
Ekonomija iz novega zornega 1238
Ekonomika handlu 3124
Ekonomika Jugoslavije 1643
Ekonomika, zájmy, politika 2091
Ekonomilitto 2378
Ekonomilitto 2629
Ekonomilitto 3607
Ekonomiści dyskutuja 3201
Ekonomisk-historiska studiee 290
Ekonomisk teori 2271
Ekonomisk tidskfrit 770
Ekonomiskās zināšanas 9162
Ekonomisti XVII i XVIII stoljeca 988

Ekonomska analiza 3608
Ekonomska efektivnost uvodenja 9503
Ekonomska nauka 9246
Ekonomska politika 9136
Ekonomska teorija 9364
Eksperymenty ekonomiczne 2310
L'élasticité de la demande 3113
Elasticité et analyse 3182
Das elastizitatsproblem 1167
The element of monopoly 3261
Elementa juris camialis 6198
Elementary aggregate 2082
Elementary economics 1380
Elementary economics 1472
Elementary economics 1577
Elementary economics 1760
Elementary economics 1866
Elementary economics 1871
Elementary lessons in logic 9722
Elementary matrices 3801
Elementary political economy 1213
Elementary price theory 1341
Elementary price theory 2238
Elementary price theory 3190
Elementary price theory 3461
Elementary principles 1407
Elementary theory of economic behavior 1495
Elementary thoughts on the bullion 5986
An elementary treatise on political 5704
Die elemente der staatskunst 1831
Elemente der staatskunst 6578
Die elemente der staatskunst 8867
Elemente der volkswirthschafts- lehre 8351
Elementi di economia 1249
Elementi di economia 1843
Elementi di economia 2020
Elementi di economia politica 1266
Elementi di economia politica 1278, 1280, 1283
Elementi di economia politica 1390
Elementi di economia politica 1453
Elementi di economia politica 1751
Elementi di economia politica 2170
Elementi di economia politica 5664
Elementi di economia politica 7676
Elementi di economia pubblica 4011
Elementi di economic com- merciale 1820
Elementi di microeconomia 2169
Elementi di politica economica 1420
Elementi di scienza 1383
Elementi di scienza dell' amministrazione 7612
Elementi socijalističke 9621
Elementos de economía 1342
Elementos de economia 2132
Elementos de economia politica 1435
Elementos de economia politica 1772
Elementos de economía política 2043
Eléments d'économie 1425
Eléments d'économie politique 1078
Eléments d'économie politique 1223
Eléments d'économie politique 1581
Eléments d'économie politique 2120
Eléments d'économie politique 6184
Eléments d'économie politique 6509
Eléments d'économie politique 7453
Eléments d'économie politique 9790
Eléments d'économiques 1795
Eléments de la police 6033
Eléments de la politique 4212
Eléments de la politique 5930
Elèments de l'économie politique 6092

Eléments de logique 9706
Eléments de science économiques 1315
Eléments de statistique 6555
Eléménts de théorie 9163
Eléments du commerce 4284
Elements of a plan for the liquidation 6189
The elements of agriculture 4217
The elements of banking 6111
The elements of banking 8243
The elements of commerce 4225
Elements of commerce 4545
The elements of commerce 4814
Elements of economic analysis 448
Elements of economic analysis 1763
Elements of economic analysis 3751
Elements of economic theory 2011
Elements of economics 1313
Elements of economics 1392
Elements of economics 1610
Elements of economics 1851
The elements of economics 2171
Elements of economics 2276
The elements of economics 8244
The elements of economics 10086
Elements of economics of industry 9839
Elements of Marxian theory 9059
Elements of medical statistics 6188
Elements of modern 1793
The elements of political 1673
Elements of political 1800
The elements of political 1987
Elements of political 6376
Elements of political 6513
The elements of political 6760
The elements of political 7227
Elements of political 8161
The elements of political 8168

Elements of political 8245
Elements of political 8422
Elements of political 8699
Elements of political science 5849
The elements of politics 8624
Elements of practical agriculture 6398
The elements of public finance 7716
The elements of railroading 8393
Elements of statistics 7554
Elements of the philosophy 7048
Die emancipationkampf 8296
Emergence and content of modern economic analysis 209
Emergence and content of modern economic analysis 1394
L'émigration européene 8177
Empire and interest 5234
An empirical principle 3611
L'emploi des mathématiques 3767
Employment and equilibrium 9861
Employment and equilibrium 10047
En analytisk presisering 10089
En gustaviansk dagbok 2384
En oversikt over betingelser 3102
En quoi consiste la prospérité 6880
En torno al concepto de alienación 9624
Enclosures a cause of improved agriculture 6251
Encouragement for seamen 4253
Encyclopaedia metropolitana 5993
An encyclopaedia of agriculture 6397
Encyclopedie 4199
Encyclopedie socialiste 9113
Encyclopoedia Britannica 5988
Encyclopoedie der kameralwissenschaften 6883
Encyklopädie die staatswissenschaften 6528
The end of laissez-faire 9985

The end of the ancient world 5026
Das ende der grenznutzentheorie 9788
Enderecos 2457
Enérgetique générale 1486
Energie, produktivitat 1706
Friedrich Engels 9149
Friedrich Engels 9428
Engineering economics 1244
Engineering economy 1314
Engineering materials 3424
The engineers and the price 8993
The engineer's approach 1329
England 7822
England and India inconsistent 4612
England in the 15th century 7736
England's calamities 4858
England's great happiness 4229
England's improvement by sea 4867
England's improvement revived 4730
Englands interest 4298
Englands interest 4532
England's interest by trade 4081
England's path to wealth 4641
England's safety 4699
Englands safety in trades encrease 4682
England's treasure 5269
Englands wants 4102
Die englische arbeiterversicherungswesen 7997
Das englische armenwesen 7395
Die englische fabrikinspection 8778
Englische freihandler vor Adam Smith 2773
Das englische recht zur zeit 2751
Das englische verfassungsgeschichte 7920
English agriculture 5665
English and American railroads 7763
English and Irish land 8619
English associations 7414

English colonisation 7595
English guilds 7013
The English improver 4031
The English labour laws 7724
English land 7570
English manual of banking 7700
English merchants 7547
The English philosophers 2732
English political economy 3911
English poor 8237
English social movements 8801
English theories 2765
English theories of foreign trade 5316
English trade and finance 8025
The English usurer 4030
The English utilitarians 2785
The English village 8599
Enige aspekt van die invloed 3885
Enige aspekte van die invloed 2925
Enige opmerkingen over de grenzen 857
Enige theoretisch-economische 9939
The enlargement of economics 3505
Les énormités du libre échange 7536
Enquête sur la banque 8415
Enquête sur le crédit 7437
Une enquête sur le prix 7858
Enquête sur les associations 8718
The enquirer 6121
An enquiry 7078
An enquiry concerning political justice 6122
An enquiry concerning the influence of tithes 6252
An enquiry concerning the principles of morals 4379
An enquiry into the causes 4269
An enquiry into the causes 4297
An enquiry into the causes of the encrease and miseries 4230
An enquiry into the conduct of our domestic affairs 4231
An enquiry into the effects

6588, 6589
An enquiry into the nature 7105
An enquiry into the nature of the corn laws 5468
An enquiry into the past and present 4232
An enquiry into the prices of wheat 4130
An enquiry into the principles of taxation 6173
An enquiry into the reasons of the advance of the price 4233
An enquiry whether a general practice of virtue 4234
Ensaios de história econômica 87
Ensayo sobre economía cuantitativa 3820
Ensayo sobre la historia 7603
Ensayos de economía poskeynesiana 10054
Die enstehung 7579
Entendons-nous 4534
Enterprise and secular change 867
Enterprise and the productive process 3651
Die entstehung der deutschen kameralwissenschaft 5270
Entstehung der volkswirtschaft 8834
Die entstehung des agrarschutzes 7824
Die entwickeln die vichzucht 7992
Entwickelung der gesetze 3237
Entwickelung der gesetze 6129
Die entwickelung der verkehrs-grundlagen 8513
Entwickelung des genossen-schaftwesens 6959
Entwickelungs-geschichte 2802
Entwickelungsgeschichte des Eigenthums 6035
Entwickelungsstufen der volkswirthschaft 8503
Entwickel. des . . . zollwesens 6257
Die entwicklung der Betriebs-wirtschaftslehre 2708
Entwicklung der gesetze 9707
Die entwicklung der kritik 9941
Entwicklung der markttheorie 5138
Die Entwicklung der national-ökonomie 3522
Die entwicklung der ökonomis-chen lehr 9520
Die entwicklung der theoretis-chen volkswirtschaftslehre 638
Die entwicklung der theorie 3433
Die entwicklung der volkswirt-schaftslehre 273
Die entwicklung zum idealtypus 8870
Entwicklungen und wandlungen 968
Der entwicklungsgang 2688
Der entwicklungsgang 2706
Die entwicklungstendenzen 9936
Entwicklungstendenzen der modernen 9307
Entwurf der land-staats 4278
Entwurf einer staatskunst 4469
Epistemological problems 3454
Epistemological problems 3757
Epistemological problems 9743
An epistle to Sir John Blount 3948
La epoca del mercantilismo 5241
La epoca del mercantilismo en Castilla 5249
Epoche svolgimenti tendenze nella storia 223
Die epochen der deutschen 2701
Epochen der dogmen- und method-dengeschichte J. C. B. Mohr 593
Epochen der dogmen- und methoden-geschichte 3835
Equality 9041
L'equilibre économique 1723
Equilibrio economico generale 3783

Equilibrium and growth 930
Erinnerungen aus meinem Leben 2498
Die erlösung der darbenden 8650
Ernährungs-statistik 8122
Erotemi di economica 1899
Erotemi di economia 3788
Die erstdrucke der werke von Marx und Engels 9048
Erték és újratermeleś 9073
Ertéktöbbletelmélet 3411
Der ertragswert 3131
Erweiterte volkswirtschaftliche 3893
Erwerbs- und wirthschaftsgenossenschaften 7698
Erzeugen, verbrauchen 3748
Esame storico-critico 6037
Esame storico-critico di economisti 212
Esbôco dos fundamentos 1974
Escritos economicos 9214
Eseje o teoriích 9618
Eseje o teoriích ekonomickeho 9175
L'Espace dans le pensée économique du XVIe aud XVIIIe siècle 178
L'espagne éclairée de la seconde moitié du XVIIIe siècle 578
Esquisse d'un ouvrage 5563
Esquisse d'une histoire 2842
Esquisse d'une histoire 5063
Esquisse d'une histoire monétaire 4899
Esquisse d'une théorie générale 9943
Esquisses de littérature politico-économique 81
Essai anlytique sur la richesse 4325
Essai comparatif sur la formation 5999
Essai concernant les armateurs 6000
Essai d'economique 729
Essai de législation 8805
Essai d'un plan de finances 6202
Essai historique et moral 6001

Essai historique et moral 6047
Essai historique sur la condition 7560
Essai historique sur les differentes situations 4235
Essai politique sur le commerce 4503
Essai politique sur le revenu 6084
Essai sur la centralisation 9889
Essai sur l'admission des navires neutres 4285
Essai sur la force 5882
Essai sur la loi de king 5214
Essai sur la marine des anciens 4194
Essai sur la nature du commerce 1214
Essai sur la nature du commerce 4078
Essai sur la partie politique 4286
Essai sur la police générale des grains 4356
Essai sur l'appréciation 6360
Essai sur la repartition 8186
Essai sur la science des finances 6005
Essai sur la science des finances 6081
Essai sur la science sociale 7636
Essai sur la théorie 795
Essai sur la théorie du salaire 7454
Essai sur le crédit commercial 6158
Essai sur le luxe 4606
Essai sur le rapport des poids etrangers 4240
Essai sur le statistique 6213
Essai sur les causes de la diversité des taux 4058
Essai sur les Colonies Francoises 4236
Essai sur les conditions 5723
Essai sur les consuls 6003
Essai sur les entraves 7121
Essai sur les intérêts du commerce maritime 4355
Essai sur les monnaies 4238
Essai sur les monnaies 6873

Essai sur les monnaies 4700
Essai sur les moyens 5566
Essai sur les moyens d'améliorer 5618
Essai sur les principes politiques 5640
Essai sur les probabilités de la durée 4239
Essai sur les qualités 6430
Essai sur les valeurs 7017
Essai sur l'établissement des hôpitaux 6391
Essai sur l'etat actuel 6004
Essai sur l'etat actuel 6103
Essai sur l'etat du commerce 4237
Essai sur l'evolution 726
Essai sur l'evolution 907
Essai sur l'histoire des comices 6154
Essai sur l'inegalité 7922
Essai sur l'influence des croisades 6193
Essai sur l'organisation du travail 6566
Essai sur l'organisation politique 8184
Essai sur quelques theories 5112
Essai sur un code maritime 6002
Essais économiques 3187
Essais sur le commerce 4380
Essais sur les etablissements 7225
Essais sur les ponts et chausses 5382
An essay concerning the multiplication 4593
An essay for lowering the gold 4241
An essay in dynamic theory 811
An essay on a registry 3982
Essay on average 7047
Essay on colonies 7335
An essay on insurances 4243
An essay on insurances 4480
An essay on Keynesian 10007
An essay on Marxian economics 9508
An essay on medals 6697

An essay on medieval 5055
An essay on money 5230
Essay on money 6006
An essay on money 6730
An essay on money 7132
An essay on probabilities 6562
Essay on relations between labour 6568
An essay on some general principles of political 6884
Essay on some unsettled questions 6518
Essay on the application of capital 7235
An essay on the best means 5861
An essay on the causes of the decline of the foreign trade 4179
An essay on the causes of the present high price 4242
An essay on the causes which regulate 5992
An essay on the circumstances 6418
An essay on the construction of roads 5975
An essay on the co-ordination 3470
An essay on the co-ordination of the laws of distribution 9803
Essay on the currency 6295
An essay on the depressed state of agriculture 5753
An essay on the distribution 6305
An essay on the distribution 6750
An essay on the East-India trade 4172
An essay on the external corn 7133
An essay on the gold and silver-coin 4024
An essay on the governing causes 4491
An essay on the history of civil society 4267
An essay on the impolicy of a bounty 6514
An essay on the influence of a low price 6852
An essay on the manufactures

7215
An essay on maritime power 4195
An essay on the national debt 4374
An essay on the nature 3814
An essay on the nature 5933
An essay on the nature 6077
An essay on the nature and method 4372
An essay on the nature and methods of trade 3945
An essay on the nature of colonies 6007
An esaay on the political 5989
An essay on the political 6008
An essay on the population 4628
An essay on the population 6721
An essay on the principle of commercial exchanges 6053
An essay on the principle of population 6447
An essay on the production of wealth 7134
An essay on the public debts 4224
Essay on the rate of wages 5690
An essay on the sinking fund 4324
An essay on the state of England 4085
An essay on the right of property 6009
Essay on the supposed advantages 6148
An essay on the theory of money 7011
An essay on the theory of money 7241
An essay on the trade 4209
Essay on the trade of Ireland 4786
An essay on the treatment 6751
An essay on the treaty of commerce with France 4246
An essay on the value of the mines 4852
An essay on trade 4055
An essay on trade and commerce 4245
An essay on ways and means 4247

An essay on ways and means 4265
An essay to ascertain the value of leases 4427
An essay towards a general history of feudal property 4167
An essay towards an historical account 4724
An essay toward deciding 4540
An essay towards illustrating 4541
An essay towards New-Coyning 4029
An essay towards regulating the trade 4086
An essay towards the recovery of the Jewish measures 4165
An essay towards the settlement 4087
An essay upon credit 4429
Essay upon industry and trade 4027
An essay upon money 4349
An essay upon projects 4188
An essay upon public credit 6182
An essay upon publick credit 4189
An essay upon the present interest of England 4248
An essay upon the probable methods 4173
An essay upon trade 4690
Essays 969
Essays 3803
Essays 5227
Essays 7309
Essays 7639
Essays about the poor, manufacturers 4013
Essays and treatises 4381
Essays in biography 2415
Essays in economic analysis 871
Essays in economic management 735
Essays in economic method 3845
Essays in economic theory 937
Essays in economic thought 985

Essays in economics 758
Essays in economics 870
Essays in economics 939
Essays in economics 941
Essays in economics 970
Essays in economics 3724
Essays in European 2625
Essays in finance 7908
Essays in Indian political 2830
Essays in mathematical economics 3842
Essays in monetary 10051
Essays in normative 9047
Essays in our changing order 8994
Essays in persuasion 9986
Essays in political 5693
Essays in political 8193
Essays in political economy 872
Essays in political economy 3728
Essays in positive 9814
Essays in positive economics 784
Essays in social economics 773
Essays in statistics 8785
Essays in taxation 8601
Essays in the history 991
Essays in the history of materialism 9490
Essays in the theory of economic growth 957
Essays in the theory of employment 958
Essays in the theory of employment 10055
Essays moral and political 4382
Essays on economic semantics 880
Essays on husbandry 4350
Essays on Maimonides 4896
Essays on Marx 9120
Essays on Marxian 9608
Essays on modern cooperation 1011
Essays on money, exchanges 6294
Essays on philosophical 7336
Essays on political 5530
Essays on political economy 7950

Essays on population 779
Essays on several subjects 4371
Essays on sociology 1018
Essays on some unsettled questions 904
Essays on the evolution of antebellum 3081
Essays on the materialist 9301
Essays on the prevention of pauperism 7499
Essays on the public debt 4249
Essays on the theory of economic growth 9079
Essays on the theory of optimal 974
Essays on trade 4044
Essays on value 3274
Essays on wealth 6971
Essays relating to agriculture 5469
The essence of finance 7367
Essential economic principles 1764
Essential economics 1969
The essential left 9385
The essential principles 6138
Essential works of Marxism 9440
Essentials 1590
Essentials of economic theory 1262
Essentials of economics 1042
Essentials of economics 1096
The essentials of economics 1498
Essentials of Marx 9386
Estado de la poblacion 6011
Estado de las Islas Filipinas 6010
An estimate of the comparative strength 5709
An estimate of the number of inhabitants 5970
Estimo con elementi di economia 3755
Estratto del progetto 4837
Estudios de economía social 8147
Estudios de historia y economia 250
Estudios políticos 7409

Estudos de economia teorica 1234
Etat actuel de la Grande-Bretagne 6627
Etat de la France 7517
Etat des colonies 6013
Etat des habitations 7591
Etat des pauvres 4417
L'état moderne 8187
L'état stationnaire 416
Ethical and economic theories 7319
The ethical foundations 9265
Ethics and economics 3640
Ethics and the economic interpretation 3707
Ethics and the materialist 9272
The ethics of competition 786
The ethics of competition 849
The ethics of competition 3293
The ethics of competition 9832
Ethik und volkswirtschaft 8832
Ethnographie moderne 7474
Etterspørselssammenhenger belyst 3270
Etude de sociologie 7542
Etude du crédit public 5932
L'étude économique 1688
Etude economique et juridical 7769
Etude historique 7696
Etude sur la banque d'Espagne 6522
Etude sur les tarifs 7381
Etude sur le travail 8317
Etudes d'économie humaiste 13
Etudes d'economie politique 774
Etudes d'économie polituque 6015
Etudes d'économie politique 7257
Etudes d'économie politique 8905
Etudes d'économie politique 9791
Etudes d'économie sociale 9792
Etudes de crédit public 6014
Etudes de crédit public 6916
Etudes de la science social 6361
Etudes de philosophie morale 5537
Etudes économique 7855
Etudes économique 8146
Etudes economiques 7859
Etudes économiques sur l'Alsace 7987
Etudes historiques 6016
Etudes sociales 7642
Etudes sur Colbert 5232
Etudes sur Colbert 6313
Etudes sur l'Angleterre 6028
Etudes sur la richesse 6943
Etudes sur l'économie politique 6999
Etudes sur l'économie sociale 8504
Etudes sur l'économique nationale 7479
Etudes sur le crédit 7538
Etudes sur le régime des manufactures 6842
Etudes sur les causes de la misère 5724
Etudes sur les économistes 6843
Etudes sur les forces productives 7081
Etudes sur les principaux économistes 185
Etudes sur les principaux économistes 7770
Etudes sur les réformateurs 6844
Etudes sur les socialistes 6845
Etudes sur les theories 2558
Etudes sur l'industrie 7825
L'etudiant economiste 2387
Die europäische Baumwollen-industrie 8088
L'Europe et ses colonies 5547
European reconstruction 9987
Evaluation of some uncertainty hypotheses 3399
Events, ideology 762
Events, ideology and economic theory 187
Everyday economics 2105
L'evidence, fondement necessaire 5371
The evident advantages to Great Britain 4254
La evolución de las ideas 94
Evolucion del pensamiento economico 65
La evolución económica 473
The evolution 954
L'e

Short Title Index   781

L'evolution de la theorie 2777
L'évolution de la théorie 3417
L'évolution économique 580
L'évolution économique 6531
The evolution of dialectical 9261
The evolution of economic thinking in India 2806
The evolution of economic thought 381
The evolution of economic thought 498
The evolution of Marshall's principles 9819
The evolution of modern capitalism 8042
Evolution of modern economics 244
The evolution of Ricardian 2725
Evolutionary economics 278
Evolutionary empiricism 3798
Evolutionary socialism 9052
The evolutionist revolt 270
Evolutionist revolt 8951
Evoluzione ed unita della teoria economica 174
An exact survey of the affaires 4255
Examen de la reponse au memoire de M. l'Abbé Morellet 4256
Examen de la réponse de M. N. (Necker) 4536
Examen de quelques questions 5679
Examen de quelques questions 5928
Examen des advantages 4287
Examen des principes les plus 5606
Examen des reflexions politiques 4581
Examen du gouvernement 6020
Examen du système commercial 5731
Examen impartial 6435
An examination and explanation of the South-Sea company's 4258
Examination of Dr. Franklin 4257

An examination of Dr. Price's essay 6253
An examination of the British 6021
An examination of the doctrines of value 3167
An examination of the doctrines of value 5834
An examination of the new tariff 6022
Exercises in economic analysis 2003
Exercises in economic analysis 3818
Exercises, political 7094
The exorbitant grant of William the III 3989
L'expansion coloniale 8155
Expectations in economic theory 934
Expectations in economics 10070
The expedience of a free exportation of corn 4872
An expedient for taking away all impositions 4157
An expedient to pay the publick debts 3994
Explication du Tableau economique 5328
The exploitation of theories 3211
Explorations in economics 775
Exposé de l'administration général 5506
Exposé des principes elémentaires 6319
Exposé elementaire 8804
Exposés et entretiens sur le marxisme 9176
Exposition abrégée 5801
External economies 1367
External economics 9813
Extrait du livre de l'Esprit des lois 4288
Extraits des enquêtes parlementaires 7683

Fabian essays 8617
Fabian essays 9553
Fabian socialism 9105
Fabian socialism and English politics 9432

The Fabian society 9106
Fabian society 9177
The Fabian society 9552
Fabian tracts 9178
Fabianism 9433
The fable of the bees 4485
Fable of the bees 7316
Fabricius 6024
Fact and metaphysics 3708
Fact and theory 8931
Factories 7079
Factors influencing the demand 3178
Factory act legislation 8095
Factory and workshop acts 8489
Facts addressed to the landholders 6025
The facts of the cotton famine 8757
Factum de la France 4036
The failure of the new economics 9958
The failures of economics 3831
Les faits contre la doctrine 9312
Les faits et la doctrine economiques en Espagne 5267
The fall of the old colonial 5288
Fallacies in progress 7993
Fallacies of Karl Marx 9498
The falling rate of profit 9206
Fal'sifikatory sotsiallizm 2545
A familiar discourse 4262
Families in different parts 5872
Family budgets 8033
The farmer's letters to the people 4873
The farmer's tour 4874
Farther considerations upon a reduction 4263
A farther examination 4264
A farther inquiry 7272
Fasal-fasal ekonomi 2326
Les faux dilemmes liberalisme 157
The federal income tax 7939
La femme 8078

Festgabe fur Friedrich Bulow 987
Festgabe fur Georg Jahn 914
Festskrift til professor, dr. polit. Jørgen Pedersen 2381
Festschrift zum 70 3533
A few doubts 6759
A few words on the corn laws 5864
Das fictive capital 8381
The field of economic dynamics 3561
Fifty years' development in ideas of human nature 8910
A fifty years' history 6413
Fifty years of international socialism 9035
Fikr al-iqtisādī fī Muqaddimat Ibn Khaldūn 481
Filosofia della statistica 6041
Filozofia ekonomii 1594
Finance and budget 8647
Finance and politics 7589
Finances and public works 8662
Les finances considerees 5383
Les finances de la France 7702
Les finances de la France 8108
Finances de la France du XIXe 8671
Les finances de l'ancien 8660
Les finances de la Russie 7258
Les finances de la Russie 8476
Les finances de l'Autriche 8332
Les finances de l'empire 8734
Les finances de l'empire de Russie 7637
Les finances de l'Italie 7703
Finances et comptabilité 8075
Les finances francaises 8347
Financial history 7523
Financial history 7741
The financial history of Baltimore 8053
Financial, monetary 5918
The financier 8672
Le financier citoyen 4557
La finanza 8323
Die finanzen 6231

Short Title Index 783

Die finanzen Frankreichs 8119
Die finanzen oesterreich 8292
Dei finanzen Oesterreichs 7458
Die finanzen oesterreichs 7867
Das finanzielle und sociale wesen 8772
Firma Burgi 4479
A first approach 1821
First Australian economist 8009
The first Indian war of independence 9387
First lessons in political 8744
The first nine years of the Bank of England 8529
A first primer 1298
First principles 7618
First principles of political 8792
First report of the commissioners 6042
First report on the commercial 5620
The first stages of the tariff 8036
Fiscal legislation 8368
Fiscal policy 9947
The fiscal policy of international 9840, 9841
The fiscal revolution 10080
Fisica economica 1896
The fisheries revived 4273
Earl Fitzwilliam 2501
Five lectures 6497
Five lectures on economic problems 992
Five reports of the committee 6045
Fluctuations, growth 1728
Fluctuations of currency 7252
Focus på nationaløkonomien 1867
Foedora 4689
Die folgen der aufhebung 7063
Folgen einer theorie 9185
Folkhushållningens grundfrågor 1781
Fondamenti e problemi 1708
Il fondamento struttural 1681
Fondateur du collectivisme d'Etat 2430

Les fondements actuels de la valeur 3315
Les fondements comptables 1053
Fondements de la critique 9388
Fonti per la storia delle dottrine 711
Footprints on the sands 2401
For Marx 9007
Force productives 5947, 5948
Forces producing disturbances 3460
Forces productives 6050
Die forderungen der arbeitenden 9511
Forecasting 3624
Foreign commerce of England 8787
The foreign-trade doctrines 5333
Foreign work 7561
Foretaget och dess 2272
Foretagets ekonomi 1067
Företagsekonomie för alla 2098
Foreward 9988
The forgotten man 995
La formation de la pensée 9353
La formation historique de l'economie politique 238
Le forme primitive 7646
Formen 9389
The formula of sacrifice 3582
Forschungskonzeptionen 3556
Die fortschritte der nationaloeconomie 6579
Fortune publique 7518
La forza contrattuale dell' impresa 3149
Foundations of economic analysis 2039
The foundations of economics 202
The foundations of the demand 9883
Founders of American 3086
The founders of political economy 401
The four consumers' surpluses 9822
450 lat krakowskiej myśli ekonomicznej 2928
Four lectures on poor laws 6393

Four lectures on the organisation 5517
Four letters to the Earl of Carlisle 6054
Four tracts on political 4813
Four tracts on political 7160
Fourier 9068
Die frage der landwirtschaft 7890
Fragen der marxistischen soziologie 9189
Fragen des preises 3203
A fragment on government 9043
The framework of economics 1356
The framework of price theory 1054
The framework of price theory 3101
La France avec ses colonies 6377
La France coloniale 8479
La France commerciale 8273
La France et l'étranger 8178
La France industrielle 8444
France shakai-keizai-shigaku 2647
France under Richelieu 5166
Benjamin Franklin 2530
Franklin's economic views 2351
Frantsuzskaia burzhuaznaia 2651
Franzosische wirtschaftsgeschichte 2652
Die frau und der sozialismus 7455
Das frauenstudium der nationalökonomie 297
A free and impartial inquiry 4851
The free and prosperous commonwealth 455
A free disquisition 4305
Free exchange papers 8255
Free land 7393
Free land and free trade 7689
Free thought 3661
Free thoughts on religion 4486
Free trade 4519
A free trade 5752
Free trade 7836

Free trade 7910
Free trade and other fundamental 305
Free trade and protection 5457
Free trade in capital 7980
Free trade in corn 6063
Free trade in land 6323
Free trade speeches 8732
Free trade vs. fair 7830
Freedom, economics and 289
Freiheit der wirtschaft 9761
Die freiheit des getreidehandels 6783
Freisinnige ansichten 8038
French and German socialism 7807
French and German socialism 9166
French excise 4306
French finances 6586
The French king's declaration 4307
French mercantilism 5177
French mercantilist doctrines 5178
French predecessor of Malthus 2653
Professor Friedman's consumption 3236
From Hegel to Marx 9239
From Karl Marx to Mao Tse-tung 9098
From Marshall to Keynes 200
From the ground up 1582
The frontiers 734
A full and clear vindication of the 'Full answer' 4310
A full and detailed catalogue 7537
A full and exact collection 4311
A full answer to the letter from a by-stander 4309
Full employment 9896
The function of China 9343
The functional economy 1321
Functionalism in the social sciences 3746
Fundament der volkswirtschaftslehre 2135
The fundamental idea of capital 8404
Fundamental methods of mathematical 3554
Fundamental thoughts 1231
Fundamental thoughts 3146

Fundamentals 1579
Fundamentals 1823
Fundamentals 2205
Fundamentals of economics 1106
Fundamentals of economics 1449
Fundamentals of Marxist political 9325
Fundamentals of model construction 3790
Fundamentals of political 1862
Fundamentals of political 2288
Fundamentos de economia marxista 9575
Fundamentos de la evolución 1990
Die funktion der wirtschaft 1130
Funktionskostnadsanalys 3228
Further considerations concerning raising the value 4461
A further justification of the present war 4772
Further observations 6190
Further reflections 6404
The future of Communism in Europe 2615
The future of economic theory 3562

Gaisetsu nihon keizai shi 2891
Gakusha shobal 2447
Ferdinando Galiani 2392
Ferdinando Galiani 5204
Der Abbé Galiani 5319
Der Abbé Galiani als nationalökonom 5161
Gandhian economic philosophy 2804
Gandhijira arthanaltika darsana 2822
Der gang des welthandels 8126
Ganzheitliche 2223
Pierre Gassendis metaphysik 5062
A gazetteer of the countries 7102
Gedanken über die wirtschaft in hundert Jahren 341

Die Gedanken zur wirtschaftlichen 2552
Gegen die Brandung 2702
Die gegenwartige krisis 2700
Der gegenwartige stand 2715
Geist der nationaloeconomie 6363
Geistige arbeit 1702
Geld und geist 3774
Geld und kredit 8855
Die geld- und kreditlehre 5187
Die geld- und kreditheorie 9193
Die geldtheoretischen 5189
Gendai keizai riron no essensu 360
Gendai keizai riron nyumon 2308
Gendai keizaigaku 2193
Gendai keizaigaku 2297
Gendai keizaigaku no kontei 686
Gendai keizaigaku nyumon 1076
Gendai keizaigaku ron 1658
Gendai no keizaigakushi 158
Gendai no keizaigakushi 3584
Gendai to shihonshugi 10037
Genealogie der wirtschaftsstile 471
General economics 707
General economics 1560
General economics 2089
General history of inland navigation 6694
The general history of socialism 9036
General maxims in trade 4405
A general medical 6300
General observations on provident 5740
General report on the agricultural state 6995
A general theory 1243
The general theory 9990
A general theory of economic process 102
The general theory of employment 9989
A general theory of the price level 2264
A general treatise of monies 4317
A general treatise of naval

trade 4318
A general view of the coal trade 5511
Generalmo, markedsteori 1494
Generating economic cycles 8320
Genesis des historischen materialismus 9263
Genesis of the marginal utility 5008
Genesis of the marginal utility 9729
The genesis of the multiplier 9959
Die genossenschaftstheorie 7906
Genshi chikuseki-kino keizai shoriron 366
A geographical, historical 5791
Géographie commerciale 7776
A geographical, statistical 6178
A geometrical political economy 1295
A geometrical political economy 3576
Geometrical theory of the determination 3456
Mr. Lloyd George's general election 9995
Die gerechtigkeit 3829
The German ideology 9390
German socialism 7726
German wage theories 2670
Gesammelte aufsatze sur sozial 675
Gesamelte schriften 1150
Gesammelte schriften 6727
Gesammelte werke 1790
Geschichte der arbeit 8651
Geschichte der burgerlichen 632
Geschichte der eisenbahnen 8669
Geschichte der erdkunde 8519
Geschichte der handelsgesellschaften 8766
Geschichte der markenverfassung 6480
Geschichte der national-oekonomik 2703
Geschichte der nationalökonomie 155
Geschichte der nationalökonomie 464
Geschichte der nationalökonomie 494
Geschichte der nationalökonomie 659
Geschichte der nationalökonomie 673
Geschichte der nationalökonomie 2930
Geschichte der nationalökonomie 8387
Geschichte der nationalökonomik 191
Geschichte der nationalökonomik 5289
Geschichte der nationalökonomik 7800
Geschichte der nationalökonomischen 7648
Geschichte der ökonomischen Lehrmeinungen 237
Geschichte der ökonomischen theorien 7877
Geschichte der produktivitatstheorie 29
Geschichte der produktivitätstheorie 3118
Geschichte der statistik 8102
Geschichte der volkswirtschaftslehre 573
Geschichte der volkswirtschaftslehre 585
Geschichte der volkswirtschaftslehre 648
Geschichte der volkswirtschaftlichen 302
Geschichte der volkswirtschaftlichen 5252
Geschichte der volkswirtschaftlichen literatur 134
Geschichte der waldeigenthums 7469
Geschichte der wirtschaftlichen 8831
Geschichte der wirtschaftlichen lehrmeinungen 672
Geschichte der wirtschaftstheorie 628
Geschichte des deutschen volkes 8091
Geschichte des eisenbahnwesens

Short Title Index 787

7975
Geschichte des hanseatischen 6932
Geschichte des kirchlichen 7875
Geschichte des socialismus 8755
Geschichte des volkswirtschafts-
 lehre 910
Geschichte die deutschen handels
 8026
Geschichte die deutschen post
 8137
Geschichte die levanthandels
 8027
Geschichte du deutsch zollwesens
 7826
Die geschichte einer grossen
 entdeckung 9632
Geschichte literatur 7665
Geschichte theoretisch 8288
Geschichte und kritische
 studien 3055
Geschichte und literatur 671
Geschichtliche darstellung
 6163
Die geschichtliche entwicklung
 der modernen werttheorien
 347
Die geschichtliche entiwcklung
 der nationaloekonomik 348
Geschichte der volkswirtschaft-
 lichen theorien 378
Gescheidenis der staathuis-
 handkunde 5880
Geschiedenis der staathuis-
 houdkunde 2922
Geschiedenis der staathuis-
 kounde 6778
Geschiedenis van het econo-
 misch denken 692
Der geschlossene handelsstaat
 6040
Gesellschaft und wirtschaft
 2243
Gesellschaftliche produktion
 9011
Gesellschaftliche wirtschaft
 3902
Die gesellschafts- und staatslehre 5355
Die gesetze die socialen 8020
Gesetzkunde und volkwirt-
 schaftslehre 7779
Gesetzmassigkeit und
 voraussehbarkeit 3671

Das gesicht der wirtschafts-
 theorie unserer zeit 589
Gestzmassigkeit in gesellschafts-
 leben 8277
Getting and spending 1287
Getting and spending 2009
Gewerb und handelsfreiheit 6375
Gewerkvereine 8208
Die gewinnbetheiligung 7872
Giammaria Ortes e la scienza
 2852
The gild merchant 7958
Das gildenwesen im mittelalter
 7248
Gindirea economica din Grecia
 5058
Gindirea social-economica 495
Giving alms no charity 4190
Glaube und wirtschaft bei Luther
 2472
Gleanings of past years 7916
Gleichgewichtswachstum 3821
Gli economisti italiani 9934
Gli economisti napoletani 2853
Gli insegnamenti economici 14
Gli sviluppi storici della
 economia politica 477
Goals of economic life 1017
Gold and debt 7840
Gold and silver money 8702
Gold in the East 7715
Gold, silver und währung 7999
H. H. Gossen 9692
Hermann Heinrich Gossen 9766
H. H. Gossen oder die geburt
 9661
Gouvernement des Romains
 5582
The government and the curren-
 cy 6510
Government revenue 8521
Goyaku 2506
Goyaku 2902
Graf Georg von Buquoy 2511
Les grains 5406
Grammar of political 8265
Grand dictionnaire 9114
La grande bourgeoisie au
 pouvoir 873
Les grande économists 235
La grande trasformazione 63
Les grandes compagnies 7530
Les grandes crises financières

7771
Les grandes fortunes 8717
Le grandi strade del commerce internazione 7643
Grandriss zum studium 132
Les grands courants de la pensee 2581
Les grands courants de la pensee 5373
Les grands économistes 792
Les grands faits économiques 8225
The graphic presentation of the laws of supply 9720
Gray's proposal 4327
The graziers advocate 4328
Great Britain arraigned 4329
Great Britain in the latest age 2790
Great Britain for the last forty years 6244
Great Britain's commercial interest explained 4616
Great Britain's glory 4353
Great Britain's poverty 4330
The great economists 435
Great economists 2439
Great ideas in economics 510
The great metallic powers 7613
Great money reformers 2396
The great transformation 529
Greece 8664
The Greek atomists and epicurus 4890
The Greek commonwealth 5146
Greek economics 5016
Greek political theory 4892
Horace Greeley and other pioneers 9578
Grenzkostenpreise 9781
Gresham on foreign exchange 5280
Groans of the plantation 4335
The groans of the poor 4367
Grondbeginselen der economie 1332
Grondbeginselen der moderne economie 1192
Grondbeginselen van communistische 9232
Grondbegrippen grondbeginselen 2208
Grondslagen van de economische analyse 1623
Die grossen dialektiker 9227
The grounds of an opinion 6448
Groundwork of economics 1996
Groundwork of economics 7739
The growing economy 1768
Growth and the economy 2289
The growth and vicissitudes 8812
Growth, employment 2234
Growth, employment 3085
Growth of capital 7909
The growth of economic thought 624
The growth of English industry 5182
Growth of English industry 7707, 7708
The growth of English industry 8837
The growth of philosophic 7301
Grundelemente der wirtschaftsgesellschaft 9237
Grundelmente der wirtschaftstheorie 1537
Grundfragen af den politiska 7424
Grundfragen der okonometrie 3903
Grundfragen der volkswirtschaftslehre 2058
Grundfragen des Rechts 8880
Die grundgedanken 2487
Die grundgedanken der sozialistischen 3278
Die grundgedanken der sozialistischen pädagogik 9269
Grundkurs zum Kapital 9542
Die grundlagen 2154
Die grundlagen der Karl Marxschen 3099
Die grundlagen der nationalokonomie 1375
Grundlagen der nationalökonomie 7679
Grundlagen der volkswirtschaft 5285
Grundlagen der volkswirtschaftspolitik 680
Die grundlagen des historismus

192
Die grundlagen des historismus 8839
Grundlagen die gesammten 7882
Grundlagen einer quantitativen 3463
Die Grundlagen eines betriebswirtschaftlichen 3413
Grundlegung der politischen 3894
Die grundlehren der volkwirthschaft 6336
Grundlehren d. v. Adam Smith 8526
Grundlinien der reinen 6100
Grundriss der allgemeinen 2054
Grundriss der allgemeinen 2263
Grundriss der allgemeinen 8881
Grundriss der politischen 1378
Grundriss der politischen 1943
Grundriss der volkswirtschaftslehre 1735
Grundriss der volkswirtschaftslehre 1832
Grundriss der volkswirthschaftslehre 6454
Grundriss einer geschichte der volkswirtschaftslehre 222
Grundriss für vorlesungen 8016
Grundriss zu vorlesunger 8874
Grundriss zum studium 7662
Grundrisse der kritik 9391
Grundsaetze der kameralwissenschaften 6067
Grundsaetze der staaten 6946
Grundsätze der nationalöekonomie 6292
Grundsätze der polizei 7019
Grundsätze der staatswirtschaft 1212
Grundsätze der volkswirtschaftlehre 1691
Grundsatze der volkswirtschaftslehre 3730
Grundsätze der volkswirtschaftslehre 6757
Grundsätze der volkswirthschaftslehre 9739
Grundsatzfragen der wirtschäftsordnung 718
Grundtraek af den praktiske statsökonomie 6631
Grundtraek af økonomikken 1692
Die grundzüge 8776
Grundzuge der allgemeinen 1782
Grundzuge der modernen 1844
Grundzuge der nationalokonomie 2284
Grundzüge der nationaloekonomie 8795
Grunzuge der neueren wirtschaftsgeschichte 606
Grundzuge der staatswirthschaft 5985
Grundzuge der theoretischen 3104
Grundzüge der theorie 3126
Grundzuge der volkswirtschaftslehre 1664
Grundzuge der wirtschaftsgeschichte 59
Grundzüge der wirtschaftslehre 7876
Grundzuge die nationalökonomie 8002
Grundzüge einer allgemeinenrechts 6337
Grundzuge einer klassifikation 3752
La guerre dans la pensee 5294
Guida allo studio dell'economia politica 137
Guide financier 8735
Guide to John Rae's life of Adam Smith 7354
A guide to Keynes 9948
Guide to marine insurances 7182
A guide to Marxism 9627
A guide to modern 1779
Guideposts in time of change 744
Le guidon de la mer 4338
Le guidon generale des finances 4316
Yves Guyot son action 759

Habitations ouvrières 8333
La hacienda castellana 2970
Hallesismo y communismo 9356
ha-Mahashavah ha-kalkalit

694, 5147
Hamilton, Alexander, als nationalism 7994
Hammurabi's code 4970
Handboek 1910
Handboek van de economie 1774
Handbook 2375
Handbook die statistik 7979
Handbook for economics 1699
Handbook of commercial geography 7623
Handbook of London bankers 8458
A handbook of Marxism 9087
Handbook of social 7359
Handbook on communism 9062
Handbook to land charters 7793
Handbuch der bankwesens 8796
Handbuch der finanzwissenschaft 6440
Handbuch der geographie 7036
Hanbuch der nationalökonomie 8738
Handbuch der ökonometrie 3872
Handbuch der politisch 8209
Handbuch der politischen 8588
Handbuch der statistick 5904
Handbuch der strassenbahnkunde 8037
Handbuch der vergleichenden 8136
Handbuch der volks-wirtschaftslehre 629
Handbuch der staatswirthschaft 6933
Handbuch zur geschichte 2345
Die handelspolit 7841
Handelsgeschichte der Griechen 6266
Die handelspolitik Englands 7873
Der handelsverkehr 7714
Handwörterbuch 7663
Handwörterbuch der staatswissenschaften 7988
Handwörterbuch der volkswirthschaftslehre 7989
Hanse towns 8817
Die Hansestädte 8570
Harmonie en conflict 1918

Harmonies économiques 5531
Harmonies et perturbations 6476
Harmony and conflict 1919
A használati érték 3198
Hat-mahashavah ha-kaikalit 690
Die hauptheorien der volkswirtschaftslehre 622
Hauptprobleme und verfahrensfrage 3905
Der haushalt 1360
Der haushaltplan des konsumenten 9659
Die hausindustrien 8563
Mr. Hawtrey on the scope 3815
Hē oikonomikē hōs epistēmē 3791
He poreia tes oikonomiskes skepseos 504
Hē theōrēsis tou problēmatos 118
W. E. Hearn: first Australian 2547
Heavens below 9016
L'hégémonie du consommateur 1674
Henry home of Kames 7176
Heraclitus 5136
Die herausbildung 9559
Lars Herlitz 9129
Herodotus 5098
The herring-busse trade 4731
Alexander Herzen 9352
Het aardige 1917
Het aardige van de economie 511
Het apriorisme 7348
Het had anders gekund 2495
Het welwaren 6779
Hiberniae leges 7563
Professor Hicks on value 3362
The high price of bullion 6853
Bruno Hildebrand gedenkworte 8843
Hints from Holland 6905
His majesties gracious patent to the goldsmiths 4359
His majesty's royal charter 4360
His speech 4684

Short Title Index

Histoire concise 6052
Histoire critique 6872
Histoire de Colbert 5174
Histoire de Colbert 5754
Histoire de fous 156
Histoire de la banque 6159
Histoire de la civilisation 6161
Histoire de l'administration 5949
Histoire de la législation 7520
Histoire de la monnaie 6090
Histoire de la navigation 5961
Histoire de la pensée 9969
Histoire de la pensée économique 166
Histoire de la pensee economique 306
Histoire de la pensée économique 338
Histoire de la pensée economique 522
Histoire de la pensee economique 3083
Une histoire de la pensee economique contemporaine 508
Histoire de la philosophie medievale 5142
Histoire de la philosophie scolastique 4977
Histoire de la population 8589
Histoire de la poste 8544
Histoire de la question coloniale 7737
Histoire de la reforme commerciale 6862
Histoire de la science politique 8086
Histoire de la société domestique 6099
Histoire de la souveraineté 7065
Histoire de l'assistance 6541
Histoire de l'association commerciale 7871
L'histoire de la vie 5173
Histoire de l'économie politique 83

Histoire de l'economie politique 171
Histoire de l'economie politique 2612
Histoire de l'economie politique 4937
Histoire de l'economie politique 5341
Histoire de l'économie politique 5593
Histoire de l'économie politique 6683
Histoire de l'economie politique 7191
Histoire de l'economie politique en Italie 2861
Histoire de l'economie sociale 4965
Histoire de l'impôt 7627
Histoire des ateliers nationaux 7092
Histoire des banques 7685
Histoire des classes agricoles 5869
Hist. des classes ouvrières 5700
Histoire des classes ouvrières 6378
Histoire des classes rurales 5913
Histoire des doctrines de la population 5208
Histoire des doctrines economiques 138
Histoire des doctrines économiques 201
Histoire des doctrines economiques 241
Histoire des doctrines economiques 251
Histoire des doctrines économiques 7823
Histoire des doctrines monétaires 252
Histoire des doctrines relatives au credit 548
Histoire des faits économiques 426
Histoire des faits économiques 466
Histoire des Français 6544
Histoire des grandes opérations 5681

Histoire des grand chemins de l'Empire Romain 4019
Histoire des impôts 6659
Histoire des impôts 6662
Histoire des institutions 5042
Histoire des monts-de-piété 4100
Histoire des Paysans 5610
Histoire des pêches 6220
Histoire des relations commerciales 6936
Histoire des sociétés coopératives 7788
Histoire des systèmes économiques 163
Histoire des theories 2733
Histoire des theories economiques 339
Histoire des théories économiques spatiales 531
Histoire du commerce 3947
Histoire du commerce 4361
Histoire du commerce 4378
Histoire du commerce 5890
Histoire du commerce 8436
Histoire du communisme 7066
Histoire du consulat 7090
Histoire du crédit hypothécaire 6899
Histoire du finances 8509
Hist. du luxe privé 5538
Histoire du saint-simonisme 9101
Histoire du socialisme 8260
Histoire du socialisme 9342
Histoire du système des finances 4213
Histoire du système des finances 4362
Histoire du système protecteur 5755
Histoire du tarif 6532
Histoire du tarif de 1664, 4215
Histoire economique 523
Histoire économique de l'Espagne 7940
Histoire economique de l'Europe 2611
Historie économique, XIXe et XXe siècles 399

Histoire et doctrines 2721
Histoire financière 5509
Histoire financière 5631
Histoire financière 6682
Histoire générale 4214
Histoire générale des finances 5479
L'histoire monétaire 8000
Histoire parlementaire 7596
Histoire philosophique 4644
Histoire philosophique 6221
Histoire raisonnée du commerce 6222
Histoire sommaire de la pensée économique 340
Histoire statistique 6223
Historia 7655
Historia crítica 9392
História das doutrinas 11
Historia das doutrinas economicas 321
Historia de la economia 133
Historia de la economia 782
Historia de la economia politica española 2967
Historia de las doctrinas 35
Historia de las doctrinas 2568
Historia de las doctrinas economicas 409
Historia del comercio 55
Historia del pensamiento económico 582
Historia do pensamento 2948
Historia economia de Europa 2610
Historia economica general 391
Historia mysli ekonomicznej 115
Historia mysli ekonomicznej do roku 1970 307
Historia politica 6444
Historia polskiej mysli 2934
Historia powszechnej myśli 2938
Historia powszechnej myśli ekonomicznej 260
Historia rozwoju 2175
Historia rozwoju ekonomiki 649
Historia y antologia 5094
Historia y antologie 610
A historian's perspective 563
Historias de los bancos 8557
An historical account 4312
An historical account of Guinea

4016
An historical account of the establishment 4363
Historical account of the navigable 6725
An historical and chronological deduction 3952
An historical and descriptive account of China 6584
An historical disquisition 6867
Historical and economic studies 844
Historical and economic studies 2817
Historical and political remarks 6224
Historical approach 8863
Historical basis of socialism 8082
The historical character 8895
Historical compendium 7184
The historical development 126
The historical development 2362
Historical dissertations on the law 5655
Historical documents 4985
An historical inquiry 6287
Historical materialism 9086
Historical materialism 9121
The historical method in ethics 8451
Historical remarks on the taxation 6495
Historical researches 6225, 6226
The historical school 8887
The historical setting of the Austrian school 9744
Historical sketch of paper currency 8428
Historical sketch of the bank 6419
Historical sketch of the distribution 7490
Historical sketch of the progress of discovery 7047
The Historical versus the deductive method 3525
Les historiens florentins 4956
Historija ekonomiskih doktrina 485
Die historische schule 8858
Die historische schule der wirtschaftswissenschaft 404
History abrégée de traités de paix 6333
The history and antiquities of the exchequer 4478
History and criticism 2792
A history and criticism 8234, 8281
History and criticism of the labor 3467
The history and description of fossil fuel 6237
The history and development 421
History and explanation of stamp duties 7765
History and principles of ancient commerce 6113
The history and principles of banking 6112
History and theories of the working-class 9215
The history and theory of money 8621
The history, civil 5979
History, conditions 6957
History de l'économie politique 7780
History de l'émigration 7792
History des origines du gouvernement 6162
History du commerce 7433
History, law 7653
History of agriculture 8530
A history of American currency 8673
History of American manufactures 7496
History of American socialisms 8378
History of bank of England 7864
The history of banking 6114, 6115
History of banking in Scotland 8123
History of banks 8429
History of bimetallism 8162
A history of Bolshevism 9516
History of boroughs 6496
History of British commerce 5851
History of British commerce

8198
History of British India 6515
A history of British socialism 9037
History of Catholic social thought 144
History of civilization 7581
History of coal, coke 7853
History of cooperation 7464
History of co-operation 8058
A history of currency 7616
A history of economic 3340
History of economic analysis 594
History of economic doctrines 236
History of economic doctrines 291
A history of economic ideas 396
A history of economic ideas 681
A history of economic theories 9393
History of economic theory 3054
A history of economic thought 19, 20
A history of economic thought 33
A history of economic thought 42
History of economic thought 168
History of economic thought 281
A history of economic thought 558
History of economic thought 572
History of economic thought 625
A history of economic thought 651
The history of economic thought 889
History of economics 172
The history of economics 420
History of economics 626
The history of economics 8246
The history of economics in Montana 3079
History of English railway 6061

History of English thought 2784
A history of epidemics 7693
History of European colonies 8412
History of free trade 8312
History of Greece 7963
A history of Greek 2798
A history of Greek economic 5122
History of Greek mathematics 4982
A history of Greek philosophy 4971
A history of Greek public finances 4884
The history of inland navigations 4364
A history of interest 3263
A history of inventions 6301
The history of Java 6745
History of labor 8929
History of land tenure 8316
The history of law of real 7752
The history of local rates 7598
A history of machine wrought hosiery 7842
A history of marginal utility 9730
The history of maritime 6228
History of money 7730
History of merchant shipping 8217
A history of modern banks 7659
History of navigation 4462
The history of our national debts 4365
History of past and present 7163
A history of political economy 124
A history of political economy 334
History of political economy 822
History of political economy in Europe 5594
A history of prices 7122
The history of prices 7126
History of prices 8331
History of protective tariff 8701

History of Russian 2954
History of saving banks 8205
The history of savings banks 6717
History of social philosophy 4944
A history of social thought 227
A history of socialism 8132
History of socialism 9235
History of socialism 9282
A history of socialism 9363
A history of socialist 9304
A history of socialist thought 9107
History of steam navigation 8455
The history of Sumatra 6466
The history of tariff 7937
History of taxation 7076
A history of taxation 7766
A history of the bank 8207
History of the British Empire 7103
History of the chartist 7883
History of the colonization 6227
History of the cotton manufacture 5510
History of the cotton 6160
History of the custom revenue 7982
A history of the economic institutions 8868
History of the English landed 7886
History of the English poor law 6606
The history of the European commerce 6437
History of the Fabian 9480
The history of the factory 6229
The history of the general doctrine of rent 8235
A history of the glove trade 6264
History of the grange 8268
A history of the greenbacks 8975
The history of the independent treasury 8127
History of the Indian archipelago 5855
History of the inductive 7243
History of the land question 8560
History of the manufacture of iron 8681
History of the middle and working 7203
History of the national debt 6145
History of the national economy of Russia 2958
History of the New York property tax 8595
The history of the origins 5075
A history of the people of Israel 5074
The history of the poor 6902
The history of the poor-laws 4063
History of the precious 7731
History of the present tariff 8686
A history of the prices 7129
History of the public revenue 4617
The history of the public revenue 6996
The history of the rise 5750
History of the Scottish poor law 6607
History of the surplus revenue 7546
A history of the theories 3143
The history of the twelve great livery 6206
History of the United States 5515
History of the United States 6217
History of the worsted 6296
The history of trade unionism 8758
The history of usury 8334
The history of Utopian 9231
History of vagrants 8506
History of wages 8806
History of wool 7585
Ho kratikos parembatismos 431
Die hochschullehrer der wirtschaftswissenschaften 2394
Hodnota a ceny 3295
Hollandische wirtschaftsges-

chichte 2919
El hombre y la economía 1711
El hombre y la rqiueza 412
Homes for London poor 8035
The homes of the working 8049
L'homme, agent du développement économique 1000
L'homme aux proportions 6031
L'homme et les richesses 1422
Un homme nouveau 2360
Hommes, besoins, activités 2032
An honest dollar 7383
An honest scheme for improving the trade 4373
Hon'iden Yoshio hakushi koki 825
Hon-iden Yoshio Hakushi koki kinen rombun shū 313
Hoofdiijnen der moderne economie 284
Hoofdstukken 2327
John Hopkin's notions 6461
The house of Adam Smith 7297
How do we want economists to behave 3628
How to discover the law of supply 3 217
How to pay for the war 9991
How will free trade 7232
Sir Albert Howard in India 2408
Hsi yang ching chi ssu hsiang 386
Hsien Ch'in ching chi ssu hsiang 2577, 2580, 2583
Hsüeh hsi Ma-k'o-ssū En-ko-ssū 9103
Human action 1806
Human behavior 8976
Human capital 358
Human capital 3119
The human condition 4887
The human investment revolution 67
Human values 3368
Human values 3665
El humanismo de Marx 9455
An humble address 4815
An humble declaration 4846
Husbandry and trade improved 4375, 4376

The husbandry of the ancients 5900
Francis Hutcheson 2490
Francis Hutcheson and David Hume 2508
Hva er marxisme 9179
The hygiene, diseases 7390
Hygiène sociale 7680
Hyŏndai kyŏngjehak 3808
Hyŏndak sasang yŏn'gu 9102
Hyŏndae ui kyŏngjehak 1258

I diritti del lavoro 2483
I fondamenti 2219
I grandi problemi 1865
Iban Khaldoun 4904
Ibnu Chaldun tentang sosial 2482
Idea gospodarstwa narodowego 569
The idea of usury 5049
The idea of value 3310
Ideal commonwealths 9254
The ideal foundations 627
The ideal foundations 3850
Idealer og regler i anvendt 1693
Idealistische und materialistische dialektik 9032
Ideas and issues 3660
Ideas economicas y fiscales 2594
Ideas of the great economists 619
Die idee der universalokonomie 2648
Die idee der wirtschaftsverfassung 5163
L'idee du juste prix 3436
L'idee du juste prix 4955
L'idee du juste salaire 944
L'idee du juste salaire 3391
Idée d'une souscription partriotique 4001
Le idee economiche degli scrittori Emiliani 2850
Ideen . . . die politik 6195
Ideen, produktionen 3673
Ideen zu einem versuch die Gränzen 6268
Les idées coloniales 5364
Idées d'un citoyen sur le administration 4002
Idées d'un citoyen sur le com-

merce d'Orient 4003
Les idees economiques de Voltaire 2357
Les idées économques d'Iha Khaldoun 5030
Les idées financieres 2514
Les idees politiques 3037
Les idées socialistes 9256
Ideologi zapadnogermanskogo 2719
Ideología y método 46
Ideological responsibility 3507
L'idéologie économique 1333
Ideologische einflüsse auf die entwicklung 362
Ideology and organization in Communist China 2590
Ideology and utopia 9357
Igirisu jushoshugi kenkyu 5171
Ihr glücklichen augen 2532
Ikonomicheskite vuzgledi 2564
Ikonomika, zájmy, politika 9560
Iktisadi dusunce 353
Iktisadi dusunce tarihi 486
Iktisadin prensipleri 1615
Iktisat. 1373
Iktisat dersleri 1659
Iktisat teorisi 1616
Ilban kyŏngjehak 1617
Ilban kyŏngjehak 2301
'Illm al-iqtisād 1567
Illusões econόmicas 1294
Illustrations and proofs 6701
Illustrations of political 6473
Immigration and emigration 8642
The impact of Marxism 9349
An impartial vindication 4396
Imperial and colonial constitution 7691
Imperial economy 5192
Impianti di riserva 3100
Implicit theorizing 3725
Importance of British plantations 4346
The importance of effectually supporting 4397
Important considerations 4398
L'impôt sur le mobilier 8725
L'impôt sur 1. pain 7856

L'impôt sur le revenue 7615
L'impôt sur le revenu 7972
L'impôt sur le revenue 8719
L'impôt territorial 6385
In defense of Heckscher 5175
In hoeverre kunen economische stellingen 3869
In memoria del manifesto 9302
In the twilight of socialism 9089
Inbjudan till de offentliga 2516
Income 1949
Income and taxation 7446
Income distribution 3135
Income, employment 828
Income, employment 1937
The income of nations 1279
The income of society 1558
Income revisited 1950
Income, saving 9925
Income tax 8751
The income-tax scrutinised 6139
Index to economic history 967
Index to periodical literature 9568
India; the land 5666
India; or, Facts Submitted 6863
Indian agriculture 8750
Indian coinage 8465
Indian currency 9992
Indian public works 7107
L'individu et l'état 5952
Individual in society 418
Individualism 7306
Individualism 8201
Individualism and economics 817
L'Individualisme 7328
L'individualisme économique 581
Inductive political 6928
Industrial and commercial supremacy 8531
Industrial arbitration 8226
Industrial arbitration 8771
Industrial biography 8638
Industrial conciliation 7695
Industrial conciliation 8807
Industrial democracy 8759
The industrial economy 1083
The industrial economy 8911
Industrial government 8930
Industrial history 7524

An industrial history of
  England 7901
The industrial progress 7401
Industrial resources of Ireland 6320
The industrial situation 8587
Industrial society 890
Industrie 6922
L'industrie nationale 6410
Der industriebetrieb 8003
Les industrieles agricoles 8534
The industries of Scotland 7565
Industry and trade 9842
Industry, income 1131
Inflation 8360
Influence and development of
  English gilds 8031
L'influence de la philosophie 9454
Influence des expériences communistes 333
The influence of events and
  policies 631
Influences of the corn 7253
The influence of rate of
  interest 9796
The influence of Veblen's 8923
The influence of Veblen 8952
Information, addressed to
  the Lords of session 4069
Information concerning the
  cost 6273
Informe de don Gaspar de
  Jovellanos 6315
Informe de la sociedad
  economica 6274
Inhaltsvergleichsregister der
  Marx-Engels 9230
Iniciacao a econômia 1787
Initiation à l'économie 2031
Initiation à l'economie générale 1251
Initiation à l'économie politique 1071
Initiation à l'éconômique 1316
Initiation economique et sociale 965
Inland waterways 8103
Inleiding in het economisch
  denken 2286
Inleiding tot de economie 1719

Inleiding tot de economische
  wetenschap 204
Inleiding tot de moderne
  economie 1193
Inleiding tot het denken 9898
Die innere französische gewerbepolitik 7827
Input-output 3726
Input-output analysis 9909
Inquiries concerning the poor 6431
An inquiry 5870
An inquiry concerning the
  population 5996
An inquiry concerning the
  rise 6174
An inquiry into economic 634
An inquiry into physiocracy 5331
An inquiry into some of the
  principal monopolies 5856
An inquiry into the causes 5521
An inquiry into the causes 5524
An inquiry into the causes 6218
An inquiry into the causes and
  modes 5828
Inquiry into the causes and
  remedies 6275
An inquiry into the causes of
  the general poverty 5875
An inquiry into the colonial 5637
An inquiry into the connection
  between the present price 3971
An inquiry into the corn trade 5908
An inquiry into the currency 7123
An inquiry into the expediency 5525
An inquiry into the expediency 6276
Inquiry into the late and
  present scarcity 5592
Inquiry into the late and
  present scarcity 6277
An inquiry into the late
  mercantile distresses 4399
An inquiry into the nature 1672
An inquiry into the nature 6353
An inquiry into the nature 6449
An inquiry into the nature 7337

Short Title Index 799

An inquiry into the nature of zemindary 6134
An inquiry into the original 4226
An inquiry into the permanent causes of decline 6704
An inquiry into the policy 5555
An inquiry into the poor-laws 5580
An inquiry into the practical working 7135
An inquiry into the present state of population 7211
An inquiry into the principles 2013
An inquiry into the principles 2145
An inquiry into the principles 2186
An inquiry into the principles 4770
An inquiry into the principles 5304
An inquiry into the principles 6886
An inquiry into the principles 7096
An inquiry into the principles of taxation 6278
An inquiry into the rise of prices 7270
An inquiry into the state of British West Indies 6401
An inquiry into the state of national subsistence 5783
An inquiry into the state of slavery 5586
An inquiry into the state of the ancient measures 4400
Inquiry into the taxation 5647
An inquiry into the various systems 6085
An inquiry into the workhouse 5628
Instinct of workmanship 8995
Institucionalismo 8906
Instituições de economia politica 1114
Institutes de droit commercial 6279
Institutes of economics 7384

Institutional adjustment 8989
The institutional approach 8955
Institutional economics 8926, 8927
Institutional economics 8932
Institutional economics 8964
Institutional economics 9002
Institutional factors 8987
Institutional revenue 8936
Institutional revenue 9686
The institutional school 8961
The institutional theory 8981
Institutionalism 8956
Institutionalism 8962
Institutionalism and contemporary price 8941
Institutionalism and empiricism 8967
Institutionalism and orthodox 8907
Der institutionalismus als epoche amerikanischer 3764
Der institutionalismus als Richtung 3047
Der institutionalismus als Richtung 8934
Institutiones Juris Cambialis 4299
Instituzioni di scienza della finanze 7947
Instructions for travellers 5313
Instructor's manual 1761
Instrumental doktrinhistoria 4
The insufficiency of the causes 6254
Insularity and cosmopolitanism 327
Insurance cyclopaedia 8740
Das integrations problem 245
The intellectual and the market place 993
The intellectual virtues 7526
Intelligence and the guidance 8977
Intelligent woman's guide 9554
El intercambio mercantil 9313
The interdependence of different sources 3388
Interdependenzen von politik 3678
Interest 4935
Interest and prices 9797
Interest and usury 4931
The interest of England 4228

The interest of Great Britain 4303
Interest of money mistaken 4401
Intérêts de la France 6339
Les interets des nations de l'Europe 4402
Intermediate economic analysis 1227
Intermediate economic analysis 1344
Intermediate economic analysis 9689
Intermediate economic theory 1372
Intermediate economic theory 1731
Intermediate economic theory 1767
International bimetallism 7425
International coinage 7416
International conference on input-output 3680
International economic papers 831
The international economics 9954
Internationale Karl-Marx-konferenz 9255
Internationale wirtschaftspolitik 363
Internationales eisenbahnfrachtrecht 8536
Interpretacion del mercantilismo 5275
The inter-state commerce act 7764
Intervencion del estado 556
Intrinsic value 9693
Introducão 2019
Introdução 2118
Introducão economia 249
Introdução à economia 1233
Introducão à economia moderna 406
Introducao a historiografia 3674
Introdução à política 1418
Introducción 1902
Introduccion a la dinamica 2312
Introducción a la economia social 526
Introduccion a las doctrinas 465

Introducción al estugio 1916
Introduction in oeconomian nationalem 6201
An introduction 1349
An introduction 1369
An introduction 1423
Introduction 1589
An introduction 1599
An introduction 1635
An introduction 1663
An introduction 1679
An introduction 1700
Introduction 1822
Introduction 1827
Introduction 1954
An introduction 1973
Introduction 2083
Introduction 2130
Introduction 2141
Introduction 2200
Introduction 2212
Introduction 2282
Introduction 3683
Introduction 3837
Introduction 7312
Introduction 8978
Introduction a l'analyse macroeconomique 1073
Introduction à l'étude 1796
Introduction a l'étude du manuele de v. Pareto 9669
Introduction a l'histiore 666
Introduction a l'histoire 3766
Introduction à une sociologie 40
Introduction allo studio 7677
Introduction aux mathématiques 3796
Introduction critique 1348
The introduction of Adam Smith's 7305
The introduction of Adam Smith's doctrine 2681
Introduction to Aristotle 5038
Introduction to contemporary microeconomics 2237
Introduction to economic analysis 1765, 1769
Introduction to economic cybernetics 3721
Introduction to economic issues 842
An introduction to economic reasoning 3819

Introduction to economic statistics 3572
Introduction to economic thinking 395
An introduction to economics 1072
An introduction to economics 1142
Introduction to economics 1206
Introduction to economics 1578
Introduction to economics 10033
Introduction to engineering 2287
An introduction to English 7398
An introduction to English 8823
Introduction to English economic history 4889
An introduction to Keynesian 10069
Introduction to Keynesian dynamics 10008
Introduction to macroeconomic 2104
An introduction to Marxism 9088
An introduction to Marxist 9354
Introduction to Marxist 9430
Introduction to merchandise 6175
An introduction to microeconomic 1310
An introduction to modern 2005
An introduction to modern demand 3484
An introduction to modern economics 1220
Introduction to microeconomic 1440
Introduction to modern microeconomics 1665
Introduction to "Notes on Malthus" 2405
An introduction to political 7808
Introduction to political 8423
An introduction to political economy 1146
An introduction to positive 1695
Introduction to public finance 8441
Introduction to Rogers 98
An introduction to some Japanese 2897
An introduction to the American economy 1473
Introduction to the new 1267
An introduction to the principles 2291
Introduction to the study 2115
Introduction to the study 7583
Introduction to the study of economics 1195
An introduction to the study of political 5604
Introduction to the theory of employment 2004
Introduction to the theory of employment 10056
An introduction to the theory of value 3428
An introduction to the theory of value 8636
An introduction to the theory of value 9773
Introduction to the total theory of labor 3296
Introduction to the use of mathematics 3669
Introduction to the world economy 1183
An introduction to West African 1883
Introductory economics 1328
Introductory economics 1338
Introductory economics 1513
Introductory economics 1607
Introductory economics 2295
An introductory lecture 6179
An introductory lecture 6498
An introductory lecture 6738
An introductory lecture on political 6306
Introductory lectures on political 7240
Introduzione 1897
Introduzione all'economia 1105
Introduzione all storia delle dottrine 2858
Introduzione alla economia politica 2222

Introduzione alla politica 1281
Introduzione alla pratica del commercio 4403
Introduzione allo studio 1904
Introduzione allo studio 6074
Introduzione allo studio della storia economica 206
An investigation of the cause 6280
Investigations in currency 9723
L'investissement et la demande 3412
Ippan keizaigaku 2304
Ire economisti Italiani 2474
Ireland before and after 6470
Irish land laws 8511
Iron kyŏngjehak 10002
Irregularity of employment 7863
Les irrigations en Egypte 7435
Der irrthumer des historismus 3753
Irrthumer des historismus 8290
Die irrhumer des historismus 8864
Is communism the next stage? 79
Is communism the next stage? 2992
Is economic theory possible 3657
Is market price determinate 3437
Is 'Utility' the most suitable 3213
Isaak Iselin 5340
Islāmī ma'ashiyāt 2838
The "isms" 248
Der isolirthe staat 7116
Istanze statiche ed istanze evolutive 3610
Istituzioni di economia politica 1480
Istituzioni di economia politica 8950
Istituzioni di scienza economica 1716
Istoriîa ekonomicheskikh 2989
Istoriîa ekonomicheskikh učhenjǐ 47

Istoriîa ėkonomićeskikh ucenii 48
Istorija ekonomiceskih učenij 335
Istoriîa ekonomicheskikh uchenĭi 689, 2983
Istoriia ekonomicheskogo 2621
Istoriia ėkonomicheskoi mysli 567
Istoriîa ekonomicheskogo byta Zapadnoi Evropy 385
Istoriia ekonomichnoi 3024
Istoriîa ekonomichnoi dumky 568
Istoriîa ėkonomisheskoĭ 1008
Istoriia na ikonomicheskata 2565
Istoriîa na ikonomicheskite ucheniîa 482
Istoriîa politicheskoĭ ekonomii 121
Istoriîa politicheskoĭ economiĭ 400
Istoriîa politicheskoĭ ėkonomii 566
Istoriia russkoi 2985
Istorija ėkonomićeskiucenij 9267
Istorija ekonomiceskih ucenij 1014
Istorija ėkonomićeskog mysli 336
Italian finances 8606
L'Italie et son développement 8551
Iz istorii antichynkh 5100
Iz istorii ėkonomicheskoĭ 18
Iz istorii russkoj 3026

Edmund J. James lectures 2411
Japanese communism 9309
Japanese communist 9541
Japanese notions of European 8254
Japanese sources on the history 9556
Japan's landwirtschaftliche 8213
Japans volkswirtschaft 8483
Le Japon de nos jours 7550
Jefferson and the physiocrats 5342
Jevons and his precursors 9767
Jevon's theory of political 9806

Short Title Index

The jewel house of art 4607
Jitsurei, fuka kachi 3238
Jitsuryoku wa oshiminaku 2895
Der joint council on economic education 3685
Richard Jones 2356
Richard Jones 2529
Richard Jones 8918
Thomas Joplin and the rate 2436
La jornada 3209
Joseph of Egypt 2347
Journal d'économie publique 6881
Journal of an embassy 5857
A journey from Madras 5648
A journey through Spain 7140
Journeys through the Upper Provinces of India 6314
Journey through utopia 9051
Jōyo kachi gakusetsu ryakushi 468
Judaism in the first centuries 5043
Die juden und das wirtschaftsleben 2707
Jugoslavska ekonomie 9586
Junogakuha chinginsetsu 5357
Junoshugi bunseki 5442
Jus maritimum 4773
Jus maritimum hanseaticum 4414
Jūshō shugi kaitaiku no kenkyō 365
The just price 4929
Just price 4932
Just price 5003
The just wage 4978
Justo y Marx 9473
Juyō riron no kenkyū 3485

K filosofické problematice 9496
K problematice socialistickych 2092
K problematice socialistickych 9561
K voprosu o predmete i zadacah 3005
K voprosu ob istorii razvitiia 3027
Kachi no riron 3425

Kachi ronsō shi ron 3283
Kachiron 3335
Kachiron to shakaishugi 3298
Kachironsō shi 3109
Kagaku, gijutsu jidai 1569
K'ai-en-ssŭ ti Chiu yeh 9928
K'ai-ên-ssŭ yü Ma-erh-sa-ssŭ 10020
Kai-yin-ssŭ ching chi hsüeh 9966
Kaiso hachijunen rekishi 2889
Kakaku to shihon no riron 3375
Kamata na investicione kredite 9606
Kameralistische encyclopadie 5153
Kapauku papuan economy 5069
Das kapital 6875
Das kapital 9394
Das kapital 9512
Kapital 9154
Das Kapital centenary volume 9266
Kapital; kryptka ekonomii 1756
Kapital und arbeit 8039
Kapital und kapitalzins 1151
Kapital und kapitalzins 7513
Kapitalismus 8573
Kapitaltheoretische 1376
Kapitoly ke studiu dějin ekonomickych teorií 78
Karakter en methode der staathuish houdkunde 8030
Die kartelle 8134
Katalog der Carl Menger 9716
Katechismus der ifanzwissenschaft 7494
Katechimsus der volkswirtschaftslehre 8585
Katedra politicke ekonomie 1977
Der katheder-sozialismus 2697
Die kaufmannische arbitrage 8682
Keiki bunseki ABC 10040
Keins--ideolog monopolisticheskogo 10099
Keinzu 9956
Keinzu-ha keizaigaku 9933
Keinzu keizaigaku kaisetsu 10003
Keinzu keizaigaku kōgi 10006
Keinzu-keizaigaku no kisen 10034
Keinzu kenkyu 10004
Keinzu koyō riron no bunseki

10087
Keinzu nyūmon 10071
Keinzu-shugi keizai riron 10041
Keio gijuku keizai gakkai 2887
Keisaigaku gaisetsu 2165
Keizai gaku shi 361
Keizai genron 107
Keizai genron 1252
Keizai genron 1543
Keizai genron 1634
Keizai genron 1846
Keizai genron 2029
Keizai genron gaisetsu 2305
Keizai hatten to shihon 10072
Keizai honshitsu ron 1878
Keizai kagaku no sōzō 303
Keizai no ronri to genjitsu 2194
Keizai riron to takei-teki 389
Keizai seichō 688
Keizai seichō no kiso riron 3891
Keizai shakai shiso shi 597
Keizai shisō shi 478
Keizai shisō no kakushin 439
Keizai shisō shi 493
Keizai shisō shi jiten 314
Keizai shisō shi zuihitsu 997
Keizai taisei no mondai 1595
Keizai taisei ron 299
Keizai tetsugaku 1847
Keizaigaku 1814
Keizaigaku 1887
Keizaigaku 2507
Keizaigaku e no susume 441
Keizaigaku e no susume 1608
Keizai-gaku 50 nen 500
Keizaigaku gairon 1545
Keizaigaku gairon 2303
Keizaigaku gaisetsu 1813
Keizaigaku genri 1544
Keizaigaku genri 2166
Keizaigaku genri 9604
Keizaigaku hattatsu-shi 1.
Keizaigaku hihan taikei no seisei 367
Keizaigaku hōhōron 3702
Keizaigaku hōhō ron 3775
Keizaigaku keieigaku o manabu 1597
Keizaigaku kogi 1876
Keizaigaku ni okeru koten 848
Keizaigaku ni okeru ningenzō 1875
Keizaigaku no hoho 917
Keizaigaku no kiso chishiki 300
Keizaigaku no kiso riron 2302
Keizaigaku no kontei 332
Keizaigaku no koten 1546
Keizaigaku no rekishi-teki 159
Keizaigaku nyūmon 1253
Keizaigaku nyūmon 1877
Keizaigaku nyūmon 2195
Keizaigaku sampo 501
Keizaigaku sampo 2454
Keizaigaku shi 111
Keizaigaku shi 368
Keizaigaku shi 371
Keizai-gaku-shi 374
Keizaigaku shi 388
Keizaigaku-shi 424
Keizaigaku shi 643
Keizaigakushi 655
Keizaigaku-shi 755
Keizaigaku shi 847
Keizaigaku-shi 861
Keizai-gaku-shi gaisetsu 604
Keizaigakushi gaisetsu jo 605
Keizaigakushi koza 1006
Keizaigakushi no kenkyu 656
Keizai-gaku-shi no Kosei 642
Keizai-gaku-shi shinko 615
Keizaigaku shi tsūron 315
Keizaigaku shinkō 2306
Keizaigaku taikō 351
Keizaigaku to rekishi 3585
Keizaigaku to Toyo shiso 2573
Keizaigaku to Toyo shiso 2618
Keizaigaku wa muzukashiku 2196
Keizaigaku; waga shi 645
Keizaigaku yōron 1621
Keizaigaku yottsu 1547
Keizaigaku zenshi 644
Keizai-riron no rekishi-sei 657
Keizaishi 2883
Keizaishi ko 2878
Keizai-shiso-shi no atarashii mikata ni tsuite 646
Kennen en keuren 1961
Kennismaking 2274
The key of wealth 5277
A key to modern economics 2290

Short Title Index 805

John Maynard Keynes 9908
John Maynard Keynes 9931
John Maynard Keynes 9952
John Maynard Keynes 9970, 9971
Lord Keynes 10063
John Maynard Keynes 10067
Keynes 10073
J. M. Keynes a soudobý kapitalismus 10060
Keynes' allgemeine theorie 9888
John Maynard Keynes als Psychologe 10066
Keynes and after 10081
Mr. Keynes and finance 10052
Keynes and his underconsumption predecessors 10025
Keynes and Marx 9929
Mr. Keynes and Mr. Marx 9887
Keynes and Proudhon 9921
Mr. Keynes and the Classics 9960
Keynes and the classics 10015
Keynes and the classics 10018
Mr. Keynes and the labour 10059
Mr. Keynes answered 9906
Keynes at Harvard 10097
Lord Keynes' central thesis 9885
Keynes, economista vulgar 9975
John Maynard Keynes, ein falscher prophet 10076
Keynes, Foster and Marx 9903
Keynes general theory 9910
Keynes' general theory 9945
Keynes' general theory 10019
Keynes's General theory 10048
Mr. J. M. Keynes' general theory 10049
Keynes' neue wirtschaftslehre 9930
Mr. Keynes on the rate of interest 9927
Mr. Keynes on underemployment 9950
The Keynes plan 10012
Lord Keynes' theorie 10068

Mr. Keynes Theory of employment 9961
Mr. Keynes' theory of money 10053
Mr. Keynes' theory of the multiplier 9944
Keynes-Triffin plans 9940
Keynes: updated or outdated 10028
J. M. Keynes, vision 10046
The Keynesian theory 10009
The Keynesian economics 10021
Keynesian economics 10030
Keynesian economics 10075
Keynesian economics 10077
Keynesian economics 10091
A Keynesian model 10090
The Keynesian reformation 9915
The Keynesian revolution 10005
The Keynesian system 10108
A Keynesian theory of employment 10103
Keynesianism--retrospect 9967
Khutut ra'isiyah fi al-iqtisad 2835
Kihon keizaigaku 1564
Kihon keizaigaku 2307
Kindal keizai riron no tenkai 304
Kindai keizai shico gaikan 2420
Kindai keizai shichō gaikan 369
Kindai keizai shisō shi 370
Kindai keizaigaku gairon 2047
Kindai keizaigaku kōgi 2085
Kindai keizaigaku kōza 2086
Kindai keizaigaku no keisei 2786
Kindai keizaigaku no seisei 1028
Kindai keizaigaku shi 636
Kindai keizaigaku yūron 2030
Kindai nihon keizai shiso 664
Kindai nihon no dochaku 5429
Kinkō riron to shiron riron 1840
Kinsei Furansu keizaigaku 2656
Kinsei keizai shisō shi ron 352
Kensei keizaigaku shi taiko 316
Kinsei no keizai shiso 2879
Kirchliche geographie 7035
Die klassische nationalökonomie 3534
Die klassische nationalökonomie 8885

Die klassische und die moderne nationalökonomie 12
Die klassische werttheorie 3185
Kleine ökonomische schriften 9399
Kleine wirtschaftskunde 1884
Kleinere schriften zur methode 9740
Karl Knies 8838
Professor Knight on psychology 3568
Kohle und eisen 8215
Kollektivismus 5148
Kolonialreiche 7729
Kolonien, kolonialpolitik 8878
Die kommunal-verwaltung 8654
Kompendium 1636
Kompendium 2319
Kompendium der nationalokonomie 2252, 2256
Kompendium der volkswirtschaftslehre 2253
La "Konjunkturforschung" 2550
La "Konjunkturforschung" 2668
Die konjunkturtheorie in Russland 2966
Consistent aggregering 3495
Konsum-und produktionstheorie 3254
Konsum und vermögen 10032
Köpfe der wirtschaft 2422
Kostensenkung durch wertanalyse 3288
Koten keizaigaku kenkyū 2202
Koten keizaigaku no tenkai 1804
Koten-keizaigaku to shoki 2756
Kotenha keizaigaku 3110
Kotenha keizaigaku no riron 2737
Koyō riron to chingin 10083
A kozgazdasagi elmelet tortenete 294
Kratak kurs političke 9218
Krazvitie ecknomicheskoi teorii 862
Des kreditwesen 8442
Der kriegswirtschaftliche 2684
Krisis der wirtschaft 2679
Kritik der politischen 9298
Kritika economickych 1864
Kritika Englise a jeho 2755

Kritika osnovyh napravlenij 571
Kritika sovremennoi burzhuaznoi 2727
Kritika sovremennyh buržuaznyh 570
Kritika teorii sovremennykh 3050
Kritika vozzrenii russkikh 3008
Kritische geschichte 7778
Kritische geschichte der nationalokonomie 182
Kritische grundlegung der volkswirthschaftslehre 183
Krizis sovremennoj buržuaznoj 49
Kronika szczecinskiego 1967
Kŭndae kyŏngjehak 1254
Kŭndae kyŏngjehak sa 311
Kuo chia chien shê ho jên 3459
Kuo fu ssu hsiang yu hsien 2293
Kuo shih shang ti li ts'ai 2579
Kuo wai uiao i ho kuo 3339
Kurzgefasste 2248
Kurzgefasste geschichte der volkswirtschaftslehre 469
Kyariko ronso shi no kenkyu 5271
Kyŏngje suhak 3907
Kyŏngje wŏllon 1255, 1257
Kyongje wollon 1596
Kyŏngje wŏllon 1894
Kyŏngje wŏllon 2124
Kyongje wollon 2299
Kyongjehak 1630
Kyongjehak immun 2125
Kyongjehak sa 312
Kyongjehak wollon 1259
Kyongjehak wollon 1618
Kyongjehak yon'gu 359
Kyongjehak yonsup 2300
Kyongjesa 116
Kyoshi no tame no keizaigaku kōgi 112
Kyōyō keizaigaku 2168

Labor in Europe 8814
Labor movement 7809
The labor movement 8282
The labor problem 7434
The labor problem 7911
Labor rewarded 7097
Labor theory of value 3269
The labor theory of value 3408

Short Title Index 807

Il laboro 7586
Labor and the popular welfare 8257
Labour defended 6233
Labour in the English economy 5179
Labour's wrongs 5626
The laird and farmer 4418
Laissez-faire and communism 9993
Das laissez-faire der physiokraten 5399
The laissez-faire doctrine 7315
Andrés Lamas 2467
Land and its rent 8745
Land and labor 8318
Land nationalization 7688
Land nationalization 8749
The land question 7894
Land revenue 7412
The land systems 7413
Land systems 8194
Land systems 8453
Land systems of Australia 7819
Landed interest 5667
Landed property 6399
Landholding 7846
Die land-kultur-gasetzgebung 5915
Die landiche arbeiterfrage 7927
Landlord and tenants 7783
Landmarks in political economy 804
Landmarks of economic thought 211
Landmarks of scientific socialism 9171
Die landwirtschaft Japans 8339
Die landwirtschaftlich 8607
Das landwirtschaftliche 2669
Lärebok i national-ekonomien 6744
Ferdinand Lassalle 7558
Ferdinand Lasalle 8443
Harold J. Laski on the communist 9310
The last of the saxons 5757
Lasting effects of economics courses 3509
Die lateinische Münz-convention 7584

Latin American 'structuralist' 3857
J. Laurance Laughlin 2441
Latviesu progresivas 2913
Die Lauterung des nationalokonomischen 2676
John Law 5229
John Law 5272
John Law 5303
The law and practice of bankruptcy 6542
Law of banks 8325
The law of domicile 7742
Law of friendly societies 8454
The law of Greco-Roman Egypt 5109
The law of joint stock 7267
The law of nations 5737
The law of population 6907
Law of railways 8045
Law of railways 8488
Law of shipping 6780
The law of supply and demand 3207
The law of value and Soviet 3277
Law relating to factories 8374
Laws and institutes 7111
Laws and the republic 4918
The laws of ancient Greece 5117
Laws of political economy 3623
Law of the United States relating to currency 7786
The laws of trade unions 7971
Laws of wages 8321
The laws of wages, profits 2197, 3443
The laws, ordinances 4423
Laws relating to the poor 4279
Leading British statisticians 9701
A learned and necessary argument 4425
Leather 4426
Lebensbilder grosser 2469
Lebensbilder grosser nationalokonomen 542
Lebensbilder grosser nationalokonomen 950
Das lebenswerk von Knut Wicksell 9774
Lecciones de economia civil 5868

Lecons d'économie politique 6679
Lecons d'économie politique 9747
Lecciones de economia politica 422
Leccciones de economía política 8250
Leçons d'économie politique 1742
Lectures notes on types 906
Lecture notes on types of economic theory 459
A lecture on human happiness 6140
A lecture on the notion of value 6388
Lectures on advanced economic theory 948
Lectures on colonization 6499
Lectures on economic principles 961
Lectures on history of protection 8674
Lectures on justice 7338
Lectures on mediaeval 8665
Lectures on modern economic 896
Lectures on political 6394
Lectures on political 6972
Lectures on political 9798
Lectures on political economy 876
Lectures on political economy 1021
Lectures on rhetoric 7339
Lectures on the coinage 5687
Lectures on the elements of political 5822
Lectures on the industrial 2788
Lectures on the industrial revolution 8708
Lectures on the industrial revolution 8896
Lectures on the labor 7562
Lectures on the nature and use of money 6141
Lectures on the restrictive 5898
Leerboek der economie 2148
Leerboek der financien 7674
Leerboek der staathuishoudkunde 8433
Leftwing social movements in Japan 9620
Legal foundations of capitalism 3164
The legal foundations of capitalism 8928
Legal obligations of dwellings 7775
La legge di popolazione 8224
Leggere il capitale 9009
Le legge dell'economia 1397, 1398
Législation charitable 7226
Législation de l'assistance 7465
Legislation des mines 7373
Législation et organisation des sociétés 7738
Législations de l'Europe 8071
Legislative and documentary history 5748
The legitimacy of economics 3529
Lehr v. modernen staat 7510
Lehrbegriff saemtlicher oeconomischer 4600
Lehrbegriff und anfang 6043
Lehrbriefe fur das fernstudium 719
Lehrbuch d. deutschen verwaltungsrecht 8293
Lehrbuch der finanzwissenschaft 6317
Lehrbuch der finanzwissenschaft 7039
Lehrbuch der finanzwissenschaft 7177
Lehrbuch der landwirthschaft 8584
Lehrbuch der nationalökonomie 1536
Lehrbuch der nationalökonomie 1622
Lehrbuch der nationalökonomie 7040
Lehrbuch der nationalökonomie 7495
Lehrbuch der nationalökonomie 8739
Lehrbuch der oeconomischen politick 6895
Lehrbuch der politischen 6758
Lehrbuch der weltgeschichte 7230
Die lehre vom gelde 6236

Die lehre vom heerwesen 7038
Die Lehre vom unternehmergewin 1736
Die lehre vom unternehmergewinn 2649
Die lehre vom unternehmergewinn 3386
Die lehre vom unternehmergewinn 6453
Die lehre vom unternehmergewinn 7959
Die lehre vom unternehmergewinn 8435
Lehre von den banken 7204
Die Lehre von der verteilung 2489
Die lehre von der wirtschaft 2016
Lehrgebaude der volkswirthschaft 8818
Die lehrmeinungen der kameralisten 5196
Lehr- und handbuch 2230
Lehr- und handbuch 8900
Das leis economicas 1788
Leistungsmessung 3314
Die lietenden sozial- 2678
Leitfaden zur wirtschaftskunde 1945
Leitura basica de O Capital 9076
Lektsii po istorii 2622
V. I. Lenin o řízení 9567
V. I. Lenin on Marxism 9322
Leninism 9324
Leninism 9445
Leninskoe issledovanie 3010
Pierre Leroux, sa vie 2512
Leonardus Lessius 2921
Lessons from central forecasting 3544
A letter 4025
A letter addressed to Rowland Burdon 5486
A letter balancing the causes 4542
A letter commercial 7254
A letter concerning the consequences of an incorporating union 4432
A letter concerning the importance of our sugar-colonies 4433
A letter concerning the naval store-bill 4434
A letter concerning the parliament's rejecting the French 4435
A letter concerning the South-Sea 4436
A letter concerning the trade 4437
A letter concerning the Tyrone collieries 4438
A letter containing some important hints 4439
A letter for re-establishing the woollen manufactures 4296
A letter from a by-stander 4543
A letter from a Fyfe gentleman 4440
A letter from a merchant 4441, 4442
A letter from Sir Richard Cox 4443
A letter of advice 4444
A letter on several proposals 4445
A letter on the abolition 7247
A letter on the corn laws 6356
A letter on the corn laws 7026
A letter on the revival of the salt duty 4446
A letter on the true principles 6371
A letter opposing the farther extension 4447
A letter to a friend concerning naturalizations 4816
A letter to a political economist 5501
Letter to Bourchier Cleeve 4492
A letter to Charles Wood 6611
A letter to Edmund Burke 4817
A letter to explain internal bills of exchange 5652
A letter to J. B. Smith 6405
A letter to Kirkman Finlay 6689
A letter to Lord Ashley 7136
A letter to Lord Grenville 7127
A letter to Lord Howick 6973

A letter to Samuel Whitbread 6288
A letter to Sir John Barnard 4451
A letter to Sir Thomas Osborn 4452
A letter to the agriculturists 7246
A letter to the chairman of the East-India 4448
A letter to the Earl of Carlisle 5973
A letter to the Earl of Liverpool 6731
A letter to the merchants 4059
A letter to the merchants 4449
A letter to the Rev. Thomas Carte 4450
A letter to the Right Honorable Lord Althorpe 6372
A letter to the Right Hon. Lord Viscount Melbourne 7137
A letter to the right honorable William Pitt 5624
A letter to the West-India 4453
A letter to the whole people 4777
A letter to Thomas Brand 5608
A letter to Thomas Paine 7207
A letter to Thomas Spring Rice 5923
A letter touching the African 4454
A letter towards enjoying the national benefit 4455
A letter with reference to the expediencey 7166
Lettere a Maffeo Pantaleoni 9754
Lettere ai Peruzzi 2860
Letters and journal of W. Stanley Jevons 9724
Letters from a farmer 4456
The letters of David Hume 4383
Letters on credit 6242
Letters on currency 5846
Letters on the corn laws 6373
Letters on the factory act 6974
Letters on the importance of the rising generation 4348
Letters on the importance 6167
Letters on the rudiments of a science 6705
Lettre à la chambre du commerce 6374
Lettre à M. F. (Freron) 4289
Letter concernant les monnaies 6136
Lettre d'un negociant 3921
Lettre sur la monnaie fictive 4015
Lettre sur la proportion 6137
Lettres a sa femme 2464
Lettres à ses concitoyens 5676
Lettres à un ami 4457
Lettres d'un citoyen 4458
Lettres, journal 8195
Lettres sur l'Amérique du nord 5732
Lettres sur l'emprunt 6865
Lettres sur l'organisation 5733
Leviathan 4366
John L. Lewis 2331
Lex mercatoria 4404
Lex mercatoria rediviva 4009
Lexicon universae 5073
Lexicon universae rei numariae veterum 6755
Lexioni di economia civile 4320
Lexique de termes 1410
Lezione delle moneta 4170
Lezioni di commercio 4319
Lezioni di economia matematica 3499
Lezioni di economia politica 1154
Lezioni di economia politica 1187
Lezioni di economia politica 1215
Lezioni di economia politica 1371
Lezioni di economia politica 1419
Lezioni di economia politica 1850
Lezioni di economia politica 1932
Lezioni di politica 1773
Lezioni di storia delle dottrine 454
Lezioni di storia delle dottrine economiche 536
Lezioni su alcuni argomenti 1235
Lezioni sul metodo 1399

The liberal dilemma 82
The liberal elements 5210
Liberalismo económico 96
Libération 1343
La liberté commerciale 5956
Liberté commerciale 8546
La liberté des banques 6248
La liberté du commerce 4460
La liberté du travail 5539
La liberté economique 9755
A library of public finance 1872
Le libre échange 5953
Les libre-échangistes 7781
Lições de economia 1828
Lições de economia circulatoria 2035
Licões de economia política 514
Liçoes de economia política 1222
Lições de economia política 1924
The life 4384
Life and correspondence of David Hume 4385
Life and epoch of Alexander Hamilton 8620
Life and labor 7535
The life and letters of Maria Edgeworth 7795
The life and teaching of Karl Marx 9038
The life and teachings of Karl Marx 9329
The life and times 6149
The life and times of Sir Edwin Chadwick 2383
The life and times of Sir Thomas Gresham 5653
Life and work 5564
Life of Adam Smith 7300, 7322
Life of Adam Smith 7334
Life of Alexander Hamilton 8675
Life of David Hume 2445
The life of Francis Place 2527
Life of Friedrich List 2402
Life of Friedrich List 8847

The life of James Deacon Hume 5499
The life of John Locke 4463
The life of John Maynard Keynes 9955
Life of John Stuart Mill 7684
The life of Richard Cobden 2443
Life of Right. Hon. William Pitt 7027
Life of Sir William Petty 5195
The life of the Hon. Sir Dudley North 4569
The life of Turgot 5418
Life of William Allen 6239
Life tables 5977
Life tables 6383
The life, times, and labours of Robert Owen 8106
Liiketaloustiellisten tutkinus-laitoksen 875
The limitations of marginal 9784
The limits of American capitalism 3061
Lineamenti di economia 1747
Lineamenti fondamentali 9400
Linear programming 3593
Linear programming 9688
Lineare wirtschaftsalgebra 3682
Liquiditäts-aequivalenz 3125
Lire le capital 9008, 9010
Frederic List 8827, 8828
Friedrich List 8856
Friedrich List in America 3072
List--Knies--von Gottl-Ottlilien-feld 8869
List of economic books 2426
Friedrich List und Deutschlands 8844
Friedrich Lists system 8894
Literary remains 838, 6307
Literature and Marxism 9183
The literature of political 6420
The literature of political economy 446
James Lithgow 2470
Litt av hvert 1571
The livelihood of man 1290
Le livre des métiers 7515
Local government 7640
Local government 8463

John Locke 5181
Locke economista 5159
Logic and expediency 3517
The logic of political-
  economy 5879
The logic of the price
  3440
Logica delle imposte 8424
Der logische charakter 3855
Die logische theorie 8879
La loi de la demande 3402
La loi naturelle 5412
Les lois d'assistance ouvrière
  7965
Les lois de patronage 7966
Lois de protection 8684
Lois forestieres de France
  4588
Les lois naturelles 6533
Lois ouvrieres 8345
Lombard street 7417
The London economist 2744
Lonely Americans 3038
The long-run supply curve
  3382
The long-term rate 3244
The long view and the short
  1013
The long view and the short
  7355
Looking backward 9042
Loon, prijis en winst
  3341
The lottery system 7174
Lugd. Batavorum 4336
Lun chung nung chu i 5427
Luxusteuer als correctiv 7486

Nicolo Machiavelli 8729
Machtungleichgewichte 3243
Macrodynamic economics
  2084
Macroeconomia 1181
Macroeconomic analysis
  1323
Macroeconomic analysis
  2079
Macroeconomic theory 1034
Macroeconomic theory 1169
Macroeconomic theory 9886
Macroeconomic theory 10105
Macro-economics 1322
Macroeconomics 1656

Macroeconomics 1678
Macroeconomics 9890
Macroeconomics before Keynes
  9913
Macromeccanica economica 1104
La magia del credito svelata
  1324
La magia del credito svelata
  6439
Magia del credito svelata 7233
Magnae Britanniae notitia 4103
Magnats polonais 5362
Main currents in modern eco-
  nomics 598
Maintenance of free trade
  4482
Majundusliku motte pohijooni
  2607
The making of economic society
  3658
Ma-k'o-ssŭ ching chi hsüeh 3155
Ma-k'ossŭ chu i p'i p'ing 3156
Makroekonomiczny rachunek
  2617
Malthus and his work 7527
Malthus and Keynes 10043
Malthus et les deux Marx 9539
Das Malthus 'sche bevölkerungs-
  gesetz 77
Gerrard de Malynes 5268
Man, economy and state 2021
Man, money, and goods 1437
Man versus society 7287
Managerial economics 1345
Managerial economics 1389
Managerial economics 1526
Managerial economics 1854
Managerial economics 2140,
  2150
The Manchester school 2746
The Manchester school of
  economic 885
Dr. Bernard Mandeville 7307
Das Manifest der Kommunistis-
  chen 9151
The manifold causes of the in-
  crease 4818
Manoscritti economico-filosofici
  9401
Man's worldy goods 320
Les manscrits economiques de
  Francois Quesnay 5435
Manu, Marx and Gandhi 9588

Manual 2044
A manual 2113
Manual de derecho 1030
Manual de derecho y economia politica 1755
Manual de economia politica 1260
Manual de economia politica 1436
A manual of historical 7366
A manual of political 1944
A manual of political 5823
A manual of political 6695
Manual of political 7006
A manual of political 8532
Manual of political economy 1391
Manual of political economy 7837
A manual of the direct and excise tax 7551
Mannuale 1933
Manuale 2049
Manuale di economia politica 1576
Manuale di economia politica 1738
Manuale di économia politica 9756
Manuale di economia pura 1900
Manuale di statistica 8733
Manual d'économie politique 1038
Manuel d'économie politique 1121
Manuel d'économie politique 2143
Manuel d'économie politique 5540
Manuel d'économique 1666
Manuel d'économique 3719
Manuel de l'histoire ancienne 6196
Manuel de l'ingénieur 7728
Manuel de morale 6752
Manuel des affaires 5838
Manuel des consuls 6456
Manuel pratique 6457
Manuel universel 6458
Manufactures, and commerce 6629
Manufactures improper subjects 6459
The manufacturing population 6095
Les manuscrits économiques 1019
Manuskripte über die polnische frage 9402
Mao Tse-tung 9359, 9360
Le marché financier 8477
La marche monétaire 8169
Marchionis hieronymi Belloni 5156
Mare clausum 4714
The maritime dicaeology 4259
The margin of profits 7402
Marginal utility 9732
Marginal utility 9770
Marginalistički 2126
The mark in Europe 7575
Market control 2588
The market planned economy of Yugoslavia 3096
The market system 3249
Der markt und seine alternativen 1533
Marks i Engels w Polsce 9638
Marks i idea pieniadza pracy 3438
Karola Marksa obraz gospodarki 9598
Marksistička teorija 9023
Marksistička teorija 9315
K. Markss, F. Engelss, V. I. Lenins 9471
Das marktomodell in hinsicht 3231
Le marquis d'Argenson 2329
Le marquis d'Argenson 5150
Der marschall Vauban 2429
Der marschall Vauban 5251
Alfred Marshall 19809
Alfred Marshall 9811
Alfred Marshall 9818
Alfred Marshall 9826
Alfred Marshall 9829
Alfred Marshall 9860
Alfred Marshall 9872, 9874, 9879
Marshall, Marx 9828
Marshall, Marx and modern 9279
Alfred Marshall on free 9875
The Marshallian demand 9815

Alfred Marshall beitrag 9825
Marshall's concept of quasi-rent 9807
Marshall's contribution to Indian 9834
Marshall's economics 9881
Dr. Marshall's eightieth 9831
Marshall's principles 9836
Alfred Marshall's principles 9873, 9882
Alfred Marshall's theory of value 9816
Marshall's theory of value 9835
Harriet Martineau 2477
Harriet Martineau's sozialpolitischen 2379
Marukusu keizaigaku 3019
Marukusu keizaigaku 9018
Marukusu keizaigaku 9592
Marukusu-keizaigaku 9613
Marukusu keizaigaku jiten 9453
Marukusu shigo gojūnen 9284
Marukusi-shugi no ronsen 2525
Marukusu-shugi no rosen 9633
Marukusu-shugi to sangyo 3088
Jenny Marx 9140
Karl Marx 9004
Karl Marx 9019
Karl Marx 9049
Karl Marx 9072
Karl Marx 9093
Karl Marx 9116, 9117
Karl Marx 9141
Karl Marx 9198, 9202, 9204, 9209
Karl Marx 9273
Karl Marx 9290
Karl Marx 9311
Karl Marx 9334, 9341
Karl Marx 9438
Karl Marx 9527
Karl Marx 9579
Karl Marx 9647
Karel Marx a Bedřich Engels 9501
Marx against Keynes 9156
Marx against Keynes 9926
Marx against the peasants 9452

Marx and America 9075
Marx and economic calculations 9061
Karl Marx and Friedrich Engels 9395, 9396
Karl Marx and Friedrich Engels 9398
Karl Marx and Friedrich Engels 9505
Marx and Keynes 9426
Marx and Keynes 10029
Marx and modern economics 9245
Karl Marx and modern socialism 9535
Karl Marx and Say's law 9557
Marx and the authentic man 9288
Karl Marx and the British 9112
Karl Marx and the close 9064
Marx and the intellectuals 9182
Marx and the Marxists 9240
Marx and the trade cycle 9571, 9572
Marx and the trade cycle 9645
Marx and the western world 9421
Marx before Marxism 9434
Karl Marx, das kapital 9226
Karl Marx; Das Kapital 9544
Karl Marx devant le bonapartisme 9525
Karl Marx dictionary 9397
Marx, die klassische 9213
Marx e Engels 9071
Marx, Engels, and Australia 9429
Marx-Engels-Lenin 9070
Marx, Engels, marxisme 9317
Marx-Engels verzeichnis 9283
Karl Marx, essai de biographie 9526
Karl Marx et Friedrich Engels 9118
Marx et marxisme 9488
Marx, his time and ours 9543
Marx in the mid-twentieth 9484
Marx keizai-gaku nyūmon 9243
Karl-Marx-kolloquium 9268
Marx, Lenin 9424
Marx, Lenin 9546
Karl Marx, man and fighter 9461

Marx, Marshall, and Keynes 2480
Marx on economics 9190
Marx on economics 9403
Marx, Proudhon 9258
Marx, sa vie, son oeuvre 9314
Karl Marx, Schöpfer 9515
Marx si Engels 9003
Marx, su pensamiento 9566
Marx vs. Russia 9404
Marxian economics 9126
Marxian influences 9074
Marxian socialism 9040
The Marxian theory 9100
Marxism 9124
Marxism 9332
Marxism 9445
Marxism 9517
Marxism 9655
Marxism: an autopsy 9477
Marxism and alienation 9014
Marxism and democracy 9015
Marxism and freedom 9150
Marxism and linguistics 9581
Marxism and modern thought 9422
Marxism and moral concepts 9017
Marxism and Soviet economy 9280
Marxism and the democratic 9305
Marxism and the general crisis 9623
Marxism and the national 9582
Marxism and the open mind 9330
Marxism, freedom 9021
Marxism in Latin America 9005
Marxism in modern France 9333
Marxism in Southeast Asia 9605
Marxism in the modern world 9144
Marxism in the twentieth 9199
Marxism, is it science 9155
The Marxism of Jean Paul Sartre 9130

Marxism, one hundred years 9646
Marxism, past and present 9248
Marxisme, communisme 9449
Le Marxisme en Union soviétique 9099
Marxismo e humanismo 9057
Marxismo y cristianismo 9653
Marxism's hostile children 9164
Marxismus und philosophie 9291
A Marxist commentary 9518
Marxist economic theory 9355
Marxist ideology 9145
Marxist-Leninist China 9201
Marxist philosophy 9303
Marxist social thought 9191
Marxist sociology 9025
Marxistische wirtschaftstheorie 9286
The Marxists 9448
Marxov zakon vrednosti 3115
Karl Marx's Capital 3324
Karl Marx's capital 9335
Marx's concept of man 9195
Marx's economic predictions 9210
Marx's economics 9024
Karl Marx's interpretation 9060
Karl Marx's interpretation of history 9031
Marx's theory of alienation 9443
Die Marxsche wert- und mehrwertlehre 9260
Die Marxsche wirtschaftslehre 9423
Más allá de la economica 1069
The master problem 2720
Mastering basic economics 1563
Masterpieces in economics 818
Masters of social thought 613
Masters of social thought 2496
Masterworks of economics 697
Matematikai modszerek 3541
Matematyka na usługach 3578
Materiali per una logica del movimento economico 162
Materialien für die Preussische 5765

Materialien zur aufstellung
5916
Materialen zur finanz-statistik
6235
Materialism and empirio-
criticism 9318
Materialismo storico 9122
The materialist conception
9181
Materiały do studiowania
9425
Mathematical analysis 3493
Mathematical analysis 3501
Mathematical economics
3494
The mathematical groundwork
3531
Mathematical investigations 3214
Mathematical investigations
3621, 3622
Mathematical methods 3542
Mathematical methods 3849
Mathematical models 3871
Mathematical models in micro-
economics 3579
Mathematical physics 9694
Mathematical physics 3601
Mathematical systems
theory 3681
Mathematics and economics
3693
Mathematics in Aristotle
4981
Mathematics in the social
sciences 3852
Mathematik und kybernetik
3747
Les mathématiques appliquées
3916
Die mathematische schule 383
Mathematische volkswirtschafts-
lehre 9795
Maxima and minima 3630
Die maxime "Laissez-faire
7321
Die maxime laissez faire
8386
J. R. McCulloch 2449
The meaning and validity of
economic theory 557
The meaning of Marx 9436
The meaning of Marx 9530
The meaning of Marxism 9108

The means to prosperity 9994
The measure of value 3337
The measurement of real
income 9901
The measurement of utility
3369
The measurement of utility
9837
Measuring benefits of govern-
ment investments 3592
Measuring business cycles 8980
Les mécanismes économiques
1293
Les mécanismes 1677
Les mécanismes 2242
El mecanismo de la vida 1819
Meccanica economica 3500
La meccania economica 9786
Il meccanismo unico 9028
The mechanism of economic
systems 2201
The mechanism of economic
systems 3875
Mediaeval socialism 4998
Medieval cities 5065
Medieval contributions 4979
Medieval panorama 4922
Medieval technology 5137
The medieval theories 4891
Medio sigli de ciencia 2771
Meditaciones sobre Keynes
10064
Meditazioni sull' economia
politica 4839
Medunarodna konferencija 839
Medunarodna konferencija o
savremenim teorijania 345
Mélanges de morale 6483
Mélanges d'économie politique
6482
Mélanges d'économie politique
6894
Mélanges d'économique
politique 7442
Melanges economiques 1785
Mélanges économiques 6680
Melanges, economiques dedies
897
Mélanges et correspondence
6939
Memahami ekonomi 1033
Le même ouvrage 4693
A memoir of Central India 6484

Memoir of Samuel Slater 7245
A memoir of Sydney Smith 7007
A memoir of the life 5695
A memoir on the visitation of neutral vessels 6485
Memoire comptes rendus 5349
Mémoire pour dinimuer 4694
Mémoire pour l'établissement 4695
Mémoire sur la compagnie des Indes 4419
Mémoire sur la mendicité 5519
Mémoire sur la situation actuelle 4506
Mémoire sur l'administration des finances 4332
Mémoire sur l'antiquité 6486
Memoire sur le bimetallisme 8524
Mémoire sur le crédit 6657
Mémoire sur les commencements 344
Memoire sur les commencements 5005
Mémoire sur les effets de l'impôt indirect 4505
Mémoire sur les effets de l'impôt indirect 4702
Mémoire sur les moyens 6487
Mémoire sur les pauvres mendiants 4696
Mémoires concernant les impositions 6488
Mémoires concernant les impositions 6552
Mémoires et considerations sur le commerce 4508
Memoires d'économie publique 6882
Memoires pour servir 6489
Mémoires pour servir à l'histoire 3988
Mémoires pour servir à l'histoire Générale des finances 4008
Mémoires relating to the state of the royal navy 4509
Mémoires sur le commerce des Hollandois 4507
Memoires sur les grandes routes 6107
Memoirs 2373
Memoirs of a banking-house 6049
Memoirs of the Dutch trade 4510
Memoirs of the life 5713
Memoirs of Thomas Papillon 4579
Mémoirs pour servir 6490
Memoira sobre los medios 5743
Memoira presantado à S. M. 5662
Memoria sobre el establecimiento 6316
Memoria sobre la union 5663
Memorial of the committee 6491
Memorials of Alfred Marshall 9843
Memorias historicas 6492
Memorias historicas sobre la marina 5683
Memorias politicas 6351
Memorie di statistica 213
Memorie economiche ed agrarie 5513
Memorie inedite de pubblica 5514
Memorie storiche sulla economia 4838
Memories of the old College of Glasgow 2446
The menace of privilege 7898
Karl Menger 9760
Karl Mengers grundsätze 9698
Mensch und wirtschaft 2324
Menschleit und kapital 8514
Mercantilism 5317
Mercantilism 5236
Mercantilism 5263
Mercantilism 5321
Mercantilism and laissez faire 5211
Mercantilism and physiocratic 5300
Mercantilism and the East India 5311
Le mercantilisme 5185
Mercantilisme 5266
Le mercantilisme liberal 5168
Mercantilismo 5206

Mercantilismo 5264
El mercantilismo en Espana 5222
The merchant's complaint 4511
The merchants mappe of commerce 4680
Merchant and poet 5198
Le Mercier de la Riviere 5414
Mere no shikiten 2890
Merenje poslovnog uspeha 3717
Merkantilismen 5218
Der merkantilismus 5188
Der merkantilismus 5235
Die merkantilistische wahrungspolitik 5320
Merkantilisty i fiziokraty 2971
Merkantilisty i fiziokraty 5158
Merkantilisty i fiziokraty 5332
Merkantilizm 5276
Merkantilizm i ego glavnye 5157
Merkantylizm i poczatki szkoły 5261
Das merkantilsystem 5286
Le métal argent 7427
Metastatics and macroeconomics 3887
Les métaux précieux 8542
A method of government 4340
The method of isolation 3731
Method of political economy 3687
A method to prevent 4512
La méthode de l'économie politique 3784
Methode scientifique 3740
Die methodenfrage in der theoretischen 3697
Methodes et doctrines coloniales 2638
Methodologie 3642
Die methodologie 8848
Methodologie der staatswissenschaften 3566
Methodologische grundfragen 3771

Methodology of economic research 3580
Methods for land economics research 3638
Methods of industrial 8580
Methods of social reform 8099
Methods of economic investigation 3895
Il metodo dell'economia 1709
Il metodo dell'economia 9091
Metodologia dell'inchiesta 3750
Metrologie 6507, 6508
Meyers handbuch 2718
Microeconomia 1661
Microeconomic analysis 1163
Microeconomic analysis 1638
Microeconomic analysis 1701
Microeconomic theory 1140
Microeconomic theory 1400
Microeconomic theory of market 3304
Microeconomics 3777
Il microbo della guerra 2841
Microstatics 3888
Miedzyuczelniane zeszyty naukowe 901
Miejsce konsumpcji 9487
Mikrøøkonomikk 1586
Mikroökonomische theorie 1077
John Stuart Mill 2437
John Stuart Mill and Harriet Taylor 2398
J. S. Mill and J. E. Cairnes 2450
Stuart Mill; textes choisis 2438
Mill to Marshall 9808
The mineral industry 8545
Mineral statistics of Great 8076
Les ministres des finances de la Russie 8633
The ministry and the sugar 6521
Miru to Marukusu 635
Miscellanea 4787
Miscellaneous views of the coins 4735
A miscellany containing several tracts 4516
The mischief of the five shillings tax 4517
La misère 8628
A missao do economista no

Brasil 2442
Misure di una economia moderna 1998
Mit welcher methode wurden 3649
W. C. Mitchell 9001
Mity ekonomiczne w NRF 2717
Mo ch'i ti tzu pen chu 9912
Mo taku-to no keizai shiso 2587
Mobility of professional economists 2332
Mode de production féodal 9476
Model building in the human sciences 3906
Modele ekonometryczne 3799
Modèles de formation des prix 3361
Les modèles dynamiques 3627
Les modèles macroéconomiques 1301
Modelldenken und operations-forschung 3617
Models of markets 3787
Modern American capitalism 3069
The modern cambist 7074
Modern currency 7599
Modern distributive process 7632
Modern economic analysis 1079
Modern economic problems 1794
Modern economic problems 2206
Modern economic theory 357
Modern economic theory 1325
Modern economic thought 3059
Modern economics 512
Modern economics 1139
Modern economics 1198
Modern economics 1520
Modern economics 1684
Modern economics 1818
Modern economics 1920
Modern economics 2172
Modern economics 2292
The modern economists 2388
The modern economy 2179
The modern economy 2240

The modern economy in action 1052
The modern law of railways 7451
Modern socialism 9174
Modern socialism 9611
La moderna economia 3822
Die moderne christliche welt 3419
Moderne deutsch 2665
Moderne eisenbahnpolitik 7852
Der moderne kapitalismus 8892
Das moderne kriegswesen 8851
Der moderne socialismus 8085
Der moderne socialismus 8559
A modest proposal 4520
Modifying institutional-legal relations 3648
Molders of the medieval mind 4911
Momenti dinamici 1724
Mon journal 9757
Monarquia Indiana 4795
Mone, historia statisticae 6540
La moneda-maiz 3242
Moneometallism 8067
Moneta e scambi nell'alto 4912
Monetäre unabhängigkeit 10022
Monetarism versus Keynesian 10093
Monetary systems 8329
Monetary theory 9949
Monetary theory 9820
Monetary theory before Adam Smith 5265
Money 8100
Money 8128
Money 8459
Money 8747
Money 9866
Money and banking 8596
Money and banking 8780
Money and civilization 7732
Money and its laws 8448
Money and its vicissitudes 5502
Money and legal tender 8214
Money and the mechanism 9725
Money and trade considered 4420
Money and morals 6347
Money and value 7986
Money answers all things 4832

Money, banking 7525
Money, banking and credit 5081
Money, credit 9844
Money economy in medieval Japan 4908
Money in its relations 8746
Money in politics 8713
Money: interest, and prices 3381
Money, its connection 7600
Money, money 2000
Money panics 8800
Money, prices 5040
Money, prices and civilization 4919
Money, prices, and wages in Valencia 4973
The money question 8105
Money, silver, and finance 7687
Money, trade and economic growth 836
Money, trade, and economic growth 908
Money weights and measures 7574
La monnaie 8170
La monnaie chez Marx 9077
La monnaie de banque 5824
La monnaie, le crédit 7391
Monographs and essays 7378
Le monopole cause de tous les maux 6628
Monopolies and the people 7423
Monopolistic competition 3305
Monopolistic competition 9733
Monopoly capital 9027
Montesquieu and the wealth 2369
The moral and physical condition 6322
La morale et la politique d'Aristote 6551
Morale et vie économique 2070
Die moralstatistik 8380
Thomas More 9097
Thomas More 9276

Morfologia economica 1898
Mori Shozaburo kyoju lei shi 2892
The motive power 720
Le mouvement agraire 8299
Le mouvement physiocratique 5436
Mouvements ouvier 9138
Les moyens de détruire 6573
Les moyens de détruire 6452
Moyens d'extirper l'usure 6720
Możliwość funkcjonowania 9346
La multiplication des manuels d'économie politique 219
Municipal corporations 8183
Municipal government 8615
Municipal taxation 8383
Das Munzwesen Mark Brandenberg 7422
The Muqaddimah 5011
Mussen wir arm bleiben? 1838
Mutualité sociale 7924
Mysl ekonomiczno-polityczna 2944
The mysteries of the counterfeiting 3942
Le mythe de l'ordre naturel 64
Le mythe de l'ordre naturel 5337

Náčrt dejin politickej 9228
Nagra anteckningar i anknytning 3320
Nantucket 7461
Národné hospodárstvo 1177
Národní hospodařstvi 916
Narrative of adventure 6585
Narysy z istorii 2987
Nassau senior and classical 2344
Native money of Palau 5078
The national and private advantages of the African 4553
National budget 8790
National consolidation 8206
The national debt 4552
National debt 5684
The national debt 6064
National debts 7447
National distress 6345
National economic policy 2188
National economic policy 3873

Short Title Index   821

De national ekonomiska 2977
National finance 8373
The national gain 5172
National income 1091
National income analysis 2059
The national merchant 4017
National product 10011
National revenues 8616
Das nationale system 8859
Nationalekonomi för alla 2099
Nationalekonomi for nyborjare 2142
Nationalekonomiens grunddrag 8777
Nationalekonomiens utvekling 5
Nationalekonomins grunder 1178
Nationalekonomisk teori 1330
The nationalisation of land 8645
Nationalität 8763
Die nationaloeconomie 7014
Nationaløkonomi 1868
Nationalökonomic 379
Nationaløkonomie 1066
Nationalökonomie 1149
Nationalokonomie 1640
Die nationalokonomie 2655
Nationalökonomie 5867
Die nationalökonomie 8574
Nationalökonomie 8789
Die nationalökonomie 8846
Die nationalokonomie der gegenwart 301
Nationalokonomie des Alltags 1531
Nationalökonomie guterlehre 8696
Nationalokonomie und philosophie 1062
Nationalökonomie, wohin 3526
Nationalökonomische studien 7648
Nationaløkonomisk forening 1852
Natural and political observations 4326
Natural and political observations 4554
The natural economic order 1455
Natural elements 1583

Natural elements of political 6298
The natural history of the raw materials 8813
The natural history of the sperm whale 5546
Natural law 4961
The natural law of money 7573
Natural resources 8410
Natural value 9804
The naturall and morall histories 3933
Naturalwirtschaft und geldwirtschaft 180
Nature and necessity of paper currency 4301
Nature and uses of money 7212
The nature of capital 3215
The nature of fermentation 4728
The nature of the charitable corporation 4555
The nature of the present excise 4556
Die naturgeschichte d. arbeit 5572
Naturgesetz und wirtschaftsgesetz 3782
Das natürliche system 1697
Der naturliche wert 3472
Der natürliche werthes 8783
Naucne tendencije i valgarnoapologetski elementi 427
Navigation and commerce 4251
Navigation laws 6594
The necessity of abating usury 4162
A neglected British economist 2452
A neglected early statement 10038
Le negoce d'Amsterdam 4676
Le négociant anglais 4290
Neighbourhood guilds 7652
Několik kapitol 2111
Nekotorye voprosy metodologii 2991
Nektere poznatky z navstevy 2782
Neocapitalisme, socialisme 2634
Neoclassical economics 9877
The neoclassical theory 3208
Neo-klâsik teoriden Keynes 10042

Le néo-libéralisme 9683
Neoliberal'noe napravlenie v sovremennoj 375
Le néo-marginalisme 517
Le neomercantilisme 5186
Neo-normativisme 285
Neue aufgaben für die führungstätigkeit 9467
Neue beitrage zur wirtschaftstheorie 883
Neue grundlegung 6263
Die neue staatsweisheit 5764
Neue untersuchung 6955
Neue wirtschaftslehre 1909
Neue wirtschaftslehre 10045
Neue wirtschaftslehren 216
Neue wirtschaftslehren 1417
Die neue wirtschaftswissenschaft 2713
Die neuen konjunkturtheorien 9897
Neuere bankwesens 7082
Die neuere nationalokonomie 451
Die neuere nationalokonomie 8295
Neuere untersuchungen 3476
Neueste darstellung der kameralwissenschaften 7020
A new account of the East Indies 4347
The new American political economy 175
A new and complete dictionary of trade 4546
New and old principles 6600
The new Cambridge curriculum 9845
The new classical versus the neo-classical 68
New currents in Soviet-type 2597
New developments in teaching 3736
A new dictionary of trade 4685
New dimensions of political economy 295
A new discourse of trade 4110
The new economic history 708
New economics 808
The new economics 1980,
The new economics 9918

Economic Thought and Analysis

The new economics 9953
New Fabian essays 9123
The new gold age 8409
A new look at institutionalism 8916
The new mercantilism 5279
A new method for valuing of annuities 4352
New methods of measuring marginal 3631
New observations, natural 4719
The new philosophy of public debt 10035
A new political economy 7952
New political economy 8535
A new prospect 2075
New prospects 3696
The new science 2131
The new statistical account of Scotland 6601
The new theories 3794
A new view of society 6641
A new view of society 9470
New views on American 3032
New world 9327
The new world of Henri Saint-Simon 9358
Newtonian classicism 7302
Newtonian classicism and 279
Professor J. S. Nicholson 3200
Niektore metodologiczne problemy 259
Nihon keizai kenkyū 918
Nihon keizai shi 663
Nihon keizai shi 2903
Nihon keizai shi gaiyo 2884
Nihon keizai shi kogi 687
Nihon keizai shi kōgi 2905
Nihon keizai shiso-shi 2880
Nihon keizai shiso-shi kenkyū 113
Nihon keisai shiso shi kenkyu 2881
Nihon keizaigaku shi 2898
Nihon keizaigaku shi no isseki 2899
Nihon ni okeru keizaigakushi 2888
Nihon ni okeru keizaishigaku 2900
Nihon no keizaigaku 2882
Nihon no Marukushu 2894
Nihon no Marukushu keizaigaku

Short Title Index 823

9233
Nihon shakai keizai shiso shi 2886
Nihon shakai no shisoshiteki 2893
Hezekiah Niles 2503
Ninagawa Torazō Sensei koki 925
La noblesse commercante 4155
Noboru 5238
Nocoës elementares 6464
Nomisma 7614
Non-Ricardian political 2395
Non-Ricardian political 2743
Die nordamerikan 8210
Nordamerikan 8668
The Norfolk scheme 4566
Normative grundlagen 3002
North American pamphlet 6613
Not over-production 6144
Notat om sammenhengen 3130
Note elementari 1335
A note on the separability 3235
Note sul marxismo 9506
Notes 9863
Notes de philosophie economique 668
Notes on elasticity 3435
Notes on Marxian economics 3800
Notes on political economy 2350
Notes on railroad accidents 7363
Notes on the determinateness of the utility 9673
Notes, on the state of Virginia 6297
Notice des principaux règlements 5896
Notice historique 5942
Notice historique 6076
Notice historique sur les finances 6614
Notices d'economie sociale 5943
Notices et portraits 2389
Notices statistiques 6615
La notion de mode de production asiatique 9207
Notions essentielles 1835
Notions fondamentales 6534

Nouveau commentaire sur l'ordonnance de la marine 4831
Nouveau cours 7443
Nouveau dictionnaire 8376
Le nouveau monde industriel 6055
Nouveau plan de culture 6616
Nouveau précis d'économique politica 7874
Nouveau schema interpretatif 5425
Nouveau traité d'économie politique 7193
Nouveau traité d'économie sociale 5939
Les nouveaux courants de la theorie 3076
Nouveaux principes 2100
Nouveaux principes 7000
Nouvel essai sur la richesse 6912
Nouvel exposé 7681
La nouvelle économique 1981
Nouvelle exposition 6784
Nouvelle théorie du calcul 6617
Nouvelle traité d'économie politique 7774
Nouvelles idées sur la population 6019
Nouvelles recherches sur la population 6503
Nouvelles transactions sociales 6576
Nové javy v súčasnej buržoaznej 26
Nove tendencie v protimarxizme sucznej 296
Novos elements 8556
Nowa postac sporu o metode 3694
Nozioni di economia 3616
Nozioni di scienza economica 1216
Nueva economía fundamental 1441
Numismata scotiae 5686
Nummi Britannici historia 4424
Nuove linee di pensiero della scienza economica 265
Nuovi documenti sulla storia 8705
Nuovo prospetto delle scienze

6119
Nuovo schema del processo
1717

O economista José Accursio 2946
O interpretacje mysli 5025
O logické struktuře Marxova Kapitálu 9654
O Ludwiku krzywickim 1645
O nekotorykh sovremennykh burzhuaznykh 373
O que devemos conhecer da economia politica 1467
O raspodeli u prelaznom periodu 942
O regime das riquezas 8270
O revizionistskih teorijah 'slijanija' buržnaznoj 186
O savremenoj ekonomskoj 1730
O sovremennoj buržuaznoj 50
O tratado do economico 4888
O vliîânîi ekonomicheskoi 2608
Ob osobennostiakh imperializma 2986
O-bei no marukusushugi 2406
O-bei no marukusushugi 9244
Objections 4481
Objectives, prejudice 3538
Objectivos immediatos 3758
The objects and methods of political economy 3602
Objekt und grundbegriffe 3497
Objekt und grundbegriffe 8821
L'objet de l'économie politique 1491
Obras 2386
Observation economique 1346
Observation économique 3595
Observations and advises oeconomical 4568
Observations concerning the increase of mankind 4302
Observations concerning the increase of mankind 4573
Observations de la chambre de commerce de Normandie 6620
Observations illustrative 6421
Observations on a late 'state of the nation' 4061
Observations on currency 5490

Observations on marriages, baptisms 4022
Observations on Mr. Asgill's brief answer 4673
Observations on Mr. Fauquier's 'Essay on ways 4493
Observations on paper money 6669
Observations on reversionary payments 4629
Observations on roads 6414
Observations on that part of a late act of parliament 3943
Observations on the case of the Northern colonies 4571
Observations on the circumstances 5526
Observations on the commerce 6984
Observations on the commerce o the American states 6621
Observations on the condition 5528
Observations on the conduct of Great Britain 4572
Observations on the corn 6985
Observations on the defects of the poor-laws 3944
Observations on the duty 6422
Observations on the effects 5588
Observations on the effects of th corn 6450
Observations on the establishmer of the bank 5522
Observations on the expediency 6677
Observations on the financial 7154
Observations on the increase 6192
Observations on the influence 6423
Observations on the land revenue 6915
Observations on the management of the poor 5459
Observations on the manufactures 6986
Observations on the mortality 6622
Observations on the nature 7214
Observations on the past

growth 4544
Observations on the present price 7264
Observations on the present state of landed 6400
Observations on the present state of our gold 4138
Observations on the present state of the highlands 6623
Observations on the principles 5589
Observations on the produce of the income tax 5554
Observations on the proposed alteration 6841
Observations on the proposed duties 6624
Observations on the publication of Walter Boyd 5523
Observations on the question of the corn 7268
Observations on the report 7104
Observations on the state of the highways 4351
Observations on the state of the population 6691
Observations on the Treaty of Seville 4574
Observations on trade 6191
Observations politiques 6716
Observations politiques et morales 6625
Observations relating to the coin 4494
Observations respecting the salmon 6626
Observations succinctes sur l'émission 4291
Observations sur la déclaration 4065
Observations sur la liberte du commerce 4357
Observations sur les finances 5672
Observations sur l'ouvrage 5607
Observations sur l'ouvrage 5673
Observations upon the growth 4464
Observations upon the report of the select 5549
Observations upon the state of 6671
Observations upon the United Provinces 4788
Obstáculos al desarrollo económico 1103
Ocherk razvitiia ekonomicheskikh 38
Ocherki economicheskoi mysii v Rosii 2957
Ocherki istorii 2803
Ocherki istorii armianskoi 272
Ocherki istorii armianskoi 2995
Ocherki istorii burzuaznoj 614
Ocherki istorii ekonomicheskikh ucheniĭ 467
Ocherki istorii ekonomicheskoi 947
Ocherki po istorii 641
Oeconomica 5056
Oeconomica varia 781
Oeconomica varia, excerpta 780
The oeconomical table 5384
Oeconomiques 2640
Oeconomiques (1745) 4118
Oekonomiske tanker 4474
L'oeuvre de John Maynard Keynes 10013
L'oeuvre economique 2524
L'Oeuvre économique de David Hume 5284
L'Oeuvre economique de David Hume 7329
Oeuvre economique de Simonde de Sismondi 2328
Oeuvres 4421
Oeuvres 5944
Oeuvres 7089
Oeuvres 9533
Oeuvres complètes 5532
Oeuvres complètes 5793
Oeuvres complètes 6056
Oeuvres completes 6733
Oeuvres complètes 6893
Oeuvres complètes 6940
Oeuvres complètes 7119
Oeuvres complètes de Charles Fourier 9186
Oeuvres de M. Turgot 6630
Oeuvres de St. Simon 6923
Oeuvres de Turgot 5431

Oeuvres economiques 5407
Oeuvres economiques choisies 6038
Of a free trade 4583
Of empty economic boxes 3558
Of population 6123
Of systems of political 5296
Of the impracticability 5798
Der öffentliche credit 6596
Die öffentlichen abgaben 6232
Official papers 9846
Ogólne problemy 9080
Ogólne problemy funkcjonowania 1189
Okenomisch-philosophische 9405
Okonometrie und makroökonomische 2153
Okonometrie und makroökonomische theorie 3856
Okonomie, interessen 2093
Okonomie, interessen 9562
Okonomische gesetze 9466
Okonomische ideologie 1045
The old and the new 2704
The old and the new 10058
The old English manor 7382
The old generation 2432
Om arbetsklassen 7984
Om het behoud van ons bestaan 1962
Om kapitalen 9165
Om økonomiens methode 3810
Om penningar och kredit 7985
Om politiska ekonomiens utvekling 280
On certain tests of a thriving 7169
On colonial intercourse 5597
On combinations of trades 6632
On commerce 6424
On commercial economy 5703
On credit, currency 6395
On economic knowledge 413
On economic knowledge 1714
On economic knowledge 3735
On economic theory 9133
On financial reform 6672
On freedom and free enterprise 9772
On Keynesian economics 10016
On labour 7108
On Marx's Capital 9172
On pareto optima 3765

On political economy 975
On political economy 5714
On population 6124
On prices, moneys 5105
On protection to agriculture 6857
On protection to West India sugar 6396
On religion 9406
On rent 9847
On re-reading Marx 9509
On some fashions in economic theory 193
On some neglected British 2780
On the accuracy of economic observations 3769
On the approaching crisis 6997
On the concept of social value 3838
On the concepts and methods 2976
On the currency 7124
On the debt of the nation 6633
On the demand and supply 3319
On the economic theory 9337
On the expediency and necessity of striking off 6023
On the falsifiability of traditional demand 3326
On the government of dependencies 6382
On the history and development of gilds 7568
On the history and method 850
On the history and method 3709
On the history of thought 3641
On the history of thought and 263
On the importance of economic science 8047
On the interpretation of the just price 4990
On the loans raised by Mr. Pitt 6605
On the nature, measure 5503
On the nature, properties 6903
On the noxious influence of authority 3532
On the philosophical method 3675
On the philosophical method 8857

Short Title Index 827

On the policy and expedience 5971
On the possibility of a scientific law of wages 3159
On the principles and doctrine of assurances 6564
On the question of operationalism 3840
On the regulation of currencies 6071
On the relations of political 9695
On the relative importance of agriculture 5560
On the rent of land 6245
On the scientific foundations of marginalism 9764
On the shifting and coincidence of taxation 8602
On the supply of employment 5570
On the theories of usury 8413
On the theory of a monetary 9922
On the theory of economic policy 654
On the timber trade 5598
On the value of annuities 6303
On wages and combinations 7138
One pound note in the rise 7942
Onze indische financien 8736
The open philosophy 9115
The open society 9497
Operations research 3863
Opere filosofiche giovanili 9407
Opinion sur le projet de loi 6343
Opinions d'un créancier 5751
Opinions of eminent lawyers 5710
The opinions of the late Mr. Ricardo and of Adam Smith 7320
The opinions of William Cobbett 2363
Opposition to Louis XIV 5282
Oppressions and cruelties of Irish 5735
Opstellenbundel ter huldiging 1882

Optimale zweig- und standortplanung 3786
The optimum quantity of money 785
Optymalizacja planów 3729
Opuscules financiers 6032
Opuscules sur les finances 6910
Opusculoi letterarii 8306
L'or et l'argent 7259
Orders for the preventing 4501
Orders in council 6634
L'ordine economico 1911
Ordnad ekonomi 1939
Ordnance memoir 6635
L'ordre naturel 5415
Maistre Nicole Oresme 5039
L'organisateur 6924
Die organisation der kredits 8590
Organisation der landwirthschaftlich kredits 8579
Organisation des bodenkredits 8013
Die organisation des Gewerbewesens 5551
L'organisation des sociétés de prévoyance 6255
Die organisation die preussen staats eisenbahnen 8138
L'organisation du travail 5590
L'organisation du travail selon 6357
Organisation industrielle de l' armée 5734
L'organisation rationnelle de la distribution 1161
Organización y operaciones 8218
The organisation of industry 5518
Organizing society for freedom 3041
Oriental commerce 6511
Orientation in the spheres of economics and business 151
Orientering i samfundsøkonomien 1143
Origens da dialética do trabalho 9205
Origin, constitution 8741
The origin of metallic currency 8516
The origin of Russian commu-

nism 9046
The origin of the law of diminishing 3144
Origin of the term 'political' 7313
Original Marxism 9197
Original papers and letters 4576
Origine des postes 4430
Origine des postes chez les anciens 4577
Origine et progres du droit 5496
Les origines du socialisme 2658
Les origines du socialisme 8087
Origines gentium antiquissimae 4578
Les origines historiques 815
Le origini della società borghese 9408
Le origini dello spirito capitalistico in Italia 2846
Origins of academic economics 3073
The origins of Marxian 9119
The origins of scientific 2763
Osnovi ekonomike 1093
Osnovi iz političke ekonomije 1465
Osnovi nauke o društvu 1637
Osnovi polititke 1797
Osnovi polititke 1927
Osnovi polititke 9262
Osnovi polititke ekonomije 1745
Osnovi teorije mezoekonomije 1644
Osnovy a literature ke studiu političke 9278
Osnovnye etapy razvitiia 3029
Osrodek informacji i dokumentacji 3897
Osservazioni preventive al piano intorno 4079
Osservazioni sopra il prezzo legale 4564
Das österreich 5550
Die österreichische handelspolitik 7459
Die osterreichischen Kameralisten 2553
Die osterreichischen kameralisten 5298
Die österreichisch-ungarische 8391
Osutoria gakuha kenkyū 9709
The other face of mercantilism 5322
Our changing American economy 3044
Our clearing system 8066
Our economic system 1525
Our economy 3040
Our free enterprise 3045
Our iron roads 8786
Our ocean railways 8233
Our present discontents 2731
Our present system of trade 8767
Our silver coinage 7954
Our standard of living 2050
The outcome of individualism 8202
The outcome of the saving-investment discussion 10023
Outline of an economic theory 1362
Outline of economic theory 1433
An outline of international price 5325
Outline of lectures 7368
An outline of the principles 1573
An outline of the science 2071
Outline study of political 8653
Outlines of a system of political 6310
Outlines of American 8860
Outlines of American political 3067
Outlines of economic theory 1308
Outlines of economics 1370
Outlines of English industrial 7711
Outlines of historical jurisprudence 5128
Outlines of political 1762
Outlines of political 6591
Outlines of political 6638
Output budgeting 3475
Output, employment, capital

Short Title Index 829

1170
Outside readings 820
L'ourvière 8630
Les ouvriers des deux mondes 6358
Over my shoulder 2468
Overpopulation 7109
Overproduction 8525
Overproduction and crises 9513
Oversight over samfunds-økonomien 3809
Overzicht der geschiedenis 7452
Overzicht vandde evolutie 122
Robert Owen 6929
Robert Owen 9110
Robert Dale Owen 9328
Robert Owen 9491
Mr. Owen's proposed arrangements for the distressed 6575
Owrvagtser hay tntsagitakan 2996

Pacific railroad legislation 7572
Le pact de famine 7489
La paix des peuples 3202
The pamphlets of Thomas Robert Malthus 884
El pansamiento economico de echeverria 497
Paper against gold 5758
Paper credit 7106
Paper money 7996
Paper money the root of evil 8262
The paper pound 7601
Papers relating to political 768
Papers relating to political 3603
Papers relating to political 9696
Papers relative to American tariffs 6652
Papers respecting emigration 6653
Papers respecting the negociation 6654
Das papiergeld in oesterrich 8140
Para comprender la economia politica 233
Para comprender la economia politica 1445
Para una economía humana 1136
The paradox of Scottish culture 7290
Un paradoxe economique 5253
Paragraphs on banks 5609
Vilfredo Pareto 9670
Vilfredo Pareto 9697
Pareto and the Marshallian constancy 9824
Pareto e Sorel 9704
Pareto revealed 9714
Pareto versus Marshall 9884
Pareto's methodological 9779
Pareto's methodological approach 3861
Parliamentary papers 6592
Partial elasticity of demand 3360
Particular answers 4043
Particularités et observations 6547
The particulars of the enquiry 4584
Past and present delusions 6108
The past and the present 195
The past, present 7222
Paths in Utopia 9082
The path-way to peace 4252
Patologia economia 1461
Patterns of economic reasoning 538
Patterns of market behavior 730
Pauperism 7838
Pauperism and poor laws 6676
Der pauperism in England 6330
Le pauperisme 2374
Le pauperisme 7436
Le paupérisme 8166
Les pays ne sort pays prosperes 154
Peasant properties 8722
Peladjaran ekonomi 1496
Pengantar untuk ekonomi 9481
El pensamiento económico 1388
El pensamiento económico 2335
El pensamiento economico 2519
El pensamiento economico

2593
El pensamiento economico
  2916-2918
El pensamiento economico
  latino-americano 2911
El pensamiento economico
  social 667
El pensamiento social-
  cristiano 437
La pensee agronomique 2635
La pensée de Karl Marx
  9092
La pensee economique 2646
Le pensée économique de
  John-Maynard Keynes 9923
La pensee economique
  liberale 2663
La pensee economique
  liberale 2716
Pensiero e azione 2854
Il pensiero economico del
  476, 900
Il pensiero economico
  moderno 670
Il pensiero filosofico di Marx
  9499
Pentagon capitalism 3068
Pénz a szocializmusban 9219
The people of Aristophanes 4941
Pequena história da economia
  410
Per la critica dell'economia
  marxistica 9012
Per un ordre politic i econòmic
  95
La période dans l'analyse
  économique 1110
Periodization in the history
  533
Persoalan ekonomi sosialis
  Indonesia 2833
Persons and periods 9109
Perspectivas do século XIX
  2952
Perspectives in economics
  3846
Perspectives on the economic
  problem 879
Pessimism in economic thought
  288
Petit cours de politique 5802
Petit manuel de le science 7506
Le petit producteur 5950

Petit volume 6941
Petite histoire des grandes
  doctrines 669
The petition and remonstrance
  4549
The petition and remonstrance
  4591
Sir William Petty 5306
Phanomen nachfrage 3246
Philosophiae moralis 4394
A philosophic approach 9069
Philosophical essays 4386
Philosophical essays 7050
The philosophical foundations
  9152
A philosophical interpretation
  1776
Philosophie de la science 7605
Philosophie de l'économie poli-
  tique 5541
Philosophie de l'économie poli-
  tique 5962
Philosophie de l'homme 5127
Philosophie in der volkswirt-
  schaftslehre 639
Philosophie rurale 5385
Philosophie und ökonomie 9192
Philosophies and economic
  theories 650
Philosophischer kongress der
  DDR 9486
Philosophy 8625
Philosophy and myth in Karl
  Marx 9610
Philosophy and political
  7528
Philosophy and political
  economy 57
The philosophy of David
  Hume 2497
The philosophy of Plato 4930
The philosophy of St.
  Thomas Aquinas 4963
The philosophy of Thorsetin
  Veblen 8933
The philosophy of trade 7054
The philosophy of Veblen's
  8968
The philosophy of wealth 1263
The philosophy of wealth 7631
The philosophy of wealth 9678
Physiocracy and the early
  5377

Les physiocrates 5336
Physiocrates 5343
Les physiocrates 5437
The physiocratic conception 5389
The physiocratic doctrine 5346
The physiocratic theory 5417
The physiocratic theory of taxation 5347
Physiocratie 5408
La physiocratie a la fin du regne 5438
La physiocratie sous les ministeres de Turgot 5439
The physiocrats 5360
The physiocrats 5392
The physiocrats 5434
The physiocrats and Say's law 5422
The physiocrats' concept 5393
Die physiokratische lehre 5356
Der physiokratismus und die entdeckung 5401
A. C. Pigou 2460
Pigou's wealth and welfare 3912
The pioneers and progress 8466
Pisma ekonomiczne 1669
The place of abstinence 7606
The place of Marshall's principles 9876
The place of science 8996
The place of value theory 3247
A plain statement of the power of the bank 6673
Plán a trh za socialismu 9294
Plan and market in Yugoslav 3095
Plan de finance 6502
Plan d'un caisse de prévoyance 6702
Plan d'une réorganisation disciplinaire 6338
A plan for reducing 5633
A plan for rendering the poor independent 5447
Plan for the better relief 6117
Plan for the establishment 6854

Plan i tržište 9338
A plan of the English commerce 4191
Plan und markt 2094
Plan und markt 9563
Planlegging under usikker horizont 3633
Planned society, yesterday 882
Planning and economic growth 3581
Planning in the Soviet 9050
Planning in Yugoslavia 3097
Planning reforms in the Soviet 3028
Plato 5107
Platon et l'economie dirigee 2795
Platon et l'economie dirigee 5014
Plato's Cretan city 5045
A plea for a perpetual copyright 5741
A plea for peasant proprietors 7110
Plein employ & socialisme 2729
Plekhanov i russkaia 2962
Plekhanov i russkaîa ekonomii--cheskaîa mysli 530
Plutology 8010
Poemi omerici ed economia antica 4946
Poglady merkantylistyczne 5209
Pogled iz svjetske perspektive 3091
Polémica en torno 1442
Polemika med ekonomisti preteklosti 607
A polgari kozgazdasagtan rovid 443
Police sur les mendiants 4531
Poliitökonoomia propagandistile 9492
Politica 4893
Politica económica 1534
Politica económica 1955, 1956
Politica economica internazionale 364
Politica economica internazionale 2769
Politica economica interna-

zionale 5257
A political account of the diminutions 4610
The political and commercial works of Charles Davenant 4175
Political and social 5656
Political and social economy 1200
Political and social ideals 9589
The political and social ideas of St. Augustine 4928
Political and statistical account of the British settlements 6602
Political arithmetic 4875, 4876
Political arithmetic 5224
Political arithmetick 4594
Political discourses 4387
The political dynamics of European 2623
Political, economic and social thought of Fidel Castro 2602
Political economy 170
Political economy 1039
Political economy 1210
Political economy 1350
Political economy 2101
Political economy 2198
Political economy 2232
The political economy 2281
Political economy 3712
Political economy 5636
Political economy 6762
Political economy 7001
Political economy 7157
Political economy 7839
Political economy 8355
Political economy 8611
Political economy 9157
Political economy 9493
Political economy 9726
Political economy and capitalism 177
Political economy club 8445
Political economy in Australia 2549
Political economy in Guatemala 2799
Political economy in the Soviet 3020

The political economy of Communist China 2589
The political economy of inland 7075
The political economy of Juan de Mariana 5243
The political economy of Mexico 2915
The political economy of the new left 407
A political enquiry 6707
A political essay upon commerce 4504
A political essay upon commerce 4611
Political essays 7331
The political history of India 6441
Political philosophy 5638
Political science 2694
Political survey 4595
A political survey of Britain 4070
Political theories 4960
Political thought in England 2762
The political thought of Plato 4894
The political thought of Thomas Aquinas 4962
Political writings 5759
Politická ekonomia 1964
Politická ekonómia socializmu 1963
Politická ekonómia socializmu 9479
Politická ekonomie 1601
Politická ekonomie 1670
Politická ekonomie 1879
Politická ekonomie 9494
Politická ekonomie 9617
Politická ekonomie socialismu 1965
Politická ekonomie socialismu 9295
Politicka ekonomija 929
Politicka ekonomija 1179
Polticka ekonomija 1299
Politicka ekonomija 1667
Politička ekonomija 1928
Politička ekonomija 1940
Politička ekonomija 2315
Politička ekonomija 9287

Politička ekonomija 9306
Politička ekonomija 9350
Politička ekonomija 9483
Politička ekonomija 9602
Politička economija kapitalizma 1966
Politička ekonomija socijalizma 9361
Politična ekonomija 1239, 1240
Politična ekonomija 2110
Politics and economics 7709
Politics and economics 955
Politics of labor 8698
The politics of mercantilism 5167
Politik und okonomie 9558
Politikai gazdaságtani 9026
Politinés ekonomijos apybraižos 9084
La politique coloniale 8411
La politique economique britannique 2757
La politique économique du directoire 160
La politique monétaire 6660
Politique tirée 5945
Das politische grundwissen 2309
Die politische oekonomie 3705
Politische oekonomie 8181
Die politische oekonomie 8591
Die politische oekonomie 8853
Politische okonomie 1040
Politische okonomie 1863
Politische okonomie 2667
Politische okonomie 9587
Die politische okonomie des rentners 3140
Politivche okonomie des sozialismus 9495
Politische okonomie-geschichte 574
Politische okonomie in kritischen Jahren 71
Die politischen anschauungen Friedrich List 8825
Politisches modell 1512
Polity and economy 7288
Die polizeiwissenschaft 6527
Polska idea ekonomiczna 2942
Polska mysl ekonomiczna 2931
Polska mysl ekonomiczna a rozwoj gospodarczy 256

Ponderibus et mensuris 4224
The poor 5997
The poor law 7388
The poor law 7862
The poor-law bill for Ireland 5660
Poor law guardian 8238
Poor law orders 7917
The poor-laws 6102
Poor laws and paupers 6474
Poor laws in foreign 7767
Poor-laws in Ireland 7218
Poor relief in foreign 8711
Popular political 6234
Popular political economy 1551
Popular prejudices against the convention 4614
La population 8639
Population and the social 8366
La population Française 6379
Les populations agricoles 5542
Les populations ouvriers 5494
Popyt i podaz 3466
The portable Veblen 8969
Porulātārac cintanai varalāru 131
Position and prophecies of bimetallists 7701
The position of the laborer 5197
"Positive" economics and 328
Positive theorie des kapitales 3127
A positive theory 3652
The positive theory of capital 9665
Die post im Auslande 8627
Post-Keynesian 10010
Post-Keynesian economics 387
Post-office reform 6219
Die post und die charakter ihrer einkunfte 7974
La poste et les moyens 7881
Postscript to a pamphlet by Dr. Price 6715
The postulates of English 2722
The postulates of English 7418
The postulates of English political economy 3511
Postwar economic growth 865
Potere democratico e forze 2863
Potere economico 499
Pour le centenaire de la

mort de Pierre-Joseph Proudhon 9216
Pour une économie du bien commun 2740
Pour une économie éclairée 932
Poverty 7923
Poverty and the state 8304
The poverty of nations 253
The poverty of philosophy 9410
Power and influence 2341
A practical arrangement of the laws relative to the excise 6215
Practical detail of the cotton 6546
Practical directions 7098
Practical economics 8773
A practical inquiry into the number 5629
Practical moral 5978
Practical observations 5616
A practical treatise on accounts 5833
A practical treatise on banking 6116
Practical treatise on bills of exchange 5738
A practical treatise on the commercial 7266
Practical treatise on the law of partnership 5777
Practical treatise on the law of partnership 6132
A practical treatise on the law of patents 6120
A practical treatise on the laws 5739
The practical utility 3547
Präferenz- und entscheidungstheorie 3301
Prawo natury u polskich fizjokratow 5397
Die praxis und die wirtschaftgeschichte 3519
Pre-capitalist economic 9409
The precipitation and fall 6718
Précis d'économie politique 1757
Précis d'économie politique 1968
Précis d'économie politique 1988
Précis d'économie politique 2192
Précis d'économie politique 6535
Précis d'économie politique 8188
Précis d'économie politique 8799
Précis de la science 5725
Précis des institutions politiques 7889
Précis d'histoire des doctrines 27
Précis du cours d'économique politique 7611
Précis élémentaire 5596
Un précurseur du socialisme 9641
Precursors in mathematical 9660
Predecessors of Adam Smith 2753
Předmět a metoda politické 1912
Predmet ekonomskih nauka 9351
Předmět politické 1913
A preface to economic history 612
A preface to economics 1245
Preface to social economics 745
Preface to social economics 8921
Pregled radova objavljenih 2517
Preguntas y respuestas 9257
Prehistoric Europe 4920
Preis (theorie) 3488
Preise und volkswirthschaftliche 8756
Pre-Malthusian doctrines 5305
Premier commis des finances 6443
Premiere introduction 5330
Première introduction à la philosophie 4005
Premières études 5430
Premiers observations 5627
Premières sociétés 9502
Premiers pas en économie 3491
The premises of political

Short Title Index 835

1907
Present condition 8230
The present condition of
 economic science 415
The present condition of
 France 4622
The present position 3742
The present position 9848
The present position and
 prospects of political 3676
The present position of political
 3506
The present state of England
 6402
The present state of Ireland
 4623
The present state of the
 British 4589
The present state of the nation
 4333
The present state of the
 national debt 4624
The present state of the
 revenue 4625
The present state of the
 tenancy 6329
The pre-Socratic philosophers
 4952
Prestige value 3284
Le prêt a l'intérêt dernière
 6524
The prevention of poverty 4339
Price and welfare theory 1539
Price economics versus 3614
Price economics vs. welfare
 3212
Price elasticities 3264
Price indexes 3644
Price stability 3384
The price system 1680
The price system 3191
Price theory 1092
Price theory 2244, 2245
Price theory 2265
The price theory 3251
Prices 4428
Prices and earnings 7555
Prices and markets 3192
Prices and production 1524
Prices and production 9710
Prices of commodities 8561
Prices of corn 7236
Pricing and equilibrium 2957

Primeiro imperio comercial
 620
A primer on economics 1459
Primi elementi di economia
 agraria 7675
Primi elementi di scienze 7704
Primitive and peasant 5048
Primitive, archaic 5067
Primitive civilization 5095
Primitive civilization 8629
Primitive money 4942
The primitive origination of
 mankind 4344
The primitive origination of
 mankind 4631
Primitive political economy
 5231
Primitive Polynesian economy
 4948
Primitive trade 3265
The principal navigations 4341
Principes d'administration
 5583
Principes d'analyse économique
 1111
Principes d'économie contem-
 poraine 1119
Principes d'economie indus-
 trielle 8467
Principes d'economie nationale
 1180
Principes d'économie politique
 242
Principes d'economie politique
 1317
Principes d'économie politique
 5677
Principes d'économie politique
 5694
Principes d'économie politique
 6960
Principes d'economie politique
 7905
Principes d'economie sociale
 1382
Principes de la jurisprudence
 Francaise 4632
Principes de la science des
 finances 7884
Principes de la théorie des
 richesses 5842
Principes de la théorie des
 richesses 9680

Principes de l'ethnologie 4898
Principes de science 1306
Principes du commerce 6106
Principes du commerce opposé
  au trafic 4703
Principes du socialisme 5803
Principes économiques de
  Louis XII 4006
Principes fondamentaux 5482
Principes fondamentaux 6975
Principes fondamentaux
  d'economie politique 1086
Principes sur la liberté 3922
Principes sur la liberté du
  commerce 4633
Principi del dinamismo 2322
Principi di civile economia
  6967
Principi di dinamica 1734
Principi di economia politica
  1075
Principi di economia politica
  1107
Principi di economia politica
  1217
Principi di economia politica
  1270
Principi di economia politica
  1462
Principi di economia politica
  2161
Principî di economia ristampa
  stereotipa 1250
Principî di logica 1992
Principi di una nuova scienza
  4841
Principi generali di logica
  1320
Principien de geld 7083
Die principien der gerechten
  8298
Principii 1901
Principii d'economia sociale
  7626
Principi del credito pubblico
  5577
Principii del economie sociale
  6961
Principii di economia politica
  7885
Principii di economia politica
  8211
Principii di economia pura
  8398
Principii di scienza 1384
Principii di scienza bancaria
  8543
Principii di scienza economica
  1155
Principios de economia 2008
Principios de economia 2068
Principios de economia
  política 5778
Principios de financas 8092
Principios fundamentales 1784
The principle of individuation
  5086
The principle of the doctrine of
  life annuities 6477
The principle of the English
  poor-laws 6643
Principles 1733
Principles 1749
Principles 1860
Principles 1914
Principles 1938
Principles 1947
Principles 2067, 2069
Principles 2157
Principles 2160, 2173, 2176
Principles 2247
Principles 2269
Principles 3684
Principles 3743
Principles and practice of
  Islamic 2837
Principles and practices
  1001
Principles and practices
  2185
Principles and problems
  1633
Principles et observations 4292
Principles of a growing
  economy 1506
The principles of Asiatic
  monarchies 6681
Principles of banking
  7990
Principles of currency 6674
The principles of currency
  7155
Principles of econometrics
  2183
Principles of economic
  sociology 4966

Short Title Index 837

Principles of economical 8247
Principles of economics 1129
Principles of economics 1133
Principles of economics 1147
Principles of economics 1156
Principles of economics 1166
Principles of economics 1201
Principles of economics 1275
Principles of economics 1319
Principles of economics 1381
Principles of economics 1401
The principles of economics 1405
Principles of economics 1430
Principles of economics 1444
Principles of economics 1447
Principles of economics 1477
Principles of economics 2022
Principles of economics 8266
Principles of economics 8389
Principles of economics 8434
Principles of economics 9727
Principles of economics 9849
Principles of free trade 6746
Principles of life annuities 6728
Principles of monetary 8768
Principles of moral 4268
Principles of moral 7051
Principles of national economy 1228
Principles of political 1770
Principles of political 1801
Principles of political 1858
Principles of political 1861
The principles of political 1994
Principles of political 2065
The principles of political 2087
The principles of political 2217
Principles of political 2779
Principles of political 5487
Principles of political 5619
Principles of political 5691
Principles of political 6425
Principles of political 6451
Principles of political 6519
Principles of political 6855
Principles of political 6966
The principles of political 7186
Principles of political 8354
Principles of political 8875
The principles of political economy 447
Principles of political economy 1219
Principles of political economy 1229
Principles of political economy 1304
Principles of political economy 1458
The principles of population 5458
The principles of population 7238
Principles of property 8129
Principles of social 7969
Principles of social science 5692
Principles of taxation 6065
Principles of the economic philosophy 7735
Principles of the new 1354
Priručnik za spremanje stručnih 1870
Private property 5091
Die privatwirtschaftslehre als wissenschaft 3643
Problem economics 1602
The problem of economic order 8912
The problem of summation 3785
The problem of the unemployed 8043
The problem of the war in nineteenth century 609
El problema de la emigración 7540
Il problema di una mizurazione 3122
Il problema ferroviario 8199
El problema social 9029
Problemas básicos 1975
Problemas fundamentais 1829
Problematische wirtschaftstheorie 293

Le problème de la theorie 3241
Die probleme der armut 2699
Probleme der betrieblichen plannung 3422
Probleme der politischen 9006
Probleme der wirtschaftsgeschichte 2662
Probleme der wohlstandsgesellschaft 537
Probleme der wohlstandsgesellschaft 1978
Le problème monétaire 7516
Le problème monétaire 8263
Les problèmes de la croissance 9180
Les problèmes de la dialectique 9523
Problèmes économiques 1743
Problemes economiques contemporains 874
Problèmes généraux 9081
Problemi della scienza sociale 7880
Problemi e pensiero economico 496
Problemi economici di ieri 21
Problemi metodologici 3514
Problemi tributari 2144
Problems in political 8676
Problems in the theory of price 1055
The problems of a great city 8779
Problems of economics 9741
Problems of modern industry 8760
Problems of monopoly 2318
Problems of poverty 8044
Problems of the American economy 3825
Problems of to-day 7810
The problems of traditional societies 5129
Problemy i kierunki rozwoju 453
Problemy i metody historii 384
Problémy teorie hodnoty 3300
Proč a jak studovat 9022
Proceedings of the national convention 3429
Proceedings of the symposium in linear programming 3878

Process engineering 2064
La production agricole 7944
Production and consumption 1532
Production and consumption 6289
Production and distribution 9778
Production and distribution 9878
Production and distribution theories 630
The production and use 3546
The production of the precious 7500
Productive labour 3166
Produkcioni odnosi 1639
Produktionstechnik, kapital 1197
Produktionstheorie 3714
Die produktionsverhaltnisse im alten Orient 5134
Produktivitat 1792
Der produktivitatsbegriff 2551
Der produktivitatsbegriff 2685
Der produktivitatsbegriff in der modernen deutschen und 308
Proeve . . . van het bankwezen 6481
Profit sharing 7587
Profit sharing 7912
Profit sharing 8693
Profit sharing precedents 8485
Profits 3120
Profits, interest 3250
Profits, interest 9711
Prognoseverfahren in der sozialistischen 9222
Prognostik und sozialismus 9158
Program analysis 3448
Programma kursa istorii 1010
Programowanie lokalizacji produkcji 3918
Les progrès de la science 52
Les progrès de la science 7507
Progress and poverty 1451
Progress and poverty 7895
Progress and profits 5312
Progress and profits in British 2789
The progress of economics 99
The progress of the nation 6712
Progress of the United States 7156

Progress of the working 8228
Die progressive einkommensteuer 8348
Progressive taxation 8603
Proizvodnja, zaposlenost 2127
Project economy 2018
Projet d'une dixme royale 4833
Projet pour rendre la paix perpétuelle 4697
Prolegomena to relativity economics 3847
Prolegomenes a une mecanique 660
Prologue to economic understanding 1753
Les promenades de Paris 7380
The promises men live by 2051
Proniknovenie idej K. Marksa 9289
Property 5070
Property 8196
Property and contract 8945
Property and progress 8258
Propheten und magier 851
Proporcje gospodarcze 2158
Propos à bâtons rompus 440
Propos économiques 432
The proposal, commonly called Sir Matthew Decker's scheme 4495
A proposal for a national bank 4551
A proposal for establishing life annuities 4634
A proposal for making a saving 4496
A proposal for making an effectual provision 4270
A proposal for payment of the publick debts 4476
A proposal for restoring 6901
The proposal for the raising of the silver coin 4635
A proposal for uniformity of weights 6732
Proposals and reasons for constituting a Council of trade 4587
Proposals for a fund 4377
Proposals for a publick coinage 4477
Proposals for an economical 6856
Proposals for national banks 4636
Proposals for raising a college of industry 4012
Proposals for settling the East-India 4637
Proposals humbly presented to his Highness Oliver Lord 4847
Proposals made by His late highness the Prince of Orange 4638
Proposals offered for the sugar planters' redress 4639
Proposals to the king 4459
Proposals to the legislature 4877
Proposed alteration of the Scottish poor-laws 6549
Proposed modifications in Austrian theory 3173
Proposed roads to freedom 9529
The proposed system of trade 6889
La proprieta 2466
La proprietà fondiaria 6285
La propriété 7666
A prospect of political 2116
A prospect of political 9573
The prospects of Britain 5919
Prospectus d'un nouveau dictionnaire de commerce 4537
Prospectus sur les finances 4293
Prosperity in crisis 9938
Protection 8687
Protection and free trade 7588
Protection and the social problem 513
Protection or free trade 7896
Protection vs. free trade 8069
Protections 5839
Protektionismens genombrott 5184
The protestant ethic 2628
The protestant ethic 8901
Il protezionismo americano 8473
Pierre Joseph Proudhon 2370
Proudhon, Hegel 9441
Pierre Joseph Proudhon, sa vie 2368

P. J. Proudhon, seine lehre 7748
P. J. Proudhon; textes choisis 2465
The proverb crossed 4640
Provision for the poor 4354
Proyecto economico 4853
Der prozess der bedarfsgestaltung 3233
Prud'hommes employés 7504
Przyspieszony wzrost 9345
Płori projevum buržoazní 1976
Public accounts of services 4859
The public debts 6110
Public debts 7369
Public economics 1587
Public economics 2026
Public economy 1274
Public economy 5781
The public economy of Athens 4900
Public finance 7440
Public goods 3426
The public regulation of railways 7723
Publication des manuscrits de Charles Fourier 9187
Pure economics 3378
Pure economics 9751
Pure theory of capital 9712
The pure theory of foreign 9850
The pure theory of utility 3271

Quantification 3567
Quaniification 9775
Quantitative analysis 3762
Quantity and quality 3727
The quantity theory 5219
Quantulumcunque concerning money 4596
Die quasirente 9854
The Queen's taxes 8369
Quelle influence on les diverses espèces d l'impòts 6548
Quelle influence ont les diverses espèces d'impòts 6741
Die Quellen der wissenschafts-auffassung Max Webers 3464
Queries relating to a national bank 4020
The querist 4021
Francois Quesnay 5421
Francois Quesnay als politischer 5378
Quesnay and physiocracy 5394
François Quesnay et la physiocratie 5405
Francois Quesnay und die idée 5372
Francois Quesnay's system 5410
Qu'es que l'economic politique 1101
The quest for Utopia 9459
Qu'est-ce que la propriété 6734
The question concerning impositions 4176
The question concerning literary property 4642
The question concerning the depreciation 6269
The question considered 5865
La question de l'or 6380
La question des habitations 7622
La question des impòts 5612
La question des propriétes primitives 7404
La question laitière 8375
Question monétaire 7260
La question monétaire 8063
La question monétaire en 1889 7682
The question of scarcity 7271
La question ouvière au xix 8189
La question sociale 546
Question sur le commerce 4294
La questione monetaria 8251
La questione sociale 7803
Questions constitutionelles 6742
Questions d'économie politique 6536
Les questions d'economie sociale 8540
Questions économiques 5613
Questions in political economy 5504
Questions monétaires 7870
Questions of the day 7802
Die quintessenz des sozialismus 8575

The radical cause of the present 7025

Radical means or counteracting 5980
Le ragioni di scambio 3177
The rate of interest 959
The rates of merchandise 4643
Rationalité et irrationalité 9208
The rationality 8979
Railroad 7364
Railroad problem 7847
The railroad question 8159
Railroad transportation 7978
Railroads 6748
Railroads: 7365
Railroads 7850
Railway economy 6349
Railway expenditures 8130
Railway problems 8093
Railway rates 7955
Railway rates 8131
Railway reform 6749
Railway secrecy 7529
Railway tariff 8604
The railways 7360-7362
The railways 8072
Rapport à la convention nationale 5676
Rapport fait au nom de la commission chargée 6753
Rapports du comité de mendicité 6754
The raproachement between east and west in mathematical 3915
The rationality of economic activity 3763
Daniel Raymond 3070
Razvitak privrednog sistema 1941
Razvitie ekonomicheskoi teorii 3009
Razvitie na burzoaznata 2563
Razvitieto na ikonomicheskata misui sied Rikardo 483
Razvoj ekonomske misli 618
Reader in Marxist philosophy 9550
The Reader's guide 7553
Readings 1503
Readings and cases 706
Readings in contemporary 2181
Readings in econometric theory 3594
Readings in economic analysis 748
Readings in economic analysis 1265
Readings in economics 699
Readings in economics 802
Readings in economics 806
Readings in economics 843
Readings in economics 915
Readings in economics 966
Readings in microeconomics 722
Readings in microeconomics 3275
Readings in money 978
Readings in price theory 3103
Readings in the development 721
Readings in the history 938
Readings in the history 952
Readings in the social control 769
Readings in the theory of income 704
Readings in the theory of income 777
Readings on the Soviet economy 2999
The real cause of the increased price 5818
Realidad economica 2036
Realidad económica 3824
Realism and relevance 9833
A re-appraisal of Cornot's 9748
A reappraisal of Marxian 9648
Reason, social myths 9241
Reasons against a registry 4646
Reasons against lowering the interest 4645
Reasons for a farther amendment of the copyright 5644
Reasons for a limited exportation 4647
Reasons for a registry 4649
Reasons for the hindering the home consumption 4691
Reasons for the more speedy lessening 4648
Reasons humbly offered 4497
The reasons of the decay of trade 4650
Reasons offer'd for erecting a bank 4502
Recent contributions to

mathematical 3605
Recent developments 123
Recent economic changes 8774
Recent literature on interest 3128
Recent trends in economic thought in Denmark 2605
Recent research in economics education 3811
Recherches critiques sur l'age 5005
Recherches et considerations 4295
Recherches et considerations 6764
Recherches et considérations sur la population 6526
Recherches historie 7460
Recherches historiques et critiques 4066
Recherches historiques 6381
Recherches historiques 6767
Recherches récentes sur la fonction de production 3812
Recherches statistiques 6556
Recherches statistiques 6772, 6773
Recherches sur la population 4651
Recherches sur la population 6125
Recherches sur la population 6770
Recherches sur la topographie de Carthage 6774
Recherches sur la valeur des monnois 4701
Recherches sur le commerce 6763
Recherches sur l'économie 8229
Recherches sur les consommations 5722
Recherches sur les Enfans-Trouvés 6765, 6766
Recherches sur les moyens 4007
Recherches sur les principes mathématiques 5844
Recherches sur les principes mathématiques 9681
Recherches sur les rentes 6771
Recherches sur les vraies causes 5492
Recherches sur l'histoire 491
Recherches sur l'histoire 2633
Recherches sur l'or 6029
Recherches sur l'origine 6176
Recherches sur l'origine de la Boussole 6768
Recherches sur l'origine de l'impôt 6769
Rechnen und usancen 7624
Das recht auf den vollen 8289
Das recht auf den vollen arbeitsertrag 450
Rechtsstaat und socialismus 7968
Recollections of Richard Cobden 7399
A reconsideration of the Tableau 5352
A reconsideration of the theory of value 3259
The reconstruction of economic theory 509
Reconstruction of economics 814
A reconstruction of economics 1159
Recopilacion de las leyes 4652
Recreacion politica 3977
Récréations économiques 4686
Recueil d'actes et piéces 4796
Recueil de mémoires 5957
Recueil des particularités 7198
Recueil des reglemens 6775
Recueil des traités de commerce 6776
Recueil . . . traités de commerce 6185
Redelijke economie 1519
Reflections on coin 4654
Reflections on relation between economic theory 3807
Reflections on the expediency of a law 4819
Reflections on the expediency of opening the trade 4820
Reflections on the government of Indostan 4709
Reflections on the present high price 4655
Reflections on the present low price 7161
Reflections on the present matters 7162

Reflections on the work 10078
Reflections suggested 6406
Reflections upon the constitution 4174
Reflections upon the East-Indy 4126
Reflexiones economico-politicas 3964
Réflexions 7237
Réflexions philosophiques sur l'impôt 4794
Réflexions politiques 4219
Reflexions sur la formation 5432
Réflexions sur la mendicité 6543
Réflexions sur la necessité 4656
Reflexions sur la police 3923
Reflexions sur la réduction 6344
Réflexions sur la richesse future 6181
Réflexions sur le commerce 5794
Réflexions sur le plan d'une régence 6656
Réflexions sur les avantages 4538
Réflexions sur l'esclavage 5795
Reflexions sur les modèles économétriques 3896
Reform der armenpflege 8655
Reform of the bank of England 8610
Reforma degl' instituti pii 6860
Réforme des caisses d'épargne 8541
Réforme des impôts 8439
La réforme sociale 6359
Réforme sociale 8478
Refresher course 1327
A refresher course 2184
Réfutation de l'éclectisme 6368
Réfutation de l'ouvrage 4539
Réfutation des dialogues 4657
Refutation des principes 6781
A refutation of the wage-fund 8221
La régime douanier 8151
Reglamento profesional 2349
Règles bibliographiques 3734
The rehabilitation of consumers' surplus 9823
Reichsgold 7428
Der Reichsmerkantilismus 5162
A reinterpretation of Ricardo's 3253
The relation of home investment 9973
The relation of the history of economic thought 214
Relation of the state to industrial 7370
The relations between the laws of Babylonia 5001
Relations du travail 5954
The relations of political 8808
The relationships between the major economic philosophies 93
Relative movements of real wages 3286
Relativist and absolutist approaches 101
The relativity of economic doctrine 3574
Religion and the rise of capitalism 5106
Religion Saint-Simonienne 9045
Religion Saint Simonienne 9504
Religion und wirtschaft 472
Remanentismo, teoría 3221
Remarkes on the husbandry 5769
Remarks on a letter to Sir John Bernard 4660
Remarks on a scandalous libel 4662
Remarks on currency 7242
Remarks on fair prices 6434
Remarks on some fundamental doctrines 143
Remarks on some fundamental doctrines 5850
Remarks on some prevalent errors 6612
Remarks on the association 5717
Remarks on the celebrated calculations 4658
Remarks on the coinage

6501
Remarks on the deficiency of grain 6987
Remarks on the English woollen 4659
Remarks on the essay 7069
Remarks on the management 6407
Remarks on the occurrences of the years 1720 and 1721 4661
Remarks on the Philippine 6785
Remarks on the poor-laws 6550
Remarks on the report of the select committee 6525
Remarks on the revenue of customs 5881
Remarks on the state of the sugar 5817
Remarks upon a late book 4422
Remarks upon Dr. Price's appeal 4664
Remarks upon Mr. Webber's scheme 4665
Remarks upon the Bank of England 4663
Remarks upon the history of the landed 6786
Remarques sur les avantages 4169
Remarques sur les avantages 4608
The remedy for unemployment 8761
La remodelacion del orden 799
El renacimiento 637
La renaissance du mercantilisme 5254
Rendiconti del Comitato per il potenziamento 751
La reorganisation cadastrale 7569
Reorganisation de la société 6925
Répartition métriques des impôts 8707
Repetitorium der geschichte der nationalokonomie 405
Repetitorium der national-oekonomie 8582
Repetitorium der theoretischen nationalökonomie 346

The reply of a member of parliament to the mayor 4666
A reply to a pamphlet 5650
Reply to Mr. Bonsanquet's 6858
A reply to the arguments 6465
Reply to the pamphlet entitled 'Proposed alteration' 5460
Reply to the reflections 6649
A reply to the treasury pamphlet 6789
A report 4670
Report 7403
Report and evidence 6790, 6791
Report by a committee 6792
Report by and evidence 6793
Report by Sir Isaac Newton 4668
Report for the directors 6794
Report from and evidence 6795-6800
Report from and minutes 6801-6802
Report from commissioners 6803
Report from the committee 6804
Report from the committee of secrecy 6665
Report from the secret committee 6805
Report from the select committee 6666
Report from the select committee 6806-6813
Report of a committee of the citizens of Boston 6814
Report of John Finlaison 6818
Report of tariff laws 8495
The report of the commissioners 4667
Report of the committee 6815
Report of the Lords 6816, 6817
The report of the Lords committees 4669
Report of the poor law 6819
Report of the secretary 6820
Report of the secretary of the treasury 5852
Report of the secretary of the treasury 6171
Report of the select committee 6821, 6822
Report on American shipping 7755
Report on comparison of

tariffs 6824
Report on friendly or benefit societies 6825
Report on funding system 5987
Report on interstate commerce 8493
Report on national bank 6169
Report on public credit 6170
Report on rates of duty 8494
Report on state of the coinage 4565
Report on the commerce 6823
Report on the commercial statistics of Syria 5621
A report on the inland 7153
Report on the Prussian commercial 5622
Report on the statistics of Tuscany 5623
Report on United States labor laws 8496
Report to Her Majesty's principal secretary 6826
Report to the British 6433
A report to the Lords of the treasury 4473
Report upon alleged combinations 8497
Report upon weights 5448
The reporting of empirical work 3865
Reports and documents 6827
Reports and evidence 6828
Reports and speeches on local taxation 7935
Reports from and evidence 6829, 6830
Reports from and minutes 6835
Reports from the Lords committee 6667
Reports from the select committee 6668
Reports from the select committee 6836-6839
Reports of cases in the high court 6831
Reports of cases in the high court 6869
Reports of central board 6832
Reports of commissioner's appointed to revise the laws 8498

Reports of consuls on streets 8499
Reports of interstate commerce 8500
Reports of the selected committee 6833
Reports of United States consuls on emigration 8501
Reports on profit sharing 8581
The reports on the agriculture 6834
Reports on the diseases 7249
A representation concerning the knowledge of commerce 4498
Representation of the lords 6840
Les representations figurees des physiocrates 5426
The representative firm 3404
The representative firm 9864
Repression and the dialectics 3900
The republic 5066
The republic of Plato 4921
République 4032
Repudiation of state debts 8597
Research methodology 3823
Researches historical 6777
Researches into the physical history 6724
Resources and development 7429
Resources of modern countries 8791
Resources of the United States 5635
The respective pleas 4821
Respuesta fiscal 4076
Respuesta fiscal sobre acopio 4526
Restablecimiento de las fabricas 4826
Restauracion política de España 4523
Resumé d'histoire des doctrines economiques 555
Résumé sur la regime 5825
Resumption and the silver 8449
Le rétablissement des manufactures 4609
Retablissement des manufactures 4671
Retail prices 7375

The retarded acceptance of the
  marginal 9731
Rethinking on Indian 2813
A retrospective view of the
  Scots fisheries 6699
Les rêves d'un homme de bien
  4698
A review and complete abstract
  6468
A review of Dr. Price's writings
  6565
A review of economic doctrines
  329
A review of economic theory 89
The review of radical political
  economics 543
A review of regional economics
  research 3543
A review of the domestic
  fisheries 6062
Review of the effect of the
  employment 5990
A review of the financial 7159
A review of the present ruined
  condition 6719
Review of the statutes 5489
A review of the universal
  remedy 4672
A revision of demand 3257
A revision of the treaty 9996
Revisions in mercantilism 5180
Revisiting Marshall's constancy
  9817
Revoliútsionnyĭ perevorot 397
The revolt of the bees 6563
Revolution and counter- 9411
La révolution du XXe siècle 444
La révolution économique 7759
Revolution, evolution 2090
La révolution française 5914
Revue d'histoire economique 544
Revue economique 545
Revue sommaire des doctrines
  1284
Revue sommaire des doctrines
  9682
Rhyme, rhythm and truth 1777
Riassunti di politica economica
  1426
Ricardian economics 2726
The Ricardian socialist 9344
The Ricardian socialists 2766
David Ricardo 2404

David Ricardo 2539
David Ricardo and Ricardian
  theory 2390
Ricardo en Marx 8723
La richesse de la Hollande 6980
La richesse de l'Angleterre 4678
Richesses et ressources 5893
Riflessioni sulla populazione 6636
Riflessioni sulle leggi
  vincolanti 7185
Le riforme leopoldine 5044
Le riforme leopoldine nel
  pensiero 2859
The right of primogeniture 5505
The right to the whole produce
  9442
The rights of industry 6864
The rights of man 6646
The rights of the people 4868
Riktig og gal planøkonomi 1604
Riqueza firme y establic 4524
Riron-keizaigaku kōgi 1302
The rise and decline of the
  Medici bank 5082
The rise and fall of the late
  projected excise 4679
Rise and progress of English
  commonwealth 6647
Rise and progress of the
  English constitution 7692
The rise of American economic
  thought 3082
Rise of economics as an aca-
  demic discipline 507
The rise of the marginal utility
  school 9719
Risk, uncertainty 1628
Risk, uncertainty 3294
Risk, uncertainty, and profit
  3710
Road legislation 8097
The road to planned economy
  2666
The road to serfdom 9225
Roads to freedom 953
Roba, novac i zakon 1929
Karl Rodbertus 7749
Rodbertus der begründer 7372
The role of comparison 653
The role of measurement 3853
The role of the economist
  2448
The role of the history of eco-

Short Title Inedx 847

nomic thought 254
The role of the history of economic thought 3639
Roman economic conditions 5057
Roman farm management 4975
Roman system of provincial 7394
Romance of the wool trade 7532
The romance of trade 2759
The Romans of Britain 7672
Ronsō, kokusai kachi ron 3287
Roscher, Wilhelm 8835
Roscher und Knies 8902
The Rothschilds 8490
Les rouages de l'économie 1046
Round table 8922
Round table conference 8946
Rousseau e Marx 9629
The royal mint 7386
The royal treasury 4769
Rozwój angielskieg mysli 2783
Rozwoj idei socjalistycznych 9347
Rozwój myśli ekonomicznej 5246
Ruckblick auf ein halbes 590
Rudimentos de derecho 1712
Rudiments of economics 1538
Ruin to ruin 4368
The ruine of the bank 4370
The rural exodus 7941
Rural recollections 6866
Russia, political 8703
Russia seit aufhebung 5705
The Russian menace 9058
La Russie, la Pologne 6952
Russische papierswahrung 7205
Russkaia ekonomicheskaia 3021
Russkaia ekonomicheskaia mysl' 3006
Russlands finanzlage 8143
Rynek sprzedawcy i rynek nabywcy 3474

Sa vie et ses oeuvres 6917
Saggi bibliografica e storici interno 189
Saggi bibliografici 2376
Saggi bibliografici 2844
Saggi critici di economia 1205
Saggi di economia 398
Saggi di economia 1173
Saggi di economia politica 152
Saggi di economia politica 1406

Saggi di economia politica 8342
Saggi di economis 7844
Saggi di storia del pensiero economico 266
Saggi di teoria e storia 3442
Saggio di bibliografia 7478
Saggi economici 6075
Saggio delle cause e delle Augustie 6650
Saggio sul buon governo 6909
Saggio sul sistema tributario 7377
Saggio sulla natura e l'importanza 550
Saint-Simon 9065
Henri, comte de Saint-Simon 9362
The Saint-Simonian portent 9104
Saint-Simonism in England 9474
Les salaires au xixme 7621
Salários, preços e lucros 3342
Salmasii de usuris liber 4704
Salt and fisher 4129
Samfundets økonomiske forhold 2010
Samfundsøkonomi for den daglige avislaeser 1144
Samfunnslaere med arbeidsoppgaver 1584
Samhällsekonomi 1454
Sammlung nationalökonomischer 7664
Professor Samuelson on theory 3738
Professor Samuelson on theory 3826
San Bernardino da Siena 5124
San Bernardino of Siena 5083
Sarvodaya, the welfare of all 2811
Saudi Arabia 3355
Savremene burzoakse teorije 3390
Savremene burżoaske teorije vrednosti i cena 527
Savremeni problemi 2149
Saxons in England 6328
Jean-Baptiste Say 2486
Jean-Baptiste Say 7327
Scarcity challenged 1632

Schein und wirkluchkeit 2249
Les schémas de reproduction 9142
A scheme for preventing a further increase 4119
A scheme for supplying industrious men with money 4026
A scheme of economic theory 2076
A scheme of the money-matters of Ireland 4057
Scheme to pay the public debt 4778
A scheme to prevent the running of Irish wools 4707
The schemes of the South Sea 4708
Schets eener geschiedenis 142
Das Schicksal der volkswirtschaft 2673
Gustav Schmoller 8833
Gustav von Schmoller 8890
Gustav von Schmoller und die probleme von heute 3836
Schmoller versus Menger 2476
Schmoller versus Menger 3813
Gustav Schmoller zur siebenzigsten 2674
Gustav Schmoller's economics 8899
The scholastic analysis of usury 5053
Scholastic economics 5084
Scholastica ed umanismo 8704
Scholasticism and politics 5034
Scholasticism and welfare 5140
Scholasticism old and new 5143
The scholastics, usury 5085
Scholastik, puritanismus 2761
The school of Salamanca 2968
Schools and streams of economic thought 682
Schule der eisenbahnwesens 8764
Schule und wirtschaft 3834
Schultze-Delitzsch 7470
Schumpeter 2397
J. A. Schumpeter and scholastic 5080
Schumpeter's theory 2416
Science and ideology 8986
Science and social welfare 2738

La science de l'économie 5452
La science de l'economie politique 1036
La science du bonhomme Richard 4304
La science economiche in Italia 8680
La science economique 7973
La science economique americaine 3077
Science économique et travail 1115
The science of finance 7649
The science of modern cotton spinnery 8182
The science of money 7733
The science of political economy 1452
The science of political economy 7897
Science of social opulence 6930
The science of wealth 1225
The science of wealth 1549
The science of wealth 2233
The science of wealth 7213
La science politique des physiocrates 5348
Science sociale 5770
Science the false messiah 8913
Les sciences économiques 243
Les sciences économiques 2642
Scienza della finance 7678
Scienza delle finanze 8271
Scienza delle finanze 8507
Scienza economica ed economisti nel momento presente 190
La scienza economica in Italia 2871
The scope and method 8626
The scope and method of economic science 3843
The scope and method of political 3699
The scope and method of political 3901
The scope of political 3797
La scoperta dell'utile nel Settecento 2641
Scotch banks 8307
The Scotch banks 8646
Scotch statistics 7101

Short Title Index 849

Scotland in the middle ages 8084
Scottish highlanders 7498
The Scottish moralists 7330
The Scottish philosophy 2433
Scriptores rei rusticae 6950
Scriptores rei rusticae 6963
Scritti di economia 7610
Scritti di teoria 2216
Scritti economici 2354
Scritti economici vari 1386
Scritti paretiani 9758
Scritti scelti di economia 1479
Scritti teorici 9759
Scritti vari di economia 1385
Scritti vari di economia 1443
Scritti varii di economia 502
Scrittori classici italiani 5863
Scrittori classici Italiani 6964
Le scuole economiche 2671
Seasonable observations 4710
A seasonable proposal 4711
Seasonable remarks on trade 4056
Second letter recommending 4713
A second letter to a friend 4822
Second thoughts 976
Le secret-des finances de France 4308
The secret history of the late directors 4789
Seichō keizaigaku 1475
Seido-shugi keizaigaku 8966
Seisan kakaku no riron 3414
Seisan to bumpai ni taisuru 3279
Seito gakuha 658
Seiyo keizai shi gaiyo 2885
Sekimon shingaku no keizai 2901
Das selbstverstandnis 3688
A select bibliography 2748
A select bibliography 4972
Select charters 8666
Selected economic writings 903
Selected essays 9412
Selected essays on political economy 713
Selected papers 1003
Selected papers 1022
Selected readings 733
Selected readings 809
Selected readings 832
Selected readings 1516
Selected readings in econometrics 3666
Selected works 9413-9415
Selected works of Dr. Chalmers 5715
Selected writings 971
Selected writings 2781
Selected writings 2812
Selected writings 9416
Selected writings 9534
Selections from the correspondence 6593
Selections illustrating economic history 949
Selections illustrating economic history 8481
Selections in economics 772
Self-help by the people 8059
Professor Seligman on the mathe-method 3604
Sengo ni okeru shakaikeizaishigaku no hattatsu 602
El sentido comun 2952
Serie economica 962
A series of answers to certain popular objections 4823
A series of tables 6590
A series of tables of annuities 6304
Serious considerations on the high duties 4180
Serious considerations on the several high duties 4715
Serious reflections on the high price 6981
A sermon against clipping 4275
Ses mémoires 4863
Seven reports 6982
Several assertions proved 3981, 3983
Several papers relating to money 4465
The several reports 4717
Shakai kagaku to shite 3508
Shakai kagaku to shite 3884
Shakai kagaku to shite 9614
Shakai keizai shiso shi 479
Shakai keizai shiso shi 2619
Shakai keizaishigaku 3874
Shakaikau nyūmon 9555

Shakaishugi keizai 9576
Shakaishugi keizaigaku 2167
Shakaishugi keizaigaku 3000
Shakaishugi keizaigaku 3013
Shakaishugi kigyo 2599
Shakaiteki shimp no genri 1614
Bernard Shaw and Karl Marx 9551
Shê hui chu i ching chi 1559
Shěng ch'an yin tsǔ lun 3321
Shihoron igo kyakunen 9299
Shihonron kenkyū 9615
Shihonron no hōhō 3760
Shihonron no keizaigaku 9616
Shihonshugi no shisō-kōzō 1007
Shihonshugi seiritsuki 5314
Shihonshugi wa do kawatta 2358
Shihouron no tenkai 9292
Shipping interest 6989
Shirtsleeve economics 1906
Shohinbetsu ni mita chōki 3285
Shoki shihonshugi no keizai 2687
A short account of England's foreign trade 7556
Short account of the Edinburgh bank 6990
A short account of the intended bank 4322
A short account of the state of our woollen 4856
A short course of political 9326
A short discourse 4369
A short history 2772
A short history of mercantilism 5225
A short history of paper money 6130
A short history of political 8460
A short history of the charitable 4720
A short inquiry into the nature of monopoly 6567
A short life of Sir James Steuart 2510
A short method to prevent the running 4781
A short tariff history 8272
Short text-book of political 8683
A short treatise 4721
A short view of Russia 3007
A short view of the apparent dangers 4722
A short view of the frauds 4723
Shorter classics 9666
A shorter working day 7976
Shotokkeizaigaku kōgi 1841
Sidelights on contemporary socialism 9580
Le siècle de fer 8158
The significance and basic postulates 330
The significance and basic postulates 3672
The significance of a changing concept of ownership 150
Signification du Marxisme 9131
Silver and gold 8060
Silver and gold 8311
The silver coins 6187
Silver coins of England 8004
Silver in Europe 8061
The silver pound 8062
Silver question 7432
The silver situation 8688
Saint Simon 7533
La simpatia nella morale 7279
A simple theory of capital 3193
Simples notions de l'ordre social 5726
Sin kyongje taeui 1660
Sin kyongje wollon 1256
Sin kyongje wollon 1556
Sin kyongje wollon 1619
Sin kyongje wollon 1891
Sin kyongje wollon 2298
Sin kyongjehak sa 114
Sin kyŏnjesa 110
The single duty project 5335
Sinking funds 8538
Sintese de evolucao 2561
Simond de Sismondi als nationalokonom 2333
El sistema economico 534
El sistema economico 2912
Sistemas económicos 1049
Sistemi finanzearii 8819
Sistemi monetari africani 5125
Situation économique de la Belgique 5485

Six centuries of work 8533
Six English economists 2758
Six lectures on political 7244
Les six livres de la republique 5334
A six month's tour 4878
Six reports 7003
A six weeks' tour 4879
Sixteen case studies in value 3134
Sketch of American finances 8121
Sketch of the civil engineering 7045
A sketch of the history of currency 8239
A sketch of the history of the East India 6135
A sketch of the life 7009
Sketch of the life 7317
A sketch of the revenue 5746
Sketch of the ryotwar system 7005
Sketches, essays 5354
Sketches on political 5938
The skills of the economist 3530
The slave power 7593
Slavery and anti-slavery 6127
Slavery in classical antiquity 4947
The slavery of the British West India 7042
Slovník světové ekonomiky 9670
Adam Smith, 7275, 7276, 7289, 7294, 7308, 7314
Adam Smith 7829
Adam Smith 8737
Adam Smith 8816
Adam Smith and David Ricardo 7258
Adam Smith and modern sociology 7333
Adam Smith and the Scotland 7292
Adam Smith and the Wealth 7352
Smith and Turgot 5351
Adam Smith as a person 7278
Adam Smith as student 7311, 7331
Adam Smith en zign onderzoek 5500
Adam Smith in Deutschland 7351
Adam Smith in laissez-faire 7353
Adam Smith on value 7282
Adam Smith, sa vie 7734
Adam Smith speaks 7295
The Adam Smith tradition 7325
Adam Smith und Immanuel Kant 8384
Adam Smith's approach 7326
Adam Smith's empiricism 7281
Adam Smith's library 7283
Adam Smith's moral and political 7277
Adam Smith's theory of economic growth 7347
Smith's theory of value 3195
Adam Smith's two views 7356
Smuggling laid open 4733
So taka svadesi 2831
Sobre alguns problemas da teoria 139
Social accounting 3854
The social and economic history of the Hellenistic 5088
The social and economic history of the Roman 5089
The social and political ideas 4980
Social and political thought 4895
The social and political thought 9020
The social and psychological 8984
A social approach 1705
Social choice 3108
Social condition and education 6324
Social credit 3194
Social Darwinism 3062
Social delusions 6299
Social-economic movements 5015
Social economics 1497
Social economics 2278
The social framework 1542
The social interpretation 9644
Social law of labor 8770
The social philosophy of Rodbertus 7931

The social possibilities 9851
Social reform 7933
Social reformers 1015
Social reformers 9635
The social revolution 9274
Social science 8700
Social science principles 3749
The social sciences 3686
Social sciences in the USSR 2984
Social struggles 9039
Social struggles in antiquity 4897
The social system 6142
Social theories of the middle ages 4997
Social value 3105
The social value of property 5037
The social welfare function 564
Social wreckage 8414
Sociale economie voor handelswetenschappelijke 1471
Die sociale frage 8040
Sociale Fragen 6258
Socialism 7811
Socialism 7851
Socialism 7943
Socialism 8118
Socialism 8259
Socialism 9167
Socialism 9594
Socialism and international 9597
Socialism and the American spirit 7913
The socialism of Shaw 9196
Socialism re-examined 9601
Socialism, Utopian 9173
Le socialisme 5591
Le socialisme 8341
Le socialisme allemagne 7544
Socialisme, communisme 7799
Le socialisme contemporain 8171
Le socialisme depuis l'antiquité 7100
Le socialisme d'état 8089
Le socialisme d'état 8567
Le socialisme devant 5804
Le socialisme intégral 8261
Les socialismes français 9146
Socialismo antico 7647

Il socialismo cattolico 8367
Socialismo, Darwinismo 8623
Socialismo e mercato 9063
Il socialismo negli stati uniti 8267
Der socialismus 7609
Der socialismus in Dänemark 8301
Socialismus und arbeiterfrage 7514
Socialist economics 1272
Socialist economics of Karl Marx 9625
The socialist economy 9637
The Socialist tradition 9211
Socjalizm ricardiański w historii 414
La sociedad economica moderna 2313
Sociedades precapitalistas 5077
Le società cooperative 8474
Le societe cooperative 8438
Les sociétés cooperative 8148
Society today 979
Society tomorrow 980
The sociological frontier 561
Sociologie und politik 7930
Werner Sombart 8871
Sombarts wiederlegung 8872
Some account of the life and writings 6240
Some account of the rise, progress 4131
Some account of the Shrewsbury 7261
Some account of the trade in slaves 5516
Some articles on the depreciation 7419
Some aspects of the acceleration principle 2283
Some aspects of the constitution . . . of Islam 2927
Some aspects of the tariff 8689
Some computations 4392
Some considerations about the raising of coin 4743
Some considerations concerning the public funds 4744
Some considerations of the

consequences of the lowering 3327
Some considerations of the consequences of the lowering 4466
Some considerations offered against 4745
Some considerations on publick credit 4746
Some considerations on the importance of the woollen 4471
Some considerations relating to the payment 4747
Some considerations upon the state 4748
Some developments of economic thought in the Netherlands 2924
Some ethical phases of the labor 8809
Some formulas encountered in the deductive analysis 3513
Some general considerations concerning the alteration 4749
Some improvements in simple geometrical methods 3169
Some improvements in simple geometrical methods 3577
Some leading principles 85
Some leading principles 1208
Some leading principles 7594
Some limitations of the value concept 3486
Some neglected aspects of Gresham's law 5194
Some neglected points in the theory 9626
Some notes on economic thought 390
Some notes on Terborgh's the bogey 9951
Some notes on the transformation problem 3348
Some observations on a direct exportation 3985
Some observations upon a paper 4751
Some observations upon a paper 4779
Some observations upon the bank 4750
Some origins of the modern 2754
Some overtures and cautions 4828
Some practical remarks 7340
Some problems of applying mathematical methods 3713
Some problems of logical method 3889
Some proposals for the imploying the poor 4272
Some relations between political 750
Some remarks on the bill for taking 4752
Some remarks on utility 3389
Some seasonable animadversions 4753
Some thoughts concerning the maintenance 4754
Some thoughts on the interest 5297
Some thoughts on the land-tax 4755
Some thoughts on the woollen 4756
Some unpublished letters of Ricardo 8054
Sommario di storia delle dottrine economiche 91
Sommario storico del pensiero economico 394
Sophismes économiques 5533
Sophisms of free trade 7590
Soren keizai ron 3018
Sosialøkonomi 1554
Sosialøkonomie 1361
Sotsialisticheskoe stroitel'stvo 3011
Sotsial'no-ekonomicheskie vozreniia 3001
Soundings of non-euclidean 3565
Soupis spisů a článků Karla Marxe 9500
Source and impact of Veblen 8939
Source readings 924
The South-Sea scheme 4758
The sovereignty of the British seas 4039
Soveschanie za "kruglym stolom" 2500
Soviet communism 9639
The Soviet economy 3016
The Soviet economy 3023,

3025
Soviet planning today 2993
Sovremennaia burzhuaznaia politicheskaia 2791
Sowjetische politische okonomie 2998
Sowjetunion 887
Sowjetunion 3012
Sŏyang kyŏngje sa 492
Soziale aufgaben 8287
Soziale bewegungen und 425
Soziale briefe au von Kirchman 9514
Die soziale Frage 2696
Soziale reform 8658
Die soziale und volkswirthschaftliche 8144
Die sozialen kernfragen 7995
Der sozialismus 7037
Sozialismus 8017
Sozialismus und social bewegung 9577
Das sozialitäre system Eugen Dührings 44
Die sozialokonomischen 2768
Sozialpolitik 8891
Sozialreform 7571
Spanisch-jesuitische 5023
Spanish mercantilism 5170
Spanish mercantilism 5216
Sparen, beleggen en investeren 691
Sparen, Horten und Zins 9924
Spatmitterlalterliche jurisprudenza 662
Special report on the customstariff 8815
The speech 6386
A speech made by Sir Robert Cotton 4759
Speech of C. Poulett Thomson 7021
Speech of C. Poulett Thomson 7099
The speech on certain transactions 6147
The speeches 6271
Speeches in the house 6270
Speeches in the house 7022
Speeches of the Right honorable Sir Robert Peel 6688
Speeches on questions of public 5760
Speiltheorie und wirtschaftswissenschaft 3363
Spiegazione economica 2017
Die K. K. Spiegelfabrik 5217
The spirit of American economics 2567
The spirit of American economics 3071
The spirit of Russian economics 3014
Spiritualita medioevale 5093
Staat, stände und der gerechte preis 3281
Staat und gesellschaft 2690
Staat und wirtschaft 919
Die staaten's Europa 7557
De staathuishoudkunde 8064
Der staatliche einfluss 8765
Der staatliche exporthandel 5302
Staatliche theorie des geldes 8850
Der staatscredit 6066
Die staatsfinanzwissenschaft 6291
Staatshaushaltung der Athener 5602
Staatsinrichting 2225
Staatslehre 6165
Die staatslehre des Aristoteles 8382
Die staatslehre des Thomas von Aquinas 7445
Das staatsschuldenproblem 36
Staatssubventionen für privatbahnen 7960
Staatswirthschaft 4410
Die staatswirthschaft 5981
Staatswirthschaft 6334
Staats-wirthschaftslehr principes 7274
Die staatswirtschaftslehre 5308
Staatswirtschaftliche untersuchungen 6207
Staatswissenschaften 8888
The stability of prices 8405
Stätdte und gilden der germanische 8014
Städtwesen des mittelalters 6267
Stagnation or growth 1463
Stand und aufgaben 2250
The standard of life 7539
State and revolution 9319
The state and the tasks of economics 3590
State enterprise 2739

Short Title Index

The state in its relation to trade 7831
The state in relation to labor 8101
State of Europe during the middle ages 6168
The state of Japanese 2874
State of prisons 8793
State of society in France 7120
A state of the British sugar-colony trade 4499
The state of the commerce 7028
A state of the English weights 4674
The state of the Island of Jamaica 4762
The state of the nation 4601
The state of the nation 4763, 4764
A state of the national debt 4765
The state of the poor 5972
The state of the public debts 4630
State of the public debts 5866
The state of the public debts 6722
The state of the science of political 5488
The state of the silk 4766
The state of the sugar trade 4767
The state of the trade 4768
State purchase of railways 8752
State railways 8050
Statement of some new principles 1984
A statement of the claim 6664
A statement of the claims 7029
A statement of the consequences 5527
Statements illustrative 6426
Staten og vore hjems 1942
Static demand theory 3280
Statik und dynamik 4989
The stationary economy 1771
La statistic humaine 7475
Statistical abstract 7030-7033

A statistical account 6427
The statistical account of Scotland 6998
A statistical and historical inquiry 6603
Statistical annals 6983
Statistical atlas 8748
Statistical testing 3870
A statistical view of the commerce 6700
Statistick uebersicht 5905
Statistics and economics 8276
Statistics and economics 8643
Statistics and geography 6214
Statistics of the colonies 6469
Die statistik als selbstandige 8854
Statistik der verkehrs 7483
Statistik des zollvereinten 7188
Statistik und gesellschaftslehre 8278
Statistique comparée des institutions financières 7857
Statistique de la France comparée 7508
Statistique de la Grande-Bretagne 6557
Statistique de l'agriculture 6558
Statistique de l'Espagne 6559
Statistique de l'industrie 6560
Statistique des peuples 6561
Statistique du paupérisme 8364
Statistique élementaire 6693
Statistique géneral 6953, 6954
Statistique générale 7034
Statistische tafeln aller länder 6261
Statutes in force relating to poor 7918
The steam-engine 6782
The steam-engine explained 6350
Die stellung des Hugo Grotius 39
Sir James Steuart 9911
The stocks examined 6026
Stoic and epicurean 4987
The stoic and epicurean philosophers 5054
Stoic, Christian and humanist 5046

Storia civile et politica 6463
Storia critica 8315
Storia critica della teoria del valore 7948
Storia d. finanza italiama 8558
Storia del commercio 6311
Storia del commercio 7058
Storia della economia pubblica 7059
Storia della economia pubblica in Italia 2862
Storia dell'economia politica 2845
Storia dell'economia politica 7821
Storia dell' economia politique 5455
Storia delle dottrine economiche 207
Storia delle dottrine economiche 267
Storia delle dottrine economiche 268
Storia delle dottrine economiche moderne 269
Storia de' principii delle massime 6412
Storia filisofica 7060
Storie delle dottrine finanziarie 2866
La storio grafia italiana 2843
The story of manual labor 8632
The story of Marxism 9540
The story of social philosophy 4943
The story of utopias 9458
Stosunki towarowe w gospodarce 1830
Strassenbahnen in Belgien 8216
Strategia economica 1387
The strategy of planning in India 2832
Strictures on the necessity 6988
Benjamin Strong 2355
Structural interdependence 3679
The structure of classical value 3347
The structure of economic science 3715
The structure of social 9856

Les structures économiques 1685
Structures et perspectives 1908
Struktur der wirtschaftsdynamik 1168
Strukturlehre 1935
A student's history 5079
Studi de storia delle dottrine economiche 92
Studi di storia del pensiero economico 417
Studi in memoria di Gino Borgatta 833
Studi in memoria di Giovanni de Francisci Gerbino 935
Studi in memoria di Rodolfo Benini 712
Studi in onore di Amintore Fanfani 994
Studi in onore di Giorgio Mortara di L. Amoroso 902
Studi in onore di Marco Fanno 3512
Studi keynesiani 10082
Studia i polemiki 1803
Studia had historia polskiej 2939
Studia nad mysla spoleczno-ekonomiczma 4939
Studia o ekonomickych zakonoch 275
Studia o ekonomickych zakonoch 2598
Studia o Fryderyku Skarbku 2505
Studien in der romanisch-kanonistischen 197
Studien in der romanisch-kanonistischen 4945
Studien über Bruno Hildebrand 8842
Studien über den amerikanischen zolltarif 6293
Studien über der weltindustrien 8577
Studien über die entwickelung 8264
Studien uber russisch-deutsche 2695
Studien uber russisch-deutsche 2960
Studien zur lehre vom geldwert 10
Studienplanung und realität 3858

Studier i ekonomi och
   historia 2155
Studier i frihetstidens 2978
Studies and exercises in
   formal logic 3700
Studies in advanced 1778
Studies in business 921
Studies in econometric
   method 3664
Studies in economics 8637
Studies in history 8667
Studies in linear and non-
   linear 3504
Studies in mathematical 9735
Studies in modern analysis
   3540
Studies in philosophy 3654
Studies in political 1836
Studies in political 8336
Studies in state taxation 8055
Studies in statistics 8222
Studies in the economics
   746
Studies in the economics of
   overhead 3163
Studies in the economics of
   the Bible 4964
Studies in the history 633
Studies in the labour theory
   3349
Studies in the labour theory
   9437
Studies in the quantity theory
   787
Studies in the theory of
   business 9974
Studies in the theory of
   economic expansion 878
Studies in the theory of
   money 5315
Studies on Marx and Hegel
   9253
Studies relating to Adam
   Smith 7332
A study in the theory of
   demand functions 3396
A study in the theory of
   economic evolution 3645
Studies in the theory of
   economic expansion 3737
A study in the theory of
   economic revolution 274
A study of agriculture 4984

The study of economic history
   741
The study of political 8163
A study of the Chinese commu-
   nist 9593
A study of the development of
   monetary theory 2775
Study of the law of the con-
   stitution 7743
A study of the refinements 31
A study of trade unionism 8056
Surveys of economic theory 705
Sub'ektivnaĭa shkola 51
Subektivnata shkola 442
The subject matter of economics
   3548
Subjective political 8640
A subsidy granted to the king
   4774
Subsistence patterns 5018
Substance of a debate 7064
Substance of economics
   1986
The substance of economics
   2097
The substance of the arguments
   for prohibiting 4775
The substance of the evidence
   4321
Substance of the Speech of the
   Right Hon. Lord Henry
   Petty 6692
Substance of two speeches 5680
Substance of two speeches 6272
Substitution and values 3306
The sugar trade 3984
Suggestions for a change 5674
Suggestions of Keynes 10098
Sul fenomeno economico 3793
Sul movimento dell' emigrazione
   7512
Sul principio economico 3571
Sul principio economico 3795
Sul problema agrario 7608
Sul riordinamento delle banche
   5600
Sulla 'Consumer's rent' 3117
Sulla economie sociale 6462
Sulla ripartizione di una risorsa
   3527
Sulle colonie 6885
Sulle leggi vinvolanti 4840
Sully, Colbert, and Turgot 5248

Sumerian economic texts 4923
Sumerian economic texts 5004
Summa theologica 4885
Summa theologia 4886
A summary, historical 4211
A summary of certain papers about wool 4082
A summary of colonial law 5747
Summary of history and law 6326
Summary of the law of bills of exchange 5545
Sunto di economia politica 8343
Suomen talouselaman johtajia 2424
Supplement of du nouveau dictionnaire 2338
A supplement to Mr. Simon's essay 4736
A supplement to the revolution in mind 6642
A supplement to the second part of the memoirs of John Ashley 3986
Supply and demand 3204
Supply and demand 3252
Supply and demand 9821
Supply curves and maximum 3350
The supply responses of African 3176
Sur l'administration de Necker 4563
Sur la legislation 4558
Sur la legislation 4562
Sur la legislation et le commerce 5391
Sur la mortalité proportionnelle 6283
Sur l'économétrie 3551
Sur le mode de production asiatique 9094
Sur les colonies agricoles 5483
Sur les moyens d'améliorer 5484
Sur les sociétés précapitalistes 9500
Sur les vices de nos procédés 6577
Surplus du consommateur 911
A survey of contemporary 703
A survey of contemporary 1368
A survey of contemporary 1505
A survey of contemporary economics 194
Survey of economic research in postwar Japan 2904
Survey of economic theory 796
A survey of primitive money 5071
A survey of the national debts 4602
A survey of trade 4864
Suspil-no-ekonomichni tendentsii 2965
Suvremena buržoaska politička 2025
Sviluppo e stabilità 3570
Svolgimento del pensiero economico 232
The swearer's-bank 4780
Sweden 2973
Sweden's economy 2980
Jonathan Swift 5324
Swift's economic views 5240
Syllabus of a course 6308
Sylva 4250
Symposium papers 3395
Les syndicats professionels 8491
Synthetic economics 1817
Synthetic economics 8322
The synthetic wealth 7299
System der communalen 8080
System der deutschen zette bankgesetzgebung 7206
System der nationaloeconomie 6619
System der nationalokonomie 1269
System der nationalökonomie 7650
System der soziologie 1881
System der staatswissenschaft 6087
System der staatswissenschaft 7041
System der volkswirthschaft 8876
System des handelsrechts 7926
System ekononji społecznéj 7487
System nauki skarbowéj 7488

Short Title Index

A system of functional
  equations 3353
System of marine insurances
  6659
System of moral philosophy
  4395
A system of political 8612
A system of the shipping
  6241
The system or theory of the
  trade 5205
Systema Africanum 4860
Systema agriculturae 4866
Systematic economics 3859
Systematischer abriss 6068
Systematisches handbuch 7228
Système de finance 5892
Systeme de la nature 4515
Système de politique positive
  5788
Die systeme der praktischen
  7196
Système des contradictions
  6735
Systeme d'un nouveau gouverne-
  ment 4408
Système financier 7406
Système financier 7541
Système financier de la France
  5493
Système industriel 6918
Système maritime 5480
Systeme universel des Arme-
  mens 5497
Systèmes et structures 1740
Systèmes généraux d'impôts
  8661
Systems of land tenure 8464
Systems of land tenures 7641
Sytuacja zawodowa 2932
A szocialista tulajdon 9184
A szocializmus politikai 9596

Ta dogmata tēs oikonomikēs 117
Tableau chronologique 7070
Tableau de la population 7071
Tableau de l'etat physique 7192
Le tableau economic de F.
  Quesnay 5395
The tableau economique 5358
The tableau économique 5402
Tableau economique 5409
The tableau economique of

Francois Quesnay 5441
Tableau général 6538
Tableau général du commerce
  6708
Tableau historique 6284
Tableau historique 7057
Tableaux comparatifs 6926
Tableaux synchroniques,
  1800-1955 354
Table des monnaies courantes
  3998
Tables for converting the
  weights 5649
Tables for renewing 4782
Tables for the purchasing
  5508
Tables of ancient coins 3972
Tables of English gold 4280
Tables of interest 4726
Tables of the revenue 6714
Tables showing the total num-
  ber of persons assured 7072
The tables turned 2728
Tablitsi za izravnĭâvane 3690
Li Ta-Chao 9439
Talmudische oekonomie 4927
T'an t'an chia chih kuei lü 3322
Tang tai ching chi 2494
The tangled bank 9251
The tariff controversy 7805
The tariff history 8690
Tariff policy 7484
Tariff question 7485
Tariffs and trade 8486
Tarifs des chemins 7405
Tavole sinottiche 3862
Taxation 6931
Taxation 7371
Taxation 7448
Taxation 8425
Taxation and anarchism 8203
Taxation in American states
  7812
Taxation of corporations 8605
Taxation of the British 8269
The taxes not grievous 4784
Taxes on knowledge 5858
The teaching of development
  3744
The teachings of Karl Marx
  9320
Tečaj politicke 1855
Technical library 3255

Technik, wirtschaft, kultur 898
Technique économique 1689
Techniques of industrial archaeology 5060
Technische revolution 9462
Technological progress 752
Der telegraph 8852
Das telegraphenrecht 8285
Die telegraphie 8227
Das telephonenrecht 8286
Temas de economîa 1292
Temelji politične ekonomije 1094
A temperate discussion 6392
Ten great economists 2488
Las tendencias actuales 2631
Tendencies in American 3080
Tendencies in American 8622
The tendency of strikes 6475
Tendenze e richerche 2864
Tenkeiki no keizai shisō 108
Tenshūgō'to keizai bunseki 3892
Tentavivo di bilancio del pensiero economico 524
La tenue des livres rendue facile 7084
Tenure and toil 7902
Teoria de metodologia 3573
La teoria del commercio 7712
La teoria del salario 2867
La teoria del salario 3400
La teoria del valore 8508
La teoria del valore 8714
Teoria económica 1097
Teoria económica 1340
Teoria economica, 1481, 1482
Teoria economica 1926
Teoria ekonomiczna J. M. Keynesa 10079
Teoria ekonomii i aktualne 1694
Teoria general 7661
Teoria generale del profitto 7949
Teoria generale della statistica 7879
Teoria marxistz do valor 3142
Teoria microeconòmica 2102

Teoria rozwoju kapitalizmu 2689
Teoria wartosci i problem 3170
Teoria wartosci i problem 9684
Teoria y practica 2189
Téorica del bisogno 2182
Teorica y practica del comercio y marina 4790
Teorie cen w radzieckich 9348
Teorie e fatti 2851
Teorie wzrostu ekonomicznego 2316
Teoriîa nakoplenîîa 9418
Teorija i merenje tražnje 3432
Teorija i praksa 9147
Terms of all loans 6146
La terre et le travail 5416
La terre ne ment pas 5353
Terrorism and communism 9275
Testamento politico 4585
A textbook 2152
A text book 2159
Textbook of economic analysis 1856
Text book of economic theory 1326
A text-book of economic theory 1651
Textbook of economics 1174
A textbook of economics 1510
A textbook of modern economics 1572
Textbooks on economic thought 382
Texte din literatura 2953
Les textes economiques de la Mouqaddima 4995
Les textes sociologiques 4996
Textile industries 7421
Textual exegesis 3851
Themes in economic anthropology 4949
Theoretical economic systems 76
The theoretical effects of rationing 3133
Theoretical problems 1085
Theoretical system of Karl Marx 9067
Theoretical welfare economics 261

Short Title Index 861

Theoretisch-historische 60
Die theoretisch national-
 okonomie 8593
Der theoretische gehalt
 5283
Theoretische nationalokonomie
 1331
Theoretische nationalokonomie
 3587
Die theoretische national-
 okonomie Italiens 2870
Theoretische socialökonomik
 1334
Theoretische sozialökonomie
 1232
Theoretische und methodolo-
 gische probleme 9599
Theoretische volkswirtschafts-
 lehre 2001
Theoretische volkswirtschafts-
 lehre 2258
La theorie de la population
 en Italie 2865
Theorie de la richesse
 2236
Théorie de la richesse
 7217
Théorie de la valeur 3403
La theorie de l'economie
 politique 5203
La théorie de l'économie
 politique 6086
Théorie de l'impôt 5386
Théorie de l'impôt 6736
Théorie de l'impôt 8547
Théorie de l'intérêt 6131
Theorie de tarifbidung 8164
Theorie der allgemeinen
 2073
Die theorie der dynamik
 2053
Theorie der ethischen 7342
Theorie der gesellschaft-
 lichen 2279
Theorie der vollbeschaftigung
 2024
Theorie der kapital markt
 1791
Theorie der wirtschaftlichen
 2012
Theorie der wirtschaftlichen
 2061
Theorie der wirtschaftsen
tsentwicklung 5223
Theorie der wirtschaftsentwick-
 lung 309
Theorie der wirtschaftsentwick-
 lung 823
Die theorie des Aussenhandels
 7341
Théorie des banques d'escompte
 6091
La théorie des besoins de Carl
 Menger 9662
Théorie des flux, monétaires
 430
Théorie des geldes 6582
Theorie des geldes 8034
Die theorie des internationalen
 handels 324
Théorie des peines 5565
Die theorie des preises 8212
Théorie des quatre mouvements
 6058
Théorie des richesses 7004
Théorie du crédit 7834
Theorie du crédit public 6203
Théorie du luxe 4067
Théorie du système 4791
Théorie économique 1113
Théorie économique 9893
Théorie économique 9914
Theorie économique notes
 2262
Théorie générale de l'adminis-
 tration 6153
Théorie générale de la valeur
 3234
Théorie mathématique 9793
Théorie nouvelle d'économie
 6687
La theorie quantitative 5239
Theorie und geschichte der
 national-oekonomik 349
Theorie und geschichtlichen
 6321
Théorie und politik 6583
Die theorien der mekantilisten
 5366
Theorien über den Mehrwert
 3343
Theorien über den mehrwert
 9417
Les théories de l'équilibre
 1957
Les théories de l'équilibre 9763

Les théories des surplus 3358
Les théories économiques 8965
Les theories economiques dans la Grece 5102
Theories of economic growth 318
Theories of imperialism 9277
Theories of population 723
Theories of population 5164
Theories of surplus value 3344
Theories of the firm 3739
Theories of the trade cycle 2767
Théorio des choix 3366
Theory and history 456
Theory and history 9745
The theory and measurement 3420
Theory and practice 9340
The theory and practice of commerce 4830
The theory and practice of communism 9249
Theory of bimetallism 7431
The theory of business enterprise 8997
The theory of capitalist 2162
The theory of capitalist 9595
The theory of competitive 3431
The theory of consumer's demand 3370
Theory of cost 2081
The theory of credit 8248
The theory of diminishing 3356
The theory of dynamic economics 8406
The theory of economic change 1605
The theory of economic change 3701
The theory of economic development 9865
Theory of economic dynamics 3689
A theory of economic history 298
Theory of economic organisation 1775

The theory of economic policy 7324
The theory of economic progress 1084
The theory of economic progress 8914
Theory of economic statics 1171
The theory of general economic equilibrium 1652
Theory of employment 2027
The theory of general static equilibrium 1421
The theory of growth 9858
The theory of human progression 5922
The theory of idle resources 9968
The theory of imperfect competition 3183
The theory of interest 3216
The theory of interest 9737
The theory of international 7441
The theory of international prices 3107
The theory of international prices 5151
The theory of investment 1718
The theory of money 7087, 7088
The theory of money 7158
The theory of money 9746
The theory of monopolistic 3153
The theory of monopolistic 9676
The theory of moral 7343
The theory of peasant 9096
The theory of political 9728
The theory of price 2146
The theory of prices 1744
The theory of prices 3338
The theory of prices 5255
The theory of prices 10027
Theory of production 225
Theory of profit in socialist 9600
The theory of prosperity 8407
Theory of reproduction 9308
The theory of social 2254
The theory of social 8903
The theory of social and economic organization 3899

Theory of social organization 6059
The theory of the balance of trade 5307
Theory of social organization 9188
A theory of the consumption 9932
A theory of the consumption function 224
The theory of the foreign exchanges 7936
Theory of the just price 5009
The theory of the leisure class 8998
The theory of unemployment 9862
The theory of valuation 3184
The theory of value 3423
Theory of value 9127
The theory of wages 3196
The theory of wages 7607
The theory of wages 8697
The theory of wages 9715
They wrote on clay 4915
A. Thier's volkswirtschaftliche 2538
Third report from the select 6669
Thirty-five years of Indian 2808
Thirty years of American finance 8377
William Thompson 2455
Those empty boxes 3816
Those having torches 913
Thoughts and details of the high 7128
Thoughts and details on scarcity 4062
Thoughts and details on scarcity 5654
Thoughts from Adam Smith 7291
Thoughts on man 6126
Thoughts on our silver coin 4792
Thoughts on political 6761
Thoughts on the causes 4407
Thoughts on the effects of the bank 7112
Thoughts on the expediency of repealing 5819
Thoughts on the separation 6408
Thoughts upon a new coinage 7113
Thoughts upon the principles of banks 7114
Threadneedle street 7638
Three essays on the state of economic science 854
Three lectures 6180
Three lectures on the cost of obtaining money 6976
Three lectures on the rate of wages 6977
Three lectures on the transmission 5292
Three lectures on the transmission of the precious 6978
Three letters relating to the South-Sea 4514
The three panics 5761
Three phases of co-operation 8754
Three reports 6608
Three reports from the select committee 7115
The three sources 9321
Three tracts on the corn trade 4727
Three views of method 3537
Three views of method 3778
Time in economics 3841
Die times und das deutsche 8861
To the long-concealed first promoter 4467
Today's economics 1470
Tōmen no bukka mondai 9963
Tools and the man 7915
Tools of economic analysis 1351
Topical comment 812
Topographisch-statistischer 8139
Total utility 3145
Total utility 3483
Totalitetskøkomien 2926
Tote und lebendige 2136
Tour in Ireland 4880
Tours of the English 4881
Toutes les classes

productives 6740
Towar i pieniądz 1970
Toward community 3066
Toward understanding institutionalism 8953
Towards a dynamic economics 813
Towards a more general theory of value 3154
Towards a new economic theory 129
Towards the understanding of Karl Marx 9242
Town life in the fifteenth 7951
Arnold Toynbee 8866
Trabalho e desenvolvimento 9482
A tract against the high rate of usurie 4163
A tract against usurie 4164
A tract on monetary reform 9997
Tractatus oeconomicó-politicus 4412
Tractatus politicus 5165
Tracts 4597
Tracts on political 7024
Trade and market in the early 5068
The trade and navigation 4315
The trade and navigation 4797
Trade and politics in ancient Greece 4976
The trade depression 8283
The trade policy 8022
Trade, population, food 7548
The tradesman's jewel 4619
The tradesman's jewel 4798
La transition 9054
La traición de los técnicos 1662
Traité complet des chemins 8388
Traité d'analyse économique 1318
Traité d'économie 7229
Traité d'économie industrielle 7967
Traité d'économie politique 66
Traite d'economie politique 714
Traité d'économie politique 4527
Traité d'économie politique 5897
Traité d'économie politique 6093
Traité d'économie publique 6913
Traité d'économie politique 6942
Traité d'économie politique 7141
Traité d'économie rurale 8437
Traité d'économie sociale 6155
Traité d'économie sociale 6637
Traité de la circulation 4068
Traité de la circulation 4605
Traité de la circulation 4799
Traité de la construction des Chemins 4801
Traité de la propriété 5790
Traité de la proprieté 7146
Traité de la richesse 7002
Traité de la richesse individuelle 6944
Traité de la science des finances 8190
Traité de l'association domestique agricole 6057
Traité de législation 5789
Traité de l'usure 4416
Traite des assurances 5991
Traité des banques 5659
Traité des banques 5797
Traité des chemins de fer 8430
Traité des contrats aléatoires 7143
Traité des droits d'auteurs 6788
Traité des finances 4107
Traite des finances 4913
Traité des finances 6094
Traité des impôts 6661
Traité des impôts 8727
Traité des mesures itineraires anciennes 4804
Traité des monnaies 4582

Short Title Index 865

Traité des monnaies 4620
Traité des monnaies, poids 7145
Traité des monnois 3999
Traité des monnoyes 4037
Traité des opérations de bourse 7686
Traité des opérations de le bourse 7580
Traite des prets du commerce 4513
Traité des richesses 6282
Traité de statistique 7147
Le traité de Versailles 9902
Traité du crédit foncier 8107
Traité électique 6012
Traite elem. 8480
Traité élémentaire 5843
Traité élémentaire 8021
Traité élémentaire 8731
Traité et commerce des nègres 4800
Traité général de pêches Maritimes 4218
Traité général des eaux 5543
Traité general du commerce 4677
Traité general du commerce 6851
Traité du contrat 7144
Traité général du Domaine de la Mer 4802
Traité historique des monnoyes 4803
Traité philosophique 6706
Traité sur les sociétés de crédit foncier 8314
Traité sur l'indigence 5911
Traité theorique 5840, 5841
Traité théorique 8191
Traite theorique et pratique 140
Traité théorique et pratique 8418
Les traités de commerce 7519
Traités de commerce 8154
Traités sur le commerce 4111
Transactions of political 8204
Le transformation des moyens 7860
The transportation question 8023
Transports et tarifs 7657
The trasure of trafficke 4681
Tratado de economia politica 1759
Tratado de economia politica 1789
Tratado de cconomía política 1880
Tratado de economia politica 2210
Tratado de hacienda publica 8431
Tratado de teoria económica 2314
Tratado elemental 8555
Tratado elemtaire 7656
Tratado juridico-politico 4409
Tratado moderno de economia 1468
Trattato dell'Abbondanza 4783
Trattato dell'assecurazione maritime 5512
Trattato delle monete considerate 4054
Trattato di economia 1466
Trattato di tasse di registro 7934
Trattato teoretico-pratico 5601
Le travail 8631
Le travail en France 7430
Travail et richesses 1182
Les travaux publics 8505
Travels 7148
Travels in France 4882
Travels in Italy 4883
The travels of Marco Polo 7149
Tre economisti italiani 2868
Treaties and tariffs 8019
A treatise 4806
A treatise concerning the causes of the magnificencie 4040
A treatise concerning the East-India 4580
A treatise concerning the properties 6569
A treatise of taxes 4598
A treatise of the canker 4484
A treatise of the law relative to merchant ships 5444
A treatise of the relative

rights 7221
A treatise of the siease 4805
A treatise of usurie 4266
A treatise on agistment tithe 5535
A treatise on agriculture 5639
Treatise on American law of landlord 8692
A treatise on civil imprisonment 6429
A treatise on coal trade 5976
A treatise on coins 6968
A treatise on contraband 7151
A treatise on currency 6747
A treatise on friendly societies 5473
A treatise on indigence 5779
A treatise on manufactures in metal 6238
A treatise on money 8361
A treatise on money 9998
A treatise on political 2048
A treatise on political 7152
A treatise on poverty 6906
A treatise on probability 9999
A treatise on railroads 7262
A treatise on roads 6674
A treatise on savings banks 8598
A treatise on sugar 6570
A treatise on the better employment 3991
A treatise on the coines 6387
A treatise on the coins 7150
A treatise on the industry 5984
A treatise on the law of insurance 6467
A treatise on the law of Scotland 5937
A treatise on the law of taxation 7671
Treatise on the laws of literary 6479
A treatise on the maritime laws 6956
A treatise on the principles 6428
A treatise on the records of the creation 7068
A treatise on the state of the currency 5862
A treatise on the steam-engine 6904

A treatise on the valuation of annuities 6520
A treatise on the wealth 5780
A treatise on trusts 8648
A treatise that the East-India trade 4112
A treatise upon money 4358
Treatises and essays on money 893
The trend of economics 1004
The trend of economics 3913
Tres siglos de pensamiento economico 611
Tribal and peasant economies 4925
Tribal economy 5047
Les tribulations du général Ken's 9919
Triebkraft bedürfnis 9134
Triebkraft Bedurrnis 3188
Trinity college, Dublin 3123
Les trois âges de l'économie 940
La troisieme phase 5190
The trouble with Marx 9650
A true and impartial account of the rise 4808
A true discovery of the projectors 4807
The true English interest 4675
True humanism 5035
The true interest and political maxims 4809
The true law of population 5917
A true narration of the royall fishings 4732
A true state of the South-Sea 4810
The true theory of rent 7095
Trusts 7668
Trusts, pools, and corners 8094
The truth about agriculture depression 7617
Tržište i cijene 3150
Tsuron keizaigaku 1842
Tudor economic documents 5309
Turgot 7444
Turgot, administration 8522
Turgot et ses doctrines 5396
Turgot et ses doctrines 8358
Turgot: his life, times 8048

Turgot, sa vie 7117
Turgot, sa vie 8274
Turgot's unknown translator 5369
Tussen beginsel en belang 856
La tutela dei diritti 4910
Tutkimuksia Suomen 2630
Twelve reports 7168
Twentieth century 826
Twentieth-century economics 1145
Twenty-two years of protection 8450
Twenty years of financial 8372
Two discourses 4276
Two discourses 6211
Two essays on political arithmetick 4599
The two last treatises published by Mr. Hutcheson 4393
Two lectures on population 6979
Two lectures on the checks to population 6389
Two lectures on the justice 6390
Two letters and several calculations 4018
Two lives 2440
Two memoirs 10000
Two reports 7171, 7172
Two reports from the select committee 4825
Two reports on the trade in corn 6290
Two thousand years of gild 8150
Two tracts on civil liberty 6723
Tworcy economji politycznej 402
Tworcy economji politycznej 5368
Tzŭ pên shêng yü chia chih 3458
Tzū pên yü shêng yü chin 3434
Types of economic theory 460
Types of institutionalism 8957
Typus und gesetz 3646

Uber aufgabe und methode 3804
Uber den gegenstand der politischen okonomie 1057
Uber den merkantilismus 5160
Uber den ursprung 3473
Uber den ursprung 8784
Uber deutsche auswanderung 7220
Uber die idee der selbstentfremdung 7280
Uber die zeitgebundenheit 9965
Uber dynamische wirtschaftsmodelle 3659
Uber finanzen und monopole 2796
Uber finanzen und monopole 5076
Uber gesetzmassigkeiten 8840
Uber posten und postregale 6478
Uber wert, kapital 9799
Uber wert, kapital und rente 3468
Die Überbeschaftigung 9900
Udvalgte kronikker 1915
Udviklingslinier i makroøkonomisk 1009
Ueber das formale prinzip 5998
Ueber das oeffentliche Schuldenwesen 5982
Ueber das verhaltniss 7750
Ueber den einfluss des Handels 6610
Ueber den heutigen begriff 7197
Ueber den merkantilismus 7482
Ueber die entwickelung der australischen 8115
Ueber die gegenwartige lage 2672
Ueber die Herabsetzung der Zinsen 6597
Ueber die mathematische methode 3716
Ueber die mittelalterliche 8340
Ueber die natur und die ursachen 6598
Ueber die ursachen 6609
Ueber encyclopedie 6101
Ueber handelsfeindseligkeit 6726
Ueber . . . methode der politischen 8427
Ueber national industrie 6411
Ueber nationaleinkommen 6069
Ueber production 6070
Uebersicht der literatur 2682
Uebersichten der weltwirtschaft 8349
Uleminek konnumistlikule 9200
The ultimate foundation of economic science 3759
The ultimate standard of value

3160
Umrisse und untersuchungen 8882
Umumî iktisada giris 1958
Una economía libre sin crisis 1135
Una neuva clasificacion 2544
Unbekannte portugiesische 2949
Unbekannte portugiesische 5193
Uncertainty in economics 973
Understanding an economy 1303
Understanding basic 1799
Understanding economics 738
Understanding economics 1089
Understanding microeconomics 1530
Understanding our economy 1825
Understanding our free economy 1379
Une histoire de la pensee 2840
Une théorie idéologique 3308
Unearned economic benefits 1020
The unearned increment 7727
The unemployed 7768
Unemployment 9895
Un'interpretazione del processo 2857
The Union Pacific railway 7723
L'union soviétique face 9153
The United States 8781
United States arts 5847
United States duties 8029
United States notes 8135
United States of America 8613
The unity of Veblen's theoretical system 8907
The universal accountant 4323
The universal cambist 6327
The universal cambist 7178
The universal dictionary of trade 4618

Economic Thought and Analysis

The universal merchant 4828
University economics 1047
The university teaching of social sciences 3877
Uno keizaigaku hōhō 1657
Uno riron to marukusu-shugi 9451
The unperfect society 9132
Unpublished papers 9794
The unseen foundations 7597
Unternehmen- und unternehmergewinn 8592
Unternehmer und arbeiter 7521
Der unternehmergewinn 8275
Untersuchungen über 7407
Untersuchungen uber Adam Smith 287
Untersuchungen über die methode 3754
Untersuchungen über die methode 9742
Untersuchungen über die theorie 1456
Untersuchungen uber die theorie 3111
Untersuchungen zum maschinenproblem 199
Untersuchungen zur geschichte 7761
Untersuchungen zur geschichte 8192
Untersuchungen zur klassischen nationalokonomie 69
Untersuchungen zur okonomischen theorie 1411
Untersuchunger über Adam Smith 7304
Untersuchunger über das kapital 8798
Untersuchunger über die methode 8865
Unto this last 2827
Unto this last 8549
Up against the American myth 740
Ursprung der deutschen stadtverfassung 7462
Der ursprung der familie 7818
Ursprung und entwickelung 8569
Us et coutumes de la mer 4120

Short Title Index

The use and abuse of money 7710
The use and abuses of money 4829
The use and abuses of money 5433
The use of mathematics 3781
The use of social research 3882
Ustřední vybor 852
Usul 'ilm al'iqtisād 8
Usul 'ilm al-iqtisād 205
The usurpations of France 4083
Usury at six per cent 4487
La utilidad marginal 3232
Utilitarianism 9619
Utility and all that 3406
Utility and all that 9867
The utility concept 9787
The utility concept in value 3452
Utility curves 3352
Utility theory 3377
Utility theory 9750
Utopia 4533
Utopia and a dialogue 9456
Utopias--old and new 9221
L'utopie et les utopies 9531
Utopie und wirtschaft 9
Der utopische sozialismus 2643
Uvahy o duševnej práci 1703
Uvahy o socialistické 9296
Uvod do bibliografie klasikov 9250
Uvod de kritice politické 9419
Uvod u političku 1869
Uvod u političku ekonomiju 1194
Uwagi do 'zarysu historii 2940
Uzroci robne proizvodnje 9622

Väärtus, hind ja hinna-politika 3136
La valeur 3180
La valeur d'après 3445
Valeur et capitalisme 3181
Valluvar tanta poruliyal 2824

Valore e distribuzione 3441
I valori spirituali 2873
Value added as a measure 3357
Value added by distribution 3152
Value analysis 3205
Value analysis 3229
Value analysis 3351
Value analysis 3376
Value and capital 3258
Value and distribution 3174
Value and distribution 3248
Value and distribution 3331
Value and distribution 8236
Value and distribution 9685
Value and the larger economics 3615
Value, capital, and growth 3449
Value, capital, and growth 3481
Value distribution theory 3416
Value engineering 3447
Value engineering analysis 3168
Value engineering in manufacturing 3450
Value in social theory 3365
The value of political 7705
Value, price and profit 9420
Value, theory and oligopolistic 3380
Value theory as a key 3393
La valutazione monetaria 3227
The Vanderblue memorial collection of Smithiana 7286
The varieties of economics 869
Vauban et Boisguillebert 5152
Vauban, seine stellung 2427
Vauban, seine stellung in der geschichte 411
Thorstein Veblen 8935, 8940, 8942, 8943
Thorsten Bunde Veblen 8947
Veblen 8959
Thorstein Veblen 8970
Thorstein Veblen 8963
Thorstein Veblen 8985
Thorstein Veblen 9000
Veblen and industrial 8915
Veblen, the analyst 8991
Veblenism 89

Veblenism 8938
Veblen's critique 8988
Vectigalium systema 4221
Vee als voorwerp van rijkdom 5123
Velstandslaere 8179
Venice and history 3720
Verbrauchen und sparen 9937
Verein fur sozialpolitik 665
Verein fur sozialpolitik 1012
Verein für sozialpolitik 2520
Verfassungs- und wirtschaftsgeschichte des mittelalters 181
Das verhältnis von wirtschaftstheorie 9457
Verhandeling over de verdiensten 2923
Verhandeling over het staathuishoudkundig 15
Die verkehrswege im dienste 7938
Vermischte historische 6197
Pietro Verri e i problemi 2428
Pietro Verri e i problemi 2856
Vers l'avenir 2224
Verspreide geschriften 943
Versuch einer apologie des physiocratischen 6072
Versuch einer bevolkerungslehre 778
Versuch einer einleitung in die kameral 4277
Versuch einer grundlehre 6318
Versuch einer kritick der gründe 5571
Versuch einer kritischen 7467
Versuch einer neuen geldtheorie 6580
Versuch eines systems 6335
Die verteilungstheorie 1609
Der vertheidigte Kornjude 4603
Die vertragsmäsige Doppelwährung 7389
Verwaltung der preussischen 8142
Verzeichniss numismatisch 6364
The vested interests 8999
Vetenskap och politik i nationalekonomien 474
Victor considerant, sa vie 2371

Economic Thought and Analysis

Victors de Riquetti 5387
Le Vie de benessere 1845
La vie économique 1237
La vie économique 2033
La vie économique 7438
Vie de Monsieur Turgot 5796
Vie litteraire de Forbonnais 5885
La vie, l'oeuvre 2523
La vie rurale 7410
View of money system 7077
A view of the art of colonisation 7210
A view of the British empire 6332
A view of the coins 4737
A view of the copper coin 4738
A view of the gold coin 4739
A view of the Greenland trade 4227
A view of the manner in which trade 4842
A view of the natural, political 6604
A view of the origin, nature 4740
A view of the present state 5859
A view of the present state of the salmon 5832
View of the progress 2627
View of the progress 7170
A view of the rise 4835
A view of the silver coin 4741, 4742
A view of the treaty of commerce 5974
A view of the treaty of commerce 7189
A view of the United States 5848
Views of the public debt 6079
Le village 7411
Village communities 8252
The vilaege community 7929
Villainage in England 8365
Villeneuve-Bargemont 2475
A vindication of commerce 4844
A vindication of commerce 5310
A vindication of the bank 4843
A vindication of some assertations relating to coin 4845
Le visiteur du pauvre 7195
Visualized citizenship 2280
Vital statistics 7828

Short Title Index 871

Vocabulario geografico-storico-statistico 8337
Vocabulario 8432
Voices of the industrial 727
Voir aussi les oeuvres completes de Xenophon 5145
Volk und volkswirtschaft 2693
Volk und wirtschaft in lehre 149
Volks- und staatswirthschaftliche 7466
Volks- und staatswirtschaftliche 2956
Volkswirtschaft 8484
Volkswirthschaftslehre 6455
Volkswirthschaftslehre 8350
Volkswirthschaftslehre 8352
Volkswirthschaftslehre 8379
Die volkswirthschaftslehre 8583
Der volkswirt als berater 8904
Der volkswirt als manager 2336
Die volkswirtschaft 255
Die volkswirtschaft 1650
Die volkswirtschaft 2055
Volkswirtschaft 5534
Volkswirtschaft 8883
Volkswirtschaft in unserer zeit 1428
Volkswirtschaft und weltwirtschaft 282
Volkswirtschaft, volkswirtschaftslehre 3830
Volkswirtschaftslehre 356
Volkswirtschaftslehre 1196
Volkswirtschaftslehre 1521
Volkswirtschaftslehre 1726
Volkswirtschaftslehre 2040
Volkswirtschaftslehre 2163
Volkswirtschaftslehre 2251
Die volkswirtschaftliche 1552
Volkswirtschaftliche gedankenstromunger 2686
Volkswirtschaftliche regelungsvorgange 1457
Volkswirtschaftliche regelungsvorgange 3637
Die volkswirtschaftlichen anschauungen 5092
Die volkswirtschaftlichen anschauungen David Hume's 2760
Die volkswirtschaftlichen artikel 5339
Volkswirtschaftstheorie 1300
Vollbeschäftigung ohne inflation 9904
Vom Geiste der ordnung in gesellschaft 1068
Von den eleménten des nationalreichthums 6934
Von den periodischen Schwankungen 6199
Von der alteren zur neueren theori 692
Von der alteren zur neueren theorie 696, 2325
Von der ordnung der fruchpreise 4827
Von marxistischer ideologie 9478
Von Thünen's isolated state 9782
Von Thünen's isolierter staat 9762
Von Thünen's theory of distribution 9736
Voor het land von belofte 2535
Voortgezet elementair leerboek 2209
Voprosy ěkonomičeskoj teorii 9630
Die voraussetzungen des sozialismus 7471
Vorlesung über midroökonomische 1603
Vorlesungen uber rechts- 7344
Vorlesunger über nationalökonomie 9800
Vortrage uber wirtschaftliche 1886
Voyage de Françoise Bernier 4849
Voyage de M. le Baron Dupin 7200
Voyages a Peking 7201
Voyages d'un philosophe 7202
Vues politiques 6409

W sprawie pogladow 4916
Wage determination 3385
Wagen, wagen, wirtschaften 2229
Wages and capital 8691
Wages of farm labor 7757
Wages policy under full 3446
Wages, price, and profit 3345

Der wahrungstreit 7820
Wakefield and Marx 2456
Der wald in nationalen wirth-
  schaftleben 7899
Léon Walras 9668
Leon Walras 9702
Walras, a reappraisal 9708
Sartorius von Waltershausen
  579
Wan Chou chu tzu ching chi
  2575
Wants and activities 9857
War and economics in history
  551
War in disguise 7043
Ware, wert und wertgesetz 3121
Die wasserstrassen 8327
A way to get wealth 4488
Ways and means for raising
  the extraordinary supplies
  4500
Ways and means of commercial
  payment 5782
Ways and means to raise the
  value of land 3946
Wealth 7602
Wealth against commonwealth
  8219
Wealth and progress 7970
Wealth and welfare 1951
Wealth-creation 8313
Wealth discovered 4158
The wealth of Great Britain
  4854
Wealth of Great Britain
  5462
The wealth of nations 7346
Wealth, virtual wealth 2119
Weber, Max 8889
Max Weber on law in economy
  3898
Daniel Webster as an economist
  2352
Wedderkopii 4857
Der weg der deutschen volks-
  wirtschaftslehre 2714
Der weg deutschen volkswirt-
  schaftslehre 1026
Wegweiser durch 8328
Der Wehrgedanke in der
  deutschen 2709
Welfare economics 28
Welfare economics 2742

The welfare state: U.S.A. 10095
Der welkverkehr 7892
Der weltbaumwollmarkt 3552
Weltgeschichte 8482
Weltwirtschaftliche essays
  800
Welvaart en historie 3138
Wendingen in de economische
  geschiedenis 72
Werke 8862
Das werkzeug der national-
  ökonomie 3718
Wert 3129
Wert, preis und zurcchnung
  3312
Wert, rente, lohn 1995
Wert- und preislehre 3262
Die wert- und preistheoretischen
  3307
Die wert- und preistheorie 3410
Wertanalyse: Grundlagen 3299
Die Wertanalyze als methode
  industrieller 3374
Der Wertbegriff in der betriebs-
  wirtschaftslehre 3477
Wertschöpfungsprozess 1620
Wesen, aufgabe 3703
Das wesen des einkommens 8297
Das wesen und der aufgabe 8562
Das wesen und der hauptinhalt
  2062
Das wesen und der hauptinhalt
  3839
Das Wesen und die aufgaben 3827
Sir Edward West 2461
The West India commonplace
  book 7273
Western civilization 5183
Western economics 951
Western European socialism 9564
A Western influence on Japan
  2896
Der wettstreit zwischen
  mikro- und makrotheorien
  881
What are riches 5645
What do economists know 821
What economics is about 1108
What economists do 2407
What is economics! 1725
What Keynes means 10036
What makes an economist
  2493

Short Title Index 873

What Marx really meant 9111
What price the history 684
What social classes owe 8677
What the friends of the people are 9323
The wheel of wealth 146
Which? Protection, free trade 7878
A whip for the smugglers 4045
The whole works of Adam Smith 7345
Wholesale prices 7376
Who's who in economics 2359
Why freedom works 716
Why had Roscher so little influence 3575
Why is economics not an evolutionary science 3886
Why is institutional economics not institutional 8954
Why is the theory of labor 3297
Knut Wicksell 9783
The Wicksellian tradition 2981
The Wicksellian tradition 9805
Philip Henry Wicksteed 9713
Wicksteed's recantation 9687
Der wirtschafende Mensch 8830
Wirtschaft un gerechtigkeit 1654
Wirtschaft und finanzen 2805
Wirtschaft und gesellschaft 922
Wirtschaft und gesellschaft 1025
Wirtschaft und gesellschaft 1363
Wirtschaft und gesellschaft 2255
Wirtschaft und gesellschaft 4934
Wirtschaft und wirtschaftswissenschaften in West-deutschland 169
Wirtschaft verständlich 2034
Wirtschaft, wirtschaftswissenschaft 8822
Wirtschaftliche entwicklung 866
Wirtschaftliche entwicklungsgesetze 9472
Der wirtschaftliche fortschritt 461
Der wirtschaftliche liberalismus 2730

Wirtschafts forschung 717
Wirtschafts- und arbeitslehre 3773
Wirtschafts- und arbeitslehre 3806
Wirtschafts- und arbeitswelt 3904
Wirtschaftsethik 2174
Wirtschaftsethik 2259
Wirtschaftsethik und monopole 4988
Wirtschaftsformen und lebensformen 1175
Wirtschaftsforschung und geographie 584
Wirtschaftsforschung und wirtschaftfuhrung 1134
Wirtschaftsgeschichte 676
Wirtschaftsgeschichte 754
Wirtschaftsgestaltung 1127
Die wirtschaftskrisen 37
Wirtschaftskunde 1646
Wirtschaftsliberalismus 2677
Wirtschaftsmechanik 2227
Die wirtschafts-philosophie 5133
Wirtschaftsphilosophie des 20. Jahrhunderts 640
Die wirtschaftspolitik 8886
Die wirtschaftspolitik der historischen schule 591
Der wirtschaftpolitische 647
Wirtschaftsprognose 9223
Das wirtschaftsprogramm der kirche des mittelalters 617
Wirtschaftstheorie 859
Die wirtschaftstheorie 891
Wirtschaftstheorie 1016
Wirtschaftstheorie 1176
Wirtschaftstheorie 1613
Wirtschaftstheorie unter dem Hakenkruez 2691
Wirtschafts-wille und wert 1088
Wirtschafts-wille und wert 3112
Wirtschaftssoziologie 1431
Der wirtschaftsstandische gedanke 323
Der wirtschaftsstandische gedanke 2750
Der wirtschaftsteil der zeitung 3704
Wirtschaftswachstum 1647

Economic Thought and Analysis

Wirtschaftswissenschaft 677
Die wirtschaftswissenschaft 724
Wirtschaftswissenschaft 1501
Wirtschaftswissenschaft 2257
Wirtschaftswissenschaft 2555
Wissenschaftstheortische uberlegungen 1122
Wo steht die nationalökonomie heute? 380
Die wohnungszustande 8564
A woolen draper's letter 7265
Work and pay 8200
Work and wealth 1550
Work and wealth 3662
Workers' councils 3093
Working class movement 7408
The working man's companion 6331
The working principles 8249
Works 6172
Works 9044
Works 9583
Works and correspondence 2473
Works and life of Walter Bagehot 8824
The works of Aristotle 5087
The works of Walter Bagehot 7420
The works of David Ricardo 6859
The works of Sydney Smith 7008
The works of Duglad Stewart 7052
The world after Keynes 10057
World economic problems 946
World economics 1585
The world of economics 2096
The world of industry 1511
The world of Adam Smith 7293
The worldy philosophers 2399
The world's economic crisis 10001
The world's economic future 877
Wörterbuch der ökonomie 9649
Wörterbuch des deutschen 8656
Writings 2536
Writings and speeches of Eugene V. Debs 9128
The writings of Albert Gallatin 6080
Writings of great economists 840
Writings on economics 2409

Writings on economics 4388
Współczesne burzuazyjne teorie 153
Wspótezesna myśl ekonomiczna 693
Wstep do ekonomii politycznej 1720
Wstep do teorii ekonomicznej Johna Maynarda Keynesa 10044
Der wucher 7604
Der wucher und seine 7509
Wybane zagadnienia ekonomii politycznej 9651
Wybor pism 2933
Wybrane zagadnienia z historii 257

The yearly journal of trade 6711
The years of high theory 601
Yijo hugi ui sahoe 2906
Yōsetsu keizaigaku 1565
The young Hegelians 9435
Yowarti kujunen 2391
Yowartari kujunen 226
Yugoslavia 3094
Yugoslavia and the new communism 3092
Yuibutsu shikau no keisei 9465

Z dziejów polskiej myśli społeczno-ekonomicznej 377
Z istorii ekonomichnoi 2988
Z novu sujbektivismus v eknomické teorii 608
Zagadnienia dochodo 2941
Die zahlungsmittel 4933
Základy hospodárskej vedy 1600
Zaklady marxistické 9264
Zakon vrijednosti i odnos 9137
Zakonitost dohotka 9631
Zaopatrzenie i zbyt 3487
Zarys dziejow mysli 2929
Zarys ekonomii politycznej 1671
Zarys ekonomii politiznej 9450
Zarys ekonomii politycznej socjalizmu 1190
Zarys historii ekonomii politycznej 258
Zarys historii polskiej 2943
Zarys teorii gospodarki 9636
Zastosowanie metod matematycznyc

Short Title Index

3914
Zatrudnienie i rozwoj gospodarczy 963
Zawod ekonomisty w Polsce Ludowej 2419
Zerlegung und losung diskreter 3625
Zeszyty naukowe 3535
Die zinsauffassungen John Maynard Keynes' 10085
Zoku keizai shisō shi 998
Die zolltarife aller länder 6260
Die zoll-tariffe 7480
Le Zollverein 6863
Zu einigen Fragen 2664
Die Zuckerindustrie 8120
Zuckerindustrie 8390
Zum socialen Frieden 8594
Die Zukunft der marktwirtschaft 2294
Die zukunft unserer 1979
Zur anschauung der antike uber handel 487
Zur anwendung der Marxschen theorie 9656
Zur beleuchtung der sozialen 6876
Zur entscheidungsfindung 9657
Zur entstehungsgeschichte 9519
Zur erkenntniss unserer 6877
Zur erklärung und abhulfe 6878
Zur gegenwartslage der deutschen 2710
Zur genesis der sozial-okonomischen 3022
Zur geschichte 2747
Zur geschichte der englischen 5282
Zur geschichte der englischen 8877
Zur geschichte der handelbilanztheorie 8028
Zur geschichte der verkehrswesens 8421
Zur geschichte der volkswirtschaft in Ungarn 2800
Zur geschichte der werttheorie in England 2764
Zur geschichte der werttheorie in England 3323
Zur geschichte des methodenstreites 3650
Zur geschichte und kritik 8125
Zur geschichte und politik 125
Zur geschichtlichen des physiocratismus 6325
Zur historischen rolle 8841
Zur interpretation des okonomischen modell-denkens 6
Zur klassischen wert- 3186
Zur krisis der statischen 3663
Zur kritik der lehre 8527
Zur kritik der preistheorie 3418
Zur kritik der sowjetischen 2994
Zur litteraturgeschichte 8884
Zur litteraturgeschichte der staats- 586
Zur methode der politischen 3518
Zur theorie des preises 3489
Zur theorie des preises 8820
Zur theorie und messung 3206
Zur würdigung der historischen schule 8826
Das Zwangssparen in der alteren 539
Zwei bucher zur socialen 8018
Zwei grundprobleme der scholastischen 5031
Zwei spanische mercantilisten 8794
Zwei spanische merkantilisten 5323
Zwischen wirtschaft un staat 2531
Zwischen wirtschaft und staat 683
Zwölf Bücher 6949